Gerald Quirchmayr Erich Schweighofer
Trevor J.M. Bench-Capon (Eds.)

Database and Expert Systems Applications

9th International Conference, DEXA'98
Vienna, Austria, August 24-28, 1998
Proceedings

Springer

Series Editors

Gerhard Goos, Karlsruhe University, Germany
Juris Hartmanis, Cornell University, NY, USA
Jan van Leeuwen, Utrecht University, The Netherlands

Volume Editors

Gerald Quirchmayr
Universität Wien
Institut für Angewandte Informatik und Informationssysteme
Liebiggasse 4/3-4, A-1010 Wien, Austria
E-mail: Gerald.Quirchmayr@univie.ac.at

Erich Schweighofer
Universität Wien
Institut für Völkerrecht und Internationale Beziehungen
Universitätsstr. 2, A-1090 Wien, Austria
E-mail: Erich.Schweighofer@univie.ac.at

Trevor J.M. Bench-Capon
The University of Liverpool, Department of Computer Science
Chadwick Building
Peach Street, Liverpool L60 7ZF, United Kingdom
E-mail: tbc@csc.liv.ac.uk

Cataloging-in-Publication data applied for

Die Deutsche Bibliothek - CIP-Einheitsaufnahme

Database and expert systems applications : 9th international conference ; proceedings / DEXA '98, Vienna, Austria, August 24 - 28, 1998. Gerald Quirchmayr ... (ed.). - Berlin ; Heidelberg ; New York ; Barcelona ; Budapest ; Hong Kong ; London ; Milan ; Paris ; Singapore ; Tokyo : Springer, 1998
(Lecture notes in computer science ; Vol. 1460)
ISBN 3-540-64950-6

CR Subject Classification (1991): H.2, I.2.1, H.3, H.4, H.5

ISSN 0302-9743
ISBN 3-540-64950-6 Springer-Verlag Berlin Heidelberg New York

Printed in Germany

Typesetting: Camera-ready by author
SPIN 10638287 06/3142 – 5 4 3 2 1 0 Printed on acid-free paper

Preface

The Database and Expert Systems Applications (DEXA) conferences are regarded as a platform for the exchange of ideas, experiences and opinions among theoreticians and practitioners and for defining requirements for the future systems in the areas of database and artificial intelligence technologies.

The scope of the papers covers the most recent and relevant topics of database and AI systems. The sessions are primarily devoted to active and object-oriented databases, object-oriented modeling, data engineering, information retrieval, workflow and cooperative systems, spatial and temporal aspects, document management, adaption and view updates, genetic algorithms, cooperative and distributed environments, interaction and communication, transactions, partitioning and fragmentation, database queries, data warehouses, knowledge discovery and data mining, knowledge extraction, and methods. More than 200 papers have been submitted from over 36 different countries in all continents, 81 of which have been accepted.

DEXA '98 is the 9th annual conference after Vienna, Berlin, Valencia, Prague, Athens, London, Zurich and Toulouse. So this year marks the return of DEXA to its place of birth, Vienna, where it was started in 1990.

We would like to express our thanks to all institutions actively sponsoring this event, namely to:
University of Vienna, Faculty of Law, DEXA-Association, OCG (Austrian Computer Society), GI (Gesellschaft für Informatik), FAW (Unversity of Linz, Austria), Austrian Airlines, City of Vienna, Bank Austria

Many persons have contributed numerous hours to organize this conference. The names of most of them will appear on the following pages.

Special thanks go to Gabriela and Roland Wagner (FAW Linz), A Min Tjoa, Andreas Kurz, and Horst Trixl (TU Vienna University of Technology), Ramona Bruckner, Dieter Scheithauer, Thomas Schierer, Werner Winiwarter, Maria Katsaros, and Barbara Maderbacher (University of Vienna). We are very indebted to all members of the PC and others who have very carefully reviewed the submitted papers.

July 1998

Gerald Quirchmayr, University of Vienna, Austria
Trevor Bench-Capon, University of Liverpool, United Kingdom
Erich Schweighofer, University of Vienna, Austria

PC Chairs

Program Committee

General Chairperson:
N. Revell, Middlesex University, UK

Publication Chairperson:
V. Marik, Czech Technical University, Czech Republic

Conference Program Chairpersons:
G. Quirchmayr, University of Vienna, Austria
T. Bench-Capon, University of Liverpool, UK
E. Schweighofer, University of Vienna, Austria

Workshop Chairperson:
R.R. Wagner, FAW, University of Linz, Austria

Program Committee Members:
H. Afsarmanesh, University of Amsterdam, The Netherlands
K. Bauknecht, University of Zurich, Switzerland
B. Bhargava, Purdue University, USA
J. Bing, NRCCL Oslo, Norway
J. Bubenko, Royal Institute of Technology, Sweden
L. Camarinha-Matos, New University of Lisbon, Portugal
W.S. Cellary, University of Poznan, Poland
S. Christodoulakis, University of Crete, Greece
B. Croft, University of Massachusetts, USA
J. Debenham, University of Technology, Sydney, Australia
P. Drazan, RIKS Maastricht, The Netherlands
J. Eder, University of Klagenfurt, Austria
T. Eiter, University of Giessen, Germany
A.L. Furtado, University of Rio de Janeiro, Brazil
G. Gardarin, INRIA, France
F. Golshani, Arizona State University, USA
G. Gottlob, Technical University of Vienna, Austria
A. Hameurlain, Université Paul Sabatier, France
J. Hammer, University of Florida, USA
I. Hawryszkiewycz, University of Technology, Sydney, Australia
S. Jajodia, George Mason University, USA
Y. Kambayashi, University of Kyoto, Japan
M. Kamel, Naval Postgraduate School, USA
N. Kamel, City University of Hongkong, Hong Kong
G. Kappel, University of Linz, Austria
D. Karagiannis, University of Vienna, Austria
M.A. Ketabchi, Santa Clara University, USA
M.H. Kim, KAIST, Korea

P. Klement, University of Linz, Austria
J. Kouloumdjian, LISI-INSA, Lyon, France
P. Kroha, Technical University of Chemnitz, Germany
J. Lazansky, Czech Technical University, Czech Republic
T.W. Ling, University of Singapore, Singapore
A. Makinouchi, Kyushu University, Japan
V. Marik, Czech Technical Univ., Czech Republic
A. Mendelzon, University of Toronto, Canada
M. Mohania, University of South Australia, Australia
J. Mylopoulos, University of Toronto, Canada
E. Neuhold, GMD-IPSI, Germany
T.W. Olle, T.W. Olle & Associates, UK
G. Ozsoyoglu, University Case Western Research, USA
G. Pangalos, University of Thessaloniki, Greece
M. Papazoglou, Queensland University of Technology, Australia
B. Pernici, Politecnico di Milano, Italy
G. Pernul, University of Essen, Germany
I. Ramos, Technical University of Valencia, Spain
C. Rolland, University Paris I, France
N. Roussopoulos, University of Maryland, USA
R. Sacks-Davis, RMIT, Australia
M. Scholl, CNAM&INRIA, Paris, France
A. Sernadas, University of Lisbon, Portugal
C. Shahabi, University of Southern California, USA
J.C. Smith, University of British Columbia, Canada
H. Sonnberger, European University Institute, Italy
B. Srinivasan, Monash University, Australia
U. Srinivasan, CIRO, Australia
R.B. Stanton, ANK, Australia
R. Studer, University of Karlsruhe, Germany
M. Takizawa, Tokyo Denki University, Japan
K. Tanaka, Kobe University, Japan
Z. Tari, RMIT, Australia
S. Teufel, University of Zurich, Switzerland
J.M. Thevenin, University Paul Sabatier, France
H.W. Thimbleby, Middlesex University, UK
C.H. Thoma, IT pro, Switzerland
A M. Tjoa, Technical University of Vienna, Austria
R. Traunmüller, University of Linz, Austria
K. Vidyasankar, Memorial University of Newfoundland, Canada
S. Zdonik, Brown University, USA

Table of Contents

Active Databases

Object-Oriented Systems

Data Engineering I

Information Retrieval I

Workflow and Cooperative Systems

Spatial and Temporal Aspects

Data Engineering II

Information Retrieval II

Document Management I

Spatial Databases

Adaptation and View Updates

Genetic Algorithms

Invited Lecture

Cooperative and Distributed Environments

Interaction and Communication

Transactions I

Advanced Applications I

Document Management II

Temporal Aspects

Transactions II

Advanced Applications II

Oriented Systems

Partitioning and Fragmentation

Database Queries

Data Warehouses

Knowledge Discovery and Data Mining

Knowledge Extraction

Knowledge Base Reduction for Comprehension and Reuse Purposes

Composite Event Management in TriGS - Concepts and Implementation

Werner Retschitzegger

Department of Information Systems (IFS)
University of Linz, Altenbergerstraße 69, A-4040 Linz, Austria
werner@ifs.uni-linz.ac.at

Abstract. Active object-oriented database systems are a commonly accepted solution for capturing the time- and context-dependent knowledge of non-standard applications. Several attempts have been made already to integrate active concepts into object-oriented database systems and to increase the expressive power of event specification languages. However, this has often been done without considering the consequences for the implementation. The present paper tries to fill this gap. The main focus is on describing design and implementation issues concerning composite event management within the active object-oriented database system TriGS. Thereby, we concentrate on the idiosyncratic features of TriGS, which are composite events spanning several transactions and even several applications, smooth integration of composite event detection with rule scheduling, and the inheritance of rules.

1 Introduction

Non-standard application areas like workflow management, multimedia and computer integrated manufacturing require *timely responses to critical situations* and *sophisticated constraint management*. For these reasons, database systems are required to be "*(re)active*" in the sense that they are able to react automatically to certain events by means of knowledge stored in terms of triggers, i.e., Event/Condition/Action rules (ECA rules), inside the database. Besides activeness, "*object-orientation*" is equally important in non-standard application areas, since it helps to intuitively model the universe of discourse and to more easily adapt to changing requirements. The need for active and object-oriented mechanisms has also emerged during an EC ESPRIT project aiming at the development of next-generation production scheduling and control systems [11]. Therefore, the active object-oriented database system TriGS (Triggersystem for GemStone) has been developed. TriGS builds upon the commercially available object-oriented database system GemStone [9] and focuses on advanced requirements of non-standard application areas. One of these requirements is the need for composite event management to model certain complex real-world situations which have to be monitored by the active system. Since composite event definition languages are well known in the literature TriGS has been based on these elaborated approaches, such as found in Ode [14], REACH [3], Samos [8] and Snoop [4]. Furthermore, TriGS has special emphasize on the following design and implementation goals for composite event management:

- **Powerful Representation of Composite Events.** The representation of composite events has to be powerful enough to express different kinds of event operators, contexts and guards. In addition, it is required that composite events are allowed to span not only several transactions but even several applications.
- **Smooth Integration with Rule Scheduling Mechanisms.** Since rule scheduling mechanisms represent the core of an active system, composite event management mechanisms have to be an integral part thereof.
- **Inheritance of Rules Incorporating Message Events.** It is often required that rules containing message events are not only able to monitor the behavior of the class they are attached to but rather to monitor the behavior of the whole class hierarchy rooted at that respective class. Thus, inheritance of rules should be supported.

In this paper, we concentrate on design and implementation issues of TriGS which were necessary to achieve these goals. For this, the paper is organized as follows: Section 2 gives a short overview of the basic concepts of the TriGS knowledge model, including the structure of rules, composite events and inheritance of rules. In Section 3, the representation and detection of composite events in TriGS is described in more detail. The integration of composite event management and rule scheduling is presented in Section 4. Section 5 discusses the mechanisms used for implementing rule inheritance. Finally, Section 6 points to ongoing research.

2 A Tour on the TriGS Knowledge Model

In the following, the basic concepts used in the TriGS knowledge model are presented. Fig. 1 visualizes these concepts and their interdependencies by means of a data model, whereas the notation is based on UML [7].

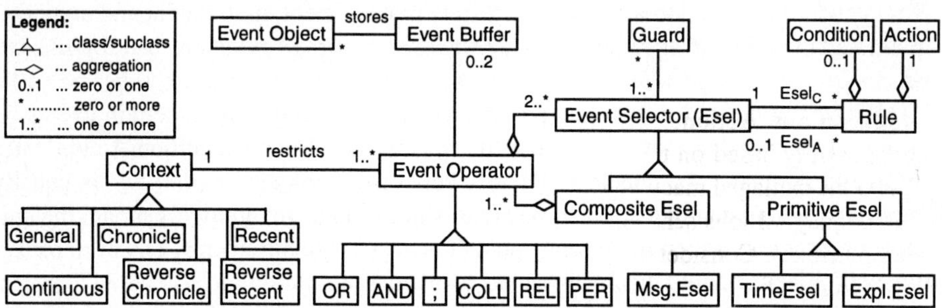

Fig. 1. Basic Concepts of the TriGS Knowledge Model

Note, in the reminder of this section these concepts are described only to the extent necessary to understand the subsequent implementation description.

2.1 Rules

Like most active systems, TriGS is designed according to the ECA paradigm [1]. Rules and their components are implemented as first-class objects allowing the definition and modification of rules during run time. Fig. 2 shows the basic syntax for specifying rules in TriGS using the Backus-Naur Form (BNF). The symbols ::= [ ] are meta symbols belonging to the BNF formalism. Angle brackets denote non-terminal symbols.

Esel$_C$ and Esel$_A$. The event part of a rule is represented by a *condition event selector (Esel$_C$)* and an optional *action event selector (Esel$_A$)* determining the events (e.g., a machine breakdown) which are able to trigger the rule's condition and action, respectively. Triggering a rule's condition (i.e., an event corresponding to the Esel$_C$ is signaled) implies that the condition has to be evaluated. If the condition evaluates to true, and an event corresponding to the Esel$_A$ is also signaled, the rule's action is executed. If the Esel$_A$ is not specified, the action is executed immediately after the condition has been evaluated to true. By default, the thread of control signaling the condition triggering event is not blocked while the triggered rule is waiting for the action triggering event to occur. Blocking can be specified by the keyword `WAIT UNTIL`. TriGS allows to monitor different kinds of *primitive events*, comprising *time events*, *explicit events* and *message events* as well as *composite events* (cf. Section 2.2). The information about each event having occurred such as the time of occurrence is stored within a so called *event object*. For each event, a *guard* similar to masks in ODE [14], i.e., a predicate over the event's parameters, may be specified, which further restricts the events able to trigger a condition or an action, respectively. Since guards are used to immediately evaluate whether an occurred event is relevant for further consideration, unnecessary rule triggering and evaluation of possibly complex conditions is avoided. For a more detailed description of primitive events it is referred to [16].

<RULE_DEFINITION> ::=	
DEFINE RULE <rule_name> **AS**	Name
ON <Esel$_C$>	Condition Event Selector (Esel$_C$)
IF <bool_expr> **THEN**	Condition (C)
[[**WAIT UNTIL**] **ON** <Esel$_A$>]	Action Event Selector (Esel$_A$)
EXECUTE [**INSTEAD**] <action>	Action (A)
[**WITH PRIORITY** <number>]	Priority
[**TRANSACTION MODES**(**C**:(serial|parallel), **A**:(serial|parallel))]	Transaction Modes
END RULE <rule_name>.	

Fig. 2. BNF of an ECA Rule in TriGS

Condition and Action. The condition part of a rule is specified by a boolean expression, possibly based on the result of a database query (e.g., are there some scheduled jobs on the damaged machine?). The action part is specified again in terms of messages (e.g., display all jobs scheduled on the damaged machine and reschedule them on another machine). Considering rules containing message events, the keyword `INSTEAD` allows to specify that the action should be executed instead of the method corresponding to the message triggering the condition evaluation. The execution order of multiple triggered rules, i.e., conditions and actions of different rules are triggered at the same time, is controlled by means of *priorities*. The *transaction mode* defines whether the condition and action, respectively, should be processed in that transaction wherein the triggering event has occurred (*serial*) or rather within an own parallel transaction (*parallel*). Note that the development of more sophisticated transaction modes is part of ongoing work (cf. Section 6). Fig. 3 shows an example rule, which is responsible for monitoring the threshold of an inventory. Condition and action descriptions are given in a self-descriptive pseudocode closely resembling Smalltalk syntax. Note that for ease of explanation it is assumed that a class automatically maintains its extent and the extent can be accessed by sending messages to the class itself (cf. `Inventory`). Every time parts are removed from the inventory (determined by the rule's $Esel_C$), the condition checks whether the remaining quantity is below a certain threshold. If true, parts are re-ordered (denoted by the rule's action) at the end of the current month (determined by the rule's $Esel_A$).

DEFINE RULE InventoryRule_1 **AS**	Name
ON POST (Inventory,remove:part quantity:quant) **DO**	$Esel_C$
IF (trgObj itemsOfType:(part category)) quant < trgObj constantThreshold **THEN**	C
ON REL (conditionEvent time, MyDateTime endOfCurrentMonth) **DO**	$Esel_A$
EXECUTE conditionEvent trgObj reorder:20 for:(part category)	A
END RULE InventoryRule_1.	

Fig. 3. Example Rule

The $Esel_A$ is represented by a relative time event (cf. REL) specifying the condition evaluation time as the initiating event and the end of the current month as the event which is finally triggering action execution.

2.2 Composite Events

As already mentioned, besides primitive events, rules in TriGS are able to monitor *composite events*. A composite event consists of so called *component events*. The event starting the detection of a composite event is called *initiating event*, the event terminating the detection is called *terminating event* or *triggering event*. Concerning the terminating event of the $Esel_A$, it has to occur after the condition evaluation has become true to be recognized by the active system. All other component events of the $Esel_A$ are recognized even if the condition has not yet been triggered.

Event Operators. *Event operators* are used to construct composite events out of two or more *component events* by establishing different relationships between them. The component events can be primitive events or again composite ones. The event operators used in TriGS are mainly based on those supported by Snoop [4]. However, there are three main modifications done in TriGS, the first two for easing implementation, the third one for increasing expressibility. First, TriGS allows to directly apply a negative event expression within the event operators *conjunction (AND)*, *sequence (;)*, *cumulation (COLL)*, *relative (REL)* and *periodic (PER)*. This is in contrast to Snoop which supports an explicit NOT-Operator. Second, whereas Snoop considers *relative* and *periodic time events* as primitive events, TriGS handles them as composite events. Third, in Snoop, the time distance necessary for relative and periodic events can be defined only statically by means of a constant. TriGS allows to define this time distance also dynamically by using a function that calculates the time distance at run-time. For a detailed description of the event operators used in TriGS it is referred to [16].

Event Consumption Modes - Contexts. So far we have defined the structure of composite events but we have not yet analyzed the occurrence of its component events. *Event consumption* determines which occurrences of a series of events are considered as component events for a certain composite event [1]. Different application categories need rather different consumption modes in order to restrict multiple occurrences of composite events of one and the same composite event selector. The mechanism introduced in [4] for realizing different consumption modes are *contexts*. A context represents a restriction for the detection of several occurrences of an event of a certain composite event selector. The contexts which are supported by TriGS are again mainly based on those of Snoop [4]. Note, that the so called *cumulative context* of Snoop is not supported by TriGS. However, TriGS supports two additional contexts, not present within Snoop called *reverse chronicle* and *reverse recent*. The *reverse chronicle context* pairs the terminating event with the most recent initiating event, and proceeds with consumption in a reverse chronological order. Thus, this context represents the counterpart to the chronicle context which pairs the terminating event with the oldest initiating event, and proceeds with consumption in a chronological order, respectively. The *reverse recent context* defines that the terminating event is paired only with the oldest initiating event instead of the most recent one as it is the case for the ordinary recent context. Note that this is in contrast to the chronicle context, where also younger initiating events are taken into account.

2.3 Inheritance of Rules Incorporating Message Events

As already mentioned, TriGS supports the notion of so called *message events* which means that any message sent to an object called *triggering object* may signal a message event. Message events can be described by event selectors consisting of the class the rule is attached to, denoted as *triggering class*, and/or the message which has been sent, called *triggering method*. Therefore it makes sense to consider such message-based rules in the context of the class hierarchy which the triggering class and the triggering method are part of. Message-based rules in TriGS are not only able to monitor the behavior of the triggering class. Rather, these rules are *subject to full inheritance* and propagated together with the structural and behavioral components of the triggering class, to all of its subclasses, denoting the *scope of the rule*. This implies that the condition and/or action part of a rule is triggered not only by invoking the triggering method on any direct instance of the triggering class but also by invoking this method on any instance of its subclasses.

Of course, additional rules can be defined in subclasses in order to monitor their behavior. Furthermore, regardless whether a triggering method is overridden in a subclass, the rules containing that method in their event selectors are still inherited. Since a rule can be inappropriate in a certain subclass, TriGS also supports *selective inheritance* meaning that the scope of the rule can be restricted to the triggering class only. The implementation mechanisms realized for supporting inheritance of rules are described in Section 5. Concerning *overriding of rules*, up to now, only some initial considerations have been made for TriGS. This topic is subject to future research and shortly discussed in Section 6.

3 Representation and Detection of Composite Events

For the representation and detection of a composite event, TriGS uses an extended syntax tree. Several syntax trees are combined to form graphs, so called extended syntax graphs (ESG), in order to avoid redundant specification of subtrees. This is since subtrees represent composite events, which themselves take part in more complex composite events as component events. An ESG consisting of the finite sets `(L,O,A,F)` can be defined as follows:

- L is a finite set of *leaf nodes,* which can accept primitive events and distribute them to the operator nodes.
- O is a finite set of *operator nodes*. The functionality of an operator node is defined by the *event operator* which is represented by the node, the *context* for event detection and a *guard.*
- A is a finite set of *arcs* connecting leaf nodes with operator nodes and operator nodes with other operator nodes.
- F is a finite set of those operator nodes (F ⊆ O) finalizing the detection of composite events and consequently triggering a rule. They have the same functionality as other operator nodes but additionally signal the detected composite event to the Rule Scheduler, as described in Section 4.

3.1 Operator Nodes and Leaf Nodes

The semantics of the event operators supported by TriGS are realized by six different operator nodes (cf. Fig. 6) [16]. The mapping between event operators and operator nodes is one to one, except for a conjunction event operator and a sequence event operator. These are mapped to several connected AND operator nodes and several connected sequence operator nodes (denoted by ";"), respectively.

Components of Operator Nodes. Each of the operator nodes contains one or more *input ports,* which are named or indexed in case of the OR operator node, where component events are injected. Thus, the set of arcs A defined above is a partial set of (LxP ∪ OxP) where P is the set of all input ports of all operator nodes. According to the semantics of the operator nodes, *event buffers* are assigned to some of these input ports. An event buffer is used to store component event objects which are waiting for the other still missing component event objects. An event buffer is realized as an ordinary array rather than as a linked list in order to minimize the performance overhead of creating a new link object. Furthermore, the *context* which was specified within the corresponding composite event selector is stored within the node and is considered in the decision of when to consume component event objects, i.e., to remove them from event buffers. *Guards* are directly stored within each operator node as GemStone executable blocks [9]. Finally, an operator node contains an arbitrary number of *output ports*, identifying all other operator nodes which are interested in the composite event represented by the operator node under consideration.

Functionality of Operator Nodes. Every time a leaf node or another operator node injects an event into an operator node, it has to be checked if all other events which are required according to the semantics of the underlying event operator have already been injected, and, if yes, the composite event object is passed on to all output ports. Otherwise, the operator node has to continue to wait. In the case of an AND node, the event object is stored within the event buffer of the port named right. For all other nodes, this event object is "forgotten", i.e., no longer considered by the operator node.

Sequence Operator Node. Let us as give an example considering the sequence operator node. The corresponding sequence operator defines that the component events have to occur in a certain order with an arbitrary time delay in between. For realizing this semantics, the sequence operator node consists of three ports named left, not, and right. The left port contains an event object buffer in order to temporarily store the event object of the first event of the sequence. The right port contains no buffer since as soon as the second event of the sequence occurs, the composite event represented by this operator node is detected and signalled to the next node. The not port contains no buffer since as soon as a not event occurs the node has to be marked as dirty (cf. Section 3.2).

Leaf Nodes. A leaf node represents a certain primitive event selector. It contains a single input port used by the RS for the injection of a primitive event. In contrast to operator nodes, a leaf node is responsible for distributing a primitive event to all the operator nodes which are interested in this event immediately after it is injected. Thus, leaf nodes contain no event buffer. As soon as a corresponding primitive event is injected by the RS it directly passes that event to those operator nodes which represent the composite event selectors which the primitive event selector is part of.

3.2 Life-Span and Consumption of Events

Life-Span of Events. The life-span of partially composed events in TriGS is, in principle, neither restricted to a single transaction, as it is the case in REACH [3] and Snoop [4], nor to an application like in SAMOS [8]. Rather, a partially composed event stays alive as long as it is not explicitly scavenged by means of a special method provided by TriGS. If the life-span would only be for a transaction, then composite events spanning several sequentially executed transactions could not be detected. If the life-span would be that of a single application only, composite events spanning sequentially executed applications could not be detected. Since in TriGS the life-span of an event is not restricted, a partially detected composite event waits an indefinite period of time for the occurrence of the terminating event. Therefore we follow the suggestion of [4] in using a timeout mechanism which can be realized with a relative or absolute event specification. This means, that to assure a composite event is scavenged after a finite period of time the rule designer has to use this timeout mechanism.

Consumption of Events. As already mentioned, each event operator can be assigned a different context. Consequently, the operator node which represents an event operator determines when events have to be scavenged by the system. Another reason for scavenging is the injection of a NOT event into an operator node. If one of these situations occurs during composite event detection, the system marks the corresponding event objects within the event buffers as dirty and remembers the affected event buffers within a set named dirtyEventBuffers. After the composite event detector has fully processed the respective event, the system traverses all event buffers within dirtyEventBuffers and scavenges the dirty event objects.

3.3 Example of Composite Event Detection

During composite event detection primitive events are injected into the leaf nodes at the bottom of the ESG. The leaf nodes distribute them upwards to operator nodes which combine them into more complex event objects and so on, until a composite event has been recognized. Fig. 4 illustrates three composite event selectors CE_1, CE_2, and CE_3, and the corresponding ESG representing these event selectors. By putting the three composite event selectors together a graph emerges since, e.g., the primitive event selectors E_1 and E_4 are used within more than one composite event selector.

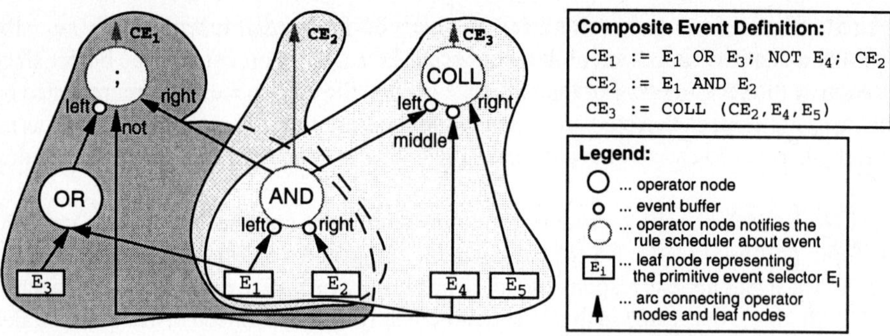

Fig. 4. Composite Event Detection Using an ESG

Within a composite event object all component event objects of a certain composite event are collected. Thus, a composite event object is realized as a hierarchical data structure.

3.4 Composite Event Detection in Other Active Systems

Both Snoop [4] and REACH [3] also use syntax trees and syntax graphs. One difference is that the syntax graphs used in TriGS take guards into account. Another difference is that unlike Snoop a NOT operator can be uniformly added to each operator node (except for OR of course) rather than having to be represented as its own operator node. Completely different approaches for the detection of composite events are followed within the systems Ode [14] and SAMOS [8]. Ode uses finite state automata which are based on the equivalence of event expressions and regular expressions. Since a finite automata can remember only the state but not the input symbols, some sentences from a context free grammar cannot be detected. Consequently, the chronological context cannot be realized [6]. SAMOS uses colored petri nets for the detection of composite events. Petri nets are best suited for detecting events in a chronological context, since the transition takes place as soon as all required tokens are available. Other contexts can be realized only by using a number of dummy place holders [6].

4 Integrating Composite Event Detection With Rule Scheduling

The present section broadens our view on composite event management by integrating composite event detection with other architectural components of TriGS where the Rule Scheduler (RS) is the most prominent one. In general, a RS in TriGS is responsible for *determining the rules triggered* by the events signalled by the primitive event detectors and by a Composite Event Detector (CED) and for *generating a schedule* for triggered rules which have to be processed. In more detail, these tasks of a TriGS RS can be described as follows (see Fig. 5):

① The RS maps the primitive event which is signalled by one of the primitive event detectors or by a rule processor in case of cascaded rule triggering to an appropriate Event Injector (EI), cf. Section 4.1.

② The RS decides on the basis of its EIs whether the primitive event is a component event of a composite event, and whether it directly triggers a rule.

③ In the first case, the event has to be injected into the corresponding CED which proceeds with composite event detection by using the new event. As soon as a composite event is fully detected the CED signals the composite event back to the RS.

④ In the second case, the primitive event can be used immediately to search for triggered rules.

⑤ For primitive as well as composite events, the RS searches for rules within the so called Active Rule Base (ARB) and inserts all triggered rules into a set called `ruleSchedule` according to their priorities. Note, that in order to be considered by the RS, rules have to be transferred from the passive rule base to the ARB, a process which is called *registering* (cf. Section 4.2).

⑥ Finally, after all rules triggered by those events having the same timestamp are scheduled, i.e., after a complete schedule is generated, the RS initiates rule processing which is done by a dynamically controllable number of rule processors.

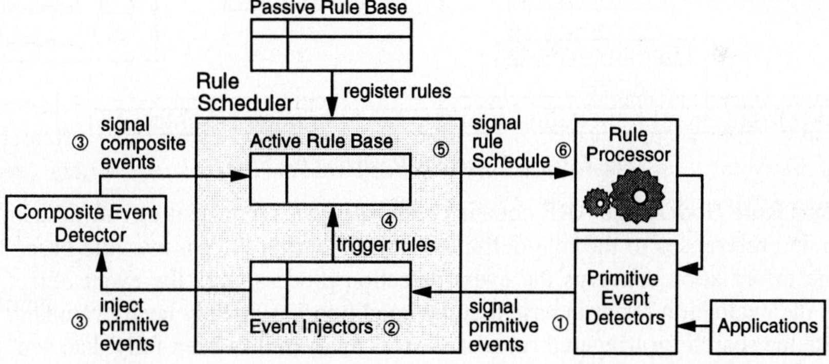

Fig. 5. Integrating Composite Event Detection with Rule Scheduling

The functionality of the RS is realized by means of an abstract class called `RuleScheduler` and its subclasses `AttachedRuleScheduler` and `DetachedRuleScheduler`. There exists a single detached rule scheduler which is responsible for scheduling rules which are defined to be processed in parallel to the triggering transaction. In addition, there exists a number of attached rule schedulers, one attached to each application process which requires active capabilities, which is responsible for scheduling rules whose transaction mode is defined to be serial. There exists an ARB for storing all rules for the detached rule scheduler as well as another ARB for holding all rules for the attached rule schedulers. Since the process of event injection and the process of scheduling triggered rules is almost the same for serial as well as parallel rules, there is no distinction made in the following description. For a more detailed discussion it is referred to [13].

4.1 Event Injection

Event injection starts as soon as a primitive event is signalled to the RS. First, a so called *injector* is selected according to the type of the signalled event. Accordingly, there are three different kinds of injectors to choose from: one for message events, one for explicit events, and one for time events. By means of the injectors, a primitive event is mapped to a leaf node of the ESG representing the respective primitive event selector. This leaf node may initiate composite event detection, or proceed it.

Representation of Injectors. Injectors are realized by instances of a GemStone symbol dictionary with hash access [9]. The key of this dictionary is the signature of the triggering method in the case of the message event injector, the name of the explicit event in the case of the explicit event injector, or a time event identifier in the case of the time event injector. A value in the message event injector dictionary represents a link to a hierarchy of triggering classes, a so called *inheritance tree*, used for realizing inheritance of rules (cf. Section 5). A value of the explicit event injector dictionary and the time event injector dictionary directly references an instance of the class `LeafNode` (cf. Fig. 6).

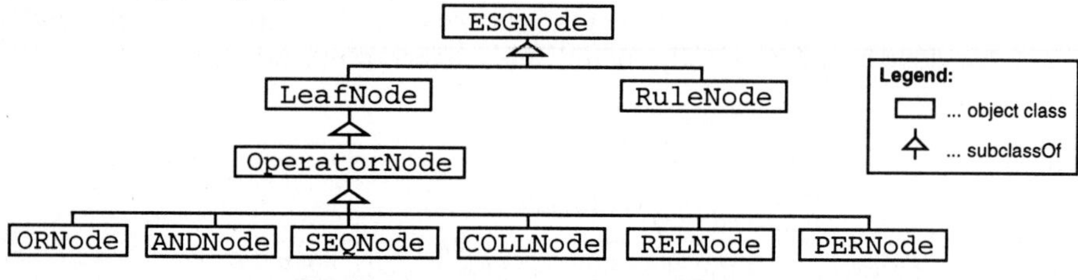

Fig. 6. Class Hierarchy Realizing the ESG

ARB and Rule Nodes. The ARB contains both *rule nodes* representing run-time information and references to the rule definition objects within the passive rule base. The run-time information concerns the event detection process, e.g., the event object, as well as the evaluation result in case that the condition has already been evaluated. To facilitate the search for triggered rules as soon as an event has been fully detected, the ESG as defined in Section 3 is extended by means of these rule nodes. For this, a rule node contains two ports, one for injecting condition triggering events and the other one for injecting action triggering events. At each of these ports either a `F` node, i.e., an operator node finalizing the detection of composite events, is allowed to inject composite events, or a leaf node is allowed to inject primitive events. The class hierarchy realizing this extended ESG is depicted in Fig. 6. Note, that the class hierarchy does not depict any specific semantic, but rather follows implementation inheritance [18].

4.2 Registering Rules - Building up EIs, ESG and ARB

As already mentioned, a rule has to be registered to a certain rule scheduler in order to be considered by that respective rule scheduler. For each rule being registered, the following steps have to be performed:

(1) A new rule node is created and inserted into the ARB together with a reference to the corresponding rule definition object which resides within the passive rule base.

(2) The rule definition object is made invariant, i.e., unchangeable. The invariance of the rule ensures that, while a rule is monitored by some RS, its definition, and thus its behaviour, remains unchanged for the RS.

(3) In case that the rule contains a composite event selector, the latter is translated into an extended syntax graph which is then merged with all existing ESGs residing

within the CED, which is attached to the RS. A reference to the rule node within the ARB is inserted into the F operator node of the composite event selector. Note that this is the root node of the extended syntax graph before merging.

(4) In case that the rule contains a primitive event selector only, that event selector is directly translated into a leaf node referencing the rule node.

The leaf node(s) generated in step 3 or in step 4 are inserted into the corresponding event injectors. In case of message event selectors, the leaf node is inserted into the appropriate position within the inheritance tree of the respective triggering method (cf. Section 5).

4.3 Example for the Collaboration Between EIs, ESG, and ARB

The collaboration between event injection, composite event detection and rule scheduling is illustrated in Fig. 7 by means of an example.

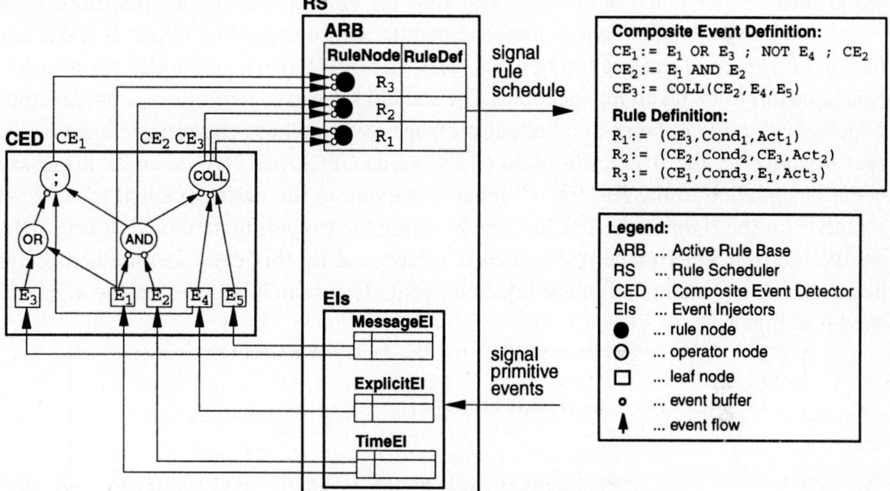

Fig. 7. Collaboration between EIs, ESG, and ARB

For this, the example ESG of Fig. 4 was extended and embedded into a broader context. Now it can be seen that E_3 and E_5 represent message event selectors, E_4 an explicit event selector, and E_1 and E_2 time event selectors, respectively. Furthermore, according to the extensions made in Section 4.1 concerning the definition of an ESG leaf nodes as well as F nodes are able to reference rule nodes. For example, the sequence operator node which is an F operator node, references the rule node R_3 depicting that the sequence operator node is able to inject the condition triggering event into R_3 which corresponds to CE_1. In addition, R_3 is referenced by the leaf node E_1, indicating that the action triggering event constitutes a primitive event. The condition triggering event and the action triggering event of R_1 are both injected by the COLL operator node, i.e., the action of R_1 is immediately processed after the condition. Finally, condition and action of R_2 are triggered by two composite events CE_2 and CE_3, respectively.

5 Realizing Inheritance of Rules Incorporating Message Events

The inheritance of rules as described in Section 2.3 is realized mainly by means of the message event injector. As already mentioned, the value of the message event injector dictionary is not a reference to a leaf node, but rather a reference to a so called *rule inheritance tree* representing all triggering classes for the triggering method which constitutes the key of the dictionary. The arcs of this tree reproduce the `subclassOf` relationships between these triggering classes. Note, that this tree needs not necessarily look the same as that of the ordinary class hierarchy of the triggering classes, since not every class is used as a triggering class. Furthermore, this tree can be seen orthogonal to the ESG.

For uniformity reasons, the root of this tree is always represented by the GemStone kernel class `Object`. Each triggering class which is part of this tree contains a list of those leaf nodes which reference the operator nodes and/or rule nodes using this triggering class within their event selectors. This list of nodes for the triggering class is divided into two disjunctive subsets. The first set (`inhRules`) contains those nodes which have to be notified about message events whose triggering object is a *direct or indirect instance* of the triggering class (`isKindOfClass`), i.e., nodes for which inheritance has to be taken into account. The second set (`notInhRules`) contains those nodes which have to be notified about message events whose triggering object is a *direct instance* of the triggering class (`isMemberOfClass`). As soon as a message event is signalled to the RS, the RS maps this event to the message event injector and searches for the right entry. This is done by using the triggering method as a key. Afterwards, the rule inheritance tree which is referenced by this entry is searched to find nodes which are interested in the injected event. This search is based on the algorithm shown in Fig. 8.

```
DO
  IF trgObject isKindOfClass Ci
    THEN notify all nodes within 'inhRules'
           IF trgObject isMemberOfClass Ci
              THEN notify all nodes within 'notInhRules'
           END IF
    ELSE GOTO notYetTraversedSibling Ci
  END IF
UNTIL trgObject isMemberOfClass Ci OR all Ci processed
```

Fig. 8. Algorithm for Realizing Inheritance of Rules

The nodes which are interested in the event are found by sending the predefined GemStone messages `isKindOfClass` and `isMemberOfClass` with the triggering class as a parameter, to the triggering object. With this, it is checked if the triggering object is an indirect or a direct instance of the class C_i. If it is only an indirect instance, then all interested nodes are within the instance variable `inhRules`. If it is both then the nodes within `notInhRules` are also interested and if it is neither, then the search continues. Fig. 9 shows a class hierarchy incorporating different rules. The rules R_1 and R_2 are defined on the triggering class `A` and the triggering method m_1. The scope of these rules includes the complete class hierarchy rooted at class `A`, namely the classes `C`, `D`, `E` and `F`. R_3 is defined on the triggering class `B` and on the triggering method m_2. R_4 is defined on the triggering class C and on the triggering method m_2 and inherited to subclass E. R_5 and R_6 are defined on triggering class D and on triggering method m_1 whereby only R_6 is defined to be inherited to subclass F. R_5 is subject to selective inheritance which means that it should not be inherited into subclass F. This is denoted by underlining R_5 in Fig. 9.

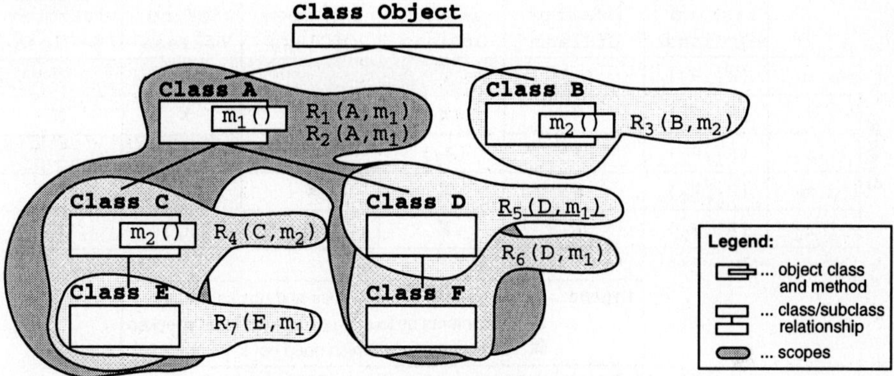

Fig. 9. Example for the Inheritance of Rules

Finally, R_7 is defined on the triggering class E and again on the triggering method m_1. Fig. 10 represents the entries within the message event injector and the referenced rule inheritance tree which are necessary in order to realize the inheritance of rules as indicated in Fig. 9. Note, that for representation convenience, the instance variables inhRules and notInhRules do not contain leaf nodes but rule nodes directly.

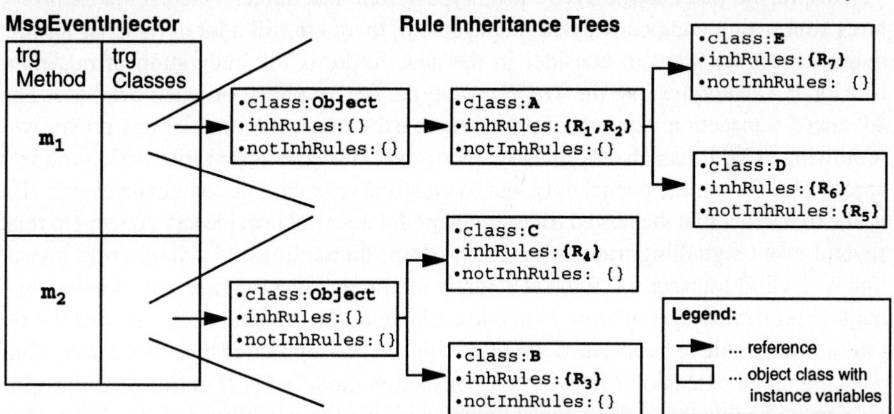

Fig. 10. Message Event Injector and Rule Inheritance Trees

Fig. 11 visualizes the output of the algorithm depicted in Fig. 8 using five different events, all concerning the rule inheritance tree referenced by the triggering method m_1. The triggering objects a, c, e, d, and f are all direct instances of the classes A, C, E, D, and F. The header of the table in Fig. 11 shows all triggering classes wherein the triggering method m_1 is known. The messages isKindOfClass and isMemberOfClass are used by the algorithm in order to check if the triggering object is an indirect and/or direct instance of the triggering classes. If it is an indirect instance only, then the rules stored within inhRules have to be triggered. If it is both an indirect and a direct instance, then the rules stored within `inhRules` and `notInhRules` have to be triggered and the algorithm stops as it is the case for `a,m1` and `e,m1` in the context of the triggering classes `A` and `E`, respectively.

Triggering Classes

Events	A		E		D	
	isKind OfClass	isMember OfClass	isKind OfClass	isMember OfClass	isKind OfClass	isMember OfClass
a, m_1	$\{R_1, R_2\}$	{ }	▒	▒	▒	▒
c, m_1	$\{R_1, R_2\}$	✘	✘	✘	✘	✘
e, m_1	$\{R_1, R_2\}$	✘	$\{R_7\}$	{ }	▒	▒
d, m_1	$\{R_1, R_2\}$	✘	✘	✘	$\{R_6\}$	$\{R_5\}$
f, m_1	$\{R_1, R_2\}$	✘	✘	✘	$\{R_6\}$	✘

Legend: { } ... contents of `inhRules` and `notInhRules`
✘ ... contents of `instVars` has not to be checked
▒ ... `trgClasses` which need not to be checked

Fig. 11. Result of the Algorithm due to Different Events

If it is neither the one nor the other, the triggering classes of another part of the hierarchy are checked.

6 Outlook

Despite the fact that the TriGS prototype system has implemented some useful features concerning composite event management, there are still a lot of open issues. One major aspect we want to consider in the near future is the integration of *additional transaction semantics* into the TriGS prototype. Active object-oriented databases need advanced transaction support, of which the nested transaction model has proven very promising [12]. It has also been shown, however, that the nested transaction model is appropriate for simple events only, but too restrictive in case of composite events. This is due to the fact that the nested transaction model does not provide any concept to relate several event signalling transactions, i.e., parent transactions, to a single rule transaction, i.e., child transaction. What is actually required is that the *rule transaction can be made a subtransaction of more than one event signalling transaction,* and, that the rule transaction is able to *cooperate with them* when accessing shared data. We are currently working on an extension of the nested transaction model of [12] in this direction since it seems to be that these extensions allow combining the reliability and flexibility of the nested transaction model with the expressive power of composite events.

The second issue we are currently investigating is *rule inheritance and overriding.* Up to now, not much work has been done in the literature concerning rule inheritance and overriding. Some systems, such as [2], [5], [14], [15], [17], propose that rules are always inherited and can never be overridden, which corresponds to *strict inheritance* [18]. Another possibility, which is followed by some systems like TriGS, is that rules are specialized arbitrarily, which is called *implementation inheritance* [18]. The motivation for using implementation inheritance in TriGS was, that the underlying object-oriented model of GemStone, which is Smalltalk, adheres to this kind of inheritance, and, in our opinion, the kind of inheritance used for rules should not contradict the kind of inheritance supported by the underlying object-oriented model [10], [16]. However, what should be investigated in the future is, how far other kinds of inheritance such as *specification inheritance* and *specialization inheritance* are useful for being applied to rules.

References

[1] ACT-NET Consortium, *The Active Database Management System Manifesto: A Rulebase of ADBMS Features*, in ACM SIGMOD Records, Vol. 25, No.3, Sept. 1996

[2] Bertino, E., Guerrini, G., Merlo, I., *Trigger Inheritance and Overriding in Active Object Database Systems*, in Proceedings of the 5th International Conference on Deductive and Object-Oriented Databases (DOOD '97), Montreux, Switzerland, December 1997.

[3] Buchmann, A.P., Zimmermann, J., Blakeley, J.A., Wells, D.L., *Building an Integrated Active OODBMS: Requirements, Architecture, and Design Decisions*, in Proceedings of the 11th International Conference on Data Engineering (ICDE '95), P. S. Yu, A. L. P. Chen (eds.), IEEE Computer Society Press, Taipeh, Taiwan, 1995.

[4] Chakravarthy, S., Krishnaprasad, V., Anwar, E., Kim, S.-K., *Composite Events for Active Databases: Semantics, Contexts, and Detection*, in Proceedings of the 20th International Conference on Very Large Data Bases (VLDB '94), J.B. Bocca, et al. (eds.), Morgan Kaufmann, Santiago, Chile, 1994.

[5] Collet, C., Coupaye, T., Svenson, T., *NAOS - Efficient and modular reactive capabilities in an Object-Oriented Database System*, in Proceedings of the 20th International Conference on Very Large Data Bases (VLDB '94), J.B. Bocca, et al. (eds.), Morgan Kaufmann, Santiago, Chile, Sept. 1994

[6] Deutsch, A., *Method and Composite Event Detection in the "REACH" Active Database System*, Master Thesis, Technical University of Darmstadt, July 1994.

[7] Fowler, M. *UML Distilled - Applying the Standard Object Modeling Language*, Addison-Wesley, 1997.

[8] Gatziu, S., *Events in an Active Object-Oriented Database System*, PhD, Kovac, 1995.

[9] *GemStone Programming Guide*, Version 4.1, 1995.

[10] Kappel, G., Rausch-Schott, S., Retschitzegger, W., Vieweg, S., *TriGS - Making a Passive Object-Oriented Database System Active*, Journal of Object-Oriented Programming (JOOP), 7(4), 1994.

[11] Kappel, G., Rausch-Schott, S., Retschitzegger, W., Tjoa, A M., Vieweg, S., Wagner, R., *Active Object-Oriented Database Systems For CIM Applications*, Information Management in Computer Integrated Manufacturing, A Comprehensive Guide to State-of-the-Art CIM Solutions, H. Adelsberger, J. Lazansky, V. Marik (eds.), Springer LNCS 973, 1995.

[12] Kappel, G., Rausch-Schott, S., Retschitzegger, W., Sakkinen, M., A *Transaction Model For Handling Composite Events,* Proceedings of the Third International Workshop of the Moscow ACM SIGMOD Chapter on Advances in Databases and Information Systems (ADBIS '96), Moscow, September 1996.

[13] Kappel, G., Rausch-Schott, S., Retschitzegger, W., *A Tour on the TriGS Active Database System - Architecture and Implementation*, ACM Symposium on Applied Computing (SAC '98).

[14] Lieuwen, D.F., Gehani, N., Arlein, R., *The Ode Active Database: Trigger Semantics and Implementation*, in Proceedings of the 12th International Conference on Data Engineering (ICDE '96), IEEE Computer Society Press, New Orleans, Louisiana, 1996.

[15] Medeiros, C. B., Pfeffer, P., *Object Integrity Using Rules,* in Proc. of the 5th European Conference on Object-Oriented Programming (ECOOP '91), P. America (ed.), Springer LNCS 512, Geneva, 1991.

[16] Retschitzegger, W., *A Tour on TriGS - Development of an Active System and Application of Rule Patterns for Active Database Design*, infix-Verlag, Germany, 1997.

[17] Shyy, Y.-M., Su, S.Y.W., *Refinement Preservation for Rule Selection in Active Object-Oriented Database Systems*, in Proceedings of the 4th International Workshop on Research Issues in Data Engineering (RIDE '94), Active Database Systems, J. Widom, et al. (eds.), IEEE-CS, Houston, Texas, Feb. 1994.

[18] Wegner, P., Zdonik, S. B., *Inheritance as an Incremental Modification Mechanism or What Like Is and Isn't Like,* in Proc. of the 2nd European Conf. on Object-Oriented Programming (ECOOP '88), S. Gjessing, et al. (eds.), Springer LNCS 322, Oslo, Norway, Aug. 1988.

Towards a Semantic Event Service for Distributed Active Database Applications

C. Collet, G. Vargas-Solar*, and H. Grazziotin-Ribeiro **
{Christine.Collet, Genoveva.Vargas, Helena.Ribeiro}@imag.fr

IMAG-LSR, University of Grenoble, BP 72 38402 Saint-Martin d'Hères, France.

Abstract. This paper proposes an approach to building event services for active database applications. It introduces dimensions to characterize distributed event definition, detection, production and notification. The core of our approach is a parametric event service called QUETZAL that has three interfaces, each of them implementing the given dimensions as parameters. Therefore, different event (detection) models may be defined simply by giving values to these parameters. Such an approach provides flexible definition, detection, production and notification of events according to application needs. Since our service is based on a consumer-producer principle, it can be combined with any producer and consumer, facilitating in this way communication and collaboration between distributed components such as classical applications, database transactions, primitive event detectors or event notification tools.

1 Introduction

The major idea in active databases is to add a reactive mechanism as ECA rules. An ECA rule is an association of an Event type, a Condition and an Action. Events types describe situations that may occur and that have to be monitored for processing a rule. They are generated internally or externally with respect to the system and detected by it. Conditions are generally predicates on database states expressed with a query language. Actions can be any sequence of operations on or outside the database. Generally speaking, rule processing is handled in a specific environment defined as an active database application including transactions.

Many active database systems models or prototypes have been proposed [WC96,Pat98]. As discussed in [CC98] it is not reasonable to provide active functionalities able to fulfill the requirements of every application. Therefore, as suggested in [GKBF98] the unbundling of active mechanisms from the DBMS should be extended to the unbundling of the active capabilities. Such an approach provides more flexibility for developing applications needing active functionality and not necessary database functionality.

* Supported by the CONACyT of the Mexican Government.
** Supported by the CAPES of the Brazilian Government.

From the wide variety of proposals for event detection and management in database systems [MZ95,Cha97,Pat98] one may find dimensions characterizing the event specification and the event detection or production processes [WC96,Dia95,DGG95,Pat98]. However distribution has not been widely introduced in active database environments and particularly in event management [Lia97]. Even if rules may reference data at multiple sites, or that each site may process rules, assumptions are made on events handling. Usually, only local visibility is achieved; global visibility may be achieved either through the existence of a central event manager to which any event of the system is communicated or by the cooperation of local event managers [Cha97].

To characterize such events, one may answer questions such as: What is an event? still a point in time ... with which global time? How to extend the event specification language for considering the "distribution" dimension? How to compose events coming from several distributed sources? How to notify them to several sources? How to define the order between events and to manage the delay in receiving events? This paper tries to give answers to these questions.

An event is a message containing a certain type of information, which is valid, depending on the events producer, during a certain period of time and within a specific context. Events allow different kinds of applications to interact with each other. Events are especially characterized by their producers and the conditions of their production. In this context, events do not simply represent instantaneous, low level operations, they become messages containing information meaningful for a group of producers and consumers.

Figure 1 illustrates event processing. It includes a definition phase during which events concerning a given application are described using an expression (type). The detection and production processes monitor the application execution to detect and recognize events. These processes detect and produce events previously described. Usually, events are explicitly signaled or detected by a monitoring (detection) mechanism. Since we place our approach within a flexible and general context, (adaptable to transactional and non transactional applications) independent from the Database Management System (DBMS) control, we consider a third operation: *notification*. It allows the notification of events under different modes and communication protocols depending on the information needs of event consumers.

For the time being, only few works have appeared proposing a framework allowing the integration and the interaction of distributed active (database) applications through an anonymous event passing communication. In this paper we introduce an event model that specifies dimensions characterizing how distributed events are defined, how they are detected and produced and also how they are notified. Our model extends related concepts defined in active database management systems for a distributed and heterogeneous context. In such a context autonomous systems exchange information to accomplish cooperative tasks. Then we present the parametric event service QUETZAL, that implements our event model. The parametric approach introduces some semantics allowing the service to be configured for adopting different event models.

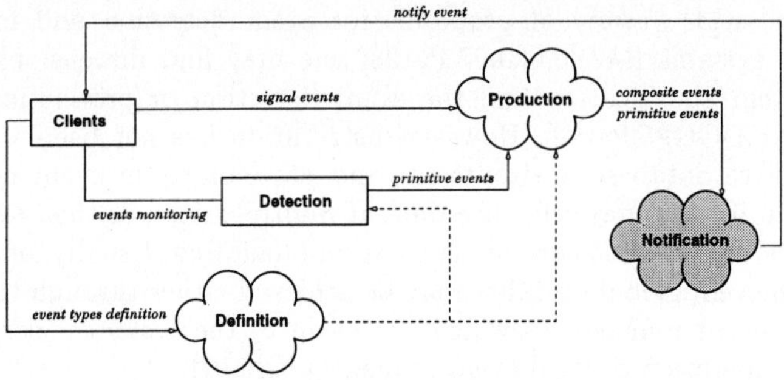

Fig. 1. Event Processing Phases

The remainder of this paper is organized as follows. We introduce dimensions of the sub-models composing our event model. The event definition model specifies basic concepts related to events in a distributed environment (Section 2). The detection and production model establishes the way events are detected and communicated by producers (Section 3). The notification model describes the communication protocols established by event consumers (Section 4). Section 5 presents the event service QUETZAL and shows how it is used to introduce distribution and the unbundling process into an existing active system. Section 6 compares our proposal with other existing works. Finally, Section 7 concludes this paper and introduces some future research directions.

2 Event Definition

Generally speaking event types are expressions for describing events and therefore events are instances of an event type. Time cannot be dissociated from events since an event occurs at a point in time. The approach to represent a point in time, is to define a reference moment and a unit (i.e. second, minute, hour, etc.). Active databases event models use a discrete representation: the Gregorian calendar and a discrete time domain isomorphic to this calendar. Each point of this domain is represented as a non-negative integer along an axis having 0 as the origin and ∞ (the indefinite time point) as the end. In distributed environments time and events acquire another dimension due to the lack of a global view of the system. Thus, events in distributed contexts are associated to global time that should be computed using methods such as those proposed in [Sch96,LMS85]. For global time we also adopt a discrete representation.

Table 1 describes dimensions associated to event definition. Events characterization and semantics depend largely on their source (dimension 1). Events may come from *internal* sources, in this case they represent operations inherent to their producer (e.g. data manipulation, transaction operations); from *abstract* sources such as the user (e.g. the mouse) or a program (e.g. exception raising); and from *external* sources such as the operating system (e.g. the clock).

Table 1. Dimensions of event definition

	Dimension	Value
1	event source	*internal* *abstract* *external*
2	event type	*primitive* *composite*
3	validity time interval	*explicit* *implicit*
4	event instance	*instantaneous* *duration-based*
5	occurrence time	*implicit* *computed*
6	event context	*yes* *no*

An event type is an expression describing a class of significant occurrences of interest (events) produced over a validity time interval [Col98], also called a monitoring interval (dimensions 2). An expression may describe *primitive* or *composite* events. Primitive event types characterize basic operations concerning data, the environment, operations execution, an application, etc. Composite event types characterize events produced by applying operators such as sequence, conjunction, disjunction, negation, parallel, etc. to other events. Composite event type expressions indicate the operators that are used and we assume some (classical) semantics for these operators. Our future work will consider the definition of semantics for each operator through specific dimensions within dimension 2.

The validity time interval defines the interval during which instances of the actual type (i.e. events) may be recognized (dimension 3). It is denoted by [s_v, e_v] where s_v and e_v correspond respectively to the starting point in time for event recognition and the ending point for event recognition. This interval can also be specified as a period (i.e., every two seconds). The validity time interval can be defined either *explicitly* at event type definition or *implicitly*, using the points of time associated with the unit of production of events (see Section 3).

Events, i.e. instances of an event type, are atomic (they completely occur or not) and may be *instantaneous* or *duration-based* (dimension 4). Let us consider the update of the attribute salary of Employee instances, denoted by UPDATE(Employee->salary, integer). When processing such an operation for an Employee instance e, i.e update(e->salary, s), the operation might be associated with an interval [t_0, t_1] that corresponds to the beginning and the end of the operation. If we consider that the validity time interval includes [t_0, t_1] then three event types may be defined depending on the granularity of significant situations we look for. We may characterize the whole update operation process (methods, programs, etc.), i.e a *duration-based event*, or the fact that the processing of an update operation is requested (finished), i.e. an *instantaneous event.*

As we already said an event is associated with a point in global time called the occurrence time (dimension 5). This point in time belongs to the validity interval of the corresponding event type. For example, (before, UPDATE(e->salary,s), t_i) is an instance of the type (before, UPDATE(Employee->salary,integer), [t_0, t_1])); [t_0, t_1] defines the interval of update processing and $t_i \in [t_0, t_1]$ is the point in time when the processing of the update starts. Due to the characteristics of time in distributed environments, the occurrence time has to be *computed.*

The above event example is an *instantaneous* event as it represents the fact that an update of the salary of Employee e is requested and does not represent the corresponding update process. Note that the occurrence time of a composite event corresponds to the moment in which it is produced. The occurrence time of a composite event e_c is by definition the occurrence time of the last primitive event that makes e_c happen. It depends on the *production mode* and on events production order. Next section gives more details on these aspects. Further, we consider that the occurrence time of *duration-based events* corresponds to the interval [s_v, e_v].

When an event is detected or produced, runtime information is collected: event type, occurrence time and actual parameters values. This information defines the event context (dimension 6).

3 Event Detection and Production

In general, to characterize event detection and production it is necessary to state - in which conditions events are produced, - how often they have to be detected, - under which protocol they are detected and produced, - what kind of operations they represent, and - for how long these events are representative. Table 2 shows the dimensions associated with event detection and production.

Events are produced under a unit of production, that corresponds to a source (application) granularity (dimension 7). Possible granularities are *session, transaction, basic operation,* and *composed operation* (program). The session corresponds to the complete execution of an application. For an object system, an operation can be a method call that can be composed by basic operations (objects creation, attributes updates, etc.). Events can be produced within ACID centralized transactions or within distributed or non classical transactions [HGM87,Mos85]. In most active systems, the validity time interval (dimension 3) is the same as the one associated with the unit of production.

Primitive events are all "detected", they are not subsumed to production modes. The production mode of events was introduced by Snoop [Cha97] under the name of parameter context (dimension 8). Different production modes depict possible compositions of primitive events with different semantics, according to application needs (dimension 8). There are four modes: *recent, chronicle, continuous, cumulative* which are largely treated in [Cha97].

Table 2. Dimensions of events detection and production

	Dimension	Value
7	unit of production	*session* *local transaction* *global transaction* *program* *basic operation*
8	production mode	*continuous* *recent* *chronological* *cumulative* *none*
9	event detection protocol	*pull* *push*
10	event detection mode	*synchronous* *asynchronous*

Combining events in different production modes is directly concerned with event ordering and consequently with global time. This can be achieved assuming that local clocks can be synchronized with a π precision. Events can then be totally ordered, provided that the granularity g of the global time-base is greater than π [Sch96].

To achieve detection it is necessary to establish interaction protocols depending on producers characteristics (dimensions 9 and 10). Events are detected under *pull* and *push* communication protocols, with a *synchronous* or an *asynchronous* event detection mode. The synchronous (asynchronous) mode implies that producer executions are (not) interrupted by the detection mechanism.

4 Event Notification

Basically, notification is characterized by notification modes, used to deliver and store event instances. Table 3 presents the dimensions associated to these operations.

Event notification takes place with respect to *event visibility* (dimension 11). The visibility of event types (also called event granularity) specifies the scope of events consumption. Events can be consumed in an *unrestricted* way: consumers are notified about all instances of an event type (e.g. every instance of UPDATE(Employee->salary, integer)). Consumers may impose restrictions over the notification of the instances of a specific event type (*restricted*) (e.g., all instances of UPDATE(Employee -> salary, integer) produced 1 hour before my login). This is achieved through filters that may be specified as masks such as in [Ron97]. These filters are conditions including predicates and temporal expressions that events should verify.

Table 3. Dimensions of events notification

	Dimension	Value
11	event visibility	*restricted* *unrestricted*
12	notification time	*transaction commit* *detection with confirmation* *detection with(out) confirmation* *derived*
13	persistence scope	*validity time interval* *unit of production* *until consumed* *until next detected* *no*
14	notification protocol	*pull* *push*
15	notification mode	*synchronous* *asynchronous*

The *notification time* dimension characterizes the time when events can be notified to consumers. Event notification can take place at:

- *transaction commit:* events of type E produced within a transaction T are notified at commit time (validated events). In this case events may be characterized with the following composite event type (sequence): ((begin_transaction T_1, E , commit_transaction T_2) where $T_1 = T_2$).
- *detection without confirmation*: events are notified as soon as they are detected. If events are produced within a transaction they are notified even though the transaction has not yet committed.
- *detection with confirmation*: events are notified as soon as they are detected and then they are validated by a confirmation event (i.e. a transaction_commit event from the producing transaction).
- *derived*: notification mode for composite events depends on the nature of the producing event. It is the last component that determines its production and its notification mode.

Note that the difference between *transaction commit* notification mode is that it only considers the notification of events produced within a transactional context i.e intra-transactional events, conversely *detection with confirmation* considers that events may be confirmed by events comming from different contexts i.e inter-transactional, or inter-application case. Notification semantics at *transaction commit* time relies upon the transaction model or on the protocol adopted. Distributed operations delimited by transactions can be achieved by a two (three) phase commit protocol. In this case, notification at *transaction commit* is done after the second phase. Under other transaction models [HGM87,Mos85] this notification mode corresponds to the end of a component transaction (SAGA).

Events can be either persistent or fugitive. Events may persist for a given period of time (persistence scope) after their detection/production and notification or they may "disappear" after notification. The persistence scope may encompass the *unit of production*, the *validity time interval*, the period of time comprised from detection *until consumption*, or until a newer instance does not arrive. In the latter case, newer instances substitute older ones.

Finally, events are notified under the *pull* and the *push* communication protocols, with a *synchronous* or an *asynchronous* event notification mode.

5 Toward QUETZAL

This section presents the main characteristics of our semantic event service QUETZAL. It follows a producer-consumer principle, where producers and consumers exchange events anonymously, under the CORBA *pull* and *push* communication protocols [OMG97]. Producers and consumers can be processes, objects, transactions, applications, operating systems. With such an approach, our service achieves the homogeneous conciliation and integration of non transactional contexts with transactional ones; and it may fulfill different information needs.

It implements models described in previous sections by turning dimensions into parameters. Different event management models may be specified by giving a *value* to some *parameters*. Parameter domains have been defined as subsets of values for the corresponding dimensions because we only consider those values that cannot be expressed in terms of others. Our service provides an event type definition language; as well as interfaces for specifying event management models and allowing subscriptions of clients (producers and consumers) to predefined event types. In this way, it allows flexible and parametric definition, detection, production and notification of events according to application needs.

Figure 2 shows how the QUETZAL introduces distribution and participates in the unbundling process of the Native Active Object System (NAOS)[Col98]. It replaces the Event Manager and allows the definition and execution of distributed active rules. Rules may be triggered by inter-transaction and inter-applicative events. Also, the event service introduces the interaction of (non) O_2 applications running on different (same) O_2 server.

The NAOS event type definition [CC96] is supported by the event definition language of QUETZAL. Further, the NAOS event detection process is based on two principles: *i)* as primitive event detection must be efficient and fine-grained, it is therefore placed inside the database it is supposed to monitor *ii)* detection is based on a subscription mechanism; only events for which an event type subscription has been submitted are signaled. Therefore, events are detected in an *asynchronous* mode. Those events concerning DBMS and transaction operations, and time are detected using the *pull* communication protocol via the event detector (*i*). On the other hand, *abstract* events have to be signaled by their producers under the *push* protocol.

NAOS introduces detection contexts that allow computation of validity intervals [CC96]. The intervals are not given explicitly and depend on the unit of

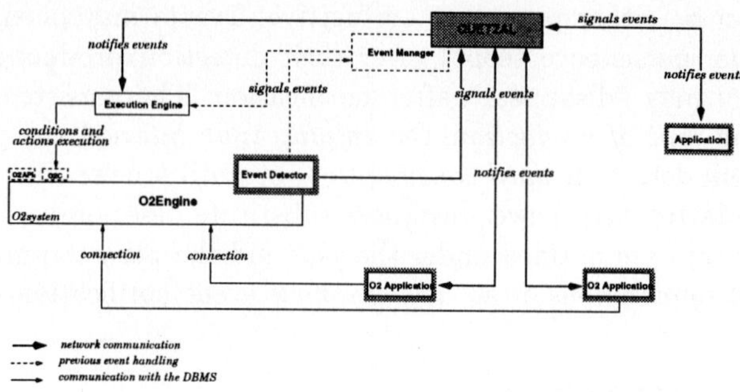

Fig. 2. Unbundling NAOS

production of events. This unit is the (triggering) *transaction*, except for temporal and user events for which it is a *session*. Futher, composite event detection depends on semantics of operators and on production modes. NAOS adopts a *continuous* production mode.

Distributed active rules consume events coming from different transactions and applications consume events coming from other applications. For this reason, includes *global transaction* and program values. This allows the detection of inter-transaction events as well as events produced during programs execution. The *unrestricted* visibility allows the construction of inter-transaction events, as well as the consumption of events coming from different transactions (by active rules) and the notification of events coming from different applications.

Distribution adds the notion of information reliability to events consumption (by active rules). How are we sure that an event consumed by a rule was produced by a transaction that finally commits? Depending on performance and information needs, events can be notified at *detection time with(out) confirmation* or at *transaction commit. Internal* events are notified either at commit transaction time or at detection time with validation. In this way, we ensure data consistency after the execution of distributed active rules. User and applicative events are notified at detection time without validation because they are not directly related to data consistency.

Due to performance needs (of active rules execution), events are notified under the *push* communication protocol. Event notification supports both *synchronous* or *asynchronous* notification modes in order to fulfill rules execution modes (e.g. for immediate rules executed in the same transaction notification is synchronous; for differed ones notification may be asynchronous).

6 Related Work

Even though events manipulation is largely extended across different domains, the event service concept has come up recently. Event services intend to answer to information exchange needs present in cooperating systems, with autonomy and generality. The range of approaches is wide, it goes from simple routing of low level signals to message delivering, respecting different communication protocols and messages processing. We do not intend to make an exhaustive list of relevant approaches, concepts and services. We focus our attention on two types of approaches : those that intend to open the scope of active functionalities to non database applications and those that are oriented towards the adding of distribution to active DBMS.

In [GKBF98] functional components of active DBMS are broken up into a number of autonomous cooperative services. They define an event service and a rule service that cooperate establishing a policy of interaction. Selected individually and configured independently, services enable the use of active functionalities in different environments. The event service records events, maintains a (persistent) event history and detects composite events. The C^{2}offein [KKB$^+$97] proposes a widely configurable service set for active functionality in CORBA-based heterogeneous, distributed systems. The system is configurable with respect to services types and features, services interaction protocols, distribution parameters, etc. The FRAMBOISE project [FGD97] proposes a construction system for the development of ECA-services, that are decoupled from a particular DBMS.

TriGS Active Database System (Trigger system for GemStone) [KRR98] supports composite event detection. Composite events are produced independently of the origin of its components. Events that occur within an application transaction are immediately signaled, independently of a proper termination of the producing transaction. [Lia97,Cha97] propose and implement a Global Event Detector for Sentinel. This system detects and manages events across applications. It communicates with local event detectors through RPC and socket-based communication to detect global events. The OMG event services [OMG97] specification defines an asynchronous communication with multiple event suppliers and consumers under the *pull* and the *push* communication models. Multiple interaction of consumers and suppliers is achieved using an event channel. Sophisticated event channel implementation is needed to provide a kind of event router or additional event semantics.

A general analysis shows that existing works may be classified into two groups. The first group focuses on unbundling active capabilities into extensible services. The second group offers concepts and mechanisms for distributed active databases. Our approach tries to integrate both aspects. It offers event management for different environments and frameworks and at the same time it introduces distribution into active database systems.

7 Conclusions and Future Work

We presented here an approach to building a flexible and semantic event service for distributed and heterogeneous systems. We first defined our event model with several dimensions that characterize event definition, detection, production and notification. This model extends event concepts used in active databases in three ways: (i) it handles different event management semantics, (ii) it considers the distribution dimension and, (iii) it opens the event model scope towards domains such as the integration of cooperative applications, interaction of heterogeneous applications, data warehousing, etc.

Then, we introduced our parametric event service named QUETZAL a powerful event broker suited for adopting different event models. The service offers different interfaces, each of them proposing parameters coming from the dimensions of our model. Event service interfaces are concerned with event specification, detection, production and notification processes. Event management for some producers and consumers can be specified simply by choosing a value for each proposed parameters among a set of already defined values. The interaction between clients and the event service is achieved via a subscription interface. We conducted an experimentation with the NAOS prototype. We specified and implemented its event manager using our event service approach. Furthermore, we showed in which way the event service introduces the distribution dimension into NAOS.

In conclusion, our main contribution is the definition of a general event service that encompasses event characterization and management in various contexts – i.e. (non) transactional, centralized, distributed, etc. Further research directions include pursuing the implementation of our event service and extend this service in order that it can cooperate with a rule execution service [CRVS98] for the processing of distributed active rules and also with other kind of tools that necessitate event monitoring. We are also interested in defining an algebra for distributed events. Another important research direction is to prove that our model is consistent – i.e., that it is defined completely, with no ambiguities nor contradictions – by formally defining it. Then, we think that it will be easier (using such a formal model) to identify several levels of event services depending on the characterization of application needs.

Acknowledgements Thanks to M. ADIBA and N. HENRY for their careful reading. Thanks also to P. HABRAKEN, T. COUPAYE and C. RONCANCIO for useful discussions about our work.

References

[CC96] C. Collet and T. Coupaye. Primitive and Composite Events in NAOS. In *Actes des 12ièmes Journées Bases de Données Avancées*, Cassis - France, September 1996.

[CC98] C. Coupaye and C. Collet. Semantics Based Implementation of Flexible Execution Models for Active Database Systems. In *les actes des 14ièmes Journées Bases de Données Avancées*, Hammamet- Tunisie, october 1998.

[Cha97] S. Chakravarthy. Sentinel : An Object-Oriented DBMS with Event-Based Rules. In *Proc. of the SIGMOD*, AZ, USA, 1997. ACM.

[Col98] C. Collet. NAOS. In Norman W. Paton, editor, *Active Rules for Databases*. Springer Verlag, 1998. to be published.

[CRVS98] C. Collet, H. Ribeiro, and G. Vargas-Solar. Towards a Flexible Execution Model for Distributed Active Rules. In preparation, March 1998.

[DGG95] K. R. Dittrich, S. Gatziu, and A. Geppert. The Active Database Management System Manifesto: A Rulebase of ADBMS Features. In T. Sellis, editor, *Proc. of the 2nd Int. Workshop on Rules in Database Systems, RIDS'95 Lecture Notes in Computer Science 985*, pages 3–17. Springer Verlag, Athens, Greece, September 1995.

[Dia95] O. Diaz. Dimensions of active database systems. In *Actes des 11èmes Journées Bases de Données Avancées*, pages 3–22, Nancy, France, septembre 1995.

[FGD97] H. Frithschi, S. Gatziu, and K.R. Dittrich. Framboise – an approach to construct active database mechanisms. Technical Report 97.04, Department of Computer Science, University of Zurich, Zurich, April 1997.

[GKBF98] S. Gatziu, A. Koschel, G. Bültzingsloewen, and H. Fritschi. Unbundling Active Functionality. *ACM SIGMOD RECORD*, March 1998.

[HGM87] K. Salem H. García-Molina. Sagas. In *Proc. of the SIGMOD International Conference on Management of Data*, pages 249–259, May 1987.

[KKB+97] A. Koschel, R. Kramer, G. Bültzingslöwen, T. Bleibel, P. Krumlinde, S. Schmuck, and C. Wein. Configuration Active Functionality for CORBA. In *Proc. of the ECOOP97 Workshop*, Jyväskulä, Finnland, June 1997.

[KRR98] G. Kappel, S. Rausch-Schott, and W. Retschitzegger. A Tour on the TriGS Active Database System - Architecture and Implementation. Technical report, Johannes Kepler Univ. of Linz, Austria, 1998.

[Lia97] H. Liao. Global events in Sentinel : Design and Implementation of a global event detector. Master's thesis, ECE University of Florida, Gainsville, USA, March 1997.

[LMS85] Lamport L. and P.M Melliar-Smith. Synchronizing Clocks in the Presence of Faults. *Journal of the ACM*, 32(1):52–78, 1985.

[Mos85] J.E.B. Moss. *Nested Transaction. An Approach to Reliable Distributed Computing.* MIT Press, Cambridge, MA, 1985.

[MZ95] I. Motakis and C. Zaniolo. Composite Temporal Events in Active Database Rules: A Logic-Oriented Approach. In *DOOD'95*, Singapore, December 1995.

[OMG97] OMG, editor. *The Common Object Request Broker Architecture and Specification.* 1997. Object Management Group.

[Pat98] N. W. Paton. *Active Rules for Databases.* Springer Verlag, 1998. to be published.

[Ron97] C.L. Roncancio. Toward duration-based, constrained and dynamic event types. In *"Workshop on Active, Real-Time and Temporal Databases (ARDBT'97)"*, Como, Italy, September 1997.

[Sch96] S. Schwiderski. *Monitoring the behavior of Distributed Systems.* PhD thesis, University of Cambridge, April 1996.

[WC96] J. Widom and S. Ceri. *Active Database systems - Triggers and Rules for Advanced Database Processing.* Morgan Kaufmann Publishers, San Francisco, California, 1996.

Involving Fuzzy Concepts in Active Mobile Databases*

Yücel Saygın, Özgür Ulusoy

Department of Computer Engineering and Information Science,
Bilkent University, Ankara 06533, TURKEY

Abstract. Current needs of industry required the development of advanced database models like mobile databases, active databases, and fuzzy databases. Fuzzy concepts are adapted to the field of databases in order to deal with ambiguous, uncertain data. Fuzziness comes into picture in mobile databases especially with moving objects. Incorporating fuzziness into rules would improve the effectiveness of active databases. Rules can be utilized in mobile databases to form a more powerful system, namely an active mobile database. In this paper we investigate the ways in which the concepts developed for fuzzy systems can be integrated to active mobile databases.

Key words: Active databases, mobile databases, rule execution, fuzzy databases, fuzzy triggers, fuzzy rule execution.

1 Introduction

Current needs of industry and business necessitated the development of advanced database models which are used to store and retrieve data in complex systems. Three of those advanced databases are of particular interest to us, namely mobile databases, active databases, and fuzzy databases. In this paper we propose an active mobile database platform and investigate the ways in which the concepts developed for fuzzy systems can be adapted to this platform. As a base for our investigation, the concepts of mobile, active and fuzzy databases are introduced in the following paragraphs, together with a description of the route which we take to achieve the proposed work.

Fuzzy concepts are incorporated to the field of databases in order to support queries closer to the natural language and to model data which is inherently fuzzy. An *active database management system (ADBMS)* allows users to specify actions to be executed when specific events are signaled [Day88]. In order for a conventional database management system to react to certain events, it should be incorporated with *rules*. Mobile database research aims to provide efficient access to data on both stationary data servers and mobile computers.

* This research is supported by the Research Council of Turkey (TÜBİTAK) under grant number EEEAG-246 and the NATO Collaborative Research Grant CRG 960648.

An *active mobile database* can be designed by incorporation of rules into a mobile database environment. We use in this paper an active mobile database platform to explain how fuzzy features can be integrated to active and mobile database systems. We adopt a battlefield environment to illustrate how the proposed approaches can be made use of in real applications. The primary contribution of our work is the incorporation of fuzziness into rule execution via fuzzy coupling modes and scenarios. We also describe how fuzzy primitive events can be combined to form fuzzy composite events, and how fuzzy rules and other fuzzy concepts can be utilized in MDBSs.

In the next section, an introduction to *fuzzy databases* is provided. Section 3 presents a mobile database system model that is supported with rules and fuzzy queries. In Section 4, a description of the current work on fuzzy triggers is provided together with our contributions. Finally in Section 5, conclusions and future work are discussed.

2 Fuzzy Databases

Uncertain nature of queries and real-life data has necessitated the development of *fuzzy databases.* Fuzzy database theory is based on the concepts of *fuzzy sets* and *fuzzy logic* which we discuss in the following.

The theory of fuzzy sets was introduced by Zadeh [Zad65]. For a crisp set (an ordinary set that we are familiar with) S, which is a subset of the universal set U, for any element $e \in U$, either $e \in S$ or $e \notin S$ where for a fuzzy set there is a degree of membership in the range $[0,1]$ for each element belonging the the universal set. Crisp set theory is a special case of the fuzzy set theory where the membership degrees of any element belonging to the universal set is either 0 or 1. A fuzzy set is characterized by its membership function. This membership function, gives us the degree of membership of each element in the universal set to the fuzzy set. Membership function of a fuzzy set F on the universal set U is generally denoted by μ_F and maps each element $x \in U$ to a real number in the range $[0,1]$, i.e.,

$$\mu_F(x) : U \rightarrow [0,1].$$

The fuzzy set theory is best understood with real life examples. Assume that we have a universal set U for all the ages a human being can have. We can define a fuzzy set *young* denoted by Y on U, and assign a membership function μ_Y to Y. A sample membership function can be defined as in Figure 1.

Similarly, fuzzy logic is an extension of crisp logic and based on fuzzy theory. Using fuzzy logic, we can reason about the degree of truth of imprecise propositions.

Fuzzy database models generally adopt the relational database model as their base since it has a well established theoretical framework. One approach by Buckles and Petry incorporates fuzziness into relational database model by replacing the ordinary equivalence relation by the notion of similarity [BP82]. Similarity relationships are constructed to allow the comparison of linguistic terms like

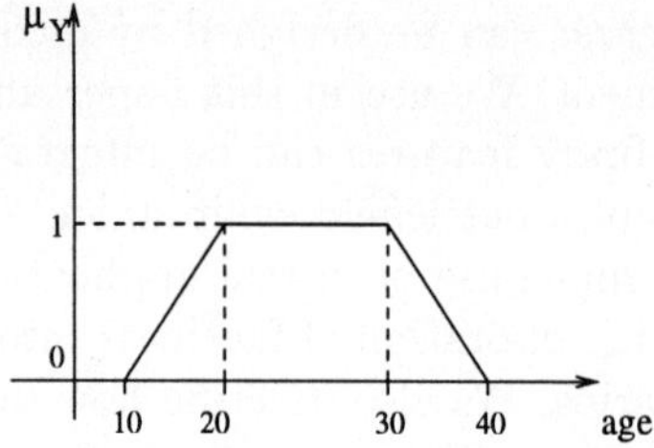

Fig. 1. Membership function of the fuzzy set young.

young, old, middle-aged in a particular domain. Similarity thresholds are explicitly defined in the queries in order to retrieve tuples in a certain similarity range.

3 Mobile and Active Databases in a Common Platform

There is a wide spectrum of applications of active mobile database management systems (AMDBMSs) from military to health and insurance. One such application in military is the management and control of vehicles in a battlefield environment [MB97], [MBM96]. In health, an active mobile computing system can be designed to reach the patients' previous records in the hospital from the moving ambulances [MB96].

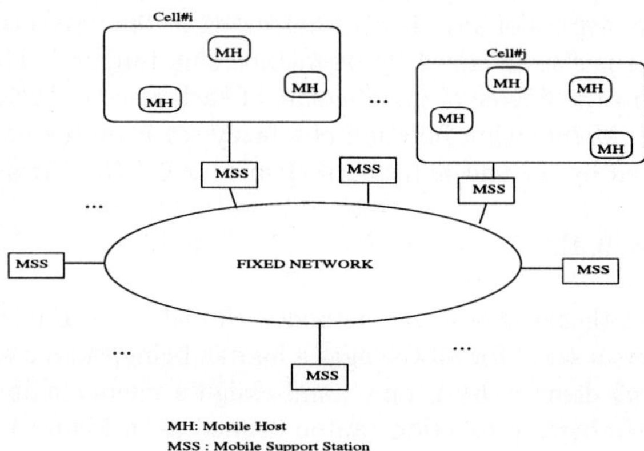

Fig. 2. A general architecture of a mobile computing system

A typical architecture for mobile computing systems which is inspired from [IB94] is depicted in Figure 2. In this architecture, there is a fixed network of Mobile Support Stations (MSSs). Mobile Hosts (MHs) are the computers which are portable and capable of mobile communication. Each MH is associated with a

MSS and MHs are connected to MSSs via wireless links. A MSS is generally fixed and it provides MHs inside a prespecified area called a cell with a wireless interface.

As an example application, a battlefield environment can be coordinated using a system based on the architecture provided in Figure 2 where the vehicles on land and aircrafts are moving objects which are also capable of issuing queries, i.e., they are MHs. In the fixed network there is a database management system supported with rules like:

- **event:** obj_1 is very close to obj_2
  condition: obj_1 belongs to enemy and obj_2 belongs to the alliances
  action: fire an alarm and inform obj_2
- **event:** send missile
  condition: there are objects close to the target that belong to the alliances
  action: move away those objects

An obvious property of the rules listed above is that they are close to natural language, and therefore very easy to write for the experts of war scenarios who are not much familiar with data management issues. These rules involve fuzzy queries on the database and some of them have fuzzy events.

4 Fuzzy Rules in Active Databases

Although incorporating fuzziness to active databases introduces much flexibility, not much attention has been paid so far to this issue. To the best of our knowledge, only a research group in VTT (Finland) has worked on fuzzy triggers [BW96], [BW97], [BKPW97]. In [BKPW97], a Condition-Action(CA) fuzzy trigger is proposed which means that fuzziness is introduced to the CA part of an ECA rule. In a later work [BW97], the concept of CA trigger is extended to a fuzzy ECA rule by introducing the notion of fuzzy events. A CA fuzzy trigger consists of a fuzzy predicate (i.e., a predicate that has linguistic hedges) on the database as its condition, and a fuzzy action where updates are performed on a fuzzy database. A rule with a fuzzy condition and a crisp (i.e., not fuzzy) action is called a C-fuzzy trigger. The C-fuzzy trigger model is based on linguistic hedges. C-fuzzy trigger is a rule which has a fuzzy predicate as its condition. Max-min inference method is applied to the rule set to determine the truth value of the fuzzy predicates. In fuzzy ECA rules, an event may fire a set of rules. Fuzzy events are defined as fuzzy sets and use linguistic hedges like *high, low,* and *strong* [BW97]. Formally a primitive fuzzy event is represented as a tuple $< e_c, e_f >$ where e_c is a crisp event, and e_f is a fuzzy event predicate. When a crisp event is signaled (such as a database update), the current value v produced upon the operation causing the crisp event is fed into the membership function of e_f. The output of the membership function is called the event match factor, and the fuzzy event is signaled only if the event match factor is greater than zero [BW97]. Upon the signaling of the fuzzy event, the corresponding rules are fired and their conditions (which are fuzzy predicates on the database) are checked. The action of a rule may be started to execute depending on the result of condition evaluation.

The methods discussed in [BW97] and [BKPW97] try to incorporate fuzziness into the event and condition of a rule. In this paper, we deal with the rules belonging to particular fuzzy sets, together with the coupling modes and scheduling of rules. The rest of this section is devoted to the detailed discussion of our approach.

4.1 Fuzzy Events

Different events and their categorization together with composite events are explained in [GGD94], [CM91], and [Buc94]. Among these references, the most comprehensive event set and composition semantics are provided in [Buc94]. Primitive events are categorized in [Buc94] as: method execution events, state transition events, temporal events, transaction and flow-control events, and abstract events. Method execution events are raised when the specified methods are executed. State transition events are signaled when the corresponding state changes occur in the database, for example location updates of moving objects. Temporal events are either absolute or relative. An absolute temporal event is something like, "at 13:45", and a relative temporal event is like "5 seconds before the firing of a missile". Transaction and flow-control events are related with the beginning, commit and abort of transactions. Finally, abstract events are defined by user and therefore signaled explicitly by the user.

Events which are important from the point of fuzzy rule execution are state transition events, and temporal events. There is a high level of potential for incorporating fuzzy concepts into those kinds of events.

Temporal events are widely used in many active database systems and can be applied to critical jobs in real time systems. Fuzzy concepts can be incorporated to temporal events by adding fuzzy modifiers to exact time values. For example, instead of the absolute temporal event, "at 13:43", we may have a fuzzy absolute temporal event like, "at about 13:43" which is more flexible. Relative temporal events can also be modified in order to convert them to fuzzy relative temporal events. Calculating the membership degrees of fuzzy temporal events can be done using the membership functions of the fuzzy terms and the concept of fuzzy numbers which is explained in more detail in [KF88]. Membership degree of crisp events is taken as one.

Primitive events can be combined to form composite events. Composition of primitive events can be done with different event constructors, like conjunction, disjunction, closure, sequence, history, and negation [Buc94], [GGD94], [CM91]. Disjunction of two events E_1 and E_2 is raised when one of E_1, or E_2 is raised. Conjunction of two events E_1 and E_2 is raised when both E_1 and E_2 have occurred, regardless of the order of occurrence. Sequence is similar to conjunction but the order of occurrence of the events is important with sequence. Closure constructor is used when multiple occurrences of the same event in a period of time (such as, during the execution of a transaction) is considered together as a composite event. History event constructor is a more restricted case of the closure event constructor where the number of occurrences of the same event is specified. Negation of an event can also be considered as a composite event and it is raised when the negated event has not occurred in a specified period of time. Events composed by multiple event constructors are composite events as well.

Fuzzy composite events can be constructed by combining crisp primitive events listed above and fuzzy primitive events (i.e., fuzzy temporal, fuzzy state change, and fuzzy method execution events). The membership values of fuzzy composite events can be calculated depending on the semantics of the event constructors. In case of the conjunction event constructor, the event with minimum membership degree among the component events is selected, and its membership degree determines the membership degree of the composite event. When disjunction is used as the event constructor, then the maximum membership value among the membership degrees of the component events determines the membership degree of the composite event. In case of negation, the membership degree, μ_n, of the composite event is calculated as,

$$\mu_n = 1 - \mu_e$$

where μ_e is the membership degree of the event being negated.

Computation of the membership degrees of composite events constructed by history and closure is done by using the following formula:

$$\mu_c = \frac{\sum_{i=1}^{i=n} \mu_{e_i}}{n}$$

where μ_c is the membership degree of the composite event, μ_{e_i} is the membership degree of the ith occurrence of event e, and n is the number of occurrences of event e. Here we should note that different occurrences of the same event may result in different membership degrees depending on the crisp parameter of the event. Membership degrees of the composite events formed by the sequence constructor are computed similar to that of the conjunction constructor.

We define the strength of a primitive or fuzzy event as the membership degree of the corresponding event parameter. For example, an event like "obj_1 is close to obj_2" can have different strengths depending on how close obj_1 is to obj_2 in a particular situation. Closer the objects, more strong is the fuzzy event.

4.2 Inter-rule Fuzziness Via Scenarios

There can exist a finite set of events that can be signaled in an active database system. We partition the whole event set E into event groups called scenarios (not necessarily disjoint). The idea of scenarios comes from the need to group rules into sets corresponding to different situations. There can be only one active scenario at a time. Switching among scenarios is performed by rules as well. Consider the battlefield application we discussed in Section 3, where there can be *emergency* situations as well as *normal* situations. An emergency situation corresponds to the events which may have serious effects like a serious damage and should urgently be handled whereas a normal situation corresponds to the events with a low level of importance. Switching from a normal scenario to an emergency scenario is performed by rules which detect emergency situations. Each rule may be subscribed to more then one scenario. If a rule is not subscribed to a scenario, then it is called an *idle rule*. Each scenario behaves like a fuzzy set, i.e., it has a membership function that maps the rules to a real number in the range $[0, 1]$. Events belonging to a scenario are fuzzy events as described in Section 4.1. Event signaling is done by considering the membership degree of the event parameter in the fuzzy event. The fuzzy event structure described in [BW97] is utilized where a primitive event is a tuple, $e :< e_c, e_f >$, consisting of a crisp part e_c which is the crisp parameter coming from the system and a fuzzy part e_f which denotes the fuzzy event set. In order to decide whether a rule r will be fired in response to the signaling of a fuzzy event $e :< e_c, e_f >$, the membership value of r is multiplied by the membership value of e_c in the fuzzy set e_f. The result is compared with a threshold value associated with the rule. If the result is greater than or equal to the threshold value, then the rule is fired. Threshold values of rules can be changed dynamically to tune to particular scenarios.

Assume that in our battlefield application, we have *emergency* and *normal* scenarios which are considered to be fuzzy sets. Each rule belongs to one or two of the scenarios with a membership degree. Consider the following rule:

event: obj_1 is very close to obj_2
condition: obj_1 belongs to enemy and obj_2 belongs to the alliances
action: fire an alarm and inform obj_2

which belongs to the emergency scenario with a membership degree of 0.9. Assume that its event is signaled, and the membership degree of the event parameter (i.e., the distance between the objects) in the fuzzy set *close* is 0.7. If the rule has a threshold value 0.6 for that scenario, then the rule will be fired since $0.9 * 0.7 = 0.63 \geq 0.6$. The threshold parameters and the membership functions for the fuzzy rules can be determined according to the results of a priori simulations.

4.3 Similarity Based Event Detection

Signaling of similar events upon an event detection is something very useful when the cost of missing events is very high in supported applications, like a nuclear reactor control system. Assume that an event such as *update in temperature level* is detected. Events with a high similarity degree, like *update in pressure level* should also be signaled automatically. This way, the risk of events escaping from detection is reduced.

In similarity based event detection, when an event is signaled, other events which are similar to it should also be fired. In order to facilitate this, each scenario has a similarity matrix, where the similarity values of the events in that scenario are stored. Similarity matrices which show the similarities between events in a pairwise manner can be provided by the experts of the particular application; in our application they are military experts. Similarity matrices can be dynamically constructed and updated by the system by examining the event history. Signaling of two events consecutively in a short period of time implies that those events may be similar. As the consecutive signaling of two events is seen more frequently in the event history, the similarity of these events should be increased in the similarity matrix. This way, system learns the similarity values as the event history grows.

An example would be helpful in explaining similarity based event detection. Assume that event e_1 is raised. Other events whose similarity to e_1 is greater than or equal to the similarity threshold for the current scenario also need to be considered. If, for example, the similarity threshold for a scenario s is 0.7, and e_1 is signaled (which belongs to s) and another event e_5 is similar to e_1 with degree 0.8, then event e_5 should also be signaled since $0.8 \geq 0.7$. But the membership value of e_5 is multiplied by its degree of similarity (in this case 0.8) in order to determine which rules are going to be fired as a result of e_5.

Grouping of rules into scenarios restricts the number of rules to be considered when an event is raised, improving the efficiency of rule execution especially in case of emergency when efficient use of resources is very important.

4.4 Fuzzy Coupling Modes

In ECA rules coupling modes between event and condition, and between condition and action determine when the condition should be executed relative to the occurrence of the event, and when the action should be executed relative to the satisfaction of the condition, respectively. There are three basic coupling modes: *immediate*, *deferred*, and *detached* (or *decoupled*) [Day88]. If the condition is specified to be evaluated in *immediate* mode, then it is executed right after the triggering operation that caused the event to be raised. If the action part is specified to be executed in immediate mode then it is executed immediately after the evaluation of the condition. In case the condition is specified to be in *deferred* mode, its evaluation is delayed until the commit point of the transaction, and similarly if the action is in deferred mode relative to the condition, again it is executed right before the transaction commits. Finally, in *detached mode*, condition is evaluated or action is executed in a separate transaction.

Coupling modes is a very important concept for rule execution in active database systems and should also be considered for fuzzy rule execution. In fuzzy ECA rules, the coupling modes between event and condition, and between condition and action can be determined depending on the strength of the event and *credibility* of the condition respectively in case the coupling mode is not specified explicitly. We define the *credibility* of a condition as the truth value of the fuzzy predicate or the combination of the fuzzy predicates. Determination of the truth values of the fuzzy predicates is explained in [KF88]. A high credibility implies immediate or detached coupling mode and a low credibility implies deferred coupling mode in case the coupling modes are not specified explicitly. Each coupling mode should be assigned a credibility threshold which will determine the coupling mode between the event and condition, and condition and action. That way, implicit priorities are assigned to the condition and action depending on the credibility of the corresponding event and condition. Strength of an event signaled due to its similarity to another event is calculated by multiplying its similarity value by its membership value. Assume that, in an emergency scenario, two of the events are $e_1 :< e_{c1}, e_f >$ and $e_2 :< e_{c2}, e_f >$. If the membership value of e_{c1} in e_f is 0.8, the membership value of e_{c2} in e_f is 0.4, threshold values for immediate, detached and deferred coupling modes are, 0.7, 0.5, and 0.0[2], respectively. Assuming that both e_1 and e_2 are signaled, the condition of the rule whose event is e_1 will be evaluated in immediate mode where the condition of the rule whose event is e_2 will be evaluated in deferred mode. The same techniques can be applied to the rules with composite events using the membership calculation methods proposed in Section 4.1.

Assume that we have a rule with the event "obj_1 is very close to obj_2" and no coupling mode was assigned for the rule. If the strength of the event is 0.95 which means that when obj_1 gets very close to obj_2, then the condition should be evaluated immediately, suspending the transaction that signaled the event, or should be evaluated in detached mode. But if the strength of the event is 0.6 then the evaluation of the condition can be deferred to the end of the transaction since obj_1 is not dangerously close to obj_2.

5 Conclusion

In this paper we have discussed the potential of adapting fuzzy database concepts in active database rules and mobile database systems. In doing this, we assumed an active mobile database management system which is a mobile database system supported with active features. In Section 4, we have tried to illustrate how fuzziness can be introduced to different aspects of rule execution. Lots of interesting research issues have been raised mostly on the incorporation of membership degrees for the dynamic determination of coupling modes of rules and priority assignment. Partitioning of the rule set into scenarios has also been discussed as an example of inter-rule fuzziness.

As a future work, a fuzzy database system can be designed for a mobile system application like a battlefield environment together with all possible types of generic queries. The concepts developed for the incorporation of fuzziness into active databases can be applied to a real active database system to measure the effectiveness of the proposed methods. Fuzzy rules may also provide a high degree of flexibility to mobile systems. Design of mobile database system applications incorporating fuzzy rules is an important research issue that requires further work.

[2] A value greater then zero as a credibility threshold for deferred mode means that some rules may not be fired even in deferred mode.

Acknowledgment

The authors wish to thank Dr. Adnan Yazıcı for his help in establishing the fuzzy concept background of this work.

References

[BKPW97] Tarik Bouaziz, Janne Karvonen, Anton Pesonen, and Antoni Wolski. Design and implementation of tempo fuzzy triggers. In *Lecture Notes in Computer Science*, volume 1308, pages 91–100, Toulouse, Fran, September 1997. Springer.

[BP82] B. Buckles and F. Petry. A fuzzy model for relational databases. *International Journal of Fuzzy Sets and Systems*, 7:213–226, 1982.

[Buc94] Alejandro Buchmann. Active Object Systems. In Asuman Dogac, M. Tamer Ozsu, Alex Biliris, and Timos Sellis, editors, *Advances in Object-Oriented Database Systems*, pages 201–224. Springer-Verlag, 1994.

[BW96] Tarik Bouaziz and Antoni Wolski. Incorporating fuzzy inference into database triggers. Technical report, VTT Information Technology, P.O. Box 1201, November 1996.

[BW97] Tarik Bouaziz and Antoni Wolski. Applying fuzzy events to appoxiamte reasoning in active databases. In *Proc. Sixth IEEE International Conference on Fuzzy Systems(FUZZ-IEEE'97)*, Barcelona, Catalonia, Spain, July 1997.

[CM91] S. Chakravarthy and D. Mishra. An event specification language (snoop) for active databases and its detection. Technical report, University of Florida at Gainesville, September 1991.

[Day88] Umeshwar Dayal. Active Database Management Systems. In *Proceedings of the Third International Conference on Data and Knowledge Bases*, pages 150–169, Jerusalem, June 1988.

[GGD94] Stella Gatziu, Andreas Geppert, and Klaus R. Dittrich. The samos active dbms prototype. Technical report, Institut fur Informatik, Universitat Zurich, October 1994.

[IB94] Tomasz Imielinski and B. R. Badrinath. Mobile wireless computing: Challenges in datata management. *Communications of the ACM*, pages 19–27, October 1994.

[KF88] George J. Klir and Tina A. Folger. *Fuzzy Sets, Uncertainty and Information.* Prentice Hall, 1988.

[MB96] S. Morton and O. Bukhres. Mobile transaction recovery in distributed medical databases. In *LASTED Eighth International Conference on Parallel and Distributed Computing and Systems*, 1996.

[MB97] S. Morton and O. Bukhres. Mobile computing in military ambulatory care. In *The 10th IEEE Symposium on Computer-Based Medical Systems(CBMS'97)*, 1997.

[MBM96] S. Morton, O. Bukhres, and M. Mossman. Mobile computing architecture for a battlefield environment. In *International Symposium on Cooperative Database Systems for Advanced Applications*, 1996.

[Zad65] L.A. Zadeh. Fuzzy sets. *Information and Control*, 8:338–353, 1965.

An Analytical Study of Object Identifier Indexing

Kjetil Nørvåg and Kjell Bratbergsengen

Department of Computer and Information Science
Norwegian University of Science and Technology
7034 Trondheim, Norway
{noervaag,kjellb}@idi.ntnu.no

Abstract. To avoid OID index retrieval becoming a bottleneck, efficient buffering strategies are needed to minimize the number of disk accesses. In this paper, we develop analytical cost models which we use to find optimal sizes of the index page buffer and the index entry cache, for different memory sizes, index sizes, and access patterns. Because existing buffer hit estimation models are not applicable for index page buffering in the case of tree based indexes, we have also developed an analytical model for index page buffer performance. The cost gain from using the results in this paper is typically in the order of 200-300%. Thus, the results should be of valuable use in optimizers and tools for configuration and tuning of object-oriented database systems.

1 Introduction

In a large OODB with logical object identifiers (OIDs), the OID index (OIDX) can be quite large, typical in the order of 20% of the size of the database itself [7]. This means that in general, only a small part of the OIDX fits in main memory, and that OIDX retrieval can become a bottleneck if efficient access and buffering strategies are not applied. As the amount of memory increases, most of the frequently accessed part of the index and database will fit in main memory, and in this case, it is the cost of the *infrequently accessed* data and index structures that will represent the disk bottleneck. In this paper, we will study OIDX retrieval analytically, and use the results to reduce the average number of disk accesses needed to retrieve an index entry, in many cases to only a fraction of the original cost.

Traditionally, the most recently used *index pages* have been kept in the buffer pool to make OID mapping efficient, usually managed as an LRU chain. However, if the index entries have low locality, which is often the case for OID indexes, only a small part of the information in the pages in the buffer is really being used. To better utilize the memory, it is possible to keep the most recently used *index entries* in an OID entry cache (OE cache), as is done in the Shore OODB [11]. This can improve performance considerably, but it is important to know how much of the memory should be used for buffering index pages, and how much should be used for caching[1] index entries. This issue has not previously been studied in detail. The OIDX access cost is also an issue that has been underestimated in research literature, the OID mapping cost have not been included into the cost models. As is evident from the results presented later in this paper, this cost can not be ignored, and we will later show that there is much to be gained by optimization.

An OIDX is usually realized as a hash file or a B-tree. Based on simulation results from a comparison study by Eickler et al. [7], and our own study of OID indexing, we believe B-trees or ISAM variants to be the best suited for OID indexing, and therefore we limit this discussion to tree based indexing. It should be noted, however, that much of this paper is still relevant to hash file indexing, the only difference is the index access equations, which are simpler for hash files.

The organization of the rest of the paper is as follows. Sect. 2 gives an overview of related work. In Sect. 3 we describe our OODB buffer model. In Sect. 4 and Sect. 5 we describe our assumptions regarding access pattern and our page access model. In Sect. 6 we present the Bhide, Dan and Dias LRU buffer model (BDD model) [2], which our index buffer model in Sect. 7 is based on. In Sect. 8 we develop an OID retrieval cost model, and in Sect. 9 we study how different memory and index sizes affects the performance. Finally, in Sect. 10, we conclude the paper.

2 Related Work

There have been several approaches to estimate the number of page accesses in the case of non-hierarchical files [3, 13, 14], and studies of the characteristics and validity of these estimates [6, 9]. However, they have not taken access pattern and buffering into account. Accesses have been assumed to be uniform, and an infinite buffer has been assumed, where only the first access to a page is counted.

Recently, other approximations have been developed, the most interesting is the work done by Bhide, Dan and Dias [2], which is an improvement of a model presented by Dan and Towsley [5]. They model requests through an LRU buffer, and the model is valid under the assumption that each request is independent of all previous requests. We will describe this model in more detail in Sect. 6.

Modeling buffer in the case of hierarchical files, where traversing the tree makes the request independency assumption invalid, complicates the situation. One modeling approach is presented in [10], where an I/O model for index scans with LRU buffer is presented. However, this model assumes a complete scan of the index, and is thus a model for uniform access to the index, all entries have the same probability of access (essentially one access during one scan).

Several cost models for OODBs have been developed, for example [1, 8], but they do not include buffer and OID mapping cost.

---

[1] In this paper, we use buffer and buffering when we talk about index *pages* in memory, and cache and caching when we talk about index *entries* in memory. This is established terminology, but apart from the naming, there is no real difference between buffering and caching techniques in this case.

3 Buffer

The buffer in a page server OODB is used for buffering object pages, index pages, and optionally, index entries, as illustrated on Fig. 1. In the rest of this paper, we will denote the index page buffer size as M_{ipages}, the OE cache size as M_{ocache}, and the sum of these as M_i, as illustrated.

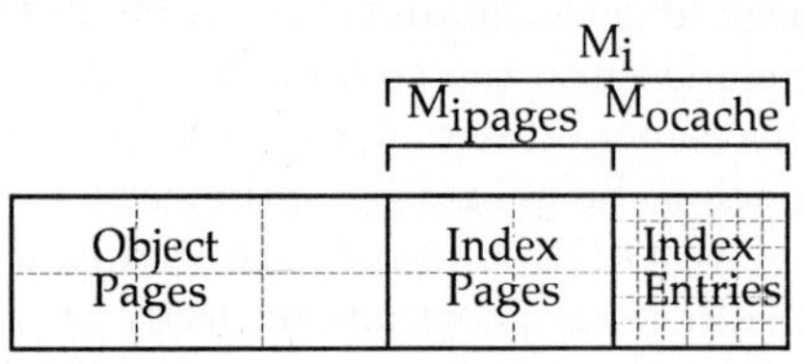

Fig. 1. Buffer in a page server OODB.

In a real implementation, there will usually not be separate buffer areas for object and index pages. All index and data pages resides in a common buffer, managed by some buffer management policy, for example DBMIN [4]. With this buffer management policy, it is possible to put restrictions on how much of the buffer a certain task/transaction can allocate. This is necessary to avoid situations where some operation do something that replaces all the pages in the buffer, e.g. a scan operation. With such a management strategy, it is also possible to control the amount of memory used for indexing, and even without such policies, it is still easy to know the amount of buffer occupied by index pages by simple bookkeeping.

The size of the OE cache can be fixed (set at system startup time), or adaptive. We will later in this paper study how an adaptive OE cache can improve performance over a fixed size OE cache.

4 Index Entry Access Model

We assume accesses to objects in the database system to be random, but skewed (some objects are more often accessed than others). We assume it is possible to (logically) partition the range of OIDs into partitions, where each partition has a certain size and access probability. This is illustrated on the bottom of Fig. 2. We consider a database in a stable condition, with N_{obj} objects (and hence, N_{obj} index entries).

In many analysis and simulations, the 80/20 model is applied, where 80% of the accesses go to 20% of the database. While this is satisfactory for analysis of some problems, it has a major shortcoming when used to estimate the number of distinct objects to be accessed. When applied, it gives a much higher number of distinct accessed objects than in a real system. The reason is that for most applications, inside the hot spot area (20% in this case), there is an even hotter and smaller area, with a much higher access probability. This has to be reflected in the model.

In the simulations and analysis described in this paper, we have employed two different partition sets, each with three partitions (note that this is accesses to OIDs, and not to pages in the index). In both partitioning sets, the 20% hot spot area from the 80/20 model is partitioned. In the first partitioning set, we

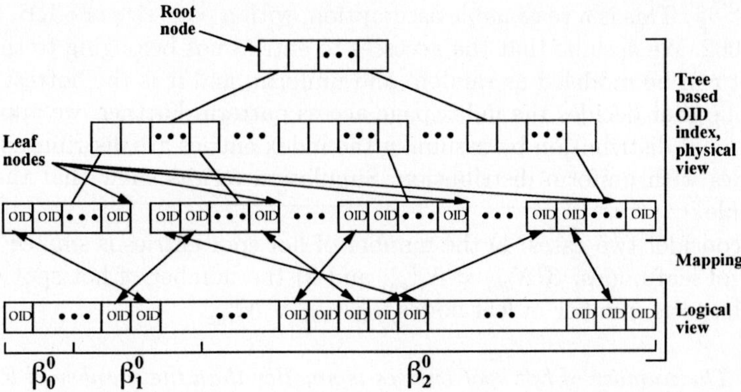

Fig. 2. OID index. The lower part shows the index from a logical view, the upper part is as an index tree, which is how it is realized physically. We have indicated with arrays how the entries are distributed over the leaf nodes.

Partition Size, Set 1	Partition Size, Set 2	Partition Access Probability
$\beta_0^0 = 0.01$	$\beta_0^0 = 0.001$	$\alpha_0^0 = 0.64$
$\beta_1^0 = 0.19$	$\beta_1^0 = 0.199$	$\alpha_1^0 = 0.16$
$\beta_2^0 = 0.80$	$\beta_2^0 = 0.80$	$\alpha_2^0 = 0.20$

Table 1. Partition sizes and partition access probabilities for two partitioning sets used in the study.

have a 1% hot spot area, in the other, a 0.1% hot spot area. The partition sizes and partition access probabilities are summarized in Table 1. β_i^0 denotes the size of partition i, as a fraction of the total database size, and α_i^0 denotes the fraction of accesses done to partition i.

5 Index Page Access Model

As noted, we can assume low locality in index pages. Because of the way OIDs are generated, entries from a certain partition are not clustered in the index. This is illustrated in Fig. 2, where a leaf node containing index entries contains unrelated entries from different partitions. This means that the access pattern for the leaf nodes is different from the access pattern to the database from a logical view.

We use the initial index entry partitioning (the index entry access pattern) as basis for deriving the index page partitioning (the index page access pattern). With a totally unclustered index, the index entries from the different partitions are distributed over the leaf nodes with binomial distribution. To simplify this analysis, we make some approximations and assumptions: The second most hot area has a number of entries sufficiently larger than the number of leaf nodes, i.e., $\beta_1^0 > \frac{1}{F}$. This is a reasonable assumption, with a page size of 8 KB, this gives $\beta_1^0 > 0.002$. We assume that the accesses to entries not belonging to the hottest hot spot can be modeled as random and uniform, and it is the hottest hot spot area alone that decides the index page access pattern. Further, we approximate the binomial distribution by assuming the index entries are distributed over the leaf nodes with uniform distribution. Simulation results show that the error is acceptable.

We consider two cases: 1) the number of hot spot entries is smaller than the number of leaf nodes, $\beta_0^0 N_{obj} < N_{\text{tree}}^0$, and 2) the number of hot spot entries is larger than the number of leaf nodes, $\beta_0^0 N_{obj} > N_{\text{tree}}^0$.

Case 1: The number of hot spot entries is smaller than the number of leaf nodes. When the number of objects in the hot spot area is less than the number of leaf nodes, pages belong to one of two partitions: Those that have an hot spot entry, and those which have not:

$$\beta_{L0} = \beta_0^0 N_{obj} / N_{\text{tree}}^0 \qquad \alpha_{L0} = \alpha_0^0 + \beta_{L0} \sum_{i=1}^{p} \alpha_i^0$$
$$\beta_{L1} = 1 - \beta_{L0} \qquad \alpha_{L1} = 1 - \alpha_{L0}$$

Case 2: The number of hot spot entries is larger than the number of leaf nodes. In the case where there is one or more hot entry in each page, we will with a uniform distribution over the pages have some of the pages with one hot index entry more than the others. Especially in the case where there are few hot index entries in each page, it is important to capture this fact in the model. We now have two partitions, one with the pages containing that extra index entry, and the other with those pages that do not:

$$\beta_{L0} = (\beta_0^0 N_{obj} - \lfloor \beta_0^0 N_{obj} / N_{\text{tree}}^0 \rfloor N_{\text{tree}}^0) / N_{\text{tree}}^0 \qquad \alpha_{L0} = \beta_{L0} N_{\text{tree}}^0 \frac{\lceil \beta_0^0 N_{obj} / N_{\text{tree}}^0 \rceil}{\beta_0^0 N_{obj}}$$
$$\beta_{L1} = 1 - \beta_{L0} \qquad \alpha_{L1} = 1 - \alpha_{L0}$$

With an increasing number of hot spot index entries in each page, the access pattern will get more and more uniform.

6 The BDD LRU Buffer Model

In our analysis, we need to estimate the buffer hit probability in an LRU managed buffer. We do this with the BDD LRU buffer model [2]. We will only briefly explain the model in this section, the derivation and details behind the equations can be found in [2]. A database in the BDD model has of size N data granules (pages or objects), partitioned into p partitions. Each partition contains β_i of the data granules, and α_i of the accesses are done to each partition. The distributions *within* each of the partitions is assumed to be uniform. All accesses are assumed to be independent.

After n accesses to the database, the number of distinct data granules (pages, objects, or index entries) from partition i that have been accessed is:

$$B_i(n) = \beta_i N(1 - (1 - \frac{1}{\beta_i N})^{\alpha_i n})$$

When the number of accesses n is such that the number of distinct data granules accessed is less than the buffer size B, $\sum_{i=1}^{p} B_i(n) \leq B$, the buffer hit probability for partition i is:

$$P_i(n) = 1 - (1 - \frac{1}{\beta_i N})^{\alpha_i n}$$

and the overall buffer hit probability is:

$$P(n) = \sum_{i=1}^{p} \alpha_i P_i(n)$$

The steady state average buffer hit probability can be approximated to the buffer hit ratio when the buffer becomes full, i.e., n is chosen as the largest n that satisfies $\sum_{i=1}^{p} B_i(n) \leq B$, where B in this case is the number of data granules that fits in the buffer:

$$P_{\text{buf}}(B, N) = P(n) \tag{1}$$

7 General Index Buffer Model

In the previous section, we presented the BDD LRU buffer model for independent, non-hierarchical, access. Modeling buffer for hierarchical access is more complicated. Even though searches to the leaf page can be considered to be random and independent, nodes accessed during traversal of the tree are *not* independent. We will in this section present a general index buffer model, where the granularity for access is a page.

In the generic tree used in this model, the size of one index page is S_P, and the size of one index entry S_{ie}. This give a fanout $F = \lfloor S_P/S_{\text{ie}} \rfloor$ and with a database consisting of N_{obj} objects to be indexed, the number of leaf nodes is $N^0_{\text{tree}} \approx \frac{N_{\text{obj}}}{\lfloor S_P/S_{\text{ie}} \rfloor}$.

Our approach to approximate the buffer hit probability, is based on the obvious observation that *each level* in the tree is accessed with the *same probability* (assuming traversal from root to leaf on every search). Thus, with a tree where the index nodes has a fanout F, the number of levels in the tree is $H = 1 + \lceil \log_F N^0_{\text{tree}} \rceil$. We initially treat each level in the tree as one partition, thus, initially we have H partitions. Each of these partitions is of size N^i_{tree}, where N^i_{tree} is the number of index pages on level i in the tree. The access probability is $\frac{1}{H}$ for each partition.

To account for hot spots, we further divide the leaf page partition into p' partitions, each with a fraction of β_{Li} of the leaf nodes, and access probability α_{Li} relative to the other leaf page partitions. Thus, in a "global" view, each of these partitions have size $\beta_{Li} N^0_{\text{tree}}$ and access probability $\frac{\alpha_{Li}}{H}$. In total, we have $p = p' + (H-1)$ partitions. The hot spots at the leaf page level make access to nodes on upper levels non-uniform, but as long as the fanout is sufficiently large, and the hot spot areas are not too narrow, we can treat accesses to nodes on upper levels as uniformly distributed within each level. With the modifications described, a tree of height H, and p' leaf page partitions, the equations for α_i and β_i (access probability and fractional size of each partition) becomes:

$$\alpha_i = \begin{cases} \frac{\alpha_{Li}}{H} & \text{if } i < p' \\ \frac{1}{H} & \text{if } p' \leq i < p \end{cases} \qquad \beta_i = \begin{cases} \frac{\beta_{Li} N^0_{\text{tree}}}{N_{\text{tree}}} & \text{if } i < p' \\ \frac{N^i_{\text{tree}}}{N_{\text{tree}}} & \text{if } p' \leq i < p \end{cases}$$

We denote the number of leaf nodes as N^0_{tree}. The total number of nodes in the tree, N_{tree}, can then be calculated as:

$$N_{\text{tree}} = \sum_{i=0}^{H-1} N^i_{\text{tree}} \quad \text{where} \quad N^i_{tree} = \left\lceil \frac{N^{i-1}_{\text{tree}}}{F} \right\rceil$$

We denote the overall buffer probability, by using the BDD buffer hit probability equation (Equation (1)) with α_i and β_i as defined above as $P_{\text{buf\_ipage}}(B, N_{\text{tree}})$ where $B = \lfloor \frac{M_{\text{ipages}}}{S_P} \rfloor$ is the buffer size, and N_{tree} is the total number of index pages in the tree.

To validate the analytical model, we have compared it with simulation results. The simulations have been performed with different index sizes, buffer sizes, index page fanouts, and access patterns. Typical deviation between model and simulations is much smaller than 1%. More details about the validation results can be found in [12].

8 An OID Retrieval Cost Model

Our OID retrieval cost model is based on the number of disk page accesses, since this is the most significant cost factor and a common bottleneck. Disk I/O is only necessary if the requested information can not be found in memory. The model includes an index page buffer, and an OE cache. It is important to note that in the general case, with an ordinary data index, an OE cache can in some situations have a very costly side effect. An increase in the OE cache size reduces the number of complete pages in the buffer, something that can make lots of costly index page installation reads necessary when the entries in the index is to be updated. In an OIDX, this issue is not so important. Index entry modification does not happen often, usually only because of object migration or schema change. A tree based OIDX is essentially an append-only structure, the only potentially troublesome operation is deletion of objects, but index modifications because of this can be done in batch and/or as a background activity.

8.1 OID Entry Cache

A certain amount of memory, M_{ocache}, is reserved for the OE cache. If we assume the size of each entry is S_{ie}, and an overhead of S_{oh} bytes is needed for each entry, the number of entries that fits in the OE cache is approximately $N_{\text{ocache}} \approx \frac{M_{\text{ocache}}}{(S_{\text{ie}}+S_{\text{oh}})}$. Accesses to the OE cache can be assumed to follow the assumptions behind the BDD model, they are independent random requests, and by applying this model with object entries as data granules, we estimate that the probability of an OE cache hit is $P_{\text{ocache}} = P_{\text{buf}}(N_{\text{ocache}}, N_{\text{obj}})$, with p' partitions as defined in Sect. 7.

The results in the following analysis are highly dependent of the amount of overhead S_{oh} needed for each entry. Of course, with a minimal overhead, it would always be beneficial to use as much as possible of the total index memory as an OE cache. The most reasonable way to implement it, and at the same time keep the CPU cost low, is to use an hash table to provide fast access to the entries. In that case, approximately two pointers are needed for each entry on average.

8.2 Total OID Retrieval Cost

With a probability of P_{ocache}, the OID entry requested is already in the OE cache, but for $(1 - P_{\text{ocache}})$ of the requests, we have to access the index pages, and one or more disk accesses might be needed. The probability of a given index page being in memory is *on average* $P_{\text{buf\_ipage}}$, with α_{Li} and β_{Li} as defined in Sect. 5. To traverse the H levels from the root to a leaf node, we need $(1 - P_{\text{buf\_ipage}})H$ disk accesses. The average cost (number of disk accesses) of an index lookup is $C_{\text{indexlookup}} = (1 - P_{\text{ocache}})(1 - P_{\text{buf\_ipage}})H$.

9 Optimizing OE Cache and Buffer Sizes

We have now derived the equations necessary to calculate the cost of an OIDX lookup. We will in this section study in detail under which conditions an OE cache is beneficial, and how much of the index memory should be reserved as an OE cache, to get optimal performance.

The optimization problem is, given a certain amount of index memory,[2] to find the combination of M_{ipages} and M_{ocache} that gives the lowest cost, given the invariant $M_i = M_{\text{ocache}} + M_{\text{ipages}}$. In the rest of this paper, we give OE cache size as a fraction of the total index memory size.

The study was done with databases of two different sizes: DB1 with 2 million objects, and DB2 with 20 million objects. *The optimal OE cache sizes were the same for both database sizes.* Unless otherwise noted, results and numbers in the next sections are from the study of DB1, with an index page size of 8 KB, and access pattern according to partitioning set 1 (Table 1).

---

[2] Note that memory needed for buffering of data pages is not included, this issue is orthogonal to the one studied here.

9.1 Optimal OE Cache Size Versus Index Size

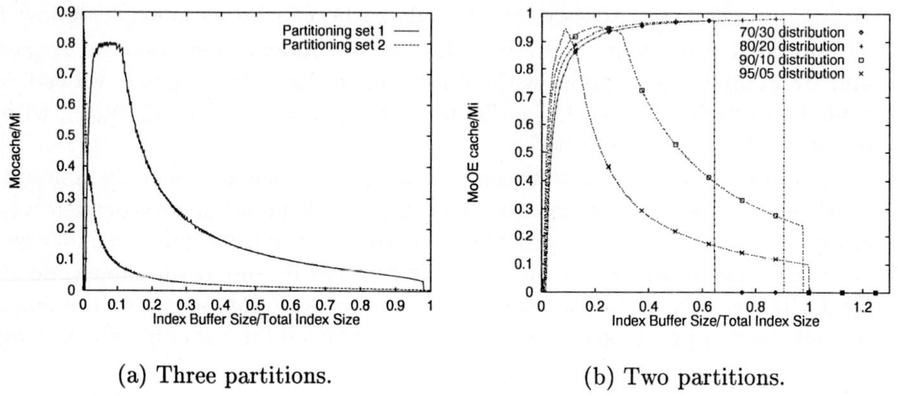

(a) Three partitions.

(b) Two partitions.

Fig. 3. Optimal OE cache size vs. amount of index memory available.

Figure 3a shows the optimal M_{ocache} for different memory sizes, where optimal M_{ocache} is the one that minimizes $C_{\text{indexlookup}}$. An interesting observation, is that the optimal M_{ocache} can be relatively large, especially for medium buffer sizes.

The OE cache is most useful for capturing the accesses to the hot and medium hot areas. This is evident from the figures. As the memory size increases beyond the size needed to capture these areas, the relative fraction of index memory useful for OE cache decreases.

When the buffer size is very small, and only a small part of the hot set fits in it, most entries in the OE cache will only be accessed once each time they are brought into the OE cache. The result is that reserving a large part of the little memory available for the OE cache can be a waste of space. In addition, to reduce retrieval cost, it will be beneficial to have as many as possible of the upper levels of the index tree in the index buffer. When the size of the index memory increases, we come to a point where most of the hot set fits in the OE cache, in addition to the most frequently accessed pages fits in the index page buffer. It is with these memory sizes (relative to the index size) we should have the largest OE cache sizes. If we increase memory even more, most of the hot set fits in the OE cache, and it is advantageous to use the extra memory for index pages. The relative size of the OE cache decreases (but the absolute size stays the same, or increases). As memory increase even more, we come to a point where the optimal OE cache size drops to zero. The reason for this, is that storing the index entries as separate entries instead of pages, incur a relatively high overhead, in the order of 50%. Stored as pages, a higher number of entries fits in the index memory,

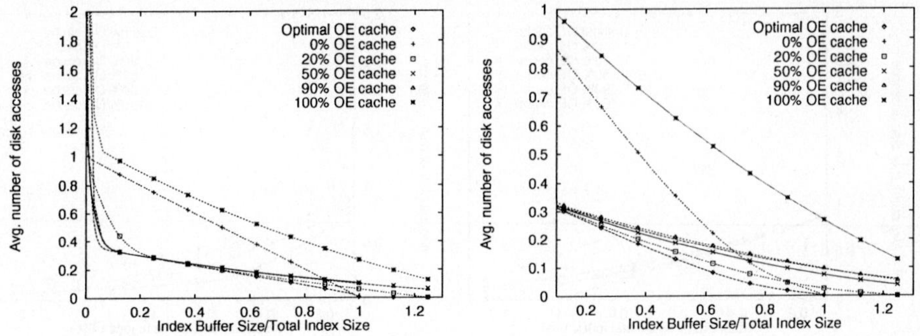

Fig. 4. Cost, partitioning set 1 to the left, partitioning set 2 to the right.

and when we come to a certain point, we get a higher buffer hit probability by storing the index entries as index pages instead of having them in the OE cache.

9.2 Mapping Cost with Different OE Cache Sizes

Figure 4 presents the average mapping costs for partitioning sets 1 and 2. It illustrates the benefits of using OE caching. It also emphasizes the importance of using the *optimal* OE cache size. It can be seen from the figure, that even though choosing a constant size of for example 50% is safe in general, if optimal performance is desired, the OE cache size should be adaptively tuned according to memory and index size. An important fact is that for most memory sizes, almost any OE cache size is better than using no OE cache at all (0% OE cache in the figures).

9.3 The Effect of Different Access Patterns

The optimal OE cache size can be highly dependent of the access pattern. Figure 3a illustrates this for the two partitioning sets. We see that as the most narrow hot spot area (0.01%) gets more narrow (0.001%), the area where a large OE cache is needed also gets smaller.

To be able to study the effect of different access patterns, we have done some studies with only two partitions, to see how the changing sizes and access probabilities affects the optimal cache size and OID retrieval cost. Figure 3b shows how the optimal OE cache size changes with different distributions. It is interesting to note that with a wide hot spot area, e.g. 70/30, it is beneficial to use almost all the available index memory for OE cache, up to a certain point. At this point, the optimal cache size drops to zero.

In the previous section, with three partitions, we had a much smaller hot spot area than in this case. The result was a drop in optimal OE cache size relative to total index memory when the OE cache was large enough to keep the hot spot, with a decline until the point where the buffer hit probability was higher with only index pages. Here we get the same result with 95/05 and 90/10

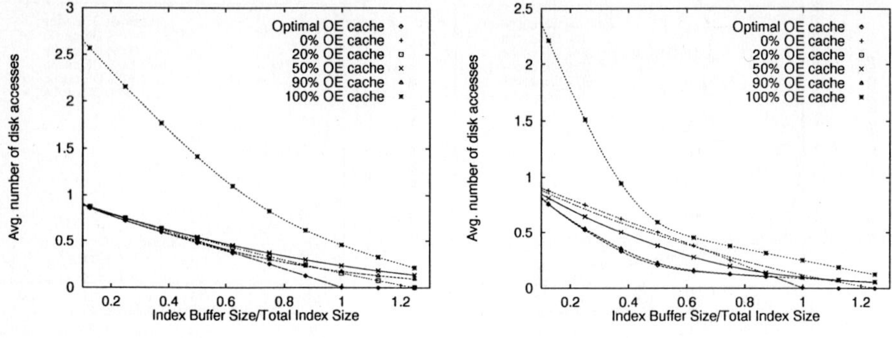

Fig. 5. Cost, 70/30 distribution of accesses to the left, 80/20 distribution of accesses to the right.

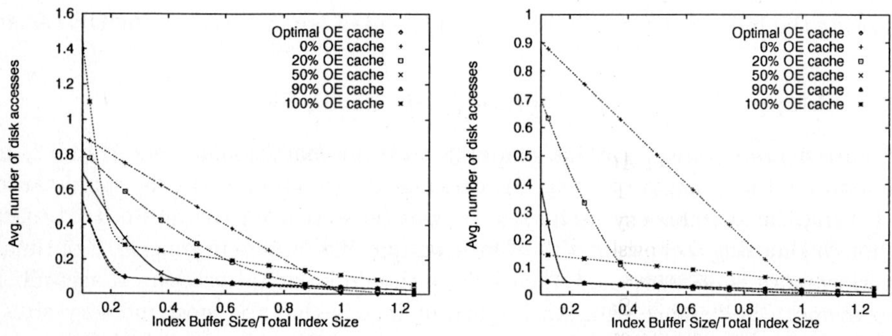

Fig. 6. Cost, 90/10 distribution of accesses to the left, 95/05 distribution of accesses to the right.

distributions, but not with the distributions with wider hot areas. The reason is that with such wide hot areas, the leaf page access distribution is almost uniform.

In Fig. 5 and 6 the mapping cost is shown for various OE cache sizes. They show how important it is to have an optimal OE cache size, and that a fixed size OE cache typically make the OID mapping process 200-300% more costly than necessary.

10 Conclusions

In this paper, we have developed an analytical model for OIDX retrieval cost which includes index buffer and OE caching. As a part of this work, we have also developed an analytical model for hierarchical index buffer performance, based on the LRU model of Bhide et al. [2]. We used the OIDX retrieval cost model to study how memory size, index size, access patterns and different OE cache sizes affects buffer hit performance. This showed that:

1. The relative amount of memory that should be reserved for OE caching is mainly dependent of the size of the index relative to the size of the index memory, not their absolute values.
2. The relative amount of memory that should be reserved for OE caching is highly dependent of the access pattern.
3. The gain from using the optimal size of the OE cache can be very high. This is very important as the size of the available memory increases. When most of the frequently used data and index structures fits in the buffer, it is the requests for the infrequently accessed items, that is not resident in memory when requested, that will use most of the disk bandwidth.

References

1. E. Bertino and P. Foscoli. On modeling cost functions for object-oriented databases. *IEEE Transactions on Knowledge and Data Engineering*, 9(3), 1997.
2. A. K. Bhide, A. Dan, and D. M. Dias. A simple analysis of the LRU buffer policy and its relationship to buffer warm-up transient. In *Proceedings of the Ninth International Conference on Data Engineering*, 1993.
3. A. F. Cardenas. Analysis and performance of inverted data base structures. *Communications of the ACM*, 18(5), 1975.
4. H. T. Chou and D. DeWitt. An evaluation of buffer management strategies for relational database systems. In *Proceedings of the 14th VLDB Conference*, 1985.
5. A. Dan and D. Towsley. An approximate analysis of the LRU and FIFO buffer replacement schemes. In *Proceedings of ACM SIGMETRICS*, 1990.
6. G. Diehr and A. N. Saharia. Estimating block accesses in database organizations. *IEEE Transactions on Knowledge and Data Engineering*, 6(3), 1994.
7. A. Eickler, C. A. Gerlhof, and D. Kossmann. Performance evaluation of OID mapping techniques. In *Proceedings of the 21st VLDB Conference*, 1995.
8. G. Gardarin, J.-R. Gruser, and Z.-H. Tang. A cost model for clustered object-oriented databases. In *Proceedings of the 21st VLDB Conference*, 1995.
9. W. S. Luk. On estimating block accesses in database organizations. *Communications of the ACM*, 26(11), 1983.
10. L. F. Mackert and G. M. Lohman. Index scans using a finite LRU buffer: A validated I/O model. *ACM Transactions on Database Systems*, 14(3), 1989.
11. M. L. McAuliffe. *Storage Management Methods for Object Database Systems.* PhD thesis, University of Wisconsin-Madison, 1997.
12. K. Nørvåg and K. Bratbergsengen. An analytical study of object identifier indexing. Technical Report IDI 4/98, Norwegian University of Science and Technology, 1998.
13. K.-Y. Whang and G. Wiederhold. Estimating block accesses in database organizations: A closed noniterative formula. *Communications of the ACM*, 26(11), 1983.
14. S. B. Yao. Approximating the number of accesses in database organizations. *Communications of the ACM*, 20(4), 1977.

DO2: Deductive Object-Oriented Database System

Tok Wang Ling, Boon Tun Wee, and Sin Yeung Lee

School of Computing
National University of Singapore
Lower Kent Ridge Road, Singapore 119260
{lingtw, weeboont, jlee}@iscs.nus.edu.sg

Abstract. *DO2* is a deductive object-oriented database developed at the National University of Singapore. The system aims to integrate deductive and object-oriented paradigms and use their advantages to overcome both the paradigms' respective weaknesses. *DO2* differs from conventional deductive object-oriented databases in its' key-based approach for OIDs, pro-active approach to resolving inheritance conflicts and natural interpretation of negation using the *not* predicates. This paper describes the structure, language, and implementation of *DO2*.

1 Introduction

Deductive and object-oriented databases are two important extensions of the traditional database technology. Deductive databases extend the expressive power of traditional databases by means of recursion and declarative querying while object-oriented databases extend their data modeling power by means of object identity, complex objects, classes, class hierarchy and inheritance. However both extensions have their shortcomings. Deductive databases lack powerful data modeling mechanisms while object-oriented databases lack logical semantics and declarative query language. Therefore, by combining the two approaches together, we can eliminate their shortcomings and reap their advantages.

There have been many proposals to integrate the two paradigms [2, 8, 13, 14, 17, 19, 18]. One method is to extend existing deductive database languages, like Datalog, with object-orientation. Other extends object-oriented database to incorporate deductive database features. Yet another approach is to build new logical theories to encompass the deductive object-oriented database features.

DO2 (Deductive Object-oriented) differs from the above approaches. We propose extending the relational database to incorporate deductive object-oriented database features. This decision is based on the fact that relational database still has many strong application pull and is likely to remain for a fairly long time. Moreover, we have seen many proposals to extend relational database to that of object-oriented databases [7, 15]. Likewise, there are also many claims that deductive database is just a natural extension of the relational database. Hence *DO2* can be considered a natural extension of the relational database which attempts to incorporate the many desirable features of deductive and object-oriented database.

In this paper, we will discuss in detail about the *DO2* system which is developed at the National University of Singapore using Oracle as the underlying database. Section 2 introduces the unique features in *DO2*. Section 3 demonstrates and explains the uniform declarative language used in *DO2*. Section 4 explains the structure and implementation of the system *DO2*. Section 5 discusses and compares *DO2* with other related works. Section 6 outlines the future direction of our project.

2 Features of *DO2*

Currently there is still no consensus on a specific object-oriented database (OODB) model or even on what components constitute an OODB model. Likewise, many DOOD also differ from each other in deductive features such as negation, query evaluation methods and optimization strategies. In the following, we will highlight the essential features which single out *DO2* from other DOOD.

2.1 Object-Identifier

Many DOOD systems, including Florid [8], Rock & Roll [2] and Rol [13] implement object-identifier in manners similar to that of an OODB. However, *DO2* has opted not to implement OIDs but instead use key values as a means to distinguish between objects. This is similar in the spirit of relational database which are key-based. Arguably this would conflict with much object-oriented issues regarding the unique nature of objects within the system. But we justify our case accordingly:

1. Ullman [18] had shown that taking OIDs seriously has converted a simple pair of logical rules, with a simple, finite, least-fixed-point semantics into something whose meaning is an infinite set. In short, using OIDs would conflict with the integration of deductive features.
2. Depending on the implementation of OIDs, Ling [12] had shown when an object migrates from one class to another, OIDs could be a very contentious issue. In fact, most OODB do not allow object migration. For example, it is possible for an object to adopt another OID when it migrates to another class, thus violating the immutability property of OID. Suppose that an employee had been promoted to manager, changing the OID of the employee to that of manager would violate the immutability property as mentioned.

OIDs are also not useful in multi-database application. Using OIDs, it is difficult to determine whether objects from different database are identical as each database could implement their OIDs differently. This is not true if key-based approach is employed. In this light, we adopt the *key-based* approach to identifying objects within the database.

2.2 ISA Hierarchies and Inheritance

In multiple inheritance systems, a conflict situation occurs when a class inherits several commonly named properties of its superclasses. Many OODBs do provide different techniques to resolve this problem, but do not examine the reasons why conflicts arise. *DO2* resolves such conflicts using a *Conflict Resolution Algorithm* adopted from [11]. We believe that inheritance conflicts are avoidable if application semantics are considered during the design stage.

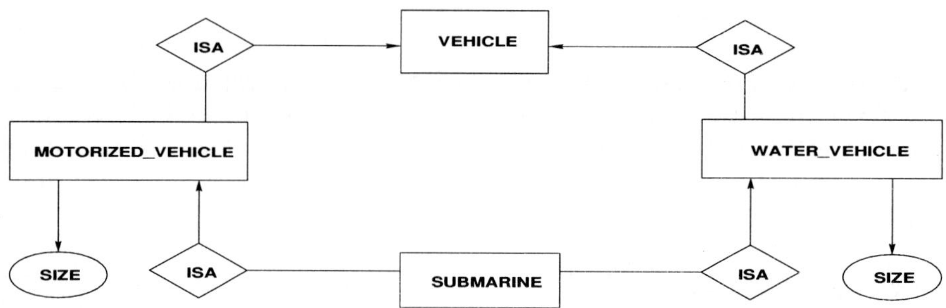

Fig. 1. Multiple Inheritance Conflicts

In Fig. 1, the class SUBMARINE needs to determine which 'SIZE' attribute to inherit from its two direct superclasses. ORION [9] chooses the first in the list of superclasses. This approach is somewhat arbitrary and may not yield the required semantics. POSTGRES [16] does not allow the creation of a subclass that inherits conflicting attributes (e.g. SUBMARINE). This approach is not flexible when compared to O_2 [6], which allows the explicit selection of the properties to inherit and emphasizes the path along which the property is to be inherited from. However, the important issue is the identity of the source class which defines (re-defines) the inherited property rather than the path. IRIS [5] uses the type information to resolve conflicts, e.g. by choosing a more specific type to inherit. It is not clear how the type specificity is determined in IRIS.

Many of these techniques examine neither the semantics of the properties involved in a conflict situation nor the reasons for the conflict. Furthermore, these techniques resolve conflicts after the schema has been completed and implemented. Clearly, they are not satisfactory. In contrast our approach is "proactive". Depending on the nature of inheritance conflicts, recommendations of conflict resolution include renaming properties, re-defining (or overriding) an overload property, removing redundant ISA relationship, explicitly selecting an inheritance class and re-designing the schema (factoring). For detail, please see [11]. Essentially, *DO2* differs from most other DOOD because we operate at semantic level rather than at syntactic level.

2.3 Methods and Late Binding

A subclass may implement a method to override that in its superclass. Method resolution that determines which implementation is associated with a given method name and class at runtime, is known as *late binding.* Suppose MANAGER ISA EMPLOYEE and *bonus()* is a method implemented in both MANAGER and EMPLOYEE. When a *bonus()* message is sent to an instance of EMPLOYEE who is also a manager, it is semantically incorrect to execute the *bonus()* method of EMPLOYEE, since a more specialized *bonus()* method exists for this particular employee who is a manager.

This issue has generally been overlooked by many DOOD systems. To address this problem, more information other than the method name and the object is required to correctly determine the class association. *DO2* resolved this problem by first determining the object's most specific subclass possible association. From which, *DO2* will be able to determine which association is semantically correct to implement the method.

2.4 Negation

To represent negation in *DO2*, we endorse the Prolog "not-predicate" instead of the usual "$\sim$" in clause negation. It had been noted in [10] that this not-predicate is not always equivalent to negation in clauses. Consider the following example where the database contains only the following two predicates:

people(name, address, sex)
married(husband, wife, marriage_date)

To query about all the bachelors within the database, we have the following,

Q1: people(NAME, ADDR, 'male'), not(married(NAME, WIFE, DATE)).

Using the not-predicate, the above query is interpreted as

get NAME and ADDR such that (people(NAME, ADDR, 'male') $\wedge$
$\sim \exists$ WIFE, $\exists$ DATE married(NAME, WIFE, DATE))

This is not the same as that if the query is written as

Q2: people(NAME, ADD, 'male'), $\sim$ married(NAME, WIFE, DATE).

In fact, *Q1* does not convey the same meaning as the *Q2.* The main difference between not-predicate and "$\sim$" lies in the interpretation of the *ungrounded variables* within the negated clause. Using not-predicate, the *ungrounded variables* are existential in nature while it is universal in the other case. Using the clause negation, queries are required to comply with Clark's safe computation rule [4], i.e. for all negated clauses, they must be ground. Realizing the difference, *DO2* has adopted the Extended Query Evaluation Procedure (EQEP) proposed in [10] to resolve negation with the "not-predicate". This is because it has more natural semantics and is more expressive. Using the not-predicate we can express certain queries easily that are difficult for the "∼" negation. To illustrate with the earlier examples, using clause negation, we cannot simply re-write *Q1* by replacing the "not-predicate" with the "∼" negation as WIFE and DATE cannot be instantiated and will therefore violate the safe computation rule. A new rule is needed to express the query as shown below:

Rule: husband(X) :- married(X, WIFE, DATE)
Query: people(X, _, 'Male'), ∼ husband(X)

Using the "∼" negation, users may need to define new rules for some simple queries. This is not acceptable as users should not need to define rules during query. Moreover in a multi-user environment, this could lead to unpredictable results if different users declare the same rule more than once differently.

3 Language Design in *DO2*

DO2's language is modeled after Prolog but with some modifications and extensions. Variables are written as any sequence of alphanumeric characters starting with a capital letter, otherwise it is constant. In *DO2*, a relation and a extennsional predicate are synonymous. The *truth value* of a predicate is *true* when it matches a fact and false when it matches no fact. The following subsections will further explain about *DO2*'s language and discuss how *DO2*'s schema, rule, method and queies are defined.

3.1 Schema Definition

Fig. 2 gives a sample schema declaration. All predicates must be declared within the schema. In this case, the four extensional predicates MARRIED, PEOPLE, EMPLOYEE, DEPARTMENT and MANAGER and the single intensional predicate BACHELOR must be declared. The notation ":" is used to delimit between the attributes and their types. This declaration is necessary for the mapping of the schema design into that for the relational database.

Class hierarchies must be declared after the delimiter *ISA Relation* within the schema file. Using ISA, we can declare that manager is the subclass of employee and that they share the corresponding key *EMPNUM* and *MGRNUM*. Similarly, the employee is also the subclass of people and shares the same corresponding key, *idnum*. Using this simple declaration, the system will also be able to detect that people is also the superclass of manager too.

3.2 Language Design

Although *DO2*'s language takes after some of the Prolog's common convention, we had modified certain properties of Prolog. We now allow user to reference

```
//Predicate Definition
manager(*MGRNUM : int[5], ALLOWANCE : int[8], PHONENUM : int[7])        // * -- indicates primary key
employee(*EMPNUM: int[5], IDNUM : char[9], DEPTNUM : int[3], PAY : int[6])
department(*DEPTNUM : int[3], DEPTNAME : char[20], BUDGET : int[8])
people(*IDNUM : char[9], NAME : char[20], SEX : char[6], ADDRESS : char[30], DOB : int[6])
married(*HNAME : char[20], *WNAME : char[20], DATE : int[6])
bachelor( *NAME : char[20] )

// Method Definition
employee( BONUS() : B, EMPNUM ) :- employee( EMPNUM, PAY : P ), B = P * 0.15.
manager( BONUS() : B, MGRNUM ) :- manager( MGRNUM, PAY : P ), B = P * 0.25.

// ISA Relation
isa( employee : IDNUM, people : IDNUM )
isa( manager : MGRNUM, employee : EMPNUM )

// Rules Definition
bachelor( NAME : X ) :- people( NAME: X,  SEX : 'Male' ), not(married( HNAME : X )).
```

Fig. 2. Sample Schema Definition

by name and *inheritance*, rather than purely by position as in Prolog. Previously in Prolog, user are forced to recall the correct position declared during the schema design for each predicate. Moreover, user must also specify "_" for variables which are not of their concern. Improving on this, *DO2* allows users to specifically name the attributes they want by using the original attribute names and ignore all other unwanted attributes within the predicate. To assign constant value or variable names to specifc attributes, they simply use the ":" notation. For example using the schema defined in Fig. 2, to reference the address of a person with idnum '12345678A'

Prolog: people('12345678A', _, _, Address, _).
DO2 : people(IDNUM : '12345678A', ADDRESS).

User can now directly reference address by quoting *ADDRESS* and use the ":" notation to assign constant value to IDNUM. This also implies users need not place the attributes according to the order they are declared in the predicate.

A unique object-oriented features of the language in *DO2*, is that users can now directly infer inherited attributes from the superclass to subclass when querying the subclass. To check the address of a manager '12345',

Prolog: manager('12345', _, _), employee('12345',IDnum, _, _),
people(IDnum, _, _, Address, _).
DO2 : manager(MGRNUM : '12345', ADDRESS).

Using normal Prolog, users must explicitly "*join*" the predicates to inquire the address. Users have to exercise caution in the order of join as it could result in very different query evaluation if placed differently. On the other hand, *DO2* recognizes that manager inherits all the attributes from people too. As such, users can directly inquire about the address of the manager straight. This is more flexible and expressive than conventional Prolog.

An extended feature in *DO2* is the implementation of aggregate functions: *max, min, count, sum* and *avg*. This had implemented in the same consideration for strong pull of field applications like [19] and the fact that such functions are readily available in most relational database. To invoke the aggregate function, users simply call the aggregate function followed by the targeted attributes enclosed in "< >" angle brackets. To illustrate, consider the following query whereby we want to sum up the pay of all employee in each department:

DO2 :   employee(DEPTNUM, sum<PAY> : SUM_PAY).

Other extensions includes the mean of projection. Previously, Prolog will output every attributes that is included within the predicate. However, *DO2* differs by providing a mean whereby users can explicitly state what attrivutes are not to be output. This is achieved by enclosing the unwanted attributes within square brackets, "[ ]". This is useful when users do not want to output attributes involved in "join" or in selection conditions. For example, to find the MGRNUM value of managers whose PAY are greater than 1000, users can query:

Prolog: manager(X, _, _), employee(X, IDnum, _, Pay), Pay > 1000.
DO2 :   manager(MGRNUM, [PAY]), PAY > 1000.

The use of "[ ]" also allows users to explicitly exclude attributes in the *GROUP-BY* clause when invoking the aggregate functions. Lastly, negation within *DO2* is represented using the original not-predicate in Prolog (See Section 2.4). In fact, *DO2* also supports nested negation too.

3.3 Rule, Method and Query Definition

In *DO2*, a *rule* is the component of a program that enables us to derive new relations from other relations. A rule is an expression of the form

$$A \quad :- \quad A_1, \ldots, A_n, B_1, B_2, \ldots, B_m$$

where $n \geq 0$ and $m \geq 0$. A is a positive literal which is called the **head** of the rule. Each of A_i is a positive literal, each of B_j is a positive literal or a negative formula, where a negative formula is of the form not$(A_1, \ldots, A_n, B_1, \ldots, B_m)$ and the commas imply conjunction. $A_1, \ldots, A_n, B_1, \ldots, B_m$ are called the **body** of the rule.

The syntax for rules follows the syntax for *DO2*'s language design. It supports recursion, (nested) negation and aggregation. Queries in *DO2* are actually rules without the heads. Therefore, the syntax for queries follows very much the same as the rule declaration.

Methods are declared according to the classes which implements them. In *DO2*, methods can be inherited like attributes from one superclass to another subclass. *DO2* supports multiple inheritance of methods too. In Fig. 2, the method *bonus()* is declared for the two classes manager and employee. Current implementation of methods do not allow for updates to the database.

4 Structure and Implementation of *DO2*

DO2 has been implemented over a relational database, namely Oracle. Oracle was chosen because it is popularity and availability on a wide variety of hardware and operating systems. *DO2* is made up of five main sections, the *user interface, schema processor, query processor, fact manager* and *database manager*. The schema processor will check for multiple inheritance conflicts within the schema design. If conflict occurs, then it will advise the users on options available to resolve the problem. At the same time, it also ensures that the rules defined are *bottom-up evaluable* and *safe*. These are in accordance to the definition in [1]. Rules declared within *DO2* must satisfy the requirement: it is range restricted and every variable in the body is secure. To cater for the negated clauses within the body, we apply the same condition in EQEP [10] to the rules too. The rules must also be further checked if they are stratifiable to ensure that all recursive rules are evaluable.

All queries are directed to the query processor. It has two main functions: 1) to evaluate the query in accordance to whether it contains intensional predicates, negated clauses, method calls or aggregate functions, etc. 2) to map the query into its SQL equivalence. The fact manager maintains a quick look-up table to enable the system to rapidly check for each instance in the database for its most specific subclass association. The table contains for all relations (classes), all records (objects) key values (OIDs) and its associated class.

The database manager performs the task of connecting the system to Oracle. Current implementation uses Java JDBC to bridge to Oracle 8. Once connected, the database manager parses the translated SQL queries to SQL and returns the answer dervied by Oracle to *DO2*.

5 Related Works

Like *DO2*, ROL [13] too supports the value-oriented approach when implementing OIDs. However, it supports both the value-oriented and object-oriented approaches to OIDs, to grant users greater flexibility. ROL also supports multiple inheritance and resolves inheritance conflicts using a similar mechanism as in O_2, allowing users to specifically state the inheritance path. *DO2* resolves this issue by providing an analytical analysis of the inheritance conflicts and makes recommendations to users the options available.

ROCK & ROLL [2] adopts a slightly different approach in that there are two different languages, one for imperative database programming and the other for logic querying. The essential difference between ROCK & ROLL and *DO2* lies in the underlying database. *DO2* engages a relational database whereas ROCK & ROLL uses an OODB. The twin programming languages approach also requires some adaptation on the part of users.

Florid [8] is memory-based. This has the disadvantage when we cannot store all data in the main memory. Florid uses trigger semantics to resolve multiple inheritance. This method is not satisfactory because it will arbitrary select the first trigger found to "deactivate" the other possible triggers. Therefore, the result is not predictable when inheritance conflict occurs. In fact, Florid does not actually detect such ambiguity until runtime.

The LDL++ [19] prototype was modeled after LDL [3]. It offers an impressive range of applications and open architecture and integration with SQL systems. In the current release, LDL++ can link with Sybase, DB2, Oracle and ESS. However, LDL++ still lacks object-oriented features whereas its main strength lies in that of deductive database processing. Also, *DO2* is unique in its evaluation of negation in queries and rules. Most DOOD have adopted the clause negation and are very much restricted when querying with negation compared to *DO2*.

6 Conclusion

In this paper, we have discussed in detail the *DO2* system. We explained the approaches and key decisions made in our system while trying to integrate the combined benefits of the object-oriented and deductive databases. The key achievement of *DO2* are as follows:

- a key-based approach for OIDs
- a powerful declarative language which incorporates object-oriented features
- an analytical approach for resolving inheritance conflict
- a more natural interpretation of negation using "not" predicates
- a simple approach for relational database to incorporate DOOD features

The simplicity of our approach allows *DO2* to be implemented over almost any existing relational database without actual changes to the database. This is similar in nature to Won Kim's work in UniSQL of extending object-oriented features into SQL except that we are extending deductive object-oriented features.

For future work, we will continue to improve on the optimization techniques in the system. We also intend to enable the storage of complex objects within our *DO2* database to enable more flexibility. Lastly, we will also attempt to look at the implementation of an active database over our system.

References

[1] F. Bancilhon and R. Ramakrishnan. An amateur's introduction to recursive query processing strategies. In *SIGMOD*, pages 16–52. ACM, 1986.

[2] M.L. Barja, A.A.A. Fernandes, N.W. Paton, and M.H. Williams. Design and Implementation of ROCK & ROLL: A Deductive Object-Oriented Database System. In *Information System*, volume 20, pages 185–211, 1995.

[3] D. Chimenti, R. Gamboa, R. Krishnamurthy, S. Naqvi, S. Tsur, and C. Zaniolo. The LDL System Prototype. In *TKDE*, volume 2. IEEE, 1990.

[4] K.L. Clark. Negation as Failure. In *Logic and Database*, pages 293–322, 1978.

[5] D. Fishman et al. IRIS: An Object Oriented Database Management System. *ACM Transaction on Office Information Systems*, 5(1):48–69, Jan 1987.

[6] O. Deux et al. The Story of O_2. *IEEE Transactions on Knowledge and Data Engineering*, 2(1):91–108, Mar 1990.

[7] C. Fahrner and G. Vossen. Transforming Relational Database Schemas into Object-Oriented Schemas according to ODMG-93. In *Deductive and Object-Oriented Databases*, pages 429–446. Springer-Verlag, 1995.

[8] P.. Kandzia and C. Schlepphorst. Florid - a prototype for F-Logic. In *German Workshop on Logic Programming*, 1997.

[9] W. Kim. *An introduction to object-oriented databases.* MIT Press, Cambridge, Mass., 1990.

[10] T.W. Ling. The Prolog not-predicate and Negation as Failure Rule. In *New Generation Computing*, volume 8, pages 5–31. Springer-Verlag, 1990.

[11] T.W. Ling and P.K. Teo. Inheritance conflicts in object-oriented systems. In *Database and Expert Systems Application*, pages 189–200, 1993.

[12] T.W. Ling and P.K. Teo. Object migration in isa hierarchies. In *Database Systems for Advanced Applications*, 1995.

[13] Mengchi Liu. The ROL Deductive Object Base Language (extended abstract). In *Database and Expert Systems Application*, pages 122–131. IEEE press, 1996.

[14] R. Ramakrishnan and J.D. Ullman. A survey of research on deductive database systems. In *J. Logic Programming*, pages 125–149, May 1995.

[15] S. Ramanathan and J. Hodges. Extraction of object-oriented structures from existing relational databases. In *SIGMOD*, volume 26. ACM, 1997.

[16] Stonebraker, M. Hanson, and E. Potamianps. A rule manager for relational database systems. Technical report, UCL Berkeley, 1987.

[17] The VALIDITY Team. Summary state of the art on deductive and deductive object-oriented databases. Deductive and Object-oriented Database, 1996.

[18] J.D. Ullman. A comparison between deductive and object-oriented database systems. In *DOOD*, pages 263–277. Springer-Verlag, 1991.

[19] C. Zaniolo. LDL++: A second-generation deductive database system. In *Computational Logic*, 1996.

Selecting Actions to Trigger in Active Database Applications*

Huang-Cheng Kuo and Gültekin Özsoyoğlu

Department of Computer Engineering and Science
Case Western Reserve University
Cleveland, OH 44106

Abstract. This paper studies the problem of selecting rules to fire in real-time active databases in order to avoid missing action deadlines. We give an algorithm that executes at every fixed time interval (called the Rule Selection Period), and satisfies three properties, namely, the Completion Property, the Duration Property, and the Priority Property. We develop a probabilistic model, and an inexpensive (polynomial-time) algorithm for the satisfaction of the Completion Property. We show that the problem of satisfying the Duration and the Priority Properties at the same time is NP-Complete. We then give two heuristic-based algorithms, and briefly summarize the associated experimental results.

1 Introduction

We consider real-time active databases with repeating[2] events, actions (transactions) with deadlines, and event-action (EA) rules with priorities. Considering actions as transactions, and utilizing the repetition history of events and actions, one can obtain fairly accurate estimates of CPU execution times and blocking times of actions.

In order to avoid missing action deadlines, a mechanism is needed to select rules to fire in the presence of currently executing actions. Due to its overhead, such a mechanism cannot be activated each time an event occurs. Thus, there is a *Rule Selection Period* $\mathcal{D}$ such that, at every $\mathcal{D}$ intervals, rules are selected and fired.

Our first goal in this paper is to give a "risk-based" algorithm, called DECIDE, for deciding whether a chosen set of rules will complete within their deadlines with a high probability. DECIDE is executed at every $\mathcal{D}$ units of time, and decides whether the completion property is satisfied.

Completion Property: If a rule is fired and the associated action is triggered, the probability that the triggered action completes within its deadline is higher than a given threshold.

---

* This research is supported by the National Science Foundation grants IRI 92-24660, IRI96-31214, and CDA95-29503.

[2] We use the term *repeating* as opposed to the term *periodic* since these events, even though they repeat over time, do not necessarily have fixed time intervals.

Duration Property: All triggered actions are expected to complete within the rule selection period. Assuming that we have[3] precise (i) context switching times for switching between action executions, and (ii) execution times for the DECIDE algorithm, we can equivalently restate the Duration Property as follows: the total CPU execution time of triggered actions is as large as possible, and smaller than the rule selection period.

Priority Property: Rules are prioritized, and high-priority rules (actions) are fired (triggered) first. Since rules can be transitively fired, in this paper, we use the criteria: "among possible sets of rules to be fired, the set with the maximum total priority value is fired."

We show that the Completion-Duration-Priority-(CDP) Satisfaction problem is NP-Complete, and present two heuristic algorithms that (use DECIDE and) choose rules to fire while attempting to satisfy all three properties. These "CHOOSE" heuristic algorithms are called CHOOSE-REGULAR and CHOOSE-ONE-AHEAD.

In section 2, we define our real-time active database model. In section 3, we develop a probabilistic model and present the DECIDE algorithm that checks whether the Completion Property is still satisfied if a new rule is fired. The algorithm is inexpensive in the sense that it runs in $O(n)$ time where n is the number of rules that are to be fired and currently executing. Section 4 discusses the policy for firing rules transitively in order to satisfy the Duration and the Priority Properties. In section 5, we formally define the CDP problem as the problem of satisfying the Completion, Duration and Priority properties, and show that the CDP problem is NP-Complete. In sections 6 and 7, we summarize two heuristic algorithms for the CDP-Satisfaction problem, and briefly report their performances using simulation.

2 Model

In the following analysis, actions are start-and-complete-transactions, and, the terms action and transaction are used interchangeably.

Let $E = \{ e_1, e_2, ..., e_n \}$ be a set of events which have occurred since the last rule selection. Let the rule set R_E^1 be the set of all eligible rules whose events form a subset of E. The action a of a rule r: $e \rightarrow a$ may fire another rule r': $a \rightarrow a'$. We call rule r the *triggering rule* of rule r'. A *triggering path* $\{ r_1 \Rightarrow r_2 \Rightarrow ... \Rightarrow r_l \}$ from r_1 to r_l is a sequence of rules, where rule r_i is the triggering rule of rule r_{i+1} for $1 \leq i \leq l-1$. The *length of a triggering path* is defined as the number of rules on the path. For the rest of this paper, we use a more restrictive definition for a triggering path in which the path starts from a rule in R_E^1. A rule set is acyclic if there are no rules that appear more than once on any triggering path.

We recursively define R_E^n as $\{ r \mid r\!: e \rightarrow a \wedge (\exists r')(r' : e' \rightarrow e) \wedge r' \in R_E^{n-1} \}$ $\cup R_E^{n-1}$ for $n > 1$. R_E^i is called the ith *level rule set of event set E*. For a given

[3] Please note that we assume that we have a repeating event environment where we have the event history information from previous executions.

rule base R without cycles on the triggering paths, the rule closure R_E^+ on the event set E is defined $R_E^+ = R_E^l$, where l is the length of the longest triggering path in R.

The following assumptions are made for the model in this paper.

- The rule set has only EA rules.
- The rule set is acyclic.
- The CPU execution time for an action (a transaction) is a random variable T_{CPU}. We assume that we have historical data about the behavior of transactions, and thus, are informed about their properties.
- At a given time, the expected CPU time to complete an action a is a random variable $T^f_{CPU\_a}$.

The mean and the standard deviation of T_{CPU} are μ_{CPU} and σ_{CPU}, which can be estimated from the execution history. Each action has a deadline $t_{deadline}$ which is the end-point of its action time interval. The random variable $T^f_{CPU\_a}$ is defined as $T_{CPU\_a} * f$, where f is the fraction of the action a which has not yet been executed at a given time t. The fraction f is a function of the system load and blocking of transactions. If the action a has not started at time t, then $f = 1$. Otherwise, the system approximates f for each currently executing transaction.

The rule manager does not process events right after they occur. Instead, events are processed periodically. The rule manager uses the CHOOSE algorithm to choose rules for firing. The rule selection period, i.e., the time duration between the two executions of the CHOOSE algorithm, is denoted by $\mathcal{D}$.

3 Deciding Whether A Chosen Rule Completes within Its Deadline

We say that a rule r and the action a of rule r have the *Completion property* with respect to a set of other initiated actions A if, in the presence of actions A, the action a can complete within its deadline with a probability higher than a given threshold ρ. For short, we will use *Completion_Probability(r, A)* for the probability that the action a of rule r completes within its deadline with respect to A. A given repeating event processing algorithm CHOOSE is said to have the *Completion property* if all the rules it fires have the Completion property with respect to A.

The probability $p(r)$ (or $p(\tau)$) that the action (transaction) τ of a rule r completes within its deadline depends on (i) the CPU execution time of the transaction τ, (ii) the starting time of the transaction τ, and (iii) the blocking time of τ due to the currently executing transactions A.

The blocking time of an action is a function of the system load, where one of the system load parameters is the number of currently executing actions. The larger the number is, the longer it takes for an action to complete. From now on, we will use the term transaction (instead of action). Because we have repeating events, the blocking time for a transaction can be estimated for a given application using the execution history. In this paper, we use a generic blocking time function.

Assume that the number of currently executing transactions is n. Let the CPU execution times to complete (started or about-to-start) transactions τ_1, τ_2, ..., τ_n be $T^f_{CPU\_\tau_1}$, ..., $T^f_{CPU\_\tau_n}$ (random variables), respectively. $T^f_{CPU\_\tau_1}$, ..., $T^f_{CPU\_\tau_n}$ are mutually independent, because the CPU execution time of a transaction has no effect on the CPU execution time of another transaction. We make the assumption that the blocking time $\mathcal{B}_i$ for transaction τ_i is a function of the CPU execution times of the currently executing transactions, and is expressed as $\mathcal{B}_i(T^f_{CPU\_\tau_1}, ..., T^f_{CPU\_\tau_n})$, which is called the *blocking time function.*

In this paper, we use the following blocking time function definition. Let T^{n-1}_{rest} be the total CPU execution times of the rest of the (n - 1) currently executing transactions, assuming that the transactions are known. We approximate $\mathcal{B}_i$ as $b_{1\_i} * T^f_{CPU\_\tau_i} + b_{2\_i} * T^{n-1}_{rest}$, where b_{1_i} and b_{2_i} are constants (blocking time factors) which represent blocking contributions of the transaction τ_i, and the rest of the transactions to $\mathcal{B}_i$, respectively. Thus, the system keeps two blocking time factors for each transaction. The blocking time factors b_{1_i} and b_{2_i} can be obtained by, say, multiple linear regression [Doug90]. The motivations for our choice of the blocking time function are (a) small number of blocking time factors need to be estimated; and (b) flexibility, since we provide altogether $2n$ application-dependent blocking time factors for n actions.

The actual completion time (relative to $now = 0$) for transaction τ_i is a function of $T^f_{CPU\_\tau_i}$ and $\mathcal{B}_i(T^f_{CPU\_\tau_1}, ..., T^f_{CPU\_\tau_n})$, and is expressed as $T_{ACTUAL\_\tau_i} = \mathcal{F}(T^f_{CPU\_\tau_i}, \mathcal{B}_i)$.

Given a set of currently executing transactions, the probability $p(\tau)$ that transaction τ completes within its deadline $t^{\tau}_{deadline}$ is then $Pr(T_{ACTUAL\_\tau} \leq t^{\tau}_{deadline})$.

3.1 Computing the Probability of Completion

First we discuss how to compute an approximation for $\bar{\mathcal{B}}_i = b_{1\_i} * T^f_{CPU\_\tau_i} + b_{2\_i} * T^{n-1}_{rest}$. $T^f_{CPU\_\tau_1}, ..., T^f_{CPU\_\tau_n}$ are random variables with their distribution parameters. In this paper, we assume that $T^f_{CPU\_\tau_1}, ..., T^f_{CPU\_\tau_n}$ are normally distributed with estimated means $\bar{\mu}_{\tau_1}$, ..., $\bar{\mu}_{\tau_n}$ and estimated standard deviations $\bar{\sigma}_1$, ..., $\bar{\sigma}_n$, respectively. Thus, $\mathcal{B}_i$ is also normally distributed since it is a combination of normally distributed random variables [Doug90]. Estimated means $\bar{\mu}_{\tau_i}$ and estimated standard deviations $\bar{\sigma}_{\tau_i}$ are initially assigned values using experimentally observed values. And, at run-time, they are updated based on the current execution history. Estimated CPU execution time means and standard deviations are updated only periodically to reduce the overhead.

Since $T^f_{CPU\_\tau_1}$, ..., $T^f_{CPU\_\tau_n}$ are independent, and $\mathcal{B}_i = b_{1\_i} * T^f_{CPU\_\tau_i} + b_{2\_i} * T^{n-1}_{rest}$, we have

$E(\mathcal{B}_i) = b_{1\_i} * E(T^f_{CPU\_\tau_i}) + b_{2\_i} * E(\sum^n_{j=1, j\neq i} T^f_{CPU\_\tau_j})$. where E denotes the expected value.

The estimated mean and variance for $\bar{\mathcal{B}}_i$ [Doug90] is $b_{1\_i} * \bar{\mu}_{\tau_i} + b_{2\_i} * \sum_{j=1, j\neq i}^{n} \bar{\mu}_{\tau_j}$ and $\sigma^2_{\mathcal{B}_i} = b^2_{1\_i} * \bar{\sigma}^2_i + b^2_{2\_i} * \sum_{j=1, j\neq i}^{n} \bar{\sigma}^2_j$

Please recall that the actual completion time (relative to $now = 0$) for transaction τ_i is $T_{ACTUAL\_\tau_i} = \mathcal{F}(\, T^f_{CPU\_\tau_i}, \mathcal{B}_i)$. We think that the choices of $\mathcal{F}$ should also be determined experimentally. As one choice, let the *completion time function* $\mathcal{F}$ be $\mathcal{F}(T^f_{CPU\_\tau_i}, \mathcal{B}_i) = T^f_{CPU\_\tau_i} + \mathcal{B}_i$. Then, the expected value for $T_{ACTUAL\_\tau_i}$ is
$\bar{\mu}_{T_{ACTUAL\_\tau_i}} = E(T_{ACTUAL\_\tau_i}) = (1 + b_{1\_i}) * \bar{\mu}_{\tau_i} + b_{2\_i} * \sum_{j=1, j\neq i}^{n} \bar{\mu}_{\tau_i}$.

The variance for $T_{ACTUAL\_\tau_i}$ is
$\bar{\sigma}^2_{T_{ACTUAL\_\tau_i}} = Var(T_{ACTUAL\_\tau_i}) = (1 + b_{1\_i})^2 * \bar{\sigma}^2_i + b^2_{2\_i} * \sum_{j=1, j\neq i}^{n} \bar{\sigma}^2_j$.

With the above approximations, the probability that the transaction τ can complete within its deadline $t^{\tau}_{deadline}$ can now be computed. T_{ACTUAL_τ} is normally distributed since both $T^f_{CPU\_\tau}$ and $\mathcal{B}_\tau$ are normally distributed. Given the threshold probability ρ value of, say .95, by looking up a normal distribution table, we can find the value 1.645 such that $Pr(X < 1.645) = .95$, where X is a standard normal distribution random variable with the mean of 0 and the standard deviation of 1. Thus, with the estimated mean $\bar{\mu}_{T_{ACTUAL\_\tau_i}}$ and the estimated standard deviation $\bar{\sigma}_{T_{ACTUAL\_\tau_i}}$, and the deadline $t^{\tau}_{deadline}$ for transaction τ, if $t^{\tau}_{deadline} \geq \bar{\mu}_{T_{ACTUAL\_\tau_i}} + 1.645 * \bar{\sigma}_{T_{ACTUAL\_\tau_i}}$, transaction τ has a probability more than .95 to complete within its deadline, i.e., transaction τ has the Completion property with respect to $\{\, \tau_1, ..., \tau_i \,\}$. Otherwise, transaction τ fails the Completion property.

Firing a newly chosen rule r increases the blocking times for the already fired rules, increases their expected completion times, and decreases their probabilities to complete actions within deadlines. Therefore, an already fired rule may fail the Completion property if the newly chosen rule r is fired. Rule r will not be fired if (i) r fails the Completion property, or (ii) any rule that is already fired fails due to the firing of r.

3.2 DECIDE Algorithm

We now present the algorithm DECIDE that determines if a transaction satisfies the Completion property with respect to a set of transactions.

Let n be the total number of earlier executions of the transaction τ. One can give an O(n) expected time complexity algorithm [Kuo97] Update-CPU-Time-Estimation which updates the estimated CPU execution time for transaction τ that has executed completely with an actual CPU execution time of t_τ. The larger the sample size n is, the more precise the estimation is.

Based on the previously-described blocking time and the completion time functions, the algorithm Compute-Trans-Comp-Time estimates the expected completion time and the standard deviation on the completion time of transaction τ. The algorithm Compute-Trans-Comp-Time computes the completion time of a transaction with respect to a fired rule set. For all the rules that are fired, this algorithm has to be executed to update estimated completion times. The attributes *MeanSum* and *VarianceSum* associated with a rule set R are the sum of the expected CPU execution times and the sum of variances on the CPU execution times of all the transactions in R.

The algorithm DECIDE (given in Figure 1) returns True if the Completion property is satisfied when the transaction τ is also fired along with the other n concurrently executing actions of the fired rule set. The algorithm returns False otherwise. Since we assume that the random variables $T^f_{CPU\_\tau_1}, ..., T^f_{CPU\_\tau_n}$, and $T^f_{CPU\_\tau}$ for transactions $\tau_1, .., \tau_n$, and τ are independent and are normally distributed, the random variable for the completion time of transaction τ (which is computed using the blocking time function and the completion time function) is also normally distributed. Therefore, if the deadline of τ is, say, more than $\bar{\mu}_\tau + 1.645 * \bar{\sigma}_\tau$, then the transaction τ has a probability of .95 or more to complete within its deadline.

Algorithm DECIDE(r, R, ρ)
Input:
  r: rule r with action (transaction) τ to be considered for firing.
  R: the fired rule set with n rules. ρ: threshold probability.
Output:
  True if the Completion pr. is satisfied for rules in R; *False* otherwise.
Body:
{*Rule r is added to the fired rule set. Each rule in R′ is tested again for the satisfaction of the Completion property.*}
  $R' := R \cup \{r\}$;
  $MeanSum := R.MeanSum + \bar{\mu}_\tau$; { $\bar{\mu}_\tau$ *is the exp. CPU time of* τ. }
   { $R.MeanSum$ *is* $\sum_{i=1}^{n} \bar{\mu}_i$, *where* $\bar{\mu}_i$ *is the exp. CPU time of* $r_i \in R$. }
  $VarianceSum := R.VarianceSum + \bar{\sigma}_\tau^2$; { $\bar{\sigma}_\tau$: *the standard deviation.* }
  for each $r' \in R'$ **do begin**
  Comp-Trans-Comp-Time (r',$\{R' - r'\}$,$MeanSum - \bar{\mu_{\tau'}}$, $VarianceSum - \bar{\sigma}^2_{\tau'}$);
   if $t^{\tau'}_{deadline} < \bar{\mu}^{\tau'}_{completion} + z * \bar{\sigma}^{\tau'}_{completion}$ **then return** *False*;
{ *If any trans fails the Completion prop wrpt R′, the alg. returns False.* τ' *is the transaction of rule* r'. $t^{\tau'}_{deadline}$ *is the deadline of* τ'. $\bar{\mu}^{\tau'}_{completion}$ *and* $\bar{\sigma}^{\tau'}_{completion}$ *are the est. mean and standard dev. on the comp. time for* τ'. *Pr*$(X \leq z) = \rho$, *where X is a standard norm. dist. rv* $z = 1.645$ *for* $\rho = 0.95$. }
  endfor
  return *True*;
EndDECIDE.

Figure 1. Algorithm DECIDE

In the worst case, the algorithm Compute-Trans-Comp-Time is called $(n + 1)$ times in the algorithm DECIDE, where n is the number of rules in the fired rule set. Since the time complexity for the algorithm Compute-Trans-Comp-Time is O(1) (*MeanSum* and *VarianceSum* are computed only once), the time complexity for DECIDE for determining the Completion property of a rule with respect to a fired rule set of n rules is O(n).

4 Issues for Duration and Completion Properties

4.1 Transitivity Issues

Definition (spanning requirement): Given the rule base R and the event set E, a rule $r \in R$ can be fired only if (i) $r \in R_E^1$, or (ii) there exists a triggering path $r_1 \Rightarrow ... \Rightarrow r_i \Rightarrow r$, where $r_1 \in R_E^1$ and $r_1, ..., r_i$ are all fired. A set of rules to be fired is said to meet the spanning requirement if one of the above two conditions holds for each of the rules in the set.

In order to satisfy the spanning requirement, the CHOOSE algorithm examines (i) whether or not the chosen rule is in R_E^1, or (ii) whether or not a triggering rule of the chosen rule

4.2 Priority Policy

Let p_i denote the priority of rule r_i. We need a policy for choosing the rule set $\{r_1(p_1), ..., r_m(p_m)\}$ to be fired in terms of rule priorities. For a given a rule set $R_i = \{r_1, ..., r_j\}$, the *priority index* $\mathcal{P}_i$ of R_i is defined as $\sum_{k=1}^{j} p_k$. In this paper, we fire the rule set with the highest priority index among all rule sets to be fired. [Kuo97] discusses other possible policies.

5 The Problem Definition and Complexity

CDP (Completion-Duration-Priority)-Satisfaction Problem:
Assume that the simple-priority-summation formula is used as the priority index. Given a prioritized rule base R, an initial event set E, a threshold probability ρ, and a rule selection period $\mathcal{D}$, find a set $R' \subseteq R$ of rules which meets the spanning requirement and
(i) $Completion\_Probability(r, R') \geq \rho$ for each rule $r \in R'$,
(ii) $\sum_{r_i \in R'} t_i \leq \mathcal{D}$, where t_i is the expected CPU execution time of r_i, and
(iii) there is no $R'' \subseteq R$ such that $\sum_{r_i \in R''} p_i > \sum_{r_j \in R'} p_j$, where p_i is the priority of r_i, and p_j is the priority of r_j.

We restate the CDP-Satisfaction problem as a decision problem:
Given a prioritized rule base R, an initial event set E, a threshold probability ρ, a rule selection period $\mathcal{D}$, and a positive integer K, is there a set $R' \subseteq R$ of rules which meets the spanning requirement and
(i) $Completion\_Probability(r, R') \geq \rho$ for each rule $r \in R'$,
(ii) $\sum_{r_i \in R'} t_i \leq \mathcal{D}$, where t_i is the expected CPU execution time of r_i, and
(iii) $\sum_{r_i \in R'} p_i \geq$ K, where p_i is the priority of r_i?

We derive a more restrictive version of the CDP-Satisfaction problem by constraining our rules as follows: no rule is triggered by the action of another rule. In this case, the rule closure $R_E^+ = R_E^1$, since no rule is triggered by another rule.

The DP-Satisfaction problem defined below does not consider the Completion property.

DP-Satisfaction Problem:
Given a prioritized rule base R where no rule is triggered by the action of another rule and no deadlocks among actions exist, an initial event set E, a rule selection period $\mathcal{D}$, and a positive integer K, is there a set R' of rules, $R' \subseteq R^1_E$, such that
(i) $\sum_{r_i \in R'} t_i < \mathcal{D}$, where t_i is the expected CPU execution time of r_i, and
(ii) $\sum_{r_i \in R'} p_i \geq K$, where p_i is the priority of r_i?

Due to space considerations, please see [Kuo97] for the proof of the theorem below.

Theorem *DP-Satisfaction* problem is NP-Complete.

Thus, to summarize, among the three properties of the CDP-Satisfaction problem, the Completion property can be satisfied in polynomial time (actually, linear in the number of rules fired). The satisfaction of the Duration property and the Priority property takes exponential time, since finding a fired rule set with the maximum priority index is an NP-Complete problem as stated above. Next we discuss heuristic algorithms.

6 Heuristic CHOOSE Algorithms for CDP-Satisfaction

Next, two CHOOSE heuristic algorithms are illustrated for choosing a rule set (to fire) with the maximum priority index. First we define the terminology used in the heuristic algorithms. A *candidate rule* is a rule which is not yet fired and which can be triggered either by an event in the event set E or by the action of a fired rule. An *outstanding candidate* is a candidate rule which has the highest rule priority among candidate rules. A candidate rule becomes a *discarded* rule if it fails the Completion property or the Duration property. A failed rule will not become a candidate any more.

6.1 CHOOSE-REGULAR Algorithm

The CHOOSE-REGULAR algorithm simply chooses the outstanding rule r with the highest rule priority among the candidate rules. If rule r satisfies both the Completion property and the Duration property, then (i) rule r is added into the rule set to be fired, and (ii) all the rules which can be triggered by r and have not been fired become candidate rules. The procedure continues until there are no more candidate rules. If rule r does not satisfy the Completion property or the Duration property, rule r is marked as *discarded*. The procedure continues until there are no more candidates, or all rules in the rule base are fired.

In the worst case, every rule is tested for the Completion and the Duration priorities. However, each rule is tested for the two properties at most once; the rule is then either fired or marked *discarded.* Therefore, the time complexity for the algorithm CHOOSE-REGULAR [Kuo97] is $O(M \times N)$ for the execution of Compute_Transaction_Completion_Time, where M is the number of rules in the rule base, and N is the number of rules in the fired rule set.

6.2 CHOOSE-ONE-AHEAD Algorithm

In the CHOOSE-ONE-AHEAD algorithm, the rules which "can" be triggered by candidate rules are considered in the choosing process. We define a *look_ahead rule* as a rule which is not fired yet and can be triggered by a candidate rule.

We define the *potential priority value* for a candidate rule (*candidate_rule*) as the average of its own rule priority value and the maximum priority value among the look_ahead rules which can be triggered by the rule *candidate_rule.* If the outstanding candidate rule has the maximum potential priority value among the candidate rules, it is fired. Else, another candidate rule with the maximum potential priority value among all candidate rules is fired.

The time complexity for the algorithm CHOOSE-ONE-AHEAD [Kuo97] is $O(M \times F) + O(N \times K \times lnK) + O(F \times (K + L))$, where M is the number of rules in the rule base, F is the number of fired rules, N is the number of distinct actions in the rule base, K is the number of rules a rule can trigger, and L is the number of rules which can trigger the same rule.

7 Experimental Results

We briefly summarize the simulation results that compare the sum of the priorities of the rules fired in the CHOOSE-REGULAR and CHOOSE-ONE-AHEAD algorithm executions.

For simulation on the heuristics, acyclic rule bases are constructed by varying the following parameters: (i) the number of rules in the rule base, (ii) the number of events in the rule base, (iii) the maximum number of rules that an event can trigger, (iv) the probability distribution for rule priority assignments, and (v) the *deadline index* γ: the ratio of the deadline over the CPU execution time t_τ of actions. The deadline of a transaction τ is normally distributed with the mean of $\gamma \times t_\tau$.

The experiments involving observations 1-4 do not consider the Completion property, and assume that the CPU execution time for each transaction is the same.

Observation 1: With either the CHOOSE-REGULAR method or the CHOOSE-ONE-AHEAD method, (a) the average rule priority of the rules fired is higher than the average rule priority of the whole rule base; and, (b) the average priority of fired rules decreases as larger number of rules have to be fired.

Observation 2: Both methods work better when rule priorities are uniformly distributed in a wide range, from 1 to 50, than when rule priorities are normally distributed with mean 25 and standard deviation 10.

Observation 3: As more rules are fired, the average priority of the fired rules drops faster in the situation where priorities are uniformly distributed than in the situation where priorities are normally distributed.

Observation 4: The average rule priority by the CHOOSE-ONE-AHEAD method is 3% to 6% higher than the average rule priority by the CHOOSE-REGULAR method when 50% of total actions are triggered.

The experiments involving observations 5-7 involve transactions with varying deadlines and varying CPU execution times, and assume that the Completion property is satisfied.

Observation 5: The average priority of fired rules decreases as more rules have to be fired.

Observation 6: The threshold probability has little effect on the average priority of the fired rules for both heuristics.

Observation 7: When priorities are normally distributed, the CHOOSE-ONE-AHEAD method outperforms the CHOOSE-REGULAR method by a range approximately from 2.5% to 3.5% for deadline indices from 15 to 50. Whereas, when priorities are uniformly distributed, the range is approximately from .7% to 2.5%.

References

[AHW95] Aiken, A., Hellerstein, J.M., and Widom, J., "Static Analysis Techniques for Predicting the Behavior of Active Database Rules", ACM TODS, Vol. 20, No. 1., March 1995.

[BCP96] Baralis, E., Ceri, S., and Paraboschi, S., "Modularization Techniques for Active Rules Design", ACM TODS, Vol. 2, No. 1, March 1996.

[Chak92] Chakravarthy, S., *Special Issue on Active Databases*, IEEE Bulletin of the TC on Data Engineering, Vol. 15, No. 1-4, December 1992.

[CKTB95] Chakravarthy, S., Krishnaprasad, V., Tamizuddin, Z., Badana, R.H., "ECA Rule Integration into an OODBMS: Architecture and Implementation", IEEE ICDE Conf., February 1995.

[Doug90] Dougherty, E.R., *Probability and Statics for the Engineering, Computing, and Physical Sciences*, Prentice-Hall, 1990.

[Kuo97] Kuo, H.-C., "A Rule-Based Cooperative Transaction Model and Event Processing in Real-Time Active Database Systems", Ph.D. Dissertation, Dept of Computer Eng. and Sci., Case Western Reserve University, Feb. 1997.

[OzSn95] Özsoyoğlu, G. and Snodgrass, R., "Temporal and Real-Time Databases: A Survey", IEEE TKDE, Vol. 7, No. 4, August 1995.

[WiCe96] Widom, J. and Ceri, S., (ed.) *Active Database Systems: Triggers and Rules For Advanced Database Processing* Morgan Kaufmann Pub., 1996.

Program Understanding in Databases Reverse Engineering

J. Henrard, V. Englebert, J-M. Hick, D. Roland, J-L. Hainaut

Institut d'Informatique, University of Namur
rue Grandgagnage, 21 - B-5000 Namur
db-main@info.fundp.ac.be

Abstract. The main argument of the paper is that *database understanding* (or reverse engineering) requires sophisticated *program understanding* techniques, and conversely. Database reverse engineering (DBRE) can be carried out following a generic methodology, one of the phases of which consists in eliciting all the implicit and untranslated data structures and constraints. Evidences of these hidden constructs can be found by analysing how the programs use and update the data. Hence the need for program analysis techniques such as searching for *clichés*, dependency analysis, program slicing and synthetic views. The paper explains how these techniques contribute to DBRE, and describes DB-MAIN, a programmable and extensible CASE environment that supports DBRE through program understanding techniques.

1. Introduction

Reverse engineering a piece of software consists, among others, in recovering or reconstructing its functional and technical specifications, starting mainly from the source text of the programs. Recovering these specifications is generally intended to redocument, convert, restructure, maintain or extend legacy applications.

The problem is particularly complex with old and ill-designed applications. In this case, not only no decent documentation (if any) can be relied on, but the lack of systematic methodologies for designing and maintaining them have led to tricky and obscure code. Therefore, reverse engineering has long been recognised as a complex, painful and prone-to-failure activity, so much so that it is simply not undertaken most of the time, leaving huge amounts of invaluable knowledge buried in the programs, and therefore definitively lost.

In information systems, or data-oriented applications, i.e., in applications the central component of which is a database (or a set of permanent files), it is generally considered that the complexity can be broken down by considering that the files or databases can be reverse engineered (almost) independently of the procedural parts, through a process called *DataBase Reverse Engineering* (DBRE in short).

This proposition to split the problem in this way can be supported by the following arguments.

- The semantic distance between the so-called conceptual specifications and the physical implementation is most often narrower for data than for procedural parts.
- The permanent data structures are generally the most stable part of applications.
- Even in very old applications, the semantic structures that underlie the file structures are mainly procedure-independent (though their physical structures are highly procedure-dependent).
- Reverse engineering the procedural part of an application is much easier when the semantic structure of the data has been elicited.

Therefore, concentrating on reverse engineering the application data components first can be much more efficient than trying to cope with the whole application.

Even if reverse engineering the data structure is "easier" than recovering the specification of the application as a whole, it is still a complex and long task. Many techniques, proposed in the literature and offered by CASE tools, appear to be limited in scope and are generally based on unrealistic assumptions about the quality and completeness of the source data structures to be reverse engineered. For instance, they often suppose that all the conceptual specifications have been declared into the DDL (data description language) and the procedural code is ignored. The schema has not been deeply restructured for performance or for any other requirements. Names have been chosen rationally.

Those conditions cannot be assumed for most large operational databases. Since 1992, some authors have recognised that the procedural part of the application programs is an essential source of information to retrieve data structures ([1], [4], [7] and [8]), and that understanding some program aspects is one of the keys to fully understand the data structures.

Program understanding is an emerging area within the software engineering field. It is the process of acquiring knowledge about an existing, generally undocumented, computer program. Increased knowledge enables such activities as error correction, enhancement, reuse, documentation and reverse engineering. A variety of approaches have been investigated to analyse programs, from straightforward textual analysis, through increasingly more complex static approaches, to the dynamic analysis of executing programs [9].

In this paper, we explain why program understanding can be useful to help understand data structures as well, and how these techniques can be used in DBRE. The paper is organised as follows. Section 2 is a synthesis of a generic DBMS-independent DBRE methodology. Section 3 discusses the need of program understanding in DBRE and the information we are looking for in programs. Section 4 describes the techniques used to analyse programs. Section 5 presents a DBRE CASE tool which is intended to support most DBRE processes, including program understanding.

2. A generic methodology for database reverse engineering

Our database reverse engineering (DBRE) methodology [4] is divided into two major processes (Fig. 1), namely *data structure extraction* and *data structure conceptualisation.* Those problems correspond to recovering two different schemas and require different concepts, reasoning and tools. In addition, these processes grossly appear as the reverse of the physical and logical design usually admitted in database design methodologies [2].

This methodology is generic in two ways. Its architecture and its processes are largely DMS-independent. Secondly, it specifies what problems have to be solved, and in which way, rather than the order in which the actions must be carried out.

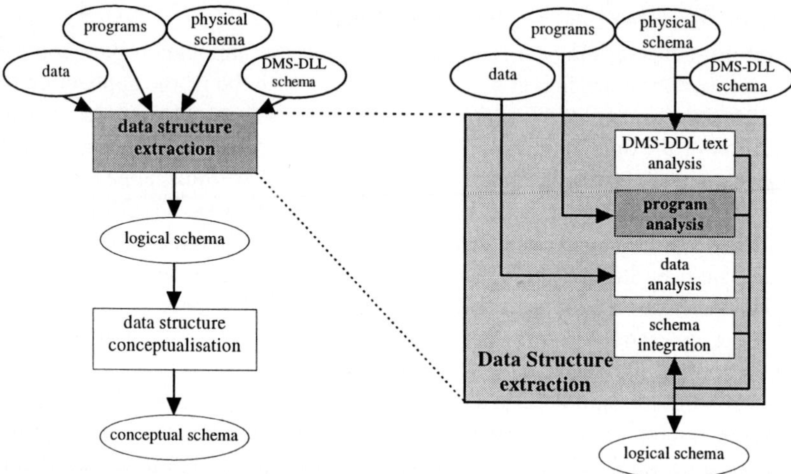

Fig. 1. Main processes of the generic DBRE methodology.

2.1 Data structure extraction

The first phase of the methodology consists in recovering the complete DMS schema, including all the implicit and explicit structures and constraints.

Some DMS, mainly the DBMS, supply a description of the global data schema. The problem is much more complex for standard files, for which no computerised description of their structure exists in most cases. The analysis of the declaration statements of each source program provides a partial view of the file and record structures. Data records and fields declaration statements provide important but partial information only. Hence the need for program and data analysis and for integration techniques.

If a construct or a constraint has not been declared explicitly in the database schema, whatever the reason, it has most of the time been translated into procedural code sections distributed and duplicated throughout the programs. Recovering undeclared, and therefore implicit, structure is a complex problem, for which no deterministic methods exist so far. A careful analysis of all the information sources (procedural sections, documentation, database content, etc.) can accumulate evidences for those specifications.

In this generic methodology, the main processes of data structure extraction are the following :

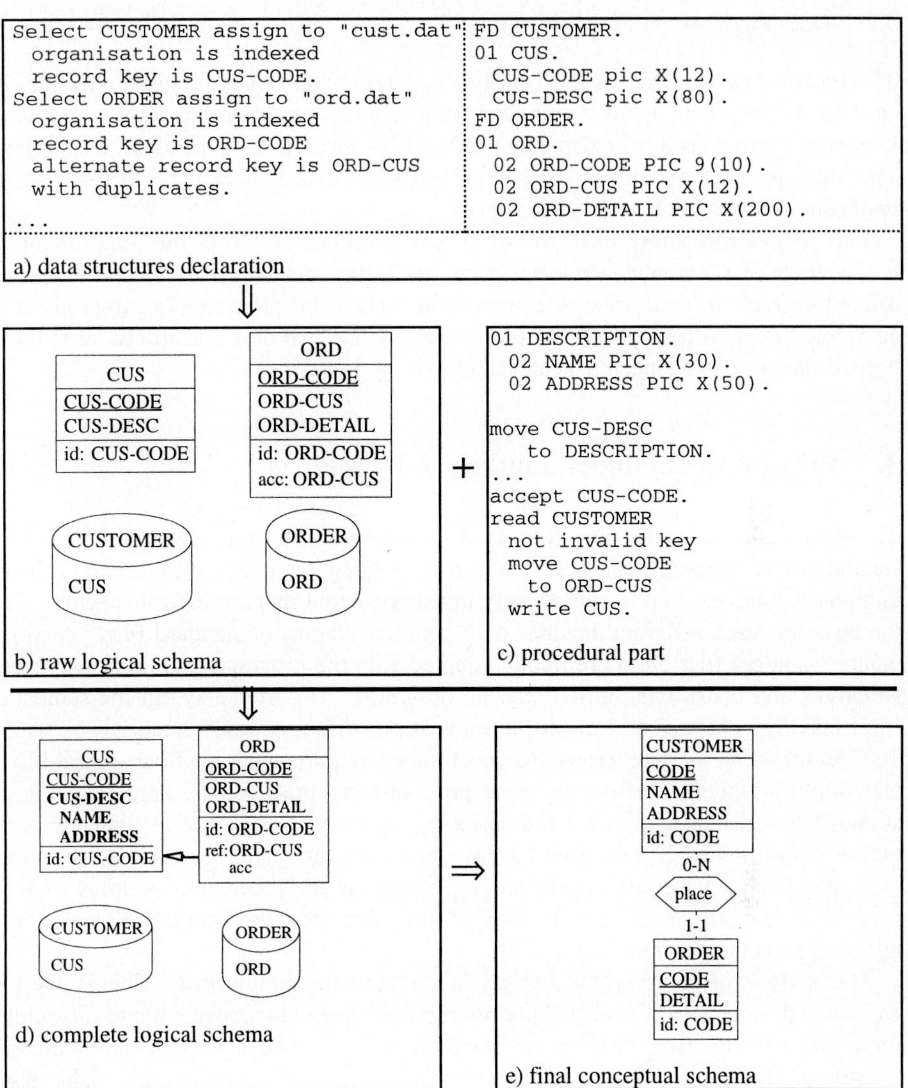

Fig. 2. Database reverse engineering example.

- *DMS-DDL text analysis*: analysing the data structure declaration statements to extract the explicit constructs and constraints, thus providing a rows logical schema.
- *Program analysis*: analysing the procedural code to detect implicit data structures.
- *Data analysis*: analysing the data in order to detect data patterns suggesting data structures and properties and to test hypotheses.
- *Schema integration*: merging the schemas obtained during the previous steps.

The final product of this phase is the complete logical schema, that includes both explicit and implicit structures and constraints.

2.2 Data structure conceptualization

The second phase addresses the conceptual interpretation of the logical schema. It consists for instance in detecting and transforming or discarding non-conceptual structures, redundancies, technical optimisations and DMS-dependent constructs. The final product of this phase is the persistent data conceptual schema of the application. More detail can be found in [5].

Fig. 2 gives a short example of a DBRE process. The files and records declarations (2.a) are analyzed to yield the raw logical schema (2.b). This schema is refined through the analysis of the procedural parts of the program (2.c) to produce a complete logical schema (2.d). This schema exhibits two new constructs. It is then transformed into the conceptual schema (2.e).

3. Why program understanding in DBRE

The data structure extraction process is often easier for true databases than for standard files. Indeed, databases have a global schema (generally a DDL text or Data dictionary contents) that is immediately translated into a first cut logical schema. On the contrary, each program includes only a partial schema of standard files. At first glance, standard files are more tightly coupled with the programs and there are more structures and constraints buried into the programs. Unfortunately, all the standard file tricks have been found in recent applications that use "real" databases as well. The reasons can be numerous: to meet other requirements such as reusability, genericity, simplicity, efficiency; poor programming practice; the application is a straightforward translation of a file-based legacy system; etc. So, in both old and recent data-oriented applications, many data structures and constraints are not explicitly declared but are coded, among others, as the procedural sections of the program. For all these reasons, one of the data structure extraction source of information is the program text source.

The analysis of the program source is a complex and tedious task. This is due to the fact that procedurally-coded data constructs are spread in a huge amount of source files, and also because there is no standard way to code a definite structure or constraint. Each programmer has his personal way(s) to express them. This also depends on the programming language, the target DBMS, the enterprise rules, the programmer skill, his mood, etc.

We do not need to retrieve the complete specification of the program, we are merely looking for information that are relevant to find the undeclared structures of persistent data. More precisely, we are looking for evidences of fields refinement and aggregation, referential constraints and exact cardinalities, to mention only a few.

We will give some informal information on how the main implicit constructs can be recovered through program analysis.

- *Field refinement* consists in associating, with a field (or a record) initially declared atomic, a new structure comprising sub-fields. *Field aggregation* is the opposite operation, according to which a collection of independent fields appear to be the components of a compound field, or the values of a multivalued field. These two constructions can be detected if there is a relation (assignment, comparison) between two variables of different structures.

- A *foreign key* consists of a field of a record that references another record. To detect a foreign key, we have to find evidences that each value of the source field belongs to the value set of the key of another record.
- The *cardinality* of an array states, through the couple I-J, that the number of active elements of the array is between I and J. The exact minimum cardinality (I) of an array can be found by the analysis of the array initialization. The maximum cardinality of an array is usually the size of the array, except if it can be found that the last elements are never used.

Several industrial projects have proved that powerful program understanding techniques and tools are essential to support the data structure extraction process in realistic size database reverse-engineering projects.

4. Program understanding techniques

In this section, we will present program understanding techniques that we use during the data structure extraction. The main techniques explained here are pattern matching, dependency graph, program slicing and program visualisation. For each of these techniques it will be shown how they can be applied to structure elicitation in database reverse engineering.

4.1 Search in text sources

The simplest way to find some definite information in a program is to search the program source text for some patterns or *clichés*. We use the term pattern and not just string, as in a text editor, because a pattern describes a set of possible strings. It can include wildcards, characters ranges, multiple structures, variables and can be based on other defined patterns. For example, we can write a pattern that match any numeric constant, or the various kind of COBOL assignment statements, or some `select-from-where` SQL queries. The pattern matching tool can be coupled with some external procedure that are triggered for each pattern match.

4.2 Dependency graph

The *dependency graph* (generalisation of dataflow diagram) is a graph where each variable of a program is represented by a node and an arc (directed or not) represents a direct relation (assignment, comparison, etc.) between two variables. Fig. 3.b illustrates the dependency graph of the program fragment of Fig. 3.a. If there is a path from variable A to variable C in the graph, then there is, in the program, a sequence of statements such that the value of A is in relation with the value of C. The very meaning of this relation between the variables is defined by the analyst: the structure of one variable is included into the structure of the other one, the variables share the same values, they denote the same real world object, etc.

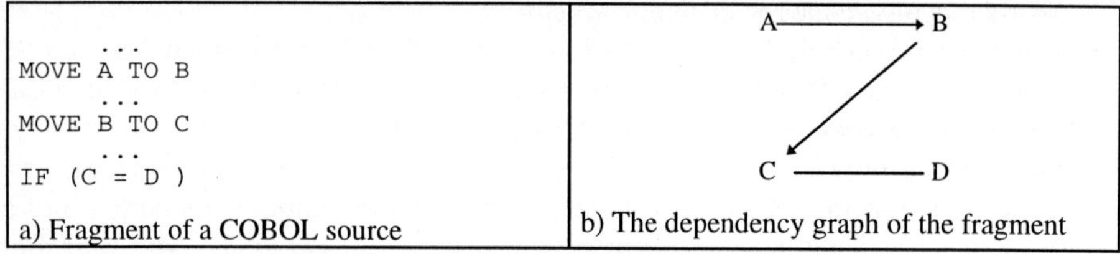

Fig. 3. The dependency graph.

The dependency graph will be used to find evidences for field refinement, field aggregation or foreign keys.

4.2 Program slicing

The slice of a program with respect to program point *p* and variable *x* consists of all the program statements and predicates that might affect the value *x* at point *p*. This concept was originally discussed by M. Weiser [10]. Since then, various slightly different notions of program slices have been proposed, as well as a number of methods to compute them.

```
FD CUSTOMER.
   01 CUS.
      02 CUS-NUM PIC 9(3).
      02 CUS-NAME PIC X(10).
      02 CUS-ORD PIC 9(2).
         OCCURS 10.
      ...
   01 ORDER PIC 9(3).
      ...
1  ACCEPT CUS-NUM.
2  READ CUS KEY IS CUS-NUM.
3  MOVE 1 TO IND.
4  MOVE 0 TO ORDER.
5  PERFORM UNTIL IND=10
6    ADD CUS-ORD(IND) TO ORDER
7    ADD 1 TO IND.
8  DISPLAY CUS-NAME.
9  DISPLAY ORDER.
```

a) COBOL program P

```
FD CUSTOMER.
   01 CUS.
      02 CUS-NUM PIC 9(3).
      02 CUS-NAME PIC X(10).

1  ACCEPT CUS-NUM.
2  READ CUS KEY IS CUS-NUM.
8  DISPLAY CUS-NAME.
```

b) Slice of P with respect to *CUS-NAME* and *line 8*

Fig.4. Example of program slicing.

Fig. 4.a is a small COBOL program that asks for a customer number (CUS-NUM) and displays the name of the customer (CUS-NAME) and the total amount of its order (ORDER). Fig. 4.b shows the slice that contains all the statements that contribute to displaying the name of the customer, that is the *slice of P with respect to CUS-NAME at line 8*.

Procedures, arbitrary control flow (Go To) and composite data types, typical to COBOL programs, make computing program slices a fairly complicated task. Our approach is based on the System Dependence Graph techniques developed by [6].

In DBRE, we use program slicing to reduce the scope of program analysis, either by visual inspection, or through the use of other tools. It is mainly used to find evidences of foreign keys, exact cardinality, local identifiers and domain constraints. The slice must be computed with respect to a statement that uses the candidate field. For example, a slice can be computed for an output statement and a candidate foreign key to see if each value of the foreign key is checked to be in the value set of the identifier of the target record.

4.3 Program representation

Program source code, even reduced through program slicing, often is too difficult to understand because the program can be huge (thousands of pages of code), poorly structured, based on poor naming conventions, and made up of hundreds of modules. To help the analyst grasp the structure of a program it is useful to give him different synthetic abstract views of it such as the *call graph* or the *input/output dataflow* of the different modules.

There are many other visualisations of a program that can be useful to help understand a program. The dependency graph can also be displayed as a graph. It is why we need a tool that can easily create new kinds of graph.

5. The tools provided by DB-MAIN

Program understanding is complex and tedious. Although the process cannot be fully automated, the analyst cannot carry it out without a powerful and flexible set of tools. These tools must be integrated and their results recorded in a common repository. In addition, the tools need to be easily extensible and customisable to fit the analyst's exact needs.

DB-MAIN is a general database engineering CASE environment that offers sophisticated reverse engineering toolsets. DB-MAIN is one of the results of a R&D project started in 1993 by the database team of the computer science department of the University of Namur (Belgium). Its purpose is to help the analyst in the design, reverse engineering, migration, maintenance and evolution of databases.

DB-MAIN offers the usual CASE functions, such as the database schema creation, management, visualisation, validation, transformation, and code and report generation. It also includes a programming language (*Voyager2*) that can manipulate the objects of the repository and allows the user to develop its own functions. More details can be found in [3] and [5].

DB-MAIN also offers some functions that are specific to DBRE. The *extractors* extract automatically the data structures declared into a source text. Extractors read the declaration part of the source text and create corresponding abstractions in the repository. The *foreign key assistant* is used to find the possible foreign keys of a schema. Giving a group of fields, that is the origin (or the target) of a foreign key, it searches a schema for all the groups of fields that can be the target (or the origin) of the first group. The search is based on a combination of matching criteria such as the group type, the length, the type and matching rules of the name of the fields.

Other reverse engineering functions use program understanding processors.

A *pattern matching* engine searches a source text for a definite pattern. Patterns are defined into a pattern description language (PDL), they can use the definition of other patterns and contain variables. Those variables can be used as parameters of a procedure to be executed for each pattern instance.

```
var ::= /g"[a-zA-Z0-9]*[a-zA-Z][-a-zA-Z0-9]*";
var_1 ::= var;
var_2 ::= var;
move ::= "MOVE" - @var_1 - "TO" - @var_2 ;
```

Fig. 5. The COBOL `move` pattern definition.

Fig. 5 shows the definition of the `move` pattern, this pattern will match with the simplest form of COBOL assignments. The PDL variables are prefixed with the '@' character and the '-' name denotes a pattern (inter-token separators) defined in a secondary library.

DB-MAIN offers a *variable dependency graph* tool. The user defines the relations between variables as a list of patterns. Each pattern must contain exactly two variables and the instances of those variables are the nodes of the graph. For example, if the pattern `move` (Fig. 6) is given then the arcs of the dependency graph will represent variables connected by a assignment statement. The dependency graph itself is displayed *in context*: the user selects a variable, then all the occurrences of this variable, and of all the variables connected to it in the dependency graph are coloured into the source text, both in the declaration and in the procedural sections. Though a graphical presentation could be thought to be more elegant and more abstract, the experience has taught us that the source code itself gives much *lateral* information, such as comments, layout and surrounding statements.

The *program slicing* tool computes the program slice with respect to the selected line of the source text and one of the variables, or component thereof, referenced at that line. When the slice is computed its statements are coloured, so that it can be examined in context. For example, some lines that do not belong to the slice (e.g., comments or error messages) may give some additional hints to understand the slice. If needed, the slice can be transformed into a new program to be processed by other analyzers.

6. Conclusion

Though the *software engineering* and *database/IS* communities most often live on different planets, experience proves that many real world problems cannot be solved without combining the concepts, techniques and reasonings belonging to each of them. Anyway, an information system mainly comprises a database and a collection of programs. Therefore, understanding these programs needs a deep understanding of the semantics of the database, while recovering this semantics cannot ignore what the programs are intended to do on/with the contents of the database.

One of the major objectives of the DB-MAIN project is the methodological and tool support for database reverse engineering processes. We have quickly learned that we needed powerful program analysis reasoning and their supporting tools, such as those that have been developed in the program understanding realm. We integrated these reasoning in a highly generic DBRE methodology, while we developed specific analyzers to include in the DB-MAIN CASE tool.

One of the great lessons we painfully learned is that they are no two similar DBRE projects. Hence the need for easily programmable, extensible and customizable tools. The DB-MAIN (meta-)CASE tool is now a mature environment that offers powerful program understanding tools dedicated, among others, to database reverse engineering, as well as sophisticated features to extend its repository and its functions. DB-MAIN has been developed in C++ for MS-Windows workstations. An education version is available at no charge for non-profit institutions (http://www.info.fundp.ac.be/~dbm).

References

1. Anderson, M.: Reverse Engineering of Legacy Systems: From Valued-Based to Object-Based Models, *PhD thesis*, Lausanne, EPFL (1997)
2. Batini, C., Ceri, S. and Navathe, S.B.: Conceptual Database Design - An Entity-Relationship Approach, Benjamin/Cummings (1992).
3. Englebert, V., Henrard J., Hick, J.-M., Roland, D. and Hainaut, J.-L.: DB-MAIN: un Atelier d'Ingénierie de Bases de Données, in *11 Journée BD Avancées*, Nancy (1995).
4. Hainaut, J.-L., Chandelon, M., Tonneau, C. and Joris M.: Contribution to a Theory of Database Reverse Engineering, in *Proc. of the IEEE Working Conf. on Reverse Engineering*, Baltimore, May 1993, IEEE Computer Society Press (1993).
5. Hainaut, J.-L, Roland, D., Hick J-M., Henrard, J. and Englebert, V.: Database Reverse Engineering: from Requirements to CARE Tools, *Journal of Automated Software Engineering*, **3**(1) (1996).
6. Horwitz, S., Reps, T. and Binkley, D. Interprocedural Slicing using Dependence Graphs, ACM Trans. on Programming Languages and Systems **12**(1), Jan. 1990, 26-60 (1990).
7. Joris, M., Van Hoe, R., Hainaut, J.-L., Chandelon, M., Tonneau, C. and Bodart, F. et al.: PHENIX: Methods and Tools for Database Reverse Engineering, in *Proc 5th Int. Conf. on Sofwazre Engieering and Applications.* Toulouse, EC2 Publish (1992).
8. Petit, J.-M., Kouloumdjian, J., Bouliaut, J.-F. and Toumani, F.: Using Queries to Improve Database Reverse Engineering, in *Proc of the 13th Int. Conf. on ER Approach*, Manchester. Springer-Verlag (1994).
9. Rugaber S. Program Comprehension. Technical report, College of Computing, Georgia Institute of Technology (1995).
10. Weiser, M.: Program Slicing, *IEEE TSE*, **10**, 352-357 (1984).

Semantics Based Schema Analysis

Nayyer Masood[1] and Barry Eaglestone[2]
[1] Database Research Group, School of Computing and Mathematics,
University of Bradford, Bradford, UK
n.masood1@comp.brad.ac.uk
[2] Department of Information Studies, University of Sheffield, Sheffield, UK
B.Eaglestone@Sheffield.ac.uk

Abstract. A new method for schema analysis is described in which reasoning is based upon the real–world semantics of schema elements. The method distinguishes between intrinsic and in–context semantics, which respectively provide a basis for shallow and deep semantic comparisons between clement. The method provides a basis for more accurate integration of component schemas within a federated database system.

1. Introduction

The schema integration (SI) process by which a federated schema is derived is critical to the effectiveness of a federated database system (FDBS) [14]. **Schema analysis** is the phase of SI in which semantic relationships between elements of component schemas are identified [2,9,12]. This requires an understanding of the semantics of those schema elements [16]. This paper therefore proposes a concept–based method of schema analysis for FDBSs which provides a basis for automated reasoning with real–world semantics. The method is based upon mapping component schema elements into common concepts and has been developed for an FDBS architecture, in which the Object Model proposed by the Object Data Management Group (ODMG) [3] is used as the canonical data model (CDM).

2. Semantic aspects of Schema Integration

Schema integration is an essential and critical phase in the design of FDBSs [14]. The effectiveness of a system is dependent on synthesis of federated schemas which correctly represent and map into relevant component schemas elements. The syntactic aspect to this problem concerns the design of federated schema elements which simultaneously represent structures of corresponding component schema elements that they integrate. This form of reconciliation is straight-forward once component schemas have been mapped into a CDM and correspondences between schema elements have been established. However, the semantic aspect, the identification of those correspondences, is problematic for three reasons: (i) Semantic integration requires knowledge of, and the ability to capture and reason with, real–world semantics of component schema elements, i.e., the phenomena in the UoD that they denote [16]. However, data models currently lack the expressiveness to represent real–world semantics within an FDBS [7]. (ii) The existence of semantic heterogeneities (SHs) between schema elements obscures semantic similarities between them [4, 2, 13, 7]. The SI process therefore involves detection and resolution of SHs [7]. (iii) In the absence of methods and tools for controlling the problem complexity, a human schema integrator may be required to analyse a prohibitively large number of component schema elements within the global context of their combined UoDs.

These major problems of SI pertain to the schema analysis phase [2,9,12,5]. The challenge is therefore to develop a semi-automated schema analysis method that compensates for a lack of semantic information in schemas and facilitates detection and resolution of SHs, in such that the problem complexity becomes manageable.

3. Related Research

Strong levels of semantic similarity determine compatibility for integration. Schema elements are considered semantically similar if they represent equivalent or related concepts [7]. Early SI methods use similarity measures based upon correspondences between attribute domains or intrinsic meanings of elements [4,9,16,12,1]. An important development was the realization of the critical role of context within which schema elements are interpreted and compared [15,13,6,8,5]. [7] identify context and concept denoted as constituents of the semantics of an element. Elements may be interpreted within multiple contexts, often represented by different structure within which they participate. Semantic similarity between schema elements depends on the context in which they are compared. Moreover, the contexts in which elements are defined and analyzed may be related to or entirely different from each other. [13,8], for example, define a taxonomy of semantic similarity based on both inter-domains mapping (as in [9]) and context(s) within which elements are compared.

The major trends in schema analysis include the approaches based entirely on schematic information [4,11,10], those which increase the semantic content of component schemas [9, 15,16,12], and the ones which base schema analysis on data element interpretations [16,12,1,5]. The basic idea in the latter is to capture the real meanings of schema elements by mapping them to the concepts they model. The concepts are taken from the shared global universe of discourse (UoD) modeled in the component dataabase systems (CDBSs) of an FDBS.

We see concept–based methods as the most promising approach to SI for FDBSs, since they provide a basis for automated reasoning with real–world semantics (rather those of the computer–world). In particular, the common concept approach (CCA) in [16] goes some way towards making explicit a common context within which comparisons can be made. Mapping and reasoning are facilitated by arranging common concepts from the UoD into a number of concept hierarchies where nodes represent concepts and edges represent semantic relationships between concepts. These hierarchies form the concept model for the UoD (CMU). However, we also see a need to apply this approach to a specific CDM and interpret its higher–level constructs (previous work considers only "attributes"). This introduces the problem of inferring schema element semantics from its structural context within the schema. Given the evolutionary nature of FDBSs and the need for consistency of schema analysis over time, we also see a need to integrate the CMU and schema element interpretations within the FDBS architecture, itself. The CCA based schema analysis method described in the remainder of this paper addresses these shortcomings.

4. An Enhanced CCA–based Schema Analysis Method

Our schema analysis methodology enhances the CCA method in [16]. We extend this method by addressing problems of SI within an FDBS architecture [14], with an ODMG–93 [3] based CDM. The architecture supports federations by exporting parts of component schemas and integrating them within federated schemas. Component, export and federated schemas all use the CDM. Our method analyses semantic similarities between elements of ODMG schemas, i.e., types (atomic and structured), instance properties (attributes, relationships), and subtype/supertype hierarchies. We have also extended the FDBS architecture to include the CMU, component schema–to–CMU bindings, and federation–specific concept models (FCM). ODMG is adopted as the CDM because of the richness of object–oriented data models and its emergence as a de–facto object database standard.

Our schema analysis methodology has three sub–processes [2, 9, 12, 5]: (i) *schema interpretation*, in which component schemas are analyzed to determine the semantics of each database by eliciting the semantics of its schema elements; (ii) *schema comparison*, in which component schemas elements are compared to identify semantic similarities between them; and (iii) *similarity analysis*, in which the nature of semantic similarities are determined and SHs are identified.

The methodology is based on the notion of schema interpretation [5], i.e., explicit mapping from schema elements to agreed representations of the concepts they denote. It is a semi-automated approach. Phase one is performed by the human integrator and produces an explicit interpretation of each component schema of the FDBS. The last two phases are performed each time a federated schema has to be developed and are automated. The output of our methodology is a set of assertions on semantic similarities between schema elements which also highlight SHs between them.

4.1 Schema Interpretation

A prerequisite to our schema analysis methodology is a concept model for the UoD (CMU). A CMU consists of a collection of instances of type *Concept* to represent general concepts from the global UoD modeled in the CDBSs. A concept represents some aspect of reality isolated by mind [1] and is represented by one or more terms; it may represent a real-world object, or a property or characteristic possessed by certain real–world objects. CMU concepts are independent of any particular application [16] and are therefore not bound to any particular structural details. Concept instances are related by is–a relationships to form hierarchies in accordance to their natural or ontological order. These are helpful in the mapping and reasoning processes. (Figures 1 and 2 respectively give an example CMU and ODMG schema which are used to illustrate the proposed schema analysis process).

The schema–to–CMU mapping process relates CDBS elements to concepts that they denote. Thus an **interpretation** is provided for each schema element. These later provide a basis for reasoning about semantic similarities between schema elements. The mapping process is similar to those in [16] and [12] but extends the scope to all mutable object types and their characteristics (not just "attributes").

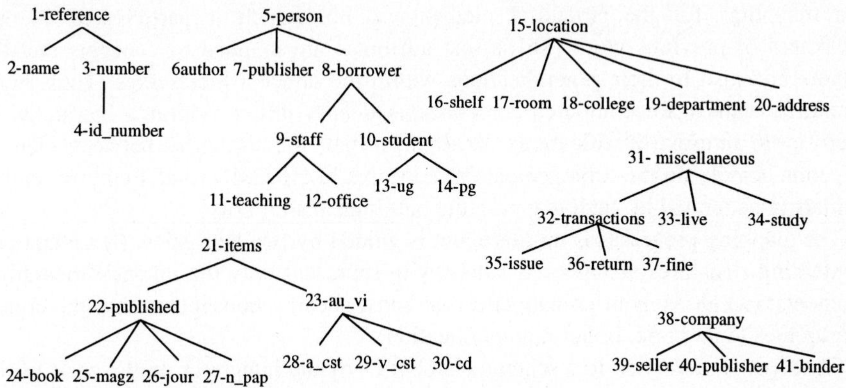

Figure 1: Example concept hierarchies from a library information system; nodes represent concepts, and edges the *is-a* relationships between concepts.

```
module UniversityLib
class Item ( extent items) {
  attribute unsigned short acc_no;
  attribute String holding;
  attribute String title;
}
class Book extends Item ( extent books) {
  attribute set<String> auth_names;
  attribute Publisher publ;
  relationship Person issued_to
        inverse Person::bk_issued
}
class Pap extends Item ( extent paps) {
  attribute String ed_name;
  attribute String pap_type;
}

class Person (extent persons) {
  attribute String name;
  relationship set <Book> bk_issued
        inverse Book::issued_to;
}
class student extends Person
        ( extent students ) {
attribute String reg_no;
attribute String dept;
attribute Structure Adress
  <string college, string r_num> d_adr;
}
class Publisher extends Person
        ( extent publishers){
  attribute String name;
  attribute String address;
}
```

Figure 2: A fragment of an ODMG library object database schema

Previous mapping approaches [16,12] do not distinguish between **intrinsic** meaning of an attribute (e.g., title denotes identity) and its **in–context** meaning by virtue of the structures within which it participates (book.title denotes a book's identity). A consequence of this representation is that the distinction between what type of fact an element represents and what it is a fact about is lost. Also, where an element participates in different structures it is not possible to distinguish between its meanings within the different contexts. We overcome this limitation by separate representations of intrinsic and in–context meanings. The former are represented as element–to–concept mappings and the latter as semantic associations between elements. Relationship subtypes represent different semantic relationships, i.e., is-a, aggregation, and association. Through navigation of the latter we can transitively assemble in–context semantics of a schema element from the element's mapping and the mappings for the structural elements within which it participates. Another weakness of previous work [16] is that attributes are mapped to concepts that they denote and also to their generalisations within the concept hierarchies. Thus, higher similarity values are computed for concepts deeply nested within a hierarchy, but there is no intuitive justifications for this. Further, the similarity between elements depends heavily on the arrangements of concepts in the CMU, that's why we call the simialrity generated by such mapping the ontological similarity.

The mapping processes is intuitive, but is guided by two heuristics: (i) semantics of containing structures are ignored; we seek to represent only the intrinsic meaning of elements; (ii) an element is mapped to the most specific concepts within the concept hierarchies (e.g., book, rather than publication).

Concepts are assigned to a schema element O_i by the integrator on the basis of their understanding of the semantics of the relevant CDBS. Intrinsic meanings of elements are defined as a function IntMean $(O_i) = \{c_i\}$, where c_i is a concept from CMU. For efficient matching, the mapping from each schema element O_i to its set of concepts in the CMU is represented as a concept vector (as in [16]). A concept vector, CV, is an n–component vector, where n is the number of concepts in the CMU, and CV(i) for $1 \leq i \leq n$, denotes the ith concept.

In-context semantics of a schema element are its specific meanings within the wider contexts within which it participates. These contexts are implicit in semantic relationships (SRs) with other elements, modeled as constructs within the schema [7]. The most common SRs are inclusion, aggregation, and association relationships [1,7,12]. These are included in most semantic data models, (e.g., the E-R data model [11]) and object-oriented (OO) data model (e.g., [2,3]). However, none of the semantic enrichment based schema analysis approaches [9,15,16,12,6,8] represent the semantics of SRs. This is a weakness, since, in many cases an SR needs an interpretation to understand the nature of associations between schema elements in a particular UoD, or even to understand the schema elements themselves. For example, the semantics of, **Person** *has* **address**, can be better established by identifying concepts denoted by the relationship, *has*, for example, as *lives_at* or *works_at.* Our methodology therefore allows the integrator to interpret SRs in situations where their names do not adequately express their meanings.

An SR, $srel_{ij}$, which relates schema elements O_i to O_j may change or elaborate the intrinsic meaning of O_i, and thus establishes the meaning of O_i within a particular context involving O_j. The meaning of a schema element O_i within the context of an association with another element O_j, via an SR $srel_{ij}$, is the in-context meaning of O_i. O_i may participate in many SRs, and therefore have different in-context meanings. However, its intrinsic meaning is invariant. Suppose a schema element O_i is related to different schema elements O_{i1}, O_{i2}, ... , O_{in}, through SRs $srel_{i1}$, $srel_{i2}$, ...$srel_{in}$. Each of O_{ij} establishes an in-context meaning of O_i through $srel_{ij}$. The Intr(O_i) function given below defines the in-context meanings of schema elements and also identifies elements related by SRs. Individual in-context meanings can be derived by aggregating together the intrinsic meanings of an element, O_i, and the intrinsic meaning of an element, O_{ij}, to which it is related via an SR, $srel_{ij}$

$Intr(O_i) = <IntMean(O_i), \{ <O_{i1}, srel_{i1}>, ... < O_{in}, srel_{in}>\}>$

where IntMean(O_i) is the intrinsic meaning of O_i, and each $<O_{ij}, srel_{ij}>$ represents a semantic relationship of type $srel_{ij}$ between two elements, $<O_i,O_j>$. Each in-context meaning of O_i can be interpreted as "IntMean(O_i) $srel_{ij}$ IntMean(O_{ij})", The application of Intr function on some of the schema elements in figure 2 is shown below:

Intr(Item) = <{*item*}, { }>
Intr(Book) = <{*book*}, {<*Item, is-a*>}>
Intr(Book.title) = < {*title*}, {<*Book, is_part_of*>}>
Intr(Book.publ> = <{*publisher, address*},<*Publisher, is_type-of*>, <*Book, is_part_of*>}>
Intr(Publisher) = < {*publisher*}, {<*Person, is_a*>}>

The schema–to–CMU binding represented by the Intr function defines a directed graph. The nodes represent schema elements and edges the associations between them within the relevant schema (figure 3). Node labels specify the concept in the CMU that are modeled by the relevant elements and edge labels describe the type of associations between them

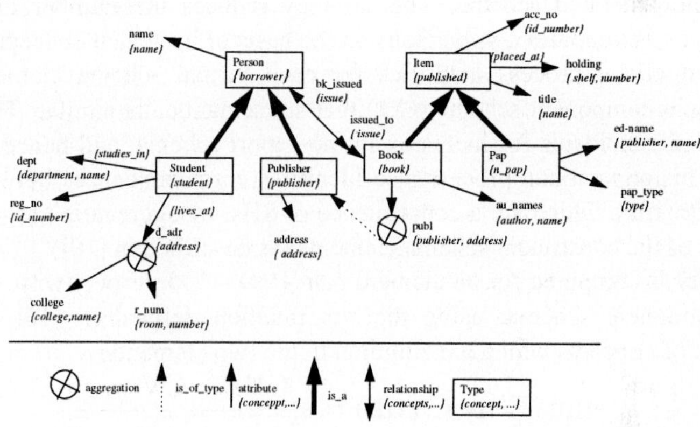

Figure 3: Directed graph for the schema fragment of Figure 4

A directed graph (as in Figure 3) provides an interpretation or component concept model (CCM) for each component schema of the FDBS. CCMs are persistent within the FDBS architecture, thus enriching its semantic content.

4.2 Schema Comparison

Schema comparison, the second phase of our schema analysis methodology, involves comparison of elements of component schemas to identify semantic similarities among them. Semantic similarities are classified as, equivalence, related or disjoint, respectively where elements model exactly the same concepts, have some concept(s) in common, and have no concept in common.

The integrator represents the context within which a federated schema is defined as a federation–specific concept model (FCM). The FCM comprises relevant concepts inter–conected by SRs. Initially, these imply virtual schema elements, since they represent what the federated schema that is being designed is required to represent, prior to its design. An example FCM is given in Figure 4.

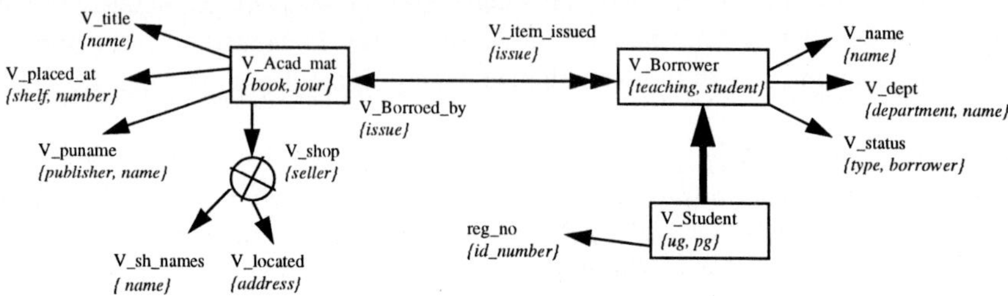

Figure 4: An example FCM

Semantics of component schema elements (from the CCM) are compared with those represented in the FCM in order to determine relevance of elements to the federation. Relevant elements are included within export schemas so that they can be integrated to form the federated schema. This strategy reduces the number of comparisons necessary, and eliminates comparisons on the basis of irrelevant concepts.

The comparison process identifies for each virtual schema element (VO_i), the elements in a component schema (CO_j) that are semantically similar. These identified elements are candidates for inclusion in the export schema, and hence, the federated schema. This comparison process also identifies correspondences between dissimilar complex structure which are a consequence of SHs, by aggregating together semantic signatures of the constituent schema elements (as described in [10]).

Similarity is computed for an element pair, (VO_i, CO_j), respectively, from the FCM and a component schema, using the *sim* function defined in [16], based on the proportion of concepts which are common to the two elements:

$$\mathrm{sim}(CV_{VOI}, CV_{COJ}) = \frac{CV_{VOI} \bullet CV_{COJ}}{\sqrt{|CV_{VOI}| \times |CV_{COJ}|}} \quad (4.1)$$

where CV_{VOi} and CV_{COj} are the concept vectors for the elements VO_i and CO_j, $\bullet$ is the dot product of two vectors and $|Z|$ is the number of ones in a vector. sim generates a value in the range [0,1] — 0 denotes semantically disjoint elements, 1 denotes semantically equivalent, and intermediate values denote semantically related elements.

The process considers intrinsic and in-context meanings of elements. Accordingly, two types of similarity are defined, **shallow** and **deep**. Shallow similarity is based on existence of one or more common concepts among intrinsic meanings of the elements. Deep similarity also takes into account concepts denoted by related elements. These are respectively computed by applying *sim* (Formula 4.1) to the intrinsic and in-context semantic signatures (as detailed below) of the elements being compared. These variants of *sim* are respectively called Ssim and Dsim. For our example CCM (figure 3) and FCM (figure 4), 44 assertions for the shallow similarity (Ssim) are generated (some example assertions are given in Figure 5).

$Ssim(VO_i, CO_j)$		VO_i Concepts	CO_j Concepts
Ssim(V_Acad_mat, C_Item)	= 0.71	book, journal	book, magz, journal, news_pap
Ssim(V_Borrower, C_Person)	= 0.87	teaching, ug, pg	teaching, office, ug, pg
Ssim(V_puname, C_dept)	= 0.50	name, publisher	name, department

Figure 5: Shallow similarity assertions and concepts associated with VOi, Coj

Schema elements cannot be integrated on the basis of shallow similarity alone, because the same concept(s) may represent properties of different real–world objects when viewed in different contexts. For instance, in figure 2 the intrinsic meanings of attributes, Item.title and Person.name are the concept *name.* On this basis, these attributes are semantically equivalent, but when viewed in the context of the respective classes in which they participate, semantic differences become apparent. We therefore introduce the notion of deep similarity: suppose VO_i is related to VO_{i1}, ..., VO_{in}, and CO_j is related to CO_{j1}, ..., CO_{jm}. Elements (VO_i, CO_j) have deep similarity if there exists a non-zero shallow similarity between (VO_i, CO_j), and also between any of their respective in-context schema elements (VO_{ix}, CO_{jy}), where x = 1,...,n, and y = 1,...,m. Testing for deep similarity between (VO_i, CO_j) therefore involves testing for shallow similarity between (VO_i, CO_j) and (VO_{ik}, CO_{jm}), separately. If both are non-zero then VO_i is said to be semantically similar to CO_j in-context of VO_{ik},. Once deep similarity between has been detected, the strength of (deep) similarity is computed by applying the *sim* function to the concepts which represent the in–context meanings of VO_i and CO_j. The in–context concepts of an element O_k with respect to some structural element are obtained by 'OR'ing the concepts for O_{k1} ,$O_{k2 \dots}$ $O_{kn,}$ when each O_{kl} is an element named within the "path" name which defines O_k within the relevant context. A Dsim assertions produced by our methodology is of the form:

$$Dsim\ (VO_i, VO_{ix}, srel_{ix}) = \{<CO_j, CO_{jy}, srel_{jy}, Sval, Dval, strn>\}$$

where VO_i and CO_j denote virtual and actual schema elements; VO_{ix}, CO_{jy} are their respective in-context through SRs $srel_{ix}$ and $srel_{jy}$ respectively. The final component "strn" denotes the strength of the assertion. An assertion states that a virtual element VO_i in-context of VO_{ix} through $srel_{ix}$ is semantically similar to CO_j in -context of CO_{jy} through $srel_{jy}$, *Sval* and *Dval* are the shallow and the deep similarity values between the two (VO_i and CO_j); *strn* is the validity of this assertion. For our example CCM and FCM 25 deep similarity assertions are generated, some of which are given in figure 6.

1 Dsim(V_Acad_mat, V_Acad_mat, -) = <C_Item, C_Item, -, 0.71, 0.71, 2 >
2 Dsim(V_Acad_mat, V_Acad_mat, -) = <C_Book, C_Item, is_a, 0.71, 0.71, 2 >
3 Dsim(V_puname, V_Acad_mat, is_part_of) = <C_title, C_Item, is_part_of , 0.71, 0.67, 2 >
4 Dsim(V_puname, V_Acad_mat, is_part_of) = <C_au_name, C_Book, is_part_of, 0.50, 0.58, 3 >
5 Dsim(V_reg_no, V_Student, is_part_of) = <C_reg_no, C_Student, is_part_of , 1.0, 1.0, 1 >
6 Dsim(V_status, V_Borrower, is_part_of) = <C_Student, C_Person, is_a, 0.0, 0.82, 4 >

Figure 6: Assertions showing deep similarity between schema elements

4.3 Similarity Analysis

In this phase, the deep similarity assertions generated in the previous phase are ranked according to the probability of validity, indicated by assertion strength value in the range 0 to 4 (see Figure 6). A strength of 1 (strongest) is assigned where there is a 'perfect' match, in which case other assertions are overridden, and assigned a 0 strength (invalid). Intermediate values are assigned where the match is less strong (the heuristics are given in [10]). Of the 25 (Dsim) assertions, 19 are generated by applying the direct mapping proposed in this paper, and the rest 5 are generated using the mapping proposed in [16], i.e., and are assigned a strength of 4. The latter therefore represent ontological similarity.

The KHOJI[1] schema analysis software tool has been developed to implement the above schema analysis tasks. When provided with an FCM and a CCM, KHOJI automatically generates assertions stating (a) schema elements from the corresponding component schema that are candidates to be included in the export schema, and hence, the target federated schema, and (b) semantic similarity between the component and the virtual schema elements.

The utility of assertions generated by KHOJI is twofold: (i) elements identified from a particular component schema as being semantically similar to the virtual ones collectively form a 'first cut' export schema, which can then be validated by the integrator; (ii) the structure and integrity constraints of the virtual and component elements associated by assertions are analyzed to identify and resolve SHs, to enable integration into the federated schema.

5. Conclusion and Future Work

A major obstacle to the automation of the SI process has been identified as the inability to represent real–world semantics within database schemas—this semantic information is necessary to identify semantically similar elements in component schemas. A semi-automatic method for partially overcoming this limitation is presented, whereby the global/shared UoD is represented as a CCM, and schemas are given interpretations by mapping schema elements to concepts within this model. Our contribution has been to extend this approach to take account of higher–level structural elements, federation–specific contexts, and to make support for the method persistent within the FDBS architecture.

Potential advantages of this approach are: (i) the performance of the schema analysis process is improved by enabling the matching algorithms to reason within the (real–world) semantic domain, rather than the (computer–world) schematic domain; (ii) the persistent concept model and schema element–to–concept mappings ensure that schema interpretations upon which SI is based are consistent between schemas and consistent over time; (iii) inclusion of the concept model and schema interpretations within the FDBS architecture provides a basis for greater automation of the SI process; and (iv) this semantic enrichment of the FDBS architecture may provide a basis for extended querying facilities, based upon schema element interpretations.

References

[1] Bonjour, M., Falquet, G., 'Concept Base: A Support to Information Systems Integration', CAISE*94, Utrecht, 1994

[1] Urdu word meaning a tracker

[2] Batini, C., Lenzerini, M., Navathe, S. B., 'A Comparative Analysis of Methodologies for Database Schema Integration', ACM Computing Surveys, 18, 4, p(323-364), Dec., 1986

[3] Cattell, R.G.C ed. 'The Object Database Standard: ODMG-93 Release 1.2', Morgan Kaufman San Francisco, 1996

[4] Dayal, U., Hwang, H., 'View Definition and Generalization for Database Integration in a Multidatabase System', IEEE Transactions on Software Engineering, p(629-645), Nov., 1984

[5] Eaglestone, B., Masood, N., 'Schema Interpretation: An Aid to the Schema Analysis in Federated Database Design', First International CAiSE'97 Workshop on Enginering Federated Database System, Barcelona, Spain, p(1-12), Jun., 1997

[6] Goh, C.H., Madnick, S.E., Siegel, M.D., 'Context Interchange: Overcoming the Challenges of Large-Scale Interoperable Database Systems in a Dynamic Environment', in Proceedings of Third International Conference on Information and Knowledge Management (CIKM), Gaithersburg, Maryland, 1994.

[7] Garcia-Solace, M., Saltor, F. Castellanos, M., 'Semantic Heterogeneity in Multidatabase Systems', Object-Oriented Multidatabase Systems A Solution for Advanced Applications, Bukhres, O. A., Elmagarmid, A., chapter 5, PHI, 1996

[8] Kashyap, V., Sheth, A., 'Semantic and Schematic Similarities between Database Objects: A Context Based approach', 22nd VLDB, Bombay, 1996

[9] Larson, J. A., Navathe, S. B., Elmasri, R., 'A theory of Attribute Equivalence in Database with Application to Schema Integration', IEEE Transactions on Software Engineering, p(449-463), Apr., 1989.

[10] Masood, N., Eaglestone, B., 'A Schema Analysis Methodology in Federated Database Systems', Technical Report TCR-0298, Database Group, Department of Computing, University of Bradford, Bradford, UK, Feb., 1998.

[11] Navathe, S., Elmasri, R., Larson, J., 'Integrating user views in database design', IEEE Computer, 19(1), p(50-62), Jan., 1986

[12] Sheth, A. P., Gala, S. K., Navathe, S. B., 'On Automatic Reasoning for Schema Integration', International Journal of Intelligent Co-operative Information Systems, 2(1), p(23-50), Mar., 1993

[13] Sheth, A., Kashyap, V., 'So Far (Schematically) yet So Near (Semantically)', Proceedings, IFIP Wg 2.6 Conference on Semantics of Interoperable Database Systems (Data Semantics 5), North Holland, Amsterdam, p(283-312), 1993

[14] Sheth, A. P., Larson, J. A., 'Federated Database Systems for Managing Distributed Heterogeneous, and Autonomous Databases', ACM Computing Surveys, 22(3), p(183-236), Sep., 1990.

[15] Siegel, M., Madnick, S. E., 'A Metadata Approach to Resolving Semantic Conflicts], 17th VLDB, Barcelona, p(133-145), 1991

[16] Yu, C., Sun, W., Dao, S., Keirsey, D., 'Determining Relationships Among Attributes for Interoperability of Multi-Databases Systems', Proceedings of the first International Workshop on Interoperability in Multidatabase Systems, IMS, Kyoto, Japan, p(251-257) Apr., 1991

Automatic Derivation of Terminological Properties from Database Schemes

L. Palopoli, D. Saccà, D. Ursino

DEIS
Univ. della Calabria
87036 Rende (CS), Italy
{palopoli,sacca,ursino}@si.deis.unical.it

Abstract. Many organizations nowadays own several information systems which represent a mine of possible information resources whose effective exploitation is becoming a key issue in many application contexts. A major problem to be faced within such contexts is the semantic normalization of scheme objects used in heterogeneous, independent and pre-existing databases as to single out differences and similitudes among data whereby a consistent, integrated view of available information can be obtained. To solve large instances of this problem, the development of automatic support tools appears to be mandatory. This paper gives a contribution in this framework by presenting algorithms for extracting useful properties holding among objects belonging to sets of pre-existing database schemes. The algorithms are capable of deriving both nominal and structural properties of scheme objects starting from database scheme descriptions.

1 Introduction

Many organizations nowadays own several information systems which can be thought of as a mine of possible information resources. However, most of these information systems are built upon heterogeneous, obsolete technologies and, therefore, not integrated within unique well structured global systems allowing users to transparently access available data. Therefore, before users can directly exploit available information resources, the construction of a global unified view of available information appears to be necessary. For scheme integration, a key problem is deriving relations among objects in schemes [1]. Thus methodologies are needed to extract these useful properties from them. Clearly, most interesting properties are *interscheme properties*, that relate objects belonging to different database schemes. In particular, an appropriate exploitation of interscheme properties is crucial for a correct synthesis of a global dictionary, describing all schemes involved in an integration problem, into a unified structure [12]. In this framework, schemes are analysed to derive reference components to be adopted in the future, to integrate data from different databases, to identify potential replications of data or inconsistencies in storing organizational information, to identify information flows and to re-engineer existing systems in order to migrate them to new architectures [9]. In all these system re-engineering problems, the process emphasis shifts away from the design and the implementation of database systems to the integration of pre-existing components and new added components [8].

In reasoning about intentional semantics of pre-existing databases, many useful properties are not explicitly encoded in databases, and so they cannot be immediately exploited. In the literature, several approaches to the extraction of these properties are described (see, e.g., [3]). [2] describes a methodology for scheme integration which is based on semantic similarities or dissimilarities between objects belonging to different schemes. [11] proposes a method based on attribute knowledge (so it is based on "syntax" and not on "semantics") and can produce unsatisfactory integrations [10].

The aim of this paper is to provide a contribution in this context. In particular we present algorithms for deriving interscheme properties not explicitly encoded with database schemes. The properties we are dealing with can be classified into Nominal and Structural. *Nominal Properties* are terminological properties stating synonymies or homonymies among objects. These properties have the form $\lfloor A, B, f \rfloor_X$ where A and B are the involved objects, f is a fuzzy coefficient which expresses the strength of the property and $X \in \{Syn, Hom\}$ denotes the kind of the property. *Structural Properties* denote subset properties. Their form is $\langle A, B, f \rangle$, meaning that A is a subset of B, and f is a fuzzy coefficient which expresses the property strength. When the number or the size of database schemes involved in the integration process is large and/or when the set of information resources changes quite frequently over time, manual derivation of interscheme properties can be very expensive and difficult. Therefore, the design of semi-automatic integration tools appears to be necessary [13].

An interesting semi-automatic approach exploiting a semantic dictionary for abstraction is described in [8]: this approach is based on three steps: (1) schema clustering, (2) abstraction of each cluster into objects called descriptors and (3) integration of similar abstract components to obtain a standard one. This method assumes that the involved schemes preliminarly undergo a terminological normalization step. [4] presents an automatic method to construct the so called *summary scheme*, which is a hierarchic structure used to allow imprecise query processing. Because of this, the method is not easily adapted to the context of heterogeneous database integration. An interesting approach is presented in [13], where a methodology is proposed to obtain the automatic resolution of structural conflicts and the integration of scheme objects.

Techniques we are presenting here are automatic and are based on semantic characterizations of involved scheme objects. Our techniques for deriving nominal and structural properties use some basic background knowledge about involved databases, which includes: (1) a set of lexicographic synonymy properties derived from a standard thesaurus, (2) a set of assertions describing inclusions between classes of objects. Possibly, such basic knowledge can be provided by the group of administrators of involved information systems. The extraction of such nominal and structural properties forms the basis for terminological normalization of involved schemes, which has a relevance on its own, and for the extraction of more complex properties [5] (Intentional Knowledge Discovery [6]). Our method requires for the DBAs to provide just an initial, typically small, set of simple terminological properties, most of the semantic properties being them automatically derived by our algorithms.

Discovering terminological and structural properties of data objects has many applications and all of them benefit from methods for automatic derivation of such assertions as the one we have presented in this paper. Applications include the design of information integration layers on the top of existing database systems, such as mediators and, more in general, the development of tools for supporting integrated access to cooperative information systems and the development of tools for accessing semistructured data, such as textual databases or Web documents. A relevant application case for our approach is the integration of Italian Central Public Administration Information Systems. In fact, the various Public Administrations have developed their own information systems mainly on an unrelated basis, yielding high replication and inconsistency of data, low interconnection and interoperability, scarce accessibility by end users to information of their own interest [1]. Our methods have been verified against this interesting application case and proved successful.

The rest of this paper is organized as follows. In the next section we illustrate an algorithm for the discovery of nominal properties. The discovery of more complex structural and nominal properties is described in Section 3.

2 Discovering Nominal Properties

In this section we illustrate an algorithm for the derivation of scheme nominal properties. Our method is based on a new algorithm for deriving synonymies among entities and relationships that considers both their attributes (taking into account their *semantic relevance* to the entity/relationship) and their context [7]. The term "context" indicates (besides attributes), entities, generalization hierarchies and relationships involving a given entity or relationship in the scheme. Exploiting the context is justified by observing that entities having the same real world semantic are usually characterized by the presence of common elements in their context. Moreover it is generally accepted that similarity techniques based on hypernimy (i.e. one term has a more general meaning than the second) and synonymy relationships between local concepts are more precise than techniques solely based on the analisys of attributes [4, 7, 11]. Finally, the necessity of taking into account the relevance of attributes to distinguish the semantics of an entity/relationship has been clearly pointed out in [10]. For instance, an attribute *Salary* works better than an attribute *Identifier* in distinguishing the entity *Employee* from the entity *Division*.

Our algorithm uses a set of basic synonymies between attributes. We assume that such synonymies are derived from a standard thesaurus. However, further synonimies more specific to the application domain can be also provided by the DBAs. Our algorithm for deriving synonymies is as follows:

Algorithm for extracting synonymy and homonymy properties
Input: a list of database schemes $\mathbf{S} = S_1, \ldots, S_n$ and a set BSA of basic synonymy properties among attributes;
Output: a set DS of derived synonymy properties among entities and relationships;
begin
  DS := *Compute_Rough_Entity_Synonymies*($S_1, \ldots, S_n$, *BSA*);
  DS := *Compute_Relationship_Synonymies*($S_1, \ldots, S_n$,*DS*,*BSA*);
  DS := *Compute_Refined_Entity_Synonymies*($S_1, \ldots, S_n$, *DS*);
  DS := *Discard_Weak_Synonymies*(*DS*)
end

The algorithm consists of four steps. The first step derives the so called *rough* synonymies among entities, starting from the set of basic attribute synonymies. Synonymies among relationships are then computed using relationship contexts as well as rough synonymies derived in the previous step and basic attribute synonymies. Further synonymies among entities are searched for by exploiting context information that can be set up through rough synonymies among entities and relationships obtained in the previous two steps. Because of the fuzzy nature of our approach, it could classify as possible synonyms entity names which are indeed distinct; so the necessity arises of a filtering phase which discards synonymies whose plausibility is under a certain threshold.

The four subprograms called in the algorithm will be illustrated in details in the following subsections.

2.1 Computing rough entity synonymies

The algorithm for computing rough entity synonymies proceeds by analysing pairs of entities belonging to different schemes. For each pair of entities, the algorithm computes a coefficient stating their synonymy degree, by using the coefficients computed in turn for each pair of attributes belonging to the two entities. Semantic normalization is also performed in order to take into account the relevance of attributes in distinguishing the semantics of the entities they belong to. Since a closure procedure is eventually executed over the set of extracted properties, it is sufficient for the algorithm to consider only scheme pairs (S_i, S_{i+1}), where $S_1, \ldots, S_n$ is the list of all involved schemes and $1 \leq i \leq (n-1)$. The algorithm is encoded in the following functions:

Function *Compute_Rough_Entity_Synonymies*($S_1, \ldots, S_n$: schemes; BSA: basic attribute synonymies): **return** *a set of rough synonimies (between entities)*
  var
   SP: a set of synonymies between attributes;
   US: a set of synonymies between entities;
  begin
   for $k := 1$ **to** $n - 1$ **do**

```
    for each pair of entities E_i ∈ S_k and E_j ∈ S_{k+1} do begin
        Clear(SP)
        for each pair of attributes A_l ∈ E_i and A_m ∈ E_j do begin
            SP_{A_l,A_m} := Weighted_Mean(A_l, A_m);
            SP_{A_l,A_m} := Normalize_Coefficient(SP_{A_l,A_m});
        end;
        SP := Filter(SP);
        SP := Compute_Characterization(SP);
        US_{E_i,E_j} := Mean(SP);
        US_{E_i,E_j} := Compute_Synonymy(US_{E_i,E_j})
    end
    return Normalization(US)
end
```

$Weighted\_Mean(A_l, A_m)$ takes two attributes as the inputs and computes the associated synonymy coefficient. $Normalize\_Coefficient(SP_{A_l,A_m})$ considers the computed coefficient SP_{A_l,A_m} and normalizes it, by setting it to zero if its value is under a certain given threshold th_v. It should be clear enough that for each pair of entities E_i and E_j and for each attribute A of E_i, A can be derived to be a synonym of at most one attribute of E_j. Therefore, the function *Filter(SP)* discards all the synonymy properties obtained for A except for one. Such a synonymy is selected taking into account both its value (higher values preferred) and the average value of the coefficients of all selected properties. The function $Compute\_Characterization(SP)$ performs a normalization of the values thus obtained which takes into account the relevance of the involved attributes in distinguishing the semantics of entities [10]. The function $Mean(SP)$ simply computes the mean of the synonymy coefficients derived by the previous function for the attributes belonging to the entities E_i and E_j. The function $Compute\_Synonymy(US_{E_i,E_j})$ finally computes the global synonymy coefficient associated to the pair of entities E_i and E_j, normalizing the mean value obtained in the previous step. The function *Normalization(US)* performs a further normalization on the set of coefficients associated to scheme entities.

2.2 Computing Relationship Synonymies

The function for computing relationship synonymies considers pairs of relationships belonging to different schemes and derives their synonymy coefficients by using information contexts provided by the topology of schemes and rough synonymies among entities derived in the previous step. The function follows:

Function *Compute_Relationship_Synonymies($S_1, \ldots, S_n$: schemes, DS: a set of synonyms, BSA: basic attribute synonymies)*: **return** *a set of synonymy properties;*

```
    var
      k : 1..n − 1; N_{R_i,R_j}, A_{R_i,R_j}, E_{R_i,R_j} : Real ∈ [0,1]
    begin
      for k := 1 to n − 1 do
        for each pair of relationships R_i ∈ S_k and R_j ∈ S_{k+1} do begin
```

```
        N_{Ri,Rj} := Compute_Lex_Synonymies(Ri, Rj);
        A_{Ri,Rj} := Compute_Attribute_Synonymies(Ri, Rj);
        E_{Ri,Rj} := Compute_Related_Entity_Synonymies(Ri, Rj);
        return Mean_Relationship(N_{Ri,Rj}, A_{Ri,Rj}, E_{Ri,Rj}) ∪ DS
    end
end
```

The function $Compute\_Lex\_Synonymies(R_i, R_j)$ simply sets to 1 only those N_{R_i,R_j} such that the names of R_i and R_j are lexical variants (i.e. are equal, one is the plural of the other and so on) and sets to 0 the remaining ones. The function $Compute\_Attribute\_Synonymies(R_i, R_j)$ computes the synonymies among attributes of the relationships. $Compute\_Related\_Entity\_Synonymies(R_i, R_j)$ returns a synonymy coefficient for all entities related to the relationships R_i and R_j. The function $Mean\_Relationship(DS_{R_i R_j}, A_{R_i R_j}, E_{R_i R_j})$ only computes the weighted mean of the various coefficients derived in previous steps.

2.3 Computing Refined Entity Synonymies

This function is devoted to derive further and/or refined nominal properties. The algorithm exploits both rough synonymies among entities and synonymies among relationships as context information to derive further interscheme knowledge. The function is as follows.

```
Function Compute_Refined_Entity_Synonymies(S1, ..., Sn: schemes; DS: a set
of synonymies): return a set of synonymies;
  var
    k : 1..n − 1; Q_{Ei,Ej}, T_{Ei,Ej}, H_{Ei,Ej}: Real ∈ [0..1]
  begin
    for k := 1 to n − 1 do
      for each pair of entities Ei ∈ Sk and Ej ∈ Sk+1 do begin
        Q_{Ei,Ej} := Compute_E_Related_Entity_Synonymies(Ei, Ej);
        T_{Ei,Ej} := Compute_E_Related_Relationship_Synonymies(Ei, Ej);
        H_{Ei,Ej} := Discover_Homonimies(Ei, Ej)
        If H_{Ei,Ej} ≠ 0 then
          DS_{Ei,Ej} := Compute_E_Synonymies(DS_{Ei,Ej}, Q_{Ei,Ej}, T_{Ei,Ej});
        else
          DS_{Ei,Ej} := 0;
      end
      return DS
end
```

Here the functions *Compute_E_Related_Entity_Synonymies*(E_i, E_j) and *Compute_E_Related_Relationship_Synonymies*(E_i, E_j) return a synonymy coefficient for all entities (resp. relationships) related to the entities E_i and E_j. The function $Discover\_Homonimies(E_i, E_j)$ examines pairs of entities looking for homonyms. $Compute\_E\_Synonymies(DS_{E_i,E_j}, Q_{E_i,E_j}, T_{E_i,E_j})$ derives synonymy coefficients between the two entities E_i and E_j as a weighted mean.

2.4 Filtering meaningful properties

The function $Discard\_Weak\_Synonymies(DS)$ considers all the synonymies among entities and relationships derived during the previous steps and computes two thresholds, one for entities and one for relationships. The threshold Th_e for entities is computed as $\frac{S_{E_{MAX}}+S_{E_{MIN}}}{2}$, where $S_{E_{MAX}}$ and $S_{E_{MIN}}$ are the maximum and the minimum synonymy coefficient of entities derived so far. The threshold Th_r for relationships is obtained similarly.

$Discard\_Weak\_Synonymies(DS)$ discards all synonymies whose coefficients are smaller than the thresholds. The final set DS of synonymy and homonymy properties produced by the algorithm is stored in the Synonymy Dictionary SD in the form of $\lfloor A, B, f \rfloor_{Syn}$ and in the Homonymy Dictionary HD in the form of $\lfloor A, B, f \rfloor_{Hom}$.

3 Extracting further structural and nominal properties

The algorithm described in Section 2 derives nominal properties and stores them in the synonymy and homonymy dictionaries. In this section, we illustrate an algorithm that derives both further nominal properties and structural ones. Structural properties state inclusions between entities or relationships.

The inputs for the algorithm are the SD (Synonymy Dictionary), plus an additional dictionary, called the Inclusion Dictionary (ID). The ID contains triplets of the form $\langle A, B, f \rangle$ where A is the included object, B is the including object and f is a fuzzy coefficient which expresses the strength of this assertion. The triplets stored in the ID represent, generally, inclusion properties between objects of the same scheme (intrascheme properties); some further inclusion properties holding between objects belonging to different schemes can be possibly stored in this dictionary by the DBAs.

The algorithm returns an enriched set of nominal and structural properties holding among objects belonging to different schemes. Both nominal and structural properties extracted in this second phase are classified either as *exact* or as *conditional*. Exact properties are always valid whereas the validity of conditional properties depends on the values of the involved coefficients. Procedures called within the algorithm add new properties to dictionaries.

The algorithm uses an associative network [10] whose nodes represent scheme objects and whose edges represent properties among objects; edge labels represent the type of the properties and their strength. Properties already included in the SD, HD and ID are thus represented as edges in the network. New properties are derived by constructing suitable closures over the network. The algorithm for deriving complex properties is the following:

Algorithm for extracting complex structural and nominal properties
Input: Synonymy and Inclusion Dictionaries SD and ID;
Output: Complex Nominal and Structural Properties;
var
    Net: an associative network

```
begin
    Net := Dictionaries_To_Network(SD,ID);
    Compute_Exact_Properties(Net);
    Compute_Conditional_Properties(Net);
    Net_To_Dictionaries(Net, SD, ID)
end
```

The function *Dictionaries_To_Network*(SD, ID) takes in input the synonymy and inclusion dictionaries and yields in output an associative network; the function *Net_To_Dictionaries(Net, SD, ID)* creates a suitable dictionary entry for each edge of the associative network in the obvious way.

3.1 Computing Exact Properties

The procedure *Compute_Exact_Properties*(Net) computes exact interscheme properties between objects. We have used a fixpoint procedure instead of the Floyd-Warshall algorithm because in this context it works much better. The function is as follows:

```
Procedure Compute_Exact_Properties(Net: an associative network)
  var
      Net: an associative network; Exists_New_Path:boolean;
      ΔNet', ΔNet : a support associative network;
  begin
      ΔNet' := Net
      repeat
          ΔNet := ΔNet';
          Net := Net ∪ ΔNet;
          for each Edge (N_i, N_j) ∈ Net do
              for each edge (N_j, N_k) ∈ ΔNet do begin
                  ΔNet' := Extend_Path(ΔNet', N_i, N_j, N_k);
                  ΔNet' := Filter(ΔNet', Net)
              end
      until ΔNet' = ∅
      return Net
end
```

The function *Extend_Path*$(\Delta Net', N_i, N_j, N_k)$ examines the edges (N_i, N_j) and (N_j, N_k) and derives one or more edges (N_i, N_k) and the associated label. This function is a modified version of the algorithm defined in [10]. To compute fuzzy coefficients in labels, we use some fuzzy operators. In particular we make use of some t-norms. We recall that t-norms are dyadic functions from $[0, 1] \times [0, 1]$ to $[0, 1]$ that are monotonic, commutative and associative and have been used to define fuzzy set intersection. We shall restrict ourselves to the t-norms $\tau_1(\alpha, \beta) = max(0, \alpha + \beta - 1)$ (exclusive t-norm), $\tau_2(\alpha, \beta) = \alpha \times \beta$ (independent t-norm) and $\tau_3(\alpha, \beta) = min(\alpha, \beta)$ (inclusive t-norm). It can easily be shown that $\tau_1(\alpha, \beta) \leq \tau_2(\alpha, \beta) \leq \tau_3(\alpha, \beta)$ holds for $0 \leq \alpha, \beta \leq 1$, and so τ_1 is the most "pessimistic" t-norm whereas τ_3 is the most "optimistic" one.

After that candidate edges from N_i to N_j are computed, $Filter(\Delta Net', Net)$ keeps one of them following some rules which can not described here for lack of space. The function *Compute_Exact_Properties*(Net) terminates when, after one run, no new edge is added or modified in the network.

3.2 Computing Conditional Properties

The procedure *Compute_Conditional_Properties*(*Net*) derives conditional interscheme properties. To give an idea of what a conditional property is, we will use an example. Suppose we have two schemes S_i and S_j; assume that the Inclusion Dictionary (ID) stores the following properties: $\langle B_{S_i}, A_{S_i}, W_{BA}\rangle$, $\langle D_{S_j}, C_{S_j}, W_{DC}\rangle$, $\langle A_{S_i}, C_{S_j}, W_{AC}\rangle$ whereas the Synonymy Dictionary (SD) stores $\lfloor A_{S_i}, C_{S_j}, V_{AC}\rfloor_{Syn}$. Now, if $W_{DC} \gg \tau_2(W_{BA}, W_{AC})$, we infer that essentially all the instances of C are also instances of D; so we can deduce that B is a subset of D with inclusion coefficient $W_{BD} = \tau_2(\tau_2(W_{BA}, W_{AC}), W_{DC})$ and synonymy coefficient $\tau_2(V_{AC}, 1)$. This property is "conditional" just because it holds only if $W_{DC} \gg \tau_2(W_{BA}, W_{AC})$.

The procedure *Compute_Conditional_Properties*(*Net*) is as follows:

```
Procedure Compute_Conditional_Properties(Net: an associative network)
    var
        CE: a set of Candidate_Edges;
        Exist_New_Path:Boolean
    begin
        repeat
            Exist_New_Path := False; CE := ∅
            for each Node N_i do
                for each Edge (N_i, N_j) representing an interscheme property
do
                    for each Inc_Edge (N_j, N_k) or (N_k, N_j) do begin
                        CE := Verify_Subset_Subset(CE, N_i, N_j, N_k);
                        CE := Verify_Superset_Superset(CE, N_i, N_j, N_k);
                        CE := Verify_Subset_Superset(CE, N_i, N_j, N_k);
                        Exist_New_Path := Conditional_Filter(CE, Net)
                    end
        until Exist_New_Path
end
```

Given a scheme S, an object A in S is called a *superset* (resp. a *subset*) if the ID stores a property $\langle C, A, f\rangle$ (resp, $\langle A, C, f\rangle$) for some C, f. There exist three kinds of conditional properties: Superset-Superset, Subset-Subset and Subset-Superset. *Superset-Superset* (resp. *Subset-Subset*) properties are derived from an interscheme property between an entity which is a superset (resp. subset) in the scheme S_i and an entity which is a superset (resp. subset) in the scheme S_j. Subset-Superset properties are derived from an interscheme property between an entity which is a subset in the scheme S_i and an entity which is a superset in the scheme S_j or vice versa.

The function *Verify_Superset_Superset*(CE, N_i, N_j, N_k) is as follows:

```
Function Verify_Superset_Superset(CE, N_i, N_j, N_k)
    begin
        if there exists an Inc_Edge between a generic node N_l and the node N_i
```

with coefficient $W_{N_l N_i}$ **then**
if there exists a *Syn_Edge* between N_i and N_j with a synonymy coefficient $V_{N_i N_j}$ **then**
if $W_{N_k N_j} \gg \tau_2(W_{N_l N_i}, W_{N_i N_j})$ **then**
add to CE an Inc_Edge with coefficient $\tau_2(\tau_2(W_{N_l N_i}, W_{N_i N_j}), W_{N_k N_j})$;
end

Verify_Superset_Subset(CE, N_i, N_j, N_k) and *Verify_Subset_Subset(CE, N_i, N_j, N_k)* behave analogously whereas the function $Conditional\_Filter(CE, Net)$ behaves similarly to the function *Filter* described above.

References

1. C. Batini, S. Castano, V. De Antonellis, M.G.Fugini, B. Pernici, Analysis of an Inventory of Information Systems in the Public Administration, *Requirement Engineering Journal* 1(1), 47-62, 1996.
2. C. Batini, M. Lenzerini, A methodology for data schema integration in the entity relationship model, *IEEE TSE*10(6), 650-664, 1984.
3. C. Batini, M. Lenzerini, S.B. Navathe, A comparative analysis of methodology for database scheme integration, *ACM CS* 18(4), 323-364, 1986.
4. M.W.Bright, A.R.Hurson, S.Pakzad, Automated Resolution of Semantic Heterogeneity in Multidatabases, *ACM Transactions on Database Systems* 19(2), 212-253, 1994.
5. A. Bonifati, L. Palopoli, D. Saccà, D. Ursino, Discovering Description Logic assertions from database schemes, *Proceedings of DL'97*,144-148, Gif Sur Yvette, 1997.
6. A. Bonifati, L.Palopoli, D. Saccà, D. Ursino, Automatic extraction of database scheme semantic properties using Knowledge Discovery techniques, *Proceedings of IADT'98*, Berlin. Forthcoming.
7. S. Castano, V. De Antonellis, Semantic Dictionary Design for Database Interoperability, *Proceedings of ICDE'97*,Birmingham, 1997.
8. S. Castano, V. De Antonellis, Reference Conceptual Architecture for Reengineering Information Systems, *International Journal of Cooperative Information Systems* 4(2-3), 213-235, 1995.
9. S. Castano, V. De Antonellis, M.G.Fugini, B.Pernici, Conceptual Schema Analysis: Techniques and Applications, *Rapporto Interno, Politecnico di Milano* 95-060, 1995.
10. P. Fankhauser, M. Kracker, E.J.Neuhold, Semantic vs. Structural Resemblance of Classes, *SIMOD RECORD*, 20(4), 1991, 59-63
11. J.A.Larson, S.B.Navathe, R. Elmastri, A Theory of Attribute Equivalence in Databases with Application to Schema Integration, *IEEE TSE* 15(4), 449-463, 1989.
12. L. Palopoli, D. Saccà, D. Ursino, Semi-automatic, semantic discovery of properties from database schemes, *Proc. of IDEAS'98*, Cardiff. Forthcoming.
13. S.Spaccapietra, C.Parent, View Integration: A Step Forward in Solving Structural Conflicts, *IEEE TKDE* 6(2), 258-274, 1994.

A Novel Integration of OODBMS and Information Retrieval Techniques for a Document Repository

Chung-Hong Lee and Lee-Feng Chien

Institute of Information Science
Academia Sinica
Taipei, Taiwan, R.O.C.
Tel: +886-2-2788-3799 ext. 1801
Fax: +886-2-2782-4814
E-mail: {leechung, lfchien}@iis.sinica.edu.tw

Abstract. Extending the usability of merged database and text-retrieval systems by building on an *object-oriented database management system* (OODBMS) can offer better and complementary advantages to both database and *information retrieval systems* (IRS). In this paper, we present a new approach for integrating OODBMSs and IRSs that maintains the flexibility and avoids overheads of mapping process, by means of wrapping the documents and encapsulating signature based IR methods into storable objects which are being stored in the database. In particular, we demonstrate how to apply such an integration approach to a special problem domain: a *multi-lingual information retrieval* system. In our framework, a sound platform and query facilities offered by the underlying object-oriented database can further enhance the original IR functions and be applicable to the construction of multimedia-document based digital libraries.

1 Introduction

Both the studies of information retrieval (IR) and database systems are concerned with the quality of queries for satisfying the user's information needs. However, although the query techniques in the database field have been well established to facilitate the retrieval of structured and pre-formatted data, little attention has been paid to support the users to retrieve the desired document, and further allow them to perform a content-based text retrieval to retrieve relevant documents from the database.

Essentially, there are two important implications in combining the information retrieval systems (IRS) and database systems. From the perspective of the information retrieval system, due to the nature that uncertainty of internal document representation, query representation and the pattern matching process during query processing, it is difficult to develop a system that can maintain perfect results of recall and precision rates to fully satisfy the user's information needs, as the querying functions performed in the database system. Therefore, to resolve the above issues, the structured and high level querying method of database systems can be acted as a complementary solution through the deployment of a information storage, in order to fully satisfy the user's information needs. On the other hand, due to the limitation caused by the pre-formatted (i.e. the data modeling process) work of unstructured data for the database development, the database content is pre-selected and limited, and therefore the queries of a developed database can only catch the data selected during the database deployment and data modeling process. In this case, the lack of a free search method for a text retrieval from a large collection of document stored in the database becomes a significant drawback, particularly for the users who are familiar with the way of accessing the internet to freely search for their required information. As a result, the integration of information retrieval and database approaches is promising for enhancing the querying function and storage of an information system.

1.1 Scope of the Proposed System

The scope of the system development is based on the scenario of an ongoing project in developing an OODBMS based multi-lingual information retrieval techniques, including English and some oriental languages, such as Chinese and Japanese. According to previous work [1,9], oriental language IR is not easily handled using conventional word-based indexing and exact match searching methods, whereas character-based indexing and best match searching methods can achieve much better performance if the design truly considers the features of oriental language IR. Since words in oriental languages are most formed by a sequence of characters, and words in a sentence are not clearly bounded by spaces as those in English, word-based indexing will cause inappropriate word breaking and proper noun identification [1,9]. On account of these difficulties, we have developed a better approach for processing natural sentences in both English and oriental languages. It adopts a statistical token-based signature extraction method. The adopted signature extraction method substitutes the use of conventional hashing functions by a corpus-based approach and a specially-designed token grouping algorithm in the determination of query and document signatures.

These documents are stored in an object-oriented database. The main aim is to integrate the existing IR technique with the OODBMS in such a way that it migrates the unstructured documents to the object database framework with regard to the integrated functionality of many existing approaches. In particular, this requires a specially designed data model which considers the requirements of both database and our specific IR queries for document retrieval. In this work, for storing Chinese data, an object-oriented database product designed particularly for Chinese data storage is employed. To avoid describing many specific product features, in this paper we will explain the object data model and queries developed in a generic way.

1.2 System Features

The features of the integrated system are highlighted as follows:

- a *wrapping* approach is applied to encapsulate the individual document and its associated IR methods to allow the textual or multimedia type of documents to be stored in the object database.

• a novel *signature file* approach particularly designed for tackling the requirements of multi-lingual information retrieval is employed to perform the functionality of document indexing and retrieval and is involved in the data modeling process for database development.

• a hierarchical query method which offers a combination of high level database queries and IR queries to enhance the expressiveness of the existing object querying technique.

In Section 2 related work is reviewed and our distinctive approach for the integration is discussed. Section 3 describes the system architecture. The functions of each module within the system are discussed in detail. Section 4 addresses our specific IR approach for multi-lingual information retrieval. Section 5 introduces the proposed hierarchical query method. Conclusions are discussed in Section 6.

2 Review of Related Work

There have been several research efforts at establishing retrieval systems that have aspects of both traditional text-retrieval systems and database systems. Some of them focused on the relational data model, such as [4,5,11], and there are also some commercial products available recently, such as Oracle SQL*TextRetrieval. However, for the management of multimedia documents, the retrieval and storage functions of the complex objects in the relational databases are relatively cumbersome and difficult. Besides, it is inefficient to satisfy the demands of semantic modeling for the complexity of document structures. Object-orient database management systems (OODBMSs), with their strengths in dealing with complex objects and close connection with the programming languages, are considered as a better solution for the development of the integration platform.

A text search extension to the ORION object-oriented database was described by Lee [6]. It described an implementation of text search capability within the ORION framework that is compatible with the general ORION query processing functionality. The integration of the INQUERY text retrieval system and the IRIS object database proposed by Croft, et al. [3] was also an earlier implementation for this. Their work employed a particular type of text (Ph.D. thesis) as a case study and modeling issues were not addressed. Several research efforts have been focused on mapping the SGML document structures into OODBMS's data models [2,8,12]. The Refus system [10] handles autonomous text stored in conventional file. In Refus, attributes are extracted from the corresponding documents and then classified class in the OODBMS. It provides searching, organizing, and browsing for the semi-structured information commonly stored in computer systems. Differing from the efforts with the aims to model only structured SGML documents in relational or object-oriented databases, our system is particularly aimed at modeling heterogeneous types of documents. That is, the underlying database platform is developed as a ***document library***, in which both the textual and multimedia documents as well as their information contents can be stored and retrieved.

2.1 Coupling Methods of the OODBMS and IRS

For comparing the OODBMS-IRS-coupling methods, a distinction between the *loose coupling* and *tight coupling* approaches has been highlighted by Volz [12]. Within a loose coupling system, the cooperating systems are more independent from each other and they normally can be used as stand alone systems individually. In particular, data has to be interchanged between the systems. While within a tight coupling, data is shared between the two systems. This is achieved by implementing existing algorithms within the integrating system in an optimized way, such as optimization of queries and data models.

Basically, the tight coupling approach requires to completely integrate the OODBMS and IRS systems and they cannot be used as a stand alone system after integration. This thus offers a better performance during query processing. It will, however, lose some flexibility for optionally adopting other IR approaches as the underlying IRS techniques to achieve some specific aims. Changing of the underlying indexing and pattern matching methods for the information retrieval subsystem, such as boolean retrieval, vector retrieval and probability models is often difficult and costly. As a result, it is determined to employ a loose coupling as our implementation approach: the system does not deal with the *query optimization* process; instead, we provide a variety of queries based on the structure and signature of documents as an extension to existing *object query language* (OQL) for document retrieval. The main reason for this is due to its flexibility in tackling the cooperation requirements with other subsystems in our project framework.

However, some differences about applying the loose coupling approach in our framework should be addressed. Although the loosely coupling technique mentioned above could be used to combine two stand alone systems for strengthening query functionality, there is still a need to map database objects to IRS documents since in these cases document bodies or representation are actually stored in two separate systems. Such a method can be considered to be less than seamless due to the overhead of required mapping process. As a result, rather than adopting the mapping methods, our integration avoid creating additional document representation in either IRS or OODBMS by means of a ***document wrapping*** approach to integrate documents and objects. This will be described later in detail.

Mixing database type of queries and text retrieval techniques allows to pose very powerful queries, being much more expressive than each mechanism by itself. By employing a query language that can effectively combine both types of queries, the retrieval quality of document databases can be further enhanced. Rather than using the embedded SQL in relational data model, the query languages of object-oriented databases, with their merits on integration with programming languages, are particularly relevant to the above issue, and avoid type system mismatch problems. Therefore, we have chosen to implement our data model of documents and query language on top of the object-orient database system.

However, the challenges are that, in an object-oriented database application system, objects are normally configured according to one particular application view, which renders sharing of information complicated. It may be difficult for another application to deal with the internal structures of complex objects retrieved from the specific object database. Besides, for complex objects, the access method to the object-oriented database may also require to be developed from scratch, since currently the supporting mechanism of the BLOB (Binary Large Objects) storage in most OODBMS are still insufficient. To resolve the above issues, a wrapper is developed and acted as a front-end of the employed object-oriented database to support access of those complex objects to the database.

3 System Architecture

The system architecture is illustrated in Fig. 1. During registration, in addition to the wrapping and insertion of new documents in the document database that is implemented by using an object-oriented database, a signature file associated with the document indexing is processed and updated. The document indexing module is used to parse the input text, perform automatic indexing, and establish the associated signature files.

It is worth meaning that, in this work the indexing task is performed to be document-specific. In practice, each document in a specific collection (i.e. class) is treated as an object with its own set of defined properties and the terms assigned to the document do not depend on terms assigned to any other document in the collection.

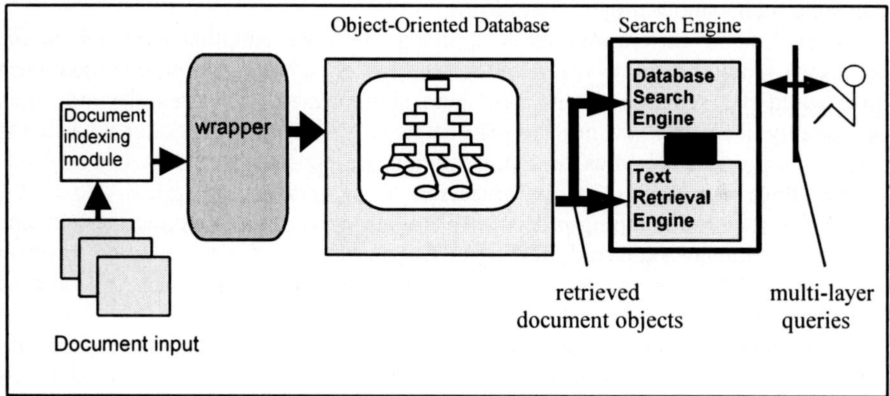

Fig. 1. System Architecture

3.1 Document Indexing Module

The indexing module is responsible for parsing documents into a set of signature representations that can be referenced in queries. It is used to produce document signatures. In order to quickly filter out non-qualifying documents and to avoid the difficulty of key word extraction, the signature-based ranking function is used. Each bit in the signatures records the existence of some certain classes and their corresponding semantics. The derived document signatures constitute a bit-slice document signature file and serves as a filter which can be used to rapidly test for the existence of any given character string.

3.2 Document Wrapping Module

As stated previously, documents may share some complex data in the form of textual documents, diagrams, photographs, even video and audio files. These data are often user-defined data types and stored in a common document database. The challenge here is in establishing an approach to handle these data types and in providing an access method to the database. The wrapper front-end runs as an input module of the database from which the complex document components can be inserted into the database. Wrapping is the process that enables the wrapped documents to become self-contained and storable objects [7].

From the perspective of OODBMS, the designed wrapper will hide the internal content of documents which are being stored in the database to convert them into objects as well as unwrapping the objects retrieved from the database to perform further viewing and editing work. In practice, the wrapper is designed for the system developers, maintainers and administrators, rather than end users. Thus, the design idea is based on the management aspects of the system.

3.3 Document Storage Module

It is worth mentioning that, differing from past efforts with the aims to model only structured text in relational or object-oriented systems such as [13], our system is particularly aimed at modeling both structured text and documents. That is, the underlying database platform is developed as a ***document library***, in which both the textual and multimedia documents as well as their information contents can be stored and retrieved. The view is taken, therefore, in this work that the data modeling should carry out textual objects and other complex objects.

3.3.1 Data Model in the Object-Oriented Database

Essentially, there are two types of information in a database: *data* and *schema*. The schema is used to describe the structure of the data. Different types of database systems have different methods to define their data and schemas and specify operations on data, just as different programming languages have different *type systems* in which their type declarations are constrained. In the database systems, these type system constraints are called the ***data model***. In general, the data model of object-oriented databases support several types of data structures, including *atomic data types* such as integer, Boolean, real, strings and bits (for bit strings), and *structural data types* such as sets and lists. Set values are unordered collections of values which must be of the same type, while list values are ordered collections of elements that also must be of the types. Note that sets and lists of objects may contain objects of a class and its subclasses.

3.3.2 Data Modeling

In this developed system, documents are stored as complex objects in an object-oriented database. It is worth mentioning that, generally speaking, a document database system should be able to store more than just textual data. Multimedia data, such as images and voices, are an important part of many documents. In our prototype system, the architecture framework is also established to manage the compound documents that contain multimedia objects. Although currently the functions of searching offered in our system are only limited to deal with the textual data, the underlying approach developed is also applicable to the multimedia type of documents. In this paper, we only report the management of the textual documents.

The core elements of the object-oriented data model are *objects (classes)* and their *relationships*. Since the continuous components are designed as to be executable independently, this enables users to employ the *generation* (*is_a*) relationship to construct the class hierarchy.

3.3.3 Modeling of Compound Documents for a Document Library

A class for a generic document model is defined as a super class for establishing a class hierarchy of a document library, as shown in Fig. 2. The class 'Document' contains six data members (e.g. title and author) which represent fundamental attributes for retrieval. In addition, we use the encapsulated text retrieval subsystem (i.e. the document-signature-representation program) as an internal method **document_signature( )** within the defined document data model. The programming capacity offered by the object query language allows both the database query engine and text-retrieval search engine to be combined within a query program and being worked together to provide users a variety of forms of queries. The approach for signature generation will be described later in detail.

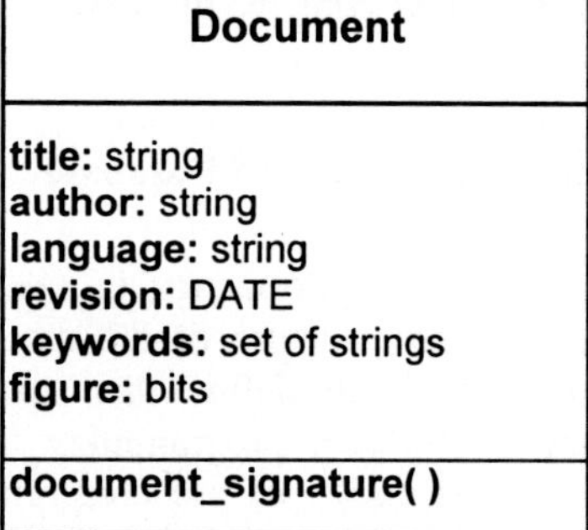

Fig. 2. Elements of the class 'Document'

3.4 Document Retrieval Module

Traditionally, documents are usually retrieved through information retrieval techniques. In these cases, documents are selected according to specific contexts relying on indexing process. They offer sophisticated pattern matching facilities such as keyword and passage searching for selecting documents, and do not require to specify the exact structure of documents. Such facilities are not provided in most OODBMS query languages. It is therefore necessary to develop extended functions for dealing with the pattern matching from a document collection based on the existing OODBMS query language.

Alone with the IR technique, the semantics of the new developed query methods will be expected to be consistent with those of the core object-oriented data model. In the proposed system, a signature based pattern matching facility was added to the underlying data model of the document library and query mechanism.

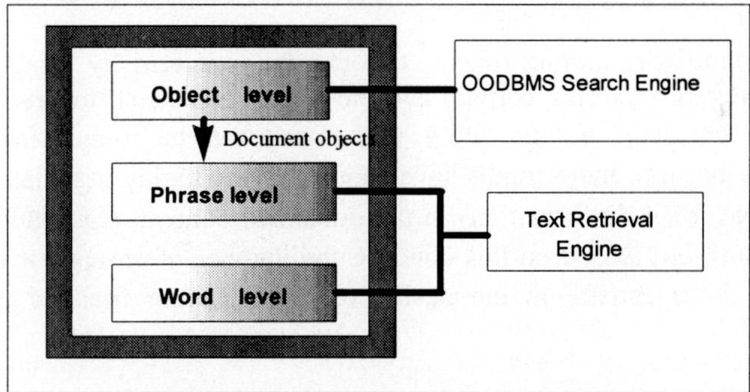

Fig. 3. Three level of information retrieval

Fig. 3 illustrates an original idea of hierarchical information retrieval. For document retrieval, since each document has been treated as an object alone with its defined attributes, it is sensible to allow a given document stored in the database to be accessible by database queries and impose the content of the document, including the portions of textual and multimedia elements, to be accessible by text-retrieval methods. The concepts of the hierarchical queries will be described in Section 5.

4 A Signature File Based Approach for Multi-lingual Information Retrieval

In the proposed approach, word, as in conventional signature file approaches, is still the basic unit (called token here) for signature generation in dealing with English documents. Nevertheless, characters and character bigrams (are tokens also) rather than words are taken as the basic units for signature generation, when the handling texts are Chinese. This is because there are about 13,053 commonly-used Chinese characters, and each Chinese word is usually composed of one or two of these characters. Although the composed words in a Chinese document are difficult to correctly segment using a computer, it is easy to extract all of the composed characters and character bigrams (each pair of adjacent characters) from texts. These characters and character bigrams hold certain semantics and form the features of the document.

4.1 Similar Token Grouping and Signature Determination

Though the composed characters and character bigrams (character tokens) can make up the features of a Chinese text, the number of possible character tokens in a database is often too large (usually exceeding 1M different tokens in a database of 100MB) and needs to be reduced. Since many of these tokens carry similar information, similar tokens can be grouped into classes and can share similar signature pattern in signature generation. In this way, it has been proved that it is possible to effectively reduce the size of the character set without losing too much information [1].

As to the similarity among tokens, this can be estimated by using the database content (or prepared training corpus) and the highly associated tokens. For example (Fig. 4), the character bigram 電腦 (computer) can be found similar to 資訊 (information), because there might have same bigrams highly associated with 電腦 (computer) and 資訊 (information) in the document context, e.g., 軟體 (software), 程式 (program), etc. Based on this concept, the number of grouped token classes is scalable and is dependent on the design of the signature file and the searching mechanism.

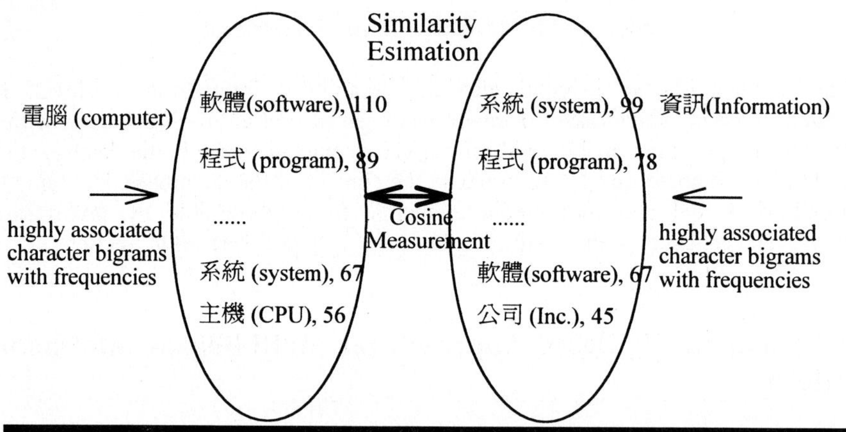

Fig. 4. An abstract diagram showing the concept of similarity estimation between tokens.

4.2 Token-based Signature Generation

With the above token grouping method, each document, which is actually a fixed block of text for simplicity, will be assigned a pre-specified three-segment bit string as its document signature (a document larger than the fixed block of text will be assigned more than one signature in a real application). The signatures are fixed binary bit strings which indicate the presence of token classes in the queries or documents. The first segment of the signature represents the occurrence of single Chinese characters, the second segment represents that of Chinese character bigrams and the third segment that of English words. The signature of a document is thus obtained by superimposing the Chinese characters, Chinese character bigrams and English words which the document is composed of. In fact, the first segment of the signature is used to indicate the existence of the frequently used Chinese characters. On the other hand, the second segment mainly records some positional information and serves as an information filter of the first segment. Moreover, the third segment is to allow the signature can also provide English search.

5 The Hierarchical Query Approach

As mentioned previously, mixing database and IR types of queries can enable to produce very powerful queries, being much more expressive than each mechanism by itself. The *hierarchical query* method developed, therefore, mainly lies on the combination of these two parts of queries. In our design, the query program written in the object query language supports retrieving document objects and further enable searching on text patterns. As the OODBMS query language employed also offer SQL-like syntax for queries, we will represent the queries based on the SQL style in this context. They are described as follows.

5.1 Object-level Queries: *document retrieval based on the original OODBMS queries*

The highest level of query is the *object-level query*. This query style employs original functions offered by the OODBMS query predicates, without additional content-based pattern matching functions. An example is presented as follows:

```
Select   a. title
from     a      in     Document
where    a. author ="Lee, C.H." and a. language = "English"
```

The use of the above query is exactly the same as utilizing the fundamental queries offered by the OODBMS system. This provides a simpler way to retrieve documents from the database. These queries are based on known attributes and structured data collections and are dominated by the database search engine, so they are regarded as the highest layer of document retrieval in our description.

5.2 Best Match Search for Quasi-Natural Language Queries

One method for text search on patterns is based on IR approach associated with a best match search approach. In addition to the database queries, the system also offer a variety of query styles, such as the *Quasi-Natural Language Queries*. The proposed best search method can be implemented using two primary modules: the fast search and the detailed search modules, as shown in Fig. 5. The purpose of the fast search module is to reduce the number of non-qualifying documents and obtain a higher recall rate. It uses a signature-based ranking function to estimate the similarity values between queries and documents. The documents which have lower similarity values can be filtered out after the fast search process is carried out. At the same time, the purpose of the detailed search module is to obtain a higher precision rate. The obtained signature-based similarity values of the remaining documents are re-estimated at this stage; the contents of the documents are scanned, the real frequencies of the composed characters and bigrams are calculated, and detailed analysis is performed.

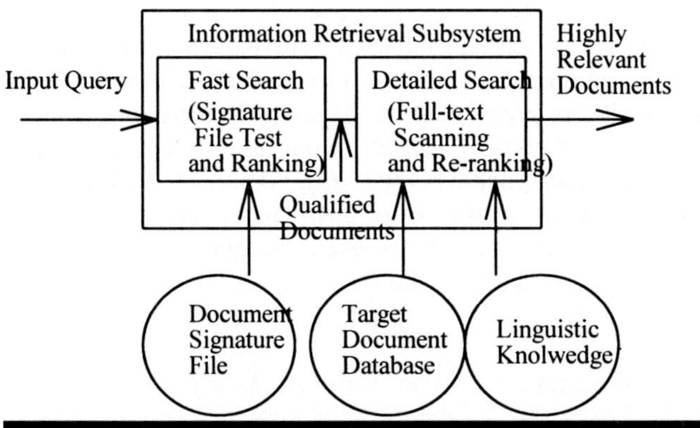

Fig. 5. Structure of the information retrieval subsystem.

5.3 Signature-based Fast Search

At the stage of the signature file test, all of the Chinese character and English word tokens in the input query will be used. Then, the fast search module generates the signature of the input query according to its composed tokens. It matches the query signature using the document signature file created by the document indexing module, calculates the similarity values using a *signature-based ranking function*, and filters out many of the non-qualifying documents [1]. In order to quickly filter out non-qualifying documents and to avoid the difficulty of key word extraction, the signature-based ranking function is used. Each bit in the signatures records the existence of some certain classes and their corresponding semantics. The derived document signatures constitute a bit-slice document signature file and serves as a filter which can be used to rapidly test for the existence of any given character string.

6 Conclusions

In this paper, we present a new approach for integrating OODBMSs and IRSs that maintains the flexibility and avoids overheads of mapping process, by means of wrapping the documents and encapsulating signature based IR methods into storable objects which are being stored in the database. In particular, we demonstrate how to apply such an integration approach to a special problem domain: a *multi-lingual information retrieval* system. In our framework, a sound platform and query facilities offered by the underlying object-oriented database can further enhance the original IR functions and be applicable to the construction of multimedia-document based digital libraries.

The main contribution of this work is a methodology to achieve the integrated functionality of OODBMSs and IRSs through an extension to the existing database queries. We use the encapsulated text retrieval system as an internal method within the defined document data model. The programming capacity offered by the object query language allows both the database query engine and text-retrieval search engine to be combined within a query program and being worked together to provide users a variety of forms of queries. The implementation addresses the advantages of flexibility, but still remains several issues with the integration architecture, mainly related to efficiency. This framework, however, is regarded as a starting point to allow for reviewing and identifying the fundamental functionality and theories of both IR and database disciplines, in order to produce quality retrieval and storage of information.

References

1. Chien, Lee-Feng: Fast and Quasi-Natural Language Search for Gigabytes of Chinese Texts. Proceedings of the 18th Annual International ACM SIGIR conference on Research and Development in Information Retrieval (1995) 112-120.
2. Christophides, V., Abiteboul, S., Cluet, S. and Scholl, M.: From Structured Documents to Novel Query Facilities. Proceedings of the ACM SIGMOD'94 (1994) 313-324.
3. Croft, W.B. Smith, L.A. and Turtle, H.R.: A Loosely-Coupled Integration of a Text Retrieval System and an Object-Oriented Database System. Proc. ACM SIGIR Conference (1992) 223-231.
4. Fuhr, Norbert.: A Probabilistic Relational Model for the Integration of IR and Databases. Proceedings of the 16th Annual International ACM/SIGIR Conference on Research and Development in Information Retrieval, Pittsburgh (1993) 309-317.
5. Fuhr, Norbert.: Integration of Information Retrieval and Database Systems. Proceedings of the 17th Annual International ACM/SIGIR Conference on Research and Development in Information Retrieval, Dublin (1994) 360.

6. Lee, W.L. and Woelk, D.: Integration of Text Research with ORION. Database Engineering, Vol. 9.(1991) 58-64.
7. Lee, C.H. and Zobel, R.N.: Representation of Simulation Models for Model Generation and a Model Library. Proceedings of the 29th Annual Simulation Symposium, New Orleans, Louisiana, USA (1996) 193-201.
8. Macleod, I.A. and Narine, D.: A Depository for Structured Text Objects. Proc. DEXA '95 (1995) 272-282.
9. Ogawa, Y.: A New Character-based Indexing Organization Using Frequency Data for Japanese Documents. Proceedings of the 18th Annual International ACM SIGIR conference on Research and Development in Information Retrieval (1995) 121-129.
10. Shoens, K. et al.: The Rufus System: Information Organization for Semi-Structured Data. Proceedings of the 19th VLDB Conference, Dublin, Ireland (1993) 97-107.
11. Stonebraker, M., Stettner, H., Lynn, N., Kalash, J. and Guttman, A.: Document Processing in a Relational Database System. ACM TOIS, 1(2) (1983) 143-158.
12. Volz, M. et al.: Applying a Flexible OODBMS-IRS-Coupling to Structured Document Handling. Proceedings of the Twelfth International Conference on Data Engineering, New Orleans, Louisiana, USA (1996) 10-19.
13. Yan, T.W. and Annevelink, J.: Integrating a Structured-Text Retrieval System with an Object-Oriented Database System. Proceedings of the 20th VLDB Conference, Santiago, Chile (1994).

Rectangular Decomposition of Signature File: Design Issues and Performance Evaluation

Khedija Arour¶, Ali Jaoua†
¶ Institut Préparatoire aux Etudes d'Ingenieur de Mateur
Route de Tabarka, Tunisie.
sadok.benyahia@fst.rnu.tn or mohamed.arour@planet.tn
† Faculté des Sciences de Tunis
Dépt. des Sciences de l'Informatique
Campus Universitaire, Tunis, Tunisie.
ali.jaoua@fst.rnu.tn

Abstract. Signature file acts as a filter to eliminate the unqualified data items for an information request. The contribution of this paper is two-fold. First, we propose a methodology for structured database. The main idea of decomposition amounts to dividing the relations of database into subrelations called *'rectangle'*. Owing to the reduction of storage overhead, rectangular decomposition has a direct benefit in a reduction of false drop probability. Second, we extend the use of rectangular decomposition to partitionning signature file called *Super-Rectangular Organisation SRO*. The choice of the criteria to cluster signatures is based upon the relationship between the associated objects. Our main concern is to study the performance of this method in terms of this ability to reduce the search space and false drop probability. We also perform simulation experiments by comparing several methods like *S-tree* and *Quick filter*. The results show that the *SRO* improves performance significantly in term of retrieval time and false drop probability.

Key words : Access method, Signature file, Clustering, Rectangular decomposition, Rectangle, Superimposed coding, Performance analysis, Information retrieval.

1 Introduction

An approach widely advocated for the unformatted as well as the formatted data is to use the signature file method. A signature file is basically an abstraction of a record file (or text). It provides an effective way of screening out records (or documents) which don't match with the query. The size of the signature file is much smaller than that of a data file. The efficiency of the signature file access method is determined by the quality of the filtering process, which is performed by the signature extraction methods and the fast query execution supported by adequate storage structures. However, searching the signature file itself may be slow this is because the size of the signature file is directly proportional to the size of the database, and performance becomes a concern for large databases. The main problem of our method is to develop a cluster scheme which allows us to search few clusters consequently few signatures. The rest of paper is organised as follows. In section 2, we describe an overwiew of signature file and various types of storage structures used for their organisation. Section 3 presents the principales ideas of rectangular decomposition. Section 4 is devoted to the description of the *SRO* method. In section 5, the we develop the analytic performance model for the proposed method. Experimental results are presented in section 6. Finally, section 7 concludes our study and gives a look at some research issues for further work.

2 Preliminaries on the signature file approach

The main idea of the signature file access method is to derive properties of data objects called *signatures* and store them in a separate file called *signature file*. Queries are assumed to be transformable to signature form. When processing a query, the signature file is scanned sequentially and many nonqualifying documents or records are discarded. Although many extraction methods for creating the signature from a term or attribute have been proposed [11]. Superimposed coding is perhaps the most common method used. Each term or attribute is hashed into a bit vector called *Word signature*, by selectiong a fixed number of bit positions from the word signature and setting them to one. A block or record signature S_i is generated by superimposing all word signatures for that block. In a query, the query terms are hasched and superimposed into a query signature S_Q in a similar way. S_Q is then compared with every signature from the signature file. A signature S_i is qualified if and only if for all bit positions in S_Q which are set to "1", the corresponding bit positions in S_i are also set to "1". Formally the set of qualified signatures is defined by $\{S_i | S_i \wedge S_Q = S_Q\}$. However, a qualified signature only means that the corresponding block is very likely to satisfy the query. That is, there is a chance that the block may not contain the term being searched for (i.e false drop). Some other methods are developped in the litterature, such that Bit block Compression BC or Run Lenght compression methods RL [5]. The difference is that the size of the signature is large and a step of compression is needed. In an earlier paper [1], we present a signature extract method that is based upon rectangular decomposition called $RSCW$. The advantage of this approach is its lower false drop probability. Even though the false drop rate is an important measure, the performance of signature files depends mainly on the I/O cost. The efficiency of filtring is determined by the storage structures and access strategies which support the filtering process. Several organisations of signature files are presented in the litterature. In single level signature methods (sequential retrieval, bit-sliced organisation) every signatures must be accessed and tested. The more objects exist the more time is spent on scanning the signature file. To support a faster access, multi-level signature organisations are suggested [9, 10, 12]. A signature in the level $'i'$ is created by superimposing the signatures contained in the level $'i-1'$. There are two problems associated with this structures. One is the density of the set bits in the parent signatures. The second problem is the rate of combinatorial errors caused by a large class of queries [3]. In [4], *S-tree* organisation is proposed. The method is based upon the clustering of signatures into cluster according to their similarity (the similarity of the positions set to $'1'$). The similar signatures are ORed to form a signature in an upper level. This method eliminates the need for examining every signatures in the signature file. Although very studies on signature techniques have been presented that is suitable to be applied to the new application environnments (i.e office systems, multimedia databases, ...). For example in [13, 8], the signature file is devided into partitions each of which holds signatures sharing the same key, and as result , we can detrmine if the signatures in a partition satisfy a query by merely examining the key, partitions not matching the key not be searched.

3 Rectangular decomposition

Rectangular decomposition allows a classification of databases presented as a binary relation, it has many applications in computer science such that data knowledge engenieering and database clustering. The problem of minimal database representation is difficult because it is $NP-Complet$. Many methods of database classification such that formatted database or documentary database have been developped to facilitate data retrieval and browsing [6, 2]. One of these methods is based on the rectangular decomposition, where a database is considered as a binary relation between a set of tuple identifiers and values attributes or between a set of documents D and a set of indexing terms T. The purpose of rectangular decomposition is to find an economical coverage of the binary relation. Starting from a binary relation R, a decomposition may help us to have a resumed database architecture.

3.1 Prelimanary concepts

Let for example D be a set of documents and T be a set of terms indexing T.

Definition 1 *A binary relation R between D and T is a subset of the cartesian product $D \times T$.*

Definition 2 *Let R be a binary relation defined between D and T. A rectangle RE of R is any cartesian product of two sets A and B. A is the domain of the rectangle $A \times B$ and B is the codomain such that $A \subseteq D, B \subseteq T$ and $A \times B \subseteq R$.*

Definition 3 *A rectangle (A, B) of R is Maximal if $A \times B \subseteq A' \times B' \subseteq R$ then $A = A'$ and $B = B'$.*

Definition 4 *The coverage is defined as a set of rectangles $CV = \{RE_1, \ldots, RE_n\}$ of R such that any element (a, b) of R is contained in at least one rectangle of CV.*

Definition 5 *A coverage CV defined by $\{RE_1, \ldots, RE_n\}$ of a relation R is economical if it is formed by a minimal number of optimal rectangles and it realises a maximum gain from space storage. This gain is measured by [6]:*

$$G = card(R) - \sum_{i=1}^{n}(card(dom(RE_i)) + card(cod(RE_i)))$$

3.2 Decomposition algorithm

The algorithm is a branch and bound one. Its idea is inspired from the maximum clique problem. In [7], a rectangle can be seen as a complete bipartie graph. Let R_D (resp. R_T) be a binary relation $\subseteq D \times D$ (resp. $\subseteq T \times T$) such that for any element e in D (resp. in T) $e.R_D = \{e' \in D | e \neq e'\}$ (resp. $e.R_T = \{e' \in T | e \neq e'\}$); and let $\Re = R \cup R_D \cup R_T$. This relation is used to ovoid a bipartie graph and with this relation a rectangle can be assimilated to a clique. Initially the algorithm considers a certain ordering of the element in $D \cup T$, say $\{e_1, \ldots, e_m\}$. When e_1 is the element such that the pseudo rectangle containing this element has the maximal gain. It has been observed that this element ordering helps us to find an economical rectangular decomposition. Without any pruning, the algorithm produces all the rectangles covering the relation. The cost of this algorithm can be taken as the number of elements for which we look for the coverage. For k incremental steps, cost is equal to the following:

$$k \times n_1 + k \times \frac{k-1}{2 \times n'} \text{ [7]}$$

Example 1 *Let be the relational schema $STUDENT$ in the table 1. The table 2 is the corresponding rectangular structure.*

3.3 Signature Extraction method

In our case the domain of a rectangle contains some values of attributes. The codomain contains the tuple identifiers that indexing these values of attributes. The signature of a rectangle is created by ORing some elementary signatures of values in the domain. To built this signature, each value of the domain yealds a bit pattern of size b, where k bits have value "1", while the others have value "0". The table 3 is the associated signature file. Query signature S_Q is generated by using the superimposed coding method. A signature S_{R_i} of a rectangle R_i is qualified if and only if $S_{R_i} \wedge S_Q = S_Q$. Accordingly, the rectangular decomposition allows us to group some values of attributes having some relationships in the same rectangle. Therefore, the signature of a rectangle reflects some semantic properties of information contained in it and almost reflects the real content of data that is represents. For this reason we expect to have less false drop. The false drop is

$$F_d = p(k) \approx [1 - (1 - \frac{k}{b})^{r_i}]^k \text{ [1]}$$

Where

Tid	Sec.	NCIN	Mod.	V	Plac.	N.	F.N.	Date
0	XC4	0272465	CB12	1	ENF.	CHRA.	AHM.	201163
1	XC4	0272465	CB14	1	ENF.	CHRA.	AHM.	201163
2	XC4	0272465	CH24	1	ENF.	CHRA.	AHM.	201163
3	XM4	0377129	MB12	0	TUN.	KHEM.	BRA.	250762
4	XM4	0377129	MB20	0	TUN.	KHEM.	BRA.	250762
5	XM4	0377129	ME11	0	TUN.	KHEM.	BRA.	250762
6	XM4	0377129	ME31	0	TUN.	KHEM.	BRA.	250762
7	XP4E	0592434	PB14	0	TUN.	FATN.	KAR.	210163
8	XP4E	0592434	PF22	0	TUN.	FATN.	KAR.	210163
9	XP4E	0592434	PF23	0	TUN.	FATN.	KAR.	210163
10	XP4E	0592434	PF24	0	TUN.	FATN.	KAR.	210163

Table 1. Instance of database STUDENT

Domaine	Codomaine
Tunis.5,0.4,XP4F.1, FATNASSI.6 KARIM.7,0592434.2,210163.8	7,8,9,10
TUNIS.5, 0.4, XM4.1, KHEMILA.6, BRAHIM.7,0377129.2,250762.8	3,4,5,6
ENFIDHA.5,1.4,XC4.1,CHRAITIA.6 AHMED.7,0272465;2,201163.6	0,1,2
PF24.3	10
PF23.3	9
PF22.3	8
PB14.3	7
ME31.3	6
ME11.3	5
MB20.3	4
MB12.3	3
CH24.3	2
CB14.3	1
CB12.3	0

Table 2. Rectangular structure of the database STUDENT

- b : lenght of signature ;
- k : weight of signature ;
- r_i : cardinality of any rectangle.

4 Super-rectangular organisation

Our method of ovoiding the linear scan is to cluster signatures by superimposing it. A query signature is first compared to the cluster signatures and if query signature does not completely cover the group signature, the entire group can be discarded without further inspection. The main idea of our approach is the use of informations contained in the rectangles and there signatures to improve the search speed. The choice of the criteria to cluster signatures is based upon the relationship between the associated rectangles. Rectangular decomposition is used to partitionning signature file. The *SRO* is a multiway tree that is hierarchy of nodes containing signatures.

S	φ
011 111 111 111 000 1	R_0
011 110 100 111 111 1	R_1
011 110 111 111 111 1	R_2
011 100 000 000 100 0	R_3
000 001 001 010 100 0	R_4
011 000 000 100 100 0	R_5
001 100 100 000 100 0	R_6
001 000 000 000 111 0	R_7
001 010 000 001 010 0	R_8
011 100 000 001 000 0	R_9
001 000 000 001 011 0	R_{10}
011 100 000 001 000 0	R_{11}
010 100 100 010 000 0	R_{12}
000 100 110 000 001 0	R_{13}

Table 3. Signature file for the rectangular structure

In the first time, we construct the binary relation associated to the signature file. Two rectangles are in relation where the intersection of their codomains is not empty.

Definition 6 *Let $R_1 = (A_1, B_1)$ and $R_2 = (A_2, B_2)$ two rectangles. R_1 and R_2 are in relation if and only if $B_1 \cap B_2 \neq \emptyset$.*

Where

- A_i : the set of attribute values ;
- B_i : the set of the tuple identifiers indexing theses values.

Therefore, if we started with the signatures of the filter, we can represent the relationship between the signatures with a binary relation. The relationship is based upon the strategy of intersection between the codomain of the associated rectangles. With this strategy, we can cluster some signatures which the corresponding rectangles have one or some values of the same tuple. To the binary relation, we apply the same heuristic of rectangular decomposition used to classify the database to obtain a minimal number of rectangles called *Super-rectangles.* A *super-rectangle* is a couple (A, B) where A (resp. B) is the domain (resp. codomain) that contains some of rectangles of the database. Let the rectangles $R_i = V_i \times T_i$ and $R_j = V_j \times T_j$ where V_i and V_j are the sets of attribute values. If there exist one tuple $t_{ik} \in T_i$ and $t_{ik} \in T_j$ then we found at least a value in V_i that is in relation with one value of V_j. With this strategy, we can cluster in the same class the signatures where the associated rectangles having some relationships.

Example 2 *In figure 1 SRO structure is presented. In table 4 the signatures of the super-rectangular organisation are elaborated.*

5 Search operation

5.1 Single term query

The signature of the super-rectangle is formed by the signature of the domain and the signature of the codomain. The signature of the domain (resp. codomain) is constructed by superimposing the

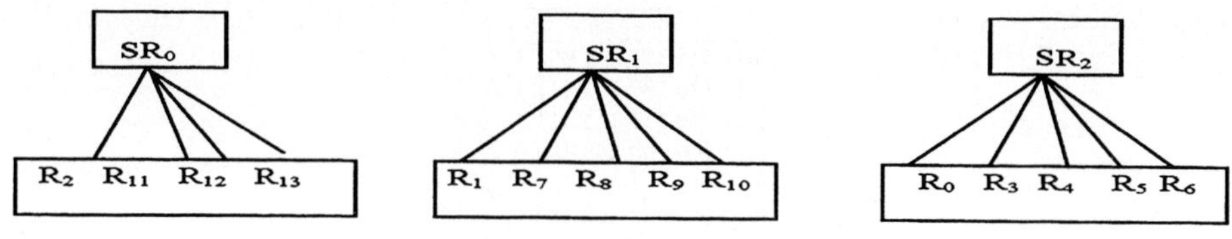

Fig. 1. Super-rectangular structure

SRid	*Domain*	*Codomain*	*Signature of the dom.*	*Signature of the cod.*
SR_0	R_2	$R_{11}R_{12}R_{13}$	*01111011111111111111*	*0111001100110010*
SR_1	R_1	$R_7R_8R_9R_{10}$	*01111010011111111111*	*0111100000010110*
SR_2	R_0	$R_3R_4R_5R_6$	*01111111111111110001*	*0111011011101000*

Table 4. *Signatures associated to the super-rectangular structure*

signatures of the associated rectangles.

Lemma 1 *One signature* $S = (S_1, S_2)$ *of the super-rectangle is qualified if and only if* $S_1 \wedge S_Q = S_Q$ *or* $S_2 \wedge S_Q = S_Q$

With mono-attribute query, the condition may appear in the domain or in the codomain of any super-rectangle and not in the two parts (per construction of the rectangles). The description of the signature based retrieval process is described in figure 2. We propose above two propositions that

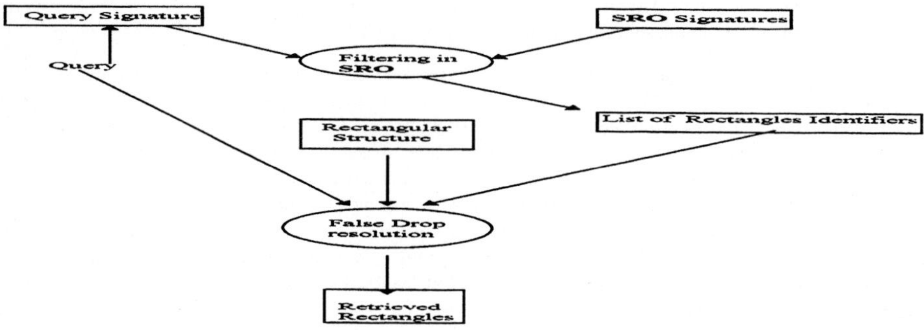

Fig. 2. Description of the process of filtering

facilate the process of retrieval.

Proposition 1 *Let* $SR = (A, B)$ *be a super-rectangle,* Q *is a query. If any rectangle* $R_i \in A$ *and the domain of* R_i *qualifies* Q *, then any rectangle of* B *not qualify* Q*.*

Proof. Let C_i be a condition of the query Q, $R_{ij} \in A$ is a rectangle that contains C_i. Let $R_{kt} \in B$ be a rectangle and $C_i \in dom(R_{kt})$. It exists a tuple t_l / $cod(R_{ij}) \cap cod(R_{kt}) = t_l$, then $C_i \in t_l$, C_i

and t_l appear in two different rectangles but the heuristic of decomposition eliminates this type of redundancy. Therefore $C_i \in R_{ij}$ or exclusively $C_i \in R_{kt}$

Proposition 2 *Let* $SR = (A, B)$ *is a super-rectangle and* C *is a condition of a query* Q*. We suppose that* $C \in dom(R_i)$ *and* $R_i \in A$*. If exist one tuple* t_j *where* $c \in t_j$ *and* $t_j \in cod(R_i)$ *then the complement of the response of the query exists in one or some rectangles of* B

Proof. The condition $C \in dom(R_i)$ and $R_i \in A$, $C \in t_j$. We suppose that $t_j \in cod(R_k)$ R_i and R_k have some common tuples. Consequently R_i appears in the domain and R_k in the codomain of the super-rectangle.

Algorithm 1 *Research algorithm*
Step1. Comparaison with the signatures of the super-rectangles
The query values are encoded using the method of superimposed coding. The query signature is compared with the super-rectangle signature S_{R_i} *where* $S_{R_i} = (S_{i_1}, S_{i_2})$*. When the bits of the query signature not cover the domain signature bits of a super-rectangle* $S_{i_1} \wedge S_Q \neq S_Q$ *then the codomain signature of the same super-rectangle is evaluated. If* $S_{i_2} \wedge S_Q = S_Q$*, then the associated rectangles are a candidat which satisfy the query. The first step constitutes a prilimary filter.*
Step 2. Second filter
In first step, some signatures of super-rectangles are qualified. The corresponding rectangles are tested using the same process. The elimination of the false drops can be done by the access of the corresonding rectangles.
Step 3. Answer completion
This step is reserved to complete the answer of the query if necessary. With proposition 2, the completion informations needed in the query is found in the rectangles that not considered in the process of the query.

To demonstrate the efficiency retrieval process of queries in the *SRO*, we consider the following example.

Example 3 *Let be the query*

Select *.*
From *STUDENT*
Where *module* = *PF23*

The query signature is $S_Q = 0000010010101000$
The second entry of the root nodes leads us to the codomain of SR_2*, since the signature of the entry contains a '1' at both the associated positions in* S_Q*. The associated rectangles included in* SR_2 *are accessed and specially the signatures of* $R_0, R_3, R4, R_5, R_6$*. The only signature that qualifies* S_Q *is* S_{R_4}*. We also need not access the rest of rectangles. The response of the query is found in* R_0*, where constitue the domain of* SR_2*. As a result the total number of block accesses is two and not including false drop.*

5.2 Multiattribute retrieval

The main problem of multiattribute retrieval in rectangular decomposition is that the attributes to be searched can appeared in many rectangles. Therefore, the propositions 1 and 2 cannot be valid. We discover that many rectangles are never retrieved nevertheless the conditions are included in the domain and the codomain. To resolve this problem, the signatures of the domain and the codomain are grouped and superimposed to form one signature for any *super-rectangle*. This idea attempts to represent all informations contained in the *super-rectangle* in one signature. We have to make sure that when any *super-rectangle* is selected further the conditions can be appeared between the rectangles of the domain and the codomain. More precisely, the signature of any super-rectangle is

$$S_{SR} = S_A \vee S_B$$

where

$$S_A = \vee_{i=1}^{r_A} S_{iA}$$

$$S_B = \vee_{i=1}^{r_B} S_{iB}$$

- r_A : cardinality of the domain (i.e number of associated rectangles) ;
- r_B : cardinality of the codomain ;
- S_{iA}, S_{iB} : signature of any rectangle.

S_{SR} is activated when $S_Q \wedge S_{SR} = S_Q$.

Example 4 *Let be the SQL query*

Select *.*   **From** *STUDENT*   **Where** *module = CB14 and section = XC4*

S_Q *is*

$$0101001000100000 \rightarrow CB14.module$$

$$\vee$$

$$\underline{0101001000000001} \rightarrow XC4.section$$

$$0101001000100001 \rightarrow S_Q$$

The signature of the super-rectangle SR_2 is qualified.

We can apply the same strategy of decomposition to construct several levels and hence signature tree is constructed from bottom to top. The process of adding an upper level continues until the weight of the generated signature is less than 50% of his lenght. The upper level signature is checked to see that it qualifies. If one signature is qualified, the corresponding branch is visited and so one.

6 Performance evaluation

6.1 Analytic cost model

The main purpose of a signature file is to reduce the search space in the database. Several parameters can affect the performances of the organisation of the signature file :

- the amount of storage required (i.e the storage overhead) ;
- the total number of signatures and super-rectangle signatures which require comparaison to the query signature.
- the number of signatures in the file
- the number of qualified signatures
- the false drop probability
- the number of signatures superimposed
- the number of conditions in the query

To estimate the performance, we assume that a partial match query with W_Q set ones should be processed. We make the following assumptions to produce our analysis.

- the structure can be formed by several levels. The number of levels is fixed to h. The construction of any level can be done by using the same process of clustering ;
- we assume that the response is found into t rectangles ;
- the number of children per cluster of signatures is fixed to d ;
- initially, we have N' recatngles. Then the relation between N' and h is $N' = d^h$.

6.2 symbols specification

- M : storage requirement ;
- h : height of the *SRO* ;
- d : degree of the hierarchic structure ;
- R_{S_F}: number of signatures searched due to false drop ;
- R_{S_Q}: number of signatures searched due to true drop ;
- R_S: number of signatures searched ;
- t: number of rectangles containing the response ;
- W_Q: weight of the query ;
- m : length of a signature ;
- N' : total number of rectangles ;
- r_R : cardinality of a rectangle ;
- k : weight of elementary signature.

6.3 Parameters evaluation

Storage overhead The hierachic construction of the structure is composed of h levels. Each signature of level i is the superposition of d rectangles signatures for the level $i-1$, each of which is of length $2 \times m$. The total storage in bits requiered is

$$M = m \sum_{i=1}^{h} d^i$$

Number of signatures in the structure The number of rectangles in the structure is N'. In the upper level, we are $\frac{N'}{d}$ signatures. The number of signatures in the new structure is

$$NS = N' \sum_{i=0}^{h} \frac{1}{d^i}$$

Number of signatures searched R_S R_S consists of two components : searches resulting from true drops R_{S_Q} and those from false drops R_{S_F}.

$$R_S = R_{S_Q} + R_{S_F}$$

At the first level, all signatures must be searched. There are t rectangles containing the query conditions. Since these rectangles are uniformly distributed into d subtrees, the probability for a subtree to contain a specific rectangle is $\frac{1}{d}$. The probability for a subtree not to contain a specific rectangle is $1 - \frac{1}{d}$. At the next level there are d sets of signatures and at max all of them must be compared each in turn containing d signatures. Thus the probability for a subtree to contain one or more of the t rectangles is $1-(1-\frac{1}{d})^t$. The total number of searched signatures at the second level due to true drop become

$$R_{S_{Q_2}} =\leq d^2(1-(1-\frac{1}{d^2})^t)$$

At level i

$$R_{S_{Q_i}} = d^i(1-(1-\frac{1}{d^i})^t)$$

then

$$R_{S_Q} = \sum_{i=1}^{h} d^i(1-(1-\frac{1}{d^i})^t)$$

In rectangular structure the false drop probability is

$$F_d = [1-(1-\frac{k}{m}^{r_R}]^k \ [1]$$

We assume that, the number of rectangles having the same cardinality is constant. Therefore, the number of values per rectangle is $\frac{N'}{r} = r_R$. A signature at the root is obtained by superimposing the corresponding child signatures at the second level and so one. Thus the cardinality of this set is ${r_R}^{d^{h-1}}$.

Hence, the false drop probability is $F_{d,1} = [1-(1-\frac{k}{m})^{r_R^{d^{h-1}}}]^{W_Q}$ and at level i is

$$F_{d,i} = [1-(1-\frac{k}{m})^{r_R^{d^{h-i}}}]^{W_Q}$$

The number of signatures resulting in false drops at level i is $d^i F_{d,i}$ then

$$R_s = \sum_{i=1}^{h} d^i(F_{d,i} + F_{t,i})$$

where

$$F_{t,i} = [1-(1-\frac{1}{d^i})^t]$$

Ratio of the number of rectangles searched to the total number of rectangles signatures The total number of signatures searched at all levels is R_S then

$$C = \frac{R_S}{NS}$$

6.4 Performance comparaison through experiments

In this section, we perform simulation experiments for the super-rectangular organisation, *S-tree* and *quick filter*. Variuos types of queries are used to evaluated the characteristics of the *SRO* and the performances of the dynamic signature file methods. We first investigate which method of organisation gives a better speed. Second, we analyse the false drop probability performance according to the signature size.

Response time versus signature size In the experiment 3, we present the results of the comparaison of the response time between super-rectangular organisation *SRO*, *S-tree* and *quick filter* for the same storage overfead. We can easly see that *SRO* response time is better for a little size of signature. Quick filter becomes better in the case of long signature. This may be explained as follows. Rectangular decomposition allows the reduction of redundancy attributes and can cluster the properties that interact highly in the same rectangle. The signatures having some relationships cannot be clustered together. Therefore the size of signature can be not very long.

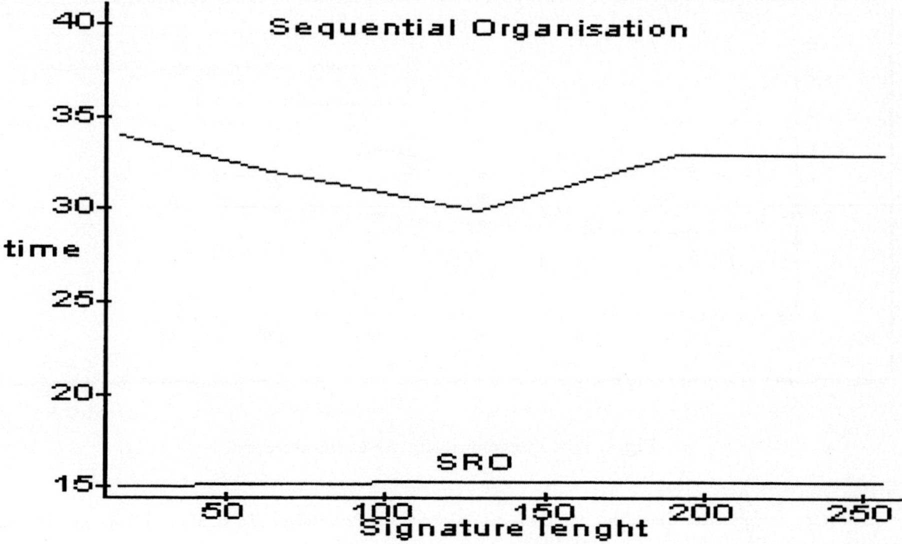

Fig. 3. Response time versus signature size

False drop probabilty versus signature size We propose in the experiment 4, the impact of the organisation of the signature file on the false drop probability. In the previous works , false drop probability is generally related to the method of how to extract signature from the objects. We can see in figure that from the same storage overhead, the *SRO* is better and more efficient. In one rectangle, we associated some values that have some properties and so one for the super-rectangle. Therefore, the signature in the same cluster have some relationships equivalent to that appear int the query. The signature of the super-rectangle reflects some semantic properties of informations contained in the corresponding rectangles. A signature at level i reflects almost the real content of data it contained.

7 conclusion

In this paper we have introduced a new access structure, called SRO for storing and retrieving signature files. We also present a methodology for structured database which has interesting performance in false drop probability. The first step is to cluster the database in some rectangles using rectangular decomposition. For the second step, we propose a new method to organise the signature files that is based upon rectangular decomposition. The choice of the criteria to cluster signatures is based upon the relationship between the associated rectangles. The advantage of this method is its response time and its lower false drop probability. In this study, we use an uniform approach to organise the database as well as the signature file to speed up the access. We have evaluated the performance of the *SRO* in terms of retrieval time, storage overhead and false drop probability. The results presented in the paper show that SRO is convenient to reduce false drop probability.

References

1. K. Arour and A. Jaoua. Signature Extraction Method in Rectangular Database. *Information Sciences*, 87(1-3):67–78, November 1995.

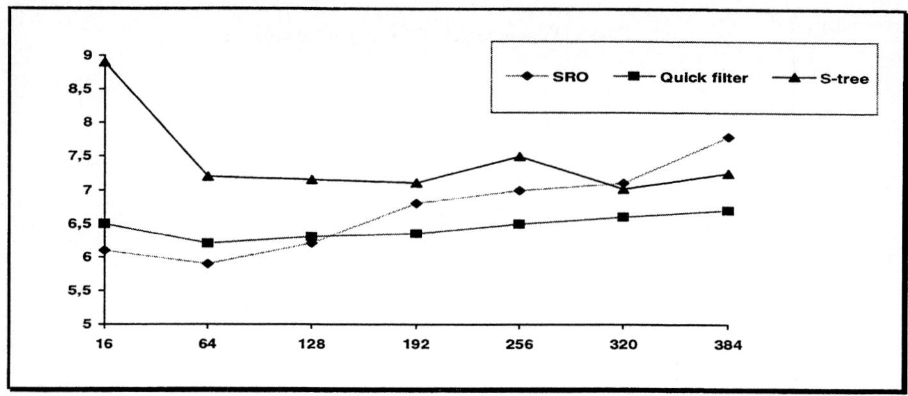

Fig. 4. False drop probability versus signature size

2. F. Can. Incremental Clustering for Dynamic Information Processing. *ACM Transactions on Information Systems*, 11(2):143–164, April 1993.
3. W.W. Chang and H.j. Schek. A Signature Access Method for the Starburst Database System. In *Proceedings of the Fifteenth International Conference on Very Large Database. Amsterdam*, pages 145–153, August 1989.
4. U. Deppisch. S-tree: A dynamic balansed signature index for office retieval. In *Proceedings of the 1986 ACM Conference on Research and Development in Information Retrieval, Pisa, Italy*, pages 77–87, September 1986.
5. C. Faloutsos. Signature Files: An Integrated Access Method for Text and Attributes Suitable for Optical Disk Storage. *BIT*, pages 736–754, 1988.
6. M.M. Gammoudi. *Méthode de décomposition Rectangulaire d'une Relation Binaire: une Base Formelle et UNiforme pour la Génération Automatique des Thesaurus et la Recherche Documentaire.* Doctorat es-sciences, spécialité informatique, Université de Nice-Sophia Antipolis, Septembre 1993.
7. R. Kcherif and A. Jaoua. Rectangular Decomposition Heuristics for Large Databases. In *Joint Conference on Information Sciences*, October 1995.
8. D.L. Lee, Y.M. Kim, and G. Patel. Efficient Signature File Methods For Text Retrieval. *IEEE Transactions On Knowledge and Data Engineering*, 7(3):423–435, June 1995.
9. F. Rabitti and P. Savino. Image Query Processing on Multilevel Signatures. In *Proceedings of the ACM SIGIR'90, International Conference, Chicago, Information Retrieval Brussels*, pages 305–314, September 1991.
10. K. Ramamohanorao, R. Sacks-Davis, and A. Kent. A Signature File Scheme Based on Multiple organizations for Indexing Very Large Database. *Information Sciences*, 41(7):508–534, 1990.
11. C.S. Roberts. Partial-Match REtrieval via the Method of Superimposed Codes. In *Proceedings of the IEEE*, volume 67, pages 1624–1642, December 1979.
12. R. Sacks-Davis, A. Kent, and K. Ramamohanorao. Multikey Access Methods Based on Superimposed Coding Techniques. *ACM Transactions on Database Systems*, 12(4):655–696, December 1987.
13. T. Zezula and F. Rabitti. Dynamic Partitionning of Signature Files. *ACM Transactions on Information Systems*, 9(4):336–369, October 1991.

Cumulative Duality in Designing Information Brokers

Bernd Wondergem, Patrick van Bommel, and Theo van der Weide

Computing Science Institute, University of Nijmegen
Toernooiveld 1, NL-6525 ED, Nijmegen, The Netherlands
bernd@cs.kun.nl

Abstract. The focus of this paper is information brokers within Information Discovery (ID). We describe Cumulative Duality matrices, an instrument to deal with design criteria for such information brokers.
ID is the synthesis of Information Retrieval and Information Filtering, where information brokers act as middle-agents. There are numerous design criteria for information brokers. Since these stem from ID, they exhibit a dual nature. The duality of the criteria is shown to be cumulative. In the form of a matrix, cumulative duality can be used as a design instrument for information brokers.

1 Introduction

In the quest for relevant information, two conceptually *dual* approaches have emerged: Information Retrieval (IR) (e.g. [12]) and Information Filtering (IF) (e.g. [2]). Where IR deals with dynamic user needs and stable collections of information, IF is concerned with stable user needs and a dynamic supply of information. See [2] for a comprehensive comparison of IR and IF.

Our paradigm Information Discovery (ID), consisting of the synthesis of IR and IF, is more powerful than their mere combination ([17]). In ID, we consider a community of possibly interconnected users, having both stable and dynamic information needs. Also, we consider a number of sources, again stable and dynamic and possibly communicating, containing documents to satisfy users' information needs. This process is facilitated by intermediaries called *information brokers*, which cooperatively compare user interests with available documents. Users and sources communicate via brokers, as depicted by solid arcs in Fig. 1. Communication between entities of the same type is depicted by dashed arcs.

The paradigm in Figure 1 is augmented in several perspectives. Firstly, the entities in the ID paradigm are modeled as intelligent agents, since agent technology (see e.g. [18]) is perfectly suited for dynamic ID environments ([16]). Secondly, information brokers essentially are *middle*-agents. Middle-agents can be designed in a variety of ways (see e.g. [9] and [8]), resulting in different instantiations of the ID paradigm. We consider design criteria for information brokers regarding ID, concerning e.g. privacy and knowledge about locations of users

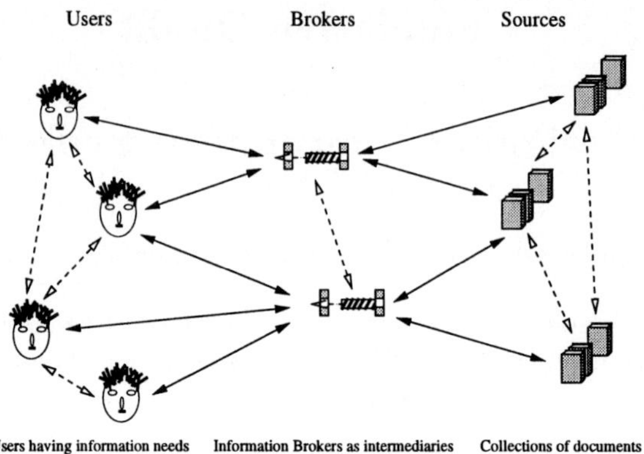

Fig. 1. Information Discovery Paradigm

and sources. These criteria exhibit a *dual* user-source nature caused by duality in ID.

The focus of this paper is on the conceptual design of information brokers in the context of the ID paradigm. Our goal is to describe Cumulative Duality matrices, an instrument which explicitly shows the influence of dual ID criteria on the design and performance of information brokers. As a consequence, this instrument provides a solid basis for analysis of duality in ID.

The duality of ID criteria is cumulative over the ID communication directions, i.e. either from user, via broker to source, or the other way around. Although the proposed application domain is ID, our approach is applicable in every paradigm that exhibits a dual nature and uses middle-agents. For instance, middle-agents in electronic commerce (see e.g. [15]) can be focused on. This also holds for numerous other applications of WWW agents, and middle-agents in general. As an example, consider BargainBot ([1]), helping users with shopping and IR, and Kasbah ([6]), aiding users in buying and selling goods.

The organisation of this paper is as follows. In Sect. 2, duality of design criteria in ID is examined and Cumulative Duality matrices (CD matrices) are introduced. Section 3 provides different applications of CD matrices, leading to different broker designs. Section 4 elaborates on other design criteria for information brokers. Finally, Sect. 5 provides concluding remarks and directions for future research.

2 Cumulative Duality in Information Discovery

2.1 Duality in Information Discovery

Duality in ID stems from the synthesis of the dual paradigms of IR and IF. On a basic level, i.e. the level of contextual assumptions, this is evident in, for instance, dynamic vs. static user needs and sources of information. On a higher level, the goals of users and sources are dual: users want only relevant information to be rendered (their preference is to receive *not too much* information), whereas sources want to deliver as much information as possible (their preference is not to distribute *not too little* information).

A result of both forms of duality between users and sources is an imbalance in the ID paradigm. To guarantee fairness in an unbalanced paradigm, neutral intermediaries are introduced: information brokers. As stated in the introduction, the more basic goal of information brokers is the matching of user interests and available documents.

A common aspect of these information brokers and Negotiated Retrieval ([11]) is the merging of documents out of several sources. However, information brokers have more goals and features. Information brokers should, for instance, be proactive to relieve the user as much as possible.

2.2 Cumulative Duality in Directed Communication

There is a clear relation with client-server architectures. Information brokers are true middle-agents, since all communication between users and sources goes through brokers (see Fig. 1). Middle-agents may be considered as an augmentation of the client-server model (see e.g. [14]). Information brokers, however, are capable of performing 2-way tasks: users and sources can act both as clients and as servers. Thus, in ID middle-agents are an extension of a double client-server model.

These 2-way tasks in ID result in a special form of duality, having a *cumulative* nature. It is cumulative over the directions of communication: either from user, via broker to source, or the other way around. Consider, for example, user privacy. Knowledge about user preferences initially is only available in the user himself and can only reach a source through a broker. The dual criterion, concerning source openness, is cumulatively communicated the other way around. Other instances of cumulative duality are considered in Sect. 3.

2.3 Cumulative Duality Matrix

Most specific ID criteria embody a cumulative user-source duality. We propose the *Cumulative Duality* matrix (CD matrix) as an instrument for representing and analysing the influences of cumulative dual criteria upon the design of information brokers. These criteria should be incorporated in a method for agent design. In, for instance, the AWIC method ([10]) the criteria influence the Interopability and Coordination models.

The general form and characteristics of CD matrices are depicted in Fig. 2. The cumulative user criterion is covered by the leftmost column. The dual cumulative source criterion is covered by the top line. The nine cells systematically enumerate the possible combinations concerning the criteria.

The upper left-most cell in Fig. 2 represents the most critical situation, since the information broker has no means to deal with neither user nor source criteria. As we go right from here, broker and user agents become capable of dealing with

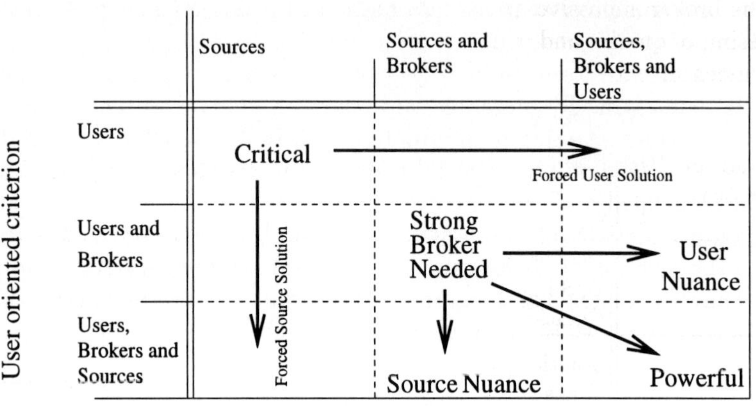

Fig. 2. General Cumulative Duality Matrix

the source criterion. Therefore, a user oriented solution is forced, i.e. one that demands most of users. If we go down from the first cell, the same occurs with respect to the user criterion.

The middle cell is the minimal cell for which the broker can cope with both the user and source criteria. Since no extra capabilities are available in either user or source, this cell demands a strong broker.

In the cell right from the middle cell, the user also is aware of the source criterion. This means that a nuance, relieving the broker's burden, towards the user can be made. Analogous remarks apply to the cell below the middle cell. The last cell represents the potentially most powerful situation since both user and source can aid or direct the broker.

The above is easily instantiated with, for example, the user criterion regarding dynamics of user interests. The first row then represents that only the user is able to deal with user dynamics. If also brokers can deal with user dynamics, we find ourself in the second row, and if sources are equally capable in the third row.

3 Instantiations of CD Matrices

3.1 Partial Environmental Knowledge

Environmental knowledge in ID concerns the locations, names, or addresses of the agents. Information brokers need this information about both users and sources. If users know the names of sources, they can send addressed queries (directed IR). If sources know the names of users they can directly send information (directed IF).

Figure 3 provides a CD matrix for the dual location criteria. First we consider the critical situation given in the upper left-most cell. In this situation, the broker initially does not know how to access either users or sources. This means that the broker is passive, i.e. both users and sources have to take the initiative. Processing of queries and incoming documents can only be based on coincidental co-occurrence.

Location of User known by	*Location of Source known by*		
	S	S+B	S+B+U
U	Passive Br U/S-initiative Coincidence Br	U-initiative (IR) S-querying	U-initiative (IR) Dir S-querying
U+B	S-initiative (IF) U-answering	Proactive Br U/S-privacy	Proactive Br Directed IR Undirected IF
U+B+S	S-initiative (IF) Dir U-answering	Proactive Br Directed IF Undirected IR	Proactive Br Directed IR Directed IF

Fig. 3. CD Matrix for Partial Environmental Knowledge

User and source initiative. Next we consider the top row of the matrix in Fig. 3. In the upper middle cell, the broker can contact sources but no users. This means that users have to take the initiative, leading to a typical IR situation with source querying. In the upper right-most cell, users can perform directed source querying, but still have to take the initiative.

Analogous situations arise in the first column. Here we have sources taking initiative, leading to a typical IF case with user answering. In the bottom cell of the first column, sources have directed user answering on the initiative of the sources themselves.

Proactive brokers. In the central cell of Fig. 3, the broker is the pivot of the system. Since it knows both user and sources, it can perform proactive IR and IF, i.e. contacting users and sources on its own initiative. Privacy of location of both users and sources is guaranteed, which also implies that users and sources cannot assist the broker.

In the cell right to the central one, the location of sources is also known by users, which therefore can also perform directed IR. Still, users privacy remains untouched (undirected IF). Analogous remarks apply to the cell below the central one. The location of users is then known by sources but not vice versa, leading to directed IF but undirected IR. The final cell is the only one totally without location privacy, resulting in fully transparent information brokers.

3.2 Privacy of Interest and Content

When searching the Internet, we would usually like to keep our profile of interest hidden for the outside world. This is an important point in designing information brokers to be treated with care. As an example, in some cases it may be required to keep our search interest private, while in other cases it may help us to make (part of) our interest known to external agents.

In this section we discuss this in the form of two dual criteria. These criteria concern privacy of user interests and source content. The resulting CD Matrix is given in Fig. 4.

User interests known by	*Source contents known by*		
	S	S+B	S+B+U
U	Naive Br Broadcaster Assembler	S-overview Hyperindexing U-guide	Selective IR Personalisation
U+B	U-overview Filter topology S-guide	True Broker Total privacy	S-recommender U-privacy
U+B+S	Selective IF Narrowed topol.	U-recommender S-privacy	Arbitrator No privacy

Fig. 4. CD Matrix for privacy of interest and Content

First we consider the upper left-most cell of Fig. 4. In this most critical case, the information broker has no instances of interest and no documents to match. The only thing left for the broker is to broadcast requests and proposals, and assemble the answers.

User and source overviews. In the middle cell of the top row, brokers can support an overview of the available information. They can, for instance, support Query by Navigation in a hyperindex (see e.g. [5], [4]). In the right cell of the top row, it is possible to perform selective IR, for example by personalising the process of hyperindexing (see e.g. [3]). Similar aspects are found in the left column.

Broker versus arbitrator. The middle cell represents a true information broker, i.e. the broker is the only one knowing about both interests and available content. Privacy for both users and sources is guaranteed. The cell to the bottom represents the broker as introducer or bodyguard. Since the user is unaware of the sources' content, it must be introduced by the broker. In the most powerful combination, the information broker can merely act as an arbitrator since users and brokers are mutually omniscient. This example is taken from [8] and adapted to ID.

3.3 Dynamical Interest and Content

Both user interests and available information are dynamic in ID. User interests are communicated cumulatively towards sources. In the dual case, the content of sources is communicated cumulatively towards users. Information brokers form intermediaries between dynamic parties. See Fig. 5 for the corresponding CD matrix, where the dual criteria concern the capability of agents to deal with user and source dynamics.

Can deal with user dynamics	*Can deal with source dynamics*		
	S	S+B	S+B+U
U	Static Intermediary	Delayed User Interest Filter ("Static User")	User Monitored Collection
U+B	Delayed Doc Provider ("Static Source")	Dynamic Interface	Dynamic Guide for Sources
U+B+S	Source Stimulated Filter	Dynamic Guide for Users	Dynamic Mutual Assistant

Fig. 5. Cumulative Duality Matrix for Dynamical Interest and Content

Delayed Interest and Content. In the most critical case, the broker is a static intermediary. This, of course, is no valid solution. Towards a forced source solution, more parties find themselves capable of dealing with user dynamics but not with source dynamics. Eventually, a source stimulated filter is obtained. Here, the source has to provide snapshots satisfying changing user needs since both users and brokers are incapable of doing so.

Interface vs. Assistant. In the middle cell, the information broker is fully responsible for the dynamics of both users and sources. It forms a dynamic interface between users and sources. The cell to the bottom of it represents a dynamic user guide, providing dynamic user access to sources. In the most powerful combination, the information broker can act as a mere assistant providing dynamic mutual support.

4 Other Cumulative Dual Criteria

Dual *time constraints* play an important role in ID. First, in IR, users have short term interests and need direct results, whereas in IF, users have long term interests and do not require results to be delivered immediately. Second, the timeliness of documents is treated differently as well. Where in IR the complete set of documents, including old ones, is queried, IF requires relatively new documents to be sent to users.

Traditionally, a user query or profile only consists of a description of the topic of interest. According to Cooper ([7]) not only topicality (logical relevance) but also *situational factors* (usability) should be taken into account. Dual criteria are obtained with respect to user interests formulated in terms of situational factors as well, and document characterisations supporting these too. The inclusion of situational factors opens the possibility for more interaction in the form of negotiation ([15]).

Agents in the ID paradigm form an *open environment*: agents can come and go when they want. This requires highly dynamic cooperation strategies without strict commitment ([13]). The electronic (ID) market stresses the importance of supporting open environment negotiation by letting only the most well adapted brokers survive.

Even more cumulative dual criteria can be formulated within ID but also more in general. The consequences of those criteria can be clearly depicted and analysed through the user of CD matrices since these give a structured overview on a conceptual level. This will make the process of broker design better structured and motivated.

5 Conclusions & Further Research

We introduced Cumulative Duality matrices as a mechanism to analyse the *role* of the information broker within the ID paradigm, and of middle-agents in dual paradigms in general. We argued that the duality in goals of users and brokers implied the need for neutral intermediaries.

Design criteria for information brokers were shown to exhibit a cumulative dual nature in Information Discovery. The sections above showed the influence of a number of dual ID criteria on the conceptual design of information brokers. A number of general conclusions can be made.

First, it appears that the information broker must be able to deal with both user and source criteria to obtain a viable broker design. This means that there are only four possible cells, i.e. those in the bottom right corner.

Second, different points of view can be adopted, resulting in different favourable broker designs and focusing on different regions of the CD matrices. The function of the information broker is to provide a transparent connection between different capabilities, needs, and knowledge. In that way the broker has to ensure a basis of equality between users and sources. Two major points of view are (1) user oriented, focusing on the cell right to the middle, and (2) source oriented, focusing on the cell below the middle.

Third, the potentially most powerful cell is in certain respects the most problematic as well. For instance, user privacy is not viable.

Finally, the dual nature of the ID criteria is visible in CD matrices as well. Taking the diagonal from top left to bottom right as a axis, the left bottom corner and right upper corner are mirror images with respect to the dual criteria used.

Further research can be focussed on a number of aspects of CD matrices. For instance on the combination of several CD matrices. The combination of CD matrices can be researched in the light of more traditional matrices. For example, by the analogy of multiplying and adding (mathematical) matrices. This will lead to the possibility to investigate and analyse hybrid brokers.

In addition, CD matrices can be combined with agent design tools. For instance, they could be included in the AWIC method as described by Mueller in [10].

Finally, the use of CD matrices for personalising brokers can be investigated. For this, we envisage CD matrices as part of advanced user interfaces in which the user can select the most appropriate broker variant.

References

1. B. Aoun. Agent Technology in Electronic Commerce and Information Retr ieval on the Internet. In *"Proceedings of AusWeb96 Second Australian World Wide Web Co nference*, Australia, 1996.
2. N.J. Belkin and W.B. Croft. Information Filtering and Information Retrieval: Two Sides of the Same Coin? *Communications of the ACM*, 35(12):29–38, December 1992.
3. F.C. Berger and P. van Bommel. Personalized Search Support for Networked Document Retrieval Using Link Inference. In A.M. Tjoa and R. Wagner, editors, *Proceedings of the Data Base and Expert System Applications Conference (DEXA 96)*, Vienna, Austria, 1996. Springer-Verlag.
4. P.D. Bruza. *Stratified Information Disclosure: A Synthesis between Information Retrieval and Hypermedia.* PhD thesis, University of Nijmegen, Nijmegen, The Netherlands, 1993.
5. P.D. Bruza and Th.P. van der Weide. Stratified Hypermedia Structures for Information Disclosure. *The Computer Journal*, 35(3):208–220, 1992.
6. A. Chavez and P. Maes. Kasbah: An Agent Marketplace for Buying and Selling Goods. In *Proceedings of PAAM 96*, pages 75–90, 1996.
7. W.S. Cooper. A Definition of Relevance for Information Retrieval. *Information Storage and Retrieval*, 7:19–37, 1971.
8. K. Decker and K. Sycara. Middle-Agents for the Internet. In *Proceedings of the 15th International Joint Conference on Artificial Intelligence*, Nagoya, Japan, August 1997.
9. D. Kuokka and L. Harrada. Matchmaking for Information Agents. In Huhns M.N. and M. Singh, editors, *Readings in Agents*, San Francisco, California, 1997. Morgan Kaufmanm Publishers.
10. H.J. Mueller. Towards agent system engineering. In *Data and Knowledge Engineering*, volume 23, pages 217–245, 1997.
11. M.V. Nagendra Prasad, V.R. Lesser, and S.E. Lander. Retrieval and Reasoning in Distributed Case Bases. In *Journal of Visual Communication and Image Representation, Sp ecial Issue on Digital Libraries*, volume 7 (1), pages 74–87, 1996.
12. C.J. van Rijsbergen. *Information Retrieval.* Butterworths, London, United Kingdom, 2nd edition, 1979.

13. T.W. Sandholm and V.R. Lesser. Automated contracting among self-interested bounded rational agents. Technical report, Computing Science Department, University of Massachusetts, Amherst, 1995.
14. G. Wiederhold. Mediators in the Architecture of Future Information Systems" . In *IEEE Computer*, pages 38–49, March 1992.
15. B.C.M. Wondergem, P. van Bommel, T.W.C. Huibers, and T. van der Weide. Opportunities for Electronic Commerce in Information Discovery. In F. Griffel, T. Tu, and W. Lamersdorf, editors, *Proceedings of the International IFIP/GI Working Conference on Trends in Distributed Systems for Electronic Commerce, TrEC 98*, pages 126–136, Hamburg, Germany, June 1998.
16. B.C.M. Wondergem, P. van Bommel, T.W.C. Huibers, and Th. van der Weide. Towards an Agent-Based Retrieval Engine. In J. Furner and D.J. Harper, editors, *Proceedings of the 19th BCS-IRSG Colloquium on IR research*, pages 126–144, Aberdeen, Scotland, April 1997.
17. B.C.M. Wondergem, P. van Bommel, T.W.C. Huibers, and Th.P. van der Weide. Agents in Cyberspace – Towards a Framework for Multi-Agent Systems in Information Discovery. In *Proceedings of the 20th BCS Colloquium on Information Retrieval, IRSG98*, Grenoble, France, March 1998.
18. M. Wooldridge and N.R. Jennings. Intelligent Agents: Theory and Practice. *Knowledge Engineering Review*, 10(2):115–152, 1995.

A Workflow System Based on Agents

Igor Hawryszkiewycz, John Debenham
School of Computing Sciences,
University of Technology, Sydney,
PO Box 123, NSW 2007, Australia
igorh, debenham@socs.uts.edu.au

Abstract. This paper describes an agent based architecture to manage workflows. The agents, rather than predefined rules, determine the flow of work, enabling them to cater for unexpected inputs. The agents in this distributed system use organisational rules, as well as the state of the decision making environment to control the flow of work. An experimental agent-based workflow system based on the World Wide Web to manage the processing of applications received by a university department from potential research students is described.

1. Introduction

Workflow management systems are gradually evolving beyond supporting planned execution of predefined tasks to become more flexible and adaptive to changes in the organizational environments and sensitive to organizational culture. Such systems can refer to an organizational knowledge base and use this knowledge base to adjust flows at execution time.

The design, implementation and evaluation of such systems is described in this paper, together with an experimental implementation, called RSA (Research Student Application). RSA manages the acceptance and processing of applications from potential research students in a university environment. Processing of these applications by the university staff requires that the staff express opinions on the applicant. Thus this workflow involves decision making. It is more complex than a simple workflow system in which specific tasks are performed completely at each step in the workflow

2. Background

The effectiveness of workflow processing is central to the success of any organisation with more effective workflow processing leading to improved corporate competitiveness. *Workflow management* is concerned with the design of workflow systems and their infrastructure so as to achieve effectiveness. Most workflow systems support planned work, which calls standard tasks at each step in the belief that this guaranteed good quality outcomes by following pre-specified rules. However, business environments are now becoming more volatile, and follow more complex processes that require workflow systems, which no longer rely on pre-specified actions (Hawryszkiewycz & Gorton, 1996). The trend from planned to situated work (Suchman, 1987) requires new kinds of workflow support. This change is due to a number of factors, including:

- individual workflows can vary and should be given appropriate treatment, there are always exceptions;
- there is increasing emphasis on the use of ad hoc groups to make decisions rather than formal statutory committees;
- if urgent workflows are being processed in a stable organisation then personnel may not always available, and
- the decision making environment is constantly changing, and workflows should adapt to these changes.

This evolution of systems is illustrated in Figure 1.

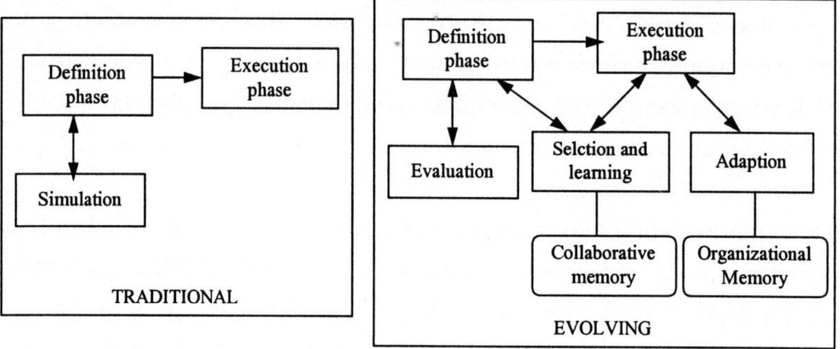

Figure 1 - Adaptive workflow systems

Thus in the traditional systems there a definition phase to define the workflow process. This is followed by the execution phase to carry out the defined process. The newer workflow forms have two extensions. One is to make execution more adaptive to organizational change. These use an organizational knowledge base to adjust particular tasks to cater for unexpected inputs or changes in the organization. The next step is to make the definition itself adaptive and allow it to change dynamically to satisfy unexpected goals. We call these workflows *adaptive workflows*. A further extension is to *learning workflows*, where workflows that are created during execution to meet emerging goals, are stored in a collaborative memory. Such stored workflows can be used later to generate workflows during definition, should those goals reappear. In this paper we are only concerned with adaptive workflows.

One important difference is in the way workflows are specified. Workflows can be specified imperatively or declaratively. A *pre-planned workflow* is usually imperative and specifies precisely how a task is to be accomplished in terms of the roles of the people involved in the workflow. Adaptive workflows are more flexible that pre-planned workflows and usually specify tasks declaratively by describing *what* has to be achieved in a workflow; it then being left to the workflow management system to deduce the 'how' from the 'what'. An adaptive workflow is specified declaratively of day-to-day changes in the environment. To more specifically define the way adaptive workflows operate we need the following definitions:

- An *instance* is the representation of pieces of information in either electronic or physical form; an instance cannot be altered as such. In other words, if an instance is altered it becomes another instance.
- A *workflow segment* as: a set of instances called the *segment inputs*, a specification of the possible outcomes of the workflow segment, an agent who is responsible for determining the correct outcome for the given segment input and for representing that outcome as a set of instances called the *segment outputs*, on the basis of specified criteria.
- A *workflow* for that segment is that segment together with the set of other workflow segments that have generated all of that segment's inputs.
- A *workflow graph* shows the agents as nodes that are joined by arcs representing the workflows. A workflow graph can be cyclic; in simple applications it may have a linear or a tree structure .

Thus a workflow segment could be specified imperatively as "the given form is sent to person X who will mark that form to show whether particular aspects of that form are correct". Alternatively, the goal of a workflow segment could be specified declaratively as "for a given form decide whether that form has been completed correctly"; it then being left to the workflow management system to determine how this goal should be achieved and who should be responsible for achieving it Such determination is made on the basis of both the goal of that segment and knowledge of the current state of the decision making environment (Kwan & Balasubramanian, 1997). Once the segment output is determined, an adaptive workflow system will derive the goal for the next workflow segment.

Adaptive workflow management systems thus rely on an understanding of the relationship of workflows to their environment. A specification of the *environment* is a specification of the "organisational rules", the "cultural factors" and the "processing capacity" of the organisation (Debenham, 1997). For each workflow segment an adaptive workflow management system will determine how the goal of that segment may be achieved. The *organisational rules* describe how an enterprise fits together and how it operates. They also describe who is authorised to do what in the name and business of the organisation and specify procedures for carrying out tasks. The *cultural factors* of an organisation are the "knowledge of how things work". This includes rules of thumb about "who is a good person to ask about certain difficult situations", or who is to be consulted so that a decision may be accepted.

2.1 Implementation

RSA has been designed as a distributed intelligent agent system based on the World Wide Web. A *distributed intelligent agent system* is a system consisting of multiple agents in which the agents are distributed in different sites of the network to be used by different users. Together these agents work cooperatively to achieve the workflow goal, which, in the case of RSA, involves making a non-trivial decision. All agents in a distributed system communicate with each other using the Agent Communication Protocol (ACP) which is described below.

Each user of the system, including the external applicant, is supported by a personal agent. Each agent acts as a "fairly dumb" assistant to support its user. In the experimental system each user's agent knows the available processing capacity of its user as well as a range of user preferences. In a distributed intelligent agent architecture each agent may be constructed separately. This eases construction and is amenable to team work. The choice of an agent architecture is a natural one, and it has the advantage that other systems may be added in subsequently by extending the knowledge of the relevant agents. In other words, if other applications are included then agents that are not effected by those other applications will remain completely unchanged.

The experimental RSA system has been implemented in Lotus Notes using a Domino Server. In this way all documents are HTML documents and the users interact with the system using a Web Browser. This ensures that the system is universally accessible.

Evaluation of the system has been carried out within a university department using test applications generated locally. The results of this evaluation are described below.

3. System Design

A highly simplified description of the external operation of the experimental RSA system follows. Prospective research students are directed to a world wide web page that contains explanatory material and a form. If the prospective student (ie the "Applicant") chooses to complete this form, the completed form is submitted. When a form is submitted it is screened automatically to check for obvious errors such as leaving the section "Please suggest a brief title for your proposed research project." blank. If the form fails the automatic screening then an email message is sent to the Applicant to request that the detected errors should be rectified. When this initial screening is complete an email message is sent to a senior academic (ie the "Supervisor") in the department advising that a form has been screened. The Supervisor will then check the form to ascertain whether the interests of the Applicant are relevant to the interests of the department. If the Supervisor indicates that the interests of the Applicant are relevant then the Supervisor marks the form with any potential supervisors who could be well suited to supervise the proposed work. The form is then released. When a form is released the system refers to a database containing the research interests of all academic staff and forms a prioritised list of appropriate candidate supervisors. The form is then circulated to these candidate supervisors until either two supervisors are found or no two supervisors can be found.

This particular application was chosen for the following reasons. The application involves three important types of interaction with players. The first type of player is the "client", ie the Applicant, who should be "kept happy" with sufficiently frequent and detailed communication to give the impression that "something is happening" whilst not giving the impression of a system that is generating unnecessary "junk mail". The second type of player is employees with whom the system communicates; the system should assist these employees to do their job with a minimum of fuss. The third type of player is the "dynamic committee" with which the system interacts during the search for a potential supervisor. In a *dynamic committee* a workflow is considered collectively by a continually changing group of people or agents whose reactions to that workflow may be influenced by the decisions already made, and by the decisions presently being made. For example, "I'll take this person on as a research student if you will" is an example of a reaction influenced by a decision that is presently being made. If any group is to be an effective decision making body then appropriate levels of communication between the active members of that group, and between the active members and any previous members, is required.

Despite its inherent interest, the application chosen is limited. First, the basic input document is an application form that is subsequently annotated but otherwise remains fixed. In other words, there is not a significant versioning problem to be managed through the workflow. Second, the flow structure involves asynchronous parallel processing but is otherwise essentially linear. Third, the RSA system is based on a "single document workflow". In a *single document workflow* the relevant sections of a single document are available to all players during processing. In a single document workflow the single document may grow during processing, and it may contain sections that are confidential to particular players. The restriction to single document workflows simplifies system design. This restriction does not prevent the use of asynchronous parallel processing.

- Figure 2 shows the overall agent architecture of the RSA system. Figure 2 shows the "Applicant", various "Academics" and three types of administrator interacting with the system. The "Diary" is a file to which each transaction is written. The Diary file is used to provide restart and recovery for the system.

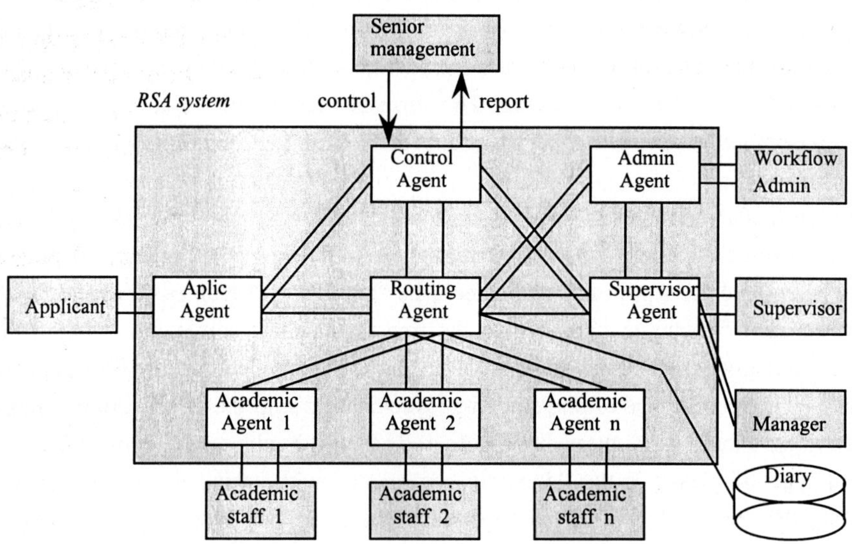

Figure 2. Architecture of the RSA system

The system agents include:

- Aplic Agent. Is responsible for presenting the application form to the Applicant, accepting the completed form, checking the completed form and returning it to the Applicant if appropriate, forwarding a checked form to the Routing Agent, and sending the final result to the Applicant.
- Control Agent. Is responsible for presenting a performance report of the system to the workflow context and accepting values.
- Routing agent. Coordinates all inter-agent communication and updates the diary file as each inter agent communication is sent.
- Academic Agent. Is responsible for alerting Academics that a form awaits their comments, accepting the Academic's reply, forwarding these replies to the Routing Agent.
- Supervisor Agent. Is responsible for presenting a new application to the Supervisor (or the Manager) to determine whether the application is appropriate for the Faculty.
- Admin Agent. Is responsible for interacting with the Workflow Administrator.

Agents are specified in the system design using a high-level language. For example, the Control Agent contains the rule:

```
IF      from_name(Aplic Agent) AND
        doc_address(xxxxx) AND
        doc_type(ResStudEnq) AND
        doc_goal(process, {YES, NO, error})
THEN
        from_name(Control Agent)
                doc_time( <date> + <interval_ResStudEnq> )
                doc_priority( <prioriity_ResStudEnq> )
                doc_confid( <confid_ResStudEnq> )
                doc_goal(check, {OK, NOK, error})
        to_name(Supervisor Agent)
```

The above rule is concerned with inter agent communication. Some rules are concerned with interacting with the external players. For example the following two rules in the Academic Agent manage one form of interaction with an Academic:

```
IF      from_name(Routing Agent) AND
        doc_address( xxxxx(q) ) AND
        doc_type(ResStudEnq) AND
        doc_goal( interested, {YES, NO, time_up} )
THEN
        from_name(Academic Agent n)
                doc_address(xxxxx)
                doc_type(ResStudEnq)
```

```
                doc_goal( you_interested, {YES, NO, time_up} )
        to_name(Academic n)
IF      from_name(Academic n) AND
        doc_address(xxxxx) AND
        doc_type(ResStudEnq) AND
        doc_goal( you_interested=YES )
THEN
        from_name(Academic Agent n)
                doc_address( xxxxx(q) )
                doc_type(ResStudEnq)
                doc_goal( interested=YES )
        to_name(Routing Agent)
```

The ACP (ie Agent Communication Protocol) draws from the structure of KQML (Finin, 1994). The basic sentence structure is:

```
        tell    (
                content<expression>;
                category<string>;
                in-reply-to<expression>;
                sender<string>;
                receiver<string>;
                )
```

Messages of this type enable one agent to "tell" something to another agent. In this message format, "content" may be a URL, an email address, a document ID or text; "category" may be a command, URL, email address, or DocID; "in-reply-to" is the address to which a message should be sent in the event of an error in communication; "sender" is the Sender's ID, and "receiver" is the Receiver's ID.

4. Implementation

RSA is implemented on the Lotus Notes/Domino platform. This platform has powerful database management, email management, script support and HTTP support. This facilitates the creation, modification and management of documents, email transformation and information sharing. The Domino server automatically translates Lotus Notes database files to HTML files. Thus the system may be used directly from the world wide web.

The overall architecture of the RSA system is shown in Figure 2. In the Lotus Notes/Domino server, every agent has its own database, mailbox and built-in knowledge base. An authorised user can access each agent as a Notes client or as an HTTP client (by URL). The RSA application form is built in the Applicant Agent and can be obtained by Interknit Applicants from an HTTP browser. Once this form has been filled out by an applicant, the RSA system begin to process the document using the agents distributed through the RSA system. The RSA system as seen from an HTTP browser is shown in Figure 3. Each RSA agent is implemented in Lotus Script. Lotus Script is a programming language that is embedded in Lotus Notes and resembles Visual Basic with Notes classes.

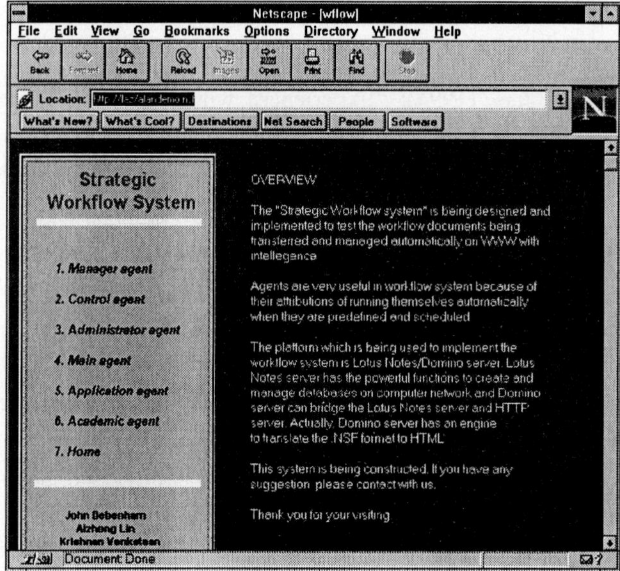

Figure 3 RSA from an HTTP browser

The description of the experimental RSA system given here has focussed on the agent-based aspects of the system. The cooperative aspects of the system are equally important and are responsible for providing a good decision making environment.

5. Conclusion

The principal conclusions from this experiment are that a simple workflow system that delivers good performance for a modest cost can be constructed using an agent-based architecture, the world wide web, email and database technologies, in reasoble time, two months in the case of RSA. Those involved in the experimental system were encouraged by the quality of the performance of the experimental system which contained approximately thirty rules; in this application a little knowledge delivered good performance.

We that that where a knowledge base is used to drive workflow systems, then the distinction between organisational rules and cultural factors is made in the design but not necessarily in the representation.

The Academic Agents in the experimental RSA system permitted academics to have limited 'control' of the way in which the system behaved. Further experiments with system useability are required.

6. References

Abbott, K.R. and Sarin, K.S. (1994): "Experiences with Workflow Management: Issues for the Next Generation" in Furuta, R., Neuwirth, C. (eds.): *proceedings Conference on Computer Supported Cooperative Work, CSCW94*, ACM Press, pp. 113-120.

Debenham, J.K. (1997) "Strategic Workflow Management", in *proceedings International Workshop Distributed Artificial Intelligence and Multi-Agent Systems DAIMAS'97*, St Petersberg, June 1997, pp553-562.

Dellen, B., Maurer, F. and Pews G. (1997) "Knowledge Based Techniques to Increase the Flexibility of Workflow Management" in *Data and Knowledge Engineering Journal* (North Holland) 1997.

Finin, T., Fritzson, R., McKay, D. and McEntire, R. (1994) "KQML as an Agent Communication Language" in *proceedings CIKM'94*, pp447-455.

Georgakopolous, D. and Hornick, M. (1995) "An Overview of Workflow Management: From Process Modelling to Workflow Automation Infrastructure" in *Distributed and Parallel Databases* 3, pp 119-153.

Hawryszkiewycz, I.T. and Gorton, I. (1996): "Workflow Support for Change Management and Concurrency" *Proceedings of the Conference on Software Engineering: Education and Practice*, Dunedin, New Zealand, pp. 181-188.

Kwan, M.M. and Balasubramanian, P.R. (1997) "Dynamic Workflow Management: A Framework for Modelling Workflows" in proceedings *Thirteenth Annual IEEE Hawaii International Conference on System Science.*

Labrou, Y. and Finin, T. (1994) "A semantics approach for KQML - a general purpose communication language for software agents" in *proceedings CIKM'94*, pp456-464.

Nwana, H.S. and Azarmi, N. (1997) "Software Agents and Soft Computing, Towards Enhancing Machine Intelligence" (Springer-Verlag Berlin Heidelberg)

Suchman, L. (1987): *"Plans and Situated Action: The Problem of Human-Machine Communication"* Cambridge University Press, Cambridge.

Multiuser Transactions for Collaborative Database Applications

Waldemar Wieczerzycki

Department of Information Technology
University of Economics at Poznań
Mansfelda 4, 60-854 Poznań, Poland
e-mail: wiecz@kti.ae.poznan.pl.

Abstract. In the paper a particular approach to transaction management in databases supporting collaborative applications is proposed. It is based on a new transaction model which allows practically unrestricted collaboration among members of the same team. The basic assumption of this model is that collaborating users try to solve their access conflicts on a higher level than the level of a database management system. Users are not mutually isolated, as it happens in classical databases. They can freely negotiate, presenting their intentions concerning future work.

1 Introduction

Majority of collaborative systems require functions and mechanisms naturally available in database management systems, e.g. data persistency, access authorization, concurrency control, consistency checking and assuring, data recovery after failures, etc. These functions, however, are generally implemented in collaborative systems from scratch, without any reference to the database technology.

Since the theory and technology of classical databases is very mature, commonly accepted and verified over many years, the following question naturally arises: can we apply this technology in collaborative systems, instead of re-implementing database functions from scratch and embedding them in collaborative systems? As usually, we can obviously try, but there is one substantial drawback we have to take into account. Almost every commercial database management system provides classical *ACID* transactions [6], which are atomic, consistent, durable, and, what is the most important, which work in isolation. The last property is the most painful, if we consider requirements of collaborative systems.

In such situation, in order to develop collaborative database applications, we have to extend database technology. There are two possible directions. The first one consists in avoiding the concept of transaction and transaction management mechanisms. Non-transactional databases, however, are generally unsafe, and it is very difficult to preserve the consistency of information stored in them. The second direction aims to avoid ACID transactions, and propose new transaction models which are more oriented for advanced database applications, especially for collaborative applications, thus preserving all advantages of transactional systems.

There are many advanced transaction models proposed in the literature [3]. Two early non-traditional models are: nested transactions and Sagas. *Nested transactions* [9] support modularity, failure handling and intra-transaction parallelism. They are very important in the development of other, more advanced models (e.g. ACTA model [2]), because they introduce the idea of structuring a transaction into a tree (or hierarchy) of subtransactions and non-vital subtransactions. *Sagas* [5], based on the compensating transactions, consist of a set of subtransactions. They relax the property of isolation by allowing a saga to reveal its partial results to other transactions before it is complete. Sagas are useful only when subtransactions are relatively independent (because of consistency problems) and each subtransaction can be successfully compensated.

There are also transaction models supporting cooperation between transactions. The most general approach proposes the *cooperative transaction hierarchy* [10] which allows to associate transactions encompassed by a transaction group with individual designers. The notion of correctness defined by serializability is substituted by the notion of user-defined serializability. Because isolation between transactions is not required, the transaction hierarchies allow cooperation between transactions and also help to alleviate the problems caused by long-lived transactions. Other transaction models from this group are not so general, since they are addressed to particular application domains, e.g. *cooperative SEE transactions* [7], *ConTract* transactions [11], *S-transactions* [4].

Taking into account the needs of generally understood collaborative work, *cooperative transaction hierarchies* [10] are very promising, since transactions from the same group are not isolated mutually and can correspond to different, though somehow related tasks. Notice, that this approach, similarly to all the other approaches mentioned above, uses a tree-structured transaction model.

An attempt to apply hierarchical transactions to databases has some disadvantages. Contrarily to flat transactions, hierarchical transactions require sophisticated transaction management methods and, as a consequence, additional system overhead which reduces its performance. Moreover, hierarchical transactions are still not sufficient, considering expectations of collaborating users, since in many situations the transaction correctness criterion restricts wide cooperation. Finally, they are not so reliable as flat transactions, since in practice commercial databases use the latter ones.

In this paper we propose a solution of problems mentioned above by the use of flat transactions, in which, in comparison to classical ACID transactions, the isolation property is relaxed. Briefly, it can be achieved by assigning the entire group of collaborating users to the same transaction, still preserving, however, the identity of individuals. The proposed transaction model is inspired by the natural perception, that a team of intensively cooperating users can be considered as a single virtual user, who has more than one brain trying to achieve the assumed goal, and more than two hands operating on keyboards.

It is worth to emphasize that both the transaction model and transaction management mechanisms have been elaborated parallel to the development of the prototype collaborative system, called *Agora.* Thus, the proposed approach is not purely theoretical, but instead, it reflects the problems and solutions which occurred during the implementation of *Agora*.

The paper is structured in the following way. In Section 2 basic concepts of the approach are introduced and the multiuser transaction model [12] is briefly reminded. Section 3 describes advanced transaction management mechanisms dedicated to multiuser transactions. In Section 3 *Agora* prototype is briefly presented and selected implementation issues concerning multiuser transactions are discussed. Section 4 concludes the paper.

2 Transaction Model

A single database can be accessed in practice by an arbitrary number of users who work independently, or collaborate with other users being members of the same working group. Depending on whether users collaborate or not, and how tight is their collaboration, we distinguish two levels of users grouping: conferences and teams. A *conference* C_i groups users who aim to achieve the common goal, e.g. to write a co-authored book, design a new version of an electronic chip. Users belonging to the same conference can communicate with each other and be informed about progress of common work by the use of typical conferencing tools, like message exchange, negotiation, etc. Conferences are logically independent, i.e. a user working in the scope of a single conference is not influenced by work being done in other conferences.

Users belonging to the same conference can collaborate tightly or loosely, depending on whether they perform the same common task, or they just aim to achieve the same final goal, respectively. Tightly collaborating users are grouped into the same team T_i. Thus, a *team* is a subset of a corresponding conference, with the restriction that a single user U_i belongs in the scope of a single conference exactly to one team, in particular, to a single-user team. Of course, if he is involved in many conferences, say n, then he belongs to n teams.

A *multiuser transaction* is a flat, ordered set of database operations performed by users of the same team, which is atomic, consistent and durable [12]. In other words, a multiuser transaction is the only unit of communication between a virtual user representing members of a single team, and the database management system.

Two multiuser transactions from two different conferences behave in the classical way, which means that they work in mutual isolation, and they are serialized by database management system. In case of access conflicts, resulting from attempts to operate on the same data item in incompatible mode, one of transactions is suspended or aborted, depending on the concurrency control policy. The same concerns two multiuser transactions which belong only to default conference C_d.

Two multiuser transactions from the same conference behave in a non-classical way, which means that the isolation property is partially relaxed for them. In case of access conflicts, so called *negotiation mechanism* is triggered by DBMS, which informs users assigned to both transactions about the conflict, giving them details concerning operations which have caused it. Then, using conferencing mechanisms provided by the system (cf. Section 3), users can consult their intended operations and negotiate on how to resolve their mutual problem. If they succeed, transactions can be continued, otherwise classical mechanisms have to be applied.

A particular mechanisms is used in case of operations of the same multiuser transaction, if they are performed by different users, and they are conflicting in a classical meaning. There is no isolation between operations of different users, however in this situation so called *notification mechanism* is triggered by DBMS, which aims to keep the users assigned to the same transaction aware of operations done by other users. We have to stress that it concerns only the situation when a user accesses data previously accessed by other users, and the modes of those two accesses are incompatible in a classical meaning. After notification, users assigned to the same transaction continue their work, as if nothing happened. Notice, that in case of users of the same team, we assume not only strict collaboration, but also deep mutual confidence.

Every multiuser transaction is started implicitly by *initialize*(T_i) operation, which is performed automatically by the system on the very beginning of a team session, after the first database operation is requested by one of team members. This team member is called a *transaction leader*.

After a multiuser transaction is initialized by the transaction leader, other team members can enter it at any moment of the transaction execution, by the use of explicit *connect*(T_i) operation, which is performed in asynchronous manner. Once connected to the transaction, any member of a team can perform *disconnect*(T_i) operation, providing there is still at least one user assigned to this transaction. *disconnect*(T_i) operation brakes the link between transaction T_i and the user.

Operations introduced up till now concern a single multiuser transaction. Next two operations: *merge*(T_i) and *split()* are special, since they concern two transactions. *Transaction* T_j can merge into transaction T_i by the use of *merge*(T_i) operation, providing the members of a team assigned to T_i allow for it. After this operation, transaction T_j is logically removed from the system, i.e. operation *abort*(T_j) is automatically triggered by the DBMS, and all T_j operations are logically re-done by transaction T_i.

Similarly to *merge* operation, *split()* operation can be used in order to avoid access conflicts (cf. Section 3). *split()* operation causes that a single multiuser transaction T_i is split into two transactions: T_i and T_j. After *split()* operation, a subset of team members, originally assigned to T_i, is re-assigned to newly created transaction T_j. Also all operations performed by re-assigned users are logically removed from transaction T_i and redone in transaction T_j directly after its creation.

Finally, there are two typical operations on transactions: *commit* and *abort* which are performed in the classical manner.

3 Transaction Management Mechanisms

Let us remind, that the main assumption of the proposed approach is to support collaboration among users to possibly maximum extent (cf. Section 1), by providing them with mechanisms for:

- simultaneous work on the same pieces of information,
- mutual awareness of the current state and progress in cooperative work, as well as notification about important operations done by members of the same team,
- negotiation, aiming at resolving potential access conflicts, resulting from incompatibility of operations requested.

The above mechanisms require additional information about intended operations and data locks implied by them to be collected by DBMS. In our approach every lock (set or requested) is represented by the following quadruple:

$$L = (lt,\ C\_id,\ t\_id,\ U\_id),$$

where *lt* denotes lock type, *C_id* and *t_id* identify, respectively, the conference and the team which encompass the transaction requesting a lock, while *U_id* identifies one of users associated to multiuser transaction.

If a transaction requests lock $L_R = (lt_R,\ C\_id_R,\ t\_id_R,\ U\_id_R)$ on a data item (tuple, object) already locked, i.e. on which $L_S = (lt_S,\ C\_id_S,\ t\_id_S,\ U\_id_S)$ lock is set, then the following intuitive algorithm is performed by DBMS.

Algorithm

```
if compatible(lt_S, lt_R) then grantLock(L_R)
else /* locks incompatible */
        if t_id_S = t_id_R then
            begin
            if U_id_S <> U_id_R then
                begin
                notify (U_id_S);
                notify (U_id_R);
                end;
            grantLock (L_R);
            end;
        else /* different teams */
            if C_id_S = C_id_R then /* the same conference */
                negotiate (t_id_S, t_id_R);
            else rejectLock (L_R);
```

Notice, that if the lock requested concerns the same team as lock set, then the mutual notification mechanism is triggered. Otherwise, there is still a chance for granting a lock, providing the locks compared concern the same conference. In this case, different negotiation mechanism are triggered which are presented further in this section.

If more than one lock is set on the requested data item, then the above algorithm has to be executed for all of them in a special way. Before the negotiation mechanisms are started, DBMS has to check whether there is a lock which definitely precludes granting a lock requested. Similarly, user notification can be triggered only if all required negotiations have succeeded. To make this procedure more efficient, all the locks set have to be ordered in the following way: locks set in different conferences (which are potentially the most conflicting), locks set by different multiuser transactions in the scope of the same conference, and locks set by other users from the same team (which are not conflicting, but require user notifications).

Now we focus on notification and negotiation mechanisms. A notification call is sent from DBMS to the collaborative application. Its scope is limited to a single multiuser transaction. When received, the application informs the respective user about the occurrence of a particular event, using available multimedia means. For example, in a collaborative writing application, user notification may consist in changing a color of a paragraph modified by a colleague and a beep signal. If the paragraph concerned is not visible on the screen of a user being notified, e.g. because he works on a different part of the co-authored book, then a special modification button may be displayed in a place visible to him. After clicking this button, a window used to work on the book is automatically scrolled to the place of modification.

When a negotiation mechanism is triggered, the following scenario is used:

1. the system informs the user holding a lock on a data item that another user attempts to access this data in incompatible mode,
2. a data item concerned is indicated on the user's screen,
3. a communication link between two negotiators is established, by the use of available multimedia and conferencing techniques,
4. the system proposes a solution which, if accepted, leads to a conflict avoidance,
5. users negotiate, giving the details about intended operations on data item concerned,
6. if the solution proposed by the system is commonly accepted, communication link is closed and negotiators continue their work; otherwise, the system repeats all the steps again proposing different solutions.

The following resolutions of access conflicts are proposed: fine-grained locking, commit request, lock release, operation embedding, transaction merge, transaction split, delayed versioning.

Fine-grained locking is a well known solution which is used in hierarchical locking methods. It consists in the conversion of a lock set on a big granule (e.g. a table, a class) into a set of locks set on smaller granules (tuples, objects). It may be applied only in particular contexts, i.e. it does not resolve every access conflict. DBMS keeps track of all operations performed by the owner of a hierarchical lock. If the lock requested is a basic lock, and if it concerns a data item which has not been yet accessed by the owner of the hierarchical lock, then there is a possibility to make a conversion of the hierarchical lock and avoid conflicts. The holder of a hierarchical lock, however, has to accept the proposed solution, and this is a subject of negotiations between the users.

Commit request. This solution is quite straightforward. As it is well-known, in the classical two-phase locking approach [6] locks are held until transaction commitment. During the negotiation, the holder of a lock is asked by his colleague to commit his updates and start a new transaction. If he agrees, a lock requested may be granted immediately after transaction commitment.

Lock release. There are two possible variants of this idea: *operation roll-back* and *operation relegation.* In the first variant, the user who requests a lock (VU_1) asks the holder of a lock (VU_2) to roll-back operations done on the data item concerned. If accepted, the operation roll-back is followed by lock release, which makes it possible for both users to continue their work. The rolled-back operation can be redone by user VU_1, or at least can influence the operations planned by user VU_1 on a conflicting data item.

In the second variant, i.e. operation relegation, if the holder of a lock (VU_2) agrees, then his operation on the data item concerned is logically removed from his transaction, and relegated to the transaction of the user requesting a lock (VU_1). In other words, user VU_2 rolls-back his operations on the data item concerned and releases his lock. Next, the rolled-back operation is automatically redone by the system in the scope of a transaction of VU_1. Both users can then continue their work with the assumption that user VU_1 is responsible for a proper state of a conflicting data.

Operation embedding. In this solution a user who can not set a lock (VU_1) informs the holder of an incompatible lock (VU_2) about his intentions. If user VU_2 accepts the operation planned by his colleague on the data item concerned, then this single operation is isolated from transaction of the user VU_1 and embedded in a transaction of the user VU_2. In such situation, there is no need for lock release by VU_2, and for lock setting by VU_1, and both users can continue their work. Notice, that this mechanism is based on a full confidence between users. When VU_1 convinces his colleague that his operation is reasonable, VU_2 allows the DBMS to embed a single operation of VU_1 into his transaction.

Let us remind that in the above discussion, saying „a user", we mean „virtual user", who corresponds to a team, which may be composed of many tightly collaborating users. Thus, in the negotiations participate in general more than two users, but the final decision is undertaken by transaction leaders (cf. Section 2). This remark is very important when we consider next two solutions.

Transaction merge. Since one transaction can not continue its execution because of lock set by another transaction in the scope of the same conference, then a natural solution is to merge those two transactions in a way presented in Section 2. During the negotiation both users: VU_1 and VU_2 consult their intended operations. If they agree that there is no conflict between their intentions, i.e. there is no conflict at the users' level, then the conflict at the DBMS level is superfluous, and the simplest way to avoid it is to merge both transactions, and continue a work in the scope of a single transaction. The merge operation implies, of course, the merge of teams.

Transaction split. This idea offers only a partial solution and can be useful if a transaction *MT* which requests an incompatible lock is assigned to a team composed of more than one user. In that case, the transaction can split into two transactions, in such way that the physical user whose operation caused a request for lock setting is assigned to the first resulting transaction (MT_1), while the rest of physical users are assigned to the second resulting transaction (MT_2). Now, transaction MT_2 can continue its execution, while transaction MT_1 has to wait until the requested data item is unlocked. Notice, that this mechanism does not require negotiations between two teams. The decision whether to split or not *MT* has to be undertaken locally, i.e. by the users composing team assigned to *MT*. Remember also, that in some cases split operation is not possible, even if users decide to do it [12].

Delayed versioning

The last mechanisms can be applied in multiversion databases in which either the entire database is a versioning granule [1], or the composite object with all its components is versionable [8]. A mechanism that can be applied to two transactions which try to set incompatible explicit locks on the same object is called *delayed versioning*. It consists in the automatic derivation of a new private and temporary version dedicated to one of the conflicting transactions (after detecting its first access conflict). The new private version is a logical copy of its parent (public) version with all non-committed updates performed by the corresponding transaction before the access conflict. These updates are also logically removed from the parent version. At this point the transaction for which the new version has been derived need not be informed about this event and can continue to access objects in the parent version. The *DBMS*, however, automatically re-addresses all the consecutive access requests to the newly created private version. Now, locking conflicts in the private version are no longer possible. If, because of some reasons (e.g. user request), transaction aborts - the private version is simply deleted. Otherwise, i.e. if transaction commits, the user is informed by the system about the new version derivation. Now, he must decide whether to promote the private version into a public one, or to merge both of them into a new public version.

4 Prototype Collaborative Database Application

Most of the concepts introduced in previous sections have been implemented in *Agora* prototype system. *Agora* is composed of two functional parts. The first one is a virtual conference tool, and the second one is a support for collaborative document writing. *Agora* provides negotiators (i.e. conference participants) with an arbitrary number of conferences and arbitrary number of collaboratively written versionable documents, with the restriction that only one document can be associated with a single conference. All negotiators discuss and present their positions by exchanging electronic messages. Each negotiator of a conference sees all the messages exchanged. A negotiator can be involved in several negotiations simultaneously, i.e. he can virtually attend different conferences. Negotiations in different conferences may concern different topics, different aspects of the same topic, or the same topic discussed by different partners.

The part of *Agora* devoted to support collaborative writing is required to prepare a final document, which is a result of negotiations. This common document is seen and accessible to all the negotiators. When a negotiator writes or modifies a paragraph of the document and commits changes, it becomes instantaneously visible to other negotiators. Next, any negotiator can modify this paragraph. *Agora* provides versioning mechanisms which additionally facilitate collaborative writing.

Agora has been implemented in Java language and connected to the Oracle database management system through Java Database Connectivity interface (JDBC) to provide persistency of both documents and negotiation history. The use of Java and JDBC provides *Agora* with platform independence, concerning hardware, operating systems and database management system.

Agora architecture is client-server. Both clients and the server are implemented as *Java* objects which communicate by *Remote Method Invocation (RMI)*. The *Agora* server is connected to a database management system by *Java-Database Connectivity (JDBC)* interface.

Concurrency control mechanisms provided by Oracle DBMS are overridden in *Agora* Server, what is necessary to validate the concept of multiuser transactions and new concurrency control mechanisms proposed in this paper.

Every document version is stored in one database table, thus if a document is available in *n* versions, then *n* tables have to be created. The first version of a document is entirely represented in a respective table, while in case of derived document versions only differences in comparison to the parent document version are represented, i.e. paragraphs explicitly modified in the child document version. This aims to avoid redundancy which can be really painful in case of documents having many slightly different versions.

Every paragraph of a document version is stored in a single raw of a corresponding table, which is composed of a paragraph content and its layout attributes. Paragraph content is modeled by a single attribute of *long raw* type. It means that a paragraph can contain not only pure text but also multimedia data (pictures, sounds, etc.). Layout attributes contain typical information about the way a paragraph is visualized to the users, e.g. color, font, size, indent.

5 Conclusion

A particular approach to transaction management in databases supporting collaborative applications has been proposed. The basic assumption of this approach is that collaborating users try to solve their access conflicts on a higher level than the level of a database management system, as it happens classically.

We feel that the proposed approach has many advantages. First of all, the multiuser transaction model is very straightforward and not complex, thus the management of transactions of this type does not cause substantial problems. Second, the model allows practically unrestricted collaboration among members of the same team. As a consequence, it fulfills their requirements and simplifies their work. Third, since the users of the same team preserve their identity, the database management system can efficiently support users' awareness and notification, which are two very important functions of every collaborative system. Finally, the proposed model is very close to the classical ACID transaction model. As we have mentioned before, it makes the model more reliable and easy to implement, since classical ACID transactions dominate at the commercial database market.

The proposed approach was verified in *Agora* prototype which is a Web-based conferencing system, offering conference participants a flexible tool for collaborative document writing. It is worth to emphasize that *Agora* is implemented on the top of a conventional and commercial database system, i.e. Oracle RDBMS, instead of another prototype specifically designed to support object versioning mechanisms. It makes the achieved results more reliable.

References

1. Cellary W., Jomier G.: Consistency of Versions in Object-Oriented Databases, Proc. 16th VLDB Conf., Brisbane, Australia, 1990.
2. Chrysanthis P.K., Ramamtitham K.: Acta - A framework for specifying and reasoning about transaction structure and behavior, Proc. of ACM-SIGMOD Int. Conference on Management of Data, 1990.
3. Elmagarmid A. (ed.): Database Transaction Models, Morgan Kaufmann, 1992.
4. Eliassen F., Veijalainen J., Tirri H.: Aspects of transaction modeling for interoperable information systems, in: Interim Report of the COST 11ter Project, 1988.
5. Garcia-Molina H, Salem K.: Sagas, Proc. of the ACM Conf. on Management of Data, 1987.
6. Gray J.: Notes on Database Operating Systems, Operating Systems: An Advanced Course, Springer-Verlag, 1978.
7. Heiler S., Haradhvala S., Zdonik S., Blaustein B., Rosenthal A.: A flexible framework for transaction management in engineering environments, in: Elmagarmid A. (ed.), Database Transaction Models, Morgan Kaufmann, 1992.
8. Katz R., Chang E., Bhateja R.: Version Modeling Concepts for CAD Databases, Proc. ACM SIGMOD Conf., 1986.
9. Moss J. E.: Nested Transactions: An Approach to Reliable Distributed Computing, The MIT Press, 1985.
10. Nodine M., Zdonik S.: Cooperative transaction hierarchies: A transaction model to support design applications, Proc. fo VLDB Conf., 1984.
11. Reuter A.: Contract: A means for extending control beyond transaction boundaries, Proc. of 2nd Workshop on High Performance Transaction Systems, 1989.
12. Wieczerzycki W.: Transaction Management in Databases Supporting Collaborative Applications, Second East-European Symposium on Advances in Databases and Information Systems - ADBIS'98, Poznań, 1998.

Modeling Phenomena in Spatiotemporal Databases: Desiderata and Solutions

Nectaria Tryfona

Department of Computer Science, Aalborg University,
Fredrik Bajers 7E, DK-9220, Aalborg Øst, Denmark
tryfona@cs.auc.dk

Abstract. This paper focuses on the database modeling of spatiotemporal phenomena. Their components and behavior are analyzed and a formal framework with a small set of concepts–namely objects, attributes, relationships, fields, and constraints, with spatial and temporal dimension–for their definition is provided. A mathematical model for the expression of spatiotemporal constraints, based on the aforementioned concepts, is presented. Next, all the described concepts are translated into modeling constructs–namely entities, attributes, relationships, fields, phenomena and constraints–to enrich the Entity-Relationship (ER) model for the conceptual design of spatiotemporal applications dealing with phenomena. We give the semantics and syntax of the prototypical extended ER; any other model augmented by the same constructs can be used for this purpose. An example demonstrates the applicability, modeling power and ease-of-use of this proposal.

1 Introduction

Phenomenon (plural: *phenomena*, from the Greek word *phainomai (φαίνομαι),* which means "to appear") is used in science to express any sign or objective symptom; any observable occurrence or fact.

Applications involving geo-referenced objects and phenomena changing over time–so-called *spatiotemporal* applications–enjoy a lot of attention in the last years. Cadastral information systems with the need to record history of land parcels existence and ownership, navigational systems computing possible routes of vehicles in time, and environmental applications, dealing with forecast prediction, especially in "sensitive" areas with typhoon and cyclone problems, are some substantial examples of this new application area.

Although in the last decade the information systems, and more specifically, the database research community gave valuable results in modeling and retrieving spatial objects [6] [11] [17], in a temporal framework [9] [12], spatiotemporal phenomena haven't really been addressed. The main reasons lie on their peculiar behavior, such as their fast evolution in space and time accompanied by the continuous change of their shape and position, involving many times fuzzy or incomplete information. These require deeper knowledge and input from the domain experts, as well as efficient tools and techniques for their representation and retrieval.

Related theoretical work fall into two disjoint modeling approaches: (a) event-based [10] or object-based [17]. The two have not met yet. On the other hand, domain experts give their own solutions and modeling techniques to these issues, mainly driven by the need for fast and applicable answers. The result is systems tightly coupled with specific software and hardware (see for example [1] for the use of Arc/Info in environmental modeling).

This paper deals with spatiotemporal phenomena from the perspective of database modeling, integrating the object- and event-based approaches. Databases are an indispensable part of spatiotemporal information systems and need to be handled as such. In order the final system to enjoy the benefits of correctness, reusability, ease-of-maintenance and portability, the complete database modeling methodology including, among others, the phases of conceptual, logical and physical design need to be followed. During the normal application development cycle, requirements describing objects, relationships among them and integrity constraints of the target environment are expressed, in turn, in: (a) the users' natural language, (b) the language (graphical or textual) of the conceptual data model, (c) the language of the logical data model and (d) finally, in the language of the specific application software package.

Our goal is, firstly, to establish a framework tailored to the needs of spatiotemporal information, in order to express phenomena without ambiguities. For this reason, we define the concepts of objects, attributes, relationships, fields and constraints with spatial and temporal dimension. Our approach is to use standard database models (object-oriented, semantic and relational) and extend them to incorporate spatiotemporal phenomena with the minimum add-ons. Spatiotemporal constraints play an important role in the development of phenomena as they act as triggers for the next action; for example "strong winds and rain" result to "storms". In each model (conceptual, logical, etc), of any development cycle, a different language must be used to express spatiotemporal constraints; however they are just different syntactic versions of the same underlying concepts we present here. Based on these concepts, we provide a language for the formal expression of spatiotemporal constraints. Next, we deal with the conceptual design of phenomena. In order to capture the semantics and represent components of spatial phenomena developing over time, all the above described spatiotemporal concepts are now incorporated–as constructs–in the Entity-Relationship Model (ER) [2]. For reasons of integrity, the new, extended ER model is accompanied by a Data Definition Language, which can be also used to express queries and constraints. We do not invite others to use the extended ER we present here; the approach is rather prototypical; the designer may use his/her favorite semantic model enriched by the discussed constructs.

The contribution of the paper is twofold: (a) a language–based on a small set of concepts–to express spatiotemporal constraints, queries and relationships, which characterize the behavior and development of phenomena. To the best of our knowledge, no other language at the conceptual or logical level for this purpose is available, (b) an extension of ER to model phenomena.

The rest of the paper is organized as follows: Section 2 gives an informal description of how phenomena behave, revealing the special modeling needs of a spatiotemporal database dealing with them. In Section 3 we give the definitions of spatiotemporal objects and fields, as well as a set operations on them and constraints among them. A formal language to express spatiotemporal constraints is presented. All the concepts of a spatiotemporal environment involving phenomena appear together in the same framework and translated into the conceptual phase of database representation. In Section 4, ER is enriched for this reason. Section 5 shows an example of usage and Section 6 concludes with the future research plans.

2 Spatiotemporal phenomena

2.1 Components and behavior

Consider the phenomenon of "rain in the city of Vienna". Rain is the result of the combination of "temperature", "pressure" and "humidity" under certain conditions or constraints, in the same area [16]. Properties like "temperature", or "pressure" are properties of space, and are called *spatial attributes* or (spatial) *properties* or *fields* [13]. Their value does not depend on the presence of any object. For example, the "temperature" of Vienna" is just a portion of the temperature in the atmosphere. As the city of Vienna expands, its (average) temperature may change, while its name (also a property) remains the same. Spatial properties have temporal dimension, i.e., they change over time.

"Rain in the city of Vienna" is a phenomenon: when the constraint (or condition) ""low temperature" and "low pressure" and "humidity"" is true for the area of Vienna, in the same time period, then, we have rain. Fig.1 shows the phenomena "rain", and "storm", their components and their interrelationships.

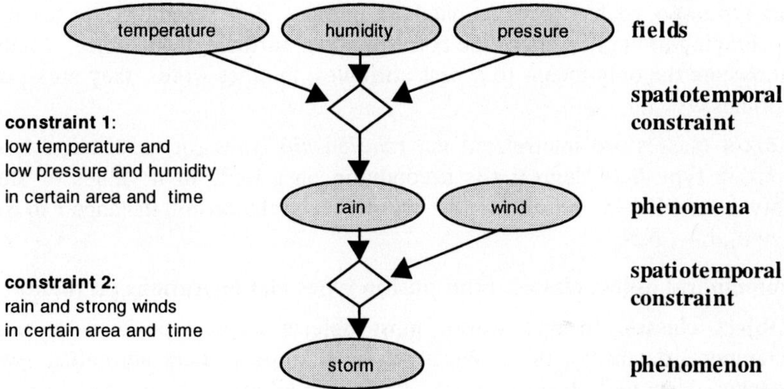

Fig. 1. Spatiotemporal phenomena, their components and interrelations

In the previous description, the concepts of objects, fields and phenomena are related to each other orthogonically. While fields (e.g., "temperature") exist all over the space, objects (e.g., "Vienna") exist in certain positions and inherit a part of fields' values; just those that refer to objects' exact location. Phenomena (e.g., "rain in Vienna") are spatial restrictions (e.g., in "Vienna" area) of virtual (or complex) fields (e.g., "rain") which are computed from others (primitive or virtual) (e.g., "temperature", "pressure" and "humidity") under certain spatiotemporal constraints). As spatiotemporal constraint or condition is defined any relationship or association between fields and/or objects relating locations in time. Notice however, that although a spatiotemporal constraint can be *user-defined* (e.g., area: Vienna), can also be *system-defined*: when temperature, humidity, pressure are combined with certain values in the same time period, then we have rain in certain areas.

The issues of objects and fields, their differences and semantics have been extensively investigated in [3] [8][17]. However, a formal framework that integrates the concepts of objects, attributes, relationships and constraints with spatial, temporal and spatiotemporal dimension is needed.

3 Definitions and the model

In this section we present the formal framework for the expression of the basic concepts related to spatiotemporal applications domain. More specifically, objects, attributes, relationships, fields and constraints, with spatiotemporal dimension are defined. This approach is based on the experience on earlier theoretical works [4][7][13], as well as applied research [15].

3.1 Spatiotemporal databases

Object classes, attributes and relationship types. A database is a collection of objects $o_1,o_2,\ldots,o_n$, which represent part of the real world; each object belongs to an object class O_1, $O_2,\ldots,O_n$. An object class O_i is characterized by a set of properties, or attributes $A_1^i,\ldots, A_m^i$ and a set of methods. Each attribute A_j^i, with $1 \leq j \leq m$, is associated with a domain $D(A_j^i)$,which is an unrestricted set of values. Domains are implemented by data types. So, each object in a database instance is represented by a set of values each belonging to the domain of the corresponding attribute of the object. Methods or operations are the only means to access attributes; in other words, they are operations of attributes.

Object classes are interrelated via *relationship types* (or association types). A relationship type R of degree n is a condition on a tuple of n values of attributes possibly from different object; in other words, each relationship instance r in R is a *n-tuple* $r<o_1,o_2,\ldots,o_n>$.

Spatiotemporal object classes, relationship types and operations on them.

(a) Object classes. In real world, most objects have a position in space. In spatiotemporal databases, these object whose position matters are called *spatial* or *geographic* object *GO*. Position *p* is a function on all and only on spatial objects; for each object, it returns parts of space which are called *geometric figures* and can be points, lines, regions or combinations thereof. (In fact, any other geometric type can be realized in this framework.) It is common to identify position with geometric figures:

$$p: GO \rightarrow G, \qquad \text{where } G \text{ is a finite set of geometric figures } g.$$

Objects with similar properties and the same kind of geometric figures belong to the same spatial or geographic object class.

(b) Relationship types. Spatial (or spatiotemporal, if they also have temporal dimension (see below)) object classes are related to each other in space. Relationship types among spatial objects are actually conditions on objects' positions and are called *spatial relationship types*. They are subdivided into *topological, directional and metric relationship* types. Topological relationships, such as *inside*, and *meet*, remain unchanged under certain transformations, like rotation. *Directional* (or cardinal) relationships refer to orientation aspects, describing the North, South, East, West and their combinations of a reference point [5] while the *metric* ones refer to distances between objects.

In spatiotemporal databases *time matters*. Object classes, attributes and relationship types can have a temporal dimension. A common technique is to capture time through valid and transaction time[1]. *Valid time*, represents the actual time in the mini-world that a particular event or change occurred, or shows when particular facts about database components (such as objects, relationships, etc.) are true, while *transaction time* shows the time a fact or an event is present in the database as stored data [12]. One approach is to record both transaction and valid time as time intervals, where a time interval $[t_s, t_e]$ is defined to be a set of consecutive time points (or *chronons*). We call t_s and t_e the *start* and the *end time* of the interval, respectively. The time interval consists of equal-sized, indivisible chronons.

(c) Operations on object classes. Operations on object classes which include objects' position are called *geometric operations*. Strictly speaking these operations are defined on objects and not on their positions. It simplifies the statement of the definitions, however, and creates no confusion if we describe them as acting on positions (see [7] for the formal treatment, on which the following set of primary geometric operations is based). The set of geometric operations includes: (a) *primary operations* whose range is real, like *distance*, (b) *primary operations* whose range is a geometric type, like *union*, (c) *derived operations* whose range is real, like *perimeter*, and (d) *derived operations,* whose range is a geometric data type, like *intersect*.

Spatial attributes or fields and operations on them.

(a) Spatial attributes or fields. Spatial attributes are properties of space which many time indirectly become properties of objects situated at some position in space, i.e., geographic objects inherit them from space; for example, "temperature" of a city. They are also called *fields* or *layers*–mainly influenced by implementation terminology.

Thus, a database dealing with spatiotemporal phenomena is not only a collection of object classes but also a collection of fields $f_1, f_2, \ldots, f_n$. A field can be seen as a function from geometric figures to the domain values of the represented attributes:

$$f_l: G \rightarrow D_1 x D_2 x \ldots x D_k$$

where G is a finite set of geometric figures g and $D_1, D_2, \ldots, D_k$ are (not necessarily distinct) domains of represented attributes. For example, the field "temperature" is a set of regions, each one of them representing the attributes "name" of the area and the "value" of temperature in this region. There are two basic types of fields: (a) those representing functions with continuous range; for example "temperature", or "erosion", and (b) those representing functions with range with discrete values; for example "classes of temperature" represented as regions. In case (a) the field represents a set of areas with different values of the same attribute or positions of objects in space, while in (b) we visualize it as homogeneous area. For spatiotemporal phenomena, such as "rain" or "pollution" we are primarily interested in the (a) field type.

(b) Operations on/among fields. Four types of operations can be performed on fields; all the others can be derived from them: (a) "attribute computation". It changes the range of a single field, but leaves the same domain, i.e., the same geometric

[1] The temporal research community has already proposed many alternatives for capturing time. Here we present one dominant approach; however our model does not depend on this.

figures. It is used to derive computable attributes, such as "population density", (b) "spatial computation". It operates geometrically on the domain of a field to produce a field with a new set of geometric figures as domain. For example: given a field representing "high noise-level" construct a field, which consists of a buffering zone around these regions, depicting the noisy areas, (c) "reclassification" which operates on a single field and concatenates adjacent figure if their range. For example, "connect areas with the same temperature", and (d) "overlay" which takes two fields (e.g., "temperature" and "humidity") and produces a new one with the geometric overlay as domain and the combination of the ranges. The resulting field keeps the descriptive attributes from both field-components.

Fields –like objects, attributes and relationships– can also have a temporal dimension.

A field type (or set) includes fields representing (or characterized by) a set of attributes. For example, field set showing "temperature". If our domain is the whole space then, the field set consists of snapshots (i.e., versions) of the same field in different time points, e.g., the "temperature" of earth in year 1997, recording it every month. But, if we refer to specific areas of space, for example "countries", then it includes different fields even at the same time-points, e.g., "temperature in Austria", "temperature in Germany" and so on. The choice of fields and their organization is outside the scope of this paper.

As mentioned in Section 2, fields, objects and phenomena are organized othrogonically. Phenomena are restrictions of fields (usually, *virtual* ones, i.e., fields computed (or derived) from others–computed or not) on specific time and space. As a consequence, they are also defined as sets of geometric figures (points, lines, regions, and combinations). A phenomenon type is a set of phenomena following the same rationale as above.

3.2 Spatiotemporal constraints

Constraints (or conditions) in databases can also have the role of relationships among database components, e.g., "strong storm is south of Vienna" or queries, e.g., "what is the meteorological status south of Vienna?". In order to express complex spatiotemporal expressions, i.e., constraints or conditions, relationships and queries, we shall use predicate calculus. A constraint is build out of atomic formulae with negation, conjunction, disjunction, and universal and existential quantification.

Definition 1. Let: O be an object class and o_1, o_2, o_3, o_4 spatial objects of class O; x,y attributes of o_1, o_2 respectively; F be a field type and f_1, f_2, f_3, f_4 fields of type F; z, ω attributes of f_1, f_2 respectively; g_1, g_2, g_3, g_4 are geometric figures of f_1, f_2, f_3, f_4 respectively; r an elementary topological relationship; Θ a geometric operation with range real (i.e., metric relationship); d a directional relationship; Δ a comparison operator; A an arithmetic operator; c a constant, $[t_s,t_e]$ a time interval, where t_s, t_e start and end time of the interval, respectively; t_i, t_j, t_k, t_m chronons of the $[t_s,t_e]$.

The following are atomic spatial, temporal and spatiotemporal formulae:

1. $o_1 \in O$ 2. $f_1 \in F$ 3. $g_1 \in f_1$

4. $r[\lambda_1, \lambda_2]$ where $\lambda_1, \lambda_2 \in \{o_1, o_2, g_1, g_2\}$

5a. $o_1.x \; \Delta \; o_2.y$ 5b. $O.o_1.x \; \Delta \; c$

6a. $g_1.z \; \Delta \; g_2.\omega$ 6b. $g_1.\, z \; \Delta \; c$

7. d $[\lambda_1, \lambda_2]$ where $\lambda_1, \lambda_2 \in \{o_1, o_2, g_1, g_2\}$

8a. $\Theta[\lambda_1]\ \Delta\ c$ 8b. $\Theta\ [\lambda_1]\ \Delta\ \Theta\ [\lambda_2]$ 8c. $\Theta[\lambda_1, \lambda_2]\ \Delta\ c$

8d. $[\lambda_1, \lambda_2]\ \Delta\ \Theta\ [\lambda_3, \lambda_4]$ where $\lambda_1, \lambda_2, \lambda_3, \lambda_4 \in \{o_1, o_2, o_3, o_4, g_1, g_2, g_3, g_4\}$

9. $t_i\ [\phi_1]\ \Delta\ t_j[\phi_2]$ where $\phi_1, \phi_2 \in \{o_1, o_2, f_1, f_2\}$

10a. $t_i\ [\phi_1]\ A\ t_j\ [\phi_2]\ \Delta\ c$ 10b. $t_i\ [\phi_1]\ A\ t_j[\phi_2]\ \Delta\ t_k\ [\phi_3]\ A\ t_m[\phi_4]$ where $\phi_1, \phi_2, \phi_3, \phi_4 \in \{o_1, o_2, o_3, o_4, f_1, f_2, f_3, f_4\}$

Definition 2. The following are spatiotemporal constraints (or expressions):

1. Every atomic formulae is a spatiotemporal constraint.
2. If P_1, P_2 are spatiotemporal constraints then so are: $\neg P_1$, (P_1), $P_1 \vee P_2$, $P_1 \wedge P_2$, $P_1 \Rightarrow P_2$, $P_1 \Leftrightarrow P_2$.
3. If P_1 (s) is a spatiotemporal constraint and s a free variable then $\exists$ s P_1 (s) and $\forall$ s P_1 (s) are spatiotemporal constraints.
4. In the absence of parentheses, operators are evaluated in the following order: $\in, \exists, \forall, \neg, \wedge, \vee, \Rightarrow, \Leftrightarrow$
5. Nothing else is a spatiotemporal constraint.

4 The extended Entity-Relationship model

After presenting a model for the formal description of spatiotemporal concepts, we proceed to the next–the conceptual (or semantic) modeling–phase of the application development cycle. Here, the main goal is to translate user requirements into an abstract representation, understandable to the user, independently of implementation issues, but formal and complete, that can be transformed into the next logical schema without ambiguities.

The Entity-Relationship Model is undoubtedly the most widely used technique for this purpose. Its main advantages are the ease of use that provides and the small set of supported constructs. In this section we extend ER to handle spatiotemporal phenomena. For this purpose, we enrich it with all the concepts showed in the Section 3, as they are the result of the understanding and experiment [15] of the spatiotemporal nature. We show the one-to-one translation of these concepts to modeling constructs of the extended ER. Central role to the extended model have the spatiotemporal constraints. The presented model is based on the GeoER [13][14] for geographic and spatiotemporal issues respectively. Issues, such as detailed conceptual representation of position of objects in space are addressed in other works [8]. We don't invite others to use this model; this is prototypical proposal: the designer can use his/her favorite semantic model and extend it with the same constructs to capture dynamics of space and time.

For reasons of integrity, the graphical representation is accompanied by the Data Definition Language (DDL): everything that can be expressed graphically, can also be expressed in DDL.

4.1 The constructs of the extended ER model

The extended ER supports the following concepts: (a) entity, which represents any autonomous object of the database, (b) relationship, which represents any association or link among entities, (c) attribute, representing characteristics or properties of entities or relationships (d) field, which represents a (complex or not) spatial attribute, and (e) phenomenon, which represents ("virtual" or computed) fields, restricted in areas, under certain constraints. Geometrically, it is a set of geometric figures[2].

Based on these concepts, the model has the following constructs:

• *Entity type*: represents a set of entities with similar structure and behavior. In spatiotemporal applications, entities have temporal dimension which is shown with the "T" (Time) in the upper right corner and spatial dimension, which is illustrated by the "G" (Geometry) in the lower right corner. "T" can be a timestamp or a time interval, with a starting and an ending point. Valid time and transaction time can be recorded in this area; in this case "T" is "VT" or "TT" respectively. If both are recorded, the "T" area is split in "VT" and "TT". "G" shows the geometric data type of the entity set and can be "Point", "Line", "Region" or any combination of these. For fuzzy objects, where the position is not accurate due to lack of information, or accuracy, or because of a mistake, "G" is a function of (x,y) showing the probability of having a specific geometric figure there.

• *Relationship type*: represents a set of associations among entity types.

• *Attribute:* static properties of entities or relationships are represented as attributes.

• *Field type*: represents a set of (complex or not) spatial attributes, showing similar spatial properties and geometry. Fields can have static attributes with different values for each geometric figure of the field. Entity types inherit parts of fields from space existing in their position. The spatial dimension of fields is shown by the "G" and the temporal dimension illustrated by the "T".

• *Phenomenon type:* represents a set of phenomena with similar properties and geometry. Phenomenon types have spatial dimension shown by the "G" and temporal dimension illustrated by the "T".

• *Constraint type:* represents a relationship among entity types and has the meaning of a trigger: whenever it is true, a phenomenon appears. One could argue that the constraint is a derived construct resulting from relationships; however, providing only the relationship type construct is not enough, as relationships don't always pre-exists the creation of constraints (e.g., in forecast-prediction systems).

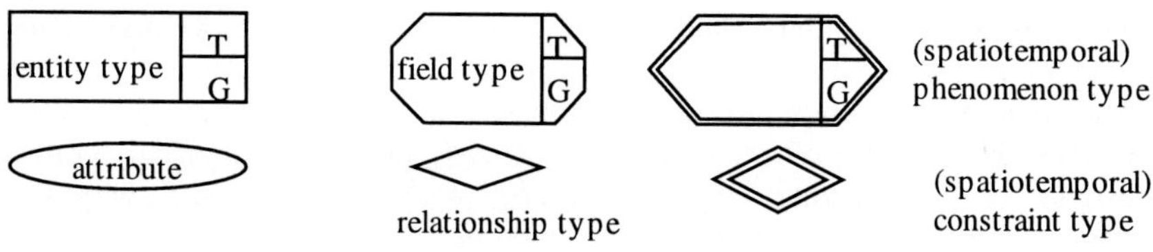

Fig. 2. The spatiotemporal constructs of the extended ER

---

[2] Usually, environmental phenomena (e.g., "storm") are captured in terms of regions represented in fields. However, for sciences dealing with liquids mixture, points and lines are observable as geometries of phenomena. Here, we took the decision to include points, lines and regions. If we want to restrict phenomena to regions, then fields are also restricted.

4.2 The formal syntax of the extended ER model

The extended ER allows for the definition of entities, attributes, relationships, fields, phenomena and constraints. Lower case words denote variables, standing for arbitrary names. Words in lower case with capitalized initial denote variables with restricted range. (e.g., Domain stands for one of STRING, DATE, etc., whereas $attr\_name_i$ is any alphanumeric string that is not a reserved word). Clauses in < > are optional arguments; in (,...) are repeatable; in { ... | ... } are alternatives (one of); in ( ) indicate grouping of arguments.

```
DEFINE ENTITY TYPE entity_type_name
<CONSTRUCT Entity_construct (entity_type_name_i,...)>
ATTR (attr_name_1, Domain_1, <KEY>),..., (attr_name_k, Domain_k, <KEY>)
<GEOMETRY Geometric_type>
<VALID TIME [start_time, end_time] >
<TRANSACTION TIME [start_time, end_time] duration >

DEFINE RELATIONSHIP TYPE rel_type_name (entity_type_name_i,...)
CARDINALITY Relationship_cardinality
<ATTRIBUTE (attr_name_j,...)>
<VALID TIME [start_time, end_time] >
<TRANSACTION TIME [start_time, end_time] duration >

DEFINE FIELD TYPE <field_type_name>
ATTR (attr_name_1^n, Domain_1^n, <KEY>),...,attr_name_mn^n, Domain_mn^n, <KEY>)
GEOMETRY Geometric_type
<VALID TIME [start_time, end_time] >
<TRANSACTION TIME [start_time, end_time] duration] >

DEFINE PHENOMENON TYPE phen_type_name
<GEOMETRY Geometric_type>
<VALID TIME [start_time, end_time] >
<TRANSACTION TIME [start_time, end_time] duration >
AMONG { entity_type_name_i,...,field_type_name_k,... }
<WITH ATTRIBUTES attr_name_1,...,attr_name_m>
<CONSTRAINT TYPE constraint_type_name>

DEFINE CONSTRAINT TYPE constraint_type_name
ON { field_type_name_j,... }
AMONG { entity_type_name_i,...,field_type_name_k,... }
AS spatiotemporal_constraint
```

5 Example of use

The reason behind the theory and the model described in Section 3 is that it can be used to express spatiotemporal integrity constraints, to define object classes and to query the database in a variety of settings. These include formal expression of user requirements, conceptual and logical modeling as well as implementation. In this section we give an explanatory example of a phenomenon and we then express it in the formal language of Section 3 and at the conceptual design phase with the use of the extended ER (Section 4).

Consider the following situation (for reasons of readability, formulas to calculate fields like "temperature" do not appear): the polluted subareas (g) in the city of

Vienna is the result of (constraint) (a) high temperature (above 25°C) in these areas (spatial constraint), and (b) in rush hours (between 13:00 and 16:00) (temporal constraint). We assume that we record temperature every hour from 8:00 to 22:00, so versions of the field "temperature" exist.

1. In the formal language proposed in Section 3, the polluted subareas can be found:

$$\{g \mid \exists t \exists c\ (t \in \text{temperature} \wedge g \in t \wedge t_s[t] \geq 13{:}00 \wedge t_e[t] \leq 16{:}00$$
$$\wedge\ c \in \text{city} \wedge c.\text{name}=\text{"Vienna"} \wedge \text{overlaps}\ [g,c] \wedge g.\text{temp\_value} \geq \text{"25°"})\ \}$$

2. In the extended ER and formal language proposed in Section 3:

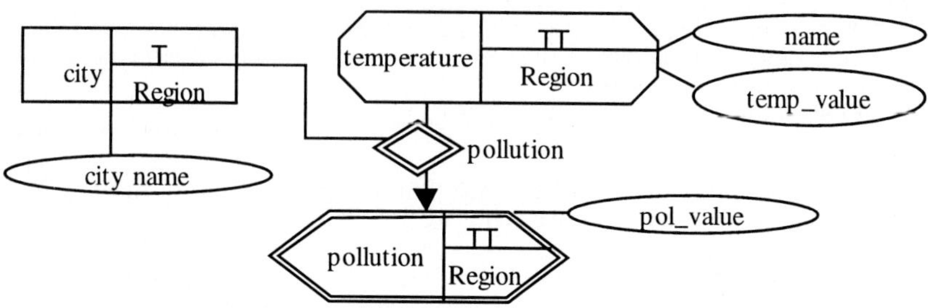

Fig. 3. An example of modeling spatiotemporal phenomena in the extended ER

```
DEFINE ENTITY TYPE city ATTR (city_name, String, KEY)
GEOMETRY Region

DEFINE FIELD TYPE temperature
ATTR (name, String, KEY) (temp_value, Int)
GEOMETRY  Region TRANSACTION TIME [8:00, 22:00] 1hr
/* temperature is recorded from 8:00 to 22:00, every hour */

DEFINE PHENOMENON TYPE pollution_in_Vienna
GEOMETRY Region TRANSACTION TIME [8:00, 22:00] 1hr
AMONG temperature, city WITH ATTRIBUTES pol_value
CONSTRAINT high_pollution

DEFINE CONSTRAINT TYPE high_pollution ON temperature
AMONG temperature, city
AS (t ∈ temperature ∧ ∃ c ∈ city ∧ ts[t]≥ 13:00 ∧ te[t] ≤16:00
        ∧ c ∈ city ∧ c.name="Vienna" ∧ overlaps [t,c] ∧ t.temp_value≥"25°")
```

6 Conclusions and further research plans

This paper addresses the conceptual design of spatiotemporal phenomena. For their efficient accommodation, a small set of concepts–namely, objects, attributes, relationships, fields, and constraints with spatial and temporal dimension–is presented. In this context, a formal language for the expression of spatiotemporal constraints, queries, and relationships referring to phenomena is discussed. The same concepts are translated into semantic constructs and incorporated into the ER model to handle spatiotemporal needs. For reasons of integrity, a DDL accompanies the extended ER. The proposed extended ER is prototypical: the designer can use his/her favorite model enriched by the same constructs to design spatiotemporal phenomena.

This is the first step to understand and represent phenomena. Several other issues are included in the future plans of this research line: the issue of fuziness of "borders" between different regions in the same phenomenon area, as well as in phenomenon itself, needs to be considered and modeled in detail. Also, there is a clear relation between applications dealing with phenomena and active databases. Another possible continuation is the transalation of spatiotemporal constraints to "event-condition-action" rules and their incorporation to the Entity-Relationship model.

Acknowledgements. This work was supported in part by the Danish Technical Research Council through grant 9700780, the Danish Natural Science Research Council through grant 9400911, and the CHOROCHRONOS project, funded by the EC DG XII Science, Research and Development, as a Network Activity of the TMR Program, contract no. FMRX-CT96-0056.

References

1. Batty, M., and Xie Y., 1994a&b. *Modeling Inside GIS: Part 1. Model Structures, Exploratory Spatial Data Analysis and Aggregation. Part 2. Selecting and Calibarting Urban Models Using Arc/Info.* IJGIS, 8, 3, 291-470.
2. Chen, P.S., 1976. *The Entity-Relationship Model: Toward a unified view of Data.* ACM TODS, 1, 9-36.
3. DeOliviera, J.L., Pires, F., and Medeiros, C.B., 1997. *An Environment for Modeling and Design of Geographic Applications.* Geoinformatica, 1,1, 29-58.
4. Delis, V., Hadzilacos, Th., and Tryfona, N. 1995. *An Introduction to Layer Algebra.* Proc. of the 6th SDH, Edinbrugh, UK, Taylor & Francis.
5. Freksa, C., 1992. *Using Orientation Information for Qualitative Spatial Reasoning.* COSIT'92. LNCS 639.
6. Guetting, R., and Schneider, M., 1995. *Realm-Based Spatial Data Types: The Rose Algebra.* VLDB Journal 4.
7. Hadzilacos, T., and Tryfona, N., 1992. *A Model for Expressing Topological Constraints in Geographic Databases.* COSIT'92. LNCS 639.
8. Hadzilacos, T., and Tryfona, N., 1997. An *Extended Entity-Relational Model for Geographic Applications*, ACM SIGMOD Record 26, 3.
9. Jensen, C.S., and Snodgrass, R.T., 1996. *Semantics of Time-Varying Applications.* Information Systems, 21, 4, 311-352.
10. Peuquet, D., and Duan, N., 1995. *An Event-Based Spatiotemporal Data Model for Temporal Analysis of Geographical Data.* International Journal of GIS, 9,1, 7-24.
11. Scholl M., and Voisard, A., 1989. *Thematic Map Modeling.* SSD'89, LNCS 409.
12. Snodgrass, R.T., 1992. *Temporal Databases.* Invited paper,COSIT'92.LNCS 639.
13. Tryfona N., and Hadzilacos, Th. 1995. *Geographic Applications Development: Models and Tools at the Conceptual Leve*l, 3rd ACM GIS, Baltimore, MD.
14. Tryfona, N., and Jensen, C. S., 1997. *Conceptual Data Modeling for Spatio-Temporal Applications.* Under submission.
15. UtilNets, [1994-1997]. Brite-Euram Project 7120, DG XII, EU, Brussels.
16. Weather Encyclopedia. http://208.134.241.135/breaking_weather/encyclopedia/
17. Worboys, M., 1994. *A Unified Model for Spatial and Temporal Information.* The Computer Journal, 37,1.

Rulebase Checking Using a Spatial Representation

Frans Coenen

Department of Computer Science, The University of Liverpool,
Chadwick Building, P.O. Box 147, Liverpool L69 3BX, England.
frans@csc.liv.ac.uk,
WWW home page: http://www.csc.liv.ac.uk/~frans/

Abstract. In this paper we describe an approach to rule base V&V founded on a N-dimensional tesseral representation of space. The advantages offered by the representation are that it is simple, concise and lends itself to computationally effective manipulation of objects (defined in the representation) using standard integer addition and subtraction. The encapsulation of a rulebase in this tesseral representation - as a multi-dimensional "arena" - then provides an appropriate mechanism for the application of spatial algorithms to address rulebase verification. The algorithms make full use of the advantages associated with the representation, and consequently offer a significant reduction in time complexity over more traditional approaches to rulebase verification. In particular this paper demonstrates the potential of tesserally encoded rulebases the full impact of which, in the author's opinion, has yet to be explored.

1 Introduction

In this paper an approach to rulebase verification and validation (V&V) using a multi-dimensional representation is described. The representation is founded on a tesseral approach ([1, 5, 6]) sometimes encountered in spatial reasoning systems ([3]). The advantages offered by this representation are that: (1) it is compact while maintaining expressiveness, (2) it is conceptually simple, and (3) it has a computationally effective integer arithmetic superimposed over it to allow objects captured in this representation to be manipulated.

The approach described also has similarities with earlier work on incidence matrices ([4]) and other similar tabular techniques. A detailed account of the representation and its usage to encapsulate the nature of rulebases is given in section 2. The discussion is illustrated using a rulebase encoded using the Horn clause sub-set of predicate calculus, however, the representation can equally well be applied to any other clausal form. A simpler approach may be used with respect to propositional rulebases. In section 3 the usage of the representation, in the context of rulebase V&V, is illustrated through that application of structural verification algorithm. This algorithm is evaluated in section 4. Some conclusions are presented in section 5.

2 Spatial Representation of Rule Bases

A Horn clause rulebase consists of a set of clauses. Each clause comprising an antecedent and a consequent such that the antecedent is represented by zero, one or more predicates and the consequent a single predicate. Predicates in turn are made up of a predicate name, and zero one or mare arguments which can be constants or variables. In Prolog terms we can describe this in terms of a set of Horn clauses. An alternative representation for such a rulebase, although not as immediately intuitive or supportive of computation, is to consider the rulebase as comprising a number of sets of numeric identifiers:

$$C = \{c \mid 0 \leq c \leq \textit{the maximum number of unique clauses in the rulebase}\}$$
$$N = \{n \mid 0 \leq n \leq \textit{the maximum number of predicates that can be contained in any clause in the rulebase}\}$$
$$P = \{p \mid 0 \leq p \leq \textit{the maimum number of unique predicates in the rulebase}\}$$
$$A = \{a \mid 0 \leq a \leq \textit{the maximum number of arguments that can be contained in any clause in the rulebase}\}$$
$$V = \{v \mid 0 \leq v \leq \textit{the maximum number of unique constants in the rulebase}\}$$

```
parent(ann,jane).
parent(jane,tom).
parent(ann,susan).

female(ann).
female(susan).
male(tom).

grandParent(X,Y):- parent(X,Z), parent(Z,Y).

grandMother(X,Y):- grandParent(X,Y), female(X).
```

Table 1. Prolog example rulebase

Let us consider the familiar (family) example rulebase given in Table 1. Here we have 8 clauses which we number from 0 to 7, the maximum number of predicates contained in a clause is 3, there are five predicate names (`parent`, `female`, `male`, `grandParent` and `grandMother`) which we number from 0 to 4, the maximum number of arguments is 2, and there are four distinct constants (`ann`, `jane`, `tom` and `susan`) which we number from 0 to 3. Thus:

$$C = \{c \mid 0 \leq c \leq 7\}$$
$$N = \{n \mid 0 \leq n \leq 2\}$$
$$P = \{p \mid 0 \leq p \leq 4\}$$
$$A = \{a \mid 0 \leq a \leq 1\}$$
$$V = \{v \mid 0 \leq v \leq 3\}$$

We now define each clause as a set whose elements are defined by 5-tuples made up of elements of C, N, P, A and V respectively. Each element of this set then describes an argument within the clause. Thus in the case of the example rulebase:

$$\begin{aligned}
Clause_0 &= \{<0,0,0,0,0>, <0,0,0,1,1>\} \\
Clause_1 &= \{<1,0,0,0,1>, <1,0,0,1,2>\} \\
Clause_2 &= \{<2,0,0,0,0>, <2,0,0,1,3>\} \\
Clause_3 &= \{<3,0,1,0,0>\} \\
Clause_4 &= \{<4,0,1,0,3>\} \\
Clause_5 &= \{<5,0,2,0,2>\} \\
Clause_6 &= \{<6,0,3,0,0>, <6,0,3,0,1>, <6,0,3,0,2>, <6,0,3,0,3>, \\
&\quad <6,0,3,0,4>, <6,0,3,1,0>, <6,0,3,1,1>, <6,0,3,1,2>, \\
&\quad <6,0,3,1,3>, <6,0,3,1,4>, <6,1,0,0,0>, <6,1,0,0,1>, \\
&\quad <6,1,0,0,2>, <6,1,0,0,3>, <6,1,0,0,4>, <6,1,0,1,0>, \\
&\quad <6,1,0,1,1>, <6,1,0,1,2>, <6,1,0,1,3>, <6,1,0,1,4>, \\
&\quad <6,2,0,0,0>, <6,2,0,0,1>, <6,2,0,0,2>, <6,2,0,0,3>, \\
&\quad <6,2,0,0,4>, <6,2,0,1,0>, <6,2,0,1,1>, <6,2,0,1,2>, \\
&\quad <6,2,0,1,3>, <6,2,0,1,4>\} \\
Clause_7 &= \{<7,0,4,0,0>, <7,0,4,0,1>, <7,0,4,0,2>, <7,0,4,0,3>, \\
&\quad <7,0,4,0,4>, <7,0,4,1,0>, <7,0,4,1,1>, <7,0,4,1,2>, \\
&\quad <7,0,4,1,3>, <7,0,4,1,4>, <7,1,3,0,0>, <7,1,3,0,1>, \\
&\quad <7,1,3,0,2>, <7,1,3,0,3>, <7,1,3,0,4>, <7,1,3,1,0>, \\
&\quad <7,1,3,1,1>, <7,1,3,1,2>, <7,1,3,1,3>, <7,1,3,1,4>, \\
&\quad <7,2,1,0,0>, <7,2,1,0,1>, <7,2,1,0,2>, <7,2,1,0,3>, \\
&\quad <7,2,1,0,4>\}
\end{aligned}$$

Note that variables can take any value contained in the set V.

The rulebase can thus be described as a set of sets where each element represents a clause:

$$Rulebase = \{Clauses_1, Clauses_2, \ ... \ Clauses_n\}$$

If we consider the sets C, N, P, A and V to each represent a dimension we can define a 5-D space described as a set, which (for reasons that will become apparent later) we will call `Positive`, that comprises a set of points each defined by a 5-tuple. Thus the set *positive* can be defined as follows:

$$Positive = \{p \mid p : \{C \times N \times P \times A \times V\}\}$$

Interestingly we can extend this concept and also identify a set $Negative$ comprising all 5-tuples where one or more of the coordinates has a negative label. Thus the set *Positive* could be more accurately described as a subset of a larger set $Universe$ (the universe of discourse) which includes the set $Negative$, i.e.

$$Universe = Positive \amalg Negative$$

(the *disjoint union* of the *Positive* and $Negative$ sets is equivalent to the set $Universe$).

From a computationally perspective points referenced by a five coordinate system are awkward and cumbersome to handle. It is therefore convenient to compress the 5-tuples into single integers referred to as addresses. We do this using a function $f_{coords2address}$ such that:

$$\begin{aligned} Dom(f_{coords2address}) &= \{< c, n, p, a, v > \mid c : C, n : N, \\ &\qquad p : P, a : A, v : V\} \\ Cod(f_{coords2address}) &= \{t \mid t : Integer\} \\ Gr(f_{coords2address}) &= \{<< c, n, p, a, v >, t > \mid t = \\ &\qquad c + 2^6 n + 2^{12} p + 2^{18} a + 2^{24} v\} \end{aligned}$$

where *Dom* indicates the domain of the function, *Cod* the codomain, and *Gr* the graph. The effect of the function is to compress the 5-tuple references into a single address with a bit pattern of the form shown in Figure 1. We also define a similar function to "translate" a given address back to a 5-tuple:

$$f_{address2coords}(t) \rightarrow < c, n, p, a, v >$$

Note that:

1. It is not necessary to associate any particular "dimension" with any particular bit grouping.
2. Any other distribution of bits could equally well have been allocated provided that each dimension of interest comprises a continuous sequence of bits.

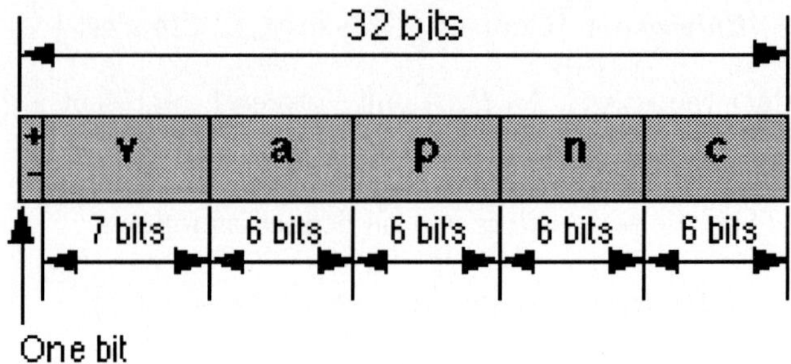

Fig. 1. Address bit pattern using a 32 bit integer

3. To accommodate a larger rulebase a 64 bit integer might be used.
4. The sign bit is included to provide for negative addressing.

In effect we have *tesselated* ([1, 5, 6]) the 5-D "argument" space. The advantages of this are as follows:

1. All references are unique and conceptually simple to generate.
2. The representation has the effect of linearising N-dimensional space which in turn has significant benefits with respect to (a) data storage, (b) comparison of sets of addresses and (c) translation through the space.

Thus, assuming the bit pattern given in Figure 1, we can now redefine the set *Universe* as follows:

$$Universe = \{u \mid f_{coords2address}(< c, n, p, a, v >) \rightarrow u,\\ < c, n, p, a, v > \in \{C \times N \times P \times A \times V\}\}$$

Returning to our example rulebase we can now express each clause in the rule base in terms of a set of addresses:

$$Clause_0 = \{0, 17039360\}$$
$$Clause_1 = \{16777217, 33816577\}$$
$$Clause_2 = \{2, 50593794\}$$
$$Clause_3 = \{4099\}$$
$$Clause_4 = \{50335748\}$$
$$Clause_5 = \{33562629\}$$
$$Clause_6 = \{12294, 16789510, 33566726, 50343942, 67121158, 274438, 17051654, 33828870, 50606086, 67383302, 70, 16777286, 33554502, 50331718, 67108934, 262214, 17039430, 33816646, 50593862, 67371078, 134, 16777350, 33554566, 50331782, 67108998, 262278, 17039494, 33816710, 50593926, 67371142\}$$

$Clause_7 = \{16391, 16793607, 33570823, 50348039, 67125255, 278535, 17055751, 33832967, 50610183, 67387399, 12359, 16789575, 33566791, 50344007, 67121223, 274503, 17051719, 33828935, 50606151, 67383367, 4231, 16781447, 33558663, 50335879, 67113095\}$

Further compression is achieved by observing that some groups of addresses collectively describe a 5-D (hyper) cube which can be defined using an appropriate infix operator indicating that the prefix operand is the corner address nearest to the origin of the positive space (the address 0), and the postfix operand is the address furthest from the origin. To this end we will use the operator '..' to indicate such a cluster. The example clauses can now be fully described as shown in Table 2. Note also that we have ordered the sets (on the prefix operand in the case of groups of addresses) according to the linear sequence which is a feature of the representation.

$Clause_0$	= {0, 17039360}
$Clause_1$	= {16777217, 33816577}
$Clause_2$	= {2, 50593794}
$Clause_3$	= {4099}
$Clause_4$	= {50335748}
$Clause_5$	= {33562629}
$Clause_6$	= {12294..67383302, 70..67371078, 134..67371142}
$Clause_7$	= {4231..67113095, 12359..67383367, 16391..67387399}

Table 2. Tessellated encoding of example rulebase

2.1 Note on tesseral addition and subtraction

Given a set of tesseral addresses of the form described above we can translate this set through the universe of discourse using simple integer addition and subtraction. To this end we define two functions, $f_{addition}$ and $f_{subtraction}$, as follows:

$$\begin{aligned} Dom(f_{addition}) &= \{< X, n > \mid X \subseteq Universe, \\ &\quad n \in Universe\} \\ Cod(f_{addition}) &= \{Y \mid Y, \subseteq Universe\} \\ Gr(f_{addition}) &= \{<< X, n >, Y > \mid \forall x : X, \exists y : Y, \\ &\quad y = x + n\} \end{aligned}$$

We define the subtraction function in a similar manner:

$$Gr(f_{subtraction}) = \{<< X, n >, Y >| \forall x : X, \exists y : Y,\\ y = x - n\}$$

The computational efficiency with which objects (encoded in the tesseral representation) can be translated through the domain of discourse, using the above $f_{addition}$ and $f_{subtraction}$ functions, is another illustration of the power of the approach.

3 V&V Algorithms

Given the spatial representation described in the forgoing section we use spatial reasoning techniques, such as those described in [3] to look for anomalies in the arguments space. We will illustrate this with an algorithm to address structural verification. Structural verification comprises the identification of anomalies such as subsumption and duplication. We define subsumption as the situation where one rule is a more specialised case of another. Duplication, where two rules are identical, is then a specialised form of subsumption.

The spatial structural verification algorithm described here is founded on ideas concerned with shape fitting, as encountered in tesseral spatial reasoning, where a "shape" described in terms of a set (*Shape*) of tesseral addresses is to be "fitted" into a "location space" also described in terms of a set (*LocationSpace*) of addresses. However, in this case it is not permissible to rotate the shape. The sets *Shape* and *LocationSpace* are defined as follows:

$$Shape = \{s \mid s : X, X \subseteq Univers \wedge 0 \in X\}$$
$$LocationSpace = \{l \mid l : Y, Y \subseteq Positive\}$$

Thus the set *Shape* comprises a set of elements belonging to the set *Univers* with one of the elements equal to the address 0. The latter acts as the reference address for the shape with respect to which it can be manipulated. The set *LocationSpace* is then some subset of the set *Positive*. With respect to structural verification the shape in question describes a clause in the rulebase and the location space the rulebase with the clause in question removed. If the shape can be fitted into the rulebase subsumption exists otherwise it does not.

The derivation of the shape is a two stage process. Given a clause we first remove references to the clause number to arrive at a set *SubShape* using a function $f_{subshape}$:

$$Dom(f_{subshape}) = \{Clause \mid Clause : Rulebase\}$$
$$Cod(f_{subshape}) = \{t \mid t : Positive\}$$
$$Gr(f_{subshape}) = \{< Clause, SubShape >| \forall t : Clause,$$

$$\exists s : SubShape, f_{coords2address}(< 0, n, p, a, v >) \rightarrow s,$$
$$f_{address2coords}(t) \rightarrow < c, n, p, a, v >\}$$

We then need to translate this set of addresses so that the zero address is included. We do this by subtracting one element of the set *SubShape* (for reasons of convenience we will use the first element encountered) from every member of the set and encapsulate this in a function f_{shape}.

$$\begin{aligned}
&Dom(f_{shape}) = SubShape \\
&Cod(f_{shape}) = Shape \\
&Gr(f_{shape}) = \{< SubShape, Shape > \mid \forall s : Shape, \\
&\quad \exists t : SubShape, s = t - n\}
\end{aligned}$$

Let us illustrate this using $clause_7$ from Table 2:

$$\begin{aligned}
Clause_7 = \{&4231..673752399, 6391..67387399, \\
&12359..67383367\}
\end{aligned}$$

then:

$$\begin{aligned}
SubShape = f_{subShape}(Clause_7) \rightarrow \{&4224..266368, \\
&12352..67383360, 16384..67387392\}
\end{aligned}$$

Note the numeric reordering of the result in line with the linear sequence that is a feature of the tesseral representation and the root of many of its principal advantages. If we now subtract the address 4224 (the first address encountered in this case) from every element we get a shape of the form:

$$\begin{aligned}
Shape = f_{shape}(< SubShape, 4224 >) \rightarrow \{&0..262144, \\
&8128..6734112, 12160..67383168\}
\end{aligned}$$

The location space set is obtained, more simply, using a function $f_{locationSpace}$:

$$\begin{aligned}
&Dom(f_{locationSpace}) = \{Clause \mid Clause : Rulebase\} \\
&Cod(f_{locationSpace}) = \{s \mid s : Clause, Clause \subseteq Rulebase\} \\
&Gr(f_{locationSpace}) = \{< Clause, LocationSpace > \mid \\
&\quad LocationSpace = Clause \setminus Rulebase\}
\end{aligned}$$

(The location space is equivalent to the complement of the set $Clause$ in the set $Rulebase$). Thus in the case of $Clause_7$ in our example rulebase (Table 2):

$$LocationSpace = f_{locationSpace}(Clause_7) \rightarrow \{0, 2, 70..67371078, 134..67371142, 4099, 12294..67383302, 16777217, 17039360, 33816577, 33562629, 50593794, 50335748, 33562629\} = Clause_7 \setminus Rulebase = \{4231..673752399, 6391..67387399, 12359..67383367\} \setminus \{0, 2, 70..67371078, 134..67371142, 4099, 4225..67113095, 12294..67383302, 12359..67383367, 16391..67387399, 16777217, 17039360, 33816577, 33562629, 50593794, 50335748, 33562629\}$$

We then use a shape fitting algorithm such as that described in [3] to determine if the shape can be "fitted" into the location space. If so subsumption exists. We can summarise this shape fitting algorithm as follows using a function $f_{subsumption}$:

$$\begin{array}{l} Dom(f_{subsumption}) = < Shape, LocationSpace > \\ Cod(f_{subsumption}) = Boolean = \{true, false\} \\ f_{subsumption}(< Shape, LocationSpace >) = \\ \quad true\ if\ \exists n : LocationSpace \\ \qquad f_{addition}(< Shape, n >) \subseteq LocationSpace \\ \quad false\ otherwise \end{array}$$

In the example the shape cannot be fitted into the location space therefore we conclude that no duplication/subsumption exists.

4 Evaluation

Intuitively, to implement structural verification, every clause in the rulebase must be compared with every other clause in the rulebase. This comparison also requires that given a pair of clauses every predicate (and every argument in every predicate) in one must be compared with every predicate (and every argument in every predicate) in the other. Given even a simple rulebase the time complexity required by such an algorithm will be significant. A crude measure of this complexity is given by:

$$\frac{NumberOfClauses^2 - NumberOfClauses}{2}$$

Using the algorithm defined in section 3 the time complexity is significantly reduced, and can be quantified as the number of clauses in the rulebase. There is of course an overhead associated with the implementation of the shape fitting mechanism but this may considered to be roughly equivalent to the overheads associated with the detailed comparison of predicates. It is therefore considered that a significant saving in time complexity is achieved when the proposed spatial algorithm is used to check for structural anomalies.

5 Conclusion

In this paper we have shown how a rulebase can be encoded using a 5-D tesseral representation, and have illustrated the advantages offered by this encoding with two "spatial" algorithms - the first to address structural verification and the second directed at inference verification. The principal advantage of the encoding is the saving in time complexity that are gained when algorithms founded on the representation are applied to address rulebase V&V. Work is currently centred on techniques to identify contradictions and inconsistencies in the rulebase by ascertaining the possible values for variables and matching this with the known set of possible values derived from a domain expert. Work to date indicates that the value passing mechanism adopted in Prolog style rulebases necessitates that an additional sixth dimension be included which encapsulates variable names. Work is also underway considering the advantages offered by the tesseral approach as a model of computation in its own right. It is also worth observing that the tesseral representation can be used to encode any tabular approach to rulebase V&V, and not just incidence matrix style approaches. Perhaps the most significant point that this paper establishes is that there my be great potential in tesserally encoded rulebases the fill impact of which has yet to be explored.

References

1. S.B.M. Bell, B.M. Diaz, F.C. Holroyd and M.J.J. Jackson (1983). Spatially Referenced Methods of Processing Raster and Vector Data. Image and Vision Computing, 1(4), pp211-220.
2. Coenen, F.P. (1995). An Advanced Binary Encoded Matrix Representation for Rulebase Verification. Journal of Knowledge-Based Systems, Vol 8, No 4, pp201-210.
3. Coenen, F.P., Beattie, B., Bench-Capon, T.J.M, Diaz, B.M. and Shave. M.J.R. (1997). A tesseral Approach to N-Dimensional Spatial Reasoning. In Hameurlain, A. and Tjoa, A.M. (Eds), Database and Expert Systems Applications, (Proceedings DEXA'97), Lecture Notes in Computer Science 1308, Springer Verlag, pp633-642.
4. Coenen, F.P. and Dunne, P.E. (1997). Verification and Validation of Rulebases using a Binary Encoded Incidence Matrix Technique. Proceedings EUROVAV'97, Katholieke Universiteit Leuven, Belgium, pp43-53.
5. B.M. Diaz and S.B.M. Bell (1986). Spatial Data Processing Using Tesseral Methods. Natural Environment Research Council publication, Swindon, England.
6. I. Gargantini (1982). Linear Octrees for Fast Processing of Three Dimensional Objects. Computer Graphics and Image Processing, 20, pp365-374.

Hypermedia Broadcasting with Temporal Links

Kazutoshi SUMIYA, Reiko NODA, and Katsumi TANAKA

Graduate School of Science and Technology, Kobe University
Rokkodai, Nada, Kobe 657-8501, JAPAN
{sumiya,noda,tanaka}@db.cs.kobe-u.ac.jp

Abstract. In this paper, we propose a temporal link mechanism for 'time-dependent' hypermedia. It has become a serious problem to maintain link information at all times according to updating. It is very important to keep consistency and maintain the updates, especially for broadcast hypermedia, which are transmitted from a server to a client via the internet or a broadcasting system. The mechanism we propose supports links in broadcast hypermedia to designate adequate anchors automatically. We also describe the implementation issues of the link mechanism.

1 Introduction

Recently, information delivery systems, via the internet or digital video broadcasting (DVB) [1], are receiving much attention, because of their potential and convenience [2]. The concept of these systems is generally based on a *push* type service instead of a *pull* type service. A pull type service, for example, is conventional Web surfing as pulling information. Users pull information from different Web sites by searching for topics that they are interested in. However, in a push type service, it is not necessary for users to access the information resources, because the required and/or updated information is transmitted automatically. That is, users register their favorite channels at a service server in advance and then the system will transmit information for each user at regular intervals.

The transmitted data contains not only simple text documents but also hypertext and hypermedia. In this paper, we discuss not only text data but also hypertext and hypermedia, especially link mechanisms for them. Hyperlinks are classified into two types: static links and dynamic links. Static links are created by an author in advance, and are never changed. On the other hand, dynamic links are generated then and there, when a user navigates the link. Several dynamic link mechanisms have been proposed[3]. There are some kinds of mechanisms: computed links [4][5][6][7] and query based links[8][9].

In actual hypertext and hypermedia, it becomes a serious problem to maintain link information at all times according to updating. This situation is much more prominent for time dependent contents because updating is carried out very frequently. The contents, for example, are current event news, on-the-spot broadcasting of sport programs, and so on. We propose a temporal hyperlink mechanism for time dependent hypertext and hypermedia to solve troublesome maintenance.

We have been developing a prototype system called *Mille-feuille* based on our proposed temporal management mechanism for hyperlinks. At the present time, the basic facilities we propose have been implemented on the system, which are a temporal management mechanism, data sending/receiving function and the user interface applications. We have ascertained the possibilities of the mechanism and discussed how the mechanism can be adapted to existing systems.

The rest of this paper is organized as follows: Section 2 describes our motivating examples of link maintenance and characteristics of broadcast hypermedia. Section 3 discusses and defines the temporal validity of anchors and links. Section 4 explains our control mechanism for time dependent links. Section 5 describes a broadcasting hypermedia system with the link control mechanism we propose. Finally, Section 6 gives a conclusion.

2 Motivating Examples

2.1 Dangling Links in Hypertexts

Hypertext is very useful for retrieving information by navigating hyperlinks interactively. Indeed, a great deal of information can be accessed through the World Wide Web (WWW). In actual data on WWW, however, some anchors in HTML documents no longer point to the target information because the documents have moved or been deleted. A "**Error 404. Not Found – file doesn't exist.**" error message of HTTP 1.0[10] is often displayed, when the target document no longer exists, while navigating Web pages. This makes hypertext frustrating and lacks consistency.

To avoid this situation, for example, Alexa[11] makes an archive of the Web which has an *eight terabyes* archive of the entire WWW constantly and saves whole archives[12]. Although this system is very useful, the maintenance of archiving is very troublesome. It may be a solution that links are automatically generated/deleted, if the concept of *life span* of documents and anchors can be introduced. Therefore, hypertext links should be extended to links with a mechanism handling its temporal aspect to solve missing links and dead links.

2.2 Broadcast Hypermedia

Recently, several push technologies, such as Pointcast 1.0[13], Castanet 2.0[14] and so on, have been developed. These systems are applied to information delivery, software distribution or document distribution. For example, Pointcast transmits current event news which users may need individually at regular intervals.

Let us consider a situation: there are two mutually-related data items in a server and each data will be transmitted separately. In this case, each piece of data does not always arrive at the same time. Only an implicit relationship between them is recognized at the server, however, each piece of data may be handled as just individual data at a client. The questions then arise about semantical consistency among transmitted data: (1) There are no explicit relationship among data, (2) It is not complete with entire consistency because of partial updates of data at a server. Therefore the requirements for push technologies are as follows:

- Automatically generating relationship among relative data
- Keeping consistency in temporal aspects

To satisfy these requirements, in a conventional way, all of the relations among data must be created manually. This gives a lot of trouble to generate links one by one. On the other hand, from the point of view of temporal management, dangling links at a client should be regarded as *upcoming links*, because these links may become valid links when related data arrives. Therefore, a framework which tolerates temporary contradiction for push type services is necessary. We call push type service, which handles hypermedia, *broadcast hypermedia.*

3 Time Dependent Link

In this section, we introduce a time dependent link (TDL) to manage dangling links and to handle the link maintenance for broadcast hypermedia. TDL are defined as a pair of anchors. We discuss and define temporal validity of anchors and links.

3.1 Anchor and Container

Anchors are all kinds of objects: keywords, paragraphs, pages and so on[1]. To be exact, all kinds of objects can be a candidate of an anchor even if the object is a page (maximum object).

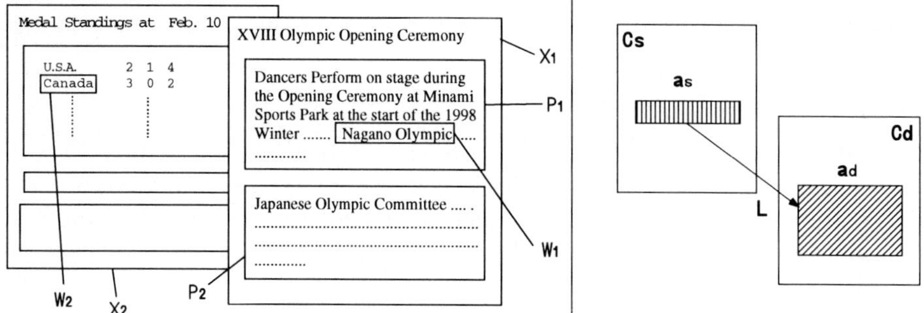

Fig. 1. (a) An example of anchors and containers, (b) Link between a_s and a_d

[1] Anchors are not necessarily text objects. Namely, animation objects, sound objects and video objects can be also anchors.

A container is the object which includes some anchors in itself. For example, a news article page is a container and a keyword is an anchor (Fig. 1(a)). Actually, the extra edition page "`XVIII Olympic Opening Ceremony`(X_1)" can be a container, the keyword "`Nagano Olympic`(W_1)" and the paragraph " `Dancers perform on stage during the ...` (P_1)" can be anchors. Of course, the page "`XVIII Olympic Opening Ceremony`(X_1)" can be an anchor.

There are two kinds of nodes in TDL: *source node* and *destination node.* A source node is a source anchor in a source container. A destination node is a destination anchor in a destination container.

3.2 Link Definition

TDLs are defined as a pair of a source anchor and a destination anchor: $L = (a_s, a_d)$. Fig. 1(b) shows a source anchor that is included in the source container and a destination anchor that is included in the destination container.

3.3 Transaction Time and Valid Time of Nodes

The transaction time and valid time of a node are defined below. Table 1 shows transaction times and valid times of nodes. Transaction time is generally defined as the time when the object is stored in a storage system. Transaction times are consistent with the serialization order of the transactions[15].

The transaction time of an anchor tr is the time when the anchor is registered in the container. In the same way, the transaction time of a container Tr is the time when the container is stored in a storage system. The transaction time values cannot be after the current time.

According to the definition of valid times by Snodgrass[15], the valid time of a fact is generally defined as the time when the fact is true in the modeled reality. The valid time of an anchor $[v_1, v_2]$ is the interval when the anchor works as an executable navigation point. In other words, valid times of the anchor is

	source		destination	
	anchor	container	anchor	container
transaction time	tr_s	Tr_s	tr_d	Tr_d
valid time	$[v_{s_1}, v_{s_2}]$	$[V_{s_1}, V_{s_2}]$	$[v_{d_1}, v_{d_2}]$	$[V_{d_1}, V_{d_2}]$

Table 1. Transaction time and valid time

its *life span.* That is, the anchor works from time v_1 to time v_2 and expires at time v_2. For example, in a definition, the valid time of the keyword "`Nagano Olympic` (X_1)" is [Feb.7, 08:00, Feb.22, 21:00], according to the period of the XVIII Olympic Winter Games.

The valid time of a container $[V_1, V_2]$ is the interval when the container is effective. This is the life span of a container. For example, the valid time of the container "Medal Standings at Feb.10(X_2)" is [Feb.10, 00:00, Feb.10, 24:00] and the container makes senses only during this period.

3.4 Temporal Validity of Links

The transaction times of a source anchor and a destination anchor are tr_s and tr_d, respectively. The transaction times of a source container and a destination container are Tr_s and Tr_d,respectively. On the other hand, the valid times of a source anchor and a destination anchor are $[v_{s_1}, v_{s_2}]$ and $[v_{d_1}, v_{d_2}]$, respectively. The valid time of a source container and a destination container are $[V_{s_1}, V_{s_2}]$ and $[V_{d_1}, V_{d_2}]$, respectively.

Therefore, the valid time of TDL is determined by the valid time of the anchors and the containers. Namely, if all of the following conditions are satisfied, the TDL is *valid*.

First, the intersection of an anchor's valid time and a container's valid time include the current time. This condition must be satisfied at both source side and destination side. This condition means that an anchor is effective in the valid container. For example, if the keyword "Nagano Olympic(W_1)" is valid as

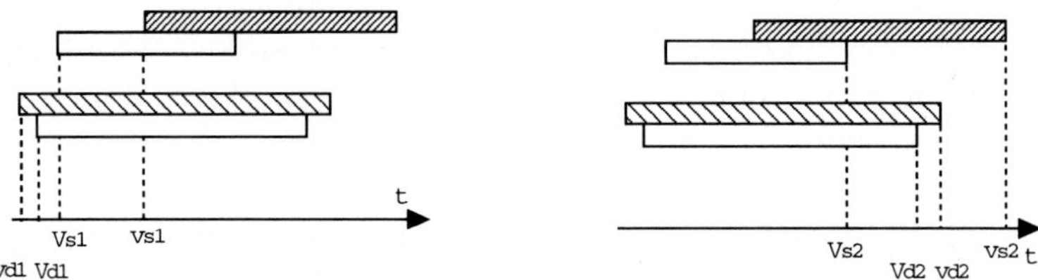

Fig. 2. Creation and expiration time of TDL

an anchor and the page "XVIII Olympic Winter Games(X_1)" is also valid as a container, the anchor is guaranteed an executable navigation point.

$$max(V_{s_1}, v_{s_1}) \leq t_{now} \leq min(V_{s_2}, v_{s_2}) \tag{1}$$

$$max(V_{d_1}, v_{d_1}) \leq t_{now} \leq min(V_{d_2}, v_{d_2}) \tag{2}$$

And next, the intersection of a source anchor's valid time and a destination anchor's valid time include the current time.

$$max(v_{s_1}, v_{d_1}) \leq t_{now} \leq min(v_{s_2}, v_{d_2}) \tag{3}$$

Finally, the intersection of a source container's valid time and a destination container's time include the current time. Of this condition, little need be said.

$$max(V_{s_1}, V_{d_1}) \leq t_{now} \leq min(V_{s_2}, V_{d_2}) \tag{4}$$

If all the conditions are satisfied for a TDL, the validity of the TDL is guaranteed at time t_{now}.

3.5 Creation and Expiration of TDL

In this section, we show creation times and expiration times of TDL and describe how the life span of TDLs is computed. Creation time L_{create} and expiration time L_{expire} of a link are determined as follows: L_{create} is the latest time in the four times, such as v_{s_1}, V_{s_1}, v_{d_1}, V_{d_1}. L_{expire} is the earliest time in the four times, such as v_{s_2}, V_{s_2}, v_{d_2}, V_{d_2}. Fig. 2 shows creation and expiration times: white rectangles and filled rectangles are containers and anchors, respectively.

$$L_{create} = max(v_{s_1}, V_{s_1}, v_{d_1}, V_{d_1})$$
$$L_{expire} = min(v_{s_2}, V_{s_2}, v_{d_2}, V_{d_2})$$

Therefore, the valid time of TDL is determined as follows: $L_{valid} = [L_{create}, L_{expire}]$. In other words, L_{valid} is the life span of a TDL. TDLs are dynamic links, because they are generated and lost automatically.

4 Link Control Mechanism

In this section, we explain the link control mechanism based on temporal validity. We have prepared several basic operations related to TDLs.

4.1 Management of Dangling Links

To maintain consistency of links among hypertext/hypermedia, we propose a management mechanism for dangling links. Let us consider the reasons why dangling links happen unexpectedly:

1. The fellow container has disappeared.
2. The fellow anchor does not make sense as an anchor.
3. 1. and 2. simultaneously

In case 1., the valid time of the container $[V_1, V_2]$ should be checked. In case 2., the valid time of the anchor $[v_1, v_2]$ should be checked. However, in both case 1. and case 2., it is necessary to check only the valid time of the link. Of course, in case 3. it is also sufficient.

Therefore, it is sufficient to check valid times of links, to avoid dangling links. Generally, it is practical to check the valid time of a link before the source container is loaded into an application/browser. Like with a Web browser, the valid anchors can be just hi-lighted (underlined or emphasized in color). Conversely, the other anchors, which have invalid links, must become normal or dismissed. Because there are individual processes to handle anchors for each application, the checking method should depend on the design policy of the application.

4.2 Features of Broadcast Hypermedia

Although dangling links should be avoided, there is an occasion on which the invalidity should be accepted. The reason for this is not hard to see: it is that the fellow anchor of the link would be *upcoming* in the near future. In this case, hypermedia are transmitted at a server and they are received at a client via the internet or broadcasting system. The features are as follows:

- Nodes and links are dynamically changed at a server
- Configurations of nodes and links are not always the same at a server and a client, because they are transmitted partially and gradually

It must be noticed that the concept of static/dynamic link is independent from whether it is broadcast type or not.

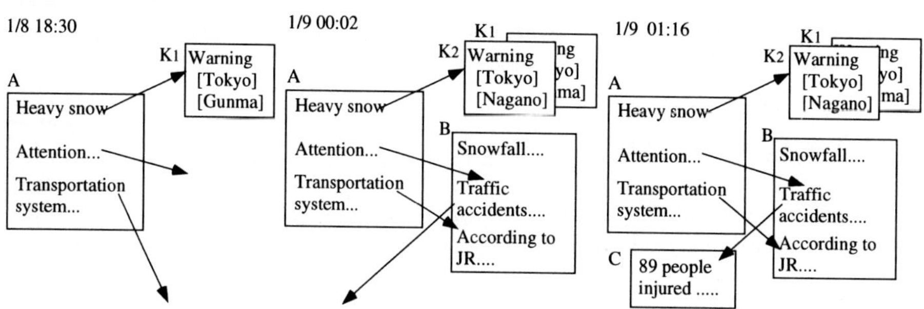

Fig. 3. Growth of broadcast hypermedia

Next, we introduce *growth* of broadcast hypermedia. Fig. 3 shows an item of current event news. In this example, the news stories say that traffic was snarled and a heavy snow warning has been issued for several places and that snow blanketed the metropolitan area in Japan in January. In this example, the left, middle and right part shows news articles at [Jan.8, 18:30], [Jan.9, 00:02] and [Jan.9, 01:16] , respectively. Rectangles are news articles and arrows are links.

- [Jan.8, 18:30]: Anchor "`Heavy snow`" in A is related with weather warning news article K_1. The link from anchor "`Transportation system...`" is an upcoming state. This is an example of an *upcoming* link.
- [Jan.9, 00:02]: News article B arrives and then upcoming links are dissolved. Also, anchor "`Heavy snow`" in page A is related to *new* weather warning news article K_2.
- [Jan.9, 01:06]: News article C arrives and then upcoming links from anchor "`Traffic accidents ...`"are dissolved.

4.3 Control of Broadcast Hypermedia

Upcoming Link Mechanism Generally, if fellow anchors or fellow containers do not exist, the links are not established. In broadcast hypermedia, however, this situation should be accepted, because the fellow anchors and containers may be transmitted partially and gradually. Therefore, the source anchors should be at a waiting state. Note that these links are not dangling links.

A waiting order is determined by the order in which users have activated the anchors. There are three types of orders: list, stack and queue. These types should be used appropriately according to the purpose of the applications.

Newest Link Mechanism In broadcast hypermedia, new version data come frequently from a server to a client. A newest link mechanism provides automatic updates which delete the link to old anchors and create a link to new anchors. In this case, transaction time would be evaluated. That is, if the transaction time of a new container which includes new anchors is later than an old one, the new link would created. In this case, we premise that all the containers at a server have a unique identifier and incremented version number.

5 Prototype System *Mille-feuille*

We are developing a prototype system for an information delivery service called *Mille-feuille*[2]. This system is implemented based on an application distributing system Castanet 2.0[14]. Castanet automatically distributes and maintains software applications and content across the internet. The Castanet transmitter (server) and tuner (client) work together to keep software and content always up-to-date.

The functionalities of a server and a client are designed as Castanet transmitter and tuner, respectively. The applications of a client are implemented as Java applications. Also, the user interface (*Mille-feuille* browser) is designed with the visual interface builder Bongo 1.1[17]. Fig. 5(a) shows the system architecture of *Mille-feuille.*

In this version of *Mille-feuille*, not all facilities we proposed are implemented: link type is limited to static link, newest link is not supported. Fig. 4 shows a screen image of an F1 racing information delivery service[3]. All the windows display anchors and the containers included in them. Of course, it is possible for users to navigate to an outside Web page using an URL.

6 Concluding Remarks

We have proposed the mechanism of time dependent links in hypermedia. The mechanism supports broadcast hypermedia because the links designate adequate

---

[2] *mille-feuille*: small rectangular pastries made of crisp layers of puff pastry and pastry cream. The word means "a thousand leaves". In our metaphor, pastry expresses nodes and cream interprets links.

[3] News source: http://www.monaco.mc/f1/97/europe/news.html#26/10/9715h45

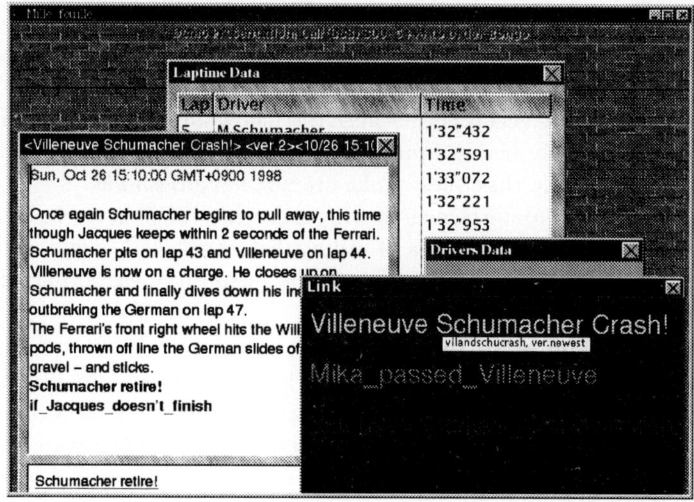

Fig. 4. Screen image of F1 racing information delivery service

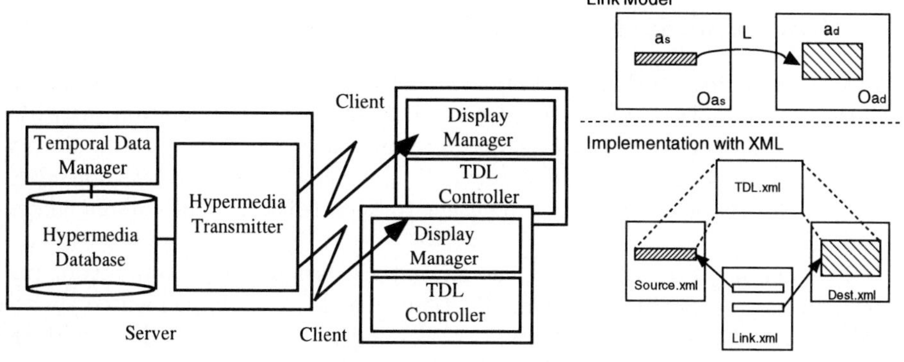

Fig. 5. (a) System architecture, (b) An implementation of TDL with XML

anchors automatically. TDL can run independently of implementation platforms. For example, the links would be defined with XML[18]. The anchors and containers would described using XML meta data. The links would be XML linking language using out-of-line link and group link[19]. We show an implementation of TDL with XML in Fig. 5(b).

There are several issues to be pursued about the temporal aspects of broadcast hypermedia. One is that we must handle the arrival time of data, as a delay time of the broadcasting period must occur in practical use. Another issue is that we must design management of historical data for necessity of retrospective search.

Acknowledgments

This research was supported by the Japanese Ministry of Education Grant-in-Aid for Scientific Research on Priority Area: "Advanced Databases," area no.275(08244103) and Research for the Future Program of Japan Society for the Promotion of Science under the project "Researches on Advanced Multimedia Contents Processing".

References

1. European Broadcasting Union. Digital video broadcasting (DVB) systems. *http://www.dvb.org/dvb_index.html.*
2. Kate Gerwig, The push technology rage...so what's next?, ACM netWorker: The Craft of Network Computing, vol.1, no.2 (1997) 13—17
3. Jemes Mayfield. Two-level models of hypertext. *Lecture Notes in Computer Science*, 1326 (1997) 90–108
4. Michael Biever. Issues in modeling a "dynamic" hypertext interface for non-hypertext systems. *Proc. of ACM Hypertext '91* (1991) 203–217
5. Frank Wm. Tompa, G. Elizabeth Blake, and Darrell R. Raymond. Hypertext by link-resolving components. *Proc. of ACM Hypertext '93* (1993) 118–130
6. Daniel T. Chang. HieNet: A user-centered approach for automatic link generation. *Proc. of ACM Hypertext '93* (1993) 145–158
7. Nipon Charenkitkarn, Jim Tam, Mark H. Chignell, and Gene Golovchinsky. Browsing through querying: Designing for electronic books. *Proc. of ACM Hypertext '93* (1993) 206–216
8. K. Tanaka, N. Nishikawa, S. Hirayama, and K. Nanba. Query pairs as hypertext links. *Proc. of IEEE International Conference on Data Engineering* (1991) 456–463
9. Daniel Cunliffe, Carl Taylor, and Douglas Tudhope. Query-based navigation in semantically indexed hypermedia. *Proc. of ACM Hypertext '97* (1997) 87–95
10. Network Working Group. Hypertext Transfer Protocol – HTTP/1.0 RFC(Request for Comments) 1945.
11. Alexa. Alexa version 1.3. *http://www.alexa.com/.*
12. Jim Rapoza. *Alexa's theory of relativity - filtering, analytical algorithms link to Web sites – relevant or not.* PC Week on line, August (1997) http://www.zdnet.com/pcweek/reviews /0818/18alexa.html.
13. PointCast. PointCast Network. *http://www.pointcast.com/ main.html.*
14. Laura Lemay. *Official Marimba Guide to Castanet.* Sams.net, Indianapolis, IN 46268, USA, (1997)
15. R. Snodgrass. Temporal databases. *IEEE Computer*, Vol.19, No.9 (1986) 35–42
16. James Clifford, Curtis E. Dyreson, Tomás Isakowitz, Christian S. Jensen, and Richard T. Snodgrass. On the semantics of "now" in databases. *ACM Transactions on Database Systems*, Vol.22, No.2 (1997) 171–214
17. Danny Goodman. *Official Marimba Guide to Bongo.* Sams.net, Indianapolis, IN 46268, USA, (1997)
18. World Wide Web Consortium(W3C). Extensible Markup Language(XML). *http://www.w3.org/TR/REC-xml.*
19. World Wide Web Consortium(W3C). XML Linking Language(Xlink) Draft 3. *http://www.w3.org/TR/WD-xlink.*

Inferring Functional Dependencies in Linearly Ordered Databases

Wilfred Ng
Department of Computing
Hong Kong Polytechnic University
email: csshng@comp.polyu.edu.hk

Abstract. We extend the relational data model to incorporate linear orderings into data domains, which we call the ordered relational model. We formally define Ordered Functional Dependencies (OFDs) for the extended model by means of two possible extensions of domains, pointwise-orderings and lexicographical orderings. We first present a sound and complete axiom system for OFDs in the case of pointwise-orderings and then establish a set of sound and complete chase rules for OFDs in the case of lexicographical orderings. Our main result shows that the implication problems for both cases of OFDs are decidable, and that it is linear time for the case of pointwise orderings.

1 Introduction

We assume that the data domains of the relational data model are linearly ordered and call the extended model the ordered relational model. Our extension is well justified, since linear ordering is essential to the existing primitive data types used in DBMSs. There is also strong evidence that ordering is inherent to the underlying structure of data in many database applications [4, 7, 11], in which linear ordering is particularly important to those advanced applications involving temporal information and scientific information [10, 8].

We formalise the notions of FDs being satisfied in an ordered database and call them *Ordered Functional Dependencies* (OFDs). Informally speaking, OFDs can capture a monotonicity property between two sets of values projected onto some attributes in a relation. The semantics of OFDs are defined by means of two possible extensions of the domain orderings: *pointwise-orderings* and *lexicographical orderings.* Pointwise-orderings require each component of a data value to be greater than its predecessors and lexicographical orderings resemble the way in which words are arranged in a dictionary. We classify OFDs according to whether we use pointwise-orderings or lexicographical orderings in their definitions, whose short forms are written as POFDs ($X \hookrightarrow Y$) and LOFDs ($X \rightsquigarrow Y$).

Consider in Figure 1 a relation called EMP_RECORD over the set of attributes {EMP, POST_TITLE, YEARS, SALARY}. The semantics of EMP_RECORD is that an EMPloyee with a given POST TITLE, who has been working in a company for some YEARS, has the present SALARY. We assume that there is a *semantic ordering* in POST_TITLE as represented by the following domain {'Junior Programmer' < 'Senior Programmer'} [11]. The relation SALARY_RECORD in Figure 1 then satisfies the POFD, {POST_TITLE, YEARS} $\hookrightarrow$ SALARY, which states the fact that the SALARY of an employee is greater than other employees who has junior post titles and less experience in the company, and the LOFD, {POST_TITLE, YEARS} $\rightsquigarrow$ SALARY, which states the fact the SALARY of an employee is greater than other employees who has junior post titles, or the same post title but less experience in the company. Note that the semantics of the POFD and the LOFD mentioned above are different. For instance, in the first case, an employee has a higher salary only if he or she has both a senior post title and more experience than another, whereas in the second, it requires only that he or she only has to have a more senior post title.

EMP	POST_TITLE	YEARS	SALARY
Mark	Senior Programmer	15	35K
Nadav	Junior Programmer	7	25K
Ethan	Junior Programmer	6	22K

Fig. 1. An employee relation EMP_RECORD

We investigate the *implication problem* arising from OFDs [14, 3]. One approach is to establish a set of *inference rules* F which constitutes the *axiom system* $\mathcal{A}$. We can use the rules of $\mathcal{A}$ to *derive* an order dependency f from F. We call $\mathcal{A}$ *sound and complete*, if we can prove that, by using $\mathcal{A}$, f can be derived from F if and only if an ordered relation r satisfies F, it also satisfies f. We adopt this approach to show that the axiom system comprising the inference rules for POFDs, a superset of Armstrong's axiom system [2]. Another approach is to develop a *chase* procedure, which consists of a set of *chase rules* as a theorem proving tool. We choose an appropriate chase rule to apply to r until a fix point is attained in order to test whether r satisfies F. The chase procedure operates on a relation containing variables as data values, known as a *tableau* [9, 3], which is basically the template for those relations that could possibly violate f. Our investigation also relates to the issues of data dependencies in those extensions of the relational data model to incorporate sequences as data types [1, 13].

In Section 2 we clarify the notion of linear order and its extensions to the Cartesian product of linearly ordered sets, and define the ordered relational model. In Section 3 we examine FDs in the context of ordered databases. In Section 4 we present the axiom system comprising the inference rules for POFDs, which is sound and complete. Also, we define the chase rules for LOFDs and, using an extended notion of tableaux for LOFDs, show that the chase is sound and complete for LOFDs. In Section 5 we give our concluding remarks.

Definition 1. (Notation) We refer to a sequence of attributes as a short hand for a sequence of distinct attributes and use the common notation for both sequences and sets. The fact that two sequences have the same elements is denoted by $X \sim Y$. The difference between two sequences of attributes, denoted as $X - Y$, is defined by the sequence resulting from removing all the common attributes in X and Y from X while maintaining the original order of the remaining attributes in X. We also denote by XY the *concatenation* of two sequences X and Y if X and Y are *disjoint*, or $X(Y - X)$ if X and Y are not disjoint.

2 The Ordered Relational Model

We assume the usual definition of a *linear ordering* $\leq$ on the set S: a binary relation on S satisfying the conditions of *reflexivity*, *anti-symmetry*, *transitivity* and *linearity*, which becomes a *partial ordering* if without the linearity condition [6]. A *linearly ordered set*, denoted as $\mathcal{S}$, is a structure $\langle S, \leq \rangle$. From now on, the term *ordered* will mean linearly ordered, unless explicitly stated otherwise. We assume that the equality predicate, =, still applies to ordered sets and use the notation < to represent the usual meaning of $\leq$ but $\neq$.

Let $D_1, \ldots, D_n$ be n ordered sets, t be an element in the Cartesian product $S = D_1 \times \cdots \times D_n$ and $t[i]$ be the ith coordinate of t. We now define *pointwise-orderings* and *lexicographical orderings* on the Cartesian product of ordered sets.

Definition 2. (Pointwise-Ordering and Lexicographical Ordering) A *pointwise-ordering* on S is defined as for all $t_1, t_2 \in S$, $t_1 \leq_S t_2$ if for all $1 \leq i \leq n$, $t_1[i] \leq_{D_i} t_2[i]$. A *lexicographical ordering* on S is defined as for all $t_1, t_2 \in S$, $t_1 \leq_S t_2$ if either (1) there exists k with $1 \leq k \leq n$ such that $t_1[k] <_{D_k} t_2[k]$, and for all $1 \leq i < k$, $t_1[i] = t_2[i]$, or (2) for all $1 \leq i \leq n$, $t_1[i] = t_2[i]$.

The idea of the pointwise-ordering extension on data domains has been commonly used to study the issues concerning incomplete information [7], but in this case we need to define partial ordering over data domains. The ordering of the domain *DATE*, called *chronological orderings*, can be viewed as the lexicographical ordering of the domains $YEAR$, $MONTH$ and DAY, if (1) the domain $MONTH$ has the ordering as $\{JAN \leq FEB \leq \cdots \leq DEC\}$ and (2) the Cartesian product of the domains are taken in the following order: $YEAR \times MONTH \times DAY$.

Let D be a countably infinite set of constant values and $\leq_D$ be an ordering on D. Without loss of generality, we assume that all attributes share the same domain D. We now give the definition of an ordered database.

Definition 3. (Attributes and Ordered Domains) We assume a countably infinite ordered set of attribute names, $\langle U, \leq_U \rangle$. For all attributes $A \in U$, the domain of A is $\langle D, \leq_D \rangle$. We call $\leq_D$ the *domain ordering* of D.

Definition 4. (Relation Schema and Database Schema) A relation schema (or simply a schema) R, is a subset of U consisting of a finite set of attributes $\{A_1, \ldots, A_m\}$ for some $m \geq 1$. A *database schema* is a finite set $\mathbf{R} = \{R_1, \ldots, R_n\}$ of relation schemas, for some $n \geq 1$.

Definition 5. (Projection) Let $X = \{A_1, \ldots, A_m\}$ be a finite subset of U where $A_i \neq A_j$ for $i \neq j$ and $A_1 \leq_U \cdots \leq_U A_m$. A *tuple* t over X is a member of D^m. We let $t[A_i]$ denote the ith coordinate of t. The *projection* of a tuple t onto a set of attributes $Y = \{A_{i_1}, \ldots, A_{i_k}\}$, where $1 \leq i_1 < \cdots < i_k \leq m$, is the tuple $t[Y] = \langle t[A_{i_1}], \ldots, t[A_{i_k}] \rangle$.

Definition 6. (Ordered Relation and Ordered Database) An *ordered relation* (or simply a relation) r defined over a schema R is a finite set of tuples over R. An *ordered database* (or simply a database) over $\mathbf{R} = \{R_1, \ldots, R_n\}$ is a finite set $d = \{r_1, \ldots, r_n\}$ such that each r_i is a relation over R_i.

We make two assumptions in our model. First, the orderings of domains can be extended to tuples so that tuples in an ordered relation are ordered according to the lexicographical ordering of the domains associated with the attributes present in the underlying relation schema. Any change in the order of attributes in a relation schema may affect the order of tuples in an ordered relation. Second, given a data domain, apart from the system ordering assumption, we can declare one or more semantic orderings which override the default system ordering.

3 Functional Dependencies (FDs) in Ordered Databases

We first formalise the notion of *logical implication* and *an axiom system*, and then briefly discuss two possible views of FDs in the context of ordered databases. Definition 7 will be repeatedly used in different contexts of data dependencies such as POFDs in Section 4.1 and LOFDs in Section 4.2.

Definition 7. (Logical Implication and Axiom System) We say that a set of data dependencies F *logically implies* a data dependency f over R, written F $\models f$, whenever for all relations r over R, if for all $f' \in$ F, $r \models f'$ holds, then $r \models f$ also holds. An *axiom system* $\mathcal{A}$ for F is a set of inference rules (or simply rules) that can be used to *derive* data dependencies from F over R. We say that f is *derivable* from F by $\mathcal{A}$, if there is a finite sequence of data dependencies over R, whose last element is f, and where each data dependency in the said sequence is either in F or follows from a finite number of previous data dependencies in the sequence by one of the inference rules. We denote by F $\vdash f$ the fact that f is *derivable* from F by a specified axiom system.

There are two possible views of FDs in the context of ordered databases. The first view is straightforward, that is, Armstrong's system can be directly carried over to ordered relations, since we assume that the equality predicate still applies to ordered domains. Another view of FDs in the context of ordering is more interesting. Let r be a relation over R and X be a sequence of attributes projected onto R. A domain ordering operator ω_X over r is a linear orderings $\leq_r$ on r such that for each for any tuples $t_1, t_2 \in r$, if $t_1[X] \leq_X t_2[X]$, then $t_1 \leq_r t_2$ (recall that $\leq_X$ is a lexicographical ordering on the Cartesian products of data domains associated with X). The semantics of FDs in an ordered relation r can be defined via the notion of ω_X as follows, an ordered relation r *satisfies* a functional dependency $X \to Y$ if $\omega_X \pi_{XY}(r)$ is unique.

4 Ordered Functional Dependencies (OFDs)

The semantics of an OFD with two or more attributes on either the left or right hand side are defined according to lexicographical orderings and pointwise-ordering on the Cartesian product of the underlying domains of the attributes in the OFD, which gives rise to POFDs and LOFDs, respectively.

4.1 OFDs Arising from Pointwise-Orderings

We give the definition of a POFD as follows.

Definition 8. (Ordered Functional Dependency Arising from Pointwise-Orderings) An *ordered functional dependency arising from pointwise-orderings* (or simply a POFD) over a relation schema R, is a statement of the form $R : X \hookrightarrow Y$ (or simply $X \hookrightarrow Y$ whenever R is understood from the context), where $X, Y \subseteq R$ are sequences of attributes. The POFD $X \hookrightarrow Y$ is said to be *standard* if $X \neq \emptyset$.

From now on, we will assume that all POFDs are standard. We now give the definition of the semantics of a POFD.

Definition 9. (Satisfaction of a POFD) A POFD, $R : X \hookrightarrow Y$, is satisfied in a relation r over R, denoted by $r \models X \hookrightarrow Y$, if for all $t_1, t_2 \in r$, $t_1[X] \leq_X t_2[X]$ implies that $t_1[Y] \leq_Y t_2[Y]$, where $\leq_X$ and $\leq_Y$ are pointwise-orderings on the Cartesian products of the respective domains of X and Y.

We next give a set of inference rules for POFDs and show that Armstrong's axiom system carries over to ordered relations with respect to POFDs.

Definition 10. (Inference Rules for POFDs) Let X, Y, Z and W be subsets of R and F be a set of POFDs over R. The inference rules for POFDs are defined as follows:

(POFD1) *Reflexivity*: if $Y \subseteq X$, then $\mathrm{F} \vdash X \hookrightarrow Y$.
(POFD2) *Augmentation*: if $\mathrm{F} \vdash X \hookrightarrow Y$ and $Z \subseteq R$, then $\mathrm{F} \vdash XZ \hookrightarrow YZ$.
(POFD3) *Transitivity*: if $\mathrm{F} \vdash X \hookrightarrow Y$ and $\mathrm{F} \vdash Y \hookrightarrow Z$, then $\mathrm{F} \vdash X \hookrightarrow Z$.
(POFD4) *Permutation*: if $\mathrm{F} \vdash X \hookrightarrow Y$, $W \sim X$ and $Z \sim Y$, then $\mathrm{F} \vdash W \hookrightarrow Z$.

We remark that POFD4 is introduced because we are dealing with sequences of attributes rather than the usual sets of attributes in FDs.

Theorem 1. The axiom system comprising from POFD1 to POFD4 is sound and complete for POFDs.

(*Proof Outline*). The underlying idea in this proof is standard [14]. We need the notion of the closure of a set of attributes X^+ in the context of POFDs, which is given by $X^+ = \{A \mid \mathrm{F} \vdash \mathrm{X} \hookrightarrow \mathrm{A}\}$. We also need to assume that each domain has at least two distinct elements, say, $0 < 1$. It is easy to show that the inference rules from POFD1 to POFD4 are sound. The completeness can be proved by showing that if $\mathrm{F} \nvdash X \hookrightarrow Y$, then $\mathrm{F} \not\models X \hookrightarrow Y$. We exhibit a relation given in Figure 2 to show that $r \models \mathrm{F}$ but $r \not\models X \hookrightarrow Y$. □

	X^+	Z
t_1	$1 \cdots 1$	$1 \cdots 1$
t_2	$1 \cdots 1$	$0 \cdots 0$

Fig. 2. A relation r showing that $r \not\models X \hookrightarrow Y$

4.2 OFDs Arising from Lexicographical Orderings

We give the definition of a LOFD as follows.

Definition 11. (Ordered Functional Dependency Arising from Lexicographical Orderings) An *ordered functional dependency arising from lexicographical orderings* (or simply a LOFD) over a relation schema R, is a statement of the form $R : X \rightsquigarrow Y$ (or simply $X \rightsquigarrow Y$ whenever R is understood from the context), $X, Y \subseteq R$ are sequences of attributes.

Similar to POFDs, we assume that all LOFDs are standard. We now give the definition of the semantics of a LOFD.

Definition 12. (Satisfaction of a LOFD) A LOFD, $R : X \rightsquigarrow Y$, is satisfied in a relation r over R, denoted by $r \models X \rightsquigarrow Y$, if for all $t_1, t_2 \in r$, $t_1[X] \leq_X t_2[X]$ implies that $t_1[Y] \leq_Y t_2[Y]$, where $\leq_X$ and $\leq_Y$ are the lexicographical orderings on the Cartesian product of the domains of X and Y, respectively.

We observe that the concept of POFDs and LOFDs are incomparable. The following example helps to illustrate this point.

$r_1 =$

A	B	C
1	3	6
2	4	5

(a)

$r_2 =$

A	B	C
1	4	6
2	3	5

(b)

Fig. 3. Relations r_1 and r_2 showing that POFDs and LOFDs are incomparable.

Example 1. Consider the relations r_1 and r_2 over $R = \{A, B, C\}$ shown in Figure 3. It is clear that in (a) $r_1 \models A \rightsquigarrow BC$ but $r_1 \not\models A \hookrightarrow BC$. On the other hand, in (b) $r_2 \models AB \hookrightarrow C$ but $r_2 \not\models AB \rightsquigarrow C$.

The chase is a fundamental theorem proving tool in relational database theory [9]. We now extend the classical chase defined over conventional relations with respect to FDs [9,3] to ordered relations with respect to LOFDs. The extended chase will be used as a sound and complete inference tool for LOFDs in Theorem 2. We need two operations, *equate* and *swap*, to manipulate values in ordered domains before presenting our chase rules.

Definition 13. (Equate and Swap Operations) We denote $min(a, b)$ and $max(a, b)$ the minimum and maximum of the values a and b, respectively. For any two distinct tuples $t_1, t_2 \in r$ over R and some $A \in R$, the *equate* of t_1 and t_2 on A, denoted as *equate*($t_1[A]$, $t_2[A]$), is defined by replacing both $t_1[A]$ and $t_2[A]$ by $min(t_1[A], t_2[A])$; the *swap* of t_1 and t_2 on A, denoted as *swap*($t_1[A]$, $t_2[A]$), is defined by replacing $t_1[A]$ by $min(t_1[A], t_2[A])$ and $t_2[A]$ by $max(t_1[A], t_2[A])$, respectively.

We now give the chase rules, which are applied to two tuples in a relation with respect to a set of LOFDs.

Definition 14. (Chase Rules for LOFDs) Let t_1 and t_2 be two tuples in r such that $t_1[X] \leq_X t_2[X]$ but $t_1[Y] \not\leq_Y t_2[Y]$, A be the first attribute in X such that $t_1[A] \neq t_2[A]$, if such an attribute exists, and B be the first attribute in Y such that $t_1[B] \neq t_2[B]$, then the *chase rules* for the LOFD $X \rightsquigarrow Y$, is defined by the following two rules:

Equate rule: if $t_1[X] = t_2[X]$ but $t_1[B] \neq t_2[B]$, then *equate*($t_1[B], t_2[B]$);

Swap rule: if $t_1[A] < t_2[A]$ but $t_2[B] < t_1[B]$, then *swap*($t_1[B], t_2[B]$), or if $t_2[A] < t_1[A]$ but $t_1[B] < t_2[B]$, then *swap*($t_1[A], t_2[A]$).

The said chase rules cater for all the possible cases when there are two tuples in a relation violating $X \rightsquigarrow Y$. In applying the chase rules we need a fixed ordering on the tuples t_1 and t_2. We will show in Lemma 1 that under such a condition the chase procedure always terminates.

Let $r = \{t_1, \ldots, t_n\}$ be an ordered relation over R and F be a set of LOFDs with $\mid R \mid= m$. We now give the pseudo-code of an algorithm designated $CHASE(r,\text{F})$, which applies the chase rules given in Definition 14 to R as long as possible and returns the resulting relation r over R, also denoted as $CHASE(r,\text{F})$.

Algorithm 1 ($CHASE(r, \text{F})$)

```
begin
    Result := r = ⟨t_1, ..., t_n⟩ ;
    Tmp:= ∅;
    while Tmp ≠ Result do
        Tmp := Result;
        if ∃X ⇝ Y ∈ F, ∃ t_p, t_q ∈ Result such that
        t_p[X] ≤_X t_q[X] but t_p[Y] ≰_Y t_q[Y] then
        Apply the appropriate chase rule to Result with
        t_1 = t_min(p,q) and t_2 = t_max(p,q);
    end while
    return Result;
end.
```

Lemma 1. $CHASE(r,\mathrm{F})$ in Algorithm 1 terminates and satisfies F.
(*Proof Outline.*) Let P_j with $1 \leq j \leq m$ be the sequence $\langle a_{1j}, \ldots, a_{nj} \rangle$, where $a_{ij} = t_i[A_j]$ (i.e., $P_j = \pi_{A_j}(Result)$), a_j^{min} be the minimum value in P_j, and P_j^{min} be the sequence $\langle a_j^{min}, \ldots, a_j^{min} \rangle$ (a sequence of n identical values). Suppose an application of a chase rule changes P_j to $P'_j = \langle a'_{1j}, \ldots, a'_{nj} \rangle$. Since the chase rules neither change the value a_j^{min} nor introduce any new values into the variable *Result*, P_j^{min} is unchanged throughout the process of the chase. It is shown that $P_j^{min} \leq_{lex} P'_j <_{lex} P_j$, where $\leq_{lex}$ is a lexicographical ordering. It follows that $CHASE(r,\mathrm{F})$ satisfies F, otherwise $CHASE(r,\mathrm{F})$ has not yet terminated, violating the assumption. □
Lemma 2. $CHASE(r,\mathrm{F})$ in Algorithm 1 can be computed in time polynomial in the size of r and F. □

We note that the result of the chase is not necessarily unique. However, we still can apply it in tackling the implication problem of LOFDs. This point is illustrated by the results shown in next theorem and Theorem 3.
Theorem 2. Let r be a relation over R and F be a set of LOFDs over R. Then $r \models \mathrm{F}$ if and only if $r = CHASE(r,\mathrm{F})$.
Proof.
(*IF:*) Assume to the contrary that $r \not\models \mathrm{F}$ and thus there exists a LOFD, $X \rightsquigarrow Y \in$ F such that $r \not\models X \rightsquigarrow Y$. It follows that there must be two rows, $t_1, t_2 \in r$, such that $t_1[X] \leq_X t_2[X]$ but $t_1[Y] \not\leq_Y t_2[Y]$; so the chase rule for $X \rightsquigarrow Y$ can be applied to r resulting in a different relation. Hence $r \neq CHASE(r, F)$.

(*ONLY IF:*) It follows from Definition 14 that a chase rule for F can be carried out only if r violates some LOFD in F. □
Lemma 1 and Theorem 2 are fundamental because they allow the chase procedure to be employed to test the satisfaction of r with respect to F in a finite number of steps. In order to provide a proof procedure for LOFDs, we now define the notion of *ordered variables*. Such variables afford us the ability to infer orderings between attribute values and to set up a set of *templates for relations.*

Definition 15. (Ordered Variables and Variable Domain) The *variable domain* of a relation schema R, denoted by $vdom(R)$, is the finite set $\{l_1, \ldots, l_m, h_1, \ldots, h_m\}$, where $m = \mid R \mid$. The variables l_i and h_i with $i \in \{1, \ldots, m\}$ are called *low ordered variables* and *high ordered variables*, respectively. We call them collectively *ordered variables*, whose ordering is given by $l_i < h_i$.

We now define a set of relations defined over variable domains with respect to a given LOFD, which basically enumerate all the possible cases for two tuples violating the LOFD.

Definition 16. (Template Relations for a LOFD) Let f be the LOFD $X \rightsquigarrow Y$ over R with $\mid X \mid= n$ and $\mid R \mid= m$. We use two short hand symbols u_i and v_i to represent one of the following three cases: (1) $u_i = l_i$ and $v_i = l_i$, (2) $u_i = l_i$ and $v_i = h_i$ or (3) $u_i = h_i$ and $v_i = l_i$. A *template relation* (or simply a template) with respect to f, denoted as r_f, is a relation consisting of two tuples, t_1 and t_2, whose underlying domain is $vdom(R)$, such that it is equal to either T_0 or T_k, where $Pre(X) = \langle x_1, \dots, x_k \rangle$ for $1 \leq k \leq n$.

$$T_0 = \begin{array}{|c|c|c|} \hline & X & R-X \\ \hline t_1 & l_1 \cdots l_n & u_{n+1} \cdots u_m \\ t_2 & l_1 \cdots l_n & v_{n+1} \cdots v_m \\ \hline \end{array} \qquad T_k = \begin{array}{|c|c|c|c|} \hline & x_1 \cdots x_{k-1} & x_k & R-Pre(X) \\ \hline t_1 & l_1 \cdots l_{k-1} & l_k & u_{k+1} \cdots u_m \\ t_2 & l_1 \cdots l_{k-1} & h_k & v_{k+1} \cdots v_m \\ \hline \end{array}$$

Fig. 4. Template relations for a LOFD

We remark that in Definition 16 the symbols u_i and v_i represent three possibilities of combinations of l_i and h_i. Therefore, it is easy to verify that there are 3^{m-n} templates defined by T_0 and 3^{m-k} templates defined by T_k for each k. Altogether there are $\frac{3^m+3^{m-n}}{2}$ templates. Note that there are some redundant templates in both T_0 and T_k, if we take into account the fact that there are two possible orderings for t_1 and t_2, but this does not affect the order of the upper bound of the number of templates, which is shown to be $O(3^m)$.

We apply the chase rules to a template relation using the ordering defined on a variable domain $vdom(R)$. The following proposition gives the result corresponding to Theorem 2.

Proposition 1. Let r_f be a template relation over R and F be a set of LOFDs over R. Then $r_f \models$ F if and only if $r_f = CHASE(r_f, F)$. □

A template relation can be viewed as a relation instance consisting of two tuples by using an ordering isomorphism mapping values in D to low ordered variables and high ordered variables, respectively. We formalise this idea by the following definition.

Definition 17. (Valuation Mapping) Let $R = \{A_1, \dots, A_m\}$ and $vdom(R)$ $= \{l_1, \dots, l_m, h_1, \dots, h_m, \}$. A *valuation mapping* ρ is a mapping from $vdom(R)$ to D such that $\rho(l_i) < \rho(h_i)$ for all $1 \leq i \leq m$. We extend ρ to a tuple t by $\rho(t) = \langle \rho(t[A_1]), \dots, \rho(t[A_m]) \rangle$. We also extend ρ to a template relations r_f by $\rho(r_f) = \{\rho(t_1), \rho(t_2)\}$.

The next proposition states that if there is a valuation mapping relating a template relation to a relation having two tuples, then they satisfy the same set of LOFDs.

Proposition 2. Let $\rho(r_f) = r$, where r is a relation over R having two tuples. Then $r_f \models X \rightsquigarrow Y$ if and only if $r \models X \rightsquigarrow Y$. □

We now extend the notion of tableaux for a LOFD f to be a set of templates. The tableaux in our case is different from that for FDs, which just requires a single template for FDs (see Theorem 4.2 in [3]). We define *tableaux*, denoted by T_f, to be the set of all template relations in Definition 16.

Definition 18. (Satisfaction and a Valuation Mapping of Tableaux) The chase of T_f, denoted as $CHASE(T_f, F)$, is defined by $CHASE(T_f, F) = \{CHASE(r_f, F) \mid r_f \in T_f\}$. $CHASE(T_f, F)$ satisfies $X \leadsto Y$, denoted by $CHASE(T_f, F) \models X \leadsto Y$, if for all $r_f \in T_f$, $CHASE(r_f, F) \models X \leadsto Y$. Furthermore, $CHASE(T_f, F)$ satisfies F, denoted by $CHASE(T_f, F) \models$ F, if for all $X \leadsto Y \in$ F, $CHASE(T_f, F) \models X \leadsto Y$. A valuation mapping of T_f is a valuation mapping of some r_f in T_f.

The following theorem shows that the chase rules can be also viewed as a sound and complete inference procedure for LOFDs.

Theorem 3. Let F be a set of LOFDs over R and f be a LOFD $X \leadsto Y$. Then $CHASE(T_f, F) \models f$ if and only if F $\models f$.

Proof.

(*IF:*) Assume $CHASE(T_f, F) \not\models f$. By Definition 18, there exists $r_f \in T_f$ such that $CHASE(r_f, F) \not\models f$ but $CHASE(r_f, F) \models$ F. Note that $CHASE(r_f, F)$ is a template which can be viewed as an instance. Therefore, we have a valuation mapping ρ to generate a relation instance $\rho(CHASE(r_f, F))$ and by Proposition 2, $\rho(CHASE(r_f, F)) \models$ F but $\rho(CHASE(r_f, F)) \not\models f$. This leads to a contradiction.

(*ONLY IF:*) We let w_1, w_2 be any two tuples in a relation r such that $w_1 \leq_X w_2$. We claim $w_1 \leq_Y w_2$. Let $s_f \in T_f$ be the template relation such that $\rho(t_1) = w_1$ and $\rho(t_2) = w_2$. We can always find such an s_f because T_f exhausts all possibilities of two tuples which satisfy the condition $w_1 \leq_X w_2$. Thus we have $\rho(s_f) = \{w_1, w_2\}$ and $\rho(s_f) \models$ F. By Proposition 2, we have $s_f \models$ F. It follows by Proposition 1 that $s_f = CHASE(s_f, F)$. Since we have assumed that $CHASE(T_f, F) \models f$, we have $CHASE(s_f, F) \models f$. Thus, $\rho(CHASE(T_f, F)) = \rho(s_f) = \{w_1, w_2\}$, which implies that $w_1 \leq_Y w_2$ as required. □

The following corollary is an immediate result of Theorem 3. It shows that the chase rules together with tableaux can be used to provide a systematic way to solve the implication problem for LOFDs.

Corollary 1. Let F be a set of LOFDs over R. The chase procedure is a decidable, sound and complete inference algorithm for LOFDs.

5 Concluding Remarks

We have extended the relational data model to incorporate linearly ordered domains. Within the extended model, we defined ordered databases in which we introduced OFDs. We have studied the implication problems of OFDs, which are classified into two categories, POFDs and LOFDs, according to whether they arise from pointwise-orderings or lexicographical orderings on the Cartesian products of underlying domains. In the special case of unary OFDs, these two categories are identical. We presented a sound and complete axiom system for

POFDs in Theorem 1. We also presented a set of sound and complete chase rules for LOFDs in Definition 14, which can be employed as a theorem proving tool for LOFDs, as indicated in Theorem 3.

Finally, we compare the satisfaction of an OFD in ordered databases introduced in this paper as the diagram given in Figure 5. We let $SAT(f)$ be a set of database instances that satisfy a data dependency f, and $f_1 = X \rightarrow Y$, $f_2 = X \hookrightarrow Y$ and $f_3 = X \rightsquigarrow Y$. We remark that if X and Y are unary, then in general we have $SAT(f_2) = SAT(f_3)$.

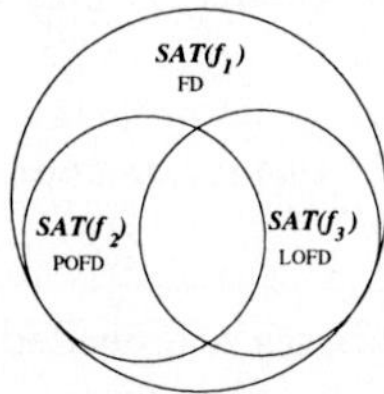

Fig. 5. Satisfaction of various OFDs in databases

References

1. S. Abiteboul and S. Ginsburg. Tuple Sequences and Lexicographical Indexes. *Journal of the Association for Computing Machinery* **33**(3), pp. 409-422 (1986).
2. W.W. Armstrong. Dependency Structures of Data Base Relationships. In *Proceedings of the IFIP Congress*, Stockholm, pp. 580-583, (1974).
3. P. Atzeni and V. De Antonellis. *Relational Database Theory.* Benjamin/Cummings Publishing Company, Inc., (1993).
4. P. Buneman, A. Jung and A. Ohori. Using Powerdomains to Generalise Relational Databases. *Theoretical Computer Science* **91**, pp. 23-55, (1991).
5. S. Ginsburg and R. Hull. Order Dependency in the Relational Model. *Theoretical Computer Science* **26**, pp. 129-195, (1983).
6. G. Gratzer. *General Lattice Theory.* NewYork: Academic Press, (1978).
7. L. Libkin. *Aspects of Partial Information in Databases.* Ph.D. Thesis, University of Pennsylvania, United States, (1996).
8. N.A. Lorentzos. DBMS Support for Time and Totally Ordered Compound Data Types. *Information Systems* **17**(5), pp. 347-358, (1992).
9. D. Maier, A.O. Mendelzon and Y. Sagiv. Testing Implication of Data Dependencies. *ACM Transactions on Database Systems* **4**, pp. 455-469, (1979).
10. D. Maier and B. Vance. A Call to Order, In *ACM symp. on Principles of Databases Systems*, pp. 1-16, (1993).
11. W. Ng and M. Levene. An Extension of OSQL to Support Ordered Domains in Relational Databases. In *IEEE Proceedings of the International Database Engineering and Applications Symposium*, Montreal, Canada, pp.358-367, (1997).
12. W. Ng and M. Levene. The Development of Ordered SQL Packages for Modelling Advanced Applications. In *LNCS 1308: DEXA '97 Conference, Proceedings,* Springer-Verlag, pp. 529-538, (1997).
13. P. Seshadri et al. The Design and Implementation of a Sequence Database System. *VLDB '96 Conference, Proceedings,* pp. 99-110, (1996).
14. J.D. Ullman. *Principles of Database and Knowledge-Base Systems, Vol. I,* Rockville, MD., Computer Science Press, (1988).

Building Consistent Sample Databases to Support Information System Evolution and Migration

Jesus Bisbal, Bing Wu, Deirdre Lawless, and Jane Grimson

Computer Science Department, Trinity College Dublin, Ireland

e-mail: *Firstname.Lastname*@cs.tcd.ie

Abstract. Prototype databases are needed in any information system development process to support data-intensive applications development. It is common practice to populate these databases using synthetic data. This data usually bears little relation to the application's domain and considers only a very reduced subset of the integrity constraints the database will hold during operation.

This paper claims that in situations where operational data is available, as is the case in information system evolution and migration, a sample of this data must be used to create a prototype database. The paper outlines a method for consistently sampling a database. This method uses a new concept, the Insertions Chain Graph, to assist in selecting instances so that the resulting Sample Database reaches a consistent state, a significant task of database sampling.

1 Introduction

When developing data-intensive applications there is a need to prototype the database that the applications will use during operation. Such a database can be used to support several stages of the development process [12]: (1) Validation of database and/or application requirements: different designs can be checked for completeness and correctness [10]. (2) User training: applications will need a database on which to operate with during training. (3) Testing: as is needed in, for example, system's functional test [4].

In this paper, the term Prototype Database refers to any database constructed to support the development of data-intensive applications. Common practice is to populate a Prototype Database with data from predefined domains (e.g. [10, 15, 11]) instead of using 'real' data. In addition, usually only a very reduced set of integrity constraints (hereafter constraints) that the database will actually hold during operation is considered (e.g. [2]). The resulting Prototype Databases cannot fully support the applications development process.

This paper presents an approach which proposes that existing operational data be used to construct Prototype Databases. This will result in Prototypes specific to the application's domain. In cases where a Prototype Database is a sample of operational data it will be called *Sample Database*. In contrast, a Prototype Database constructed from predefined domains will be called *Test Database*.

The Sampling method presented in this paper is being developed as part of the MILESTONE project, which is developing a methodology for legacy system migration. A Sample Database has been identified as essential to support the migration process [14].

The remainder of the paper is organised as follows. The next section provides a brief overview of related work. Section 3 states the problems consistently sampling a database can rise. Section 4 defines the concept of *Insertions Chain Graph*, required by the method outlined in Sect. 5. The final section summarises the paper and indicates a number of intended future directions for this research.

2 Related Work

Most of the work on Prototype Databases found in the literature is based on the construction of Test Databases. The general mechanism for test data generation involves inserting data values into the database and then testing-and-repairing this data by adding/deleting data so that it meets the specified constraints. Most solutions proposed for test data generation deal with a very reduced set of constraint types (e.g. [11, 15, 2]), tipically functional dependencies and inclusion dependencies only.

A notable exception is found in [10] where a subset of First-Order-Logic (FOL) is used to define the set of constraints that the generated test data must meet. However using an approach based on FOL the whole set of constraints must be explicitly uncovered, a non-trivial task when dealing with large databases. This set of constraints must then be expressed using a FOL language which can result in an obscure set of formulas. This set of formulas must be consistent, otherwise no database can satisfy this set of constraints. It is well-known that to prove consistency in FOL is a semi-decidable problem [6]. It is also necessary to perform some kind of logical inference in order to maintain consistency. Neufeld [10] proved that such approach does not scale.

A different approach is presented in [15]. This method firstly checks for the consistency of an Extended Entity-Relationship (EER) schema defined for the database being prototyped, considering cardinality constraints only. Once the design has been proved consistent, a Test Database is generated. To guide the generation process, a so-called general Dependency Graph is created from the EER diagram. This graph represents the set of referential integrity constraints that must hold in the database and is used to define a partial order between the entities of the EER diagram. The test data generation process populates the database entities following this partial order. Löhr-Richter [9] further develops the test data generation step used by this method, and recognises the need for additional information in order to generate application's domain relevant data.The most significant drawback of this approach is that it considers cardinality and referential integrity constraints only.

3 The Problem of Consistent Sample Database Extraction

This section outlines the main desirable properties to be satisfied by Prototype Databases and describes the issues involved in consistently sampling a database.

3.1 Properties of Prototype Databases

Considering the three uses of Prototype Databases, i.e. validation of requirements, user training and testing, such databases should satisfy two main properties:

P1. Faithfully represent operational data. For both user training and testing purposes, applications should be subjected to conditions as similar as possible to those which they will encounter during operation. Thus a Prototype Database must be 'similar' to the operational data. Testing will be more effective as errors which would otherwise have occurred after the applications were placed in production are more likely to be detected during testing.

To achieve good similarity with operational data, a Prototype Database must be constructed with two features in mind: (a) it must satisfy the same constraints as the operational data; and (b) it must include all the 'data-diversity' found in the operational data, i.e. not being restricted to only one consistent part of the database.

P2. Efficiently constructed. For requirements validation and testing purposes, several Prototype Databases may be required in order to test different possible designs, use different testing data, etc. Therefore the Prototype Database construction process should be efficient.

3.2 The Faculty Database Example

Fig. 1 shows a possible EER schema [3] for a Faculty Database example, which will be used throughout the paper to illustrate the sampling process. This database stores data about Courses, with Students who follow them and Lecturers who lecture these Courses. Every Course must have only one Lecturer, and a given Lecturer can teach several Courses. Each student must follow between two and eight Courses. The faculty is composed by Persons, which can be either Students or Lecturers. The entity Full Time Students represents a subset of Students, those that follow four or more Courses.

Fig. 2 represents a logical relational design[1] for the database example that could be developed from Fig. 1 (see [3]).

3.3 Challenges in the Database Sampling Process

The most important aspect to consider when sampling from an existing database regards the correctness of the resulting database. The Sample Database must be

[1] Primary keys are underlined and foreign keys marked with asterisk (*).

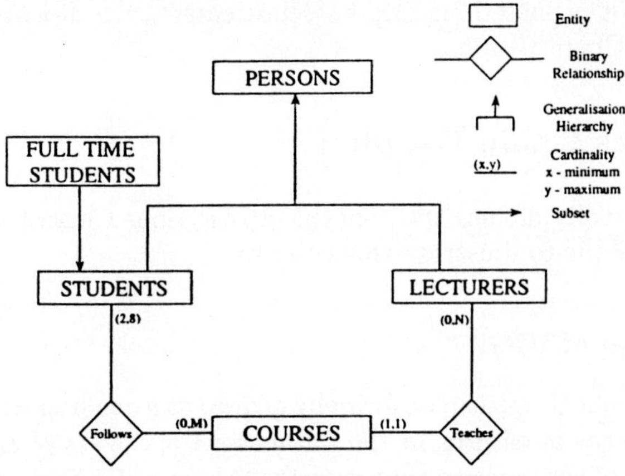

Fig. 1. Extended Entity-Relationship Schema for the Faculty Database

consistent with the same constraints held by the Source Database (term used to refer to the database being sampled). The extraction of such a sample requires knowledge about the set of constraints that the Sample must meet since this information is used to guide the sampling process. Therefore, the first challenge is to extract the set of constraints held by the database (There is a large body of research on database reverse-engineering, e.g. [8], while few database prototyping methods have been reported). This set of constraints is buried within both the database schema (hereafter, schema) and the applications.

Persons(IDPerson, Role, ...)
Students(IDStudent* REFERS TO Persons(IDPerson), ...)
Lecturers(IDLecturer* REFERS TO Persons(IDPerson), ...)
Courses(IDCourse, IDLecturer* REFERS TO Lecturers(IDLecturer), ...)
Follow(IDStudent* REFERS TO Students(IDStudent),
    IDCourse* REFERS TO Courses(IDCourse), ...)
FullTimeStudents(IDStudent* REFERS TO Students(IDStudent), ...)

Fig. 2. Logical Relational Design for the Faculty Database

The second challenge posed by consistent database sampling is that due to constraints the inclusion of one instance[2] in the Sample may require the inclusion of other instances[3] before the resulting Sample Database reaches a consistent

[2] Hereafter, terms *entity* and *instance* will be used in descriptions which do not refer to a concrete data model. Terms *table* and *tuple* will refer to the relational model used in the Faculty Database example.

[3] It is well known that updates must be propagated [7] to keep any database in a consistent state after any data manipulation. The same discipline also applies to the construction of a Sample Database.

state. This chain of insertions can be represented by a directed graph, called here Insertions Chain Graph.

4 Insertions Chain Graph

This section formally defines the concept of Insertions Chain Graph (ICG) and presents an example to illustrate this concept.

4.1 Definition of ICG

An Insertions Chain Graph can be formally defined as a quadruple ICG=(Q,I,T,δ), where: **Q** is the set of entities in the database; **I** is the set of arrow identifiers; and **T** is the set of arrow types that describe the type of consequence of inserting an instance into the Sample, as described in Table 1 (Partial arrows subsume all other arrow types. However, the other arrow types are kept because they simplify the resulting ICG). δ is the Insertions Function. For each entity in the

Arrow Type	Required Information	Semantics	Constraint Type
Total	None	One insertion in the target entity is required every time an instance is inserted into the source entity	Referential Integrity Constraints
Quantified	Number of additional instances	The specified number of refered intances must be present in the target entity after inserting the referring instance into the source entity	Cardinality Constaints
OR	Target Entity Names: P$\in 2^Q$, and Criterion to select between them	One instance must be inserted in (some of) the specified entities, after inserting one instance into the source entity	Generalisation Constarint
Partial	Condition	Only when the condition evaluates to true will the insertion be required	General Constraint

Table 1. Arrow Types in an Insertions Chain Graph

database, it describes the set of arrows in the ICG that start at this entity. It is defined as

$$\delta : Q \rightarrow 2^{I \times 2^Q \times T \times C} \tag{1}$$

and thus each arrow in the graph can be described by a quadruple: **<i, P, t, c>** where **i** $\in$ **I**, **P** $\in 2^Q$, **t** $\in$ **T**, and **c** $\in$ C = $\mathbb{N} \bigcup$ **Predicate** $\bigcup$ Selector-**Predicate**. **c** represents the additional information required for some arrow types, as detailed in Table 1. It must be interpreted in different ways depending on which arrow type it is associated to (see Sect. 4.2 for examples): (1) QUANTIFIED arrows: c $\in \mathbb{N}$; (2) PARTIAL arrows: c $\in$ **Predicate** must express a condition to be satisfied by the databases before a new insertion into the target entity is required. For each entity E in the database, there are two entity names that may appear in this predicate, Source-E and Sample-E, referring to this entity in the Source and Sample databases respectively. Using the Faculty Database example, and thus the relational model, the language used to express this predicate is assumed to be a well-formed SQL predicate (see [5] for a possible syntax of such a predicate); (3) TOTAL arrows: c has no meaning in this case; and (4) OR arrows: c $\in$ Selector-Predicate is a criterion to select which of the possible target entities a new instance must be inserted into. It consists of a list of predicates, defined as for Partial arrows, each one associated with an entity in the Sample Database. When a predicate evaluates to true, a new insertion into its associated entity will be required. The syntax to express this criterion is:

Selector-Predicate ::= **Predicate** $\rightarrow$ Name
|**Predicate** $\rightarrow$ Name, **Selector-Predicate**
Name ::= **Sample-*EntityName***

The rationale behind these four arrow types is that they are able to express much of a Source Database's semantics. The constraint type each arrow type expresses is shown in Table 1 in column Constraint Type.

4.2 Example of ICG

Fig. 3 represents an ICG that includes all semantics of the Faculty Database. Each node of this graph represents one table of the logical design (Fig. 2), and its edges represent database semantics relevant to the sampling process[4].

Arrows starting or ending at entity Persons represent the generalisation hierarchy shown in Fig. 1. A partial arrow from Students to Full Time Students ensures that the semantics of this entity are kept consistent, which also requires a quantified arrow from Full Time Students to Follow to ensure that all Full Time Students actually follow at least four courses. When a tuple from table Follow is sampled, related tuples from Course and Student tables must also be sampled. A quantified arrow from Students to Follow represents the fact that all students must follow at least two courses. Finally, since all Courses must have one lecturer, a total arrow is required from table Courses to Lecturers.

Table 2 contains the definition of all conditions used in Fig. 3. C_1 is associated with a partial arrow and thus it must return a boolean value. It queries the Sample Database to count how many courses a given student follows. If (s)he follows more than four courses (s)he is a full time student. C_2 is associated with an OR arrow and is used to decide whether a given person is a student or lecturer. It queries the Source Database and checks whether the identifier of a given person also appears in table Students or Lecturers (being x the identifier).

Instead of using a graphical representation, an ICG could also be described using its formal definition, in terms of a quadruple ICG=(Q,I,T,δ).

[4] Maximum cardinality constraints have not been represented as their absence cannot lead to an inconsistent Sample Database.

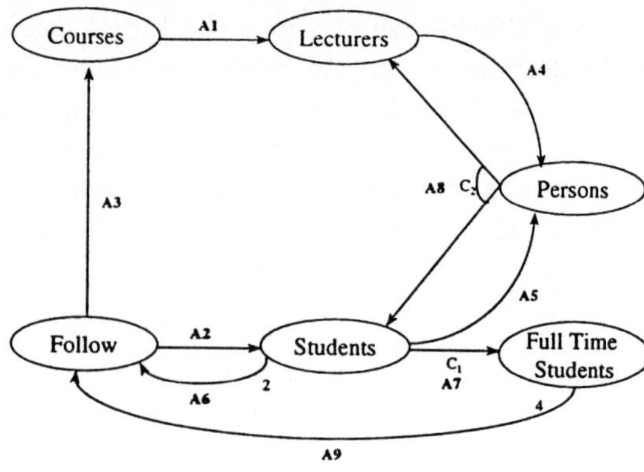

Fig. 3. (Complete) Insertion Chain Graph for the Faculty Database

4.3 Expressiveness of ICG

ICG can be seen as a language to express integrity constraints (it expresses the consequences of these constraints rather than the constraints themselves). As for any language, its expressiveness could be assessed [1]. Since it is based on the query language used by the Source Database, its expressiveness depends on that language. More precisely, the example given above is SQL-based, so its expressiveness is limited by the expressiveness of SQL (which is, in turn, a proper subset of FOL).

Condition Name	Definition
C_1	**Select** count(*) **From Sample**-Follow **Where** IDStudent = x) $\geq$ 4
C_2	**Exists (Select** IDLecturer **From Source**-Lecturers **Where** IDLecturer = x) $\rightarrow$ **Sample**-Lecturers, **Exists (Select** IDStudent **From Source**-Students **Where** IDStudent = x) $\rightarrow$ **Sample**-Students

Table 2. Conditions Table for the ICG Shown in Fig. 3

In spite of the fact that some constraints cannot be expressed (e.g. instance-based constraints), as is the case for any other language [1], ICG allows for the definition of a wide range of commonly used constraints.

5 Consistent Database Sampling Method

This section describes a method for consistently sampling a database based on the use of an ICG. For testing purposes it is commonly agreed that random sampling will lead to adequate test data [13]. For this reason tuples will be selected randomly[5] from the Source Database.

5.1 Algorithm

The following information is required as input to the sampling process:

1. Insertions Chain Graph for the database being sampled.
2. Minimum number of instances for each entity that should appear in the Sample Database. This information provides a condition to stop sampling.
3. The number of different entities that each entity points to and is pointed by in the ICG, referred to as Fan-out and Fan-in values (see *SelectEntity* below).

Fig. 4 outlines the algorithm for extracting a Sample Database consistent with an Insertions Chain Graph introduced as input parameter. In order to

```
/*NotFullEntities represents the set of entity names which still have not reached
the minimum number of instances in the Sample Database. Initially it would be
the set of entities with a minimum number greater than zero.
SampleDatabase represents the contents of the Sample Database being extracted.*/
begin
      while ¬ (NotFullEntities = ∅ ) do
            entity := SelectEntity (); /* Based on Fan-in and Fan-out values */
            instance := SampleInstance (entity); /* Randomly */
♣           InsertInstance(SampleDatabase,entity,instance,NotFullEntities);
♣                       /* It also modifies NotFullEntities */
♣           TargetEntities := ICG.δ(entity)|P;
♣                       /* Set of entities to be considered as */
♣                       /* a consequence of the current insertion*/
♣           for each target_entity ∈ TargetEntities do
♣               new_instance := SelectInstance ( target_entity, instance );
♣               KeepConsistent ( target_entity, new_instance, NotFullEntities );
♣           endfor
      endwhile
end
/* OUTPUT: SampleDatabase */
```

Fig. 4. Algorithm for Consistent Sample Database Extraction

simplify the description of the algorithm only those parameters essential to the meaning of each function call are shown.

[5] It must be decided which probability distribution to use. For simplicity, it can be used a uniform distribution. Another option is to use a so-called Operational Distribution [13], where instances frequently accessed when the database is in production will be more likely to become part of the Sample.

• *SelectEntity*: using the ICG, and restricted to the entities in *NotFullEntities*, select the entity with the biggest Fan-out value; if equal, select the entity with smallest Fan-in. If equal again, choose randomly. This heuristic aims to lead to the maximum possible consequences and additional insertions, which will keep the Sample Database consistent.

• *SampleInstance*: randomly samples an instance of the input entity.

• *InsertInstance*: inserts the sampled instance into the Sample Database. It also checks if this entity has already reached the minimum number of instances required in the Sample Database. If so, its name is removed from *NotFullEntities.*

• *ICG.δ(entity)*$|_P$: ICG.δ() is the Insertions Function, and $|_P$ denotes the restriction the resulting quadruple to its second element, P.

• *SelectInstance*: selects from the Source Database the appropriate instance of the *target_entity.* It must be an instance not yet in the Sample.

• *KeepConsistent*: (recursive function) The instance selected when calling to *SelectInstance* must be inserted into the Sample, and this insertion must also be kept consistent. This function implements the part of Fig. 4 marked with ♣.

The reader should note the randomness involved in function *SampleInstance.* Although the starting entity selected in *SelectEntity* is based on the ICG, in *SampleIntance* concrete instances are selected randomly from the Source Database. This procedure will, potentially, lead to the selection of all interesting portions of the Source Database, which refers back to Sect. 3.1, property P1(b).

5.2 Termination and Correctness

The termination of the alrgorithm shown in Fig. 4 can be guaranteed: (1) The outer loop terminates because the number of entities in the set *NotFullEntities* will decrease (function *InsertInstance*) as new instances are inserted into the Sample. Eventually, it becomes the empty set and the algorithm terminates. (2) The chain of recursive calls (function *KeepConsistent*) also terminates due to the workings of function *SelectInstance.* It ensures that infinite loops cannot be created because it only selects instances not yet in the Sample.

This algorithm is correct with regard to the set of constraints represented in the ICG given as input parameter: the Sample Database satisfies those constraints. The size of the resulting Sample is predefined by the user. Additional insertions may be required in order to satisfy the entire set of constraints.

6 Conclusions and Future Research

This paper has analysed the construction of databases used to support the development of database applications. A method for consistent Sample Database extraction has been developed based on an alternative representation of database constraints, the Insertions Chain Graph (ICG). This graph has been formally defined and its role in the sampling process clearly stated.

Future work will focus on adding new constructs to the language (ICG) so that it gains in expressiveness, particularly regarding to the limitations outlined in Sect. 4.3. As seen in Sect. 4.2 not all constraints need to be expressed in order to arrive at a consistent Sample. A characterisation of such constraints will be investigated. Another direction is concerned with the existence of a Minimal Insertions Chain Graph. That is, whether given an ICG an 'equivalent' ICG may be constructed such that it has the minimum possible number of arrows, without omitting any constraint. A minimal ICG will allow for a more efficient sampling process, because only those arrows that actually lead to additional insertions in the Sample Database would be part of the graph.

References

[1] S. Abiteboul and V. Vianu. *Theoretical Studies in Computer Science*, chapter Expressive Power of Query Languages, pages 207–251. Academic Press, 1992.

[2] C. Bates, I. Jelly, and J. Kerridge. Modelling test data for performace evaluation of large parallel database machines. *Distributed and Parallel Databases*, pages 5–23, January 1996.

[3] C. Batini, S. Ceri, and S. B. Navathe. *Conceptual Database Design: an Entity-Relationship Approach.* The Benjamin/Cummings Publishing Company, 1992.

[4] B. Beizer. *Software Testing Techniques.* Van Nostrand Reinhold, second edition, 1990.

[5] S. Ceri and J. Widom. Deriving production rules for constraint maintenance. In *Proceedings of the 16th Very Large Databases Conference*, pages 566–577, 1990.

[6] A. Church. An unsolvable problem of elementary number theory. *American Journal of Mathematics*, 58:345–363, 1936.

[7] C. J. Date. *An Introduction to Database Systems.* Addison-Wesley Publishing Company, 1990.

[8] J-L. Hainaut, J. Henrard, J-M. Hick, D. Roland, and V. Englebert. Database design recovery. In *Proceedings 8th Conference on Advanced Information Systems Engineering (CAiSE'96)*, volume 1250 of *Lecture Notes in Computer Science*, pages 272–300. Springer-Verlag, May 1996.

[9] P. Lohr-Richter and A. Zamperoni. Validating database components of software systems. Technical Report 94–24, Leiden University, Department of Computer Science, 1994.

[10] A. Neufeld, G. Moerkotte, and P. C. Lokemann. Generating consistent test data: Restricting the search space by a generator formula. *VLDB Journal*, 2(2):173–213, April 1993.

[11] H. Noble. The automatic generation of test data for a relational database. *Information Systems*, 8(2):79–86, 1983.

[12] I. Sommerville. *Software Engineering.* Addison-Wesley, fifth edition, 1995.

[13] E. J. Weyuker and B. Jeng. Analyzing partition testing techniques. *IEEE Transactions on Software Engineering*, 17(7):703–711, July 1991.

[14] B. Wu, D. Lawless, J. Bisbal, R. Richardson, J. Grimson, V. Wade, and D. O'Sullivan. The butterfly methodology: A gateway-free approach for migrating legacy information systems. In *Proceedings of the 3rd IEEE Conference on Engineering of Complex Computer Systems*, pages 200–205, 1997.

[15] A. Zamperoni and P. Lohr-Richter. Enhancing the quality of conceptual database specifications through validation. In *Proceedings of the 12th International Conference on Entity-Relationship Approach*, volume 823 of *Lecture Notes in Computer Science*, pages 85–98. Springer-Verlag, 1993.

Process Centred Approach for Developing Tool Support of Situated Methods

Carine Souveyet, Mustapha Tawbi

CRI - Université Paris 1 - Sorbonne90, rue de Tolbiac. 75013 Paris - France

{souveyet, tawbi}@univ-paris1.fr

Abstract : A reuse based approach to construct software tool supporting a specific method built « on the fly » is presented in this paper. Its originality is to apply a process view on the reusable component which is either method chunk or software chunk. Our process view leads to construct method and software tool by assembling chunks. Chunks which are either method or software ones can be assembled in different ways depending on the situation of the project at hand. One of these ways is called a method or a software path. Our aim is to support the construction of a specific method path and its use in a CASE environment. The paper focuses on (i) the description of a process centred approach for software tool development (ii) its use in the development of the tool « l'écritoire » .

1 Introduction

Reuse is nowadays a way of working which applies in many situations. Reuse was initially introduced by the software engineering community [1] in order to avoid repetitions in coding. As a technique, reuse was introduced in object oriented programming languages through concepts such as class, class template and inheritance.

However, reuse has crossed the boundaries of programming and demonstrates its effectiveness in most of the steps of the system development life cycle. In fact it is argued that the effectiveness of reuse is increased in the early stages of the software development. Following this line reuse is introduced in domain analysis [6,7], [8] with the purpose of capturing and storing domain knowledge in a domain knowledge base. Reuse of this domain knowledge facilitates eliciting the requirements imposed to the system to be developed. Reuse based approaches have been recently introduced in the Information System Engineering (ISE) community [3] [2] [5] to construct methods « on the fly » by assembling method chunks stored in a method base. The aim in this case is to avoid the use of a method which is inappropriate to the situation of the project at hand. Reuse is combined with capitalisation of chunks of good practice and constitutes a means to benefit from past experiences in a given project.

In the context of the CREWS[1] project, we have defined a collection of method chunks to support elicitation of requirement engineering (RE) by coupling goal modelling and scenario authoring [12] [13]. These chunks can be assembled in different ways depending on the situation of the RE project at hand. We will refer to one of this way as a method path. The aim of the project is complementarily to support the construction of a specific path and its use in a CASE environment. In order to fulfil this objective we developed a process centred approach for software tool development which is the subject of this paper. We associate to each method chunk a software chunk and by analogy with the notion of method path we view the software tool as a path among software chunks. For each specific situation, one of the predefined path can be reused or a new one can be constructed by assembling the predefined software chunks. A software chunk is a module which is composed of two parts : a body which codes the method guidelines and an interface which defines the adaptation parameters. We shall see that its use requires two types of parameter : the method related ones to ensure method chunks (MC) coupling and the technical ones to ensure he interoperability of the tool with the technical environment in which it functions.

2 The notions of method chunk and method path

2.1 Method chunk

The notions of a method chunk and method path are presented in section 2 whereas the corresponding notions of software chunk and software path are developed in section 3. Section 4 presents the current implementation of « L'écritoire », the prototype implementing the CREWS situated method. Finally, some conclusive remarks are made in section 5.

A *method chunk* is a reusable component embedding guidelines to achieve a specific intention (or goal). As shown in figure 1, a method chunk has an interface and a body.

The chunk interface is a pair <situation, intention>. The situation is the part of the product required as a pre-requisite for the fulfilment of the intention. The intention is the goal to be achieved in that particular situation. For example the following interface <situation=(*Goal* : *g*) intention=*Elicit scenario using CREWS authoring guidelines*> expresses the fact that a *Goal* is a required product part for achieving the intention to elicit a *Scenario*. The interface <situation=(*Scenario* : *s*), intention=*verify scenario by checking the vocabulary*> characterises a method chunk to guide the *verification of a scenario by checking the vocabulary* which is applicable in a situation where a *scenario* has been already elicited. As shown by these two examples, the interface of a method chunk situates its context of application. The body chunk contains the guidelines to be applied when the chunk actually used. For capturing a large range of guidelines, the body is either formal or informal.

---

[1] This partly funded by the Basic Research Action CREWS (ESPRIT n°21.903). CREWS stands for Cooperative Requirement Engineering With Scenarios.

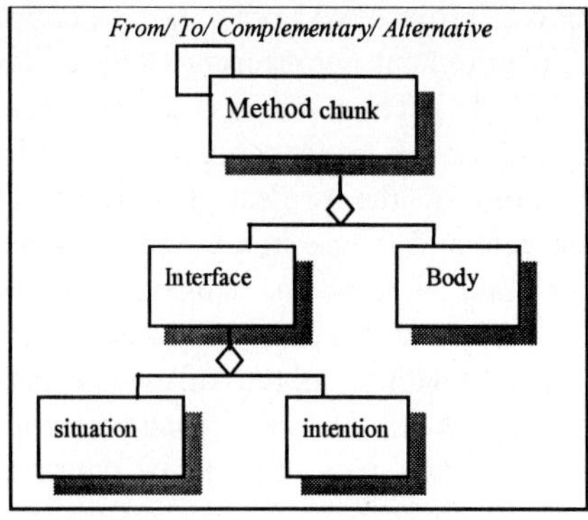

Fig. 1. Content of a method chunk.

The former implies to define guidelines as proposed by the Nature process formalism [9] [4]. Detailed examples of such a description can be found in [Rolland 96], [14]. The latter describes guidelines in natural language.

In addition to facilitate the selection of a chunk when constructing a situated path a method chunk includes contextual information. These are expressed (see figure 1) by three types of relationships *from/to, alternative and complementary.*

The *from/to* relationships indicates chunks which can be used before or after a given chunk. For example, <situation=(*Scenario : s*), intention=*verify scenario by using linguistic completion rules*> may be preceded by a chunk analysing the semantics of a scenario content. The interface of the chunk is as follows :

< situation=(*Scenario : s*), intention=*analyse scenario semantics with a linguistic case grammar*>. Therefore, a *from* relationship is used to connect the first chunk(*verify*) to the second one (*analyse*) and a *to* relationship is used to related the « *analyse* » chunk to the « *verify* » chunk.

The *alternative* and *complementary* relationships allow to classify method chunks achieving the same goal with different manners. For example, « *elicit scenario in full prose* », « *elicit scenario with template* » and « *elicit scenario by using CREWS authoring guidelines* » are three chunks with the same goal (*write a scenario*) but several manners to achieve the goal. The first chunk supports a free text approach whereas the second constraints its user a template text approach and the last one promotes an intermediate approach with authoring guidelines.

A *complementary* relationship is used between two chunks when their ways of achieving the same goal are complementary. For example, « *Verify scenario by checking the scenario vocabulary* », « *verify scenario by using linguistic completion rules* » and « *verify scenario by disambiguating anaphoric references* » are complementary manners to verifying a scenario. These chunks can be used in the same method in order to achieve scenario verification. Consequently, *complementary way* relationships can be used between these three chunks.

2.2 Method path

A method path is based on the distinction between two types of method chunks : step chunk and flow chunk (figure 2). The former helps in the satisfaction of an intention impacting the product under development whereas the latter helps in selecting the next intention to make the process proceed. In this view, we consider a process as being intentional. The process performance is a route between steps that we called the process flow. Steps achieve intentions and result in product transformation whereas the flow represents the sequence of intentions that have been considered [15]. Our claim is that a method must support the engineer by providing guidelines to both help fulfilling an intention and selecting the most appropriate intention to be achieved in the next step.

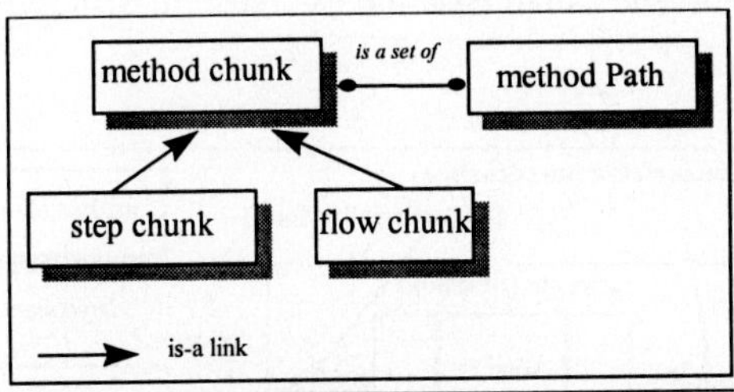

Fig. 2. Method path definition.

As illustrated in the previous example a *step chunk* supports the fulfilment of an intention in a specific situation. For example, <situation=(*Goal : g*), intention=*elicit scenario using CREWS authoring guidelines*>.

A *flow chunk* guides the progression in the process. The chunk <situation=(*Scenario : s / state(s)=conceptualised*), intention= *progress by goal discovery strategy*> is a flow chunk which provides guidelines to select a way of progressing from a step where a scenario has been conceptualised. The different ways for progressing proposed by a chunk all followed the same strategy, namely a goal discovery strategy.

A *method path* is defined by a collection of step and flow chunks. For instance, the method path associated to the intention « Author a scenario specification » is defined by a collection of steps :

<(Goal :g), elicit scenario by using CREWS authoring guidelines>, <(Scenario :s), analyse scenario semantic with a linguistic case grammar>, <(Scenario : s), verify scenario by checking terminology>, <(Scenario : s), verify scenario by using linguistic completion rules>,<(Scenario : s), verify scenario by disambiguating anaphoric references>,<(Scenario : s), conceptualise scenario>.

and a collection of flows

(<(Scenario s / state(s)=elicited), progress by analysing its semantic>, <(Scenario s / state(s)=elicited), progress by applying a verification strategy>, (Scenario s / state(s)=elicited), progress by conceptualising it>).

3 The notions of Software chunk and Software path

3.1 Software chunk (SC)

A method chunk is implemented in a software chunk (see figure 3). A software chunk is reused when a new method path has been conceived and required to be implemented in a tool environment. In order to minimise the activity of reusing software chunk we propose to package its code according to a predefined template presented in figure 3.

The template has been designed in order to make the software code inter-operable with different product managers. Indeed a software chunk manipulates product parts and it is important to make its code as independent as possible of a particular product manager. This independence shall ease the SC reuse in different repository managers and/or DBMS.

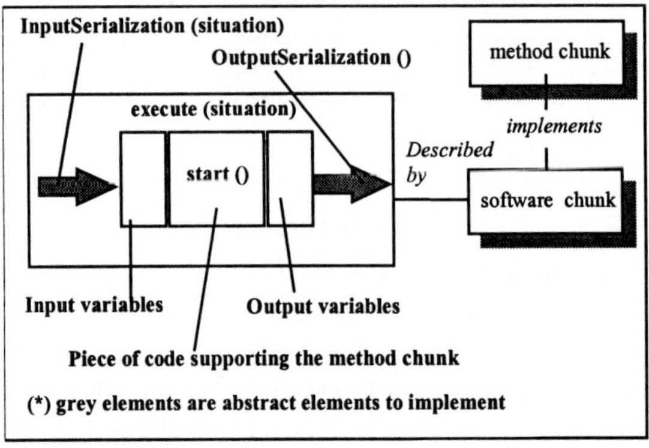

Fig. 3. Template of a software chunk.

In order to fulfil this inter-operability goal, the template separates the body of the software chunk from its input and output variables.

Input and Output variables correspond to the product parts which are used as inputs and outputs of the chunk body. Complementarily, the *InputSerialization* and *OutputSerialization* procedures are required to map the product structure as managed by the product manager into the variables format adapted to the SC body. The *InputSerialization* procedure allows to initialise the input variables from the « product manager » whereas the *OutputSerialization* procedure aims at transferring the output variables to the « product manager ». These two procedures are abstract procedures which are not implemented in the software chunk but must be developed when the chunk is reused. The body of the software chunk is an abstract module as it is shown in figure 3. This abstract module is defined as follows :

- the definition of variables which are local to the software chunk,
- the signature and the code of the procedure *execute (<situation>)*. The situation given as input parameter is the situation of the related method chunk,

- the signature and the code of the function *start*() returning a boolean expressing if the goal of the related method chunk is achieved or not,
- the signature of the two abstract procedures *OutputSerialization* (), *InputSerialization (<situation>)*. The situation given as input parameter is the situation of the related method chunk,

Invocation of the function *execute* provokes the SC execution. This includes the execution of the *InputSerialization* procedure, the *start* function and the *OutputSerialization* procedure when the intention assigned to the method chunk has been achieved. The function start is used to return a boolean value telling if the chunk has been completely executed and thus if the intention has been achieved.

3.2 Software path

A software path implements a method path. Therefore it is composed of a collection of software flow chunks and software step chunks. The former define possible orderings of the latter. A software path is realised by including in every step chunk the invocation of the flow chunk which corresponds to the possible way of progressing from this step. In order to guide the software engineer in the realisation of the path, we propose the template presented in figure 4.

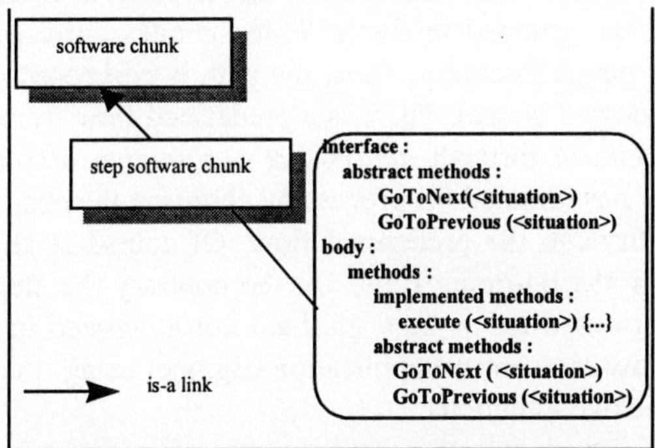

Fig. 4. Definition of a step software chunk.

The template shows that we propose to overload the *execute* function of every step chunk. This corresponds to two abstract procedures *goToNext*() and *goToPrevious*(). These two procedures will have to be implemented by the software engineer. The *goToNext* procedure invokes the flow chunk supporting the selection of the next step intention whereas the *goToPrevious* procedure permits backtracking to the previous step. The former corresponds to the normal process proceeding. The latter occurs when the performance of the step chunk has been aborted. These two procedures are abstract because the step software chunk must be independent of what it is performed before or after it. Their implementations are made when the software chunk has to be customised according to the software path it is reused.

We are going to illustrate the use of this component-based approach for designing the software tool named « l'écritoire ».

4 Illustration of one CREWS method path in *L'écritoire* software tool

Figure 5 visualises one of the CREWS method paths which is implemented in the software prototype called « l'écritoire ».

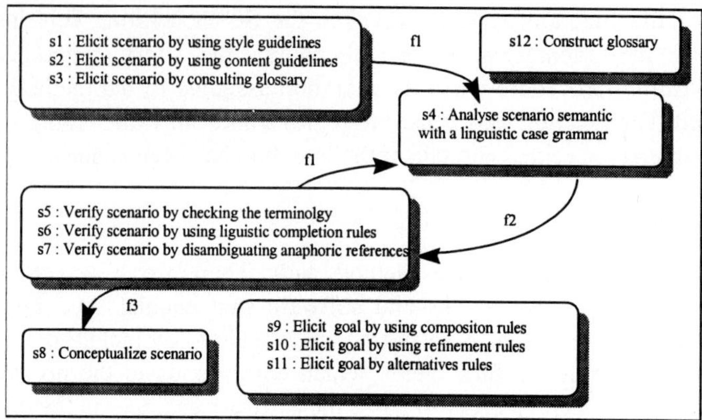

Fig. 5. Example of method paths.

The path is composed of twelve step chunks and three flow chunks (f1, f2, f3). For sake of readability, we grouped in figure 5 step chunks corresponding to different ways of fulfilling a single intention. Thus, the path is composed of, sort to speak, 6 macro steps (in shadowed boxes). There is a predefined flow from the *elicit scenario* to *conceptualise scenario* through *analysis & verification of scenarios*. When the application engineer has initiated the process by choosing the elicit scenario intention, he will be guided through the predefined flow. Of course at any moment, he can decide to not follow the on-going flow. On the contrary the steps to *construct the glossary* and the various ways to *elicit goal* are not integrated in a predefined flow. This means that at any moment the application engineer using l'écritoire may decide to select any of these two intentions.

The programming environment we have chosen to explore the framework and to implement l'écritoire in Visual Basic. The product manager we have selected is Access DBMS because of its inter-operability with Visual Basic. The product handled by the method path shown in figure 5 is described by the following set of schema relations :

Verb (name)
Object (name)
Actor(name)
RC (sid, RcName, goal, manner, type, LNText, semanticPatterns, state)
Action (sid, actid, actionType)
Flow (sid, actid, flowType, flowcondition, action1, action2)
Atomic (sid, actid, verb, from, to, parameter, text)

The software chunks of this software path have been adapted to this product manager. It means that *InputSerialization* and *OutputSerialization* procedures of each software chunk have been implemented in order to get (resp. to transfer) product parts from (resp. to) the product manager. It implies the implementation of the *GoToNext* and *GoToPrevious* procedures of each step chunk.

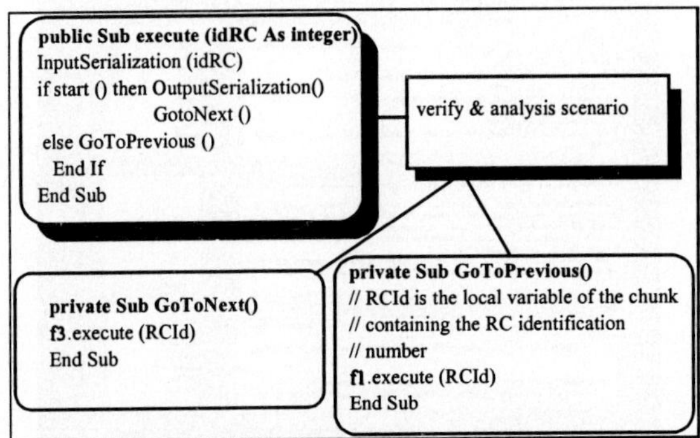

Fig. 6. Adaptation of the step chunk s4.

In addition each step chunk of this software path has been connected to the flow chunk helping to progress from it or to backtrack to its previous step. The adaptation of the step chunk to the method path is illustrated in figure 6 by showing the code of the *GoToPrevious* and *GoToNext* procedures.

The flow chunks invoked are mentioned in a shadow style. As a reminder, we give the code of the *execute* procedure which is similar to all the steps. Figure 7, 8 and 9 illustrate three steps namely to *elicit, to analyse and to conceptualise a scenario*. In figure 7, the three ways of eliciting a scenario implemented in s1,s2 and s3 by the corresponding button. The figure shows an excerpt of a textual scenario produced by the application engineer using the style guidelines. When the application engineer pushes the OK button, the f1 flow chunk is executed and the window presented in figure 7 is displayed.

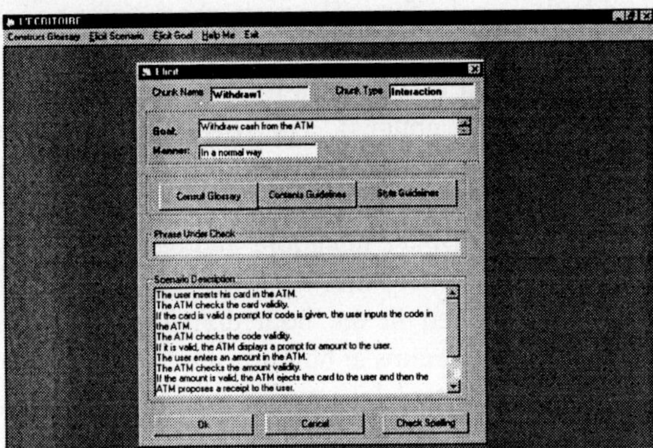

Fig. 7. The *elicit scenario* chunk.

The scenario elicited in the previous step appears in the upper text field of the window. In order to perform the s4 chunk, the application engineer has to pushed the button « linguistic check ». This trigger the analysis performed using a linguistic case grammar. The result appears in the two text fields as shown in figure 8.

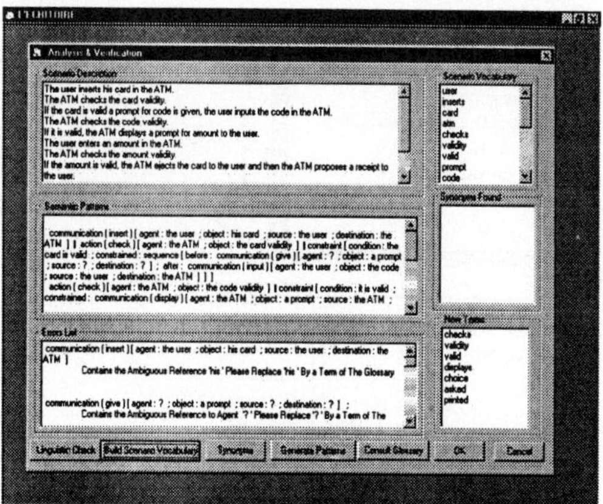

Fig. 8. The *analysis* step chunk.

They correspond to (a) the instantiated case patterns and (b) the errors detected by the semantic analysis. By pressing the OK button, the verify scenario step is suggested by the f2 flow chunk. Let assume that the verification has been performed and that following f3 flow chunk the « *conceptualise* » step is triggered. The conceptualisation step generates a formalised scenario description presented in an indented format. This formalisation uses the semantic patterns instances generated in the previous step.

Finally, the main menu of the tool is composed of the three top level intentions of the path namely elicit scenario, construct glossary and elicit goal.

5 Conclusion

The paper has presented a component-based approach for developing software tool supporting a method built « on the fly ». The main characteristic of this approach is to be a reuse-centric approach for constructing the method and its software tool. It means that the method as well as the software tool are constructed by assembling method chunks (resp. software chunks). The originality of this component-based approach is to propose a process centred framework which considers process as being intentional. And the process performance in this view is a route between steps that we called the process flow. Steps achieve intentions and result in product transformation whereas the flow represents the sequence of intentions that have been considered. This novelty approach is applied in the both domains method engineering and software engineering. The former aims at building methods « on the fly » whereas the latter leads to build a software tool by reusing, assembling and adapting software chunks. This approach has been experimented in the CREWS project by developing one of the CREWS method paths in the software tool « l'écritoire ». The experimentation has led that the process centred approach can be generalised to built faster software tool of a specific method path. But it also shown that Visual Basic is not the best programming environment for supporting the definition of abstract modules, their adaptation and their reuse. We will shift to a more appropriate programming environment such as Java because it manages abstract classes, classes, inheritance and its portability is a strong criteria to take into account.

In addition, a design for reuse will be also defined in order to support method engineer as well as software engineer in the method base improvement.

References

1. G. Booch : « Software components with ADA : structures, tools and sub-systems », Benjamin Cummings, 1987.
2. F. Harmsen, S. Brinkkemper, H. Oei : « Situational Method Engineering for Information System Project Approaches », Proc of the conference on Methods and Associated Tools for Information Systems Life Cycle, eds A.A. Verrijn-Stuart and T.W. Olle, pub. North Holland, IFIP WG. 8.1, 1994.
3. Proc. Of the Conference on Method Engineering , IFIP WG 8.1, ed. Chapman & all, Atlanta 1996.
4. V. Plihon, C. Rolland : « Modelling Ways of Working », Proc. Of the 7th International Conference on Advanced Information Systems Engineering, CAiSE'95.
5. V Plihon, J. Ralyte, A. Benjamen, N.A.M. Maiden, A. Sutcliffe, E. Dubois, P. Heymans : « A reuse-Oriented Approach for the Construction of Scenario Based Methods »,ICSP'98 (submitted).
6. R. Priéto-Diaz : « Domain Analysis for reusability », Proc. Of COMPSAC'97, Tokyo, Japan, 1987.
7. R. Priéto-Diaz , P. Freeman : « Classifying software for reusability », IEEE software, vol 4, n°1, january 1987.
8. R. Priéto-Diaz: Domain Analysis : an introduction », ACM SIGSOFT software engineering, vol 15, n°2, april 1990.
9. C Rolland, G. Grosz : « A General Framework for describing the requirement engineering Process », IEEE conference on Systems, Man & Cybernetics, CSMC'94, San Antonio, Texas, 1994.
10. C Rolland, C. Souveyet, M.Moreno : « An approach for defining Ways of Working », Information Systems Journal, Vol 20, N°4, pp337-359,1995.
11. C Rolland, V. Plihon : « Using generic chunks to generate process model fragments », Proc. Of the 2nd Conference on Requirements Engineering, ICRE'96, Colorado Springs, 1996.
12. C. Rolland, C. Ben Achour : « Guiding the construction of textual use case specifications », accepted to Data Knowledge Engineering Journal.
13. C Rolland, C. Souveyet, C. Ben Achour : « Guiding », submitted to TSE journal.
14. C Rolland, V. Plihon, J. Ralyte : « Specifying the reuse context of Scenario Method chunks », paper accepted to the Conference on Advanced System Engineering (CAiSE'98), 1998.
15. S. Si Said : « Guidance for requirements engineering process », Proc. Of the 8th conference on Databases & Expert Systems Applications, DEXA'97, Toulouse, 1-5 September 1997.

A Retrieval Language for Historical Documents

María José Aramburu Cabo and Rafael Berlanga Llavori

Departament d'Informàtica
Campus Penyeta Roja, Universitat Jaume I,
E-12071 Castellón, SPAIN
e-mail: {berlanga,aramburu}@inf.uji.es

Abstract. This paper focuses on a set of structured document applications that we have denoted databases of *historical documents*. The information into these documents is closely related to the time in which they are created while being still of great usefulness in the future. The main contribution of this paper is the formulation of a group of operators and predicates that express retrieval conditions over the temporal features of documents. Additionally, the resulting retrieval language supports the construction of time series of documents, here named chronicles, which are regarded as a preliminary step towards the implementation of more complex data mining operations over historical document repositories.

1 Introduction

This paper deals with a particular kind of structured document applications, namely, databases of *historical documents*. Broadly speaking, we consider historical documents as those that keep information related with the time instant at which they were published at the same time that are still useful in the future [1]. Among them, we can identify newspapers, periodicals, patents, manuals and so on. All these types of documents have in common that the meaning of their contents must be located in some time period during which they are up-to-date. Afterwards they become obsolete, although yet useful for some applications such as researching, elaboration of reports and data discovery.

A database of historical documents is intended to store a large amount of documents organised into classes with the purpose of being retrieved in the future. Then, for example, we can have a database of newspapers, where the issues of several classes of newspapers are inserted every day. The users of these applications will be interested in finding out elaborated information from the database. That is, instead of retrieving certain issues by their attributes as in current information retrieval systems, the users will discover information about how things happened in the past. In this way, the retrieval mechanisms should allow for the specification of temporal relationships of cause/effect, or correlation among various concepts.

In our previous work, the modelling requirements of this kind of documents have been deeply analysed, resulting in the TOODOR (*Temporal Object-Oriented Document Organisation and Retrieval*) database model [1] [2] [3]. Relying on TOODOR, we have also developed a new declarative retrieval language for historical documents which is presented in this paper. The purpose of this language is to facilitate the specification of complex conditions so that historical documents can be retrieved by their contents, structure and temporal relationships. As a consequence, users will be able to extract the maximum profit from the historical information in a way that current systems do not allow.

The paper is organised as follows. Section 1.1 reviews the TOODOR data model and analyses the modelling requirements of historical documents. Section 2 introduces the syntax, predicates and temporal operators of the Temporal Document Retrieval Language (TDRL). Finally, Section 3 presents some conclusions.

1.1 An Overview to the TOODOR Data Model

Historical documents present complex structures, where the elements of information are organised into deep hierarchies of composition whose shape is previously defined but in which many irregularities use to appear. By this reason, the data model of TOODOR includes a flexible type system with the usual type constructors for complex data plus a set of constructors specially suited for structured documents type definition [1]. These special constructors are ordered tuples that represent the ordering of the components of documents, and others that allow for the variations that can occur in the structure of the documents of a class. In this set, we have included constructors to represent the repetition of the components of a section, the option of some elements and the union of types. Every class of objects in the database will have assigned one or several types to express the structure of its instances. Given the flexibility of this type system, it is not necessary that all the objects of a class present exactly the same structure.

In order to represent the temporal behaviour of historical documents, TOODOR includes two temporal dimensions [3]. In the first temporal dimension, every object has associated a period named *valid time* that refers to the time of relevance of the information contained in the document that represents. These time periods serve to locate and relate the information of each object, which is very useful for retrieval purposes.

In the second dimension, the sequence of versions of document classes is represented by means of an interval that indicates its lifespan in the database, and which is partitioned into so many subintervals as different type definitions have been assigned to the class [1]. As a result, when the editors of a publication decide to reorganise its structure, a new type can be assigned to the corresponding class of documents. Finally, objects have a component, named *insertion time*, that states at which instant and under which type definition they were inserted into the database. In this way, when an object is inserted into the database it must conform to the type definition of its class that is current at that moment.

Additionally, TOODOR presents some differences with respect to other temporal object oriented data models [4] [8].The main one is that in the intended applications, documents are not modified once inserted into the database. Consequently, in TOODOR every object is of a non-temporal data type, and the database only stores a single value for each object attribute. On the other hand, the insertion time of an object and its components must coincide. It should be noted that this property implies that at the instant at which an object is created, a definition for all the classes that it references must be current.

2 The Temporal Document Retrieval Language

Relying on the TOODOR data model, we have developed a temporal retrieval language to be used by its final applications which is specially suited for retrieving documents and document portions according to their structural and temporal features. This declarative language is denoted TDRL (Temporal Document Retrieval Language) and, in order to provide it with a maximum of uniformity with respect to previous object-oriented query languages, we have designed it by adopting the main features of the Object Query Language proposed by ODMG-93 standard [7]. This standard has been here chosen because its features were in conformance with the requirements of TDRL in many senses, including the structure of the queries, the treatment of path expressions, and its extendibility to new predicates.

2.1 TDRL Syntax

The general schema of a query in TDRL follows the usual select-from-where profile, where variables ranging over sets of objects can be specified in the from clause and then used elsewhere in the query. The result of a query consists of a set of object instances belonging to one or several predefined classes or alternatively, a projection of the values associated to these objects.

Since TOODOR classes can have different types associated and such types are flexible, the instances of a class can present different structures. In this way, when some objects in the query do not conform with the specified trajectory, they are discarded from the answer without producing any failure. However, in some cases users may find difficult to specify the precise structure of documents, or simply they are only interested on documents that satisfy some weak containment condition. For these purposes, we have included in TDRL a predicate denoted contains which expresses that one object takes part of another through any path expression in the object aggregation hierarchy. Query 1 illustrates how to use this predicate to retrieve photos of *Berlin* within some article about *pollution* published in any of the sections of *The Times*.

Query 1: select a **from** Times t, Article a, Photograph p
where t contains a **and** a contains p
and 'Pollution' ∈ a.key-index **and** 'Berlin' ∈ p.key-index

Like in this query, conditions on document contents are always stated by means of different object attributes included in the user class definition for indexing purposes, e.g. key-index and subject.

Regarding the temporal features of TDRL, the first one consists of projecting the database over some period of time by means of a clause at. This clause establishes the time at which the query should be evaluated so that it restricts the set of objects to be considered to those whose insertion time belongs to the provided time slice. For instance, Query 2 retrieves those articles of *Ana Sacks* inserted during the fifth month of the year 1995. When a query does not contain a clause at, its temporal projection is associated to the whole database life (i.e. [0, now]).

Query 2: select a **from** Article **as** a
where 'Ana Sacks' ∈ a.author **at** [1/5/1995, 31/5/1995]

2.2 Temporal Predicates

The clause at just concerns with the insertion time of objects, which are directly related to their dates of publication. However, more interesting queries are those that concern with the valid time of objects because this can be used to relate the documents by the temporal location of their contents.

In this way, the predicate intersects allows checking if the information of documents coincide somehow along time. Apart from evaluating temporal coincidence of documents, other queries that consider ordering relationships between them can be formulated. For this purpose, TDRL includes a group of predicates that only takes into account the starting point of the intervals of valid time. As an example, Query 3 shows how to retrieve those articles about the *public surveys on political trends* after the new *regulation for taxes on houses* of *June 95*.

Query 3: select a **from** Article **as** a, b
where 'public survey on political trends' = a.subject **and**
'new regulation for taxes on houses' = b.subject **and**
start-after(a, b) **and** intersects(b, [1/6/1995, 30/6/1995])

In Table 1 the formal semantics of all the temporal predicates of TDRL are presented. In this table, *a* and *b* denote objects whose valid time component is stated by *vt* and *c* denotes a span of time. Furthermore, the superscripts - and + indicate respectively the lower and upper bounds of an interval, and the functions *inc* and *dec* can be applied to shift a time point forwards and backwards respectively according to the corresponding calendar [3]. The reasons why we have selected this group of temporal predicates for TDRL are that they satisfy the requirements of the applications for which TOODOR is intended at the same time that facilitate the specification of a large range of temporal conditions.

Table 1. Semantics of the temporal predicates of TDRL

Predicate	Definition
intersects(a, b)	$a.vt \cap b.vt \neq \emptyset$
starts-after(a,b)	$a.vt^{-} > b.vt^{-}$
starts-before(a, b)	$a.vt^{-} < b.vt^{-}$
after-span(c, a, b)	$a.vt^{-} > inc(b.vt^{-}, c)$
before-span(c, a, b)	$a.vt^{-} < dec(b.vt^{-}, c)$
after-within(c, a, b)	$a.vt^{-} > b.vt^{-} \wedge a.vt^{-} < inc(b.vt^{-}, c)$
before-within(c, a, b)	$a.vt^{-} < b.vt^{-} \wedge a.vt^{-} > dec(b.vt^{-}, c)$

2.3 Granularity

So far, we have presented a group of temporal predicates which are evaluated at the temporal granularity of one day, which is the granularity at which TOODOR represents the temporal information of documents. Nevertheless, TDRL allows for higher levels of granularity, and thus, the predicates intersects, starts-before and starts-after can be extended with a third attribute specifying the temporal granularity at which they should be evaluated. The possible calendar granularities are: day, week, month, quarter, semester, year and decade.

Supporting different calendar granularities makes possible to evaluate temporal queries in a coarse mode and in this way, withdraw conclusions that are not explicit in the stored temporal data or to relax the evaluation of the predicates. For example, we can relate documents that occur during the same quarter despite the fact that their intervals of valid time do not coincide at all. Query 4 shows how to apply such features. It finds the articles about *mass meetings against racism* during the months before to the celebration of the *World Congress against Racism.* The meetings celebrated the same month than the congress will not be retrieved.

Query 4: select a **from** Article a, b
where a.subject = 'mass meeting against racism'
and b.header.title = 'World Congress against Racism'
and before (a, b, month)

For the evaluation of these predicates the interval of valid time assigned to each object in the query must be translated to other time interval over which it is possible to check the indicated condition. For example, if the valid times of two objects a and b are respectively [12/4/1997, 20/5/1997] and [30/5/1997, 10/6/1997], then to evaluate the predicate intersects(a, b, semester) the two periods are translated into the intervals [1/1/1997, 30/6/1997] and [1/1/1997, 31/12/1997], and the condition is evaluated over them. In [3] a theory of time has been defined for TOODOR which indicates among other things how to perform this translation.

2.4 Chronicles

In order to obtain more comprehensive information from the database, we have included in TDRL the capacity of elaborating and relating what we have named *chronicles*. Broadly speaking, a chronicle is defined as an aggregation of objects whose valid times keep some kind of temporal structure. The ways in which these temporal structures can be stated produce several types of chronicles with different application meanings.

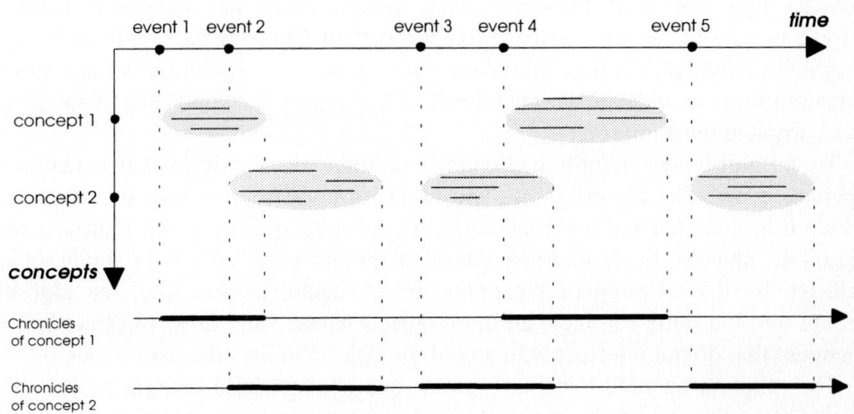

Fig. 1. The valid time of the event chronicles on two different concepts

Let us suppose that some information about the *international offences* that have coincided in time with the celebration of some *peace conference* is required. Initially, Query 5 could be formulated so that a set of articles about *international offences*, grouped by time intersecting articles about *peace conferences* was obtained. Nevertheless, it should be noted that all the Article instances in the database that report certain event, like a conference, produce a group of valid time intervals whose composition determines a single interval that can be considered as the period during which the event is up-to-date (see Fig.1). The set of objects whose valid times determine this time interval constitutes a chronicle instance whose valid time is the same interval.

In this way, alternatively to Query 5, TDRL allows the definition of the Query 6 that includes the elaboration of two groups of chronicles: one to see when a *conference of peace* has been held, and another to see which *international offences* have occurred. Afterwards, the resulting chronicles are related by means of the predicate intersects to evaluate which occurrences have coincided along time. As a result, the user will obtain a set of chronicle objects where each one consists of a set of Article instances. All the instances in a chronicle refer to the same international offence but moreover, this offence coincide along time with the celebration of some peace conference.

Query 5: select a **from** Article a, b
where 'international offence' ∈ a.index **and** 'peace conference' ∈ b.index
and intersects(a, b, month) **group by** b

Query 6: select a **from** Article **as** x, y, event(x, day) **as** a, event(y, day) **as** b
where 'international offence' ∈ x.index **and** 'peace conference' ∈ y.index
and intersects(a, b, month)

This example has introduced the first kind of chronicles. They are called event because they are used to know when certain event has happened from the information stored in the database. Notice that in Query 6 the elaboration of the chronicles is based on a time granularity. In this way, the operation is more flexible because users can indicate at which level of granularity the valid time of the objects in a chronicle must intersect.

To formalise this definition, Figure 2 presents an algorithm that executes the operator event. The algorithm has two input parameters for the set of objects over which it is executed and the granularity that must be applied, and it returns a set of chronicle objects. Each returned chronicle points to a set of the input objects selected by the criterion of the predicate intersects. In this way, the algorithm groups into the same chronicle all those objects whose valid times intersect between them but that do not intersect with any of the objects in the other chronicles.

The function denoted minimum returns one object whose interval of valid time starts before the rest of objects in the set that it takes as input. The function denoted cover builds a time interval equivalent to [minimum(S).vt^-, maximum(S).vt^+], where maximum is the inverse of minimum and S is the argument of cover. Finally, it should be noted that a chronicle must consist at least of two object elements.

```
EVENT(input P, g; output Ch)
      Aux ← ∅ Aux2 ← ∅ Ch ← ∅
      while P ≠ ∅ do
         begin
            Aux ← {minimum(P)}
            repeat
               Aux2 ← SELECT_intersects(p, a, g)(P(p), Aux(a))
               Aux ← Aux ∪ Aux2
               P ← P — Aux2
            until Aux2 = ∅
            if |Aux| > 1 then
               begin
                  vt ← cover(Aux)
                  Ch ← Ch ∪ create-chronicle(vt, Aux)
               end
         end
```

Fig. 2. An algorithm to generate chronicles of events

2.4.1 Other Types of Chronicles

Taking into account other interesting time structures, TDRL includes three other kinds of chronicles presented in this section. To define their formal semantics we need three further temporal predicates which are introduced in Table 2. The function *abs* translates time periods to higher levels of granularity by means of the procedure depicted in section 2.3 and formally defined in [3].

Table 2.: Predicates for the Evaluation of Chronicle Objects

Chronicle Type	Definition	Predicate Definition
cascade	*overlap(a,b,g)*	$abs(a.vt,g)^- < abs(b.vt,g)^- \wedge$ $abs(a.vt,g)^+ < abs(b.vt,g)^+ \wedge$ $abs(a.vt,g)^+ > abs(b.vt,g)^-$
sequence	*start(a,b,g)*	$abs(a.vt, g)^+ = abs(b.vt, g)^-$
hierarchy	*include(a,b,g)*	$abs(a.vt, g)^- < abs(b.vt, g)^- \wedge$ $abs(a.vt, g)^+ > abs(b.vt,g)^+$

In the definitions below, consider P(p) as the input set of objects of the operation, and g as the level of granularity at which the chronicle should be evaluated. Each one of the Chronicle objects created by the operation is denoted by c.

- CASCADE(P(p), g, Ch(c)), which creates the chronicle objects c that group those objects in P into cascades at granularity g. Formally, any chronicle object c must satisfy $\forall$ o $\in$ c, $\exists$ o' $\in$ c such that o $\neq$ o' and *overlap*(o, o', g) $\vee$ *overlap*(o', o, g) is true.
- SEQUENCE(P(p), g, Ch(c)), which creates the chronicle objecs c that group those objects in P into sequences at granularity g. Formally, any chronicle object c must satisfy $\forall$ o $\in$ c, $\exists$ o' $\in$ c such that o $\neq$ o' and *start*(o, o', g) $\vee$ *start*(o', o, g) is true.
- HIERARCHY(P(p), g, Ch(c)), that creates the chronicle objects c grouping those objects in P into hierarchies at granularity g. Formally, any chronicle object c satisfies $\forall$ o $\in$ c, $\exists$ o' $\in$ c such that o $\neq$ o' and *include*(o, o', g) $\vee$ *include*(o', o, g) is true.

In the three cases, it is possible for an object to be part of several chronicles. For this reason, the algorithms that evaluate them are different from the previous one. To specify their semantics, we are going to employ the terminology of directed acyclic graphs.

We can consider that each object in the input set P is a node of a directed graph. Then, there will exist an edge between two nodes when the corresponding chronicle criterion between them holds. For example, if we are evaluating chronicles of cascades, then the criterion is the predicate *overlap*, and we will insert an edge from *a* to *b* if *overlap(a, b, g)* is true. Notice that given the semantics of the three predicates of Table 2, cycles cannot occur in the graph.

Once the corresponding graph is completed, it only remains to find out which chronicles can be constructed. The way to construct chronicles also differs in the three cases. For cascades and sequences, each chronicle is formed by all those nodes (i.e. objects) that participate in a directed path of maximum length inside the graph. In the case of hierarchies, the edges are interpreted as precedence relationships between nodes. Then, each chronicle is formed by a node without predecessors together with all its successors.

3 Conclusions

The main contribution of this paper is a set of predicates and operators that relate document contents by their temporal features. Currently, we are developing a group of indexing and retrieval strategies plus a query processing method to evaluate efficiently TDRL queries. Furthermore, a first prototype of this query processor has been implemented on MegaLog [6] in the context of the work presented in [3].

From the user point of view, the most relevant feature of the TDRL is that it should be regarded rather as an information retrieval language than as a conventional database query language. This feature mainly stems from imprecision in answers due to the presence of document content conditions into the queries (e.g. key-words, subject and valid time). Another source of imprecision is the use of time granularities in query statements (answers obtained for a given time granularity may be refined or abstracted to adjust the results to the user requirements). Considered as an information retrieval system, TDRL can improve the effectiveness of traditional approaches since it specifies temporal and structural conditions over documents.

Concerning the predicates we have designed, they allow the specification of complex temporal conditions in a quite straightforward way. Furthermore, it can be stated that TDRL is the first temporal query language that has used time granularity for information retrieval purposes. This is a feature that has shown very useful for extracting relevant information in the context of the intended applications. In particular, we are analysing the usefulness of these predicates for a real database of newspapers, which is the main case study of TOODOR.

On the other hand, although the elaboration of chronicles may seem a costly operation we are working on a group of algorithms that can optimise their evaluation. Nevertheless, chronicles constitute an original idea that provides to the retrieval language some temporal reasoning capabilities. In this context, the use of chronicles can be regarded as a preliminary step towards the implementation of more complex data mining procedures over repositories of historical documents [5].

Finally, as can be noted in the provided examples for the specification of conditions on the contents of documents, we have relied on the existence of some key-word indexing for every object. In this sense, we identify the need for further investigation on new indexing mechanisms for object-oriented databases of documents.

Acknowledgments

This work has been partially funded by the Spanish CICYT project with contract number TEL97-1119 and BANCAIXA project P1A97-17. We are also very grateful to the reviewers of the paper by their useful comments.

References

1. Aramburu, M.J. and Berlanga, R.: Metadata for a Digital Library of Historical Documents. Proceedings of the 8th DEXA International Conference. LNCS Series 1308 Springer Verlag, Toulouse (1997) pp 409--418.
2. Aramburu, M. and Berlanga, R.: An Approach to a Digital Library of Newspapers. Information Processing & Management, Special Issue on Electronic News. Pergamon Press Publishers, Vol 33(5) (1997) pp 645-661.
3. Aramburu Cabo, M. J. TOODOR : A Temporal Database Model for Historical Documents PhD Thesis, (1998), School of Computer Science, The University of Birmingham, UK.
4. Bertino, E., Ferrari, E. and Guerrini, G.: A Formal Temporal Object-Oriented Data Model Proceedings of the Fourth International Conference on Extending Database Technology (EDBT), Avignon France (1996) ACM Press pp 342-356.
5. Berlanga, R., Aramburu, M.J. and Barber, F.: Discovering Temporal Relationships in Databases of Newspapers International Conference on Industrial & Engineering Applications of Artifical Intelligence & Expert Systems. Springer Verlag, Benicasim, Spain (1998) pp 36--45.
6. Bocca, J.: MegaLog: A Platform for Developing Knowledge Base Management Systems. Proceedings of the International Symposium of Database Systems for Advanced Applications, Tokyo, April (1991) pp. 374-380.
7. Cattell, R.G.G. (eds.).: The Object Database Standard: ODMG-93 Release 1.2. Morgan Kaufmann Publishers (1996) San Francisco.
8. Özsu, M.T., Straube, D. and Peters, R.: Query Processing Issues in Object-Oriented Knowledge Base Systems. Emerging Landscape of Intelligence in Database and Information Systems. Petry, F. and Delcambre, L. (eds.), JAI Press (1994) pp. 79--144.

Modeling, Indexing and Retrieving Images Using Conceptual Graphs

Iadh Ounis, Marius Paşca

CLIPS-IMAG, MRIM team, University of Grenoble
BP 53, 38041 Grenoble Cedex, France
E-mail: {Iadh.Ounis, Marius.Pasca}@imag.fr

Abstract. When dealing with the complexity of an image as part of the indexing process, keywords are not sufficient to obtain an index that is a faithful representation of the image content. We propose to use the conceptual graphs formalism as the indexing language, which allows to use not only keywords, but also relations between them. The obtained indexes are more precise, and retrieval effectiveness is thus improved. Our paper presents a system that provides a computer-assisted image indexing process, which is performed according to a formal image model. The result of the indexing process, which is a set of conceptual graphs, is then organized so that to improve retrieval execution times. Our image retrieval system, called RELIEF, is implemented on an object-oriented DBMS and is available on the Web. It ensures the management of an image test collection and gives good results, with respect to both execution time and quality of answers.

1 Introduction: Towards Precision-Oriented Systems

In the evaluation of an information retrieval (IR) system, two widely used measurements are *precision* and *recall*. They correspond respectively to the ability of the system to retrieve only relevant documents and to its capacity to retrieve all the documents that are relevant to the user's query. In addition, two other evaluation parameters are often considered. The notion of *noise* refers to the proportion of non-relevant documents amongst the system's answers and is complementary to precision. Analogously, the inability of the system to retrieve relevant documents is measured by *silence*, which is therefore complementary to recall. An IR system attempts to maximize recall and precision. However, it has been shown experimentally that these criteria interact with each other in a way similar to the expressiveness-tractability trade-off [1]. We share the opinion that the explosive growth of the available information and its complexity suggest that precision would be more and more important as compared to recall [2]. Indeed, when the system's answer is very large, the noise becomes intolerable.

Usually, the indexes of the documents consist in a set of keywords. In spite of advantages such as ease of implementation and fast algorithms, keywords have a few less desirable properties when used for document representation. Indeed, let us consider that the user is searching AltaVista for documents about *heart disease* or *cardiac disease*. This information need is to be formulated as a query, in one of the different ways supported by the advanced search option of AltaVista. The queries shown in figure 1 [1] are

[1] We launched these queries on March 16, 1998.

five ways of formulation. The first query illustrates the noise problem, because many of the retrieved documents are not relevant to the information need. This is due to the occurrence of the two keywords in different parts of the same document. More precisely, the noise is due to the fact that there is no semantic relationship between the words *heart* and *disease* found in the document. This suggests that a formalism that supports explicitly the relationships between keywords would give a better precision than simple keywords.

The user can artificially specify the relationship between *heart* and *disease* by introducing the second query. In this case, the precision is maximum: all the retrieved documents contain the corresponding string, so they are relevant. It is worth mentioning that the quotes are in fact a means for expressing relationships between words, hence they are a primitive substitute for a semantic relation. More specifically, the primitive adjacency relation is a substitute for the *bears-on* semantic relation (the *disease* bears-on the *heart*). However, the retrieved documents do not include those that are about *cardiac disease*, nor those containing the string "*heart disease*s". Introducing an advanced boolean query, such as the third one, only makes things worse, by increasing the noise.

The importance of the linguistic and semantic treatments in retrieval effectiveness is illustrated by the fourth query. To obtain the documents that contain "heart diseases" (linguistic extension) or "cardiac disease" (semantic extension) or "cardiac diseases", the knowledge about their relation to the information need have to be identified, and then made explicit in the user's query. The last query shows that the lack of control of the Web search engines indexers, on the one hand, and the grammar and spelling errors of the Web page designers, on the other hand, represent a source of noise. The problems encountered for the above example could be corrected if the indexes would be obtained by using a richer indexing language. Such a language would allow to detect relations such as synonymy between "heart disease" and "cardiac disease", as well as the inflection rules involved in the construction of plural noun forms.

No.	*Query submitted to AltaVista*	*Retrieved documents*
1	heart AND disease	229,382
2	"heart disease"	88,778
3	(heart OR cardiac) AND (disease OR diseases)	267,324
4	"heart disease" OR "heart diseases" OR "cardiac disease" OR "cardiac diseases"	92,921
5	heart AND desease	745

Fig. 1. Searching for a *heart disease* on AltaVista

The need to express semantic indexes becomes more evident when documents are not texts but are images, as we will show in the next section. In this paper, we choose Sowa's conceptual graphs (*CGs*) formalism [3] as the indexing language. After introducing a formal image indexing model in section 3, we show how the *CGs* formalism permits to index images according to this model. Indexing is performed semi-automatically, through a process described in section 4; its result is a conceptual graph associated to each image. The next step of our indexing phase is motivated by the retrieval time performance requirements. In section 5, we propose an organization of the conceptual graphs into an inverted-file based structure. This allows to perform retrieval through set intersections, as we briefly describe in an example. Section 6 presents our experimental results, both in quality of results and execution time. A conclusion is given in section 7.

2 The Necessity of a More Powerful Formalism

A particular characteristic of images is their richness. Images are two-dimension documents, which introduce new types of information that have to be considered in indexing. We consider the first two images in figure 2 to review some of these types of information. Both images contain objects, that can be identified and represented at first view by the same set of keywords {MAN, TABLE, HAT, BEARD}. In this case, whatever the user's query, the two images will be either both retrieved or not retrieved at all. Nevertheless, the two images contain further information that permits to refine their description, and thus to differentiate them. For example, our objects have different relative positions. In the first image, the MAN is on the left of the TABLE, while the inverse relation holds for the second image. Moreover, the BEARD does not appear independently in each image, but it is the MAN which has it. The position of the MAN also makes the difference: he is seated in the first image, but is standing in the second image. We would also like to introduce attributes such as the name of the two different photographs who took the two images or the identification of the photographed persons.

As a consequence, we need a formalism that supports relations, which offers a precise indexing process. Among other possible choices, we choose Sowa's conceptual graphs [3]. The reason of this choice is that this formalism allows to represent uniformly all the components of an IR system, i.e. indexing, interrogation and the matching function [4]. Furthermore, as introduced by Sowa, this formalism can be easily extended to accommodate new domain knowledge and needs, without a specific revision of its semantics [5]. We also need a consistent indexing model, supporting relations and attributes such as those identified here.

Fig. 2. Three images from our PARYSIS collection. The rightmost image includes the contours of the polygons delimiting the image objects.

3 The Indexing Model

In our example of section 2, we identified different relations that our image indexing model must take into account. These relations include composition relations between objects appearing in the image, spatial relations between objects, semantic or symbolic relations that refine the image contents, and database-like attributes such as author, date etc. They were identified in the general model developed at the University of Grenoble [6, 7]. We adapted this image model, such that each index consists of the following views:

- the *structural view* based on the composition relation (Comp) between the image objects. The structural view of an image contains a set of relations of the form: [Concept]→(Comp)→[Concept].
- the *symbolic view* is mainly given as a sequence of arches of the form: [ImageObject]→ (IsA) → [Specific Concept] and/or [ImageObject] → (HasAttribute) → [Specific Attribute] and/or [Concept] → (SymbolicRelation) → [Concept].
  It associates semantic descriptions to the image or to the image objects.
- the *spatial view* describes the shape and the relative position of the image objects; this view is also given as a set of relations, of the form : [Polygon] → (Spatialrelation) → [Polygon] or [ImageObject] → (VueSpa) → [Polygon].

As an illustration, the views for the first image of figure 2 are represented below in the form of a conceptual graph. A conceptual graph is a graph formed by two kinds of nodes, concepts and relations [2]. The different views are combined together in the indexing model, so that to obtain one conceptual graph (see figure 3), as an index for our image. The relations of the index given in this figure have different colours, according to the view to which they belong.

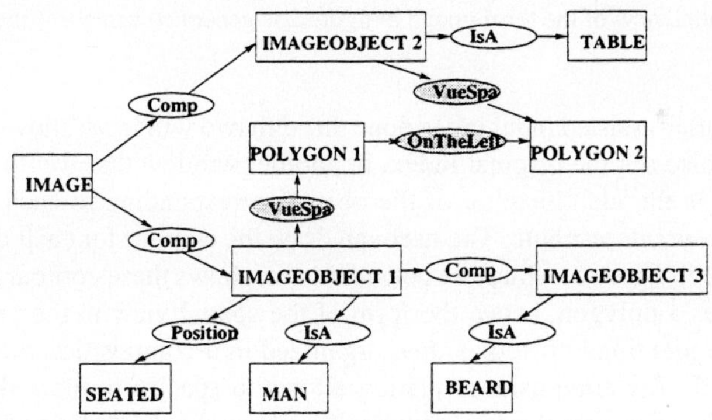

Fig. 3. A partial index for the first image of figure 2

[2] Concepts are represented graphically by rectangles and syntactically by brackets. Relations are represented graphically by ovals and syntactically by parentheses.

4 Indexing Each Image by a Conceptual Graph: A Computer-Assisted Process

In our case, images are provided with original descriptions of their contents, in the form of keywords and textual descriptions. These original descriptions were given by specialists of the French Ministry of Culture. We have a total of 650 images, grouped together in a collection called PARISYS [8, 9]. The images of the PARISYS collection are photographs taken mainly in Paris, at the beginning of the century. An original index contains attributes such as *author*, *image type*, *contents* and *title*. In this section, we consider for illustration the third image of figure 2. The *contents* attribute refers to the semantic content of the image. This attribute was carefully chosen by the French specialists. Our image includes, for example, a woman (Femme), a man (Homme), a dress (Robe), a staircase (Escalier) etc.

Starting from the original indexes, the indexing process provides tools for computer-assisted indexing in the form of conceptual graphs. The idea behind is to give priority to the choice of specialists and *not add any concepts* during the process. Instead, we can *specify only relations between concepts*. These relations may include spatial, composition, and semantic or symbolic relationships. The resulting image index will be a conceptual graph that conforms to the image model presented above.

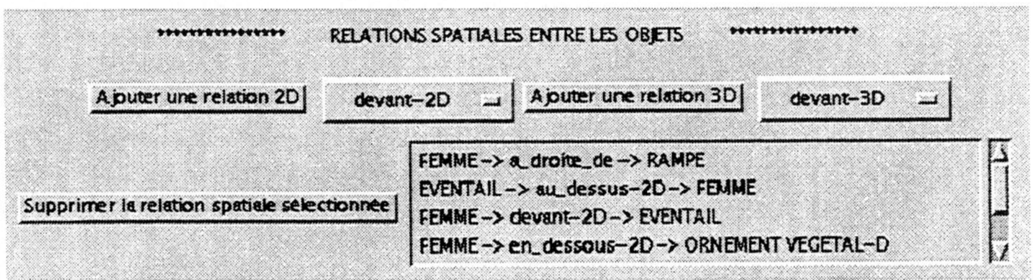

Fig. 4. The spatial view of the third image in figure 2 is generated using this interface window.

The computer-assisted indexing is done through two windows, shown in figures 4, 5. The user can also see the original index, in another window that we do not show here. The first step is the identification of the object corresponding to each keyword mentioned in the *contents* attribute. The user can draw the contour for each of these objects. The last image in figure 2, which we consider here, shows these contours in white. Each contour defines a polygon, hence the form of the spatial view in the previous section. The set of the identified objects is then organized in a composition hierarchy, such as that in figure 5. The composition relation allows to specify in more detail the image content. The interface generates automatically a composition relation between a common image object (Image) and each previously identified object. Then the user selects an object from the hierarchy, e.g. leg (Pied), drags and drops it on the object to which it belongs, in our case woman (Femme). Thus we can arrive to the final hierarchy shown in figure 5, where a composition path connects in a chain the ramp (Rampe) to the staircases (Escalier) to the photograph accessory (Accessoire de Pose) and finally to the image (Image). What we obtain is the structural view of the image. The next step is the introduction of spatial relationships between the objects, using the buttons shown in figure 4. For example, we can introduce the first spatial relationship of figure 4 by clicking in figure 5 firstly on the woman (Femme) and secondly on the ramp (Rampe), in this order, and then selecting the on-the-right (a-droite-de) relation. In addition to this facility, the interface also handles possible inconsistencies.

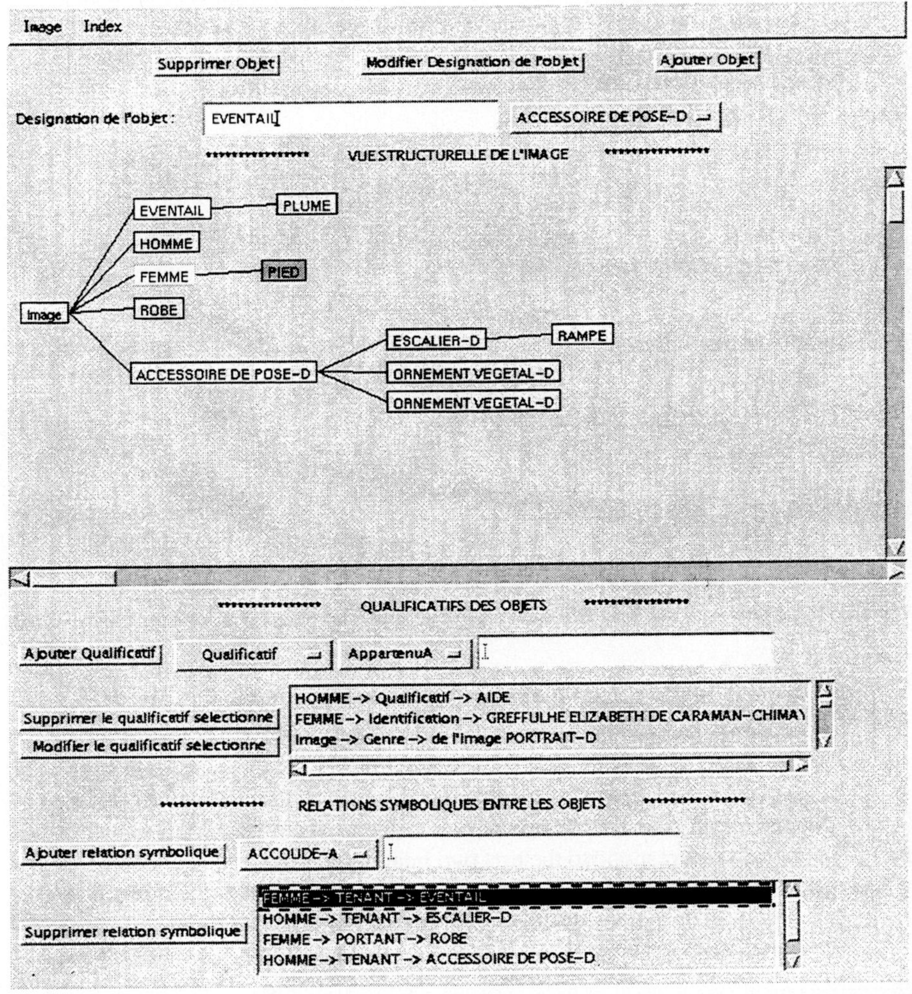

Fig. 5. This interface window allows for the generation of the structural and symbolic views of the third image in figure 2

The index can be further refined using the lower part of the interface of figure 5. This allows to express easily that not only are there a woman and a robe in our image, but the woman is wearing the robe (Femme→portant→Robe, in the third line of the lower part of figure 5). This part of the interface introduces the symbolic view of the image. Together with the structural and spatial views, it completes the computer-assisted indexing process, according to the supporting image model. A last internal operation, which is automatically performed by the interface once the indexing process is finished, is the gathering of the information introduced by the user. A single connected conceptual graph is generated by the interface. We note that our computer-assisted indexing process permits to reduce the indexing to about 5 minutes for each image, as the existence of the objects is already asserted by the original descriptions. Given the considerable size of an average indexing graph, we estimate that this value is quite reasonable.

5 An Optimized Index Organization: an Algebraic Approach

The conceptual graphs obtained by the process described in the previous section constitute a rich but also complicate representation of the image content. Therefore, we finalize the indexing by organizing the conceptual graphs into an algebraic structure that will permit to speed-up the retrieval process. This structure consists in an inverted file, whose entries associate, to each relation of the indexes, the documents in which it appears, as well as its precise position in the graph. We do this by grouping together the relations that are syntactically equal in one entry of the inverted file.

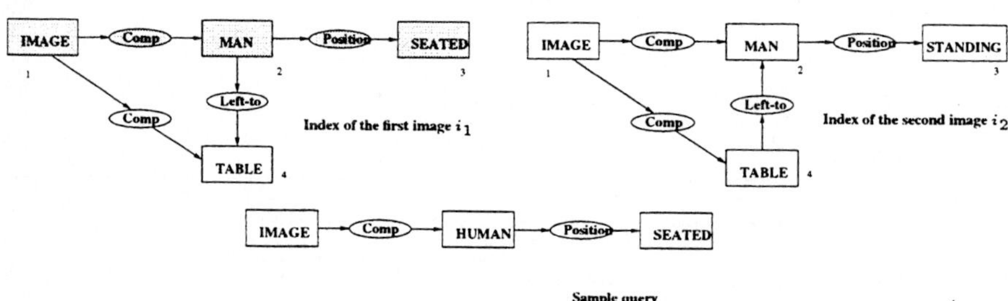

Fig. 6. The simplified indexes of the first two images in figure 2 and a sample query

An example of an inverted file obtained for the graphs in figure 6 is shown in figure 7. These graphs correspond to the first two images in figure 2 [3]. We can note the use of distinct identifiers, that are uniquely associated to each concept of each graph (see figure 6) to preserve the graph structure. [4] This functionality can be illustrated for the concept MAN of the first index. The identifier $i_1 : [2]$ uniquely identifies it and serves

[3] For a clearer presentation, we do not strictly follow the indexing model that we presented in section 4. Instead, we use simplified indexes in figure 6.

[4] We note $i_2 : [1]$ for the identifier 1 of the index of the second image.

to join the relations Comp (the upper one), Left-To and Position. Therefore it has to be stored in the corresponding position in the inverted file.

To build the inverted file, each relation of the indexes in figure 6 is taken, together with the identifiers associated to the concepts. It is put into its corresponding entry of the inverted file. For instance, the first relation of the first index is Image→Comp→Man. It is put in the first entry of the inverted file, and the identifiers are put in their corresponding position: $i_1 : [1]$ next to Image and $i_1 : [2]$ next to Man. The first relation of the second index is the same, therefore the identifiers $i_2 : [1]$ and $i_2 : [2]$ are also put in the first entry of the inverted file, next to the others. The rest of the relations in the indexes are introduced into the inverted file in the same way. The construction of the inverted file finishes the indexing process.

In the case of conceptual graphs, the matching function is provided by the so-called projection operator. Given a query in the form of a conceptual graph, this operator consists in searching for a sub-graph in each of the indexes, such that this sub-graph is equal to the query graph, up to some concept specializations. For instance, in figure 6, there is a darkened sub-graph in the first index, which corresponds to the query graph, up to the specialization of Human into Man.

Generally, the projection operator is applied from the query to each index. For a large collection, this becomes a time-consuming operation. Moreover, independently of this repeated application, the operator itself is considered to be complex and giving bad time performance [10]. Our structure reduces this projection operator between graphs to an algebraic sequence of set intersections, therefore the complexity of our matching function is polynomial.

Indeed, assume that the user is looking for images showing *a seated human*. In this case, the query will be represented by the graph in figure 6, in which we have two relations. For each relation we must find all the relations in the inverted file that are equal to it, up to concept specializations. To this effect, we use a set of additional structures called acceleration tables, which we presented in [5]. As an illustration of their functionality, for the first relation of the query, Image→Comp→Human, the acceleration tables give directly the row 1 of the inverted file. For the second relation of the query, Human→Position→Seated, the acceleration tables give us the row 5 of the inverted file.

The two query relations are joined by the concept Human. Therefore, the solution to our query is found by intersecting the sets of identifiers associated to the concept Man (the specialization of Human) in rows 1 and 5. We obtain $[i_1 : [2], i_2 : [2]] \cap [i_1 : [2]]$, which gives $i_1 : [2]$. This indicates that the first image is relevant to our query. Indeed, we obtain as the projection of the query the sub-graph in the first index of figure 6 mentioned above.

The soundness and completeness of our new matching function, according to the projection operator, are ensured by an underlying logical interpretation for conceptual graphs, that we gave in [11]. This logical interpretation uses a classical technique in first order logic, called the witness technique [12]. The latter fulfills all the requirements of the conceptual graphs model, while being a speed-up factor [13].

Row	Relation	Concepts	Witnesses	Row	Relation	Concepts	Witnesses
1	*Comp*	Image:	$i_1 : [1], i_2 : [1]$	4	*Left-to*	Table:	$i_2 : [4]$
		Man:	$i_1 : [2], i_2 : [2]$			Man:	$i_2 : [2]$
2	*Comp*	Image:	$i_1 : [1], i_2 : [1]$	5	*Position*	Man:	$i_1 : [2]$
		Table:	$i_1 : [4], i_2 : [4]$			Seated:	$i_1 : [3]$
3	*Left-to*	Man:	$i_1 : [2]$	6	*Position*	Man:	$i_2 : [2]$
		Table:	$i_1 : [4]$			Standing:	$i_2 : [3]$

Fig. 7. The inverted file structure corresponding to the indexes of figure 6

6 Experimentation and Results

In the previous sections, we presented a computer-assisted indexing process, which is based on a formal image model and results in indexes in the form of conceptual graphs. We proposed an index organization that allows for faster retrieval. In this section, we illustrate the impact of the use of the conceptual graphs formalism on the precision of our RELIEF system, as well as the benefits of our organization on the rapidity of retrieval. RELIEF is implemented on top of the O_2 object-oriented database management system [14]. The availability of recent advances in the object-oriented database domain and the support of database connections via Web browsers are the main reasons for the choice of O_2. RELIEF is a system proposed as a solution to the integration of object-oriented modeling and Web technologies in the IR domain [9].

6.1 An Improved Precision

For the general case, the information need can be formulated in our system through an interface accessible from any Web browsers supporting JAVA, which provides a structured interrogation. We consider the query formulated as shown in figure 8. Similarly to the case of the indexing process, when the user submits the query, the latter is transformed into a conceptual graph by a process that gathers the information introduced for the different image model views. Now, if we used a boolean model, independently of the complexity of the underlying system, the flexibility in the query formulation would be limited from the beginning, as we showed in section 1. For our case, the query would be reduced to *human AND table*, and the spatial relation present in the user's information need could not be taken into consideration. It is worth mentioning that our system can be assimilated to a boolean one, if no relations are specified (that is, only the structural view of the model would be used) [5].

[5] In figure 8, the spatial relation Humain→a-droite-de→Table would not exist for a boolean-like query

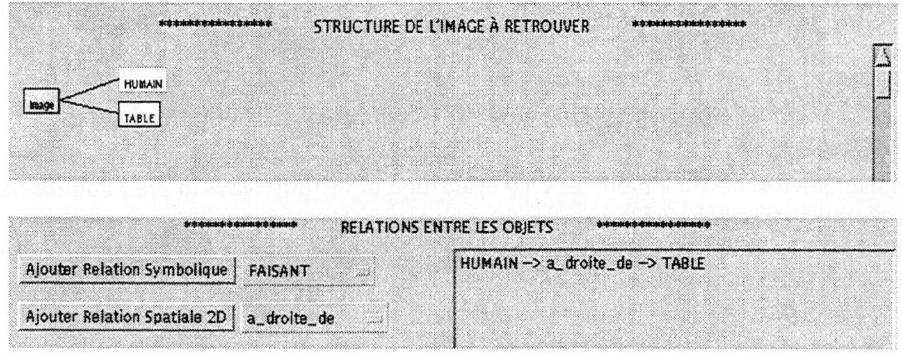

Fig. 8. Zooms on two parts of the Web query interface, if the user is looking for images showing *a human on the right of a table*. The interface is very similar to that in figure 5. The "Qualificatifs des objets" interface part in figure 5 is empty for this query.

The results obtained for such a boolean-like query are shown in the first caption of figure 10. A user that would search through the retrieved images would find that only 6 out of 17 are really relevant to his information need (images 4676, 4678, 4449, 4448, 4683, 4675). The additional 11 images only introduce noise and consequently a low precision is obtained.

If the spatial relation is added and therefore all the user's information need is taken into account, the system returns 6 images in a first result class, and other 11 images in a second classes (see the second caption in figure 10). As one can see, the first 6 images are the exact answers to the query. They are really relevant to the information need. The other 11 are provided by the system only in search of more flexibility; they are obtained from the original query by removing a certain part of it (though this part only concerns the relations; objects themselves are never removed). In this case, the relation Humain→a-droite-de→Table is removed; the objects themselves, Humain and Table are maintained in the query.

As opposed to the boolean-like query where all the 17 images are shown in the same class, there is no noise here for the first class [6]. The system presents the relevant images *separated* from the approximately relevant ones, thus contributing to the effectiveness of the interrogation. At the time of interrogation, other relations could be specified using buttons similar to those in figure 5, if the user wants to further specify, for example, that the man in the retrieved images must be seated. Consequently, we note that the introduction of the spatial relation has a clear impact on the precision of the system. The use of a rich indexing language, which allows for the formulation of different kinds of relations, proves its usefulness.

It is worth mentioning that, while it can be envisaged that the user might have the time to go through 17 retrieved images and choose the relevant ones, this would hold no longer if the collection scaled-up. The experiments presented here were performed

[6] Precision and recall are obviously computed according to the first class, which corresponds to the projection operator.

on our PARISYS test collection of 650 images [8]. If the collection size increased to, say, 65000 images, having the user go through all of them and choose the (supposedly) 1700 relevant images is not a practical hypothesis. Even for the 17 images retrieved by the boolean-like query on the PARISYS collection, one can see that choosing the good 6 relevant images is not obvious (see figure 10).

In order to obtain a more detailed evaluation of the difference in precision for our conceptual graphs-based system as opposed to a boolean system, we ran some of the PARISYS queries, whose results were given in advance by specialists of the French Ministry of Culture. Figure 9 gives an idea of the importance of the use of relations in a precision-oriented system. In the worst case, when no relation is used except that of composition (which is generated internally by the interface for the structural view), our system cannot obtain results worse than those of a boolean system. Adding relations results in increasing precision or, correspondingly, reducing noise.

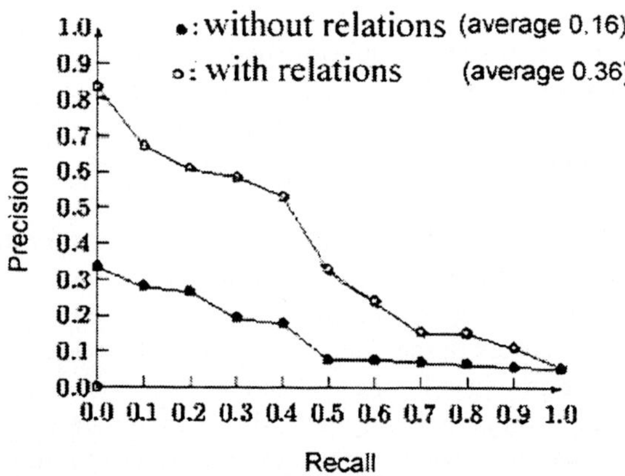

Fig. 9. Precision improvement by using relations in the query formulation, as opposed to the boolean-like query formulation.

The RELIEF system is an implementation of a logical IR model. This stems from the fact that the projection operator for conceptual graphs can be assimilated to a logical implication from the document to the query [3]. Indeed, in the general logical IR model, a document is retrieved if it logically implies the query. This gives a powerful flexible model, and it leads to retrieval effectiveness which is better, in terms of precision, than that of previously introduced IR models (boolean, vector-based or probabilistic models), as it was proven that the logical IR model can be instantiated to the other models [15, 16]. The increased precision of our system confirms this theoretical result. Furthermore, the opinion (never verified in practice) that the logical IR model is not practicable due to its complexity is not necessarily true. Our logically-based index organization allows to achieve important speed-up, as we show in the next sub-section.

6.2 A Faster Retrieval

Using a classic approach, the query conceptual graph would have to be matched against each index of the 650 images. This is done in search of a projection of the query into each of the indexes. To avoid the practically proven negative impact of such an approach on the retrieval rapidity [10], we illustrate here the importance of our structures in the improvement of execution time. By running the PARISYS queries, we found that our index organization reduces execution times by a factor of 10. Indeed, we have an execution time between 6 and 53 seconds for the projection operator, and between 1 and 3 seconds for our algebraic approach. This gives an average of 17.6 versus 1.8 seconds. The speed improvement illustrates another contribution of this paper. By using an algebraic approach to solve a logical implication, that is, using set operations on an inverted-file structure instead of the projection inference itself, we achieve much better retrieval time performance. We believe that an algebraic solution can be found for each logic-based indexing language. It is the case of conceptual graphs, as shown here, but it may also be the case of formalisms such as terminological logics.

7 Conclusion

We presented a complete solution to the problem of modeling, indexing and retrieving images. We use the conceptual graphs formalism to this effect and illustrate how this choice reduces the noise and therefore improves overall retrieval effectiveness (precision).

This paper's contribution is its being a proof that the logical model for information retrieval is not only a powerful theoretical model that contains the other ones previously developed, thus obtaining at least the quality given by such models, but it can also be implemented for efficient retrieval.

We achieve reasonable time performance thanks to an adequate organization of conceptual graphs. Though our execution times are of the order of seconds, while boolean systems may perform retrieval in several milliseconds, we think that our early results are encouraging. It may be a personal opinion, but we would prefer to wait some more seconds each time we submit queries to AltaVista, if the proportion of relevant documents amongst those retrieved were larger. Search engines are very useful for the Internet users community, but notions such as relevance and ranking are not actually taken into account into the present-day versions [2]. The importance of precision for an image retrieval system, as well as the support offered by the conceptual graphs for expressing accurately the original information need, should not be under-estimated. Moreover, we estimate that, by improving the algorithms used for our early implementation, we can significantly cut down execution times.

Future work includes the introduction of ranking in our system. As we already mentioned, the current version only provides classification of images into classes, without further ranking within a class. We are going to extend the $tf \times idf$ method [17], which was mainly developed for text, in order to take into account parameters depending on other types of media, such as images. For instance, such an image parameter would be the area of the objects, computed from the contours of the objects identified during

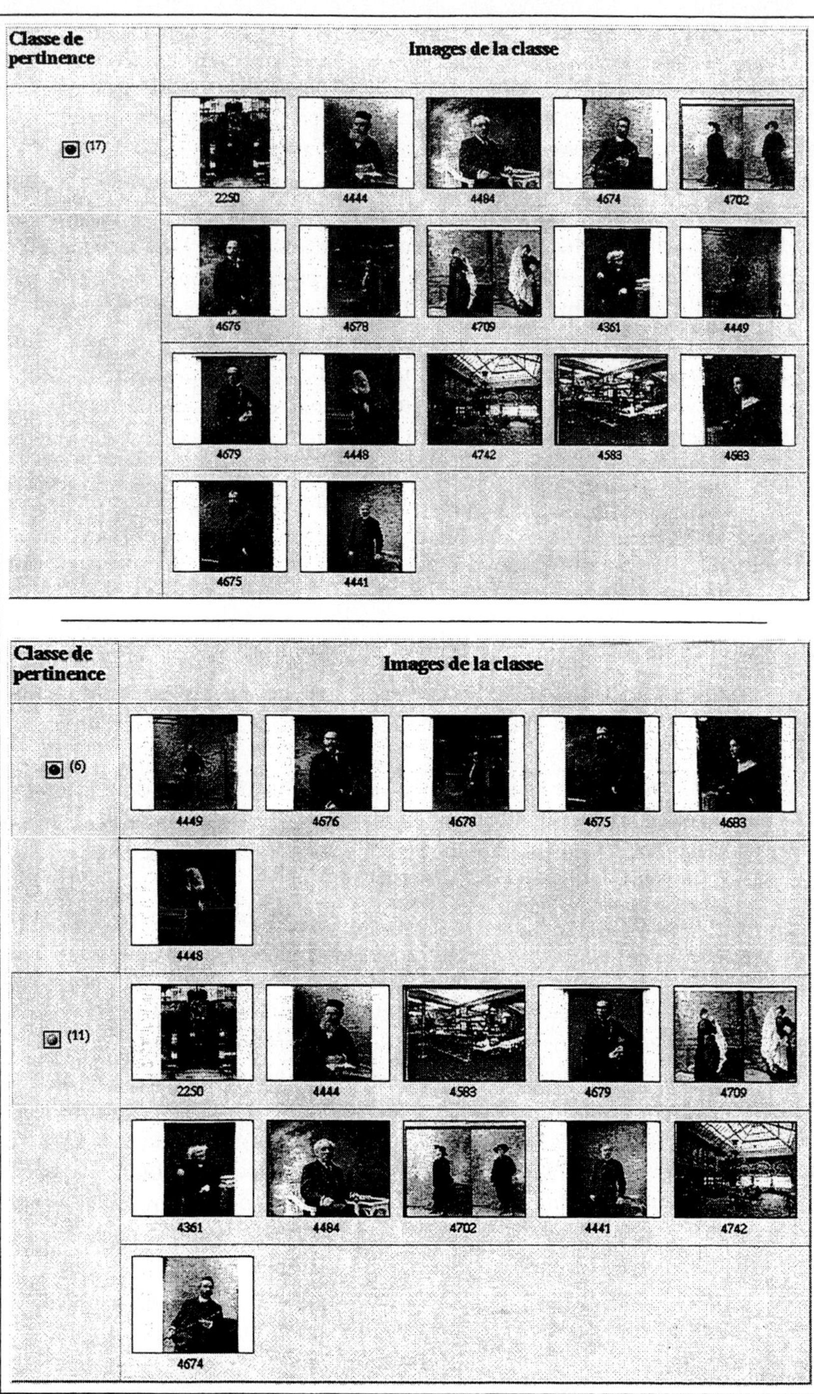

Fig. 10. Images retrieved for the queries *images showing a human and a table* (upper Web interface caption) and *images showing a human on the right of a table* (lower Web interface caption)

indexing. It would allow, for a query looking for a man, to rank the first image in figure 2 before the second one, in decreasing order of the object areas. We identified other parameters as well, which are now being implemented in the system.

References

1. H.J. Levesque and R.J. Brachman. *A fundamental tradeoff in knowledge representation and reasoning*, pages 42–70. Morgan Kaufmann Publishers, Los Atlos, California, 1985.
2. O. Andrieu. *Trouver l'info sur l'internet.* Eyrolles, Paris, France, 1998.
3. J.F. Sowa. *Conceptual Structures : Information Processing in Mind and Machine.* Addison-Wesley Publishing Company, 1984.
4. T.W.C. Huibers, I. Ounis, and J.P. Chevallet. Conceptual graphs aboutness. In P.W. Eklund, G. Ellis, and G. Mann, editors, *Proceedings of the 4th International Conference on Conceptual Structures, ICCS'96*, volume 1115 of *Lecture Notes in Artificial Intelligence*, pages 130–144, Sydney, August 1996. Springer-Verlag, Berlin.
5. I. Ounis and M. Pasca. Effective and efficient relational query processing using conceptual graphs. In *20th Annual BCS-IRSG Colloquium on IR Research, Autrans, France.* EWIC, Springer-Verlag, 25–27 March 1998.
6. M. Mechkour. *EMIR2. Un Modèle étendu de représentation et de correspondance d'images pour la recherche d'informations. Application à un corpus d'image historiques.* PhD thesis, Université Joseph Fourier, Grenoble, 1995.
7. M. Mechkour. EMIR2. An extended model for image representation and retrieval. In *DEXA'95. Database and EXpert system Applications, London.*, pages 395–404, September 1995.
8. Y. Chiaramella and M. Mechkour. Indexing an image test collection. Technical report, FERMI BRA 8134, April 1997.
9. I. Ounis and M. Pasca. The RELIEF retrieval system. In *The IEEE Knowledge and Data Engineering Exchange Workshop (KDEX'97), Newport Beach, California, U.S.A.* IEEE Computer Society Press, November 1997.
10. M. Chein and M.L. Mugnier. Conceptual graphs: fundamental notions. *Revue d'Intelligence Artificielle*, 6(4):365–406, 1992.
11. I. Ounis and M. Pasca. RELIEF: Combining expressiveness and rapidity into a single system. Accepted at the ACM SIGIR'98 conference, Melbourne, Australia, 1998.
12. C.C. Chang and H.J. Keisler. *Model Theory.* North-Holland, 1973.
13. I. Ounis and M. Pasca. A promising retrieval algorithm for systems based on the conceptual graphs formalism. In *International Database Engineering & Applications Symposium (IDEAS'98), Cardiff, UK.* IEEE Computer Society Press, July 1998.
14. Deux O. and al. The o2 system. *Communications of the ACM*, 34(10):34–48, 1991.
15. J. Nie. *Un Modèle Logique général pour les systèmes de recherche d'informations. Application au prototype RIME.* PhD thesis, Université Joseph Fourier, Grenoble, 1990.
16. Y. Chiaramella and J.P. Chevallet. About retrieval models and logic. *The Computer Journal*, 35(3), 1992.
17. G. Salton and C. Buckley. Term-weighting approaches in automatic text retrieval. *Information Processing & Management*, 24(5):513–523, 1988.

Applying Document Retrieval Techniques in Software Engineering Environments

Andreas Henrich

Praktische Informatik, Fakultät Sozial- und Wirtschaftswissenschaften, Otto-Friedrich-Universität Bamberg, D-96045 Bamberg, Germany, e-mail: andreas.henrich@sowi.uni-bamberg.de

Abstract. In previous papers we have proposed the integration of content-based document retrieval facilities into the repository underlying a software engineering environment. In the present paper we describe the application of these facilities in typical application areas, such as searching reusable components or identifying project dependencies. Furthermore we describe the integration of the facilities into a concrete software engineering environment.

1 Introduction

Most modern software engineering environments utilize something which might be called an *object base* as the repository for the data used by the tools of the environment. The main objective of the repository is data integration, i.e. the sharing of data/documents between multiple tools. As a side effect a valuable information pool accrues. This information pool comprises documents of various types from various projects. Unfortunately repositories usually provide only limited query facilities to exploit this information pool. For example the ISO repository standard PCTE [6] provides only navigational access to the data and other repositories based on relational database technology provide an SQL query language. However, various situations can arise where more powerful retrieval facilities would be useful. Two typical scenarios are as follows:

- The sales department states the request for a new information system supporting their field service representatives, and the IT department has to draw up a prestudy for the intended project. In this case it would be desirable, to search the repository for relevant and/or reusable documents from other projects. To this end, a search by content would be useful. For example, a short description of the new project could be used to search for documents with similar content in the repository.
- To avoid possible inconsistencies the quality assurance group of a company wants to search for redundant class definitions in the repository. To this end, it would be useful, to determine the most similar pairs of classes, which are no relatives of each other in the inheritance hierarchy. The similarity can for example be defined on the content of the class definitions, on the associated attributes and on the signatures of the associated methods.

In practice information needs like those mentioned in the first example above are often addressed using pattern matching facilities like the `grep` command in UNIX. Although these pattern matching facilities are useful in many situations they have certain drawbacks: (1) They do not consider different forms of a word or synonyms, (2) they do not allow for the definition of a content-based similarity measure between documents, and (3) they do not allow for a ranking of the documents with respect to their relevance for the information need.

To overcome these problems content-based search techniques have been developed in the field of information retrieval. The techniques developed allow for example to search for the documents most similar to a given query text, where similarity is defined content-based. The abstraction from the concrete wording of a document is achieved for example using stemming techniques and techniques to exploit the correlation between different terms.

In [4] we have presented P-OQL, an OQL-oriented query language for PCTE combining the usual declarative access ("`select` ... `from` ... `where`") with content-based retrieval facilities (cf. section 2). Furthermore in [3] and [5] we have proposed special access structures for the efficient evaluation of corresponding queries. The main contribution of the present paper is to describe the application of these retrieval facilities in a broad variety of situations (cf. section 3) and to sketch their integration in a software engineering environment (cf. section 4). In particular we will describe the various opportunities to combine similarity-based queries with additional conditions and to define new application specific similarity measures dynamically.

2 The Repository

PCTE (*Portable Common Tool Environment*) is the ISO and ECMA standard for a public tool interface (PTI) for an open repository [6]. As one of its major components PCTE contains a structurally object-oriented object management system (OMS). The data model of the PCTE OMS can be seen as an extension of the binary Entity-Relationship Model. The object base contains objects and relationships. Relationships are normally bidirectional. Each relationship is realized by a pair of directed links, which are reverse links of each other. PCTE offers five different link categories: *composition* (defining the destination object as a component of the origin object), *existence* (keeping the destination object in existence), *reference* (assuring referential integrity and representing a property of the origin object), *implicit* (assuring referential integrity) and *designation* (without referential integrity).

Let us consider the example schema for OOA-diagrams in figure 1. As usual, object types are given in rectangles, attribute types are given in ovals, and link types are indicated by arrows. A double arrowhead at the end of a link indicates that the link has cardinality *many*. Links with cardinality *many* must have a key attribute. In the example the numeric attribute *no* is used for this purpose. A *"C"* or *"R"* in the triangles at the center of the line representing a pair of links, indicates that the link has category *composition* or *reference*.

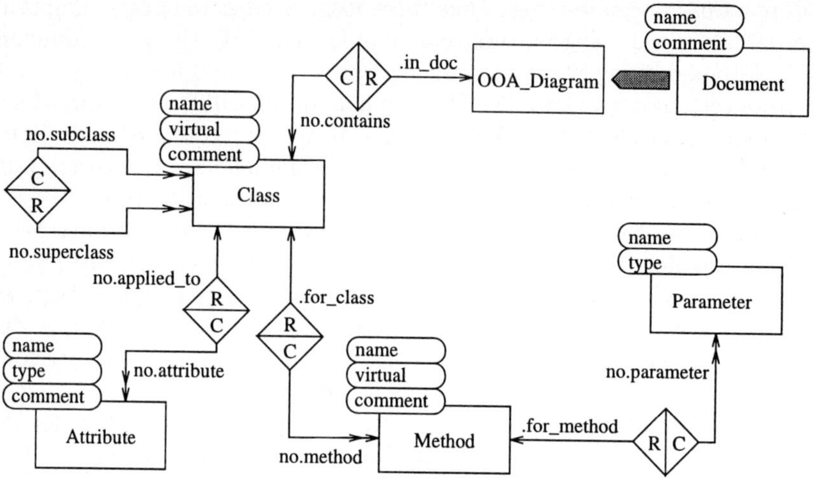

Fig. 1. Simplified example schema for OOA-diagrams

Finally the schema contains a subtype relationship between the object types *Document* and *OOA_Diagram* which is indicated by a broad shaded arrow.

P-OQL [2] is an OQL-oriented query language for PCTE. Assume that we search for the name and the applicable methods of all classes in the OOA-diagram named *"Clearing"*. The following query in P-OQL yields this information:

```
select C:name, normalize C:[_.superclass]*/_.method/->name
  from D in OOA_Diagram, C in (D:_.contains/->.)
  where D:name = "Clearing"
```

In the **from-clause** two base sets are defined: Base set `D` addressing all OOA-diagrams and base set `C` addressing all objects which can be reached from the actual object of base set `D` via a path matching the regular path expression "`D:_.contains/->.`". In this path expression the prefix "`D:`" addresses the actual element of base set `D`. "`_.contains`" means that exactly one link of type *contains* must be traversed. The underscore ("`_`") is used as a wildcard for numerical key attributes. "`/->`" is used to address the destination object of the path. In addition "`->`" can be used to address the last link of the path. The "`.`" at the end of the regular path expression means that the object under concern is addressed. It is also possible, to address an attribute or a tuple of values.

In the **where-clause** of our example query the considered combinations of OOA-diagrams and classes are restricted to those for which the *name* attribute of the OOA-diagram has the value *"Clearing"*.

The **select-clause** states that a multiset of pairs is requested. Each pair consists of the name of the class and a set containing the names of the methods which can be applied to instances of the class. Since methods defined for superclasses of the class under concern can also be applied to instances of the class, we have to address these methods as well. To this end, the regular path expression "`C:[_.superclass]*/_.method/->name`" is used. "`[_.superclass]*`" defines that zero or more links matching the link definition "`_.superclass`" have to be traversed. Alternatively P-OQL knows the iteration facilities "`[` *path_definition* `]+`" to indicate that a path matching *path_definition* has to be traversed at least once and "`[` *path_definition* `]`" to indicate that a path matching *path_definition* is optional. Summarizing, the regular path expression "`C:[_.superclass]*/_.method/->name`" determines a multiset containing the names of all methods which can be reached from the class object under concern traversing an arbitrary number of *superclass* links and exactly one link of type *method*. This multiset is transformed into a set using the unary operator `normalize`.

In addition to the link definitions used in the above example P-OQL allows the specification of a set of link categories with the meaning that all links having one of the given categories fulfill this link definition. E.g. the expression "`[{c, e}]+/->.`" addresses all objects which can be reached via a path consisting only of links with category *composition* or *existence*. Finally an additional `shield`-option can be used to prevent traversing a link of a given type or a link with a destination object of a given type. For example the link definition "`{c shield subclass}`" allows to traverse arbitrary *composition* links except those of type *subclass*.

As mentioned in the introduction one main feature of P-OQL is the integrated **document retrieval facilities**. These facilities implement the vector space model [9, 7]. This model assumes that an available term set (vocabulary) is used to identify both, maintained documents and information requests. Queries and documents are represented as *term vectors* of the form $D_i = (a_{i1}, a_{i2}, \ldots, a_{it})$ and $Q_j = (q_{j1}, q_{j2}, \ldots, q_{jt})$ where t is the number of the terms in the term set and where the coefficients a_{ik} and q_{jk} represent the relevance of document D_i or query Q_j, respectively, with respect to term k. In the literature various term-weighting formulas have been proposed to calculate the a_{ik} and q_{jk}. In P-OQL we employ the formulas presented in [8] which have been proved to be competitive e.g. in [1].

To integrate these formulas into P-OQL, we use three operators. First there are the unary operators `D_vector` and `Q_vector` which determine a document or query description vector, respectively. Roughly spoken these operators calculate the vector components for the terms based (1) on the term frequency of the term in the document under concern and (2) on the inverse collection frequency which is high for terms occurring in only a few documents and low for terms occurring in many documents (see [4] for the details). The third operator is the binary operator `sim` calculating the conventional vector product of a document and a query description vector. This yields high values for "similar" documents and low values for "unrelated" documents.

The operator `D_vector` can be applied to *document definitions*. A *document definition* can e.g. be (1) a string attribute, (2) an object (in this case all string attributes of the object are considered), or (3) a collection (set, multiset, list, or structure) of the before-mentioned entities. Such a collection can e.g. be defined by a regular path expression.

If we are e.g. looking for non-virtual class definitions similar to a given textual class description, it would be appropriate to consider each *Class* object together with the associated attribute and method definitions as a *"class definition document"*. This is done in the following query applying `D_vector` to a set of objects determined by the path expression "`[{c shield subclass}]*/->.`". The query determines the 10 classes most similar to the textual class description:

```
head[10]
  sort-
    (select (Q_vector "<textual class description>"
             sim D_vector [{c shield subclass}]*/->.),
             name
       from Class
       where virtual = FALSE)
```

In this query the query text is given as a string constant. The `Q_vector` operator is applied to this query text to create the query description vector. The document description vectors are determined applying the `D_vector` operator to the *"class definition documents"*.

The select-statement yields a multiset of pairs, where the first component contains the similarity value for the actual *"document"* and the second component contains the value of the *name* attribute of the *"document"*. The `sort-` operator is applied to the result of the select-statement yielding a list with the pairs sorted descendingly according to their similarity values. Then the `head` operator is used to extract the 10 elements at the beginning of this list.

3 Application Examples

3.1 Addressing Documents of Various Types

In software development projects situations are common, where someone searches for documents dealing with a specific topic. Assume for example that a new project is set up for a specific problem. In this case the project leader will be interested in all documents created by previous projects which address this problem area. In this situation the type of these documents is of minor importance. Fortunately the generic path definitions based on link categories allow for such type independent queries in P-OQL. For a given query text — for example a short description of the new project might be used for this purpose — the following query searches the 25 most similar documents in the repository:

```
head[25]
  sort-
    (select (Q_vector "query text" sim D_vector [{c}]*/->.),
            .,
            type of .
       from Document^)
```

In the from-clause of this query "Document^" defines that all objects are addressed which are either of type *Document* or of an arbitrary subtype. In the select-clause the result items are defined as triples. In the first component the similarity value is calculated. For the calculation of the description vector for the document we consider all string attributes of objects which can be reached traversing zero or more *composition* links. In the second component the dot defines that an object reference of the object under concern is required. This object reference can be used to apply other PCTE operations and it can be passed to a tool which deals with objects/documents of the corresponding type. Finally in the third component the type of the document under concern is determined.

3.2 Content-Based Retrieval with Additional Conditions

Besides the broad queries described in the previous section, precisely restricted queries are as well needed during software development. One usual requirement in this respect is to combine a content-based query with additional conditions. For example one might be interested only in documents created by a certain person or after a certain date, or one might be interested in method definitions with a special signature. Due to the homogeneous integration of the document retrieval facilities into P-OQL the query language provides unlimited freedom in this respect. As an example, we can search for the classes most similar to a given query text and in addition demand that the classes should not be virtual and have an attribute named *"state"*:

```
head[25]
  sort-
    (select (Q_vector "query text"
             sim D_vector [{c shield subclass}]*/->.),
             .
       from Class
       where virtual = false
         and exists A in _.attribute/->. with A:name =[1] "state")
```

In the exists quantifier all attributes of the actual class are addressed and it is demanded that at least one name of an attribute has an edit distance to *"state"* of at most 1.

Another opportunity is to address the structure of the complex objects under concern. For example we can search for the methods most similar to a given query text which have at least two parameters of type *"float"* and one parameter of type *"integer"* (note that constant multisets are defined as `M{ ... }` in P-OQL):

```
head[25]
  sort-
    (select (Q_vector "query text" sim D_vector [{c}]*/->.), .
       from Method
       where M{"float", "float", "integer"} <= _.parameter/->type)
```

3.3 User-Defined Similarity Measures

One obvious drawback of the document retrieval facilities integrated in P-OQL is that they address only the content-based similarity of the textual parts of the documents. On the other hand, we can utilize the expressive power of P-OQL to define new similarity measures. Assume for example that we are interested in methods. Obviously there are different ways to define the similarity of methods. One opportunity would be to address the signatures, another opportunity might be to address the control structures and last but not least the similarity can be defined on the text written in the comment attribute. Depending on the concrete situation it might be useful to combine multiple similarity measures. As an example the following query combines the content-based similarity of the comment attributes and the similarity of the signatures, where the desired signature consists of two float parameters and one integer parameter:

```
head[25]
  sort-
    (select ((Q_vector "query text" sim D_vector comment)
            * count (M{"float", "float", "integer"}
                     intersect _.parameter/->type)),
            .
      from Method)
```

In this query the cardinality of the intersection of the desired signature and the actual signature is multiplied by the content-based similarity of a given query text and the comment attribute. This way we yield a symmetric combined measure where a higher similarity with respect to one basic similarity measure can compensate a lower similarity with respect to the other similarity measure. It is also possible to combine similarity measures in a hierarchical way. Assume for example that the signature-based similarity should be the dominant one. Then the similarity for the comment attribute should be considered only for methods which have the same signature-based similarity value. Since "`Q_vector "query text" sim D_vector comment`" yields results in the interval $[0,1]$ and "`count (M{"float", "float", "integer"} intersect _.parameter/->type)`" yields values out of $\{0, 1, 2, 3\}$ this can be achieved by the following query:

```
head[25]
 sort-
  (select (count (M{"float", "float", "integer"}
                 intersect _.parameter/->type)
          + 0.5 * (Q_vector "query text" sim D_vector comment)),
          .
     from Method)
```

3.4 Selecting Similar Pairs

As mentioned in the introduction, the information retrieval facilities can also be used to search for redundant documents indicating double work and potential inconsistencies. Assume for example that we are trying to avoid unrelated classes implementing similar things. In this case we could search for pairs of classes with a high similarity, which are not related to each other in the inheritance graph:

```
head[25]
  sort-
    (select (D_vector A:[{c shield subclass}]/->.
             sim D_vector B:[{c shield subclass}]/->.),
            A:.,
            B:.
       from A in Class, B in Class
       where A:. < B:.
         and A:. !in B:[_.subclass]+/->.
         and B:. !in A:[_.subclass]+/->.)
```

The first condition in the qualification-clause of this query assures that (1) no pair containing the same class in both components is returned and that (2) the pairs are not reported twice — as (a, b) and as (b, a). The second and the third condition assure that neither a is a subclass of b nor b is a subclass of a.

Summarizing, the above query yields the 25 most similar pairs of classes which are not related in the inheritance graph. For these pairs an expert might now consider if the classes should be in some inheritance relation or if they are really independent.

4 Integrating the Retrieval Facilities into a CASE Tool

The major aim of PCTE and P-OQL is to support tool developers. Tool developers should use the high level functionality of PCTE and P-OQL via the application programming interface (API) to develop new tools with a reasonable effort. Nevertheless, it seems to be worthwhile, to integrate a special tool into a software engineering environment which enables the user of the software engineering environment to state similarity searches directly.

Figure 2 shows the user interface of our tool. The main window comprises three subwindows.

- In the subwindow *"Addressed Entity"* the *root objects* of the addressed documents are defined. To this end, an object type can be selected from a menu. This menu also shows the inheritance relations between the object types. In addition the user can define that objects of subtypes should be addressed as well, and he can state a selection predicate in the usual P-OQL syntax.
- In the subwindow *"Address As Document"* the attributes or objects containing the content of each document can be defined. The user can either select one of the three standard opportunities or he can state a regular path expression in the P-OQL syntax.
- In the subwindow *"Query"* the information need can be defined either by a query text, or by selecting and weighting terms from the vocabulary, or by a regular expression.

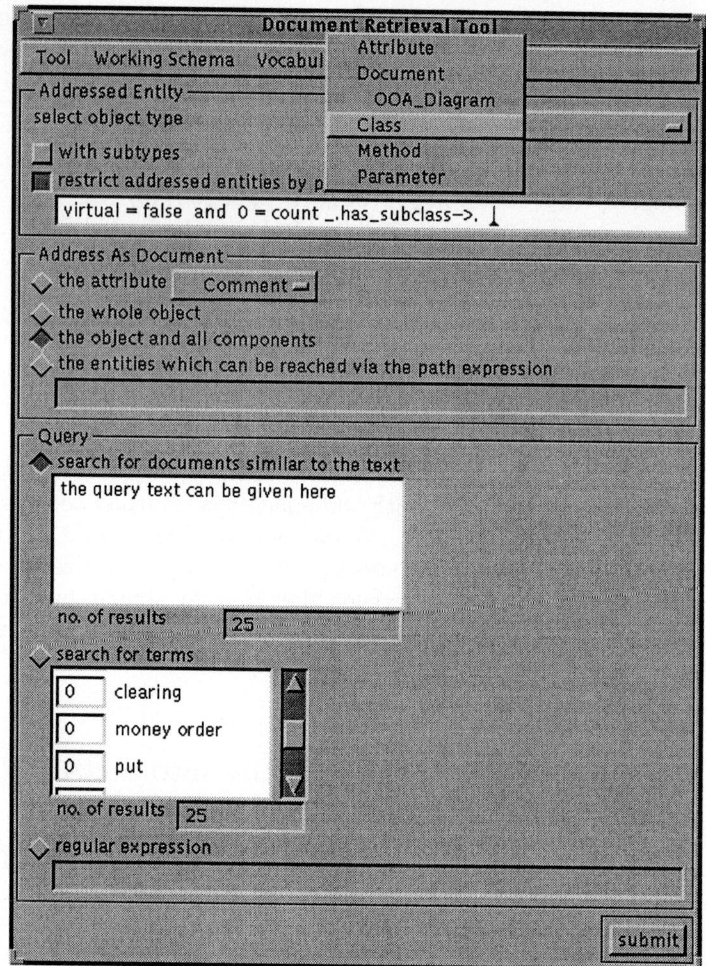

Fig. 2. An end-user interface for the document retrieval facilities

When the *"submit"*-button is pushed, a P-OQL query is created based on the selections of the user. In addition the tool searches for an attribute *name* or *Name* applied to the selected type for the object representing the document. If such an attribute exists, it is integrated into the query result to enhance the readability of the result. Furthermore the type of the object is addressed using the `type of` operator.

In case the option *"search for terms"* is chosen in the subwindow *"Query"*, the application of the `Q_vector` operator is replaced by an explicitly given query vector (which is stated in an abbreviating notation). If the option *"regular expression"* is chosen in the subwindow *"Query"*, the query is transformed into a query applying the pattern matching facilities of P-OQL described in [4].

Once a query is submitted, the next problem is the presentation of the query result. To this end, we employ a standard result viewer. In this viewer all values except of link references and object references are presented in a formatted way. Link and object references are represented by buttons. If a button representing an object is pushed, the viewer creates a list with all objects in the repository containing the object under concern as a component. In this list the objects are sorted with respect to the length of the paths connecting the object in the list and the object under concern. Then the tool registration module of the software engineering environment is asked for each element in the list if there are tools registered for the corresponding object type. If exactly one tool exists for all elements in the list, this tool is started. If more than one tool exists, a tool selection menu is displayed where the user can choose the tool he wants to start in order to work with the selected object. If no tool exists, a standard object browser is opened. This browser displays the attributes and links of the object under concern and allows to navigate across the links. While navigating with the browser, the browser always asks the tool registration module of the software engineering environment for the tools available for the actual object and the user can start these tools from the menu bar.

Obviously similar interfaces can be built for other types of queries. Furthermore the presented tool allows to state queries in plain P-OQL. Since queries can be saved, this allows experienced users to compose queries for different purposes, which can be utilized by other users.

References

1. D. Harman. Overview of the second text retrieval conference (TREC-2). *Information Processing and Management*, 31(3):271–289, 1995.
2. A. Henrich. P-OQL: an OQL-oriented query language for PCTE. In *Proc. 7th Conf. on Software Engineering Environments (SEE '95)*, pages 48–60, Noordwijkerhout, Netherlands, 1995. IEEE Computer Society Press.
3. A. Henrich. Adapting a spatial access structure for document representations in vector space. In *Proc. 5th Intl. Conf. on Information and Knowledge Management*, pages 19–26, Rockville, Md., USA, 1996.
4. A. Henrich. Document retrieval facilities for repository-based system development environments. In *Proc. 19th Annual Intl. ACM SIGIR Conf. on Research and Development in Information Retrieval*, pages 101–109, Zürich, 1996.
5. A. Henrich. A homogeneous access structure for standard attributes and document representations in vector space. In *Proc. 3rd Intl. Workshop on Next Generation Information Technologies and Systems*, Neve Ilan, Jerusalem, Israel, June 1997.
6. Portable Common Tool Environment - Abstract Specification / C Bindings / Ada Bindings. Standards ECMA-149/-158/-165, 3rd edition, and ISO IS 13719-1/-2/-3, 1994.
7. G. Salton. *Automatic Text Processing: the Transformation, Analysis, and Retrieval of Information by Computer.* Addison-Wesley, Reading, Mass., USA, 1989.
8. G. Salton and C. Buckley. Term-weighting approaches in automatic text retrieval. *Information Processing & Management*, 24(5):513–523, 1988.
9. G. Salton, A. Wong, and C.S. Yang. A vector space model for automatic indexing. *Communications of the ACM*, 18(11):613–620, November 1975.

Browsing SGML Documents with Maps: The French "Inventaire" Experience*

Bernd Amann[1], Dan Vodislav[1], Julio Fernandes[1] and Georges Coste[2]

[1] Cedric CNAM, 292 Rue St. Martin
75141 Paris Cedex 03 France
{amann, vodislav, fernandj}@cnam.fr

[2] DRAC Poitou-Charentes, Service Régional de l'Inventaire, 102 Grand-Rue BP 553
86020 Poitiers Cedex France
coste@culture.fr

Abstract. For GIS, SGML document servers and other highly specialized application domains, the systems integration problem is essential since the available software often is complex and would be costly to reimplement or to modify. In this paper we describe a two-level architecture for integrating software components based on partial data integration and user interface synchronization. We also present a prototype implementation of this architecture.

1 Introduction

The growing facility to access distributed data via the World Wide Web has opened the horizon to new software environments integrating related information from different application domains. Real-world entities often share addresses or other geo-referencing attributes which might be exploited for the integration of data. For example, a document archive might store a collection of structured SGML (Standard Generalized Markup Language) [11] documents which describe historical buildings of the 18th century. The address of each building is contained in the document and corresponds to a point or a region on a map stored in a Geographic Information System (GIS). This spatial property might then be used in different ways starting from the simple graphical display on a map interface to complex query processing about the document contents and the positions of the buildings they describe.

Standard database technology supplies efficient storage and query processing of strongly typed complex objects and relations. But it also suffers from the lack of flexibility for storing and manipulating *complex, non-standard application specific data*. Examples of such data are structured documents (SGML, HTML, XML), computer-aided design (CAD) diagrams, spatial maps and images. A common solution to this problem is to extend the logical database model by some application specific Abstract Data Types (ADT) which are implemented

* This work has been supported by the French *Ministère de la Culture (Direction du Patrimoine)* Grant 97 5620 024

by highly-specialized software components. These components allow query processing on both standard and application specific data and range from specific index structures to adapted user interfaces.

The ADT approach has several serious drawbacks. First, its implementation relies on a strict separation between the logical database model and the application specific abstract data types and leads to a *non-uniform processing* of "standard" and "non-standard" data. Second, whereas recent versions of commercially available Database Management Systems (DBMS) such as Oracle [10] or O_2 [9] provide extensions devoted to spatial data or other application specific information structures such as SGML documents [6], it still remains difficult to implement applications integrating for example SGML documents and spatial maps. The display and manipulation of complex data structures such as GIS maps, CAD diagrams or SGML documents generally need *adapted user interfaces.* Application specific data and software is *rapidly changing* with respect to new needs, architectures and algorithms. As it is the case for user interfaces, this is orthogonal to the development of standard application independent database software.

In this paper we describe the integration of two complex software components, i.e. an SGML document server and a GIS component. Our approach is based on the interoperation of these two components at the data level and the user interface level. Section 2 presents the French "Inventaire" (Inventory) project. In Section 3 we describe the motivation for extending standard document querying and browsing with spatial functionalities. Section 4 presents a general architecture for integrating an SGML document server with a GIS component. The prototype implementation on top of a SGML document server based on the O_2 Object-Oriented DBMS and ESRI's commercially available ArcView system is presented in Section 5. Future perspectives based on a mediated approach and related work are described in Section 6 and Section 7.

2 The French "Inventaire" project

The "Inventaire" (Inventory) project, realized by the French *Ministère de la Culture*, the *Conservatoire national des Arts et Métiers* (CNAM), the *Institut National de Recherche en Informatique et Automatique* (INRIA) and the Euroclid company, aims the creation of structured documents on French historical monuments and the definition of access methods to this information through the Web. Currently, information about historical monuments is scattered. Textual descriptions, photos, sketches, maps are separately managed and only the paper form of the document puts all the elements together. The main goals of the project are (1) the definition of the SGML structure (DTD) and the representation of inventory documents, (2) the definition of the stages and the procedure for the creation of such documents (document workflow), (3) the creation of export interfaces to other formats, and (4) the support of an on-line access for consulting the documents through the Web [18]. This paper presents our approach to the last issue.

Inventory data, organized in documents and folders, has a rather complex structure. Documents concern objects, buildings, aggregates of buildings and contain textual information, photos, plans, maps, etc. Folders may group documents on spatial (e.g. all monuments in Paris) or spatio-thematic criteria (e.g. all monuments of the 15th century in Paris). Several types of links may relate documents and folders : membership of documents to folders, inclusion of folders, relations among documents (e.g. a crucifix is located within a church, a cathedral has similar characteristics to another one).

An important property of monuments is their spatial location which is described by a geometric form (point, line, polygon) in the geographic space. Location plays a structuring role in the creation of inventory documents and folders, because spatial criteria are used to group elements and to build links between documents. Therefore, the geographic dimension is essential in browsing and querying documents. The user must be able to display maps, to navigate through the geographic space, to visualize monuments as spatial objects on the map, to express spatial queries on the location of monuments.

This paper focus on the integration of spatial clues for browsing and consulting of inventory documents through the Web. Visualization of SGML documents and navigation through links is completed with the display of monuments as spatial objects on maps and navigation through the geographic space. Queries on the contents and the structure of documents are enriched with spatial criteria on the location of monuments. We study the problems raised by the integration, we propose some possible solutions, and we describe the current implementation.

3 Extending User Interaction

The user interacts with two distinct system components : a SGML Document Server and a GIS Map Server.

The SGML Document Server stores inventory documents and folders as complex objects in some O_2 object-oriented database. The "Inventaire" project has adopted the SGML standard [11] for the internal representation of documents and folders and uses Euroclid's O_2/SGML system [7, 18] for the storage of these documents in the O_2 object-oriented DBMS. The user interface is typically a standard Web browser (e.g. Netscape) and communicates with O_2 via the O_2Web interface. O_2Web allows to the publisher the creation and customization of HTML documents from complex objects. Object relationships are translated into virtual hypertext links (URLs) encapsulating OQL queries which are evaluated at link traversal. The user can (1) display SGML documents describing buildings and artifacts, (2) navigate through documents connected by hypertext links, and (3) query the contents and the structure (e.g. title of the first section) of documents and folders using the OQL query language [6].

The Map Server stores maps and spatial objects based on the location and the extent of monuments. Spatial data handling is realized with ESRI's ArcView System. The Web interface is implemented by the ArcView Internet Map Server (AVIMS). As for the Document Server, the user interface is a standard Web browser providing the user with (1) the display of thematic maps (administrative regions, cities, districts, buildings, etc.), (2) navigation in thematic maps, using zoom and pan operations, and (3) evaluation of spatial (intersection, distance, etc.) and relational SQL queries using the Avenue script language.

It is easy to see that the integration of these functionalities not only represents the sum of the both user environments but adds new functionalities to the user interaction model :

Geo-referenced Document Browsing : Spatial relationships between documents and spatial objects are converted to bi-directional hypertext links for obtaining those documents which correspond to some spatial object or vice-versa. For example, a user might first display a map of Paris, zoom into the third district and then click on the graphical representation (button) of some spatial object, e.g. the Museum of the Conservatoire National des Arts et Métiers, for displaying all documents describing this building. This mechanism "synchronizes" the information displayed by both interfaces.

Spatial Document Querying : Spatial relationships might be exploited for querying both SGML documents and spatial maps simultaneously. For example the user might ask to display all spatial objects corresponding to museums in the third district of Paris. In fact, this corresponds to the dynamic definition of map layers depending on the document contents. Spatial selection of documents (e.g. display all documents describing churches of the 15th century at a distance of less than 500 meters to the Louvre museum) is also possible.

Each subsystem has its own specific Web user interface for browsing and querying data. Therefore, the problem of integrating structured documents and maps has to be handled at the data and the user interface level. In our case, the data model and the Web user interface for the two system components (SGML and GIS) are quite complex and different in nature. Therefore, it is very difficult to build a system for browsing spatially located structured documents by only extending one of both components. Actually, ArcView stores non-spatial data in relational tables, but this is not enough for querying and browsing SGML structures. In the same way, a structured documents system based on an object-oriented database could store some spatial data (points, lines, ...) or even maps, but lacks the support for spatial queries and map browsing.

4 Two-Level Interoperability Architectures

In this section we will describe an architecture for integrating two commercially available software components, i.e. a SGML document server based on O_2 and the ArcView Geographic Information System.

4.1 Partial data integration

During the past several years an important effort on standardizing application interfaces has been undertaken. Among these standards, the most popular are

OMG/Corba [14] for general object services, JDBC/ODBC [17] for relational DBMS and ODMG [15] for Object-Oriented DBMS. All of these standards are based on a client-server architecture and uniform logical data models for describing and exchanging data between different applications.

The O_2 DBMS implements a number of standard interfaces (e.g. ODMG, ODBC, Java Binding) for integrating external application software with O_2 database functionalities. ArcView can store spatial and non-spatial data in commercially available relational DBMS (Oracle, Sybase) via ODBC. A two-tier architecture using the ODBC standard for connecting O_2/SGML and ArcView is shown in Figure 1. In this architecture, O_2 and ArcView can exchange SQL

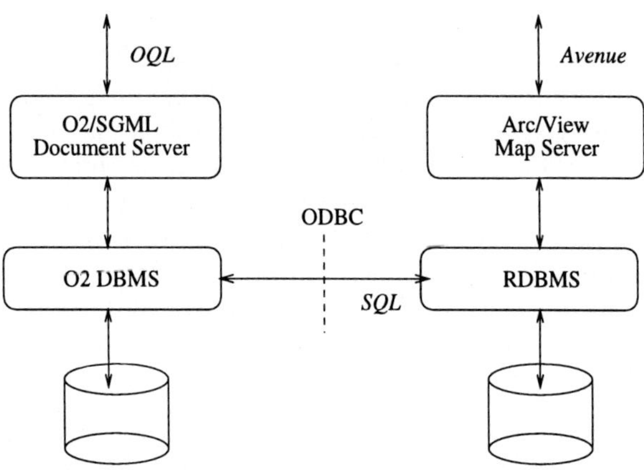

Fig. 1. Two-Tier Architecture : ArcView's relational DBMS and O_2 access external data via the ODBC interface.

queries via ODBC. Whereas this feature is useful for the evaluation of simple SQL queries on external relational tables, it is insufficient for more complex queries on both SGML documents and geographical maps. For example, it is not possible to find all photos of churches at less than 100 meters from the Seine river at Paris. This query has to be decomposed into two complex subqueries. The first subquery is an OQL query on the contents and structure of documents and finds all photos within documents describing churches. The second subquery is a spatial restriction of the distance between churches and the Seine river and must be evaluated by ArcView.

Another problem which is not solved by this architecture concerns the user interface. Since both Web interfaces (O_2Web and AVIMS) are specially conceived for the underlying data structures they are insufficient for browsing and querying external data such as SGML documents in the case of AVIMS or geographical maps in the case of O_2Web. We will present a solution to this problem in the following section.

4.2 User interface integration

The approach proposed in this section is based on the fact that complex data needs adapted user interfaces which are strongly-coupled to the underlying data structures. In order to display and to manipulate both structured documents and spatial data, one needs to integrate existing user interfaces.

The proposed architecture is described in Figure 2. The Document Server and the GIS are both accessed through their own Web user interface which are synchronized by some global synchronization mechanism. At a given time, the user works within one of the two environments and is able to switch to the other one while keeping up the context. Typically, the user browses and queries SGML documents, and asks to display on the map the location of the artifact described in some displayed document. Reversely, the user may ask some spatial queries to the GIS and then access a SGML document by selecting a point on the resulting map.

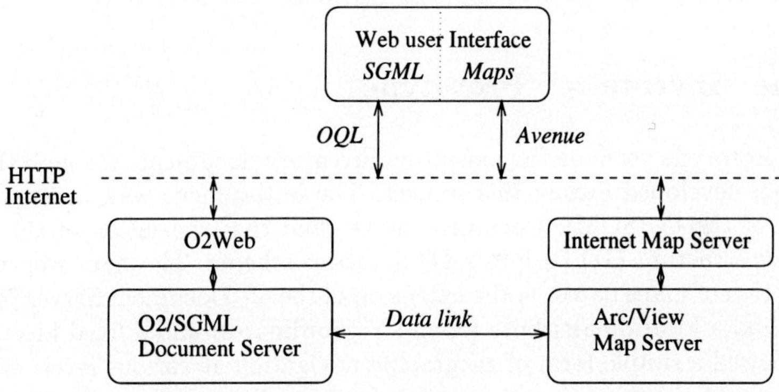

Fig. 2. User Interface Integration Architecture

Each document within the Document Server has a unique, implementation independent identifier (e.g. the value of an attribute). The same value identifies the corresponding spatial object within the GIS. The connection between documents and maps is based on this unique identifier. The global interface keeps the context of the browsing process by storing the identifiers of current accessed objects (in structured document or spatial object form).

Keeping the current context of browsing within the interface allows an easy switching from documents to maps. This favors an user-oriented strategy for asking complex queries on both the description and location of an artifact. For example, the user is searching for photos of 15th century churches within a distance of less than 10 kms of the A6 highway. He will first ask the GIS for monuments at less than 10 kms of the A6 highway. The result of this search is displayed on the map and the corresponding identifiers will form the new context. The user switches then to the SGML interface and asks to the Document

Server only the photos of selected monuments that are 15th century churches. Of course, the way this query is processed depends on the way data is distributed between the GIS and the Document Server, but the principle does not change. For example, if the GIS stores some additional information about monuments (e.g. type of monument, century), the first query is more precise : find 15th century churches with the given spatial condition.

In conclusion, the interface is an active participant to the browsing and querying process. By storing the current context, it allows a transparent communication between its two data-specific parts. More functionalities can be added to the interface by using a vector representation of maps (currently, the ArcView Web interface uses JPEG images for displaying maps). In this case, selecting a spatial object or highlighting the location of a document on the map can be done locally, i.e. within the user interface client.

The main disadvantage of this approach is that complex queries (concerning both document contents and location) have to be split by the user into a spatial part and a structured document part. Future work will consider a *mediated* three-tier architecture for avoiding this drawback (see Section 6).

5 The "Inventaire" Prototype

Several prototype versions for consulting inventory documents through the Web have been developed during this project. The initial focus was directed to the creation of the O_2 SGML Document Server and the translation of the SGML document structure (DTD) into a O_2 database schema. The next step was the introduction of maps based on the extension of the O_2 Document Server [7]. Each artifact had a location attribute (X and Y coordinates) and a fixed hierarchy of maps allowed a simple form of geographic navigation at various levels of detail. The poor spatial browsing and querying functionalities of the second prototype revealed the need of using a GIS.

The current prototype uses ESRI's ArcView GIS and its Web interface ArcView Internet Map Server (AVIMS). The advantage of the interface oriented integration is that the existing O_2 SGML Document Server is reused with minor user interface modifications. The ArcView GIS Server stores several layers of French vector maps (administrative borders, roads, rivers,...) and the spatial inventory data about monuments. This spatial data is extracted from the same SGML documents that feed the O_2 Document Server.

For each spatial object, besides its geometry, ArcView may store and query usual alphanumeric attributes in relational tables. In the current prototype, partial data integration (Section 4.1) has been implemented by data replication. Instead of a dynamic SQL link between ArcView and O_2 (Figure 1) the main alphanumeric attributes (monument type, date, materials, etc.) are replicated in O_2 and ArcView's relational DBMS.

The access to the ArcView GIS is done by launching internal ArcView application scripts, written in the Avenue script language. Scripts implement application behavior within ArcView, by using any of its GIS capabilities (map navigation, spatial queries, etc). AVIMS provides Web client software with HTML, Java or ActiveX access for Web clients to ArcView. The existing prototype uses the Avenue script language for generating raster maps (JPEG images) included in standard HTML documents. A Java interface, based on the AVIMS MapCafé applet, is currently under preparation.

The global user interface combines the Web user interfaces for ArcView and for the O_2 Document Server. The GIS part of the user interface allows for map browsing by zooming and panning, spatial and alphanumeric querying, and object identification. Selecting an object on the map will display the corresponding document in the structured document browser. Reversely, the user may display on the map the location of the current document in the SGML browser.

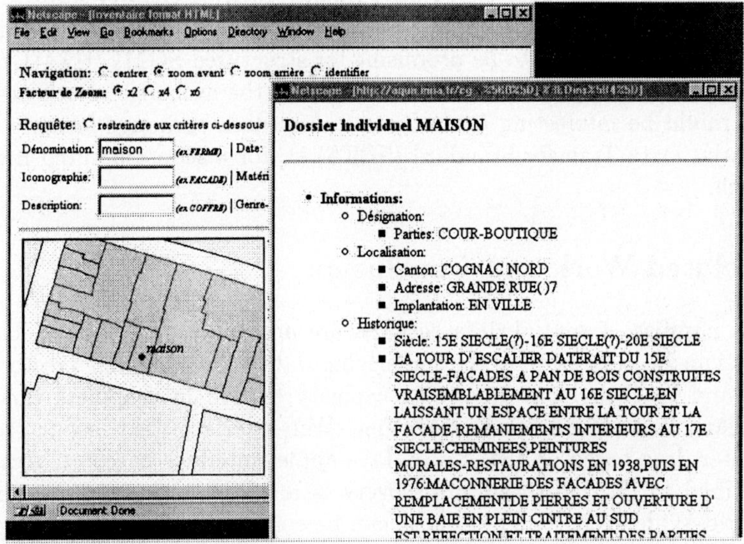

Fig. 3. Screen Snapshot

The screen snapshot shown in Figure 3 is the result of several user actions. The user selected a geographical zone of interest by zooming and panning a thematic map with French administrative borders. The selected zone displays a part of the city of Cognac and all points corresponding to houses built in the 15th century. The new map is the result of an overlay of the old map and the query result. By clicking on the point with label *maison*, the user obtains the SGML document displayed in a different window.

6 Future Work - The Mediated Perspective

A different solution to the problem of integrating software components is the definition of a mediator-based architectures [19]. Mediators break the strong coupling between servers and clients, caused by low-level interfaces allowing only restricted forms of abstraction. They are generally based on common data models restricted to some application domain and include various information processing tasks like format conversion, data access, selection and integration.

The main issue is the definition of a mediation model and query language which are general enough to describe such diverse data as SGML documents and geographical maps and specific enough to be implemented efficiently. Recent work on data mediation proposes different approaches based on the ODMG [5] standard, on description logics [4] or semi-structured data models [2]. The authors are not aware of any evaluation or implementation using one of these approaches for integrating spatial data with other complex data structures. Reference [3] describes a spatial mediator architecture based on the ODMG standard. Nevertheless strongly typed data models such as ODMG seem to be too rigid for the integration of complex data. The approach based on a semistructured view of data seems to be promising for structured SGML/HTML or XML documents. Similar to these standards based on the exchange of self-describing data it might be interesting to evaluate spatial data exchange formats such as the Spatial Data Transfer Standard (SDTS) [1] for a semistructured mediation approach.

7 Related Work and Conclusion

A large number of spatial data services are accessible on Internet. These interfaces can be classified by the underlying data representation (vector versus raster) and by their local processing capacity (active Java applets versus passive HTML ISMAP [13, 8]) The ArcView Web interface used in our prototype uses raster data based on ISMAP. A Java applet interface based on vector data is described in [3]. Information discovery is a major issue for users browsing the World-Wide Web. Our prototype can be considered as a Spatial Digital Library [12] for patrimonial data. On the one hand, the document subsystem represents a catalogue service containing descriptive meta-information for spatial data and, on the other hand, it is possible to find relevant documents with respect to the spatial properties of the buildings they describe. The Open Geodata Interoperability Specification (OGIS) framework [16] achieves "data interoperability" by an extensible information model describing real world space/time phenomena at different abstraction levels (real-world, specification, implementation). This framework has been conceived for spatio-temporal data and does not address the problem of integrating complex data from different application domains.

Acknowledgments

We wish to thank Michel Scholl who set up this work in our group. We would like also to acknowledge O. Toche, H. Verdier, J.Y. Riou and P. Brihaye of the French *Ministère de la Culture* for their support and fruitful discussions.

References

1. Sdts home page. U.S. Geological Survey, Feb. 1998. Online information available: `http://mcmcweb.er.usgs.gov/sdts`.
2. Abiteboul, S. Querying semi-structured data. In *6th Int. Conf. on Database Theory (ICDT)* (1997), vol. 1186 of *LNCS*, Springer, pp. 1–18.
3. Amann, B. Integrating GIS components with mediators and CORBA. Tech. Rep. 97-09, Cedric, CNAM, Paris, May 1997. Online version available: `ftp://sikkim.cnam.fr/pub/Reports/GISMed.ps.gz`.
4. A.Y. Levy, A. Rajaraman, J. O. Querying heterogeneous information sources using source descriptions. In *Proc. of the 22th International Conf. on Very Large Data Bases (VLDB)* (Bombay, India, Sept. 1996), Morgan Kaufmann, pp. 251–262.
5. Carey, M., Haas, L., Schwarz, P., Arya, M., Cody, W., Fagin, R., Flickner, M., Luniewski, A., Niblack, W., Petkovic, D., Thomas, J., Williams, J., and Wimmers, E. Towards heterogeneous multimedia information systems: The Garlic approach. In *5th Int. Workshop on Research Issues in Data Engineering - Distributed Object Management (RIDE-DOM)* (Taipei, Taiwan, Mar. 1995), e. O.A. Bukhres, Ed., pp. 124–131.
6. Christophides, V., and Rizk, A. Querying structured documents with hypertext links using OODBMS. In *Proc. of the ACM European Conf. on Hypermedia Technology (ECHT)* (Edinburgh, Scotland, 1994), pp. 186–197.
7. Cornetti, J. Médiaculture : les dossiers de l'Inventaire Général sur le réseau Internet. Master's thesis, Conservatoire National des Arts et Métiers (CNAM), Paris, France, 1998. in French.
8. Crossley, D., and Boston, T. A generic map interface to query geographic information using the World Wide Web. In *The Fourth International World Wide Web Conf.* (Boston, Massachusetts, USA, 1995).
9. Fleximage. URL `http://www.fleximage.fr/produits/o2geo/o2geoa.htm`.
10. Herring, J. The ORACLE 7 spatial data option. Tech. rep., ORACLE, 1996.
11. ISO. Information processing – text and office systems – Standard Generalized Markup Language (SGML). Tech. Rep. 8879, ISO, 1986.
12. Kacmar, C., Hruska, S., Lacher, C., Jue, D., Koontz, C., Gluck, M., and Weibel, S. An architecture and operation model for a spatial digital library. In *Proc. of the 1st Conf. on the Theory and Practice of Digital Libraries (DL)* (1994).
13. Li, C., Bree, D., Moss, A., and Petch, J. Developing internet-based user interfaces for improving spatial data access and usability. In *Third Int. Conf. on Integrating GIS and Environmental Modeling* (Santa Fe, New Mexico, Jan. 1996).
14. Mowbray, T., and Zahavi, R. *The Essential CORBA: Systems Integration Using Distributed Objects.* Wiley/OMG, 1995.
15. ODMG. *The Object Database Standard : ODMG-93 : Release 1.1.* Morgan Kaufmann series in data management systems. Morgan Kaufmann, 1994.
16. OGIS. *The OpenGIS Guide.* No. 96-001 in OGIS TC Document. OGIS Project Technical Committee, Open GIS Cons., Inc., 1996.
17. Reese, G. *Database Programming With JDBC and Java.* Java series. O'Reilly & Associates, Inc., Newton, MA 02164, USA, July 1997. Java 1.1.
18. Rizk, A., Malécieux, F., and Scholl, M. Recommondations pour la chaîne d'édition des dossiers d'inventaire. Projet Médiaculture, July 1996. rapport de la phase 2 (in French).
19. Wiederhold, G. Mediaton in information systems. *ACM Computing Surveys 27*, 2 (June 1995), 265–267.

An Application-Oriented Approach for HyTime Structured Document Management

Frederic Andres[1], John Buford[2], and Kinji Ono[1]

[1] NAtional Center for Science Information Systems (NACSIS) - R&D Department
Otsuka , Bunkyo-ku Tokyo 112, Japan
{andres,ono}@rd.nacsis.ac.jp
[2] GTE Laboratories 40 Sylvan Road, Waltham, MA 02254, USA
jb01@gte.com

Abstract. In this article, we point out the important functionality needed by emerging multimedia applications such hypermedia presentations or digital library retrieval systems to prepare the next generation database systems. Uniform management of hypermedia data is required to be suitable to various kinds of applications: different data types, different data model, varied data format or i/o devices. DBMSs provide efficient data storage facilities but still lack of customizability according to the target applications. Moreover, content-based and structure-based retrieval management are required by modern information retrieval systems. In order to combine the requirements of information retrieval systems and opened DBMS, we have implemented information retrieval functions inside the Application-Oriented DBMS Phasme. The document representation is either SGML or HyTime. SGML or HyTime documents are stored inside Phasme and are accessed using full text retrieval functionality. Such functionality are implemented as Phasme plug-ins and are stored inside Phasme. The storage management of the documents is independent from the way the user application will retrieve them. The developments achieved so far inside the AHYDS project (Active HYpermedia Delivery System) currently under process at NACSIS illustrate the chosen architecture design of the retrieval system. The performance of the current prototype is evaluated against a 40 GB document Benchmark showing that our approach yields excellent results.

1 Introduction

During the last years, multimedia information systems based on client/server architecture have integrated various kinds of user tools such as authoring tools, browsers, presentation tools, or animation tools. Information themselves are also various (e.g. various types, various formats). Meanwhile, hypermedia information relate multimedia data by linking them together and enable navigation through links.
Existing systems do not yet provide all the functionality required by the hypermedia information systems. As an example, it is necessary to support content-based and

structure-based retrieval [7] as well as database query mechanisms for hypermedia document management. Moreover, information retrieval issues are a key input for document management as it is mentioned in [12]. Also database services (concurrency control, recovery, versioning) are very important for efficient multimedia management.

The contribution of this paper is twofold: first we present the implementation of an hypermedia retrieval system using Phasme DBMS, and second we evaluate the performance of this implementation and compared to the ORBDMS technology.

We shows how the hypermedia document description using HyTime[9] and the retrieval functions can be mapped inside the application-oriented system Phasme[3], a state of the art, parallel database micro-kernel. Phasme stores data in a uniform way independently of the various kinds of user applications (different data formats, data types and semantics). Moreover, it provides traditional DBMS services such as persistency, concurrency control, recovery and versioning. The vertical customizability (from the data definition to the execution model) enables the Application-Oriented DBMS to be tailored according to the requirements of the application (e.g. index types, word matching algorithm).

This paper presents a system that performs information retrieval with high performance. This system translates the hypermedia document description (in HyTime) into the Phasme EBG data structure. Phasme is used as a back-end for the information retrieval execution. The demonstration of the performance has been done using the Binary Document Management[2] benchmark and managing from 5GB to 40GB sets of hypermedia documents. The data set, and the queries of this benchmark illustrate the performance of our system.

Object-relational databases typically bring together relational table storage and query processing, and the object-orientation of object-oriented DBMSs. Object-Relational systems with a capability of vertical customizability (adaptability from the data definition to the execution model) and with a uniform data storage will be able to adapt themselves dynamically according to the application requirements and to provide high performance.

The end-goals of the AHYDS project is to demonstrate a system with all these features inside an hypermedia application. The work described in this paper is limited to document retrieval management.

The organization of the remainder of the paper is as follows. Section 2 describes the architecture of the AHYDS platform. In Section 3, technical aspects of the hypermedia delivery system are sketched, while Section 4 analyses the performance experiments and results. Some related works are presented in Section 5. Finally, Section 6 summaries and concludes the paper.

2 The Active HYpermedia Delivery System (AHYDS)

This section reminds the major requirement of hypermedia retrieval systems. Then the management of SGML/HyTime Documents within an AODBMS is discussed. Finally the architecture of the AHYDS platform is described.

2.1 Requirements of Hypermedia Document Retrieval Applications

Hypermedia document management in many library applications requires the following features from the information server:

Support for structured document management.
Such documents can include only text or text and media information such as audio, images, and moving pictures. Several document languages such as SGML, HyTime, or ODA have been developed in order to satisfy this requirement.

Support of DBMS services
Transaction control, data integrity and data sharing, and version control are required for handling a large amount of multimedia data under dynamic multi-user environments.

Uniform data management independently of the application data model.
Uniform storage structure is appropriate to deliver information to different kinds of multimedia applications (presentational type, conversational type) based on different kinds of data models (relational, object oriented).

Durability against the standardization.
Several standard generalized markup languages have been proposed. SQL/MM is now emerging to support full text retrieval functions. The interface of the multimedia server must be flexible and customizable enough to support new languages.

Efficiency and quality of service for the data delivery.
Combining functionality with efficiency and quality of services is mandatory in order to support both time-dependent and resolution-dependent media data.

2.2 Handling SGML/HyTime Documents within an AODBMS

We have chosen to focus on the integration of the information retrieval functionality inside the AODBMS for the following reasons: (1) it allows a greater flexibility and extensibility with regards to the information retrieval system‘s requirements in terms of standards (e.g. information manipulation languages, information representation, application data models, data exchange); and (2) it provides high performance and customizability mechanisms for durable hypermedia systems.
The advantages of such a coupling are a) process structure-based and content-based query processing closed to the stored data, b) high degree of concurrency, and c) update management inside the DBMS. Such an integration reduces the number of layers between the application and the document storage manager.
The advantages are: a) a full AODBMS functionality, e.g. vertical customizability of the kernel to support efficiently information retrieval functionality, an uniform storage

management independently of the application's semantics; b) no overhead due to the traditional mapping between application data and database storage and c) the durability of the information system against the evolution of standards, and the hardware trends.
The overall architecture is shown in Fig. 1. Information about the SGML/HyTime support can be found in [16]. It defined the framework to store and to retrieve SGML and HyTime documents. A short overview is given in the next section, further details can be found at the web site http://www.rd.nacsis.ac.jp/~andres/db/ahys.html.
One of the objectives of the AHYDS (Active Hypermedia Delivery System) Project is to demonstrate the great interest of an application-oriented database application framework for structured and hypermedia document storage. The data representation is based on the Extended Binary Graph structure (EBG) of the Phasme DBMS[3]. Each component of the document corresponds to an EBG. The EBGs corresponding to a document's elements make up a hierarchy. Leaf EBGs contain text or media information.

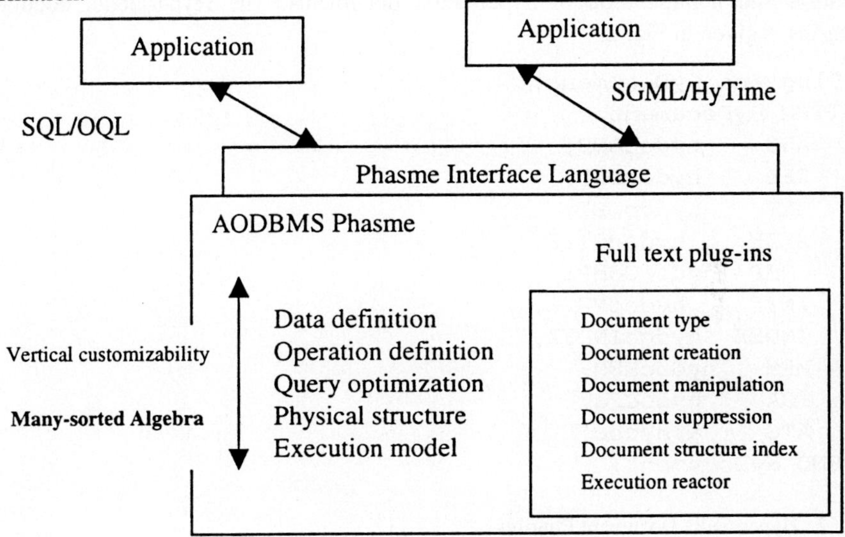

Fig. 1. System Architecture

2.3 Architecture of the AHYDS Platform

We applied the application-oriented approach to the SGML/HyTime framework described in the previous section. The integration of the IR-functionality with the AODBMS requires the design and the development of plug-ins in order to customize vertically the Phasme DBMS. On the one hand, hypermedia document retrieval processing is done inside the DBMS kernel closed to the data storage manager. On the other hand, the plug-ins mechanism enables to adapt the DBMS according to the real application requirements. The Active Hypermedia Delivery System allows a dynamic creation of new components of hypermedia documents. Combined structure and content-oriented queries are done within the user query language or following the user application requirements.

3 Technical Aspects of the Hypermedia Document Management

3.1 The HyTime plugins

SGML/HyTime support has been provided by the HyMinder Library[14]. SGML/HyTime documents are stored in the Phasme DBMS. Each SGML/HyTime element is stored as a SGML/HyTime item of Phasme. It enables various granularity creation and manipulation of hypermedia documents. The Hypermedia document plug-ins is given in Fig. 2.

```
Plug-ins HyDocument;
ITEM HyDocument
  ADD     hydocADD;
  DEL     hydocDEL;
  GET     hydocGET;
  SIZE     hydocSIZE;
  COMP   hydocCOMP;
  INIT     hydocNULL;
  INDEX  hydocINDEX;
  MEM    hydocMEM;
  TOA     hydoc2a;
  ATO     a2hydoc;
END HyDocument;
```

Fig. 2. Hypermedia Document Plug-ins

The plug-ins includes both hypermedia document manipulations, conversion from EBG format to ascii format, and index management. For example, the operations *hydocADD* and *hydocDEL* respectively inserts into the Phasme data structure and deletes a document from the Phasme data structure. The operation *hydocGET* retrieves a document or some parts of it from the database.

3.2 Document Retrieval Queries

Document retrieval queries enable both structural and content-based accesses. To illustrate our approach, the document retrieval query part is formulated as arguments of the plug-ins operation *hydocGET*. The examples of queries are based on the many-sorted algebra of the Phasme EBG data structure. Here is two examples of the query formulation:

"Select all the paragraphs of documents having an image and an audio summary about 'Austria Culture'" :

```
hydocGET(hydoc.paragraph,hydoc.image.isabout("Kamakura
temples")and hydoc.audio.isabout("Austria Culture"));
```

"Select the title and the abstract of documents created in 1996 containing a paragraph about 'World Cup Soccer'":

```
hydocGET((hydoc.title,hydoc.abstract,hydoc.datecreation
(1996)and hydoc.paragraph.isabout("World Cup Soccer"));
```

4 Performance Experiments

This section describes the results of experiments that measure the efficiency of the hypermedia document manipulation inside the AHYDS platform compared to a commercial ORDBMS.

4.1 Configuration

Our server platform was a SPARC 1000 with 128 Mb of main memory and 8 SPARC processors. It has a RAID disk (level 0) with 60GB as capacity. The document set includes tags such as title, author, abstract, keywords, and at least 3 chapters with image and video. Complete details are given in the full report[4]. The test-bed server of the Phasme DBMS version 2.02 used as the data storage manager of AHYDS. The client test software just retrieves the document from the server.

4.2 Performance results

Performance evaluation of the Response Time

The first set of measurements evaluates the performance of the access method of the hypermedia document in the context of the text retrieval issues. Fig. 3 shows the average elapsed time of document retrieval queries varying the number of documents from 10000 to 200000. The hypermedia document identifier is randomly chosen for one couple of measures from the Hypermedia application running on the ADHYDS platform and on the ORDBMS platform. The average size of a document is 0.2 MB. The maximum size of documents managed inside both the AHYDS platform and the ORDBMS is 40 GB of documents.

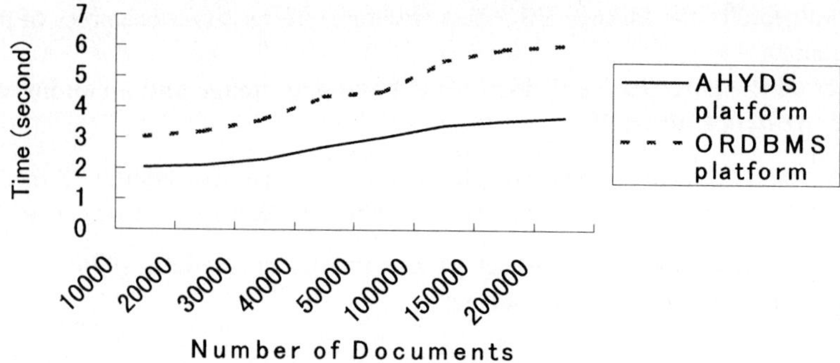

Fig. 3. Performance Evaluation of the AHYDS DBMS and an ORDBMS.

Inter-operation parallel

Fig. 4 shows the influence of the intra-operation parallelism of the Phasme DBMS on a document retrieval access. Database is set to 200 000 documents. This experience was run on a SUN ULTRA 2 workstation. We varied the number of threads from 1 to 8 threads. The set of hypermedia documents has been vertically clustered. In this way, the set of threads can be dynamically associated to the set of hypermedia document buckets. The mechanism for intra-operation parallelism of the execution model considerably improves the performance of the document retrieval.

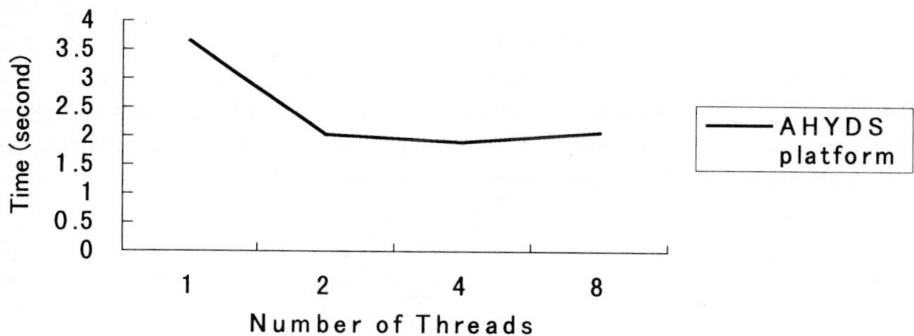

Fig. 4. Hypermedia Retrieval and Intra-operation Parallelism.

The multi-threading management using more than 4 threads produces an overhead due to the small number of processors. There are overheads due to the thread swapping over the processors. Some improvements will be introduced due using pattern programming approach.

User scalability and Elapsed Time

An important issue is the scalability and the influence of the increase of the number of users on the elapse time in order to receive a complete document. Fig. 5 shows the variation of the performance (elapsed time) of the AHYDS platform increasing the number of users. We verified that the system supports the increase of users. The ORDBMS is becoming better when the number of users increase due to caching effects. Then the elapsed time is increasing as the caching effect is no more improving the elapsed time according to the number of users.

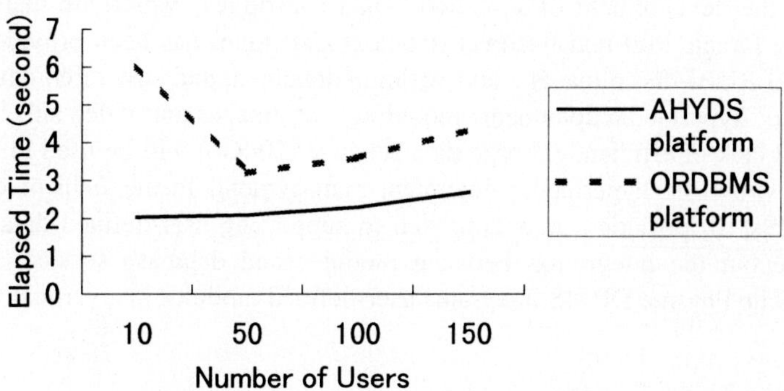

Fig. 5. Influence of the Number of Users on the Elapsed Time

User scalability and number of documents delivered per second
An important issue is the behavior of a delivery system related to the number of delivered documents according to the number of users querying the system.

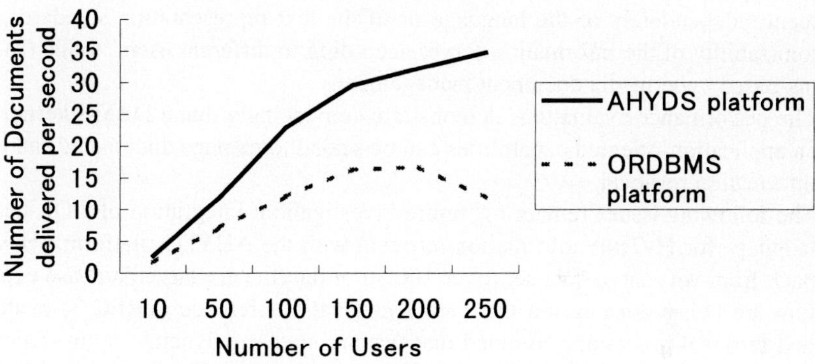

Fig. 6. Evaluation of the Number of Documents Delivered per Second

Fig. 6 shows the variation of the number of documents delivered per second for both the AHYDS platform and the ORDBMS-based platform when increasing the number of users. The ORDBMS platform does not support the scalability when we increase the number of users. Our AHYDS supports the increase of users even if the number of users goes over 200.

5 Related Works

Quite a number of research prototypes of hypermedia database management systems[1, 6, 8, 11, 13, 15] have been developed over the last years, mostly on OODBMS platforms.
As an example of commercial development, the Oracle Universal Server[13] is extensible for the development of so-called “Data Cartridges” which are manageable objects. The Oracle Full text retrieval (Context Cartridge) has been provided to extend traditional RDBMSs to manage text within a document and structured data. The management of hypermedia documents including text, images and video still lack of flexibility and lack of efficiency. Large data set (over 100Go) will be used in the future in order to stress the hypermedia document management. In the field of extensibility, ORBDMSs[10] provide a new approach to supporting user-defined data types using datablade but the integration between modules and database services is still very loosely. The Phasme DBMS integrates user-defined modules in a vertical tight way.

6 Conclusion

In this paper, we have described an information delivery system providing the integrated functionality of information retrieval system based on non query languages (SGML, HyTime) inside the Phasme Application-oriented DBMS. We have pointed out the problems that arose when traditional DBMSs are used. Further, we believe that our approach is rather flexible for the following reasons: (1) Uniform data management independently of the language or of the text representation standards. (2) Customizability of the information server according to different users' tools. (3) the plug-ins-based hypermedia document management.
The performance evaluations demonstrate convincingly that a DBMS kernel based on an application-oriented capabilities can be scaled to manage documents and to support information retrieval.
The following issues remain for future investigation: integration of OQL-based query language for HyTime information retrieval with the AHYDS platform, relevant feedback from very large data set (over 100Go of data). Very large database experimentation are being done inside the Text REtrieval Conference (TREC-7) evaluation for text retrieval processing. Beyond that, we are studying dynamic optimization rules to provide high performance for full text performance. Finally, the management of emerging representation languages such as XML, full text SQL or SMIL are investigated as extensions of the current retrieval and delivery system.

Acknowledgement

We thank TechnoTeacher for their support and help in the implementation of the HyTime plug-ins for the Phasme DBMS.

References

1. Andrews K., Kappe F., and Maurer H. "The Hyper-G network Information System", Information Processing and Management, Special Issue: Selected Proceedings of the Workshop on Distributed Multimedia Systems, Graz, Austria, (1994)
2. Andres F., and Asada K. "The BDM Benchmark: an Example of Use on G-BASE", IEICE'95, Fukuoka, Japan, (1995)
3. Andres F., and Ono K. "Phasme: A High Performance Parallel Application-oriented DBMS" in Informatica Journal, Special issue on Parallel and Distributed Database Systems (1997)
4. Andres F., and Ono K. "An Application-oriented Approach for HyTime Structured Document Management" NACSIS report, 1998.
5. Buford J.F., and Rutledge L. "Third generation Distributed Hypermedia Systems" in *Multimedia Information Management Handbook* (ed. W. Grozky), Prentice Hall, (1997)
6. Christophides V., Abiteboul S., Cluet S., and Scholl M. "From Structured Documents to Novel Query Facilities", in Proceedings on ACM SIGMOD International Conference on Management of Data, (1994) 313-324
7. DeFasio S., Daoud A., Smith L.A., and Srinivasan J. "Integrating IR and RDBMS using cooperative indexing" in Proc. of the 18th Annual Int. SIGIR Conf. on Research and Development in Information Retrieval, (1995) 84-92
8. Hara Y., Hirata K., Takano H., and Kawasaki S. "Hypermedia Database "Himotoki" and Its Application" in Proc. Int'l Conference on ICDE, (1996) 372-379
9. HyTime ISO/IEC 10744, (1997)
10. "Developing DataBladeR Modules for InformixR-Universal Server" White Paper, (1998)
11. Kim H., Zhoo Z., Shin H., and Chang J. "An Object-oriented Hypermedia System for Structured Documents" in Proc. Pacific DBMS'96, Hong Kong, (1996) 286-295
12. Kowalski Gerald "Information Retrieval Systems Theory and Implementation", Kluwer Academic Publishers, second printing, (1998)
13. "Managing Text with Oracle8^{TM} ConText Cartridge, An Oracle White Paper, (1997)
14. Ozsu M. T., Iglinski Paul, Szafron Duane, El-Medani Sherine, and Junghanns Manuela, "An Object-oriented SGML/Hytime Compliant Multimedia Database Management System", in Proc. 5th International Multimedia Conference (ACM Multimedia 97), Seattle, WA, (1997) 239-249
15. Volz M., Aberer K., and Bohm K. "An OODBMS-IRS Coupling for Structured Documents" in Proc. IEEE ICDE, (1996) 10-19
16. Technoteacher "HyMinder User Guide", (1996)

Qualitative Spatial Relationships Representation IO&T and Its Retrieval

Chuan Heng Ang, Tok Wang Ling and Xiao Ming Zhou

Department of Information System and Computer Science
National University of Singapore
Lower Kent Ridge, Singapore 119260
{angch, lingtw, zhouxm}@iscs.nus.edu.sg

Abstract. We present in this paper, a qualitative spatial relationships representation scheme called IO&T which combines fuzzy Intrinsic Orientation and Topological spatial relationships, and a similarity measure based on this representation. This scheme is invariant under translation and rotation. In addition, the proposed picture similarity retrieval approach, which is based on dominant objects, is especially useful for similarity retrieval involving a small number of dominant objects.

1 Introduction

Pictorial spatial databases have been used more widely recently ([6], [9], [10], [12], and [14] etc.). Most research results focus on qualitative spatial relationship representation. However, qualitative similarity retrieval is still in its budding stage. In this paper, we describe a comprehensive similarity retrieval approach that is made possible with the use of a new representation scheme which is called *fuzzy Intrinsic Orientation and Topological relationships representation (IO&T).*

The research on qualitative spatial relationships can be grouped as follows:
(1). *Topological relationships* which are invariant under topological transformation of the reference objects[3].

Egenhofer[3] proposed a model called 4-Intersection to formally define the topological relationships which stay invariant under topological transformation such as translation, rotation, and scaling. According to this model, each object is represented in 2D space as a point set which has an interior and boundary. Eight meaningful relationships can be defined in this model, which are disjoint(dt), touch(to), overlap(ov), covers(co), inside(in), coveredby(cb), contains(ct), and equal(eq).
(2). *Directional relationships* which concern partial and total orientation relationships among objects. In [2], [13], and [10], several different models have been developed.

Recently, some work has been done on combining these two representation methods. The typical work includes [4], [8] and [9]. However, they can't solve the rotation-invariant of picture representation issue which is becoming another hot topic recently. This issue can be solved by the proposals of 2D R-string ([11], [12]) and RS-string[6] which all make use of polar coordinates system based on a designated center (or origin). However, to find an appropriate polar center is the main difficulty as the center chosen may not appear in all database pictures. This means that the reference frame is changed from picture to picture. In addition, the rotation of objects have not been considered by any approaches just discussed.

The remainder of this paper is structured as follows: Section 2 introduces our qualitative spatial relationship representation IO&T. Section 3 discusses the similarity retrieval based on IO&T. Section 4 concludes and discusses some further issues.

2 IO&T representation

Our proposed representation is a combination *of fuzzy Intrinsic Orientation relationship and Topological relationship*, and hence it is called *IO&T* in short. We make use of Egenhofer's topological category to describe the topological relationship between the objects and a variant of range representation of [5] for the orientation representation.

2.1 Fuzzy orientation category

Fig. 1. The common level of the range representation of orientations (adapted from [5])

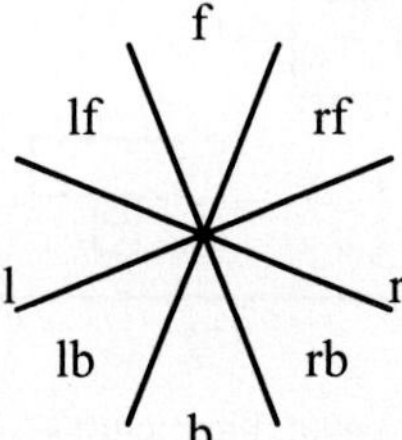

Fig. 2. The level 3 representation of [5]

Hogg and Schwarzer[5] propose to divide the orientation into 16 sectors(Fig.1) to express the 3 levels of details in orientation as a range of sectors. To facilitate the understanding of the proposed orientation category, we use the level 3 representation of [5] in the following discussion, and substitute different ranges with 8 orientation codes {f, rf, r, rb, b, lb,l, lf} which represent front, right-front, right, right-back, back, left-back, left, and left-front respectively as shown in Fig.2. It is clear that every sector in the common level (Fig.1) is included in only one orientation sector in Fig.2. However, we introduce fuzziness to the normal eight orientation relationships in Fig.3 to allow the categories of orientation relationships to be overlapped. Given two neighboring relationships R and S, the overlap part between them is denoted as R|S. Interpreting the overlap part R|S as either sector R or sector S are both acceptable. Using this notation, the new sector codes are r|rf, rf|f, f|lf, lf|l, l|lb, lb|b, b|rb, rb|r.

Fig.3 shows clearly the effect of fuzziness to each of the 8 normal orientations and how the overlapping induce the eight fuzzy relationships.

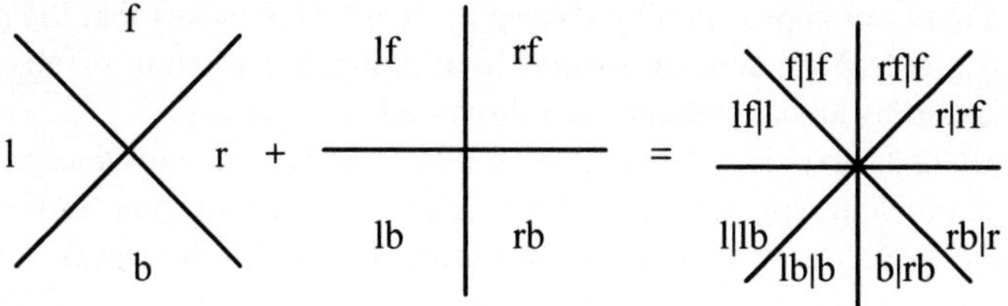

Fig. 3. The fuzzy category

With the use of the fuzzy category in describing the orientation relationship, we overcome the problem of sudden change in the orientation of the objects to be described. We endow an application the flexibility to interpret the orientation codes according to its need.

2.2 Intrinsic orientation

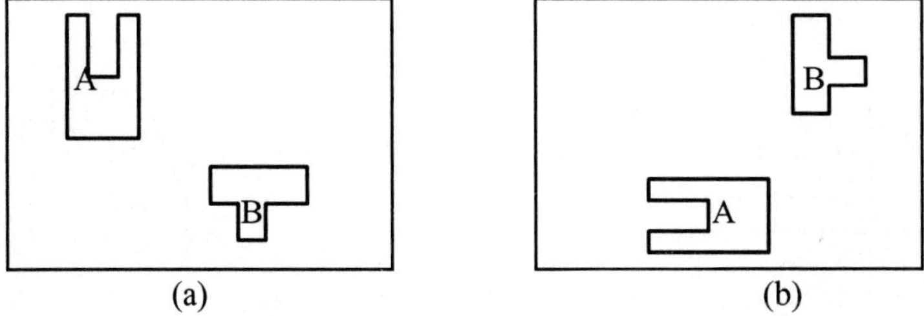

Fig. 4. Two example pictures ((b) is a rotated version of (a))

The intrinsic orientation is the most natural framework of reference that can be used to define the relative orientations among objects. The intrinsic orientation of an object has to be defined before it can be used as the reference object to describe others. The picture in Fig.4(b) is a rotated version of the picture in Fig.4(a). Their representations are totally different if we use those existing representation approaches that we have discussed. However, they are the same if the representation is based on the intrinsic orientations of objects because the relative orientation of objects remain the same when a picture is rotated. The position of object B relative to object A in Fig.4(a) is the same as that in Fig.4(b) if we use A's intrinsic orientation as a reference, and vice verse.

2.3 IO&T representation scheme

The spatial relationship (including topological and orientation) between two objects A and B is usually represented as <A, [TR, OR], B> where TR is a topological relationship from the set{dt, to, ct, in, ov, co, eq, cb}which is invariant under translation and rotation, and OR is an orientation relationship from the set {f, rf, r, rb, b, lb, l, lf, r|rf, rf|f, f|lf, lf|l, l|lb, lb|b, b|rb, rb|r} which can also be invariant under translation and rotation after using intrinsic orientation. However, an important observation is that the orientation relationship of object A to object B is not necessary the complement or the opposite of the orientation relationship of B to A when intrinsic orientation is involved. This is because of A's intrinsic orientation (e.g. its intrinsic front) may be different from B's intrinsic orientation. We define the spatial relationship between two objects as follow:

Definition 1: The spatial relationship between two objects A and B is <A, [TR, OR1, OR2], B> where TR is the topological relationship between object A and object B, OR1 represents the orientation relationship of A to B based on A's intrinsic orientation, and OR2 represents the orientation relationship of B to A based on B's intrinsic orientation.

Since a tuple in the IO&T representation involves two objects, a picture with n objects ordered alphabetically in their names will have to be represented by n*(n-1)/2 tuples <Oi, [TRij, OR1ij, OR2ij], Oj> where Oi, Oj are objects, the set of objects are linearly ordered with Oi<Oj, and [TRij, OR1ij, OR2ij] are relationships between Oi and Oj. If V is a finite nonempty set of symbols representing the objects in the picture and R is a set of IO&T tuples, then a picture can be represented as (V, R). With the use of intrinsic orientation, when we rotate the whole picture, the IO&T representation of the picture won't change. Therefore, the IO&T representation is invariant with respect to translation and rotation of the picture.

3 Picture retrieval

There are two kinds of picture retrieval: exact matching and similarity retrieval, with the former a special case of the latter. In similarity retrieval, we are to retrieve from the pictorial database those pictures that are similar to the query picture given by a user. For example, there are four pictures P1, P2, P3, and P4 in Fig.5. P1 is a query picture, and P2, P3, and P4 are database pictures. To find which picture among P2, P3, and P4 is most similar to P1, we must design a real-valued function that can measure the similarity of every pair of pictures. For the ease of discussion, we assume that all objects involved are distinct in each picture. We ignore the situations in which there are multiple instances of the same object within a picture. It has been proved in [15] that the similarity retrieval problem is NP-hard when multiplicity of objects is allowed in picture matching.

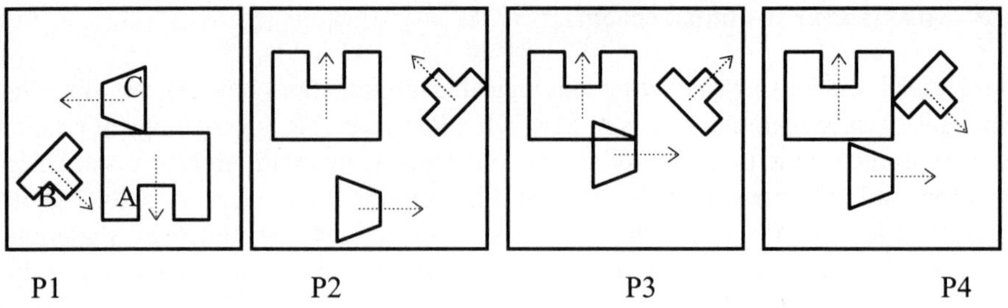

Fig. 5. Example pictures (All arrows represent intrinsic fronts of objects)

3.1 Similarity functions

Several functions are used to measure the degree of similarity between two pictures ([7], [14] and [9]). Basically, these functions measure certain aspect of similarity as follows:

1. How many objects have changed their spatial relationships (Some spatial relationships have been changed due to the movements of these objects);
2. How many pairwise spatial relationships have changed (The number of changed pairwise spatial relationships);
3. To what degree the pairwise spatial relationships have changed (The extent of the changes based on a defined measure).

For example, in [7], the number of objects that have changed their spatial relationships is used as a measure of similarity. Using graph representation, the similarity problem can be transformed to finding a common maximal clique between two graphs of the corresponding two pictures.

The measure of [7] is well-defined. Unfortunately, the complexity of the maximal clique problem is NP-hard. Researchers turn to other measures recently. For example, in [14], to calculate the number of pairwise relationships that are different between two pictures, some complicated deduction and reduction sets are constructed. In [9], a neighborhood metric is used to measure the degree of pairwise spatial relationships changes. Experimental results have shown that their similarity functions are effective in some application areas.

However the measures of [14] and [9] have also been found inapplicable sometimes. The number of changes in pairwise relationships multiplies even when only very few objects change their positions.

3.2 Object based similarity

A database picture is considered to be most similar to a query picture when the former can be changed to the latter with the minimum number of operations (translations, rotations, or scaling), assuming they have the same set of objects. However, the complexity of this matching process is quite high. To make it tractable, we may retrieve the similar pictures by object based similarity.

A query is always issued with reference to some dominant objects. We may base on the first dominant object O1 to retrieve the set S1 of similar pictures within a tolerance, and then the second dominant object O2 to retrieve similar pictures from S1 to form S2. This process is repeated until the last dominant object has been considered. The last set obtained is the answer set of pictures that are similar to the query picture based on all the dominant objects.

3.3 IO&T similarity measure

The IO&T similarity measure is used to determine the similarity between a database picture P and a query picture Q. To understand how the changes in spatial relationships can be measured, we begin with the notion of topological neighborhood as follow.

Definition 2: Two topological relationships between two spatial objects are neighbors if one of the relationship can be directly transformed into the other without going through any other intermediate topological relationships by continuously deforming(scaling, moving, rotating) the objects concerned.

For example, disjoint and touch are neighbors. However, disjoint can not be directly transformed to overlap without passing the intermediate state touch. So they are not neighbors.

According to the definition, we may construct a neighborhood graph as in Fig.6. Given two topological relationships TRi and TRj. The length of the shortest path in the topological neighborhood graph from TRi to TRj is defined as the topological distance Dt(TRi, TRj) between them. The topological distances among the eight topological relationships are shown in Table 1.

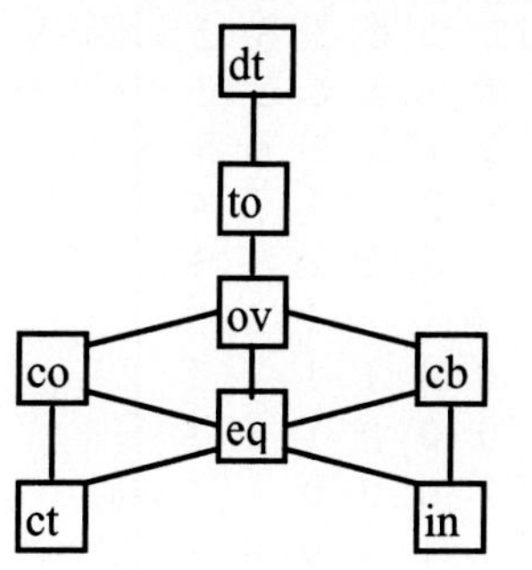

Fig. 6. Topological neighborhood graph

Table 1. Topological distances Dt(TR_i, TR_j)

TR_i \ TR_j	dt	to	ov	co	cb	eq	ct	in
dt	0	1	2	3	3	3	4	4
to	1	0	1	2	2	2	3	3
ov	2	1	0	1	1	1	2	2
co	3	2	1	0	2	1	1	2
cb	3	2	1	2	0	1	2	1
eq	3	2	1	1	1	0	1	1
ct	4	3	2	1	2	1	0	2
in	4	3	2	2	1	1	2	0

As for the fuzzy orientation relationships, the notion of the orientation neighborhood is defined as follows.

Definition 3: Two normal (fuzzy) orientation relationships are neighbors if anyone of them can be transformed into the other by continuously deforming the objects without going through an intermediate normal (fuzzy) orientation relationship.

Definition 4: A normal orientation relationship and a fuzzy orientation relationship are kin if they are partially overlapped.

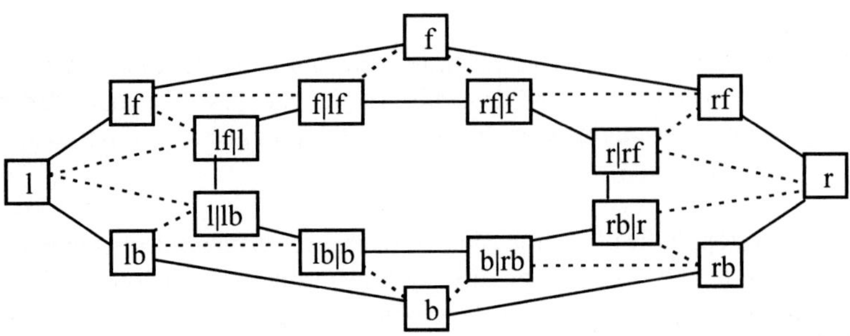

Fig. 7. Orientation neighborhood graph

Table 2. Orientation distances Do(OR_i, OR_j)

OR_i \ OR_j	r	r|rf	rf	rf|f	f	f|lf	lf	lf|l	l	l|lb	lb	lb|b	b	b|rb	rb	rb|r
r	0	0	1	1	2	2	3	3	4	3	3	2	2	1	1	0
r|rf	0	0	0	1	1	2	2	3	3	4	3	3	2	2	1	1
rf	1	0	0	0	1	1	2	2	3	3	4	3	3	2	2	1
rf|f	1	1	0	0	0	1	1	2	2	3	3	4	3	3	2	2
f	2	1	1	0	0	0	1	1	2	2	3	3	4	3	3	2
f|lf	2	2	1	1	0	0	0	1	1	2	2	3	3	4	3	3
lf	3	2	2	1	1	0	0	0	1	1	2	2	3	3	4	3
lf|l	3	3	2	2	1	1	0	0	0	1	1	2	2	3	3	4
l	4	3	3	2	2	1	1	0	0	0	1	1	2	2	3	3
l|lb	3	4	3	3	2	2	1	1	0	0	0	1	1	2	2	3
lb	3	3	4	3	3	2	2	1	1	0	0	0	1	1	2	2
lb|b	2	3	3	4	3	3	2	2	1	1	0	0	0	1	1	2
b	2	2	3	3	4	3	3	2	2	1	1	0	0	0	1	1
b|rb	1	2	2	3	3	4	3	3	2	2	1	1	0	0	0	1
rb	1	1	2	2	3	3	4	3	3	2	2	1	1	0	0	0
rb|r	0	1	1	2	2	3	3	4	3	3	2	2	1	1	0	0

According to the above definitions, the orientation neighborhood and kin graph and the orientation distance table can be constructed as in Fig.7 and Table.2 respectively. A solid line in Fig.7 represents being a neighbor, and a dotted line represents being a kin. We use Do(ORi, ORj) to represent the orientation distance between two orientation relationships ORi and ORj. If both ORi and ORj are the normal relationships or both are fuzzy relationships, Do(ORi, ORj) is defined as the length of the shortest path from ORi to ORj. However, if only one of ORi and ORj is a fuzzy relationship, then Do(ORi, ORj) is defined to have a value which is one less than the length of the shortest path between ORi and ORj. This is because we allow two kin nodes to be overlapped, and hence the distance between them should be defined as zero. For example, both r|rf and rf|f are overlapped with the orientation rf. Therefore Do(r|rf, rf)=0, and Do(rf|f, rf)=0. Similarly, we have Do(r|rf, r)=0.

Now, we are ready to compute the tuple distance DTP(T1, T2) between two IO&T tuples T1= <Oi,[TRij, OR1ij, OR2ij],Oj> and T2=<Ox, [TRxy,OR1xy,OR2xy],Oy>, where Oi and Oj, and Ox and Oy are the same objects respectively and the pairs are probably in two different pictures. It is defined as follow:

$$DTP(T1, T2)= \partial 1 * Dt(TRij, TRxy)+ \partial 2 *(Do(OR1ij, OR1xy)+ Do(OR2ij, OR2xy))$$

Where $\partial 1$ and $\partial 2$ are two constants which are dependent on applications. For the ease of discussion, we will set both $\partial 1$ and $\partial 2$ to 1 by default in the following.

3.4 Similarity retrieval approach

So far, we have a distance measure to compare two IO&T tuples. To compare the similarity between two symbolic pictures based on one dominant object, we need to use all the corresponding IO&T tuples related to this dominant object.

Definition 5: The IO&T similarity measure DP is a vector function that is defined for a database picture P, a query picture Q and a dominant object O such that DP(O, Q, P)=(D1(O, Q, P), D2(O, Q, P)) where D1(O, Q, P) is the number of objects that have changed their relationships with respect to O and D2(O, Q, P) measures the total extent of changes that have taken place.

D1( ) and D2( ) are closely related to the function DTP( ) used to measure the distance between two IO&T tuples. Let pictures P and Q be represented by (Vp, Rp) and (Vq, Rq) respectively where Vp and Vq are sets of object symbols, and Rp and Rq are sets of IO&T relationships tuples. The following algorithm can be used to calculate the IO&T similarity measure.

Algorithm I: Function for similarity measure DP(O,Q,P)
Input: O, a dominant object;
(Vq, Rq) and (Vp, Rp), the IO&T representations of the query picture Q and a database picture P.

Output: D1(O,Q,P), the number of objects that have changed their relationships with respect to the dominant object O in Q and P;
D2(O, Q, P), the total extent of changes with respective to the dominant object O.
begin
1. D1=0, D2=0
2. if VqÍVp then
3. for each T1=<Vi, [TRij, OR1ij, OR2ij], Vj> in Rq
4. if Vi or Vj = O then begin
5 find T2=<Um,[TRmn, OR1mn, OR2mn],Un> in Rp
such that Um=Vi, and Un=Vj
6. compute DTP(T1, T2)
7. if DTP(T1, T2)<>0 then add 1 to D1 and add DTP(T1, T2) to D2
8. endif
9. elseif set D1 and D2 to μ
10. return D1 and D2
end

When D1 and D2 are both smaller than their respective tolerance, then P will be accepted. When there are k dominant objects, the same algorithm will be invoked k times with each invocation working on the output list of similar pictures from the previous invocation.

It is easy to see that the complexity of this algorithm is $O(N^2)$ where N is the number of objects in Q. Compared with the common clique algorithm adopted by [7], our algorithm is certainly more practical.

3.5 An example and experiments

Lets refer to the example in Fig.5 and assume A to be the only dominant object. After removing all the IO&T tuples not related to A, P1, P2, P3, and P4 will contain the following tuples:

P1: <A, [dt, r, lf|l], B>, <A, [to, b|rb, l|lb], C>
P2: <A, [dt, r, lf|l], B>, <A, [dt, b|rb, l|lb], C>
P3: <A, [dt, r, lb|b], B>, <A, [ov, b|rb, l|lb], C>
P4: <A, [to, r|rf, rb|r], B>, <A, [to, b|rb, l|lb], C>

Using Algorithm I, the distances between P1 and other pictures are:

D1(A, P1, P2)=1, D2(A, P1, P2)=1;
D1(A, P1, P3)=2, D2(A, P1, P3)=3;
D1(A, P1, P4)=1, D2(A, P1, P4)=5;

Because D1(A, P1, P2) and D1(A, P1, P4) are both 1 and D2(A, P1, P2) is smaller than D2(A, P1, P4), we conclude that P2 is the most similar picture to P1.

We have implemented the similarity retrieval algorithm and carried out a number of experiments. We find that the percentage of pictures retrieved from groups with fewer object changes are always higher. When we relax both the tolerances for D1 and D2, there are more and more pictures being retrieved.

4 Conclusion and future work

In summary, we have proposed in this paper:

- A set of directional relationships to cater for the fuzziness of human perception.
- The IO&T representation to represent the spatial knowledge qualitatively.
- IO&T similarity measure.
- An object based similarity retrieval approach.

Our approach is based on the intrinsic orientations of objects. However, it is not always possible to define the intrinsic orientation for an object. This issue will be taken into consideration in our ongoing research on refining the IO&T representation.

References

1. Allen, J.F.: Maintaining knowledge about temporal intervals. Comm. ACM, Vol. 26. No. 11, (1983) 832-843
2. Chang, S.K., Shi Q.Y., Yan C.W.: Iconic indexing by 2D strings. IEEE Transaction on Pattern Recognition and Machine Intelligence, Vol. 9. No.3, (1987) 413-428
3. Egenhofer, M.J.: Point-set topological spatial relations. International Journal of Geographical Information Systems. Vol. 5. No.2, (1991) 161-174
4. Hernandez, D.: Qualitative representation of spatial knowledge. Lecture Notes in Artificial Intelligence no. 804, Springer -Verlag, (1994).
5. Hogg, S., Schwarzer, I.: Composition of spatial relations. Forschungsberichte Kunstliche Intelligenz FKI-163-91, Institut fur Informatik, Technishe Universitat Munchen. 44, (1991)
6. Huang, P.W., Jean, Y.R.: Spatial reasoning and similarity retrieval for image database systems based on RS-string, Pattern Recognition, Vol. 29, No. 12, (1996).2103-2114
7. Lee, S.Y., Shan, M.K., Yang, W.P.: Similarity retrieval of iconic image databases. Pattern Recognition, Vol. 22, No. 6, (1989) 675-682
8. Nabil, M., Sheperd, J., Ngu, A.H.H.: 2D projection interval relationships: A symbolic representation of spatial relationships. Advances in Spatial Databases: Fourth Int'l Symp., SSD'95, Lecture Notes in Computer Science no.951, (1995)292-309, Springer-Verlag
9. Nabil, M. Ngu, A.H.H., Sheperd, J.: Picture similarity retrieval using 2D projection interval representation. IEEE TKDE. Vol.8, No.4, (1996) 533-539
10. Papadias, D., Sellis, T.: A pictorial language for the retrieval of spatial relations from the image databases. Proc. Of the 6th International Symposium on Spatial Data Handling. Taylor Francis, (1994)
11. Petraglia, G., Sebillo, M., Tucci, M., Tortora, G.: Towards normalized iconic indexing. Proc. of the 1993 IEEE Symposium on Visual Language, Bergen, Norway, (1993) 392-394
12. Petraglia, G., Sebillo, M., Tucci, M., Tortora, G.: Rotation invariant iconic indexing for image database retrieval. Progress in Image Analysis and Processing III (edited by S. Impedovo), World Scientific, (1994) 271-278
13. Peuquet, D.J., Ci-Xiang, Z.: An algorithm to determine the directional relationship between arbitrary-shaped polygons in the plane. Pattern Recognition, Vol. 20. No. 1, (1987) 65-74
14. Sistla, A.P., Yu, C., Liu, C., Liu, K.: Similarity based retrieval of pictures using indices on spatial relationships. Proc of the 21th VLDB Conference, Zurich, Switzerland (1995)
15. Tucci, M., Costagliola, G., Chang, S.K.: A remark on NP-completeness of picture matching, IPL (1991)

A Qualitative Approach to Integration in Spatial Databases

Baher A. El-Geresy and Alia I. Abdelmoty

School of Computing, University of Glamorgan,
Treforest, Mid Glamorgan, CF37 1DL, Wales, U.K.
bageresy,aiabdel@glam.ac.uk

Abstract. This paper considers the problem of integrating data sets which hold information about the same features in space. The approach proposed is based on allowing inconsistent data sets to coexist in the database and explicitly representing the nature of inconsistencies among those sets. A qualitative level of representation is created where the data sets can be integrated and manipulated using qualitative reasoning techniques. A systematic approach is used to identify classes and levels of consistency which can be checked in isolation. This provides the flexibility for two data sets to be integrated without necessarily being totally consistent in every aspect. The method is simple and can be used in many applications which incorporates the modelling and manipulation of spatial entities such as GIS, CAD and image databases.

1 Introduction

One of the main functions of spatial information systems such as GISs is the unification and integration of different data sets and making them available for coherent manipulation and analysis by different applications [1]. Huge amounts of information have become available on regular basis which can be used for a lot of different applications such as in studying global environmental phenomena (e.g. global warming). Integrating geographic information is also needed for transferring data across systems and organisations.

Integrating data in these systems involves the integration of diverse types of information drawn from a variety of sources requiring effective matching of similar entities and information consistency across data sets. The problem of integration is further complicated as the data may be collected in incompatible ways and may vary in reliability. Some details may be missing or undefined. Two possible approaches can be identified for handling the integration problem:

1. Convert all the data sets to a single format and store the most detailed representation of the data (at one scale) [2].
2. Permit inconsistent data to co-exist with explicit information being provided on the inconsistencies between the data sets [3].

In this paper the approach proposed combines ideas from both of the above approaches where the inconsistent data sets are allowed to co-exist in the database and a common (qualitative) level of representation is created where all the data sets can be integrated. The issues in this paper are discussed using geographic information in GISs as example, but are also applicable to other types of spatial information systems and applications. The paper is structured as follows. The general approach is described in section 2. In section 3 the qualitative level of representation is discussed. A novel qualitative structure for capturing topological and orientation relationships is described. Different consistency classes and levels are proposed in section 4 and an example is given to illustrate qualitative data integration in section 5. Conclusions are given in section 6.

2 The Approach

Spatial knowledge that can be inferred from a scene can be either: ***object-based*** or *relation-based. Object-based* information include object descriptions through their location, shape, dimension and size. *Relation-based* information are object descriptions through their spatial relationships to others. Four main types of spatial relationships can be identified [4]: a) topological, or connectivity of the objects components (e.g. touch, inside), b) orientation, or the relative organisation of the objects in space, c) proximity, relative distance between objects (e.g. far, near) and d) size, (larger, smaller, or equal).

The object-based spatial knowledge can differ among data sets and are dependent on the scale, accuracy and format of representation. They represent the main sources of incompatibility which needs to be handled in integrating data sets quantitatively. Relation-based knowledge however, can remain consistent among data sets even with discrepancies in object location, size, dimension and shape and hence can be used with spatial reasoning techniques in integrating spatial data sets [4, 5, 6].

In this paper, the approach used to handle the integration problem is based on two steps:

1. **Build a qualitative level of representation:** where relation-based information are stored and manipulated using qualitative reasoning techniques [5, 6, 7, 8].
2. **Explicit representation of the set of consistent knowledge between data sets [4].** This can be achieved by identifying the different aspects and measures of equivalence between the data sets. This provides the flexibility for two data sets to be integrated without necessarily being totally consistent in every aspect. Also, the ambiguity or uncertainty inherent in this knowledge needs to be represented.

This approach is aimed at providing a clear view of the nature of the data sets manipulated in the spatial information system, including the extent of consistent knowledge that can be retrieved as well as the nature and measure of any inconsistency that may result.

3 The Qualitative Level of Representation

A novel structure is proposed to capture and represent relation-based spatial knowledge in the form of a matrix. The matrix is used to represent both the topological and orientation relations as well as the relationships around the map edge.

3.1 Assumptions

Given a space S and a set of spatial entities $O_1, \cdots, O_n$ embedded in it.

1. Space S is dense and infinite.
2. The spatial entitles are connected. If an entity is not connected, each of its components will be considered separately.
3. The entities jointly cover the whole space, i.e. $S = O_1 \cup \cdots O_n \cup S_0$, where S_0 is the complement of the entities in space S. The inclusion of S_0 is necessary for two reasons: a) to avoid mis-interpretation of space topology and b) to provide an explicit representation of the edges of the scene (or map).
4. The spatial entities don't overlap, i.e. $O_i \cap O_j = \phi$ for all $1 \leq i \neq j \leq n$.

3.2 Capturing Topology- The Adjacency Matrix

The adjacency matrix is a qualitative spatial structure used to describe the topological distibution of objects in the map scene by capturing the adjacency relations between objects in the scene. In figure 1(b) the adjacency between the four objects in 1(a) are encoded in a matrix. The fact that two entities are adjacent is represented by a value of (1) in the matrix and by a (0) otherwise. For example, A is adjacent to B and D but not to C, and D is adjacent to all others. Since adjacency is a symmetric relation, the resulting matrix will be symmetric around the diagonal. Hence, only half the matrix is sufficient for the representation of the space topology and the matrix can be collapsed to the structure in figure 1(c). The complement of the objects in question shall be considered to be infinite. The suffix 0 (S_0) is used to represent this component. As seen in the figure, the map edges are explicitly represented by the adjacency relations of S_0 (complement of objects in S). Objects B and C do not touch any of the map edges.

3.3 Capturing Orientation: The Matrix Map

The adjacency matrix captures the topology of space under consideration. Orientation relations can be added by explicitly representing those relations between adjacent objects in the scene. Orientation relations are order relations and have converses. Hence, half the matrix is still enough to capture these relations. Other relations between non-adjacent entities can then be deduced using qualitative reasoning techniques.

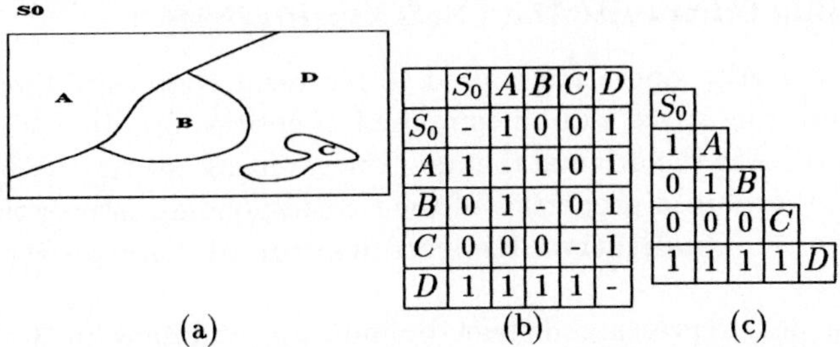

	S_0	A	B	C	D
S_0	-	1	0	0	1
A	1	-	1	0	1
B	0	1	-	0	1
C	0	0	0	-	1
D	1	1	1	1	-

S_0				
1	A			
0	1	B		
0	0	0	C	
1	1	1	1	D

Fig. 1. (a) Space represented by four objects. (b) Adjacency matrix. (c) Half the symmetric adjacency matrix is sufficient to capture the scene representation.

The convention of orientation relations is $R(column, row)$. For example, the relationships in figure 2 are $West(A, B)$ and $South(A, C)$. Different granularities of the orientation relations can be defined, e.g. $south - west(A, D)$. In the figure, the following orientation relations are defined between adjacent objects. $W(A, B), N(A, C), S(A, D) \wedge SW(A, D), S(B, D), W(B, E), W(C, D), W(D, E)$. [1] The matrix in figure 2(b) contain the orientation relations between adjacent objects only. The rest of the orientation relations can then be derived using the rules:

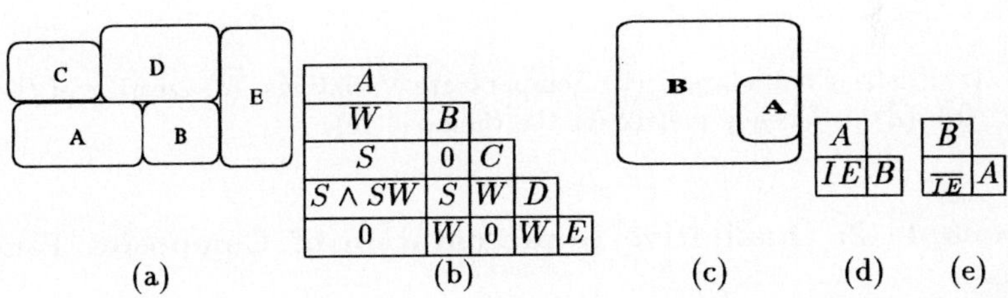

A				
W	B			
S	0	C		
$S \wedge SW$	S	W	D	
0	W	0	W	E

A	
IE	B

B	
$\overline{IE}$	A

Fig. 2. (a) Set of adjacent regions. (b) Matrix map for the map in (a). Orientation relations are represented only between adjacent regions. (c) Representing part-whole relationships -$Inside(A, B) \wedge East(A, B)$. (d) Matrix map for (c). (e) Matrix map with the order of the objects reversed.

$W(A, B) \wedge W(B, E) \rightarrow W(A, E)$.
$S(A, D) \wedge W(D, E) \rightarrow S(A, E) \vee SW(A, E) \vee W(A, E)$.
$SW(A, D) \wedge W(D, E) \rightarrow W(A, E) \vee SW(A, E)$.
The combined adjacency and orientation relations is denoted the *Matrix Map*.

[1] S denotes *South*, W denotes *West*, etc.

3.4 Defining Composite Data Sets Qualitatively

A qualitative overlay operation is used to represent composite thematic layers, where the resulting space will be composed of entities resulting from the intersection of entities in the original themes. The resulting entities are homogeneous and carry the combined properties of their corresponding intersecting ones.

Example 1: Qualitative Representation of Composite Thematic Fields

The map in 3(a) represents district boundaries, and that in 3(b) represents temperature variations. The map in 3(c) represents the temperature variations across the districts by overlaying 3(a) and (b).

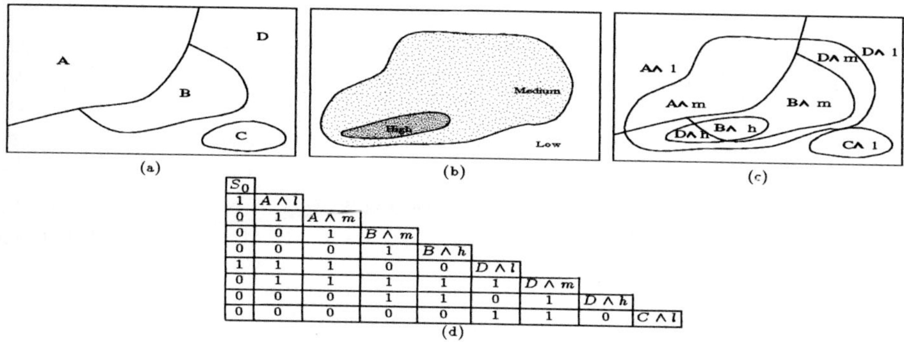

S_0								
1	$A \wedge l$							
0	1	$A \wedge m$						
0	0	1	$B \wedge m$					
0	0	0	1	$B \wedge h$				
1	1	1	0	0	$D \wedge l$			
0	1	1	1	1	1	$D \wedge m$		
0	0	0	1	1	0	1	$D \wedge h$	
0	0	0	0	0	1	1	0	$C \wedge l$

Fig. 3. (a) District boundaries. (b) Temperature Variations. (c) Overlay of themes in (a) and (b). (d) Adjacency matrix for the theme in (c).

Example 2: Qualitative Representation of Composite Temporal Fields

A similar approach as used above can be used here to capture *change* in space. In particular, a qualitative structure can be built which represents the sequence of changes that occured for the objects in the spatial scene considered. In this case the space will be represented by entities whose values are the sequence of values of entities that occupied that space. This sequence shall be denoted in the matrix by a (,). Hence (A, B) denotes that the space occupied by that entity changed from A to B.

In figure 4 a map at different instances in time is shown. The composite *temporal map* is shown in figure 4. The boundaries of object B has changed affecting the extension of objects A and D. Also object C disappeared at time t_2. Representation of more than two temporal changes can be achieved in a similar manner. For example if at t_3 the spatial entity represented by the value (A, B) retained the value A then the entity on the temporal map becomes (A, B, A) and so on. This temporal adjacency represents the dynamic behaviour of the fields in space and it can capture dynamic events such as ecological variations,

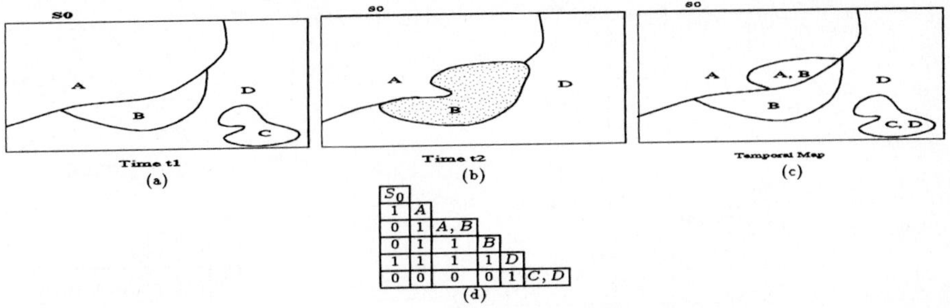

S_0					
1	A				
0	1	A, B			
0	1	1	B		
1	1	1	1	D	
0	0	0	0	1	C, D

Fig. 4. (a) Space at time t1. (b) Space at time t2. (c) The composite temporal map of the considered space at t_1 and t_2. (d) Adjacency matrix for the map in (c).

political boundary changes or prediction of natural disasters such as floods. The global relations between changes can be easily recorded by arranging a temporal sequence for example $(A, B) < (C, D)$.

3.5 Representation of Ambiguity or Inconsistency

Spatial data sets, such as geographic data in GISs typically contain error. Details may be missing or undefined. Errors in this data can lead to ambiguity in the resulting relationships between objects in space. Objects may be disjoint when they are meant to touch, or the relative direction of object may change. Relationships between objects in different data sets can therefore differ. This makes the task of data integration quite complex. The example in figure 5 shows two maps (1) and (2) for the same area in space. There is ambiguity in the extension of the object B and uncertainty in the location of object C. The overlay of the two maps in 5(a) and (b) result in the map in (c). The spatial entities in the result map hold the identities (or values) of the possible entities that occupied that space according to the original data sets. The adjacency matrix for the map in (c) is given in (d). The adjacency structure (or matrix map) can also be used to represent the common consistent set of knowledge in two scenes. For example, the structure in 5(e) is informative of the common consistent topological knowledge between the two data sets.

4 Representing the Consistent Set of Knoweldge

Equivalence of two representations of a spatial object can be studied using an absolute frame of reference, an object-based frame of reference and a relation-based frame of reference. Three classes of spatial equivalence can therefore be identified as follows.

I. Positional Equivalence: Two objects from two different data sets match only if their representative sets of coordinates match exactly and two data sets

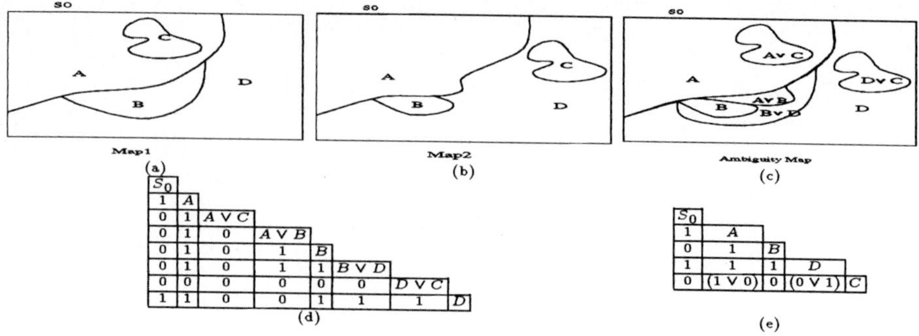

S_0							
1	A						
0	1	$A \vee C$					
0	1	0	$A \vee B$				
0	1	0	1	B			
0	1	0	1	1	$B \vee D$		
0	0	0	0	0	0	$D \vee C$	
1	1	0	0	1	1	1	D

(d)

S_0				
1	A			
0	1	B		
1	1	1	D	
0	$(1 \vee 0)$	0	$(0 \vee 1)$	C

(e)

Fig. 5. (a) Data set in Map 1. (b) Same data set from different source in Map 2. (c) The composite ambiguity map. (d) The adjacency matrix for the map in (c). (e) Common set of consistent knowledge in the map1 and map2.

can be considered as locationally consistent if any position (x,y,z) corresponds to the same object in both sets.

II. Object-Based Equivalence Classes: Here, properties of the spatial object define several consistency classes. These classes include: a) object existence equivalence, b) object dimension equivalence, c) object shape equivalence, d) object size equivalence, and e) object detail equivalence. Two data sets can be said to be object-based consistent of a certain class if for each object in both sets this consistency is achieved. Other object-equivalence classes may exist, but the above set are possibly the most important from a general point of view. Note that the above classes may not be mutually exclusive.

III. Relation-Based Equivalence Classes The third type of consistency measures is based on the spatial relationships between objects in the data sets considered. Three classes of equivalence can be classified according to the types of spatial relationships.

(A) Topological Equivalence: Two data sets can be regarded as topologically consistent if the set of topological relationships derived from one set are the same as those derived from the other. The two sets in figure 6(a) are topologically inconsistent. Object B crosses object C in the first map and is disjoint from C in the second.

(B) Direction or Orientation Equivalence: Two data sets can be regarded as directionally consistent if the relative direction relationship in one set is the same as the other set. The two sets in figure 6(b) are directionally inconsistent.

(C) Relative Size Equivalence: Two data sets can be regarded as consistent with reference to relative size relationships if the qualitative size relations of larger and smaller are maintained between corresponding sets of objects in the two sets. Objects in 6(c) are relative size inconsistent. $A > B > C$ in (a) and $A > B < C$ in (b).

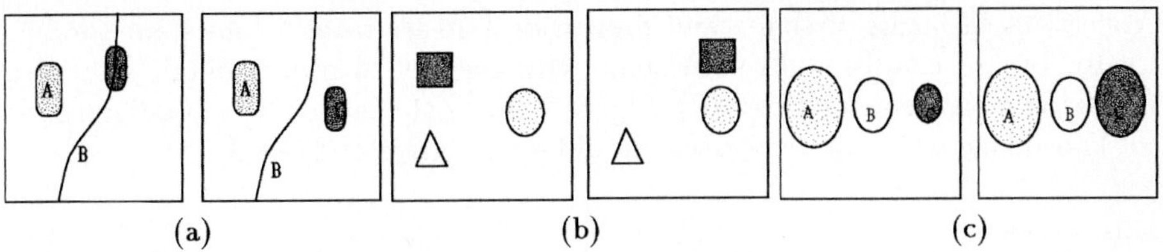

Fig. 6. (a) Topological inconsistency. (b) Directional inconsistency. (c) Relative size inconsistency.

4.1 Different Levels of Spatial Consistency

Two spatial data sets can be consistent in more than one class of those defined above. For example, the data sets can be topologically and dimensionally equivalent, or consistent with reference to dimension, detail and category, etc. In reality, only a subset of objects in the different data sets would conform to a specific consistency class and different subsets would conform to different consistency classes. Ranking the level of consistency for the different classes identified is important as it would provide the user of the spatial database an initial measure of the nature of the data sets in his use. Further processing of this ranking would be to identify how the data sets compare and which parts of the data sets are consistent, i.e. the nature of such consistency.

Three levels of consistency can be identified.

(A) Total Consistency

Two data sets S_1 and S_2 can be said to be totally consistent with reference to a certain consistency class i, if $S_{1i} \cap S_{2i} = S_{1i} \vee S_{2i}$, i.e. $S_{1i} = S_{2i}$. In this case a query to the GIS involving only properties of class i shall return identical results if posed to either S_1 or S_2.

(B) Partial Consistency

Two data sets S_1 and S_2 can be said to be partially consistent with reference to a certain consistency class i, if $S_{1i} \cap S_{2i} = C_i$ and $C_i \subset S_{1i} \wedge C_i \subset S_{2i}$. In this case only part of class i knowledge is consistent in the two sets. If the two data sets are to be used together, then it is important to know which subsets of the different classes of knowledge can be manipulated interchangeably between sets.

(C) Conditional Consistency

Two data sets S_1 and S_2 are said to be conditionally consistent with reference to a certain consistency class i, if there exists a set of functions F which when applied to S_{1i} makes it totally consistent with S_{2i}, i.e. $S_{2i} = F(S_{1i})$. This can also represent the case where S_{1i} is consistent with S_{2i} but S_{2i} is not consistent with S_{1i}, i.e. $(S_{1i} \cap S_{2i} = S_{1i}) \wedge (S_{1i} \subset S_{2i})$, (an asymmetric consistency). The set of functions F must be non-ad-hoc, i.e. predefined. For example, the set of cartographic generalisation rules used to produce maps at different scales or a set of predefined rules used to produce a schematic from a faithful representation of a map. In most cases the data sets which need to be integrated relate to a combination of classes and levels. For example, two data sets can be partially consistent in terms of shape and dimension but are totally consistent topologically, or are conditionally consistent with respect to object detail as well as partially consistent topologically. Figure 7 shows the integration of different sets of knowledge which are consistent in different classes and levels.

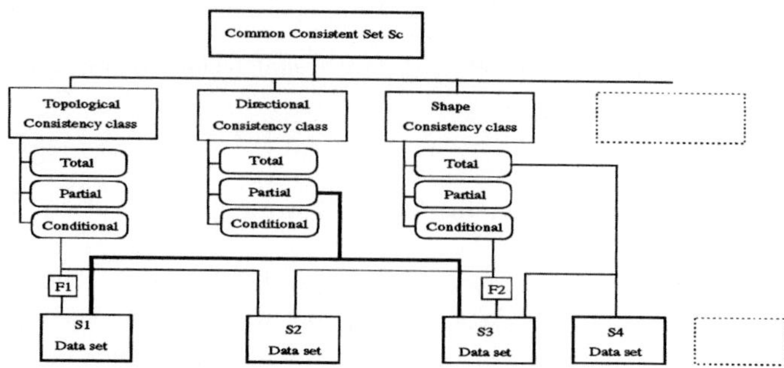

Fig. 7. Integrating different data sets with different classes and levels of consistency to produce a common set of consistent knowledge. $F1$ and $F2$ represent sets of predefined functions for conditional consistency.

5 An Example

In carrying out some analysis using a GIS, it was required to manipulate certain objects details. No one data set was found to contain all the required details and hence data sets needed to be integrated. The sets required had to be consistent in topology and orientation and together contain all the objects details. Two data sets were found to comply with the above; one, a remotely sensed image in raster format and the other a digitised map in vector format. Parts of both maps are shown in figure 8 along with their corresponding matrix maps. In what follows, we 'll show how to integrate the two data sets using the matrix maps and qualitative reasoning. Note that the alternative method for integrating the data sets is to overlay them and calculate their exact intersections, which is a computationally expensive and error-prone process.

From the object matching process we have: $A = (D \cup F)$ and $E = (C \cup B)$. From matrix map (b): $\neg adjacent(D, E) \rightarrow \neg adjacent(D, C) \wedge \neg adjacent(D, B)$ (1). To define the relations between F and both B and C. From matrix map (a): $adjacent(A, B) \rightarrow adjacent((D \cup F), B)$ (2). From (1) and (2) we get: $adjacent(F, B)$ (3). Also, $adjacent(C, A) \rightarrow adjacent(C, (D \cup F))$ (4). From (1) and (4) we get: $adjacent(C, F)$ (5). From the matrix maps we have: $IE(F, D) \wedge \overline{IW(B, C)}$ To deduce the orientation relations: $W(A, C) \rightarrow W((D \cup F), C) \rightarrow W(F, C) \rightarrow E(C, F)$ Also, $E(E, F) \rightarrow E((B \cup C), F) \rightarrow E(B, F)$ The full integrated matrix map is shown in figure 8(c).

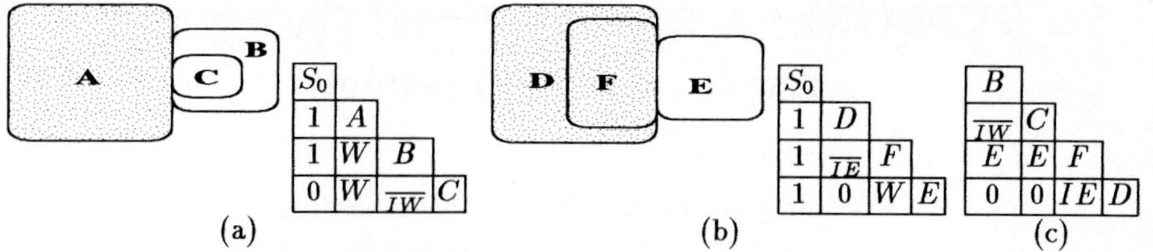

Fig. 8. (a) Data set (1) with details B and C and its matrix map. (b) Data set (2) with details D and F and its matrix map. Note that S_0 represent the union of the rest of the object space. (c) Integrated Matrix Map for (a) and (b).

6 Conclusions

A qualitative approach is proposed for the integration of data in spatial databases. The approach consists of two main parts.

1. Building a qualitative level of representation: where relation-based information are stored and manipulated using qualitative reasoning techniques.
2. Explicit representation of the set of consistent knowledge between data sets using predefined consistency classes and levels. This provides the flexibility for two data sets to be integrated without necessarily being totally consistent in every aspect.

The paper shows how topological and orientation information can be explicitly represented using a simple structure (map matrix), and how the structure can be used in integrating different data sets irrespective of their relative level of consistency and format of representation.

References

1. Flowerdew, R.: Spatial Data Integration. Geographic Information Systems. **1** (1991), 375–387
2. Nyerges, T.: Schema Integration Analysis for the Development of GIS Databases. Int. J. GIS. **3(2)** (1989), 153–183
3. Shepherd, I.D.H.: Information Integration and GIS. Geographic Information Systems, Longman Scientific. **1** (1991), 337–60
4. Abdelmoty, A. I., Jones, C.B.: Towards Maintaining Consistency in Spatial Databases. CIKM'97, ACM Press. (1997), 293–300
5. El-Geresy, B.A., Abdelmoty, A.I.: Order in Space: A General Formalism for Spatial Reasoning. IJAIT, World Scientific Publishing. **6(4)**, 423–450
6. El-Geresy, B.A.: The Space Algebra: Spatial Reasoning without Composition Tables. TAI'97, IEEE Computer Society Press. (1997), 67–74
7. Egenhofer, M.J., Clementini, E., Di Felice, P.: Evaluating Inconsistencies among Multiple Representations. SDH'94, IGU Commission of GIS. **2**, (1994), 901–918
8. Kuijpers, B., Paredaens, J., den Bussche, J.V.: On topological elementary equivalence of spatial databases. ICDT '97, Springer Verlag. **LNCS-1186**, (1997), 432–446

SVIQUEL: A Spatial Visual Query and Exploration Language

Sudhir Kaushik and Elke A. Rundensteiner

Department of Computer Science
Worcester Polytechnic Institute, Worcester, MA 01609
sudhir@cs.wpi.edu, rundenst@cs.wpi.edu
http://davis.wpi.edu/dsrg/index.html

Abstract. *This paper represents the first effort to apply direct-manipulation (VIS) techniques to spatial data exploration providing mechanisms for visually querying as well as browsing spatial data and for reviewing the visual results for trend discovery. We present a visual query language (SVIQUEL) which allows us to specify the relative spatial position (both topology and direction) between objects using direct manipulation of spatial query filters, called S-sliders. The S-sliders for the selection of precise numeric ranges for query dimensions are complimented by Active-Picture-for-Querying (APIQ), a qualitative direct-manipulation query paradigm. SVIQUEL thus supports spatial browsing and spatial trend discovery with no particular query in mind. The tight coupling between the quantitative S-sliders and qualitative APIQ allows the users to work either qualitatively or quantitatively depending on his/her particular needs and freely switch between the two while working in a continuous data exploration mode.*

1 Introduction

The exploration of large information spaces remains a challenging task especially with the growth of the World Wide Web and other such huge repositories [1]. Many users are not able to cope with the flood of information. Visual Information Seeking (VIS) addresses this problem by recognizing the enormous capacity of human visual information processing [1]. By presenting information visually and allowing user interaction through direct-manipulation, users can traverse larger information spaces in shorter time. Our goal is to apply the concept of VIS to *special-purpose data types* such as *spatial* and *temporal* data, as to the best of our knowledge VIS has up to now only been applied to simple numeric data types [1] [18]. Our previous work focussed on designing a direct manipulation environment for *one-dimensional temporal data*, called TVQL [8] [7] [6] [9], that allowed a user to visually specify temporal queries over video data giving an instantaneous visualization of the results of the query. Formal user studies of TVQL show that users could more accurately specify and more quickly adjust queries using TVQL than using forms [8] [9], indicating the promise of our approach.

In this paper, we study the extension of the above concepts for *two-dimensional* spatial data. In particular, our contributions are:

- An integrated framework for spatial data analysis incorporating both direction and topology queries into one uniform exploration environment.
- A visual query interface for spatial data (SVIQUEL) over this integration of direction and topology expanding VIS to more complex data types (spatial in this case) which has not been attempted before.
- An active picture (APIQ) for query specification at the qualitative level and for visual query disambiguation of the quantitative S-sliders.
- Mapping functions between quantitative settings of S-sliders to qualitative query semantics in APIQ, providing for a tight coupling between the two[13].
- A working implementation of SVIQUEL implemented using the AWT library of JDK1.1.3 (http://davis.wpi.edu/dsrg/MMVIS/svql/svql.html).

Section 2 reviews related work. Section 3 gives an overview of our approach. The primitive spatial relations and the integrated neighborhood concept are introduced in Section 4 while APIQ is introduced in Section 5. Section 6 concludes the paper.

2 Related Work

Surprisingly little has been done thus far in applying the direct manipulation paradigm to spatial environments. Visual query environments based on VIS [18] are typically restricted to simple numeric domains. The Dynamic Homefinder, a Real Estate Information Exploration System based on VIS [18], allows users to search for a house that meets their criteria by manipulating sliders for different input parameters (such as number of rooms, price, distance from a fixed point, etc). However, it does not allow the user to specify the relative *spatial* position of two objects. Our goal is to provide a new class of dynamic filters tuned for continuous spatial querying.

Most spatial query languages are textual (SQL-based) [3]. The possibly most popular GIS system MapInfo [1] uses an SQL-style language to specify queries to query primarily over non-spatial and a few spatial attributes such as area and distance of the underlying data. This language however is neither incremental nor direct-manipulation based and thus our proposed interface is complimentary to such technology.

Cigales [17] takes a Query by Example approach that specifies the query using an actual drawing, while GEO-QUEL [2] uses an image depicting the relationship as means for query specification.

3 Overview of Our Spatial Exploration Environment

The four major components of our system include the spatial slider interface (S-sliders), the Active Picture for Querying interface (APIQ), the Spatial Query Processor and the Spatial Visualization of results (SVIZ) [12, 15, 14]. A user

[1] More information about MapInfo can be found at "http://www.mapinfo.com"

specifies a query using a combination of the S-sliders and APIQ interfaces. The S-slider interface is tightly coupled to APIQ allowing both qualitative and quantitative spatial data exploration. APIQ also presents a valuable aid in confirming the query specified in a visually intuitive manner. The quantitative queries expressed by the S-sliders are mapped to range queries to be processed by the query processor [6] [10]. Once processed against the spatial database, a graphical visualization of the results is presented to the user via SVIZ. The visualization is immediately updated whenever users manipulate one of the interfaces, giving the users a sense of causality between adjusting a query interface and the visualization of the results.

4 SVIQUEL Interface

The following are the goals in designing SVIQUEL:

- a visual interface to specify relative position spatial queries of any type such as topological or directional relationships in a precise yet simple manner via direct manipulation.
- ability to quickly adjust and incrementally refine spatial queries via direct manipulation.
- power to both specify particular queries as well as to browse over spatial relationships, with no particular query in mind.
- support for composing complex queries such as a combination of spatial relationships in a simple manner.

Given two spatial objects A and B, the spatial (topological, directional or distance) relationship between the two objects can be inferred from the relationships between the extremities of each object along both the X and Y dimension [2]. Fully constraining relative object placement gives complete information about how B is spatially placed with respect to A, such as whether B is to the north and overlaps with A. Our interface constrains the placement of one object B called the *primary* object with respect to the second object A that serves as the *reference* object [16, 11]. To query over the relative spatial position, we design our SVIQUEL language to specify any primitive spatial relationship as well as combinations of these primitive relationships as discussed below.

4.1 Relative Spatial Queries

Given two spatial objects A and B, our SVIQUEL interface distinguishes between eight possible primitive topological relationships *(disjoint, meet, overlap, covers, coveredBy, contains, inside and equal)* [4] and eight possible directional

[2] One important assumption here is that we are approximating each object by its Minimum Bounding Rectangle (MBR) with its sides oriented along the X and Y axes, and the spatial relationship between the two objects is expressed in terms of its MBR.

relationships *(north, south, east, west, north east, north west, south east and south west)* between the two objects and two special relationships of same-longitude and same-latitude. Since it is possible for two regions to have both kinds of relationships, each combination of a topology and a direction forms a *primitive* spatial relation (a SPRIM).

In our model, we have identified 45 meaningful primitives among the 64 possible ones (Fig. 1), which capture both the topological and the directional relationship between the regions. The reason we have 45 spatial primitives (SPRIMs) and not 64 is that for certain topologies like *inside*, *contains* or *equals* having a directional component is not meaningful [5].

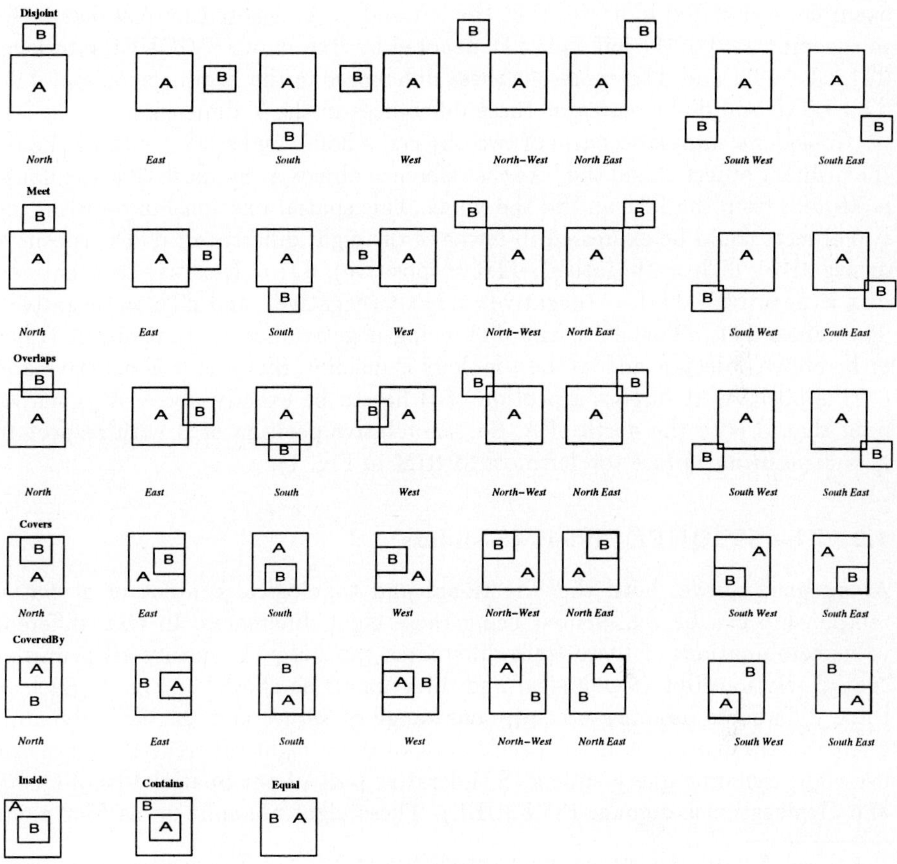

Fig. 1. Spatial Primitives (SPRIMs) with Topology and Direction Combined.

The SPRIMs as depicted in Fig. 1 can be defined in terms of the differences between the left and right ends in the X dimension and the top and bottom ends in the Y dimension of the two objects A and B. The left and right ends of an object are its extremities in the X dimension while the top and bottom ends are its extremities in the Y dimension. Consider two objects A and B with the extremities for each object along the X dimension given by Axl, Axr, Bxl, Bxr [3]. The spatial relationship between the two objects is defined by a conjunction of the eight pairwise relationships between the extremities in each dimension. In many cases, fewer than eight differences are sufficient to represent the relative spatial position of two objects: ((Axl θ Bxl) AND (Axl θ Bxr) AND (Axr θ Bxl) AND (Axr θ Bxr)) AND ((Ayt θ Byt) AND (Ayt θ Byb) AND (Ayb θ Byt) AND (Ayb θ Byb)) where $\theta = \{ <, >, = \}$. [4] [5]

Each of these eight expressions combined by the AND operator shows the relative spatial position of the corresponding extremity of the two objects. For example, Axl < Bxl indicates that the left end of A, denoted by Axl, has to be to the left ("<") of the left end of B, denoted by Bxl. In our SVIQUEL interface, dTl, dTr, dTlr and dTrl represent these differences in the X dimension and dTt, dTb, dTtb and dTbt represent these differences in the Y dimension.

Consider a sample scenario of two objects, a house and a lake, with the house the primary object B and the lake the reference object A. Suppose that the house is *disjoint* from the lake and to the *north*. This spatial relationship between the two objects could be expressed in terms of the eight differences: dTl = (positive or negative); dTlr = (negative); dTrl = (positive); dTr = (positive or negative); dTt =(negative); dTtb = (negative); dTbt =(negative); and dTb = (negative). The values dTt, dTbt, dTtb and dTb being negative implies that object B has to be above object A and so the topology is disjoint. Since dTlr is negative and dTrl is positive, it implies a portion of B has to be exactly above A. Thus we infer that B is to the north of A. So, the relative position of B with respect to A is *disjoint-north* (see top leftmost SPRIM in Fig. 1).

4.2 The SVIQUEL Sliders (S-sliders)

As outlined above, both the directional and topological content of a spatial relationship can be represented using these eight differences. In fact, different value combinations of these eight differences can uniquely specify all primitive spatial relationships (topological and directional) as shown in Fig. 1. Each of these differences assumes a continuous range of values and therefore dynamic query sliders can be used to specify each of these eight differences. Hence, we use eight dynamic query sliders (S-sliders) as part of our Spatial Visual Query and Exploration Language (SVIQUEL). These eight are split up as four along

[3] Axl and Axr are the left and right extremities of A in the X dimension respectively and the same holds true for B also and along the Y dimension given by Ayt, Ayb, Byt, Byb. Ayt and Ayb are the top and bottom extremities of A in the Y dimension respectively and the same holds true for B also.

[4] We assume that each object has a finite non-zero width and height and also Axl < Axr, Ayt < Ayb, Bxl < Bxr, Byt < Byb always.

[5] The sizes of A and B do not convey any information about the size of the actual objects that they represent.

each dimension as each of the two 2D objects has two endpoints along each dimension (see Fig. 2).

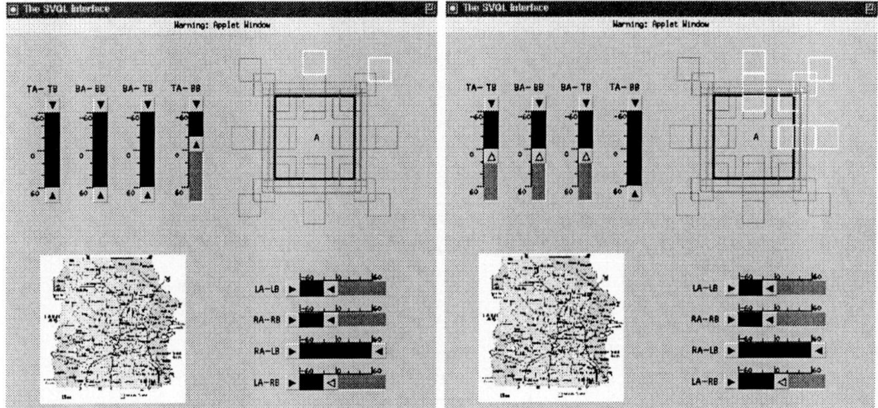

Fig. 2. APIQ for Query "Find all cases where B is disjoint from A and north or north east of A"

Fig. 3. APIQ for Query "Find all cases where B is disjoint from A and north, north east or east of A"

In order to prevent the specification of illegal queries, constraints and dependencies are introduced between the sliders so that only legal combinations of values can be specified using our interface [13]. There are two main advantages of creating such dependencies: it avoids the specification of illegal queries by users, and it simplifies the process of query specification whenever possible.

4.3 Integrated Neighborhood Concept for Topology and Direction

In addition to selecting one SPRIM among the 45 distinct possible spatial primitives, our SVIQUEL interface is designed to also allow the user to specify a combination of these primitives. Since our sliders enable us to specify a range of values for each of the sliders, we can also use them to specify combinations of spatial relations by adjusting the sliders to include a larger set of values. [6] Let us consider the scenario where we have a number of houses in the vicinity of a lake and the user is interested in buying a house in the region. Suppose he asks the query, "Give me those houses which are to the *north* or the *north east* of the lake". In our example above, the user essentially has two spatial relations specified between the house and the lake, one is the *north* directional relation and the other is the *north east* directional relation. Since the sliders specify a range

[6] For simplicity, we follow the common approach of modeling both the primary and the reference objects as two rectangles (the Minimum Bounding Rectangles of the two objects). The sliders can be used to manipulate the left, right, top and bottom extremities of the rectangle.

of values, the user could ask for these two relations in a single query by proper adjustment of the appropriate sliders. This way, the user is actually querying for combinations of spatial relations. If the user now adjusts the slider "Right A - Left B" to also include negative values, the configuration *disjoint-north east* is also included (see Fig. 2).

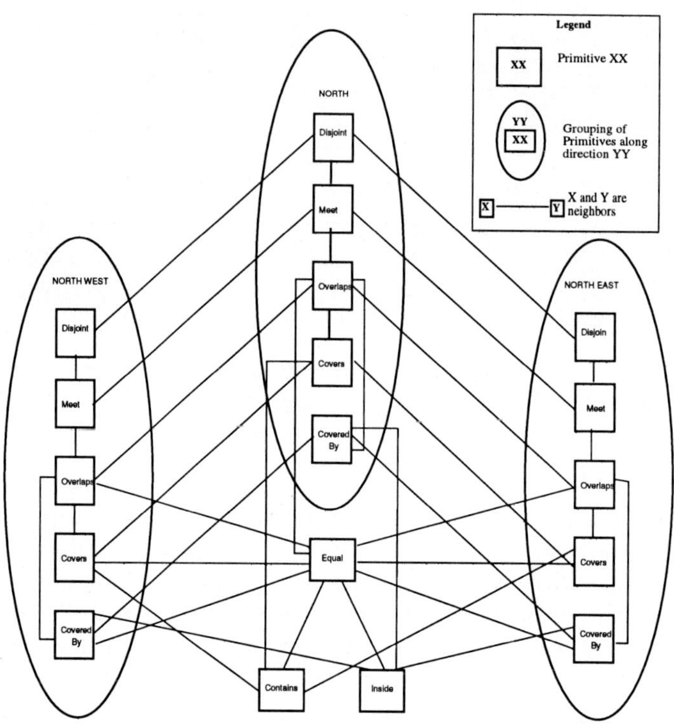

Fig. 4. Our Neighborhood Model Combining Topology and Direction Relations.

However, since the sliders operate over continuous ranges of values, they can only be used to specify those combinations of relations which are 'neighbors' of each other. The specification of continuous ranges of values by the sliders enables us to go from one spatial relation to the one closest to it by the simple move of the mouse and thus fosters rapid yet continuous exploration of the data set. Going to any arbitrary relation from the current one would require the skipping of values in the middle which is not supported by our query paradigm.

This observation requires us to establish a precise definition for this intuitive concept of neighborhood viz the relations closest to a given relation form a neighborhood. For topology, we borrow the concept of neighborhoods among topological spatial relations between a line and a region [4]. This model considers the intersections between the interior, boundary and the exterior of the line and the region, and differentiates between the topologies based on these 9 intersection values. For direction, we use the concept of neighborhood as developed by Hernandez [5].

Given our goal of querying over both topology and direction, we developed a neighborhood model for an aggregate relationship integrating both direction and topology [5]. Our neighborhood model is a natural extension of the two individual models. In the sense, when we ignore one of the two spatial components (direction or topology), our model defaults to the individual known model. The neighbors for a particular SPRIM can be obtained in our model using the knowledge of its neighbors with respect to topology and with respect to direction. So, the neighbors for a particular spatial primitive can be deduced as follows:

- Those relations which have the same topology but are neighbors with respect to direction.
- Those relations which have the same direction but are neighbors with respect to topology.

The underlying assumption here is that the user is allowed to go from one spatial primitive to the other only by moving along the two axes of our 2D space, one at a time, i.e., he is not allowed to move diagonally along the two axes. [7] The chart showing the neighborhood relations of the SPRIMs in the *north*, *north east* and *north west* directions are shown in Fig. 4. The other neighborhood relationships can also be derived in a similar manner and are omitted here for space reasons. The configurations *same-longitude* and *same-latitude* are special cases. This formal model of neighborhood enables us to specify all legal combinations of relative spatial positions that could be specified by SVIQUEL as well as incremental transitions between them. Thus, each SVIQUEL query corresponds to a set of neighboring SPRIMs and the interface allows to move from one SPRIM to another if and only if they form a neighborhood set.

5 APIQ: An Active Picture for Qualitative Querying

5.1 Direct Manipulation in APIQ

The APIQ environment is used to specify a qualitative relative position spatial query. In our system, the user selects and de-selects the primitives which are a part of the query using mouse clicks. For example, given the APIQ depicted in Fig. 2, if the user wishes to specify the primitive *disjoint east* as part of the query, then a mouse click on that primitive results in including that primitive as part of the query. The resulting APIQ and S-sliders, consistent with the integrated neighborhood model, are shown in Fig. 3. The tight coupling between the S-sliders and APIQ achieved by our mapping functions between the two gives the new setting of the S-sliders as a result of the direct manipulation of APIQ [13].

[7] The configuration *same-longitude* is the neighbor of *overlap-north* and *overlap-south* and also to all neighbors of these two configurations. In the case of *same-latitude*, its neighbors are *overlap-east*, *overlap-west* and all the neighbors of these configurations.

After the user has specified the qualitative query using the APIQ, the S-sliders could be used to set precise numeric values and thus specify the relative position query quantitatively.

5.2 APIQ: Qualitative Query Representation

Formal user studies of temporal queries in MMVIS have shown that a graphical depiction of a slider-based query for query disambiguation results in better performance and easier comprehension for the users [8]. Borrowing this idea of qualitative query disambiguation of MMVIS [6], the Active Picture for Querying (APIQ) also provides visual *qualitative* representations of the query to the user. APIQ represents a valuable aid for confirming the specified query to the users in a visually intuitive manner.

APIQ is the natural compliment to the S-slider query model as it corresponds to the union of all neighboring SPRIMs specified by the user in the SVIQUEL query. In other words, APIQ shows all the primitive positions B could occupy with respect to a reference object A - each position graphically depicted by one SPRIM primitive.

This should increase the speed and the certainty with which the users modify and construct complex queries. Another advantage of APIQ is that it increases the utility of the SVIQUEL interface for spatial browsing of the data with no particular query in mind. That is, both APIQ and the visualization of the results (SVIZ) are dynamically updated as users manipulate the sliders, thereby enabling the users to simply slide the sliders front and back until an interesting result appears and then see from APIQ what query was specified.

6 Conclusions

In this paper, we have presented a framework for applying the direct manipulation paradigm to spatial data. In our work, we have defined a Spatial Visual Query and Exploration Language (SVIQUEL) for specifying relative spatial position queries. SVIQUEL enables users to specify any primitive spatial relation, with both direction and topology combined, as well as conceptual neighborhood combinations of them. Our SVIQUEL interface provides users with a visual paradigm for browsing the spatial data through direct manipulation and in a spatially continuous manner. SVIQUEL introduces a qualitative active picture for querying (APIQ) which allows the user to qualitatively specify spatial queries. We have a working implementation of the complete system in Java using JDK1.1.3 at the following URL ("http://davis.wpi.edu/dsrg/MMVIS/svql/svql.html").

Acknowledgments: Special thanks goes to Stacie Hibino, who had developed the initial MMVIS framework including TVQL, for providing us with TVQL source code on which we based our implementation. We would also like to thank the Database Systems Research Group (DSRG) at WPI whose feedback was very valuable to us at every stage of our research.

References

1. C. Ahlberg and B. Shneiderman. Visual information seeking: Tight coupling of dynamic query filters with starfield displays. *CHI'94*, pages 313–317, Apr 1994.
2. R. Berman and M. Stonebraker. Geo-Quel, a system for the manipulation and display of geometric data. *ACM Computer Graphics*, 11(2):186–191, 1977.
3. M. Egenhofer. Spatial SQL: A query and presentation language. *IEEE Trans. on Knowledge and Data Eng.*, 6:86–95, Feb 1994.
4. M. Egenhofer and D. Mark. Modeling conceptual neighborhoods of topological line region relations. *International Journal of Geographic Information Systems*, 9:555–565, 1995.
5. D. Hernandez. Qualitative representation of spatial knowledge. In *Lecture Notes in Artificial Intelligence*, volume 804. Springer Verlag, Feb 1994.
6. S. Hibino and E. Rundensteiner. MMVIS: Design and implementation of a multimedia VIS environment. *ACM Multimedia*, pages 75–86, 1996.
7. S. Hibino and E. A. Rundensteiner. A visual multimedia query language for temporal analysis of video data. In *MultiMedia Database Systems*, pages 123–159. Kluwer Aca, 1996.
8. S. Hibino and E. A. Rundensteiner. User study evaluation of direct-manipulation temporal interfaces. *ACM Multimedia*, pages 99–109, Nov 1997.
9. S. Hibino and E. A. Rundensteiner. Comparing MMVIS to a timeline for temporal trend analysis of video data. *Advanced Visual Interfaces*, May 1998.
10. S. Hibino and E. A. Rundensteiner. Processing incremental multidim. range queries in a direct manipulation paradigms. *IEEE Int. Conf. on Data Eng.*, pages 458–465, Feb 1998.
11. Z. John, M. Tamer, and D. Szarfon. Spatial reasoning rules in multimedia management systems. Multimedia Technical Report TR96-05, Department of Computer Science, University of Alberta, Mar 1996.
12. S. Kaushik. Direct-manipulation spatial exploration using SVIQUEL. Master's thesis, Computer Science Department, Worcester Polytechnic Institute, May 1998.
13. S. Kaushik and E. A. Rundensteiner. SVIQUEL: A spatial visual query and exploration language. Technical Report CS-TR-97-10, Comp. Science Dept, Worcester Polytechnic Institute, 1997.
14. S. Kaushik and E. A. Rundensteiner. Direct-manipulation spatial exploration using SVIQUEL. In *Visual Database Systems Conference'98.* Short paper and software system demonstration, Acquia, Italy, Springer Verlag, May 1998.
15. S. Kaushik and E. A. Rundensteiner. SEE: A spatial exploration environment based on a direct-manipulation paradigm. Technical Report CS-TR-98-7, Computer Science Department, Worcester Polytechnic Institute, May 1998.
16. D. Papadias, Y. Theodoridis, T. Sellis, and M. Egenhofer. Topological relations in the world of minimum bounding rectangles: A study with R-trees. *Proceedings of SIGMOD*, 24, June 1995.
17. A. B. Wansek, D. Calcinelli, B. Languou, C. Lecocq, and M. Mainguenaud. CIGALES: A visual query language for GIS: The user interface. *International Journal of Visual Languages and Computing*, 5:113–132, 1994.
18. C. Williamson and B. Shneiderman. The Dynamic HomeFinder: Evaluating dynamic queries in a real-estate information exploration system. Technical Report CS-TR2819, Dept. of Computer Science,Univ. of Maryland, Jan 1992.

View Adaptation in Data Warehousing Systems

Zohra Bellahsene

LIRMM UMR 55060 CNRS - Montpellier II
161 rue ADA 34392 Montpellier Cedex 5, France
e-mail : bella@lirmm.fr

Abstract

An important aspect of a data warehouse system should be its ability to evolve according the user and organization needs. The reason being that the schema of a data warehouse can evolve for integrating new requirements resulting from analysis or data mining processing, schema changes on information sources etc. More precisely, schema changes arising on information sources should be propagated to the related views in order to maintain consistency between the sources and the derived views. In this paper, we present a view model extending the relational view model. And we show how this extended view definition language allows to support view schema changes enforcing consistency and without causing disruptions or modifications to existing views and application programs.

Keywords: data warehouse, relational views, data warehouse evolution.

1 Introduction

A data warehouse is a repository integrating information from heterogeneous and autonomous sources. Fig. 1 illustrates a functional architecture of a data warehouse system based on the one proposed in [15]. The information sources could be heterogeneous and may include relational tables, legacy systems, object schema, flat files, HTML documents, etc. A wrapper component provides the information translation from the native format of a data source into the relational data model format. The next phase encompasses issues concerning the integration of the different sources schemas, such as the data inconsistency and structural or semantic conflicts. We have to note that the translation problem is not a specific problem of a data warehouse but inherent to data integration process in a heterogeneous environment. The integrator task consists in merging sources schemata into an integrated schema (called also the data warehouse conceptual schema) and defining views from the resulting integrated schema.

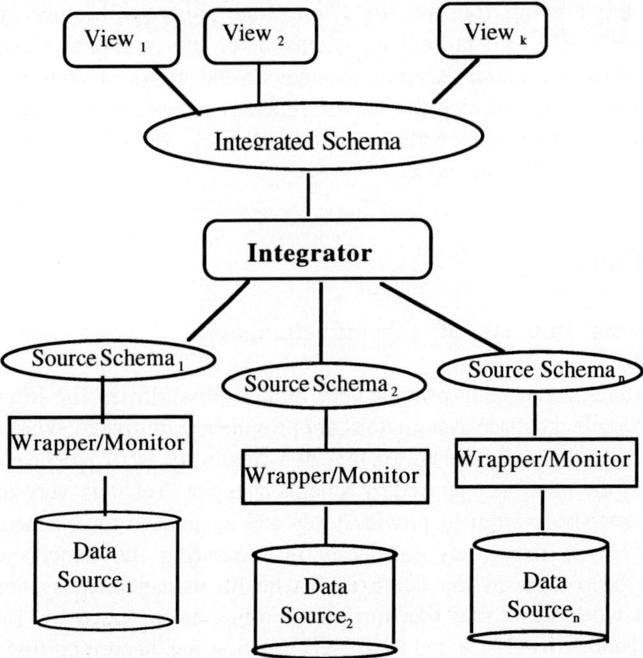

Fig. 1. A Schema Architecture of a Data Warehouse

The data of a data warehouse is used primarily in organisational decision-making and it may be strategic. Consequently, we argue that schema changes should be handled without causing information loss or disruptions to application programs. In this paper, we focus on the issue of supporting view schema changes in a relational data warehouse with materialized views. More precisely, we show how a view definition language can be used to support both structural modifications of views according the changes arising on the information sources and direct schema changes on views. In both cases, the issue is to maintain the coherence between the data sources and the data warehouse and to maintain the compatibility of existing programs in the data warehouse. Although in the first case, the schema changes arising on the data sources should be propagated to the views. While in the case of direct schema changes arising on views, the schema changes are not propagated to the data sources since the sources are autonomous and independent from the data warehouse. Program compatibility is provided by maintaining multiple versions of the views. However, only, schema changes that do not entail a risk of incompatibility, are actually performed and propagated to the derived views. In this way, our approach avoids the proliferation of versions of views. In summary, the main contributions of our work are:

- an extended relational view model to take into account the specific requirements in a relational data warehouse and to support schema evolution,
- a structural evolution of the data warehouse maintaining data coherence, and which also preserves application programs.

This paper is organised as follows. In section 2 are presented the motivations of our work. In the section 3, we present an extension of the relational view model. We examine the impact of sources schema changes on the views in section 4. Section 5 describes a strategy for updating the views' schemas independently from information sources. Section 6 gives an overview of related work. Finally, section 7 contains concluding remarks and future work.

2 Motivations

2.1 Minimizing impacts of schema changes

The relational database systems provide very limited possibilities for schema changes. For instance, Oracle database system does not provide a primitive to express directly an attribute deletion. The main reason of this non-flexibility is to preserve the database from the risk of inconsistency caused by schema changes. Yet it is very important for any advanced database system to provide tools and techniques for a schema evolution support [9], [11]. A first study consisting in measuring the frequency of schema evolution has been done in the context of a health management system [11]. The results of this work show that the number of relations increased by 139% and the number of attributes by 274% and that every relation has been modified. The second report [9] concludes that 59% of attributes are changed on the average.

Schema evolution, in the context of a data warehousing system, may arise from schema changes on information sources or from direct schema changes on the views schemata. The changes performed on information sources may modify existing views, therefore, the application programs referencing the views can no longer run. To ovoid this problem, we propose to use the view mechanism to simulate the schema changes. Thus performing a schema change with our approach, consists in creating a new view which reflects the semantics of the schema change. Furthermore, our approach is based on enforcing two requirements

(i) maintaining consistency between the data sources and the data warehouse and

(ii) preserving the existing views and programs from incompatibility caused by schema changes.

2.2 Modeling specific requirements

In relational database systems, a view is a derived relation, (i.e. table) which includes a subset of attributes belonging to the database schema. We propose to extend the relational view definition language to allow the specification of views with non-derived attributes. The first interest of including additional (non-derived) attributes in a view independently of the source relations allows the integration of new requirements resulting from analysis or data mining processing in the data warehouse. The second interest of including additional (non-derived) attributes in a view is to achieve the simulation of schema changes that augment the underlying schema.

3 Extending the relational view definition language

3.1 Terminology

Definition. A view
Let Q be an SQL query over a set R of relations. Let A be a set of attributes introduced in the view for modelling the data warehouse specific requirements. We call these attributes *specific attributes*. Then, we denote a view V as a tuple (Q(R), A).

3.2 The sample schema

Fig.1 describes a data warehouse conceptual schema from which some views will be derived. It describes an application performing analyses of trends in sales and supply. It contains information about articles, customers and their suppliers.

Articles (anum: integer, price: number, type: string, name: string, custnum: number, numsup: number)

Customers (custnum: number, name: string, addr_id: number, country: string)

Address (addr_id: number, num: integer, street: string, city: string, zip_code: integer)

Suppliers (numsup: number , name: string, addr_id: string, country: string,)

Fig. 1. Example of a data warehouse conceptual schema.

3.3 The extended view definition language

Defining a view consists in specifying what information derived from the database relations (or from other views) should be visible. In a relational database system, this feature is performed with the project operation which includes all attributes that should be visible. As it has been noted in [1], this approach presents the disadvantage that the definition of the view should be changed according the schema changes of the root relation even if the view attributes are not affected by these changes. Consequently, we propose to allow the direct expression of hiding attributes by using the *Hide attribute* primitive. Therefore, the database administrator can use alternatively the *Hide* operator or the *projection.* In fact, the former is suitable when the number of attributes to be hidden is small and vice versa the *projection* is more appropriate in the inverse case and when the result of the view query includes an *aggregate* function or a *group by* clause. Furthermore, as we will see in the next section, the *Hide* operator is very appropriate for expressing the simulation of a delete operation. Finally, a view definition has the following structure:

```
[Create] view  <view name> As
Query : <query  expression>; /* this is an SQL like query */
[Add Attribute  <attribute name>: <query expression>/<type>]
[Hide Attribute  <attribute name>]
End <view name>;
```

The semantics of this statement is creating a view. The *add attribute* clause allows a view to own specific attributes (i.e. non derived attributes). The type of the added attribute is inferred if a query expression is given or explicitly specified if it is a new specific attribute (i.e. non-derived from sources data). Thus, this statement allows for example to define historical information although source information does not. This possibility is also useful for simulating schema extension or modification operations. Finally, it is possible to render invisible some properties in a view by using the *Hide attribute* clause.

Example 3.3.1

We imagine now the DWA wants to provide users with a view providing a special treatment for computer articles sold only in France. The corresponding view is defined with our view language as follows :

```
Create View French_Computers  As
query:Select A.anum, A.name, A.price
       From articles A, customers C
       Where A.type = 'computer' and C.country = 'France' and
              A.custnum = C.custnum;
End French_Computers;
```

4 Impact of the sources schema changes on Views

An important feature in a data warehouse is taking into account the changes arising in the data sources. In the literature, only data updates are taken into account [15]. The schema changes arising on information sources should be propagated to the data warehouse schema in order to ensure consistency between the data warehouse and the information sources. In this section, we examine the impact of sources schema changes on the related views. In our approach, the adopted strategy consists in propagating actually these changes if only if they do not entail a risk of incompatibility of existing programs or the existing views. Otherwise the propagation consists in creating implicit versions[1] of the affected views. However, the created views should be materialized.

---

[1] The user is unaware of the schema changes therefore the version is transparent for him.

4.1 Propagation of the schema extension

The relevant issue of propagating an *add attribute* operation arising in data source schema concerns the visibility of the added attribute respectively to the corresponding views if the affected relation is a derivation root. However, this operation does not entail a risk of incompatibility of the existing programs. The decision to integrate the new added attribute in the existing views is application context dependent. And it is of the responsibility of the DWA to appreciate the pertinence of the added attribute and to determine which views are potentially concerned.

4.2 Propagation of delete an attribute

The semantics of the propagation of the delete operation is to remove the specified attribute from the type of the concerned views in the data warehouse only if the related attribute is not currently referenced by an application program in the data warehouse. For this purpose, we define a function named "fused(x)" which returns a Boolean (true if the variable x is currently used and false otherwise). The first usage of "fused" is to avoid keeping indefinitely an attribute when the user whiches to delete it and is not actually used. Programming languages, for instance Smalltalk, also provides this kind of function. If the attribute to be deleted entails a risk of incompatibility, the update operation is not actually performed: a version of the view operand will be created and does not include the deleted attribute. The deletion of an attribute may also entail the deletion of a view if this attribute is included in a view query predicate. Here is a procedure for performing the propagation of the deleted attribute on a view. Before executing this procedure, the system has to determine the affected views.

```
Propagation_Delete (A, V) /* propagate the deletion of an attribute A at the
                                        data source level to a view V */
If A is not involved in a query predicate of V
        Then If (not (fused(V))
                Then remove V
        Else If not(fused(A)) and V is not a derivation root
                Then    Delete A from the view V;
                Else    create view V' As
                        query : select * from V;
                        Hide attribute A ;
                        end;
                        Rename V' as V;
                        Materialize V;
End Delete;
```

Example 4.2

We imagine the database administrator of the related information sources wants to delete the attribute name in the relation Article, in the schema presented in fig. 1.

Remember, this attribute is included within the view French_computers. Thus, if this attribute is currently referenced by an application program, the deletion of this attribute will not be actually performed but simulated by creating a new view as follows:

```
Create View French_computers_V1 As
query : select * from French_computers;
Hide attribute name;
end;
Rename French_computers_V1 as French_computers;
```

The result of this query is a version (i.e. a view) of the view French_ computers which does not involve the attribute name. However, the existing applications continue to use it since the deletion is virtual and the old version of the view is kept by the system.

4.3 Propagation of an attribute type modification

The adopted strategy is similar to the delete propagation strategy previously presented.

```
Propagate_Modification (A, T, V) /* Attempt to propagate the effect of modifying the
attribute A at the data source level to a view V */
If not(fused(A)) and V is not a derivation root
        Then Modify A: T in view V;
        Else Create View V' As
             query : Felect * From V;
             Hide attribute A;
             Add attribute A : T   /* Now A has the new type T in V' */
        end;
        Rename V' as V;
End Modification;
```

5 Direct view schema changes

In this section, we examine the direct schema evolution: the clients or the DWA can invoke update operations on the data warehouse schema independently of the information sources. The modification and deletion of an attribute type in a view schema can entail an incoherence with regard to the data source schema. Consequently, such schema changes will not be actually performed but simulated by creating specific views. However, the created view should not be materialized since the data maintenance is performed on the old version which is computed from the data sources. Furthermore, the user is aware of the created view version.

5.1 Extension of a view

The semantics of an add attribute operation is to augment the type of a view with the specified attribute. However, this operation does not entail a risk of incoherence with regard to the data source schema or the existing views.
The specific attribute introduced by the Add Attribute clause is persistently stored and its values will be explicitly inserted by the user or the DWA.

5.2 Delete an attribute in a view schema

Deleting an attribute must not produce side-effects on other existing views. Furthermore, existing programs must be preserved from incompatibility. This new view is assigned by the system to the user and the old one is kept as long as programs continue to run on it.
The semantics of the delete operation is to remove the specified attribute from the type of the specified view V. The algorithm dealing with the delete attribute operation is similar to the delete algorithm presented for the deletion propagation described in the previous section. However, the main difference lies in the fact that the new view is an explicit version: it will be visible by the user and it will not be materialized.

5.3 Modify an attribute type

The semantics of this operation consists in modifying the type of an attribute in a view. The strategy of a modification operation consists in actually performing the modification only if there is no derived views from the operand view. Otherwise, the modification will be simulated by creating first a view which does not involve the specified attribute. The second step consists in adding in the previously created view an attribute with the same name and having the specified new type. The created view will not be materialized.

Example 5.3

Suppose the DWA wants to modify the type of the attribute price in the view French_Computers. Because in this view, the articles of interest are only sold in France, He (She) would like to compute the computers price according the French VAT amount (which is 20.6 per cent). The corresponding view is defined with our view language as follows :

```
Create View French_Computers_V1 As
query:    Select * From French_Computers;
Hide price;
Add attribute price : {Select price*0.206
                               From French_Computers}
End French_Computers_V1;
```

6 Related work

The work we present in this paper is closely related to research in two fields: data warehousing and schema changes. We discuss each in turn.
Research problems in data warehousing systems are clearly identified in [13]. This paper was the first one emphasizing research directions according the state of the art in the data warehouse topic. In the related work we are aware of, the view specification languages for data warehouse schema design are based on the relational model [7], [8]. A conceptual model based on graphical representation to build a data warehouse from the pre-existing E/R schemes, has been proposed in [6]. Commercial data warehousing systems are organized according the multidimensional data model. This representation is appropriate for complex analysis and visualization of the data [4].

An alternative approach to overcome the drawbacks of the direct schema changes approach (time consuming, a risk of information loss, etc.), consists in using the view mechanism to simulate schema modifications. The main advantage of the view approach is to allow schema changes without database reorganization, since the definition of a view does not affect the underlying schema [2], [3], [10], [12]. In this paper, we focus on adapting this approach in the context of a relational data warehousing systems. Furthermore, our approach avoids the proliferation of versions of views since a version of the original view is created if and only if the schema evolution operation entails a risk of incoherence of either the existing views or application programs.

7 Conclusion

In this paper, we have defined an extension of the relational view model in order to take into account the modeling of specific requirements of a data warehouse and to support schema changes without reorganization. However, this extension does not need the extension of the data manipulation language since a view in our model is a derived relation. Furthermore, we have shown how our view definition language can be used to support structural evolution of a data warehouse without disrupting existing views and application programs. We note our view definition language can be used to support simulate schema evolution in classical relational database systems.

The presence of historical information is a very important feature in a data warehouse. Thus, providing a version mechanism of views may contribute to support different type of analysis and to maintain historical information. Therefore our approach allows to take into account the temporal dimension in a way.

An open issue concerns the detection of structural changes and the delay of their propagation on the data warehouse. The change detection is dependent from the type of the information source. Consequently, we plan to develop algorithms for this purpose.

References

1. Abiteboul, S., Bonner, A.: Objects and Views. in Proc. ACM SIGMOD, Conference on Management of Data, pp 238-247, Denver, Colorado, May 1991.
2. Bellahsene, Z.: Views for Schema Evolution in Object-oriented Database Systems. British National Conference on Database BNCOD-14. Lectures Notes in Computer Science of Springer Verlag, Edinburgh, July, 1996.
3. Bertino, E.: A View Mechanism for Object-oriented Database. 3rd International Conference on Extending Database Technology, March 23-24, Vienna (Austria),1992.
4. Chaudhuri, S., Dayal U.: An Overview of Data Warehousing and OLAP Technology. SIGMOD Record, Vol.26, N01, March 1997.
5. Ferrandina ,F., Meyer, T., Zicari, R., Ferran, G., Madec, J.: Schema and Database Evolution in the O2 Object Database System. Proc. of VLDB Conference Zurich, Switzerland, pp. 65-74, September, 1995.
6. Golfarelli, M., Maio, D., Rizzi, S.: Conceptual design of data Warehouses from E/R Schemes. Proc. of Hawaii International Conference on System Sciences, IEEE society press, Kona, Hawaii, January 6-9, 1998.
7. Hammer, J., Garcia-Molina, H., Widom, J., Labio, W., and. Zhuge, Y. The Stanford Data Warehouse Project. IEEE Data Engineering Bulletin, in Proc. Special Issue -48, June 1995.
8. Hull, R., Zhou, G.: A Framework for supporting Data Integration using the Materialized and Virtual Approaches. Proc. of SIGMOD'96 Conference, Montreal, Canada, 1996.
9. Marche, J.: Measuring the Stability of Data Models. European Journal of Information Systems, Vol. 2, N0 1, pp. 37-47, 1993.
10. Ra, Y.G., Rundensteiner E. A: A transparent object-oriented Schema Changes Approach Using View Evolution. IEEE Int. Conf. on Data Engineering, Taipei, Taiwan, 1995.
11 Sjoberg D.: Quantifying Schema Evolution. Information and Software Technology Journal, Vol. 35, N0 1, pp. 34-44, January 1993.
12. Tresch, M., Scholl, M.H, "Schema Transformation without Database Reorganization. in SIGMOD Record, 22(1), March, 1993.
13. Widom, J., "Research Problems in Data Warehouse. Proc. of 4th international Conference on Information and Knowledge Management (CIKM), November, 1995.
14. Wiener, J.L et al: A System Prototype for Warehouse View Maintenance. Proceedings of the Workshop on Materialised Views : Techniques and Applications, Montreal, June 7, 1996.
15. Zhuge, Y., Garcia-Molina, H., Wiener, J.: Consistency Algorithms for Multi-Source Warehouse View Maintenance. Journal of Distributed and Parallel Information Systems, Kluwer Academic Publishers, pp 1-36, December 1996.

Query Containment Checking as a View Updating Problem

Carles Farré, Ernest Teniente, Toni Urpí

Universitat Politècnica de Catalunya
E-08034 Barcelona -- Catalonia
[farre | teniente | urpi]@lsi.upc.es

Abstract. In this paper we present a new approach that handles Query Containemnt problems by expressing them as a view updating problem. Since this approach is independent of any particular view updating method, it provides a general framework that joins research efforts in both the Query Containment checking and view updating fields. In particular, the larger development of current view updating technology allows us to check properly Query Containment when considering negative-derived literals or integrity constraints. Existing methods for Query Containment checking that deal with these cases do not check actually containment but another related property called uniform containment, which is a sufficient but not necessary condition for containment.

1 Introduction

Query Containment (QC) [Ull89] is the problem concerned with checking whether the answers that a query obtains on a database are a subset of the answers obtained by another query on the same database, regardless of the specific content of the database.

An important amount of research has been devoted to QC checking over the last 20 years [CM77, ASU79, JK83, Klu88, Sag88, Ull89, CV92, LMSS93, LS93, ZO93, LS95, DS96, ST96, CR97]. Although they are different in many aspects, these methods seem to share a common base: they are intended to solve containment by first identifying and constraining themselves to a subclass of queries according to some syntactic conditions on the language the queries are expressed with. Then they propose an optimised solution using this syntactic knowledge.

However, existing methods that deal with queries having negated-derived atoms in their rule bodies [LS93, ST96] do not check actually QC but another related property called Uniform Containment [Sag88].

Consider, for instance, a deductive database consisting of two base predicates. *Emp*(x, d, s), indicates that employee x works at department d with a salary s. *Manager*(x, d) indicates that x is a manager of the department d. There are also two view predicates: *Boss*(x), which defines who is manager of some department, and *Chief*(x), defining who is manager and employee at the same department:

$Boss(x) \leftarrow Manager(x, d)$

$Chief(x) \leftarrow Emp(x, d, s) \wedge Manager(x, d)$

We define two queries, $\mathbf{Q_1}$ and $\mathbf{Q_2}$, with the same predicate query:

$\mathbf{Q_1}$: $Subordinate(x) \leftarrow Emp(x, d, s) \wedge \neg Boss(x)$

$\mathbf{Q_2}$: $Subordinate(x) \leftarrow Emp(x, d, s) \wedge \neg Chief(x)$

The intuition behind these queries is that the first query retrieves those employees that are not managers anywhere, while the second one retrieves those employees that are not employees and managers at some department at the same time. Clearly, $\mathbf{Q_1}$ is more restrictive than $\mathbf{Q_2}$, that is, all the answers that can be obtained by $\mathbf{Q_1}$ are also answers to $\mathbf{Q_2}$. Thus we say that $\mathbf{Q_1}$ is contained in $\mathbf{Q_2}$, written $\mathbf{Q_1} \sqsubseteq \mathbf{Q_2}$.

This simple example cannot be solved in a satisfactory way by the methods proposed in [LS93, ST96]. These methods would check whether $\mathbf{Q_1}$ is uniform contained in $\mathbf{Q_2}$, written $\mathbf{Q_1} \sqsubseteq^u \mathbf{Q_2}$. Uniform containment is a sufficient but not necessary condition for QC: uniform containment implies containment, but the inverse is not true. In this example, [LS93, ST96] would prove that $\mathbf{Q_1}$ is not uniform contained in $\mathbf{Q_2}$[1], but this result does not prove whether $\mathbf{Q_1} \sqsubseteq \mathbf{Q_2}$ is true.

When considering the integrity constraints defined in a database, the containment relationship between two queries does not need to hold for any state of the database but only for those that satisfy the integrity constraints. This idea is captured by the notion of **IC**-compliant Query Containment. Again, the current methods that handle **IC**-compliant QC [Sag88, ST96, DS96] take the uniform containment approach.

In this paper we present a new approach that reformulates the containment properties (QC and **IC**-compliant QC) in terms of a view updating problem. Roughly, the main idea of our approach is to express the accomplishment of the QC relationship between two queries in terms of a derived (view) predicate. Then, checking QC is performed by requesting the insertion of that predicate. If some solution exists the predicate can be satisfied and, therefore, the expressed relationship holds.

This new approach is based on the seminal work of [DTU96], which uses view updating to perform database schema validation tasks. The reformulation of the containment problem we propose is similar to that of [LMSS93, LS95], which translates QC to the problem of query satisfiability, i.e. a query is satisfiable if there is some database state in which the answer to the query is not empty. However, the query-satisfiability methods that are provided by [LMSS93, LS95] impose stronger restrictions on the cases that they handle, and they do not consider **IC**-compliant QC.

The main contributions of our approach are:

- To the best of our knowledge, it is the first approach that tackles QC and IC-compliant QC problems for queries with negated-derived atoms in the rule bodies, by checking "true" QC instead of uniform query containment.
- Our approach provides also a general framework that unifies research efforts in both the QC checking and view updating fields. In our case, the larger development of the current view updating technology, with respect to the treatment of negation and integrity constraints, has allowed us to obtain new results for QC checking.

---

[1] For more details, see section 6 below.

- Moreover, this framework is generic enough to be independent of any particular view updating method. In this way, any future advance in the view updating technology can be also applied in the QC checking field.

This paper is organised as follows. Next section reviews basic concepts needed in the rest of the paper. Section 3 presents our approach to check QC by view updating. Section 4 shows how to use view updating to check **IC**-compliant QC. Section 5 considers some aspects of the view updating technology to be used for QC checking. Section 6 discuses related work. Finally, section 7 presents our conclusions and points out further work.

2 Base Concepts

In this section, we briefly review some definitions related to Deductive Databases, Queries, QC and View Updating [LT84, BR86, Llo87, Ull88, Sag88, Ull89, TO95].

2.1 Deductive databases

Throughout the paper, we consider a first order language with a universe of constants -a, b, c, a_1, b_1, ...-, a set of variables -x, y, z, x_1, y_1, ...-, a set of predicate names -P, Q, V, P_1, Q_1, ...-. A *term* is a variable or a constant. If P is a n-ary predicate and t_1, ..., t_n are terms, then $P(t_1, ..., t_n)$ is an *atom*. The atom is *ground* if every $t_{i = 1,...,n}$ is a constant. A *literal* is defined as either an atom or a negated atom.

A *fact* is a formula of the form: $P(t_1, ..., t_n) \leftarrow$, where $P(t_1, ..., t_n)$ is a ground atom. A *deductive rule* is a formula of the form:

$P(t_1, ..., t_n) \leftarrow L_1 \wedge ... \wedge L_m$ with $n \geq 0$, $m \geq 1$

where $P(t_1, ..., t_n)$ is called the *head* and $L_1 \wedge ... \wedge L_m$ the is the *body*. Variables are assumed to be universally quantified over the whole formula.

An *integrity constraint* is a formula that every state of the deductive database is required to satisfy. We deal with constraints in *denial* form:

$\leftarrow L_1 \wedge ... \wedge L_m$ with $m \geq 1$

For the sake of uniformity, we associate to each integrity constraint an inconsistency predicate *Icn* . Then, we would rewrite the former denial as an *integrity rule* $Ic1 \leftarrow L_1 \wedge ... \wedge L_m$. We also define an standard auxiliary predicate *Ic* with the following rules: $Ic \leftarrow Ic1$, ..., $Ic \leftarrow Icn$, one for each integrity constraint of the database. A fact *Ic* will indicate that there is an integrity constraint that is violated.

A *deductive database* **D** is a triple **D** = (**EDB**, **DR**, **IC**) where **EDB** is a finite set of facts, **DR** a finite set of deductive rules, and **IC** a finite set of integrity constraints. The set **EDB** of facts is called the *extensional* part of the deductive database and the set **DR** of deductive rules is called the *intensional* part.

Predicates in the body of deductive rules may be *ordinary*, base and derived predicates, or *evaluable* ("built-in"), e.g. comparison and arithmetic predicates. *Base* predicates appear only in the extensional part and (eventually) in the body of deductive rules. *Derived* (view) predicates appear only in the intensional part. Evaluable predicates can be evaluated without accessing the database

A set of deductive rules is *recursive* if there is one ore more cycles in its *dependency graph*, which is built by drawing one edge between each pair of ordinary predicates appearing, respectively, in the head and the body of the same rule. As usual, we do not admit negative literals of a derived predicate defined in a recursive way (*stratified negation*), and the variables appearing in negated atoms, as well as in evaluable ones, must also appear in a ordinary positive literal in the same rule body (*safeness*).

2.2 Queries, Query Containment and IC-compliant Query Containment

A *query* **Q** for a deductive database **D** is a finite set of deductive rules that defines a dedicated n-ary *query predicate Q*. We assume without loss of generality that the only derived predicate heading the deductive rules in **Q** is *Q* and that all predicates, base or derived, other than *Q* appearing in the bodies of the rules belong to **D**.

The *answer* to the query is the set of all ground facts about *Q* obtained as a result of evaluating the deductive rules from both **Q** and **DR** on **EDB**:

$$\{Q(a^i_1,\ldots,a^i_n) \mid Q(a^i_1,\ldots,a^i_n) \in (\mathbf{Q} \cup \mathbf{DR})(\mathbf{EDB})\}$$

where (**Q** ∪ **DR**)(**EDB**) is the result of evalutating the deductive rules in **Q** ∪ **DR** on **EDB**. Notice that, in particular, **Q** could be a subset of **DR**, i.e. a derived predicate defined in **DR** may also play the role of the query predicate.

A query $\mathbf{Q_1}$ is *contained* in an another query $\mathbf{Q_2}$ when the set of ground facts answering $\mathbf{Q_1}$ is a subset of the set of ground facts answering $\mathbf{Q_2}$, regardless of the underlying **EDB**.

Definition 2.1 Let $\mathbf{Q_1}$ and $\mathbf{Q_2}$ be two queries defining the same n-ary query predicate *Q* on a deductive database **D** = (**EDB**, **DR**, **IC**). $\mathbf{Q_1}$ *is contained in* $\mathbf{Q_2}$, written $\mathbf{Q_1} \sqsubseteq \mathbf{Q_2}$, if

$$\{Q(a^i_1,\ldots,a^i_n) \mid Q(a^i_1,\ldots,a^i_n) \in (\mathbf{Q_1} \cup \mathbf{DR})(\mathbf{EDB})\}$$
$$\subseteq \{Q(a^k_1,\ldots,a^k_n) \mid Q(a^k_1,\ldots,a^k_n) \in (\mathbf{Q_2} \cup \mathbf{DR})(\mathbf{EDB})\}$$

for any **EDB**. □

When considering integrity constraints, the containment relationship between two queries must not hold for any **EDB** but only for consistent **EDB**'s, i.e. those that satisfy the integrity constraints. As stated before, we assume that the database contains an inconsistency predicate *Ic* that holds whenever some integrity constraint is violated. Thus, consistent **EDB**'s are those where the fact *Ic* does not hold.

Definition 2.2 Let $\mathbf{Q_1}$ and $\mathbf{Q_2}$ be two queries defining the same n-ary query predicate *Q* on a deductive database **D** = (**EDB**, **DR**, **IC**). $\mathbf{Q_1}$ *is IC-compliant contained in* $\mathbf{Q_2}$, written $\mathbf{Q_1} \sqsubseteq_{\mathbf{IC}} \mathbf{Q_2}$, if

$$\{Q(a^i_1,\ldots,a^i_n) \mid Q(a^i_1,\ldots,a^i_n) \in (\mathbf{Q_1} \cup \mathbf{DR})(\mathbf{EDB})\}$$
$$\subseteq \{Q(a^k_1,\ldots,a^k_n) \mid Q(a^k_1,\ldots,a^k_n) \in (\mathbf{Q_2} \cup \mathbf{DR})(\mathbf{EDB})\}$$

for any **EDB** such that *Ic* ∉ (**IC** ∪ **DR**)(**EDB**). □

2.3 View Updating

For a deductive database **D** = (**EDB**, **DR**, **IC**), an *update* is a bipartite set **U** = **Ins** ∪ **Del** of ground facts about base predicates which defines a new deductive database **U**(**D**) = (**EDB'**, **DR**, **IC**) such that **EDB'** = (**EDB** - **Del**) ∪ **Ins**.

View updating is concerned with determining how a request to update a view (i.e. derived) fact should be appropriately translated into updates of the underlying base facts. For a deductive database **D** = (**EDB**, **DR**, **IC**) and a n-ary derived (view) predicate V defined in **DR**, a *view update request* is a formula of the form ← *Insert*(V(a_1, ..., a_n)) [or ← *Delete*(V(a_1, ..., a_n))]. An update **U** is a *translation* satisfying the view update request if the ground derived fact $V(a_1, \ldots, a_n)$ is evaluated true [or false] in **U**(**D**). A view update request *succeeds* when there is at least one translation, otherwise the view update request *fails*. In general, several translations may exist for a given view update request.

3 Query Containment Checking by View Updating

As we have just seen, we can request to update an **EDB** indirectly in terms of an insertion or a deletion of a view (derived) fact, by using a view updating method that translates the view update request into insertions and/or deletions of base facts. In this way, we can see the request to insert some view fact as an intent to change the underlying **EDB** in order to satisfy and make true the property (or the relationship) expressed by that view fact.

Taking this into account, we may express the non-containment relationship between two queries in terms of a derived predicate. We do this by defining a new derived predicate, *Not_Cont_*Q_1*_in_*Q_2, such that its defining rule(s) expresses that the answers to the query $\mathbf{Q_1}$ are not a subset of the answers to $\mathbf{Q_2}$. When we request to insert the *Not_Cont_*Q_1*_in_*Q_2 view fact on an **EDB** we indeed want to find whether there is some **EDB'** (reachable through some translation) on which $\mathbf{Q_1}$ is not contained in $\mathbf{Q_2}$. If there is some translation that satisfies the view update request ← *Insert*(*Not_Cont_*Q_1*_in_*Q_2), then $\mathbf{Q_1}$ is not contained in $\mathbf{Q_2}$. Otherwise, $\mathbf{Q_1} \sqsubseteq \mathbf{Q_2}$.

We use view updating to check whether $\mathbf{Q_1}$ is not contained in $\mathbf{Q_2}$, written $\mathbf{Q_1} \not\sqsubseteq \mathbf{Q_2}$, since non-containment is proved by finding just one **EDB** on which the answers to $\mathbf{Q_1}$ are not a subset of the answers to $\mathbf{Q_2}$. Since containment is a property that needs to be fulfilled on every **EDB**, this non-containment test based on a view-updating formalism is nothing but a way to check QC by a refuting prove.

Therefore, and in contrast with the preceding "syntactic" methods and proposals, our approach can be seen as a kind of simulation of how queries and the whole database behave, in the sense that view updating traces explicit and implicit relationships among rules in their intend to obtain translations leading to target database extensions, i.e. those on which the *Not_Cont_*Q_1*_in_*Q_2 is true.

Lemma 3.1 Let $\mathbf{Q}_1$ and $\mathbf{Q}_2$ be two queries defining the same n-ary query predicate Q on a deductive database **D** = (**EDB**, **DR**, **IC**).

$\mathbf{Q}_1 \sqsubseteq \mathbf{Q}_2$ iff the view update request $\leftarrow$ *Insert*($Not\_Cont\_Q_1\_in\_Q_2$)
fails on **D'** = (Ø, **DR'**, Ø)

where Ø stands for both empty **EDB** and **IC**,

$\mathbf{DR'} = \mathbf{DR} \cup \mathbf{Q}_1' \cup \mathbf{Q}_2' \cup \{Not\_Cont\_Q_1\_in\_Q_2 \leftarrow Q_1(x_1,\ldots,x_n) \wedge \neg Q_2(x_1,\ldots,x_n)\}$

$\mathbf{Q}_1'$ is the result of changing the query-predicate name Q for Q_1 in $\mathbf{Q}_1$, and

$\mathbf{Q}_2'$ is the result of changing the query-predicate name Q for Q_2 in $\mathbf{Q}_2$ □

Note that we do not take into account the database integrity constraints -the **IC** set- to check QC, because the definition itself of containment requires such a property to be held on every **EDB** regardless of its consistency.

Example 3.1 Let us review the example we presented in the introduction, where we had a database **D** = (**EDB**, **DR**, **IC**) where

EDB is a set of ground facts about two base predicates *Emp*(*emp_name*, *department*, *salary*) and *Manager*(*emp_name*, *department*),

DR = { $Boss(x) \leftarrow Manager(x, d)$
$Chief(x) \leftarrow Emp(x, d, s) \wedge Manager(x, d)$ }

and **IC** = Ø.

We define two queries with the same predicate query:

$\mathbf{Q}_1$: $Subordinate(x) \leftarrow Emp(x, d, s) \wedge \neg Boss(x)$

$\mathbf{Q}_2$: $Subordinate(x) \leftarrow Emp(x, d, s) \wedge \neg Chief(x)$

As we saw in the introduction, intuitively, $\mathbf{Q}_1$ is more restrictive than $\mathbf{Q}_2$, so we say that $\mathbf{Q}_1$ is contained in $\mathbf{Q}_2$. In order to check that $\mathbf{Q}_1 \sqsubseteq \mathbf{Q}_2$ actually holds within our new framework, we first build the new database **D'** = (Ø, **DR'**, Ø) where

DR' = {$Not\_Cont\_Q_1\_in\_Q_2 \leftarrow Subordinate_1(x) \wedge \neg Subordinate_2(x)$
$Subordinate_1(x) \leftarrow Emp(x, d, s) \wedge \neg Boss(x)$
$Subordinate_2(x) \leftarrow Emp(x, d, s) \wedge \neg Chief(x)$
$Boss(x) \leftarrow Manager(x, d)$
$Chief(x) \leftarrow Emp(x, d, s) \wedge Manager(x, d)$ }

The next step is to perform the view update request $\leftarrow$ *Insert*($Not\_Cont\_Q_1\_in\_Q_2$) on **D'** using a view updating method. In this case, such a request fails to succeed. Hence, $\mathbf{Q}_1 \sqsubseteq \mathbf{Q}_2$ is true. Roughly, the main idea is that to satisfy $Subordinate_1(x)$ we have to insert $Emp(x, d, s)$. This insertion induces an insertion of $Subordinate_2(x)$, which can only be falsified by considering an additional insertion of $Manager(x, d)$. However, this new insertion falsifies at the same time $Subordinate_1(x)$. Therefore, it is not possible to find a translation leading to an **EDB** where $Subordinate_1(x)$ is true and $Subordinate_2(x)$ is false.

On the contrary, let us consider the opposite case: to check whether $\mathbf{Q}_2 \sqsubseteq \mathbf{Q}_1$ holds. Again, we first need to build a new database **D''** = (Ø, **DR''**, Ø) where

DR'' = {$Not\_Cont\_Q_2\_in\_Q_1 \leftarrow Subordinate_2(x) \wedge \neg Subordinate_1(x)$
$Subordinate_1(x) \leftarrow Emp(x, d, s) \wedge \neg Boss(x)$
$Subordinate_2(x) \leftarrow Emp(x, d, s) \wedge \neg Chief(x)$
$Boss(x) \leftarrow Manager(x, d)$
$Chief(x) \leftarrow Emp(x, d, s) \wedge Manager(x, d)$ }

Now, the view update request ← *Insert(Not_Cont_Q_2_in_Q_1)* succeeds on **D''**. A possible translation might be: {*Insert*(*Emp*(joan, sales, 70000)), *Insert*(*Manager*(joan, accounting))}, so in the new **EDB** *Chief*(joan) is not true (joan is manager at a department other than the department where she is employee), but *Boss*(joan) is true. Therefore, we have found a translation that leads to an **EDB** where $Subordinate_2(x)$ is true but $Subordinate_1(x)$ is not. Thus we conclude that $\mathbf{Q_2} \not\sqsubseteq \mathbf{Q_1}$. □

4 IC-compliant Query Containment by View Updating

Due to the expressiveness of our approach, we can easily adapt it to take also into account the integrity constraints defined on the database. As we stated in section 2.2, **IC**-compliant QC between two queries holds when the answers to one query are a subset of the answers obtained by the other query on any consistent **EDB**, i.e. on every **EDB** where no integrity constraint is violated. Translating this concept to our framework, we use view updating to check whether $\mathbf{Q_1}$ is not **IC**-compliant contained in $\mathbf{Q_2}$, written $\mathbf{Q_1} \not\sqsubseteq_{IC} \mathbf{Q_2}$, since non-containment is proved by finding just one consistent **EDB** on which the answers to $\mathbf{Q_1}$ are not a subset of the answers to $\mathbf{Q_2}$. As we stated in section 2, a consistent **EDB** is that where the fact *Ic* does not hold, assuming that the database contains an inconsistency predicate *Ic* that holds whenever some integrity constraint is violated. So now we define a new derived predicate, *Not_IC_Cont_Q_1_in_Q_2*, such that its defining rule(s) expresses that the answers to the query $\mathbf{Q_1}$ are not a subset of the answers to $\mathbf{Q_2}$, enforcing that *Ic* does not hold at the same time. If there is some translation that satisfies the view update request ← *Insert(Not_IC_Cont_Q_1_in_Q_2)*, then $\mathbf{Q_1}$ is not **IC**-compliant contained in $\mathbf{Q_2}$. Otherwise, $\mathbf{Q_1} \sqsubseteq_{IC} \mathbf{Q_2}$.

Lemma 4.1 Let $\mathbf{Q_1}$ and $\mathbf{Q_2}$ be two queries defining the same n-ary query predicate *Q* on a deductive database **D** = (**EDB**, **DR**, **IC**).

$\mathbf{Q_1} \sqsubseteq_{IC} \mathbf{Q_2}$ iff the view update request ← *Insert(Not_IC_Cont_Q_1_in_Q_2)* fails on **D'** = (Ø, **DR'**, **IC**)

where Ø stands for an empty **EDB**

DR' = **DR** ∪ $\mathbf{Q_1}$' ∪ $\mathbf{Q_2}$'

∪ {*Not_IC_Cont_Q_1_in_Q_2* ← $Q_1(x_1,\dots,x_n) \wedge \neg Q_2(x_1,\dots,x_n) \wedge \neg Ic$ },

$\mathbf{Q_1}$' is the result of changing the query-predicate name *Q* for Q_1 in $\mathbf{Q_1}$, and

$\mathbf{Q_2}$' is the result of changing the query-predicate name *Q* for Q_2 in $\mathbf{Q_2}$ □

Example 4.1 Let us consider again the example 3.1 with

EDB is a set of ground facts about two base predicates *Emp*(*emp_name*, *department*, *salary*) and *Manager*(*emp_name*, *department*),

DR = { *Boss*(*x*) ← *Manager*(*x*, *d*)

Chief(*x*) ← *Emp*(*x*, *d*, *s*) ∧ *Manager*(*x*, *d*) }

IC = { *Ic1* ←*Emp*(*x*, *d1*, *s*) ∧ *Manager*(*x*, *d2*) ∧ d1 ≠ d2, *Ic* ← *Ic1* }

And the two queries that we have been defined before:

$\mathbf{Q_1}$: *Subordinate*(*x*) ← *Emp*(*x*, *d*, *s*) ∧ ¬*Boss*(*x*)

$\mathbf{Q_2}$: *Subordinate*(*x*) ← *Emp*(*x*, *d*, *s*) ∧ ¬*Chief*(*x*)

So, we have introduced an integrity constraint, *Ic1*, forbidding any person to be employee and manager at different departments. If we do not take this integrity constraint into account, the query containment results we obtained in example 3.1 also hold, i.e. $\mathbf{Q_1} \sqsubseteq \mathbf{Q_2}$ and $\mathbf{Q_2} \not\sqsubseteq \mathbf{Q_1}$.

Since the answers to $\mathbf{Q_1}$ are always a subset of the answers obtained by $\mathbf{Q_2}$ on any **EDB** independently of its consistency, $\mathbf{Q_1} \sqsubseteq_{IC} \mathbf{Q_2}$ also holds. On the contrary, although $\mathbf{Q_2} \not\sqsubseteq \mathbf{Q_1}$, we are going to demonstrate that $\mathbf{Q_2} \sqsubseteq_{IC} \mathbf{Q_1}$ is true.

We check whether $\mathbf{Q_2} \sqsubseteq_{IC} \mathbf{Q_1}$ holds by making the view update request $\leftarrow$ *Insert*(*Not_IC_Cont_*Q_2*_in_*Q_1) on **D''** = (Ø, **DR''**, **IC**) where

$$\mathbf{DR''} = \{\ Not\_IC\_Cont\_Q_2\_in\_Q_1 \leftarrow Subordinate_2(x) \wedge \neg Subordinate_1(x) \wedge \neg Ic$$
$$Subordinate_1(x) \leftarrow Emp(x, d, s) \wedge \neg Boss(x)$$
$$Subordinate_2(x) \leftarrow Emp(x, d, s) \wedge \neg Chief(x)$$
$$Boss(x) \leftarrow Manager(x, d)$$
$$Chief(x) \leftarrow Emp(x, d, s) \wedge Manager(x, d)\ \}$$

In this case the view update request fails and, then, $\mathbf{Q_2} \sqsubseteq_{IC} \mathbf{Q_1}$ is true. Roughly, the fact is that all possible translations obtained before when checking $\mathbf{Q_2} \sqsubseteq \mathbf{Q_1}$, {*Insert*(*Emp*(joan, sales, 70000)), *Insert*(*Manager*(joan, accounting))} for instance, are not valid translations now because all of them require somebody to be manager of a department other that the department where she or he is assigned as employee, and this requirement violates necessarily the integrity constraint *Ic1*. □

5 View Updating Methods for Containment Checking

Our approach to handle QC checking by using view updating is independent of the particular method used to perform the requested view update. However, a method able to deal with view updates in a certain class of deductive databases should satisfy the following requirements in order to be used to check QC:

1. The class of deductive databases considered by the method must allow to express the declarative definitions of the non-containment relationships that we have defined in sections 3 and 4. In particular, it involves to handle stratified negation.
2. If there exists some translation that satisfies a given request, the method obtains one such translation, but not necessarily several or even all of them. Otherwise, if no translation exists, the method must terminate.

The Events Method [TO95], for instance, is a view updating method that fits well in these requirements. All the examples we show in this paper are performed successfully by this method and, thus, the containment problems they pose are solved in a satisfactory way.

6 Related Work

Most research has been concerned with containment checking of conjunctive queries [CM77, ASU79, JK83, Klu88, Ull89, ZO93, CR97] and different results are obtained according to the syntactic features they considered. However, our aims have not been addressed to provide more efficient algorithms for these cases, but to set up a widespread framework where we can handle as many cases as possible, including those cases that had never been dealt properly before.

The main point is that our approach has allowed us to tackle containment in the presence of negation and integrity constraints in a proper way. So in the next (sub-) sections we review the related work according to these two topics.

6.1 Query Containment with Safe Stratified Negation

In this section we show how our approach handles queries with (safe stratified) negated-derived literals and (safe) built-in atoms, i.e. covering entirely all the features of our data model as we have defined it in section 2. We want to point out that our approach keeps checking "true" containment. We remark the word "true" to refer to the concept of containment such as we have dealt with it in the previous sections and it was defined in section 2, in contrast to the concept of uniform containment that we will review below.

Since we express the noncontainment relationship between two queries by defining a view predicate with a deductive rule of the form $Not\_Cont\_Q_1\_in\_Q_2 \leftarrow Q_1(x_1,\ldots,x_n) \wedge \neg Q_2(x_1,\ldots,x_n)$, dealing with stratified negation is always a necessary requirement for our approach and for the view updating methods we can use, even when no rule in $\mathbf{Q_1}$, $\mathbf{Q_2}$ or **DR** has negated derived atoms.

As usual, safe stratified negation was first tackled inside well-defined boundaries: [LMSS93] proves that containment for queries with only 1-ary base predicates and stratified negation is decidable; and [LS95] provides an algorithm to check predicate satisfiability that can also be used to check containment of a datalog query, i.e. without negation, in a union of conjunctive queries having local negated-base and inequality atoms (a negated-base or inequality atom is local when all its variables appear in at least one base atom).

In contrast, other research works tackle broadly datalog extensions from the "uniform-containment" point of view: [LS93] provides an algorithm to check Uniform Query Equivalence (i.e. whether both $\mathbf{Q_1} \sqsubseteq^u \mathbf{Q_2}$ and $\mathbf{Q_2} \sqsubseteq^u \mathbf{Q_1}$ hold) for datalog queries with stratified negation and safe built-in atoms; and [ST96] propose a more efficient but incomplete algorithm to perform uniform query containment checking for queries with stratified negation.

Uniform Query Containment was coined in [Sag88] as an alternative concept to QC and proved it to be decidable for Datalog queries. Let $\mathbf{Q_1}$ and $\mathbf{Q_2}$ be two queries defining the same n-ary query predicate Q on a deductive database $\mathbf{D}$ = (**EDB**, **DR**, **IC**). $\mathbf{Q_1}$ *is uniform contained in* $\mathbf{Q_2}$, written $\mathbf{Q_1} \sqsubseteq^u \mathbf{Q_2}$, if

$$\{Q(a^i_1,\ldots,a^i_n) \mid Q(a^i_1,\ldots,a^i_n) \in (\mathbf{Q_1} \cup \mathbf{DR})(\mathbf{I})\}$$
$$\subseteq \{Q(a^k_1,\ldots,a^k_n) \mid Q(a^k_1,\ldots,a^k_n) \in (\mathbf{Q_2} \cup \mathbf{DR})(\mathbf{I})\}$$

for every **I** being an arbitrary set of ground facts about base and derived (query or view) predicates. Note that, in contrast to "true" QC, derived facts in **I** are independent from and may not be related to the ones computed by applying the rules in **DR** (and/or the ones from the queries) on the base facts only.

As pointed out in [Sag88], uniform query containment provides a sufficient but not necessary condition for QC. Hence if the uniform query containment test fails, i.e. $\mathbf{Q_1} \not\sqsubseteq^u \mathbf{Q_2}$, nothing can be said about whether $\mathbf{Q_1} \sqsubseteq \mathbf{Q_2}$ holds.

Example 6.1 Let us review again our working example. As we proved in the example 3.1, $\mathbf{Q_1} \sqsubseteq \mathbf{Q_2}$ holds because no translation exists for the view update request $\leftarrow$ *Insert(Not_Cont_Q_1_in_Q_2)* that we performed on the database **D'** such as we defined them according to our approach.

However, this example does not fall into the query subclasses that handle [LMSS93] and [LS95], so their proposals cannot be applied to this example.

On the other hand, any uniform-containment based method, either [LS93] or [ST96], would have to demonstrate that $\mathbf{Q_1} \sqsubseteq^u \mathbf{Q_2}$ holds in order to prove that $\mathbf{Q_1} \sqsubseteq \mathbf{Q_2}$ is true. However, the fact is that $\mathbf{Q_1} \sqsubseteq^u \mathbf{Q_2}$ does not hold. For example, let us consider **I** = { *Emp*(rose, sales, 9000), *Chief*(rose) }, according to the definition of uniform containment that allows **I** to contain also ground facts about derived predicates. Computing the answers for each query on **I** we obtain:

- ($\mathbf{Q_1} \cup$ **DR**)(**I**) = { *Emp*(rose, sales, 9000), *Chief*(rose), *Subordinate*(rose) }, from applying **DR** = {$Boss(x) \leftarrow Manager(x, d)$
  $Chief(x) \leftarrow Emp(x, d, s) \wedge Manager(x, d)$ } and
  $\mathbf{Q_1}$: $Subordinate(x) \leftarrow Emp(x, d, s) \wedge \neg Boss(x)$
  so the answer to $\mathbf{Q_1}$ on **I** is *Subordinate*(rose). Note that the single rule from $\mathbf{Q_1}$ produces the fact *Subordinate*(rose) because *Boss*(rose) does not appear in **I**.
- ($\mathbf{Q_2} \cup$ **DR**)(**I**) = { *Emp*(rose, sales, 9000), *Chief*(rose) }, from applying **DR** and
  $\mathbf{Q_2}$: $Subordinate(x) \leftarrow Emp(x, d, s) \wedge \neg Chief(x)$
  so the answer to $\mathbf{Q_2}$ on **I** is Ø. Note that here the fact *Chief*(rose) in **I** does not allow the query rule from $\mathbf{Q_2}$ to produce *Subordinate*(rose).

Therefore any uniform-containment based method would fail to prove that $\mathbf{Q_1} \sqsubseteq^u \mathbf{Q_2}$ and, thus, it would not be able to show that $\mathbf{Q_1} \sqsubseteq \mathbf{Q_2}$ in this example. □

6.2 IC-compliant Query Containment

Integrity constraints as the so called tuple generating dependencies (TGD's) were already considered in [Sag88] to check **IC**-compliant QC for datalog queries. Moreover, [ST96] extends [Sag88] by taking also equality generating dependencies into account and [DS96] provides a method to check **IC**-compliant QC for conjunctive queries and disjunctive-datalog integrity rules. However, all those proposals tackle the problem from the uniform-containment approach, i.e. they do not check **IC**-compliant QC but "**IC**-compliant uniform query containment". In section 6.1 we have already discussed the "weaknesses" of the uniform-containment approach, so our major contribution is that our proposal checks actually **IC**-compliant QC in contrast to the other related work.

7 Conclusions and Further Work

We have presented a new approach for checking QC that is based on the use of view updating. The idea is to define a view expressing the non-containment relationship between two queries. Then, a request to insert that view allows us to determine whether the non-containment relationship holds.

Our approach is independent of any particular method for view updating and, in this way, we can take advantage of the current and future advances in the view updating research area. Moreover, it handles in a uniform way all query subclasses that have been identified up to now in the literature of deductive databases. Hence, we set up a new framework that unifies both QC checking and view updating research areas.

The application of the advances of the current view updating technology in this framework yields to another main contribution of our approach, which is that of checking properly "true" QC in the presence of negation and integrity constraints for the first time.

As further work, we are going to implement a new view updating method according to the approachs proposed in [TO95, CTU97], in order to use it efficiently for containment checking.

Other possible extensions of our work would be to consider QC in the presence of aggregate functions, queries over bags, or in object oriented databases as addressed in [LS97, CV93, BH97, BJNS94], to mention some previous work.

Acknowledgements

We would like to thank Antoni Olivé and the FOLRE group for their hepful comments and suggestions.

This work has been partially supported by PRONTIC CICYT program project TIC97-1157.

References

[ASU79] A.V. Aho, Y. Sagiv, J.D. Ullman: "Efficient Optimization of a Class of Relational Expressions". *ACM TODS*, Vol. 4, No. 4, 1979, pp. 435-454.

[BH97] N.R. Brisaboa, H.J. Hernández: "Testing Bag-Containment of Conjunctive Queries". *Acta Informatica*, Vol. 34, No.7, 1997, pp. 557-578.

[BJNS94] M. Buchheit, M.A. Jeusfeld, W. Nutt, M. Staudt: "Subsumption of queries in object-oriented databases". *Information Systems*, Vol. 19, No. 1, 1994.

[BR86] F. Bancilhon, R. Ramakrishnan: "An amateur's introduction to recursive query processing strategies". *Proceedings of the 1986 ACM SIGMOD International Conference*. SIGMOD Record, Vol. 15, No. 2, 1986, pp. 16-52.

[CM77] A.K. Chandra, P.M. Merlin: "Optimal Implementation of Conjunctive Queries in Relational Data Bases", *Proceedings of the 9th ACM SIGACT Symposium on Theory of Computing*. 1977, pp. 77-90.

[CR97] C. Chekuri, A. Rajaraman: "Conjunctive Query Containment Revisited". *Proceedings of ICDT'97.* LNCS, Vol. 1186, Springer, 1997, pp. 56-70.

[CTU97] D. Costal, E. Teniente, T. Urpí: "An Approach to Obtain Intensional Translations for Consistent View Updating". *Proocedings of the DOOD'97.* LNCS, Vol. 1341, Springer, 1997, pp. 175-192.

[CV92] S. Chaudhuri, M.Y. Vardi: "On the Equivalence of Recursive and Nonrecursive Datalog Programs". *Proc. of the PoDS'92.* ACM Press, 1992, pp. 55-66.

[CV93] S. Chaudhuri, M. Vardi: "Optimizing real conjunctive queries". *Proceedings of the PoDS'93.* ACM Press, 1993, pp. 59-70.

[DS96] G. Dong, J. Su: "Conjunctive QC with respect to views and constraints". *Information Processing Letters*, No. 57, pp. 95-102, 1996.

[DTU96] H. Decker, E. Teniente, T. Urpí: "How to tackle schema validation by view updating". *Proc. of the EDBT'96.* LNCS 1057, Springer, 1996, pp. 535-549.

[JK83] D.S. Johnson, A. Klug: "Optimizing conjunctive queries that contain untyped variables". *SIAM Journal on Conputing*, Vol. 12, No. 4, pp. 616-640, 1983.

[Klu88] A. Klug: "On Conjunctive Queries Containing Inequalities". *Journal of the ACM*, Vol. 35, No. 1, 1988, pp. 146-160.

[Llo87] J.W. Lloyd: *Foundations of Logic Programming.* Springer, 1987.

[LMSS93] A. Levy, I.S. Mumick, Y. Sagiv, O. Shmueli: "Equivalence, query-reachability and satisfiability in Datalog extensions". *Proceedings of the PoDS'93.* ACM Press, 1993, pp. 109-122.

[LS93] A. Levy, Y. Sagiv: "Queries Independent of Updates". *Proceedings of the VLDB'93.* Morgan Kaufmann, 1993, pp. 171-181.

[LS95] A. Levy, Y. Sagiv: "Semantic Query Optimization in Datalog Programs". *Proceedings of the PoDS'95.* ACM Press, 1995, pp. 163-173.

[LS97] A. Levy, D. Suciu: "Deciding Containment for Queries with Complex Objects". *Proceedings of the PoDS'97.* ACM Press, 1995, pp. 20-31

[LT84] J.W. Lloyd, R.W. Topor: "Making Prolog More Expressive". *Journal of Logic Programming*, 1984, No. 3, pp. 225-240.

[Oli91] A. Olivé: "Integrity Checking in Deductive Databases". *Proceedings of the VLDB'91.* Morgan Kaufmann, 1991, pp. 513-523.

[Sag88] Y. Sagiv: "Optimizing Datalog Programs". In J. Minker (Ed.): *Foundations of Deductive Databases and Logic Programming.* Morgan Kaufmann, Los Altos, CA, 1988, pp. 659-698.

[ST96] M. Staudt, K.v. Thadden: "A Generic Subsumption Testing Toolkit for Knowledge Base Queries". *Proceedings of the DEXA'96.* LNCS, Vol. 1134, Springer, 1996, pp. 834-844.

[TO95] E. Teniente, A. Olivé: "Updating Knowledge Bases while Maintaining their Consistency". *The VLDB Journal*, Vol. 4, No. 2, 1995, 193-241.

[Ull88] J.D. Ullman: *Principles of Database an Knowledge-Base Systems, Volume 1.* Computer Science Press, Rockville, MD, 1988.

[Ull89] J.D. Ullman: *Principles of Database an Knowledge-Base Systems, Volume 2: The New Technologies.* Computer Science Press, Rockville, MD, 1989.

[ZO93] X. Zhang, M.Z. Ozsoyoglu: "On efficient reasoning with implication constraints". *Proc. of the DOOD'93.* LNCS 760, Springer, 1993, pp. 236-252.

View Updates Translations in Relational Databases

Fadila Bentayeb[1] and Dominique Laurent[2]

[1] LIFO - Université d'Orléans, BP 6759, F-45067 Orléans Cedex 02 - France
bentayeb@lifo.univ-orleans.fr,
[2] LI/E3I - Université de Tours, 3, place Jean Jaurès F-41000 Blois - France
laurent@univ-tours.fr

Abstract. Views over databases have been studied in various directions for many years. Among these directions, translating view updates in terms of updates on the base relations has motivated many research efforts. In this paper, we propose a method for characterizing translations of view updates, based on the notion of inverse of a relational expressions. Moreover, we characterize two kinds of updates: (1) deterministic updates regardless to the database state, and (2) deterministic updates according to some database state.

1 Introduction

In relational databases, non materialized views are seen as query definitions whose names are stored in the database dictionary, and whose evaluations are *computed* each time the views are used. The user interacts with a view by issuing queries and update requests. The view definition mapping is sufficient to translate queries on views into queries on the underlying database. View updates, however, present a difficulty, referred to as non-determinism in the literature [4, 3, 2, 11] which can be stated as follows: Given a view v and an update $\mathcal{U}$ on v, there exists in general more than one way to translate $\mathcal{U}$ into updates on the relations explicitly stored in the database.

The objective of this paper is to study the view update translations in the context of the relational model and not only, as in [3, 10, 11], in the context of weak instances. Moreover, two kinds of updates are characterized: (1) deterministic view updates regardless to the database state, called strongly deterministic updates, and (2) deterministic updates according to some database state, called weakly deterministic updates.

We consider view updates which are insertions or deletions of a given tuple over the view. Let us illustrate our approach by an example that we shall use as our running example throughout the paper.

Running Example: Consider an employee relation *emp* with attributes *Ename*, *Pname* and a department relation *dept* with attributes *Ename*, *Dname*.

Let $emp = \{\langle John, P \rangle\}$ and $dept = \{\langle John, M \rangle\}$, meaning that employee $John$ works in project P and that employee $John$ works in department M, resp. Consider now the view v defined by $\Pi_{Ename,Dname}(\sigma_{Pname=P}(emp \bowtie dept))$.

First, consider inserting in v the tuple $\langle Mary, CS\rangle$ (meaning: employee Mary works in department CS). Since the view v concerns employees working in project P, the *only* way to perform this update is as follows: (1) insert $\langle Mary, P\rangle$ in *emp*, and (2) insert $\langle Mary, CS\rangle$ in *dept*. The database updates (1) and (2) form the update translation. In this case, the insert view update is deterministic, since there is a unique translation to perform it. Note that $(\langle Mary, P\rangle, \langle Mary, CS\rangle)$ is the inverse-image of $\langle Mary, CS\rangle$ wrt v, in the sense that computing v with these two tuples as input, produces the tuple to be inserted in the view.

Next, consider deleting from v the tuple $\langle John, M\rangle$, meaning that it is no more true that $John$ works in project P and in department M. There are three ways to perform this deletion: either (1) delete $\langle John, P\rangle$ from *emp*, or (2) delete $\langle John, M\rangle$ from *dept*, or (3) delete both $\langle John, P\rangle$ and $\langle John, M\rangle$ from *emp* and *dept* resp. Although, this solution is discarded because of the minimal change in databases, the translation is not unique.

Suppose now that $emp = \{\langle John, P\rangle\}$ and $dept = \emptyset$ and consider previous deletion. With respect to minimal change, and according to translations (1) and (2) above, the second translation changes the database instance less than the first one. Then, the deletion is deterministic wrt the database instance because, according to the current database state, there is a unique translation (namely translation 2) which guarantees minimal change.

The organization of this paper is as follows: We first recall some basic definitions concerning the relational database model in Section 2, then we present the notion of view update translation in Section 3. In Section 4, we introduce our formalism about the inversion of the relational algebra (excluding the difference). In Section 5, we present our method for characterizing the set of translations of a given view update, and we consider two kinds of deterministic updates. We conclude with some perspectives in Section 6. The proofs are omitted due to luck of space, the interested reader is referred to [5, 6].

2 Basic Definitions and Notation

We consider here a relational database model with a *fixed* database scheme, where several views can be created, possibly over the same relation scheme. We first give basic definitions of the relational model that slightly differ from the classical approach [1, 12, 13].

Definition 1. *A universe is a finite set U whose elements are called attributes. Each attribute A of U is associated with a domain dom_A, and with a set of variables var_A. The values of dom_A are denoted by v_A, v'_A, v^1_A, etc ..., and the variables of var_A are denoted by x_A, x'_A, x^1_A, etc ... For each A in U, let $\Sigma_A = dom_A \cup var_A$, $dom = \bigcup_{A \in U} dom_A$, $var = \bigcup_{A \in U} var_A$, and $\Sigma = dom \cup var$.*

Let X be a relation scheme (i.e. a subset of U), a tuple t over X is a function from X to $\bigcup_{A \in X} \Sigma_A$ such that for every A in X, $t(A) \in \Sigma_A$. The tuple t is total if for each A of X, $t(A) \in dom_A$.

As usual, $t(A)$ is denoted $t.A$, and ϵ denotes the "empty" tuple (over any relation scheme). In the database definition below, we distinguish *relation symbol* from its effective value, called *relation instance* or *relation* for short.

Definition 2. *Given a relation symbol R over relation scheme $\mathcal{R}$, we call relation instance, or relation for short, of R any finite set of tuples r over $\mathcal{R}$.*

A database $\mathcal{D}$ defined on the universe U is a set of relation symbols $R_1, R_2, \ldots, R_n$, where each R_i is associated with a relation scheme $\mathcal{R}_i$. An instance of $\mathcal{D}$ is a set of relations $r_1, r_2, \ldots, r_n$ where each r_i is an instance of R_i.

A relational expression E defined from the relation symbols $R_1, \ldots, R_n$ in this order is denoted by $E(R_1, \ldots, R_n)$. Moreover, given instances $r_1, \ldots, r_n$ of $R_1, \ldots, R_n$ resp., the result of the evaluation of $E(R_1, \ldots, R_n)$, denoted by $\mathcal{E}(r_1, \ldots, r_n)$, is obtained by replacing each R_i in E with the relation r_i. The relation scheme of the resulting relation is denoted by $sch(E)$.

3 View Update Translation

Based on [13], we formally define a transaction as follows:

Definition 3. *Let $\mathcal{D}$ be a database and $R_1, \ldots, R_n$ be n relation symbols. A transaction is a finite sequence of updates $T = u_1 \ldots u_m$ where each u_i is a single update which consists in inserting (or deleting) a set of tuples τ_i in (from) R_i and denoted by $ins(\tau, R_i)$ ($del(\tau, R_i)$).*

If $T = u_1 \ldots u_k$ is a transaction, R a relational symbol associated with $\mathcal{R}$, and τ a set of tuples over $\mathcal{R}$, then:
- Let r be an instance of R. $u = ins(\tau, R)$ (resp. $u = del(\tau, R)$) is called a *single update over* R. The effect of u over r denoted by $ins(\tau, r)$ (resp. $del(\tau, r)$) is $r := r \cup \tau$ (resp. $r := r - \tau$). (Note that τ may be empty).
- $T' = u'_1.u'_2.\ldots.u'_k$ is called sub-transaction of $T = u_1 \ldots u_k$ if for every $i = 1, \ldots, k$, $u_i = upd(\tau_i, R_i)$, $u'_i = upd(\tau'_i, R'_i)$, $R'_i = R_i$, $\tau'_i \subseteq \tau_i$, and $upd = ins$ or $upd = del$ (we draw attention on the fact that our notion of sub-transaction differs from that usually defined in the literature).
- T_R is called the R-transaction of T if: (a) T_R is a sub-transaction of T, (b) T_R contains all the single updates over R in T, and (c) for every $R_i \neq R$, $u_i = upd(\tau_i, R_i)$ implies $\tau_i = \emptyset$.
- We denote by $eff(T_R, r)$, the effect of T_R on an instance r of R. Moreover if R does not occur in a given transaction T, and if r is an instance of R, then T_R is an empty transaction and $eff(T_R, r)$ is r.
- We call insert-transaction (resp. delete-transaction), a transaction which contains only insert (resp. delete) updates.

Given a relational expression $E(R_1, \ldots, R_n)$ and a tuple t over $sch(E)$, the insertion or the deletion of t in the view defined by E is called *view update of t over E* and denoted by $\mathcal{U}(t, E)$, where $\mathcal{U}$ stands for Ins or Del.

Definition 4. *Let $E(R_1, \ldots, R_n)$ be a relational expression and t a tuple over $sch(E)$. A* translation *of the view update $\mathcal{U}(t, E)$ is a transaction $T = u_1.u_2 \ldots u_n$ such that:*

1. *$u_i = upd(\tau_i, R_i)$ where, for $i = 1, \ldots, n$, $upd = ins$, or $upd = del$*
2. *(a) If $\mathcal{U}(t, E)$ is an insertion, then for all instances $r_1, \ldots, r_n$, of $R_1, \ldots, R_n$ resp., $t \in \mathcal{E}(eff(T_{R_1}, r_1), \ldots, eff(T_{R_n}, r_n))$,*
   (b) if $\mathcal{U}(t, E)$ is a deletion, then for all instances $r_1, \ldots, r_n$, of $R_1, \ldots, R_n$ resp., $t \notin \mathcal{E}(eff(T_{R_1}, r_1), \ldots, eff(T_{R_n}, r_n))$.
3. *For each sub-transaction T' of T, point 2 above does not hold.*

Let $E(R_1, \ldots, R_n)$ be a relational expression not containing the difference operator. It can be seen that, if $\mathcal{U}(t, E)$ is an update of a tuple t over E, then:
1. If $\mathcal{U}(t, E)$ is an insertion, then every translation $T = u_1 \ldots u_n$ of $\mathcal{U}(t, E)$ is an insert-transaction such that, for every $i = 1, \ldots, n$, $u_i = ins(t_i, R_i)$, where t_i is a tuple over $\mathcal{R}_i$.
2. If $\mathcal{U}(t, E)$ is a deletion, then every translation $T = u_1 \ldots u_n$ of $\mathcal{U}(t, E)$ is a delete-transaction such that, for every $i = 1, \ldots, n$, $u_i = del(\tau_i, R_i)$, where τ_i is a set of tuples over $\mathcal{R}_i$.

As a consequence under the restriction that E does not contain the set difference operator, every translation of $\mathcal{U}(t, E)$ is written as $T = upd((\tau_1, R_1), \ldots, (\tau_n, R_n))$, where τ_i $(i = 1, \ldots, n)$ is a set of tuples over the relation scheme $\mathcal{R}_i$ associated to R_i, and where $upd = ins$ or del, depending on whether $\mathcal{U}(t, E)$ is an insertion or a deletion. We note that, as a consequence of this notation, item 3 of Definition 4 can be expressed as follows:
3': For each $T' \neq T$ such that $T' = upd((\tau'_1, R_1), \ldots, (\tau'_n, R_n))$ with $\tau'_i \subseteq \tau_i$ $(i = 1, \ldots, n)$ and $\tau'_{i_0} \neq \tau_{i_0}$ for one i_0, item 2 of Definition 4 does not hold.

Example 1. Consider the insert view update $\mathcal{U}(\langle Mary, CS\rangle, E)$ over the view v of our Running Example. According to Definition 4, $T = ins((\{\langle Mary, P\rangle\}), (\{\langle Mary, CS\rangle\}))$ is a translation of $\mathcal{U}(\langle Mary, CS\rangle, E)$ since $\mathcal{E}(\{\langle Mary, P\rangle\}, \{\langle Mary, CS\rangle\}) = \{\langle Mary, CS\rangle\}$ and since no sub-transaction of T is a translation of $\mathcal{U}(\langle Mary, CS\rangle, E)$.

We note that if E contains the set difference operator, then translations of updates such as $\mathcal{U}(t, E)$ are neither insert- nor delete-transactions. In the remainder of this paper, we consider *only* relational expressions not containing the set difference operator, usually referred to as *positive* relational expressions.

4 Inverse-images: Formalism and Computation

The problem of inverting (positive) relational expressions in a relational database model has already been studied in [9] in the context of view equivalence and where inverses are represented by tables. In our approach, inverses are represented by means of tuples of tuples (k-tuples) associated with linear equations (c-k-tuples). Solutions of this equations are called inverse-images and are used to translate view updates.

4.1 Definitions, Notation

Definition 5. *k-tuple: A k-tuple is a tuple of tuples denoted by* $(t_1, t_2, \ldots, t_n)$, *where* $n \geq 1$ *and* t_i $(i = 1, \ldots, n)$ *is a tuple.*

Note that a single tuple t can be seen as the k-tuple (t). A k-tuple of the form (t) or of the form $(\epsilon, \ldots, \epsilon, t, \epsilon, \ldots, \epsilon)$, where $t \neq \epsilon$, is called *unary.* Moreover, any k-tuple of the form $(\epsilon, \ldots, \epsilon)$ is simply denoted by ϵ whenever no ambiguity is possible.

Definition 6. *An elementary constraint is a boolean expression c of the form:* $\top$ *(true),* $\bot$ *(false) or* $x\theta y$ *where x and y are variables or constants of* Σ *and* $\theta \in \{<, >, \geq, \leq, =\}$.

A constraint is a boolean expression $C = c_1 \wedge c_2 \wedge \ldots \wedge c_l$ $(l \geq 1)$ *such that for each* $i = 1, \ldots, l$, c_i *is an elementary constraint.*

A constrained k-tuple, or c-k-tuple, is a pair $P = [N, C]$ *where N is a k-tuple and C a constraint over N. The c-k-tuple P is called unary if N is unary.*

Selection conditions are associated with constraints as follows: Without loss of generality, we consider that any selection condition Γ is of the form $\Gamma = \Gamma_1 \vee \Gamma_2 \vee \ldots \vee \Gamma_k$, where $\Gamma_i = \gamma_i^1 \wedge \gamma_i^2 \wedge \ldots \wedge \gamma_i^l$ and where $\gamma_i^j = X\theta Y$ or $\gamma_i^j = \neg(X\theta Y)$, X is an attribute and Y is either an attribute or a constant, and $\theta \in \{<, >, \geq, \leq, =\}$. Let Γ be a selection condition and let t be a tuple over $\mathcal{R}$ such that all attributes occurring in Γ are in $\mathcal{R}$. We associate Γ with a set $\bar{\Gamma} = \{\bar{\Gamma}_1, \ldots, \bar{\Gamma}_k\}$ where, for every $i = 1, \ldots, k$, $\bar{\Gamma}_i$ is obtained from Γ_i as follows: $\bar{\Gamma}_i = c_i^1 \wedge c_i^2 \wedge \ldots \wedge c_i^l$ $(l \geq 1)$ where for each $j = 1, \ldots, l$, c_i^j is obtained from γ_i^j in the following way: If X_i^j (resp. Y_i^j) is an attribute, then X_i^j (resp. Y_i^j) is replaced by $t.X_i^j$ (resp. $t.Y_i^j$), else X_i^j (resp. Y_i^j) does not change.
Clearly, we have the following: $t \models \Gamma$ iff there exists i such that $\bar{\Gamma}_i$ is true.

4.2 Inverting the Relational Algebra

Definition 7. *Let* $E(R_1, R_2, \ldots, R_n)$ *be a relational expression and t be a tuple over sch(E). The set of the inverse-images of t by E, denoted by Inv(t, E), is the set of all k-tuples* $(t_1, t_2, \ldots, t_n)$ *such that:*
1. $\mathcal{E}(\{t_1\}, \{t_2\}, \ldots, \{t_n\}) = \{t\}$ *where, for* $i = 1, \ldots, n$, $sch(t_i) = sch(r_i)$
2. $\forall\, i = 1, \ldots, n$, *if* $t_i \neq \epsilon$ *then* $\mathcal{E}(\{t_1\}, \ldots, \{t_{i-1}\}, \{\}, \{t_{i+1}\}, \ldots, \{t_n\}) \neq \{t\}$

Example 2. For $E = \Pi_{AC}(\sigma_{(B=b)}(R \bowtie R'))$, where R and R' are defined over the schemes AB and BC resp., and for $t = ac$, we have $Inv(t, E) = \{(ab, bc)\}$.

Because of the monotonicity of relational algebra excluding the difference operator, Definition 7 is independent of the database state, that is, if $(t_1, t_2, \ldots, t_n)$ $\in Inv(t, E)$, then for all instances $r_1, r_2, \ldots, r_n$, $\mathcal{E}(r_1 \cup \{t_1\}, r_2 \cup \{t_2\}, \ldots, r_n \cup \{t_n\}) = \{t\}$. We note that, if relational expressions are allowed to contain the difference operator, this does not hold.

In order to compute the set of inverse for a given relational expression, we define the following four operators:

Definition 8. *Let $P = [(t), C]$ be a unary c-k-tuple, let t be a tuple over $\mathcal{R}$, and let $\mathcal{R}'$ be a relation scheme such that:*
1. If $\mathcal{R}' \subseteq \mathcal{R}$, then the projection operator of P over $\mathcal{R}'$, denoted by $proj(P, \mathcal{R}')$, is: $proj(P, \mathcal{R}') = [(t.\mathcal{R}'), C]$.
2. If $\mathcal{R} \subseteq \mathcal{R}'$, then the extension operator of P over $\mathcal{R}'$, denoted by $ext(P, \mathcal{R}')$, is: $ext(P, \mathcal{R}') = [(N\bar{N}), C]$ such that $N = (t)$ and $N' = (t')$ where t' is a tuple of variables defined over $\mathcal{R}' - \mathcal{R}$. (At each application of the extension operator, ext generates new variables).

Definition 9. *Let $P = [(t_1, t_2, \ldots, t_m), C]$ and $P' = [(t'_1, t'_2, \ldots, t'_n), C']$ be two c-k-tuples. The append operator and the completion operator of P and P', denoted resp. by $P \odot P'$ and $P \diamond P'$ are defined as follows:*
3. $P \odot P' = [(N, N'), C \wedge C']$ where $(N, N') = (t_1, t_2, \ldots, t_m, t'_1, t'_2, \ldots, t'_n)$.
4. $P \diamond P' = \{[(t_1, t_2, \ldots, t_m, \underbrace{\epsilon, \ldots, \epsilon}_{n\ times}), C], [(\underbrace{\epsilon, \ldots, \epsilon}_{m\ times}, t'_1, t'_2, \ldots, t'_n), C']\}$.

The operators $Proj$, Ext, $\bigodot$ and $\Diamond$ extend the operators $proj$, ext, $\odot$ and $\diamond$ as follows: Let $\mathcal{P}$ and $\mathcal{P}'$ be two sets of c-k-tuples and let $\mathcal{R}$ be a relation scheme.
– $Proj(\mathcal{P}, \mathcal{R}) = \{proj(P, \mathcal{R}) \mid P \in \mathcal{P}\}$, and $Ext(\mathcal{P}, \mathcal{R}) = \{ext(P, \mathcal{R}) \mid P \in \mathcal{P}\}$.
– $\mathcal{P} \bigodot \mathcal{P}' = \{P \odot P' \mid P \in \mathcal{P}, P' \in \mathcal{P}'\}$, and $\mathcal{P} \Diamond \mathcal{P}' = \{P \diamond P' \mid P \in \mathcal{P}, P' \in \mathcal{P}'\}$.

Based on these definitions, it can be shown ([5]) that the inverse of a given relational expression can be computed according to the following definition.

Definition 10. *Let E, E', E'' be relational expressions and let $\mathcal{P}$ be a set of unary c-k-tuples. We call inverse of $\mathcal{P}$ wrt E the following set of c-k-tuples, denoted by $\widetilde{E}(\mathcal{P})$:*
- *If $E = R$, where R is a relation symbol, then $\widetilde{E}(\mathcal{P}) = \mathcal{P}$.*
- *If $E = \sigma_\Gamma(E')$, where $\Gamma = \Gamma_1 \vee, \ldots \vee \Gamma_k$, then $\widetilde{E}(\mathcal{P}) = \widetilde{E'}(\{[N, C \wedge \bar{\Gamma}_i]) \mid [N, C] \in \mathcal{P}, \bar{\Gamma}_i \in \bar{\Gamma}\})$, where $\bar{\Gamma} = \{\bar{\Gamma}_1, \ldots, \bar{\Gamma}_k\}$ is the set of constraints associated with Γ.*
- *If $E = \Pi_X(E')$, then $\widetilde{E}(\mathcal{P}) = \widetilde{E'}(Ext(\mathcal{P}, sch(E')))$.*
- *If $E = E' \bowtie E''$, then, $\widetilde{E}(\mathcal{P}) = \widetilde{E'}(Proj(\mathcal{P}, sch(E'))) \bigodot \widetilde{E''}(Proj(\mathcal{P}, sch(E'')))$.*
- *If $E = E' \cup E''$, then $\widetilde{E}(\mathcal{P}) = \widetilde{E'}(\mathcal{P}) \Diamond \widetilde{E''}(\mathcal{P})$.*

The following basic theorem states that, given a relational expression, the set of inverses coincides with the corresponding set of inverse-images.

Theorem 1. *Let E be a relational expression, and let t be a tuple defined over $sch(E)$. Then: $Inv(t, E) = \{(N\psi) \mid [N, C] \in \widetilde{E}([(t), \top])$ and $C\psi = \top$ where ψ is an instantiation of all variables in $[N, C]\}$.*

Example 3. We recall that in our Running Example the view v is defined by $E = \Pi_{Ename,Dname}(\sigma_{Pname=P}(Emp \bowtie Dept))$. If $t = \langle Mary, CS\rangle$ is a tuple over the relation scheme $Ename\ Dname$, then: $\widetilde{E}(\langle Mary, CS\rangle, \top) = \{[(\langle Mary, x_{Pname}\rangle, \langle x_{Pname}, CS\rangle), x_{Pname} = P]\}$. Hence, $Inv(t, E) = \{(\langle Mary, P\rangle, \langle P, CS\rangle)\}$.

5 View Update Translations using Inverse

5.1 Relationship between Translations and Inverses

The next two propositions sate the relationship between $Inv(t, E)$ and translations of $\mathcal{U}(t, E)$.

Proposition 1. *Let $E(R_1, \ldots, R_n)$ be a relational expression and $\mathcal{U}(t, E)$ a view update of a tuple t over E. If $\mathcal{U}(t, E)$ is an insertion, then: $T = ins((t_1, R_1), \ldots, (t_n, R_n))$ is a translation of $\mathcal{U}(t, E)$ iff $(t_1, \ldots, t_n) \in Inv(t, E)$.*

Example 4. In the context of our Running Example, consider the following view update: $Ins(\langle Mary, CS\rangle, E)$ where $E = \Pi_{Ename,Dname}\ (\sigma_{Pname=P}(Emp \bowtie Dept))$. According to Definition 4, $ins(\ ((\langle Mary,\ P\rangle,\ Emp), ((\langle Mary,\ CS\rangle, Dept))$ is a translation of $Ins(\langle Mary, CS\rangle, E)$. On the other hand, as seen in Example 3, $((\langle Mary, P\rangle, \langle Mary,\ CS\rangle) \in Inv((\langle Mary,\ CS\rangle, E)$.

In order to translate delete updates, we need the following additional notation. Let $E(R_1, \ldots, R_n)$ be a relational expression and let t be a tuple over $sch(E)$. For all sets of tuples $\tau_1, \ldots, \tau_n$ defined resp. over $\mathcal{R}_1, \ldots, \mathcal{R}_n$, for $i = 1, \ldots, n$, we denote by Inv_i the set $\{N \in Inv(t, E) \mid \tau_i \neq \emptyset, N_i \in \tau_i\}$ (where N_i is the $i-th$ tuple of N).

Proposition 2. *Let $E(R_1, \ldots, R_n)$ be a relational expression and $\mathcal{U}(t, E)$ a view update of a tuple t defined over $sch(E)$ over E. If $\mathcal{U}(t, E)$ is a deletion , then: $T = del((\tau_1, r_1\rangle, \ldots, (\tau_n, r_n\rangle)$ is a translation of $\mathcal{U}(t, E)$ iff $\{Inv_i \mid i = 1, \ldots, n\}$ is a partition of $Inv(t, E)$.*

Example 5. In the context of our Running Example, consider the following view update: $Del(\langle John, M\rangle, E)$ where $E = \Pi_{Ename,Dname}\ (\sigma_{Pname=P}(Emp \bowtie Dept))$. Clearly, the two translations of $Del(\ ((\langle John, M\rangle, E)$ are $T = del(((\langle John, P\rangle, Emp),\ (\emptyset, Dept))$, and $T' = del((\emptyset,\ Emp), (\langle P, M\rangle, Dept))$. In this case, T and T' are associated with the following partition of $Inv(\langle John, M\rangle, E)$: $\{(\langle John, P\rangle, \langle P, M\rangle)\}$.

It should be clear that, given a relational expression $E(R_1, \ldots, R_n)$ and a tuple t defined over $sch(E)$, a partition of $Inv(t, E)$ does not always correspond to a translation of $Del(t, E)$.

Given a relational expression $E(R_1, \ldots, R_n)$, a tuple t defined over $sch(E)$ and a view update $\mathcal{U}(t, E)$, a translation of $\mathcal{U}(t, E)$ is built from the set $Inv(t, E)$ in the following way:
(1) If $\mathcal{U}(t, E)$ is an insert view update, based on Proposition 1, the computation of $Inv(t, E)$ allows for obtaining all translations of $\mathcal{U}(t, E)$.
(2) If $\mathcal{U}(t, E)$ is a delete view update, based on Proposition 2, every partition of $Inv(t, E)$ of the form $\{Inv_1, \ldots, Inv_n\}$ corresponds to a translation of the form $del((\tau_1, R_1), \ldots, (\tau_n, R_n))$. Moreover, the sets τ_i can be built up as follows:

Begin

$\tau_l := \emptyset$, $Inv_l := \emptyset$, for $l = 1, \ldots, n$

While $Inv(t, E) \neq \emptyset$ *Do*

choose ν in $Inv(t, E)$ and let i_0 be such that $\nu_{i_0} \neq \epsilon$

$\tau_{i_0} := \tau_{i_0} \cup \{N_{i_0}\}$

$Inv_i := Inv_i \cup \{N \in Inv(t, E) \mid N_i = \nu_{i_0}\}$

$Inv(t, E) := Inv(t, E) - Inv_i$

EndWhile

End

5.2 View Update Determinism

In this section, we characterize two kinds of deterministic updates based on translations: (1) deterministic updates regardless to the database state, called strongly deterministic updates, and (2) deterministic updates according to some database state, called weakly deterministic updates. It is important to note that results in this section are stated under the following restrictions: relational expressions are positive, and moreover, contain no more than one occurrence of any relation symbol.

Strongly deterministic view updates are defined as follows.

Definition 11. *Let $E(R_1, \ldots, R_n)$ be a relational expression, t a tuple defined on $sch(E)$, and $\mathcal{U}(t, E)$ a view update over E. $\mathcal{U}(t, E)$ is strongly deterministic, if for all instances $r_1, \ldots, r_n$ of $R_1, \ldots, R_n$ resp., and for all translations T and T' of $\mathcal{U}(t, E)$, $eff(T_{R_i}, r_i) = eff(T'_{R_i}, r_i)$, $i = 1, \ldots, n$.*

Based on Propositions 1 and 2 , strongly deterministic view updates are defined as follows.

Proposition 3. *Let $E(R_1, \ldots, R_n)$ be a relational expression and let t be a tuple defined on $sch(E)$. If for all i and j such that $i \neq j$, $R_i \neq R_j$, then:*
- *$Ins(t, E)$ is strongly deterministic iff $|Inv(t, E)| = 1$.*
- *$Del(t, E)$ is strongly deterministic iff every N in $Inv(t, E)$ is unary.*

Now, in order to define weakly deterministic view updates, we need the following definition.

Definition 12. *Let $E(R_1, \ldots, R_n)$ be a relational expression, t a tuple defined on $sch(E)$, and $T = upd((\tau_1, R_1), \ldots, (\tau_n, R_n))$ a translation of $\mathcal{U}(t, E)$. Given n instances $r_1, \ldots, r_n$ of $R_1, \ldots, R_n$ resp., the quantity of change, called measure, of T is defined by:*
- *$\phi(T) = |\tau_1 - r_1| + \ldots + |\tau_n - r_n|$ if T is an insert-transaction.*
- *$\phi(T) = |\tau_1 \cap r_1| + \ldots + |\tau_n \cap r_n|$ if T is a delete-transaction.*

Definition 13. *Let $E(R_1, \ldots, R_n)$ be a relational expression, t be a tuple defined on $sch(E)$, $I = (r_1, \ldots, r_n)$ be an instance of $(R_1, \ldots, R_n)$ and $\mathcal{U}(t, E)$ be a view update of t over E. If $\mathcal{T}$ is the set of translations of $\mathcal{U}(t, E)$ then a translation T_0 of $\mathcal{T}$ guarantees the minimal change on I if, for every T in $\mathcal{T}$, we have: $\phi(T_0) \leq \phi(T)$.*

Based on the above definition, the weak determinism is defined as follows:

Definition 14. *Let $E(R_1, \ldots, R_n)$ be a relational expression, let $\mathcal{U}(t, E)$ be a view update, and let $I = (r_1, \ldots, r_n)$ be an instance of $(R_1, \ldots, R_n)$. $\mathcal{U}(t, E)$ is weakly deterministic according to I if for all translations T and T' of $\mathcal{U}(t, E)$ which guarantee the minimal change on I, $T = T'$.*

Example 6. Let $E = \Pi_{AC}(\sigma_{B \geq b}(R_1 \bowtie R_2))$ be a relational expression such that $r_1 = \{ab\}$ and $r_2 = \emptyset$ are two instances of R_1 and R_2 defined resp. on the schemes AB and BC, and let ac be a tuple over $sch(E)$. Let $dom_B = \{b, b'\}$ with $b' \geq b$. As $Inv(t, E) = \{(ab, bc), (ab', b'c)\}$, $T_1 = ins((ab, R_1), (bc, R_2))$ and $T_2 = ins((ab', R_1), (b'c, R_2))$ are the only translations of $Ins(ac, E)$. Moreover, $\phi(T_1) = 1$, and $\phi(T_2) = 2$. As $\phi(T_1) < \phi(T_2)$, T_1 is the unique translation which guarantees the minimal change on the instance $(\{ab\}, \emptyset)$. Hence, $Ins(ac, E)$ is weakly deterministic according to $(\{ab\}, \emptyset)$.

5.3 Performing View Updates: An Overview

In the traditional relational model, where the views are not stored, when the view update has more than one translation, this view update is simply rejected. In our approach, given a relational expression $E(R_1, \ldots, R_n)$ over a database $\mathcal{D}$, and a tuple t over $sch(E)$, we propose a method to perform a view update $\mathcal{U}(t, E)$ under the restriction that $Inv(t, E)$ is a finite set. To this end, we consider the following three steps:

Step 1. Strong determinism of the view updates

(a) $\mathcal{U}(t, E) = Ins(t, E)$: If $|Inv(t, E)| = 1$, i.e. if $Inv(t, E) = \{(t_1, \ldots, t_n)\}$, then perform the database updates $ins((t_1, R_1), \ldots, (t_n, R_n))$.

(b) $\mathcal{U}(t, E) = Del(t, E)$: If every k-tuple in $Inv(t, E)$ is unary, then build the unique translation from $Inv(t, E)$ using the algorithm described in Section 5.1 and perform the database updates $del((\tau_1, R_1), \ldots, (\tau_n, R_n))$.

Step 2. If the test in item 1 above has failed, then test the weak determinism of the view update according to Definition 14. If there exists a unique view update translation T which guarantees minimal change of the database instance $r_1, \ldots, r_n$, then execute T on the database.

Step 3. If steps 1 and 2 fail, then apply the method of [5] where the tuple to be inserted or deleted is explicitly stored in the view. We note that this step is closely related to the problem of view maintenance in the context of *materialized* views [7,8].

We note that testing weak determinism is polynomial in the size of the database. Indeed, computing the measure of change is achieved through a query (which is polynomial in the size of the database), moreover, in the case of an insertion, this computation has to be done for each element of $Inv(t, E)$. However, in the case of deletion, all translations are obtained by applying the algorithm of Section 5.1 for all possible choices in the while-loop, which leads to an exponential number of computations. We are currently considering the characterization of cases under which this number of computations is polynomial.

6 Conclusion

We have presented a method for translating view updates into database updates using the inversion of relational algebra under the following restrictions: relational expressions are positive and, contain no more than one occurrence of any relation symbol. We have proposed a way to compute the set of inverses of a given relational expression, and we have shown that this set coincides with the corresponding set of inverse-images. Moreover, we have characterized the notion of a view update translation and shown that there is a strong link between the set of translations and the set of inverses of the relational expression defining the view. We are currently studying the generalization of our results to the case of any relational expression, possibly containing set difference and several occurrences of the same relation.

We have characterized two kinds of updates: (1) deterministic updates regardless to the database state, called strongly deterministic updates, and (2) deterministic updates according to some database state, called weakly deterministic updates. We are investigating particular cases where the test of weak determinism is polynomial.

References

1. S. Abiteboul, R. Hull, and V. Vianu. *Foundations of Databases.* ADDISON-WESLEY, 1995.
2. P. Atzeni and R. Torlone. Updating Intensional Predicates in Datalog. *Data and Knowledge Engineering*, 8, 1992.
3. P. Atzeni and R. Torlone. Updating Relational Databases through Weak Instance Interfaces. *ACM TODS*, 17:718–745, 1992.
4. F. Bancilhon and N. Spyratos. Update Semantics of Relational Views. *ACM Trans. on Database Syst.*, 6(4):557–575, December 1981.
5. F. Bentayeb and D. Laurent. Inversion de l'Algèbre Relationnelle et Mises à jour (french). Technical Report 97-09, LIFO, Orléans, France, Juin 1997.
6. F. Bentayeb and D. Laurent. Translating View Updates Using Inversion of Relational Algebra. Technical Report 98-03, LIFO, Orléans, France, February 1998.
7. J. A. Blakeley, P.-A. Larson, and F. W. Tompa. Efficiently Updating Materialized Views. *ACM SIGMOD*, 1986.
8. S. Ceri and J. Widom. Deriving Production Rules for Incremental View Maintenance. In *Proceedings of the 17th International conference on Very Large Data Bases*, Barcelona, September 1991.
9. T. Imielinski and W. Lipski. Inverting Relational expressions - A Uniform and Natural Technique For Various Database Problems. *ACM SIGACT-SIGMOD*, 1983.
10. D. Laurent, V. Phan Luong, and N. Spyratos. Deleted Tuples are Useful when Updating through Universal Scheme Interfaces. In *8th IEEE ICDE*, USA, 1992.
11. D. Laurent and N. Spyratos. A Partition Model Approach to Updating Universal Scheme Interfaces. *IEEE TKDE*, 6(2), Avril 1994.
12. J. Ullman. *Principles of Database and Kowledge-Base Systems*, volume 2. Computer Science Press, 1989.
13. G. Vossen. *Data Models, Database Languages and Database Management Systems.* ADDISON-WESLEY, 1990.

Optimisation of Active Rule Agents Using a Genetic Algorithm Approach

Evaggelos Nonas[1] and Alexandra Poulovassilis[2]

[1] Department of Computer Science, King's College London, Strand, London WC2R 2LS, U.K.
vagelis@dcs.kcl.ac.uk

[2] Department of Computer Science, King's College London, Strand, London WC2R 2LS, U.K.
alex@dcs.kcl.ac.uk

Abstract. *Intelligent agents and active databases have a number of common characteristics, the most important of which is that they both execute actions by firing rules upon events occurring provided certain conditions hold. This paper assumes that the knowledge of an intelligent agent is expressed using a set of active rules and proposes a method for optimising the rule-base of such an agent using a Genetic Algorithm. We illustrate the applicability of this method by using it to optimise the performance of a self-adaptive network. The benefits of our approach are simplified design and reduced development and maintenance times of rule-based agents in the face of dynamically evolving environments.*

1 Introduction

Beliefs-desires-intentions (BDI) agents have been around for some years now and have been extensively studied ([5], [9], [11], [2]). A BDI agent has the following components:

- Beliefs Database: Contains facts about the sate of the world, as well as about the agent's internal state.
- Desires: Contains agent's goals expressed as conditions over some interval of time and are described by applying various temporal operators to state descriptions.
- Plans: Actions the agent has to take in order to fulfill its goals. They have an invocation condition which specifies upon which events the plan should be fired and a context condition which specifies under what condition the plan applies.
- Intentions: Plans that are valid for firing are placed in an intentions structure where they are executed. They can be hierarchically ordered.

Active databases are also based upon an Event-Action architecture [4]. An active database system consists of the "traditional" components of a database system plus a component that is concerned with the firing of ECA (event, condition, action) rules. The meaning of an ECA rule is: "when an event occurs check the condition and if it is true execute the action". There is an event language for defining events and for specifying composite events from a set of primitive ones. The condition part of an ECA rule formulates in which state the database has to be, in order for the action to be executed. The action part of an ECA rule usually starts a new transaction which when executed may trigger new ECA rules. In this way we can have trees of triggering and triggered transactions.

Similarities and differences between BDI agents and active databases are discussed in [1], [12], where characteristics such as events, actions, consistency, query expressiveness, goal achievement, responsiveness and others are compared. The most important of their common characteristics is the way actions are executed, in that upon a certain event occurring, if a condition holds a rule is fired. There may be cases where more than one rule may be triggered by the same event occurrence. The system will then select the rule with the highest priority to fire, or will arbitrarily select a rule to fire if there are more than one with the same priority.

In this paper we assume that the knowledge of an intelligent agent is expressed using a set of active rules, and that a genetic algorithm determines the "best" rule to fire if more than one rule is triggered. Genetic algorithms and genetic programming have been used before in the design of agent systems [8], [10]. The novelty of our work is that we are using GAs to select the "best" rule to be fired and also to automatically respond to changes in the environment.

The outline of this paper is as follows: In section 2 GAs are described and their use in optimising rule based agents is proposed. In section 3 we apply our methods to the problem of optimising a self-adaptive network. In section 4 some results of our application are presented. Finally, some conclusions and possible directions for further research are presented.

2 GAs and Rule-Based Agents

Genetic algorithms ([7], [3], [6]) are methods of solving problems based upon an abstraction of the process of Natural Selection. They attempt to mimic nature by evolving solutions to problems rather than designing them. Genetic algorithms work by analogy with Natural Selection as follows. First, a population pool of chromosomes is maintained. The chromosomes are strings of symbols or numbers. They might be as simple as strings of bits - the simplest type of string possible. There is good precedence for this since humans are defined in DNA using a four-symbol alphabet. The chromosomes are also called the genotype (the coding of the solution), as opposed to the phenotype (the solution itself). In the Genetic algorithm we maintain a pool of chromosomes, which are strings. These chromosomes must be evaluated for fitness. Poor solutions are purged and small changes are made to existing solutions. We then allow "natural selection" to take its course, evolving the gene pool so that steadily better solutions are discovered.

The basic outline of a Genetic Algorithm is as follows:

```
Initialise pool randomly
for each generation
{
  Select good solutions to breed new population
  Create new solutions from parents
  Evaluate new solutions for fitness
  Replace old population with new ones
}
```

The randomly assigned initial pool is presumably pretty poor. However, successive generations improve, for a number of reasons:

- Selection. On each generation parents are selected to produce new children. The selection of parents is biased by fitness, so that fit parents produce more children; very unfit solutions produce no children. This is known as selection. The genes of good solutions thus begin to proliferate through the population.
- Mutation. Small changes (mutations) are made to at least some of the newly created children. Some of these mutations may be harmful. However, this doesn't matter as bad mutations will soon be purged by selection. Good mutations, on the other hand, will succeed, causing further increases in fitness.
- Crossover. It combines the genetic material from parents in order to produce children, during breeding. Since only the good solutions are picked for breeding, during the selection procedure, the crossover operator mixes the genetic material, in order to produce children with even greater fitness. For example, if we assume single point crossover at position 3 two binary chromosomes with values (000000, 111111) will produce (000111, 111000) as children. Moreover, there can be multiple point crossover.

What we propose here, is an "automatic" way of selecting the best action to execute upon an event occurring. The action is selected by a genetic algorithm. For the moment we do not support conditions in our active rules, although we plan to add a condition part in the future. When an event has occurred the system can take several actions. For each of possible events, the system holds an ordered set of possible actions that can be taken when the event occurs. The first action is always selected, but a genetic algorithm running in parallel may dynamically change the order of the actions. Obviously this approach requires a measure of the performance of the agent, which must be available at run-time, to be given to the genetic algorithm.

Since the genetic algorithm controls the way the agents respond to events, we can say that the reactive behaviour of the agent is controlled by the genetic algorithm. But there can also be another "level" (the "rational" level) to control the agent, especially if our architecture is part of an agent built partially using another method and controlled partially by the constructs this method provides. If for instance the agent is built conforming to the BDI model, it will have facts, goals, plans and intentions (plans that have been selected for execution). Some of the plans will be selected for execution using the traditional approach, but some others using the GA approach. This rational part of the agent can also control several parameters of the GA, restart it when needed, or schedule it to be run when the load is low.

Our architecture can also be embedded in more complex systems. When an event/action language is necessary for the building of an agent type system, our method can be used for a subset of the events and the actions of the system. This simplifies the design and reduces testing and maintenance times when compared to a deterministic rule-set with many conditions and checks.

3 An Example Application: Self-Adaptive Networks

A self adaptive network is a network that can automatically adapt to changes in its environment without human intervention being necessary. While load conditions change and nodes and links may fail, the network continues to operate near the optimum state requiring little or no assistance from its operators. In other words, the network must be autonomous, intelligent and have distributed control. There should be no global knowledge for the network. On the contrary all information must be kept as local as possible.

Our network model is a simple yet powerful one. The network is composed of a set of nodes and a set of connections between them. Each node can exchange messages only with the ones it is connected with. There is no global knowledge of the topology of the network stored in any node. There is a set of services provided by the network and each node can provide some or all of the services. The task for every node is to provide the services requested from it with the minimum cost. The cost can be a function of the number of intermediate nodes and links the service is using, as well as the load and the spare capacity of those nodes and links respectively. Obviously, the bigger the number of intermediate nodes and links a service is using, the bigger the cost for the provision of that service is.

Messages are exchanged between nodes to allow service establishment and service canceling. Messages can be exchanged only between connected nodes. For the time being we use three kinds of messages, but we intend to add more in the future. The first requests a service from a node and has as parameters the requesting node, the service number as well as the hop-count (number of intermediate nodes the request has used). Messages with a hop-count greater than a specific number are canceled automatically, to avoid flooding the network with cyclic or very long requests. The second type of message concerns the answer to a request for a service. If the service can be provided, the cost is returned, otherwise the message just rejects the request. The third kind of message cancels services already provided.

Table 1. A Simple Example

Events	Actions
On provide any service	Local, Remote
On send request for service 1	Send to node 2, Send to node 3, Send to node 4
On send request for service 2	Send to node 2, Send to node 3, Send to node 4
On send request for service 3	Send to node 2, Send to node 3, Send to node 4

In each node of the network there is an agent running which is built using the proposed architecture. For the time being only the reactive part of the agent has been built, although in the future we intend to build a rational part, together with event and action languages. There is a set of events and a set of actions for each event. An event occurs when a service is requested. There are two actions that can be triggered for this event: the service can be provided either remotely or locally. When a request for a service is to be sent to another node a separate event is generated for each service. The actions corresponding to this event are all the nodes that the requesting node is connected with. For instance, if node 1 is connected with nodes 2, 3 and 4 and the network provides 3 services, the events and actions for node 1 are shown in Table 1 (no order is shown, just all the events and all the possible actions for each event).

A simple genetic algorithm is used to try out several permutations of the rule set and finally find thc best rule set for each node. Permutations of actions for each event are enumerated and placed in the chromosome one after the other. We define a correspondence between all possible permutations of the actions for an event and an integer in the range [0..n!-1], where n is the number of actions. The binary representation of this number is placed in the chromosome to encode the ordered set of actions for an event. The whole chromosome is composed of K (where K is the number of events) numbers placed in it, in their binary representation, one after the other. In this way one chromosome can encode the rule set with which each agent works.

Each agent has a chromosome pool which is initially randomly instantiated. Then the chromosomes in the chromosome pool are evolved by the genetic algorithm to better solutions. We use a constant population size, selection proportional to fitness

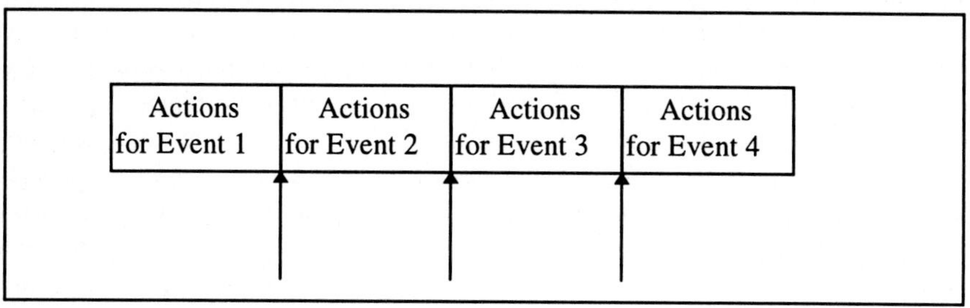

Fig. 1. Chromosome Encoding

and full replacement of parents by their children. Multiple point crossover is used for breeding. Crossover points are set at the end of each event in the chromosome. The chromosome for the example of Table 1 is shown in Figure 1, where arrows show the positions of the crossover points.

The fitness of each rule is calculated as follows: When a node provides a service to another node, it also sends to it the cost of this service. This cost, is a function of the number of intermediate nodes and links the service is using as well as their load and free capacity respectively. Obviously, when the service is provided locally, the cost is minimum. Each rule in the chromosome pool is used for service provision for some time and the costs of the services provided using this rule are averaged. The fitness, then, for this rule is inversely proportional to this average cost. So the bigger the cost, the smaller the fitness of the rule and vice-versa.

The current implementation of our architecture is in Borland C++ Builder and runs under the Win32 platform (Windows 95 and Windows NT). A network simulator as well as the actual agents running on each node of the network have been built. Finally the genetic algorithms used by the agents have also been programmed. There is a graphical user interface that provides for the design of the network, the design of the rules the agents are using and the fine-tuning of the genetic algorithm that each agent runs.

4 Experiments and Results

In this section we present some results for several network configurations. In all the graphs the Y axis shows the average of the mean fitness of the chromosome pools over all the nodes. The X axis shows the number of generations the genetic algorithm has been run. While nodes are being trained service requests have a uniform distribution as far as type of service is concerned, across all nodes. Of course, real traffic data can ultimately be used for more effective training.

Our first experiment is concerned with a network of 100 nodes and 200 links. The topology has been randomly created by our software. In total there are 40 services provided across the network. We examine three different cases with varying service distribution across nodes. In the first case all 40 services are provided by all the nodes. In the second case there is a random distribution of services across nodes. The number of different services provided by each node is drawn randomly from the range [1..40]. In the third case, services and nodes are split into 5 disjoint sets and eight services are provided by each node. For example, nodes 1 to 20 provide services 1 to 8, nodes 21 to 40 provide services 9 to 16, etc. Graphs for all three cases are shown in Figure 2 under the legends Totally Replicated, Random and Partitioned respectively.

As we would expect, the best performance is achieved when services are totally replicated across all nodes. The worst performance is achieved when services and nodes are partitioned into disjoint sets. This is because only a few of the total number of services can be provided locally, or with a small hop-count. Random distribution of services results in a performance between the two “extreme” cases.

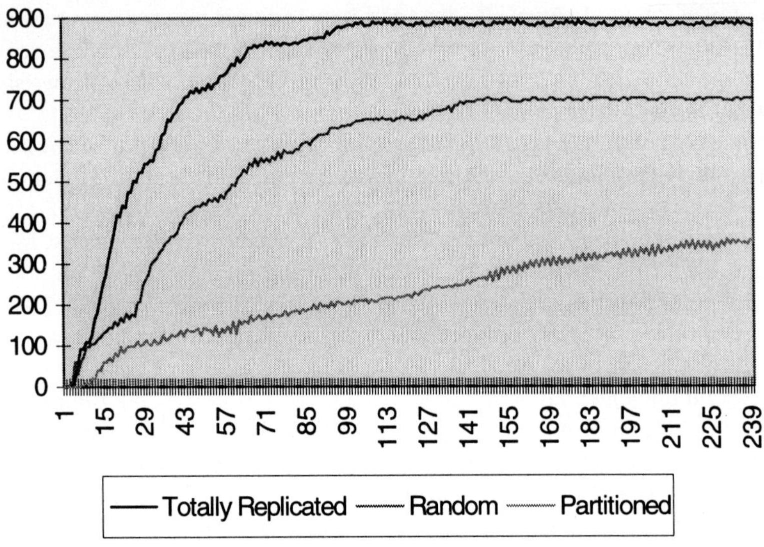

Fig. 2. Varying the Distribution of Services

Our second experiment demonstrates the fault tolerance of the network and its behaviour is illustrated in Figure 3. There is a network of 11 nodes and 10 services. 10 of the nodes are connected in a ring and provide only 3 services each, which vary from node to node. The 11th node provides all 10 services and is connected with all the other nodes. So it is the most important node of the network. The GAs are run and at generation 150, this 11th node of the network goes down. We see initially a

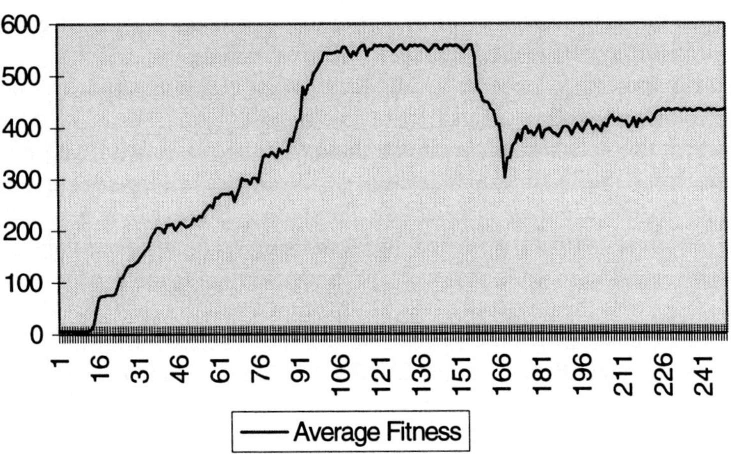

Fig. 3. Fault Tolerance Demonstration

decrease in the fitness of the rule-sets in the remaining 10 nodes, since the services that were provided by node 11 to these nodes cannot now be provided. But the GAs quickly evolve better rule-sets and their fitness increases again. Not surprisingly, it cannot be restored to its original value, since services that were before provided in only one hop-count from node 11 (since node 11 was connected to every other node) now have to be provided with a bigger hop-count from other nodes.

5 Conclusions

In this paper we have described how sets of active rules can be used to express the knowledge of intelligent agents, and how a genetic algorithm can be used to dynamically prioritise rules in the face of dynamically evolving environments. To our knowledge, this is the first time that GAs have been used for this purpose. We have illustrated the applicability of our method by using it to optimise the performance of a self-adaptive network. The advantages of our approach to optimising self-adaptive networks are apparent: distributed solution, load balancing and sharing, and self adaptation to varying load conditions and fault situations.

One could argue that the genetic algorithm can find a local optimum and then stop. This is always a danger with a genetic algorithm, but again it depends on the search space. In a network where service distribution across nodes is done in such way that neighbouring nodes have some services in common there are many good solutions and the genetic algorithm will find one of them. In extreme cases where there is only one good solution the genetic algorithm may fail, but again it can be restarted by the rational part of the agent with many chances to find a better solution. Finally, in such cases the advantages of adaptation, autonomy and distributed operation are more important than the discovery of the best solution, especially in a dynamic and continually changing environment where keeping track of global information would be difficult if not impossible.

One could also argue that this architecture is not powerful enough since it does not work based on an event/action language. However there is nothing to prevent this architecture from being a subset of a rich and powerful event/action language. In such a case it can be used to pick the rule to be fired when there are no other criteria available for rule selection. In other cases it may be better to let the genetic algorithm pick the rule to be fired, instead of having many conditions which will complicate the active rule set and consequently increase design, test and maintenance times.

For further work we plan to construct the rational part of the agent. This too will be based on active rules. It will schedule, restart and fine tune the genetic algorithm. It will also feed it with a good initial population and will provide for knowledge exchange between neighboring nodes. We believe that this combination of intelligence and heuristic search methods like genetic algorithms will lead to a much better performance than use of the latter alone.

We will also explore different types of genetic algorithms, for example ones with overlapping populations such as steady state or incremental GAs. In such cases, we can have a small replacement percentage, so that the GA could be used for driving the nodes at real time (once an initial good state has been reached) and not just training them. The above would be useful mostly for relatively stable environments. We also plan to investigate other methods for finding the optimum rule set (for example, neural networks or other heuristic search methods like simulated annealing) and to formally compare our results with theoretical results obtained by a statistical analysis of the network.

Acknowledgments

E. Nonas is sponsored by B.T. Laboratories, Systems and Software Unit, Martlesham Heath, Ipswich.

References

1. J. Bailey, M. Georgeff, D. B. Kemp, and D. Kinny, "Active databases and agent systems --- A comparison", Lecture Notes in Computer Science, 985, 342-356, (1995).
2. Michael Bratman, Intention, plans, and practical reason, Harvard University press, 1987.
3. Lawrence Davis, Handbook of Genetic Algorithms, Van Nostrand Reinhold, New York, 1991.
4. K. R. Dittrich, S. Gatziu, and A. Geppert, "The active database management system manifesto: A rulebase of ADBMS features", Lecture Notes in Computer Science, 985, 3-17, (1995).
5. Klaus Fischer, Jorg P. Muller, and Markus Pischel, "A pragmatic BDI architecture", in Proceedings on the IJCAI Workshop on Intelligent Agents II : Agent Theories, Architectures, and Languages, volume 1037 of LNAI, pp. 203-218, Berlin, (19-20 August 1996). Springer Verlag.
6. D. E. Goldberg, Genetic Algorithms in Search, Optimization, and Machine Learning, Addison-Wesley, Reading, Mass., 1989.
7. David Goldberg, Genetic Algorithms, Addison Wesley, Reading, 1989.
8. Thomas Haynes and Sandip Sen, "Evolving behavioral strategies in predators and prey", in IJCAI-95 Workshop on Adaptation and Learning in Multiagent Systems, pp. 32-37, (1995).
9. David Kinny, Michael Georgeff, and Anand Rao, "A methodology and modelling technique for systems of BDI agents", in Proceedings of the 7th European Workshop on Modelling Autonomous Agents in a Multi-Agent World, volume 1038 of LNAI, pp. 56-71, Berlin, (22-25 January 1996). Springer Verlag.
10. Mauro Manela and J. A. Campbell, "Designing good pursuit problems as testbeds for distributed AI: A novel application of genetic algorithms, in Proceedings of the 5th European Workshop on Modelling Autonomous Agents in a Multi-Agend World (MAAMAW'93), volume 957 of LNAI, pp. 231-252, Berlin, GER, (August 1995). Springer.
11. Anand S. Rao and Michael P. Georgeff, "BDI agents: from theory to practice", in Proceedings of the First International Conference on Multi—Agent Systems, pp. 312-319, San Francisco, CA, (1995). MIT Press.

12.Johan van den Akker and Arno Siebes, "Enriching active databases with agent technology", in Proceedings ot the First International Workshop on Cooperative Information Agents, volume 1202 of LNAI, pp. 116--125, Berlin, (February26--28 1997). Springer.

Optimization of Constrained Queries with a Hybrid Genetic Algorithm

Augustine Chidi Ikeji[1], Farshad Fotouhi[2]

[1]Computer Science Department
Eastern Michigan University
Ypsilanti, MI 48197
ikeji@emunix.emich.edu
(734) 487-1063

[2]Computer Science Department
Wayne State University
Detroit, MI 48202
faf@cs.wayne.edu
(313) 577-3107

Abstract. Optimization of constrained queries is a growing area of DBMS. Databases are getting larger and users are demanding fast and efficient algorithms for processing queries. Users want the ability to limit the query output set, processing time, or number of records analyzed. Processors have self-imposed constraints which force them to process queries with as little resource as possible. Under these constraints, processors may not be able to produce an entire result, and have to render an optimal partial result. We propose an algorithm that combines statistical sampling and the genetic algorithms idea of survival of the fittest to identify and concentrate in areas of the relation "better fit" for the query result. Our algorithm is also compared to the conventional ones.

Keywords: Query Optimization, Genetic Algorithms, Statistical Sampling, Constrained Queries.

1 Introduction

Databases are becoming very large and users are demanding fast and efficient algorithms for query processing. A typical example is the enormous amount of information on the World Wide Web (WWW) that is spread over thousands if not millions of sites. Most users do not have the time, patience or need to wait for all applicable data to be processed before getting their result. Users want the ability to limit the query output set, processing time, or number of records analyzed in a query. An example of a constraint query is to identify five hundred companies with the word "computer" in their name, or to identify as many such companies as possible in one minute.

Faced with these constraints or other self-imposed constraints, a query processor may not be able to produce all the tuples in the result set and thus will have to render a partial result under the circumstances. The issue then is for the processor to generate an optimal result under the constraints. The conventional techniques [1], [2], [9] for processing this class of queries do not work quite well - they either require a-priori information which may not be used frequently enough to justify its existence or they use statistical sampling without much modification to help identify an optimal result set.

In this paper, we propose an algorithm that requires no a-priori information except for the data necessary to identify all the tuples in the target relation i.e. the relation from which the tuples in the result are obtained. Also we show that the proposed algorithm performs better than the conventional algorithms for processing constrained queries. The algorithm we propose employs the ideas of statistical sampling and genetic algorithms to divide the target relation of a query into several segments, which we call chromosomes. Initially, each chromosome is sampled and the fitness value evaluated. Those chromosomes that are better fit i.e. contain more of the query result get to move on to an active population while those less fit are placed in an inactive population. As chromosomes in the active population are sampled from, their fitness values are re-evaluated. A chromosome is demoted to the inactive population if its fitness value is not high enough. The better performing chromosomes from the inactive population replace the chromosomes demoted from the active population. The net effect is that sampling is concentrated on the better performing chromosomes (active population) which increases the likelihood of obtaining most of the query results in a lesser amount of time or record accesses.

The rest of this paper is organized as follows. Section 2 is a summary of the conventional techniques for processing constrained queries. Genetic algorithms is summarized in section 3, and in section 4, we present our algorithm and compare it to the conventional ones. A conclusion and areas of future work is given in Section 5.

2 Processing of Constrained Queries

There are different types of constraints that a client can place on a query. For example, the constraints may be a limit on the time taken to process the query, a limit on the number of records to be accessed while processing the query, or a limit on the size of the query result. These constraints may be explicit i.e. specified as part of the query or implicit where the query processor always strives to use a limited amount of resources when processing queries. There are two schools of thought for processing constrained queries - the use of a-priori information, and sampling a subset of the target relation to minimize the cost of query processing. In this section, we discuss these two techniques and also present their pros and cons.

2.1 A-Priori Information

A-priori information may be kept on all or some attributes in the database, and whenever applicable, the a-priori information is used to process a query.

The cost of maintaining the information is justified by distributing it across all queries that use it. Different types of a-priori information may be maintained on a database. Some systems maintain what is traditionally known as an index structure. An index is used to classify the tuples of a relation on a particular attribute, which makes it easier to locate tuples when the query discriminant is the same attribute used in building the index.

There are DBMSs that track the distribution of the values of an attribute or break the values down into ranges like 1 to 100, 101 to 200, and keep track of the frequencies of the ranges only. When information is desired for a range that does not exist, say 50 to 150 in the above example, it may be estimated by averaging the ranges that span it. It takes time and space to maintain a-priori information. As long as the information is used frequently enough, the gains can exceed the cost. However, a-priori information such as indexes are not always maintained on all query selection conditions so when a query involves a discriminant that does not have an index, the query processor would have to process the query without much help from the index.

2.2 Brute Force (Linear Search), Binary Search and Hashing

When there is no index, nor are there other a-priori statistics to guide a search on an attribute, the query processor may process the tuples by brute force[5]. This means that the processor may retrieve each tuple in the relation and test whether or not it satisfies the query conditions.

The drawback with this technique is that the query processor makes no attempt to dynamically locate pockets of concentration of the tuples that satisfy the query condition and process such pockets first. This is especially damaging when there is not enough resource such as time to process the entire relation. Also in situations where clients want some partial result to keep them occupied while the rest is gathered such as in WWW searches, it is desirable to find as much of the query result as possible in the early stages of the query processing. This will keep the client engaged long enough for the rest of the result to be obtained.

For binary search or hashing to work, the tuples in the relation have to be arranged in an order that supports the selection condition. It is impossible to build and keep an ordering for all possible selection conditions that can appear in a query, unless we disallow selection conditions for which there is no ordering. Also, any ordering maintained in the database should be used frequently enough to justify its existence.

2.3 Sampling

First, we will present some background information on statistical sampling and estimation. Statistics is defined as the scientific study of techniques for collecting, analyzing, and drawing conclusions from data. Statistical procedures may be applied to a variety of areas in which observations are made. Procedures that are developed for use in one area may be adapted for use in other areas. Probabilities can be applied to statistical information and used to predict the likelihood of an outcome. Probability models can be constructed and used to predict events in the real world.

A population consists of the whole set of attributes or events to be analyzed. A sample consists of n elements from a population of say size N. Randomly selected samples give the assurance that the laws of probabilities will hold. If one is interested in a particular attribute, each occurrence of the attribute is an event. Based on the number or distribution of events in the sample, a conclusion (inference) can be reached on the number or distribution of the events in the population. If the number of events in the sample is the population. If the number of events in the sample is k, then $\hat{p} = k/n$ is the proportion. $\hat{p}$ is used to estimate P, the true proportion of the population. The members of one sample may vary from the members of another sample although the samples are drawn from the same population. This is known as sampling variability. Due to sampling variability, it is unlikely that $\hat{p}$ will be equal to P, therefore probability theory is used to state a confidence interval for the estimate.

The sample size used in sampling is no indication of the precision of the estimate. If the sample elements are carefully chosen, then an increase in the sample size may yield some gains but the point of diminishing returns is reached rapidly [15]. For example, about the same sample size may be used for a population of 50,000 and for a population of 50,000,000 if the two populations have similar characteristics.

Precise predetermined sample sizes are not always possible. However, there are techniques for estimating the required sample size depending on the degree of precision desired.

2.4 Sampling for Processing Constrained Queries

There are different sampling techniques that statisticians use depending on the characteristics of the data among other things. We are going to discuss the technique known as simple random sampling which is the most generic of the sampling techniques. Simple random sampling may be used in selectivity estimations, processing of constrained queries and estimating aggregate queries [8].

Simple random sampling is also the most straightforward of the sampling techniques. A simple random sample is a sample in which every member of the population has an equal likelihood of being included in the sample, or a sample of size n is a simple random sample if all samples of size n in the population have an equal likelihood of being chosen. The population is treated as one unit when samples are drawn from it.

For example, when sampling is used in join selectivity estimation, the population will consist of the Cartesian product of the relations in the join query. The tuples in the population are numbered from 1 to N (the population size). After estimating the sample size n, a random number generator is used to generate n integers between 1 and N. The population members that match the generated random numbers will make up the sample. Next the proportion $(\hat{p})$ of the sample is used as the estimate of the join selectivity of the population.

When sampling is used to process time constrained queries, the processor may estimate how many tuples that may be sampled under the time constraints and use that many tuples to evaluate the query. If it is not possible to estimate the sample size under the constraints, the processor may perform an initial sample and based on how much resources this initial sample took, the amount of remaining samples to take can then be estimated. Yet another way is to incrementally sample in small amounts until the constraints are reached.

The main advantage of simple random sampling is its simplicity. It is quite easy to use a random number generator and put together the indexes corresponding to the sample elements. A major drawback of simple random sampling is the fact that every element of the population should have an equal likelihood of being selected. In a DBMS, this can prove to be very costly because the cost of retrieving the elements may not be equal. The tuples may reside at different storage mediums such as main memory, disk, tape, or even at physically different sites. Ideally, one would like to favor those tuples that are relatively cheaper to retrieve, such as those in main memory as opposed to secondary memory or remote sites.

3 Genetic Algorithms (GAs) for Search and Optimization Problems

David Goldberg pioneered GAs while under the tutelage of John Holland. GAs are based on adaptive systems. They model the process of natural evolution in solving search, optimization and other kinds of problems. Given a problem, the parameters usually containing some solutions to the problem are encoded into binary strings called chromosomes. These chromosomes constitute the population. The next step involves the evaluation of the fitness of each chromosome in the population and the formation of new chromosomes using the reproduction operators such as mutation and crossover. The better fit chromosomes have a higher chance of reproducing and the newly produced chromosomes may replace the less fit chromosomes in the population. The process of selection, mutation, crossover and replacement is repeated for as long as necessary. The hope is that at the end, the current generation will contain mostly fit chromosomes and the process would have wedded out the weaker ones. Also, while going through the generations, the better fit chromosomes are identified along the way. The problem to be solved is related to the GA through the fitness evaluator i.e. the fitness evaluator will vary from problem to problem.

The template for a simple GA is as follows:

1. Formulate and initialize the population of chromosomes for the first generation.
2. Compute the fitness value of each chromosome in the current population.
3. Reproduce new chromosomes and create a new population with the newly formed chromosomes and possibly some old ones.
4. If not done, go to step 2.

3.1 Variations of GAs

Some of the variations are based on the selection process for identifying chromosomes for reproduction, or on the crossover and mutation techniques themselves. The variations based on how chromosomes are selected for reproduction are as follows.

1. Proportionate Selection: The selection of a chromosome for reproduction is directly related (proportional) to its fitness value. The draw back of this technique is that the presence of a few highly fit chromosomes may result in domination and extinction.
2. Selection based on scaled fitness values: Scaling may be used to reduce the differences in the fitness values of the chromosomes before the selection is applied.
3. Selection based on ranks: In ranked selection, the chromosomes are ranked in order of their fitness values and the selection is directly related to the ranks.

For example, if there are three chromosomes C1, C2, and C3 with fitness values of 0.9, 0.2, and 0.1 respectively. With proportionate allocation, C1 will be nine times as likely as C3 to be selected. With scaled fitness values, the huge discrepancy between C1 and C3 can be reduced. Under Ranked selection, C1 will be ranked first, C2 second and C3 third. This makes C1 three times as likely as C3 to be selected.

These are not the only selection criteria used in GAs, but they are the ones that closely relate to the work presented in this paper.

3.2 Hybrid Algorithms

A hybrid algorithm combines the best features of two or more algorithms in hopes of producing an even better algorithm. This approach is particularly useful when the individual algorithms have very unique features that can not be easily represented in the new approach or will weaken the performance of the new algorithm if changed. What happens then is that such unique features are preserved and combined with other new features to produce a new algorithm. Hybrid GAs preserve the best features of an existing technique and tailor the GA methodology to take advantage of these features. The combinatorial problem of graph coloring is an example of how a GA can be combined with greedy algorithms to produce a better performing algorithm [13], [14].

4 Our Algorithm - (Hybrid-GA)

Our algorithm is a hybrid one that combines the ideas of statistical sampling and genetic algorithms. If a query is over a target relation R with 10000 tuples, the chromosomes may be constructed by placing tuples 1 to 1000 of R in C_1, tuples 1001 to 2000 in C_2, etc. The chromosomes do not have to be of equal sizes. If the target relation is distributed over several nodes, it may be too costly to access the tuple members of a chromosome if they are split into multiple nodes, so this should be avoided if possible. The structure of a chromosome consists of:

- The tuples in the chromosome. If these tuples lie contiguously in memory, all we represent is the starting address and the number of tuples. When they are not contiguous, we represent the starting address of each group and how many tuples in each group.
- The number of samples drawn from the chromosome.
- The number of events (matches) made in the chromosome.
- The fitness value of the chromosome which is the number of events in the chromosome over the number of samples drawn from the chromosome.

Initially, all chromosomes are sampled and their fitness values evaluated. Those chromosomes that are better fit i.e. contain more of the query result get placed in an active population while those less fit are placed in an inactive population. As chromosomes in the active population are sampled from, their fitness values are re-evaluated. A chromosome is demoted to the inactive population if its fitness value is not high enough. The better performing chromosomes from the inactive population replace chromosomes demoted from the active population. This process is repeated until the constraints are reached. The net effect is that sampling is concentrated on the better performing chromosomes which increases the likelihood of obtaining most of the query results in a lesser amount of time or record accesses.

In a DBMS segmentation may already exist such as in partitioned or distributed databases. Even if segmentation does not already exist, or is not in the desired form, it can be induced. For example in a database of bank accounts, if one is interested in the daily balances, s/he may use each bank location as a chromosome. Also our algorithm yields information about each segment (chromosome), which may be useful.

The algorithm can be summarized as follows.

1. Initialization
   (a) Let $S = \emptyset$
   /* S is the accumulated query result so far */
   (b) Let $R =$ The target relation
   /* R is the relation from which the query results are obtained */
   (c) Divide R into k segments (chromosomes)
   /* C_1, C_2, ..., C_k. Not necessary equal segments */
   (d) Let $P = \{C_1, C_2, \ldots, C_k\}$
   /* P is the population of all chromosomes */
   (e) Let $P_{lf} = \emptyset$
   /* P_{lf} is the population of less fit (those possessing less of the query result) chromosomes. P_{lf} is empty because at the beginning, no chromosome is less fit yet */

(f) Let $P_{bf} = P$
/* P_{bf} is the set of better fit chromosomes. $P_{bf} = P$ because every chromosome is better fit at the beginning */
(g) for $i = 1$ to $|P|$ { $S_i = \emptyset$ }
/* S_i is the accumulated query result from C_i */

2. Sample each chromosome in P_{bf}, and use the proportion $numberOfEventsInC_i/numberOfSamplesFromC_i$ as the fitness value of C_i.
   (a) sample each better fit chromosome
       for $i = 1$ to $|P_{bf}|$ {
         $S_i = S_i + \{$the query result tuples present in the latest sample from C_i of $P_{bf}\}$
         Re-compute the fitness value of C_i
       }
   (b) Tag all sampled tuples from P_{bf} so no tuple is sampled more than once.
   (c) Let $S = S \bigcup_{i=1}^{k} S_i$
       /* i.e. accumulate query result in one set */
3. Generate new population of lesss fit and better fit chromosomes.
   (a) Let P_{lf} = All currently less fit chromosomes in P. This may be defined as those chromosomes that rank in the bottom half of the fitness values.
   (b) Let $P_{bf} = P - P_{lf}$
       /* i.e. chromosomes with fitness values ranked in the top half */
4. If not done, go to Step 2
   /* A condition for not done may be when the requested number of tuples has not been matched or time has not expired */
5. S is the final accumulated query result

4.1 Experimental Results of Hybrid-GA

This section presents the experimental results of the performance of our algorithm. Each experiment is summarized as follows:

1. $nTuples = 5000$
2. $tuple_i = i$ with $1 \leq i \leq nTuples$
   /* i.e the relation has only one attribute and i is the value of that attribute for $tuple_i$ */
3. for $k = 1$ to $nTuples$ {
   /* randomly scramble the tuples */
   - Generate two random numbers i and j
   - swap($tuple_i$,$tuple_j$) in R

   }
4. Assuming the query selectivity is x%,
   - Generate a random numbers r_1 such that $(1 - r_1/nTuples) \geq x$.
     /* i.e. we want to make sure that at least x% of the tuples have values of r_1 or higher. */

- Let $r_2 = r_1 + (x/100 * nTuples) - 1$
  Note that $(r_2 - r_1 + 1)$ is the result of the query $COUNT_{r_1 \leq tupleValue \leq r_2}(R)$ and $(r_2 - r_1 + 1)/nTuples$ is the query selectivity. We experimented with different selectivities and the results are presented later. */

5. Compute the sample size n, number of chromosomes k, and reduction factor f. f is how much of the sample size spent at each stage. One approach is to do less sampling at the early stages, and increase the sub-sample size at the later stages when the lesser fit chromosomes have been weeded out. If a time constraint is given as opposed to a sample size, we estimate the sample size possible with the given time.
6. Run all the algorithms Hybrid-GA, Sampling, and Brute Force with the above values and the query $COUNT_{r_1 \leq tupleValue \leq r_2}(R)$. By replacing COUNT with $SELECT$, one will get the set of tuples with values in the range r_1 to r_2. This does not change the performance of the algorithm.

The experiment was repeated with varying parameters - $nTuples$, r_1, r_2, n, k, and f. In Brute Force, the sample was chosen as the first n tuples in the target relation. For Sampling, the samples used were obtained using the Simple Random Sampling technique outlined in the previous section on sampling. The performance of each algorithm was based on how much of the query result was found in the tuples that were compared while using that algorithm. The bigger the size of the result obtained, the better the algorithm.

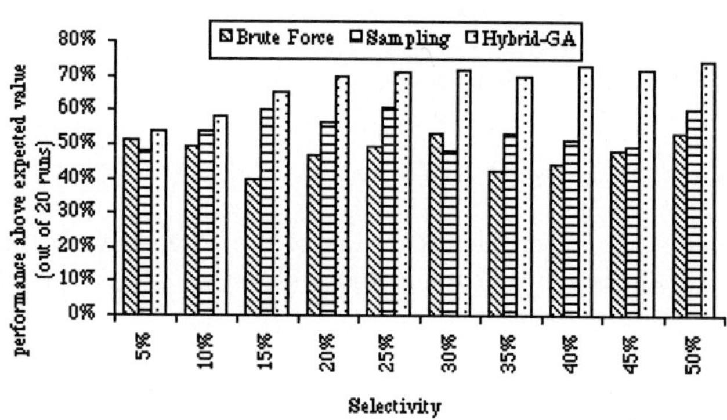

Fig. 1. Hybrid-GA, Brute Force and Sampling with different selectivities

Figure 1 shows the performance of our algorithm for some of the experiments. The y-axis represents the number of times (in percentage) that each of the algorithms yielded a query result that contained more tuples than were expected. We used a target relation with 50000 tuples, 20 chromosomes of 2500 tuples each, and 5% Sample size. In a population of 50000 tuples with uniformly distributed tuple values in the range 1 to 50000, if $r_1 = 1000$ and $r_2 = 5999$, the actual value expected in the query $COUNT_{r_1 \leq tupleValue \leq r_2}(R)$ is 5000 tuples i.e. 5000 tuples will be in the range 1000 to 5999 in the relation. So in a sample of 5%, 5000 * 5% which is 250 is the expected count for that sample. To be thorough, each point on the y axis is the percentage out of 20 runs. The x-axis represents the selectivity of the query. The figure compares our algorithm Hybrid-GA to the others. And it shows that Hybrid-GA yielded a larger query result than the others especially as the query selectivity increases. For example, the bars above a selectivity of 5% show that Brute Force was above the expected value about 50% of the time, Sampling was a little less than 50%, and Hybrid-GA was above the expected value about 55% of the time.

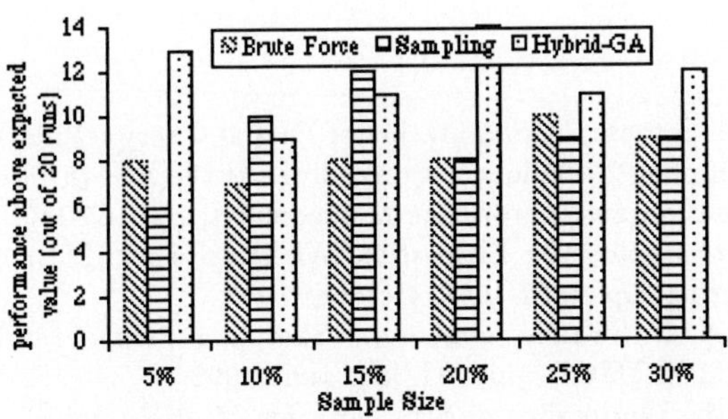

Fig. 2. Hybrid-GA, Brute Force and Sampling with different sample sizes

In figure 2, we compare the behavior of our algorithm and the two others with a relation of size 20000, selectivity of 10% and varying sample. The y-axis of figure 2 represents the number of times each algorithm yielded a result with more tuples than expected out of 20 runs. Each run uses the same relation size, selectivity and sample size, but a different randomly scrambled tuples in the target relation. The expected number of tuples is computed as illustrated in the explanation for figure 1. The bars above a sample size of 5% show that Brute Force was above the expected value 8 times, Sampling 6 times and Hybrid-GA 13 times.

5 Conclusion and Future Work

In this paper, we described different techniques for computing constrained queries. We also presented our own algorithm Hybrid-GA that is a combination of genetic algorithms and statistical sampling. The expected performance of our algorithm was shown to be better than the conventional ones, namely, Simple Random Sampling and Brute Force or Linear Search. Our algorithm requires a little bit more space than the others do because it has to keep track of the parameters of each chromosome. When the time requirements are compared, our algorithm takes about the same time as the others. Most of the time is spent accessing tuples, and the three algorithms access the same amount of tuples.

Currently, we are incorporating Hybrid-GA with the World Wide Web search engines. In future, we plan on applying it to scientific or realtime database systems. For WWW searches on keys without indexes, the pages or addresses to search will serve as the population. They may be segmented based on host locations or alphabetical order to form the chromosomes. The better fit chromosomes could be identified and more processing will concentrate in the area where they most occur. This should help in reducing the query response time, and in generating more matching links in a smaller time frame. The user will have the option of indicating a time limit or sample size with the query and the result is computed within those constraints.

References

1. A. C. Ikeji, and F. Fotouhi, "Computation of Partial Query results With An Adaptive Stratified Sampling Technique", Proceedings of the Fourth International Conference on Information and Knowledge Management, pp. 145-149, 1995
2. N. C. Rowe, "Antisampling for Estimation: An Over-view", IEEE transactions on Software Engineering, pp. 1081-1091, October 1985
3. P. J. Haas, and A. N. Swami, "Sequential Sampling Procedures For Query Size Estimation", ACM SIGMOD, pp. 341-350, June 1992
4. Y. C. Tay, "On the Optimality of Strategies for Multiple Joins", Journal of the ACM, 40, 5, pp. 1067-1086, November 1993
5. E. Ramez, and S. B. Navathe, "Fundamentals of Database Systems", The Benjamin/Cummings Publishing Company, Inc., Redwood City, California, 1989
6. R. Lipton, J. Naughton, and D. Schneider, "Practical Selectivity Estimation through Adaptive Sampling", Proceedings of the ACM SIGMOD, pp. 1-11, 1990
7. G. T. Henry, "Practical Sampling", SAGE Publications, Inc., Newbury Park, California, 1990
8. F. Olken, and D. Rotem, "Random Sampling from B+ trees", Proceedings of the 5th International Conference on VLDB, pp. 269-278, August 1989
9. Y. Ling, and W. Sun, "A supplement to Sampling-Based Methods for Query Size Estimation in Database System", Proceedings of the ACM SIGMOD, pp. 12-15, 1992
10. L. D. Whitley, "Foundations of Genetic Algorithms 2", Morgan Kaufman Publishers, California, 1993
11. P.G. Selfridge, D. Srivastava, and L.O. Wilson, "Interactive Data Exploration And Analysis", Proceeding of SIGMOD-96, ACM Press, New York, pp. 24-34, Montreal, June 1996.
12. M. Schwartz, "Theory of Statistics", Springer-Verlag, New York, 1995.
13. L. Davis, "Handbook of Genetic Algorithms", Van Nostrand Reinhold, New York, 1991
14. D. Goldberg, "Genetic Algorithms in Search, Optimization, and Machine Learning", Addison-Wesley Publishing Company, Inc., Massachusetts, 1989
15. A. J. Wilburn, "Practical Statistical Sampling for Auditors", Marcel Dekker, Inc., New York, 1984

Highlights of the SAMMOA Framework for Object Oriented Application Modelling

Wolfgang Hesse[1] and Heinrich C. Mayr[2]

[1] Univ. of Marburg, Dept. of Informatics,
Hans Meerwein-Str., D-35032 Marburg
hesse@informatik.uni-marburg.de

[2] Univ. of Klagenfurt, Inst. for Business Informatics and Information Systems,
Universitätsstr., A-9022 Klagenfurt
mayr@ifi.uni-klu.ac.at

Abstract There is a variety of modelling methods and tools for software (application) system development. Nevertheless, the field still lacks a set of well-defined, commonly understood and solidly anchored basic concepts which can be used as a uniform referential framework to build upon more specialised and sophisticated models and systems. This paper is intended to put into discussion the kernel of such a conceptual framework which comprises elements of static modelling as well as elements of dynamic modelling. In order to meet formal requirements such as systematics, consistency, orthogonality and disambiguity as well as requirements of practitioners like readability, transparency and applicability, a (semi-formal) meta-model approach has been chosen for presenting the framework.

1 Introduction: Goals, requirements, notations

Methods and tools for object oriented design (e.g., [1,2,3,4,5,6]) have passed their adolescence stage and are increasingly employed by professional producers of software (application) systems (SAS). A closer look at these methods, however, brings out some considerable weaknesses and problems which still are unsolved. E.g.,

- there is no clear and uniform philosophical basis (and no appropriate terminology) that might be referred to for answering open questions. Think, for example, about the relation of perceived things (to be modelled) and mentally constructed things (used for modelling). Most methodologies just start with the latter, leave their relation to the "real world" open or treat it in a very "intuitive", i.e. vague and unspecified way. I.e., there is a "philosophical gap".
- there is no common, unambiguous naming and understanding of fundamental concepts like *type, feature, class, component, method, operation, state, event etc.* - not to speak about the buzzword *object* itself. Numerous object oriented methodologies seem to compete with each other giving such concepts new names,

meanings or both. Thus, dubious or even contradictory definitions and explanations may be found. I.e., we live in an "Object-Babylon".

Both problems affect the stability, comparability, compatibility and practical effectiveness of methods and tools since they cause a lot of vagueness, misunderstandings, confusion, and discomfort for non-experts and, sometimes, even for experts in the field.

From a technical point of view, OO methods and tools have been surveyed and compared several times, e.g. in [6,7,8,9,10]. Terminological surveys, comparisons and proposals for conceptual frameworks or at least for a harmonised terminology, however, are much rarer. Well-known glossaries like [11] do not aim at a uniform, coherent term system and do not yet reflect the new "object oriented world". The glossary of the OMG gives a good survey and explanation of many important terms but is restricted to an alphabetical list of terms accompanied by informal explanations using natural language exclusively.

The FRISCO report [12] offers a very recent conceptual and terminological framework based on semiotics, ontology and a constructivist philosophical approach. But it is restricted to the information systems field as well and puts its focus more on the general fundaments of information system development than on detailed definitions of the kernel concepts of OO modelling. The FRISCO results had, however, a significant influence on the work presented here.

The authors of UML "Unified Modelling Language" [13,14,15] put their focus on unifying different approaches, i.e. attack the second problem mentioned before. However, UML has not yet succeeded in settling fundamental problems like clarifying the *class, type* and *object* concepts or introducing a universally acceptable abstraction mechanism for OO application models.

In this paper we present results of the work of a German/Austrian task group consisting of practitioners and scientists and aiming at a better understanding and clarification of principles and techniques in the field of OO analysis and modelling. Former publications of the group were concerned with the OO modelling of business processes [16] and the architecture of object oriented systems.

For both, a sufficiently rigid and readable presentation of our framework, we have chosen a metamodel approach. A *metamodel* is a set of interrelated modelling concepts that may be used for constructing models for certain domains (i.e. parts of the real world, often called Universes of Discourse) .

In principle, the metamodel consists of two levels:

(1) a collection of basic notions taken from every-day language which are mainly used for referring to things belonging to the domains to be modelled. Being part of every-day language, these notions cannot be defined in a formal way but are

explained via so-called "assumptions" using natural language in order to achieve a common understanding of the starting points of our approach.

(2) a set of notions given by more formal definitions which follow certain rules as e.g. excluding homonyms or circular definitions. These definitions may only build upon notions from earlier definitions or those introduced in the assumption part. Clearly, this is a semantic modelling approach.

The development of the metamodel has been guided by the following *requirements:*

- *Universality:* The metamodel has to be independent from particular application areas and be compatible with the conceptual structures and terminology of most widespread methodologies.
- *Semantic power and practicability:* The metamodel has to enable and support the modelling of practical (technical or commercial) universes of discourse according to their particular project requirements.
- *Clarity, scientific soundness and (semi-) formality:* The metamodel has to meet the needs of system developers and tool providers as well as of professionals in the application domain.

What distinguishes our approach from others known from the literature?

- We do not intend to provide a glossary of the object-oriented terminology. Instead we have tried to define a coherent and consistent system of interrelated concepts and terms for modelling static and dynamic aspects.
- Rather than introducing a new modelling or specification language we concentrate on presenting a conceptual framework in (semi-formal) textual and graphical form. Further we use an ad hoc-notation for representing some short, illustrating examples. Cross references between single definitions are facilitated by a simple, coherent numbering scheme.
- For reasons of orthogonality and clarity we propose a clear distinction between the concepts of type (object type, data type) and class. The former is used in an intensional sense, the latter in an extensional.
- The most central concepts of the approach, i.e., type and feature are interwoven by a twofold relationship that reflects the fact, that types are ‘constituted’ by some features (= attributes and operations) and that, in turn, they ‘characterize’ some other (if not recursive) features, e.g., being their definition or target domain. This leads to a rather stringent and systematic metamodel.
- The concept of cardinality, as proposed within this paper, offers (together with so-called ‘counter-cardinalities’) a rather powerful means for specifying relationships of all kinds (attributes, object references, associations, aggregations).
- Besides of abstractions (generalisation and aggregation) we propose two kind of relationships between objects: object references and association types, where the

latter again may have object references besides of the 'classical' roles. This leads to a very powerful means for application modelling.

In this presentation, we concentrate on the definition of a few, in our view fundamental concepts of the OO analysis and modelling field and their interrelationships. A more comprising and detailed version of the metamodel (in German language) is [17].

2 The kernel model: Things, types and features

In order to distinguish the two levels of our metamodel, we deliberately use different terms for ontological concepts and for modelling. Therefore, we start with some rudimentary basic assumptions and conventions on universes of discourse (as parts of real world) introducing notions like *thing, property, action*, or *association* located at what we call the ontological level. We then proceed by introducing the kernel of our metamodel in a bottom-up manner: starting with features (attributes and operations) and types, instances and classes are formed and types are classified into data and object types.

2.1 Basic assumptions: Things, properties, actions and associations

Our basic assumptions and conventions contain several distinguished notions (highlighted by italics in bold font) which are to be used in the following, more formal definitions:

(2.1.1) Some distinguished part of the real world constitutes an ***universe of discourse (UoD).***

(2.1.2) We consider an UoD being composed of a collection of (real or imagined) well-distinguished ***things***.

Examples of things are the *Town Hall of Munich;* the *number 4;* the *colour grey;* the *person called Charles Brown,* the *insurance contract identified by the number 345567 of the insurance company called XYZ* (short: *contract no. 345567*).

(2.1.3) Every thing has an ***identity*** and (usually) ***properties*** which *characterise* it.

Example: The town of Frankfurt/M is a unique thing - thus it has an identity. Some of its properties are: being situated at the Main river, having an airport, having between 500.000 and 1.000.000 inhabitants, having the name „Frankfurt“. This name is, however, not sufficient for unique identification.

Some properties of a thing may change over time (as for example, the number of inhabitants of Frankfurt), others do not (as, for example, the property of being situated at the Main river).

Things which are characterised by the same or comparable properties are said to be of the same ***kind***.

Example: The town of Munich is of the same kind as the town of Frankfurt/M. We can denote this kind by the notion *town*.

(2.1.4) Things may perform ***actions*** or be involved in ***processes***.

Examples: The client Brown moves (changes his address from Isarstraße 24 in Munich to Garden Road 28 in Manchester; the contract no. 345567 is terminated)

(2.1.5) Things can be related to each other. A relationship may be *permanen*t (unlimited in time) or *temporary* (limited in time).

Examples: The client Charles Brown *is son of* Anne Brown (permanent relationship), and *owes the bank ABC* 10.000 DM (temporary relationship).

Systems, elements and components

We introduce some notions to deal with complex things, i.e. those consisting of other things which are combined by close or multiple relationships.

(2.1.6) A collection of things which are conceived to be interrelated in such way that they form together a whole, having its own, "emergent" properties, is called a ***system.***

A system has a boundary separating it from its ***environment*** (i.e. the collection of all things not belonging to the system itself).

All parts constituting a system (in a direct or recursive way) are called its ***components***. Components which are not be considered as (sub-) systems may be called ***elements***.

2.2 Features and types

In this and the following subsections, the kernel of the SAMMOA metamodel will be established. Our goal is to define a uniform, encompassing type system covering data types as well as object types. Type definitions are based on features (= attributes and operations) the value domains of which in turn are defined by means of types. Obviously, a mutually recursive definition of features and types is required to meet this goal. As a starting point, we define domains formed by (primitive or composed) values. These are needed as value domains for the attributes to be defined next. Types are composed of attributes and can now be used to generalise the definition of attribute domains. In a next step, operations and features are introduced The feature concept generalises the attribute and operation concepts and is used for the definition of object types. All these definitions reflect an intensional view on the elements of OO application modelling. To complete this by an extensional view, the concepts of instance, object and class are introduced in the last subsection.

We have illustrated some of our definitions by a few (very common) examples. The notation used there is ad-hoc, i.e. we do *not* intend to introduce a new notation. Our focus stays on the metamodel.

Figures 1 and 2 show (in a self-explanatory fashion) a graphical representation of the kernel of our metamodel.

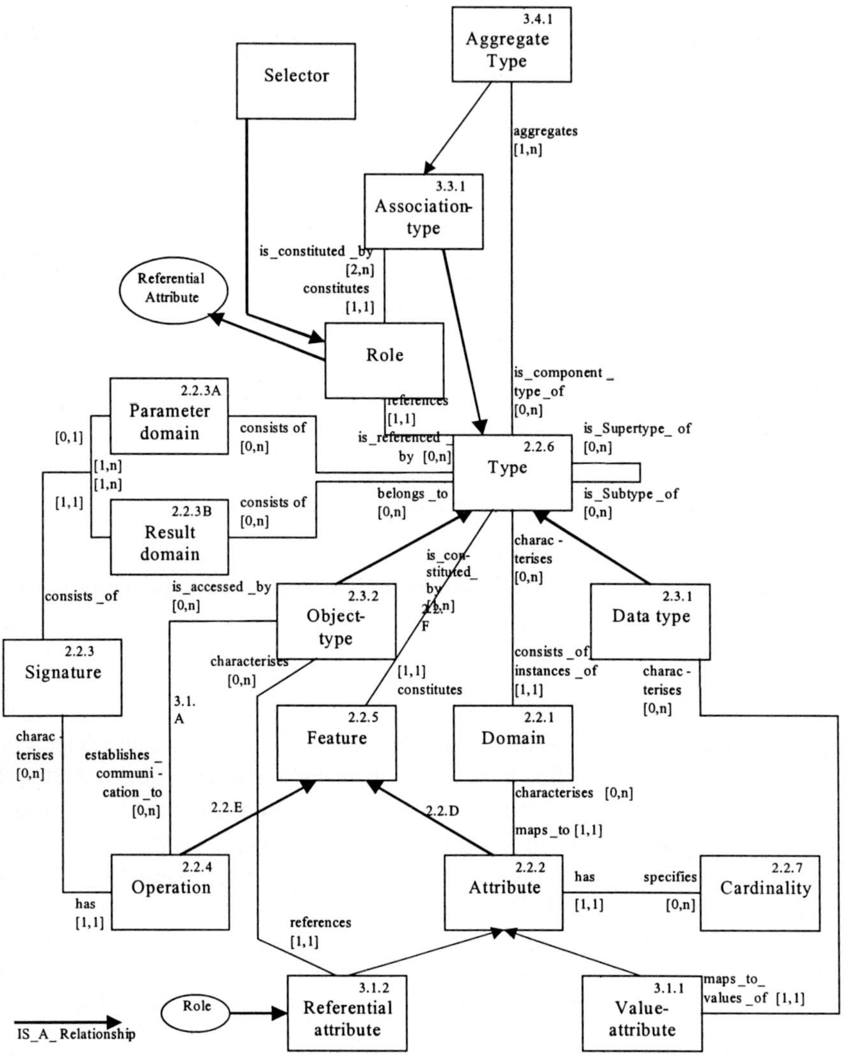

Figure 1 Graphical representation of the SAMMOA concepts for modelling static UOD aspects.

Domains and attributes

(2.2.1) ***Domain:*** A (finite or infinite) set of primitive or composed ***values*** which are used to describe properties of things. Values may be composed of (primitive or other composed) values.

The metamodel notion *attribute* is used to express properties of things which may change in time.

(2.2.2) ***Attribute:*** A function mapping time to a domain. Its values are called ***attribute values***. The domain is said to ***characterise*** the attribute. Each attribute is identified by a ***attribute designator.***

Example: The property of some city to have 98.340 inhabitants on Jan 1st, 1998 is modelled by associating an instance of the *attribute No_of_inhabitants: Time → Integer* with that city, that maps the (example) value '1.1.1998' to 98340:
No_of_inhabitants(1.1.1998) = 98340.

No_of_inhabitants is *characterised* by its domain *Integer.*

For reasons of practicability we will use, in what follows, the terms attribute and attribute instance synonymously as long as the concrete meaning becomes clear from the context.

Signatures, parameters and operations

In our ontology, we can observe things having passive and active properties. The first relate to the *state* of a thing, the latter make up its *behaviour*. In the metamodel, state is represented by attributes, whereas behaviour is represented by operations to be defined next.

Operations are used to model actions which a thing can perform to alter its own properties or those of other things. Each operation is defined by one or several *routines* (i.e. functions). If we look in an analogous way to operations as we did to attributes, routines can be considered the values of operations. The domain of a routine is just the interface part of an operation definition consisting of the list of its parameter and result domains (its *signature*) .

(2.2.3) ***Signature:*** A pair of two (possibly empty) domain specifications to be used for describing the functionality of an operation. Each domain specification consists of one or several domain or type designators **(2.2.A).** The first is called the ***Parameter domain*** and the second the ***Result domain***. **(2.2.B).**

(2.2.4) ***Operation*:** Operations are used to represent active properties of things, i.e. actions to be performed on or performed by them. An operation is defined by its (unique) signature and by one or several routines (strings of text describing the action in detail). A signature *characterises* one or several operations **(2.2.C)**. In case that there are several (alternative) routines, one has to be selected depending on the context. In this case, the operation is called *polymorphic*.

Features and types

Having defined both operations and attributes for modelling active and resp. passive properties of things we can now generalise these to form the *feature* concept, based on which the type concept is defined.

(2.2.5) ***Feature:*** A feature is either an attribute **(2.2.D)** or an operation **(2.2.E)**. A feature is identified by a ***feature designator***. It is either characterised by a type designator or by a signature.

(2.2.6) ***Type:*** A collection of *features* which is used for describing a particular kind of things. The features concerned are said to ***constitute*** the type **(2.2.F)**. A type is identified by a ***type designator***.

Example: **type** Client = Name: String,
First_name: String,
Date_of_birth: Date, ...;
Change_credit_limit: Client x Credit_limit --> Client.
endtype

In this definition *Client* is a type *constituted* by several features. The attribute *Name* is *characterised by* its domain *String* which refers to its possible values. A possible value of the operation *change_credit_limit* is a routine which takes two instances of the types *Client* and *Credit_limit* as input and yields an instance of the type *Client* as result.

Note that in our example notation attributes are merely specified by their characterising type (omitting the stereotype *Time* → part of their definition). For the definition of operations and routines several methods and notations are used as, for example, the axiomatic, algebraic or algorithmic specification. These are, however, beyond the scope of this article.

We use the usual dot notation to denote the selection of attributes from types, e.g., *Client.First_name*

Cardinalities

(2.2.7) ***Cardinality:*** Attributes are characterised not only by their domain but also by their *cardinality*. The cardinality indicates the minimal and maximal number of possible values. *Counter-cardinalities* indicate the minimal/maximal number a domain value might be referred to by an attribute.

We denote a cardinality by [min, max], i.e.

A [m,n]: [k,l] d

means: At the same time, the attribute A may have at least m and not more than n instances of domain d, m <= n. A value of domain d may be, at the same time, value of at least k and at most l attribute instances).

Example: *Insurance_contract.start_date [1,1]:[0,n]Date.* The attribute *start_date* has exactly one value (of the type *Date*), an element of date may be value of 0 or any *start_date* instances.

Several attributes may be characterised by the same type and thus get values of the same sets of instances.

2.3 Data types and object types

The type concept comprises the full power of conventional and of so called "abstract" data types as they are normally used in an OO environment. For convenience (and for further use in section 3) we distinguish two kinds of types:

(2.3.1) ***Data type:*** A type constituted only by constant features (operations and/or constant attributes).

(2.3.2) ***Object type:*** A type constituted by features, from which at least one may change its value(s) over time

Examples:

- The type *Natural* of natural numbers is constituted by the features *0, succ, +,* where *0* is a 0-ary, *succ* a unary and + is a binary function. It is a data type, since all its features are constant.
- The type *Client* describing a sort of persons is constituted by the features *Name, First Name,* .. etc. It is an object type, since there are features as e.g. *Client_no* which may change in time.

type Client =
Name: String,
First_name: String,
Date_of_birth: Date,
Client_no: Natural,
Change_address:(Client x Addr) → Client; ....;

Standard data types (as e.g. *String* or *Integer*) may be considered to be pre-defined and imported from another model (component), e.g. for introducing domains and their values. This way, the domain concept can be subsumed under the type concept - domains just being represented by standard data types.

On the twofold relationship between types and features

As was pointed out in section 2.2, types and features (= attributes and operations) are interwoven by a twofold relationship. In the SAMMOA metamodel we explicitly distinguish the "constitutes" and "characterises" relationships: Each type is *constituted by* features (attributes and operations) but each attribute and each operation parameter or result are *characterised by* a type. This distinction reflects the fact that a type designator may occur in either context: (a) defining a new type (by *constituting* it through features), (b) referring to a (known) type definition when an attribute, operation parameter or result is *characterised* (cf. also the example below).

In the above examples, *Client* is a type *constituted* by several features. The feature *Name* is *characterised by* the type designator *String* which refers to the domain of its possible values. *Client* is an object type which may be used for characterising a feature *Account_owner: Client* in an object type *Account.*

2.4 Instances and classes

The above definition of "type" is an intensional one. In contrast to that, an extensional definition would consider a type as a set of things, called "instances". Each instance represents a thing of the real world. Since we want to make a terminological difference between these two points of view, we will use the terms *type* (with an intensional meaning) and *class* (with an extensional meaning) in the sequel.

Instances

The identity of things (cf. 2.1.3) is modelled assuming a global mechanism which assigns to each instance a unique *identifier* (i.e. some sort of global token which may be assumed to be taken from a particular domain of identifiers.

(2.4.1) ***Instance identifier:*** A token which is used for uniquely representing a thing in an application system.

Example: The client Brown is identified by a token id_{Brown}. This should not be confused with a feature *client_no* (see last section) which is meant to be an application specific identifier (“key”) for clients.

Remark: The identifiers introduced here are normally not visible for the users. In database implementations they correspond to (internally administered) *tuple identifiers* or *object identifiers.*

(2.4.2) ***Instance of type T:*** A pair consisting of an instance identifier and the collection of feature instances of T.

Note that in contrast to "thing" (part of the real world) "instance" is introduced as part of the model world. It can be imagined as some sort of ‘container’ (similar to a ‘frame’ in AI approaches) for possible values of its features that may be determined at any point in time. An instance of a data type is by definition constant, thus it can be identified through its value and does not need a particular instance identifier.

Example: *(idBrown· , (Name: String,*
First_name: String,
Date_of_birth: Date,
Client_no: Natural,
Change_address:(Client x Addr) → Client; ...));

is an instance of the object type *Client.*

(2.4.3) ***Valued feature:*** A feature together with an instance of its characterising type. The instance is associated to it at a certain point of time.

Note that there are constant features (e.g. operations) having the same value at all points of time (following their initialisation)

Examples: *First_name: String → Brown* and

Client_no: Natural→123456

are valued features of type *Client.*

(2.4.4) ***Valued instance of type T:*** A pair consisting of an instance identifier and the collection of valued features of T.

Example: *(idBrown· , (Name: String→ 'Brown',*
First_name: String → 'John',
Date_of_birth: Date→ '3.12.45',
Client_no: Natural, → 123456,
Change_address:(Client x Addr) → Client; ...));

is an valued instance of type *Client* representing its state at a certain point of time.

Objects and classes

As we have seen, instances of data types and object types can be subsumed under a common instance concept. However, they behave differently which justifies the following terminological distinction: Instances of data types are called ***values,*** instances of object types are called ***objects***.

The set of all instances of a data type (values) had already called its ***domain*** (cf. 2.2.1).

(2.4.5) ***Object:*** Instance of an object type

Of course, we can also speak of *valued objects* using definition 2.4.4.

Classes are used to model sets of somehow related things (e.g. things of the same kind) which are to be treated jointly for certain application purposes.

(2.4.6) ***Class:*** A set of instances of one or several types.

Examples: All clients of the company ABC; all contracts of the insurance company XYZ which have been signed prior than 1.1.1993.

Note that this definition differs from the "class" notion in many methodologies where it is an intensional concept, i.e. corresponds much more to our "type" concept. We have chosen the extensional meaning for its close relation to mathematics and data base theory.

Further note that this is a rather liberal definition. Normally, all instances of a class have the same type.

3 Relationships

In this section, we will consider several kinds of relationships between types (and their instances). These are: referential attributes and operations, generalisation/specialisation types, association types, aggregation types and clusters.

3.1 Referential features

Starting with one given type T, a relationship to one or several other types T' may be modelled in two ways: by specifying an attribute characterised by T' or by an operation having T' in its signature.

Referential attributes

We distinguish two cases depending on the kind of the type T characterising an attribute A:

(1) T is a data type, i.e., A (and thus instances of its constituting type) is associated with values of the domain of T.

(2) T is an object type, A (and thus instances of its constituting type) is associated with values (objects) of type T and thus *refers to* instances of T.

For terminological distinction, we call attributes of the first kind *value attributes*, and those of the second kind *referential attributes*. Referential attributes serve for establishing simple (often static or persistent) relationships between objects. If a relationship is to be established between object types A and B, this can be done by a referential attribute of A referring t B or vice versa.

(3.1.1) ***Value attribute:*** Attribute characterised by a data type. Its values are instances of that type.

(3.1.2) ***Referential attribute:*** Attribute characterised by an object type. Its values are references to instances (objects) of that type.

Examples: *Person.Age [1,1]: Natural*

Account.Owner [1,n]: Client

Person.Spouse [0,1]: Person

An object type may also contain *recursive attributes.* A recursive attribute is characterised by the same type of which it is a constituting feature.

Example: ***type*** *Employee = Name: string, ..., Boss: Employee;*

References through operations

Another possibility to build relationships between types is by means of operations. An operation may be used to establish a ***communication relationship*** between instances of the concerned types **(3.1.A)**.

Example: The object type *Client* has a communication relationship to the object type *Teller_machine* through its operation *Draw_mane.* which embodies a call of an operation *Accept_card* of *Teller_machine..*

An object may establish a communication to objects of various object types. On the other hand, objects of a given type may be accessed by various operations (of any type).

3.2 Generalisation and specialisation

In order to facilitate a finer characterisation of values and objects types are admitted to have a subtype/supertype relationship to each other. Type A is said to be a supertype of type B (B is subtype of A), iff each instance of type B is also instance of type A. If B_1, .., B_n are subtypes of A, we could also say: "B_1, .., B_n *are generalised to* A" or "A *is specialised to* B_1, .., B_n".

As a consequence of this, an object is no longer characterised by exclusively one type but (possibly) by several ones. This implies to view one particular object under various aspects - expressed by different types.

For example, one particular person may be viewed as employee, as patient, as tax payer, as car license holder etc. and be characterised by corresponding types. By the way, we see no necessity to distinguish between "abstract" and "concrete" types. In principle, each type may have instances.

By the subtype-/supertype relationship, a hierarchy of types is established. If to each subtype there exists at most one supertype, we have a tree-like hierarchy, otherwise its structure corresponds to a directed acyclic graph.

Subtype relationships may be further characterised by the following properties:

Disjointness: If a supertype has several subtypes, each instance of the supertype may be an instance of at most one of its subtypes - i.e. the subtypes are disjoint.

Coverage: Each instance of the supertype is at the same time also an instance of at least one of its subtypes, i.e. all the subtypes together cover the supertype.

Subtype/supertype relationships may come along with inheritance mechanisms but this is not mandatory. In practice, however, both mechanisms are often interlinked. If there is an inheritance relationship between a supertype and a subtype, each feature of the supertype is automatically also a feature of the subtype.

Data types my be specialised to object types - but not vice versa.

3.3 Associations and roles

As we have outlined in section 3.1, relationship between objects may be established either by referential attributes (cf. 3.1.D) or by means of operations and inter-object communication (cf 3.1.E). In both cases the relationship is implicit, i.e. it is not considered an object itself. Sometimes this is, however, intended by the analyst, e.g. for ternary (or more complex) relationships. Then, a special kind of type is needed which we call *association type*, its instances being called *associations.*

As is true for other types, association types are characterised by features. Among the features of an association type are:

- at least two referential attributes, the so-called *roles* which establish the references to the corresponding object types involving certain cardinalities (note that the constraint to have at least two roles will be released later on for aggregations, cf. section 3.4),
- possibly further attributes and operations (the so-called *emergent features*).

(3.3.1) ***Association type***: Object type which is constituted by at least two referential attributes - called ***roles*** - and a possible empty set of (further) features. Instances of association types are called ***Associations***.

Associations are objects, i.e., they are uniquely accessed by an object identifier.

Notation: Roles are denoted by the symbol '>'. Thus an n-ary association Z which links the object types T_1, .., T_n through the roles R_1, .., R_n having the cardinalities W_1, .., W_n is denoted as follows:

type Z =

> S_1 W_1: T_1,
...,
> S_n W_n: T_n
.... *{further features}*;

Remark: The cardinalities W_i indicate the minimal and maximal number of objects of type T_i participating at an Z-association. This implies the case that each object of type T_i may occur in arbitrarily many instances of the association type.

Example: The association type *purchase* is constituted by the roles *Buyer* and *Good* which establish an association between the object types *Customer* and *Product.* Further features of the association type are the attributes *Price* and *Quantity.* In this association, *Customer* plays the role of *Buyer* and *Product* plays the role of *Goods.*

type *Purchase* =
> Buyer [1,1]: Customer,
> Good [1,1]: Product,
Price [1,1]: Integer,
Quantity [1,1]: Integer;

Note that a maximum cardinality greater than 1 leads to a grouping of referenced objects.

If an object is restricted to occur in a limited number of association instances, this can be specified by an additional cardinality - the so called ***counter- cardinality***:

type Z =

> A_1 W_1 : W_1' T_1,
...,
> A_n W_n : W_n' T_n
.... *{further features}*;

Example: ***type*** *Project_work* =
> Team_member [1,1] : [0,n] Person,
> Work_subject [1,1] : [1,n] Project;

For reasons of simplicity (especially in the case of binary association types), we can omit

- the identifiers A_1 and A_2, if not required,
- the cardinalities W_1 and W_2 if they are [1,1]
- the counter-cardinalities W_1' and W_2' if they are [0,n].

Remarks:

- If a role has the minimal cardinality 0, it is called *optional*. This means it may have no reference object for a certain time since this, for example, is not (yet) determined or not (yet) known.
- It should be clear by now, that this kind of cardinality definition is more powerful than what is usually found in literature. Clearly we could allow free set definitions instead of intervals (as is proposed, e.g., in UML). For reasons of readability, however, we refrained from that for the scope of this paper.

3.4 Aggregation

A specific kind of association is the *aggregation*. Whereas an association allows to establish a relationship between several things, an aggregation is meant to combine several instances (of possibly different types) to more complex objects - the so-called *aggregates*.

(3.4.1) ***Aggregate type***: A type defined by aggregating types $B_1,..., B_n$ (n >= 1, see 3.3). The types $B_1,..,B_n$ are called *Component types of the Aggregate type* A.

A type may be component type of several aggregate types. An instance of a component type occurring in an aggregate is called *component* of that aggregate. A component type may be instantiated by no, one or several instances. In the latter case we call it a *grouping*. If there is at least one object component type in an aggregate type, the whole aggregate type is an object type (no data type).

Aggregates are objects which are composed of other objects (the components). Like other objects they are addressed by identifiers. Components are addressable themselves (e.g. by their own identifier). By considering an aggregation as a specific kind of association, we gain the possibility to address single components of an aggregate using the (identifiers of the) roles of an association. These role identifiers are called ***selectors***. Shortly, selectors are used to address components via the aggregate.

Notation: In order to contrast the particular properties of an aggregation with those of associations we denote the links of an aggregate type to its components by ">>":

type *A* =

$>> S_1\ W_1 : W_1'\ T_1,$

...,

$>> S_n\ W_n : W_n'\ T_n,$

...

$> S_r\ W_r : W_r'\ T_n$ *{further associations}*;

...

m: T ... {further features};

Cardinalities are defined as in association types. Usually, selectors have the counter-cardinality [0,1], i.e. an instance of a component type is a component of no or exactly one aggregate. In this case, the counter-cardinality may be omitted.

Example: The object type *Truck* is defined by aggregating the types *lorry* and *trailer*.

> ***type*** *Lorry_train =*
>
> > *>> Lorry [1,1]: Tractor,*
> > *>> Trailer [0,10]: Non_tractor,*
> > *License [1,1]: Vehicle_Id;*

In the other case, i.e. if a component is admitted to be member of several aggregates, this has to be specified by counter-cardinalities.

Example: The type *Hexagon* is defined by group (exactly six instances) of the type *Point*.

> ***type*** *Hexagon = >> Vertex [6,6] : [0,n] Point;*

Aggregation types may be used to model complex things in a more "natural", problem-oriented form. If a thing is modelled as an aggregate, this has several consequences:

- Aggregates are objects themselves. The existence of the components is not necessarily bound to the existence of the aggregate. This means: Components of a no longer present (e.g. deleted) aggregate may "survive" - they do not necessarily "die" with the aggregate.
- Components are objects themselves - which implies to be addressable from outside. Additionally, they may be accessed by a two-level (or n-level in case of a more complex aggregation) identifier including the selector. If *Id* is the identifier of an aggregate and S_i is its i-th selector, $Id.S_i$ is a complete identifier of the i-th component(s) of the aggregate.
- The rules given above represent a relatively "liberal" kind of aggregation. We call it "weak aggregation". There are, however, also stronger kinds of aggregation requiring, for example, that each component must not belong to more than one aggregate.

Further examples:

- The object type *School_class* is defined by aggregating (more exactly: grouping) the type *Pupil* with a cardinality of, say, *[3,28]:*

  type *School_class = >> Class_members [3,28]: Pupil;*

- The object type *Department* is defined by aggregating (more exactly: grouping) the type *Employee* with several selectors:

- ***type*** *Department* =

  >> Dept_Director [1,1]: Employee,
  >> Dept_Secretary [0,1]: Employee,
  >> Dept_Member [2,n]: Employee,
  Dept_Name [1,1]: String;

4 Elements for modelling system dynamics

In the previous sections we have presented concepts for modelling the static aspects of a universe of discourse. Our metamodel comprises concepts for modelling *dynamic UoD aspects (system dynamics)* as well. However, it would go beyond the scope of this paper to introduce them in the same detail as before. We therefore restrict ourselves, in order to give some impression, to name these concepts, namely ***message***, ***event***, ***communication potential***, ***state***, ***state transition*** and ***state model***, and to show their integration into the metamodel in figure 1. A detailed study of that part of the metamodel that also includes concepts for modelling business processes is devoted to another paper.

The most important notions and their effect on the corresponding object types are:

Dynamic model element	**means for the correponding object type:**
State	Behaviour potential
State transition	Behaviour change potential
Message	Communication potential
Event	Reaction potential

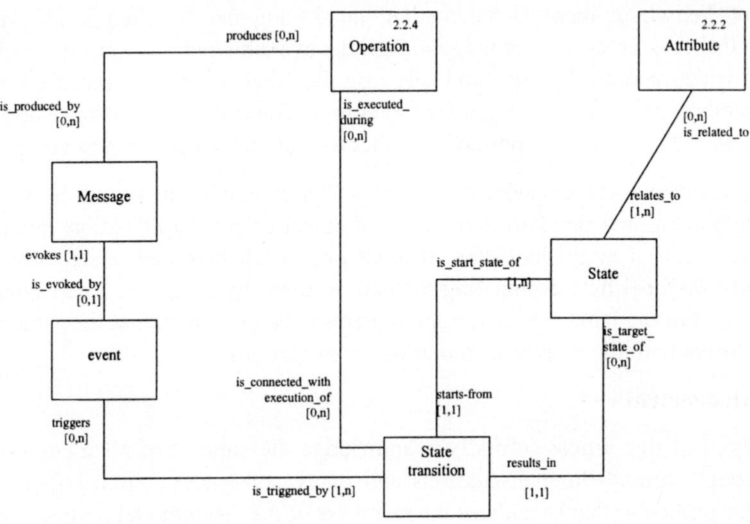

Figure 2 Graphical representation of the SAMMOA concepts for modelling dynamic UoD aspects

5 Conclusions and summary

In the preceding sections, we have presented a collection of concepts in the area of object oriented application modelling and explained them in the context of a coherent metamodel. The focus of our work is more on the coherent and consistent definition of some kernel concepts than on a cataloguing or even compete presentation.

Particular attention has been paid to the innermost kernel consisting of the concepts type and feature and their mutual dependency through characterisation and characterisability (section 2.1). Further we have put emphasis on a modular structure of the metamodel in order to facilitate possible extensions, for example for defining further type constructors, extended cardinalities or introducing business processes as metamodel elements without any extra effort.

With our metamodel we have deliberately not followed one particular method but concentrated on those general concepts which we believe are in the kernel of most existing methods. In this point we deviate from must current parallel approaches. The most well-known of these is the method underlying the "Unified Modelling Language" UML. As far as we can judge it from the available publications, it is richer and covers a wider area on the one hand side - on the other it is concentrated on one particular method and does not try a terminological foundation as we have tried. This way, we would rate the two approaches rather as complementary than as competing.

At the moment, we still consider it an open question whether there will be a terminological and notational standard in the field of object oriented application development and, if yes, how it might look like. It is also open whether such a standard will be established *de facto* by a dominating method or rather by a method-independent standardisation. For the latter we have tried to prepare the ground and, at the same time, to be compatible with the current methodological evolution.

Acknowledgement

The authors of this article cordially acknowledge the support of all members of the "OO Group" through long discussions and many constructive contributions to that work. Our particular thanks address the members of the "metamodel review subgroup" Ruth Breu, Günther Müller-Luschnat, Thomas Naefe and Michael Rohloff.

While discussing that approach, the group met several times in the stimulating Bavarian region of Samerberg; therefore, the metamodel was called the 'SAmerberg Meta-Model for Object oriented Application modelling", SAMMOA.

References

[1] Booch, G.: *Object-Oriented Analysis and Design with Applications;* Second Edition, Benjamin/Cummings Publ. Comp. 1994.

[2] Coad, P., Yourdon, E.: *Object-oriented analysis;* 2nd ed., Yourdon Press 1990.

[3] Ferstl, O., Sinz, E.: *Objektmodellierung betrieblicher Informationssysteme im Semantischen Objektmodell (SOM);* Wirtschaftsinformatik 32.6, pp. 566 - 581, Dez. 1991.

[4] Jacobson, I.: *Object-Oriented Software Engineering - A Use Case Driven Approach,* Revised Printing, Addison- Wesley 1993.

[5] Meyer, B.: *Object-oriented software construction;* Prentice Hall 1988.

[6] Rumbaugh, J., Blaha, M., Premerlani, W., Eddy, F., Lorensen, W.: *Object-Oriented Modelling and Design;* Prentice Hall 1991.

[7] Kaschek, R., Mayr, H.C.: *A Characterization of OOA-Tools*; In: O. Frieder, J. Wigglesworth (Eds.): Proceedings of the Fourth International Symposium on Assessment of Software Tools. IEEE Computer Society Press. Los Alamitos, California et al.. 1996. p.: 59-67.

[8] Martin, J., Odell, J.: *Object Oriented Methods: A Foundation*; Prentice Hall 1995.

[9] Stein,W.: *Objektorientierte Analysemethoden – Vergleich, Bewertung, Auswahl*, Wissenschaftsverlag Mannheim-Leipzig-Wien-Zürich, 1994.

[10] Fowler, M.: *A survey of object-oriented analysis and design methods*; A tutorial for ICSE 18, M.Fowler 1996, email: 00031.3311@compuserv. com,1996.

[11] *IEEE Standard Glossary of Software Engineering Terminology*, IEEE Standard 61012-1990; IEEE Society Press 1990.

[12] Falkenberg, E. et al.: *FRISCO – A framework of information system concepts*, The FRISCO Report; Draft version, Univ. of Leiden, Dec. 1996.

[13] Booch, G., Rumbaugh J.: *Unified Method for Object Oriented Development, Documentation Set;* Version 0.8, Rational Software Corp., 1995.

[14] Booch, G., Rumbaugh J., Jacobsion, I.: *The Unified Modelling Language for object-oriented development, Documentation Set;* Version 0.9 Addendum, Rational Software Corp. 1996.

[15] Rational Software Corp.: *UML-documentation*, http://www.rational.com/uml/.

[16] Müller-Luschnat, G., Hesse, W., Heydenreich, N.: *Objektorientierte Analyse und Geschäftsvorfallsmodellierung;* in: *Proc. GI-EMISA-Fachtagung „Objektorientierte Methoden für Informationssysteme";* Klagenfurt 1993.

[17] Hesse, W., Mayr, H.C., Breu, R.: *SAMMOA - Ein universelles Metamodell für die objektorientierte Anwendungsentwicklung*. Technical Report, FB Mathematik & Informatik, Univ. Marburg, 1997.

Virtual Enterprises and Federated Information Sharing

Hamideh Afsarmanesh, César Garita, L.O. Hertzberger

University of Amsterdam, Computer Science Department, Kruislaan 403, 1098 SJ Amsterdam, The Netherlands
{hamideh, cesar, bob}@wins.uva.nl

Abstract. In general, a Virtual Enterprise (VE) is an interoperable network of pre-existing enterprises with a common goal, where the enterprises can function together as a single organization. With the objective of developing a reference architecture and a support infrastructure for VEs, the Esprit project PRODNET II[1] (Production Planning and Management in an Extended Enterprise) is conceived. In the PRODNET architecture, the Distributed Information Management System (DIMS) component supports the VE information management requirements and provides a framework to exchange and cooperatively manage data between VE-member enterprises, while preserving the autonomy of individual enterprises. The DIMS design is based on an object-oriented federated/distributed information management architecture, specifically tailored for the VE paradigm. The focus of this paper is on describing the design of the federated architecture of the DIMS component.

1 Introduction

Most business enterprises nowadays find themselves in a very aggressive environment set by the global competition and fast commercialization streams. To ensure their survival under these hard conditions, enterprises must reevaluate and optimize the way they do their business and probably change or adopt new systems, tools, and methodologies in their internal information processing. Paradigms such as Virtual Enterprises (VEs) represent a promising solution for those enterprises eager to adapt to the current market trends, as well as an active area of research and technological development [3],[6],[9],[12].

In spite of the lack of a common definition in the literature, a VE can be generally defined as a network of enterprises that constitute a temporary alliance, in order to share their costs, skills, and resources, in supporting certain activities. The PRODNET II project focuses on the design and development of a VE platform to support the basic important requirements of a number of Small and Medium size Enterprises (SMEs) that may join efforts to form and function as a Virtual Enterprise.

---

[1] This research is partially supported by the ESPRIT project-22647, PRODNET II of the European Commission, http://cupido.uninova.pt/~prodnet.

The focus of this paper is basically on describing the general design and necessary architecture and support environment for efficient information sharing among VE nodes. Here, the issue of enterprise autonomy and different levels of access rights to shared data are emphasized. It is clear that the degree of trust among enterprises is limited, and that every enterprise needs to precisely define the specific information access rights and visibility levels for every other VE partner. As a result, the support for the security of shared data and provision of different access rights to shared data -based on other enterprise's role in the VE- are mandatory to be supported and reinforced.

In the remaining sections of this paper, the PRODNET II system architecture and the current design stage of its Distributed Information Management Subsystem (DIMS) are described. In particular, Section 2 characterizes the main components of the PRODNET II architecture. Section 3 describes the management of the shared information in PRODNET II, supported by the DIMS, including the distributed information analysis process and the current design of the DIMS integrated schema. Section 4 focuses on the details of the DIMS federated approach, where the import/export mechanisms and the query processing issues are addressed and properly described. Finally, Section 5 contains the major conclusions about the work presented in this paper.

2 The PRODNET II Supporting Platform for VEs

In previous publications a large number of functional and information-handling requirements for VEs support have been identified [1], [4]. From this wide range of functionalities, a selected set has been carefully specified for the design of the PRODNET II reference architecture. In the PRODNET II architecture, every enterprise in the network of potential VE-members is considered as a "node", where each node may play the role of a material supplier, a producer, or a final consumer of goods or services. Every PRODNET II node is composed of: an "Internal Module", a "PRODNET Cooperation Layer (PCL)", and an "Advanced VE Coordination" module, as depicted in Fig. 1 [2],[4].

The Internal Module (IM) of a node consists of the company's information management systems, its internal decision making processes -namely its Production Planning and Control systems (PPC), and other engineering systems necessary to accomplish its local tasks. The Internal Module is extended with a Mapping Module (MM), which supports all the interactions between the Internal Module of an enterprise and its PCL.

The PCL supports the functionalities for inter-operation between a given node and other nodes in the network. All the data sharing and exchange among different nodes is handled through the PCL. The cooperation layer itself consists of several internal *components* as illustrated in Fig. 1, and described briefly below.

A PCL internal workflow, specifying the desired cooperation behavior of each enterprise, will be executed and controlled by its Local Coordination Module (LCM). Thus, the LCM of an enterprise handles all Cooperation Events between this enterprise and other enterprises according to the specified rules defined by this enterprise.

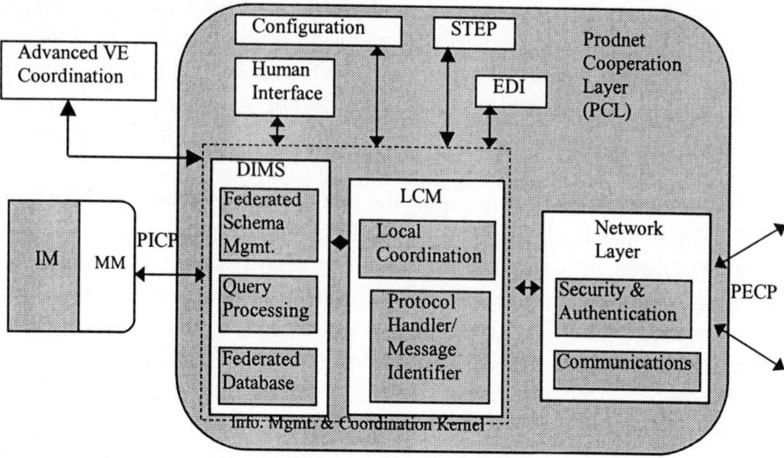

Fig. 1. Description of the PRODNET II general architecture.

The STEP and EDI components primarily support the exchange of technical product data and the commercial order-related data respectively. The Human Interface module supports the enterprise's end-users interaction with the PCL. The Configuration component determines the necessary elements and functionality of the enterprise within every VE in which it is involved.

The PRODNET II Distributed Information Management System (DIMS) cooperatively supports all VE information management requirements, and provides an interoperability platform to exchange and cooperatively manage large amounts of data between VE-members.

The Advanced Coordination Functionalities (ACFs) module provides some additional functionalities to extend the scope of the PCL, including the advanced coordination of VE-related activities, and supporting tools for logistics operations.

The Network Layer component supports the communication of this node with other nodes in the VE. Two different communication protocols are defined: PRODNET Internal Communications Protocol (PICP), and the PRODNET External Communications Protocol (PECP). The PICP supports all interactions between the PCL and both the Internal Module and the Advanced VE Coordination module of the enterprise. The PECP supports all interactions between a given PCL and all the other nodes in the network. This protocol supports the exchange of security and authenticity parameters among nodes.

3 Management of Shared Information in PRODNET II

In this section we first discuss the results of the analysis of the information which is shared and exchanged among VE member nodes, and then we describe the high-level PCL integrated schema that captures all the information needed to support the proper PCL operation.

3.1 Analyzing the Shared and Exchanged Information

In general terms, the Virtual Enterprise domain constitutes a fractal-shaped network of interrelated nodes with complex functional and information management requirements. Analyzing the wide variety of shared and exchanged information among VE member nodes, and achieving a comprehensive description and classification of this information, are some of the difficult tasks tackled within PRODNET II. We have followed a step-wise approach in this analysis that is described below:

1. Definition and study of several distinct focus areas. First, we divided the study domain into three focus areas that represent the main kinds of interactions and exchange of information between different elements of the PRODNET II architecture. The three focus areas consist of: a) the exchange of information between the Internal Module and its cooperation layer PCL; b) the exchange of information within the PCL needed by the PCL components in order to operate properly and provide the expected functionality; c) the exchange of information between every two nodes in the virtual enterprise.
2. Identification of the local, imported and exported information. As a first step towards modeling this diverse information for every enterprise, we divided the enterprise information into three categories of *Self, Acquaintance,* and *Virtual Enterprise* information with corresponding intuitive meanings (the details of this classification approach and their further division into private, restricted and public information, are outside the scope of this paper). As a result of the performed analysis, it was possible to determine: a) which part of the information is generated and stored in this enterprise and thus becomes *local* (i.e. *Self* and some local part of the *Virtual Enterprise* information); b) which part of the information needs to be accessed from the other nodes and thus needs to be *imported* from other enterprises (i.e. *Acquaintance* and some other enterprises information related to the *Virtual Enterprise*); c) which part of the local information needs to be shared with other enterprises and thus needs to be *exported* to other enterprises (a part of the *Self* information and some local part of the *Virtual Enterprise* information).

Sections 4.1 and 4.2 describe the federated architecture of the DIMS that handles the local, import and export schemas for the enterprise, while supporting the expected data location transparency for the user, distributed query processing, site autonomy, access security, and reliability, among other requirements. However, every enterprise needs to have access to both its local information and the information imported from other enterprises, and thus the two parts of information need to be integrated into one coherent schema for the sake of enterprise's convenience of access and retrieval of information. Then clearly, always a part of this integrated schema represents the local schema (of which a part is also exported), and the other part represents the imported schemas at the node.

3.2 General Schema Design for the PCL Information

Based on the initial analysis and identification of different variety of information, an *integrated* object-oriented database schema for enterprise information has been designed [2], as depicted in Fig. 2. The schema represents a uniform class hierarchy and association relationships representing only the high-level categories of information handle within the PCL. Since the design stage of the DIMS for PRODNET II is still an on-going task, different parts of this schema are still being extended as long as the other components of the PCL are being progressively defined. This schema diagram is described in the style of the Object Modeling Technique (OMT) notation [7].

The class definition representing the integrating point in this schema is the PCL (in the middle of the schema). The PCL information is basically composed of three major parts: local PCL components' information (on the left side of the diagram), VE-related information (on the bottom right side of the schema diagram), and directory information (at the lower right side of this schema diagram). The detailed description of the schema components is beyond the scope of this paper, and only the relevant information classes are described when necessary.

4 Design of the DIMS Federated Architecture

In order to support the information management requirements, and proper interoperation among PCLs in different nodes, a federated database architecture is designed for the DIMS module in PRODNET II [1], [4].

The federated architecture approach has proved to adequately facilitate and support the sharing of information between enterprises, while providing the necessary visibility levels to ensure their own autonomy and information privacy. The designed federated architecture has its roots in the PEER federated database system, developed at the University of Amsterdam [11]. A survey of other related work on federated database system is described in [8]. Other approaches for distributed information management in the context of VE support platforms can be found in other related projects such as NIIIP [5] and VEGA [12].

In NIIIP, the information is uniformly modeled in an object-oriented framework. A number of object-oriented local conceptual schemas are defined; one for every individual VE member organization. However, the detailed specification of NIIIP data management services is still under development and so far there is still little information available.

In VEGA, the Distributed Information System (DIS) is supported by a "CORBA access to STEP" layer. Through the CORBA architecture the physical distribution of the documents is handled. The DIS works on a single data model: the STEP data model. The DIS is a distributed database and in comparison to the federated approach chosen for PRODNET II, the concepts of export, import, and integrated schemas, and the support for information security and hierarchy of information visibility and access levels, are not directly addressed in this system architecture.

The remaining of this section focuses on the two main functions of the federated DIMS system for PRODNET II: support of data exportation/importation, and the distributed query processing.

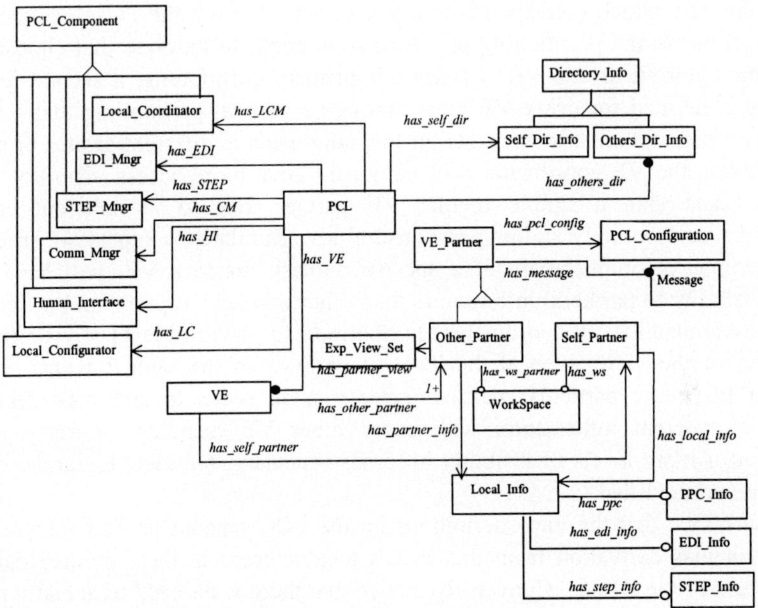

Fig. 2. High-level integrated schema for the PCL of an enterprise.

4.1 Data Exportation/Importation and Visibility Rights

Since different enterprises must have different visibility levels and access rights to other nodes' information, every node in the federation must decide what part of the information to make available to every other partner in a particular VE. Namely, the level of visibility and access that other partners have on the local PCL schema of a given node must be clearly determined by that node. To accomplish this objective, every node can preserve its autonomy and privacy by defining one detailed *individual view* on its PCL local schema, for every other node with which it shares information. The individual view defines the corresponding access right of other nodes to this node's local data. Furthermore, for every class defined in the local schema, the individual view determines which instances (i.e. horizontal class partitioning) and which attributes (i.e. vertical class partitioning) of those instances will be made available to the other node.

The concept of individual view definition on the local schema for every external "user", is the basic idea. However, we have generalized the basic idea of an individual view to the definition of a complete *hierarchy of views.* The hierarchy of views allows the grouping and classification of common view characteristics, facilitating in this way the task of individual view definitions. As an example, let us assume that there are three different kinds of roles that a given node can play in a VE: *coordinator*, *supervisor* (subordinated to coordinator but enabled to monitor certain VE activities), and *regular* VE partner. At the first level of visibility, it is needed to extract the data which corresponds to every given VE from the PCL local schema. Namely, a horizontal partitioning of information needs to be done that chooses "all information related to one VE". After this primary partitioning, a second level of visibility is defined for every VE view, through a vertical partitioning that supports the proper information "access rights for the individuals in different groups of users". For instance, the VE coordinator will obviously have more access visibility to VE partners' data than a simple regular VE partner, due to its inherent control, monitoring, and possibly auditing responsibilities. Similarly, a supervisor in charge of the proper accomplishment of a specific subtask inside a VE, will have more access visibility to partners' information than other regular VE partners, but certainly more limited than the VE coordinator. Furthermore, at the third level of visibility, the definition of the view, even at the level of partners of the same VE, can still be different for every particular partner, since a node needs to and may decide to exchange different information with every other VE member. Clearly, if the definition of more levels of visibility becomes necessary, the view hierarchy can be extended and modified.

Please notice that the view definitions on the PCL schema, in fact represent the export schemas derivation from that PCL's local schema in the federated database architecture of the DIMS. Conversely, notice that there is no need to actually import any schema structure from other nodes. No import schemas required due to the fact that the base schema structure is the same for both the exported and imported at every PCL, at the same time not all the information is available to every given node due to the visibility levels defined by their view definitions.

In Fig. 2, the export views are encapsulated in the class Exp_View_Set, associated with every other VE-partner (Other_Partner class) of this enterprise in a particular VE.

4.2 General Design for Distributed/Federated Query Processing

In general, there are two kinds of queries that need to be handled. In the first place, a query can be issued at this node against the integrated schema. This query in turn can be a local query which can be answered without acquiring any information from other nodes, or it can be a query to external nodes (distributed query) which involves the retrieving of information from one or a specific set of nodes. When a locally issued query arrives to the DIMS, it must be determined if the query is a local query or a distributed query. To make this distinction, the query must be parsed and analyzed in search of for instance, specifications of partners' ID corresponding to Other_Partners. The processing of a distributed query may involve the decomposition of the queries in a set of subqueries which need to be sent to other nodes. For example, any query on the Local_Info involving other partners, must be sent to the corresponding nodes, where the query will be evaluated against the view definition (for this node) and the results (if any) will be sent back.

The second kind of queries arriving to the DIMS represent the subqueries sent from another DIMS in order to solve a query against its integrated schema. At the receiving node, these queries can be seen as remote queries which need to be evaluated against the corresponding export schema according to the requesting node. The remote queries comply with a given format to facilitate the processing at the target node. An initial query format is presented in Fig. 3. First of all, since there are many different kinds of messages exchanged between enterprises' PCLs, there is a *msg_type* field in every message that identifies if the message is actually a DIMS query message. The second field is a unique identifier for the query, set by the originator DIMS. The third and fourth fields correspond to the identifications of the origin and the target nodes, respectively. The fifth field identifies the VE (if any) to which the query is related and for which the information is requested. Finally, the last field is reserved for the content of the query itself.

msg_type	query_id	sender_id	receiver_id	VE_id	query

Fig. 3. Structure of an inter-PCL query message.

In summary, in all cases that a query is issued by a user or an application to the DIMS (local queries against integrated schema), the federated query processor of the DIMS involves the following steps:

1. Determine if the SQL query can be answered locally (local query)
2. If the query is a local query then
   2.1. Evaluate the local query and prepare the result
3. If the query is a distributed query then
   3.1. Identify the external nodes that must receive the query
   3.2. Decompose the query into subquery messages involving only one partner
   3.3. Send a PECP to every partner node with the corresponding subquery msg.
   3.4. Wait for the results of the subqueries evaluation at the different nodes
   3.5. Merge the partial results and prepare the final result
4. Return the result

msg_type	query_id	sender_id	receiver_id	result

Fig. 4. Structure of an inter-PCL query-result message

On the other hand, when a query arrives from another node, a number of steps must be followed to convert the incoming remote query into a local query. As described earlier, the PCL schema definition is the same in all nodes. Therefore, any node can issue a query against the "imported" part of this schema. But clearly (from previous descriptions), the access rights of every node to the data that it can import from a second node are precisely specified in the export (individual) view defined for the origin node in the target node. Therefore, the arriving query will be evaluated against the corresponding view. However, before this query evaluation step, first the specification of the query needs to be altered (rewritten) according to the particular view definition. For example, the class names in the individual views will definitely be different than the actual class names (the views cannot have the same name as the original table, because the table and view names must be unique). Since the actual class names are the ones used by the incoming query, these names need to be replaced by the names for the corresponding local view. After this, the query can be evaluated locally, and all the visibility access constraints are preserved. When the result is obtained, it must be returned to the sender of the query, using the node identification that is contained in the PECP DIMS message.

More specifically and following the PCL schema and the view mechanism details introduced earlier in this paper, the sequence of steps that must be followed to process an external query includes:

1. Identify the VE(s) involved in the query
2. Identify the Other_Partner instance corresponding to the sender partner, which is associated with the VE
3. Get the specific partner view associated with the partner
4. Rewrite the incoming query replacing the specified table names with the view table names (defined in the partner view)
5. Evaluate the rewritten query (it is evaluated on the locally defined views)
6. Find the results
7. Create a "query-result DIMS message" with the results
8. Embed the query result in a PECP message and send it back to the original node

The format of a DIMS query-result message is represented in Fig. 4. The target node for the query places the corresponding query_id, places its ID as sender_id, places the ID of the sender node in the field receiver_id, and appends to it the result of the query. As mentioned before, these messages will also be embedded in PECP messages (all PECP messages are properly encrypted and secured by the Network Communication Layer Component of the PCL).

5 Conclusions

The paradigm of cooperative virtual organization represents a very broad research area with a large growing potential. Federated databases have proved to provide particularly attractive features for handling some open-issues in information management for the virtual organization domain. In this paper, special emphasis was given to several of these federated information management issues in VEs, through a description of the general design of the DIMS for the PRODNET II project.

The proposed DIMS approach properly supports the main information management requirements identified in PRODNET II for the VE paradigm, such as the cooperative information sharing and exchange, node autonomy, information visibility and access rights for a wide variety of kinds of exchanged data among VE nodes. In general, the presented DIMS design represents a federated architecture, which has been specifically tailored to handle the complex interoperability and functionality requirements set by the VE paradigm. One novel feature of the DIMS approach presented in this paper is its unique architecture, in which the "PCL schema" is shared in all nodes but the data is imported/exported according to proper access privileges defined in the hierarchy of export schemas for external nodes.

References

[1] Afsarmanesh, H; Camarinha, L. - Federated Information Management for Cooperative Information - in proceedings of the 8th Int. Conf. on Database and Expert Systems Applications (DEXA'97), September 97.

[2] Afsarmanesh, H; Garita, C; Hertzberger, L.O.; Santos, V. - Management of Distributed Information in Virtual Enterprises : The PRODNET Approach – in proceedings of the Int. Conf. on Concurrent Enterprising (ICE'97), October 97.

[3] Browne, J.; Sackett, P.J.; Wortmann, J.C (1994) - The system of manufacturing: A prospective study, Report to the DG XII of the CEC.

[4] Camarinha, L; Afsarmanesh, H; Garita, C; Lima, C - Towards an Architecture for Virtual Enterprises; The Second World Congress On Intelligent Manufacturing Processes & Systems, Budapest, Hungary, June 1997.

[5] The NIIIP Reference Architecture, 1996, http://www. niiip.org.

[6] Rabelo, R.; Camarinha-Matos, L.M. - Towards agile scheduling in extended enterprise, in Balanced Automation Systems II, L.M. Camarinha-Matos, H. Afsarmanesh (Eds.), Chapman & Hall, June 1996.

[7] Rumbaugh, J. et al - Object-Oriented Modeling and Design, Prentice Hall, 1991.

[8] Sheth, A. et al. – Federated database systems for managing distributed, heterogeneous and autonomous databases. ACM Computing Surveys, Vol. 22, No. 3, September 1990.

[9] Silberschatz, A. et al – Database Systems: Breaking Out the Box. SIGMOD Record, Vol. 26, No. 3, September 1997.

[10] Walton, J.; Whicker, L. - Virtual Enterprise: Myth & Reality, Journal of Control, October 96.

[11] Wiedijk, M.; Afsarmanesh, H.; Hertzberger, L.O. - Co-working and Management of Federated Information-Clusters. 7th Int. Conf. on Database and Expert Systems (DEXA'96), Lecture Notes in Computer Science 1134, pp 446-455. Springer Verlag, September 96.

[12] Zarli, A. et al – Integrating Emerging IT Paradigms for the Virtual Enterprise: Ghe VEGA platform. In proceedings of the Int. Conf. on Concurrent Enterprising (ICE'97), Nottingham, England, October 97.

Facilitating Virtual Representation of CAD Data through a Learning Based Approach to Conceptual Database Evolution Employing Direct Instance Sharing

Awais Rashid[1], Peter Sawyer[1]
[1]Computing Department, Lancaster University, Lancaster, LA1 4YR, UK
{marash, sawyer} @comp.lancs.ac.uk

Abstract. This paper presents a framework for a learning based approach to dynamically evolve the conceptual structure of a database in order to facilitate virtual representation of data in a CAD environment. A generic object model is presented which spans applications from a wide range of engineering design domains. The object model is complemented with a schema model. The object model and the schema model are justified through several sample cases depicting the mapping from the object model to the schema model.

1 Introduction

Object databases are considered to be well-suited to computer aided design applications which cannot be easily supported through the built-in data types in relational databases. In CAD applications, progressively more enhanced versions of a design object are created from existing multiple versions of the same. The very nature of CAD applications, however, not only requires the design objects to change but also the design templates. Therefore, not only the objects residing in the database but also the schema of the database needs to evolve when supporting CAD applications. The highly interactive nature of design applications further requires that any such schema changes be dynamic.

In this paper we present a framework for the application of learning techniques to dynamically evolve the conceptual structure of a database in order to facilitate virtual representation of data in a computer aided engineering design environment.

Rule induction and knowledge acquisition from databases [13], [15] are not new concepts. Work has been carried out both for knowledge discovery in databases [9], [16] and to allow the specification and implementation of autonomous reactive behavior in databases [3]. We, however, scope our approach to make use of the knowledge inherent in engineering design data and use this knowledge for database evolution through semi-autonomous learning in a manner that will facilitate virtual representation and manipulation of both the design objects and their templates.

2 The Object Model

This section presents the object model for our application. Data models for CAD applications have mainly been product specific [1]. The drawback for these models is that they are based on relevant information for the particular product and cannot be generalized to fit all or most of the CAD applications. Product models are mostly static in nature and don't incorporate a great deal of flexibility for dynamic evolution. Our object model, GOMCAD - Generic Object Model for CAD - is based on the observation that objects are *molecular* in nature with each *molecule* consisting of more primitive molecules, the most primitive ones being the *atoms* [4]. Although CAD data is highly diverse in nature, still certain generic graphical objects can be identified that form the basic building blocks for virtual representation of data in most engineering applications. Consider figure 1, for instance, which provides an example from electronic circuit design. Shown in the figure is the virtual representation of a capacitor, which has been built using three cylinders.

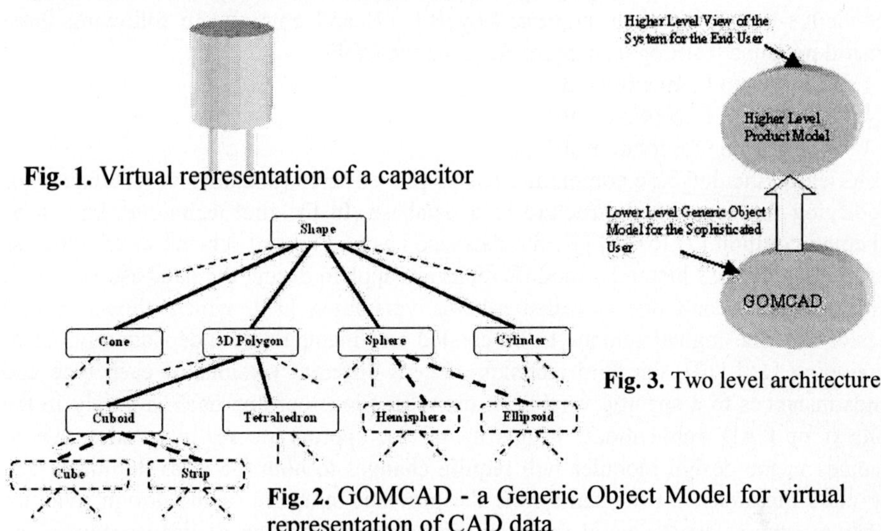

Fig. 1. Virtual representation of a capacitor

Fig. 3. Two level architecture

Fig. 2. GOMCAD - a Generic Object Model for virtual representation of CAD data

Our object model is presented in figure 2. GOMCAD provides inherent flexibility for dynamic evolution. As shown in figure 2 the *shape* objects that act as the basic building blocks are *cone, cuboid, tetrahedron, sphere* and *cylinder*. Note that the classes *shape* and *3D Polygon* are abstract classes. The solid lines between the objects show inheritance relationships while the dotted lines indicate that there can be further sub-classes. The thick dashed lines show derivation relationships. The objects shown dotted are obtained by applying, to the basic objects, one of six operations three of which are categorized as *linear* the other three being *non-linear*. The three linear operations are *scale*, *rotate* and *reflect* while the three non-linear operations are *cut, trim* and *shear*. These six operations can be used to create further atomic objects such as *cube, strip* (through the application of the *scale* operation to a *cuboid*), *hemisphere* (by applying the *cut* operation to a sphere) and *ellipsoid* (obtained by using the *shear* operation on a sphere). The *join* and *merge* operations can then be applied to the basic or derived atomic objects to form molecular objects which are further *joined* or *merged* to form higher level molecular objects.

GOMCAD is well suited for virtual representation of data from several engineering domains such as power plant design, electronic circuit design, mechanical engineering design, architecture, city & regional planning and chemical plant design. As shown in figure 3 above, GOMCAD can act as an underlying object model for defining higher level product models in order to facilitate virtual representation of data for a wide range of engineering design applications at the same time providing end user isolation from the underlying database evolution process.

3 Conceptual Database Evolution (CDE)

This section describes our approach to conceptual database evolution and how it facilitates CAD applications. Work has been carried out previously to evolve, both statically and dynamically, the conceptual structure of a database. The approaches have been both passive [2], [10], [11], [12] and active [6], [7]. We take the knowledge-based approach suggested by [6], [7] and employ the following three general machine learning techniques for dynamic CDE.

- Learning from Instruction (LFI)
- Learning from Exception (LFE)
- Learning from Observation (LFO)

Historically, the database community has employed three fundamental techniques for modifying the conceptual structure of a database. In the first technique, known as schema evolution [2] [5] [6] [7], the database has one logical schema to which class definition and class hierarchy modifications are applied during the database evolution process. The second one is called schema versioning [11], which allows several versions of one logical schema to be created and manipulated independently. Class versioning [10] [12], the third technique, keeps different versions of each type and binds instances to a specific version of the type. Since our approach is purely in the context of CAD applications, triggering of the appropriate learning rules due to changes in the design modules will require changes to both the class definition and the class hierarchy. At the same time the previous structure of the design modules needs to remain intact should the user choose to revert to an earlier version of the design module. Our approach, therefore, superimposes schema evolution on class versioning and views conceptual database evolution as a composition of the following four components:

1. Class hierarchy evolution
2. Class versioning
3. Object versioning
4. Knowledge-base/rule-base evolution

From this point onwards we use the term *database evolution* to refer to any changes in the conceptual structure of the database. The evolution of the knowledge-base/rule-base must form part of the CDE process since we suggest that the knowledge-base resides within the OODBMS itself in order to guarantee consistency between the rules and the data and to achieve performance improvements [14]. We do not suggest the use of a front-end expert system shell [14] since we want the learning processes to make use of the rich semantics of CAD data. In addition, new knowledge will keep on entering the database due to the highly diverse nature of CAD data. Conceptual evolution of the knowledge-base/rule-base is therefore necessary.

3.1 The Schema Model

This section presents the schema model underlying our CDE framework presented in the following section. The conceptual database schema in our system is a fully connected directed acyclic graph (DAG) depicting the class hierarchy in the system (note that our system allows multiple inheritance). Each node in the DAG is a *class version derivation graph* [8]. Each node in the class version derivation graph (CVDG) has the following structure:

- Reference(s) to predecessor(s)
- Reference(s) to successor(s)
- Pointer to the versioned class object
- Descriptive information about the class version such as creation time, creator's identification, etc.
- Pointer(s) to super-class(es) version(s)
- Pointer(s) to sub-class(es) version(s)
- A set of reference(s) to object version derivation graph(s)

The reason why each node of the CVDG must keep pointers to the super-class(es) and sub-class(es) can be observed from figure 4 which presents two nodes of the hierarchy graph along with their associated CVDGs. It should be noted that the dashed arrows inside each node represent the derivation path for the class versions. The solid lines show the conceptual inheritance relationship between the two classes while the dashed lines represent the actual inheritance relationship between various versions of these classes. Note that version *B1* of class *B* has as its super-class version *A3* of class *A* while both versions *B2* and *B3* inherit from the version *A2*. Conceptually, the sub-class can only inherit from the super-class (assuming that the class has only one super-class) but each version of the sub-class might be inheriting from a separate version of the super-class. Also, we can see that version *B2* of class *B* in figure 4 might be the result of changing its super-class to be version *A2* and not *A3*. Pointers to sub-classes need to be maintained to make sure that correct sub-class instances are substituted for the class under consideration. For example, only an instance of the sub-class version *B1* can be substituted where an instance of class version *A3* is required. This does not mean that instances associated with one class version are not compatible with the others. Later in this section we provide an underlying framework for converting instances from one class version to another.

Each node of a CVDG keeps a set of reference(s) to some object version derivation graph(s) (OVDG). Each OVDG node has the following structure [8]:

- Reference(s) to predecessor(s)
- Reference(s) to successor(s)
- Pointer to the versioned instance
- Descriptive information about the instance version such as creation time, creator's identification, etc.

Since an OVDG is generated for each instance associated with a class version, a set of OVDGs results when a class version has more than one instance associated with it. As a result a CVDG node keeps a set of references to all these OVDGs. Figure 5 above shows the structure of a CVDG node with references to two OVDGs.

Note that our schema model allows maintenance of a logical database schema while at the same time keeping track of the historical version derivation paths without storing the information within the versioned types and instances. In the context of CAD applications it will not normally be desirable to convert instances of one class version to another. However, in cases where such a behavior might be expected of the system, missing information must be added or additional information must be removed from the instance version being manipulated. The resulting instance will then be stored in the database as a new instance version of the class version it was made compatible to. Note that this should not affect the older instance version from which the new instance version was derived.

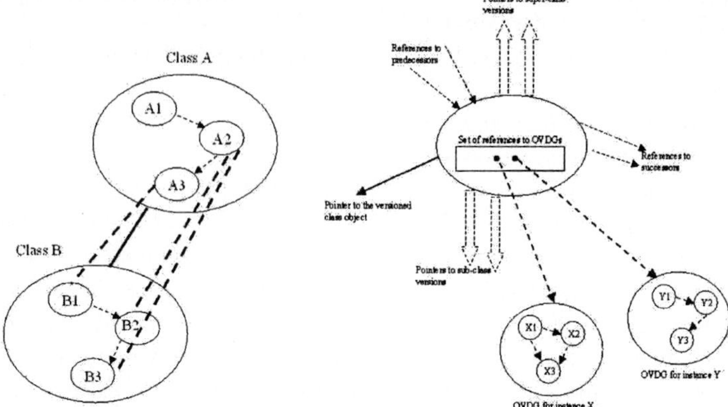

Fig. 4. A simple class hierarchy with super-class sub-class links between various nodes of the CVDGs

Fig. 5. A CVDG node with references to two OVDGs

It should also be noted that in our approach each instance version is associated with a particular class version and derivation of a new class version does not, by default, require instance versions associated with older class versions to be updated to form instance versions associated with the new class version. Any such action is performed on specific demand. We, therefore, have only one copy of each instance version in the system. As a result, instance versions are directly shared by all the class versions. This is known as *direct instance sharing* [11].

4 Mapping from the Object Model to the Schema Model

In this section we present several sample situations which depict the mapping from our lower level generic object model, GOMCAD, to the schema model through the application of the above mentioned learning techniques. We use the schema change taxonomy presented by [2] as a basis to further classify the four components of conceptual database evolution that we identified above. However, some of the cases, such as manipulating the shared value of an instance variable, in the taxonomy are specific to the ORION data model. We, therefore, support only the general cases identified by [2].

The learning processes are triggered when a design object is *checked in* to the database. Dependent upon the degree of modification of this design object, the LFO (learning from observation) process employs one of the following three rules in order to resolve the default type of evolution which the conceptual structure of the database undergoes:

- Any non-linear changes in the structure of any atomic or molecular object, such as those caused through the application of the *cut*, *trim* or *shear* operations, lead, by default, to the creation of a new version of the class with the object being bound to the newly created class version (addition of a CVDG node: Class Versioning)

- Any linear changes in the structure of any atomic or molecular object, such as those caused through the application of the *scale*, *rotate* or *reflect* operations, by default lead to the creation of a new version of the object (addition of an OVDG node: Object Versioning)
- Creation of higher level molecular objects, such as through *joining* and *merging* lower level molecular or atomic objects or both, or transition to lower level molecular objects because of the removal of molecular or atomic objects, by default, leads to changes in conceptual class hierarchy (changes to the DAG: Class Hierarchy Evolution)

Referring to figure 2 the above rules suggest that *cube*s and *strip*s (obtained through the application of the linear operation *scale* to a *cuboid*) will be treated as instances of *cuboid* while both *hemisphere* and *ellipsoid* (obtained by applying the non-linear operations *cut* and *shear* to a *sphere* respectively) will be treated as versions of the class *sphere*. However, the semantics of *cube & strip* and *hemisphere & ellipsoid* can be conceptually well understood if these are sub-classes of *cuboid* and *sphere* respectively. This implies that there can be certain situations where the default behavior described in the above three general rules might be undesirable in order to maintain the conceptual integrity of various classes in the system. Human guidance has, therefore, been incorporated into the system since there exists a trade-off between autonomy and versatility [9].

4.1 Example CDE Cases

For our example CDE cases we choose electronic circuit design as our application domain. The four evolution cases are presented below:

Case # 1: Creation of a new atomic type

Type of Change and Object: Linear change to an atomic object

Sample Situation: Suppose that the user takes an instance of the generic class *cylinder* and scales it with an intention to create a *wire*. When the modified object is checked in to the database the LFO process will, by default, consider that it be checked in as a new instance or instance version of the class *cylinder* depending on whether the object was newly created or checked out of the database. However, the user would like *wires* to be instances of a separate class. The user, therefore, instructs the system to create a new class *wire* and check the object in as an instance of that class. The existing knowledge in the knowledge-base informs the system that the new class to be created has the same properties as the class *cylinder*. With the user's approval, it therefore, checks the object in as a new instance of the newly created sub-class *wire* of the class *cylinder*. The whole evolution process is depicted in figure 6 below.

Learning Techniques Applied: LFO, LFI

Type and Semantics of Evolution: Class Hierarchy Evolution i.e. addition of a new DAG node. Also, by default, the addition of a new class creates a new CVDG node and the addition of a new instance creates a new OVDG node.

Case # 2: Creation of a new molecular type

Type of Change and Object: Creation of a molecular object from atomic objects subject to linear change

Sample Situation: Suppose that the user wants to create a capacitor. For this purpose the user will create a *cylinder* instance and *merge* with it two new instances of the class *wire* in order to form a capacitor. When the newly created object is checked in to the database the LFO process observes a new molecular object and uses the knowledge in the knowledge-base to check for existing classes with possible similarities to the new object being checked in. Failing to find any such molecular classes the LFO process suggests creating a new sub-class - an aggregation of *cylinder* and *wire* - of the class *shape* and checking the new object in as an instance of the newly created class. Under instructions from the user the system creates a new sub-class *capacitor* of the class *shape* and checks the new object in as an instance of the newly created *capacitor* class. Note that the cylinder instance that forms part of the capacitor will automatically be stored as an instance of the class *cylinder* while the two associated *wire* instances will be stored as new instances of the class *wire* since these are new instances and have undergone only linear changes. The evolution process is shown in figure 7 below.

Learning Techniques Applied: LFO, LFI

Type and Semantics of Evolution: Class Hierarchy Evolution i.e. addition of a new DAG node. Also, by default, the addition of a new class creates a new CVDG node and the addition of a new instance creates a new OVDG node. Also the storage of new atomic instances results in changes to the CVDG nodes these instances are associated with.

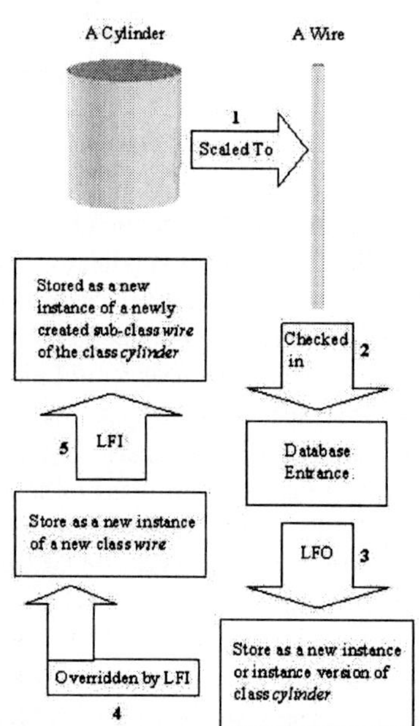

Fig. 6. The database evolution process for evolution case # 1

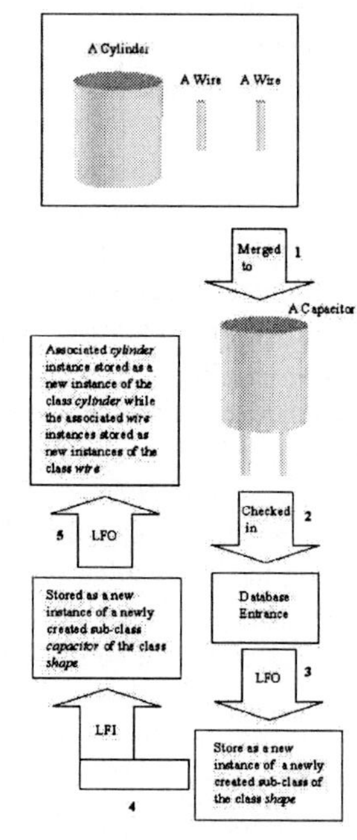

Fig. 7. The database evolution process for evolution case # 2

Case # 3: Creation of a new molecular type similar in structure to an existing one

Type of Change and Object: Creation of a molecular object from atomic objects subject to both linear and non-linear changes

Sample Situation: Suppose that the user wants to create a resistor. For this purpose the user will create a *cylinder* instance and *scale* and *rotate* it so that it lies horizontally. Then the user will create two instances of class *wire* and *scale* and *shear* them in order to form terminals for the resistor. The above three instances will then be *merged* together to form a resistor. When the newly created object is checked in to the database the LFO process observes a new molecular object and uses the knowledge residing in the knowledge-base to check for any existing classes with possible similarities. Since a resistor contains the same components as a capacitor but with some linear and non-linear changes the LFO process suggests creating a new version of the class *capacitor* and storing the new object as an instance of this class version. However, a resistor is conceptually different from a capacitor so the LFI process guides the system to create a new class *resistor* and store the object as an instance of this class. The system, finding no other similarities to the *resistor* class within the existing classes, with the user's approval creates a new sub-class *resistor* of the class *shape* and stores the new object as an instance of this newly created class. Note that the cylinder instance that forms part of the resistor will automatically be stored as an instance of the class *cylinder* since it has undergone a linear change only (*rotation*). On the other hand the two associated *wire* instances have undergone non-linear changes. However they are mere reflections of each other. The LFO process will, therefore, create a new class version of the class *wire* and associate both the instances with this new version of the class.

Learning Techniques Used: LFO, LFI

Type and Semantics of Evolution: Class Hierarchy Evolution i.e. addition of a new DAG node. Also, class versioning takes place since a new CVDG node has been added to the atomic class *wire*. Also, by default, the addition of a new class creates a new CVDG node and the addition of a new instance creates a new OVDG node. Figure 8 below presents the conceptual database schema after the evolution. The database schema before the evolution can be seen in figure 10.

Case # 4: Generalization of an existing and a newly created molecular type into a super-type

Type of Change and Object: Creation of a molecular object from atomic objects subject to linear change

Sample Situation: Suppose that the user wants to create another form of capacitor but one that is flat rather than cylindrical. For this purpose the user creates an instance of the generic class *cuboid* and scales it to form a strip. The user then creates two new instances of the class *wire* and *merges* them together with the strip in order to form the flat capacitor. When the newly created object is checked in to the database the LFO process detects a new molecular object and finding no existing class to which the newly created object can belong to, suggests creating a new sub-class of the class *shape* and storing the newly created object as an instance of this class. With the user's approval the LFO process goes ahead to create a new class *capacitor*. However, the class *capacitor* already exists in the system. Here the LFE (learning from exception) process suggests combining the common features of both the new and old type of *capacitor* into a super-class with the specialized features incorporated into two sub-classes of this new super-class. With the user's guidance the system then renames the existing *capacitor* class to *cylindrical capacitor* and adds a newly created class *capacitor* as its super-class. Note that the new *capacitor* class will be an abstract class. The system also creates another sub-class of *capacitor* named *flat capacitor*. The system then stores the newly created object as an instance of the class *flat capacitor*. Also note that this will result in the common features of both *cylindrical capacitor* and *flat capacitor* being combined into the new *capacitor* class and any instances associated with the older *capacitor* class will now be associated with the class *cylindrical capacitor*. Note that the cuboid instance that forms part of the newly created flat capacitor will automatically be stored as an instance of the class *cuboid* while the two associated *wire* instances will be stored as new instances of the class *wire* since these are new instances and have undergone only linear changes.

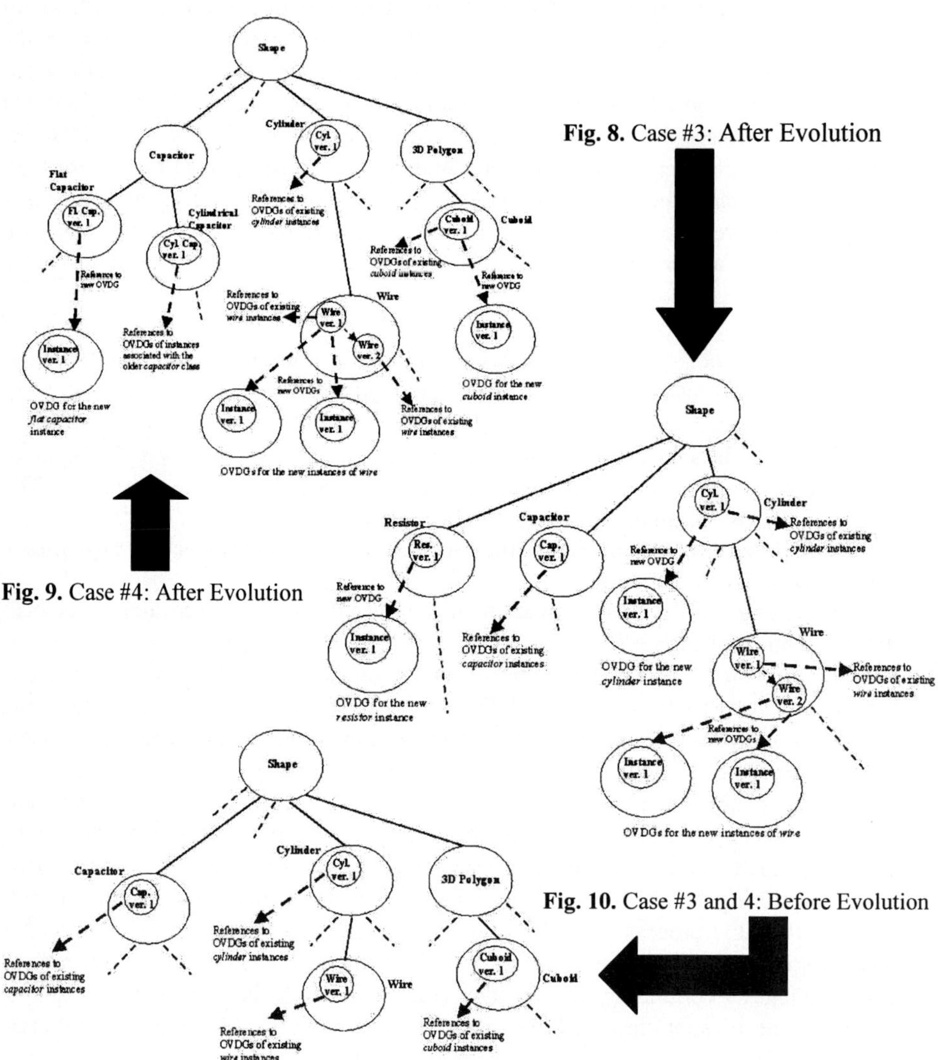

Fig. 8. Case #3: After Evolution

Fig. 9. Case #4: After Evolution

Fig. 10. Case #3 and 4: Before Evolution

Learning Techniques Used: LFO, LFI, LFE
Type and Semantics of Evolution: Class Hierarchy Evolution i.e. name of an existing DAG node has been changed while both a new leaf and non-leaf node have been added. Also, by default, the addition of a new class creates a new CVDG node and the addition of a new instance creates a new OVDG node. Figure 9 above shows the conceptual database schema after the evolution. The database schema before the evolution can be seen in figure 10.

5 Summary and Conclusions

We have presented a semi-autonomous learning approach to dynamically evolve the conceptual structure of an object oriented database. However, unlike earlier work on database evolution, our approach is specifically in the context of CAD applications. We observe that despite the highly diverse and complex nature of CAD data, several generic graphical objects can be identified that act as the basic building blocks in various engineering design applications. We have complemented our generic object model with a schema model and have provided several example evolution cases depicting how our learning approach makes use of the knowledge inherent in CAD data in order to facilitate dynamic database evolution. The work, at present, is in the early stages of implementation with the overall system architecture being designed. We are building our database evolution system on top of the OODBMS *O2* from *O2 Technology*.

References

1. Anumba, C. J.: Data Structures and DBMS for CAD Systems. Advances in Engineering Software, Vol. 25, No. 2-3, 1996, pp. 123-129
2. Banerjee, J. *et al.*: Data Model Issues for Object-Oriented Applications. ACM Transactions on Office Information Systems, Vol. 5, No. 1, Jan. 1987, pp. 3-26
3. Dittrich, K. R. *et al.*: The Active Database Management System Manifesto: A Rulebase of ADBMS Features. Proceedings of the 2nd Workshop on Rules in Databases, Sept. 1995, Lecture Notes in Computer Science, T. Sellis (ed.), Vol. 985, pp. 3-20
4. Harder, T. *et al.*: PRIMA - a DBMS Prototype Supporting Engineering Applications. Proceedings of the 13th International Conference on Very Large Databases, Sept. 1987, pp. 433-442
5. Kim, W. *et al.*: Architecture of the ORION Next-Generation Database System. IEEE Transactions on Knowledge and Data Engineering, Vol. 2, No. 1, March 1990, pp. 109-124
6. Li, Q. & McLeod, D.: Conceptual Database Evolution through Learning. Object Oriented Databases with Applications to CASE, Networks, and VLSI CAD, Edited by: Gupta, R. & Horowitz, E., c1991 Prentice Hall Inc., pp. 62-74
7. Li, Q. & McLeod, D.: Conceptual Database Evolution through Learning in Object Databases. IEEE Transactions on Knowledge and Data Engineering, Vol. 6, No.2, April 1994, pp. 205-224
8. Loomis, M. E. S.: Object Versioning. Journal of Object Oriented Programming, Jan. 1992, pp. 40-43
9. Matheus, C. J. *et al.*: Systems for Knowledge Discovery in Databases. IEEE Transactions on Knowledge and Data Engineering, Vol.5, No.6, Dec. 1993, pp.903-913
10. Monk, S. & Sommerville, I.: Schema Evolution in OODBs Using Class Versioning. SIGMOD Record, Vol. 22, No. 3, Sept. 1993, pp. 16-22
11. Ra., Y.-G. & Rundensteiner, E. A.: A Transparent Schema-Evolution System Based on Object-Oriented View Technology. IEEE Transactions on Knowledge and Data Engineering, Vol.9, No.4, July/Aug.1997, pp.600-624
12. Skarra, A. H. & Zdonik, S. B.: The Management of Changing Types in an Object-Oriented Database. Proceedings of the 1st OOPSLA Conference, Sept. 1986, pp.483-495
13. Smyth, P. & Goodman, R. M.: An Information Theoretic Approach to Rule Induction from Databases. IEEE Transactions on Knowledge and Data Engineering, Vol.4, No.4, Aug. 1992, pp.301-316
14. Stonebraker, M.: The Integration of Rule Systems and Database Systems. IEEE Transactions on Knowledge and Data Engineering, Vol.4, No.5, Oct. 1992, pp.415-423
15. Yasdi, R.: Learning Classification Rules from Database in the Context of Knowledge Acquisition and Representation. IEEE Transactions on Knowledge and Data Engineering, Vol.3, No.3, Sept. 1991, pp.293-306
16. Yoon, J. P. & Kerschberg, L.: A Framework for Knowledge Discovery and Evolution in Databases. IEEE Transactions on Knowledge and Data Engineering, Vol.5, No.6, Dec. 1993, pp.973-979

Evaluation of the Strength of Computer Aided Method Engineering for Product Development Process Modeling

A.N.W. Dahanayake

Faculty of Information Technology and Systems, Department of Information Systems, Delft University of Technology, P.O. Box 356, 2600 AJ Delft, The Netherlands
A.N.W.Dahanayake@is.twi.tudelft.nl

Abstract. Even though it is common now a days that the product development process is fully automated, the decision making factors and information about the product development process is not properly coordinated. An approach carried out for the generation of a generic data model of the product development process and the population of company specific work floor information with the use of the Computer Aided Method Engineering environment is evaluated and results and conclusions are presented in this paper.

1 Introduction

Today the production organizations are forced to improve their product development process mainly due to the consumer demands and the increasing competition within the industry partners. There are many tools and techniques such as work floor management, planning, and decision support, available in the market claiming their capacity to improve the product development process. The main problem confronted with the introduction of such tools and techniques in the production industry is that the vast unstructuredness of the work floor information and the integration of the work floor information with such tools.

At the moment there are no tools available to structure the work floor information such that decision support tools can be integrated into product development process. As the plug in tools are difficult to integrate and the use of separate tools for specific tasks with no integration with other active tools were disadvantageous, Computer Aided Method Engineering (CAME) technology was considered to solve this problem. The research presented in this paper discuss the advantages of using CAME in the production industry to structure the work floor information, as well as the integration of specific decision support tools used in the production industry using this platform.

2 The Product Development Process

To gain more insight into this problem a study was carried out in co-operation with a set of Dutch industrial partners, Inalfa at Venray, IKU at Montfoort, and

Texas Instruments Holland at Almelo. The companies are automotive suppliers who engineer and produce products, including mechanical and electrical components to order. These companies have similar product and process development processes, and were increasingly suffering from enormous time and quality pressures. This made them realize that the traditional, isolated, sequential method of product development was no longer appropriate. Prior to this study the situation was dealt with by making small adjustments to the product development process. This form of adjustment became inadequate given the current demands. It was realized that multiple company functions must be brought in at an early stage of the development process, to process a customers demands with an optimum time to market interval, with the highest possible product quality, and at a competitive price.

A central issue of early involvement in the product development process is optimization of the supply information to the user rather than to the product producer. The production information must be available in time, at right moment and in the right format for its users, who are not necessarily the production department. To achieve this it is necessary to determine and chart the information that is created and/or used by the industrial engineering designs and then to determine where, when and how to structure the product development process to realize company goals. For detailed specifications and extensive background information refer to [3] and [10].

2.1 The Product Development Process Modeling Approach

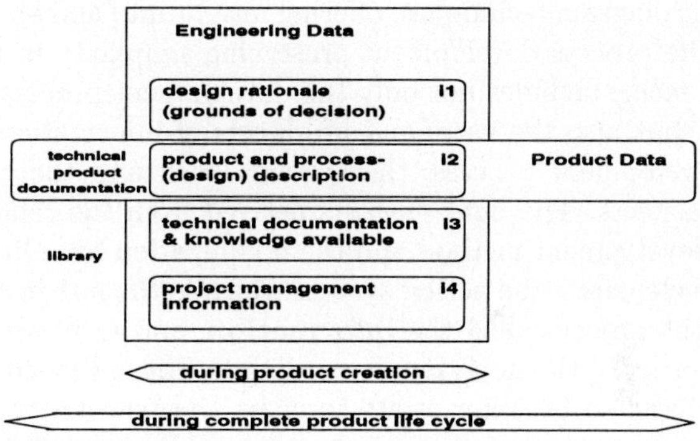

Fig. 1. Designing a company specific data model

The *way of thinking* behind this approach of structuring the work floor information is that there is a distinction between product information and engineering information and this is based on four *types* of information contained in a generic model that describes the entire information involved in product development processes (see figure 1). These four types of information can be represented in a generic model to be charted in the required form using a set of automated tools to improve information access, by the person who requires the information and to present it where the user requires it. The development process, which is also described in the models, can be improved by tuning the development process to the information requirements and by tuning the activities of the process to each other.

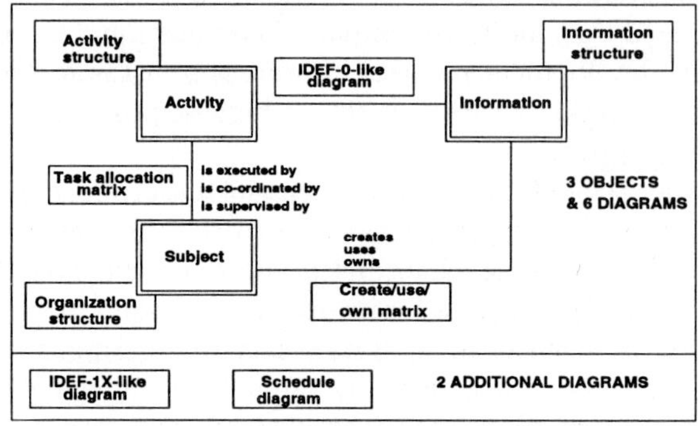

Fig. 2. The way of modeling

The *way of modeling* as summarized in figure 2 determines the contents of a company specific data model and the way this data is represented and analyzed using eight diagram techniques, offering insight into and an overview of the product and the process development preserving simplicity in the resulting models. The *data model* includes not only the development process and the information structure, but also the users and producers of information, the time consumed in the development process, the systems used and the relationships between all these aspects. The *data model* is derived from the relationship between the product development method and the organization by splitting the organization into three elements: the acting system which is the **subject**, the treated system which is the object called the **information**, and in between these two lies the action or process, the **activity**. According to this approach, these three elements are considered to be appropriate to chart the relevant aspects of product and process development process, and they form the main building blocks of the data model. The database building blocks are modeled in an object oriented manner including attributes and relationships between the objects. A set of eight diagram techniques are defined. Three of them representing the relationships *within* the objects (one dimensional) Organizational Structure Chart (OSC), Activity Structure Chart (ASC), and Information Structure Chart (ISC). Another three representing the relationships *between* the objects (two dimensional) IDEF[1]-O-like diagram (IDEF-O), Create/Use/Own Matrix (CUOM), and Task Allocation

[1] Integrated computer-aided manufacturing DEFinition

Matrix (TAM). Further, two additional diagrams are given: Scheduler-like Diagram (SD), IDEF-1X-like diagram (IDEF-1X).

The *way of working* of this approach is first to populate the database using the company specific data model and to generate automatically the above mentioned diagrams, this approach does not include a *way of control*.

The *way of support* is a software tool generated using the CAME environment to ease and accelerate the use of the data models and diagram techniques. This tool is called the 'Graphical Database Presentation Tool' (GDPT) and the main function of the tool is clearly to present the contents of the objects in the database, and it is the only tool available for this approach.

3 The CAME Environment and its Architecture

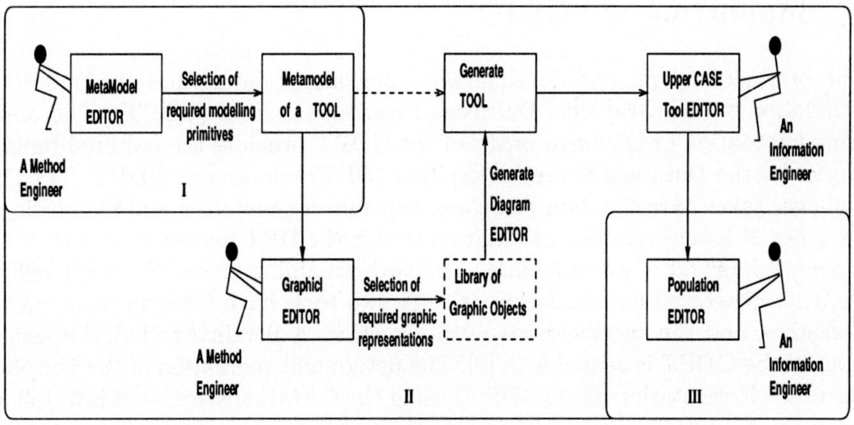

Fig. 3. The main support functions of the CAME environment

The global philosophy behind a CAME environment is that such an environment has to provide the required design tools according to the chosen method particular to a problem situation (see figure 3). The CAME environment functions as a service based object oriented MetaCASE environment, which offers services required for modeling tools by a mechanism interpreting the required modeling knowledge and changing the visual representations to the required form with the use of a graphic object binding mechanism. Further, this environment offers mechanism for population of models specified according to such designed tools. The general architecture of a service based CAME environment and a detailed description is available in [3].

The environment is a layered database architecture based on the principle of service objects [4]. This approach differs from other MetaCASE approaches which focus more on the representation of the methods as first order logical theories, or graphical behavior of design objects. The approach has some similarity to the MetaEdit+ [5] approach from the viewpoint of conceptual modeling where the design of a method specification is akin to the development of a conceptual schema of a software repository, and the design of a CASE tool resembles the design of an external view to a conceptual schema [1]. A specific difference of this approach with respect to the MetaEdit+ approach is the ability to define arbitrary process description and to support arbitrary process specification, which is important for selecting the suitable method or its parts for a specific problem area [4].

The prototype based on this generic model is implemented on NeXTstep/ Objective C platform, integrating the research areas of MetaCASE and object-oriented service specifications. A detailed specifications of this prototype are available in [3], [6], [7], [9] and [2].

4 Supporting the GDPT

The product and process development information determines the underlying foundation to the Graphical Database Presentation Tool (GDPT). The underlying foundation or the *meta model* of the GDPT provides the required building blocks for the Database Presentation Tool (DPT) manager of GDPT. The DPT manager takes over the *data modeling, population generation* and facilitation of six types of *tool generation.* In addition to this the DPT manager includes a *synonyms editor* and a *query facility.* The two remaining tools, SD and IDEF-1X were not generated for evaluation as these two tools have a strong planning tool character, and the specifications were not clear. A detailed technical specifications of the GDPT is available in [2]. The design and generation of the Graphical Database Presentation Tool (GDPT) using the CAME environment is as follows:

4.1 Data Modeling and Population Generation

The general data model of the participating companies was composed of three building block objects: **activity**, **information** and **subject**, with each object having several levels. The objects were used to determine the appropriate detail level of an example model and internal structure of the objects. A level is identified by a number that represents the position of the level within the structure of the object. The numbering used is similar to that used in the Structured Analysis and Design Technique (SADT) [8], a technique that is frequently used in the manufacturing industry and is sometimes called Integrated computer-aided manufacturing DEFinition (IDEF). For example, A0 is the main IDEF diagram in which the activities such as A1,A2,··Am, are presented. Subsequently, the activities are divided into A11,A12,··· and A21,A22,A23, etc., taking into account the hierarchical relationships between the activities. Each object is characterized by its type and is included at one level of an object and is represented by a *type* attribute.

4.2 Activity Object

Figure 4 illustrates an **activity object** with its hierarchical structure of five levels; *area of analysis*, *subdivision of analysis area*, *producer*, *task* and *activity or decision*, and the attributes of each level. Each level describes *processes* with the lower level representing the same process in more detail. The attributes that appear in the *levels of activities* include the relationships between **activity object** and the other two main objects. The relationship between the **activity object** and the **information object** are included in the *task* level as *required information* and *delivered information.* All attributed levels of activities contain relationships between **activity object** and **subject object**, as the contents of these relationships are considered to be different, and these relationships are concerned with responsibility, coordination and execution activities.

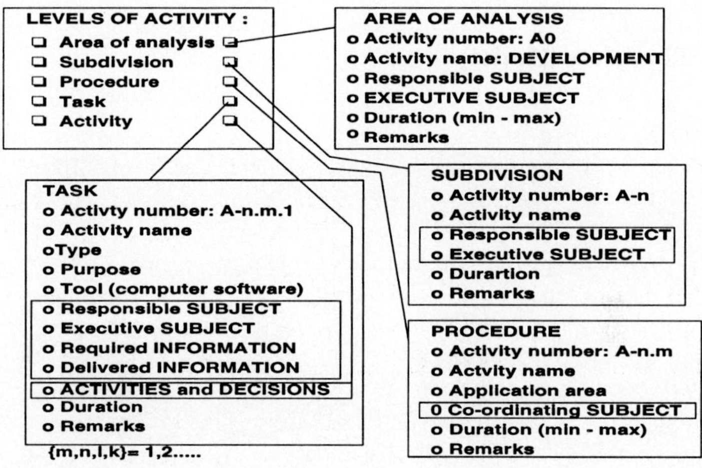

Fig. 4. Levels of the activity object

4.3 Information Object

The **information object** is composed of four levels; *group of information carriers*, *information carriers*, *group of information elements* and *information element.* In the **information object**, the attribute *type*, is used mainly at the *group of information element* level and the *information carrier* level inherits the value of the *type* attribute and is used to characterize the information. Figure 1 gives the *types* of information which have to be managed differently. The relationships between the **information object** and the **subject object** are represented by the attributes at different *levels of information.* The **information object** does not visualize the relationships with the **activity object** as they are already incorporated within the **activity object**.

4.4 Subject Object

The **subject object** has five levels and in addition to these levels, there are external subjects such as, *client*, *supplier*, *competitor* and *external diverse*. The *external diverse* subjects include such subjects as, authors of books or articles and standardization committees, and no attributes are attached to them other than a *subject number* to enable storage of the relationships between these subjects and the other objects. The attribute *type* distinguishes the line and the staff of departments, and no characterization is made at other levels as it is of no importance to the structure within the **subject object**. The relationships between the **subject object** and other two objects are not taken into account as they are already available within the structures of other two objects. Depending on the size of a company, the level of *man/machine* can be a functional group instead of an individual.

4.5 The Meta Model

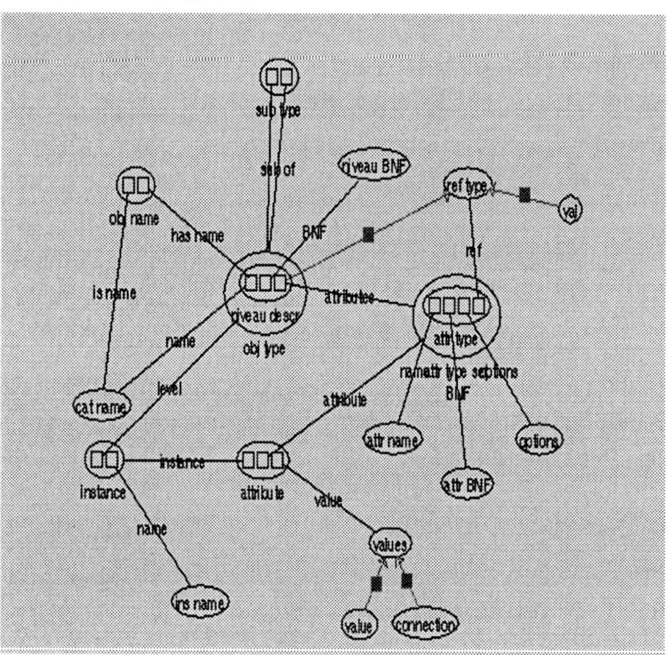

Fig. 5. The meta model of product development process

The concepts discussed under the three main building blocks were translated accordingly to define the meta model of the product development process using the *meta model editor*, see figure 5. Before generating the GDPTools, the data model must be designed and populated. As the tools were intended to be used to present data, a DPT manager was introduced to make a separation between the design tools of Information Systems (IS) analysis and design activities. Therefore, a simple *data model editor* was designed within the DPT manager. This *data model editor* is a menu driven text editor, where multiple levels of required main objects are allowed to be defined. It enables the selection of relationships and attributes according to the company situations at each level of the three objects. The concepts that are required to appear in the *data model editor* are those of characters, and therefore, the *Concept* to *graphic_object* counterpart definition was simple. The only difference was that a simple selection oriented *data model editor* was required. The *data model editor* allows the user to add the company specific data model, and this was designed specifically to the taste of the problem solver.

Population generation is associated with a *population editor* that allows the user to enter, modify or delete instances to the data model and is coupled to the *DPT manger* (see figure 6) which takes control of the main activities of the GDPTool. Multiple levels of main objects defined in the data model are described by a number of attributes. The *population editor* assigns values to each attribute and characterize a main object instance at a certain level. Population editing is menu driven, and the user selects a main object, the level of the object, and then the desired operation to be performed. For example, after an *add* operation, a form appears on the screen in which the attributes can be given a value to characterize the instance. This way straightforward add, delete, or modify operations are included according to the problem owners requirements. The *population editor* also consists a *synonym editor* which enables the user to stream line the jargon usage. The synonyms can be defined and the preferred synonym option can be given. The 'check synonyms option' can be selected for automatically translating the term used into preferred synonyms during the addition or modification of an instance.

In addition to *population generation* the *DPT manager* gives the user access to extract and present the entered data in several ways, including simple listings, user defined listings, graphics, trees and matrices. The simplest way to extract data from the database uses the list option. The *list* button generates a list of all instances in the database. The query facility is associated with the *query* button, for selectively extracting instances of any kind to be put on a list for further investigation. These additional options were built into the *DPT manager* to fulfill user requirements.

4.6 Activity Structure Chart

The Activity Structure Chart (ASC), is a one dimensional tree structure of activity hierarchy relationships within the **activity object**. The attribute *activity number* of the **activity object** is the identification that determines the position in the ASC. The components that must appear in the ASC are the instances of

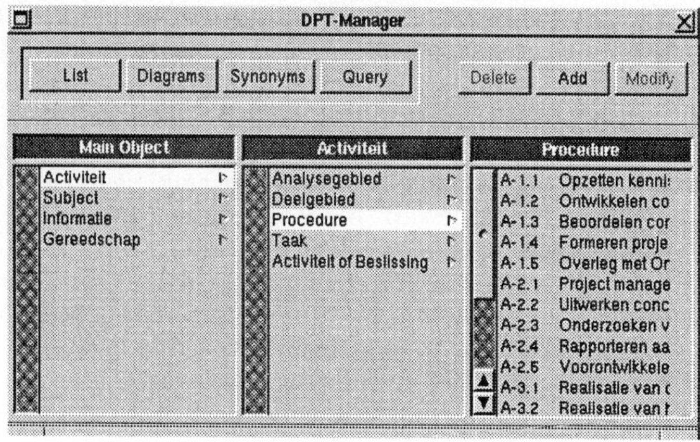

Fig. 6. The DPT manager

activity object and its *subtype relationships*. The activity structure is maintained in the *activity number* attribute, and must be sorted out by extracting the required instances.

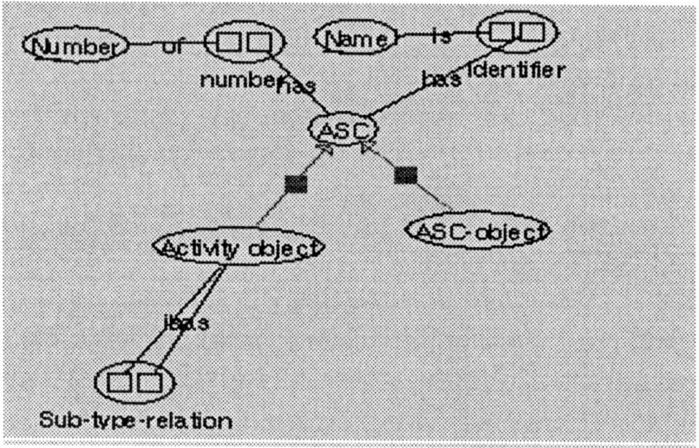

Fig. 7. Meta model of the ASC

Figure 7 shows the meta model that described the information architecture of the ASC. ASC_object is introduced to derive the activity structure chart together with a graphic object called tree_object. The tree_object is provided with the algorithm to calculate the positioning of the Activity_object instances in the hierarchy tree and for including the Sub_type_relationships and positioning rules. The tree_object places the tree chart from left to right on a page and is used for very large tree charts. The required *Concepts*, *graphic_object* counterparts and their *visual shapes* including the calculation to generate activity structure charts are shown in table 1. Figure 8 shows a part of an ASC generated using the CAME environment. The ASC is quite large owing to the number of object instances in the database and is not presented fully as it contains classified information.

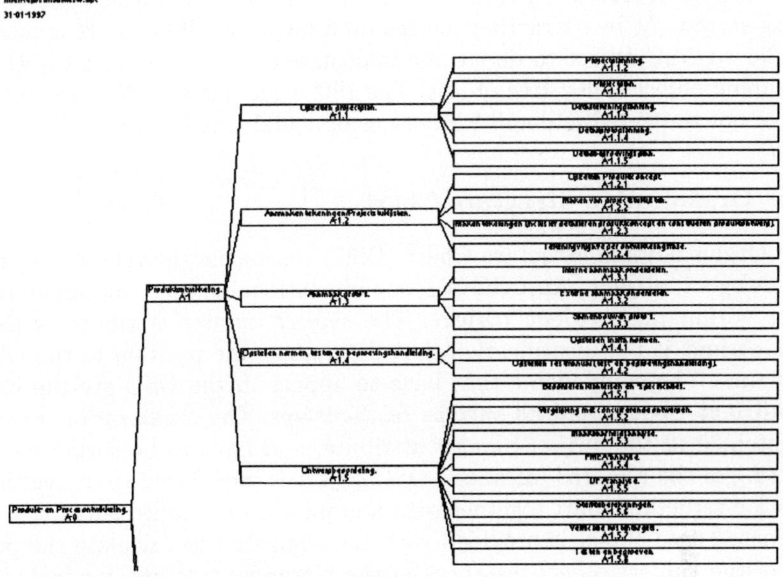

Fig. 8. Part of an activity structure chart

OS_object	*graphic_object*	*shape*
Activity_object	activity_object	a square with activity name and number
Sub_type_relation	sub_type_relation	a line; connecting path in the activity hierarchy
ASC_object	tree_object	a tree chart spreading left to right

Table 1. ACS components of the meta model and their graphic counter parts.

4.7 Information Structure Chart

The Information Structure Chart (ISC) shows the relationships between the levels of the **information object**. This hierarchical tree structure does not exist for the *group of information carriers* level as one *information carrier* can be a part of more than one group or may not be in a group at all. The ISC is a one dimensional information hierarchy relationships within the **information object**. The *information number* attribute of the **information object** is the identification that determines position in the ISC. The components that appear in the ISC are the instances of **information object** and its *subtype relationships*. The information structure is maintained in the *information number* attribute, and being sorted out by extracting the required instances. ISC_object is introduced similar to ASC_object to derive the information structure chart together with a graphic object called tree_object. The ISC is similar to ASC and quite large, but is not presented in detail for reasons of confidentiality.

4.8 Organization Structure Chart

The Organizational Structure Chart (OSC) represents the relationships within the **subject object**. An OSC is a one dimensional subject hierarchy relationships within the **subject object**. The *subject number* attribute of the **subject object** is the identification that determines the position in the OSC tree structure. The components that have to appear in the OSC are the instances of **subject object** and its *subtype relationships*. The organization structure is maintained in the *subject number* attribute, and have to be sorted out by extracting of the required instances. OSC_object is introduced to derive the organization structure chart together with a graphic object called small_tree_object. The small_tree_object is provided with the algorithm to calculate the positioning of the subject_object instances in the hierarchy tree and for including the Sub_type_relationships and positioning rules. The small_tree_object places the tree chart from top to bottom on a page and is used for relatively small tree charts. The OSC is not so large as other two structure charts, but full details are not presented for reasons of confidentiality.

4.9 Create/Use/Own Matrix

The Create/Use/Own Matrix (CUOM) represents the relationships between the **subject** and **information object**. This is a matrix that indicates whether a subject, is an information creator, user and/or owner using the letters C, U and O[2]. Creator, user and owner are attributes of **information object**. The components that have to appear in the CUOM are the instances of **subject** and **information object** and the *relationships* between these are selected at each level of **information object** according to *create, own* and *user* attributes. The matrix maintains the *number and name* of **subject** and **information object**, and they have to be sorted out by extracting of the required instances. The meta model that described the information architecture of the CUOM is given in figure 9.

[2] The GDPT uses M, G and E for Creator, User and Owner as the tool was developed for a Dutch problem owner this stands for Maker, Gebruiker and Eigenaar in Dutch.

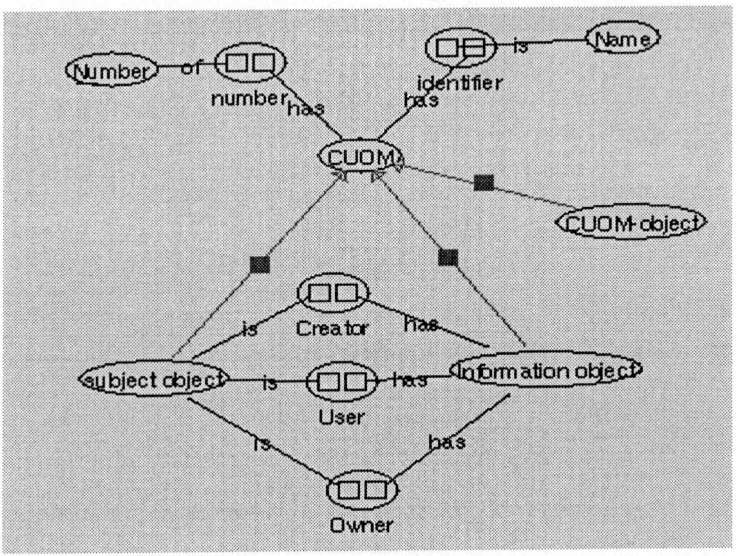

Fig. 9. Meta model of the CUOM

The CUOM matrix is generated using the following graphic object coupling. CUOM_object is introduced to derive a create/user/own matrix together with a graphic object called the matrix_object. The matrix_object is provided with the algorithm to calculate the positioning of the subject and information object instances. The subject and information objects are given graphic text objects to include their name and number. The subject object instances with their name and number are placed horizontally one after another, top to bottom and the information object instances with their name and number are placed vertically from left to right. The matrix_object calculates the maximum number of subject and information object instances involved and the relationships between creator, user and owner attributes of the information object and place this information in the matrix. The matrix_object also takes care of drawing vertical and horizontal lines according to the maximum number of selected object instances. Figure 10 shows a part of a CUOM generated with the use of the CAME environment. The CUOM is quite large owing to the number of object instances of the database and is not included due to the confidential nature of the data.

4.10 Task Allocation Matrix

The Task Allocation Matrix (TAM) is similar to CUOM matrix except for the fact that it represents the relationships between the **subject** and **activity object**. This is a matrix that indicates whether a subject has a task, responsibility, coordination and/or execution with letters R, C and E. Responsible, co-ordination and executive are task level attributes of an **activity object**. The

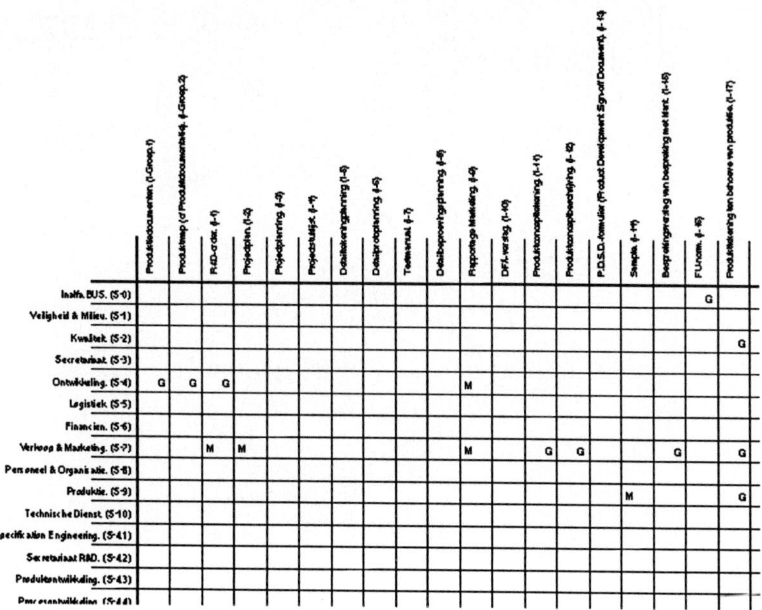

Fig. 10. Part of a create/use/own matrix

components that have to appear in the TAM are the instances of **subject** and **activity object** and the *relationships* between these are selected at each level of **activity object** according to *responsible, co-ordination* and *executor* attributes. The matrix maintains the *number and name* attributes of **subject** and **activity object**, and theses have to be sorted out by extracting of the required instances. The TAM is similar to CUOM, is quite large and detailed matrices are not given for reasons of confidentiality.

4.11 IDEF-0 like Diagram

The Integrated computer-aided manufacturing DEFinition (IDEF)-0-like diagram represents the relationships between the **information** and **activity object**. This diagram is used to represent the relationships in a surveyable manner, and is slightly different from the original IDEF-0 diagram and therefore it is called an IDEF-0-like diagram. The boxes represent the instances of the **activity object** and arrows represent the instances of the **information object**. The incoming arrows to the left of the activity box represent the information *required* to carry out an activity, while the outgoing arrows to the right of the activity box represent the information *delivered* by the activity. The reaching the activity box from the bottom indicate the *tools* used in the activity, each activity carries its decomposition up to the task level and maintains a hierarchy structure, is similar to Data Flow Diagram (DFD) technique.

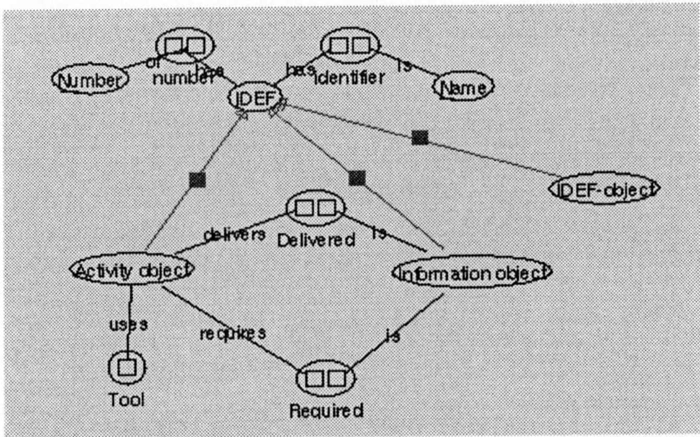

Fig. 11. The meta model of the IDEF-0-like technique

The components that have to appear in an IDEF-0-like diagram are the instances of **information** and **activity object** and the *relationships* between these are selected at each level of **activity object** according to *required* and *delivered* attributes. The diagram maintains the *number and name* attributes of **information** and **activity object**, and these have to be sorted out by extracting of the required instances. The meta model that described the information architecture of the IDEF-0-like technique is given in figure 11.

To generate the IDEF-0 like diagram the following graphic objects were used: Activity_object is provided with a graphic object an IDEF_activity graphic object as an adjustable box with activity name and number including an algorithm to calculate the activity decomposition up to task level. Information_object is provided with text graphic object to represent the name and number of the information object instance. The required relationship is given a graphic object with an arrow and a dot at the begin point. The delivered relationship provided with a graphic object, out going arrow. The tool relationship is provided with a graphic object, upward_arrow to indicate the value of the tool attribute. IDFE_object is introduced to derive a IDEF-0 like schema together with a graphic object IDEF_graphic_object. The IDEF_graphic_object is provided with an algorithm to calculate positioning of the activity object and information object instances in relation to the required and delivered attributes of the activity object. The IDEF_graphic_object places the required and delivered graphic objects by calculating their relative position, and also places the upward_arrow in the correct position to indicate the tool attribute.

Figure 12 shows a part of an IDEF-0-like diagram generated using the CAME environment. The amount of information in one diagram is quite large owing to the number of object instances of the database population. Usually these diagrams are printed on large sheets of paper, detailed models are not presented for reasons of confidentiality.

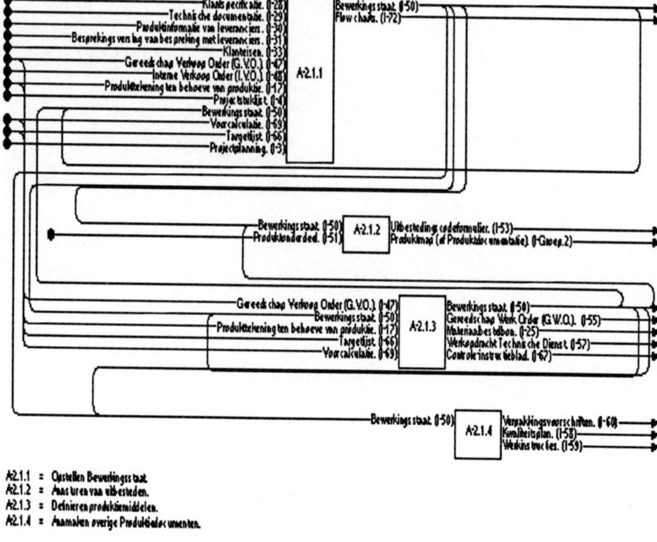

Fig. 12. Part of an IDEF-0-like diagram

5 The Conclusions and Discussion

The detailed evaluation of the GDPT carried out by Vroom [10] on the strength of the CAME technology as a supporting platform for structuring the work floor information for optimizing the supply information can be summarized as follows. The modeling tools required to structure the production process of three production organizations were generated successfully. This was achieved by first modeling the schema description of the product development process and generating six tools to present data in the required form. The databases were populated with real information from the production processes of the participating organizations and each database contained around 3500 object instances. Performance was low but reliable, as the experiment was conducted using an index structure instead of an Object Oriented database. The experiment proved the ability of the environment to support multiple methods, in this case, data modeling and six modeling techniques. The resulting models gave a method integration level as required and a reliable information retrieval and computational facility. At the same time the degree of representational independence was demonstrated by providing, IDEF-0-like graphic representations as well as matrix and tree structures.

The CAME environment proved to be tailorable to product development process modeling requirements. The experiment results lead to the conclusion that the service object based CAME architecture can provide problem specific modeling support to structure product development process data. It showed a stable tool set integration, multi-tool, and multi-method support by the performances of the service object based CAME prototype in real-life situations of product development process modeling. The meta modeling technique described within the CAME environment supported the demands of integrity and consistency of repository and this is guaranteed in the architectural specifications of the environment data during concurrent access by different tools. The novel method specification and generation mechanism answered the needs of the highly diverse representational paradigms, i.e., graphic, tree and matrix structures and information processing requirements.

The requirement of not only the Database Presentation tools but also the ability to experiment with presented results was seen as one of the important issues. The ability to couple computational facilities within the architectural specifications by associating graphic objects with algorithms and procedures is a good indication that the platform is extendable to generate decision support tools. Even though this is not an elegant solution. Therefore, it is being considered as a future research objective. The CAME principle proved a step forward in conceptual modeling. It proved that the conceptual modeling is not limited to information systems development but also applicable to other engineering disciplines, when coupled with Computer Aided Method Engineering facility.

So far we elaborated on the success story of this approach, but there is a long way to go. During a business process redesign and organizational change project there are number of factors have to considered other than the technological capabilities. Computer supported modeling and presentation approaches of many kinds are becoming increasingly important to cross-functional teams charged with understanding business processes and developing solutions. These teams are often composed of members from many disciplines and backgrounds. Many of the members may be unfamiliar with formal modeling approaches, such as those used with structured systems analysis, discrete event simulations, system dynamics, action work-flow, process modeling methods such as IDEF, object-oriented modeling, knowledge modeling, and others. The gap between specialists who are familiar with the modeling tools in use, and the team members who have little or no such background, but are deeply engaged in and knowledgeable about the subject matter of the modeling effort such as business process redesign or an organizational change project has to be addressed. The participatory design of runnable models, such as simulation models and design in a CASE tool, where participants represent their subject matter domain using simulation and representational conventions associated with a modeling tool need to be explored and supported within CAME environments. A consistent way for a team to view, work with, discuss, understand, validate, and apply the results of their design work will be considered in future. The dimension of the interplay between modeling specialists and domain experts or participants being collapsed together in a given project situation remains a research challenge for Computer Aided Method Engineering.

References

1. ANSI Study Group on Data Base Management Systems.: Interim Report 75-02-08. ACM SIGMOND Newsletter **7(2)** (1975)
2. Bouma, H.: Ontwikkeling van een database-presentation tool. Technical Report. School voor Communicatiesystemen, The Netherlands (In Dutch). (1995)
3. Dahanayake, A.N.W.: An environment to support flexible information systems modeling. PhD thesis, Delft University of Technology, The Netherlands. (1997)
4. Dahanayake, A.N.W., Sol, H.G., Dietz, J.L.G.: A fully flexible CAME in a CASE environment. In proc. of 16th International Conference on Conceptual Modeling - ER,97, L.A., California, USA, Springer-Verlag, Lecture Notes in Computer Science. (1997)
5. Kelly, S., Lyytinen, K., Rossi, M.: MetaEdit+ a fully configurable multi-user and multi-tool CASE and CAME environment. In proc. of 8th International Conference CAISE'96, Advance Information Systems Engineering, Springer-Verlag. (1996)
6. van Lohuizen, M., van't Hoff, P., Ammerlaan, M.: Adding Populations to Meta. Technical report, Delft University of Technology, The Netherlands. (1994)
7. van Mourik, D., van Dalen, R.: Building a User Interface to Meta. Technical report, Delft University of Technology, The Netherlands. (1995)
8. Marca, D.A., McGrowan, C.L.: SADT Structured Analysis and Design techniques. McGraw-Hill. (1987)
9. Salazar-Zarate, M.G.: Development of a diagram editor to support modeling techniques used in Upper CASE tools. Master's thesis, Delft University of Technology, The Netherlands. (1996)
10. Vroom, R.W.: A general example model for automotive suppliers of the development process and its related information. Computers in industry (310), 255-280. (1996)

Distributed Light-Weight Persistence in Java - A Tour on RMI- and CORBA-based Solutions

Gerti Kappel, Birgit Schröder

Department of Information Systems
University of Linz, AUSTRIA
{gerti, birgits}@ifs.uni-linz.ac.at

Abstract. Java has potential to support the development of distributed and autonomous though collaborating components in a network computing environment. To provide for the flow of objects between these components some kind of distributed shared memory is needed. So far, Java offers distributed shared memory aka distributed persistence by employing database systems. However, since the main features of database systems, such as transaction management and query languages, are often not needed for these applications, a so called light-weight solution is preferred. In this paper, we introduce the Persistence API supporting a distributed container structure for handling sets of structured data and objects. Distribution is realized both by means of Java's Remote Method Invocation and on top of the CORBA compliant Visibroker for Java. We highlight implementation differences and efforts for migrating between these two technologies.

1 Introduction

Persistence is becoming more and more a primary feature of programming languages, not least due to the requirements of nowadays distributed application scenarios. Such a scenario includes distributed asynchronous communication between autonomous components, where a distributed store acts as an anonymous, distributed shared memory. Java has potential to support the development of such distributed applications, however, there is no persistence model built into Java yet. In the following, we shed some light on various efforts for incorporating persistence into Java, we discuss why database systems do not provide the optimal solution, and what is proposed instead in this paper.

Persistence. There are many research efforts underway to provide any form of persistence for Java. Concerning object persistence, research interest focuses on forms following three determinant principles [2]:

- Orthogonal persistence
- Transitive persistence
- Transparent persistence

Orthogonal persistence implies that any type in an application may be transient or persistent. In terms of Java that means that objects as well as classes and methods may be made persistent.

Transitive persistence implies persistence by reachability, i.e., any instance contained in the object graph rooted at a persistent instance is also meant to be persistent.

Moreover, transitive persistence implies automatic persistence in the sense that objects do not have to be explicitly read from or written to disk.

Transparent persistence implies that code should work independently of whether it is operating on a transient or persistent object. That means that there may be a "store mode" and a "non store mode" for applications as a single indication for persistent or transient behaviour.

There are two main approaches for realizing persistence for Java in the literature [6,3,10]. The first "camp" is providing orthogonal persistence as described above by means of replacing the standard Java Virtual Machine (JVM) with a persistence capable extension. This camp is most prominently lead by the PJama Team [17], and also well supported by Sun Microsystems itself. If these efforts lead to an integration with the standard JVM the upgrading problem may be alleviated. The second "camp" is lead by commercial database companies, which add persistence by changing either the Java source files by means of a preprocessor (e.g., POET 5.0 by POET Software), or the Java class files by means of a postprocessor (ObjectStore PSE by ObjectDesign [7]). Changing source files and class files, however, implies reduced transparent persistence, while by adding hooks into the JVM full transparent persistence is preserved. At the same time, adding distribution and concurrent access is easier for the database camp due to the inherent features of distributed database systems.

Distributed Persistence. While there is a distribution model planned for PJama [12], currently, the main efforts are undertaken with regards to extending the JVM in a single, local address space. For realizing the proposed distribution model for PJama it seems that it will be based on top of Java's Remote Method Invocation (RMI) [11]. The distribution group at JavaSoft favours the principle of exposure of distribution [19], which fits the decision to give PJama a non location transparent global naming scheme in form of an extended URL. The so called Persistent Object Locator (POL) contains a composite of a protocol name, a DNS name as well as a store name followed by an object name ("pol://hostname/storename.objectname"). This naming scheme is scalable, and - last but not least - can easily be implemented on top of Java RMI. In addition, there is also proposed a location transparent naming scheme for applications requiring a more closely coupled cooperation of a limited number of stores. In such cases, a so called Persistent Object Name (PON) is to be used, which contains just a protocol identifier followed by a store name and an object name ("pon://storename.objectname"). While a location transparent naming scheme requires more efforts in supporting uniqueness of names, with CORBA it may be possible to get location transparent functionality at a reasonable effort.

Distributed Light-Weight Persistence. By now, distributed persistence in Java is mainly available by "heavy-weight" database systems with more or less transparent persistence. Database systems are called heavy-weight since they offer a lot of features which are not needed for many applications at hand. At the same time, these features make database systems less flexible and less adaptable to changing requirements. Thus, we favour a distributed "light-weight" persistence model, where we trade heavy-weight database features such as query management and consistency management with access to distributed storage by means of Java RMI [15] and CORBA [8].

Related Work. Most closely related to our work, the JavaSpaces Technology [13] proposed by Sun Microsystems provides a distributed persistence and object exchange mechanism for Java (there is no public beta release of JavaSpaces available yet). Objects are written in entries that provide a typed grouping of relevant fields. Clients can perform simple operations on a JavaSpace server to write new entries, lookup existing entries, and remove entries from the space. With its "flow of objects" approach, a JavaSpace may be used to implement cooperative, distributed applications, which communicate just by connecting to a common distributed JavaSpace and by passing objects through that space. So, a JavaSpace is like a distributed shared memory in a loosely coupled system. JavaSpaces do not provide transparent persistence, since they rely on the Java Object Serialization mechanism [14]. They work only on copies of entries in contrast to object databases with full transparent persistence.

Focus of this paper. We have implemented a persistence model similar to JavaSpaces, while providing less consistency and integrity because no transaction mechanism is supported yet. The model is built upon a flat data structure - a single table containing attributes of some predefined data types. Such a restricted data model is easy to implement and the resulting base application can be used to investigate further distribution strategies. In addition, the proposed distributed light-weight persistence model is also applicable in any situation, where the features of a heavy-weight database system such as query and consistency management cause too much overhead. A usage scenario might be a network computer environment [1] where a network computer has little or no persistent store, thus one is looking for other ways than heavy-weight database systems to provide network computing applications with distributed persistence. Another, very similar scenario are cooperative applications needing a simple asynchronous communication mechanism to park some data another application will fetch some time later. Using a database system for that purpose results in too complicated solutions and is therefore just overkill. A Network File System may provide an appropriate solution but may not always be available.

The main contribution of this paper lies in analyzing two architectures for distributed object computing with respect to their practicability and usability for implementing distributed persistence for Java, namely Java RMI and CORBA. In addition, the investment required to migrate between these two technologies is investigated.

In the following section, we describe the proposed architecture called Persistence API and provide a simple though intuitive example demonstrating the usability of the proposed light-weight persistence in a cooperative distributed environment. In Section 3, we present the implementation of the Persistence API in a local as well as in a distributed environment by means of Java RMI. Section 4 discusses the realization of the distributed Persistence API on top of a CORBA ORB, to make these two distribution mechanisms comparable, and to highlight the migration effort between RMI and CORBA. A final comparison concludes the paper.

2 Architecture of Persistence API

Suppose you are working in a small group (up to 10 persons) of researchers with workstations bundled together in a LAN and having an intranet connected to some databases for the administration of lectures, research papers, and a small library. The library contains about 2000 books, which are - for historical reasons - recorded in a single file formatted like

```
%n 2049
%a ORFALI, R./HARKEY, D.
%t Client/Server Programming with Java and CORBA
%y 1997
```

Access is granted to anybody having a login belonging to the researchers' group. So anyone may read and edit the file. The file is linked from the department's web server, so students may look up the library with the browser's built-in text search utility.

Moving that data file to - for instance - Oracle8 and adding a web user interface for updating and querying is one alternative for migrating the library file into a more user-friendly environment, while a heavy-weight one. The other one is building a small Java applet or application connecting to a distributed light-weight persistence mechanism maintaining a single table with four attributes, namely number, author, title, and year. No database features other than persistence are required, and the application can handle the persistent data almost like any other, but transient data structure.

In this case, the distributed light-weight persistence mechanism proposed in the following sections could be applied as follows. The application has to define the table structure:

```
public class LibraryStructure
   extends persistence.RecordDefinition{
   public LibraryStructure(){
      alias = "library";
      attributes ={"number","author","title","year"};
      types ={"INTEGER","STRING","STRING","STRING(4)"};
   }
}
```

The next step is connecting to the location of the table:

```
RecordDefinition libRecord =
   new LibraryStructure();
// if the table resides on the local host:
// TableIfc library = new Table("library.jps",libRecord);
// if the table resides on a remote host:
TableIfc library = new Table("rmi://panther:2001/ifs-library/library.jps",
   libRecord);
```

Afterwards the library instance may be updated or queried like

```
library.get("title","Java and CORBA");
```

Additionally, there is the attribute type OBJECT available, as an extension to the classical table-oriented relational data model containing numerical and character types only. The here presented persistence mechanism just catches any Java object and uses the built-in Java Object Serialization mechanism to produce a byte stream representation of the object's state to be stored in the table's file. Querying for two objects to be equal results in the equals() method to be executed as provided by the runtime types of the instances. While method equals of Java's root Object does check for object identity, subclasses of Object typically override the equals method to provide a value-based comparison operation. So, querying of OBJECT typed attributes in a table does only return correct results, if the object's class overrides the equals operation accordingly.

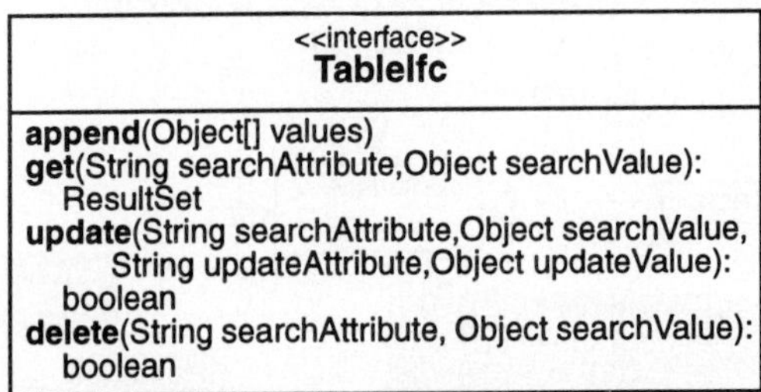

Fig. 2-1. Persistence operations defined in interface Tablelfc

As a summary, Persistence API allows the following types to be used as attribute types: BYTE, INTEGER, LONG, DOUBLE, FLOAT, BOOLEAN, STRING [(fixed length)], BYTE_ARRAY [(fixed length)], and OBJECT. A table given a set of attribute names and corresponding attribute types can then be manipulated through operations defined in the interface Tablelfc described in Fig. 2-1. Note, get, update, and delete operations are overloaded operations and work also with set-valued input parameters.

The interface defining the operational functionality of Persistence API is realized by one of the following architectural components (cf. Fig. 2-2):

- A single user implementation operating on a local random access file.
- An implementation making remote method invocations to a server, which is controlling concurrent accesses to a random access file residing on the server's host. As shown in Fig. 2-2, remote method invocation requires a stub on the client side and a skeleton on the server side.
- Any future implementation mapping the persistence operations of the interface to a full-fledged database system by means of JDBC [5]. This alternative is not followed in detail here, as the white components in Fig. 2-2 indicate.

We have implemented the first two of these architectural alternatives: The component operating purely locally, and the component operating in a remote file system. For the latter, both Java RMI and a CORBA compliant Java ORB have been used. The next sections will guide the reader through both solutions.

Java Application
Persistence API
local file system
Stub | Stub | JDBC
Skeleton | Skeleton | native Driver | Net Bridge
remote file system
JDBC
Middle-ware

Fig. 2-2. Architecture of Persistence API

3 RMI Persistence API

This section first describes the local solution in short, i.e., how access operations on a local random access file are realized. Thereafter, reuse of the local component within a distributed environment by means of Java RMI is shown.

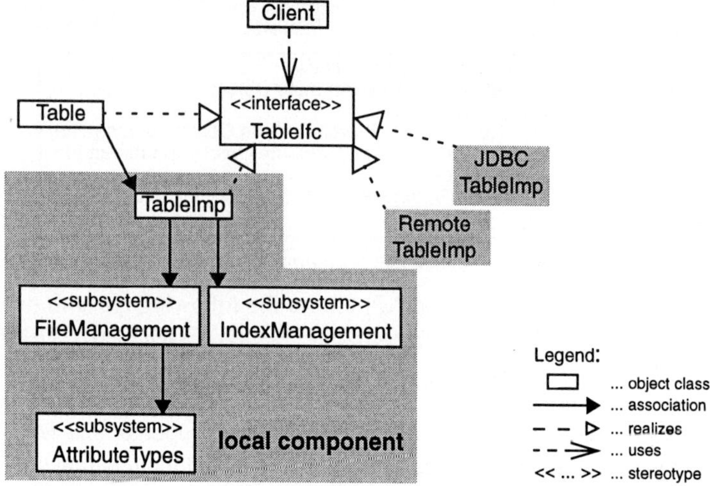

Fig. 3-1. Local and remote implementation of TableIfc

The local component in the proposed architecture is represented by one single class called TableImp encapsulating and directing three subsystems; File Management, Attribute Types, and Index Management (cf. Fig. 3-1)

1. The subsystem File Management fulfills tasks like positioning, reading from, and writing to the file, which has been indicated through the constructor of class Table as shown in the previous section.
2. The subsystem Attribute Types supplements the File Management subsystem by defining read and write operations for all available attribute types. Any extensions with regards to available types are to be added here.
3. The subsystem Index Management is active if the user has specified one or more attributes to be indexed. Then the TableImp class consults the Index Management each time a query request is made for all record positions matching the indexed attribute(s), and if new records are to be indexed. This way, lookup performance may be increased significantly.

Clients just handle instances of Table via its interface TableIfc. In addition, a table contains an instance implementing either the local or the remote component of the Persistence API. One can say that Table acts as a proxy (cf. the proxy pattern in [4]) for any implementation of interface TableIfc. This proxy has to do additional mappings depending on the used - local or remote - implementation.

For the remote component, the natural aim is to reuse the local component unchanged at a large degree. In order to be available for remote method invocation, RMI requires a local implementation to declare that it implements an application specific subtype of the common superinterface java.rmi.Remote, next to any other local interface the class may implement. So we would like to define a subinterface of TableIfc to be also a subinterface of java.rmi.Remote via Java multiple interface inheritance, and let any remote implementation declare that it implements the so derived interface RemoteTableIfc. However, this is not allowed with Java RMI. Due to the principle of exposure of distribution, any client using a java.rmi.Remote interface has to be aware that she is dealing with a non-local interface.Therefore the client must always be prepared to handle special exceptions of type java.rmi.RemoteException representing network and other failures resulting from a non-local execution of code. So, an application specific interface may never have multiple, local and remote supertypes. Thus, we have to declare an additional interface RemoteTableIfc with all the operations as declared by the interface TableIfc, but extending java.rmi.Remote.

The first step to make our application RMI-capable is done. The next step is to define the implementation of interface RemoteTableIfc. There are two alternatives. First, one may leave an existing class totally unchanged and wrap it into a RMI-capable class delegating all remote method invocations to its aggregate, resulting in an additional class required. Alternatively, the existing local implementation has to declare an additional - remote - interface in its implements clause. This is done for class TableImp. So the first lines of its class definition read like this:

```
public class TableImp
   implements TableIfc, RemoteTableIfc{...}
```

Class Table acts now as a proxy for TableImp in a twofold way. First, via an instance variable of type TableIfc, and second, via an additional instance variable of type RemoteTableIfc (cf Fig. 3-2). Since Table may not use one single, polymorphic variable, it must statically distinguish those two instance variables. Main differences in handling the two variables are found when creating the corresponding objects. While in the local case a client constructs an instance of class Table, which results in a local instance of class TableImp to be created (via the Java new-operator), a remote instance of class TableImp has to be created via a Factory object residing on the same remote host as the user-specified remote table. Therefore we have declared a class TableServerImpl implementing a remote interface TableServer with just one operation called open. This single method is implemented to return any already existing instance of TableImp handling the required file, otherwise it creates a new one. The underlying RMI runtime system is responsible for connection management and multi-threading; managing concurrent accesses is also up to the RMI runtime system. The user defined implementation has just to define any remote method as synchronized. This keyword signals the Java built-in exclusive lock mechanism to be active, so multiple requests on the object are executed sequentially.

As we have seen, any existing, local implementation can be made RMI-capable by just declaring an additional, but Remote interface in its implements clause. Further, the RMI compiler rmic has to be run against any implementation of a remote interface, in order to get the stub and skeleton classes required for client-server communication via RMI. In our case, rmic generates the client side stub named TableImp_Stub.class - to be deployed on the client host - and the server side skeleton named TableImp_Skel.class (cf. Fig. 3-3). All the basic network communication is initiated and done on behalf of these two classes. From an application programmer's view they are the only visible components of the RMI system.

In our example, a Table instance holding a remote reference to a remote TableImp instance is built as depicted in Fig. 3-2. You have to keep in mind that the variable remotePerformer is declared as type RemoteTableIfc and receives an object of class TableImp_Stub. Because this is done via a remote method invocation itself, the stub object has to be shipped across the network. For that purpose, the RMI runtime system uses the standard Java Object Serialization mechanism. The stub object is serialized into a byte stream on the server side, sent to the client, and then deserialized into a newly created instance of the stub class on the client host. The same way any parameter or return value passed by some remote method invocation is shipped. This implies that only serializable Java types can take part in a remote method invocation. The TableServer's method open, e.g., receives an instance of a String as well as an instance of a RecordDefinition as parameters. While String is serializable by default, class RecordDefinition has to declare to implement java.io.Serializable explicitly.

```
public class Table{
   TableIfc performer;
   RemoteTableIfc remotePerformer;
   Table(String url,RecordDefinition struct){
      ...
      // if url contains  rmi://host:2001/tablename
   TableServer factory = (TableServer)Naming.lookup("host:2001/TableServer");
   remotePerformer = factory.open(tablename,struct);
   }
```

Fig. 3-2. Implementation of class Table

Fig. 3-3 shows the relationship between a stub and a TableImp. This relationship again exploits the proxy pattern described in [4], because the stub hides the fact, that it operates the request of the table client on the real subject by delegating to it. With a network connection in between, the stub knows how to connect to its real subject (the remote TableImp instance), and marshalls the parameter to be shipped to the real subject's skeleton (TableImp_Skel). The skeleton on the server side unmarshalls the parameters, calls the real subject, and marshalls the returned value to be shipped back to the client.

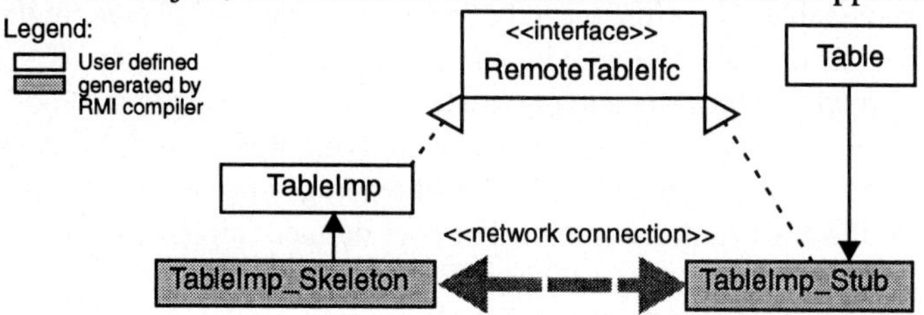

Fig. 3-3. Table uses TableImp_Stub as proxy for TableImp

There are some words remaining to be spoken about the Naming class used in Fig. 3-2. As mentioned already in the introduction, the Java RMI Naming Service is built in a location-dependent manner. There has to run a separate RMI registry process on any host offering remotely available objects, and this process has two main purposes. First, a RMI object has to be bound in the local RMI registry in order to become available for remote clients. If a RMI object is bound in a RMI registry, that registry maintains the stub of the RMI object to be shipped to remote clients. Second, lookup operations are allowed for both local and remote clients. The lookup consists of an URL string indicating the name under which a RMI object is bound in the registry, and it results in the stub of the bound RMI object to be shipped to the client. A remote client typically uses the Naming class providing the client with an URL based naming interface to a registry - this time adding a hostname and a portnumber in front of the name of the searched RMI object.

To summarize the implementation process, distributing an instance of class TableImp requires the following steps.

1. Define any method to be invoked remotely in interface RemoteTableIfc extending the interface java.rmi.Remote (cf. Fig. 3-2.).
2. Define class TableImp to implement interface RemoteTableIfc.
3. Build TableImp_Stub and TableImp_Skel by means of the RMI compiler rmic (cf. Fig. 3-3.).
4. Define the factory interface TableServer with one method open to maintain any TableImp instances on a single host.
5. Define implementation class TableServerImpl as subtype of java.rmi.server.UnicastRemoteObject. This class builds the server application by implementing the main() method, where an instance of the class binds itself in the local RMI registry and then awaits client requests. Method open() checks the filename and the structure of a table requested by a client and dynamically creates a new TableImp_Stub to be shipped to the client.
6. Class Table must delegate all persistence operations to either the local or the remote implementation it contains, and it must catch any RemoteException, if it uses a RMI object.

4 CORBA Persistence API

Migrating the RMI Persistence API to a solution based on CORBA first of all enrolls the question which product to use. CORBA is just an abstract specification of the common tasks a distributed object bus brokering requests and responses between various applications in an heterogeneous environment has to fulfill.

While operations on a standard CORBA object have to be defined in a corresponding IDL interface, and any IDL language binding can then be used to implement that IDL interface, we just need an homogenous Java solution. Therefore, Visigenic's (now Borland's) Visibroker for Java [18] comes at hand, with Caffeine compiler as an optional feature, which may be used to define operations on a CORBA object already in Java leaving IDL behind. Another advantage is that with Caffeine full object-oriented semantic of RMI remote method invocation is preserved, while IDL just allows parameters of predefined basic or constructed data types to be used in a call. This restriction is due to the fact that in favour of maximum heterogeneity CORBA has to define a least common denominator of data types of a large amount of programming languages in order to be shipped across a common object bus.

Visibroker's Caffeine uses an IDL extension called extensible struct as type for parameters destinated for CORBA objects implemented in a 100% pure Java environment, lacking therefore interoperability with CORBA objects residing on the same bus, but written in other languages. Analogous to RMI, any serializable Java object may then be used as a parameter or return value in a remote method invocation, rapidly simplifying the migration effort between RMI and CORBA. Thus, necessary changes to the RMI solution for realizing distributed light-weight persistence based on the Visibroker ORB are reduced to some architectural differences between these two mechanisms, which are covered in the following.

First, the Naming service of Visibroker is realized in a location transparent manner by means of the ORB Smart Agent (osagent). While multiple osagents maintaining registered CORBA objects find each other inside a LAN via UDP broadcasting, osagents have to be configured statically to find other osagents residing in "foreign" TCP/IP based LANs. In principle, it is possible to register and lookup a CORBA object by just specifying an interface name and an optional instance name, which has been given at instantiation, and it's the osagent's task to locate a suiting CORBA object wherever it resides. Of course, one can also specify a host indicating the location of the CORBA object.

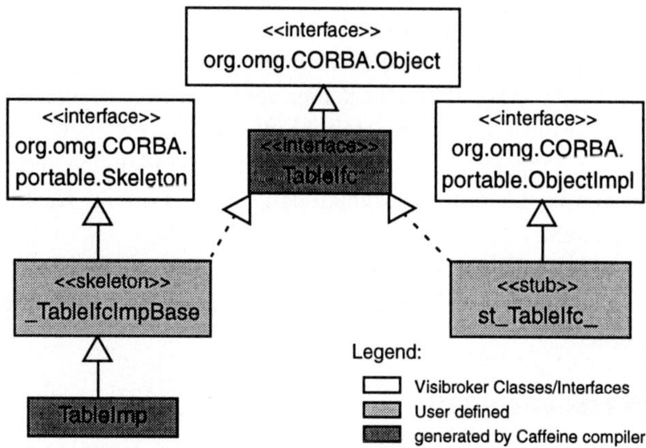

Fig. 4-1. Developing a Table as CORBA Object

Second, if the osagent locates a requested CORBA object on the same host as the client, a local pointer is returned to the client instead of initiating a network connection based on sockets, while RMI initializes interprocess communication via sockets in any case.

In the following, the migration process from the RMI solution shown in the previous section to Visibroker's ORB supported by Visibroker's Caffeine compiler java2iiop is outlined (Note: No IDL interface has to be defined!).

1. Derive both interfaces TableIfc and TableServer from org.omg.CORBA.Object instead of from java.rmi.Remote. As a restriction, any used Java Exception has to be redefined to extend just org.omg.CORBA.UserException, without any further inheritance.
2. Run the Caffeine compiler java2iiop against those two Java interfaces. There is a considerable large amount of Java source files generated, at least two source files per Java class that is used as a parameter or return value in the above interfaces, for providing all necessary conversions between a first class Java type and its corresponding IIOP format. Source files of further interest are those forming the base for implementing the interfaces, as shown in the next step.

3. For reuse of the local component Tablelmp, a different way to RMI is possible. Deriving Tablelmp class from the Skeleton class _TablelfclmplBase generated in step 2 (cf. Fig. 4-1) rules out the usage of an instance outside the CORBA runtime. This implies that class Table no more needs two separate instance variables to distinguish between an implementation of Tablelfc, and of RemoteTablelfc, respectively. The Tablelmp instance would be either remote or local, depending on whether the client and the table requested by the client reside on the same host or not. However, the standard Java interpreter may not be used, but the Visibroker runtime vbj encapsulating the Java interpreter.
4. Implement TableServerlmpl through extending the also generated Skeleton class _TableServerlmplBase. In addition, perform all the same tasks as its sibling class in the RMI Persistence API has performed, despite the dynamic creation of a Tablelmp instance, which is now done by the following lines of code inside method open():

   ```
   Tablelfc table;
   ...
   table = new Tablelmp(filename, struct);
   boa().obj_is_ready(table);      // Registering with the Basic Object Adapter (boa)
   ...
   return table;
   ...
   ```

   In contrast to RMI where the variable of type RemoteTablelfc receives a stub instance, a CORBA reference is not shipped via Object Serialization of a stub, but via an Interoperable Object Reference (IOR), a very large alphanumerical character chain identifying any registered CORBA object.
5. What's on the client side left to do? Look at the following lines of code.

   ```
   public class Table{
      Tablelfc performer;
      ...
      public Table(String url,RecordDefinition struct){
         TableServer factory;
         // if url contains a location
         // factory =TableServerHelper.bind(orb,"TableServer",location, null);
         // else (if no host is specified)
         factory =TableServerHelper.bind(orb,"TableServer");
         // use the factory to connect to the Tablelmp
         performer = factory.open(filename,struct);
         ...
      }
   ...
   }
   ```

The important difference here is that if someone does not specify a location, then there should be just one TableServer instance active in the whole LAN. The host where that TableServer object resides is the same for all dynamically created Tablelmps.

5 Comparison and Outlook

Distributed light-weight persistence is useful for cooperative network computing environments, within the context of the flow of objects approach, requiring a loosely coupled, distributed shared memory. Unlike JavaSpaces, we have investigated in distributed light-weight persistence by means of Java RMI, as well as by using a CORBA-compliant ORB, namely Visibroker for Java offering the Caffeine Compiler.

Table 5-1: RMI versus CORBA

	RMI	CORBA
Parameter passing	• in • call-by-value for local parameters, call-by-reference for RMI objects	• in, out, inout • call-by-reference, but without Visibroker's Caffeine only IDL types may pass a call
Polymorphism	• Supported, but stubs always depend on the remote implementation	• Supported, for CORBA objects (stubs are independent on remote implementation) but not supported for local parameters (just flat IDL types)
Persistent References	• Since JDK 1.2 (Remote Object Activation)	• Supported (through implementation repository)
Location transparency	Not supported: • host specific RMI registry, • no multiple, local and remote mixed inheritance of Remote interfaces allowed • always interprocess communication via Sockets	Supported, with Visibroker: • agent based name service • no sockets for client and server on same host
Connection management	• not user configurable	• flexible
Communication modes	• synchronous	• synchronous • asynchronous oneway • deferred synchronous
Usability	• simple	• complex environment, IDL mapping
Availability	• free (included in Sun JDK's Java Core API)	• to be acquired
Standardization	• Through Sun (infiltrated by Microsoft)	• OMG: Well accepted industry standard

For comparison of both the RMI and the CORBA solutions as remote components of the Persistence API, we have considered three dimensions, namely the programming model, differences between infrastructures supported by RMI and a CORBA ORB, and some practical considerations regarding usability, availability, and standardization (see Table 5-1).

Migrating the here presented RMI Persistence API to Visibroker's ORB envolved the process of pulling CORBA down to a RPC system's level. This perhaps provocative statement is based on the following considerations:

1. *Object-oriented semantics*: The conceiveable point of view, that preserving full Java object-oriented semantics in a remote method invocation is better than using flat IDL, is to be faced with the therefore lost heterogeneity. A serialized Java object is transportable via CORBA's IIOP (Internet Inter-ORB Protocol) [8], but senseless for any non-Java receiver. Otherwise, the here presented Persistence API could be leveraged to contain all but the OBJECT type, and the mappings that are to be done in order to pull Java objects into a random access file may be reused for pulling them also onto IIOP.
2. *Implementation versus interface inheritance:* A CORBA stub depends solely on its IDL Interface, while a RMI stub depends on the actual implementation of a Remote interface. When it comes to inheritance, any CORBA stub on the client side may be used to invoke methods on any subtype of its interface, while RMI requires the stub built upon the subclass implementing the subinterface to be available on the client host. While RMI offers dynamic stub loading instead, there is an overhead with the time needed for downloading as well as with possible exeption handling.
3. *Transparency:* A CORBA ORB may not only offer location transparency, but also relocation and migration transparency, and finally full language transparency, while RMI is limited to be non location transparent. RMI requires an homogenous language environment (100 % pure Java).
4. *Parameter passing:* CORBA IDL allows parameters to be declared as in, out, and inout, whereas Java RMI parameters are always passed as in. Therefore CORBA parameters are called by reference, and RMI parameters called by value (via Java Object Serialization).
5. *Communication modes:* CORBA offers synchronous communication by default, but also oneway (client does not block for server) and a deferred (future) synchronous mode.
6. *Connection management and multi-threading:* RMI has a closed connection management mechanism and offers no means for user configuration. CORBA allows 4 different activation strategies which are also related to the underlying connection management.
7. *Standardization:* The broad standardization body formed by the OMG lets expect a higher quality assurance and user acceptance than available for Java RMI with a single vendor giving licences.

The main advantage of RMI lies in its ease of use and free availability. For rather simple applications requiring an homogenous Java environment, Java RMI may do it perfectly, while applications with special requirements, such as for integrating legacy systems, may need to invest in CORBA.

However, there is a process for melding these two technologies for interoperating based on CORBA IIOP, as mentioned in [9,16]. We believe, that there are major movements in the field of distributed object computing, and especially its integration with distributed information systems underway, so further investigations are urgently needed.

References

[1] APPLE, IBM, NETSCAPE, ORACLE, SUN, 1996. Network Computer Reference Profile, http://www.nc.ihost.com/nc_ref_profile.html.

[2] ATKINSON, M.P., DAYNES, L., JORDAN, M.J., SPENCE, S., 1996. Design Issues For Persistent Java: A Type-safe, Object-oriented, Orthogonally Persistent System. In Proceedings of the Seventh Workshop on Persistent Object Systems, New Jersey, May 1996.

[3] First International Workshop on Persistence and Java (PJ1), Glasgow, September 1996. http://www.dcs.gla.ac.uk/~carol/Workshops/PJSAbstracts.html.

[4] GAMMA, E., HELM, R., JOHNSON, R., VLISSIDES, J., 1995. Design Patterns: Elements of Reusable Object-Oriented Software. Addison-Wesley 1995.

[5] HAMILTON, G., CATTELL, R., 1997. JDBC: A Java SQL API, JavaSoft, January 10, 1997.

[6] JORDAN, D., 1998. Stimulating Java Persistence: A Report on the Second International Workshop on Persistence and Java. In Java Report, SIGS Publications, Vol.2(1), January 1998.

[7] OBJECTDESIGN INC. ObjectStore PSE for Java. http://www.odi.com/content/products/pse/doc_120/doc/

[8] OBJECT MANAGEMENT GROUP, The Common Object Request Broker: Architecture and Specification, 2.0. ed., July 1995.

[9] ORFALI, R., HARKEY, D., 1997. Client/Server Programming with Java and Corba, John Wiley & Sons.

[10] Second International Workshop on Persistence and Java (PJ2), San Francisco, August 1997. http://www.sunlabs.com/research/forest/COM.Sun.Labs.Forest.PJava.PJW2.pjw2.html.

[11] SPENCE, S. A Scalable Model of Distribution Strategies for Persistent Java. In [3].

[12] SPENCE, S., ATKINSON, M.P. A Scalable Model of Distribution Promoting Autonomy of and Cooperation between PJava Object Stores. In Proceedings of the Hawaii International Conference on System Sciences, Aston Wailea Resort, Wailea, Hawaii, USA, January 1997.

[13] SUN MICROSYSTEMS, JavaSpaces Specification, http://chatsubo.javasoft.com/specs/index.html.

[14] SUN MICROSYSTEMS, Object Serialization Specification, http://www.javasoft.com/products/jdk/1.1/docs/guide/serialization/spec/serialTOC.doc.html.

[15] SUN MICROSYSTEMS, Remote Method Invocation Specification, http://www.javasoft.com/products/jdk/1.1/docs/guide/rmi/spec/rmiTOC.doc.html.

[16] SUN MICROSYSTEMS, RMI and IIOP in Java, June 1997. http://www.javasoft.com/pr/1997/june/statement970626-01.html.

[17] The PJama Project, University of Glasgow, Department of Computing Science, http://www.dcs.gla.ac.uk/.

[18] Visibroker for Java: Programmer's Guide, Version 3.0. Borland, http://www.visigenic.com.

[19] WALDO, J., WYANT, G., WOLLRATH, A., KENDALL, S., 1994. A Note on Distributed Computing. Sun Micorsystems Technical Report (SMLI TR-94-29), November 1994.

Specifying the Interaction Between Information Sources

T.J.M. Bench-Capon

Department of Computer Science, The University of Liverpool,
Chadwick Building, P.O. Box 147, Liverpool L69 3BX, England.
tbc@csc.liv.ac.uk

Abstract. Recently there have been proposals for sophisticated informations systems which require a number of information sources to communicate with each other autonomously. In this paper we discuss how such interactions might be specified, using performatives specified in terms of preconditions, postconditions and completion conditions, identified with respect to conversation classes. Full specification requires additional conditions deriving from the policies and strategies of particular agents. The result is an approach to the specification of interaction between information sources which is uniform, and so permits generic handling of the different sources, but which provides sufficient flexibility to allow for different styles of conversation, and customised agent behaviour.

1 Introduction

Today, through the Internet and World Wide Web, information is more accessible than ever before. Users can get information from distant databases and other information sources. One influential suggestion for an architecture to support the automated collection of this information is that proposed in Wiederhold (1992), which introduced the notion of a *mediator* as a program which when presented with an information need would locate, extract and combine information from a variety of sources to provide a value added service. There is now a considerable body of work following these aims, perhaps most notably the group of projects which go under the umbrella title of the Knowledge Sharing Effort (Neches et al 1991). Other approaches share many of these ideas, perhaps most generally systems based on co-operating communicating agents (e.g. Wooldridge and Jennings 1995).

In all these systems is that we have a collection of software programs able to communicate with one another under their own control. Since the various systems will have been built in different styles and for different purposes, they must be extended in some way to give them these common communication facilities. The architectural solution in the Wiederhold style of system is to provide each system with a *wrapper*, which supplies common communication protocols, performs language translation and the like. (In an agent system this would correspond to the communication layer, but I shall use "wrapper" henceforth in this paper, and "agent" to refer to any wrapped resource, with no commitment to what lies behind the wrapper.) When the systems are wrapped in this way they present a uniform appearance to each other: the precise nature of the system is hidden behind the wrapper. In this paper I want to look at how we might specify the communication capabilities of these wrappers.

The main tool for talking about these communication facilities is the notion of a *speech act* or *performative*. The key elements in the theory for our purposes are:

- Different speech acts can use the same propositional content: thus the same utterance can be used both to make an assertion and to ask a question. In speech we can indicate the difference with tone of voice, and in writing by punctuation. In this way we can separate the speech acts from their content, and see the speech acts as the focus with their content as a set of parameters.
- Speech acts are intended to have effects, and are characterised by these intended effects. Thus an assertion is intended to cause the beliefs of its addressee to be modified, while a question is intended to cause the addressee to supply information. Thus when uttering a speech act, the utterer has the intention to bring about some effect, and our linguistic conventions supply the necessary causal link between utterance and desired effect.

Speech acts have become rather dominant in considering how to effect the wrapper layer of the systems we are interested in. The most developed use is in the Knowledge Query and Manipulation Language (KQML), as set out in Finin et al (1994). KQML provides a set of speech acts which are intended to provide an extensible core for communication between the different systems in a knowledge sharing network. We will follow this approach, but focus more closely on how such speech acts can be specified. KQML uses the term *performatives* rather than "speech acts", and we will follow this in the remainder of this paper.

2 Specification of Performatives

The starting point for our investigation is the thesis of Labrou (1996). Labrou provides semantics for KQML performatives by giving, for each performative:

- A natural language description of the performative's intuitive meaning;
- An expression that describes the performative, essentially a formalisation of (1) using certain primitives (discussed below);
- Preconditions which must be satisfied if the sender is to issue the performative and the receiver is to accept it;
- Postconditions that describe the states of sender and receiver after the performative has been issued;
- Completion conditions that indicate the final state (possibly after some additional conversation) after the intention which led to the issue of the performative has been fulfilled;
- Comments to enhance understanding of the description of the performative.

The primitives used in the specification above refer to the cognitive states of agents, and are *believe*, *know*, *want* and *intend*. These primitives obviously rely heavily on the terminology of agents, and might be thought inappropriate to a system which is intended to include more conventional systems such as databases among its communicating systems. If we wish to adopt this style of specification we would need to operationalise these states in the wrapper in a way appropriate to a wrapped system; for example, in the case of a database, *bel(A,P)* means that P is in the database A, whereas *knows(A,P)* means that P is such that its truth or falsity can be confirmed by the database A.

As an example of this style of specification consider Labrou's specification of the speech act *tell*, which has three parameters: the sender, (A); the recipient, (B), and the propositional content, (X).

- A states to B that A believes X to be true.
- bel(A,X).
- Preconditions for A: bel(A,X) and know(A, want(B,know(B,bel(A,X))))
- Preconditions for B: intend(B,know(B, bel(A,X)))
- Postcondition for A: know(A,know(B,bel(A,X)))
- Postcondition for B: know(B, bel(A,X))
- Completion: know(B, bel(A,X))
- The completion holds unless B cannot acknowledge the tell correctly.

There are several points to note about this definition:

- There is some commitment to a particular use of *tell*. The preconditions on A mean that it can only be issued if A thinks B wants to know X, and so cannot be used to broadcast information or to volunteer it in case the recipient might be interested. This already suggests the notion of some conventions regulating the conduct of the conversation, but which are implicit in the semantics as given by Labrou.
- There is no guidance on whether A should issue the performative or not. Here there is a number of issues which need to be considered, such as whether it is in A's interests to tell B that X, whether A has the authority to tell B that X, and the like. Labrou understandably does not consider these issues, but if we are to move to a practical system they become of high importance.
- The primitives require the various agents to have beliefs about the other agents, as well as themselves and the conversation they are engaged in. This is a complicating factor: is it really necessary? In fact, I believe it is not, and will introduce a way of eliminating these iterated modalities in section 5.

Labrou offers us a very promising starting point for specifying performatives. It does, however, leave out a number of factors which need to be specified if we are to equip our agents with the required communication ability. It provides no more than the barest semantics for the performative, does not dictate their use sufficiently in some cases, and perhaps over constrains their use in others. We will consider what more we need to be specify in the next section.

3 Specifying the Use of Performatives

Recent work on dialogues (see Bench-Capon 1997 for an overview) has observed that arguments can be evaluated in several ways; as well as argument being *sound*, we can also consider whether it is *correct*, which is judged by whether it accords to the conventions of the particular argument situation. This is what gives rise to different argument "games", At a third level we can argue *well*; within the rules of a particular type of argument, there may often be choices to be made amongst different moves, and one choice will typically be better than the others. Just as we may play chess in accordance with the rules and lose because we make bad moves, so too we can argue soundly and correctly, and yet fail to persuade because we argue badly.

These points about argument can be generalised to conversation in general. As well as knowing how to speak a language, we must also be aware of the different conventions that apply to different conventions, and how to use the conventions to maximum effect.

The importance of conventions governing the use of performatives is recognised in work such as that on COOL (Barbuceanu and Fox 1995). Their approach is to distinguish a number of *conversation classes*, each characterised by a state transition diagram which reflects the way in which performatives can be issued within the particular conversation class.

This addition, however, suffers from the drawbacks:

- It is not integrated with the specification of the performatives themselves;
- The state transition diagram may reveal a number of choice points at which the conversation rules leave the performative to be issued undetermined. In other words it says only how to play the game, not how to play it well.

From the above discussion, I conclude that in order to be in a position to give a full specification of performatives, capable of being implemented in a determinate manner, we need to specify material at three levels:

- The intrinsic level - corresponding to understanding the performative in general
- The conversation level - corresponding to how the performative *can* be used in conversations
- The heuristic level - corresponding to how the performative *should* be used to make the conversation as good as it can be.

In the next section I shall introduce some motivating examples.

4 Example Information Sharing Conversations

In this section I shall introduce some related conversations, concerned with the obtaining of information from a database. I shall use a state transition diagram notation for the conversation.

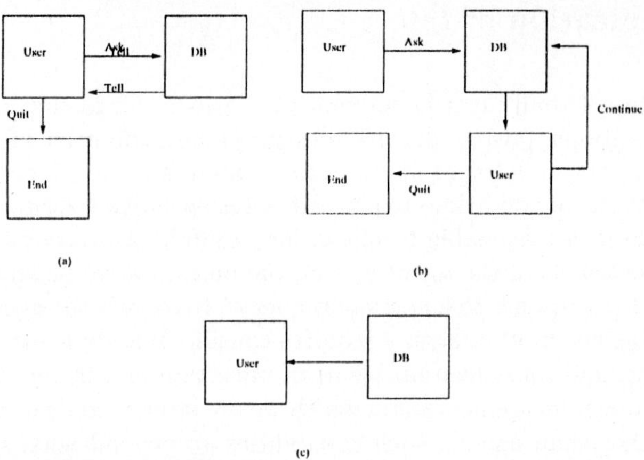

Fig. 1. (a) Conversation 1 - Simple Database Query: (b) Conversation 2 - Query with updates: (c)Conversation 3 - Unsolicited Information

The simplest case is where a user simply queries a database, as shown in Figure 1a.

This is probably what is in mind in Labrou's definition of *tell* given in section 2. However, it is by no means the only possibility for *tell*: consider the following cases, depicted in Figure 1b and Figure 1c. Figure 1b represents a conversation in which once a question has been posed, the user can request up-dates until he chooses to quit, useful, for example, for keeping track of a sporting event which is currently happening, or for share prices. In order for *tell* as required here we need to change Labrou's specification. Now the *tell* is not complete until the user explicitly quits - the query remains live until no longer required. Also it is a further precondition on the issue of the second and subsequent *tells* that such *tells* are only issued when the information changes.

Figure 1c illustrates the case where information is supplied without being solicited. Again this is excluded by Labrou's specification in that the precondition requires A to know that B wants this information. The specification given in section 3 gives only one interpretation of *tell*, and yet the other interpretations seem quite natural.

We can also raise other questions. Suppose for example that A is not permitted to reveal its beliefs to all and sundry, but only if the recipient has appropriate authorisation. Here we would need another precondition on A, namely that B satisfies these authorisation requirements. This is orthogonal to which of the three conversations we are in.

What is emerging from this is that all three elements of good conversation identified at the end of the last section can contribute preconditions, post conditions and completion conditions to the specification of the performative. In the next section I shall consider some of the various elements that could be used in the specification of *tell*.

5 Specification of *tell*

In this section I shall identify some of the various things that might be used to give preconditions, postconditions and completion conditions for *tell*. I shall, in giving these, attempt to eliminate iterated modalities on the cognitive states of agents in favour of conditions expressed in terms which refer to the conversation itself. While it is reasonable to allow, for example, a precondition expressed in terms of the beliefs of the agent issuing the performative (easily operationalised in terms of the response to a particular query), to require the agent to have beliefs about the beliefs of other agents requires considerable sophistication on the part of the agent, and must face problems of uncertain and incomplete information. Moreover, since the application in which we are interested deals with information sources rather than agents, such capabilities go beyond what we would expect of, for example, a database.

In any case, I believe this approach is preferable on other grounds. For example if someone asserts that P, I cannot infer that he believes that P; he may be lying, or introducing it to expose a contradiction, or whatever. I can, however, conclude that *for the purposes of the conversation* he is committed to P. Thus restricting knowledge of other agents to what is manifested in the conversation seems both sensible and right.

To support this we will need to maintain information on several things:

- The performatives issued in the conversation so far
- The commitments of the participants as a result of the conversation so far
- The goals manifested by the agents in the conversation so far. In fact I shall not use goals in this paper, but they are mentioned for completeness.

5.1 Conditions Derived From the Conversation Classes

In this subsection I shall look at the preconditions, postconditions, and completion conditions that are implied by the three conversation classes depicted previously in Figures 1 to 3.

Tell in Conversation 1 In conversation 1 a *tell* can be issued only in response to an ask. Thus letting S be sender, R be recipient and X be content:

```
Precondition: R has issued an ask(X) to S
Postcondition: S is committed to X
Completion: none
```

Note that S need not believe that X; S may have other reasons for giving this reply. Nor need R believe that X or that S believes that X. What R chooses to do with S depends on additional considerations.

Tell in Conversation 2 In conversation 2, S may issue updates to the information supplied. The general question here is X, and X' are successive answers to that question. The conditions for tell(X') are:

```
Preconditions: R has issued an ask(X) to S,
               S has not issued a tell(X'),
               There are no uncompleted tell performatives
Postconditions: S is not committed to any previous answer to X
                S is committed to X'
Completion: R has issued a continue, or R has issued a quit
```

The second precondition, together with the completion condition ensures that the same information is not supplied twice and the third that it is the sender's "turn" to speak. The postconditions replace the commitment to the old answer with the later one.

Tell in Conversation 3 Here the information is unsolicited, so there are no preconditions imposed on *tell* by the conversation.

```
Preconditions: none
Postcondition: S is committed to X
Completion conditions: None
```

Note that here there are no preconditions or completion conditions imposed by the conversation class: this is a one performative conversation, always available to the agent.

Summary of Conditions From Conversation Classes From the above we note that there is only one element common to all three conversation classes, namely that S is committed to X. This does indeed capture the core notion of *tell*, that it is used to commit the speaker to a proposition, for the purposes of the conversation. Making such a commitment is an important feature of any information related conversation, and so we will expect to find some form of *tell* in any such conversation. The remainder of the conditions identify when such a commitment can be made in the context of a particular conversation. By themselves, however, these conditions are insufficient to determine when an agent should issue the performative, and what use will be made of the commitment it brings about. We must therefore now consider supplementary conditions that will be individual to an agent, and derive from policies and heuristics.

5.2 Conditions Derived From Policies and Heuristics

In this section I shall consider a number of possible additional conditions that can supplement those from the conversation class and which will personalise the behaviour of the agents.

Preconditions Consider first a precondition, found in Labrou's specification,

```
believes(S,X).
```

If we have this as a precondition, an agent will only be able to commit to a proposition that it believes to be true. Adding this precondition thus gives us an *honest* agent. Sometimes this may well be desirable, depending on the role of the agent within the overall system. It is not, however, always desirable, particularly in some more complicated conversations in which propositions must be advanced "for the sake of the argument".

Next consider a situation where the agent has sensitive information which can only be issued to a restricted group. Here we will need a precondition expressing that the receiver is allowed to receive the information, for example:

```
permitted_to_receive(R,X).
```

We will need to supply a definition of what it means for a resourse to be permitted to receive a piece of information. For example the information source may maintain a list of registered users, and the precondition would be satisfied if the recipient was on that list. Or the conversation might have been preceded by another conversation in which the recipient supplies a valid password. The details are unimportant; what is important is that we can effect the restriction on information through the precondition.

As an example of a heuristic precondition consider conversation 2. If the information is constantly being updated, we may wish to issue updates at periodic intervals, rather than every time there is a change. This could be effected by a precondition stating that a certain period of time must have elapsed since the last *tell*.

Postconditions Postconditions help us to specify what the effect of a performative is, and this will very often depend on the stance of the recipient. For example, the recipient could also choose to commit to X, in which case we could add the postcondition

```
R is committed to X
```

This gives us a *weakly credulous* agent, which is willing to commit to the proposition for the purposes of the conversation, but which does not modify its actual beliefs. We could, however, give a *strongly credulous* agent, but adding the postcondition

```
believes(R,X)
```

This would cause the receiver to be updated. This would be useful, for example in a stock trading system, which is waiting for the price to reach a certain level before selling. In order to determine this, the information received must be believed so the appropriate tests can be applied, and this information will in turn determine whether a *continue* or a *quit* is issued.

Note here that these postconditions are entirely independent of the conversation class. The other agent need not be aware of what use is being made of the information, and only the receiving agent can be in a position to know what use is appropriate.

Completion conditions Policies and heuristics are less fruitful as a source of completion conditions, since when a performative is complete is something that must be agreed between the participants in the conversation. Therefore we should expect that these conditions derive always from the conversation class, and cannot, unlike preconditions and postconditions, be personal to an agent.

6 Discussion

It has emerged from the above that the concept of a conversation class is essential to permit communication between information sources of the sort envisaged in knowledge sharing applications. The notion of performatives is useful, but a performative needs to be given the context of a particular conversation class to be properly understood. In the context of different conversations a given performative may have different conditions associated with it. The conversation class tells us how a performative *can* be used, and sharing the conversation class harmonises the use of the performative across agents. In order for effective communication to be possible, the communicators must be operating within the same conversation class, so using the same conventions.

Additionally, however, agents will need to know how they *should* use the performatives. These conditions can be expressed in the same way as the conditions deriving from the the conversation class in a uniform framework of preconditions, postconditions and completion conditions. These conditions, however, need not be shared by both parties to the conversation. Since they do not affect the validity of the conversation, but rather the moves that will be chosen within it, the communicating agents are free to operate according to different policies and with different heuristics, as best befits their reasons for entering into the conversation.

We should not, therefore look for *the* specification of a performative. Rather what we need is to specify conversation classes. The specification of each conversation will comprise:

- A set of performatives which can be used in the conversations belonging to this class;
- For each such performative, a set of preconditions, postconditions and completion conditions regulating the use of that performative within the conversation class.

Two agents will be able to communicate if they have a conversation class in common. The conditions for the speech acts within a conversation class can then be augmented by additional conditions, which may be different for the two different agents, governing the moves they make in the particular conversation.

These conditions may also be different for a single agent in different instances of the conversation class. This gives a great deal of flexibility to the behaviour of agents within a conversation class.

An important feature of the method of specification given in this paper, is that conditions are expressed explicitly in terms of moves in the conversation rather than in terms of iterated cognitive modalities. This step towards an operationalisation may well be more appropriate to the kinds of information sources used in the application we took as a starting point, as it makes no commitment to the agents as full blown cognitive entities.

7 Conclusion

In this paper we have:

- Identified the need to specify autonomous communication between information sources in a generic manner;
- Given a framework for such specifications using performatives defined in terms of preconditions, postconditions and completion conditions.
- Distinguished between conditions which arise from the nature of the conversation, and which must be common to the communicating agents, and conditions which can be personal to the agents;
- Shown how we can replace iterated cognitive modalities by explicit reference to the conversation history.

We believe this framework provides a simple, and flexible but uniform, framework for the specification of communication between information sources in knowledge sharing applications.

References

1. Barbuceanu, M., and Fox, M.S., (1995), COOL: A Language for Communication in Multi Agent Systems in Lesser, V., (ed), Proceedings of the First International Conference on Multiagent Systems, MIT Press, Cambridge, Mass.
2. Bench-Capon, T.J.M., Argument in Artificial Intelligence and Law Artificial Intelligence and Law, 5(4), 249-61.
3. Finin, T., McKay, D., Fritzon, R., and McEntire, R., (1994) KQML: An Information and Knowledge Exchange Protocol in Fuchi, K., add Yokoi, T., (eds), Knowledge Building and Knowledge Sharing, Omsha and IOS Press.
4. Labrou, Y., (1996) Semantics for an Agent Communication Language, PhD Thesis, University of Maryland.
5. Neches,R., Fikes, R., Finin, T., Gruber, T., Patil, R., Senatir, T., and Swartout, W., (1991) Enabling Technology for Knowledge Sharing, AI Magazine 12(3), pp36-56.
6. Wiederhold (1992) Mediators in the Architecture of Future Information Systems, IEEE Commuter, 25(3), pp38-49.
7. Wooldrige, M., and Jennings, N., (1995). Intelligent Agents: Theory and Practice, Knowledge Engineering Review 10(2).

HEROS: A Heterogeneous Object Oriented Database System

Elvira Maria Antunes Uchôa, Sérgio Lifschitz and Rubens Nascimento Melo

Departamento de Informática, Pontifícia Universidade Católica do Rio de Janeiro, Brasil

{elvira, lifschitz, rubens}@ inf.puc-rio.br

Abstract. This work provides an overview of HEROS, a heterogeneous object oriented database management system, with emphasis in its architecture and transaction model. A detailed discussion of its implementation using CORBA for components interoperability is also given.

1. Introduction

The coexistence of many different database systems seems natural and inevitable through large organizations. These multiple database systems are operated and administrated under autonomous and local rules, possibly running in different computational environments, with several data models and languages, for similar information [LMR90]. A possible approach to deal with this situation would be another database management system level, giving access to existing database systems that are different from each other and are distributed throughout a network, without requiring neither changes in databases nor reprogramming the DBMSs (Database Management Systems) involved. The systems that consider these requirements are entitled Heterogeneous Database Management Systems (HDBMSs). Frequently, in the literature, the HDBS (Heterogeneous Database System) is used as synonym of federated database system and multidatabase system.

This paper describes HEROS, which is a tightly coupled object oriented HDBMS. HEROS gives support to the operations of its database systems (DBS) components, besides managing its own database. With respect to the latter, HEROS manages both the schema and data, whereas with relation to the others, it provides only access to but no data materialization from their databases. The systems integrated by HEROS may differ on their DBMS, data model, computational environment and physical location.

HEROS' main properties are [Ucho94]: full implementation of location and data models transparency; minimum interference on the processing of its DBS components; multiple data abstractions to better represent the semantics of its DBS components; consistency maintenance of replicated data when these data are mapped into the global schema, and; physical data independence, since the global schema imposes a logical layer on top of HEROS DBS components.

The purpose of this paper is to describe some project choices made for HEROS as a HDBMS. Particularly, we present the HEROS scheme integration mechanisms, global transaction model and the way HEROS deals with some kinds of heterogeneity, such as hardware, operating systems and data models.

The remaining sections are organized as follows. In sections 2, 3 and 4, the HEROS project and its main components are detailed. The implementation of HEROS using CORBA is discussed in section 5. In section 6, some important systems related to this work are discussed. Finally, in section 7, the current status of the work and its continuation are commented upon.

2. An Overview of HEROS

HDBMS have been proposed for the management of many distributed, autonomous and heterogeneous databases. The analysis about the kind of integration that exists among the HDBS components allows HDBSs to be classified into tightly coupled or loosely coupled federated database systems [SL90].

Tightly coupled HDBSs are made of a set of database systems components, heterogeneous, co-operative but autonomous. These components are integrated into a federation, so that any request can be done independently of data location and access paths. Such transparency is made possible by translating and integrating different component schemas into a common data model, building a so-called global schema. Every transaction that involves more than one database is defined in terms of this global schema.

Object oriented standards have been used as a strategy for a flexible coordination and integration of information resources. In HDBMS architecture, these standards may be used for the integration and interaction of the federation components, increasing flexibility and expansion capacity.

HEROS - HEteRogeneous Object System is a tightly coupled object oriented HDBMS, which has been built in PUC-Rio Computer Sciences Department, using one object oriented standard (CORBA) to make its internal components interoperate. HEROS DBS components may differ on their DBMS, data model, computational environment and physical location. The main issues in the HEROS project were the global data model, the scheme integration mechanisms, the global transaction model and the management and treatment of heterogeneity.

3. Schema Architecture

HEROS has a global schema that integrates the several component database schemas [PSDM93]. The data model globally used is an object-oriented data model, specified in [Ucho94]. The four-level schema architecture used by HEROS is one that is typically found in tightly coupled HDBS and it is composed of local schemas and export schemas, one for each DBS component, global schema and external schemas.

Each local schema has a description of its objects that will be shared by the federation, according to the data model used by the respective DBMS. The export schema of each local database contains the description of the local shared objects, expressed in terms of the HEROS' global data model. The global schema contains the integrated description of the objects shared by the DBS components. Each external schema represents an application view of the global schema.

The schemas are represented as classes in Figure 1. In this diagram, only the services related to the global transaction management are presented, and the services related to the schema integration are omitted. The Class Diagram used in this work is based on the one proposed in [RBP+91]. The marked classes mean that they are detailed in another diagram.

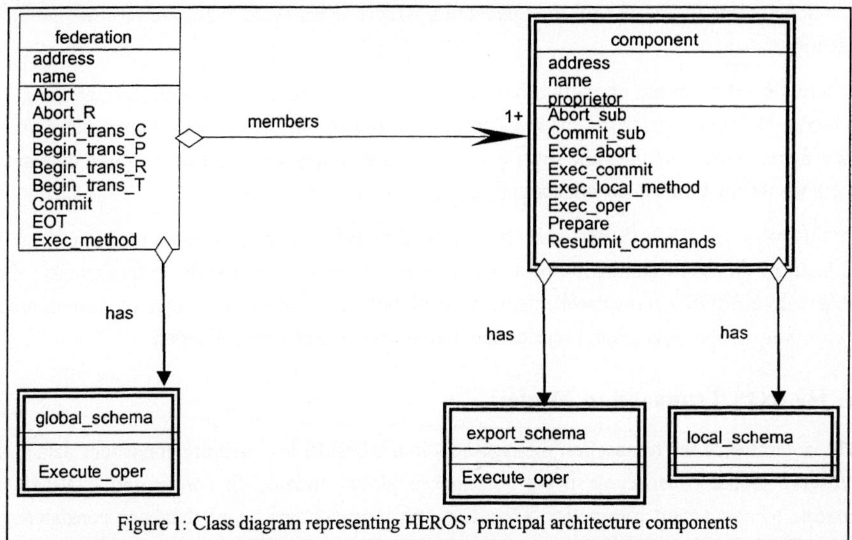

Figure 1: Class diagram representing HEROS' principal architecture components

The integration of the component systems is achieved with the definition of the export scheme [Ucho94]. These are generated automatically at insertion time of a system component into the federation, according to three types of definition: the environment, the database and the translation rules definitions.

The first type is illustrated in Figure 2 by the *Relational-DB* class, which represents an environment definition, while the second type is exemplified by the *Oracle* class, representing the specific DBMSs level. These classes are specialization of the *Component* class that has generic information of all federation components. The third type consists of the translation rule definitions to map the local schema properties into HEROS data model elements. The mapping rules are associated to the class that represents the environment, while the class related to the DBMS defines the specific access forms to a particular software. This hierarchy of classes is used, in HEROS, to represent the meta-information associated to each component system. The instantiation of these classes, with specific information about the structures and applications of each system to be integrated,

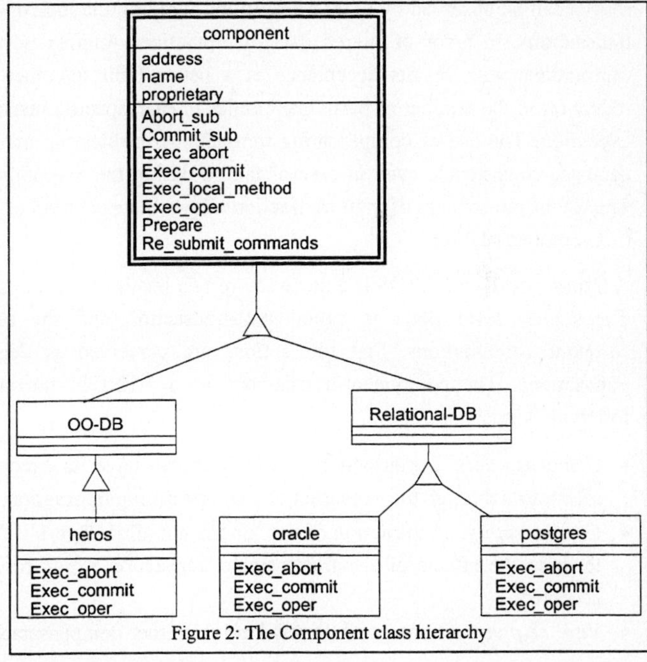

Figure 2: The Component class hierarchy

is made automatically through rule execution whenever an event associated to the operations execution occurs.

Whenever a data access or operation over a component system is requested through the global schema, HEROS queries the mapping information stored in the export schema, determines a path for the requested data and retrieves it for update, query or execution, through data access methods defined for the component system.

In this version, HEROS performs the translation between data models and leaves to the federation database administrator the detection of possible semantic heterogeneity. Once detected, HEROS offers mechanisms to deal with the following kinds of heterogeneity: synonyms, homonyms, object replication, measure units and generalization.

4. HEROS Transaction Model

The objective of the transaction management in a HDBMS is to acquire consistent data and to preserve global consistency in the presence of global updates. In conventional DBMS, the control of concurrent transaction execution and the maintenance of database consistency in case of failures are well-defined problems with several solutions. However, these solutions have presented restrictions in the HDBS environment, due to the fact that transactions tend to be long and the control structure, implicit in the traditional transaction model, would result in the maintenance of data access restrictions during long periods of time, reducing the concurrency level.

The HEROS transaction model uses the concepts of compensatable and compensating transactions, presented in the Sagas model [CR92], vital transactions, as in the nested transaction model. A HEROS' transaction is an open nested transaction. The model permits the modular composition of transactions, allowing the visibility of partial results. These results can be observed by other transactions avoiding the lock of data access in case of long transactions, in favor of shared data manipulation. Another advantage of the use of sub-transactions with results acceptance is a better fault tolerance schema, once there is a reduction in the number of participant nodes in each specific instant of the global transaction execution. The use of compensating transactions enables the maintenance of the integrated database consistency, even in case of failure during the execution of a distributed protocol. The use of the concept of vital transaction allows the execution of traditional flat transactions (non-compensatable).

A transaction R in HEROS is a hierarchy of two levels of sub-transactions, with open nesting. The higher level node is called root-transaction and the remaining nodes represent component-transactions. Flat transactions are perceived as degenerated cases of nested transactions. The component-transactions of a HEROS' transaction can be one of the following kinds:

- *Compensatable*: a transaction of this kind can have its execution accepted and undone afterwards through the execution of a compensating transaction;
- *Compensating*: a transaction of this kind is not allowed to fail. The transaction is executed to undo the effects of a compensatable transaction which results have being previously accepted;
- *Vital or pivot*: a transaction of this kind is neither compensatable nor compensating. Once

accepted, its results are not undone by the execution of a compensating transaction.

A transaction may have any number of compensatable transactions, plus the corresponding compensating transactions, and will always present a single vital (or pivot) transaction -Fig 3.

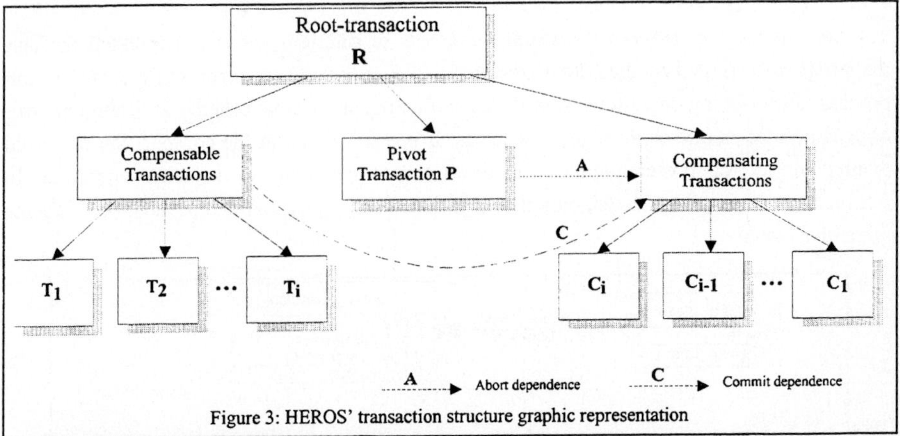

Figure 3: HEROS' transaction structure graphic representation

Each compensatable transaction has the results of its execution accepted as soon as its actions are completed. If the transaction that the compensatable transaction belongs to is canceled, it is necessary to re-position the global database in a consistent state, dropping the effects of the actions that were executed and accepted. The approach used is the one that executes the compensating transaction to semantically undo the mentioned effects.

The pivot transaction should always be executed and its result can only be accepted after the execution of all the compensatable transactions. The acceptance of the pivot transaction execution implies total acceptance of the transaction.

The specification of the semantic operation of the HEROS transaction model was made with the use of the ACTA formalism and is presented in [Silv94].

HEROS transactions are executed by the class called *Federation* (Figure 1), that is responsible for the global management of transactions, and by a set of classes that are specialization of the *Component* class (Figure 2), responsible for the local management of transactions. The operations of a global transaction are executed one by one. A new operation is only submitted after the *Federation* class returns the corresponding result to the execution of the precedent operation.

The *Federation* class is responsible for the interaction of HEROS and the applications, implementing an interface that consists of basic operations {*Begin_trans_R, Begin_trans_T, Begin_trans_P, Begin_trans_C, Exec_method, Commit, Abort, Abort_R, EOT*}. A compensating transaction is derived by the transaction management from the operations executed by a compensatable transaction that completed with success. The compensating transaction is executed when there is a need to semantically undo the effects of an original compensatable transaction over the global database.

The specialized classes of the *Component* class are responsible for the interaction with the local DBMS. They represent, in each place, the global system controlling the submission of commands to be executed by the respective DBMS and representing the DBMS in the process of acceptance of global subtransactions, in a similar way as the method of agents 2PCA. From the transaction execution point of view, in order to integrate a new type of component system to the federation, it is sufficient to create a new class that is a specialization of the *Component* class, and implement the three basic operations for it: {*Exec_oper, Exec_commit, Exec_abort*}.

The correspondence between the schema concepts of different levels is expressed through mappings, represented by the *Global Tree* class in Figure 4. These mappings are used in the process of translating operations over objects defined in an external schema to operations over objects defined in one or more local schemas. It is also needed in the composition of partial results and in the presentation of the result that corresponds to a global operation. In transaction management design, only the operations over objects defined in the global schema were considered.

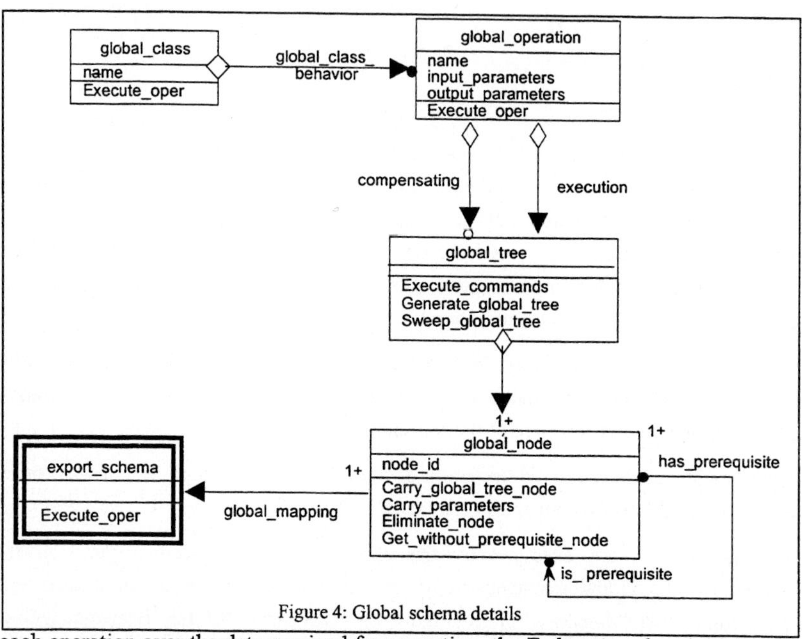

Figure 4: Global schema details

For each operation over the data received for execution, the *Federation* class initially uses the mapping data stored in the global schema and generates a corresponding operation tree. This tree contains, in its nodes, operations over the local databases systems, expressed in concepts of the export schema, and the composition operations with the response presentation to the global operation. The operations in this tree are submitted to the respective classes that are specialization of the *Component* class, which represent local DBMS. The specialized class of the *Component* class uses the mapping data stored in the export schema, represented by the *Local Tree* class in Figure 5 and generates a tree with corresponding operations. This tree contains, in its nodes, operations over the local databases systems, expressed in concepts of the local schema and the composition operations with the response presentation to the operation submitted by the *Federation* class. Since the mappings between global and local schemas are transparent to the user, it is possible to have data dependencies between two local subtransactions derived by the transaction management.

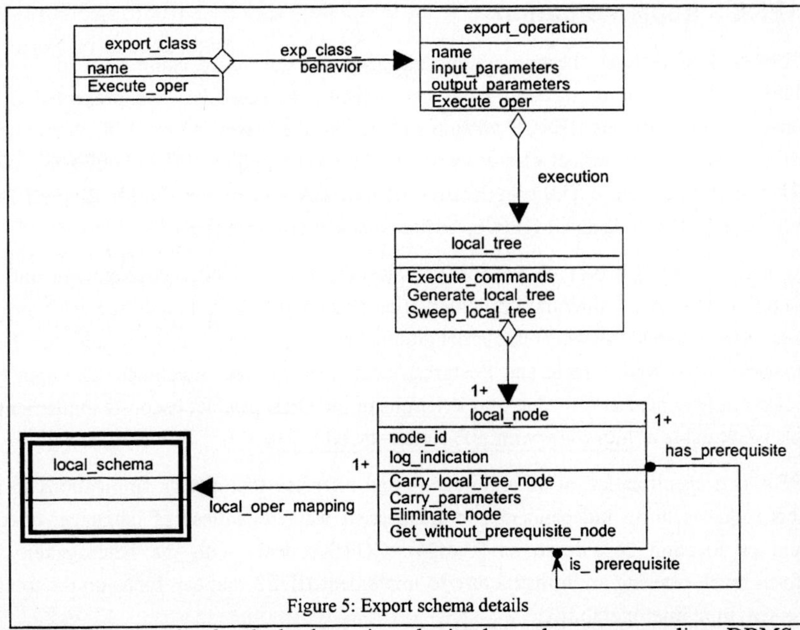

Figure 5: Export schema details

Each operation on the local database is submitted to the corresponding DBMS as a component of a local subtransaction. For each global transaction there is at most one subtransaction per node. The local subtransactions are executed by the corresponding DBMS in the same way of ordinary local transactions; *i.e.*, a local DBMS does not distinguish between global and local transactions.

In the transaction management specification, it is assumed that each DBMS uses the strict 2PL protocol for the concurrency control to guarantee serializable and recoverable schedules on all executed transactions. When a sub-transaction is cancelled by the local DBMS - as in the case of the solution of multiple locks - the information about the cancellation is supplied. The DBMS is not responsible for the resubmission of the subtransaction.

The execution of a global statement is preceded by the acquisition of locks for the ongoing transaction. The possibility of semantic conflicts between the operations is verified through the examination of compatibility tables defined for each object class by the global database administrator at the time of the global schema creation. These tables are created with the use of the commutative principle of operations, *i.e.*, verifying that the final effect is the same, independently of the execution order.

One operation over one object may result in the indirect execution of other operations over the same or other object. The descriptions of which object classes are affected and which operations are indirectly executed as part of each method specification. The access restriction granularity at the global level corresponds to the one of the object class that the operation belongs to. When the access requirements of a global operation can not be fully accepted, the operation is placed in a waiting queue until it can be executed. The detailed description of functional components of transaction management and the formal specification of the transaction execution model are described in [Silv94].

5. HEROS Implementation

In HEROS' first version, the transactions manager was developed using a set of functional modules, communicating through RPC mechanisms. In [UML96] we presented a short summary of this previous HEROS version and studied the feasibility of HEROS architecture based on restructuring object classes, with its remote components communicating using a CORBA implementation. The specification of CORBA - Common Object Request Broker Architecture [OHE96] is an OMG (Object Management Group) product.

The current HEROS prototype version was developed on a UNIX environment and used ORBeline (CORBA commercial implementation [Post94]) to link its architecture component classes. The classes' services implementations were developed in C++ and the DBMS components used were Oracle and Postgres, located in different machines. The application was also implemented in C++ due to restrictions of the ORB product used. Its implementation details is available at http://www.inf.puc-rio.br/~tecbd/heros.

CORBA is a specification of an architecture and interface that allows applications to make objects requests in an independent and transparent way, regardless of language, operating system or location considerations [Catt94]. CORBA deals with the heterogeneity in a platform level, offering an infrastructure to implement HDBS that can focus on the treatment of the semantic interoperability.

The use of CORBA in the HEROS architecture brings the following advantages:

1. A better comprehension of all components and its functionality with an object representation;
2. Encapsulation of HEROS components promotes refinement and evolution, as long as the interface is kept unchanged and the actual implementation is hidden;
3. Particular execution managers, as required by new federation DBS components, may be easily integrated by specializing one generic definition of a execution manager through inheritance;
4. When under OMG standards, any application, defined in any programming language, may use HEROS, *i.e.*, run on a federation without worrying about redundancy checking, semantic representation conflicts and physical location;
5. As CORBA objects, HEROS' components may reside in any physical location and may be replaced. CORBA is responsible to administrate this action. This increases HEROS extensibility, in the sense that it is adaptable to new requirements and communication structures, with no internal changes;
6. Both HEROS application and global component may reside anywhere, communicating in a heterogeneous (or not) way, again under responsibility of CORBA administration;

The prototype's classes (detailed in [ULM97]) were implemented as C++ classes. The interactions between classes for global transaction management were designed based on Jacobson's Interaction Diagram [JCJO92] and can be found at [ULM97].

Over the ORBeline structure were declared three classes, which objects were accessed through the ORB (Object Request Broker), providing the system with location and operation system transparency. The refered classes are (Figure 6): *Federation*, *Component* and *Factory*. Only the services to be called by ORB were specified using IDL.

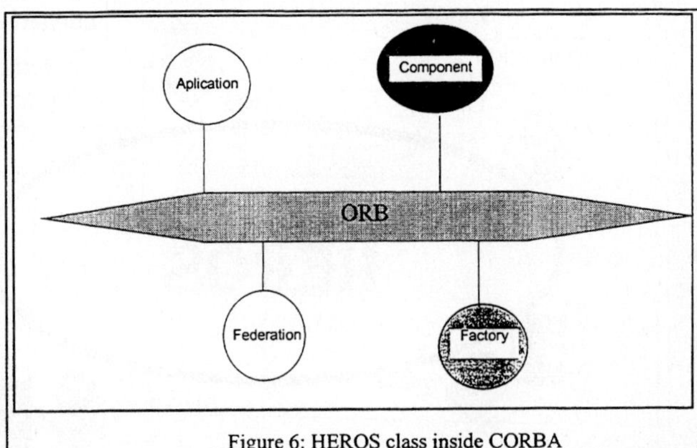

Figure 6: HEROS class inside CORBA

The *Federation* class is responsible for HEROS interactions with applications, by implementing an interface that consists of the basic operations {*Begin_trans_R, Begin_trans_T, Begin_trans_P, Begin_trans_C, Exec_method, Commit, Abort, Abort_R, EOT*} as discussed in section 3.2.2. Its implementation covers the following classes in C++: *Federation, Global Class, Global Operation, Global Tree, Global Node, Root Transaction, Subtransaction, Compensating Command, Compensating Process, Concurrency Control* and *Global Log*. In order to re-use the code from HEROS first version and to maintain the implementation independent of communication's mechanisms,*mediators* were developed to convert data types generated by ORBeline to data types used in methods.

The *Component* class is responsible for the *Federation* class interaction with local DBMS, implementing an interface that consists of basic operations {*Exec_local_method, Commit_sub, Abort_sub, Prepare*} as discussed in section 3.2.2. Its implementation covers the following classes in C++: *Component, Export Class, Export Operation, Local Schema, Local Tree, Local Node, Local Process* and *Local Log*. In our prototype, there are three different implementations to the *Component* class corresponding to *Postgres, Oracle* and *HEROS* classes (Figure 2).

The implementation covers all the above mentioned classes differing each other only in the services code {*Exec_oper, Exec_commit, Exec_abort*}, responsible for the DBMS access. In order to create an object of the *Component* class, one must indicate the implementation to be used.

The need for the *Factory* class was due to the ORBeline implementation, which requires an object to exist before it can be referenced. This class is responsible for creating and listing the objects whose services can be requested through ORB.

In the application, the ORBeline *bind* function was used for activating an ORB object. Once this function is called, the ORBeline finds the object's implementation, activates it and returns an object reference to the application, which uses it to request services.

In Figure 7, we see HEROS' components distribution architecture.

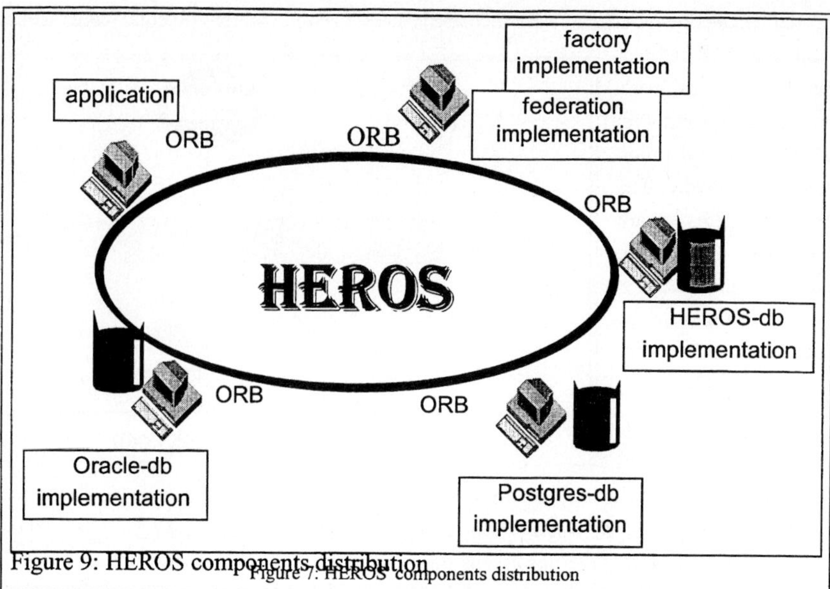

Figure 9: HEROS components distribution
Figure 7: HEROS components distribution

The main implementation issues assumed in the context of this prototype are:

- *Object Granularity*: In CORBA, objects can be defined in various granularity levels. In HEROS, objects correspond to federations managed by HEROS and to the components systems that are part of these federations. HEROS provides only access to the component databases without data materialization.
- *Invocation Style*: CORBA allows clients to invoke interfaces either statically or dynamically. In our current implementation, only static interface invocation was considered, once objects were already known to the system and interface changes are not expected.
- *Object Types*: ORBeline supports two types of objects: persistent and transient. Our prototype used persistent objects only, since objects managed by ORBeline need to be registered so to be activated later by the applications.
- *Object Life Cycle*: ORB's objects need to be created or installed to become available to clients. ORBeline offers three create/delete persistent objects mechanisms: the object activation daemon, the BOA's (Basic Object Adapter) services or to instance/destroy C++ classes. We decided to use the daemon mechanism through the *Factory* class. This choice enabled the created object server to be activated automatically upon a client service request. The BOA's services correspond to the daemon's programmable interface but it does not work with the ORBeline version installed.
- *Object Identification*: A client application needs a reference to an object to make a request. In CORBA, an object's reference can be obtained when: i) the client obtains an object reference from an external source. The external source can be a file or a database that contains object's references in string format; ii) the objects can be named and this name used by services requests. In ORBeline the unique way for clients to access a specific class is by specifying the object's name. As so, every object in HEROS is named.
- *Activation Policy*: Each object to be registered in CORBA specifies its activation policy. The policy defines the rules an implementation follows when multiple objects or

implementations are to be activated. There are four different activation in CORBA [OHE96]: shared server, unshared server, server by method and persistent server. In the Factory class we can find those objects that are shared, *i.e.*, various active objects of a specific implementation share the same server. All other objects are activated in unshared mode, with the exception of an object in an implementation that can be active in a single moment in a server. With respect to the Federation class, the unshared mode server allows a multi user environment, with various clients requesting the Federation services simultaneously. In the Component class the unshared policy allows exploring parallelism in local execution of global procedures.

- *Mapping between client and server requests*: In order to associate a client request with a server method, CORBA offers the following alternatives: one interface to one particular implementation, one interface to one implementation among several ones and one interface to several implementations. In the *Federation* class we used the first one, considering the lack of different implementations. For the *Component* class the more adequate alternative would be the third one, with each implementation supplying part of the interface. This alternative would only request for new component type to be incorporated to HEROS the implementation of the services $\{Exec\_oper, Exec\_commit, Exec\_abort\}$. As the ORBeline version used does not offer this option, the second alternative was rather chosen.

6. Related Work

A HDBMS may offer a list of functionalities, which include scheme integration, global query evaluation, global transaction management and the possibility of dealing with different types of heterogeneity. Several federated database systems have already been proposed and they offer different functionality. They can be distinguished for the data model used to integrate the various data sources. Most previous federated DBMSs were built around the relational model [SL90], using a relational global schema and SQL as language to access global data. To provide a better integration platform for applications, Multibase [LI82] adopts the functional model and Jupiter [MG94] uses a formal object model, described in Z notation.

With the advent of non-standard data types, richer data model integrating complex attributes and methods are required. Some projects are also considering semi-structured data models, as TSIMMIS [GHI+95] and Information Manifold [KLS+95]. Typically these systems have their main focus on query optimization.

Recently, several research projects have used object-oriented techniques to facilitate the building of federated database systems. Selecting a specific object-oriented model is an important question. Some systems, such as Pegasus [SAD+95], VODAK [GMD95] and GARLIC [CH+95], use their particular object model. Another possibility is to choose a standard model, for example, the OMG object model. This is the case of IRO-DB [KW97] and MIND [KOD+95] which use the ODMG'93 standard [Catt94] as a common object model supporting the ODL definition language and the OQL query.

HEROS also uses its own object-oriented model. It works with a class collection, which represents metadata. The HEROS metaclasses are organized in a multilevel specialization hierarchy (*component*, *environment type* and *commercial product*) in order to facilitate component integration. The MIND project reports only the *Database Object* class creation for this finality.

The DBMSs particularities are treated by the implementation development, one to each DBMS that will be integrated to the federation.. Some systems use mediators for this objective, as TSIMMIS and Information Manifold. MIND, Jupiter, IRO-DB and HEROS utilize CORBA for integrating new systems. The issue of global transaction management addressed by HEROS is also treated in VODAK, Pegasus, IRO-DB and MIND projects. .

Major differences between HEROS and other systems are the heterogeneity treatment and schema translation. HEROS uses a rule system (where rules are also objects), while others projects use another kind of solution, such as view mechanisms, mapping functions and conversion tables.

7. Final Comments

The implementation of HEROS is still under development in a UNIX environment. A current version uses Oracle and Postgres and the HEROS native DBMS as components. Details of this implementation is available at http://www.inf.puc-rio.br/~tecbd/heros. Currently, HEROS is being extended with a *legacy component* to allow the integration of legacy systems and with a component for integrate metadata of heterogeneous information available in intranets. They correspond to new classes in Figure 2.

The fact that HDBMSs need adequate components depending upon the application domain suggests the necessity of developing an environment where the components can be defined and chosen to cope with each situation. As a consequence, the HEROS project is now evolving to a new project called ECOHOOD - **E**nvironment of **CO**nfigurable **H**eterogeneous **O**riented **O**bject **D**atabase Management Systems. The ECOHOOD goal is to provide an environment that contains component versions which, when assembled, become a specific HDBMS. The main objective of this new architecture is to provide flexible configurations that are able to respond efficiently to different application areas. The researches in object oriented interoperability standards area and, specially, the experience acquired in the development of previous projects (HEROS and EITIS - Environment of Integrated Tools for Interactive Systems [Melo87]) form the basis for this new project.

Acknowledgments

We thank Fernanda Lima, Fábio André Machado Porto and Álvaro César Pereira Barbosa, for their revision of this current version.

References

[Catt94] Cattell R.G.G., "The Object Databases Standard: ODMG-93", Morgan Kaufmann, 1994.

[CH+95] Carey M.J., Haas L.M., Schwarz P.M., Arya M., Cody W.F., Fagin R., Flickner M., Luniewski A., Niblack W., Petkovic D., Thomas II J., Williams J.H. & Wimmers E.L.. "Towards Heterogeneous Multimedia Information Systems: the Garlic Approach", in RIDE-DOM'95: 5th Intl. Workshop on Research Issues in Data Engineering: Distributed Object Management, Taiwan, Mar. 1995, pp. 124-131.

[CR92] Chrysanthis P.K. & Ramamritham K., "ACTA: The Saga Continues", in Database Transaction Models for Advanced Applications, (A. K. Elmagarmid, editor), Morgan Kaufmann, 1992.

[GHI+95] Garcia-Molina H., Hammer J., Ireland K., Papakonstantinou Y., Ullman J. & Widom J., "Integrating and Accessing Heterogeneous Information Sources in TSIMMIS", in Proc of the AAAI Symposium on Information Gathering, Stanford, Mar. 1995, pp. 61-64.

[GMD95] Gesellschaft fuer Mathematik und Datenverarbeitung mbH, "VODAK V4.0 User

Manual". Arbeitspapiere der GMD - GMD Technical Report n° 910, German National Research Center for Information Technology, Darmstadt, Germany, April 1995, 107 p.

[JCJO92] Jacobson I., Christerson M., Jonsson P. & Övergaard G., "Object-Oriented Software Engineering - A Use Case Driven Approach". Addison-Wesley, 1992.

[KLS+95] Kirk T., Levy A.Y., Sagiv Y. & Srivastava D., "The Information Manifold", in Proc of the AAAI Spring Symposium on Information Gathering in Distributed Heterogeneous Environments, Stanford, Mar. 1995.

[KOD+95] Kilic E., Özhan G., Dengi C., Kesim N., Koksal P. & Dogac A., "Experiences in Using CORBA for a Multidatabase Implementation", in Proc of the 6th Intl Workshop and Conference on Database and Expert Systems Applications DEXA'95, London, UK, Sept. 1995, pp. 223-230.

[KW97] Kapsammer E. & Wagner R.R., "The IRO-DB Approach Processing Queries in Federated Database Systems", in Proc of 8th Intl Workshop on Database and Expert Systems Applications DEXA'97, Toulouse, France, Sept. 1997, pp. 713-718.

[LI82] Landers T. & Iosenberg R., "An Overview of Multibase", in Distributed Database. H. J. Schneider Ed., North-Holland, The Netherlands, 1982.

[LMR90] Litwin W., Mark L. & Roussopoulos N., "Interoperability of Multiple Autonomous Databases", in ACM Computing Surveys, 22(3), 1990.

[Melo87] Melo R.N., "EITIS - Environment of Integrated Tools for Interactive Systems" (in Portuguese), in Proc I Brazilian Symposium on Software Engineering, Petrópolis, Rio de Janeiro, Brasil, 1987.

[MG94] Murphy J. & Grimson J., "The Jupiter System: An Environment for Multidatabase Interoperability", Tech. Rep. Dublin City University and Trinity College Dublin, Jan. 94.

[OHE96] Orfali R., Harkey D. & Edwards E., "The Essential Distributed Objects - Survival Guide", John Wiley &Sons, 1996.

[Post94] PostModern Computing Technologies, "ORBeline User's Guide". 1994.

[PSDM93] Pacitti E., Silva S.D., Duarte C.H.C. & Melo R.N., "HEROS: An Object-oriented Heterogeneous Database System" (in Portuguese), in Proc of VIII Brazilian Symposium on Databases, Campina Grande, Paraíba, Brasil, 1993.

[RBP+91] Rumbaugh J., Blaha M., Premerlani W., Eddy F. & Lorensen W., "Object-Oriented Modeling and Design", Prentice-Hall, 1991.

[SAD+95] Shan M., Ahmed R., Davis J., DU W., Kent W., "Pegasus: A Heterogeneous Information Management System", in Modern Database Systems, Addison Wesley, 1995.

[Silv94] Silva S.D., "Heterogeneous Database Systems: a Transactions Management Execution Model" (in Portuguese), Ph.D. Thesis, Departamento de Informática, Pontifícia Universidade Católica do Rio de Janeiro, 1994.

[SL90] Sheth A.P. & Larson J.A., "Federated Database Systems for Managing Distributed Heterogeneous and Autonomous Databases", in ACM Computing Surveys, 22(3), 1990.

[Ucho94] Uchôa E.M.A., "HEROS - A Heterogeneous Database System: Scheme Integration" (in Portuguese), M.Sc. Thesis, Departamento de Informática, Pontifícia Universidade Católica do Rio de Janeiro, 1994.

[ULM97] Uchôa E.M.A., Lifschitz S. & Melo R.N., "HEROS: a Heterogeneous Database System using CORBA" (in Portuguese), Technical Report MCC42/97, Departamento de Informática, Pontifícia Universidade Católica do Rio de Janeiro, 1997.

[UML96] Uchôa E.M.A., Melo R.N & Lifschitz S., "Object Interoperability in Heterogeneous Database Systems" (in Portuguese), Technical Report MCC45/96, Departamento de Informática, Pontifícia Universidade Católica do Rio de Janeiro, 1996.

An Architecture for Nested Transaction Support on Standard Database Systems*

Erik M. Boertjes, Paul W.P.J. Grefen, Jochem Vonk, Peter M.G. Apers

Center for Telematics and Information Technology
University of Twente
{boertjes,grefen,vonk,apers}@cs.utwente.nl

Abstract. Many applications dealing with complex processes require database support for nested transactions. Current commercial database systems lack this kind of support, offering flat, non-nested transactions only. This paper presents a three-layer architecture for implementing nested transaction support on a commercial multi-database environment. The architecture is directed at high portability and flexibility. The modular approach and the simple, event driven interfaces between the layers of the architecture enable the nested transaction support to be adapted to various applications, nested transaction models and database management systems. The architecture has been implemented to support a prototype of a commercial next-generation workflow management system.

1 Introduction

There is an increasing use of database management systems (DBMS's) in advanced applications that deal with complex processes. In the WIDE Esprit project [Cas96a, Cas96b, Cer97, Gre97], a multi-level process model is adopted, allowing hierarchical decomposition of such complex processes (e.g. workflow processes). The process semantics of the higher levels of the process hierarchy are usually different from those in the lower levels of the hierarchy. To comply with these process semantics, extended transaction support is needed that goes beyond the standard transaction support offered by standard, commercial DBMS's.

Higher level processes are in general long running processes with cooperative characteristics. These characteristics demand that these processes should not be executed in strict isolation. Strict isolation would prevent cooperation between processes as they would not be able to share information. Strict atomicity of long running processes is not desirable either. A process failure (e.g. a system crash) would cause the loss of all work done so far by the process. Processes lower in the hierarchy are relatively short living processes requiring strict transactional semantics. The separation between the higher and lower levels is formed by the notion of business transaction in the workflow application, being a subprocess that is composed of subprocesses that together form an atomic unit of work from an application point of view. This atomicity is not completely strict however, because of the notion of *critical* and *non-critical* subprocesses. In general there will be subprocesses whose successful completion is not a nec-

---

* The work presented in this paper is supported by the European Commission in the WIDE Project (ESPRIT No. 20280). Partners in WIDE are Sema Group sae and Hospital General de Manresa in Spain, Politecnico di Milano in Italy, ING Bank and University of Twente in the Netherlands.

essary condition for the successful completion of their parent. We call such subprocesses non-critical. Critical subprocesses are processes that have to be completed successfully in order to let their parent complete successfully. Business transactions need to be strictly isolated from each other as intermediate results of business transactions have no semantics. Since subprocesses within business transactions in general share data, isolation within business transactions is relaxed.

Traditional flat transaction models fail to model the process semantics of both levels described above because they do not allow transactions to be nested neither do they support relaxed atomicity nor relaxed isolation. Therefore, extended transaction support is desired. As current applied research shows [Cosa, Reu95, Sar96], there is a commercial and scientific interest in extended transaction support. Meanwhile, [Alo96, Bar95, Chr94] state that actual implementations of such support are hard to find. In WIDE, a combination of modified existing transaction models is used to cope with the transactional requirements posed by complex processes [Gre97]. The higher level processes are mapped onto a Saga-like transaction model providing relaxed transactional semantics [Gre98]. The lower level processes, i.e. business transactions and the processes below them, are mapped onto the nested transaction model, providing atomicity of business transactions, full isolation between business transactions and relaxed isolation within them.

This paper focuses on transaction support for the lower level processes. We propose to build nested transaction support on top of existing standard commercial DBMS's. Taking commercial DBMS's as a basis will facilitate introduction of the nested transaction support in business environments. Main focus of this paper is a highly portable and flexible architecture for the implementation of a nested transaction support server. To obtain portability and flexibility, the architecture is composed of three independent layers. The upper layer of the architecture translates process events from the client application to nested transaction primitives. The middle layer maps these nested transaction primitives to abstract, DBMS-independent flat transaction primitives. The lower layer maps the abstract flat transaction primitives on DBMS-specific transaction primitives in a multi-DBMS environment. Because of the simple event based communication between the layers a highly modular architecture is obtained resulting in high portability and flexibility. The lower layer, for instance, can be adapted individually to various DBMS's. Various nested transaction models can be handled by adapting the middle layer. The architecture has been realized in a next generation workflow system, as part of the WIDE Esprit project.

In section 2 we give an overview of related work in the area of nested transaction support. Section 3 describes the adopted nested transaction model as well as the mapping process from nested transactions to flat transactions. Section 4 gives an architecture for nested transaction support, an implementation of which is discussed in section 5. Conclusions and directions for further work are given in section 6.

2 Related Work

A model for nested transactions is first introduced in [Mos85]. It is proposed to overcome the limitations of the traditional flat transaction model in dealing with complex processes. Different variations on the model can be found in [Elm92]. We aim at the implementation of nested transaction support rather than introducing another nested transaction model. The work in [Chr94] describes how ACTA is used as a tool for the synthesis of extended transaction models. Although the framework could be used to show the correctness of a particular implementation, it does not discuss the implementation itself nor does it give an architecture for it. In the approach given in [Kan95], each leaf transaction of a nested transaction tree is mapped on a separate flat transaction. All changes made by a subtransaction become visible to the parent transaction and its children upon the subtransaction's commit. Not before then, the updates are made durable. One sibling can use the results of the other sibling only after the latter has committed. This approach prevents data sharing between concurrent subtransactions. In our view however, data sharing between concurrent subtransactions within a business transaction is required, as stated in the previous section. [Day92] gives another approach to map long running activities onto transactions. They also break down the process in transactions, comparable to business transactions. Main difference is their use of rules and triggers to express and manage control flows. An extended nested transaction model is used to govern the execution of these rules rather than giving nested transaction support to complex processes, as we do.

In [Alo96] it is shown how several transaction models can be implemented using a Workflow Management System (WFMS). They propose to implement extended transaction support as part of the workflow application. In WIDE however, we aim at extended transaction support orthogonal to workflow management functionality by building a separate module that provides extended transaction support. An example of a commercial WFMS is COSA [Cosa]. In COSA the concept of transaction is included, but contrary to our approach, only flat traditional transactions are supported. Thus COSA does not offer extended transaction semantics.

In the Reflexive Transaction Framework [Bar95] transaction support is built on top of a Transaction Processing (TP) monitor. In our approach, the transaction support is built directly on top of a commercial DBMS. This seems to be more attractive for practical use because it does not require a TP monitor to be configured. Furthermore, only a small part of our architecture is DBMS-specific. This makes it more easily portable to other DBMS environments than architectures conforming to the Reflexive Transaction Framework.

3 Nested Transaction Support

In section 1 we have given the requirements posed on transaction management to cope with nesting in complex processes. This section specifies the nested transaction support that fulfills the requirements of section 1. Section 3.1 gives a description of our nested transaction model. Section 3.2 describes how complex processes are mapped onto nested transactions. Section 3.3 discusses the mapping from nested transactions to flat, DBMS-independent transactions. Section 3.4 presents the last mapping step, describing the mapping from DBMS-independent flat transactions to DBMS-specific flat transactions.

3.1 Nested Transaction Model

The nested transaction model has been proposed in [Mos85] to overcome the limitations of the flat transaction model in dealing with complex processes. Nested transactions allow for safe concurrency within transactions and offer a modular approach to realize both intra-transaction and inter-transaction parallelism. Furthermore, nested transactions allow for a finer grained recovery mechanism than flat transactions, localizing the effects of failures and faults (see [Elm92]).

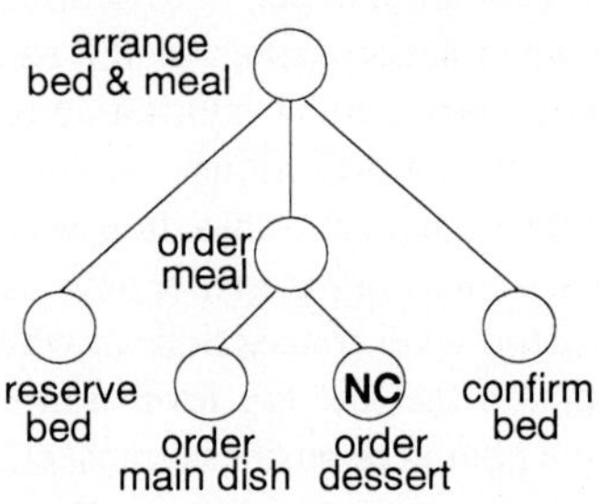

Figure 1: Example nested transaction

Our nested transaction model is based on the nested transaction model given in [Mos85] and allows for hierarchical decomposition of transactions, flexible notion of atomicity and flexible notion of isolation. We use the concepts of *critical* and *non-critical* transactions (called *vital* and *non-vital* in [Elm92]) to localize the effect of failures. Nested transactions are strictly isolated from each other. The isolation mechanisms we adopt in our model to provide safe concurrency *within* a nested transaction are simpler than those proposed in [Mos85]. We allow all subtransactions within a nested transaction to share data concurrently, while models described in [Mos85, Elm92, Kan95] allow datasharing between siblings only. For reasons of brevity, we will not discuss details of the isolation aspects of our model.

Figure 1 gives an example of a nested transaction that is part of a real-life workflow application in a hospital. The top level transaction 'arrange bed & meal' is decomposed into subtransactions 'order meal', 'reserve bed' and 'confirm bed'. Subtransaction 'order meal' is in turn decomposed into subtransactions 'order main dish' and 'order dessert'. The leaves of the tree (e.g. 'order main dish') represent transactions that are no further decomposed. Leaf transactions are strictly atomic.

When a subtransaction completes successfully, it is said to have committed, even though it is not a top-level transaction. Such commitment is relative: any updates become permanent only if all subtransactions containing the committed subtransaction also commit, and the enclosing top-level transaction completes. Thus, top-level transactions are special: they are the only irrevocable transactions.

Flexible atomicity is acquired by allowing a transaction to commit although not all its subtransactions have completed successfully. This flexible atomicity is specified by labeling each subtransaction as being either critical or non-critical. A subtransaction is labeled critical when its successful ending is a necessary (but not sufficient) condition for the successful ending of its parent transaction. A subtransaction is labeled non-critical when its success does not affect the success of its parent. A transaction may commit even when its non-critical children have not ended successfully. Thus, the atomicity of the transaction is relaxed.

In Figure 1, all subtransactions are critical except those marked 'NC' (non-critical). The subtransaction 'order meal' cannot commit when its subtransaction 'order main dish', which is critical, has not ended successfully. But 'order meal' can commit even when its subtransaction 'order dessert', which is non-critical, has ended unsuccessfully. This makes 'order meal' non-atomic.

3.2 Mapping Processes onto Nested Transactions

The mapping step from processes onto nested transactions is rather straightforward. Because of their process characteristics, business transactions are mapped onto top level nested transactions. This yields the required strict isolation between business transactions. Processes below the business transaction level are mapped onto subtransactions. This gives the required relaxed isolation between subprocesses of the same business transaction. Critical subprocesses are mapped onto critical subtransactions and non-critical subprocesses are mapped onto non-critical subtransactions.

Each time a new business transaction is started, a new top level transaction is created. Likewise, each time a subprocess of a business transaction starts, a new subtransaction is started. This subtransaction is part of the top level transaction on which the business transaction is mapped. The nested transaction (i.e. the top level transaction and all subtransactions) is committed only when the complete business transaction ends successfully.

3.3 Mapping from Nested Transaction Model to Flat Transaction Model

As stated in section 3.1, we adopt strict *inter*-nested transaction isolation while having relaxed *intra*-nested transaction isolation. The mapping from nested transactions to flat transactions has to preserve these isolation characteristics. To preserve inter-nested transaction isolation, different nested transactions are mapped onto different flat transactions. Accesses in different top-level nested transactions are mapped onto different flat ACID transactions. To preserve intra-nested transaction isolation, an entire nested transaction is mapped onto the same flat transaction. This means that each database access of a nested transaction is done within the same flat ACID transaction, allowing data sharing. A result of this is that accesses in concurrent subtransactions within the same nested transaction are executed in an interleaved fashion in the corresponding flat transaction. The flat transaction is committed if and only if the corresponding top level nested transaction is committed.

Relaxed atomicity is realized by using savepoints in the flat transaction model. Rolling back a subtransaction in the nested transaction model corresponds to rolling back to a savepoint in the flat transaction model. Because of the above mentioned interleaving of accesses in the flat transaction, rolling back one subtransaction in the nested transaction model might require other subtransactions to be rolled back as well. An algorithm has been developed that determines the minimum amount of subtransactions to be rolled back.

Any time a non-critical subtransaction starts, a savepoint in the flat transaction is set. When a failure occurs in a *non-critical* subtransaction, the flat transaction is at least rolled back to that savepoint. The flat transaction has to be rolled back even further when other subtransactions performed accesses concurrently with the failed subtransaction. When a failure occurs in a *critical* subtransaction, its parent should be rolled back. If the parent is critical as well, the parent's parent should be rolled back in turn. As a result of the failure, either a non-critical ancestor of the failing transaction is rolled back or the whole nested transaction is rolled back. In the flat transaction model this corresponds with either aborting the whole flat transaction or rolling back to the savepoint coinciding with the start of the non-critical ancestor. Again, concurrency aspects have to be taken into account.

Figure 2 shows the progress in time of the nested transaction of Figure 1 up to the point where subtransaction 'order dessert' fails. Figure 2 also shows the mapping of the nested transaction onto a flat transaction. Subtransactions 'reserve bed' and 'order main dish' have ended. Subtransaction 'confirm bed' is still active and is concurrent with 'order dessert'. Because 'order dessert' is non-critical, a savepoint has been set at its start. At failure of 'order dessert' the flat transaction is rolled back to this savepoint. Subtransaction 'confirm bed' however, has done database accesses that are interleaved with those of 'order dessert'. Therefore 'confirm bed' should be aborted as well. Because 'confirm bed' is critical, its parent 'order meal' is aborted as well. Subtransaction 'order meal' is a critical child of the top level transaction 'arrange bed & meal'. Thus, the whole nested transaction is canceled and the flat transaction is aborted.

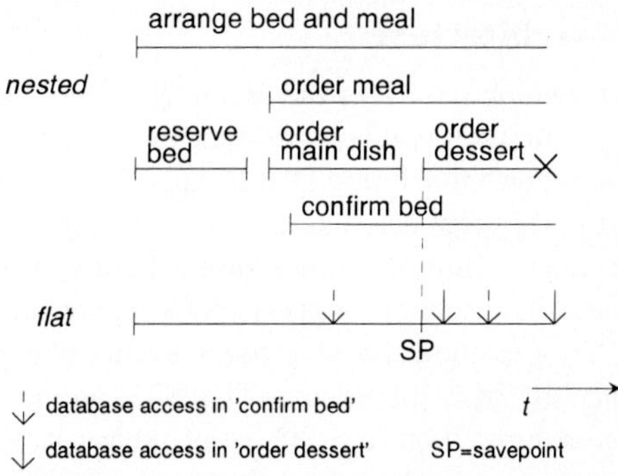

Figure 2: Example of mapping a nested transaction onto a flat transaction

3.4 Mapping from Flat Transaction Model to Database Specific Transactions

The final step in the mapping process involves mapping of abstract, database independent transaction operations to database specific operations. Operations like starting a new flat transaction, setting savepoints, and rolling back to savepoints are mapped onto the functions that the DBMS offers. Table 1 gives examples of DBMS-specific operations, in this case those of the Oracle DBMS. The left column contains abstract flat transaction operations that are mapped on the operations of the Oracle OCI library [Ora96] listed in the right column. Note that this mapping is not a one-to-one mapping. There are no OCI primitives for setting savepoints or for rolling back to savepoints. In those cases SQL-statements are used, parsed and executed by the OCI primitives OPARSE and OEXEC.

Abstract operations	Oracle OCI functions
start transaction	OOPEN
commit	OCOM, OCLOSE
abort	OROL
rollback to savepoint	OPARSE, OEXEC
set savepoint	OPARSE, OEXEC

Table 1: Abstract and Oracle specific flat transaction operations

4 Architecture

This section describes the architecture of a software component that offers the nested transaction support as specified in section 3. It maps nested processes via a nested transaction model onto DBMS-specific flat transactions. The Nested Transaction Support component acts like a server and can handle multiple clients simultaneously, and per client multiple transactions. Figure 3 shows the communication between the Nested Transaction Support (NTS) server and its client, a Process Engine (PE). The PE notifies the NTS of process events like the start of a business transaction or the canceling of a subprocess. The NTS provides the PE with status information on the nested transaction (e.g. the list of subtransactions that have been rolled back due to the canceling of a subprocess). In case a new business transaction or subprocess is started, the NTS returns the identifier of the transaction on which it has mapped the new business transaction or subprocess. This identifier is used by the PE when performing database accesses. These accesses are performed outside the NTS. When the PE wants to access the database during a subprocess, it requests a physical database context from the NTS, providing the NTS with the transaction identifier on which the subprocess is mapped. The NTS returns the physical database context in which the PE should perform the database access.

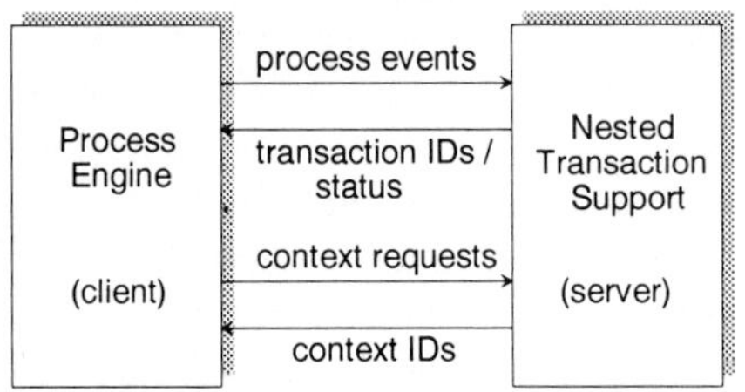

Figure 3: Communication between NTS server and its client

The architecture of the NTS consists of three layers, each performing one of the mapping steps. The interfaces of the layers are kept simple by using event based communication, resulting in a modular architecture of independent layers, which makes the architecture portable and flexible. Portability allows the architecture to be implemented in different DBMS environments with little adaptation, while flexibility allows it to be easily adapted to various nested transaction models. Modularity of the architecture allows the layers to be used separately in various applications. The lower layer, for instance, can be used independently in environments with flat transactions only. Another example is the use of the lower two layers separately from the top layer in situations where there is at most one business transaction active at a time.

Figure 4 gives a global overview of the architecture. The sections below each describe one of the architecture's layers.

4.1 Nested Transaction Manager

The Nested Transaction Manager (NTM) performs the first mapping step as described in section 3.2. It acts as a nested transaction support server and can handle multiple clients simultaneously. It receives notifications of process events (like 'start subprocess' and 'cancel subprocess') from clients and maps these events to nested transaction operations (like 'start subtransaction' and 'cancel subtransaction').

The NTM takes care of passing each nested transaction operation to the transaction object that represents the corresponding nested transaction in the Nested Transaction

Object layer. The NTM manages those objects: it creates and removes top-level transaction objects when needed by a process (see section 4.2).

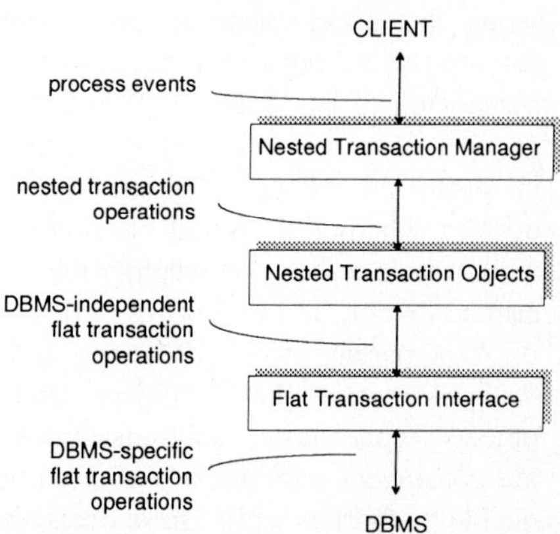

Figure 4: Internal architecture of NTS

4.2 Nested Transaction Objects

The middle layer of the architecture consists of Nested Transaction Objects (NTO's). There are two kinds of objects: each Top-level Transaction (TT) object represents a top-level transaction, while each Subtransaction Object (ST) represents a subtransaction. Figure 5 shows the internal architecture of this layer, with a hierarchical arrangement of the objects.

Top-level transaction objects are responsible for the mapping from the nested transaction model to the abstract flat transaction model. They use the ST objects to keep track of (1) the hierarchical decomposition of the top-level nested transaction and (2) concurrency between subtransactions within the nested transaction.

There is no centralized administration of this decomposition or concurrency: this knowledge is distributed among the objects. Each object applies the same algorithms on the part of the nested transaction's state that it represents. Each object takes care of creating and deleting its own children. The TT objects are created and deleted by the NTO-layer's client (the Nested Transaction Manager).

A nested transaction operation enters the NTO-layer at a TT object. This object passes the message to each of its children, which in turn pass it further to their children until it reaches the proper object. This object takes care of handling the operation, by performing an action like creating or deleting a child or by changing its status (e.g. to 'ended' or 'canceled'). Objects update their own administration of hierarchical structure and concurrency. Decisions concerning the canceling of subtransactions are taken locally by the objects corresponding to the subtransactions. The notification of the action or decision is sent back up the tree until it reaches the TT object. Based on the notifications it gets from its children, the TT object maps the operation to the proper flat transaction operation.

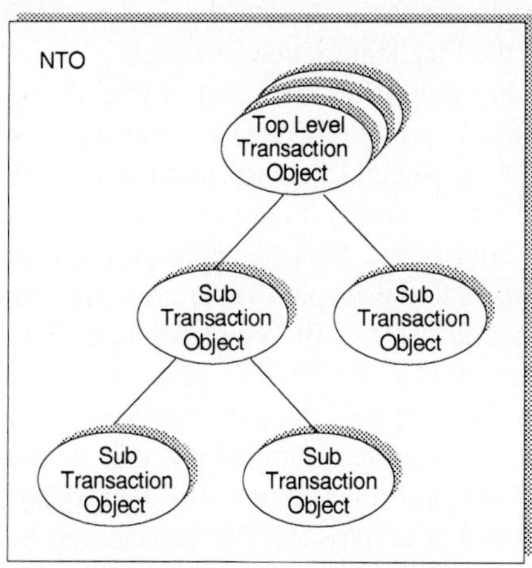

Figure 5: Objects in the NTO layer

As an example we take the nested transaction operation 'abort subtransaction'. This operation is sent by the NTM layer to the TT object containing the subtransaction. The TT object sends the abort message down until it reaches the ST object representing the subtransaction to be canceled. This ST object changes its status to 'canceled' and informs its parent of the cancellation. The parent decides whether it should be canceled as well, which depends on whether the child is critical or not. The parent, in turn, notifies its own parent of the decision, until the decision reaches the TT object. Other ST objects representing subtransactions that are concurrent with the one aborted, might decide to abort as well. These decisions are also passed up to the TT object. Based on all notifications coming from down the hierarchy, the TT object maps the 'abort subtransaction' operation either on the flat transaction operation 'rollback to savepoint' or on the flat transaction operation 'abort flat transaction'. The latter one is chosen when one of the critical children (if any) of the TT object has decided to abort itself.

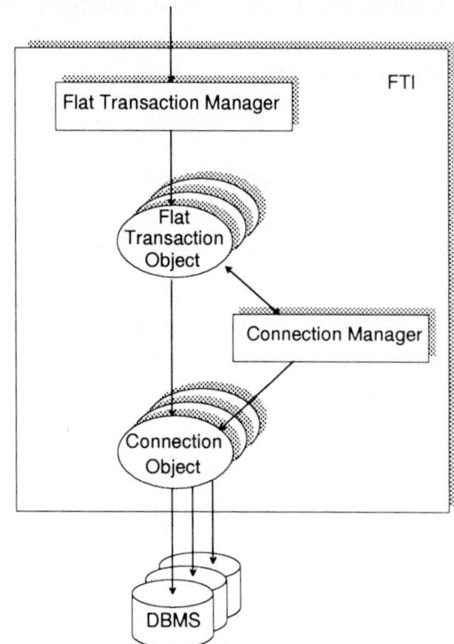

Figure 6: Internal architecture of the FTI

4.3 Flat Transaction Interface

The Flat Transaction Interface (FTI), which forms the lower layer of the architecture, is responsible for the third mapping step (see section 3.4). It translates abstract flat transaction primitives to database specific flat transaction operations. This layer thus forms the interface to the DBMS for the other two, DBMS-independent layers, shielding them from DBMS-specific issues. By adapting the FTI, the nested transaction support can be ported to different DBMS's. Besides the mapping process, the FTI also takes care of handling the client-server connections with the various DBMS's. Figure 6 shows the internal architecture of the Flat Transaction Interface.

The Flat Transaction Manager handles the creation and removal of Flat Transaction Objects. Each time it is notified (by a Nested Transaction Object) of the start of a new flat transaction, it creates a new flat transaction object. Likewise, when it is notified of the end of a flat transaction (either by commit or cancel) it removes the corresponding Flat Transaction object. Besides, the Flat Transaction Manager is responsible for dispatching the abstract flat transaction primitives to the proper Flat Transaction Objects.

A Flat Transaction Object represents one abstract, DBMS-independent, flat transaction. In practical applications, there is sometimes the need to perform accesses on different DBMS's within the same business transaction. As each business transaction is mapped on one flat abstract transaction (via a nested transaction), this abstract flat transaction should be mapped on *multiple* physical transactions. The Flat Transaction Object takes care of this mapping. It ensures that all physical flat transactions belonging to the same abstract flat transaction are committed, aborted or partially rolled back simultaneously. Flat transactions that are mapped onto more than one physical transaction are pseudo-atomic however. Imagine a flat transaction being mapped onto two different physical transactions T1 and T2. When the flat transaction commits, the Flat Transaction Object signals T1 and T2 to commit. T1 might commit successfully while committing T2 might fail because of a DBMS failure, leaving the flat transaction only partially committed.

The Connection Manager (CM) provides its clients (the Flat Transaction Objects) with connections to the DBMS. When a Flat Transaction Object asks for a new physical transaction, the CM provides a free connection that is not in use by a Flat Transaction object. If there is no free connection, the CM opens a new one by creating a new Connection Object representing a client-server connection with the DBMS. The Connection manager returns a reference to this Connection Object.

The X/A protocol [XOp96] allows multiple concurrent physical transactions to use the same connection, but is not part of standard DBMS functionality. Since our goal is to build transaction support on standard DBMS functionality, we assume that a connection can be used by at most one physical transaction at a time. The actual opening and closing of connections is done by the Connection Objects, as they contain the DBMS-specific knowledge required to do so. Each Connection Object represents a client-server connection to a DBMS. Connection Objects contain DBMS-specific methods for opening and closing connections. They also perform the mapping from DBMS-independent transaction primitives to DBMS-specific transaction operations. Thus, all DBMS-specific knowledge is kept locally in the Connection Objects. For each DBMS there must be defined a Connection Object class, from which the Connection Manager can instantiate Connection Objects. The CM picks the class depending on the DBMS to which the CM's client requires a connection.

5 Implementation

The architecture specified in section 4 has been implemented in the WIDE Esprit project [Cas96a, Cas96b, Cer97, Gre97]. Goal of WIDE (Workflow on Intelligent Distributed database Environment) is to develop extended database technology as the basis for a commercial next-generation workflow management system. In WIDE, extending database technology focuses on extended transaction management and active rule support.

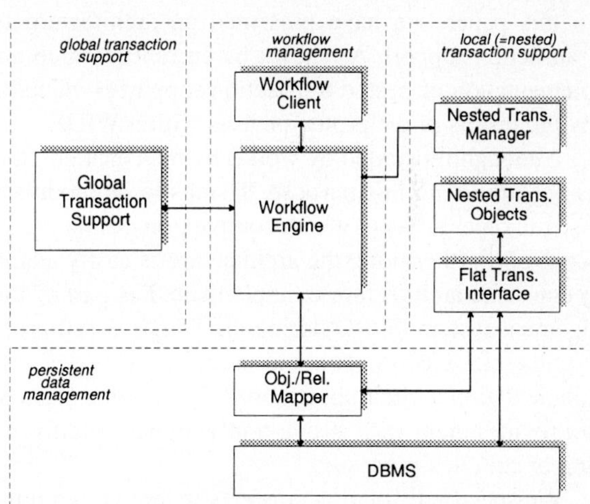

Figure 7: WIDE transaction support architecture

Figure 7 shows how the nested transaction support architecture is embedded in the overall WIDE architecture. In WIDE, the nested transaction support is called

'Local Transaction Support'. The Saga based transaction support for the higher level processes (see section 1) is called Global Transaction Support. The terms Global and Local do not refer to distribution aspects but rather to being below or above the business transaction level. As can be observed from the architecture, the two modules of transaction support are completely orthogonal. For a detailed description of the WIDE architecture, see [Cer97].

The Workflow Engine (WFE) is the core of the Workflow Management System. It takes care of scheduling and assigning processes. It provides the Nested Transaction Manager with the process events of the processes on and below the level of business transactions. The Nested Transaction Support performs the mapping as described in section 3. It provides the WFE with transaction identifiers, that are used by the WFE to access the DBMS. Database accesses go through the Object/Relational Mapper. This Mapper provides an object-oriented database access interface to its clients and maps this to the relational interface of the DBMS. It requests the physical database context in which it performs the accesses from the FTI layer, providing it with the transaction identifier. In case a subprocess is canceled by the Workflow Client, the WFE notifies the Nested Transaction Manager (NTM) accordingly. The NTM provides the WFE with the IDs of the subprocesses that have been canceled by the Nested Transaction Support. The WFE can then adapt its scheduling and can notify its clients. The architecture allows multiple clients per NTM (see section 4.1). For reasons of simplicity, however, there is a separate NTM per WFE in the current implementation. Each NTM is capable of handling multiple transactions simultaneously though.

The WIDE WFMS has been built on top of the Oracle v.7.3 DBMS. Connection Objects in the Flat Transaction Interface take care of mapping abstract flat transaction primitives to Oracle specific function calls from the Oracle Call Interface (OCI) library [Ora96]. In the current implementation the Flat Transaction objects map each abstract flat transaction on one physical transaction only.

6 Conclusions

In this paper, we have presented an architecture for the implementation of nested transaction support. As shown by current research and commercial developments, implementation of nested transaction support is valued important. This is also confirmed by the results of the prototype tests within WIDE.

Although illustrated by workflow management, the use of the architecture presented is not limited to this purpose. Thanks to its modularity, the architecture can be easily used in other areas in which complex processes are important, like CSCW and Process Control. Furthermore, the architecture is easily adaptable to different DBMS environments. The architecture is implemented as part of the next generation workflow management system FORO during the WIDE Esprit project, with Oracle as the underlying commercial DBMS. The end users in the WIDE consortium used and tested the implementation in their applications. They value Nested Transaction Support useful since it provides them with strong transactional primitives which they can use in the modeling of complex processes.

We specified isolation concepts within nested transactions on the level of workflow data objects. Further work will be aimed on implementing this intra-nested transaction isolation. Other future work will focus on the formalization of the algorithms used in nested transaction support. As some of these algorithms take possibly critical decisions about abortion of processes, formalization is desired to show the correctness of the behavior of the Nested Transaction Support to advanced application designers.

References

[Alo96] G. Alonso, D. Agrawal et al.; *Advanced Transaction Models in Workflow Contexts*; Procs. Int. Conf. on Data Engineering, 1996.

[Bar95] R. Barga & C. Pu; *A Practical and Modular Method to Implement Extended Transaction Models*; Procs. 21st Int. Conf. on Very Large Data Bases; Zürich, Switzerland, 1995.

[Cas96a] F. Casati, S. Ceri, B. Pernici, G. Pozzi; *Deriving Active Rules for Workflow Enactment*; Procs. 7th Int. Conf. on Database and Expert Systems Applications; Zürich, Switzerland, 1996.

[Cas96b] F. Casati, P. Grefen, B. Pernici, G. Pozzi, G. Sánchez; *WIDE: Workflow Model and Architecture*; CTIT Technical Report 96-19; University of Twente, 1996.

[Cer97] S. Ceri, P. Grefen, G. Sánchez; *WIDE - A Distributed Architecture for Workflow Management*; Procs. 7th Int. Workshop on Research Issues in Data Engineering (RIDE); Birmingham, UK, 1997; pp. 76-79.

[Chr94] P.K. Chrysanthis, K. Ramamritham; *Synthesis of Extended Transaction Models using ACTA*; ACM Transactions on Database Systems, vol. 19(3), 1994, pp. 450-491.

[Cosa] COSA Solutions Gmbh; *Cosa Solutions: Turning Workflow into Cashflow;* http://www.cosa.de.

[Day92] U. Dayal, M. Hsu, R. Ladin; *A Transactional Model for Long-Running Activities*; Procs. 17th Int. Conf. on Very Large Databases, 1991.

[Elm92] A. Elmagarmid, ed.; *Database Transaction Models for Advanced Applications*; Morgan Kaufmann; USA, 1992.

[Gre97] P. Grefen, J. Vonk, E. Boertjes, P. Apers; *Two-Layer Transaction Management for Workflow Management Applications*; Procs. 8th Int. Conf. on Database and Expert Systems Applications; Toulouse, France, 1997.

[Gre98] P. Grefen, J. Vonk, E. Boertjes, P. Apers; *Global Transaction Support: Formal Specification and Practical Application*; CTIT Technical Report 98-10; University of Twente, 1998.

[Kan95] I.E. Kang & T.F. Keefe; *Reliable Nested Transaction Processing for Multidatabase Systems*; Integrated Computer-Aided Engineering, vol. 2(1), 1995, pp. 49-67.

[Mos85] J. E. B. Moss; *Nested Transactions: An Approach to Reliable Distributed Computing*; The MIT Press, Cambridge, Massachusetts, 1985.

[Ora96] Oracle Corporation; *Programmer's Guide to the Oracle Call Interface, release 7.3*; Oracle Corporation, 1996.

[Reu95] A. Reuter, F. Schwenkreis; *ConTracts - A Low-Level Mechanism for Building General-Purpose Workflow Management Systems*; IEEE Data Engineering Bulletin; vol. 18(1), 1995, pp. 4-10.

[Sar96] S.K. Sarin; *Workflow and Data Management in InConcert*; Procs. 12th Int. Conf. on Data Engineering; New Orleans, USA, 1996.

[XOp96] X/Open Company; X/Open Guide: Dis*tributed Transaction Processing: Reference Model, version 3*; X/Open Company, 1996.

Transaction-Based Coordination of Software Agents

Evaggelia Pitoura

Department of Computer Science, University of Ioannina, GR 45110 Ioannina, Greece
EMAIL: pitoura@cs.uoi.gr WWW: hhtp://www.cs.uoi.gr/~ pitoura

Abstract. Cooperative software agents provide a novel framework for building distributed applications. Central to the model is the support for sophisticated coordination and close cooperation among different agents working together towards accomplishing a specified task. In this paper, we focus on expressing and enforcing correctness properties of the coordination and interaction among agents. We build on transaction concepts from database systems to formalize the proposed correctness properties and introduce methods for enforcing them in the context of mobile object systems.

1 Introduction

Mobile agents are programs which may be dispatched from a client computer and transported to a remote server computer for execution. With the rapid development of network-centered applications and web-based technologies, this new model of distributed computing has attracted much attention. The mobile agent model provides an efficient, asynchronous method for attaining information or services in rapidly evolving networks: mobile agents are launched into the unstructured network and roam around to accomplish their task. Agents simplify the necessary distribution of computation and overcome the communication barrier by minimizing the interchanged messages. In addition, mobile agents support intermittent connectivity, slow networks, and light-weight devices which is the case in wireless computing. In this context, mobile agents can be used to offload functionality from wireless components to the fixed network [16].

Most current research on agent-based models [18, 2, 1] focuses on aspects related to intelligence and security, both critical for the realization and success of mobile agent systems. In this paper, we address another issue, that of consistency. Agents model long-lived computations, own local resources, and access data at remote systems. There is a need to ensure that the concurrent execution of multiple agents does not violate the consistency of the data accessed. Besides their own data, agents access two types of data. First, they access data owned by other cooperative mobile agents, that is data that belong to the context of other concurrently executing agents. This form of interference among agents must be controlled to ensure the consistency of each agent's context in the presence of concurrent accesses. Second, agents query and modify data that belong to remote systems. Remote systems may include persistent data stores such as databases. Ensuring consistency in the context of the agent model is hard since there is no central point for the coordination of agents. In addition, the behavior of agents is dynamic, and there may be no prior knowledge of their potential interaction.

In this paper, we consider agents in the context of object systems. An agent is an active object with its own methods and data. Our approach is based on associating with each agent an *agent manager* to coordinate its execution. An agent manager provides a focal point for the coordination of each mobile agent. Each agent manager is itself an agent that may be mobile and distributed at different sites. The special methods that the agent manager supports form a small and uniform for all managers set of primitives. Thus, this set can be implemented as part of an agent library. Agent managers are the analog to transaction managers in traditional database concurrency control. They cooperate with each other to enforce the serialization of the executions of their associated agents. The proposed technique provides fine-grained control over agent execution at the level of each agent's method execution.

The remainder of this paper is organized as follows. In Section 2, the structure of the execution of an agent is defined as well as constructs to provide cooperation between agents. In Section 3, a transaction model for agents is presented, and in Section 4, protocols for enforcing it are advanced. Finally, in Section 5, we present related work and offer our conclusions.

2 Concurrency and Synchronization

Mobile agents are processes dispatched from a source computer to accomplish a specified task [9]. Each *mobile agent* is a computation with its local data and execution state. After its submission, the mobile agent proceeds autonomously and independently of the sending client. When the agent reaches its destination processing unit, it is delivered to an agent execution environment. Then, if the agent possesses necessary authentication credentials, its executable parts are started. To accomplish its task, a mobile agent can transport itself to another computer, spawn new agents, or interact with other agents. Upon completion, the mobile agent delivers the results to the sending client or to another server. In the following section, we abstract the constituting parts of an agent, and formalize intra-agent and inter-agent synchronization.

2.1 The Model

An *agent* is an active object encapsulating the state, behavior and location of a computation. The state of an agent is the set of values of a set of local to the computation variables; its behavior is the set of methods it provides; and its location is the context of its execution. Computation starts by invoking an appropriate agent. For a processing unit to execute an agent, it must provide an agent execution environment. The agent may be executed as an operating system process, an operating system thread or it may be managed by a thread package within the agent execution environment. The methods that build the agent program may correspond to local to the agent functions, functions of other agents, or functions of remote systems.

To develop our model, we distinguish the methods of an agent as simple and composite. Composite methods consist of a number of other simple or composite methods. A simple method is either a primitive or a basic method. *Primitive* is a method that only accesses the state of the agent, that is a method that manipulates only local variables. *Basic* is a method that accesses non-local to the agent resources. Such methods are either methods that access resources of another mobile agent or resources of the remote system where the agent is transmitted. Each agent has a top-most method, called *Compute*, that encodes the intended computation.

Agents are instances of a system-defined class called *Agent_Class*, thus all agents have similar behavior and structure. Upon activation of an agent, the agent creates an Agent Manager (*AM*) to coordinate its execution. *AM*s are special agents, instances of a system class called *AM_Class*. Specific local variables of an *AM* represent the execution state of each method of the corresponding agent. An additional local variable records the history of the execution of the agent, in particular the order of method invocations.

2.2 Intra-agent Concurrency and Synchronization

Concurrency inside an agent is achieved through asynchronous invocations of more than one of its methods. Synchronization mechanisms are necessary to control the interaction among the execution of the agent's methods. Intra-agent synchronization is based on defining a set of dependencies on the ordering of the execution of methods [17]. Such dependencies are called structural and are expressed in terms of the controllable states of the methods of the agent. Defining flow of control and data using dependencies among states of methods provides fine-grained control over the execution of an agent. It also allows for a large degree of parallelism in the agent's execution, which is very important since different parts (methods) of the agent may be executed at different network sites.

The states of a method include the submission, execution and completion of the method. When a method is invoked, it enters the ready state and moves to the submitted state when it is actually submitted for execution. In terms of basic methods, the agent manager of an agent may delay the submission of a method to another agent or system to ensure correctness. When its execution starts, the method enters the running state and remains in this state until its completion. Upon completion, the method may be either accepted or aborted. If accepted, the results of the method become permanent and the method enters the committed state. The committed state may either correspond to failure or success depending on whether the expected result was accomplished or not. If aborted, the results of the method are not recorded, and the method has no effect on data.

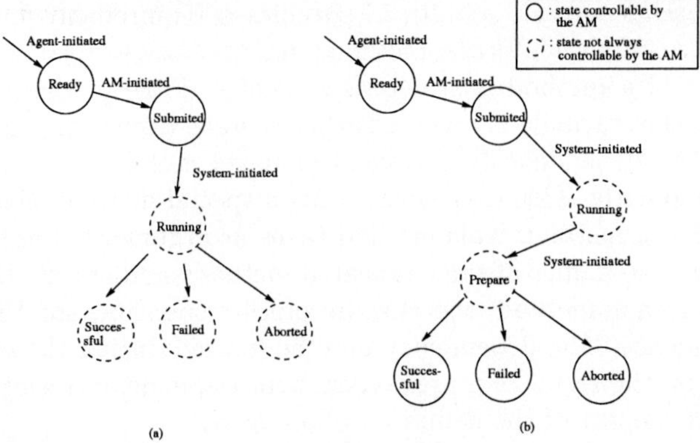

Fig. 1. Controllable states for basic methods, when: (a) there is no prepare-to-commit state, and (b) there is a prepare-to-commit state.

A state of a method is controllable, if the agent that submitted the method or its agent manager can cause a transition of the method into this state. Although, the agent that invokes a primitive method and its manager can control all states of a method, they can control only the submission of a basic method. The actual execution time of a basic method is under the control of the corresponding remote mobile agent or system that receives the agent. The same holds for the completion of a basic method. Some remote systems may provide a prepare-to-commit state that indicates that a method has completed execution and its results are about to become permanent. If this feature is available, then the agent or its manager can also decide on the completion of the method. Figure 1 summarizes the controllable states of a basic method. The following definition formalizes the concept of a structural dependency among states:

Definition 1. *A* structural dependency *SD is a triple (C, $\mathcal{M}$, $\mathcal{S}$), where C is a specification, $\mathcal{M}$ is a set of methods M, and $\mathcal{S}$ is a set of controllable states of the methods $M \in \mathcal{M}$.*

There are three types of structural dependencies based on the form of C: order, existence, and real-time dependencies in accordance with the primitives defined in [14]. In an *order structural dependency* (C, $\mathcal{M}$, $\mathcal{S}$), C has one of the following forms: M_i can enter state s_i only after M_j has entered state s_j, or M_i cannot enter state s_i after M_j has entered state s_j, where M_i, $M_j \in \mathcal{M}$ and s_i, $s_j \in \mathcal{S}$. Ordering dependencies can be used to enforce a serial execution of a number of methods, by forcing a method to begin only after the commitment of the previous one. In an *existence structural dependency* (C, $\mathcal{M}$, $\mathcal{S}$), C has the following form: if M_i enters state s_i, then M_j must enter state s_j, where M_i, $M_j \in \mathcal{M}$ and s_i, $s_j \in \mathcal{S}$. A special case of an existence structural dependency is a *compensation method*: a method that is executed to semantically undo the effect of a committed method when some other method aborts. Finally, in a *real-time structural dependency* $(C, \mathcal{M}, \mathcal{S})$, C specifies a requirement for the real time submission or completion of the methods in $\mathcal{M}$.

The state of a method is stored as a local variable of the associated AM. The value of this variable is modified when a state transition occurs. To implement structural dependencies, the agent manager handles the controllable state transitions explicitly. This is achieved using a special method of the AMs called *form_dependency* method. This method takes as arguments the type of the dependency and the names of the associated methods and states. Upon receipt of a *form_dependency* method, the AM becomes responsible for the enforcement of the dependency. The dependency may be formed during the execution of an agent based on the result of a previous action. Dependencies may also be specified statically as part of the definition of an agent.

2.3 Inter-agent Communication and Synchronization

Concurrency at the inter-agent level is achieved by allowing more than one agent enactment. Agents interact with each other to accomplish a common goal. Moreover, the execution of an agent may interfere with the execution of another agent indirectly when they both access the same data concurrently. There is a need to define and control both the desirable and indirect interactions among agents that are executed concurrently.

Inter-agent synchronization and communication can be achieved either by message passing or through shared memory. Message passing provides explicit control on the visibility of an agent's data, since an agent explicitly sends information about its local data to other agents or accepts similar information from them. Interaction through shared memory relies on the observation of partial changes in an agent's local data caused by other agents. This interaction can be controlled by defining specific points in the execution of an agent where other agents are allowed to observe its partial results through modifications in the agent's local data. This may be accomplished by explicitly defining break [12] or permit [7] points within the execution of an agent where other agents are allowed to interleave.

Definition 2. *A* breakpoint *B of an agent T is a triple $(B_s, B_e, \{(T_i, M_j)\})$ where $\{(T_i, M_j)\}$ is a set of pairs of agents (T_i) and methods (M_j) of these agents, and $B_s = (M_s, s_c)$, $B_e = (M_e, s_e)$ are pairs of methods along with corresponding controllable states of the agent T which allow members of $\{(T_i, M_j)\}$ to be executed between B_s and B_e of T.*

Another form of inter-agent communication is *delegation*, where an agent delegates responsibility of the execution of a method to another agent.

Definition 3. *A* delegation *of an agent T is a pair (M_i, T_j) that denotes that the method M_i invoked by T will be executed as part of agent T_j.*

To implement breakpoints and delegation, two special methods, called *breakpoint* and *delegation*, are used. A *breakpoint* method is sent to the Agent Managers of the agents that are involved in the breakpoint. The *delegation* method is sent to the Agent Manager of the agent to which the execution of the method is delegated.

Interaction among agents can also be achieved by defining a common to all agents data storage. Agents can then communicate by importing and exporting data from this common storage. The techniques in this paper are applicable to this scenario as well by considering the common storage as the local data of a special agent.

3 The Agent Transaction Model

Attributing to agents the properties of traditional transactions is too restrictive. In particular, the execution of each agent is not isolated from the execution of other agents, since agents can see the intermediate results of execution of other agents by accessing their local data. Furthermore, the execution of an agent is not necessarily atomic, since while a method of the agent may be aborted, some other method may be accepted. In this section, we define what is a correct execution of an agent as well as a correct execution of a number of concurrently executing agents.

3.1 Well-Structured Agent Execution

Two methods of an agent conflict if they do not commute, that is if the order of their execution affects the final state of data. A commutativity relation is defined for each pair of methods. Two methods conflict if they do not commute. For example, two methods conflict if they access the same data item and one of them updates it. We assume that a commutativity relation is defined for both simple and composite methods. Alternatively, we could define commutativity only for simple (primitive and basic) methods and let the commutativity of composite methods be inferred from the commutativity of their constituting simple methods. The computation of an agent is extended to include the methods that are delegated to it. In particular, the execution of an agent is modeled as a sequence of its breakpoints and of state transitions of the methods that it invokes or are delegated to it.

Definition 4. *An* agent execution *is a pair* $(\Sigma, <)$ *where* Σ *is a set of events and* $<$ *is a partial order. An event in an agent execution is either a breakpoint* B *in the Compute of the agent or a pair* (M, S) *where* M *is a non-delegated method invoked by the Compute method of the agent or a method delegated to it and* S *is a state of* M*. The partial order* $<$ *is such that for all non commutable methods* M_i *and* M_j *either* $(M_i, E) < (M_j, E)$ *or* $(M_j, E) < (M_i, E)$*, where* E *stands for the running state of the method.*

Thus, the execution of an agent is a partially-ordered sequence of method executions and breakpoint events. This partial order must respect the structural dependencies among the methods of an agent as expressed in the following definition.

Definition 5. *An agent execution is* well-structured *in terms of a set D of structural dependencies if the partial order $<$ on its events does not violate any of the dependencies in D.*

3.2 Schedule Correctness

A schedule is an interleaved execution of methods and breakpoints of a set of agents. Formally,

Definition 6. *A* schedule *of a set $\{T_1, T_2, ..., T_n\}$ of agents executions $T_i = (\Sigma_i, <_i)$ is a pair $(\Sigma, <_h)$ where $\Sigma = \bigcup \Sigma_i$ and $<_h$ is a partial order such that: (1) if, for any events s_k and $s_l \in \Sigma_i$, $s_k <_i s_l$ then $s_k <_h s_l$, and (2) for all non commutable methods M_i and M_j of two different agent executions either $(M_i, E) <_h (M_j, E)$ or $(M_j, E) <_h (M_i, E)$, where E stands for the running state.*

The first condition states that, the interleaved execution of a set of agents preserves the execution order of each of the agents. The second condition imposes a relative order between the non-commutable methods of two different agent executions.

Each agent or remote system observes the execution of agents by changes in the state of its local data. The *projection* of a schedule S on the local data of agent T_i is the schedule that results if we exclude from S all but the primitive methods on data of T_i and the breakpoints, if any, that immediately precede each of them. Similarly, the *projection* of a schedule S on the local data of a remote system DB_i is the schedule that results if we exclude from S all but the basic methods on data of DB_i and the breakpoints, if any, that immediately precede each of them.

To enforce that the concurrent execution of transactions (agents) does not violate the consistency of data, the most common approach is to ensure that the corresponding schedule is *conflict-serializable*, that is conflict equivalent to a serial schedule [6]. Two schedules are conflict equivalent, if they consist of the same events and order conflicting operations in the same manner. This is based on the assumption that each transaction (agent) maintains data consistency if executed alone. In the case of breakpoints, serializability is extended to relative serializability [12].

A *step* of an agent execution T is a subsequence of T that includes exactly the events between two consecutive breakpoints in T. A method interleaves with a step if it executed before an event E of the step and after another event E' of the step. We use a modified model of relatively serializability [12] that allows for efficient, i.e., polynomial, serializability testing [3]. We say that, in a schedule S, a method M_2 *directly depends on* a method M_1 if $(M_1, E) <_h (M_2, E)$, where E stands for the running state. The *depends on* relation is defined as the transitive closure of the directly depends on relation.

A schedule is *relatively serial* if, for all pairs of agents, T_i and T_j, if a method M of T_i is interleaved with a step of T_j starting with breakpoint $(B_s, B_e,$

$\{(T_k, M_l)\}$) then at least one of the following is true: (a) M does not depend on any method pair of an event of the step and no method of an event of the step depends on M, or (b) $(T_i, M) \in \{(T_k, M_l)\}$.

Definition 7. *A schedule is* correct *if (1) all the execution of its agents are well-structured, and (2) it is conflict equivalent to a relatively serial schedule.*

As the following theorem shows, to ensure that a schedule is conflict equivalent to some serial schedule, it suffices to ensure that its projections are conflict serializable with consistent orders:

Theorem 1. *If each agent and remote system projection of a schedule S is conflict equivalent to a relatively serial schedule, and there is an order $<_o$ consistent with the serialization orders assumed by each projection, S is conflict equivalent to a relatively serial schedule.*

Proof. (Sketch) The schedule S_o that has order $<_o$ and the same set of agents as S orders conflicting operations the same way with schedule S, so it is conflict-equivalent to it. It is also relatively serial. To prove that, suppose it is not, then one of its projections is not relatively serial, a contradiction. □

4 Managing Agents at Run-Time

Ensuring the correctness of the interleaved execution of agents is the responsibility of different units, (Figure 2):

- *agent managers* (AM) of all agents involved
  The AMs are created upon the activation of each agent to ensure its structural correctness. They decompose the top-most method (*Compute*) of their associated agents into basic and primitive methods and take care of submitting the basic methods to the appropriate *AMs* or *DGTMs* at remote sites.
- *distributed transaction managers* (DGTMs) located on top of each remote system
  Each DGTM coordinates the submission of agents to its system. Each DGTM receives methods from the various AMs, schedules them to control concurrency and inter-agent synchronization and submits them to the corresponding LTMs.
- *pre-existing local transaction managers* (LTMs) at each remote system
  An LTM at a remote system controls the execution of the basic methods submitted to the corresponding remote system. The properties that an LTM ensures for the execution of a method vary based on the requirements of each system. For example, LTMs for database systems ensure the ACID properties of each basic method, that is, that each method is executed as an atomic, consistent, isolated and durable unit.

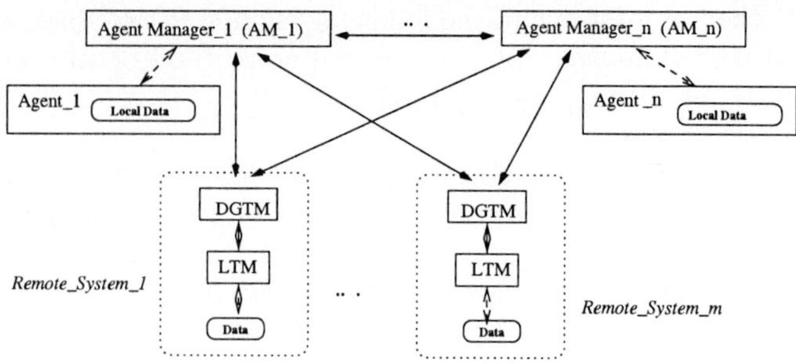

Fig. 2. Agent execution.

In summary, each AM ensures that the execution of its agent is well structured using either graph-based methods [7] or automata-based techniques [4]. It also ensures that the projection of all operations on its agent's data is relatively serializable by deploying for instance a timestamp-based protocol. Each $DGTM_i$ ensures that the execution of all basic methods at its corresponding site i is relatively serializable based on the timestamp order.

5 Conclusions and Related Work

In this paper, we have presented a scheme for ensuring correctness of the concurrent execution of agents. The properties ascribe to the execution of an agent is that of advanced transactions. In particular, the structure of an agent is defined through dependencies between the execution state of its methods. Furthermore, agents can cooperate with each other by sharing their intermediate results or by delegating the responsibility of specific actions to each other. The enforcement of the structural properties of an agent and the control of the interaction of agents with other agents and remote resources is assigned to per agent agent managers that accomplish this task through a well-defined small set of primitives. These primitives can be efficiently implemented in the form of library support for concurrency.

The techniques for supporting consistency in mobile object models presented in this paper combine concepts from multidatabase concurrency control, advanced transaction models, and workflow management. While distribution is central to mobile agents, the majority of multidatabase transaction management systems (see [8] for an excellent survey) adopt a centralized approach; [19, 5] are possible exceptions. Many advanced transaction models have been proposed (see [11] for examples). ACTA [10] provides a framework based on first-order logic for reasoning about extended transaction models. This model is low-level; a higher-level model based on transaction primitives is described in [7]. These two models can be used to express and implement respectively the structural characteristics of agents. On the basis of extended transaction models, many researchers have defined workflow specifications [17, 13] similar to the agent structural dependencies. A very preliminary presentation of some ideas in this paper has appeared in [15].

References

1. Special Issue on Intelligent Agents. *Communications of the ACM*, 37(7), 1994.
2. Special Issue on Internet-based Agents. *IEEE Internet Computing*, 1(4), 1997.
3. D. Agrawal, J. Bruno, A. Abbadi, and V. Krishnaswamy. Relative Serializability: An Approach for Relaxing the Atomicity of Transactions. In *Proceedings of the 13th ACM Symposium on Principles of Database Systems*, pages 139–149, 1994.
4. P. Attie, M. Singh, A. Sheth, and M. Rusinkiewicz. Specifying and Enforcing Intertask Dependencies. In *Proceedings of the 9th International Conference on Very Large Database Systems*, pages 134–144, 1993.
5. P. K. Batra, M. Rusinkiewics, and D. Georgakopoulos. A Decentralized Deadlock-free Concurrency Control Method for Multidatabase Transactions. In *Proceedings of the 12th International Conference on Distributed Computing Systems*, June 1992.
6. P. A. Bernstein, V. Hadjilacos, and N. Goodman. *Concurrency Control and Recovery in Database Systems.* Addisson-Wesley, 1987.
7. A. Biliris, S. Dar, N. Gehani, H. V. Jagadish, and K. Ramamritham. ASSET: A System for Supporting Extended Transactions. In *Proceedings of the 1994 SIGMOD Conference*, pages 44–54, May 1994.
8. Y. Breitbart, H. Garcia-Molina, and A. Silberschatz. Overview of Multidatabase Transaction Management. *VLDB Journal*, 1(2):181–239, 1992.
9. D. Chess, B. Grosof, C. Harrison, D. Levine, C. Parris, and G. Tsudik. Itinerant Agents for Mobile Computing. *IEEE Personal Communications*, 2(5), 1995.
10. P. K. Chrysanthis and K. Ramamritham. Synthesis of extended transaction models using acta. *ACM Transactions on Database Systems*, 19(3):450–491, 1994.
11. A. K. Elmagarmid, editor. *Database Transaction Models for Advanced Applications.* Morgan Kaufmann, 1992.
12. A. A. Farrag and M. T. Ozsu. Using Semantic Knowledge of Transactions to Increase Concurrency. *ACM Transactions on Database Systems*, 14(4):503–525, 1989.
13. D. Georgakopoulos, M. F. Hornick, and A. P. Sheth. An Overview of Workflow Management: From Process Modeling to Workflow Automation Infrastructure. *Distributed and Parallel Databases*, 3(2), 1995.
14. J. Klein. Advanced Rule Driven Transaction Management. In *Proceedings of the IEEE COMPCON*, 1991.
15. E. Pitoura and B. Bhargava. A Framework for Providing Consistent and Recoverable Agent-Based Access to Heterogeneous Mobile Databases . *ACM SIGMOD Record*, 24(3):44–49, September 1995.
16. E. Pitoura and G. Samaras. *Data Management for Mobile Computing.* Kluwer Academic Publishers, 1998.
17. M. Rusinkiewicz and A. Sheth. Specification and Execution of Transactional Workflows. In W. Kim, editor, *Modern Database Systems*, pages 592–620. Addison Wesley, 1995.
18. J. Vitek and C. Tschudin, editors. *Mobile Object Systems: Towards the Programmable Internet.* Springer Verlag, LNCS 1222, 1997.
19. A. Wolski and J. Veijalainen. Achieving Serializability in Presence of Failures in a Heterogeneous Multidatabase. In *Proceedings of the Parbase90 Conference*, 1990.

Object-Based Group Protocol

Tomoya Enokido, Hiroaki Higaki, and Makoto Takizawa

Dept. of Computers and Systems Engineering
Tokyo Denki University
Ishizaka, Hatoyama, Saitama 350-0394, Japan
E-mail {eno, hig, taki}@takilab.k.dendai.ac.jp

Abstract. In traditional group protocols, messages are causally delivered at the network level. In order to reduce the protocol overhead, only messages required to be causally delivered at the application level have to be ordered. The state of the object depends on in what order the requests and responses are exchanged and the requests are computed. In this paper, we define a novel significant precedence order of messages based on the conflicting relation among the requests. We discuss a protocol which supports the significantly ordered delivery of request and response messages.

1 Introduction

Distributed applications like teleconferences are realized by a *group* of multiple application objects. Many papers [3, 7, 11–13] have discussed so far how to support the causally ordered delivery of messages at the network level in the presence of message loss and stop faults of the objects. $O(n^2)$ processing overhead and $O(n)$ to $O(n^2)$ communication overhead are implied for number n of objects in the group [11]. On the other hand, Cheriton *et al.* [4] point out that it is meaningless at the application level to support the causally ordered delivery of all messages transmitted in the network. Only messages required by the applications have to be causally delivered in order to reduce the overhead. Ravindran *et al.* [14] discuss how to support the ordered delivery of messages based on the precedence relation among messages explicitly specified by the application. Agrawal *et al.* [9] define *significant* messages on receipt of which the state of the object is changed. Raynal *et al.* [1] discuss a group protocol for replicas of file where write–write semantics of messages are considered. Enokido and Takizawa [6] discuss a group protocol for replicas where a transaction concept is introduced.

An object o is an encapsulate of data and *abstract* operations for manipulating the data. On receipt of a *request* message with an operation op, o computes op and sends back a response message with the result of op. Here, op may invoke another operations, i.e. nested invocation. The states of the objects depend on in what order the operations are computed. The *conflicting* relation [2] among the operations is defined for each object based on the semantics of the object. If two operations sending and receiving messages conflict in an object, the messages have to be received in the computation order of the operations. Thus, the *significant precedence relation* among request and response messages can be defined based on the conflicting relation. In this paper, we present an *Object-based*

Group (OG) protocol which supports the significantly preceded delivery of messages where only messages to be ordered are delivered to the application objects in the order. Tachikawa and Takizawa [16] show a protocol which uses the real time clock. However, it is not easy to synchronize real time clocks in distributed objects. We propose *object vectors* to causally order messages.

In section 2, we present the system model. In section 3, we discuss the significant precedency among messages. In section 4, the protocol for supporting the significantly ordered delivery of messages in the group is discussed.

2 System Model

The distributed application is realized by cooperation of multiple objects which exchange messages in the network. An object o can be manipulated only through an operation supported by o. Let $op(s)$ denote a state obtained by applying an operation op to a state s of o. Two operations op_1 and op_2 of an object o are *compatible* iff $op_1(op_2(s)) = op_2(op_1(s))$ for every state s of o. op_1 and op_2 *conflict* iff they are not compatible. The *conflicting* relation among the operations is specified when o is defined. Suppose that op_1 is issued to o while op_2 is being computed in o. If op_1 is compatible with op_2 in o, op_1 can be computed. Otherwise, op_1 has to wait until op_2 completes.

Each time o receives a request of op, a thread is created for op. In the thread, *actions* of op are sequentially computed in o. An action is a primitive unit of computation in o. The thread is an *instance* of op in o. Only if all the actions computed in op complete successfully, the instance of op completes successfully, i.e. *commits*. If some action in op fails, no action in op is computed, i.e. *aborts*. That is, op is *atomically* computed. op_i may further invoke operations. Thus, the computation of op is *nested*.

A *group* G is a collection of objects $o_1, \ldots, o_n$ ($n \geq 2$) which are cooperating by exchanging requests and responses through the network. We assume that the network is *less reliable* and *not synchronous*, i.e. messages sent by each object are delivered to the destinations with message loss not in the sending order and the delay time among objects is not bounded.

3 Significant Precedence

3.1 Precedence of operations

It is critical to consider in what order the operations are computed in the objects. Let op^h denote an instance of an operation op in an object o_h. Here, op_1^i *precedes* op_2^i ($op_1^i \Rightarrow_i op_2^i$) iff op_2^i is computed after op_1^i completes in o_i.

[Definition] op_1^i *precedes* op_2^j ($op_1^i \Rightarrow op_2^j$) iff $op_1^i \Rightarrow_i op_2^j$ for $i = j$, op_1^i invokes op_2^j, or $op_1^i \Rightarrow op_3^k \Rightarrow op_2^j$ for some op_3^k. □

op_1^i and op_2^j are *concurrent* ($op_1^i \parallel op_2^j$) iff neither $op_1^i \Rightarrow op_2^j$ nor $op_2^j \Rightarrow op_1^i$. In Figure 1, $op_1^i \Rightarrow op_2^i \Rightarrow op_4^j$, $op_1^i \Rightarrow op_3^i$, and $op_2^i \parallel op_3^i$.

3.2 Significant precedence

A message m_1 *causally precedes* m_2 if the sending event of m_1 precedes the sending event of m_2 [3,8]. Suppose an object o_i sends a message m_1 to o_j, and o_k and o_j sends m_2 to o_k after receiving m_1. o_k has to receive m_1 before m_2 because m_1 causally precedes m_2. For example, if m_1 is a question and m_2 is

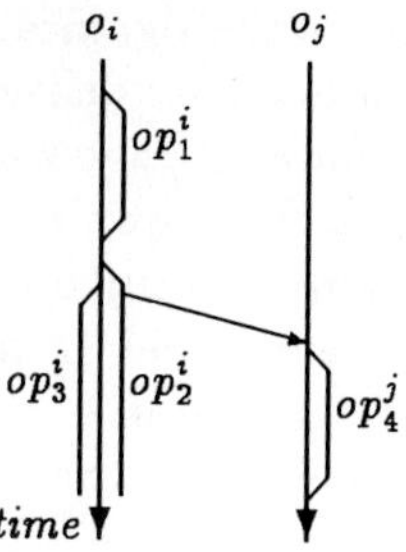

Fig. 1. Precedence of operations

the answer of m_1, m_1 has to be received before m_2. However, if m_1 and m_2 are independent questions, m_1 and m_2 can be received in any order. Thus, it is critical to consider what messages are required to be ordered in the application. We define a *significant* precedence relation "$\rightarrow$" among m_1 and m_2 based on the concept of objects. There are the following cases.

S. o_i sends m_2 after m_1 [Figure 2].

S1. m_1 and m_2 are sent by op_1^i.

S2. m_1 and m_2 are sent by op_1^i and op_2^i, respectively:

- **S2.1.** op_1^i precedes op_2^i ($op_1^i \Rightarrow op_2^i$).
- **S2.2.** op_1^i and op_2^i are concurrent ($op_1^i \parallel op_2^i$).

R. o_i sends m_2 after receiving m_1 [Figure 3].

R1. m_1 and m_2 are received and sent by op_1^i.

R2. m_1 is received by op_1^i and m_2 is sent by op_2^i:

R2.1. $op_1^i \Rightarrow op_2^i$. **R2.2.** $op_1^i \parallel op_2^i$.

First, let us consider a case that an object o_i sends m_2 after m_1 [Figure 2]. In S1, m_1 *significantly precedes* m_2 ($m_1 \rightarrow m_2$) since m_1 and m_2 are sent by the same instance op_1^i. In S2, m_1 and m_2 are sent by different instances op_1^i and op_2^i in o_i. In S2.1, op_1^i and op_2^i are not concurrent, i.e. op_1^i precedes op_2^i ($op_1^i \Rightarrow op_2^i$). Unless op_1^i and op_2^i conflict, there is no relation between op_1^i and op_2^i. Hence, neither $m_1 \rightarrow m_2$ nor $m_2 \rightarrow m_1$. Here, m_1 and m_2 are *significantly concurrent* ($m_1 \parallel m_2$). Suppose op_1^i and op_2^i conflict. If $op_2^i \Rightarrow op_1^i$, the output data carried by m_1 and m_2 may be different from $op_1^i \Rightarrow op_2^i$ because the state obtained by applying op_1^i and op_2^i depends on the computation order of op_1^i and op_2^i. Thus, if op_1^i and op_2^i conflict, the messages sent by op_1^i have to be received before the messages sent by op_2^i, i.e. $m_1 \rightarrow m_2$. In S2.2, $op_1^i \parallel op_2^i$. Since op_1^i and op_2^i are not related, $m_1 \parallel m_2$.

Next, let us consider a case that an object o_i sends a message m_2 after receiving m_1 [Figure 3]. In R1, $m_1 \rightarrow m_2$ since m_1 is received and m_2 is sent by op_1^i. Here, m_1 is the request of op_1^i or a response of an operation invoked by op_1^i. m_2 is the response of op_1^i or a request of an operation invoked by op_1^i. For example, suppose m_1 is a response of op_2 invoked by op_1^i and m_2 is a request of op_3. The output data of op_2 may be the input of m_1. In R2, m_1 is received by op_1^i and m_2 is sent by op_2^i ($\neq op_1^i$). In R2.1, $op_1^i \Rightarrow op_2^i$. If op_1^i and op_2^i conflict, $m_1 \rightarrow m_2$. Unless op_1^i and op_2^i conflict, $m_1 \parallel m_2$. In R2.2, $m_1 \parallel m_2$.

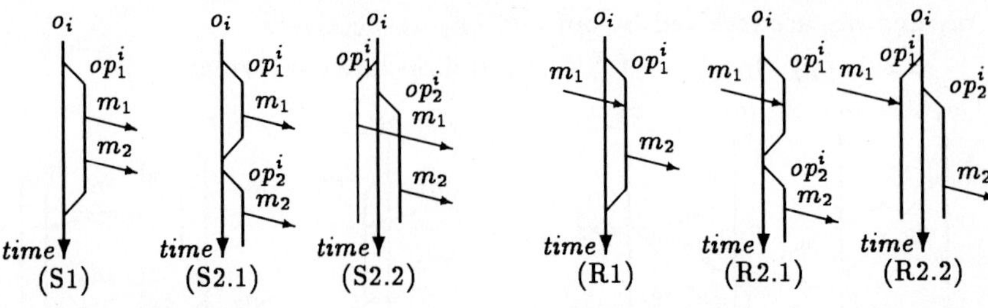

Fig. 2. Send-send precedence **Fig. 3.** Receive-send precedence

[Definition] m_1 ***significantly precedes*** m_2 ($m_1 \rightarrow m_2$) iff one of the following conditions holds:

(1) m_1 is sent before m_2 by an object o_i and
 (1-1) m_1 and m_2 are sent by the same operation instance, or
 (1-2) an operation sending m_1 conflicts with an operation sending m_2 in o_i.

(2) m_1 is received before sending m_2 by o_i and
 (2-1) m_1 and m_2 are received and sent by the same operation instance, or
 (2-2) an operation receiving m_1 conflicts with an operation sending m_2.

(3) $m_1 \rightarrow m_3 \rightarrow m_2$ for some message m_3. □

[Proposition] A message m_1 causally precedes m_2 if $m_1 \rightarrow m_2$. □

A message m is causally preceded by all messages which o_i has received and sent before sending m. However, m is significantly preceded by only messages which are related with m, not necessarily all the messages.

3.3 Ordered delivery

Suppose o_h sends a message m_1 to o_i and o_j, and o_k sends m_2 to o_h, o_i, and o_j [Figure 4]. There are the following cases on m_1 and m_2 :

C1. m_1 and m_2 are requests.

C2. One of m_1 and m_2 is a request and the other is a response.

C3. m_1 and m_2 are responses.

In C1, suppose m_1 and m_2 are requests of op_1 and op_2, respectively, which conflict in o_i and o_j. If $m_1 \parallel m_2$, m_1 may be delivered before m_2 in o_i and m_2 before m_1 in o_j. That is, $op_1^i \Rightarrow op_2^i$ and $op_2^j \Rightarrow op_1^j$ may hold. The state of o_i obtained by the computations may be inconsistent with o_j because op_1 and op_2 conflict in o_i and o_j. In order to keep o_i and o_j mutually consistent, m_1 and m_2 have to be delivered to o_i and o_j in the same order. Request messages m_1 and m_2 have to be delivered in every pair of the common destinations o_i and o_j in the same order if the requests conflict in o_i and o_j. In C2 and C3, m_1 and m_2 can be delivered in any order.

Suppose o_i receives two messages m_1 and m_2. If m_1 and m_2 are requests sent to one object and $m_1 \parallel m_2$, o_i can receive m_1 and m_2 in any order. Next, Suppose $m_1 \rightarrow m_2$. There are the following cases.

T. o_i receives m_2 before m_1 [Figure 5].

T1. m_1 and m_2 are received by an instance op_1^i.

T2. m_1 and m_2 are received by op_1^i and op_2^i, respectively.

T2.1. $op_2^i \Rightarrow op_1^i$. **T2.2.** op_1^i and op_2^i are concurrent.

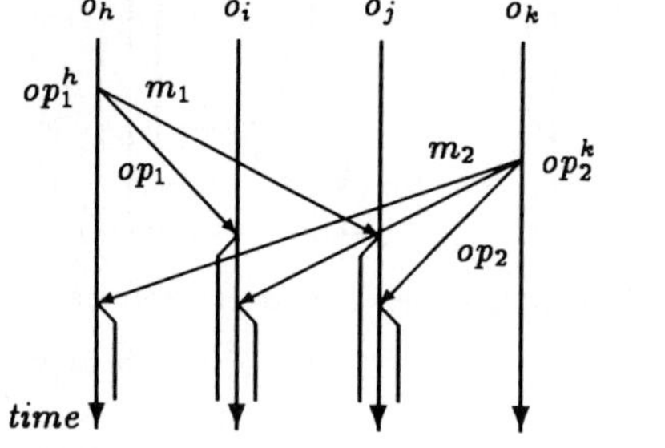

Fig. 4. Receive-receive precedence

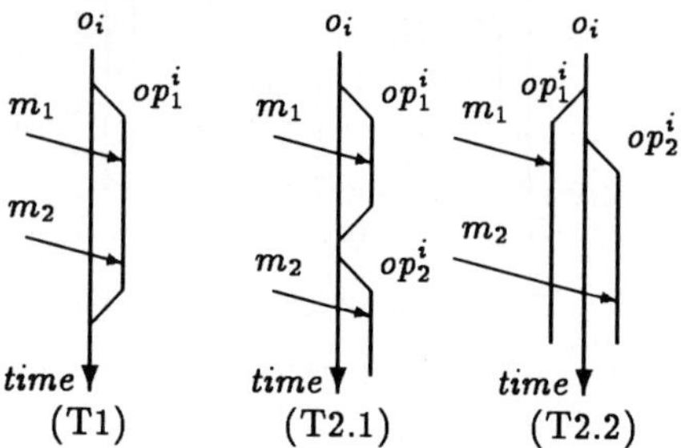

Fig. 5. Receive-receive precedence

In T1, m_1 has to be delivered to o_i before m_2 since m_1 significant precedes m_2 ($m_1 \rightarrow m_2$). In T2, m_1 and m_2 are received by different instances op_1^i and op_2^i. If op_1^i and op_2^i are concurrent in T2.2, m_1 and m_2 can be independently delivered to op_1^i and op_2^i. In T2.1, first suppose op_1^i and op_2^i conflict. If m_1 or m_2 is a request, m_1 has to be delivered before m_2 since $m_1 \rightarrow m_2$. Next, suppose m_1 and m_2 are responses. Unless m_1 is delivered before m_2, op_1^i waits for m_1 and op_2^i is not computed since op_1^i does not complete. That is, deadlock among op_1^i and op_2^i occurs. Furthermore, suppose m_3 is sent to op_1^i and m_4 to op_2^i and $m_4 \rightarrow m_3$. Even if op_1^i precedes op_2^i ($op_1^i \Rightarrow op_2^i$) and m_1 is delivered before m_2, the deadlock occurs because $m_4 \rightarrow m_3$. Thus, the messages destined to different instances cannot be delivered to o_i in the order $\rightarrow$ unless at least one of the messages is a request. Unless op_1^i and op_2^i conflict, m_1 and m_2 can be delivered in any order.

[Significantly ordered delivery (SO)] A message m_1 is delivered before m_2 in a common destination o_i of m_1 and m_2 if

(1) if $m_1 \rightarrow m_2$,

 (1-1) m_1 and m_2 are received by the same operation instance, or

 (1-2) an operation instance op_1^i receiving m_1 conflicts with op_2^i receiving m_2 in o_i, and one of m_1 and m_2 is a request,

(2) if $m_1 \parallel m_2$ and both of m_1 and m_2 are conflicting requests, m_1 is delivered before m_2 in another common destination of m_1 and m_2. □

[Theorem] No communication deadlock occurs if every message is delivered by the SO rule.

[Proof] Suppose op_1^i receives m_1 and op_2^i receives m_2. If op_1^i and op_2^i are compatible or one of m_1 and m_2 is a response, m_1 and m_2 can be received in any order. Next, suppose op_1^i and op_2^i conflict. Suppose m_1 and m_2 are delivered by the SO rule but deadlock occurs. Since the deadlock occurs, $op_2^i \Rightarrow op_1^i$ and $m_1 \rightarrow m_2$. From the SO rule (1-2), $op_1^i \Rightarrow op_2^i$. It contradicts the assumption. □

[Theorem] The system is consistent if messages are delivered by the SO rule.

[Proof] First, suppose $m_1 \parallel m_2$. If request messages m_1 and m_2 are sent to multiple objects and the operations of m_1 and m_2 conflict, the operations are computed in the same order by the SO rule Next, suppose $m_1 \rightarrow m_2$. By the

SO rule, m_1 is delivered before m_2 if m_1 or m_2 is a request and op_1^i and op_2^i receiving m_1 and m_2 conflict. Here, $op_1^i \Rightarrow op_2^i$. □

4 Protocol

4.1 Object vector

The *vector clock* [10] $V = \langle V_1, \ldots, V_n \rangle$ is used to causally order messages received. Each V_i is initially 0. An object o_i increments V_i by one each time o_i sends a message m. m carries the vector clock $m.V$ ($= V$). On receipt of m, o_i changes V as $V_j := \max(V_j, m.V_j)$ for $j = 1, \ldots, n$ and $j \neq i$. m_1 causally precedes m_2 iff $m_1.V < m_2.V$.

Significant messages are defined in context of operations instances and in nested invocations. That is, a group is considered to be composed of instances. The membership of the group changes if instances are initiated and terminated. If the vector clock is used, the group has to be frequently resynchronized [3,4,8–10,16]. The vector clock can be used to causally order messages sent by objects but not by operation instances. In this paper, we propose an *object vector* to causally order only the significant messages sent by the operation instances.

Each instance op_t^i is given a unique instance identifier $t(op_t^i)$ satisfying the following properties :

I1. If op_t^i starts after op_u^i in an object o_i, $t(op_t^i) > t(op_u^i)$.

I2. If o_i initiates op_t^i after receiving a request op_t from op_u^j, $t(op_t^i) > t(op_u^j)$.

o_i manipulates a variable *oid* showing the linear clock [8] as follows :

- Initially, $oid := 0$. $oid := oid + 1$ if an instance op_t^i is initiated in o_i.
- On receipt of a message from op_u^j, $oid := \max(oid, oid(op_u^j))$.

When op_t^i is initiated in o_i, $oid(op_t^i) := oid$. Then, $t(op_t^i)$ is given a concatenation of $oid(op_t^i)$ and the object number $ono(o_i)$ of o_i. $t(op_t^i) > t(op_u^j)$ if (1) $oid(op_t^i) > oid(op_u^j)$ or (2) $oid(op_t^i) = oid(op_u^j)$ and $ono(o_i) > ono(o_j)$. It is clear that the instance identifiers satisfy I1 and I2.

Each action e in op_t^i is given an event number $no(e)$. o_i manipulates a variable no_i to give the event number to each event e in o_i as follows :

- Initially, $no_i := 0$.
- $no_i := no_i + 1$ if e is a sending action. $no(e) := no_i$;

That is, the event number is incremented by one each time a sending event occurs. Each action e in op_t^i is given a global event number $tno(e)$ as the concatenation of $t(op_t^i)$ and $no(e)$.

o_i has a vector of variables $V^i = \langle V_1^i, \ldots, V_n^i \rangle$ where each V_j^i is defined for an object o_j for $j = 1, \ldots, n$. Each V_j^i is initially 0. Each time an operation instance op_t^i is initiated in o_i, op_t^i is given a vector $V_t^i = \langle V_{t1}^i, \ldots, V_{tn}^i \rangle$ where $V_{tj}^i := V_j^i$ for $j = 1, \ldots, n$. op_t^i manipulates V_t^i as follows :

- If op_t^i sends a message m, m carries the vector V_t^i as $m.V$ where $m.V_j := V_{tj}^i$ for $j = 1, \ldots, n$, $no_i := no_i + 1$, and $V_{ti}^i := no_i$;
- If op_t^i receives a message m from o_j, $V_{tj}^i := m.V_j$;
- If op_t^i commits, $V_j^i := \max(V_j^i, V_{tj}^i)$ for $j = 1, \ldots, n$;

Figure 6 shows two objects o_i and o_j. Initially, the vectors $V_i = V_j = \langle\ 0,\ 0\ \rangle$. An instance op_1^i is initiated in o_i where $V_1^i = \langle\ 0,\ 0\ \rangle$. After sending m to op_2^j, V_1^i is changed to $\langle\ 1i0,\ 0\ \rangle$ where $1i0$ is the event number of the sending event of m. m carries the vector $\langle\ 1i0,\ 0\ \rangle$ to op_2^j. On receipt of m, op_2^j changes V_2^j to $\langle\ 1i0,\ 0\ \rangle$. After op_2^j commits, V_j of o_j is changed to be $\langle\ 1i0,\ 0\ \rangle$.

4.2 Message transmission and receipt

A message m is composed of the following fields:

$m.src$ = sender object of m.
$m.dst$ = set of destination objects.
$m.type$ = message type, i.e. *request*, *responce*, *commit*, *abort*.
$m.op$ = operation.
$m.tno$ = global event number $\langle\ m.t,\ m.no\ \rangle$, i.e. $tno(m)$.
$m.V$ = *object vector* $\langle\ V_1,\ \ldots,\ V_n\ \rangle$.
$m.SQ$ = vector of sequence numbers $\langle sq_1,\ \ldots,\ sq_n\rangle$.
$m.d$ = data.

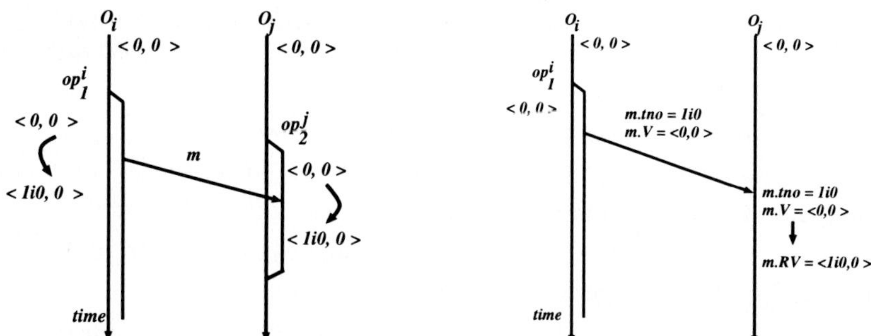

Fig. 6. Object vector

Fig. 7. Receipt vector

If m is a response message of a request m', $m.tno = m'.tno$ and $m.op = m'.op$.

o_i manipulates variables $sq_1,\ \ldots,\ sq_n$ in order to detect a message gap, i.e. messages lost or unexpectedly delayed. Each time o_i sends a message to o_j, sq_j is incremented by one. Then, o_i sends m to every destination o_j in $m.dst$. o_j can detect a gap between messages received from o_i by checking the sequence number sq_j. o_j manipulates variables $rsq_1,\ \ldots,\ rsq_n$ to receive messages. rsq_j shows a sequence number of message which o_i expects to receive next from o_j. On receipt of m from o_i, there is no gap between m and messages sent before m if $m.sq_j = rsq_i$. If $m.sq_j > rsq_i$, there is a gap m' where $m.sq_j > m'.sq_j \geq rsq_i$. That is, o_j has not yet received m' which is sent by o_i. m is *correctly* received by o_j if o_j receives every message m' where $m'.sq_j < m.sq_j$. That is, o_j receives every message which o_i sends to o_j before m. We adopt the selective retransmission to recover from the message loss. If o_i does not receive a gap message m in some time units after the gap is detected, o_i requires o_j to send m again. o_j enqueues m in the receipt queue RQ_j.

Suppose op_t^i sends a request op^j. o_i constructs a message m as follows :

$m.src := o_i$; $m.dst :=$ set of destinations;
$m.type := request$; $m.op := op^j$; $m.tno = \langle m.t, m.no\rangle = \langle t(op_t^i), no_i\rangle$);

$m.V_j := V^i_{tj}$ for $j = 1, \ldots, n$;
$sq_j := sq_j + 1$ for every o_j in $m.dst$; $m.sq_j := sq_j$ for $j = 1, \ldots, n$;

An additional *receipt* vector $RV = \langle RV_1, \ldots, RV_n \rangle$ is given to each message m received from o_i in the receipt queue RQ_i as follows :

- $m.RV_i := m.tno$;
- $m.RV_h := m.V_h$ for $h = 1, \ldots, n$ $(h \neq i)$;

In Figure 7, op^i_1 sends a message m to o_j where $m.tno = 1i0$ and $m.V = \langle 0, 0 \rangle$. On receipt of m, o_j enqueues m into RQ_j. Here, o_j gives an additional vector RV to m, i.e. $m.RV = \langle 1i0, 0 \rangle$ while $m.V$ is still $\langle 0, 0 \rangle$.

4.3 Message delivery

A pair of messages m_1 and m_2 are ordered by the following ordering rule.

[Ordering rule] A message m_1 precedes m_2 $(m_1 \Rightarrow m_2)$ if

(1) If $m_1.V < m_2.V$ and $m_1.RV < m_2.RV$,
    (1.1) $m_1.op = m_2.op$, or
    (1.2) $m_1.op$ conflicts with $m_2.op$.

(2) else $m_1.type = m_2.type = request$, $m_1.op$ conflicts with $m_2.op$, and $m_1.tno < m_2.tno$. □

It is straightforward for the following relation to hold :

[Theorem] m_1 significantly precedes m_2 $(m_1 \rightarrow m_2)$ iff $m_1 \Rightarrow m_2$. □

The messages in RQ_i are ordered in $\Rightarrow$. Messages not ordered in $\Rightarrow$ are stored in RQ_i in the receipt order.

[Stable operation] Let m be a message which o_i sends to o_j and is stored in RQ_j. m is *stable* iff one of the following conditions holds :

(1) there exists such a message m_1 in RQ_j that $m_1.sq_j = m.sq_j + 1$ and m_1 is sent by o_i.

(2) o_j receives at least one message m_1 from every object such that $m \rightarrow m_1$. □

The top message m in RQ_j can be delivered if m is stable, because every message significantly preceding m is surely delivered in RQ_j.

[Definition] A message m in RQ_j is *ready* in o_j if no operation conflicting with $m.op$ is being computed in o_j. □

In addition, only significant messages in RQ_j are delivered by the following procedure in order to reduce time for delivering messages.

[Delivery procedure] While each top message in RQ_j is stable and ready, {m is delivered from RQ_j;}. □

[Theorem] The TBCO protocol delivers a message m_1 before m_2 if m_1 significantly precedes m_2 $(m_1 \rightarrow m_2)$. □

If an object o_i sends no message to o_j, messages in RQ_j cannot be stable. In order to resolve this problem, o_i sends o_j a message without data if o_i had sent no message to o_j for some predetermined δ time units. δ is defined to be proportional to delay time between o_i and o_j. o_j considers that o_j loses a message from o_i if o_j receives no message from o_i for δ or o_j detects a gap in the receipt sequence of messages. Here, o_j requires o_i to resend m. o_i also considers that o_j loses m unless o_i receives the receipt confirmation of m from o_j in 2δ after o_i sends m to o_j.

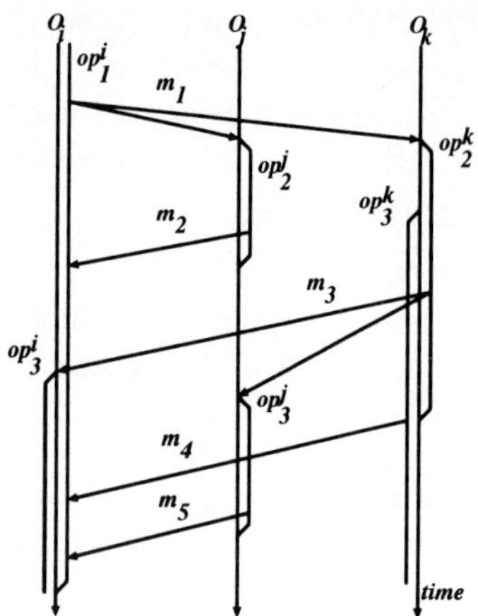

Fig. 8. Example.

Table 1. Object vectors

m	$m.tno$	$m.V$	$m.RV$
m_1	$1i0$	$\langle 0, 0, 0\rangle$	$\langle 1i0, 0, 0\rangle$
m_2	$2j0$	$\langle 1i0, 0, 0\rangle$	$\langle 1i0, 2j0, 0\rangle$
m_3	$2k0$	$\langle 1i0, 0, 0\rangle$	$\langle 1i0, 0, 2k0\rangle$
m_4	$3k0$	$\langle 0, 0, 0\rangle$	$\langle 0, 0, 3k0\rangle$
m_5	$3j0$	$\langle 1i0, 0, 2k0\rangle$	$\langle 1i0, 3j0, 2k0\rangle$

[Example] Figure 8 shows three objects o_i, o_j, and o_k. op_1^i is computed in o_i and sends a request message m_1 to o_j and o_k. On receipt of m_1, o_j computes op_2^j and o_k computes op_2^k. op_2^k sends a request m_3 to o_i and o_j. o_i and o_j compute op_3^i and op_3^j on receipt of m_3, respectively. op_2^j and op_3^j send responses m_2 and m_5, respectively. op_2^k and op_3^k are concurrent in o_k. op_3^k sends a response m_4 to o_i. Suppose op_2^j and op_3^j conflict in o_j. Each message m carries $m.tno$, $m.V$, and $m.RV$ as shown in Table 1. Here, m_3 causally precedes m_4. o_i has to receive m_3 before m_4. In this paper, messages received in a receipt queue RQ_i are ordered by using the ordering rule. Since $m_3.V(=\langle 1i0, 0, 0\rangle) > m_4.V\ (=\langle 0, 0, 0\rangle)$ but $m_3.RV\ (=\langle 1i0, 0, 2k0\rangle)$ and $m_4.RV(=\langle 0, 0, 3k0\rangle)$ are not compared, m_3 and m_4 are not ordered in o_i. Therefore, if o_i receives m_4 before m_3, o_i delivers m_4 to the application object without waiting for m_3. □

5 Concluding Remarks

In this paper, we have discussed how to support the causally ordered delivery of messages from the application point of view named the ***significant precedence*** while most group protocols are discussed at the network level. Only messages to be causally ordered at the application level are delivered in the significant precedence order. The system is modeled to be a collection of objects. Based on the conflicting relation among abstract operations, we have defined the significant precedence among request and response messages. We have presented a group protocol which supports the significantly ordered delivery of messages by using the object vector in the object-based systems.

References

1. Ahamad, M., Raynal, M., and Thia-Kime, G., An Adaptive Protocol for Implementing Causally Consistent Distributed Services. *Proc. of the 18th IEEE Int'l Conf. on Distributed Computing Systems (ICDCS-18)*, 1998, pp.86–93.
2. Bernstein, P. A., Hadzilacos, V., Goodman, N., "Concurrency Control and Recovery in Database Systems," *Addison-Wesley Publishing Company*, 1987.

3. Birman, K., Schiper, A., and Stephenson, P., "Lightweight Causal and Atomic Group Multicast," *ACM Trans. Computer Systems*, Vol.9, No.3, 1991, pp.272-314.
4. Cheriton, D. R. and Skeen, D., "Understanding the Limitations of Causally and Totally Ordered Communication," *Proc. of the ACM SIGOPS'93*, 1993, pp.44–57.
5. Enokido, T., Tachikawa, T., and Takizawa, M., "Transaction-Based Causally Ordered Protocol for Distributed Replicated Objects" *Proc. of IEEE ICPADS'97*, 1997, pp.210–215.
6. Enokido, T., Higaki, H., and Takizawa, M., "Group Protocol for Distributed Replicated Objects" *to appear in Proc. of IEEE ICPP'98*, 1997.
7. Garcia-Molina, H. and Spauster, A., "Ordered and Reliable Multicast Communication," *ACM Trans. Computer Systems*, Vol.9, No.3, 1991, pp.242–271.
8. Lamport, L., "Time, Clocks, and the Ordering of Events in a Distributed System," *Comm. ACM*, Vol.21, No.7, 1978, pp.558–565.
9. Leong, H. V. and Agrawal, D., "Using Message Semantics to Reduce Rollback in Optimistic Message Logging Recovery Schemes," *Proc. of IEEE ICDCS-14*, 1994, pp.227–234.
10. Mattern, F., "Virtual Time and Global States of Distributed Systems," *Parallel and Distributed Algorithms* (Cosnard, M. and Quinton, P. eds.), *North-Holland*, 1989, pp.215–226.
11. Nakamura, A. and Takizawa, M., "Reliable Broadcast Protocol for Selectively Ordering PDUs," *Proc. of IEEE ICDCS-11*, 1991, pp.239–246.
12. Nakamura, A. and Takizawa, M., "Priority-Based Total and Semi-Total Ordering Broadcast Protocols," *Proc. of IEEE ICDCS-12*, 1992, pp.178–185.
13. Nakamura, A. and Takizawa, M., "Causally Ordering Broadcast Protocol," *Proc. of IEEE ICDCS-14*, 1994, pp.48–55.
14. Ravindran, K. and Shah, K., "Causal Broadcasting and Consistency of Distributed Shared Data," *Proc. of IEEE ICDCS-14*, 1994, pp.40-47.
15. Tachikawa, T. and Takizawa, M., "Distributed Protocol for Selective Intra-group Communication," *Proc. of IEEE ICNP-95*, 1995, pp.234–241.
16. Tachikawa, T. and Takizawa, M., "Significantly Ordered Delivery of Messages in Group Communication," *Computer Communications Journal*, Vol. 20, 1997, pp. 724–731.
17. Tachikawa, T., Higaki, H., and Takizawa, M., "Group Communication Protocol for Realtime Applications," *Proc. of IEEE ICDCS–18*, 1998, pp.40–47.
18. Tanaka, K., Higaki, H., and Takizawa, M. "Object-Based Checkpoints in Distributed Systems", *Computer Systems Science and Engineering, CRL Publishing Company*, Vol. 13, No.3, May 1998, pp.125–131.

Aurora: An Architecture for Dynamic and Adaptive Work Sessions in Open Environments

Manolis Marazakis, Dimitris Papadakis, and Christos Nikolaou

Department of Computer Science, University of Crete
and
Institute of Computer Science, FORTH,
PO Box 1385, GR 71110 Heraklion, Greece.
e-mail: {maraz,dimpapa,nikolau}@ics.forth.gr
WWW: `http://www.ics.forth.gr/pleiades/projects/Aurora`

Abstract. This paper presents the Aurora architecture for network-centric applications, complementing the CORBA and WWW/Java frameworks with support for composition of services. The architecture addresses the requirements of dynamic open environments with multiple autonomous service providers. The paper presents a detailed technical design of the run-time infrastructure that enables on-demand composition of services. Aurora is based on a *container framework*, which provides the basis for dynamic and adaptive composition, as well as detailed monitoring and tracking. Work sessions are implemented as networks of active containers. A distinguishing feauture of Aurora is that such networks can be inspected and manipulated at run-time.

1 Introduction

In open and dynamic environments, such as the Internet, a *network-centric* application paradigm is becoming popular, as a means to utilize widely distributed application components and information resources that are made available by autonomous providers. In such environments, dynamic configuration and composition are key requirements, as the basis for both *coordination*, which entails structured processes involving mainly automated activities, and *collaboration*, which entails mainly unstructured processes with significant human interaction. Current distributed application frameworks do not adequately support these requirements, as they assume well-structured applications where software components are developed according to given specifications and interact in predefined configurations. Applications are structured as networks of components with static interconnections and there is no support for dynamic adaptation.

CORBA [1] is a comprehensive distributed application framework that provides mechanisms and support services for developing applications as collections of distributed objects. The World Wide Web (WWW) [2], although it started as a distributed service over the Internet facilitating the dissemination of documents, is evolving towards becoming a complete platform for applications that combine the functionality and services of multiple components, which are owned and managed by autonomous authorities. The introduction of the Java programming language [3] has contributed to this objective by offering support for *active content.* Furthermore, several vendors have proposed development frameworks (see for example Netscape's ONE, IBM's NCF, and Oracle's NCA) that extend the CORBA and the WWW/Java functionality by introducing additional middleware services.

We view all such approaches as being to a large extent complementary, each being more suitable for certain applications. Therefore, we propose a framework within which they can be combined, and extended towards supporting coordination and collaboration and accommodating the dynamic aspects of open environments. *Aurora* [4] is an architecture we are developing towards that end, aiming for a unified treatment of the problem of supporting network-centric applications via a set of common middleware services [5].

The remainder of this paper is organized as follows: In Section 2 overviews the *Aurora* architecture and application model. Section 3 describes the *Aurora* session management infrastructure, which relies on a container framework and a scripting language, and supports dynamic and adaptive work sessions. Section 4 provides a comparison of our approach with related research. Finally, Section 5 summarizes the ideas expressed in this paper, and reports on the current state of our development effort.

2 Overview of *Aurora*

Dynamic open environments exhibit certain distinguishing features related to autonomy, consistency requirements, dynamics of the execution, and human factors [6]. Each service provider is *autonomous* in the way it provides services to a task that is part of a workflow. It is to be treated as a "black box" whose details of operation are not known to, and cannot be controlled by, its clients. Each service provider is responsible and can manage only its own services.

By providing a publicly accessible interface, a service provider allows unpredictable interactions between its local application programs that implement its services with *any* other program that is aware of this interface and the way to use it. A client may have to determine where a service provider is located before using its services. A service provider may allow different access privileges to different clients. Therefore, a service provider encapsulates services and resources in software components which export well-defined interfaces for use by clients who, in general, do not know, and cannot control, the details of operation. Clients can be either users, represented by interaction tools (such as WWW browsers) or other service components, when complex services have to be composed of "primitive" services.

Aurora is an open architecture for network-centric applications that supports dynamic configuration and composition of components, as well as detailed on-line monitoring. Figure 1 illustrates the basic components of the *Aurora* architecture. The following subsections describe these components.

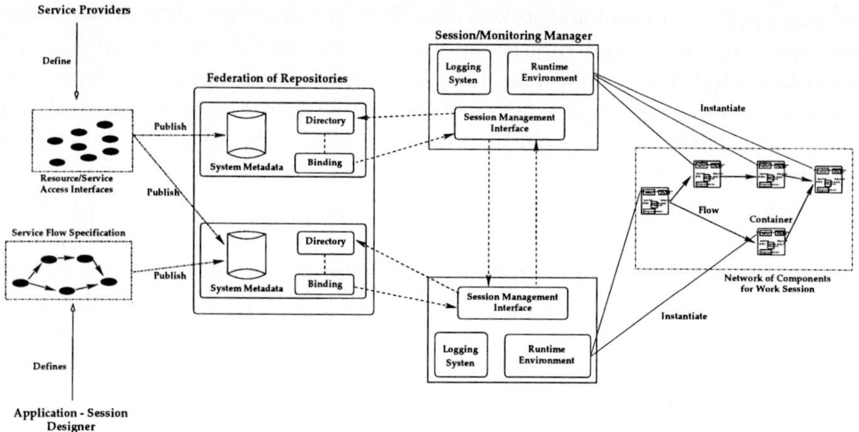

Fig. 1. Overview of *Aurora* Architecture.

2.1 Uniform Containers for Plug-Compatibility

In *Aurora*, the developer's task is to identify appropriate components and "plug" them together, via a form of *scripting* as in [7]. The execution model supports *peer-to-peer* interactions between *loosely coupled* participants, covering both coordination and collaboration. In *Aurora*, we achieve plug-compatibility by encapsulating services offered by resources in software component *containers* which export a uniform management interface. We can synthesize on-demand composite services by linking the appropriate input and output communication ports, and thus implement a composite service as a network of cooperating components, in a run-time environment provided by a session manager and supervised by a monitor. A *container* is an extensible shell combining application-specific code that implements a step in a work session with an application-independent management interface, which enables *external control* of containers in a manner that is independent of the work session context. Work sessions are implemented by establishing a network of active containers. Containers also export a uniform interface for task/component management, which enables them to participate in work sessions supervised by a session manager. Details are given in Section 3. While a task (encapsulated in a container) remains active, it can retrieve data from its input port and forward data to its output port. Input and output are in the form of *streams*, which represent a flow of data as well as operation (action) invocations from a producer task to one or more consumer tasks. Each component is also expected to provide some form of instrumentation for monitoring and control purposes. The *Aurora* model assumes that application components encapsulated in containers export for these purposes part of their state, in the form of a list of attribute-value pairs. The uniform management interface provides methods for initializing, enabling, and disabling the instrumentation within an application component encapsulated in a container, and methods for retrieving and modifying the values of state variables exposed by the application component. This information is made available by the application component by registering with the *Aurora* monitor service [4]. Each encapsulated component in a container exports a description (in CORBA IDL) of the state variables and control operation that it supports.

2.2 Communication Infrastructure

Support for dynamic configuration of the network of active containers involved in a multi-party distributed work session requires a flexible communication infrastructure, that supports event-driven interactions between *dynamic* sets of participants. The session manager of *Aurora* relies on a communication infrastructure that supports, apart from the standard request/reply mode of communication, a *publish/subscribe* mode [8]. Communication channels between active containers may be established, destroyed and reset in order to effect a reconfiguration of the work session. The session manager instructs each container, through the uniform management interface, to subscribe (or unsubscribe) to specific subjects. The subjects are determined, for each work session, by the session manager. Subscribing to a common subject enables multiple containers to receive all data published on that subject. Messages can represent requests, or can simply be data objects. The run-time environment does not enforce strict typing on the objects exchanged via channels.

2.3 Specification of Composition

We have designed a scripting language, HERMES, to express scripts for work sessions. Control and data flow are driven by events that are a combination of service request messages, state transition signals associated with tasks, as well as system-generated or application-specific notifications. Event-Condition-Action (ECA) rules [9] specify the events and conditions that activate a task. The course of a workflow may change dynamically, as the "next" actions to execute are determined by rule triggering. Data and operation invocations flow among components through streams which are established as a result of rule triggering. Optionally, a component can provide additional state information by producing application-specific events. Thus, the results of automated tasks as well as the actions of humans may affect the workflow.

A list of *service flow rules* are specified in the definition of each compound task. Such rules have the form `WHEN(c)` { `Sequence-of-Actions` }. An activation condition `c`, involving one or more events that are combined using Boolean operators, is to be evaluated in order to decide whether to execute the `Sequence-of-Actions`. HERMES only enforces a standard format for *containers* of metadata (attribute-value pairs). However, it defines specific semantics for *service flow rules.* The semantics is defined in terms of the events considered in the evaluation of the condition in the rule, and the effects produced by the execution of the actions associated with the rule. Actions are triggered when the condition in a rule evaluates to `TRUE`, and their effects include the generation of events and possible modifications to the settings of communication channels between tasks. A channel setting operation can be described as a port pair (w, z), where communication port w is to be linked to port z. A pair of communication ports defines a communication channel between the tasks that own the ports. The result of triggering a service flow rule is to generate appropriate event notifications and channel setting operations that affect the network of components involved in a work session. The *Aurora* run-time can then be viewed as an abstract machine that computes this semantics incrementally during the course of a work session.

2.4 Service Composition and Work Session Management

Aurora introduces a *service flow* paradigm, where composite services are realized in the context of *work sessions* as flows of primitive service requests among components. Scripts describe the desired configuration of components for realizing a work process; however, this configuration can be inspected and manipulated at run-time. Dynamic configuration is achieved by invoking state inspection and control operations exported by the components encapsulated in containers. By allowing manipulation of components and their interconnections at run-time, workflow becomes more adaptive to the dynamics of the execution environment.

Each task is required to notify its run-time environment when a significant state transition is to take place, particularly when the task begins execution (`START`), and when it terminates, either with success (`DONE`) or with failure (`FAIL`). Task execution may generate events for itself, as well as cause other tasks in a service flow to generate events. Optionally, a task can provide notification of the beginning and end of *phases* during its execution. Notification about the beginning and end of phases may be taken into account in the specification of work sessions. The *Aurora* run-time allows a task to be instructed to reset its original communication channels settings, and, furthermore, load dynamically a new application component. Thus, phase transitions allow run-time adaptation, which is essential for supporting dynamic and adaptive work sessions. Moreover, phase transitions allow the developer of an application component to expose task structure and state in detail, thus enabling monitoring of the task.

Since we are considering open environments with multiple autonomous service providers, we cannot assume that all the providers involved in a session are able or even willing to participate in a distributed transaction under the supervision of a single (mutually trusted) transaction coordinator. Therefore, HERMES cannot be a fully transactional specification language, as we cannot enforce desired semantics on work session participants. We only require that service providers provide notifications about significant state transactions for the requests that they execute. Such events can be coupled appropriately using Boolean operators to express activation conditions for actions that need to be taken in order to handle partial failures. Provided that service providers export compensating actions to handle failures, it is possible to specify rules that emulate transaction commitment protocols (such as two-phase commit) or even to handle partial failures in an application-specific manner. Therefore, rather than focusing on global consistency requirements, we provide mechanisms enabling *compensation* and *event tracking* via the *Aurora* monitor service [4].

2.5 Repository Service

HERMES also provides containers of metadata about the generic concepts of the *Aurora* application model: resources, events, tasks and task groups. Metadata is expressed as lists of attribute-value pairs. This enables the definition of the application domain-specific metadata that describe resource capabilities and task requirements. For each object defined, HERMES requires the declaration of a unique name, and a *type*, which identifies the "standard" according to which the attribute-value pairs assigned to the object are to be interpreted. Rather than assuming a single metadata standard, we support a two-level framework, that defines generic concepts (resources, events, tasks) and application domain-specific attribute-value pairs.

Aurora provides a repository service for managing the metadata that enables interoperation and management of components. This repository provides a *directory* that allows providers to publish their services and resources, users and applications to locate components that satisfy their requirements (which are expressed as lists of attribute-value pairs), and a *binding service* for *dynamic binding* of resources to tasks. This is essential for dynamic environments, with evolving user needs and service offers, and enables an *open market* for service providers. The repository is based on the CORBA Trader Service [10], making use of the trader's functionality to establish a federated network of autonomous cooperating directories of information related to available services. This information includes metadata for describing access methods, access control restrictions, and the service's expected behavior in terms of exception handling and performance [4].

3 Work Session Management

While processing a client request, the session manager may initiate a new work session, shutdown a session, join or leave an ongoing session, inquire about the current status of an ongoing session, or perform a search over the list of ongoing sessions. The run-time environment provided by the session manager can be decomposed into four major functional components: Interface, Scheduler Run-Time Environment, Container Run-Time Environment, and Logging System.

The *Interface* component interprets work session specifications, expressed in the HERMES scripting language and stored in the repository, and generates scheduling requests to its local Scheduler Run-Time and possibly to remote session managers. By establishing a network of containers to implement a work session, the session manager distributes the information required for sequencing the execution among multiple management components. There is no single scheduling component responsible for coordinating execution.

The *Scheduler Run-Time Environment:* provides a run-time environment for task scheduling components. For each service flow rule, the Scheduler Run-Time environment hosts a thread that is responsible for receiving specific event notifications and evaluating the activation condition of the rule, as specified by the Interface component. This thread registers with the *Aurora* monitor as a consumer of event notifications, for each of the events involved in the activation condition to be evaluated. As event notifications are received, it incrementally evaluates the activation condition. When the condition becomes `TRUE`, the Container Run-Time Environment is instructed to instantiate one or more containers encapsulating the tasks enabled by the rule's triggering. Furthermore, the task scheduling thread generates all the required configuration operations, through the management interface of containers. Configuration involves determining the application code to be executed and establishing appropriate input/output channels. An important aspect is that the application-specific code in a container is dynamically loaded, thus allowing extending its functionality on-demand. An example application of this feature is to allow access to a resource by dynamically loading the resource's access interface. An example of such an interface is a *wrapper object* that allows access to the functions provided by a legacy information system. This allows extending the functionality of a container on-demand.

For each instantiation of a task, in the context of different service flows, there is a corresponding active container encapsulating the task. However, there is a *single* task scheduling component for this task, shared by all active task instances (containers).

The *Container Run-Time Environment* is the host environment for containers instantiated in the context of a service flow. Each active container is associated with the scheduling thread that is responsible for the task encapsulated in the container. All active instances of the same task share the same scheduling component. The session manager uses the uniform management interface of containers for configuration operations to manage the network of containers involved in a work session. Having established such a network, the task/component interface of containers allows them to perform work in the context of a session. This interface is presented later in this section, in Figure 2.

The *Logging System* collects log records related to "significant" workflow events, which are produced by containers and session managers. These events include service requests and responses, state transitions, and application-specific events. The latter type of events allow application code to selectively expose its internal state. The logging system is the foundation of the *Aurora* monitor service [4]. Logging and correlation of requests and responses can be implemented in an application-independent manner, by treating log records provided by application components as *opaque* objects, which however share a common format (consisting of a unique ID and a component-specific record that is structured a list of attribute-value pairs).

Figure 2 defines the task/component interface exported by containers, which allows them to perform work and interact with each other and the session manager in the context of a work session. It includes methods for issuing and manip-

```
interface TaskComponent {
 RequestID BeginRequest(string name, SessionID sid, TaskID tid,
          AttrValuePairList args);
 ErrCode AbortRequest(RequestID rid);
 ErrCode SuspendRequest(RequestID rid);
 ErrCode ResumeRequest(RequestID rid, AttrValuePairList state);
 ErrCode CompletedRequest(RequestID rid, AttrValuePairList state);
 ErrCode AbortedRequest(RequestID rid, AttrValuePairList state);
 AttrValuePairList WaitRequest(RequestID rid);
 ErrCode RefuseRequest(RequestID rid);
 ErrCode AcceptRequest(RequestID rid);
 AttrValuePairList QueryRequestStatus(RequestID rid);
 RequestIDList ListRequests(SessionID sid);
 RequestIDList GetRequest(SessionID sid, TaskID tid);
 RequestIDList GetRequestByAttributes(SessionID sid,
               AttrValuePairList attrs);
};
```

Fig. 2. *Aurora* Container: Task/Component Interface.

ulating *asynchronous* requests to other containers, as well as methods for other containers to signal the completion (successful or unsuccessful) of a previously issued request. A container can begin, abort, suspend, or resume a request. Requests are identified by *persistent* identifiers of type `RequestID`. A container (or an external entity such as the monitor) can inquire about a pending request (using the `QueryRequestStatus` method). In most of the methods of this interface, *state* related to a request is passed as an argument or returned as a result, in the form of a sequence of attribute-value pairs. It is important to note that the `BeginRequest` method, by which a client issues a request for a service, is *generic*, in other words the container's task/component interface is *not* aware of the details of how this request is implemented. Therefore, the session manager is able, through this interface, to manage the flow of requests, without imposing any restrictions on service providers, apart from the requirement that their (proprietary) application components that implement services can be encapsulated inside the uniform containers of the *Aurora* run-time environment. Using the CORBA Dynamic Invocation Interface (DII) [1], clients (which can be containers or the session manager) can on-demand construct a method call at run-time, supplying all required parameters as elements of a list. This is in contrast to the more common approach of using the stubs generated at compile-time for the methods (using the CORBA IDL compiler). Since requests are asynchronous, the `WaitRequest` is provided to allow a component issuing a request to block waiting for a response. It is also possible to specify "callbacks" to be called by the component that served a request upon terminating the processing of a request, either successfully or unsuccessfully (methods `CompletedRequest` and `AbortedRequest`, respectively).

An important aspect of the task/component interface of containers is that a container can browse (method `ListRequests`) or perform searches over the pending requests in its work-list (methods `GetRequest, GetRequestByAttributes`). This provides flexibility in selecting among pending requests, and enables *late-binding* of resources to tasks. A consequence of late-binding is that the actual flow of control and data does not have to be fully (and statically) specified during the definition of the work session. Participants, particularly humans, are allowed to *refine* the specification by decomposing the request into further requests to other service providers. The originator of the request is not necessarily informed about this decomposition. A participant must explicitly accept or refuse a request (methods `AcceptRequest` and `RefuseRequest`, respectively).

4 Related Work

In this section, we review related research and compare it with the *Aurora* approach in terms of objectives, approach, and scope. We focus mainly on research related to workflow [11, 12], as this has been the main theme of this paper, and in particular distributed workflow system implementations. It must be noted that most workflow systems to-date have been centralized, with a single component responsible for sequencing workflow execution.

Exotica/FMQM [13] and WIDE [14] present distributed architectures for workflow enactment based on middleware technologies. Exotica/FMQM is layered on top of a transactional persistent queue system. Each node synchronizes with other nodes by communication over the network of persistent queues. WIDE is distributed CORBA-based architecture for workflow management, based on a database management system with active rule support. Each workflow engine maintains an event database, and includes a scheduler component that matches events to rules. Selected rules are recorded in a "to-execute" list, which is polled by a rule interpreter component. Both approaches seem to be more appropriate for the private networks of enterprises, since the dependence on specific middleware components imposes restrictions on the autonomy of service providers.

A major aspect of our approach is that the *Aurora* application model assumes autonomous service providers (authorities), in contrast to implicitly assuming tight integration, according to a static configuration schema, and a single authority responsible for maintaining integrity. Furthermore, *Aurora* provides a run-time environment for component composition, with detailed monitoring (provided that components export appropriate state inspection and control operations), and supports dynamic configuration and adaptation. Rather than hard-coding component configurations and interconnections, *Aurora* encapsulates components in *containers* which expose a uniform interface for inspection and manipulation and enables cooperation by establishing subject-addressable communication streams to carry the flow of operation invocations and data between components. This container framework, which enables detailed monitoring and control of active tasks and long-running compositions of tasks, is a major distinguishing feature of our approach.

[15] describes a Java-based system that supports peer-to-peer communication among distributed processes. Each process is implemented as a multithreaded object with a set of queues for incoming and outgoing messages. Such objects can be composed into sessions, by binding output queues to to one or more input queues. This is also supported by *Aurora*, with additional emphasis on supporting dynamic configuration and detailed monitoring. [16] describes the WebFlow environment that supports distributed, multi-server coordination by extending standard WWW servers with *resource managers* and by providing *coordination agents*. WebFlow is based on the Coordination Language Facility (CLF), a transactional rule-based scripting language for specifying client/server interactions. As in *Aurora*, scripts are interpreted rather than compiled, thus enabling flexible resource binding.

This is also a major difference with the workflow architecture proposed by the $METEOR_2$ project [17], which relies on a code generator to produce task management components and 'wrappers" (both for human and automated tasks) that need to be manually installed at each participating site. Each wrapper includes a hard-wired specification of the immediate predecessors and successors of the task that it manages, as well as code for evaluating the task's activation condition, invoking the task, and handling error recovery. This is a robust approach for *production workflow*, but it is too restrictive for more open-ended interactions as in the context of network-centric applications in open environments. The *Aurora* architecture relies on explicitly establishing communication channels among components, in response to events, accomodates dynamic configuration changes, and supports on-line monitoring.

Network-centric applications stretch traditional transaction processing concepts in several directions, mainly due to fact that transactions involve multiple autonomous service providers. None of the previously described related projects has addressed the issue of autonomy. Autonomy is addressed by the INCA (*Information Carriers*) model [6], under which work is carried out as interactions between an INCA, encapsulating an activity, and processing stations, which are assumed to be autonomous and may be only partially automated. The INCA contains private data for the activity, which define the context shared by activity steps, a log of all actions (together their parameters) executed so far, and a set of rules defining the the control and data flow among activity steps. Each processing station, upon receiving an INCA, performs the service requested and routes the INCA to the next destination(s). Rules encode control and data flow, as well as failure atomicity requirements. It is possible for a processing station to modify, add, or delete the data and the rules in an INCA. Autonomy is also addressed in [18], which presents the *service transactions* model, based on the notion of service actions implementing persistent conversations and a compensation paradigm to maintain integrity. This reference argues that for transactions involving multiple autonomous service provider the main integrity requirement is that the parties involved respect *pair-wise legal agreements* with each other. This is an important abstraction for service-level management, which we consider to be a major area of research for open systems.

5 Conclusions

Dynamic composition of services emerges as a key common requirement for several network-centric applications in open environments, such as digital libraries, electronic commerce, and scientific collaborative work [5]. The *Aurora* architecture presented in this paper supports an application paradigm based on the concept of *service flow*. Composition of services is achieved by interconnecting general-purpose *containers* which encapsulate "primitive" services, in a run-time environment provided by a session manager and supervised by a monitor. A repository service maintains the required metadata and handles the details of binding tasks to resources on-demand. Service flow is event-driven, and occurs through a network of active containers. This network may be inspected and reconfigured at run-time, thus supporting adaptation and monitoring.

Our ongoing work in developing the *Aurora* architecture for network-centric applications aims to provide a shared workspace as the basis for collaboration among participants in a work session. This workspace allows participants to invoke services and "publish" the results they get in response to their requests. Complex tasks, specified as service flows, can be fully automated. Such structured processes can then be represented as objects for manipulation in the shared workspace. This broadens the scope of both sets of tools, to cover extremely diverse application requirements. A similar view is taken in [19], which argues for the integration of coordination and collaboration technologies with information management to support more dynamic and adaptive processes, and provide more effective support for human-intensive work.

We are developing a prototype of the *Aurora* architecture based on the Java, WWW, and CORBA technologies, as a testbed for our research in the area of decentralized control according to the *open market paradigm*. This is closely related to research in the area of *service level management*, which aims to support a form of contracts that bind service providers to offer a predictable and measurable quality of service to their clients, which in turn have to respect the access and usage terms specified by the providers. These two research areas are fundamental for current-generation distributed systems to become more adaptive and manageable, in dynamic open environments.

References

1. *"The Common Object Request Broker: Architecture and Specification"*. Object Management Group, Framingham, Mass., 1994. Revision 2.0.
2. T. Berners-Lee and R. Cailliau and A. Luotonen and H. Frystyk-Nielsen and A. Secret. "The World Wide Web". *Communications of the ACM*, 37(8):76–82, August 1994.
3. K. Arnold and J. Gosling. *The Java Programming Language.* Java Series. Addison-Wesley, May 1996.
4. M. Marazakis, D. Papadakis, and C. Nikolaou. "The Aurora Architecture for Developing Network-Centric Applications by Dynamic Composition of Services". Technical Report TR 213, FORTH/ICS, 1997.

5. C. Nikolaou, M. Marazakis, D. Papadakis, Y. Yeorgiannakis, and J. Sairamesh. "Towards a Common Infrastructure to Support Large-Scale Distributed Applications". In *Proc. European Conference on Advanced Technologies for Digital Libraries*, 1997.
6. D. Barbara, S. Mehrotra, and M. Rusinkiewicz. "INCAs: Managing Dynamic Workflows in Distributed Environment". *Journal of Database Management*, 7(1), 1996. Special Issue on Multidatabases.
7. O. Nierstrasz, D. Tsichritzis, V. deMey, and M. Stadelmann. "Object + Scripts = Applications". In D. Tsichritzis, editor, *Object Composition*. University of Geneva, 1991.
8. B. Oki, M. Pfluegl, A. Siegel, and D. Skeen. "The Information Bus - An Architecture for Extensible Distributed Systems". In *Proc. ACM Symposium on Operating System Pronciples*, 1993.
9. U. Dayal, M. Hsu, and R. Ladin. "Organizing Long-Running Activities with Triggers and Transactions". In *Proceedings of the ACM SIGMOD Conference on Management of Data*, 1993.
10. "Trading Object Service Specification". In *CORBAservices: Common Object Services Specification*. Object Management Group, Framingham, Mass., 1996.
11. D. Georgakopoulos, M. Hornik, and A. Sheth. "An Overview of Workflow Management: From Process Modeling to Workflow Automation Infrastructure". *Distributed and Parallel Databases*, 3(2):119–154, April 1995.
12. N. Krishnakumar and A. Sheth. "Managing Heterogeneous Multi-System Tasks to Support Enterprise-Wide Operations". *Distributed and Parallel Databases*, 3(2), April 1995.
13. G. Alonso, D. Agrawal, A. El Abbadi, C. Mohan, M. Kamath, and R. Guenthoer. "Exotica/FMQM: A Persistent Message-Based Architecture for Distributed Workflow Management". In *Proc. IFIP Working Conference on Information Systems Development for Decentralized Organizations*, 1995.
14. S. Ceri, P. Grefen, and G. Sanchez. "WIDE: A Distributed Architecture for Workflow Management". In *Proc. 7th Int'l Workshop on Research Issues in Data Engineering*, 1997.
15. K.M. Chandy, A. Chelian, B. Dimitrov, H. Le, J. Mandelson, M. Richardson, A. Rifkin, P.A.G. Sivilotti, W. Tanaka, and L. Weisman. "A World-Wide Distributed System Using Java and the Internet". In *Proc. 5th IEEE Int'l Symposium on High Performance Distributed Computing*, 1996.
16. A. Grasso, J.L. Meunier, D. Pagani, and R. Pareschi. "Distributed Coordination and Workflow on the World Wide Web". *Computer Supported Cooperative Work*, 6:175–200, 1997.
17. A. Sheth, K. Kochut, J. Miller, D. Worah, S. Das, C. Lin, D. Palaniswami, J. Lynch, and I. Shevchenko. "Supporting State-Wide Immunization Tracking using Multi-Paradigm Workflow Technology". In *Proc. VLDB Conference*, 1996.
18. D. Asit and F. Parr. "The Coyote Approach for Network-Centric Service Applications: Conversational Service Transactions, a Monitor and an Application Style". In *Proc. High Performance Transaction Processing (HTPS) Workshop*, 1997.
19. A. Sheth. "From Contemporary Workflow Process Automation to Adaptive and Dynamic Work Activity Coordination and Collaboration". In *Proc. Workshop on Workflow Management in Scientific and Engineering Applications*, 1997.

Design of Secure Distributed Medical Database Systems

Marie Khair[1], Ioannis Mavridis[2] and George Pangalos[2]

[1] Dept of Computer Science, Faculty of Natural and Applied Sciences, Notre Dame University, Louaize, Lebanon
mkhair@ndu.edu.lb

[2] Informatics Lab., Computers Div., Faculty of Technology, Aristotle University of Thessaloniki, 54006, Greece
imav@eng.auth.gr, gip@eng.auth.gr

Abstract. Security is an important issue in health care environments where large amounts of highly sensitive personal data are processed. It is therefore important that both the technical considerations and the security requirements (availability, integrity and confidentiality) are taken into account as main design objectives when designing a distributed medical database system. The aim of this paper has been to describe a step-by-step methodology for the design of a secure distributed medical database system. The methodology is based on the combination of mandatory and discretionary security approaches and uses hierarchies of user roles, data sets and sites in order to decide the secure distribution of the application. An experimental implementation of the proposed methodology in a major Greek hospital has shown the usefulness of the proposals as well as their effectiveness in limiting the unauthorized access to the medical database, without severely restricting the capabilities of the system.

1 Introduction

The design of a distributed database usually takes into account several objectives; for example the processing locality, the availability and reliability of distributed data, the workload distribution and storage costs versus availability, etc. However, using all these criteria at the same time is usually very difficult since it often leads to complex optimization models. So the trend has been to take only the most important objectives into consideration, for example maximizing processing locality, and to consider the other features as constraints ([3]). During the design of distributed database systems, parameters related to performance and reliability is usually taken into account in order to decide the allocation and replication scheme. Security is however another important issue which must also be taken into account from the very first steps of the design process, especially in security critical environments as is the health care one ([5,8]). For example, while replication seems to be generally advantageous because it can localize the access to the data, if not well handled it may create several problems related to the preservation of the confidentiality of the data residing on the sites.

The proposed design methodology takes into account and handles all three components of security (availability, integrity, confidentiality). Although adding yet another objective may further increase the complexity of the design procedure, this is necessary, especially in health care environments where large amounts of highly sensitive personal data are to be processed. The security problem becomes even more important when the distributed system includes mobile sites ([7]).

2 The Fragmentation and Allocation Problem

As opposed to the case of centralized databases, the design of a distributed database usually includes two additional important design decisions: the fragmentation of the data and the allocation and replication of the fragments. During fragmentation data are divided horizontally, vertically or mixed in sets, so that the fragments can be allocated at different sites. A fragment consists of a group of tuples (in case of horizontal fragmentation) or attributes (in case of vertical fragmentation) which have the same properties from the viewpoint of their allocation ([3]). The correctness of the fragmentation depends on the disjointness (no fragment overlap), completeness (every subpart is covered), and reconstruction (nothing lost) of the whole data schema. During allocation it is decided where to fit the fragments, and also whether to support redundant or nonredundant allocation. In our case we start with nonredundant and continue with redundant allocation since replicating a fragment through several sites, if well handled, may increase the availability of the application.

The following method can be used to determine the nonredundant allocation of fragments [3]:

- A measure is associated with each possible allocation and the site with the best measure is selected ('best fit' approach).

Either of the following two methods can be used for the redundant allocation of fragments [3]:

- Determine the set of all sites where the benefit of allocating one copy of the fragment is higher than the cost, and allocate a copy of the fragment to each element of this set ('all beneficial sites').
- Determine first the solution of the nonreplicated problem, and then progressively introduce replicated copies starting from the most beneficial ('additional replication').

Since we support replication, a study has to be made in order to decide, for each site, whether to replicate the fragment under study or not. This can be done, for example, in the following two ways.

Let i be the fragment index, j is the site index, k is the application index, f_{kj} is the frequency of application k at site j, r_{ki} is the number of retrieval references of application k to fragment i, u_{ki} is the number of update references of application k to fragment i and $n_{ki} = r_{ki} + u_{ki}$. Then:

i. The 'best-fit' approach

For a nonreplicated allocation, we place fragment R_i at the site j where the number of references (Reads and Updates) to R_i is maximum. The number of local references of R_i at site j is:

$$B_{ij} = \sum_k f_{kj} n_{ki} \qquad \textbf{(1)}$$

R_i is allocated at site j^* such that B_{ij^*} is maximum.

ii. The 'All beneficial sites' approach

Using the 'all beneficial sites' method for replicating allocation, we place fragment R_i at all sites j where the cost of retrieval references (Reads) of applications is larger than the cost of update references (Updates) to R_i from applications at any other site. The B_{ij} is evaluated as the difference:

$$B_{ij} = \sum_k f_{kj}\, r_{ki} \;-\; C \times \sum_k \sum_{j' \neq j} f_{kj'}\, u_{ki} \qquad \textbf{(2)}$$

C is a constant which measures the ratio between the cost of an update and a retrieval access. Typically, update accesses are more expensive, since they require a larger number of control messages and local operations (thus $C \geq 1$). R_i is allocated at all sites j^* such that B_{ij^*} is positive; when all B_{ij} are negative, a single copy of R_i is placed at the site such that B_{ij^*} is maximum.

3 A Step-by-Step Secure Conceptual Design Phase Methodology

In the proposed methodology ([5,9]), that is based on an RBAC-oriented approach ([10]) for health care environments, the secure conceptual design phase is usually the most critical in the overall process of designing a distributed secure medical database system. The secure conceptual design phase includes the following steps:

- *Step 1*: Identification of sites, subjects, objects, and permitted actions (identification process).
- *Step 2*: Assignment of security labels (labeling process).

- *Step 3*: Fragmentation and allocation of data (distribution process).
- *Step 4*: Processing of security constraints.
- *Step 5*: Definition of permitted actions.

In the remaining of this section we outline a step-by-step design methodology for the implementation of the secure conceptual design phase of a distributed database.

Step 1: Identification of subjects, objects, sites and permitted actions (identification process).

Substep 1.1: Identification of the subjects.
As was previously mentioned, we have chosen to support the concept of user roles for the representation of the security subjects. So, characterization of the different user roles within the application must be performed in the first place. This is performed by studying the duties of the users within the application and the possible grouping of these duties into a user role, that can have different sensitivities that depend on the need-to-know of the persons playing this role.

The responsibilities of the individuals are characterized into two distinct levels of abstraction for the development of a User Role Hierarchy (URH): user roles and user categories. User roles allow the security designer to allow particular privileges to individual roles. To represent similarities that exist among user roles, a user category can be defined. Different categories can be grouped into categories of higher level. The highest category, represented as the root, contains all user roles. Privileges that are supplied to each role are passed on to its categories. The grouping of user roles into user categories is very application dependent. This step can be further divided into the following substeps:

1. Define all the user roles that exist within an application.
2. Group the existing user roles under the corresponding user category depending on the task of the user in the application.
3. Repeat step (2), grouping all user categories into higher category, until reaching the root category.

As a result of these actions, the security designer obtains an initial characterization of the URH.

Substep 1.2: Identification of the objects.
The security objects are the target of the security protection, and are in another sense the data contained in the application. Generally, data are characterized by high complexity and heterogeneity in both the nature and the sensitivity levels of the different data sets included in them (especially in environments where sensitivity is not easily defined as for example in healthcare ones). Organizing these data in a structured manner is necessary for the development of the appropriate user views, which in its turn is a required step in the design and implementation of the application.

Data is grouped into data sets, that will be target for the labeling process later. Data sets represent data with a common use. These data sets are grouped into a number of data categories. A data category characterizes common characteristics among related data sets. In turn, the different data categories can be grouped into one or more data categories of higher levels.

Substep 1.3: Identification of the sites.
This step consists on studying the sites where data will be distributed. This study should identify the following characteristics:

- the function of each site in the context of the whole application,
- the technical characteristics of the site (storage capacity, processing power, etc.), especially if they may constitute a constraint,
- the type of connection of the site to the network (LAN, Internet, dial-up, etc.),
- whether the site is mobile or not and the degree of mobility, since this may have a significant impact on the design,

- the security threats to each site,
- any special requirements and conditions of the site.

Substep 1.4: Identification of the permitted actions.
Since we have chosen to support both DAC and MAC security policies, there are different types of accesses that can be executed by subjects to objects. These operations are not defined only by the sensitivity levels of both (for example the *-property of Bell-Lapadula), but they also depend on the needs of the user roles, with respect to the security policy.

The basic well defined actions in most DBMSs are 'Select', 'Update' which includes 'Insert' and 'Delete'. In a medical database, deletion of sensitive data must be prohibited for follow up reasons.

Step 2: Assignment of security labels (labeling process).

Since our security policy supports MAC, the reading and writing of data by individuals is based on their authorized security clearance label. And since, the DAC security policy is supported too, a richer set of access modes that are specific to the particular type or category of information is granted to the individuals based on their need-to-know requirements. For this reason, we have first to define the security labels, assigned to users, data and sites, and then to define the type of permitted access.

The security label has two parts: The level and the category. The category of a user depends on his position in the User Role Hierarchy (URH). The highest category that corresponds to the root of the URH tree contains all sub categories and roles defined in the application. The category of data depends on its usage and corresponds to the needs of some categories of users. The category of a site depends on its use (what categories of users use it and what categories of data they need to use) and on its type (whether it is standalone, internet connected, mobile, stationary, etc).

The security levels assigned to each one of the users, data and sites are defined after an initial study that results in a rating of the clearance of users, the sensitivity of data and the trustworthiness of sites.

Substep 2.1: Assignment of security labels to the subjects
Having obtained an initial characterization of the user roles (URH), this substep allows us to assign a security label to each user role starting from the root and moving to the last level before the leaves (that form the user roles) of the tree. More specifically:
1. assign the category of the user role, as represented in the URH, then
2. assign a level to the user role that represents the level part of the label. This level depends on the trustworthiness of the user, and on his/her responsibility as defined in [5], [9].

By completing this substep, the security designer obtains an initial characterization (overall structure) of the User Role Hierarchy, and a primary assignment of labels to users.

Substep 2.2: Assignment of security labels to the objects
After the overall structure of the User Role Hierarchy (URH) has been established, the security designer can then proceed to assign data sets to the URH leaves which correspond to the data that needs to be accessed by the user roles. In this process, the designer uses the information accessing requirements as a guide for ensuring that the correct privileges are given. The procedure is repeated until reaching the root.

This step can be sub-divided into the following substeps:
1. Assign data sets starting with the user roles under a user category.
2. Move data sets shared by all user roles to their common user category.
3. Move data sets shared by all user categories to their common super categories. This procedure is repeated till reaching the root.
4. The label to be assigned to the data set then consists of:
   - a category that corresponds to the category of the node or the leaf already assigned in the URH.

– a level that corresponds to the lowest clearance level of the user roles contained in the category.
5. Repeat this process for all the data sets within each user role, and then within their user categories.

As a security check for this substep, a stand-alone classification of the sensitivity of the data can be processed. This classification is dependent on both the content and the context of the data. In the case where the levels differ, the security designer must check and decide which level to assign. By completing this substep, the designer obtains an initial identification of privileges of each URH node and an initial label assigned to each data set.

Substep 2.3: Assignment of security labels to the sites
As in the case of users and data, each site should also be labeled with a level and a category. The security label of each site is derived from a function of physical and operational parameters of the site, as well as the type of connection and the grade of its mobility.

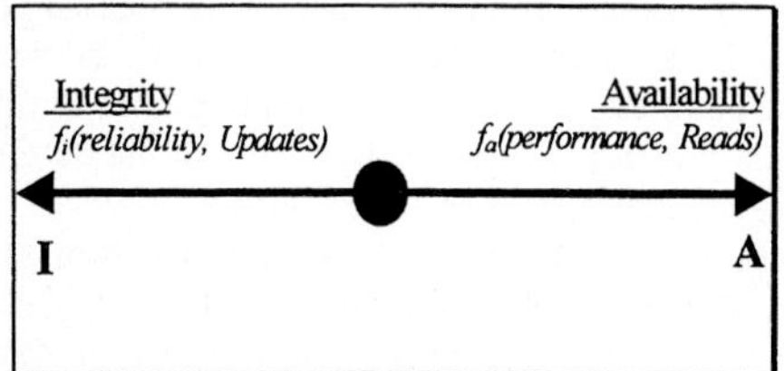

Fig. 1.

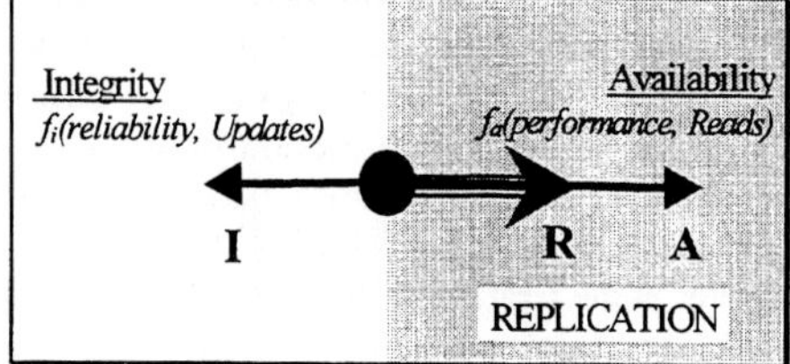

Fig. 2.

The category of the site depends on its use, i.e. the category of local users accessing the site (local users include all users having direct access to the site).

The security level of the site depends on several parameters related to the site, for example the vulnerability of the O.S. and the DBMS, the physical environment, and nature of the site, etc. The vulnerability of the O.S. and DBMS can be rated by using national or international security evaluation criteria and methods ([9]). A very significant characteristic of the site is also whether it is mobile or stationary since vulnerabilities in both categories differ strongly ([7]).

Step 3: Fragmentation and allocation of data (distribution process).

Having identified the subjects, the objects, the sites and the various types of access and assigned the security labels, this step focuses on the study of how data will be distributed on these sites. This distribution process can be divided into 2 substeps: fragmentation and allocation.

Substep 3.1: Fragmentation.
In our model, the fragmentation of the global schema is driven by two factors: the different users' needs (data should be distributed to several sites), and the different sensitivities of the data (data should be confined only in some sites).

First, depending on the users' needs the data sets are examined. Since we support the need-to-know principle, no user should have access to data that is not needed to perform his task. This results to an initial vertical and/or horizontal fragmentation of the initial data sets ([1]).

Then, we begin to look for all the security constraints that have been formally defined during the requirements analysis. As soon as the security designer begins to add the security constraints (generally prohibited tasks), the conflicts' identification analysis process begin ([9]), to notify the designer when assigned/prohibited actions contrast. Different types of conflicts can be found depending on the type of constraints to be inserted. In fact, in order to prohibit an unauthorized access from a user to a data set, an upgrade of the part of the data set involved must be performed ([9]).

Depending on the type of the security constraint, and since we have chosen the tuple level granularity, this can lead to one of the following actions:

1. If the part to be upgraded is the whole table, then all the table and all its rows are upgraded.
2. If the part to be upgraded is just some rows of the table, then just these rows are assigned a higher security label.

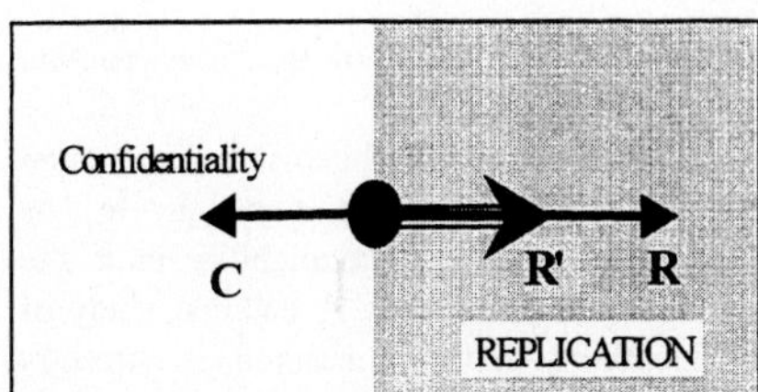

Fig. 3.

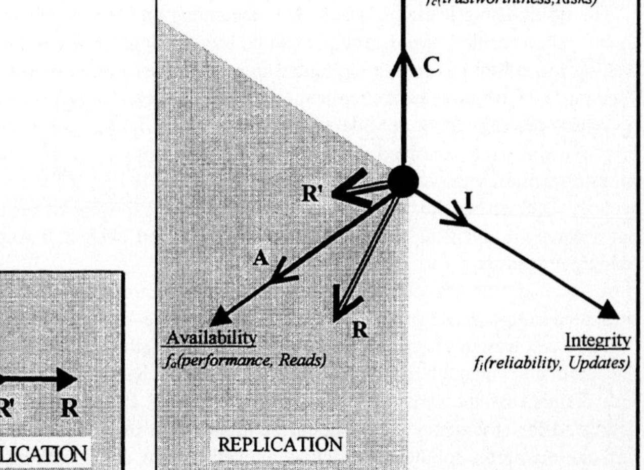

Fig. 4.

3. In the case that the part to be upgraded is only some fields of a table, then this causes the initial table to be fragmented into two tables. One part is assigned a low and another a strictly higher level.

The final fragmentation and allocation scheme is obtained only after completion of step 4 below, when all the security constraints have been processed. As a result, each tuple of these fragments is assigned a security label and can be accessed by one or more user roles.

Substep 3.2: Allocation and replication

One of the important factors that may affect system performance is the replication of the fragments through the sites. The replication scheme determines how many replicas are created for each fragment, and to which sites these replicas are allocated. This affects for example the performance of the distributed system since reading locally is faster and less costly than reading from a remote site. The decision of whether to replicate or not is usually based on two factors: the number of reads versus the number of updates (or, as seen below, the availability versus the integrity (Fig. 1)).

More precisely, if a fragment is frequently accessed in a read mode, a widely distribution is mandated in order to increase the number of local reads and to decrease the load on the network, which can be understood as increasing the availability of the whole system. On the other hand, an update of a fragment can be written to all or to a majority of the replicas (depending on the algorithm supported by the DDBMS). In this case, a wide distribution slows down each write and increases its communication cost. Therefore, if a fragment is sufficiently accessed in update mode, a narrowly distribution is mandated. This can be understood as balancing the cost of integrity that is increased by the replication with the cost of availability that is increased now by the non replication. So the decision whether to replicate or not should be driven by this two contrary forces (*A* for availability and *I* for integrity) that can be seen as vectors. The result of replicating or not is then depending on the area where the resultant *R* of the two vectors resides (Fig. 2).

There is however also another important factor to be examined. This is the confidentiality issue which is particularly important in environments containing sensitive data, as for example the health care ones. Confidentiality acts as a contrary force C against the resultant R of the figure 2. The final decision whether to replicate or not, taking into consideration the confidentiality requirements of the specific site, should be based on the area where the resultant R' of the two vectors resides (Fig. 3).

Concluding the above observations and placing all the facts together, we can say that the final decision whether to replicate or not should be driven by the combination of three forces (A for availability, I for integrity and C confidentiality) that can be seen as vectors.

The result of replicating or not is then depending on the area where the common resultant R' of the three vectors resides, as for example can be seen in figure 4 where the overall scheme of the decision making procedure has been represented in a two-dimension perspective and an initial estimation has been made of the cases where replication should be preferred (gray area).

When speaking about confidentiality in the above figures, we mean the need for confidentiality to be provided by the examined site in the case of allocating a specific fragment of data. In fact, the need for confidentiality depends mainly on both the estimated risks for exposure of sensitive data and the security level of the site. For example, if the risk for exposure of sensitive data is high and the site is not secure, the decision tends towards non replication even if it would have been beneficial in the reading procedure.

A summary of the objectives and depending factors for evaluating each of the three vectors presented in figure 4, is proposed in the following table 1.

The exact way in which the above objectives and factors participate in the final decision depends on the particular characteristics of the site. These characteristics contribute as a weight in the measurement of the three security components. For example, the weight of availability in a site dedicated for emergency cases should be higher than that of the confidentiality. A detailed study of how these weights should be assigned, as well as how confidentiality may be measured, is currently under further study.

Table 1. Summary of objectives and factors for replication decision.

	OBJECTIVE	FACTORS
CONFIDENTIALITY	Minimum Exposure Risks (maximum secrecy)	– Estimation of risks for exposure of sensitive data – Trustworthiness rate of the site
AVAILABILITY	Maximum Locality of READS (minimum remote access)	– Frequency of READ-accesses – Performance rate of the site
INTEGRITY	Minimum Remote UPDATES (maximum data consistency)	– Frequency of UPDATE-accesses – Reliability rate of the site

In our methodology we use an extension of the combination of the 'best-fit' and the 'all beneficial sites' methods for the allocation and replication of data, respectively. Following is a step by step explanation of how we use it, taking as objective the optimization of the three security components.

Substep 3.2.1: Allocation

We support the 'best-fit' approach for a nonreplicated allocation. This step can be seen as studying how to obtain the minimum remote access of the data in case of non replication. The value of B_{ij} in our methodology depends on the total number of reads and updates and on the trustworthiness of the site.

$$B_{ij} = \sum_k f_{kj} n_{ki} + f(\textit{trustworthiness of the site}) \quad (3)$$

Substep 3.2.2: Replication

To apply replication, we must decide, for each site, whether to replicate the fragment under study or not. Using the 'all beneficial sites' method for replicating allocation, we place fragment R_i at all sites j where the resultant of the three vectors falls in the shaded area of the figure 4.

$$
\begin{aligned}
B_{ij} &= f_{confidentiality}(trustworthiness,\ Risks) \\
&\quad + f_{availability}(performance,\ Reads) \\
&\quad\quad + f_{integrity}(reliability,\ Updates)
\end{aligned} \tag{4}
$$

Steps 4 - 5: Processing of security constraints - Definition of permitted access types.

After the identification, labeling and distribution processes, the different security constraints should be examined. For each constraint, checking must be performed to ensure its obedience. In case of conflict, the security designer should be notified to decide about the implementation procedure ([9]). Since we have chosen also to support DAC security policy, the permitted access types must be defined for all subjects to the data sets under their clearance. This definition depends on the need-to-know requirements of the subjects dominated by their clearance and their responsibilities in the application.

4 The Experimental Implementation

The AHEPA University Hospital, which has been used as our test-bed for designing secure database systems, is a general hospital which is part of the Aristotelian University of Thessaloniki. The following figures describe briefly the hospital: 16 clinics including the reference and hospitalization center for AIDS patients from all Northern Greece; 40 laboratories; a radiological department including M.R.I., C.T., U.S., D.S.A, X-rays, etc.; a nuclear medicine department (SPECT, Gamma-Camera); 705 beds; 520 medical doctors including consultants; 762 nursing personnel; 466 personnel for financial and general support; 28,000 inpatients per year; 2,500 surgical procedures per year; 107,000 outpatients per year; 2,345,000 laboratory tests per year (1993).

For the purposes of the experimental implementation a set of appropriate data flow diagrams (DFDs) and entity relationship models (ERMs) for the representation of data and functions, concerning the drugs delivery and the examinations orders and results in AHEPA, have been developed. For the identification of the sites, a general model of the Health Information System architecture has been utilized. Eight different user roles have been identified and grouped in a five-level-deep URH. Nineteen data sets have also been identified and have been grouped in a six-level-deep tree. An initial fragmentation of the data sets has been obtained, based on the different user needs and sensitivities of the data. Further fragmentation has been provided by the examination of the security constraints. The allocation and replication of the fragments has been based on the 'best fit' and 'all beneficial sites' approaches, respectively. Specific work is currently taking place on the area of measuring the trustworthiness, performance and reliability of the sites. An additional study has also started on the implications of the location and specific situation parameters on the design.

5 Conclusion

During the design of distributed database systems, parameters related to performance and reliability are usually taken into account in order to decide the allocation and replication scheme. Security is however another very important issue that should also be taken into account when designing a distributed medical database system.

This paper describes a step-by-step methodology for the design of a secure distributed medical database system. The methodology is based on the combination of mandatory and discretionary security models and uses hierarchies of user roles (RBAC based approach), data sets and sites in order to decide the secure distribution of the application.

An experimental implementation of the proposed methodology in a major Greek hospital has shown the usefulness of the proposals as well as their effectiveness in limiting the unauthorized access to the medical database, without severely restricting the capabilities of the system.

6 References

1. Ozsu, T., Valduriez, P.: Principles of distributed database systems. Prentice Hall (1991)
2. Bell, D.: Distributed database systems. Addison Wesley (1993)
3. Ceri, S., Pelagatti, G.: Distributed Databases: Principles and Systems. NY, McGraw-Hill (1985)
4. Castano, S., Fugini, M., Martella, G., Samarati, P.: Database security. Addison Wesley (1994)
5. Pangalos, G., Khair, M.: Design of a secure medical database systems. IFIP/SEC'96, 12th International Information Security Conference (1996)
6. Wolfson, O., Jajodia, S. and Huang Y.: An Adaptive Data Replication Algorithm. ACM Transactions on Database Systems, Vol. 22, No. 2 (June 1997) 255-314
7. Mavridis, I., Pangalos, G.: Security Issues in a Mobile Computing Paradigm. Communications and Multimedia Security (CMS'97). Vol.3 (1997) 60-76
8. Fugini, M.: Secure database development methodologies, in Database security. Landwehr (ed.) (1988)
9. Pangalos, G., Khair, M., Bozios, L.: An integrated secure design of a medical database system. MEDINFO'95, The 8th world congress on medical informatics, Canada (1995)
10. Ferraiolo, D. and Kuhn R.: Role-based access controls. 15th NIST-NCSC National Computer Security Conference. Baltimore, MD, October 13-16 (1992) 554-563

Modeling of Subjective Interpretation for Street Landscape Image

Tatsuya Shibata[1,2] and Toshikazu Kato[1,3]

[1] Electrotechnical Laboratory, 1-1-4 Umezono, Tsukuba, Ibaraki, 305-8568, Japan
{tshibata, kato}@etl.go.jp
[2] Japan Science and Technology Corporation, 4-1-8 Honmachi, Kawaguchi, Saitama, 332-0012, Japan
[3] Dept. of Industrial and Systems Engineering, Chuo University, 1-13-27 Kasuga, Bunkyo-ku, Tokyo, 112-0003, Japan

Abstract. Our hypothesis is that the model of subjective interpretation is based on rough information process. We analyze a relationship between adjectives and three graphical attributes of color, direction, and position in order to model the subjective interpretation for streetscape images. We focus especially on the graphical descriptors such as Lab color space, Lab auto-correlation and rough image segmentation, which correspond to the graphical attributes. Our psychological experiment indicates that subjective interpretations consist partly of "evaluation", "texture", and "openness". By analyzing the relationships between these three factors and the graphical descriptors, we find that subjective interpretation relates to the combination of the three graphical descriptors.

1 Introduction

Architects and urban planners are required to understand clients' impression of present or future urban scenes (urban landscape) and to obtain their consensus concerning landscape design. Virtual and augmented reality systems have been applied to show 3d urban landscape to clients or to create films. Virtual reality constructs blocks of shopping areas and augmented reality systems compose a client's house or building with a residential area. So, the client can experience and evaluate planned environments before the development is executed.

Virtual and augmented reality technology focuses on the presentation of 3d space and image processing on description and measurement of 3d space in images. These applications can not promote clients' consensus concerning landscape design because they are just tools to build 3d spaces. The client's subjective interpretation of the design is not reflected in such a system.

On the other hand, architecture and town planning researchers model subjective interpretation for urban design using simplified physical measurement such as road width and building height. Landscape is regarded not as composite information such as color, texture, and form but as physical environments humanbeings recognize. Psychology deals with conceptual models of subjective interpretation based on not physical measurement but concepts such as complexity and coherence, so it is difficult to construct a model on computers.

The main problems are:

- no application of graphical description based on subjective interpretation in virtual and augmented reality and image processing, and
- no application of composite graphical description of images in architecture, town planning, and psychology.

Our purpose is to model subjective interpretation based on a composite graphical description. Once a model is established, subjective interpretation of unknown information such as image data can be predicted. A process to establish the model is one to discriminate subjective interpretation of our environments and to find graphical descriptors which cause the discrimination of the subjective interpretation. Statistical analysis is applied to obtain the relationship between subjective responses and still image data of landscapes. Finally we examine the model of simplified graphical descriptors (color, direction, and position) which relate to discriminated subjective interpretation.

2 Modeling of subjective interpretation for landscape assessment

2.1 Definition

Figure 1 indicates a model of subjective interpretation. The semantic differential (SD) method [1] clarifies that we have discriminated concepts for our environments such as "evaluation", "potency" and "openness" and that the discriminated concepts can be represented by groups of adjective pairs such as like-dislike and soft-hard. The definition of a subjective interpretation is a discriminated concepts represented by adjectives. We also define a graphical description as a graphical representation of visual functions and attributes such as color, direction and position and a graphical descriptor as an index representing color, direction and position.

2.2 Methodology

SD method quantifies subjective responses to stimuli of landscape images to analyze subjective interpretation. A multiple regression analysis is applied to find the relationship between graphical descriptions and adjective pairs. A canonical analysis is also applied to construct a composite model between graphical descriptors and groups of adjective pairs [2]. Finally, an experiment of street landscape image retrieval is carried out to examine the model constructed by the canonical analysis.

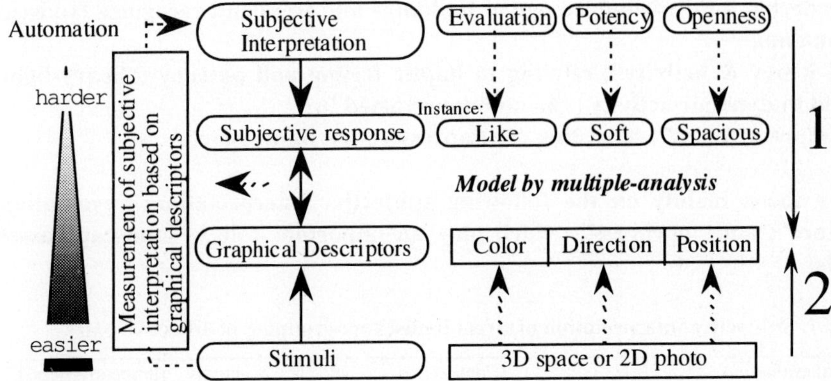

Problems:
1. Image processing-no measurement relating to subjective response
2. Architecture & psychology-no measurement using image processing skills

Solution:
To find graphical descriptions relating to subjective interpretation by using image processing skills

Fig. 1. Model of subjective interpretation

3 Subjective interpretation for landscape assessment

Experiment 1. The following experiment is carried out to analyze factors of the subjective interpretation by discriminating adjective pairs. Thirty samples, the representatives of 240 street-landscape images in Tokyo, were selected after a provisional experiment. A questionnaire was prepared using 23 well-used paired adjectives and a 7-point scaling. The selection of these scales was based on previous research [3-5].

Result. Values from 1 to 7 were allocated respectively to each point on the questionnaire's horizontal scale. The factor analysis (the principal component method and the varimax rotation) is applied to analyze the 30 samples. The number of factors are determined by the eigenvalue greater than 1.0 and a factor composition is determined by including a factor loading greater than |0.45|. Four factors are predicted: (table 1):

1. "General evaluation", representing 13 adjective pairs, which can be categorized into positive "evaluation" (e.g. like, comfortable), "texture" (e.g. unified and soft), representing attributes of 2d surfaces and edges of buildings and a road, and "openness" (e.g. spacious), representing characteristics of 3d space,
2. "Context", representing five adjective pairs like "new-old" and "historical-modern". Subjects judged age of buildings and trees and recognize landscape contents,
3. "Potency & activity", relating to haptic feeling and potency ("heavy-light") and to dynamic activity ("monotonous-varied"),
4. "Impressiveness", consisting of "impressive-not impressive".

We focus mainly on the following subjective interpretation: "evaluation", "texture", and "openness", which play an important role in landscape assessments.

Table 1. Subjective interpretation of street landscape: grouping of adjective pairs

General evaluation			Context	Potency & activity	Impressiveness
Evaluation	Texture	Openness			
Like-dislike	Unified-not unified	Dispersed-crowded	Historical-modern	Heavy-light	Impressive- not impressive
Comfortable-uncomfortable	Orderly-disorderly	Spacious-confined	Old-fashioned-novel	Monotonous-varied	
Beautiful-ugly	Soft-hard	Deep-shallow	Blurred-clear	Masculine-feminine	
Relaxed-tense	Warm-cool		Small-large-scale	Hard-soft	
Reliable-anxious			Gloomy-cheerful		
Calm-restless					

4 Relationship between graphical descriptors and adjectives

4.1 Graphical descriptors relating to subjective interpretation

An analysis of street landscape indicates that sky and foliage visibility and road width play an important role in landscape assessment [6]. A psychological experiment shows subjects draw boundary lines as if they segment images into sky, road and building areas [7].

According to Zeki [8], visual cortex has specialized functions: color, direction(form), and position. Our hypothesis is that different interpretations relate to different compositions of visual functions and attributes. We analyze: color space for color, color auto-correlation for direction and regularity, and rough segmentation for position.

Figure 2 is an image which composes RGB averages of the 30 image samples. This indicates how to segment a landscape image, which means sky, road, and buildings are segmented by a shape of triangles rather than square-grids.

The following sections analyze graphical descriptors related to subjective interpretation and examine graphical descriptions for discriminated subjective interpretations: "evaluation", "texture", and "openness".

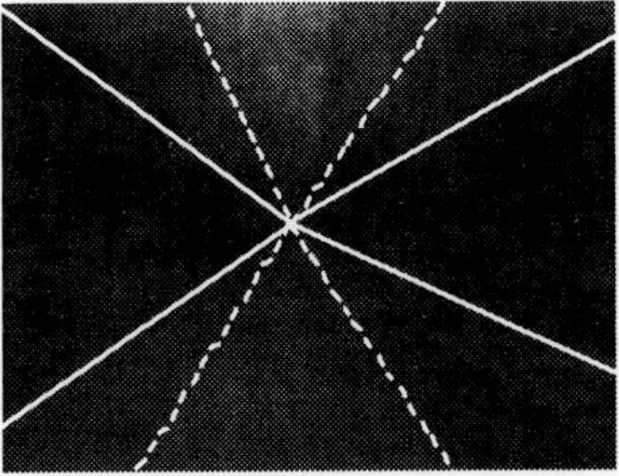

Fig. 2. Composite image of 30 samples

Table 2. Correlation between adjective groups and graphical descriptors

(a) Evaluation

Adjective pairs	R-square coefficient			
Segmentation method	3x3 squares		9 triangles (a)	
Color space	(1)RGB	(2)Lab	(3)RGB	(4)Lab
Like-dislike	0.14	0.37	0.31	0.84
Comfortable-uncomfortable	0.13	0.36	0.32	0.92
Beautiful-ugly	-	0.41	0.29	0.79
Relaxed-tense	-	0.52	0.41	0.74
Reliable-anxious	-	0.58	0.22	0.84
Calm-restless	-	0.45	0.44	0.78

(b) Texture

Adjective pairs	R2 coefficient		
Color or auto-correlation	Color		Auto
Segmentation method	(a)	(b)	(b)
Unified-not unified	0.62	0.67	0.83
Orderly-disorderly	0.52	0.74	0.94
Soft-hard	0.74	0.66	0.96
Warm-cool	0.73	0.81	0.96

(c) Openness

Adjective pairs	R2 coefficient		
Color or/and auto-cor.	Color		Both
Segmentation method	(a)	(c)	(c)
Spacious-confined	0.69	0.70	0.87
Dispersed-crowded	0.40	0.45	0.87
Deep-shallow	0.78	0.86	0.90

4.2 Graphical descriptors: evaluation

A regression analysis is applied to find the relationship between graphical descriptors and "evaluation". Table 2a shows R-square correlation (the forward-procedure step-wise method, F-value: more than 4.0) to compare an Lab color space with an RGB one and the square-grids (3x3) pattern segmentation with the triangle one (figure 3a). Figure 2 gives us a hint of how to deal with 3d space in images. The triangle pattern drawn in figure 2 can approximate boundaries between buildings/fences and road as well as sky. and it seems that buildings on the left-hand side are closer to the view points than those on the right-hand side. So the pattern in figure 3a obtains better results than the one in figure 3b as far as "evaluation" is concerned. The combination of color (RGB or Lab average) and position (grid-squares or triangles) are analyzed as color attributes.

Table 2a indicates that the Lab color space with the triangle segmentation is suitable as graphical descriptions to analyze the street landscape images. This means that brightness and hue, which is independent of each other, play a significant role in "evaluation".

Let Li, ai, bi (i=1, ..., 9) denote the Lab color averages in the nine triangles. The adjectives underlined in table 1 have more than 0.7 (R-square correlation), so "general evaluation" relates to the Lab color space with the triangle segmentation

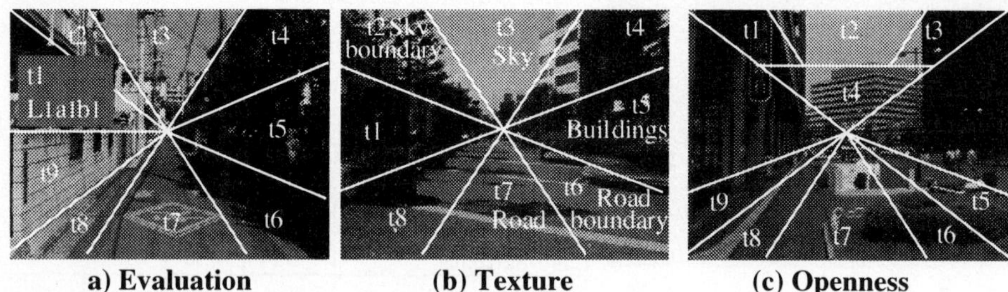

a) Evaluation (b) Texture (c) Openness

Fig. 3. Meshes for rough image segmentation

4.3 Graphical descriptors: texture

The same regression analysis is applied as "evaluation". We assume that "unified" and "orderly" relate to skylines, road boundaries and building surfaces, so the segmentation pattern is changed as figure 3b shows. Table 2b shows the R-square correlation result. The alphabetical indexes in tables 2b-c correspond to the segmentation patterns in figure 3.

The fewer number of variables(27->24), the better for models, so the segmentation pattern in figure 3b is finally selected. Table 2b also indicates that the Lab color auto-correlation [2] is a better descriptor than the Lab color average. The auto-correlation represents directions in images and is applied in 3d measurement and pattern recognition. It is found that "texture" relates to the Lab color auto-correlation rather than the Lab color average.

4.4 Graphical descriptors: openness

The same regression analysis is applied as "evaluation". In section 4.2, the "deep-shallow" adjective pair have the relationship with not buildings but sky and road parts, and frontal buildings also create compression, so the segmentation method is changed as figure 3c shows. Table 2c shows the R-square correlation to compare the Lab color average only with the Lab color average and auto-correlation both. This indicates that graphical descriptors for "openness" are the Lab color average and auto-correlation in upper and lower parts of images. It is found that all the data in images are not always necessary and this depends on the discriminated subjective interpretation.

5 Relationship between graphical descriptors and subjective interpretations

Canonical analysis can not only construct a composite model which consists of two different groups of variables: subjective responses to adjectives and graphical descriptors but also analyze the relationship between the two groups. The canonical factor loading represents the correlation between subjective interpretations and adjectives as well as graphical descriptors. We analyze the Lab color average and auto-correlation in the eight triangle-pattern areas (figure 3b) as graphical descriptor variables and the data of the 23 adjective pairs in experiment 1. The canonical analysis predicts the same subjective interpretations ("general evaluation", "context", "potency and activity" and "impressiveness") as the factor analysis and shows the relationship between the subjective interpretations and the graphical descriptors.

Figure 4 indicates the areas and graphical descriptors relating to each subjective interpretation. "General evaluation" relates to green color in areas t1, t3, which represents foliage and direction in area t7, which represents a road. The main focus of "general evaluation" is on foliage and open space. "Context" relates to the direction in the upper part (areas t1, t2, t4) and green color in only area t3, which represents the abundance of foliage in an image because of the continuation of foliage from areas t1, t2 or t4, t5. "Potency and activity" relates mainly to direction and regularity in areas t1, t5, t8, which represent texture and edges of foliage, fences and buildings. "Impressiveness" relates mainly to the average and the variance of color: red color in areas t5, t6, t7 and color variation in areas t3, t7.

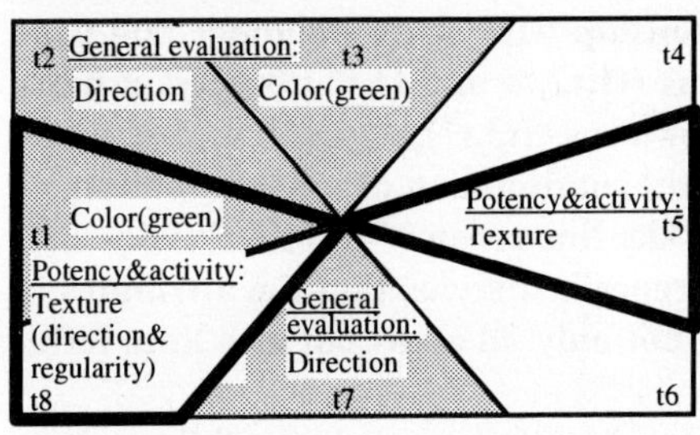

(a) Evaluation and potency & activity

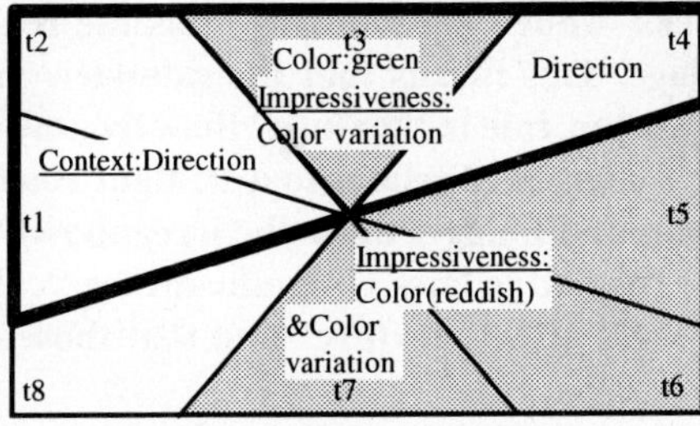

(b) Context and Impressiveness

Fig. 4. Graphical descriptors relating to subjective interpretation

In conclusion, different graphical description are required for discriminated subjective interpretations.

6 Experiment 2: test of image retrieval system

Experiment 2 has been done to test the image retrieval system based on the model of subjective interpretation. The canonical analysis [2] is applied to construct the image retrieval system. The 30 samples of experiment 1 are used for learning. And 68 images of old towns and new towns in England, Tokyo, and Tsukuba Science-city are added. The model uses the Lab color average and autocorrelation in the eight triangle-pattern segmentation (figure 3b) as 144 graphical descriptor variables and the data of the 23 adjective pairs in experiment 1.

The adjectives tested are:

1. "positive evaluation": like, comfortable, beautiful, relaxed, reliable and calm,
2. "negative evaluation": dislike, uncomfortable, ugly, tense, anxious and restless,
3. "soft texture": soft and warm,
4. "hard texture": hard and cold,
5. "coherence": unified and orderly,
6. "disorder": not-unified and disorderly,
7. "openness": dispersed, spacious and deep,
8. "depth": deep, and
9. "potency & activity": light.

Top ten images out of the 98 images, which include unknown images, are retrieved by the above adjectives. We analyze characteristics of each subjective interpretation judging from the ten images.

"Positive evaluation" relates to abundant foliage and open space, while "negative evaluation" has the relationship with little foliage and compressed space. So foliage and open space play an important role in the "evaluation" of street landscape.

"Soft texture" relates to foliage, brightness, and reddish objects such as bricks, while "hard texture" has the relationship with office buildings and little foliage. This means that the side-view areas (t1,t2,t8 and t4,t5,t6) plays a more important role in "texture" than frontal-view areas (t3,t7).

"Coherence" relates to a straight road and continuation of uniform buildings, fences and foliage, while the irregularity of sky line creates "disorder". Sky lines and road edge lines is significant for "coherence". It seems that the attributes of 2d areas affect "texture" and that those of not only 2d areas but also lines influence "coherence".

"Openness" relates to a wide road and abundant foliage and "depth" to a long continuous road and abundant foliage. "Potency & activity" has the relationship with a straight road with a focal point far from the viewpoint. Figure 5 shows the top two images retrieved by the nine subjective interpretations.

Fig. 5. Top two images retrieved using adjectives

6 Conclusion

Our purpose was to model the subjective interpretation based on composite graphical description. Our conclusions are that:

- graphical descriptions eligible for discriminated subjective interpretation exist and
- subjective interpretation segmentation for street landscapes relates to graphical descriptors of the Lab color space , the color auto-correlation, and the rough triangle.

Based on these two points, we have developed an application that can measure subjective interpretation of landscape design and can retrieve images by key adjectives. This application can automatically give us images eligible for our subjective interpretation by typing words.

References

1. Osgood, C. E., Suci, G. J., Tannenbaum, P. H.: The Measurement of Meaning, University of Illinois, Urbana (1957).
2. Kurita, T., Kato T., Fukuda, I., Sakakura, A.: Sense Retrieval on a Image Database of Full Color Paintings, J. of Information Processing of Japan (Japan), Vol. 33, No. 11, (1992) 1373-1383.
3. Funakoshi, T., Tsumita, H.: A Study of Physical-analysis on Street Spaces—Study on Street Spaces (Part II)—, J. of Architecture, Planning and Environmental Engineering (Transactions of AIJ) (Japan), no. 364, (1986) 102-111.
4. Funakoshi, T., Tsumita, H.: A Study of Correlation-analysis on Street Spaces—Study on Street Spaces (Part III)—, J. of Architecture, Planning and Environmental Engineering (Transactions of AIJ) (Japan), no. 378, (1987) 49-57.
5. N. Matsumoto et al.. A Study on the Development of the Simulation Media for Perception and Judgement of Architectural Space—Studies on the Planning of Exterior Spaces, 5—, J. of Architecture, Planning and Environmental Engineering (Transactions of AIJ) (Japan), no. 403, (1989) 43-51.
6. Shibata, T: Subjective Response to Depicted Urban Space, Doctoral Thesis, University of London (1996).
7. Oku, T.: Components of Townscape by Tachistoscopic Experiment: Experimental Study on Visual Characteristics and Feelings of Townscape Part 1. J. of Architecture, Planning and Environmental Engineering (Transactions of AIJ) (Japan), no. 321, (1982) 117-124.
8. Zeki, S: A Vision of the Brain, Blackwell Science, Oxford (1993).

Extend *Dexter* Model to Capture More Semantics of Hypermedia

Bing Wang

Computer Science Department, University of Hull, Hull, HU6 7RX, United Kingdom

Abstract. The hypermedia technology has been widely used in both industrial and academic areas for many years. The most successful example of using this technology is the Internet Web application. However, beyond such success, we still have not reached an agreement on what the formal structure of hypermedia is and we have not had an international standard for defining a hypermedia system. The lack of a standard data model for hypermedia prevents us from further studying and understanding the hypermedia fundamental structure. In 1990, Halasz and Schwartz[HM90] proposed a reference model called *Dexter* which is the first attempt to try to provide a standard structure for understanding hypermedia. Since then, *Dexter* has been widely used as a *de facto* standard for hypermedia. In this paper, we describe how to extend *Dexter* by adding several semantic constructors. As the result of such extension, the extended data model can provide not only the constructors to define nodes but also the semantic connectors to represent semantic relationships among defined nodes.

1 Introduction

What is the data model of a hypermedia system? It can be simply defined as a node-link structure. That is, a set of nodes to store multimedia information and a set of links to connect nodes. However, if we use this data structure to compare the existing hypermedia systems, we can immediately find out that it is difficult to list the common and different features of the existing systems. This is because different systems provide users different facilities to define, create and manipulate nodes and links. There is not an unified definition of the data model for a hypermedia system. Consequently, the lack of such definition prevent us from designing a open, extensible and distributed multiuser hypermedia system. Since 1990's, the importance to establish a formal data model for hypermedia system is realized, and studies have focused on the aspects of hyperbase and hypermedia interface. As a result, the concept of an open hypermedia system came out[CG88] and researches to link hypermedia and database has been carried out since then[SS90, HW92, WH95]. At DEXA96 and DEXA97 conferences, the author used formal methods to separately define an integrated data model and a unified data model for the hypermedia system design[Wan96, Wan97]. As a continuation of these researches, and most importantly, to provide a comprehensive definition for an open and object oriented hypermedia system, the author, in this paper, further extend the *Dexter* data model by adding several semantic constructors. The whole paper is organized as follows. Section 2 analyse *Dexter* model in order to illustrate the way of how to enhance it by adding several semantic constructors. In section 3, an extended *Dexter* model will be discussed on the basis of the previous section, and in the final section, we conclude and summerize the research.

2 Dexter Model and Its Semantics

The *Dexter* model is formulated in Z[1]. By using a set theory based mathematic method to abstract a hypertext structure, it will be possible for us to extend the existing definitions and add more new constructors to enhance semantics of the existing model.

2.1 The Node and Link Structure

There is no common definition of what a hypermedia system looks like, and different systems have different architectures. In this paper, a hypermedia system is defined as an information processing system which consists of two parts: one to receive the user's input and to display the result; the other to store the node and link information. Thus, a typical architecture of a hypermedia system can be represented as follows:

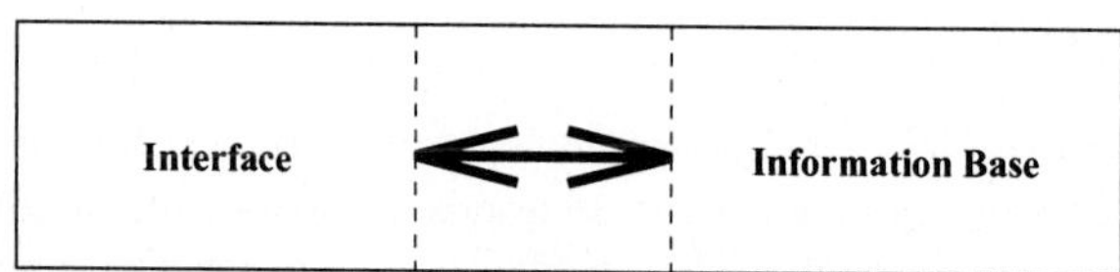

Fig. 1. The General Architecture of a Hypermedia System

The dashed lines separate the hypermedia system into two parts, and the double headed arrow indicates that there exists an information exchange between them. However, the general architecture described above can be refined further to produce a more detailed architecture. This is illustrated by the *Dexter* reference model[HM90], in which three layers are defined. These are, the *run time layer, the storage layer* and the *within-component layer*. The run time layer describes the behaviour of the interaction between the user and hypermedia, the storage layer describes the information base which stores nodes and links, and the within-component describes the structures and contents of nodes.

[1] Z is a formal specification language developed by Oxford University and it is widely used in both industrial and academic areas for defining large software systems.

Storage Layer Among these three layers, the storage layer is the most important part of a hypermedia system. It defines the data structure for nodes and links. Its importance are, firstly, it acts as a *data-store* for the long term storage of any type of data. Secondly, it is a *data-organizer*, allocating certain structures to the stored data, such as a hierarchical or network structure. This allows the designer to perform operations on the stored data with a great degree of flexibility. In the following description we shall discuss the two major structures of the components in the storage layer, i.e. *node structure* and *link structure*.

Node Architecture A node in *Dexter* is defined by the concept component. A component can be an atom, a link or a complex object. The traditional definition of a hypertext node is a atomic component defined in *Dexter*. Thus, an atomic component is the basic constructor. An object oriented concept, object identifier, is assigned to each component. The purpose for doing so is that an object identifier provide a guaranteed mechanism for addressing any component in hypertext. Finally, the component is defined as the following Z schema:

```
┌─ COMPONENT ─────────────────────────
│ compBase : BASE_COMPONENT
│ compInfo : COMP_INFO
└─────────────────────────────────────
```

In the above schema definition, the *Dexter* model illustrates a simple fact that a component has two attributes. The first attribute says that a component is a member belonging to the set of a base component. A base component is actually a general definition for all possible types of components. These types are atom, link or composition. Thus, a component can either be a basic hypermedia node which only stores a chunk of data, or a link or a composite node which contains other components. This is abstracted by a free type definition in Z as illustrated below:

$$BASE\_COMPONENT ::= atom\langle\langle ATOM\rangle\rangle \mid link\langle\langle LINK\rangle\rangle$$
$$\mid composite\langle\langle \mathrm{seq}\, BASE\_COMPONENT\rangle\rangle$$

The second attribute explains that a component has also some additional information to describe its properties. These additional information does not describe the actual content of the information stored in the node. It only specifies those physical information which are used to identify anchors and location information for displaying node's contents. This is further defined by the following Z schema.[2]

[2] To understand fully this Z schema, readers need to read books described Z formal specification such as the book by[Wor92].

$$\begin{array}{|l}
\hline
\textit{COMP_INFO} \\
\textit{attributes} : \textit{ATTRIBUTE} \rightarrowtail \textit{VALUE} \\
\textit{anchors} : \operatorname{seq} \textit{ANCHOR} \\
\textit{presentSpec} : \textit{PRESENT_SPEC} \\
\hline
\#\textit{anchors} = \#(\textit{first} (\!| \operatorname{ran} \textit{anchors} |\!)) \\
\hline
\end{array}$$

The above schema illustrates a fact that the defined attribute pairs will provide enough information to runtime layer of how to present a component to a user.

The *Dexter* model uses the above two basic schemata to describe the fundamental mechanism of the node structure. It is simple and straightforward. Clearly, it does not reveal any semantics between nodes. We will further discuss semantics of the *Dexter* node structure after discussing its link architecture illustrated below.

Link Architecture The meaning of a link defined in *Dexter* is the same as the link definition illustrated at the beginning of this section. In order to specify a link between components, *Dexter* proposed a supporting concept—anchor to describe how to make a connection within components. An anchor is composed of anchor id and anchor value. The anchor id acts as object identifier which is uniquely assigned for each anchor within a component. The anchor value is actually a set of values to describe an anchor's location, region or substructure information. It is defined as follows:

$$ANCHOR \mathrel{\widehat=} ANCHOR\_ID \times ANCHOR\_VALUE$$

The end of a link is defined by another schema called specifier. The purpose for a specifier is to describe a point of an anchor within a component. It therefore contains information such as component specification, anchor id, presentation information and direction. One of the advantages of using Z is that we can use a given set to describe a pre-defined object since we do not need to know the detailed structure of the type. So, the specifier schema is defined on the basis of the given sets of COMPONENT_SPEC, ANCHOR_ID, and PRESENT_SPEC, and a finite set DIRECTION which describe the direction of a link such as FROM, TO and BYDIRECT.

$$\begin{array}{|l}
\hline
\textit{SPECIFIER} \\
\textit{componentSpec} : \textit{COMPONENT_SPEC} \\
\textit{anchorSpec} : \textit{ANCHOR_ID} \\
\textit{presentSpec} : \textit{PRESENT_SPEC} \\
\textit{direction} : \textit{DIRECTION} \\
\hline
\end{array}$$

By using this specifier schema, a link is then defined as follows by *Dexter*.

LINK

$specifiers : \text{seq}\, SPECIFIER$

$\#specifiers \geq 2$
$\exists\, s : \text{ran}\, specifiers \bullet s.direction = TO$

This schema defines that a link must have at least two specifiers. However, the relationship between nodes is not specified by the above schema. To summerize the node architecture of the *Dexter* model, we can get the following results:

1. A node may have several attributes predefined by the system, which are used to describe the properties of the defined node. Nevertheless, among these defined attributes, the most important is a *type* definition, which characterises the nature of a set of nodes. The node type allows us to identify different nodes and so satisfy varied aims. Currently, few hypermedia systems provide a type mechanism, i.e. all nodes have the same type such as the node definition of *Dexter*.
2. The size of a node is another important property of a node structure. There are two different interpretations of the size of the node in hypermedia systems, these being physical size and logical size. The ***physical size*** of nodes may or may not be restricted. The ***logical size*** of a node may be interpreted as the amount of stored information in a node. This second meaning of node size is important when hypermedia is used to maintain a complex structured document. In such cases, nodes are not only the physical platform used to contain information, but are also ***logical units*** through which long unstructured information may be divided into more structured elements, each of which has a clear and complete logical meaning. The *Dexter* model, however, failed to provide any facility to specify a logical size of a node.

2.2 Semantics of the Node Structure

Nodes and links are used to construct the *network* in a hypermedia application. The goal of this network is to represent and organize the unstructured information involved in the application. However, the above node structure gives us a very little change to present the logical structure of an application. Normally, a hypermedia data model means a network consisting of nodes, and links which connect the nodes, to represent semantic meanings. The *Dexter* model is too simple to reveal the rationale behind a hypermedia data model although it is said that such semantic description is defined in a within component layer. To study a hypermedia data model, three issues need to be concerned: the definitions of the basic constructors, semantic constraints, and data operations. These issues tell us what the basic constructors mean, how to use them to describe a document structure, and how to create a new structure on the basis of an existing one. The *Dexter* model only defines the physical architecture of the node and link structure. It does not specifies semantic constraints upon the defined nodes and links. Thus, there is no any semantic facility provided by *Dexter* to model a logical structure of an application.

3 Extended Hypermedia Model

A hypermedia data model should also provide facilities to present the logical structure of a real world enterprise. The more semantic concepts a data model can express, the more powerful it is. An abstraction is a model of the real world enterprise in which certain structure details are omitted. The goal of abstraction is to ignore those aspects which are not important for some purposes and to abstract those aspects which are important for other purposes.

3.1 Static Type Abstractions

A static type abstraction is one which represents a semantic relationship between defined object types. Such a relationship is automatically held between object types.

- **Generalization/Specialization**
  Generalization is a mechanism which allows an object type to become a more general object type, *super-type*, of another object type, *sub-type*. The reverse of generalization is specialization. Furthermore, generalization/specialization can also be regarded as a *semantic constructor* which can ignore the differences between similar object types in order to build a semantic relationship between them.
- **Aggregation/Decomposition**
  Aggregation is "*the means by which relationships between low-level types can be considered a higher level type*" [PM88]. The reverse of aggregation is decomposition. The aggregation/decomposition mechanism of a data model supports the transformation of a set of objects into a higher level aggregate (super-type) object.

3.2 Operation Abstractions

A data model which supports the above abstraction mechanisms allows us to model *statically* a complex situation based on the existing object types. Thus, it is a requirement of such a data model that corresponding operations should be defined to support such semantic constraints.

- **Operation Sharing**
  Operation sharing mechanisms defined in a data model are more like the operation polymorphism defined in object oriented systems. In a data modelling context, operation sharing not only means that the same operation can be applied to all the elementary object types but also implies that we can get different results according to different situations.

- **Integrity Checking**
  Relationships between the defined object types in a semantic supported data model are complicated. The integrity checking mechanism in such data models guarantees that whenever an operation is performed on an object, its related objects will be reported to the user so that the user can do the same operation on them in order to maintain integrity constraints between them.

3.3 Extending Component Structure

The first approach to extend the *Dexter* model is to enhance its component structure by re-defining it as a structured node. This is to be done by using the structured node types defined by the *InterSect_DM* approach[WH95]. In this approach, a structured node type is introduced and used as both the logical unit and physical node to present an unstructured information. It defined as follows in Z:

$$\begin{array}{l} \mathit{Structured\_Node} ::= \mathit{null\_structured\_node} \mid \\ \mathit{structured\_control\_node} \langle\!\langle \mathit{Without\_Contents} \rangle\!\rangle \\ \mid \mathit{structured\_node} \langle\!\langle \mathit{With\_Contents} \rangle\!\rangle \end{array}$$

In this schema, a structured node can be either a structured node with content or a structured control node without contents attached or a null node. This is a structural approach for defining a node type. If we use this structured node type to replace the component schema defined in *Dexter*. Immediately, we can have the following additional semantics in *Dexter*.

1. A structured node type is an abstract data type which is used to describe the structure of the intra-relationship between the components and the document.
2. The structured node types have the following three important features:
   - All node types belong to two types: structured *control* node type or structured node type.
   - All node types are defined as structured node types with versions;
   - Each node type is recursively defined. That is, a node can contain a number of sub-nodes.

In the *Dexter* approach, nodes only represent the concept of information holder. Such a constraint restricts us in our representation of the structures of complex documentation environments. This weakness is overcome by replacing the component schema with the structured node type. Thus, we allow users to define a structured node without contents which which belongs to the *structured control node type*. The structured control node type plays two significant roles in a complex documentation application environment:

1. It is used as the existence constraint to determine the existence of other nodes in order to maintain referential integrity.

2. It acts as a semantic connection to link two node types.

To construct the structured node type, we have the following simplified schemata definitions which describe the features of both structured and structured control nodes.

$$\begin{array}{|l}\hline \textit{With\_Contents} \\ \textit{version}_n\textit{umber} : \mathbb{P}\,\mathbb{N} \\ \textit{attributes} : \mathbb{P}\,\textit{Attribute} \\ \textit{contents} : \mathrm{seq}\,\textit{Multimedia} \\ \textit{struct\_node} : \mathbb{P}\,\textit{Structure\_Node} \\ \hline \end{array}$$

This schema defines a structured node has a contents attached. For a node without contents, its schema definition is defined as follows:

$$\begin{array}{|l}\hline \textit{Without\_Contents} \\ \textit{version\_number} : \mathbb{P}\,\mathbb{N} \\ \textit{attributes} : \mathbb{P}\,\textit{Attribute} \\ \textit{struct\_node} : \mathbb{P}\,\textit{Structure\_Node} \\ \hline \end{array}$$

In the *Dexter* model, a link is simply a connection between two components. It does not reveal semantics among nodes. We introduce the relationship constructor to *Dexter* in order to represent different semantic means among nodes. The relationship constructor allows the user to define any explicit named relationship between two structured nodes, which is defined as follows:

$$\begin{array}{|l}\hline \textit{Relationship}[\textit{Node\_Type}1, \textit{Node\_Type}2] \\ \textit{relation\_name} : \textit{Name} \\ \textit{relationship} : \textit{Node\_Type}1 \leftrightarrow \textit{Node\_Type}2 \\ \hline \end{array}$$

However, by replacing component with node type definition and adding more semantic constructors in the *Dexter* model, we still cannot provide users a comprehensive supporting mechanism since users' requirements are dynamical. This means that we need such a hypermedia data model that has powerful functions to dynamically model users' needs. Thus, we can try again to link the *Dexter* model with the unified hypermedia model developed by the author[Wan97]. This is the second way to enhance the semantics of *Dexter* model.

3.4 Adding Schema Constructors

A concept, schema constructor, was introduced to model a hypermedia application from an object oriented database point of view. More details can be found in [Wan97]. In the *Dexter* model, we do not have a general schema definition to describe the whole application structure. One of the advantages of using databases is that we can define a global view of an application structure. The schema constructor acts as the global hypermedia application definition and it is defined as follows:

$$
\begin{array}{|l}
\hline
\textit{Scheme\_Constructor} \\
\textit{Node\_Constructor} \\
\textit{Composite\_Node\_Constructor} \\
\textit{node\_object} : \textit{Node\_Type} \nrightarrow \textit{ObjectType} \\
\hline
\forall \textit{nodes} : \mathbb{P}\,\textit{Node\_Type} \bullet \forall n : \textit{nodes} \bullet \exists o : \textit{ObjectType}; \\
N_1 : \textit{Node\_Constructor};\ N_2 : \textit{Composite\_Node\_Constructor} \mid \\
n = \textit{InheritableNode}\ N_1 \lor n = \textit{CompositeNode}\ N_2 \bullet o = \textit{node\_object}\ n \\
\hline
\end{array}
$$

The above definition reveals the following facts. Firstly, it is a constructor which arranges the defined node types. Secondly, all nodes defined by a user must have object types associated, and finally, a database can be used as the information base for supporting hypermedia. Thus, by introducing the schema constructor, we can naturally relate hypermedia with an object oriented database. The significant benefit of this enhancement is that we can fully use database facilities such as semantic integrity checking, concurrency control and query processing without making any extra effort to design a new database specifically for hypermedia.

So far, we have enhanced the semantics of *Dexter* by replacing the node structure definition and adding a schema constructor. After doing these changes in the *Dexter* model, we can achieve the following aims.

1. *The Model Enhances the Abilities of Current Hypertext Data Models by Its Complex Node Definition.* The new structured node type can contain other structured nodes which are regarded as sub-nodes.
2. *The Model Supports Versions of Defined Nodes.* User defined nodes can be version-ed according to need.
3. *The Model Provides Semantic Relationship Definition Ability to Allow Users to Define Semantic Relationships between Defined Node Types.* A semantic relationship between two node types can be defined by the user. This is achieved by the relationship type constructor.
4. *The Model Allows Users to Define the Structure of Nodes in a Hierarchical Way.* Aggregation abstraction is supported by the extended *Dexter* model. The structured node represents an *is-part-of* relationship between the node and its components. These components can themselves contain nodes which represent a hierarchical structure for the defined nodes.
5. *The Model Provides Users a Global Application Definition.* The schema constructor is built on the basis of the database facilities to provide users an overall application definition mechanism for managing the defined nodes and links. It can also provide local views for different users. Most importantly, users can evaluate the defined schema according to their needs.

There are also corresponding changes for the operations defined in the extended *Dexter* model. These operations mainly describe how to define, create and update nodes, links and schemata. For the limited length of this paper, they will be not discussed here as the aim of this paper is to illustrate how we can enhance the semantics of *Dexter* by using the approaches described above.

4 Conclusion

Formal specification is widely recognized as a precise way to define the structure of a complex software system. Z specifications can be unambiguously, precisely and concisely proven. The *Dexter* model and its extension further prove such a fact that the formal specification of hypertext structures can provide the foundation for understanding the essentials of hypertext systems. In particular, this paper focuses on the formal definitions of semantic constructors to enhance the *Dexter* reference model. Z makes it possible for us to give a full and accurate description of the semantics of a hypermedia data model, which is very difficult to realize using plain sentences. The importance of this research is that it not only reveals the nature of a hypermedia data model but also explores the possibility to link database systems. Finally, as the result of the author's efforts in recent years, we hope that through this formal approach the proposed formal model can be used both as the fundamental mechanism for hybrid system integration and a basis for the definition of the next generation hypermedia systems.

References

[CG88] B Campbell and J Goodman. Ham: A general-purpose hypermedia abstract machine. *Communications of ACM*, 31(7):856–861, July 1988.

[HM90] F. G. Halasz and S. Maye. The dexter hypertext reference model. *Proceedings of the Hypertext Standardization Workshop*, pages 95–131, January 16-18, 1990.

[HW92] P. Hitchcock and B. Wang. Formal approach to hypertext system based on object oriented database systyem. *Information and Software Technology*, 34(9):573–592, September 1992.

[PM88] J Peckham and F Maryanski. Semantic data models. *ACM Computer Surveys*, 20(3):154–187, September 1988.

[SS90] H A Schutt and N A Streitz. Hyperbase: A hypermedia engine based on a relational database management system. In *Proceedings of the First European Conference on Hypertext*, pages 95–108, France, November 1990.

[Wan96] B. Wang. The design of an integrated information system. In Roland R. Wagner and Helmut Thomas, editors, *Database and Expert System Applications (DEXA'96), Lecture Notes in Computer Science No. 685*, pages 479–488, Zurich, Switzerland, September 1996. Springer-Verlag.

[Wan97] B. Wang. Toward a unified data model for large hypermedia applications. In Ab delkader Hameurlain and A Ming Tjoa, editors, *Database and Expert System Applications (DEXA'97), Lecture Notes in Computer Science No. 1308*, pages 142–152, Toulouse, France, September 1997. Springer-Verlag.

[WH95] B. Wang and P. Hitchcock. *InterSect_DM*: a hypertext data model based on oodbms. *Information and Software Technology*, 37(3):573–592, March 1995.

[Wor92] J. B Wordsworth. *Software Development with Z.* Addison-Wesley, 1992.

A Generic Framework for Structured Document Access

Franck Fourel, Philippe Mulhem, and Marie-France Bruandet

Université Joseph Fourier, Laboratoire CLIPS - IMAG
BP 53, 38041 Grenoble Cedex 9 - France

Abstract. Current electronic document retrieval systems, i.e., database systems or information retrieval systems, do not handle enough the richness related to the document structures. Based on a classical model of structured documents, our approach intends to integrate propagation mechanisms related to document structure. These machanisms, called "scopes of attributes", have two goals: they exhibit information that is usually kept implicit in documents, and they address dependencies between the values of the attributes used for the retrieval of the documents. The model of documents, the propagation and retrieval mechanisms compose a generic framework for the retrieval of structured documents.

1 Introduction

Electronic document management is a challenging problem for new information systems, for instance digital libraries. New problems related to the storage and the retrieval of such electronic documents issue from their structural features. Documents are often structured and can be generally viewed as an organization of entities, the document parts. We address here the problem of accessing information from a collection of structured documents. Because of the multiple features of such documents, the retrieval model used has to be adaptable to fit the user's information needs. Most of the time, this retrieval model depends on the "type" of the system: database management system, information retrieval system or hypermedia system, and this model is too strict. We describe here the relevant features of these systems for our context.

Database technology provides sophisticated data management capabilities and query languages. The query results are strict and *A la* SQL queries are structurally oriented; so it is quite impossible to write queries without knowing the structure of the queried data.

Information retrieval systems allow to find a set of relevant information objects, such as documents, corresponding to a user's information need expressed by a query. A "retrievable" document is any information part related to a system internal content representation (called the index). Usual IRSs query languages are closed to natural language, and their matching process compute similarity between the document index and the user's query. Then, IRSs address more flexible retrieval from the content document point of views.

Hypermedia systems manage navigation on any related information parts. With such systems, the retrieval of a document can fail because of the hypermedia size, or by a distraction of the user.

Using the respective advantages of DBMSs and IRSs, we intend then to define a generic framework for efficient and flexible retrieval of structured documents. We address also, at a lower extend, the navigation into the proposed framework.

The framework involves three fundamental elements. We define first which features of documents are interesting for their retrieval (Section2). Then, we express how to declare the mechanisms related to implicit attributes and to the dependencies of the attribute values along the document structures (Section 3). This point is the core of our framework and is dedicated to help the retrieval process of documents that is then defined according to the above elements of the framework (Section 4). An application that implements the framework is then described in Section 5. Finally, the conclusions are given in Section 6.

2 Related works

2.1 Retrieval of structured documents

We discuss here the two connected research topics related to our works: databases and information retrieval on structured documents. Traditional information access in databases are guided by the underlying data structure. In a similar way, structural access corresponds to the location of a specific item in the document structure. For instance, if a user looks for the title and the abstract of scientific papers, he expresses the path in the document structure to reach these items. It is also possible to retrieve items by specifying their related data, their attributes. Such data are for instance the authors of a book chapter or the publication date of a paper and such attribute access is usually provided by DBMSs.

In SGML [Her90], the structure and the attributes are defined in the Document Type Definitions (DTD). So, to formulate a query, a user needs to know some features of the DTD: the attribute names (and their semantic), the types of the document parts described by the attribute and their related position in the whole structure of the documents. To provide these accesses, traditional database query languages have to consider novel operators allowing the definition of structural path. The MULTOS [BR90] and MAESTRO [Mac90] systems offered these operators in the early 90s. More recent work attempts to query structured documents without exact knowledge of their structure using generalized path expressions and path variables [ACC+97].

Access to documents according to their semantic content is related to the retrieval of documents or document parts based on their topic. This retrieval is traditionally provided by IRSs, and requires an indexing process to extract and represent the content of the documents. When managing structured documents to be indexed and retrieved, parts of documents have also to be indexed.

Researches in IR provides results about modeling of structured document content. Passage retrieval, as explained in [Cal94], uses a segmentation of documents that is different from the one provided by the document authors. We consider that the original segmentation of a document by the authors has to be used in such a way to produce sensible results for the user. For that reason, our framework defines the features of the indexing process according to a *semantic structure* of the document directly derived from the syntactic structure of the document.

To define the content modeling, we use studies on the relationships defined in the discourse structure of documents. Two major relationships are exhibited in [Par95]: the *dominance relationship*, and the *intention relationship.* In the discourse structure, each document part corresponds to a set of themes (the themes that appear in the part). The dominance relationships indicates that the composition relationships between document parts are related to the aggregation in the component part of the themes of the composing parts. The intention relationship describes explicit declarations, in the content of one document part, of one or several themes present in another document part. Such intention relationships are usually supported by references between document parts. We want to consider these relations as propagation mechanisms in our works.

2.2 Synthesis

To handle the structural access, our model gives a representation of the documents parts organization, namely the *syntactical structure.* We consider three structural relations: the composition relation defines the aggregation of document parts, the sequence relation expresses the progression of document parts and the reference relation describes the others links between parts (cf figure 1).

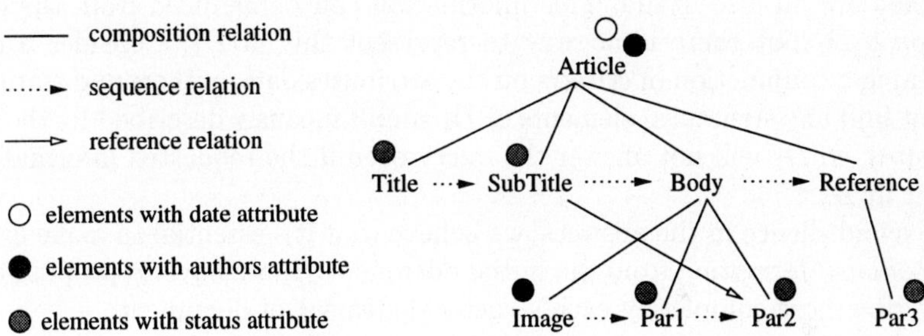

Fig. 1. The attributes of the document D_1

Attribute-based retrieval needs to have integrated attributes within the document model. As we noted above, structural elements admit an attribute if and only if their type allows this attribute. The description is then based on the type of the structural elements. However we will show in the following sections some deficiencies due to the use of such attributes during the querying processing.

We have stated that the data related to a document part is supported by attributes. To be consistent, we also represent the semantic content of document by a specific attribute that depends on the reference and composition structural relationships. These dependencies aim at making explicit the semantic organization of the documents.

Going backwards, can dependencies between attribute values be generalized to other attributes of structured documents ? We show in the following that such dependencies are of great interest and we propose propagation mechanisms on attributes to represent them.

3 Propagation mechanisms in structured documents

The current structured document retrieval systems have some drawbacks due to two essential aspects related to attributes: *coverage* and *dependencies*. We study these and propose to introduce the *scope* of the structured document attributes to address these weaknesses. We show the benefits of the scope of attributes through an example. Then, we describe the whole process that takes into account these scopes : *the structural indexing process.*

3.1 Coverage and dependencies

Some searches on attributes of the initial document D_1 of figure 1 reveal several problems related to the implicit information that occurs in the initial document and the relationships between attribute values.

If we consider that the status attribute defined on the element Par1 is valued by "draft", we shall say intuitively that the elements Body and Article have the same status. While one of their component is a draft, it is sensible to state that they are all also drafts. This information can be deduced from the initial document D_1 but there is no way to represent this in D_1. Consider a query containing a conjunction of criteria on the attributes date, authors and status. We will not find any structural elements of D_1 simultaneously described by the three attributes; so D_1 will not answer the query even if the requested information is present in D_1.

To avoid silence in the answers, we believe that it's essential to make explicit the *implicit information* from the initial document. So we have to propose a way to describe more completely each structural element of document.

In the semantic structure, we have shown which kind of dependencies exist between the semantic description of the structural elements. These dependencies are based on the structural relationships, but they are not defined in the initial document D_1. Here, our aim is to *produce dependencies between attribute values* by the use of the structural relations defined in the syntactic structure: composition, sequence and reference. We want to produce dependencies not only for the semantic content attributes but also for other attributes (date, authors, status, etc).

We are now able to describe more precisely requirements to allow the querying by attributes of structured documents. These requirements are expressed under two essential notions: the coverage and the dependencies of attributes, that correspond to two different processes.

1. We have to create attributes in order to make explicit the implicit informations and to make clear which structural elements are "reachable" (i.e., characterized in any way) by which attributes. That is the *coverage of the attributes*
2. We have then to define which values will be assign to these new attributes. That is the dependencies between the attributes values.

We introduce the scope of attributes in structured documents to tackle these two essential points.

3.2 The scope of attributes

The scopes of attributes in structured documents can be seen as inheritance mechanisms, because they define which structural elements share the same properties. Moreover they make explicit the dependencies between the attribute values.

The *scope of the attribute* α that describes the structural element o of the document D determines the set of structural elements which are concerned by the value of the attribute α on o. The members of this set share the same information source: the attribute α of element o. The scope can be defined by the following tuple :

$$\mathcal{P}^{o}_{\alpha,rel} = (\alpha, o, rel, cat, v_\alpha, f_\alpha, cond)$$

Here, α is an attribute name, o is a structural element, rel is one of the three syntactical relations and cat is a propagation category. We use the syntactical relation and the propagation category to build the set of structural elements concerned by the value of the attribute α of o. If we consider that the predecessors (successors) among rel are candidates to be memberships of the scope of the attribute α, we will have $cat = pred$ (resp. $cat = succ$).

To specify conditions that must be fulfilled by the candidates to the scope of an attribute, we introduce memberships conditions (*cond*. For instance,it's possible to specify that an attribute only concerns some structural types. We specially use these conditions to control which structural elements admit a semantic content attribute.

In the scope, we define not only which elements are concerned by an attribute (coverage), but also the behavior of the values (dependencies): v_α is the initial value of the attribute α and f_α is the propagation function. This last function determines the behavior of the value v_α among the structural relation rel. Using this function, we assign values to the new attributes.

According to the definition of the attributes scope, we have defined four major attribute classes [Fou98]. We will limit our description to two of them : 1) A **static attribute** is a traditional DBMS attribute. Its value describes only the structural element having the attribute ($cat = static$). 2) An **ascending (descending) compositional attribute** (and its value) propagates along the structural composition relationship in a bottom-up way i.e., $rel = comp$ and

$cat = pred$ (resp. in a top-down way, i.e., $rel = comp$ and $cat = succ$). The status and semantic content attributes are ascending compositional, and date and author are descending compositional.

The description above addresses one attribute and one structural element. We focus now on the whole set of scopes on a whole structured document. We introduce the triplet $\mathcal{D}_{\alpha,rel}$ for one document D and one attribute name α: this contains the set OS_α of all the elements of the document D involved in the scopes of α, the set $\mathcal{P}_{\alpha,rel}$ of the scope definitions for α and a relationship rel in D, and finally a combination function, called $combine_\alpha$:

$$\mathcal{D}_{\alpha,rel} = (OS_\alpha, \mathcal{P}_{\alpha,rel}, combine_\alpha)$$

The combination function comes from the facts that i) one structural element has at most one attribute named α, and ii) one structural element may belong to several scopes for α. We must then process a combination of the propagated values from multiple sources, to compute a unique "combinated" value for α. This function is used during the conflict resolution process explained in detail in [Fou98]. The combination function also generates dependencies between the attributes values.

3.3 One example of scope of attribute

Consider the semantic content attribute, called *content*, defined as an ascending compositional attribute on structural type title, subtitle, image, and paragraph, in the document D_1 (figure 1). Its scope for the Image structural element is:

$$\mathcal{P}^{Image}_{content,comp} = (content, Image, comp, pred, Image.content, id_{content}, \emptyset)$$

Image.content represents the original value of the attribute for the Image. The propagation function $id_{content}$ is the identity function, expressing the fact that the elements of the scope receive all the information of *Image.content*. There is no membership condition. This definition states that the Body and the Article elements have a *content* attribute, and the value of their respective *content* attributes depend on the *content* of the Image.

Consider that the others scopes of the *content* attribute are similar for the Title, Subtitle, each Paragraph of D_1. The first step of the process is dedicated to the creation of the *content* attribute on the predecessors of the elements. So, the *content* attribute is created for the Body, Article and Reference elements of D_1 (see figure 2).

The second step assigns values to these new attributes, using the propagation and the combination functions. These functions depend on the attribute domain (the indexing language). We first give the general case where the combination operator is noted $\oplus$ and we show two examples: i) the *content* attribute is a set of keywords, and ii) the attribute is a conceptual graph.

According to the definition of the content scope, we obtain the following relations : Body.content = Image.content $\oplus$ Par1.content $\oplus$ Par2.content, Reference.content = Par3.content and Article.content = Title.content $\oplus$ SubTitle.content $\oplus$ Body.content $\oplus$ Reference.content.

1. If the attribute value is a set of keywords, the combination is then the union set operator. There is then an inclusion dependency relationship between the attribute values, as we show in figure 2.
2. If the attribute value is a conceptual graph, the combination function is then a maximum joint. We used this approach in a medical context with PRIME-GC [MMFB97]. The dependency relationship between the attributes is then a first order logical implication (noted $\phi(a) \rightarrow \phi(b)$).

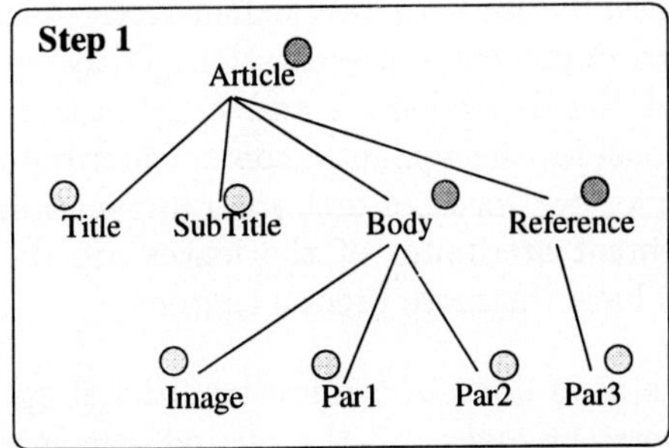

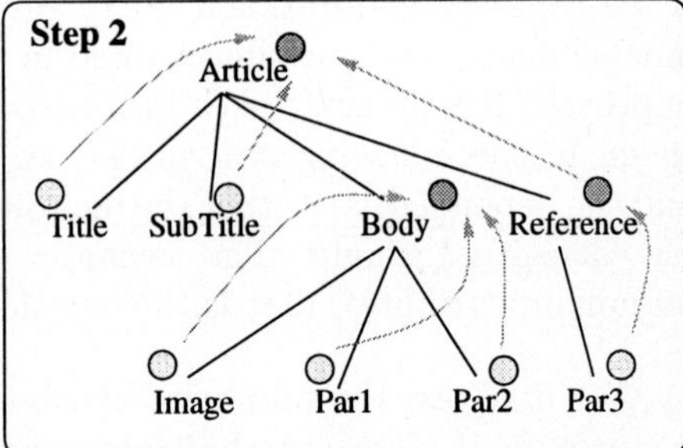

○ semantic content attribute

● new semantic content attribute

a ⇢ b : $a \subseteq b$ or $\phi(a) \rightarrow \phi(b)$

Fig. 2. Scope of semantic content attribute

The use of the scope defines firstly the coverage of the attributes, and secondly computes the attributes values. This last computation uses the propagation function, and possibly a combination function in case of scope conflicts.

3.4 The structural indexing process

The introduction of the scope has some consequences on the document model that we have to manage. In the initial structured document model, we specify the types of the elements that can have given attributes. The use of the scope generates new attributes, and these attributes may not be consistent with the document model. The final document does not now conform any more to the initial document model and so we have to define a final document model to which each final document conforms. The whole structural indexing process is then splitted into two steps :

Step 1: the extension of the initial structured document model, using the attributes scope definitions to be sure that the final documents conform the extended structured document model. The extension is type-related.

Step 2: we apply the scopes of the attributes in the two steps previously described: we create the required attributes and we propagate the attribute values.

The result of this structural indexing process has two majors advantages for the retrieval of structured documents: i) implicit information about the scope of attributes has been made explicit and can then be used during query processing, and ii) the dependencies between attributes can be used to optimize query processing as well as to explain to a user the results obtained by the system.

4 The retrieval strategy

If we consider a traditional query process, we have to test exhaustively and independently each attribute value in the document representation. With our approach, the process takes into account the dependencies and benefits from them. In the following description, we consider the semantic content attribute and the dependency is either the inclusion for keywords, or first order implication for conceptual graphs. The semantic content attributes of the leaves are the minimum attributes, that is the one that have the more precise content.

1. We first test the minimum attributes as is done in a more traditional approach. If a structural element answers the query, all the related elements that include it's semantic content attributes also answer the query. For instance, if the semantic content attribute of the image answers, than the body and the article are also relevant to the query.
2. If the tests on minimum attributes failed, we test the attributes for which all the predecessors (according to the dependency relation) have been tested. For instance, if no minimum attributes of document D_1 have answered, we will first compare to the query, attributes of the Body and the Reference. There is no relevant element if we reach the root of the attributes, In this case the whole article.

Our general retrieval strategy is based on the use of the dependencies created by the structural indexing process. It also depends on the attribute classification. In fact, we develop specific strategies for each attributes classes. The strategy described above concerns an ascending compositional attribute, and starts from the minimum attributes to reach the maximum ones. We define a strategy for each attribute class and each kind of dependency in [Fou98].

5 Application : *My Personal Daily News*

5.1 Overview of the application

We have developed the prototype *My Personal Daily News* devoted to the management of a collection of daily newspapers, on top of the OODBMS O_2. We have chosen an object oriented DBMS because it is argued in [ACC+97] that object database technology is well suited for structured document management. Moreover, we use the O_2Web utility to browse the rough content information stored in any O_2 database with any WWW client.

Our prototype manages newspapers available on Internet and coming from the Liberation server [1]. These documents share the same structure and they involve multimedia data, i.e. texts and still images. We have collected these documents initially as HTML files and we load these into the database as complex objects according to their structure. We store documents in the database as a hierarchy of structural elements and with the raw data attached to the leaves of the hierarchy. Aggregation and list constructors represent syntactic relationships. This approach allows us to keep within the database, the whole structure.

We have automatically indexed the semantic content of the structural leaves of the documents by keywords. For each element, its semantic content is represented by an instance of a subclass of the class ascending compositional attribute. We have defined properties on this subclass to manage the scope of the attribute, that is the propagation function, the memberships conditions and the combination function. So the scope conflicts are handled by these properties.

5.2 Querying and browsing documents

As others have found, we consider that the combination of access by query and by navigation is promising when we deal with a collection of structured documents. In our prototype, we combine the navigation and search processes. Query processing benefits from the results of the structural indexing process.

We have distinguished the queries based on the structural aspects of the document, the queries on the attributes of the document and finally the mixed queries, i.e., queries combining structural aspects and attributes. We deal with *queries by structure* by traditional approaches based on paths access in the syntactical structure. The *queries by attributes* address the attributes that describes the structural elements (classical DB attributes) and also a semantic content attribute. Their computation takes advantages of the generated dependencies between attributes values and we are now able to retrieve elements that classical approaches don't reach. Finally, we allow to combine structure and attributes in queries. The user can specify any kind of criteria and mixes them by conjunction, disjunctions and negations. We handle these queries using sets operators (union, intersection and difference). We have especially focused on the presentation of the query results. We want that the users keep in mind the structural context of these results by showing them the structural position of the relevant items.

We allow users to both browse the whole collection and to complete their access by queries, answers to queries are then considered as starting points in the collection. The *structural navigation* uses the relationships of the syntactical structure to provide hypertext links. On the other hand, the search engine produces hypertext links between the relevant parts. The building of these links is based on the original relationships between document parts. For instance, if two different articles of a newspaper are relevant and even if these ones are not related by the sequence relationships, the matching process relates them to make easier the browsing in the answers.

---

[1] Libération is a French daily newspaper: http://www.liberation.com

6 Conclusion and Outlook

In this paper, we have defined a generic framework for the retrieval of structured documents that integrates a model of the information flows within structured documents. Within this, new structural elements can be retrieved, and the reasons why documents have been retrieved by the system are clearer for a user.

The retrieval of the good "information" is becoming a salient point with the current communication facilities, we will then focus in the future on the following points: the kind of answers given to the user, and a better integration of the user.

In some contexts, like electronic newspapers for instance, a same information can be presented under different points of views with different newspapers. It is then interesting to give as an answer documents built-up by relevant parts of documents. The same approach can be used to generate relevant documents if not any exists in the document base.

On the other hand, we intend to bring back the user into the core of the retrieval process. We consider that indications provided by a user about the relevance of the retrieved documents should allow an evaluation of the information flow within structured documents. Such results could improve the overall system quality by tailoring the scopes in a way to satisfy the user.

Acknowledgements: We would like to thank Pr. Alan Smeaton for his help in polishing the english version of this paper.

References

[ACC+97] Serge Abiteboul, Sophie Cluet, Vassilis Christophides, Tova Milo, Guido Moerkotte, and Jerom Simeon. Querying structured documents in object databases. *International Journal on Digital Libraries*, 1(1):5–19, April 1997.

[BR90] Elisa Bertino and Fausto Rabitti. *The MULTOS Query Language*, chapter 4, pages 53–74. North-Holland, 1990.

[Cal94] James P. Callan. Passage-level evidence in document retrieval. In W.B. Croft and C.J. van Rijsbergen, editors, *Proceedings of ACM SIGIR'94*, pages 302–310, Dublin, Ireland, July 1994. ACM.

[Fou98] Franck Fourel. *Modélisation, indexation et recherche de documents structurés*. PhD thesis, Université Joseph Fourier, February 1998.

[Her90] Eric Van Herwijnen. *Practical SGML*. Kluwer, 1990.

[Mac90] I.A. Macleod. Storage and retrieval of structured documents. *Information Processing & Management*, 26(2):197–208, 1990.

[MMFB97] Mourad Mechkour, Philippe Mulhem, Franck Fourel, and Catherine Berrut. PRIME-GC: a Medical Information Retrieval Prototype on the WEB. In *RIDE'97. Seventh International Workshop on Research Issues in Data Engineering*, Birmingham, England, April 7–8 1997.

[Par95] François Paradis. Using linguistic and discourse structures to derive topics. In *Fourth International Conference on Information and Knowledge Management (CIKM)*, pages 44–49, Baltimore, Maryland, USA, November 1995.

An Evolvable Personal Advisor to optimize Internet Search Technologies

M.Montebello, W.A.Gray, S.Hurley

Computer Science Department, Cardiff University, Wales.
(m.montebello,w.a.gray,s.hurley)@cs.cf.ac.uk

Abstract. The use of AI and the application of machine learning techniques to optimize services provided by existing internet search technologies is one way to control and manage the immense and ever-increasing volume of data published on the WWW. Users demand effective and efficient on-line information access to reduce information overload. In this paper we present a novel approach to achieve these objectives by generating information which is of a high recall quality - by reusing the output generated from major search engines and other previously developed systems; and of a high precision calibre - by generating specific user profiles after several interactions with the system. This paper discusses the design issues involved, as well as practical issues such as evolvability, profile generation, and the graphic user interface.

1 Introduction

The immense size of the distributed World-Wide Web (WWW) [1] knowledge-base and the dramatic rapid increase in the volume of data on the Internet, requires techniques and tools that reduce users' information overload and improves the effectiveness of online information access. The size of the Internet is exploding and an exponential increase in the number of users and web servers is no surprise, resulting in an eventual feedback loop. As more users come on the net, they provide their own information which in turn encourages even more people to join in. With this massive increase of the Internet usage, a vast array of networks services is growing up around the Internet and huge amounts of information is added everyday. Users can now access enormous amounts of information in various forms, thereby creating an equally massive problem. This rapid growth in data volume, user base, and data diversity render Internet-accessible information increasingly difficult to be used effectively, thereby rendering the task of resource and knowledge discovery highly critical. It also limits the benefits that users can expect from their interaction, which triggered off the development of techniques for building indexes, such as Lycos[2], WebCrawler[3], and Excite[4], to help users direct their search.

It is well documented that traditional search engines provide services which are far from satisfactory [5–7]. Users are faced with the problem of these search engines being too generalized and not focused enough to their real and specific needs. This triggered further research to develop more sophisticated techniques and agent like systems that make use of the user profile to personalize the service they provide and add value to the information they presented [8–10].

In this paper we address the profile generation techniques employed within a system we developed in an attempt to improve the search engines' recall/precision scores. The Personal Evolvable Advisor (PEA) reuses information generated by search engines and other previously developed retrieval systems. Conceptually, it is similar to a meta-search engine, but with the major difference that it employs user profiling to specifically target documents for individual users. In this way duplication and redundancy of information is significantly reduced, while the real needs and interests of the users are fully addressed in a more focused retrieval.

The remainder of the paper is organized as follows. In Section 2, we overview related work, followed by a description of PEA in the next section. Section 4 goes into some detail on user profile generation, document feature extraction and machine learning techniques employed. Finally, our conclusions and future work are presented in Section 5.

2 Related Work

There has been much research and work in two main areas which are specifically related to the system we developed. Meta-search engines are the first type of related systems because of the fact that they use and depend upon information generated from other external systems, particularly the major search engines that roam the WWW. The MetaCrawler[11] and SavvySearch [12], for example, take one query and send it to several major sites, receive the results back, aggregate the results and display them. Other off-the-shelf commercial front-end meta-search systems, like Surfbot[13], WebCompass[14] and Metafind[15], have very similar capabilities plus additional features such as monitoring specific documents, verifying links and matching results returned from the various search engines. All these systems have their advantages and disadvantages. The biggest advantage (which is the reason PEA uses the same technique) is the saving in time and the assurance that the all the hits that several major search engine can return have been collated. The downside of these systems are various. First of all, with no standardization in query format among the various search engines on the WWW the search of the individual search engines defaults to the lowest common denominator. PEA overcomes this problem by making use of wrappers which have the ability to translate a complex query into the command language of each constituent search site. In this way a single query is transformed into its optimum form for each search engine or retrieval system that it employs. Secondly, meta-search systems, have a high recall record, but a low precision one. This due to the fact that just like the search engines they depend upon, the results returned are not focused enough resulting in the users having to check through the documents returned and identify which ones are of interest. We overcome this problem by making use of the capabilities offered by a second type of related system - ones that employ user profiling to assist, advise and adapt to individual users during the exploration of the WWW. Some examples are LIRA [16], Letizia[17], Sulla[18] and Personal WebWatcher [10]. All these systems are academic research systems which in one way or another automatically generate a user profile in an attempt to be as precise as possible to the users' needs and interests. None of them deal with results generated from the various search engines, as a result of which their recall score tends to be significantly low. PEA combines the optimization of both recall and precision by extracting the benefits which both kind of systems have to offer.

3 The Personal Evolvable Advisor

Our goal with PEA is to achieve a high recall and high precision performance score on the information presented to the user. The processes required by an information retrieval and filtering system include several tasks that PEA decomposes into a number of simpler tasks. Figure 1 shows the major components of the system: the WWW and the external systems at the bottom level, the middle application software on the next level up, and the GUI at the top.

The WWW is one of the components over which we have no control. It requires no local development, but its heterogeneous, unstructured and uncensored nature causes developers to face awkward coding situations in order to be able to cater for all the kinds of data found on the WWW. The WWW can be assumed to be a very large heterogeneous distributed digital information database. In order to optimize the management and exploit the potential of the WWW's vast knowledge-base we require to search and retrieve efficiently and effectively specific information for users.

The external systems utilised include some of the major search engines and also some other retrieving systems that have been developed by other research groups[10, 11, 18]. They use the WWW as their source of input and we use their output as the input for PEA. All the external systems are considered to be black boxes and action is taken upon the information they output. Wrappers are used to manage the appropriate and proper handshaking between the diverse search engines and the other retrieving systems and the application layer.

Query terms are used to locate documents and retrieve results from the external systems. These results need substantial re-formatting as they usually include completely useless information like advertisements, local links and site specific information.

The application software layer has the difficult task of performing all the work required, transparently from the user. It makes use of the information retrieved from the external systems and attempts to improve on the recall/precision metrics mentioned earlier.

PEA requires an administrator to manage the general needs and demands of a specific interest group of users. Search terms tailored to any type of interest group can be initialised by the administrator and furthermore users will be able to suggest any other terms to add to the main search list. Documents relevant to the specific area of interest are retrieved and stored by the application software

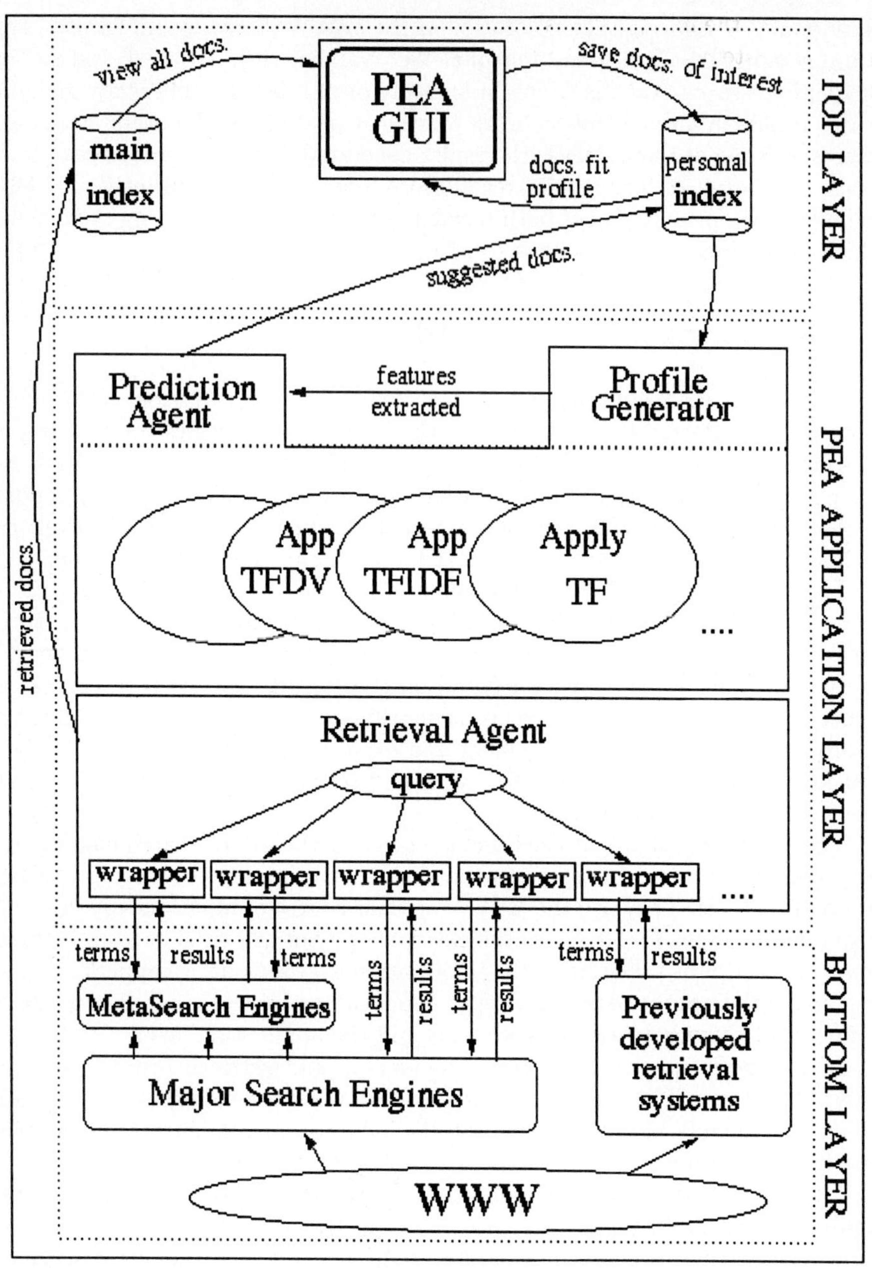

Fig. 1. PEA Architecture

layer within the main database, and when a user logs-in he/she is able to benefit from the systems' high recall fidelity. Having analysed the documents, individual users can bookmark and highlight specific items as interesting and appealing. These will be saved inside their personal database. At this stage the application layer plays another important role in attaining precise targeting of documents to individual users by generating a profile from the documents within the personal database and predicting other documents from within the main database. Users can decide to add the suggested documents to their personal database or remove them completely. As new and suggested documents are entered in the personal database the user profile becomes more focused and finely tuned, as a result of which higher precision results will be achieved.

The retrieval agent, is responsible for aggregating all the hits returned by the external systems. It collates the results, by removing duplicates and ensuring integrity, and stores the formatted and pre-ranked results as a single list in the main database. This agent interacts with the external systems via appropriate wrappers which translate a complex query into the command language of each constituent search site. In this way a single query is transformed into its optimum form for each search engine or retrieval system that it employs. It then locates and retrieves documents from the local indices and returns related results.

These results are basically a series of document addresses (URLs - Universal Resource Locator) which are listed within an HTML page that the external system returns. A scan through the WWW page will quickly identify the URL links and list them. Some of the links maybe useless to the user, so the retrieval agent initially removes adverts, duplicates, and site specific links. It then analyses the vetted URLs and accesses the document on-line. This will identify whether the link is still accessible, has been changed or removed completely. If the document is valid, then an initial paragraph from the document is extracted and saved locally in the main database together with the reference search term, its reference within the index, the URL, and the document title. All these details will be available to the user through the GUI, and also to the prediction agent to identify if the particular document is relevant to a particular user or not.

The task that the profile generator sets out to achieve is to analyse each users' personal database and generate a *profile*. If users have different interests stored in their personal index, then a separate profile is required and generated for each interest. The machine learning techniques used will be discussed in some detail in section 4. Users are able to select which technique they would like to use to generate their profile, and predict other relevant documents in future interactions.

The user interest profile generated by the profile generator will be used by the prediction agent in combination with the extracted features from documents in order to predict and suggest new interesting documents to a user. Documents that have been retrieved and stored within the main database by the retrieval agent will have their features extracted and compared to the profile of each individual user generated by the profile generator. This is performed on every item a user has shown interest in, and if any of the documents from the main index happen to fit the user's interests or needs, then they will be eventually suggested to the user the next time the user logs in. Each suggestion, if considered interesting, may be explicitly added to the personal database by the user, or deleted completely. The user might even prefer that he/she is notified, via email, that documents of interest have been located. The machine learning techniques employed to generate the user profile is also applied to extract features from documents. In this way the targetted documents reflect, and are consistent, with the specific user profile generated.

An important point to make here is about the evolvability of PEA. The choice of external systems coupled with the appropriate wrapper within the retrieval agent, and the machine learning technique employed in the application layer can be selected from a list of systems and techniques incorporated in the system. PEA allows this list to be augmented and hence other systems and techniques that might be developed in the future can be easily incorporated. The use of available systems means the system evolves as the external systems evolve. The only amendments to PEA being if a new wrapper is required.

4 User Interest Profile

Three approaches can be identified as being adopted by different systems in order to generate a user profile:

- *Rule-Based* approach[19] where users supply information directly by applying scripting languages to embody their needs within the code. Oval [20] is an example that employs this approach;
- *Knowledge-Based* approach[21, 22] consists of endowing the system with domain-specific background knowledge about its application and about the user. UCEgo [22] is one of the earliest systems that employed this approach;
- *Machine Learning* [23, 24, 9, 25] automatically generates a user profile by extracting information from documents which the user gives feedback on. It achieves a level of personalisation impossible to attain with previous systems, except through user intervention because it adapts over time as new information is processed by the system. The user profile is continually being refined and augmented, thereby improving the targeted end-user requirements. Several systems described in [26] employed the machine learning technique.

In our present implementation of PEA we make use of three machine learning techniques (Section 4.1) in order to be able to compare their performance and also their effectiveness when applied to the WWW.

Learning algorithms require a set of positive examples which will form part of the user interest profile generation. The three different measures of term significance which have been applied so far are *term frequency, term frequency/inverse document frequency*, and *term frequency/discrimination value* [27].

The following notations are used in the rest of the paper:

W_i is weight of the term i	F_i is number of occurrences of term i
N_w is total number of words	D_T is total number of documents
D_i is number of documents containing term i	DV_i is difference between the space densities before and after term i is added

The term frequency (TF) measure (Equation 1) assumes that the importance of a term is directly proportional to the frequency with which it appears within a document.

$$W_i = \frac{F_i}{N_w} \tag{1}$$

The second technique applied is the term frequency inverse document frequency (TFIDF) measure (Equation 2) which assigns a greater significance to terms that are good discriminators between documents in a collection. It compares how frequently a term appears in a document against the number of other documents which contain that term.

$$W_i = F_i * ln \frac{D_T}{D_i} \tag{2}$$

Finally, the term frequency discrimination value (TFDV) measure (Equation 3) is based on the hypothesis that a good term is one which on removal from the collection of documents leads to an decrease in the average dissimilarity (adding it would hence lead to an increase), whereas a bad term is one which leads on removal to an increase.

$$W_i = F_i * DV_i \tag{3}$$

After that each technique is implemented in PEA, a prediction threshold is calculated out of the average of all the item weights extracted from the documents. This threshold will eventually be used by the prediction agent to suggest and recommend documents to the user.

$$W_a = \frac{1}{n} \sum_{i=1}^{n} W_i \tag{4}$$

$$PT = W_a + \frac{1}{n} \tag{5}$$

The profile generator extracts features from all the documents from within the personal database, and applying Equation 5 works out the prediction threshold. Any documents from within the main database whose weighing measure is above this threshold, are recommended to the user.

To compare the three feature extraction techniques employed and assess the overall performance of PEA we ran a set of data tests on three different topics, once on documents returned from a single search engine and consecutively on PEA. AltaVista was selected during the tests because it averaged most frequently

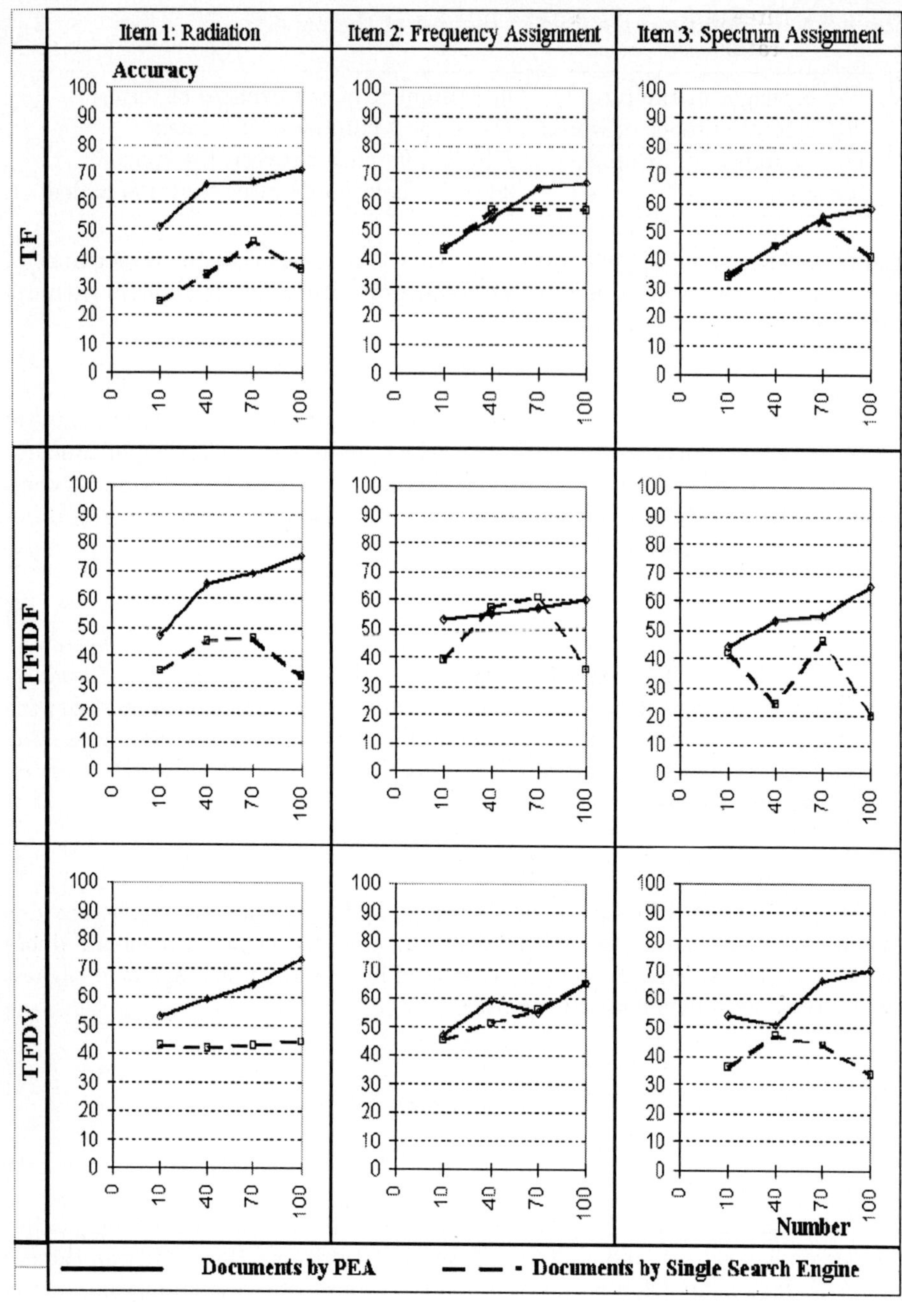

Fig. 2. Tests on Machine Learning Techniques employed in PEA

in the top three search engines ranking list of the Search Engine Watch[28]. The profile generation and prediction was repeatedly done by PEA over a number of documents selected (starting from 10 to 100 in steps of 30) from the documents returned in both cases. Then the quality and accuracy of the prediction in each case was assessed on the relevance, correct domain, and user interest. The results (Figure 2) indicate that the feature extraction techniques employed did not outperform each other, but rather complemented one another.

Clearly, as the number of documents selected by the user increased then the profile generator could progressively improve the predictions. To note that some inconsistencies in the graphs on the left (the single search engine) due to the fact that even though the recall is high the precision starts to drop as the number of documents increased. This will automatically reflect in the quality of predictions made by PEA due to the decline in the quality of documents retrieved by the single search engine.

5 Conclusion

In this paper we have presented a system, PEA, that adds value to the information traditional search engines generate from the WWW. We argue that by using the output from several retrieving/indexing systems we ensure a high recall score, while generating a specific user profile to predict and target other documents to specific users, we also ensure a high precision score. Users are able to select their own profile generator/prediction agent from a number of alternatives, reflecting different machine learning techniques employed. New techniques can be integrated into this evolvable system by the system administrator, who can also easily maintain the system's resources and update the search terms specific to a user group. In the future we will be investigating the integration of other machine learning techniques that have been developed and employed by other systems. This will help us to continue to evaluate which technique is best suited to cater for the needs of different users. Evaluation of the recall/precision scores has been demonstrated to ensure that value has been added to the normal services provided by the search engines and the meta-search engines. This will continue to be done by analysing more feedback given from a group of users who are presently making use of the system and who will eventually assess the extent to which the information presented is of high recall/precision quality.

References

1. T Berners-Lee, R Caillian, A Luotonen, H F Nielsen, and A Secret. The World-Wide Web. *Communications of the ACM*, 37(8):76–82, 1994.
2. Lycos Inc. *Welcome to Lycos.* http://www.lycos.com/.
3. Excite Inc. *WebCrawler Searching.* http://webcrawler.com/.
4. Excite Inc. *Excite.* http://www.excite.com/.
5. P M E DeBra and R D J Post. Searching for arbitrary information in the WWW: the fish-search for mosaic. In *Proceedings of the 2nd. international world wide web conference*, 1994.

6. V N Gudivada and S Tolety. A multiagent architecture for information retrieval on the world-wide web. *Proceedings of the 5th. RIAO conference Computer Assisted Information Searching on the Internet.*, 1997.
7. S Spetka. The TkWWW Robot: Beyond browsing. In *Proceedings of the 2nd. WWW conference '94: Mosaic and the Web*, 1994.
8. M Pazzani, J Muramatsu, and D Billsus. Syskill and Webert: Identifying Interesting Web Sites. *AAAI Conference*, 1996.
9. C L Green and P Edwards. Using Machine Learning to enhance software tools for internet information management. In A Franz and H Kitamo, editors, *AAAI-96, Workshop on Internet-Based Information Systems*, pages 48–55. AAAI Press, 1996.
10. D Mladenic. Personal WebWatcher: Implementation and Design. Technical Report IJS-DP-7472, J Stefan Institute, Llubljana, Slovenia, 1996.
11. E Selberg and O Etzioni. Multi-service search and comparison using the metacrawler. *The Web Revolution. Proceedings of the 4th. international world wide web conference*, 1995.
12. D Dreilinger and A E Howe. An information gathering agent for querying web search engines. Technical Report CS-96-111, Computer Science Department, Colorado State University, 1996.
13. Surflogic. Surfbot. http://www.surflogic.com/.
14. Quarterdeck. Webcompass. http://www.quarterdeck.com/qdeck/products/webcompass/.
15. Metafind. Metafind. http://www.metafind.com/.
16. M Balabanović and Y Shoham. Learning Information Retrieval Agents: Experiments with Automated Web Browsing. *AAAI Spring Symposeum on Information Gathering*, 1995.
17. H Lieberman. Letizia: An Agent that assists Web Browsing. In *International Joint Conference on Artificial Intelligence*, 1995.
18. D Eichmann and J Wu. Sulla - a user agent for the web. In *5th. International World Wide Web Conference*, 1996.
19. T Malone, K Grant, F Turbak, S Brobst, and M Cohen. Intelligent Information-Sharing Systems. *Communications of the ACM*, 30(5):390–402, 1987.
20. K Lai, T Malone, and K Yu. Object Lens: A "spreadsheet" for cooperative work. *ACM transactions on Office systems*, 5(4):297–326, 1988.
21. J W Sullivan and S W Tyler. *Intelligent User Interfaces.* ACM Press, 1991.
22. D N Chin. Intelligent Interfaces As Agents. In Sullivan J W Tyler S W, editor, *Intelligent User Interfaces.* ACM Press, New York, 1991.
23. H Chen. Information retrieval: Neural networks, symbolic learning, and genetic algorithms. *Journal of the American Society on Information Sciences*, 43(3):194–216, 1995.
24. D Goldberg, D Nichols, B M Oki, and D Terry. Using Collaborative Filtering to weave an Information Tapestry. *Communications of the ACM*, 35(12):61–70, 1992.
25. T Joachims, T Mitchell, D Freitag, and R Armstrong. WebWatcher: Machine Learning and Hypertext. In Morik K and Herrmann J, editors, *Fachgruppen treffen Maschinelles Lernen.* University of Dortmund, 1995.
26. P Edwards, C L Green, P C Lockier, and T C Lukins. Exploiting Learning Technologies for World Wide Web Agents. *IEE Colloqium on Intelligent World Wide Web Agents*, 1997. Digest No 97/118, IEE, Savoy Place, London.
27. G Salton and M J McGill. *Introduction to Modern Information Retrieval.* McGraw-Hill, 1983.
28. *Search Engine Watch.* http://searchenginewatch.internet.com/.

Indexing Valid Time Intervals*

Tolga Bozkaya and Meral Ozsoyoglu

Computer Engineering and Science Department
Case Western Reserve University
email:{bozkaya, ozsoy}@ces.cwru.edu

Abstract. To support temporal operators and to increase the efficiency of temporal queries, indexing based on temporal attributes is required. We consider the problem of indexing the temporal dimension in valid time databases where the temporal information of data objects are represented as valid time intervals that need to be managed dynamically by an efficient index structure. We propose an indexing scheme that uses augmented B+trees called Interval B+trees for indexing a dynamic set of valid time intervals. We apply time-splits at the leaf level of the IB+tree that would partition long valid time intervals into disjoint subintervals and distribute them among several leaf nodes to increase efficiency of search operation, especially for *timeslice* queries. We compared IB+trees with time-splits to one dimensional R-trees and observed that while their performances for *timeslice* queries are comparable, IB+trees are far more superior for many temporal queries that are based on beginning points of time intervals.

1 Introduction

In this paper, we are concerned with indexing a dynamic set of valid time intervals. Valid time intervals represent the time span in which the data entities exist in real life. The use of valid time notion is very common in many database applications, such as banking, scientific experiments, payroll databases, multimedia databases, etc.. In valid time databases, necessary tools are provided to model, maintain, and query the information that varies over time. To efficiently handle queries on the temporal dimension of data in valid time databases, indexing time intervals that correspond to lifespans of temporal object versions is required.

Majority of research on indexing temporal databases concentrates on designing efficient index structures for transaction time databases [ST95]. In transaction time databases, temporal objects are inserted into the database in an append only fashion, and modifications or deletions to historical data are not allowed.

* This work has been partially supported by NSF grants IRI 92-24660, IRI 96-31214, and the NSF FAW Award IRI-90-24152.

Indexing valid time intervals in a temporal database is quite a different problem than indexing transaction time intervals. First of all, the append-only behavior cannot be assumed in valid time databases. In valid time databases, it is possible to insert, update or delete past and future information whenever the information becomes available. Modifications and deletions are possible also due to corrections. In short, valid time intervals have to be managed dynamically, unlike transaction time intervals. Second, valid time intervals may extend into future indefinitely (making them open ended), or they may have end points that move along the current timeline. Coupled with the fact that these intervals have to be managed dynamically, the problem of indexing valid time databases becomes a problem with different requirements. In this paper, since our focus is on valid time databases, unless otherwise specified, we use "intervals" to refer to "valid time intervals".

Temporal information can be queried in a variety of ways. Conventionally, a temporal index is supposed to support *timeslice* queries. Since we focus on indexing the temporal dimension only, we are mainly interested in answering *pure-timeslice* queries efficiently. A *pure timeslice* query asks for all temporal objects whose time intervals intersect a given query time point (query time interval, in the general case). Other variations of *timeslice* queries may include specifications on the *key* dimension such as asking for temporal objects whose key values fall in a given key range/value and whose time intervals intersect a given time instant (*range-timeslice queries / pure-key-timeslice queries*). In the most general case, temporal queries may employ any of the temporal operators that specify various relationships between intervals [AH85] such as *covers, met-by, before, after*. Particular index orders among the beginning points, or the end time points of the intervals may come in handy in efficiently answering queries that employ these temporal operators.

We propose an indexing scheme that uses B+trees on beginning points of the intervals augmented with maximum end time points of intervals in the internal nodes. We call this augmented structure as the Interval B+tree [BO98][1] (IB+tree for short). Since the basic structure of the IB+tree is the B+tree, it can efficiently index a dynamic set of valid time intervals. The keys of the IB+tree are beginning points of the intervals, which makes it useful for temporal queries that employ temporal operators that capture temporal relationships based on beginning points of intervals. The augmented information in the internal nodes helps to trim the search for *timeslice* queries, and may be useful for queries that employ other temporal operators.

In IB+trees, the augmented information in an internal node is simply the maximum end points of intervals that are indexed in the subtrees below that node. This information will not be very useful when there are several long intervals distributed over the timeline causing the maximum end points in the subtrees to be too high to trim the search efficiently. To handle this situation, we propose a time-split algorithm to be applied to the intervals in the leaves. These time-splits in the leaves partition long intervals into several shorter parts making the augmented information

[1] In [BO98], we used IB+trees to index transaction time intervals of historical object versions where the transaction time database was divided into two states keeping past (historical) and currently valid object versions separately.

very useful in trimming the search path. The time-splits do not require any extra operation on the IB+trees, although they increase storage requirements as the split parts have to be reinserted to the tree. We should also note that time-splits can be applied off-line during non-peak hours of operation.

We compared IB+trees (with time-splits) with one dimensional R-trees and observed that their performances for timeslice queries are very close. Note that, R-trees do not directly support search operations based on beginning points of the intervals. Most of the time, they require a timeslice search for these operations. We also experimented on queries that employ *covered by*, and *met by* operators to demonstrate this point.

The rest of the paper is organized as follows. In the next section, we discuss the related work on indexing temporal intervals, and dynamic interval management. In section 3, we describe the IB+tree structure. Time-splits are explained in section 4. Section 5 shows the results of our experimental work on comparing one dimensional R-trees and IB+trees with time-splits. Section 6 concludes.

2 Related Work

There are quite a number of index structures designed for transaction time databases (See [ST95] for a recent survey) including [EWK90, EWK93, SG93, TK95, BO98, Ram97, LS90, BGO+93, ST95]. We do not elaborate much on these structures due to limited space.

There are also index structures that are used for dynamic management of time intervals. Segment R-trees [KS91], R-trees [Gut84], TP-index [SOL94] are some of them to name a few. These structures are mostly multidimensional index structures that can be directly used (such as R-trees) to index time intervals, or variations of multidimensional index structures tailored for indexing temporal domains (such as TP-index). Being a popular spatial index structure, R-trees have been heavily used for dynamic interval management and comparison to its efficiency has been a common practice for new index structures. We take the same approach in this paper, and compare the performance of IB+trees with time-splits to one dimensional R-trees. General purpose index structures are also used for indexing valid time data by transforming intervals into one dimensional points. In [GLOT96] and [ND97], valid time intervals are mapped to one-dimensional values by different transformations, and these values are then indexed by using regular B+trees.

3 Interval B+trees

In this section we briefly explain the Interval B+tree structure. There are several structures in the literature for indexing interval (not necessarily temporal) data such as Priority Search trees [Mc85], Segment trees [PS85], Interval-trees [CLR90]. Although they are not suitable for secondary storage as they are binary tree structures, they have been the inspiration for many secondary storage index structures for database applications. The interval B+tree (IB+tree) is a direct generalization of the Interval-tree to a multi-way B+tree structure. It is, basically, a B+tree where each node is augmented with the same kind of information as in the binary Interval-trees. While the properties of the B+tree structure are kept invariant, the internal nodes of an IB+tree keep the maximum end point of the intervals indexed by its subtrees. So, an internal node of order *k* (with *k* children) has *k* maximum points for each of its children as the augmented information. The leaves of the tree keep the data items and have no children, so they do not have any extra information.

Insertion and deletion operations for IB+tree are similar to those for B+trees, with the only exception of a little overhead to maintain the augmented information. However, this overhead does not change the complexity of the operations. Most of the time, only the *maximum* fields of *some* of the nodes visited (in the worst case, all of them) along the path from the root to the leaf (the leaf where the insertion or the deletion is made) may need to be updated. The complexity of insertion and deletion operations for IB+trees is $O(\log_k n)$ (the same as B+trees), where n is the number of leaf nodes, and k is the average fanout of a node in the tree.

The internal node structure of an IB+tree with *k* keys $a_1, a_2, .., a_k$, and *k* child pointers $c_1, .., c_k$, and with *k* maximum end points (we will shortly refer them as *maximums*) $m_1, .., m_k$ of the subtrees rooted for each child. .

The difference from the Interval-trees is that the maximum end points for each of the children are kept in the parent node. So, the children nodes need not be accessed to check the maximum end points in their subtrees, as required in Interval-trees. Since an IB+tree is a generalization of the binary Interval tree, we can use the interval search algorithm for interval trees [CLR90] with minor modifications for an IB+tree.

```
INTERVAL-SEARCH (N, I)    (for Interval B+trees)

(For a given search interval I[i_s, i_e] (where i_s and i_e are the
starting end the ending points of I), find an interval that
intersects with I in the Interval B+tree T. Here, N is a node of
the Interval B+tree and the initial call is INTERVAL-SEARCH(
root(T), I))

(Let us assume that N has k children (internal node), or k data
items (leaf))

     1) if  N is a leaf node then check if there is an
        intersecting interval with I
                     among the  intervals in N.
     2) else if  N is an internal node then
          2.1) i=0;
          2.2) if I intersects [a_i , m_i] then
                     INTERVAL-SEARCH(c_i , I)
          2.3) else if  i< k  then  i = i + 1, goto 2.2
```

As the keys of the IB+tree are the beginning points of the indexed intervals, any query on the beginning points of intervals can be answered efficiently using the search algorithms of B+trees. This structure does not fully support the queries that are based on the end points of the intervals, but, it is still helpful in many cases.

Note that INTERVAL-SEARCH algorithm returns *one* interval (if there exists at least one) that intersects with the given search interval. Actually, that interval is also the one with the minimum beginning point. To find all the intervals that intersect a given query interval, we can still use the INTERVAL-SEARCH to find the first intersecting interval (the one with the minimum beginning point), and then we can use the links between the leaf nodes for a sequential search from that point on. Or, we can follow all the child pointers that satisfy the condition in step 2.2 of the algorithm to find all the intersecting intervals, hoping that we will be able to trim some high level branches of the search tree, which will help us to be faster in answering the query. We refer to this search algorithm described above as ALL-INTERVAL-SEARCH algorithm.

Example 3.1: In Figure 3.2, we see an IB+tree of height 2 and of order 3. Let's assume we want to find all the intervals that intersect with the search interval [18, 25]. We can answer this query in two ways. In the first one, we can use INTERVAL-SEARCH algorithm to find the first intersection interval with the minimum starting point ([4, 22]) and then carry out a sequential search following the links between the leaf nodes. For this we have to visit the nodes R, C_1, C_2, C_3 in order. In the second way we can use the ALL-INTERVAL-SEARCH algorithm, in which case we visit the nodes R, C_1, C_3, but not C_2.

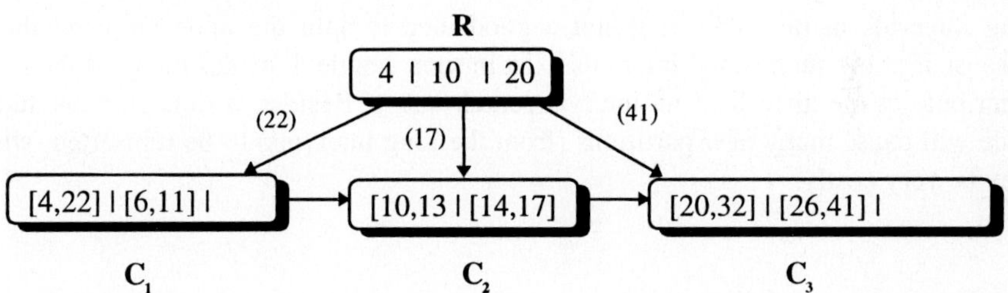

Fig. 1. The IB+tree used in Example 3.1

4 Time-Splits

Although the IB+tree structure is a simple structure that allows dynamic management of valid time intervals, the efficiency of the IB+trees (for *timeslice* queries) very much depends on how much the augmented information can be used to trim the search. To improve efficiency, we suggest to apply *time-splits* at the leaf level that will partition long intervals into disjoint subintervals and distribute them over several leaf nodes.

If a time-split operation is to be applied to a leaf node at time instant *t*, all data intervals whose end points extend beyond *t* are split at point *t*. The split parts are reinserted into the IB+tree, *t* is marked to be the new maximum end point of the intervals in the leaf. The maximum end point information is posted to the parent level and this may proceed further up the tree if necessary. Let us give a simple example:

Example 4.1: Assume that there is a leaf node L accommodating the intervals [2, 6], [3, 46], [4, 10], [6, 58], [8, 11], [12, 14]. The maximum end point for L is 58 which is kept at its parent node as the augmented end point information.

If we decide to time-split this node at time point 14 the intervals [3, 46] and [6, 58] will each be separated to two partitions at time point 14 ([3, 46] will be split to [3, 14] [15, 46], and [6, 58] will be split to [6, 14] and [15, 58]). After the split, L= ([2, 6], [3, 14], [4, 10], [6, 14], [8, 11], [12, 14]) with its maximum end point being 14. The intervals [15, 36], and [15, 58] will be reinserted into another node with respect to their beginning points (which is 15).

Algorithms to decide when to apply a time-split to a node, and then if a time-split is to be applied, to determine the point of time-split (i.e. to find the index to the interval whose end point is the split point with the minimum cost) are given in [B98]. The cost of finding such a best split point is O(klogk), where k is the number of intervals in a leaf node [B98].

In order to decrease the number of disk accesses during search queries, it is important to avoid cases where a search query retrieves a leaf node and finds only one interval to put into the result from that leaf. As it is discussed in [B98], a leaf node is not necessarily split whenever it has long intervals. If there are too many of these long intervals in the node, it is not a good idea to split the node anyway; that is because if many such (long) intervals exist in such a node, it means many of them will contribute to the answer of an interval search query. Besides, a time-split on such a node will cause many new partitions (from the long intervals) to be reinserted, which may be very costly.

5 Experimental Results

In this section, we briefly summarize our experimental results with IB+trees and one dimensional R-trees. Full discussion can be found in [B98]. In the experiments, we compare the search efficiency of IB+trees and R-trees in terms of the number of nodes read during search operations.

The experiments are done using five different data sets. Each data set contains 100,000 intervals whose beginning points are distributed randomly in the range 0 to 250,000. The distribution of the duration of the intervals are different in each of the five different data sets, D1, ... D5. D1 and D2 consist of intervals distributed exponentialy with means 100 and 2000 respectively. D3 is created by merging D1 and D2, where 20% are from D2, and the rest are from D1. D4 and D5 consist of intervals distributed normallly with means 200 and 2000 and standard deviations 200 and 1000 respectively. The queries are evaluated after all data intervals are inserted in each test case.

We compared three structures, the IB+tree, the IB+tree with time-splits, and the one-dimensional R-tree. All of these structures have a maximum fanout of 51 and a minimum fanout of 26 for both internal nodes and the leaves. All of these structures have the same node structure. The IB+tree (with and without time-splits) keep a key, the maximum end point of the subtree below, and a pointer in each entry of an internal node. An R-tree node entry has a minimum bounding interval (a beginning and an end point) and a pointer. So, having the same fanout for both structures is a fair assumption.

In terms of storage requirements, one dimensional R-tree and IB+tree without time-splits are about the same. IB+trees with time-splits require more storage due to the increased number of intervals because of splits. For data sets D1, D2, D4, and D5; IB+tree with time-splits require 50-60% more storage. For data set D3, storage requirement is around 85% more as the intervals in D3 have a considerable number of long intervals stored together with short intervals, causing more splits to take place. The query performance results for these index structures are discussed below. These results are obtained by taking averages of 20 different queries. Each query consists of a query interval and the type of temporal relationship employed for the query.

To compare the search performances of the index structures, first, we tested the performances of the index structures for *interval timeslice* queries, (i.e., all data intervals intersecting a query interval are retrieved as the result). The midpoints of the query points are picked randomly, and their durations are normally distributed with $\mu=100$ and $\sigma=50$. Two types of search strategies are available for IB+trees. The first one is *(Sequential Search)* finding the first interval (with minimum beginning point) that intersects the query interval using INTERVAL-SEARCH() algorithm of section 3, and then looking at consecutive leaf nodes sequentially to find others. The second one is *(Range Search)* using ALL-INTERVAL-SEARCH() algorithm of section 3. Generally, *Range Search* strategy is superior, but *Sequential Search* strategy can be chosen when the leaf nodes are physically clustered in the secondary storage. Both strategies can be used for both IB+tree variants, with or without splits.

Average numbers of internal node accesses per timeslice query: For all of the three index structures, the height was 4 (3 internal + 1 leaf level). That means the *sequential search* method for IB+tree variants will make 3 internal node accesses for each query. For the *range search* method. IB+trees with time-splits make less number of internal node accesses than R-trees for data sets D2 and D3 due to the large number of splits applied on mostly long intervals). In these data sets, IB+trees with time-splits packs the resulting set of data intervals (after splits) more tightly into the leaf nodes. For data sets D1 and D5, R-trees make slightly less number of node accesses than IB+trees with time-splits. IB+trees without time-splits perform the most number of internal node accesses in every data set.

Average numbers of leaf node accesses for the three index structures: When the durations of the intervals are small (D1) and relatively close to each other (D4 and D5), IB+trees with time-splits perform close to IB+trees without time-splits, having a slight edge over them. The difference comes into surface when there are long intervals distributed with short intervals (data sets D2 and especially D3). *Sequential search* methods for IB+trees without time-splits perform very poorly in such cases.

Range search methods perform better, but still it does not get close to the performance of IB+trees with time-splits. *Sequential* and *range search* methods give close performances in IB+trees with time-splits in every case.

Although IB+trees do not perform better than one dimensional R-trees for *timeslice* queries, they keep the list of intervals ordered with respect to their beginning points, making them superior to R-trees for other temporal query operators such as *right-covered by, equals, right-covers, covered by, left-covered by, right overlaps, met by*. These operators are either totally based on beginning points of intervals, or they specify a range for the beginning points of the intervals. R-trees cannot handle such queries as well as they handle *timeslice* queries. For example, a simple *met by* query can be answered by an IB+tree in O(logn) time while one dimensional R-trees have to make a point inclusion search to answer the same query. To make this point clear, we experimented on these three index structures for *covered by* and *met by* operators.

Covered by operator specifies the inclusion relationship between intervals (actually, between data intervals and the query interval). For this, as the beginning points of the qualifying data intervals should fall in the range specified by the query interval, *covered by* queries can be considered to be partially based on beginning points. Such queries can be answered by IB+trees by checking all data intervals whose beginning time points fall into the specified range, which requires a range search on beginning points. For R-trees, the search strategy is not any different than the strategy for *interval timeslice* queries, i.e., all nodes (leaf or internal) with minimum bounding intervals intersecting the query interval should be accessed.

Average number of internal node accesses for IB+trees and one dimensional R-trees for covered by queries: For both IB+trees with time-splits and IB+trees without time-splits the number of internal nodes accesses required is the same as *covered by* queries are answered by checking the intervals whose beginning points fall into the query range. R-trees make more internal node accesses, especially when the data intervals have large durations (data sets D1, D3, and D5).

Average number of leaf node accesses for *covered by* queries for different query sets: When the data intervals are relatively long (D2, D3, and D5), one dimensional R-trees had very poor performance, especially for short query intervals. It performs slightly better than IB+trees with time-splits when the data intervals are short (D1 and D4) but the query intervals are long. IB+trees without time-splits always give the best performances, which is an expected result.

Performances of the three structures for *met by* queries: *Met by* operator is completely based on beginning points of intervals. For IB+trees, it is simply a key-based point search. For R-trees it is not simpler than a *point timeslice* search, since all nodes whose minimum bounding intervals include the end point of the query interval have to be accessed. While the IB+trees make slightly more than one leaf access per query on the average, one dimensional R-trees have to make an order of magnitude more leaf node accesses.

7 Conclusion

In this paper, we considered the problem of indexing time intervals in valid time databases. Valid time intervals should be indexed dynamically, since updates and deletions are possible in valid time databases unlike the case for transaction time databases where intervals are inserted in an append-only fashion with time order..

We suggest to use Interval B+trees to index valid time intervals. Interval B+trees can easily handle dynamic operations as they are basically B+trees built on beginning points of the valid time intervals, whose internal nodes are augmented with maximum end point information of the subtrees below them. To efficiently handle skewed distributions, we introduce a time-split algorithm to be applied to the leaf nodes of the IB+tree to increase efficiency in search operations. Time-splits help partition relatively long intervals and distribute those partitions among different leaf nodes, so that all the leaves accommodate intervals of comparable lengths. Experimental results show that using time-splits in IB+trees considerably improve search performance, although causing some increase in storage due to the increased number of intervals because of partitions. Comparison with one-dimensional R-trees showed that IB+trees with time-splits give very close performance to R-trees for *timeslice* queries, however IB+trees perform far more superior for many temporal queries that are based on beginning points of time intervals (such as *met by, covered by*). This result was expected since IB+trees index the intervals with respect to their beginning points. In [B98] we have also shown modifications to IB+trees for handling valid time intervals that have moving (*now*) or indefinite (*infinity*) ending points. Since the beginning point of any valid time interval is always a fixed point, these modifications just concern the handling of augmented data and do not make any changes to the underlying B+tree structure. On the other hand, it is not clear how useful R-trees can be when open ended intervals are indexed together with intervals with fixed end points, especially in terms of controlling the overlap.

References

[AH85] J.F. Allen, P.J. Hayes, "A Common-sense Theory of Time", *Proceedings of the International Joint Conference on Artificial Intelligence*, August 1985.

[B98] T. Bozkaya, "Index Structures for Temporal and Multimedia Databases", PHD Thesis, CES Dept., Case Western Reserve University, Cleveland, Ohio, May 1998.

[BGO+93] B. Becker, S. Gschwind, T. Ohler, B. Seeger, P. Widmayer, "On Optimal Multiversion Access Structures", *Proceedings of Symposium on Large Spatial Databases, in LNCS, Vol* 692, *pages* 123-141, *Singapore* 1993.

[BO98] T. Bozkaya, M.Ozsoyoglu, "Indexing Transaction Time Databases", *to appear in Information Sciences.*

[CLR90] T. H. Cormen, C. E. Leiserson, R.L. Rivest "Introduction to Algorithms", *MCGraw-Hill 1992.*

[EWK90] R. Elmasri, G.T.J. Wuu, Y. Kim, "The Time-Index: An Access Structure for Temporal Data", *Proc. VLDB'90* , *pages* 1-12, August 1990.

[EWK93] R. Elmasri, G. T. J. Wuu, V. Kouramajiam, "The Time-Index and The Monotonic B+tree", *In* [T93], *chapter* 18.

[GLOT96] C.H. Goh, H. Lu, B.C. Ooi, K-L. Tan, "Indexing Temporal Data Using Existing B+-Trees", *Data and Knowledge Engineering, vol* 18, *no* 2, *pages* 147-165, March 1996.

[Gut84] A. Guttman, "R-trees: A Dynamic Index Structure for Spatial Searching", *Proc. ACM SIGMOD'84,* pages 47-57, May 1984.

[KTF95] A. Kumar, V.J. Tsotras, C. Faloutsos, "Access Methods for Bi-Temporal Databases", *Proc. International Workshop on Temporal Databases, Zurich, Switzerland, pages* 235-254, 17-18 September 1995.

[KS91] C. Kolovson, M. Stonebraker, "Segment Indexes: Dynamic Indexing Techniques for Multi-dimensional Interval Data", *Proc. ACM SIGMOD, pages* 138-147, May 1991.

[LS90] D.B. Lomet, B. Salzberg, "The Performance of a Multiversion Access Method", *Proc. ACM SIGMOD'90, pages* 353-363, June 1990.

[Mc85] E.M. McCreight, "Priority Search Trees", *SIAM Journal on Computing, pages* 257-277, 1985.

[ND97] M.A. Nascimento and M.H. Dunham, "Indexing Valid Time Databases Via B+-Trees - The MAP21 Approach", *Technical Report 97-CSE-08, Southern Methodist University.*

[PS85] F.P. Preparata, M.I. Shamos, "Computational Geometry, An Introduction", *Springer-Verlag,* 1985.

[Ram97] S. Ramaswamy, "Efficient Indexing for Constraint and Temporal Databases", *Proc. ICDT'97,* January 1997.

[SG93] A. Segev, H. Gunadhi, "Efficient Indexing Method for Temporal Relations", *IEEE Transactions on Knowledge and Data Engineering,*5(3), *pages* 496-509, 1993.

[SOL94] H. Shen, B. C. Ooi, H. Lu, " The TP-Index: A Dynamic and Efficient Indexing Mechanism for Temporal Databases", Proc. *IEEE DE, pages* 274-281, 1994.

[ST95] B. Salzberg, V.J.Tsotras, "A Comparison of Access Methods for Time Evolving Data", *To appear in ACM Computing Surveys.*

[T93] A. U. Tansel et. al. "Temporal Databases, Theory, Design and Implementation", *Benjamin /Cummings* (1993).

[TK95] V. J. Tsotras, N. Kangelaris, " The Snapshot Index: An I/O Optimal Access Method For Timeslice Queries", *Information Systems,* 20(3), *pages* 237-260, 1995.

Indexing Time-Series Databases for Inverse Queries *

Alexandros Nanopoulos Yannis Manolopoulos
Dept. of Informatics, Aristotle University, Thessaloniki 54006, Greece
tel: ++3031-996363, fax: ++3031-998419,
email: {ananopou,manolopo}@athena.auth.gr

Abstract. In this paper we examine the problem of indexing time sequences in order to answer inverse queries. An inverse query computes all the time points at which the sequence contains values equal to the query value. The presented method is based on [7] in order to represent each time sequence with a few ranges of values, which are in fact one dimensional minimum bounding rectangles. We compare the proposed method with the IP-index which has been presented in [8] as an indexing mechanism for answering inverse queries. As it is shown, the proposed method outperforms the IP-index for very large time sequences.

1 Introduction

Time series databases consist of discrete sequences representing the values of one or several variables as a function of time. This function may be discrete or continuous. In the case of a continuous function, the values of the sequence are produced by a sampling procedure and, if it is desirable, the intermediate values can be obtained through an interpolation function (linear, step-wise constant, splines).

Time sequences have found applications in temporal and historical databases [10] and in scientific databases which store several phenomena measurements. In data mining applications, time sequences are used in order to discover sequential patterns [3]. All these applications require the time sequences to be dynamically updated and that all the past values should be maintained.

The two basic categories of queries for time series data are the similarity queries and the retrieval queries. The first category has been already studied thoroughly [1, 7, 2]. Retrieval queries ask for the value at a particular time point, or for the range of values for a time span. These queries can be handled efficiently by several type of indexes [5].

Lin et al. [8] have proposed a method for answering inverse queries, i.e. queries that ask for the time points where the sequence contains values equal to the query value. Figure 1a illustrates an example of an inverse query. The approach of [8] is based on the association of each inserted value with all its covering segments.

* Work supported by the European Union's TMR program ("Chorochronos" project, contract number ERBFMRX-CT96-0056 (DG 12 - BDCN)).

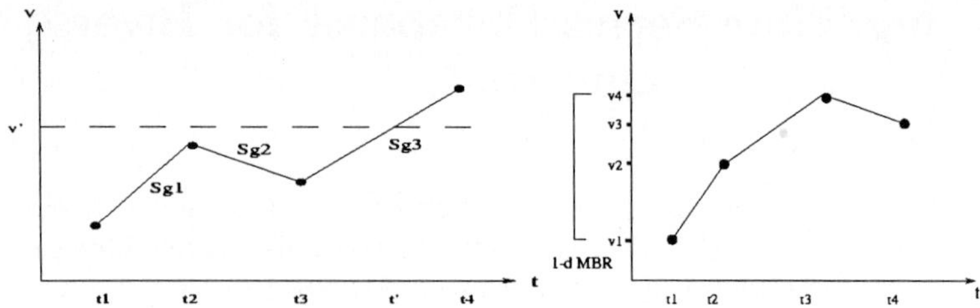

Fig. 1. a. An example of an inverse query : value v' is equal to the value at t'. **b.** An 1-d MBR of 4 successive values.

A segment is defined as the line segment that joins two consecutive values (in Figure 1a all segments are represented as Sg_i). In the same figure, we remark that the value at the time point t_2 is covered by the segment Sg_3 (a segment Sg_i covers a value v, if v is between the values of the bounding points of Sg_i). This indexing scheme is called IP-index, and compared to sequential scanning results in a performance improvement of more than two orders of magnitude.

As it is mentioned in [8], the insertion time and the space requirements are heavily depended on the number of covering segments which, as it is shown in the sequel, for very large time series grows rapidly, resulting in an increase in the above requirements. Therefore, for very large time sequences, which are stored in the secondary memory, we have to take into consideration the fact that successive values are likely to be covered by a large number of common segments. Thus, we propose the representation of successive values of the time sequence by their covering range of values, which is in fact their one dimensional minimum bounding rectangle (1-d MBR). Figure 1b presents a number of successive values and the corresponding MBR. The collection of the resulting MBRs can be efficiently stored in an R*-tree [4]. This idea was successfully used in [7], where the values of the Fourier Transformation of time series are indexed, in order to answer subsequence matching similarity queries. It will be shown that this approach correctly finds all the qualifying time points. As a result, we have to store a much smaller number of entries, yielding to reduced space overhead and processing costs as it is validated by the experimental results.

The rest of this paper is organized as follows. In Section 2 we present a description of the IP-index and the way it can be implemented in secondary storage. Section 3 presents the proposed approach and Section 4 describes the experimental evaluation of both approaches. We summarize in Section 5 by giving some brief conclusions.

2 Related Work and Motivation

In this section, we present the implementation of the IP-index [8] for secondary storage. Lin et al. have proposed that for time sequences of one value, each pair of a time point t_i and a value v_i (a point in the two-dimensional t-v plane)

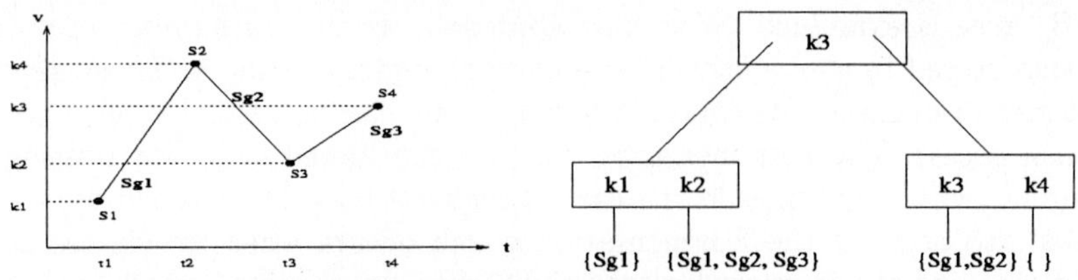

k1 k2 k3 k4

{Sg1} {Sg1, Sg2, Sg3} {Sg1,Sg2} { }

Fig. 2. a. A sequence of 4 time points and the projections of the values on the v-axis. **b.** The corresponding B$^+$-tree and the attached segment lists.

defines a state S_i. Two consecutive states S_i and S_{i+1} define a line segment Sg_i. Then the problem of answering an inverse query for a value v' is equivalent to finding all the segments Sg_i that are intersected by the line $v = v'$ (see Figure 1a). The corresponding time points can be found by applying any interpolation function (e.g. linear interpolation is used in the example of Figure 1a).

In order to answer an inverse query without scanning the hole time sequence, each line segment Sg_i is projected on the v-axis. The collection of all the projections for all states S_i forms a set of non-overlapping intervals $[k_j, k_{j+1})$ (see Figure 2a). Each k_j corresponds to one (more than one in case of equal values) value v_i. Then, all the values that belong in the interval $[k_j, k_{j+1})$ are covered by the same segments. The IP-index associates each interval $[k_j, k_{j+1})$ with the corresponding list of covering segments $< Sg_i >$. Since intervals are successive, each interval can be represented only with its starting value, i.e. k_j.

In [8], the IP-index was implemented in main memory by using an AVL-tree. For secondary storage, the IP-index has to be implemented as a B$^+$-tree, where every leaf node entry contains a pointer to its corresponding segment list. Figure 2b gives the resulting B$^+$-tree for the example of Figure 2a. To answer an inverse query for a value v' using the IP-index, we have to search the B$^+$-tree (or any other implementation) to find the interval $[k_j, k_{j+1})$ that v' belongs to. This is achieved by finding the maximum value k_j that is less than or equal to v'. Then, the list of the covering segments for that interval, contains all the segments that intersect the line $v = v'$.

The performance of the IP-index method is affected by the total number of entries and especially the number of covering segments, which in very large sequences tend to increase rapidly. In [8], this problem is addressed by limiting the precision of the measured values. This results into the reduction of the number of index entries due to the fact that several time points will have the same value for the reduced precision, while this is not the case of the original precision. Apparently, the reduction of the precision is application depended and cannot be applied in general.

Since the IP-index has been proposed as a main memory index, the search time is linear with respect to the length of the segment lists. However, for secondary storage, extra disk access cost is required to traverse these lists. For the implementation of those lists in secondary storage, we follow the approach proposed in [6], where the problem of the efficient handling of posting records in a B^+-tree is examined. With this approach, we have a number of covering segments stored in consecutive positions in secondary memory. These segments are stored in buckets, the contents of which one can be retrieved with one logical disk access. The cost measures that are considered in [6] for posting lists are similar with those ones in the case of segment lists. More precisely, we have to take into account the fragmentation which occurs when we choose a large bucket size and the increased search time when we choose a small bucket size. We have to note that we use a constant bucket size. Although the other method described in [6] achieves improved search time, it requires total reorganization of the bucket entries. This would had a great impact on the insertion time due to the large number of bucket entries which the IP-index requires.

3 Proposed Method

The problem of answering inverse queries translates to finding a way to index the values of the time sequence in order to discard irrelevant parts of the sequence and search only the ones that contain values satisfying the query condition and thus, avoiding the straightforward solution to search the entire sequence for finding the time points which answer the query.

As it has been mentioned previously, the IP-index divides the set of all values into intervals of values which contain values that are all covered by the same segments. This method gains at instances of time sequences that contain the same values at several time points. As it is mentioned in [8], the IP-index performs extremely well for periodic time sequences with values of reduced precision. However, in most cases, time sequences are not periodic and may contain values of high precision. This fact leads to a point where we have to store as many intervals as the number of points in the time sequence. Moreover, the problem is enhanced due to the fact that several intervals are covered by the same segments. As a consequence, there is a large number of duplicates stored in the segments lists. Since, as it will be shown later, for very large time series the overlapping between covering segments is also large, the IP-index leads to a large space overhead. This also affects the insertion and search times.

The inefficiency in terms of space and insertion time stems from the fact that every interval is explicitly stored. The proposed method is based on the property that consecutive time points will probably have similar values. This approach was followed in [7], in order to answer subsequence similarity queries. Therefore, we can divide the sequence into subsequences of consecutive time points that do not have values with large differences. The collection of these points corresponds to a range of values and all included values can be represented only with that range. An inverse query has to retrieve only the ranges that contain values satisfying the query condition. It is easy to show that if an inverse query intersects some of the values inside the range then it has to intersect the range itself. The time points of all the subsequences which take values inside the retrieved ranges have to be computed by examing the contents of each subsequence. As it will be shown in the sequel, the proposed method correctly finds all the time points which

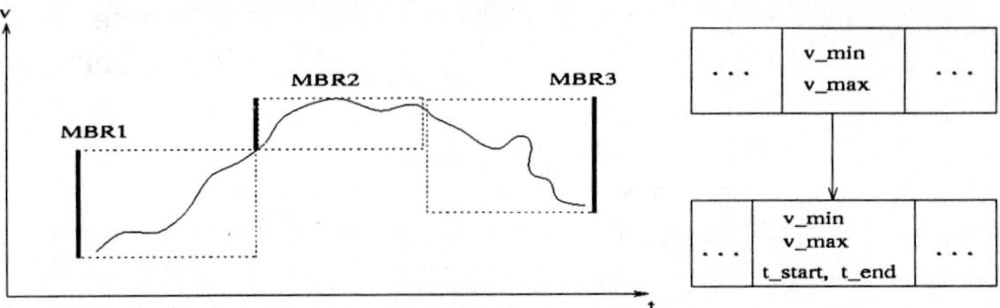

Fig. 3. a. A sequence divided into 3 parts and the corresponding MBRs. **b.** The structure of an internal and of a leaf node of the R*-tree.

satisfy the query condition. Such a range of values represents the one dimensional minimum bounding rectangle (MBR) of the values it includes. Therefore, the proposed index method can be implemented with an 1-d R*-tree, storing these MBRs.

Figure 3a presents an example of a time sequence which is divided into three subsequences. For each one of them the corresponding 1-d MBR is depicted with a solid line (for illustration reasons each subsequence is bounded by a rectangle). In the same figure it is shown that different MBRs may have overlapped projections on the v-axis. Notice that the R*-tree has to store at the leaf nodes the starting time and the ending time of each subsequence. Figure 3b illustrates the structure of an internal and an external node of the R*-tree.

3.1 Insertion

Following the previously described approach, we have to define a way such that several consecutive values will be included in the same MBR, forming one subsequence. As it is mentioned in [7], the criterion whether a value will belong to a subsequence or not is based on the fact that it does not increase the probability that the corresponding MBR is going to be accessed. As it can be easily shown for data normalized to the range $[0, 1]$, the probability P that an MBR (1-d in our case) of length L will be accessed by the average range query is equal to $P = L + 0.5$ (it is assumed that an average range query is of length equal to 0.5). Also, notice that this criterion requires that the values are normalized to the range $[0, 1]$. In [7] for an MBR consisting of k values the marginal cost mc of this MBR is defined as $mc = (L + 0.5)/k$ which means that the probability of accessing the MBR is divided by the number of values that this MBR includes.

Hence, the criterion to include (or not) a new value in a subsequence is based on the comparison of the new marginal cost mc_a of the MBR produced in case of insertion of the new value into the specific subsequence, with the marginal cost mc_b of the MBR before the insertion. More precisely if the MBR length before the insertion was L_b, whereas after the insertion it changes to L_a (notice that L_a may be equal to L_b if there is no expansion), then we have to test if $L_a/(k + 1) \leq L_b/k$

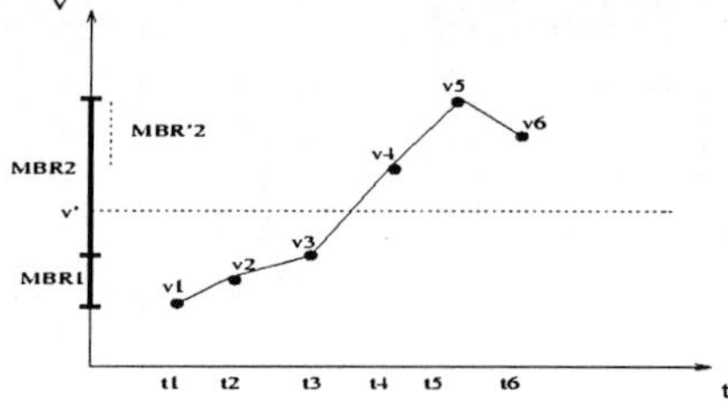

Fig. 4. MBR_2 is involved in inverse query v' while MBR'_2 (with dotted line) does not.

Therefore, we start with the first value of the whole sequence and we form a subsequence by including all the successive values, as long as these values preserve the above inequality. In case that the inequality does not hold, we have to start a new subsequence. At this point, our approach differs from that in [7] in order to include a special case. Figure 4 illustrates this case. In this figure values v_1, v_2 and v_3 belong to the same subsequence and they are represented by their 1-d minimum bounding rectangle MBR_1. Value v_4 is such that it has to be excluded from the previous subsequence and to start a new subsequence. In this new subsequence, values v_5 and v_6 will also be included. In order to be able to answer correctly an inverse query with a value v' such that $v_3 < v' < v_4$, we have to define as starting value of the second subsequence the value v_3 and not v_4. As a consequence, the 1-d minimum bounding rectangle MBR_2 of the second subsequence, as it is drawn in Figure 4, will be intersected by values of inverse queries like the value v'. Otherwise, if we started the new subsequence from the value v_4 (forming the MBR'_2) then the indexing method could not guarantee safe satisfaction of inverse queries. Finally, notice that the proposed method supports the dynamic appending of new values at the end of the sequence, since these new values can be the starting points of new subsequences.

3.2 Search

Here, we examine how we have to search the index for the time points that correspond to an inverse query. First, for a given inverse query that asks for all the time points that the time sequence takes values equal to v', we perform a point query within the R*-tree to retrieve all the leaf MBRs that totally enclose the value v'. The retrieved MBRs, as it was described before, represent ranges of values in subsequences of the original sequence. The fact that an MBR encloses the value v' means that the corresponding subsequence includes values, where some of them are equal to v'.

In the sequel we have to examine all the subsequences that are represented with an MBR that has been retrieved in the previous step. Thus, we perform sequential scanning, but only inside each subsequence, in order to find the exact time points that the time sequence takes values equal to v'. As it has been

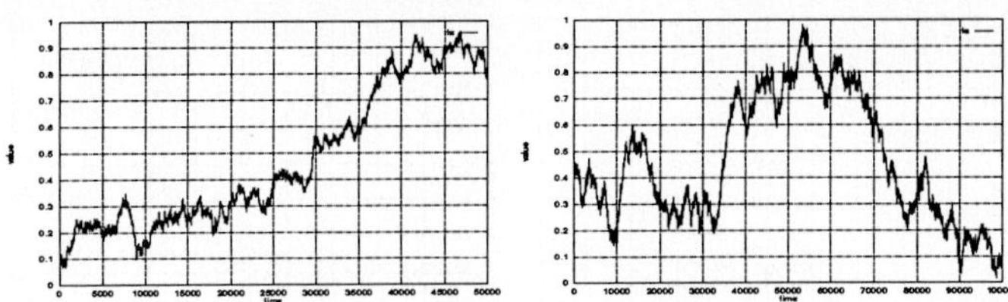

Fig. 5. Synthetic Time Sequences

described, the boundaries of each subsequence, i.e. its starting and its finishing time, are stored within the corresponding MBR. This way for each query we can quickly select only the interesting subsequences, and then we can exactly answer the query by searching only inside these subsequences.

3.3 Correctness

The following lemma proves the correctness of the proposed method.

Lemma 1. *The proposed method correctly finds all the time points that the time sequence contains values equal to the query value.*

Proof. Let an inverse query of value v'. Then for any interval of consecutive values $[v_1, v_2]$ which satisfies the condition : $v_1 \leq v' \leq v_2$, values v_1 and v_2 will either belong to the same or to consecutive subsequences. In the first case, the MBR that represents the subsequence they belong to, will enclose that interval and thus, the MBR will be retrieved by the query. In the second case, as it was explained in subsection 3.1, the MBR of the second subsequence will enclose the interval $[v_1, v_2]$ and so it will also be retrieved by the query. Since these cases are the only ones, the proposed method correctly answers inverse queries. □

4 Performance Evaluation

We implemented both the IP-index structure and the proposed one in C++ and we carried out experiments on a Ultra Sparc under Solaris 2.5.1. We used synthetic data of various lengths and characteristics. According to [8], the IP-index is by far better than the sequential method, henceforth we do not study the sequential scanning any more. We measured the performance of the IP-index and the proposed method, which we will refer to as SIQ-index (denoting indexing Sequences for Inverse Queries). More precisely we performed measurements of space overhead, insertion time and search time.

The synthetic data were modeled as *random walks* [9]. A random walk, also called brown noise, can be generated by using the following formula [1]:

$$x_t = x_{t-1} + z_t$$

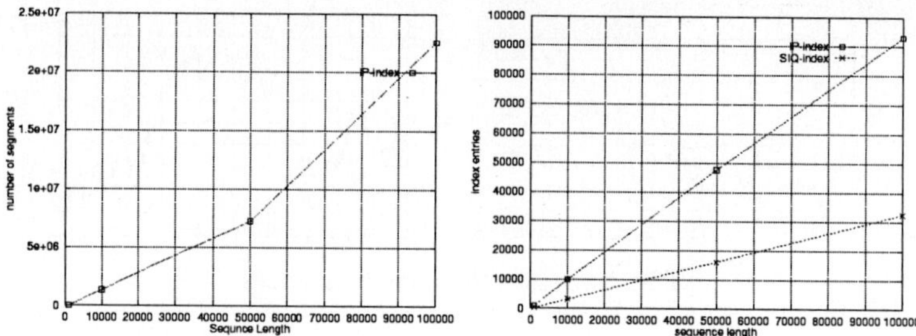

Fig. 6. a. Number of segments IP-stores versus sequence length. **b.** Number of index entries versus sequence length.

where z_t, $t = 0, 1, \ldots$ are IID random variables following uniform distribution. Figure 5 shows examples of the produced synthetic time sequences. These sequences have lengths equal to 50000 and 100000 respectively. Each value was represented with a float number and no limit to the precision was applied.

The page size for the B$^+$-tree and R*-tree access methods is equal to 4K. Hence, the B$^+$-tree has a larger fan-out because, as it was explained earlier, the SIQ-index requires some additional information to be stored in the leaf nodes of the R*-tree. On the other hand, for the implementation of the segment lists for the IP-index, we chose the buckets containing the elements of the lists (the covering segments) to be of constant size equal to 1K. As it is mentioned in [8], each segment is represented with only one integer denoting the time point of its staring value. Note that if we chose a larger bucket size, e.g. 4K, then this would result in severe fragmentation and, as a consequence, in large space waste. In all our experiments, a bucket of 1K was large enough to hold the average number of entries of the segment list for each entry in the B$^+$-tree.

4.1 Space overhead

We first measured the number of covering segments that the IP-index requires to store. This is the total number of covering segments for all index entries, including the duplicates which the IP-index requires to store. Figure 6a gives the results with respect to the time sequence length. As it is illustrated, the number of covering segments grows rapidly with respect to the size of the sequences.

For the same sequences, we measured the number of index entries for the IP and SIQ indexes. Since the IP-index requires the storage of almost every individual value, whereas the SIQ-index stores only ranges which include more than one values, the SIQ-index has much less index entries. Figure 6b illustrates the number of entries for each index. Therefore, the SIQ-index requires much less space overhead since it stores less index entries and moreover, it does not require the storage of the covering segments.

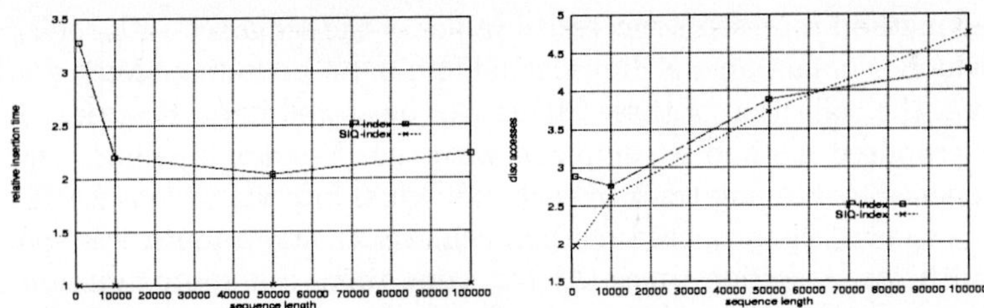

Fig. 7. a. Relative insertion time versus sequence length. **b.** Required disk accesses versus sequence length for the search operation.

4.2 Insertion time

Next we measured the insertion time for both indexing methods. Figure 7a illustrates the results with respect to the sequence length. In Figure 7a, the insertion time of the IP-index is given relatively to the insertion time of the SIQ-index. As it is clearly shown by these results, the SIQ-index outperforms the IP-index due to the fact that it involves the insertion of a much smaller number of entries and moreover, it does not require the manipulation of the covering segments that the IP-index does.

4.3 Search time

Finally, we measured the search time which both methods require in order to answer inverse queries. We carried out the measurement by producing 100 random query values. As a cost measure we choose the number of required disk accesses. Since both the IP-index and SIQ-index involve a post-processing phase (the former in order to do the interpolation and the latter in order to discard all intervals that are not intersected by the query value), this measure does not include the post-processing time which is considered to be negligible since it is a main memory operation.

Figure 7b illustrates the results of this measurement (the vertical axis depicts the average disk accesses for one query). As it shown in this figure, in most cases the SIQ-index is slightly better than the IP-index, except some cases where IP-index performs a little better. This is due to the fact that in these cases, the overlapping between the MBRs is quite large, so the R*-tree requires more than one leaf MBR to be searched in order to answer the query. On the other hand, the IP-index can answer the query by accessing only one leaf node because it divides all values into non-overlapping intervals. The price paid for this is a very large space overhead.

5 Conclusions

We have presented a method to index time series databases in order to efficiently answer inverse queries. This method is based on [7], where the problem of indexing time series databases for subsequence similarity queries is examined. The proposed method represents successive values of the sequence with their range of values which is in fact an one dimensional minimum bounding rectangle (MBR). Therefore, the collection of these MBRs can be stored in an R*-tree.

The proposed method is compared with the IP-index [8] which organizes a time sequence by keeping track of each individual interval of consecutive values. As it was shown, the proposed method achieves clearly a much less space overhead and better insertion times. At the same time, the approximation of time values by ranges of values does not lead to worse search time.

Future work may include the examination of the proposed method for indexing collections of time sequences. Also, one other interesting topic is the examination of the method for time sequences of more than one dimensions. Finally, future research could involve the generalization of the proposed method for queries which find the intersection points between time sequences.

References

[1] R. Agrawal, C. Faloutsos, and A. Swami. "Efficient Similarity Search in Sequence Databases". *Proc. of the Fourth International Conference on Foundations of Data Organization and Algorithms"*, Chicago, USA, October 1993.

[2] R. Agrawal, K. Lin, H. Sawhney, and K. Shim. "Fast Similarity Search in the Presence of Noise, Scaling, and Translation in Time-Series Databases". *Proc. of the 21st VLDB Conference*, Zurich, Switzerland, 1995.

[3] R. Agrawal, and R. Srikant. "Mining Sequential Patterns". *Proc. of the 11th Int'l Conference on Data Engineering*, Taipei, Taiwan, March 1995.

[4] N. Beckmann, H. Kriegel, R. Schneider, and B. Seeger. "The R*-tree: An Efficient and Robust Access Method for Points and Rectangles". *Proc. of the ACM SIGMOD Conference on Management of Data*, Atlantic City, USA, May, 1990.

[5] R. Elmasri, G. Wuu, and Y. Kim. "The Time Index: An access structure for temporal data". *Proc. of the 16th VLDB Conference*, Brisbane, Australia, 1990.

[6] C. Faloutsos and H. Jagadish. "On B-tree Indices for Skewed Distributions". *Proc. of the 18th VLDB Conference*, Vancouver, Canada, 1992.

[7] C. Faloutsos, M. Raganathan, and Y. Manolopoulos. "Fast Subsequence Matching in Time-Series Databases". *Proc. of the ACM SIGMOD Conference on Management of Data*, Minnesota, USA, May 1994.

[8] L. Lin, T. Risch, M. Skold, and D. Badal. "Indexing Values of Time Sequences". *Proc. of the Int'l Conference on Information and Knowledge Management (CIKM)*, Rockville, USA, 1996.

[9] M. Schroeder. "Fractal, Chaos, Power Laws : Minutes from an Infinite Paradise". *W.H. Freeman and Company*. New York, USA, 1991.

[10] R. Stam and R. Snodgrass. "A bibliography on temporal databases". *IEEE Bulletin on Data Engineering, 11(4)*, December 1998.

Implementing Embedded Valid Time Query Languages

Costas Vassilakis[1], Panagiotis Georgiadis[1], Timos Sellis[2]

[1] Univ. of Athens, Dept. of Informatics, Panepistimiopolis, TYPA Buildings
GR-157 71 Athens Greece
{costas, georgiad}@di.uoa.gr
[2] National Technical University of Athens, Dept. of Electrical and Computer Engineering,
Computer Science Division, GR -157 73 Zografou, Greece
timos@cs.ntua.gr

Abstract. Application development on top of database systems is heavily based on the existence of embedded and 4GL languages. However, the issue of designing and implementing embedded or 4GL temporal languages has not been addressed insofar. In this paper, we present a design approach for implementing an embedded temporal language that supports valid time. Furthermore, we introduce implementation techniques that can be used for implementing any embedded temporal language that supports valid time on top of a DBMS.

1 Introduction

In the past years temporal databases have received substantial research attention, and numerous application areas which would benefit from the introduction of the time dimension have been identified (e.g. [2], [5], [6], [7]). However, little has been reported on the implementation of temporal applications using the temporal database management systems (TDBMSs) implemented, with the exception of time series-oriented applications: in [8] an application for managing medical temporal data is presented, while [16] reports on a temporal application which was developed for Clinica Puerto de Hierro of Spain. One of the main reasons for this shortage, is the absence of suitable development tools: database application development is based on embedded and 4GL languages (usually complemented by graphical user interface libraries), and none of the temporal database systems implemented insofar ([3]) is reported to provide such tools. Some of these systems provide graphical user interfaces ([4], [8], [19]), but these interfaces are oriented towards assisting query formulation, and not targeted for general-purpose application development. TSQL2 ([22]) includes specifications for cursors, but no implementations for TSQL2 cursors has been reported insofar. Time series applications, on the other hand, can be easily developed since there do exist database systems whose development packages support the time series concept ([15], [17]). This paper presents a design approach to the implementation of an embedded temporal language for a TDBMS supporting valid time (VTDBMS). We will not focus on a specific temporal language but, rather, we will identify *categories of statements* that appear in VTDBMSs, and outline algorithms for handling such statements. The design is based on the following assumptions:

- The non-temporal part of the valid time query language (denoted as VTQL, hereafter) is pure SQL, or can be mapped to it. For simplicity, in our discussion we will assume that the non-temporal part is pure SQL.
- A *terminal monitor* application that accepts and processes interactive VTQL statements has been developed. The terminal monitor uses certain algorithms to evaluate queries with temporal aspects. The design of embedded VTQL (denoted as VTQL, hereafter) does not rely on the existence of *specific* algorithms, but requires that such algorithms *do exist*.
- EVTQL will be implemented on top of a DBMS that supports embedded SQL. This implies that a *layered architecture* is adopted, as suggested in [20], [21] and [23].

Finally, for simplicity in our discussion, we will assume that *homogeneous valid time* and *tuple timestamping* ([13]) is used, although the techniques presented here may easily be adapted to handle heterogeneous valid time and attribute timestamping.

The remnant of this paper is organised as follows: section 2 outlines the syntax and semantics of EVTQL, and the categories of statements that may appear in a VTDBMS are identified. Section 3 presents a design approach to the implementation of EVTQL, discussing the software modules that compose it, the role of each module and the algorithms it employs. Although the design has been completed for both static and dynamic

EVTQL statements, only static statements are presented in this paper, for brevity reasons. Section 4 concludes and outlines future work.

2 An Embedded Valid Time Query Language

EVTQL should obey the *dual-mode principle* ([10]), i.e. every VTQL statement that can be used interactively, may be executed as part of an application program. Embedded VTQL statements, however, may use a number of extensions not available to interactive statements (the prefix `EXEC VTQL` that is used to distinguish embedded VTQL statements from host language statements is a trivial issue, and will not be addressed in the rest of this document):

1. embedded VTQL statements may contain references to host language variables, which must be prefixed with a colon (`:`). Variable references may appear in any place of a VTQL DML statement that a literal can be used, and in the `INTO` clause.
2. the embedded `SELECT` statement is augmented with an `INTO` clause, which specifies the host variables into which data will be retrieved.
3. a number of statements (or *statement forms*) associated with *cursors* is available (`DECLARE CURSOR`, `OPEN`, `FETCH`, etc.), providing a *row-at-a-time* interface to the database.

In the remainder of section 0 EVTQL DML statements will be presented. DDL statements are not discussed, since their syntax and semantics is identical to their interactive VTQL counterparts. The `CONNECT`, `DISCONNECT` and `BEGIN/END DECLARE SECTION` statements are also excluded from the discussion, since they are identical to their embedded SQL counterparts ([9]). Each of the `SELECT`, `INSERT`, `DELETE` and `UPDATE` statements are subdivided into two categories, which will be used in the discussion in section 0:

- *Snapshot-transformable statements*. This category includes VTQL statements that can be mapped to a *single SQL statement*. Statements that include operations on data types representing time may fall in this category, even if the underlying DBMS does not directly support these operations: indeed, for a DBMS not supporting the TSQL2 `PRECEDES` predicate, the expression `instant1 PRECEDES instant2` may be rewritten as `instant1 < instant2` or even `precedes(instant1, instant2)`, if the underlying DBMS implements the *precedes* predicate as an operator or a function, respectively.
- *Non snapshot-transformable statements*. This category includes VTQL statements that require the application of a set operation not directly supported by the underlying DBMS. Such operators are coalescing operators ([13]), operators converting between instant and period timestamping, as well as the SL and SP_p operators introduced in [22] (chapter 27). If data are stored in the base tables in coalesced form, `INSERT`, `DELETE` and `UPDATE` statements against valid time tables always fall in this category.

2.1 Operations not involving cursors

The DML statements of VTQL that do not involve cursors are the "singleton" form of `SELECT`, the `INSERT` statement, and the `DELETE` and `UPDATE` statements, except for their the `WHERE CURRENT OF` forms, which will be presented later. These statements are described in the following paragraphs.

The SELECT Statement ("singleton" form).
The "singleton" form of the embedded VTQL `SELECT` statement is used to fetch at most one tuple from the database. Its syntax is identical to the interactive counterpart, except that the `INTO` clause may precede the `FROM` clause, specifying the host language variables into which the query results will be stored. For example the TSQL2 ([22]) query

```
SELECT Name
INTO :emp_name
FROM Employee E1
WHERE VALID(E1) CONTAINS PERIOD(DATE '01/01/1991', DATE '12/31/1991');
```

can be used to fetch the name of the employee that has worked during all of 1991 (assuming that only one such employee exists).

The INSERT Statement.
The syntax of the EVTQL INSERT statement is identical to the corresponding statement of SQL, with two exceptions:

1. If the values to be inserted are specified via a *select*-query, the query may include temporal features.
2. If the column storing the tuple's valid time is *implicit* (as in TSQL2), a specific clause must be introduced to specify the tuple's valid time, when inserting data into a valid time clause using the values clause.

The DELETE and UPDATE Statements (non-Cursor Forms).
The DELETE and UPDATE statements of embedded VTQL are used to delete and update either whole tuples, or specific periods of the valid time data stored in a table. The syntax of the embedded VTQL DELETE and UPDATE statements is identical to their SQL counterparts, with the following exceptions:

1. The WHERE clause in both statements may use temporal extensions.
2. When deleting or updating valid time tables, the valid time period to which the operation applies must be specified. If the column storing the tuple's valid time is implicit, special provision for modifying the tuple's valid time must also be included.

2.2 Operations involving cursors

Cursors provide a *row-at-a-time* interface to the database. Using cursors, an application may obtain addressability to tuples stored in the database (one tuple at a time), fetch data values into its address space, as well as delete or modify the tuples.

Before any cursor is used, it must be *declared*, i.e. associated with a VTQL SELECT statement. The syntax for cursor declaration is

```
EXEC VTQL DECLARE cursor_name CURSOR FOR VTQL-Select-Statement;
```

Cursor declaration does not trigger the evaluation of the associated query. The query is evaluated only when the cursor is *opened*, which is accomplished via the statement

```
EXEC VTQL OPEN cursor_name;
```

Upon opening, a cursor does not point to any tuple in the result set. In order to position the cursor to the next tuple (marking it as the *current tuple* of the cursor) and fetch the values of the selected attributes into host language variables, the statement

```
EXEC VTQL FETCH cursor_name INTO host-variable-list;
```

must be used. If no more data is available in the result set to be fetched, the *vtqlca.vtqlcode* variable (which is implicitly declared in all programs using embedded VTQL) is assigned a special value to indicate the error. Finally, a cursor may be closed using the statement

```
EXEC VTQL CLOSE cursor_name;
```

Two issues are worth noting here, with respect to TSQL2:

1. TSQL2 introduces *nested cursors* for valid time tables. *Outer-level* cursors provide addressability to *explicit attributes*; the *inner level* cursors provide access to the valid timestamps of the tuple, while the outer level cursor points to a specific tuple. In a relational environment, this implies that valid timestamps are stored in a different table, necessitating thus the need for joins in query processing. Since such a scheme is inefficient to implement in a relational environment, we will not consider nested cursors; instead, standard single-level cursors provide access *both* to the explicit attributes *and* the valid time of the tuple.
2. The cursor versions of the DELETE and UPDATE statements in TSQL2 apply only to *complete tuples*; the design presented in this paper provides with means to specify that the operation applies only to *a specific part* of the valid time of the tuple that is pointed to by the cursor.

The DELETE Statement (Cursor Version).
The syntax of the cursor version of the DELETE statement is

```
DELETE FROM table_name WHERE CURRENT OF cursor_name [VT_selection];
```

where *VT_selection* is a syntactic construct (probably a clause, such as the VALID clause in the non-cursor form of TSQL2's DELETE statement), specifying the valid time period to which the deletion applies. There is no particular reason why this syntactic construct should be placed last in the query: it may be positioned in any place, provided it does not introduce syntactic ambiguities.

If *VT_selection* is used, the cursor does not point to a *current tuple* after the UPDATE statement is executed, and thus is not qualified for further deletions and updates, until a new FETCH statement is executed for that cursor. If this specification is omitted, the deletion applies to the whole tuple that is current for the designated cursor.

The cursor version of the DELETE statement may be used only if the cursor points to an *updatable result tuple set*. The cases for which a result tuple set is updatable practically depend on the underlying DBMS ([12], [14], [18]). The SQL standard ([9]) specifies a minimal set of queries yielding updatable results (roughly, this includes queries which apply only SELECT and PROJECT relational algebra operations, with no duplicates removal, on a single base table; joins are permitted but only when expressed via a subquery), but various RDBMSs allow updates on the results of a wider range of queries. We will consider updatable only the result sets which are designated as updatable by the SQL standard. The usage of the coalescing operators, operators converting between period and instant timestamping as well as the SL and SP_p operators destroys the physical one-to-one mapping of result tuples to stored tuples (i.e. a tuple in the result set does not correspond to a single stored tuple), and thus renders the result set not updatable.

The UPDATE Statement (Cursor Version).
The syntax of the cursor version of the UPDATE statement is

```
UPDATE table_name SET col = value {, col = value}
WHERE CURRENT OF cursor_name [VT_selection];
```

When using this form of the UPDATE statement (which is permitted only if the cursor points to an updatable result tuple set), the update applies to the tuple that is current for cursor *cursor_name*. Again, *VT_selection* specifies the valid time period to which the operation applies. If *VT_selection* is used, the cursor does not point to a *current tuple* after the UPDATE statement is executed, and thus is not qualified for further deletions and updates, until a new FETCH statement is executed for that cursor.

3 Design of an EVTQL Architecture

In this section we describe the design of an architecture for the embedded VTQL language, which may be implemented on top of any relational DBMS. The proposed architecture follows the approach taken by embedded SQL packages, but introduces two additional modules, the *EVTQL preprocessor* and the *EVTQL library*. The application programmer develops the temporal application in some host language (e.g. C, C++ etc.), using embedded VTQL statements to interact with the database. Each file written by the programmer is then processed by the EVTQL preprocessor, which translates EVTQL statements to calls to the EVTQL library. Calls to the EVTQL library may need to be supported by data structures and/or embedded SQL statements, thus the output of the EVTQL preprocessor is an intermediate file conferment to the embedded SQL syntax rules. These intermediate files are fed to the DBMS's embedded SQL preprocessor, whose output is processed by the host language compiler, producing object files. Finally, object files are linked with the host language's libraries, the DBMS libraries, the EVTQL library and any other libraries specified by the programmer (e.g. GUI libraries), in order to produce the application executable file.

The EVTQL library is a collection of procedures, providing support for the execution of EVTQL statements and for temporal cursors. It is developed in some host language, and uses embedded SQL to interact with the database. The files containing the EVTQL library's source code are processed by the DBMS's embedded SQL preprocessor and are then compiled to object files, using the host language compiler. Finally, the system library manager is used to bundle these object files into a single library file. Only this library file is needed in the linking phase of temporal applications.

Figure 1 illustrates the overall process of temporal application development, using embedded VTQL.

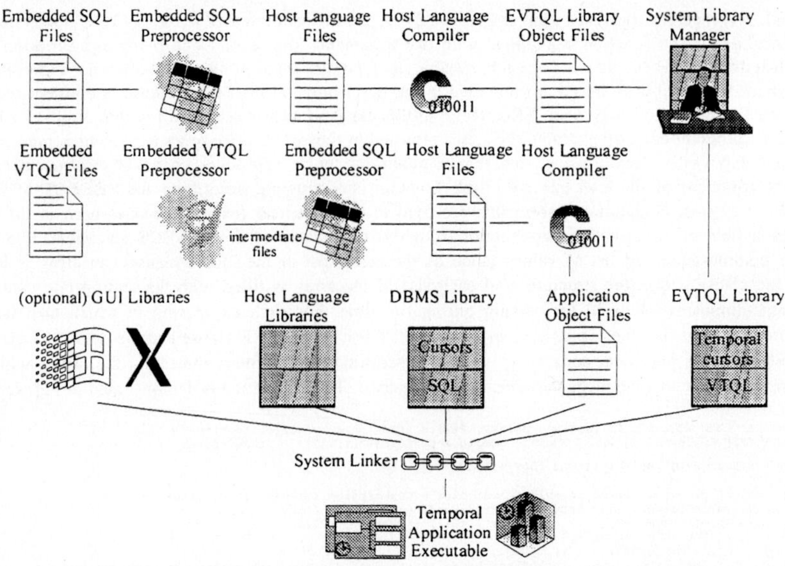

Fig. 1. Embedded VTQL architecture

In the following paragraphs, the operation of the EVTQL preprocessor and the algorithms employed by the EVTQL library are presented.

3.1 The EVTQL Preprocessor

The EVTQL preprocessor operates on files containing host language statements and embedded VTQL statements. For each input file, the embedded VTQL preprocessor generates an output file, which contains host language, embedded SQL statements and calls to the EVTQL library, and is then processed by theDBMS's embedded SQL preprocessor and the host language compiler, to produce object files. More specifically, the embedded VTQL preprocessor is responsible for the following actions:

1. analyse syntactically the embedded VTQL statements, verifying that they conform to the EVTQL syntax rules.
2. determine the types of the host language variables which are used within embedded VTQL statements, so as to facilitate information exchange between the VTDBMS and the application program.
3. translate embedded VTQL statements to appropriate calls to the EVTQL library. Each call must be supplied with parameters, which provide adequate information for the statement execution. Some statements need additional data structures and/or code to be introduced; the EVTQL preprocessor is responsible for planting these data structures and the appropriate pieces of code into the output file.
4. insert pieces of code to implement the `WHENEVER` statements[1].

In order to perform these tasks, the EVTQL preprocessor must be aware of the host language syntax and semantics rules, so as to tailor its behaviour to the specific host language (type analysis of variable declarations, code emission etc). In this paper, we focus on the EVTQL preprocessor for the"C" language, since C (along with C++) is the dominant third generation language for application development. The techniques presented, however, can be used for implementing preprocessors for other host languages. Since statement parsing is covered in detail elsewhere (e.g. [1], [11]), we focus only on the VTQL-specific aspects of the preprocessor, i.e. the translation of embedded VTQL statements and the implementation of the `WHENEVER` statements.

Embedded VTQL statement translation.

The SELECT statement ("singleton" form).

[1] Analogous to the embedded SQL WHENEVER statements.

The EVTQL preprocessor translates each singleton SELECT statement to a call to the EVTQL library function `evtql_select`. The function is supplied with two arguments, the second one being a description of the variables listed in the INTO clause. For each variable, its type, its length in bytes and a pointer to the memory location where the variable is stored are included in the description. If the INTO clause is omitted, a special value is used for the second argument. Effectively, in this case, no data is retrieved into the program's address space, but the program can still examine the status returned in the *vtqlca.vtqlcode* variable, which may indicate that the statement was successfully executed, that no qualifying tuples were found or that an error occurred.

The first argument of the `evtql_select` function is a structure describing the SELECT statement, together with the host language variables that are used in the statement (except the ones used in the INTO clause). Each field of the structure corresponds (roughly) to a clause of the SELECT statement. If a clause contains a comma-separated list of values (such as the select list or the FROM clause), an array is used to represent the clause within the structure, and each slot of the array is filled with the appropriate value. This arrangement eliminates the need for parsing during run time. For each expression in which host language variables may be used (i.e. the expressions in the SELECT list, the WHERE clause and the HAVING clause), a supplemental array is provided, containing variable descriptions and pointers indicating the offset, within the expression, where the host language variable must be inserted. This translation is demonstrated in **Fig. 2.**[2]:

```
/* EXEC VTQL SELECT EmpName, Salary, Period INTO :name, :salary, :period
FROM Employees E1 WHERE EmpId = :empid and BEGIN(VALID(E1)) = :targetDate; */

static evtql_select_struct vtql_sel_001 = {
{
   /* Number of items in select list plus a description for each item. Since no host
   variables are used here, the corresponding lists are empty. */
   {3, {{"EmpName", {0}}, {"Salary", {0}}, {"Period", {0}}},
   /* The FROM clause */
   {1, {"Employee", "E1"}},
   /* The WHERE clause, including the description of the two host variables. Each description
   contains the offset within the string, where the variable value must be inserted. Notice
   the translation of VALID(E1) to E1.VT. */
   {"EmpId =  and BEGIN(E1.VT) = ",
       {2, {VTQL_CHAR, 5, NULL, 8}, {VTQL_DATE, 10, NULL, 29}}}
};

/* Structure describing the INTO clause. */
static evtql_varlist vtql_varlist_001 = {
3, {{VTQL_CHAR, 20, NULL}, {VTQL_INT, 4, NULL}, {VTQL_INTERVAL, 25, NULL}}
};

/* data structure initialisation */
vtql_sel_001.where.vars[0].ptr = empid;
vtql_sel_001.where.vars[2].ptr = targetdate; vtsl_varlist_001.vars[0].ptr = name;
vtql_varlist_001.vars[1].ptr = &salary; vtql_varlist_001.vars[2].ptr = period;

/* call to the library */
evtql_select(&vtql_sel_001, &vtql_varlist_001);
```

Fig. 2. - Translation of a singleton SELECT statement

The first comment in **Fig. 2.** shows the original EVTQL statement. The following two declarations are generated by the EVTQL preprocessor and are inserted at the beginning of the output file, whereas the executable statements that follow are inserted at the place where the embedded VTQL statement was located in the original file. The first group of statements fixes the pointers to the host variables, which are contained in the data structures. Data structure declaration cannot include pointer initialisation, because host variables may be either local or global, and data structures are declared at global level. Declaring the data structures at global level is required, since the declarations include initialisations, and many compilers reject such declarations at local (function) level. Additionally, using global declarations avoids unnecessary initialisation upon every entry to the function. Data structures are declared with *static* storage class, to avoid clashes with variables in other preprocessed files.

The INSERT, DELETE and UPDATE statements.

Data insertion and the non-cursor forms of the DELETE and UPDATE statements are handled by calls to EVTQL library functions. Data deletion and update is performed by the `evtql_delete` and `evtql_update` functions, respectively, whereas for data insertion, one of the functions `evtql_insert_values` and `evtql_insert_query` is called, depending on whether the data to be

[2] A number of fields which are not used in the example is omitted (e.g. the field describing the GROUP BY clause) for brevity reasons, but they are actually emitted by the preprocessor. Additionally, arrays are initialised in separate declarations, but in this example their initialisation is merged with the declaration of the data structure which includes them.

inserted are specified via the VALUES clause or a query. In all cases, data structures formulation follows the rules described for the SELECT statement. Each function call is supplied with parameters that describe the requested operation.

The DECLARE CURSOR statement.
The DECLARE CURSOR statement is not directly translated to a call to the EVTQL library. The preprocessor memorises the cursor name and the associated SELECT statement, and this data are used when the corresponding OPEN statement is processed. At this point, however, the SELECT statement is syntactically analysed, errors (if any) are reported and appropriate data structures are formulated in the preprocessor's memory.

To each cursor that is declared in a source file, the EVTQL preprocessor assigns a *DBMS statement name* and a *DBMS cursor name* (these are unique, system-generated identifiers). Additionally, for each declared cursor the preprocessor generates four functions, which are appended to the output file. The first function is named `evtql_open_CName` (*CName* is the name of the VTQL cursor) and contains the following embedded SQL statements:

```
EXEC SQL PREPARE dbms_statement FROM :host_string;
EXEC SQL DECLARE dbms_cursor CURSOR FOR dbms_statement;
EXEC SQL OPEN dbms_cursor;
```

(*dbms_cursor* and *dbms_statement* are the DBMS cursor name and statement name which are assigned to the cursor by the EVTQL preprocessor; *host_string* is a parameter passed to the function.) This function is called by the `evtql_open_cursor` EVTQL library function (presented later) to open the DBMS cursor, because embedded SQL packages do not allow cursor declarations via dynamic statements, or declarations in which the cursor name is stored in a host language variable.

The following two functions, namely `evtql_fetch_CName` and `evtql_close_CName`, are generated for analogous reasons. `evtql_fetch_CName` contains the embedded SQL statement

```
EXEC SQL FETCH dbms_cursor INTO :descriptor;
```

where *descriptor* is a parameter of type *DBMS_descriptor*, which is passed to the function. Function `evtql_fetch_CName` is called by the `evtql_fetch` and `evtql_fetch_descriptor` EVTQL library functions, when data fetching through the VTQL cursor is required. The `evtql_close_CName` function contains the embedded SQL statement

```
EXEC SQL CLOSE dbms_cursor;
```

and is called by the `evtql_close_cursor` EVTQL library function.

The fourth function generated for each declared cursor is named `evtql_exec_CName`, and contains the embedded SQL statement

```
EXEC SQL EXECUTE IMMEDIATE :cursor_statement;
```

This function is called whenever deletions or updates must be performed through the RDBMS cursor and is used because some DBMSs (e.g. Ingres [12]) require that all operations through a cursor must be performed from within the file that the cursor has been declared. *cursor_statement* is a dynamically formulated SQL statement (by some function in the EVTQL library), which is passed as a parameter to the `evtql_exec_CName` function.

In order to maintain the association between the EVTQL cursor name and the elements constructed by the EVTQL preprocessor (the DBMS statement name, the DBMS cursor name and the four functions) during run-time, the EVTQL preprocessor must be invoked in a special mode. When the EVTQL preprocessor operates in this mode, it processes all embedded VTQL source files compiles in a separate file a *table of cursors*, which is a host language array of records, containing an entry for every declared cursor. Each entry contains the EVTQL cursor name, the DBMS cursor and statement names, plus pointers to the four preprocessor-generated functions. This file must be processed by the host language compiler to produce an object file, which should be linked into the temporal application executable file.

The OPEN statement.
The OPEN statement prepares a cursor so that it can be used for data fetching. It is translated by the EVTQL preprocessor to a call to the `evtql_open_cursor` EVTQL library function. The function accepts two arguments, the first one being the name of the cursor, whereas the second argument is a structure describing the

SELECT statement. If the SELECT statement includes references to host language variables, then appropriate assignment statements are inserted before the call to the EVTQL library function, so as to adjust the pointers to these variables.

The FETCH statement.
The EVTQL FETCH statement is translated by the preprocessor to a call to the evtql_fetch EVTQL library function. The function is supplied with two parameters, the first one being the cursor name, whereas the second parameter is an array of host language variable descriptors. Each descriptor contains the type and the size of each variable, and a slot for the pointer to the actual memory location of the variable. This slot is filled by assignment statements which are inserted by the preprocessor, before the call to the evtql_fetch EVTQL library function.

The DELETE statement (cursor form).
The cursor form of the EVTQL DELETE statement is translated by the EVTQL preprocessor to a call to the evtql_delete_cur library function. The function is supplied with three parameters, the first two being the cursor name and the name of the target table, respectively. The third parameter describes the *VT_selection*, and its structure is identical to the respective parameter used in the non-cursor form of the DELETE statement. If the *VT_selection* syntactic construct is specified and the right hand side expression of the assignment contains references to host language variables, then appropriate assignment statements are inserted before the call to the EVTQL library function, so as to adjust the pointers to these variables.

The UPDATE statement (cursor form).
The cursor form of the EVTQL UPDATE statement is translated by the EVTQL preprocessor to a call to the evtql_update_cur library function. Four parameters are passed to the library function, the first two being the name of the cursor, the name of the table to be updated, respectively. The third and fourth parameters describe the *VT_selection* syntactic construct and SET clause, respectively. If these clauses contain references to host variables, then appropriate assignment statements are emitted by the preprocessor, in order to adjust the pointers to the variables.

The CLOSE statement.
The CLOSE statement is translated by the preprocessor to a call to the VTQL library function evtql_close_cursor, which is provided with a single parameter, designating the name of the cursor to be closed.

Implementing the WHENEVER statements.
The WHENEVER statement may be used in an embedded VTQL program to simplify the database error handling process. The EVTQL preprocessor supports three flavours of the WHENEVER statement, which may be used to specify the action to be taken in the event of an error (VTQLERROR), a warning (VTQLWARNING) or when a select statement could not return any data (NOT FOUND). If a source file contains WHENEVER statements, then the VTQL preprocessor automatically inserts after the code implementing each translated statement appropriate host language statements which test the value of the *vtqlca.vtqlcode* variable and perform the designated action as needed. This procedure is illustrated in **Fig. 3.**.

```
/* EXEC VTQL WHENEVER VTSQLERROR GOTO error_handler; */
/* EXEC VTQL WHENEVER VTSQLWARNING CONTINUE; */
/* EXEC VTQL WHENEVER NOT FOUND PERFORM no_more_data_dialog; */

/* EXEC VTQL SELECT Name, Salary INTO :name, :salary FROM employee; */
evtql_select(...);
if (vtqlca.vtqlcode < 0) /* VTQLERROR */
        goto error_handler;
/* Since the "continue" action is specified for the VTQLWARNING
event, no tests are performed for this event class */
if (vtqlca.vtqlcode == VTQL_NO_MORE_DATA) /* NOT FOUND */
        no_more_data_dialog();
```

Fig. 3. - Implementation of the WHENEVER statements

3.2 The EVTQL Library

The EVTQL library is a collection of procedures which implement the embedded VTQL statements. In the following paragraphs, the algorithms employed by these procedures to perform the requested operations, are described. For brevity reasons, details of reporting the status of the operations' execution to the application are not discussed; this is always done by means of the *vtqlca.vtqlcode* status variable, which the procedures set to 0, for successful completion, or to a non-zero value, to indicate an error.

The SELECT statement ("singleton" form).
The singleton selection operation is performed via the `evtql_select` library procedure, which accepts two arguments, the first one describing the SELECT statement, whereas the second argument describes the variable list into which the values will be fetched. The `evtql_select` library procedure processes the request using the following algorithm:

1. If the SELECT statement is *snapshot-transformable* (see page 2), the `evtql_select` library procedure reconstructs the original select statement and prepares a *descriptor* (a DBMS-specific data structure) which is actually a list of variable descriptions (type, size and memory address). The prepared descriptor contains one entry for each variable that appears in the original INTO clause. The data pointer of each entry is set to the memory location of the host language variable, so that the data will be directly placed into the desired memory area, with no additional data copying. The reconstructed SELECT statement is executed and the variables are fetched into the host language variables using the following embedded SQL statement:

```
EXEC SQL PREPARE dbms_stmt FROM :stmt;
EXEC SQL DECLARE tmp_cursor CURSOR FOR dbms_stmt;
EXEC SQL OPEN tmp_cursor;
EXEC SQL FETCH tmp_cursor USING DESCRIPTOR :dl;
EXEC SQL EXECUTE IMMEDIATE :stmt USING DESCRIPTOR :dl;
```

   where the host variable *stmt* contains the reconstructed statement and *dl* is the prepared descriptor.
2. If the query is not snapshot-transformable, the EVTQL library uses the algorithms employed by the terminal monitor application to evaluate the query. Results, however, are not output to the screen, but stored in a temporary table *tmp_table*. Finally, the batch of embedded SQL statements described in case (1) is executed to fetch the data into a suitably prepared descriptor. In this case the host variable *stmt* contains the SQL statement

```
SELECT * FROM tmp_table;
```

   Finally, the intermediate table is dropped.

The INSERT statement and the non-cursor versions of the DELETE and UPDATE statements.
Data insertion is implemented through two functions in the EVTQL library, namely `evtql_insert_values` and `evtql_insert_query`, which are invoked when the data to be inserted are specified by means of the VALUES clause or an select subquery, respectively. Data deletion and update are handled by the `evtql_delete` and `evtql_update` EVTQL library functions. In all cases, the EVTQL library functions employ the algorithms used by the terminal monitor application to handle the user request.

The OPEN statement.
When a cursor is *opened* using the EXEC VTQL OPEN statement, the execution of the VTQL SELECT query which is associated with the statement is actually triggered. The `evtql_open_cursor` EVTQL library procedure distinguishes three cases for the processing of the request:

1. the SELECT statement is snapshot-transformable and results either to a non-updatable tuple set, or to an updatable tuple set, which is not derived from a valid time table. In this case, the original statement is reconstructed into a host language string variable, and the preprocessor-generated `evtql_open_CName` function is called. The reconstructed statement is used as an argument to this call. This invocation triggers the preparation of a statement and the opening of a cursor at the DBMS level.
   The procedure completes by modifying the relevant entry in the table of cursors. Flags are set to designate that the cursor is currently open, whether it points to an updatable tuple set or not and the current status of the cursor, which is initially set to NO_CURRENT (no tuple is current for the cursor). If the tuple set is

updatable, an additional flag is set within the entry, indicating that the tuple set is not derived from a table with valid time semantics.

2. the SELECT statement is snapshot-transformable and results to an updatable tuple set, which is derived from a table with valid time semantics. In this case, the EVTQL library constructs into a host language string variable an SQL query, which is identical to the original one but its SELECT-list is extended to include all columns which are part of the table's schema, but are not listed in the original select list. These extraneous columns are necessary for the implementation of the cursor forms of the DELETE and UPDATE statements, which are described later. The steps of opening the RDBMS cursor and registering the entry in the table of open cursors are identical to the ones described for case (1), except that the "result set updatability" and "valid time semantics" flags are set to TRUE. Additionally, memory for fetching the extra columns is allocated in the EVTQL library's private memory pool.
3. the SELECT statement is not snapshot-transformable. In this case, the `evtql_open_cursor` procedure applies the algorithms used in the terminal monitor application to evaluate the query, but stores the results in a temporary table tmp_table, rather than displaying them on the screen. The query

```
SELECT * FROM tmp_table
```

is stored into a host language string, and passed to the preprocessor-generated function `evtql_open_CName`, so as to open the DBMS-level cursor. Finally, the appropriate flags are set in the EVTQL library's table of cursors, as in case (1). However, in this case the "result set updatability" flag is set to FALSE (since the operations query involves at least one set operation that renders the query result not updatable), and the name of the temporary table is stored in the cursor's entry.

The FETCH statement.
When a FETCH command is processed, the `evtql_fetch` function locates into the table of cursors the entry for the cursor through which data fetching is requested and verifies that it is open. Afterwards, data are fetched through the DBMS-level cursor into the EVTQL library's memory calling the preprocessor-generated `evtql_fetch_CName` function. An appropriately prepared descriptor is passed as an argument to this function. The fetched data are subsequently copied into the variable list designated by the second parameter of the `evtql_fetch` function (note that extraneous columns that are fetched for updatable tuple sets that are derived from tables with valid time semantics are not copied). If no more data can be fetched (as indicated by the *sqlca.sqlcode* status variable), the status field of the cursor entry is set to *DATA_EXHAUSTED*, and the error is reported to the application through the *vtqlca.vtqlcode* status variable. If, however, data fetching is successful, the cursor status is set to *HAS_CURRENT* and control is returned to the application.

The DELETE statement (cursor form).
The `evtql_delete_cur` EVTQL library function initially examines if the cursor points to an updatable tuple set. If the result set is not updatable or the cursor status is found to be different than *HAS_CURRENT*, control is immediately returned to the application. If both tests succeed, then the second parameter is examined to determine if the *VT_selection* syntactic construct was used in the original statement, designating that only *part of the tuple* is to be removed. If this syntactic construct was not specified, the whole tuple is deleted by formulating into a host language string variable the embedded SQL statement

```
DELETE FROM table_name WHERE CURRENT OF dbms_cursor_name;
```

and passing it to the preprocessor-generated `evtql_execute_CName` function. If, however, the *VT_selection* syntactic construct was specified, it is verified that table *table_name* actually has valid time semantics (an error is raised if this is not the case) and one of the following actions is taken, depending on the relative position of the tuple's valid time (denoted as T_{vt}) and the value of the expression used in *VT_selection* (denoted as T_{del}):

1. if T_{del} *contains* T_{vt}, then the whole tuple is deleted from the table.
2. if the time points included in T_{vt} but not in T_{del} are consecutive, then the tuple's valid time is set to the difference T_{vt} - T_{del}, by building the statement

   ```
   UPDATE TableName SET valid_column = Tnew WHERE CURRENT OF dbms_cursor_name
   ```

   into a host language string variable and calling the function `evtql_execute_CName` (T_{new} is set to T_{vt} - T_{del}).
3. if the time points included in T_{vt} but not in T_{del} are not consecutive, requiring thus two periods for their representation (denoted as p_1 and p_2), then the tuple's valid time is set to p_1, as described in case (2) and a

new tuple is inserted in the target table. All columns of the new tuple are equal to the modified tuple's corresponding columns, except for the valid time, which is set to p_2.

4. if T_{vt} and T_{del} do not overlap, no action is taken.

In all cases, the status field of the cursor entry is set to *NO_CURRENT*, disallowing further deletions and/or updates, until the next tuple of the result set is fetched.

The UPDATE statement (cursor form).

Analogously to the `evtql_delete_cur` function, the `evtql_update_cur` EVTQL library function initially verifies that the cursor actually points to an updatable tuple set and that a current tuple exists, terminating prematurely if any of these conditions is not met. If both checks succeed, one of the following actions is taken, depending on whether the *VT_selection* syntactic construct was used in the original statement:

1. *VT_selection was not used.* In this case, the EVTQL library examines if the target table has valid time semantics or not, and takes one of the following actions:
   A. *the table does not have valid time semantics.* In this case, the current tuple is updated, as specified in the `SET` clause, by using the cursor form of the embedded SQL `UPDATE` statement (an appropriate `UPDATE` statement is formulated in a host language string and passed to the `evtql_execute_CName` function). Errors reported by the DBMS are trapped by the EVTQL library and reported back to the application.
   B. *the table has valid time semantics.* In this case, the current tuple is removed from the table, the new values of the columns designated in the `SET` clause are computed, and the updated version of the current tuple is constructed. If *value-equivalent tuples* ([13]) with overlapping valid timestamps are not allowed for the updated table, the table is scanned for tuples whose data columns are identical to the updated tuple's corresponding columns and whose valid time overlaps with the updated tuple's valid time. If such a tuple exists, the update violates this constraint, thus changes to the database state made by this statement are undone and control is returned to the application.
   If no such tuple is found, the update procedure continues normally. In the case that valid time tables are not stored in a coalesced form, the tuple may be flushed to the database immediately. If, however, valid time tables are not stored in a coalesced format, the updated tuple *can not* be inserted into the table at this point, since this insertion might have the effect of altering the values of a tuple in the result set which has not been fetched through the cursor yet. In other words, there may exist a tuple *res_tuple* in the result set that has not been yet processed and can be coalesced with the updated tuple (*upd_tuple).* Thus, inserting the tuple at this point will lead to replacing *res_tuple* with the result of *COALESCE*(*res_tuple*, *upd_part*), which is undesirable. Instead of inserting the updated tuple in the table at this point, it is stored in a *pending tuple list*, which is associated with the cursor. These tuples are inserted to the database (and possibly coalesced with other tuples) when the cursor is closed. However, the list is scanned when the violation of primary key uniqueness is checked, to ensure that an update does not clash with previous modification operations.

   In both cases, the update operation completes by setting the status flag of the cursor to *NO_CURRENT*, disallowing any further updates through this cursor until the next tuple is fetched.
2. *VT_selection was used.* In this case, it is verified that the updated table is a valid time table, and if it is not, control is immediately returned to the application with an appropriate error indication. Subsequently, the part of the tuple which is subject to update is removed from the database, following the procedure described for the cursor version of the `DELETE` statement (paragraph 0). The removed part of the tuple is modified as specified in the `SET` clause and, primary key uniqueness checks are conducted as needed (see case (B) above) and the updated tuple is either flushed to the database or inserted in the pending tuple list of the cursor, depending on whether a coalesced storage scheme is used for valid time tables. Finally, the status flag of the cursor is set to *NO_CURRENT*, disallowing further updates through this cursor until the next tuple is fetched.

The CLOSE statement.

Cursor closing is handled by the `evtql_close_cursor` EVTQL library function, which closes the DBMS-level cursor (by calling the `evtql_close_CName` function, which has been created by the preprocessor), destroys the temporary table created during the `SELECT` statement's evaluation (if any), frees memory that was used for storage of extraneous columns (for updatable results) and removes the corresponding entry from the EVTQL library's table of open cursors. If the list of pending tuples associated with the cursor is not empty, then the tuples in the pending list are inserted in the table, performing any necessary coalescing. Constraint violation checks (for value equivalent tuples with overlapping valid timestamps) need not be conducted at this point, since all tuples in the pending list have been checked when the corresponding UPDATE statement was processed.

4 Conclusions-Future Work

In this paper, we presented an embedded temporal language, and proposed an architecture for its implementation, on top of a relational DBMS. The software modules comprising the development environment were presented (the *preprocessor* and the *EVTQL library*), and the algorithms employed by the software modules were discussed. Future work will focus on the development of the EVTQL preprocessor and the EVTQL library for the TSQL2 language. Optimisation issues will be also studied, along with techniques for enhancing concurrency control within multi-user environments.

References

[1] A. V. Aho, R. Sethi and J. Ullman, "Compilers: Principles, Techniques and Tools", Addison-Wesley, 1985.

[2] G. Ariav, "Information Systems for Managerial Planning and Control: A Conceptual Examination of their Temporal Structure", Journal of MIS, vol. 8, 1992.

[3] M. Böhlen, "Temporal Database System Implementations", SIGMOD RECORD Vol. 24, No. 4, December 1995.

[4] M. Böhlen, "TimeDB Software", Department of Mathematics and Computer Science, Aalborg University, 1995.

[5] R. Chandra and A. Segev, "Using Next Generation Databases to Develop Financial Applications", Proceedings of the First International Conference on Application of Databases (ADB), Vadstena, Sweden, June 1994.

[6] J. Clifford, C. Jensen, R. Snodgrass, M. Böhlen, H. Dewand and D. Schmidt, "Panel: The State-of-the-Art in Temporal Database Management: Perspectives from the Research and Financial Application Communities", Proceedings of the VLDB International Workshop on Temporal Databases, Zurich 1995.

[7] C. Combi, F. Pinciroli, G. Musazzi and C. Ponti, "Managing and Displaying Different Time Granularities of Clinical Information", Eighteenth Annual Symposium on Computer Applications in Medical Care, Washington DC, U.S.A. 1994.

[8] C. Combi, F. Pinciroli, M. Cavallaro and G. Cucchi, "Querying Temporal Clinical Databases with Different Time Granularities: The GCH-OSQL Language", Nineteenth Annual Symposium on Computer Applications in Medical Care, New Orleans, U.S.A., 1995.

[9] C. J. Date and H. Darwen, "A Guide to the SQL Standard" (third edition), Reading, Massachusetts, Addison-Wesley, 1993.

[10] C. J. Date, "An Introduction to Database Systems" (sixth edition), Addison-Wesley Publishing Company Inc., 1995.

[11] R. Hunter, "Compilers: Their Design and Construction Using Pascal", Wiley and Sons, 1985.

[12] Ingres Corporation, "Ingres SQL and ESQL Reference Manual" (for release 6.4), 1991.

[13] C. S. Jensen, J.Clifford, R. Elmarsi et al. "A Consensus Glossary of Temporal Database Concepts", SIGMOD Record, 23(1), pp. 52-64, March 1994.

[14] Oracle Corporation., "SQL Language Reference Manual" (for release 7), 1993.

[15] Oracle Corporation, "ORACLE8 Time Series Cartridge User's Guide", November 1997.

[16] ORES Project (ESPRIT III P7224) Deliverable D4.2: "Application Manual", edited by 01 Pliroforiki, University of Athens, Agricultural University of Athens and Information Dynamics, 1993. Available at ftp://ftp.di.uoa.gr/pub/ores/rep/d4_2.ps.gz.

[17] D. Schmidt and R. Mari, "Time Series, a Neglected Issue in Temporal Database Research?", Proceedings of the VLDB International Workshop on Temporal Databases, Zurich 1995.

[18] Sybase Inc., "Transact SQL User's Guide" (for release 10), 1994.

[19] B. Theodoulidis, A. Ait-Braham and G. Karvelis, "The ORES Temporal DBMS and the ERT-SQL Query Language", Proceedings of the 5th International Conference on Database and Expert System Applications, Athens 1994.

[20] K. Torp, C. Jensen and M. Böhlen, "Layered Implementation of Temporal DBMSs-Concepts and Techniques", TimeCenter Technical Report TR-2, 1997 available from http://www.cs.auc.dk/general/DBS/tdb/TimeCenter/publications.html

[21] K. Torp, C. Jensen and R. T. Snodgrass, "Stratum Approaches to Temporal DBMS Implementations", TimeCenter Technical Report TR-5, 1997, available from http://www.cs.auc.dk/general/DBS/tdb/TimeCenter/publications.html

[22] The TSQL2 Language Design Committee, "The TSQL2 Temporal Query Language", Edited by R.T. Snodgrass, Kluwer Academic Publishers, 1995.

[23] C. Vassilakis, P. Georgiadis and A. Sotiropoulou, "A Comparative Study of Temporal DBMS Architectures", Proceedings of the 7th International DEXA Workshop, pp. 153-164, Zurich, 1996.

On the Correctness of a Transaction Model for Mobile Computing[1]

Sanjay Kumar Madria[2], Centre of Advanced Information Systems, School of Applied Science, Nanyang Technological University, Singapore. askumar@ntu.edu.sg.

Bharat Bhargava, Department of Computer Sciences, Purdue University, West Lafayette, IN, USA. bb@cs.purdue.edu.

Abstract. We discuss and prove the correctness of a transaction model for mobile computing. In our transaction model, we incorporate a prewrite operation (before a write) which does not update the state of a data object but makes visible the value that the data object will have after the commit of the transaction. Once a transaction read all the values and declares all the prewrite values, it pre-commits at mobile host. A pre-committed transaction's prewrite values are made visible both at mobile and stationary hosts before the final commit. Thus, increases data availability. A pre-committed transaction's remaining execution (i..e, writes on database) is delayed and shifted to the mobile service station to reduce the computing expenses at mobile host. We have analysed various cases of running transactions concurrently both at mobile and stationary hosts. We have proved that our algorithm produces only serializable schedules.

1 Introduction

In a mobile computing environment, the network consists of stationary and mobile hosts [5,17]. A mobile host (MH) changes its location and network connections while computations are being processed. While in motion, a mobile host retain its network connections through the support of stationary hosts with wireless connections. These stationary hosts are called mobile support stations (MSS). Each MSS is responsible for all the mobile hosts within a given small geographical area, known as a cell. At any given instant, a MH communicates only with the MSS responsible for its cell. When a MH leaves a cell serviced by a MSS, a hand-off protocol is used to transfer the responsibility of mobile transaction and data support to the MSS of the new cell.

Wide area and wireless computing [5,17] suggest that there will be more competition for shared data since it provide users with ability to access information and services through wireless connections. Further, mobile users will have to share their data with others. The task of ensuring consistency of shared data becomes more difficult in mobile computing because of limitations of wireless communication channels and restrictions imposed due to mobility and portability. A transaction in mobile environment is different than the transactions in the centralized or distributed databases in many ways [9]. To support mobile computing, the transaction processing models should accommodate the limitations of mobile computing [17]. Mobile computations should minimize aborts due to disconnection. Operations on shared data must ensure correctness of transactions executed on both stationary and mobile hosts.

---

[1] This research is partly supported by a grant from NSF under NCR-9405931.

[2] This work was performed during author's visit as Research Consultant to Department of Computer Sciences, Purdue University, USA in summer of 1997.

The blocking of a transaction's execution on either the stationary or mobile hosts must be minimized to reduce communication cost and to increase concurrency. Proper support for mobile transactions must provide for local autonomy to allow transactions to be processed and committed on the mobile host despite temporary disconnection.

Our objective in this paper is to discuss a transaction model to increase data availability both at mobile and stationary hosts. Our transaction model makes visible the value before it commits, but still ensures serializability and ACID properties [1]. We divide transaction in to parts and run the parts concurrently at MH and MSS. We have discussed the locking algorithm for our mobile transaction model. We have also proved that our mobile transaction model produces only serializable schedules.

2 Related Work

Semantic based transaction processing models [2,19] have been extended for mobile computing in [20] to increase concurrency by exploiting commutative operations. In [20], fragments of data objects have been used to facilitate semantic based transaction processing in mobile databases. In optimistic concurrency control based schemes [6], cached objects on mobile hosts can be updated without any co-ordination but the updates need to be propagated and validated at the database servers for the commitment of transactions. This scheme leads to aborts of mobile transactions unless the conflicts are rare. In pessimistic schemes, cached objects can be locked exclusively and mobile transactions can be committed locally. The pessimistic schemes lead to unnecessary transaction blocking since mobile hosts can not release any cached objects while it is disconnected. Dynamic object clustering has been proposed in mobile computing in [15,16] using weak-read, weak-write, strict-read and strict-write. Strict-read and strict-write have the same semantics as normal read and write operations invoked by transactions satisfying ACID properties. [7] presents a new transaction model using isolation-only transactions (IOT). IOTs do not provide failure atomicity and are similar to weak transactions of [15]. An open nested transaction model [8] has been proposed in [3] for modelling mobile transactions as a set of subtransactions. The model allows transactions to be executed on disconnection. It supports unilateral commitment of subtransactions and compensating transactions. However, not all the operations are compensated [3], and compensation is costly in mobile computing. A kangaroo transaction (KT) model was given in [4]. It incorporates the property that transactions in a mobile computing hop from a base station to another as the mobile unity moves. The mobility of the transaction model is captured by the use of split transaction [18]. Transaction models for mobile computing that perform updates at mobile computers have been developed in [3,15]. These efforts propose a new correctness criterion [3] that are weaker than the serializability [14]. They can cope more efficiently with the restrictions of mobile and wireless communications. In [10,11,12], we have presented transaction models using prewrites. A review of the existing transaction models for mobile computing appears in [9].

3. Our Mobile Transaction Model

Definition 1: A *prewrite* operation announces the value that the data object will have after the commit of the corresponding write operation.

Definition 2: A transaction is called *pre-committed* if it has announced all the prewrites values and read all the required data objects, but the transaction has not been finally committed.
Definition 3: A *pre-read* returns a prewrite value of the data object whereas a read returns the result of a write operation. A pre-read becomes a *weak-read* (in case the data objects involved are not simple) if it returns a prewrite value even though the transaction who announced the last prewrite has been finally committed. However, this weak-read should not to be aborted. This makes our weak-read different from the weak-read of [15].

Each prewrite operation at MH makes visible the value the transaction will eventually write on database at MSS. Once the required data objects are read or pre-read and prewrites are computed, the transaction pre-commits at MH. A transaction is required to read or pre-read all the required data objects before pre-commit because after a transaction releases a lock for a prewrite operation, it can not get a lock for read operation due to the condition of two phase locking [1]. After a pre-commit, the prewrites are made visible to other transactions both at MH and MSS for processing. The prewrites are handled at the transaction manager level whereas physical writes are handled at the data manager level.

The transactions's commit order in the serilaizable transactions's execution history is decided at the order of pre-commit action. A transaction is not allowed to abort after pre-commit. Thus, the prewrites provide non-strict execution without cascading aborts. In case the pre-committed transaction is forced to abort due to system dependent reasons such as system crash, the transaction can restart on system revival. To restart a failed pre-committed transaction from the last consistent state, prewrite and write logs can be saved on stable storage [13]. Our model relaxes the *isolation* property among ACID properties as the prewrites are made visible to others after pre-commit but before the transaction is finally committed at MSS. Also, durability of prewrites is guaranteed at the pre-commit point.

3.1 Prewrite Processing in Mobile Computing Environment

Here, we discuss how prewrites can be adopted in mobile applications to increase availability. We discuss the following two cases:
Case 1: MH has limited server capability to do concurrency control, logging, and to execute pre-commit.
In our mobile transaction model, a transaction begins its execution at mobile host. When a transaction arrives at MH, the transaction's read requests are processed at MH in case it has the consistent cached data objects. Otherwise, the MH sends request for some of the reads (for which the MH has no consistent cached data objects) to the MSS. When a read access transaction arrives at MSS, it analyses the transaction and returns the prewrite values in response. If a prewrite is not available, the write values are returned. The MSS identifies that the return value is a prewrite value. In case the transaction needs the final write, it has to initiate a read again. Once all the requested values are returned by MSS to MH, the transaction pre-commits at MH after declaring all the prewrite values for the data objects. A pre-committed transaction's execution is then shifted from mobile host to the stationary host for the completion of its remaining execution involving database updates. This moves the expensive part of the mobile

transaction execution to the static network. At the stationary host, the transaction actually updates all the data objects for which the prewrite values have been declared earlier and commits thereafter (see figure 1). Thus, the prewrite value of the data object is made visible by MSS to other mobile hosts in that cell before the data object is updated at the stationary host. This increases availability. Prewrites are stored in the transaction's private workspace at MH and once the transaction pre-commits, they are moved to the MSS.

Start____ Reads/Prewrites______ Pre-commit _______ Writes ______ Commit
Part of transaction executed at MH Part of transaction executed at MSS

Fig.1. Transaction Processing in Mobile Computing

Case 2: MH has very slow CPU and small memory, thus acts as an I/O device only.
In case the mobile host can not execute the transaction at MH (i.e., MH only acts as I/O), it can submit the transaction to the MSS. The MSS server returns all the required values and declares all the prewrite values corresponding to the write operations. After the transaction pre-commits, the prewrite values are send to the mobile host and at the same time, the rest of the transaction starts executing at the MSS.

4. Concurrent Operations and Locking

In our model, a pre-read operation can be executed at both MH and MSS at the same time. A pre-read can be executed at MH (MSS) while a write can take place at MSS (MH) concurrently. Similarly, a read can be executed concurrently with a prewrite. A prewrite operation can also be executed concurrently with another write operation since prewrites are managed at TM level whereas writes at DM level.

Case 1: A pre-read is currently being executed at MH and at the same time, another transaction which has announced the prewrite values finally commits at MSS.
See Figure 2(a), the pre-read will return a prewrite value that might be different than the last write value. For example, if the data object x is the simple data object, the read transaction T2 can commit as the prewrite and write values will be same. In case x is a design object, the system designate the read T2 as a weak-read since the final design may differ from the prewrite design model. The transaction T2 can resubmit its read request later to MSS if it needs the latest complete model of the design.

T1 ____ r(x), pw(x) ______ pc _____ w(x) ______ c At MSS
T2 _____ pr(x) ______ c At MH

Fig. 2(a). Situation in Case 1

Case 2: A read transaction commits at MH after the transaction (who announced the prewrite operation) has been pre-committed. Note that a read operation is compatible with a prewrite.
The read in this situation will return an old value. However, this is not a significant problem because the transaction can still be serialized (see section 5). For example, transaction T2 returns a write value, however it commits after T1 has pre-committed. The transaction T2 can be serialized before T1.

T1_____ r(x), pw(x) _____ pc ______ w(x) __________ c At MSS
T2 _____ r(x) ____________ c At MH

Fig. 2(b). Situation in Case 2

The concurrency control algorithm in our model is executed in two phases. In the first phase, the concurrency control for controlling prewrite and pre-read operations is performed at the transaction manager (DM) level at MSS. In the second phase, the concurrency control for controlling write and read operations (to access write values) is performed at the data manager (DM) level at MSS mainly since the data managers are accessed only while performing updates on the databases. Since prewrite values are made visible after pre-commit, the lock-type held by the prewrite operation is converted to the lock-type for write operation after pre-commit provided no conflicting locks are held by other transactions. The lock acquired for a prewrite operation is not released after pre-commit because the two phase locking [1] does not allow a transaction to acquire a lock after the transaction has released some locks.

We use read-lock for read, pre-read-lock for pre-read, prewrite-lock for prewrite, and write-lock for write operations, respectively. A prewrite-lock conflicts with other pre-read- and prewrite-locks, however, it does not conflict with read- and write-locks. A prewrite-lock can not be released after pre-commit as the transaction has to still get a write-lock for final updates. A prewrite-lock acquired by a pre-committed transaction is converted to a write-lock provided no other transaction holds the conflicting locks. Once a prewrite-lock is updated to a write-lock, the same transaction can not acquire any other lock (see section 5, case 1). However, pre-read-locks can be acquired by others to access prewrite values. The locking protocols are given in figure 3. The formal mobile transaction-processing algorithm is given in figure 4.

Pre-Read-Lock(X): Grant the requested pre-read-lock to a transaction T on X if no other transaction holds a prewrite-lock on X.
Read-Lock(X): Grant the requested read-lock to a transaction T on X if no other transaction holds a write-lock on X.
Prewrite-Lock(X): Grant the prewrite-lock to a transaction T on X if no other transaction holds a Prewrite- or pre-read-lock on X.
Write-Lock(X): update a prewrite-lock on X held by a transaction T to write-lock if

```
Begin
 If  the write-lock-wait queue for X is empty then
  Begin
   If the transaction T is pre-committed and no other transaction holds a read- or
   write-lock on X then
   convert prewrite-lock to write-lock;
 End;
    else
     Begin
     put the transaction T in a write-lock-wait queue for X;
     End;
End.
```

Fig. 3. The Locking Protocol

---

1. A transaction T is submitted to the mobile host.
2. Mobile host analyzes the transaction T to find out about its read, pre-read and write requests (we assume here that MH has some server capability).
   (/*pre-commit part of the transaction executed at MH*/)

3. If the transaction T has pre-read, read and write operations then
 Begin
  For all pre-read, reads and writes $\in$ T
  MH sends a request to MSS for all the required pre-read, read and prewrite locks;
  After MSS acquirs the necessary locks, it returns pre-read, read values to MH (Only for those pre-read and read values that are not available locally at MH, however in that case, locks need to acquire)
For all writes $\in$ T
  Begin
   Announce all the prewrite values at MH (without waiting for prewrite-locks);
   Store the prewrite logs at MH;
   Write pre-commit log record and destination move log record;
   Send prewrite values, prewrite logs and other log records to MSS;
   If MSS acquired all prewrite-locks for all the data objects for which prewrite values have been announced then
    Begin
    MSS accepts the prewrite values and logs;
    MSS update the prewrite-lock to write-lock provided no other transaction holds conflicting locks (see figure 3);
    End;
   else the prewrite values and corresponding logs are discarded at MH;
  End;
 End;
4. For each prewrite announced (/*post pre-commit algorithm executed at MSS*/)
  Begin
   Update those data objects in the database for which prewrites have been announced;
   Store necessary log records;
  End;

Fig. 4. Mobile Transaction Processing Algorithm

5 Serializable Schedules in Mobile Transaction Processing

In this section, we formalize our mobile transaction model and discuss some interesting cases of concurrent execution of two transactions at MH and MSS.

A read operation executed by a transaction T_i on a data object x is denoted as r_i(x), write as w_i(x), pre-read as pr_i(x) and prewrite as pw_i(x). The pre-commit is denoted as pc_i, commit as c_i and an abort as a_i. A serial history is one where for every pair of transactions T_i and T_j either all the operations executed by T_i precede all the operations executed by T_j or vice-versa. Two histories H and H′ are equivalent if they are defined over the same set of transactions and if p and q conflict and $p <_H q$ then $p <_{H'} q$. A history is conflict serializable [14] if it is equivalent to some serial history. To determine whether a history is conflict serializable, we analyze the graph derived from the history called serialization graph. The serialization graph of H, denoted by SG(H), is a directed graph whose nodes are transactions in T and has edges $T_i \rightarrow T_j$ if one of the T_ií s operations precede and conflict with one of the T_jí s operation. A history H is conflict serializable if and only if SG(H) is acyclic [1,14]. The transactions execution history will include lock and unlock operations. Each operation p_i (x) is preceded by a lock operation pl_i (x) and followed by an un-lock operation $pul_i(x)$. Also in the history, $pwl_i(x) \rightarrow wl_i(x)$ implies that a prewrite-lock obtained by transaction T_i on object x is converted to a write-lock.

Case 1: In this case we consider simple data objects and see that a history with a prewrite is same as the history without a prewrite.

Consider the following history H :

$$pwl_1(x)pw_1(x)rl_2(x)r_2(x)rul_2(x)c_2pc_1(pwl_1(x) \rightarrow wl_1(x))prl_3(x)pr_3(x)$$
$$prul_3(x)c_3w_1(x)wul_1(x)c_1$$

The serialization graph of the above history will have an edge $T_1 \rightarrow T_3$ due to conflicting operations $pw_1(x)$ and $pr_3(x)$ and an another edge $T_2 \rightarrow T_1$ due to conflicting operations $r_2(x)$ (denotes the reading of the initial write value of x) and $w_1(x)$. Therefore, the above history is conflict serializable in the order $T_2 \rightarrow T_1 \rightarrow T_3$. It is equal to a serial schedule $T_2\ T_1\ T_3$. However, the above history is not strict since T_3 reads the value from T_1 but commits before T_1. According to our algorithm, a transaction T_1 can not abort after its pre-commit operation is executed. In case of a failure after pre-commit, the transaction T_1 will restart from the failure point. Therefore, it will not introduce cascading aborts [1]. Hence, it is safe to allow non-strict executions in our algorithm. We observe that the above history has commutative operations $pw_1(x)$ and $r_2(x)$. That is, $pw_1(x)r_2(x)$ is same $r_2(x)pw_1(x)$. This is because a read returns the value from the write-buffer and therefore, a read before or after a prewrite will return the same value. We note that pre-read and write operations are also commutative in case the data objects involved are simple. In this case, a pre-read after a prewrite or a read after its associated final write will return the same value. However, after the write, a pre-read may not be same as read since a write value (final value) may differ from its prewrite value (working copy) in case of design objects. After taking into account these commutative operations, the above history will be equivalent to:

$$rl_2(x)r_2(x)rul_2(x)c_2pwl_1(x)pw_1(x)pc_1(pwl_1(x) \rightarrow wl_1(x))prl_3(x)pr_3(x)$$
$$prul_3(x)c_3w_1(x)wul_1(x)c_1$$

The above history provides a serial history $T_2\ T_1\ T_3$. If we remove the prewrite operations from the above history, it will be a serial history consisting of only read and write operations. Thus, we have shown that in the case of simple data objects, any history with prewrites will be equivalent to a history without prewrites. That is, any system which permits pre-read, read, prewrite and write is same as the system with read and write operations in the sense that reads in both the systems will return the same value. However, the system with prewrites permits more concurrency than the system with normal read and writes.

Consider another history H' :

$$pwl_1(x)pw_1(x)rl_2(x)r_2(x)rul_2(x)c_2pc_1(pwl_1(x) \rightarrow wl_1(x))pwl_3(x)$$
$$pw_3(x)pc_3w_1(x)wul_1(x)c_1(pwl_3(x) \rightarrow wl_3(x))w_3(x)wul_3(x)c_3$$

The serialization graph of the above history has an edge $T_1 \rightarrow T_3$ due to conflicting prewrite and write operations. The graph also has an edge $T_2 \rightarrow T_1$ due to coflicting read and write operations. Therefore, the above history is conflict serializable in the order $T_2 \rightarrow T_1 \rightarrow T_3$. Observe that the ordering $T_1 \rightarrow T_3$ for two prewrites and writes are same. This is required so that the prewrites and writes of two different transactions are performed in the same relative order. Also, the transaction T_3 sets the prewrite-lock after T_1 has converted its prewrite-lock to write-lock. Since two write-locks conflict, and also T_1 completes its prewrite before T_3's prewrite, therefore, T_3 has to wait until T_1 completes its final write.

Case 2: In this case we see that once a transaction's prewrite-lock is updated to the write-lock, it can not acquire any other lock.

Consider the following history :

$$pwl_1(x)pw_1(x)pc_1(pwl_1(x) \rightarrow wl_1(x))prl_2(x)pr_2(x)pwl_2(y)pw_2(y)pc_2$$
$$(pwl_2(y) \rightarrow wl_2(y))w_2(y)prul_2(x)wul_2(x)c_2w_1(x)rl_1(y)r_1(y)rul_1(y)wul_1(x)c_1$$

The above history is not conflict serializable though it satisfies our locking protocols and two phase locking. The schedule has a cycle since T_1 preceds T_2 on x and T_2 precedes T_1 on y. As stated in figure 3, additional restrictions must be introduced to disallow such an execution. Therefore, if a transaction's prewrite-lock is updated to a write-lock then the transaction can not acquire any other lock on any data object.

When this rule is introduced in the above history, T_1 can not acquire the lock on the data object y, therefore, there will not be a cycle.

Case 3: In this case, we see that a prewrite-lock can not be updated to a write-lock if some other transaction is holding a conflicting lock.

Consider a partial history:

$$rl_1(x)r_1(x)pwl_1(x)pw_1(x)rl_2(x)r_2(x)pc_1(pwl_1(x) \rightarrow wl_1(x))$$

The above history is not allowed as T_2 holds a read-lock on x and conflicts with the write-lock acquired by T_1 after pre-commit. Thus, the prewrite-lock is updated to write-lock only if there is no conflicting lock (see write-lock rules in Figure 3).

Consider another partial history:

$$pwl_1(x)pw_1(x)pc_1(pwl_1(x) \rightarrow wl_1(x))plw_2(x)pw_2(x)w_1(x)pc_2$$
$$(pwl_2(x) \rightarrow w_2(x))$$

The above history is not allowed as T_1 and T_2 now hold conflicting locks. However, if $wul_1(x)$ appears before pc_2 then the history is allowed.

Case 4: In this case, we see that a transaction which returns an old value can be serialized in the history.
Consider another history:

$$rl_1(x)r_1(x)pwl_1(x)pw_1(x)rl_2(x)r_2(x)pc_1rul_2(x)c_2(pwl_1(x) \rightarrow wl_1(x))$$

The above history is allowed. T returns an old-value since T_1 has pre-committed before T_2 commits. However, this history can be serialized if we move T_2 operations before T_1.

5.1 Proof of Correctness

In this section, we present the outlines of the proof of the correctness of our algorithm and the locking protocols. We prove that the schedule produced by our locking protocols is conflict serializable [14].
Property 1: If o is an operation then ol(x) < o(x) < ou(x).
From two phase locking rule, we have the following property :
Property 2: If p_i (x) and q_i (y) are two operations under T_i then pl_i (x) < qul_i (y), i.e., for all lock operations $l_i \in T_i$ and un-lock operations $ul_i \in T_i$, $l_i < ul_i$.
From the lock-upgrading rule, we have the following property :
Property 3: If $(pwl_i(x) \rightarrow wl_i(x)) \in T_i$ then
(1) for any operation $ol_i \in T_i$, $ol_i(x) <_i (pwl_i(x) \rightarrow wl_i(x))$. That is, once a prewrite-lock is converted to a write -lock, no other operation can lock any data object.
(2) for any operation $pul_i \in T_i$, $(pwl_i(x) \rightarrow wl_i(x)) <$ $pul_i(x)$. That is, a prewrite-lock is converted to a write-lock before any lock is released.
Property 4: If $p_i(x)$ and $q_j(x)$ are two conflicting operations then either

1. $pul_i(x) <_H ql_j(x)$. If $p_i(x)$ is a prewrite operation then $(pwl_i(x) \rightarrow wl_i(x)) <_H ql_j(x)$. If $p_i(x)$ is read operation then $pul_i(x) <_H (pwl_j(x) \rightarrow wl_j(x))$. Or
2. $qul_j(x) <_H pl_i(x)$. If $q_j(x)$ is a prewrite operation then $(pwl_j(x) \rightarrow wl_j(x)) <_H pl_i(x)$. If $q_j(x)$ is a read then $qul_j(x) <_H (pwl_i(x) \rightarrow wl_i(x))$.

Property 5: If pc_i and c_i are pre-commit and commit then $pc_i <_i c_i$ in T_i and for any pc_j, if $pc_i <$ pc_j then $c_i < c_j$. However, if the transaction T_j is a read-only transaction and $pc_i < pr_j$ then $c_i < c_j$ or $c_j < c_i$.
Property 6: If pc_i $\in T_i$ then no $a_i \in T_i$.
Property 7: If $pw_i(x)$, $w_i(x) \in T_i$ and $pw_j(x), w_j(x) \in T_j$ and if $T_i \rightarrow T_j$ then
(1) if $pwl_i(x) < pwl_j(x)$ then $wl_i(x) < wl_j(x)$.

(2) If $wl_i(x) < pwl_j(x)$ then $pwl_j(x) < w_i(x) < wl_j(x)$ or $wl_i(x) < pw_j(x) < w_j(x)$.

we now prove that any history that satisfies the above properties has an acyclic serialization graph. for a history H, SG(H) has a node for each transaction and an edge $T_i \to T_j$ if T_i has an operation p_i that conflicts with an operation $q_j \in T_j$.

Lemma 1: If $T_1 \to T_2$ in SG(H) then there exists an unlock operation $pul_1 \in T_1$ or a lock convert operation $(pwl_1 \to wl_1) \in T_1$ such that for all lock operations $ql_2 \in T_2$ or a lock convert operation $(pwl_2 \to wl_2) \in T_2$, $pul_1(x) < ql_2(x)$ or $(pwl_1(x) \to wl_1(x)) < ql_2(x)$ or $pul_1(x) < (pwl_2(x) \to wl_2(x))$.

Lemma 2: Let $T_1 \to T_2 \to \ldots \to T_n$ be a path in SG(H) where n>1. Then for data objects x and y and some operations $p_1(x)$ and $q_n(y)$ in H, $pu_1(x) < ql_n(y)$ or $(pwl_1(x) \to wl_1(x)) < ql_n(y)$ or $pul_1(x) < (pwl_n(y) \to wl_n(y))$.

Theorem: Every history H obtained by the locking protocols given before is serializable.

6. Conclusion

We have presented a mobile transaction model using prewrites and its proof of correctness. Prewrites help in increasing availability as transactions can be executed concurrently during disconnections both at MH and MSS without blocking. The model allows a transaction's execution to shift from the MH to MSS for database updates. Thus, reduces the computing expenses. We have discussed some cases of concurrently running transactions at MH and MSS. We have designed a locking protocol for our transaction model. We have proved that our transaction model produces only serializable schedules.

References

[1] Bernstein P., Hadzilacos, V., and Goodman, N., Concurrency Control and Recovery in Database Systems, Addison-wesley Publishing Co.,1987.

[2] Barghouti, N., and Kaiser G., Concurrency Control in Advanced Database Applications, ACM Computing Surveys, 23(3):269-317,1991.

[3] Chrysanthis, P.K., Transaction Processing in a Mobile Computing Environment, Proceedings of IEEE workshop on Advances in Parallel and Distributed Systems, pp.77-82, Oct.1993.

[4] Eich, M. H. and Helal, A., A Mobile Transaction Model That Captures Both Data and Movement Behaviour, ACM/Baltzer Journal on Special Topics on Mobile Networks and Applications,1997.

[5] Imielinksi T. and Badrinath B. R., Wireless Mobile Computing:Challenges in Data Management, Communications of ACM, 37(10), October 1994.

[6] Kisler J. and M. Satyanarayanan, Disconnected Operation in the Coda File System, ACM Transactions on Computer Systems, 10(1), 1992.

[7] Lu Q. and Satyanaraynan, M., Improving Data Consistency in Mobile Computing Using Isolation-Only Transactions, in proceedings of the fifth workshop on Hot Topics in Operating Systems, Orcas Island, Washington, May 1995.

[8] Madria, S. K., A Study of Concurrency Control and Recovery Algorithms in Nested Transaction Environment, The Computer Journal, Vol. 40, No. 10, 1997.

[9] Madria, S. K., Transaction Models for Mobile Computing, in proceedings of 6th IEEE Singapore International Conference on Network, World Scientific, Singapore, July, 1998.

[10] Madria S. K., A Prewrite Transaction Model, in the proceedings of 3rd International Baltic Workshop on Database and Information Systems, Riga, Latvia, April, 1998.

[11] Madria, S. K. and Bhargava, B., System Defined Prewrites to Increase Concurrency in Databases, accepted for First East-Europian Symposium on Advances in Databases and Information Systems (in co-operation with ACM-SIGMOD), St.-Petersburg (Russia), Sept.97.

[12] Madria, S. K. and Bhargava, B., A Transaction Model for Mobile Computing, in proceedings 2nd IEEE International Database and Engineering Application Symposium (IDEAS'98), Cardiff, U.K., 1998.

[13] Madria, S. K., Maheshwari, S.N, Chandra, B., Bhargava, B., Crash Recovery Algorithm in an Open and Safe Nested Transaction Model, 8th International Conference on Database and Expert System Applications (DEXA'97), France, Sept.97. Lecture Notes in Computer Science, Vol. 1308.

[14] Papadimitriou, C. H., The Serializability of Concurrent Database Updates, J. ACM, 26:4, pp.631-653, 1979.

[15] Pitoura E. and B. Bhargava, Building Information Systems for Mobile Environments, Proceedings of 3rd International Conference on Information and Knowledge Management, pp.371-378, 1994.

[16] Pitoura E. and B. Bhargava, Maintaining Consistency of Data in Mobile Computing Environments, in proceedings of 15th International Conference on Distributed Computing Systems, June,1995.

[17] Pitoura E. and B. Bhargava, Dealing with Mobility: Issues and Research Challenges, Technical Report TR-93-070, Department of Computer Sciences, Purdue University, 1993.

[18] Pu C., Kaiser G., and Hutchinson, Split-transactions for Open-ended Activities, in proceedings of the 14th VLDB Conference, 1988.

[19] Ramamritham K. and Chrysanthis. P. K., A Taxonomy of Correctness Criterion in Database Applications, Journal of Very Large Databases, 4(1), Jan.1996.

[20] Walborn, G. D., Chrysanthis, P. K., Supporting Semantics-Based Transaction Processing in Mobile Database Applications, in proceedings of 14th IEEE Symposium on Reliable Distributed Systems, pp.31-40, Sept.1995.

A Single-Phase Non-blocking Atomic Commitment Protocol[1]

Maha Abdallah, Philippe Pucheral

University of Versailles, PRiSM Laboratory
45, avenue des Etats-Unis
78035 Versailles - France
{Maha.Abdallah, Philippe.Pucheral}@prism.uvsq.fr

Abstract. Transactional standards have been promoted by OMG and X/Open to allow heterogeneous resources to participate in an Atomic Commitment Protocol (ACP), namely the two-phase commit protocol (2PC). Although widely accepted, 2PC is a blocking protocol and it introduces a substantial time delay (two phases to commit). Several optimized protocols and non-blocking protocols have been proposed. Optimized protocols generally violate site autonomy while non-blocking protocols are inherently more costly in time and increase communication overhead. This paper proposes a new ACP that provides the non-blocking property while (1) having a lower latency than other ACPs (one phase to commit), and (2) preserving site autonomy, which makes it compatible with existing DBMSs. This protocol relies on the assumption that all participants are ruled by a rigorous concurrency control protocol. Performance analysis shows that our protocol is more efficient in terms of time delay and message complexity than other ACPs.

1 Introduction

Recently, much emphasis has been laid on the development of distributed systems integrating several data sources. Standards like DTP from X/Open [6] and OTS from OMG [8] define transactional interfaces that allow distributed data sources to participate in a two-phase commit (2PC) protocol [7], generally coordinated by TP-Monitors. 2PC is used to preserve the atomicity of distributed transactions even in the presence of failures. Although 2PC is the most widely used A*tomic Commit Protocol* (ACP), it has two major drawbacks. First, it is *blocking:* if the coordinator crashes between the *vote* phase and the *decision* phase, a transaction can hold system resources for an unbounded period. Second, it incurs three sequences of message rounds (request for vote, vote and decision) that introduce a substantial delay in the system even in the absence of failures. This makes 2PC not adequate to today's highly reliable distributed platforms.

---

[1] This work has been partially funded by the CEC under the OpenDREAMS Esprit project n°20843.

Several solutions have been proposed to eliminate the voting phase of the 2PC. The *early prepare* protocol [9] forces each participant to enter in a *prepare* state after the execution of each operation. A participant is thus ready to commit a transaction at any time thereby making its vote implicit. The main drawback comes from the fact that each operation has to be registered in the participant's log on disk, thus introducing a blocking I/O. The *coordinator log* protocol [9] exploits the *early prepare* idea and avoids the blocking I/O on the participants by centralizing the participant's log on the coordinator. However, this violates site autonomy by forcing participants to externalize their log records. More recently, the IYV (*implicit yes-vote*) protocol [1] has been proposed to exploit the performance and reliability properties of future gigabit-networked database systems. IYV capitalizes on the *early prepare* and *coordinator log* protocols. The underlying assumption in IYV is that all sites employ a rigorous concurrency control protocol [4]. Participants in a transaction pass in the acknowledgment messages their redo log files and read locks to the coordinator. Thus the coordinator can forward recover a transaction on failed participants. Although well adapted to gigabit-networked DBMSs, this protocol (i) does not preserve site autonomy by forcing participants to externalize logging and locking information, (ii) puts strong hypothesis on the network bandwidth and (iii) increases the probability of blocking since a coordinator crash that occurs at any time during the transaction processing will block the participants until the coordinator's recovery.

A number of non-blocking commit protocols have been proposed in the literature. The simplest is the *three phase commit protocol* (3PC) [10]. 3PC is non blocking at the expense of two extra message rounds needed to terminate a transaction even in the absence of failures. This high latency makes 3PC not adapted to today's systems with long mean time between failures. To avoid this problem, a new protocol, noted ACP-UTRB, was proposed [5]. ACP-UTRB shares the basic structure of 2PC (two phases to commit) and achieves non-blocking in synchronous systems by exploiting the properties of the underlying communication primitive it uses to broadcast decision messages.

In this paper, we propose a new atomic commitment protocol, noted NB-SPAC (Non-Blocking Single-Phase Atomic Commit). NB-SPAC has a *low latency* (one phase to commit), is *non-blocking* and preserves *site autonomy*. During normal execution as well as in case of one or more site failures, a transaction is committed in a single phase under the assumption that participating DBMSs are ruled by a rigorous concurrency control protocol [4]. This assumption is exploited to eliminate the voting phase of 2PC and to guarantee that our recovery mechanism preserves serializability. Non blocking is achieved by using a reliable broadcast primitive to deliver the decision messages [5]. Finally, NB-SPAC preserves site autonomy by exploiting techniques introduced in multidatabase systems to recover from failures [3].

This paper is organized as follows. Section 2 introduces the distributed transaction model we consider. Section 3 presents SPAC, our single phase atomic commitment protocol. Section 4 details NB-SPAC, the non-blocking version of SPAC. The two protocols share the same structure but differ in the way communications between the sites are handled. Section 5 introduces the recovery protocol, common to SPAC and NB-SPAC, needed to recover after site failures. In section 6, we compare the performance of NB-SPAC with other well known ACP protocols. Finally, section 7 summarizes the main contributions of this work.

2 Distributed Transaction Model

We consider distributed database systems built from pre-existing and independent local DBMSs located at different sites. Distributed transactions are allowed to access objects residing at these DBMSs under the control of a Global Transaction Manager (GTM). Each distributed transaction is decomposed by the GTM into one branch per accessed site. There is no restriction on parallel or sequential processing by the GTM of the operations belonging to the same transaction or to different distributed transactions. However, we consider that each operation is acknowledged by the local DBMS executing it. Each operation is sent to and executed by a single DBMS.

An important objective of the considered distributed transaction model is the preservation of *site autonomy*. This means that : (i) participating DBMSs do not have to be aware of the distribution, (ii) local DBMS information (e.g., log records or lock tables) is not externalized and cannot be exploited by the GTM. Site autonomy is a preliminary condition to the integration of existing systems [3]. Each participating DBMS is assumed to guarantee, by means of a local transaction manager (LTM), serializability and fault tolerance of all transactions (i.e., GTM's transaction branches) submitted to it. The GTM is responsible for the global serializability and the global atomicity of distributed transactions. A local GTM agent, noted GTMAgent, can be used to ease the integration of each local DBMS. This doesn't violate site autonomy as far as the existing interface of each local DBMS is preserved. To simplify notations, we consider a single DBMS per site (i.e., site S_k is synonym of $DBMS_k$) and a single GTM in the architecture. A typical example of a GTM is a TP-monitor. Clearly, several instances of GTMs can co-exist in the same architecture and may share the same GTMAgents. Note that the presence of several GTMs does not impact the algorithms. The distributed transaction model we consider is presented in Fig. 1.

We summarize below notations that will be used all along the paper :

• $op1_i$, $op2_i$, ..., opn_i is the sequence of operations performed by transaction T_i.

• ack(op) refers to the acknowledgment of a given operation op.

• T_{ik} refers to the branch of transaction T_i executed on site S_k.

• $commit_i$ (resp., $abort_i$) refers to the commit (resp., abort) of the transaction T_i.

• $commit_{ik}$ (resp., $abort_{ik}$) refers to the commit (resp., abort) of T_{ik}.

• $send_k(m)$ and $receive_k(m)$ respectively refer to the sending to site S_k and the receipt from site S_k of a given message m.

• $T_i \xrightarrow{RW} T_j$ represents a dependency between T_i and T_j due to a Read/Write conflict, that is T_j performed a write operation on a given object O which conflicts with a preceding T_i read operation on O. Similar notations are used to express Write/Write (WW) and Write/Read (WR) conflicts. $T_i \rightarrow T_j$ represents any dependency between T_i and T_j.

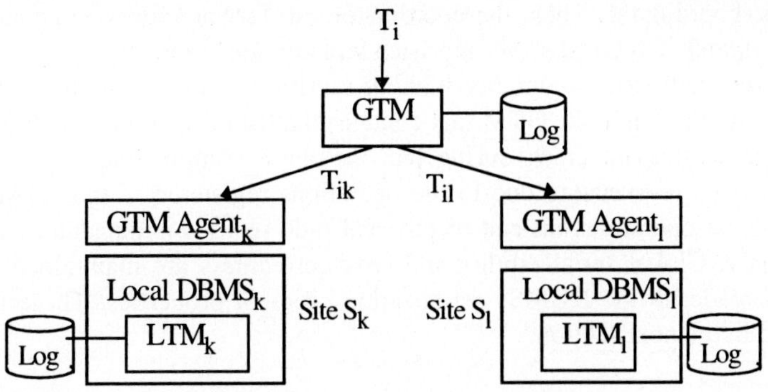

Fig. 1. Distributed transaction model

3 The Single-Phase Atomic Commit Protocol

3.1 Informal Description

The objective of this section is to introduce a Single-Phase Atomic Commitment protocol, noted SPAC, that preserves site autonomy (i.e., that can be used with existing DBMSs). For the rest of the paper, the words GTM (resp., GTM agents) and coordinator (resp., participants) will be used interchangeably to designate the coordinator (resp., participants) of the atomic commitment protocol.

The basic idea on which SPAC relies is eliminating the voting phase of 2PC by exploiting the properties of the local DBMSs serialization protocols. Let us assume that all participating DBMSs serialize their transactions using a pessimistic concurrency control protocol and that this protocol avoids cascading aborts (e.g., strict 2-Phase Locking protocol [4]). In this context, a transaction that executes successfully all its operations can no longer be aborted due to a serialization problem. Thus, this transaction is guaranteed to be committed in a failure free environment. When the acknowledgments of all operations of a transaction T_i are received, this means that all the transaction branches T_{ik} have been successfully executed till completion. At this point, the application submits its commit demand to the GTM which can directly ask each site accessed by the transaction T_i to commit, with no synchronization between the sites. If a transaction branch, say T_{ik} is aborted by S_k during its execution for any problem (e.g., integrity constraint violation or non serializability), the GTM simply asks each accessed site to abort that transaction.

While the SPAC and the IYV protocols [1] share the same assumption concerning the serialization policies of the local DBMSs, they strongly differ in the way failures are handled. Assume that site S_k crashes during the one-phase commit of transaction T_i. Meanwhile, T_i may have been committed at other sites. To guarantee T_i atomicity, the effects of the transaction branch T_{ik} have to be forward recovered on S_k. In the IYV protocol, participants in a transaction pass their redo log files and read locks to the coordinator. Thus, the coordinator can forward recover a transaction on failed participants. Obviously, this approach violates site autonomy.

To enforce transaction atomicity without sacrificing site autonomy, SPAC maintains a logical redo log at the GTM that contains the list of operations sent to each site. In case of a participant crash during the one-phase commit, the failed transaction branches will be re-executed due to the operations registered in the GTM redo log. Logging logical operations instead of physical redo records is mandatory to preserve site autonomy. Global serializability and redo correctness are maintained due to the hypotheses made on the DBMSs serialization protocol properties. These hypotheses are detailed in the next section.

3.2 Hypotheses on Participating DBMSs

In order for our protocol to work properly, the participating DBMSs must satisfy the two following properties:

P1: If all operations of T_{ik} have been acknowledged by S_k, then T_{ik} is serializable on S_k

P2: Local transactions are strongly isolated

Assuming all sites satisfy property *P1* guarantees that if the GTM receives the acknowledgment of all operations of transaction T_i, T_i is serializable on all sites. Property *P2* means that local schedules are cascadeless. Moreover, *P2* is necessary in order to handle failures properly (see Section 5). If both *P1* and *P2* are satisfied and if the commit decision is submitted after having received the acknowledgment of all operations, the assertion *A1* given below is true. It follows that a single-phase commit protocol is sufficient to guarantee the atomicity of distributed transactions in a failure free environment.

A1: [$\forall$k, $send_k(commit_i)$] by the GTM => T_{ik} will be committed if S_k doesn't crash

In [2], we showed that only rigorous DBMSs (i.e., DBMSs ruled by a rigorous concurrency control protocol) satisfy *P1* and *P2*. This restriction is not so strong since almost all today's DBMSs (either relational or object oriented) are ruled by strict 2PL which is a rigorous serialization protocol. However, commercial relational DBMSs are likely to use levels of isolation standardized by SQL2 [11]. These DBMSs do not satisfy properties *P1* and *P2* since they accept some non serializable schedules. In [2], we showed that NB-SPAC can be extended to deal with DBMSs providing levels of isolation.

3.3 Protocol Description

The standard scenario induced by the SPAC protocol is depicted in Fig. 2. To simplify the figure, we show the actions executed by a single GTM and a single site, assuming that all GTMs and sites follow the same scenario.

Step 1 represents the sequence of operations executed on behalf of T_{ik}. The coordinator registers in its log each operation that is to be executed. Note that this registration is done by a non-forced write. Non-forced writes are buffered in main memory and do not generate blocking I/O. Operations are then sent to and locally executed by $DBMS_k$. Every operation is acknowledged up to the application.

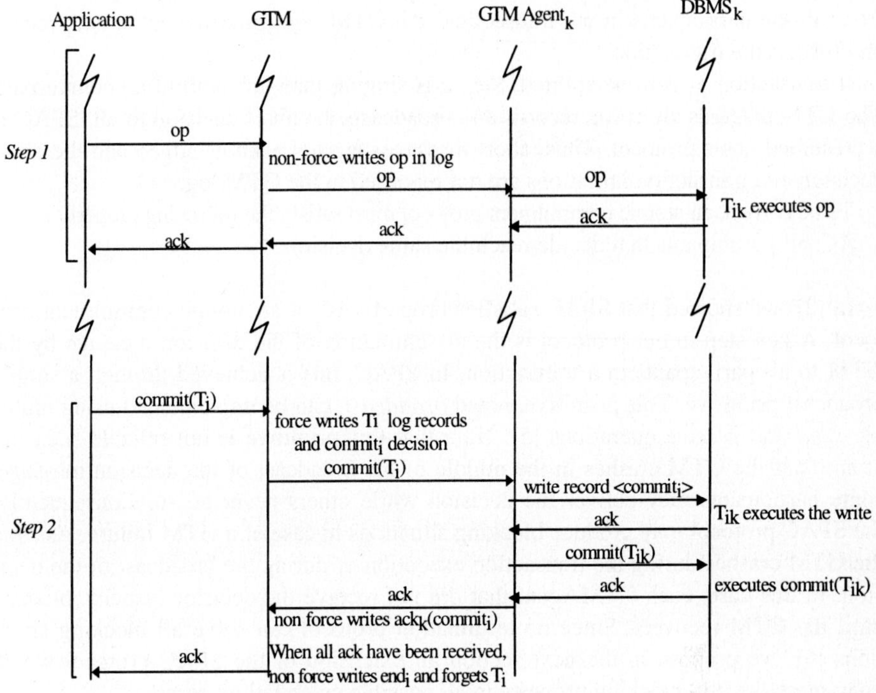

Fig. 2. Basic SPAC protocol scenario

Step 2 concerns the atomic commitment of T_i. If the application issues a commit request to the GTM, this means that all operations of T_i have been successfully executed (consequently T_i is serializable at all sites). The GTM can thus take the commit decision. First, the GTM force writes all T_i log records along with its commit decision on stable storage in the same step. Assuming that the GTM log is a sequential file, this step will generate a single blocking I/O, the size of which depends on the activity of T_i. Second, the GTM asks its agents to commit T_i by broadcasting the commit decision to all.

In order to be able to know whether or not a failed DBMS has effectively committed a transaction and without violating the DBMS autonomy, each agent creates in the local database a special record containing the commit decision for T_i. This record is created by means of an ordinary write operation inside T_i.[2] This operation will be treated by the DBMS in exactly the same manner as the other operations belonging to T_i, that is either all committed or all aborted atomically. Once the write operation of the commit decision record has been acknowledged by the DBMS, the GTM agent

[2] Note that this operation cannot generate a dependency cycle since it is the last operation executed in any transaction that has to be committed.

asks the local DBMS to commit T_i. In a failure free environment, this commit always succeeds and is acknowledged up to the GTM. For every transaction T_i, the GTM non-force writes each $ack_k(commit_i)$ in its log. When the acknowledgment is received from all the participants in the transaction, the GTM non-force writes an end_i record and forgets the transaction.

If transaction T_i is to be aborted, Step 2 is simpler than its committing counterpart. The GTM discards all T_i log records and broadcasts the abort decision to all. SPAC is a presumed abort protocol. Thus, abort messages are not acknowledged and the abort decision and transaction initiations are not recorded in the GTM log.

To be correct, an atomic commitment protocol must satisfy the following property :

AC: all participants that decide reach the same decision.

In [2], we showed that SPAC satisfies property *AC* of an atomic commitment protocol. A key step in our protocol is the dissemination of the decision message by the GTM to all participants in a transaction. In SPAC, this is achieved through a simple broadcast primitive. This primitive, noted *broadcast*, can be implemented using multiple *send* and *receive* operations [5]. Note that this primitive is not reliable (i.e., not atomic): if the GTM crashes in the middle of the broadcast of the decision message, some participants may deliver the decision while others never do so. Consequently, the SPAC protocol may produce blocking situations in case of a GTM failure. Assume the GTM crashes during the transaction execution or during the broadcast of the decision. In this case, each GTMAgent that did not receive the decision remains blocked until the GTM recovers. Since no termination protocol can solve all blocking situations [5], we propose in the next section an extension of the SPAC protocol which guarantees the non-blocking property in all possible crash failure cases.

4 Achieving Non-blocking

4.1 System Model

In the previous section, we made no assumptions whatsoever concerning message transfer delays or communication failures since the SPAC protocol can be used in systems that are subject to site failures, communication failures as well as unknown time delays to transport messages. In order to achieve non-blocking, we follow the model and terminology used in [5] and assume, for the rest of the paper, a synchronous system composed of a set of DBMSs completely connected through a set of communication channels.[3] Since it is well known that distributed systems with unreliable communication do not admit non-blocking solutions to the atomic commitment problem [7], we also assume a reliable communication between the sites. A synchronous system means that there is a known upper bound on communication delays, that is each message is received within δ time units after being sent. In such a model, site failures can be reliably detected by any *reliable failure detector* and reported to any

[3] An adaptation of our non-blocking protocol to asynchronous systems is currently being studied.

operational site. Reliable failure detectors can be easily implemented by means of time-out. At any given time, a site may be *operational* or *down*. Operational sites may go down due to crash failures. A site that is down may become operational again by executing a recovery protocol. Finally, we say that a site is *correct* if it has never crashed ; otherwise it is *faulty*.[4]

4.2 The Non-blocking Single-Phase ACP Algorithm

SPAC has failure scenarios for which no termination protocol can lead to a decision. This is due to the unreliability of the broadcast primitive used in SPAC, which allows faulty GTMAgents to deliver a message that is never delivered by correct ones. To solve this problem, we need a broadcast primitive, called Reliable Broadcast [5], which guarantees the following properties :

Uniform Agreement : if any GTMAgent, correct or not, delivers a message *m*, then all correct GTMAgents will eventually deliver *m*.

Δ-Timeliness : There exists a known constant Δ such that if the broadcast of a message *m* is initiated at time t, then no participant receives *m* after time t+Δ.

This primitive, noted *R_broadcast*, can be implemented as follows [5]. Every participant (GTMAgent) relays the message it receives for the first time to all the others before delivering it to the local DBMS. It is obvious that this implementation satisfies the Uniform Agreement property. To prove that it satisfies the Δ-Timeliness property, [5] showed that there exists a constant delay $\Delta = (F+1)\delta$, where F denotes the maximum number of sites that may crash during the execution of the atomic commitment protocol, by which the delivery of *m* must occur.

The blocking SPAC can be made non-blocking by replacing the unreliable broadcast primitive used by the GTM to disseminate its decision message with the reliable primitive *R_broadcast*. Fig. 4 illustrates the algorithm implementing the Non-Blocking Single-Phase Atomic Commit protocol, noted NB-SPAC.

GTM algorithm

```
do forever
    wait for (receipt of a message m from the application)
        case(m) of:
            op1_i():      send_GTMAgent_k(op1_i) ;
            opn_i():      send_GTMAgent_k(opn_i) ;
            abort_i:      R_broadcast_A(abort_i) ;^5
            commit_i:     force write Ti log records and
                              T_i commit decision in GTM's log ;
                          R_broadcast_A(commit_i) ;
```

---

[4] The period of interest of these definitions is the duration of the atomic commitment protocol.

[5] A stands for the set of all GTM agents participating in transaction T_i.

GTMAgent$_k$ algorithm

```
do forever
    wait for (receipt of a message m from the GTM or delivery of a decision message m
                    by the broadcast or receipt of GTM crash notification )
        if (receipt or delivery of m) then treat message m
        else set time-out to Δ ;                                    // GTM crash notification
              wait until (delivery of a decision by the broadcast or time-out expiration )
                  if (delivery of a decision) then send_localDBMS(decision_ik)
                  else send_localDBMS(abort_ik) ;
```

Fig. 4. NB-SPAC algorithm

An atomic commitment protocol is said to be non-blocking if it satisfies the following property in addition to property *AC*:

NBAC: Every correct participant involved in the atomic commitment protocol eventually decides.

We showed in [2] that NB-SPAC satisfies properties *AC* and *NBAC* of an atomic commitment protocol.

5 Recovering Failures

To preserve global atomicity even in the presence of site failures, we need to forward recover a globally committed transaction on participants that failed during the commit procedure. This section describes the recovery algorithm executed after a participant crash, that allows such a recovery. The GTM recovery algorithm was presented in [2]. Due to space limitations, we omit its presentation in this paper. Fig. 5 details the participant's recovery algorithm common to SPAC and NB-SPAC. For the sake of clarity, step numbers correspond here to the steps ordering.

Step 1 and Step 2 represent the standard recovery procedure executed by the local DBMS on the crashed site. To preserve site autonomy, we make no assumptions on the way these steps are handled. Anyway, we assume that each local DBMS integrates a Local Transaction Manager that guarantees atomicity and durability of all transactions submitted to it. Since the GTM agents do not maintain a private log, Step 3 is necessary to determine if some globally committed transactions have to be locally re-executed at the crashed site S_k. A GTMAgent$_k$ must contact all GTMs that may have run transactions on site S_k. To simplify, we assume that each active instance of GTM is recorded by each GTM agent by means of records stored in the local DBMS. This can be done at the first connection of a GTM to the GTMAgent in order to avoid, during a transaction processing, the blocking I/O needed to record the GTM associated with the transaction. Other solutions are possible to record active GTMs.[6] Anyway, they do not impact the rest of the recovery procedure.

[6] In practical situations, a local DBMS is often under the control of a single GTM (e.g., TP-monitor) recorded statically. In more general situations, active GTMs may be registered by external traders in distributed platforms.

In Step 4, the GTM aborts all still active transactions in which the crashed site S_k participates. Step 5 checks if there exists some globally committed transaction T_i for which the GTMAgent$_k$ did not acknowledge the commit. This may happen in two situations. Either the participant crashed before the commit of T_{ik} was achieved and T_{ik} has been backward recovered during Step 2, or T_{ik} is locally committed but the crash occurred before the acknowledgment was sent to the GTM. Note that these two situations must be carefully differentiated. Re-executing T_{ik} in the latter case may lead to inconsistencies if T_{ik} contains non-idempotent operations (i.e., $op(op(x)) \neq op(x)$). Thus, the GTM must ask the GTMAgent$_k$ about the status of T_{ik} (Step 6). During Step 7, if GTMAgent$_k$ finds a record <commit$_i$> in the underlying database, this proves that T_{ik} has been successfully committed by the local DBMS, since write<commit$_i$> is an operation performed on behalf of T_{ik}. If, on the other hand, <commit$_i$> is not present in the database, this means that T_{ik} has been backward recovered during Step 2 and must be entirely re-executed. This re-execution is performed by exploiting the GTM log (Step 8). In both cases, the GTMAgent$_k$ informs the GTM about the status of T_{ik}. Once the recovery procedure is completed, new distributed transactions are accepted by the GTM (Step 9) and by the GTM agent (Step 10).

Local DBMS algorithm

1- forward recover the transactions that reached their commit state before the crash.

2- backward recover all other transactions

GTM agent algorithm

3- once the local DBMS has restored a consistent state, contact the GTM(s)

7- if the GTM asks about the local status of a transaction branch during step 6,
check the corresponding commit decision record and answer the GTM

10- accept new transactions

GTM algorithm

If contacted by the GTM agent of site S_k during step 3, do:

for each transaction T_i in which S_k participates

4- if (commit$_i$) $\notin$ GTM_log then

broadcast (abort$_i$) to all other T_i participants and forget T_i

5- if (commit$_i$) $\in$ GTM_log,

if ack$_k$(commit$_i$) $\notin$ GTM_log, then

6- ask GTMAgent$_k$ for the exact state of T_{ik}

8- if T_{ik} has not been locally committed, then

restart a new transaction T'_{ik} on S_k

re-execute all T_{ik} operations within T'_{ik}

9- accept new distributed transactions

Fig. 5. Participant recovery algorithm

This recovery algorithm guarantees that re-executing the concerned transaction branches in Step 8: (i) will not produce undesirable conflicts and (ii) will generate exactly the same database state than after their first execution.

Let us call φ the set of all transaction branches that have to be re-executed at S_k during Step 8.

$\varphi = \{T_{ik}$ / $commit_i \in$ GTM_log $\wedge$ $ack_k(commit_i) \notin$ GTM_log $\wedge$ <$commit_i$> $\notin S_k$ database$\}$.

Proof of condition (i): Since local DBMSs are rigorous, $\forall T_{ik}, T_{jk} \in \varphi, \neg\exists(T_{jk} \rightarrow T_{ik})$. Otherwise, T_{ik} would have been blocked during its first execution, waiting for the termination of T_{jk}, and would not have complete all its operations, which contradicts $T_{ik} \in \varphi$. This means that T_{ik} and T_{jk} do not compete on the same resources, thereby precluding the possibility of conflict occurrence.

Proof of condition (ii): Step 2 of the recovery algorithm guarantees that all resources accessed by any $T_{ik} \in \varphi$ are restored to their initial state (i.e., the state before T_{ik} execution). The re-execution of all other transaction branches belonging to φ cannot change this state due to condition (i). Since Step 8 precedes Step 9 and Step 10, new transactions that may modify T_{ik} resources are executed only after T_{ik} re-execution. Consequently, T_{ik} is guaranteed to re-access the same state of its resources and consequently, will generate the same database state as after its first execution.

Since the recovery procedure may lead to a decision, we need to prove that this decision is not in conflict with any decision taken by correct participants or by the GTM. We showed in [2] that the recovery algorithms guarantee property *AC* stating that all participants (faulty or not) that decide, reach the same decision.

6 Performance Analysis

In this section, we compare the performance of SPAC and NB-SPAC with 2PC, the most well-known *blocking* ACP, and ACP-UTRB, the most efficient *non-blocking* protocol for synchronous systems, respectively. In Table1, *n* denotes the number of participants in the transaction. The performance of NB-SPAC and ACP-UTRB depends on the performance of the reliable broadcast primitive. [5] proposed different optimizations to this primitive that reduce the number of messages from quadratic to linear. These optimizations can be directly used in NB-SPAC, making it even more efficient than 2PC.

Table 1. Steps, time delay and message complexity for SPAC, 2PC, NB-SPAC and ACP-UTRB

Protocol	*Number of steps*	*Time Delay*	*Message Complexity*
SPAC	1	δ	n
2PC	2	3δ	3n
NB-SPAC	1	Δ	n^2
ACP-UTRB	2	$2\delta+\Delta$	$2n+n^2$

7 Conclusion

In this paper, we proposed an atomic commitment protocol, named NB-SPAC, which provides the non-blocking property while having the lowest latency possible for an ACP (one phase to commit). The underlying assumption in NB-SPAC is that all participants are ruled by a rigorous concurrency control protocol. In [2], we showed that this assumption can be relaxed to accept participants supporting SQL2 levels of isolation [11], making it practical for most commercial DBMSs. It is worth noting that NB-SPAC preserves site autonomy making it compatible with existing DBMSs.

While SPAC requires no assumption on the underlying network, we considered a synchronous communication system in the implementation of NB-SPAC. We are currently studying the possibility of extending NB-SPAC to deal with asynchronous systems.

References

1. Y. Al-Houmaily and P. Chrysanthis. Two-phase Commit in Gigabit-Networked Distributed Databases. In *Proceedings of the 8th International Conference on Parallel and Distributed Computing Systems*, September 1995
2. M. Abdallah and P. Pucheral. A Single-Phase Non-Blocking Atomic Commitment Protocol. Technical Report 97/019, PRiSM Laboratory, University of Versailles, November 1997. Available from ftp ://ftp.prism.uvsq.fr/pub/reports/1997/1997.019.ps.gz
3. Y. Breitbart, H. Garcia-Molina, and A. Silberschatz. Overview of Multidatabase Transaction Management. *VLDB Journal*, October 1992
4. P. A. Bernstein, V. Hadzilacos, and N. Goodman. *Concurrency Control and Recovery in Database Systems*, Addison Wesley, 1987
5. O. Babaoglu and S.Toueg. Non-Blocking Atomic Commitment. In Sape Mullender, editor, *Distributed Systems*, ACM Press, 1993
6. CAE Specification, *Distributed Transaction Processing: the XA Specification*, XO/CAE/91/300, 1991
7. J. Gray. Notes on Database Operating Systems. In *Operating Systems: An Advanced Course*. R. Bayer, R.M. Graham and G. Seegmuller editors, LNCS 60, Springer Verlag, 1978
8. *Object Transaction Service,* OMG Document 94.8.4, OMG editor, August 1994.
9. J. Stamos and F. Cristian. A Low-Cost Atomic Commit Protocol. In *Proceedings of ninth Symposium on Reliable Distributed Systems,* October 1990
10. D. Skeen. Non-Blocking Commit Protocols. In *Proceedings of the ACM-SIGMOD International Conference on Management of Data,* 1981
11. International Standardization Organization IS, *Information Processing Systems - Database Language SQL,* ISO/IEC 9075, 1992

A Global Garbage Collector for Federated Database Management Systems

Frédéric Mulatéro[1], Jean-Marc Thévenin[2], Pierre Bazex[3]

[1] Université Toulouse II, 5 Allée A. Machado, 31 058 Toulouse Cedex, France
mulatero@cict.fr
[2] Université Toulouse I, Place A. France, 31 042 Toulouse Cedex, France
thevenin@univ-tlse1.fr
[3] IRIT, Université Toulouse III, 118, route de Narbonne, 31 062 Toulouse Cedex 04, France
bazex@irit.fr

Abstract. This paper presents a global Garbage Collector (GC) integrated in a MultiDataBase System architecture which preserves DataBase Management Systems (DBMS) autonomy. Each DBMS is supposed to have its own local GC and none assumption is made on the behavior of the local GC. There is no interaction between the global GC and the local GC. The global GC proposed is an adaptation of reference listing combined with a reverse mark and sweep technique. It has the following properties: it is incremental and requires few interactions with transactions; the reverse mark and sweep technique is able to detect dead object cycles that are frequent in a DBMS context; it is able to collect objects without accessing the whole database and global synchronization of DBMS sites is not required. The Global GC works exclusively on entry and exit items without accessing global object cells stored in DBMS. Consequently it implies few I/O overhead for the DBMS.

1 Introduction

MultiDataBase System (MDBS) [20] provides uniform access to data managed by autonomous DBMS that can be heterogeneous and that are distributed across a network. Data being distributed and shared, it may be impossible for an application to determine which data are still in use and which data should be discarded. Referential persistency models conjointly used with a garbage collector provide a nice solution to ease this process.

Referential persistency models [1] rely on the following rules. The user is allowed to give names to objects. Named objects are so called *persistency roots*. Each object referenced through a persistency root directly or indirectly is *persistent*. Other objects are transient and should be destroyed by the GC if they are no more used by any application. Thus the role of the GC is to detect objects that are neither connected to persistency roots nor connected to objects in the stacks of applications, in order to discard them.

A lot of works have been dedicated to GC in charge to collect objects in centralized environments [23] and distributed environments [4, 15, 21, 22]. Some works have also been dedicated to GC in charge to collect database objects [2, 6, 9, 13, 17, 24]. The specificity of database objects is that they have to respect the ACID properties [11], namely : Atomicity, Coherency, Isolation and Durability. Consequently, database objects are manipulated through transactions that run concurrently with the GC.

A new trend is to federate existing and independent DBMS into MDBS. In this approach it is fundamental to preserve the autonomy of the federated DBMS. Indeed, the emergency of global applications should not disturb the preexisting local application running on each local DBMS. In this paper we propose a solution to implement a global GC for a MDBS composed of federated DBMS. This solution aims at respecting DBMS autonomy and supposes that each DBMS has its own local GC. The data of the MDBS are complex in the sense that there is no restriction in the localization of global objects in order to combine them.

The algorithm proposed for the global GC is based on reference listing [17], a variant of reference counting [8]. Such algorithms do not detect object cycles which are quite frequent in object DBMS [2]. To solve the problem, the proposed algorithm implements reverse mark and sweep based on inverse reference lists. This technique has two main advantages compared to regular mark and sweep techniques [16]: it is able to collect objects without accessing the whole database and objects are accessed only once. In addition, while running in a distributed context, it does not require global synchronization between DBMS sites.

The following of the paper is organized as follows. Section 2 introduces our vocabulary and gives the main issues concerning global and local objects. Section 3 describes the architecture that supports these concepts. Section 4 presents the global GC protocol. Section 5 concludes.

2 Global and local objects

Two types of applications coexist in a federated MDBS. *Local applications* are limited to the manipulation of local objects stored in one DBMS. These manipulations escape to the control of the MDBS. *Global applications* transparently access to shared data located in the different DBMS federated by the MDBS.

For each DBMS involved in the federation, objects are partitioned into three disjoint sets. *Local objects* are only accessed by local applications. References between local objects are local to one DBMS. Global objects are shared by global applications under the control of the MDBS. A *global object* may contain external references, that is references to global objects located in remote DBMS. *Shared local objects* are accessed both by local and global applications. Such objects are local objects that are made visible to the global applications. They do not contain external references. Thus local application not under the control of the MDBS can not reach a global object through a shared local object.

Applying referential persistency, objects are said to be persistent if they are named or referenced through a named object. In order to preserve DBMS autonomy, each DBMS manages its own set of *local names* for persistency roots of local objects and the federated MDBS manages a unique set of *global names* for persistency roots of global objects.

As mentioned above, two types of reference coexist in the federated MDBS. *Local references* are used to identify or send operations to local and shared local objects inside a local DBMS. *External references* are necessary to access global and shared local objects in the federated MDBS context. While local references provide direct access to objects inside a DBMS, external reference provide indirect access to objects across the network. As in [15], an external reference to object o is composed of (see Fig. 1) a local reference to an *exit item* stored in the local DBMS, which in turn references an *entry item* stored in the DBMS containing object o, which itself contains a local reference to object o.

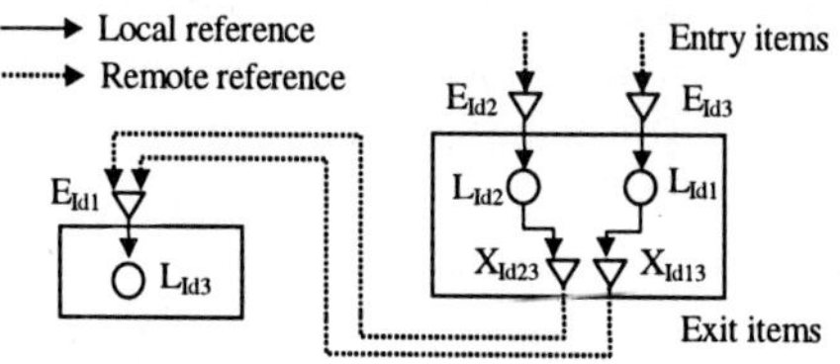

Fig. 1. Entry and Exit Items

The reference between an entry item and an exit item is a *remote reference* that can be implemented as the concatenation of a DBMS identifier and a local reference. In the following, if o_i denotes a global object then Eid_i, Xid_{ij} and Lid_i respectively denote the external reference of o_i which is also the reference of the entry item of o_i, the reference of exit item from o_j to o_i, and the local reference of object o_i.

The operations defined on external references are the following : create external reference, assign external reference, traverse external reference, return external reference, and unassign external reference. These operations are implemented through operations on exit and entry items so that the use of external references is transparent to global applications. Operations on local references are defined by the DBMS involved in the federation.

3 General Architecture

It was mentioned in the introduction that there is no restriction in combining global objects to construct complex objects. For instance global object o1 stored in DBMS1 can be composed of global object o2 stored in DBMS2 in turn composed of object o3 stored in DBMS3 in turn composed of object o4 stored in DBMS1. There is no limitation in the length of the composition string of complex objects and there is no hierarchy between the DBMS involved in the composition. As a consequence, the same DBMS can in turn play the role of a client or a server. It is considered as a client when it calls the interface of a global object stored in a remote DBMS, while it is considered as a server when it implements the interface of a global object. In order to integrate a new DBMS into the federation, two modules have to be developed, namely the DBMS client module and the DBMS server module, so that the DBMS can play its two roles (see Fig. 2).

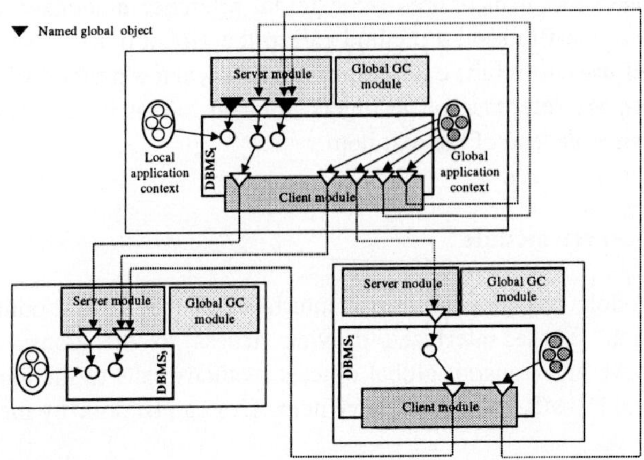

Fig. 2. General Architecture

3.1 DBMS client module

The client module is in charge to provide both the MDBS interface to global applications and the global object interface. The MDBS interface is composed of the following operations: connection to the federated MDBS, disconnection, commit of a transaction and abort of a transaction. The transactional aspects of this interface are further discussed in section 3.4.

The global object interface consists in sending global object method calls to the appropriate DBMS server module as well as to provide access to the list of global names. This can be done following CORBA by mean of proxy whose objective is to encapsulate object method calls through exit items. It is important to mention here that since we are in a transactional context, each global object operation is performed for one transaction whose identifier is transmitted somehow.

Exit items are managed by the client module. Exit items are implemented as a class of local objects stored in the DBMS associated to the client module so that they can be referenced through a local reference. The main operations of this class are : create exit item, assign exit item, traverse exit item and unassign exit item. *Create exit item* is used each time an external reference is returned by a method so that an external reference is always encapsulated into an exit item. The result exit item is then bind to the application context (see Fig. 2). *Assign exit item* and *unassign exit item* are used respectively to link and unlink a global object to an exit item. If the exit item is already assigned to a global object the assign exit item operation creates a new exit item so that there is one exit item per external references held in the DBMS even if they refer to the same object (see Fig. 1). Having several exit items pointing to the same object avoids contention on exit items due to the DBMS transaction management mechanism (an exit item updated by one transaction is locked for the whole transaction). Recall that exit item should not be assigned to local shared objects. *Traverse exit item* returns the external reference associated to an exit item. This interface is used to send a method call to the global object associated to an exit item. It is also used to return external references: when a method of global object o needs to return the reference of an object affected to o it is necessary to return the external reference instead of the exit item.

3.2 DBMS server module

The server module provides the mirror interfaces of the client module interfaces on the server side. These interfaces provide access to the transactional facilities mentioned above and transmit global objects methods calls to the appropriate object stored in a local DBMS through an entry item. This can be done by mean of stubs like in CORBA.

Entry items are managed by the server module. Entry items can be implemented as a class that should provide the following interface: create entry item, traverse entry item, delete entry item. *Create entry item* is used both by the method which creates global objects and to change the status of a local object into shared local object. *Traverse entry item* is used to send a method to call the appropriate object. *Delete entry item* is used by the global GC to collect entry items.

Contrarily to exit items, entry items are not stored in the local DBMS. In this way it is easier to provide uniform remote references in each server module. Another advantage of implementing entry items outside DBMS is to ensure that coherent parallel updates can be performed on entry items by mean of latches [18] instead of transactions. Latches are instant duration locks that guarantee the coherency property of parallel updates without providing the atomicity property of transactions. Latches are used to minimize synchronization between the global GC and transactions. Indeed next sections show that transactions and the global GC are run concurrently and that both update entry items. However, the global GC does not require the atomicity property for its updates.

3.3 Garbage Collection

The global GC proposed aims at respecting DBMS autonomy. Consequently each DBMS is supposed to have its own local GC and none assumption is made on the behavior of the local GC. In addition, there should not be interactions between the global GC and the local GC of the DBMS involved in the federation. The purpose of the global GC is to make sure that entry items, global object cells and exit items are destroyed when no more used. On the other side, the purpose of a local GC is to collect the local objects no more used in a DBMS. We detail below how these tasks are run independently.

Exit items and global objects cells are implemented as local objects and their destruction is under the responsibility of the local GC of the DBMS in which they are stored. However, only the global GC of the MDBS can decide whether a global object is alive or dead. Exit items and global objects cells are kept alive in the DBMS context by mean of local names allocated to them at creation time. The local name of an exit item can be directly stored in the exit item cell. As an exit item is unassigned, its local name is destroyed so that the local CG can collect the exit item. The local name of a global object cell is stored in the associated entry item. The global GC collect a global objects o_i as follows. First each exit item Xid_{ji} pointed by o_i is unassigned from the exit item of o_i so that it is collected as mentioned above. Then the local name of o_i stored in the entry item Eid_j is destroyed so that the local GC can collect the global object's cell. Finally the entry item can be destroyed directly by the global GC since it is stored outside the DBMS.

The global GC algorithm is a distributed algorithm implemented by global GC modules associated to each DBMS. This algorithm is detailed in section 4.

3.4 About Transaction Management and Garbage Collection

Global objects as well as local objects must satisfy ACID properties. Consequently objects can only be accessed through transactions. Transaction management is not the purpose of this paper however a few hypothesis have to be stated. The federated MDBS distinguish global transactions accessing global and shared local objects from local transactions executed on each DBMS. A global transaction is supported by one local transaction per DBMS involved in the global transaction. As a global transaction commits, the commitment of the involved local transactions is synchronized though a two phase commit protocol [11]. Commercial DBMS provide a standard interface for the two phase commit protocol. However this interface is encapsulated by the DBMS client and server modules interface for synchronization between global transactions and the global GC.

The global GC algorithm is incremental so that it runs concurrently with transactions. A first difficulty for the GC is to consider as alive volatile objects created by active transactions and not yet linked to any persistency root. The ACID properties of transactions bring the following problems [2]. Atomicity brings the problem that a transaction which cuts a link between two global objects can be rolled back. This violates the fundamental assumption that dead objects always remain dead. Coherency and Isolation introduce overhead and contention problems in transaction execution. The GC should not increase this overhead and should avoid to interfere with transactions. It should not be considered as a transaction. Durability invalidates the hypothesis of some GC algorithms that the number of alive objects is small. In addition, objects visited by the GC may be stored on disk which introduce undesirable I/O overhead. Finally to enforce Durability the DBMS provide recovery mechanism that are able to re-execute actions of committed transaction in case of system crash or disk crash. The GC actions are not taken into account by the DBMS recovery mechanisms and may be lost after a crash. This may have consequences on the database recovery.

The atomicity problem and the problem of volatile objects are solved using a read barrier [3] implemented by the interface of entry items. The purpose of the read barrier in this context is to mark with a transaction identifier the entry item of each global object involved in a global transaction. These marks allow the global GC to considerate as alive both newly created objects and objects whose external reference have been unassigned by an active transaction. As a global transaction commits all its marks must be removed. Exit items bind to the transaction and that have not been affected to a global object are also collected by the commit operation.

For each global object o_i, a link is maintained between the entry item of o_i and the set of exit items referenced by o_i so that the global GC can traverse global object graphs without accessing the global object cells stored in the DBMS. The benefit is that the global CG works exclusively on entry and exit items without accessing the objects manipulated by DBMS transactions. In addition, the global GC doesn't need to be a transaction. Indeed exit items are only accessed in read mode by the global GC and entry items are stored outside the DBMS. A last advantage is that exit items are very small objects that can be clustered together so that accessing exit items should imply few I/O overhead for DBMS.

As mentioned in the previous section, the global GC does not update or destroy DBMS objects directly. It simply destroys local names of objects that can be collected by a local GC. Consequently, the interactions with the recovery mechanism of a local DBMS are postponed to its local GC. However, transactions update entry items that are not stored in the DBMS. The server module should implement a recovery mechanism for entry items in order to ensure their durability. This aspect is not detailed in this paper.

4 Global Garbage Collector

The global GC algorithm proposed is a variant of GC algorithms based on reference counting [3]. In this context, each object maintains a *reference counter* set to the number of objects which reference it. Objects to be collected are unnamed objects with a reference counter set to zero. GC algorithms based on reference counting have the following advantages in a DBMS context. They are incremental by nature and do not require a complete scan of all the database objects for dead object detection. They also have the following drawbacks. It is impossible to detect dead object cycles, that is objects referencing each other without being reachable from a persistency root, using reference counters. Indeed, objects involved in a dead cycle have their reference counters at least set to one. A second problem is propagation. As the reference counter of object o is set to zero, it is necessary to send a decrement message to each object referenced by o before to collect o. This process can be recursive. A last drawback in a distributed context is that increment and decrement messages are not idempotent if the network does not guarantee that messages are not lost nor duplicated. As a consequence, objects could be collected while still alive.

The main solution to solve the cycle detection problem is to use a complementary mark and sweep technique [12, 15, 22]. The mark and sweep techniques are based on two steps [16]: a first step starts from roots and marks all reachable objects. Then a second step scans all objects and collects unmarked objects. To avoid that these two steps scan all the objects, some solutions are proposed to cluster object referencing each other into disjoint partitions. These two steps can then be performed independently on distinct partitions. However mark and sweep techniques do not work in perfect harmony with reference counting techniques. Several solutions have been proposed to solve the message problem [4, 6, 14, 15, 17, 22]. Most of these solutions replace reference counters by reference lists taking into account the fact that the insert and the delete messages used to update lists are idempotent. Objects are collected when their reference lists are empty.

The global GC algorithm is an adaptation of the solutions mentioned above. It combines the use of inverse reference lists with a *reverse* mark and sweep algorithm in order to solve both the dead object cycles and the propagation problems. An inverse reference list is assigned to each object. The inverse reference list of object o_j is augmented with the global reference of o_i when the external reference of o_j is assigned to o_i. When a link between o_i and o_j is cut, the corresponding exit item associated with o_i is unaffected without propagating the update to the inverse reference list of o_j. The reverse mark and sweep algorithm selects an object suspected to be dead and checks through its inverse references if it is reachable from a persistent root or a global transaction. If not, the suspected object and its predecessors are collected. Inverse reference lists are updated during this process. An important advantage of the reverse mark and sweep algorithm compared to other mark and sweep techniques is that it does not require a complete scan of the database objects for dead object detection and then keeps the advantage of reference counting techniques.

The following of this section presents the data structures used by the global GC, explains how they are updated during object management and then details the reverse mark and sweep algorithm.

4.1 Entry and Exit Item Data Structures

It was mentioned section 3.3 that the global GC can traverse global object graphs accessing only entry and exit items. Indeed all the data necessary for the GC are stored in entry and exit items in order to minimize interactions between the global GC and the DBMS transactions. Entry and Exit items are implemented as class. The main operations of these class have been presented in section 3.1 and 3.2. This section details additional operations of these required by the GC to access its data.

Let us consider the entry item instance associated to global object o_i. The entry item class must provide access to the following data: the local reference of o_i namely Lid_i; the local name of o_i; the inverse reference list of objects connected to o_i; the list of transactions that accessed o_i and the status of o_i. The local reference of o_i is not used by the global GC but is required to traverse the exit item associated to o_i. The local name of o_i is required by the global GC to collect o_i. The inverse reference list is used by the global GC to check if o_i is reachable through its predecessors. The list of transaction identifiers is used to check if o_i is reachable through an application transaction. This list implements the transaction marks mentioned in section 3.4. The status of o_i is an information used by the reverse mark and sweep algorithm to detect objects involved in a cycle. This status initiated to *quiet* can change successively into *suspected* then *cycle detector* or *cycle*. An operation is also required to check if an exit item previously affected to o_i still exists. This operation is required by the reverse mark and sweep algorithm to update the inverse reference list of o_j when reference from o_i to o_j has been cut. Finally operations on the set of entry items managed by DBMS server are required to select the suspected objects that should be inspect by the reverse mark and sweep algorithm.

Let us consider an exit item instance affected to object o_i and which references object o_j. The exit item class must provide access to the following data: the external reference of o_j namely Eid_j (traverse exit item); the local name of the exit item and the local reference to the o_i entry item namely Eid_i. Eid_j is used to traverse the exit item. The local name is used to delete the local name of the exit item. Eid_i is used conjointly with Eid_j by the global GC to check if the exit item referencing o_j previously affected to o_i still exists.

4.2 Updating Entry and Exit Item

Let us first consider the updates performed on entry and exit items by transaction T during the following operations: create o_i, assign external reference of o_j to o_i, unassign external reference of o_j in o_i, traverse external reference of o_i, return external reference of o_i and commit or rollback. Operation create o_i implies a call to create entry item with parameter Lid_i. Local reference Lid_i is affected to Eid_i and T is inserted in the transaction list of Eid_i. Operation assign external reference of o_j to o_i implies a call to assign exit item Xid_{ij} with parameter Eid_i. This operation ask the server containing o_j to insert Eid_i in the inverse reference list of Eid_j. It is not necessary to put T in the transaction list of Eid_j since it is already in the transaction list of Eid_i. Operation unassign external reference of o_j in o_i implies a call to unassign exit item Xid_{ij}. The reference Eid_i is simply removed from exit item Xid_{ij}. The inverse reference list is not updated. Operation traverse external reference of o_i implies a call to traverse exit item Xid_{ki} then to traverse entry item Eid_i. Operation traverse entry item put T in the transaction list of Eid_i. Operation return external reference of o_i implies a call to traverse exit item Xid_{ki} which does not perform any update. The commit and rollback operations remove T from the transaction list of each entry item traversed by T. They also unname each exit items created by T which are not assigned.

The global GC only performs two types of updates on entry items. The first one consists in updating inverse reference lists of entry items associated to global objects whose reference has been unaffected. The second one consists in changing the status of objects during the reverse mark and sweep process. It is important to note that these updates are never performed on objects marked by transactions. Thus there is very little interactions between transactions and the global GC for updating entry items.

4.3 Reverse Mark and Sweep Algorithm

The reverse mark and sweep algorithm exploits a diffusing computation [7, 10] initiated at any global object suspected to be dead. It exploits inverse reference lists to find if the predecessors of the suspected object are either connected to persistency root or used by an application. In order to ease the presentation, the algorithm is first presented without considering object cycles. Adaptations of this algorithm are then proposed to collect dead object cycles. The algorithm is based on the following rules:

rule 0: the initiating object takes the status *suspected*;
rule 1: a suspected object sends a question to each of its predecessors according to its inverse reference list;
rule 2: a queried object that is named or marked by a transaction answers *alive*;
rule 3: a queried object that does not satisfy rule 2 and having unaffected the exit item corresponding to the query answers *disconnected*;
rule 4: a queried object that does not satisfy rule 3 and with no predecessor answers *dead* and is collected;
rule 5: a queried object that does not satisfy rule 4 takes the status *suspected*;
rule 6: as soon as an object receives an *alive* answer, it takes the status *quiet* and answers *alive*;
rule 7: as an object receives a *disconnected* answer, it removes the corresponding reference from its inverse reference list;
rule 8: if all answers are *dead* or *disconnected*, the object answers *dead* and is collected;
rule 9: when the initiating object has received all its answers, the computation is done. A new initiating object is selected.

The reverse mark and sweep algorithm is composed of two steps. The first step consists in choosing an initiating object. This step can be done locally by a GC module. An initiating object must satisfy the two following conditions : (i) it is not named; (ii) it is not used by application processes. Such objects are selected through the entry items managed by the DBMS server module associated to the GC module. A global object satisfying conditions (i), (ii) and without predecessor is destroyed directly without initiating the computation (reference counting).
The second step is a distributed computation that can be implemented by two operations associated with entry items in charge respectively to answer a question addressed to an entry item and to send questions to the entry item's predecessors

according to rules 0 to 9. This process is illustrated in Fig. 3 for the initiator o1.

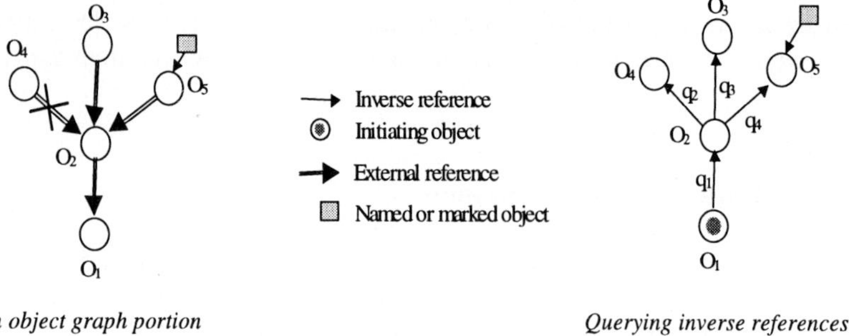

An object graph portion *Querying inverse references*

Fig. 3. Reverse Mark and Sweep Starting from O_1

Object o1 takes the status suspected according to rule 0. Then o1 sends question q1 to its predecessor o2 according to rule 1. Object o2 is not named nor marked by a transaction but has three predecessors. According to rule 5 o2 takes the status suspected and sends question q2 to its first predecessor o4. The link between o4 and o2 has been cut (the exit item associated to o4 and referencing o2 has been suppressed) and o4 answers disconnected to q2 according to rule 3. According to rule 7, o2 removes o4 from its inverse reference list. Then object o2 sends question q3 to object o3. Object o3 answers dead and is collected according to rule 4 because it is unnamed and has no predecessor. Then object o2 sends question q4 to object o5. Object o5 is named or marked by a transaction and answers alive according to rule 2. As o2 receives the answer alive to question 4, o2 takes the status quiet again and answers alive to q1 according to rule 6. As o1 receives the answer alive to question q1, o1 takes the status quiet again and the process stops according to rule 9. Note that the rules supervising step 2 are ordered. This order is important. Let us consider the example of Fig. 3 again. If the transaction which has cut the link between o4 and o2 was not completed, o4 would be marked and would have answered alive to q2 according to rule 2. Indeed such a transaction can abort which would have the consequence to reintroduce the link between o4 and o2.

This example shows that the global GC must be *conservative* (i.e. an object is not collected as soon as it becomes unreachable) which is the case due to rule 2. Rules 0 to 9 guarantee that the global GC satisfies the properties of *safety* that is: objects reachable from persistent roots or from active transactions must not be reclaimed. First, rule 2 guarantees that an object which is named or used by an application is not suspected. Then, rule 6 guarantees that a suspected object which has at least one reachable predecessor is not collected. Finally, rule 8 guarantees that a suspected object is collected if and only if all its predecessors answered dead (unreachable). Consequently if an answer message is lost the corresponding object is not collected. The global GC also satisfies the *liveness* property that is: unreachable objects should be reclaimed eventually. An unreachable object can be suspected then collected for the following reasons. The first step of the global GC can select any object as initiator using the set of entry items. All the marks inserted by a transaction in entry item's transaction lists are removed when the transaction ends (commit or abort). Rules 3 and 7 guarantee that the inverse reference list of a suspected object which has been unaffected by a commited transaction is updated. Finally an unreachable object which is queried is either directly collected according to rule 4 or suspected then collected according to rules 5 and 8.

Compared to mark and sweep algorithms of the literature, the reverse mark and sweep algorithm has several important properties. Dead objects are collected during the marking phase so that the sweep phase is unnecessary. Consequently objects are accessed only once. In addition, a complete marking phase starting from an initiator access a small portion of the database and stops before reaching named objects if objects are marked by transactions. Due to these properties the reverse mark and sweep algorithm is well adapted to a DBMS context where number of alive objects is important. In addition it works in harmony with the reference counting technique aimed by the global GC.

Cycle Collection

A cycle is detected as a suspected object receives a question. This is illustrated in Fig. 4 with the cycle between o2 and o3. Object o2 receives a first question q1. It takes the status suspected and sends question q2 to object o3. Object o3 takes the status suspected and sends question q3 to object o2. Object o2 receives a question while being in suspected state, the cycle is detected.

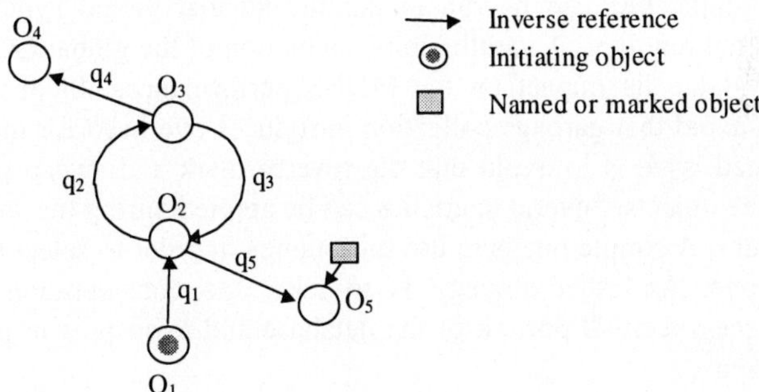

Fig. 4. Cycle Detection

In order to manage the cycle, the object that detects a cycle change its state from suspected to *cycle detector* and answers *cycle*. An object that receives a cycle answer can be in one of the two following situations (see Fig. 4): either all its predecessor are dead (case of o3) or it has a predecessor not yet queried which is alive (case of o2). In the first case the object cannot answer that it is dead because an other object involved in the cycle can be alive (objects have not yet queried all their predecessors). In this case the object propagates the cycle answer. In the second case the object answers alive and is responsible to change the state from cycle to quiet for all the objects having already answered cycle (except for the cycle detector which will receive the alive answer). If the cycle detector does not receive an alive answer from one of its predecessors it is in charge to collect all the objects involved in the cycle. Note that only the cycle detector can start the cycle collection because it knows all the answers of its predecessors. These adaptations to the original algorithm are taken into account by extending the rules 5, 6 and 8 as detailed in [19].

5 Conclusion

This paper has presented a global GC integrated in a MultiDataBase System architecture which preserves DBMS autonomy. None assumption is made on the behavior of the DBMS's local GC and the global GC works independently of the local GC. The global GC proposed is an adaptation of reference listing combined with a reverse mark and sweep technique. It has the following interesting properties: it is incremental and requires few interactions with transactions; the reverse mark and sweep technique is able to detect object cycles that are frequent in a DBMS context; it is able to collect objects without accessing the whole database. The global GC works exclusively on entry and exit items without accessing global object cells stored in DBMS. Consequently it implies few I/O overhead for the DBMS. In addition the global GC satisfies the fundamental properties of safety and liveness.

Performance issues have not been directly addressed in this paper. The global GC algorithm can have several behaviors depending on how the first step is managed [19]. Several global GC can be run in parallel so that global synchronization of DBMS sites is not required. A parallel implementation of the global GC is in progress in order to evaluate its impact on the MDBS performances. Indeed an important objective is to avoid that garbage collection introduces overhead for the DBMS sites. An other opened issue is to avoid that the reverse mark and sweep process always inspect the same objects. Several heuristics can be applied during the step in charge to select an initiator. A simple one is to use timestamps in order to select the object with the smallest one. An other strategy is to take into consideration the fact that applications access a small portion of the database and to suspect in priority objects recently accessed.

References

1. M. Atkinson, P. Bailey, K. Chisholm, P. Cockshott, R. Morrison, *An Approach to Persistent Programming,* Computer Journal, 26(4), 1983.
2. L. Amsaleg, M. Franklin, O. Gruber, *Efficient Incremental Garbage Collection for Client-Server Object Database Systems,* In Proc. of the 21th VLDB Int. Conf., Zurich, Switzerland, September 1995.
3. H. G. Baker, *List Processing in Real Time on a Serial Computer,* CACM, 21(4):280-294, April 1978.
4. A. Birrell, D. Evers, G. Nelson, S. Owicki, E. Wobber, *Distributed Garbage Collection for Network Object,* Digital System Research Center Technical Report 115, 1994.

5. P. B. Bishop, Computer System with a Very Large Address Space and Garbage Collection, PhD Thesis, MIT, Laboratory for Computer Science, Cambridge, MA, USA, May 1977, MIT/LCS/TR-178.
6. A. Björnerstedt, *Secondary Storage Garbage Collection for Decentralized Object-Based Systems,* Tsichritzis D. C. Editor Object Oriented Development, Genève, Centre Universitaire d'Informatique, 1989.
7. K. M. Chandy, J. Misra, L. M. Haas, *Distributed Deadlock Detection,* ACM TOCS, 1(2), 1983.
8. G. E. Collins, *A Method for Overlapping and Erasure of Lists,* CACM, 2(12), December, 1960.
9. J. Cook, A. Wolf, B. Zorn, *Partition Selection Policies in Object Database Garbage Collection,* In SIGMOD Conf., Mineapolis, MN, May 1994.
10. E. W. D. Dijkstra, C. S. Scholten, *Termination Detection for Diffusing Computations,* Information Processing Letters, 11(4), 1980.
11. J. Gray, A. Reuter, *Transaction Processing: Concepts and Techniques,* Morgan Kaufmann, 1993.
12. J. Hugues, *A Distributed Garbage Collection Algorithm,* In ACM Conf. on Functional Programming Languages and Computer Architecture, LNCS 201, Springer-Verlag, September 1985.
13. E. Kolodner, W. Weihl, *Atomic Incremental Garbage Collection and Recovery for Large Stable Heap,* In Proc. of the ACM SIGMOD Int. Conf., Washington D. C., June 1993.
14. S. Louboutin, V. Cahill, *Lazy per Cluster Log-Keeping Mechanism for Global Garbage Detection on Amadeus,* Distributed System Group, Trinity College, Dublin, Ireland, Technical Report TCD-CS-95-13, 1995.
15. B. Lang, C. Queinnec, J. Piquer, *Garbage Collecting the World,* Conf. Record of the Nineteenth Annual ACM Symposium of Principles of Programming Languages, 1992.
16. J. McCarthy, *Recursive Functions of Symbolic Expressions and their Computation by Machine,* CACM, 3(4), April 1960.
17. U. Maheshwari, B. Liskov, *Fault-Tolerant Garbage Collection in a Client-Server Object-Oriented Database,* In Proc. of the 3rd PDIS Int. Conf., Austin Texas, September 1994.
18. C. Mohan, F. Levine, *ARIES/IM: An Efficient and High Concurrency Index Management Method Using Write-Ahead,* IBM Research Report RJ6846, IBM Almaden Research Center, August 1989.
19. F. Mulatéro, J. M. Thévenin, P. Bazex, *A Global Garbage Collector for Multidabase Systems,* 14èmes Journées Bases de Données Avancées, Hammamet, Tunisia, October 1998.
20. M. T. Özsu, P. Valduriez, *Principles of Distributed Database Systems,* Prentice-Hall Int. Editions, 1991.
21. D. Plaifossé, M. Shapiro, *A Survey of Distributed Garbage Collection Techniques,* Int. Workshop on Memory Management, Kinross Scotland, September 1995.
22. M. Shapiro, P. Dickman, D. Plainfossé, *Robust Distributed References and Acyclic Garbage Collection,* Symposium on Principles of Distributed Computing, Vancouver Canada, August 1992.
23. P. R. Wilson, *Uniprocessor Garbage Collection Techniques,* In Proc. of the Int. Workshop on Memory Management, Number 637 in Lecture Notes in Computer Science, Springer-Verlag, Saint-Malo France, September 1992.
24. V. Yong., J. Naughton, J. Yu, *Storage Reclamation and Reorganization in Client-Server Persistent Object Stores,* In Proc. of the Data Engineering Int. Conf., Houston Texas, February 1994.

Rule-Based Management of Routing Plans in CIM Systems

Wolfram Wöß

Institute for Applied Knowledge Processing (FAW)
Johannes Kepler University Linz, Austria
e-mail: wwoess@faw.uni-linz.ac.at

Abstract. Today many enterprises have already introduced CIM systems. In many cases such enterprises are characterized by heterogeneous EDP concepts because each CIM component administrates its own databases. Due to this situation, now many CIM enterprises are confronted with high data redundancies and many inconsistencies. Data exchange between several CIM components is impossible or results in complex systems of interfaces between CIM components. In addition many enterprises have to administrate a great number of different variants of a product to fulfill today`s customers` demands. If frequent updates of such a great number of variant parts are necessary, the maintenance of the corresponding data with conventional methods and software systems is often made to expensive or sometimes even impossible. The introduced rule-based routing plan processor extends conventional relational database systems with rules and operations for the dynamic generation of routing plans. Moreover, it allows the transformation of dependencies between bill of material data and routing plan data into a database. With this approach an efficient management of routing plans is provided and redundancy and inconsistency are prevented.

1 Introduction

In the last years quality and price have been the most important competition factors of an enterprise. Today many enterprises are in addition confronted with comprehensive changes of customer requirements. Many sectors changed from a provider- to a buyer-market [1] [2].

To meet these new requirements, many enterprises introduced CIM systems, hoping to fulfill customer requirements by using powerful CAD systems, PPS, customer order management systems and many other important CIM components.

Normally, this leaded to heterogeneous EDP concepts which are characterized by autonomous CIM components, each with its own database and with only few possibilities for interoperability and data exchange with other CIM components in the enterprise [3].

Due to this situation, now many CIM enterprises are confronted with the following problems:

- Individual customer production results in a huge number of different variant parts of a product again resulting in a huge number of product data. This situation is best illustrated by exemplary looking at the production statistics of the enterprise ALNO, a German furniture manufacturer. ALNO produces 4.000 final products, 70.000 (sub)parts and manages 270.000 bills of material [4].
- Due to this great amount of data, the maintenance of each individual database of a CIM component with conventional methods and software systems is to expensive or even impossible [2]. High data redundancies and many inconsistencies between different databases are the consequences.
- Beside this quantity problem there are also some quality aspects. Different CIM components are often characterized by different structural views on the same product data, especially of bill of material data. The consequence is, that the interoperability between different CIM components is often impossible and data exchange has to be done manually.
- Planning algorithms and knowledge about bill of material processing, operations planning etc. are only implicitly defined within the whole set of variant parts. Since this knowledge is not explicitly available the planning of demands and the production planning process require many interactions and decisions of the operations planner or of another specialist of the enterprise.
- Production planning systems and routing plans depend on bill of material data. Such dependencies are still *not* available or managed in CIM databases.

Since CIM components store and administrate different types of data but most of them administrate some kind of product data it can be expected, that especially a powerful and integrated management of product data results in a significant improvement of the whole CIM system.

In general there are two kinds of product data necessary to plan the production of a product:

- Bill of material data specifies material requirements.
- Routing plans specify the sequence of operations which are necessary to produce a product.

At our institute the development of a powerful management of product data started with the introduction of a concept for transformation and processing of bill of material data [5] [6].

General data structures for the administration of routing plans and production operations are available and implemented in many systems [9]. In contrast to existing concepts this paper focuses on the administration of dependencies between bill of material data and routing plans on the one hand and dependencies between operations within a routing plan on the other hand. The presented approach completes the development of the product data manager (ProMan) [8] and therefore this is a further step to improve the management of product data.

This approach on the one hand significantly reduces the amount of data that has to be administrated and on the other hand reduces the necessary interaction between the operations planner and the CIM software. Dependencies and planning algorithms are transformed into a rule base which is stored within a relational database. Additionally each operation of the rule-based routing plan processor is stored within the database and therefore these operations are globally available for each CIM component.

The paper proceeds as follows: Section 2 starts with a discussion of general problems with the administration of routing plans in CIM systems which are characterized by a great number of variant products. In Section 3 the concept of the rule-based routing plan processor is introduced. This section includes a description of the system architecture and the main modules of the rule-based routing plan processor. Section 4 concludes and gives an outlook on future research.

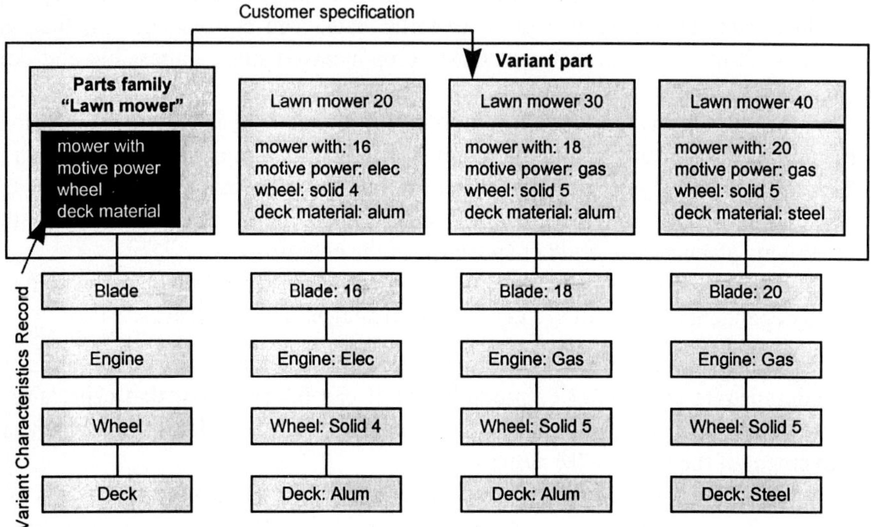

Fig. 1. Parts family, variant part and variant characteristics record.

2 General Problems with the Administration of Routing Plans

This section gives a survey of general considerations and solutions for the administration of routing plans. Before going into detail, the most important terms used in this paper are defined.

2.1 Important Terms in the Field of Routing Plans

A variant part or a variant is defined as a customer specific shape, design, etc. of a final product. The customer specifies a set of variant characteristics which describe a variant part. The set of all variant characteristics of a single variant is called variant characteristics record. The variant specification is the set of customer-specified characteristics of a variant part. That means, that the variant specification is the description of a customer specific final product. The parts family is a set of similar parts in the sense of their manufacturing technology and/or construction. Each parts family possesses its own variant characteristics record which is a valid combination of variant characteristics for the parts family at hand (Figure 1).

Technical operations and resources which are necessary to produce a product are described by using routing plans. A routing plan consists of some heading information and of a sequence of product operations [7], [8]. The heading information consists of a routing plan number, generation- and update-information, employee information (responsibility), CAD references, etc. The sequence of operations contains attributes like a technical operation number, a description, production equipment, operation time, etc. for each operation.

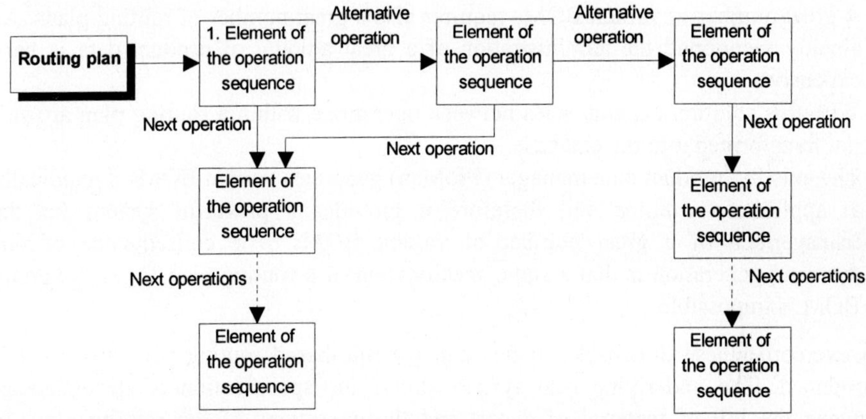

Fig. 2. Routing plans, sequences of operations and alternative operations.

Routing plans are represented by a logical sequence of (technical) operations with clear "previous" and "next" relationships between the operations (Figure 2). For each element of the operation sequence a set of alternatives may be defined. An alternative may itself be a sequence of operations or it may be a single operation. Figure 2 illustrates the connections between routing plans, sequences of operations and alternative operations [9]. Each element of the sequence of operations references a technical operation.

In general there are two reasons for the definition of alternatives within the sequence of operations:

- Alternative operations may be equivalent and therefore they are valid for every variant of a product.
- The production of different variants requires different production operations and this dependency is implicitly defined as an alternative operation. The operations planner has to choose the correct alternative for the actual variant part. To prevent incorrect decisions of the operations planner the definition of a routing plan for every variant parts is necessary. Therefore this concept is not suitable for the administration of a great number of variant parts and (variant) routing plans.

2.2 Administration of Variant Specific Routing Plans

The customer specification of a final product determines the variant bill of material of the corresponding product. The material requirements for the production are exactly derived from the variant bill of material. Now the production planner determines which operations are necessary to produce this product. In many cases these operations depend on the variant bill of material (BOM). For example, if the customer requires an electrical lawn mower a cable has to be assembled otherwise a gas tank has to be assembled.

A possible solution for the transformation of such dependencies into a database would be the specification of a routing plan for each variant BOM. In this case three aspects have to be considered:

- A great number of variant BOMs requires also a great number of routing plans. As already mentioned the administration of a great amount of product data is very expensive.
- With this solution dependencies between operations within a routing plan are still not transformed into the database.
- The existing product data manager (ProMan) generates variant BOMs dynamically at application runtime and therefore it provides a powerful system for the management of a great number of variant BOMs. The consequence of this dynamic generation is that a static specification of a routing plan for each variant BOM is impossible.

To overcome these drawbacks in this paper a rule-based routing plan processor is introduced. The underlying rule system allows the specification of dependencies between the bill of material of a part and the operations of the routing plan. In addition also dependencies between operations within a routing plan may be defined.

In cooperation with other modules of ProMan the rule-based routing plan processor dynamically generates the corresponding routing plan for a customer specific final product at application runtime. As a consequence the number of routing plans that has to be administrated is dramatically reduced and therefore redundancies and inconsistencies are prevented.

3 The Concept of the Rule-based Routing Plan Processor

The introduced rule-based routing plan processor (RPP) is an extension of ProMan, a rule-based product data manager [5] [6]. ProMan enables efficient management of product data in particular bill of material data. ProMan is divided into two main modules: the generator for variants and variant bills of material and the transformation processor for bill of material data.

- The main functionality of the *rule-based generator for variants* is that it determines the variant subpart of each subposition of the BOM of the final product. This determination is based on a customer specified set of final product characteristics.
- The *rule-based transformation processor for bill of material data* creates an individual type of bill of material for each organization unit of an enterprise.

ProMan integrates different variant parts of a product to a parts family and it integrates different variant bills of material of a parts family to a basic bill of material (Figure 3). In order to establish a rule-based routing plan processor variant-BOM-depending routing plans of a parts family are integrated to basic routing plan (Figure 3). These data structures are independent from a *customer specific* variant part. The basic routing plan covers all production instructions for every variant part of a parts family. Different operation instructions for different variants are expressed by alternatives within the sequence of operations of a routing plan.

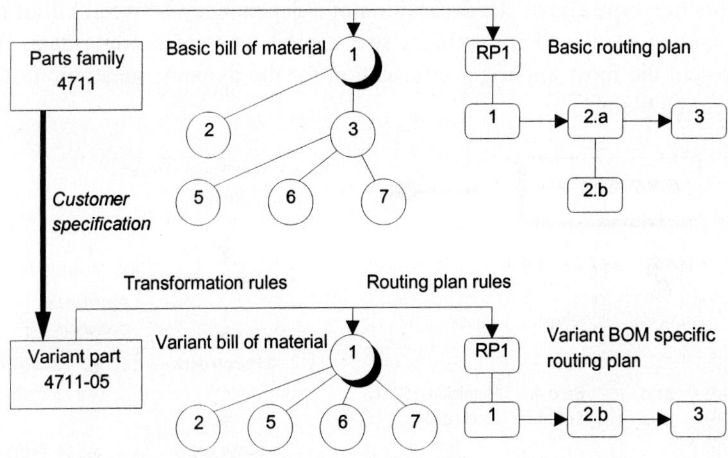

Fig. 3. Generation of a variant specific routing plan.

The procedures of ProMan derive the variant bill of material from both, the parts family and the basic bill of material by using transformation rules (Figure 3). In the next step the rule-based routing plan processor derives a variant specific routing plan from the variant bill of material and the basic routing plan by processing the corresponding routing plan rules.

Based on the customer specific variant part the set of alternative operations of a routing plan may be reduced to a single element. Hence, the operation at this position (routing plan element) within the routing plan is exactly defined. If the resulting set of alternative operations consists of more than one element, the operations planner has to determine interactively which operation is valid.

The dependencies between the bill of material and the set of alternative operations within the routing plan are defined by means of "IF-THEN" rules. Figure 4 shows an example of a simple bill of material tree of a lawn mower and its corresponding routing plan. In this example the lawn mower is made of an aluminium deck (part number 1237) or made of a steel deck (part number 2354). If the customer orders an aluminium deck then the holes of the deck are punched. In case of a steel deck holes have to be drilled. These dependencies are expresses by the following rules:

(1) IF 1208.pos4 = 1237 THEN RP10.2
(2) IF 1208.pos4 = 2354 THEN RP10.27

To transform dependencies between bill of material data and routing plans on the one hand and dependencies between operations within a routing plan on the other hand into a database two rule types are necessary:

- bill of material to routing plan rules (BOMRP rules),
- routing plan rules (RP rules).

In the IF clause a BOMRP rule references the variant bill of material of a variant part and in the THEN clause it references the routing plan of the corresponding parts family. This rule type allows the description of a dependency between bill of material data and routing plans and it combines two central types of product data. BOMRP rules represent the most important information for the dynamic generation of variant specific routing plans.

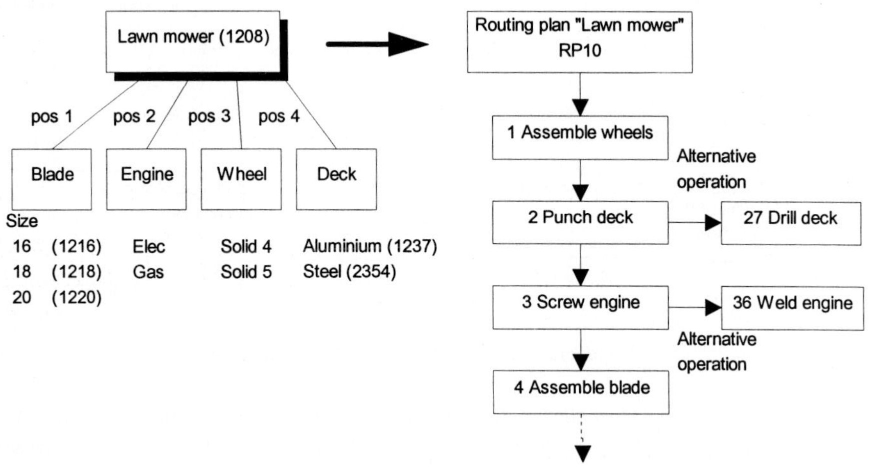

Fig. 4. Example of a bill of material and a routing plan.

RP rules are necessary for the description of dependencies between operations within a routing plan. For example, if in Figure 4 the customer orders a lawn mower with a steel deck then the necessary holes are drilled. In this case the engine of the lawn mower is screwed on the deck. The following dependency is valid: if the holes are drilled then the engine has to be screwed. This fact is expresses by the following RP rule:

(3) IF RP10.27 THEN RP10.3

For both rule types, it is possible to use logical operations OR and AND within the IF or the THEN clause. Rule 4, 5, 6 and 7 are examples of BOMRP rules, rule 8 is an examples of a RP rule.

(4) IF (1208.pos4 = 1237) OR (1208.pos4 = 2354) THEN RP10.1
(5) IF (1208.pos1 = 1216) AND (1208.pos4 = 1237) THEN RP10.27
(6) IF 1208.pos1 = 1216 THEN RP10.2 OR RP10.27
(7) IF 1208.pos1 = 1216 THEN RP10.27 AND RP10.4
(8) IF RP10.2 OR RP10.27 THEN RP10.4

Logical OR and AND operations are realized with the following database tables for BOMRP- and RP rules:

rule	*IF clause*				*THEN clause*		
	parts_family	*BOM_pos*	*variant_part*	*log_IF*	*routing_plan*	*rp_element*	*log_THEN*
6	1208	1	1216	S	10	2	O
6	1208	1	1216	S	10	27	O
4	1208	4	1237	O	10	1	S
4	1208	4	2354	O	10	1	S
5	1208	1	1216	A	10	27	S
5	1208	4	1237	A	10	27	S
7	1208	1	1216	S	10	27	A
7	1208	1	1216	S	10	4	A
1	1208	4	1237	S	10	2	S

rule	*IF clause*			*THEN clause*		
	rp_IF	*rp_element_IF*	*log_IF*	*rp_THEN*	*rp_element_THEN*	*log_THEN*
8	10	2	O	10	4	S
8	10	27	O	10	4	S

Rules with logical OR and AND operations are identified by the same rule number. Logical operations are represented by O (OR), A (AND) or S (single rule). Based on the following specification possible logical combinations of rules are transformed into the database table:

- OR within the THEN clause: log_IF=S, log_THEN=O,
- OR within the IF clause: log_IF=O, log_THEN=S,
- AND within the THEN clause: log_IF=S, log_THEN=A,
- AND within the IF clause: log_IF=O, log_THEN=S,
- AND within the IF clause, OR within the THEN clause: log_IF=A, log_THEN=O,
- ...
- no logical operation: log_IF=S, log_THEN=S.

The rule-based routing plan processor is divided into four modules. The first module allows the administration of routing plans. The modules *administration of BOMRP rules* and *administration of RP rules* are user interfaces for the administration both rule types. Depending on the customer specification of a final product and depending on the variant BOM (generated with the generator for variants and variant bills of material) the routing plan processor module generates the routing plan for this final product.

The product database contains all product specific data like part families, storage quantity, statistics, etc. Database tables for storing the different rule types of the routing plan processor are part of the rule database. Finally Figure 5 shows the rule-based routing plan processor as extension of ProMan.

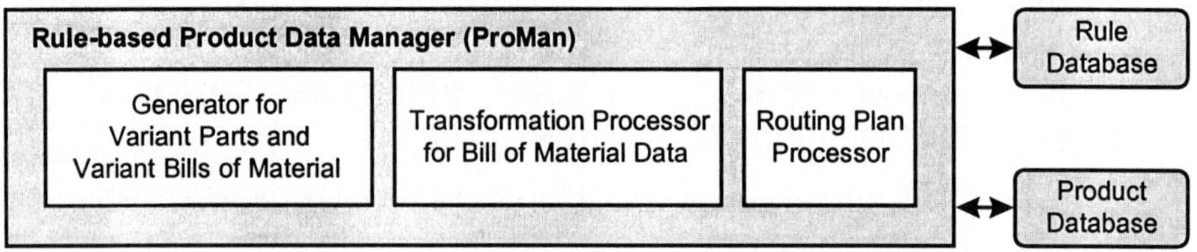

Fig. 5. The routing plan processor as an extension of ProMan.

4 Conclusions

As discussed in Section 1 and Section 2, today many enterprises are still confronted with unsolved problems in the field of product data management. Therefore this paper focuses on three aspects of the management of product data:

- Efficient management of a large number of variant specific routing plans without redundancy.
- Efficient management of dependencies between BOM data and routing plans.
- Expert-independent availability of planning algorithms and knowledge about bill of material processing, operations planning etc.

To offer a solution for these problem areas a rule-based routing plan processor is introduced which completes the previously developed product data manager. The main functionality of the proposed routing plan processor is that it determines the variant specific routing plan of a product, based on a customer specified set of final product characteristics.

In order to establish a rule-based routing plan processor variant-BOM-depending routing plans of a parts family are integrated to basic routing plan. Its data structures are independent from a customer specific variant part. The basic routing plan covers all production instructions for every variant part of a parts family. Different operation instructions for different variants are expressed by alternatives within the sequence of operations of a routing plan. The transformation of the basic routing plan into the variant specific routing plan is specified by using transformation rules.

The procedures of ProMan derive the variant bill of material from both, the parts family and the basic bill of material by using transformation rules. In the next step the rule-based routing plan processor derives a variant specific routing plan from the variant bill of material and the basic routing plan by processing the corresponding routing plan rules. As a consequence, this dynamic generation dramatically reduces the number of routing plans. With this system it is possible to generate variant specific routing plans depending on customer specifications at runtime.

The approach presented in this paper on the one hand significantly reduces the amount of data that has to be administrated and on the other hand reduces the necessary interaction between the operations planner and the CIM software. Dependencies and planning algorithms are transformed into a rulebase which is stored within a relational database. Additionally each operation of the rule-based routing plan processor is stored within the database and therefore these operations are globally available for each CIM component.

With the product data manager a system is provided that helps to bridge the gap between bill of material data and production planning systems within a CIM factory. A prototype of the introduced routing plan processor is already implemented.

Further work will be concentrated on the implementation of tools that help to structure existing product data within an enterprise. After that it is planned to develop concepts for standardized data interchange between CIM-systems based on Internet/Intranet technology. This will be a further step to improve the efficiency of CIM-systems.

References

1. Poensgen, Walter: "Prozeßorientierter Lösungsansatz für die Integration von Vertrieb und PPS bei variantenreichen Produkten", CIM-Management, Ed.: Prof. Dr. Hermann Krallmann, R. Oldenbourg Verlag München, 1994 (10) Nr. 1.
2. Thomas, R.: "Varianten - Herausforderung für Fertigungsunternehmen", ZWF Zeitschrift für wirtschaftliche Fertigung und Automatisierung, Hrsg.: Prof. Dr. Günter Spur, Carl Hanser Verlag München, 1992 (87) Nr. 11, BRD.
3. Heinen, Edmund: "Industriebetriebslehre: Entscheidungen im Industriebetrieb", Gabler Verlag, Wiesbaden, BRD 1985, (8. Auflage).
4. Straub, Egon: "CIM-gerechte Organisation der Produktionsdaten: Eine moderne PPS-Lösung für Variantenfertiger ALNO", Informationstechnik, Hrsg.: Becker-Berke K. / Färber G. / Kroneberg D. / Lipp H. M. / Louis H. P. / Rogge H./ Schuchmann H.-R. / Straßer W. / Zemanek H., R. Oldenbourg Verlag München, 1990 (32) Nr. 5, BRD.
5. Küng, Josef / Wagner, Roland / Wöß, Wolfram: "A Rule-Driven Transformation Processor for Bill of Material Data", Lecture Notes in Computer Science: Database and Expert Systems Applications, 6th International Conference DEXA 1995, Ed. Norman Revell, A Min Tjoa, Springer-Verlag Berlin Heidelberg New York Barcelona Budapest Hong Kong London Milan Paris Tokyo, London 1995. ISBN 3-540-60303-4.
6. Wöß, Wolfram: "A Rule-driven Generator for Variant Parts and Variant Bills of Material", Proceedings of the Eighth International Workshop on Database and Expert Systems Applications 1997, Ed. Roland R. Wagner, IEEE Computer Society, Los Alamitos 1997.
7. Kurbel, Karl: "Produktions- planung und -steuerung: Methodische Grundlagen von PPS-Systemen und Erweiterungen", Oldenbourg München Wien, 2. Auflage 1995.
8. Scheer, August-Wilhelm: "Wirtschaftsinformatik, Referenzmodelle für industrielle Geschäftprozesse", Springer Verlag Berlin, Heidelberg, New York (5. Auflage).
9. Meynert, Jürgen: "PPS*STAR/L1 - ein PPS-System für mittel-ständische Einzel- und Auftragsfertiger", CIM-Management, Ed.: Prof. Dr. Hermann Krallmann, R. Oldenbourg Verlag München, 1990 (6) Nr. 1.

Applications of Model-Based Co-operative Agents in Production Planning

Olga Štěpánková, Michal Pěchouček, Vladimír Mařík, Jiří Lažanský

The Gerstner Laboratory for Intelligent Decision Making and Control
Department of Control Engineering
Czech Technical University, Faculty of Electrical Engineering
Technická 2, CZ 166 27 Prague 6, Czech Republic

e-mail: {step, pechouc, marik, lazan}@labe.felk.cvut.cz

The tri-base acquaintance model of the agent's behaviour is presented in this paper. This represents an extension of the twin-base model [Cao 97]. Based on practical experience, the new model tries to cope with parallel processing, precedence constraints, and sparse resources. The idea of substituting the inter-agent negotiation processes by the internal planning activity of the agents is stressed. This strategy is enabled by periodic revisions of the knowledge and data contained in the tri-base knowledge/data bases.

1 Introduction and Motivation

The growing complexity of problems to be solved in industry requires new software system architectures integrating the already existing "islands" of well-working algorithms into more robust global systems. Currently ill-suited information flows, lack of communication among different production units and far from full utilisation of available information processing tools is what makes all of the production processes difficult to understand, model, plan and consequently optimise. Attempts to create a global, monolithic software solution, no matter how well hierarchically structured, fail.

We have been invited to participate in design of a production-planning system for the TESLA-TV factory within the framework of EUREKA No. 1439 project. TESLA-TV is a Czech manufacturing enterprise assembling TV and FM transmitters. The manufacturing process can be classified as a project-oriented production. Consequently, rather than planning and simulation of a flow of semi-products to be assembled, there is a need for a solution which would facilitate simple planning and subsequent optimisation of the discrete manufacturing of the unique final product.

After a thorough analysis of the plant it became obvious that one has to suggest a method how to integrate partial software solutions ("legacy" software systems). On the other hand the flexibility and frequent changes in the production facility inevitably require highly distributed solution. The results of the analysis strongly supported the choice of a multi-agent system as a suitable technology for building *ProPlanT* (*Prod*uction *Plan*ning *T*ool) system [Mařík 98].

There is a wide range of possible multi-agent systems' architectures. The mass of identical, conform agents and a highly granular community of deeply specialised agents are the extreme cases in this spectrum. Whereas in the case of a large community of identical agents *(collective architecture)* the "social" and "sociological" aspects of behaviour play a dominant role, in the latter case the community is expected to be strongly internally organised and co-ordinated. The latter architectures (*integration architectures*) are seem suitable for (legacy) system integration purposes, for designing and implementing highly distributed modelling, decision making and control algorithms.

The integration architectures usually involve a small number of well-developed agents with a clearly defined, highly specialised functionality. Each agent, in our understanding, consists of a *functional body* (usually a stand-alone, already well running program with a precisely specified functionality) and a *wrapper* which is responsible for agent's engagement in the agents' community. The wrapper contains a *model of the agent's behaviour* [Nwana 97]. The wrapper also "translates" the inter-agent communication into the instructions for the activity of the functional body and mediates the results of the body activity into the agents' community.

There can be found various kinds of models of agent's behaviour exploring different communication strategies [Wooldridge 95], [Lashkari 94]. Some are based on *broadcasting of task-announcement messages* or on the presence of a *central communication agent*. Another solution is offered by so called *acquaintance models* [Jennings 93] that create a wide group of behavioural models: Here, information on the capabilities and behaviour of the given agent as well as the relevant pieces of information about the other agents is stored in the wrappers of individual agents. Thus, the information is not concentrated in a central agent but kept highly distributed (but well organised and co-ordinated) across the community. The acquaintance models help to decrease necessary communication when an agent is searching for the best-qualified agent(s) for co-operation.

For system integration purposes in industrial tasks, each existing software system/module can be understood as a body of one agent - if appropriate methods for communication and co-operation among the agents are defined and corresponding techniques are implemented inside the wrappers, a highly integrated global solution can be achieved.

2 Twin-Base Acquaintance Model

A specific acquaintance model technique, called a twin-base approach was proposed recently [Cao 96]. This approach suggests organising the relevant information about co-operating agents in two separate information bases in the wrapper, namely in

- the CO-OPERATOR BASE which has an auxiliary nature and which contains/collects information concerning the other agents. It can provide information on the data and message formats used by the other agents, their addresses, statistics concerning the other agents' efficiency, trust values etc.

- the TASK BASE which contains relevant particular information on possible task decomposition and problem solving process in the form of triples

  ⟨*Task_Description*, *Agent*, *Dependence*⟩.

  Each triple represents a possible allocation of the co-ordination role when solving the given task (*Task_Description*) to one of the agents (*Agent*) as well as a description of a sequence of sub-tasks which have to be solved consequently (*Dependence*).

Another notation of the triples which was used by the system *ViSe2* [Cao 97] is

$$\langle T_j, A_i, \cup_{k=1}^{m} \langle T_{jk}, A_{ik} \rangle \rangle$$

where T_j denotes the task, A_i represents the agent co-ordinator and the third member of the triple is the decomposition of the task T_j into m subtasks fulfilled by the helping agents.

An integral part of the twin-base model is a revision process aimed at keeping the contents of the bases fresh. This way, the task-base always contains up-to-date information on the current capabilities of the peers. This facilitates directing the co-operation requests to the most suitable agent in the community. As a result, the communication traffic is significantly reduced and the system responses are very fast.

3 Tri-Base Acquaintance Model

The efficiency of a good solution of any task depends on the *current* and *future* availability of agents within the community. The notion of *future* has to be regarded mainly when considering planning and scheduling tasks mentioned in the introductory remarks of this paper. In order to cope with this aspect, we have introduced a *tri-base model* [Mařík 97]as a powerful enhancement of the *twin-base model*. The novel idea is based on the strict separation of data, and permanent and transient knowledge, which each agent maintains within its wrapper.

3.1 Tri-Base Model as an Extension of the Twin-Base Model

In the tri-base approach, the original CO-OPERATOR BASE has been split into two separate bases: the CO-OPERATOR BASE and the STATE BASE. The CO-OPERATOR BASE keeps rather static information concerning the peers while the STATE BASE is updated very frequently reflecting the changes of the other agents' activities.

The tri-base model consists of three information bases the information flow of which is shown in Fig. 1. and described in the following.

The three bases are used as follows.

- CO-OPERATOR BASE collects static information on the peer agents.
- TASK BASE contains knowledge concerning possible task decomposition with respect to problem solving processes. The *problem section* contains general knowledge on possible task decomposition and contingent time precedence and

prerequisites (if any). There is a *plan section* that stores deduced plans on how to co-ordinate particular tasks.

- STATE BASE reflects the peer agents' states that may evolve rapidly in time. The *agent section* of the STATE BASE reflects the internal states of the peer agents like their current load, reachability and trust. The *task section* describes the current states of the solution of the tasks that have been contracted and are co-ordinated by the agent. The peers are expected to report the solution progress.

Whenever a new task reaches a particular agent, the activities within the tri-base model can be roughly gathered in the following steps.

1. The general rules in the *problem section* of the TASK BASE are applied to suggest some decompo-sition of the task (if any - it can happen that the agent itself is capable to solve the task).
2. The proposed decompo-sitions are matched with the CO-OPERATOR BASE from where the additional parameters (addresses, formats, etc.) are taken. Proposed collaborators are confronted with the STATE BASE and evaluated to find the best peer to ask for help. The resulting plan is stored in the *plan section* of the TASK BASE.

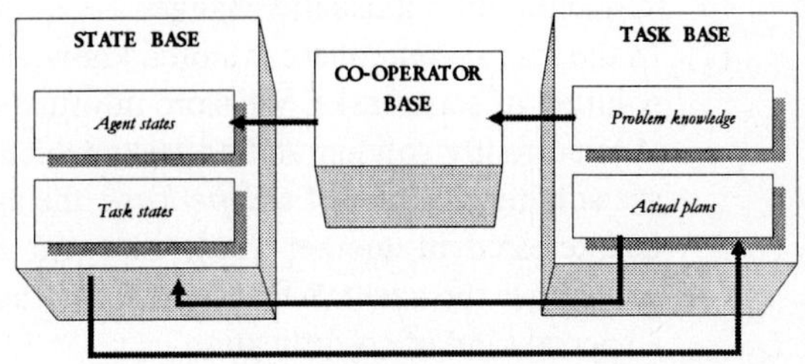

Fig. 1.

3.2 Structure of Bases within the Model

In the following we define in more detail what the bases in the wrapper of an individual agent ***A*** contain.

- CO-OPERATOR BASE - All the permanent data about co-operating agents are located within this base. For any agent ***a*** there appear three main kinds of data - agent's ***a*** address, message format, and predefined responsibility. Quadruples as follows are proposed to be used:

$$\langle \boldsymbol{a}, Address_{\boldsymbol{a}}, Language_{\boldsymbol{a}}, \mathrm{T}_{\boldsymbol{a}} \rangle,$$

  where agent ***a*** is a particular co-operating agent, $Address_a$ specifies its physical location such as IP address, port etc., $Language_a$ is its communication format used, and the set T_a specifies responsibilities of the agent ***a***, i.e. the tasks the agent ***a*** is designed to be accountable for. The agent ***a*** is accountable for any task $T \in \mathrm{T}_a$ whenever it is able to solve the task T itself or by decomposition (decomposition of the task T is suggested in the TASK BASE of the agent ***a***).
- STATE BASE - An agent's STATE BASE does not have to contain information on the entire community. It reports on load and capability of those agents and on tasks that belong to the scope of reasoning of the agent ***A***. The STATE BASE is divided into the *agent section* and the *task section*. This base comprises the non-permanent information:

(1) The agent section provides data on the status of co-operating agents regarding their load and reliability. Triples as follows are proposed to be used for this purpose:

$$\langle \boldsymbol{a}, Load_a, Trust_a \rangle,$$

where ***a*** stands for the particular agent, $Load_a$ specifies its load, and $Trust_a$ is the level of confidence of the agent ***A*** into such information. The proper meaning of agent load differs. It can be simply a flag with values of engaged/vacant, a number of requests per time unit, or the agent's agenda, specifying the nearest available time-slot in future. The level of confidence $Trust_a$ may be for instance information on how old the triple is, and/or how frequently does it usually change.

(2) In the *task section*, there is stored knowledge related to the actual state of the solution of some tasks. We store information on those tasks, which the agent ***A*** is currently solving and on tasks which agents contracted by the agent ***A*** are solving as a part of a *SuperTask*, the agent ***A*** co-ordinates. If the agent ***A*** is interested in another *Task*, an agent ***B*** is responsible for, the agent ***A*** *subscribes* the agent ***B*** for this piece of information. We see *subscription* as a special kind of co-ordination.

The quadruple for this purpose may look as follows:

$$\langle Task, Agent, Solution, Trust \rangle,$$

where the content of *Solution* specifies the status of the *Task* solved by *Agent*. Information on whether the task has been already solved and on possible time and cost requirements may be included.

- TASK BASE - This structure contains knowledge on possible decomposition of tasks considered. The decomposition can be used to devise various plans how to fulfil a requested task either by means of actions of the agent's body, or by contracting appropriate agents with a request for help. Creation of plans has to be based on fresh information on capabilities of co-operating agents with respect to the relevant goal. As mentioned above, the TASK BASE is divided into its *problem* and *plan* section.

(1) The *problem* section of the TASK BASE comprises information on possible decomposition of the tasks. Triples as follows are proposed to be used within this sub-base:

$$\langle SuperTask, \langle \{T_j\}, Precedence \rangle, Constraints \rangle,$$

This triple claims: "provided *Constraints* are met, the *SuperTask* can be successfully accomplished by performing all the tasks from the set $\{T_j\}$ in such a way that all the time *Precedence* constraints are respected". (Note that there are often no precedence constraints.) *Constraints* specify the agents' related applicability conditions for the given decomposition (for instance, requirements on maximal number of agents engaged in the problem solving or requirements on the memory consumption, etc.) If the agent ***A*** does not decompose the given task (***A*** does not delegate it further) and it solves the task itself the triple looks as follows

$$\langle SuperTask, \varnothing, Constraints \rangle.$$

(2) The *plan* section comprises production rules representing plans how a given task can be accomplished under actual configuration of the considered distributed community. Quadruples as an extension of twin-base triples have been proposed within the philosophy of the tri-base model.

$\langle SuperTask, \langle\{Agent_j, T_j\}, Precedence\rangle, Constraints, Trust\rangle$

If the applicability *Constraints* hold, the agent ***A*** plans to address the *SuperTask* so that the set of sub-tasks $\{Agent_j, T_j\}$ will be carried out. The agent ***A*** chooses an appropriate peer $Agent_j$ for each of the considered subtasks T_j. The last argument stands for the Trust of the agent ***A*** in successful accomplishment of the *SuperTask* using suggested decomposition. How to elaborate the plan is described in paragraph 0.

3.3 Process of Updating the Model

Let us review how to maintain the content of the given bases. One option is to use a special agent called *facilitator* devoted to maintain the content of the agents' bases by *periodical revisions*. In idle times it keeps checking agents' load, using the pre-defined information in the CO-OPERATOR BASEs and computes the most up-to-date information of agents' current capabilities. This information is to be represented in the form of trust in plans to be used by an agent, so that the best suitable plan gets the highest value.

This approach looses its transparency as soon as we want to deal with parallel processing and sparse resources. That is why we search for another solution based on more active role of each agent in the community. An agent can either find out all relevant information itself, or it can get it from the contracted or subscribed agents. The first method is considered expensive in terms of communication, as an agent would have to ask the collaborator every time it would go for revision. This revision must be done periodically whereas the subscribing approach makes the agent to revise its information only if necessary. That is why we prefer the second possibility. This approach tries to avoid need to rely on a kind of central communication agent, the *facilitator*, that is in charge of updating agents' plans - this kind of comparatively complex reasoning. Responsibility for the *plan section* of the TASK BASE re-computation was shifted to the agent itself. Each agent uses its idle time so that it combines its knowledge in the CO-OPERATOR BASE, the STATE BASE and permanent information on decomposition in the TASK BASE in order to create up-to-date plans. This process will be described later in section 4.1.

The planning agent has to be aware of the state of its peers. This is a necessary condition for the success of the suggested approach. To be kept informed the agent could subscribe some agents for information on their state. In this way the agent gets the relevant data directly without being forced to rely on the facilitator. Nevertheless we do not remove the central agent entirely. Our meta-agent is in charge of monitoring an overall load and communication traffic. The main aim of the meta-agent is to reason about these data in order to identify knowledge, which might prove useful for conduct of the community. The meta-agent searches for example for possible mutual relations among some seemingly independent tasks. Such explicit knowledge can significantly extend the strength of the agent community by making it able to cope with more tasks or to solve them more efficiently. The meta-agent can update knowledge in all the bases of the agents.

Let us review the updating process in each of the three bases more carefully:

TASK BASE: The problem section concerning decomposition of tasks can be understood as permanent. Changes in the problem section reflect the results of the meta-agent's reasoning mostly. Updating of the *plan section* consists of checking the available plans and in construction of the new ones – cf. section 4.1.

STATE BASE: Reliable information in the STATE BASE of an agent represents its awareness about the activity of the co-operating agents. This knowledge becomes the central issue of our approach. The STATE BASE as the changing resource of the planning process has to be well updated and maintained. Any agent contracts all of its collaborators from the CO-OPERATOR BASE and subscribes these for reporting on their status. Every time the state gets changed the collaborator sends a message to the original agent in order to let it know that the STATE BASE is to be updated.

CO-OPERATOR BASE: There are basically permanent data regarding collaborating agents stored within the CO-OPERATOR BASE. These do not require any often updates. The meta-agent that is in charge of monitoring the agent's operation may detect some of suspicious irregularities or changes in its activity. Either loss or enhancement of an agent capabilities are viewed as examples. So the meta-agent is supposed to update the CO-OPERATOR BASEs of the agents.

4 Community Lifecycle

The multi-agent community may be in charge of a number of parallel problem-solving projects (tasks). There are three distinct stages of the community operation with respect to a single project. The system may be engaged in *planning*, *re-planning*, and *execution*.

- PLANNING - When planning, the community creates a plan and elaborates an estimation of the resources (time, cost) requirements under supervision of a single agent responsible for the given task.
- EXECUTION - When executing, the system triggers the activity stored in the TASK BASEs of particular agents. Occasionally re-planning has to be evoked if an obstacle in the execution appears.
- RE-PLANNING - When re-planning, each agent reacts to any of relevant changes within the STATE BASE and thus makes the plan the most up-to-date.

4.1 Generation of Plans

Suppose an agent *A* is in charge of a *SuperTask*. The agent can either

1. use an existing plan stored in the *plan section* of its TASK BASE or
2. elaborate a new plan using its own methods and skills.

In the latter case the agent A takes problem knowledge found in the *problem* section of the TASK BASE of the agent A. Here it finds a piece of general decomposition knowledge for the considered *SuperTask* in the form

$$\langle SuperTask, \langle \{T_i\}, Precedence \rangle, Constraints \rangle,$$

where $\{T_i\}$ is the set of tasks the *SuperTask* is to be decomposed into.

For simplicity let us suppose that the set *Precedence* is empty. We will return to the more general case later. The agent A consults the CO-OPERATOR BASE of the agent A in order to detect the possible collaborators for all the tasks in $\{Ti\}$. The agent A is supposed to find a good match for each task from the set $\{T_i\}$, i.e. to complement each task T_i with the name of an agent A_j that is ready to cope with that particular task. The requested result is a set of couples $\{\langle A_j, T_j \rangle\}$ meeting the following requirements:

- For each task T_j the agent A finds an agent A_j such that there is a $\langle A_j, \_, \_, \{T_k\} \rangle$[1] stored in the CO-OPERATOR BASE of agent A and $T_j \in \{T_k\}$.
- For the set $\{\langle A_j, T_j \rangle\}$ the applicability *Constraints* get checked. Only those couples, which meet the constraints, are evaluated further.
- The evaluation of the trust *Trust* is carried out under consideration of the $Load_{Aj}$ and $Trust_{Aj}$ of the agents A_j as parameters, where $\langle A_j, Load_{Aj}, Trust_{Aj} \rangle$ is contained in the STATE BASE of A. Just those couples $\langle \{\langle A_j, T_j \rangle\}, Precedence \rangle$ with best evaluation are considered and they form possible plans:

  $$\langle SuperTask, Agent, \langle \{\langle A_j, T_j \rangle\}, Precedence \rangle, Constraints, Trust \rangle.$$

  Trust can be either minimal trust of all the agents the task is delegated to, average, or weighted average. The quadruple with the highest trust *Trust* is viewed as the actual plan.

If the content of the STATE BASE (the agent section of which is an important resource for the plan construction) gets updated, *Trust* is to be re-computed and each of quadruples is to be re-evaluated consequently. This kind of re-planning activity makes the plan the most up-to-date and bridges the planning and execution stages of the problem solving process.

Now let us consider the general case, where precedence constraints for some tasks apply. One possibility how to address this is based on the idea of planning without any scheduling mechanism, which is one of the options offered within the tri-base model. In this case we substitute planning by the negotiation process. An agent simply has to find out when the required preceding task, specified in the precedence constraints, is due to. Instead of contracting the responsible agent, it just consults its own STATE BASE - *task section* in order to find out the time when it can start planning the task T_j. If no such information is found in the STATE BASE, the agent finds an appropriate collaborator in its CO-OPERATOR BASE and *subscribes* it for such information.

If the agent is to delegate the task T_j further on to other agents it has to let them know the starting time given by the preceding task. This piece of information is usually stored in the *task section* of the STATE BASE.

---

[1] The symbol '_' stands for an anonymous variable the value of which is not relevant

The suggested approach can obviously result in plans, which are far from optimal. This can happen namely if there are some tasks in the community, which can be accomplished by a single agent only (this agent becomes a bottleneck of the solution). To avoid it more sophisticated algorithm of partitioning the set of subtasks with respect to *Precedence* constraints has to be elaborated. Our solution tries to create the relevant part of the partition within the limits generated by *lazy* and *eager* strategies [Mařík 98].

4.2 Communication Traffic

Using the tri-base acquaintance model within the wrapper of each of the agents significantly reduces the need of inter-agent communication. As it was seen above, substantial part of negotiation processes is replaced by planning carried out internally - without any vast communication with the others - by the agents responsible for the given task. Instead of the necessity to communicate, the agent consults its STATE BASE to find the best peer to co-operate.

Four kinds of messages used in the inter-agent communication remain:

1. When the plan starts to be executed, the task co-ordinator sends requests to the collaborating agents to carry out their jobs. The task co-ordinator receives messages confirming "the job is done" later. These messages up-date the task section of the STATE BASE of the task co-ordinator.
2. In the case, some information about the other agent (like the processing time or readiness to start) is missing, a message subscribing for the corresponding answer is sent out. These messages are used to certify information required for the precedence handling.
3. When the state or capabilities of an agent are changed, the agent itself sends this information to change the content of the STATE BASE or CO-OPERATOR BASEs of its peers.
4. The messages from the meta-agent represent a special category of messages, which is analysed in more detail below.

Some of the messages noted in the points 3. and 4. may be transmitted to the entire community.

6 Tri-Base Model in the Production-Planning Domain

ProPlanT is a tool aimed at production planning and simulation in factories with project-oriented profile of production [Mařík 98]. Three kinds of agents have been designed and implemented in ProPlanT, all with tri-base models within their wrappers, namely

- PPA agent simulating the activity of a project planner,
- PMA agent representing the activities of a production manager acting on any managerial level within the enterprise, and

- PA agent that models behaviour of a workshop foreman who is responsible for job-shop related activities.

The inter-agent communication uses KQML convention with the message content in the KIF format. The entire system has been implemented in C++ in Optima++ development environment. The system has been tested on parallel PC machines running Windows NT operating system. All three kinds of agents plan locally using the tri-based model. Of course, the agent's types differ in the contents of their bases. Bases of the agents' tri-base models have been implemented in Sybase SQL Anywhere DBMS. The tri-based approach proved to be transparent and efficient for being applied in the multi-agent system for production planning.

7 Conclusions

The tri-base acquaintance model of the agent's behaviour aimed at problem solving is presented in this paper. This represents a substantial extension of the twin-base model [Cao, 1996]. Let's stress some features of the model extension.

The CO-OPERATOR BASE in the original twin-base model was split into a CO-OPERATOR BASE containing permanent or semi-permanent knowledge and a STATE BASE collecting non-permanent, temporal data in the tri-base model.

The general planning knowledge is represented by quadruples in comparison to triples in the original twin-base model. The *trust* parameter was added. Moreover, the items of each quadruple are structured in more detail. Precedence constraints useful for parallel problem solving are considered. Each particular solution (plan) is inferred from

a) general knowledge in the TASK BASE,
b) knowledge about the other agents' capabilities in the CO-OPERATOR BASE, and
c) the state of the STATE BASE.

Similarly as in the twin-base model, the inter-agent negotiation processes are substituted by the internal planning activity of the agent that is responsible for the given task. This strategy is enabled by periodic revisions of the knowledge and data contained in the agents' tri-base models.

Our approach has been motivated by the problems of production planning, which are of slightly different nature compared to the secretarial administration treated in [Cao 96, 97]. This fact led us to tackle the task precedence problem as well as to design a specific community life cycle. We expect the proposed methods to have more general validity. As the tri-base acquaintance model explores various pieces of knowledge contained in its three bases and its activity is driven by the global goal to solve a specific super-task, it is possible (acceptable) to call the behaviour of agents based on this model as Knowledge-based Goal-driven Behaviour (KGB).

The work presented in this paper was carried out under the support of the EUREKA PVS'98 project (no.1439), and the grants GAČR no.102/96/0382 and MŠMT no.VS 96047.

References

[Cao 96] Cao W., Bian C.-G., Hartvigsen G.: *Cooperator Base and Task Base for Agent Modeling: The Virtual Secretary Approach.* In: Proc. of AAAI-96 Workshop on Agent Modeling, AAAI Press,1996, pp.105-111

[Cao 97] Cao W., Bian C.-G., Hartvigsen G.: *Achieving Efficient Cooperation in a Multi-Agent System: The Twin-Base Modelling.* In: Cooperative Information Agents (Kandzia P., Klusch M. eds.), LNAI 1202, Springer-Verlag, Heidelberg, 1997, pp. 210-221

[Genesereth 94] Genesereth M.R., Ketchpel S.P.: *Software Agents.* Com. of ACM, 31(7),1994, pp. 48-53

[Jennings 93] Jennings N.R., Wittig T.: *ARCHON: Theory and Practice.* In: Distributed AI: Theory and Praxis (Avouris M., Gasser L. eds.), Kluver Academic Publishers, Dordrecht,1993, pp.179-195

[Kiss 96] Kiss G.: *Agent Dynamics.* In: Foundations of Distributed AI (O'Hare G. M. P., Jennings N. R. Eds.), John Wiley & Sons,1996, pp. 247-267

[Lashkari 94] Lashkari Y., Metral M., Maes P.: *Collaborative Interface Agents.* In: Proc. of l2th National Conf on AI, AAAI Press,1994

[Mařík 96] Mařík V., Štěpánková O., Flek O.: *Multi-Agent System with Qualitative Simulation Unit.* In: Proc. of the XIIIth European Meeting on Cybernetics and Systems Research, Vienna,1996, pp.1138-1188

[Mařík 97] Mařík V., Štěpánková O., Lažanský J.: *Role of Qualitative Reasoning in a Multi-Agent System.* In Proceedings of EUROCAST'97, (Pichler F., Mo-reno-Diaz R. eds.) LNCS No. 1333, Springer Verlag, Heidelberg, 1997, pp. 380 - 393

[Mařík 98] Mařík V., Pěchouček M., Hazdra T., Štěpánková O.: *ProPlanT – Multi-Agent System for Production Planning.* In: Proc. of the XVth European Meeting on Cybernetics and Systems Research, Vienna,1998, to appear.

[Nwana 97] Nwana H.S., Ndumu D.T.: *An Introduction to Agent Technology.* In: Software Agents and Softcomputing (Nwana H.S. and Azarmi N. eds.), LNAI 1198, Springer-Verlag, Heidelberg,1997, pp. 3-26

[Štěpánková 96] Štěpánková O., Mařík V., Lažanský J.: *Improving Cooperative Behaviour in Multiagent Systems.* In: Advanced IT Tools, Chapman and Hall London,1996, pp. 293-302

[Wooldridge 95] Wooldridge M., Jennings N.: *Intelligent Agents: Theory and Practice.* The Knowledge Engineering Review, 10 (1995), No. 2, pp.115-152

[Zhong 97] Zhong N., Kakemoto Y., Ohsuga S.: *An Organized Society of Autonomous Discovery Agents.* In: Cooperative Information Agents (Kandzia P., Klusch M. eds.), LNAI 1202, Springer-Verlag, Heidelberg,1997, pp.183-194

Open Architecture for Natural Language Distributed Systems

A. Yamani, A. Al-Zobaidie, and M. Ibrahim

School of Computing & Mathematical Sciences
The University of Greenwich
Wellington Street
London SE18 6PF, UK

Tel: (+) 44 181 331 8530
Fax: (+) 44 181 331 8665

E-mail: a.yamani@greenwich.ac.uk
E-mail: a.alzobaidie@greenwich.ac.uk
E-mail: m.ibrahim@greenwich.ac.uk

Abstract

Current information retrieval systems focus on or are limited to the use of key words recognition rather than full Natural Language interface. This paper presents an open architecture for Natural Language interface to specific domain. We describe the requirements and the design objectives of a Natural Language interface to an object model that can retrieve answers from a knowledge base.

The novelty of the proposed work is that it is based on Computational Linguistic theory, namely, the Lexical-Functional Grammar theory. The linguistic presentation structures of this theory have been formulated into linguistic rules to enhance the understanding of user queries.

In addition, common-sense domain specific knowledge has been investigated and proved to be a suitable approach for eliminating some Natural Language ambiguities found within specific domain. The adoption of the developed prototype into an open architecture is also investigated. This should provide a framework for building similar applications within the chosen domain.

The framework has been tested using several newspaper stories to prove the accuracy of our approach.

1. Introduction and Natural Language Understanding

Currently, the use of Natural Language (NL) in industrial frameworks lack of semantics can lead to ambiguities across multiple frameworks application domains [4]. This weakness is due to the absence of linguistic understanding in the user interface of these frameworks. Although the main aim of these frameworks is to maximise the effectiveness of providing a good user interface, to date no attempt has been made to boost NL processing to generate a proper and correct interpretation of NL in order to eliminate ambiguities. The main focus was on processing the NL rather than understanding it.

In order to develop syntactic, semantic analysis for any NL, a powerful formal system for representing syntactic and semantic knowledge must be provided. One of the most suitable candidates for dealing with this analysis and representation is the Lexical-Functional Grammar theory (LFG) [3].

The LFG theory has been developed with the intention of serving as a grammatical basis for a precise computationally and psychologically related model of human languages [03]. Another distinguishing feature of the LFG theory is that it is one of the theories that accords the traditional notion of Subject and Object and can be applied to any language such as English or Arabic to describe agreement systems as will as word orders. The adoption of the LFG theory in our new proposed approach has been fully described in [9]. As a consequence, the framework has the ability to provide a model of interface using both languages English and Arabic.

The LFG assumes three levels of computational linguistic representations. These are:

1. Constituent Structure: deals with the syntactic level and produced the C-Structures that corresponds to the "surface" representation of the utterances and is language dependent [10].

2. Functional Structure: deals with the syntactic level and produced the F-Structures that is language independent and express linguistic "universals" [10].

3. Semantic Structure: deals with the semantic level and produced the S-Structures which correspond to the meaning of words and its' relationship with each other (e.g. agreement system) [11].

This paper is organised as follows. In section 2, we show how common-sense domain knowledge, and frames are applied in our work. We then outline an architecture framework based on MVC to design the components in our prototype NL system in section 3. In section 4, an account is given on natural language understanding framework based on LFG. This is followed, in section 5, by detailed design and the object model and implementation details. Conclusions and further work are given in section 6, followed by a list of references.

2. Common-sense Domain Knowledge

The fundamental difficulties facing research in the field of knowledge representation today are not limitations due to hardware, but rather questions about how to represent large amounts of knowledge in ways that still allow the effective use of individual facts.

As for Common-sense domain knowledge, the problem is beyond just processing NL, it involves spanning human consensus knowledge [12]. Despite many successes, AI software growing too fast and too ambitious. It seems to be that perhaps the only way forward is to limit our ambitions by narrowing the general common-sense knowledge into common-sense *domain* knowledge. Therefore, in this paper, we follow a different approach to structuring common-sense domain knowledge within the presentation structures of the LFG theory.

Adding to the three presentation levels of the LFG [3], we proposed *Common Sense Domain Knowledge Structure,* which refereed to as K-Structure [2]. K-Structure is a natural extension of the S-Structure, it determines not only the semantic knowledge features of a sentence, but it also determines rather how this knowledge can trigger another knowledge associated with it i.e. event-action system. The basic principle in structuring such knowledge is not on the question of formal power of the understanding theory, but rather on the represented knowledge. The knowledge structure presentations are organised into a hierarchy of Grammar Rules and Intelligent Domain Knowledge Rules within the structure of the proposed Lexicon. Furthermore, and due to the inheritance of knowledge between concepts (an advantage gained from using the Object-Oriented paradigm in the system). Objects follow their super-classes for their static and dynamic aspects. For example, categories dealing with feminine verbs (only for Arabic) are grouped together so that they have common syntactic features. As for the agreement between these concepts, rules have to be enforced to determine agreement system between these concepts.

2.1 Common-sense Domain Knowledge and Frames

One way to represent Common-sense domain knowledge is to use Frame structure [7]. In our proposed work, this means translating the sentences into a representation, which is compatible in its structure to frame structure. What makes frame-based representation rather an attractive option to use, is the fact that it is well suited to a wide variety of domains.

A frame has a set of slots. Each slot can provide knowledge of a particular aspect or attribute of the object with which the frame is concerned. Frames can capture a great deal of knowledge [7], but for our purpose we need to apply frames to capture detailed knowledge about how acts happen. In NL, this involves how verbs and nouns appear in typical sentences using Thematic-object [6]. The overall goal achieved by understanding that frames make it possible to capture and exploit knowledge that exist both explicitly and implicitly in any NL.

The Slot in a frame has a Name and Value (SN, SV) representing a unit of knowledge about a particular conceptual objects or class of objects [1]. We usually consider frames in a set known as a frame system; a frame system is simply a set of interrelated class, sub-class and instances. Frames provide a mechanism for structuring what is known and for substituting for what is not known. Moreover, the addition of event-action representation (i.e. Production Rules) to the frame representation system makes our knowledge representation paradigm quite a powerful and flexible one.

3. Design Framework and Open Architecture

Brown et al [15] outline a framework for an open architecture for a distributed system based on the MVC paradigm. This is indeed a 'generic' paradigm which can be used in many situations [16-19]. We are proposing in our system to apply a similar approach and architecture to that followed in [15]. The major benefits and rationale for such an approach will not be repeated here as details are given in [15] and elsewhere [16-18]. However, for completeness we present here a brief overview of MVC (Model-View-Controller) and similar paradigms, e.g. MVP [18].

In order to be show how to apply a distributed open architecture in our NL framework, we start by identifying in a top-down manner, the major components that exist in such domains or indeed many other similar domains. But before that, we show in Fig. 1, the components and structure of an MVC model. Only one view and one controller are shown but there can be several views for each model;

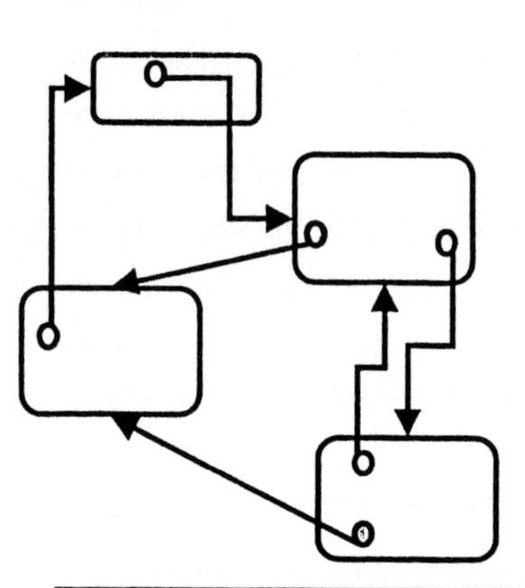

Fig. 1 The MVC Model & Interfaces

there is at least one controller per view. The MVC system as implemented in Smalltalk and others systems, relies on a broadcast-dependency mechanism. When the model changes in any way, it sends itself a message "*changed*". This results in triggering a 'change occurred' *broadcast* to all dependants in the collection object, which can contain several objects. Each view object will then respond by sending an *update* message to its model. The output result, returned by the model, of the update message will then be used to update the affected view. This seems to us to be a suitable mechanism to apply to keep the views synchronised with an application model. We simulated the dependency/broadcast mechanism in our system using Kappa, frames and slot facets. In the following subsection we explain how our architecture maps onto this model as shown in Fig.2.

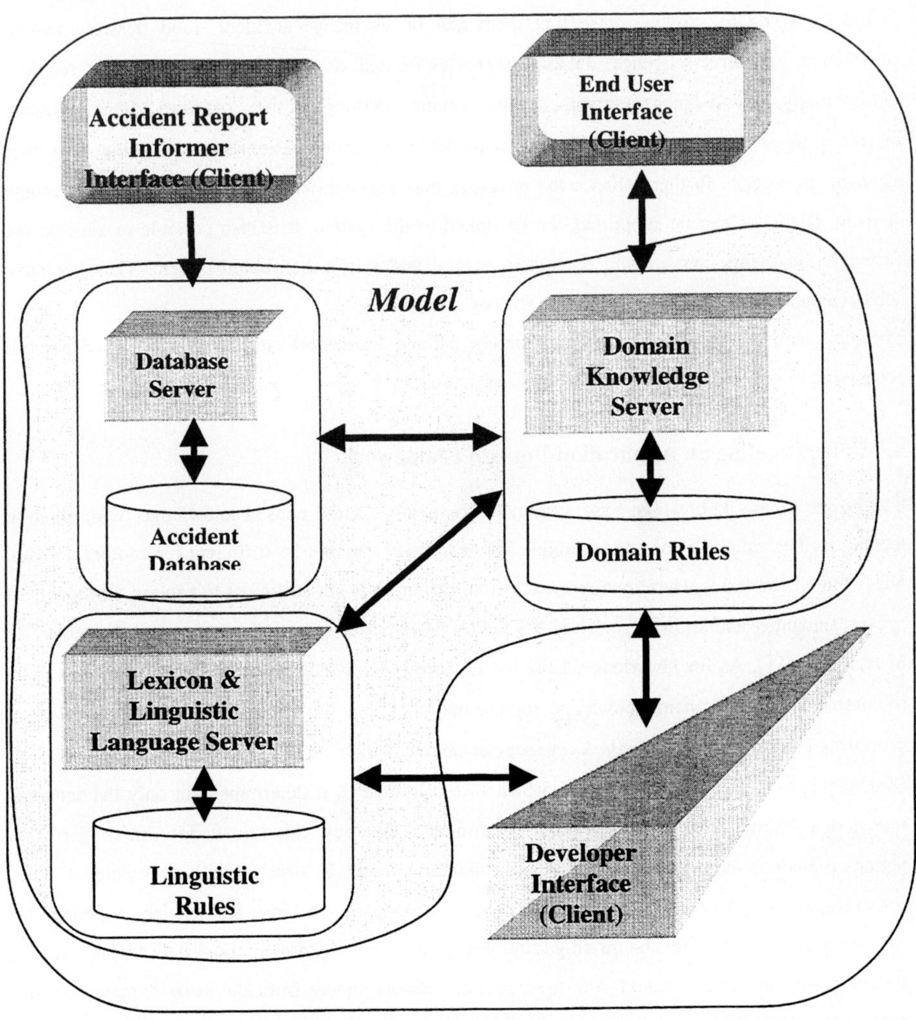

Fig.2 The Component Architecture

3.1 The Architecture and the components

Fig, 2 depict our framework architecture, its components and their interactions. This is a mapping from the MVC pattern in the following way. The model (M) is made up of the domain knowledge base component (domain knowledge server and domain rules), the accident database and its server and the language server/lexicon. The view and controller (i.e. our V and C) are represented in the user interfaces. The display screens represent the views to its users; the control is effected via commands input using of a keyboard and/or a mouse.

It should be pointed out the diagram represents a block diagram view. This design may be viewed as an *open architecture* in the sense that there can be as many 'accident' (and possibly related information, e.g. drivers licence) database server as needed, as many language servers as required and as many knowledgebase servers as appropriate. As long as they conform to the interface specification of the system, they can be seamlessly integrated. The notion of using a 'Server manager' in order to further enhance the openness may also applied as described in [15]. Of course as many clients as can be supported can be linked to the system. It is also possible to allocate the various components (servers and clients) to several nodes in a distributed system. Thus, we have achieved an open distributed architecture for our system.
The next section considers the NL application domain framework, its object model and the NL processing in general and in particular the K-structures.

4. Understanding an Application Domain Framework

The power of any knowledge base system relies mainly on the chosen knowledge representation technique. The suitability of one technique in one domain may not be sufficient for another domain. NL is one of the fields where one representation technique is not sufficient to capture all aspects of syntax, semantic, and knowledge. The LFG theory deals perfectly with the syntax and the semantics of NL [10], [11]. As for knowledge, LFG has no formal knowledge representation. Therefore, as a requirement of the domain knowledge representation within the framework of the LFG, we are proposing *Common-sense Domain Knowledge Structure,* which we shall refer to as (K-Structure). K-Structure is a natural extension of the S-Structure of the LFG, it determines not only the semantic knowledge features of a sentence, but it determines rather how this knowledge can trigger other actions to deduce more knowledge. The main objective of the K-Structure is to complement the S-Structure, and the way to achieve that is to use Domain Common-sense Knowledge to identify the missing attributes and infer the missing relationships between objects. In our system this is achieved by comparing the analysed text with a general framework model from the same domain, as Fig.1 shows, and captures all possible scenarios that may have happened in that specific application but was not directly stored an input from analysed text.

The following subsection gives a formal example of how the newly formed K-Structure can be represented. The representation shows a NL Domain as an Object Model based on the LFG theory. In addition, the representation proposes new theoretical methodology to model NL interrogative as an application Domain, where the mapping of the LFG analysis to the Object database, modelling and the structure of the LFG promote a better understanding of NL. Let us look at the property of the proposed K-Structure.

In fig. 3, we show a detailed object model of our chosen application-specific domain – traffic accidents. This model consists of the many classes that exist in such a domain, their relationships and the tow natural language parts - NL-LFG component and the LFG-OM.

4.1 The Property of the K-Structure for the Interrogatives

Figure 4 shows the property of skeleton interrogative K-Structure. Within the LFG theory, each interrogative must have a main predicate, either verb or noun. By mapping argument two (ARG-2) of the S-Structure, this will determine the main predicate/Theme of the K-Structure. Therefore, the components of the K-Structure have the following representation:

PRED<(↑Interrogative Nucleus) (↑Domain Rules)>

Every interrogative must follow the above representation i.e. every interrogative must have **↑Interrogative Nucleus** and **↑Domain Rules**. **↑Interrogative Nucleus** has two main nucleus, **Nucleus-1** and **Nucleus-2**, where:

Nucleus-1: deals with **↑Theme, ↑Relation, and ↑Thematic-object,** where:

↑Theme: is the interrogative theme e.g. *policeman.*

↑Relation: is the relation between two objects in the object model e.g. *works-for*

↑Thematic-object: is the object name from the object model e.g. Police Station.

Nucleus-2: deals with **↑ Words, ↑ Semantic Features,** and **↑ Thematic-object** where:

↑ Words: is a list of words of the interrogative.

↑ Semantic Features: is a list of semantic features of the words.

↑ Thematic-object: is a list of thematic-objects of these words.

The (↑Domain Rules)

The task of the **(↑Domain Rules)** is to select the particle from the interrogative and then the appropriate rule set which can perform a deduction in order to retrieve answers. Having got an interrogative, which required deduction to obtain an answer, the Domain rules will trigger the appropriate rule for such interrogative.

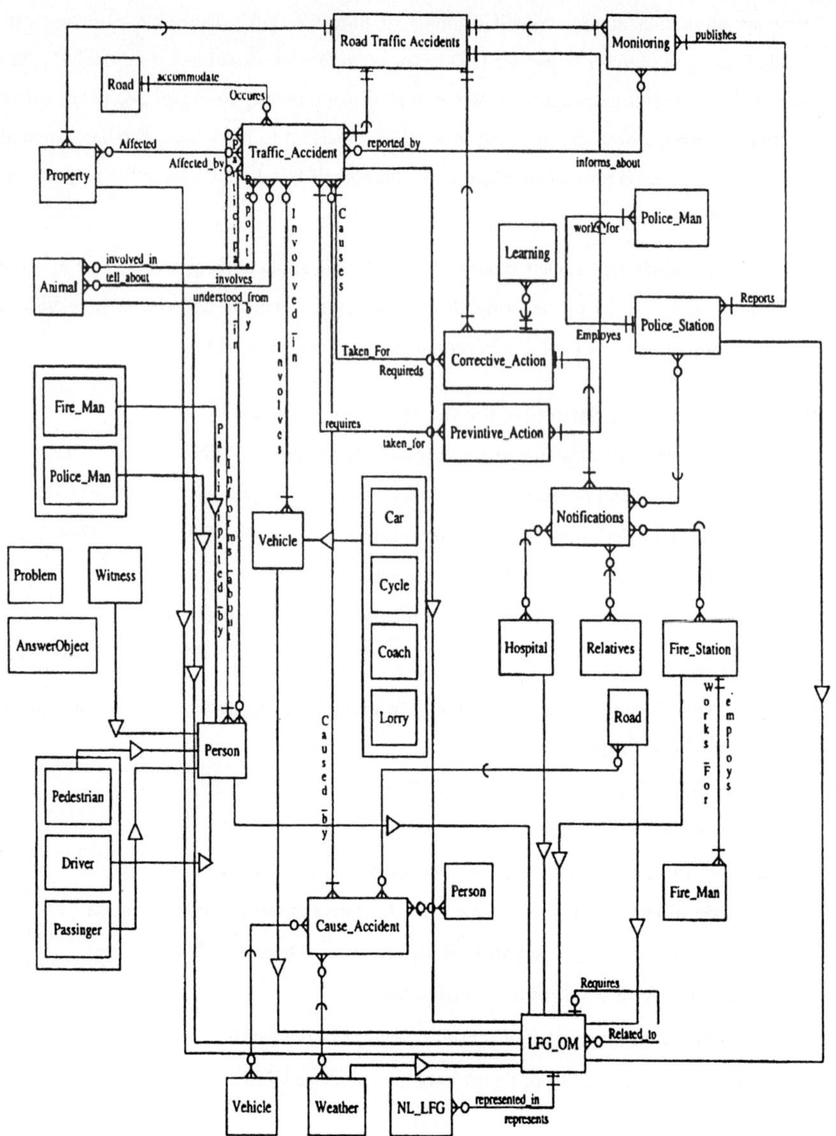

Fig. 3 The Object Domain Model

PRED <↑ Interrogative Nucleus, ↑ Domain Rules >

Interrogative Nucleus

Nucleus-1

PRED < ↑ Theme, ↑ Relations, ↑ Thematic-object >
Theme:
Relations:
Thematic-object:

Nucleus-2

PRED < ↑ Words, ↑ Semantic Features, ↑ Thematic-object >
Words:
Semantic Features:
Thematic-object:

Domain Rules

Particle Types

If Particle type = where **Then** Answer in Set A# **Where** Set A# is as follows:
If Particle type = when **Then** Answer in Set B# **Where** Set B# is as follows:
If Particle type = X **Then** Answer in Set Y#

Rule Sets

SET A: *A1#* **If** Nucleus-1 Relation is in the set of Nucleus-2 Semantic Features
Then Answer = Nucleus-1 Thematic-object Location.
A2# **Else** Build new Relation between Nucleus-1Thematic-object and
Nucleus-2 Thematic-object.
Answer = Nucleus-1 Thematic-object Location.

SET B:
B1# **If** Nucleus-1 Relation is in the set of Nucleus-2 Semantic Features
Then Answer = Nucleus-1 Thematic-object Date/Time.
B2# **Else** Build new Relation between Nucleus-1 Thematic-object and
Nucleus-2 Thematic-object.
Answer = Nucleus-1 Thematic-object Date/Time.

Figure 4. The property of skeleton interrogative K-Structure

5. Description of the proposed Lexicon and Object Model

5.1 The Functional Behaviour of Verbs, Nouns, and their Linguistic Associations

The lexicon entries are classified into three main categories, namely, the Nouns, the Verbs, and the Particles. This has been built using the Object Modelling Workbench (OMW) tools. The lexicon model captures all common Arabic verbs, nouns, particles and their linguistic categories and their associations, [14], which are important for our domain and any other domains.

The English and Arabic nouns are subcategorised into subject, verbal, complements, pronouns, adjectives, proper, source, and circumstances. The proper nouns are further subdivided into animal, static, human, numeral, tool, determinative, and location. The circumstances are also subdivided into temporal - which deals with time, and location. These are considered to be under the category of Noun Phrases (NPs).

The English and Arabic verbs are subcategorise into Intransitive, (one role), which required a subject, and the LFG theory Oblige Argument (OBL_ARG). Transitive, (two roles), which required a subject, an object, and an OBL-ARG. Di-transitive, (three roles), which required a subject, two objects, and an OBL_ARG. Tri-transitive, (four roles), which required a subject, three objects, and an OBL-ARG.

The English and the Arabic particles are subcategorised into conjunction, continuation, proposition, and interrogative. The interrogatives are subdivided into interrogative-H such as the word *how*, interrogative-WH such as the word *where*, and finally interrogative-Y/N which is Yes or No.

Each of the above categories has a further linguistic associate, for instance, within the lexicon, each word has a set of linguistic features values such as gender features, syntactic features, semantic features, etc. For instance, the functionality of the predicate verb *happen* in the lexicon has masculine gender feature (for Arabic only), and it takes two arguments, a Subject and an Obl-Argument in the F-Structure. The word such as *accident* has masculine gender feature, and can be a qualified subject. The word *where* has masculine/feminine gender feature, and can be a qualified OBL-Argument.

5.2 The Relationships Between the Object Domain Model and the LFG Structures

The LFG Structures and their content representations are all contained in the Lexicon. The Lexicon also contains the necessary linguistic features i.e. syntactic and semantic features that help to identify the target Objects and their Attributes. These words can be Nouns, Verbs, or Particles. These can be either an Instance of an Object or an Attribute of an Instance depending on its entry in the Lexicon.

For example, a Subject or WH-Question-Type can be an Instance while an Adjective or Location can be an Attribute.

The model contains the object domain model, and the relationships between objects. The Thematic-objects, Syntax, and the Semantic features of each word indicate whether that word can be mapped into one or more object names, or attribute names in order to find the correct answer. Furthermore, the combination of objects behaviour in the domain model with the LFG linguistic structures rules, resolves most, if not all, of the common ambiguities found in this domain and subsequently enhances the understanding ability of the interrogative, in order to select the right path leading to the right answer.

The powerful knowledge representation techniques available in Kappa e.g. Frames and Rules, makes the tool an attractive one. The object model has been build to the proposed prototype using Object Modelling Workbench (OMW) tools. The model captures the most common object in the domain, and also can be accommodated to include any object instances from the domain framework (e.g. text story). The prototype - through its intelligence rules, have the capabilities of tuning the object model and integrate the new extension when new object class is met that is not covered initially. This is done with the user consultation and advice. This extension will automatically be integrated within the model framework so similar future application will be dealt with no problem.

The Framework model within the traffic accident domain is extendible to include any missing classes of objects that may emerge from the analysis of a new application text. For example, a plane class may be added if the accident involves a crash between a plane and a vehicle on the road. During the inheritance of knowledge between concepts, sets of features have to be common between these concepts. As for the agreements between these concepts, rules have to be enforced to determine the Arabic agreement system between these concepts.

Although English and Arabic interrogatives are different in their structures, they are, during processing, follow the same behaviour pattern in obtaining answers. They are being utilised as specimens to prove the implementation of proposed theoretical work in order to retrieve answers. There are two methods in which the system retrieves the answer from, namely, a Pre-Determined or On-line deduction.

The used inferencing technique is Forward Chaining, where Rules are grouped into sets. Predetermined answers are stored directly from text after passing the first three LFG phases. On-line Deduction answers are performed when stored data triggers associated domain-specific Rules for further information. The system has been tested by sets of queries from different stories and produced the expected results.

In Fig.5, we show a even flow diagram of processing a NL language sentence which shows the sequence of events that has been triggered (solid colour) and also the F-, S- and K-structures.

In Fig .6, we capture the result of processing a simple natural Arabic sentence 'ayna wagga alhadeth' meaning 'where did the accident happen'. Note, however that 'accident' in Arabic has both masculine gender 'hadeth' and feminine one 'hadetha'. Notice the result "All words has been recognised" in the last text box in Fig.6. We also show in Fig.7, the processing of the semantic structure together with the arguments.

6. Conclusion and Further Developments

In this paper, we have argued for the extension of the LFG theory to form the proposed K-Structure. This extension is based on Frame structure and Thematic-object Frame representation [07]. It has been shown that the LFG theory and its three representation structures, namely, the C-Structure, F-Structure, and S-Structure required to be extended [08]. The main objective of the K-Structure is to complement the S-Structure of the interrogative, and the way to achieve this is to apply the domain common-sense knowledge to identify the missing attributes and draw the missing relationships between the object instances through the deduction and reasoning rules.

This paper presents a prototype model, which has been conducted by developing a general Object Model for the traffic accident domain. This model has been used to capture the functional behaviour of objects, the related verbal interactions and their linguistic associations in a given query. The combination of object's behaviour in the Domain Model with the LFG Structures rules, resolved most, if not all, of the common ambiguities found in NL for that domain and enhances the understanding ability of the proposed framework.

7. References

[1]. Intellicorp Inc. 1996b, Kappa/OMW Product Information. World Wide Web pages on the Internet, 'http://www.intellicorp.com/'.

[2]. Al-Zobaidie A., Al-Khonaizi M., Yamani A., al-A'ali M, Common Sense Knowledge Representation for Natural Language Processing: An LFG approach, in Processing Arabic Journal, Report 8, Nijmegen 1995, Ditters E. (Ed.), Institute for the Languages & Cultures of the Middle East, Nijmegen University Holland, ISSN 0921-9145, Pp 47-78.

[3]. Bresnan J. and Kaplan R. 1985 The mental representation of grammatical relation, Lexical Functional Grammar. The MIT Press, 1985, pp 173-281.

[4]. Fayed M. and Schmidt D.C., Object-Oriented Application Frameworks, Communication of the ACM. Oct. 1997 Volume 40, number 10, Pp 32-38.

[5]. Gazdar G. and Mellish C. Natural Language Processing in Prolog. An Introduction to computational Linguistics, 1989, Addison Wesley.

[6]. Yamani A. and Al-Zobaidie A., Natural Language Understanding for Question Answering System. In the Fourth IEEE International Conference Electronics, Circuits, and Systems, ICECS 1997.

[7]. Winston H. Artificial Intelligence. 3ed ed. Addison-Wesley, 1992.

[8]. Yamani A. and Al-Zobaidie A., Computational Linguistics Approach to Question-Answering System for Arabic. In the 5th International Conference and Exhibition on Multi-lingual Computing, ICEMCO-96, Cambridge University, April 1996.

[9]. Yamani A. and Al-Zobaidie A., Interrogative Common-sense Domain Knowledge for Enhancing the Intelligence of Question - Answering System. (To appear) in the 6th International Conference and Exhibition on Multi-lingual Computing, ICEMCO-98, Cambridge University, April 1998.

[10]. Yamani A. and Al-Zobaidie A., Long-Distance Dependencies and Coordination Phenomena in Arabic Interrogatives: An LFG Treatment. The Second International Conference on Artificial Intelligence, Cairo, 1994, Pp 166-188.

[11]. Yamani A. and Al-Zobaidie A., Semantic Structures for Arabic Interrogatives and Coordinated Arabic Interrogatives: An LFG Treatment. The Second International Conference on Artificial Intelligence, Cairo, 1994, Pp 189-205.

[12]. Lenat D. CYC: A Large-Scale Investment in Knowledge Infrastructure. Communication of the ACM Vol. 38. No. 11, Nov. 1995.

[13]. Johnson M. 1991 Features and Formulae. Computational Linguistics, ACL, 1991, pp. 131.

[14]. Ántoine El-Dahdah, 1994 El-Dahdah Encyclopaedia of Arabic Grammar: A dictionary of Arabic Grammar in Chart and Tables. Revised by G.M. Abdul - Massih, Librairie du Liban Publishers.

[15]. Brown, S., Vallas, R., Ibrahim M.T, and Al-Zobaidie, A., 1998, " Object Design and implementation of a Distributed Client/Server System, paper submitted to Dexa'98.Erich Gamma, Richard Helm, Ralph Johnson, and John Vlisside, 1995, Design Patterns: Elements of Reusable Object-Oriented Software, Addison-Wesley

[16]. Ward Cunningham and Kent Beck, 1987, "Using Pattern Languages for Object-Oriented Programs", in Proceedings of OOPSLA'87, Orlando, Florida, USA, pp. ?

[17]. Potel M., *"MVP: Model-View-Presenter: The Taligent Programming Model for C++ and Java"*, http:// ? potel@taligent.com

[18]. Brown, A.W. (Ed), 1996, Component-Based Software Engineering, IEEE Computer Society

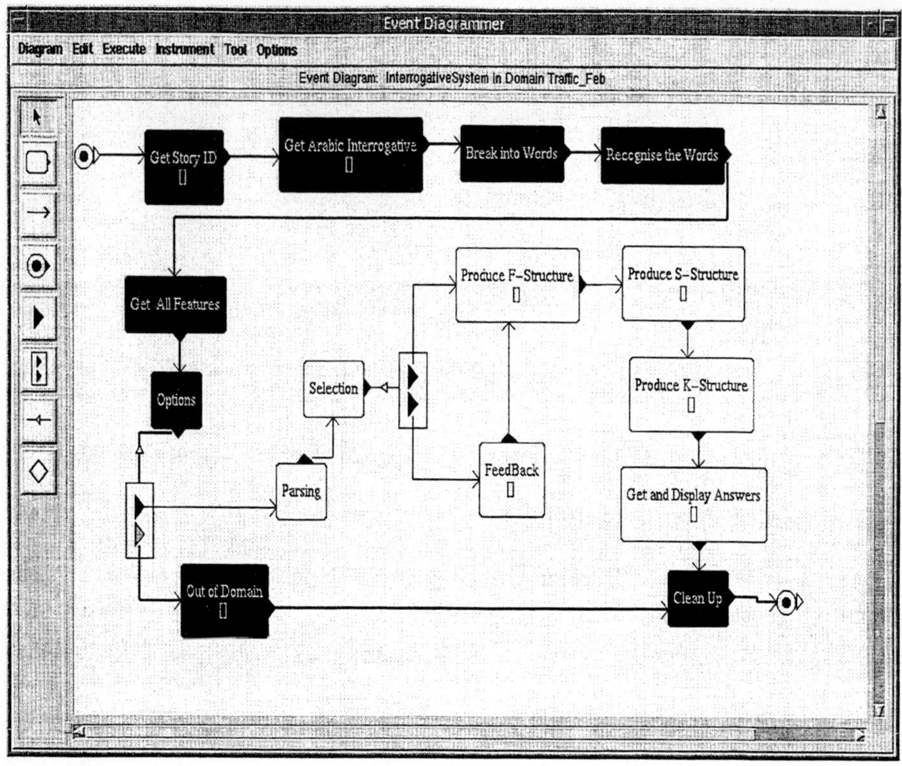

Fig 5: The Event-Diagrammer

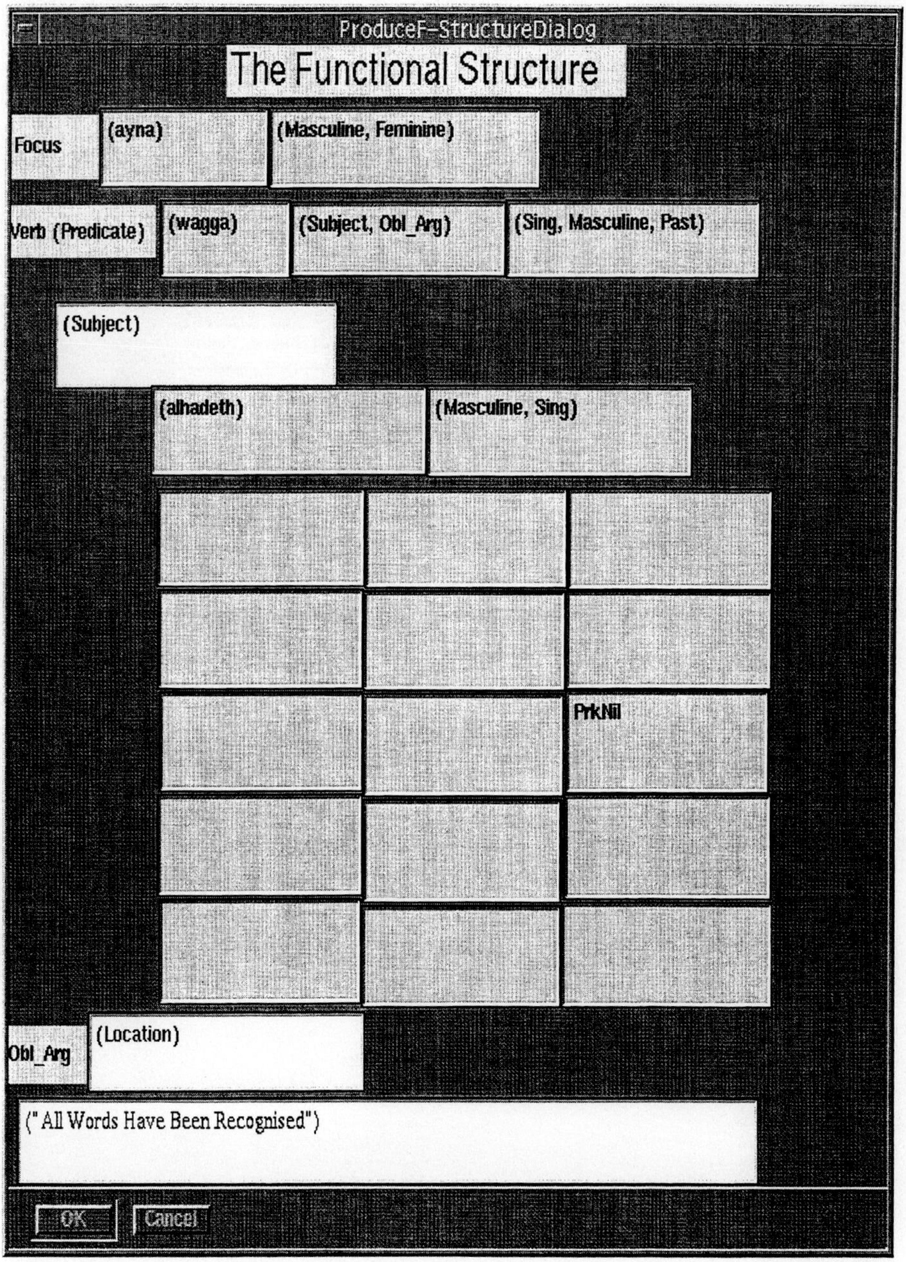

ProduceF-StructureDialog

The Functional Structure

Focus (ayna) (Masculine, Feminine)

Verb (Predicate) (wagga) (Subject, Obl_Arg) (Sing, Masculine, Past)

(Subject)

(alhadeth) (Masculine, Sing)

PrkNil

Obl_Arg (Location)

("All Words Have Been Recognised")

OK Cancel

Fig. 6: The F-structure and results

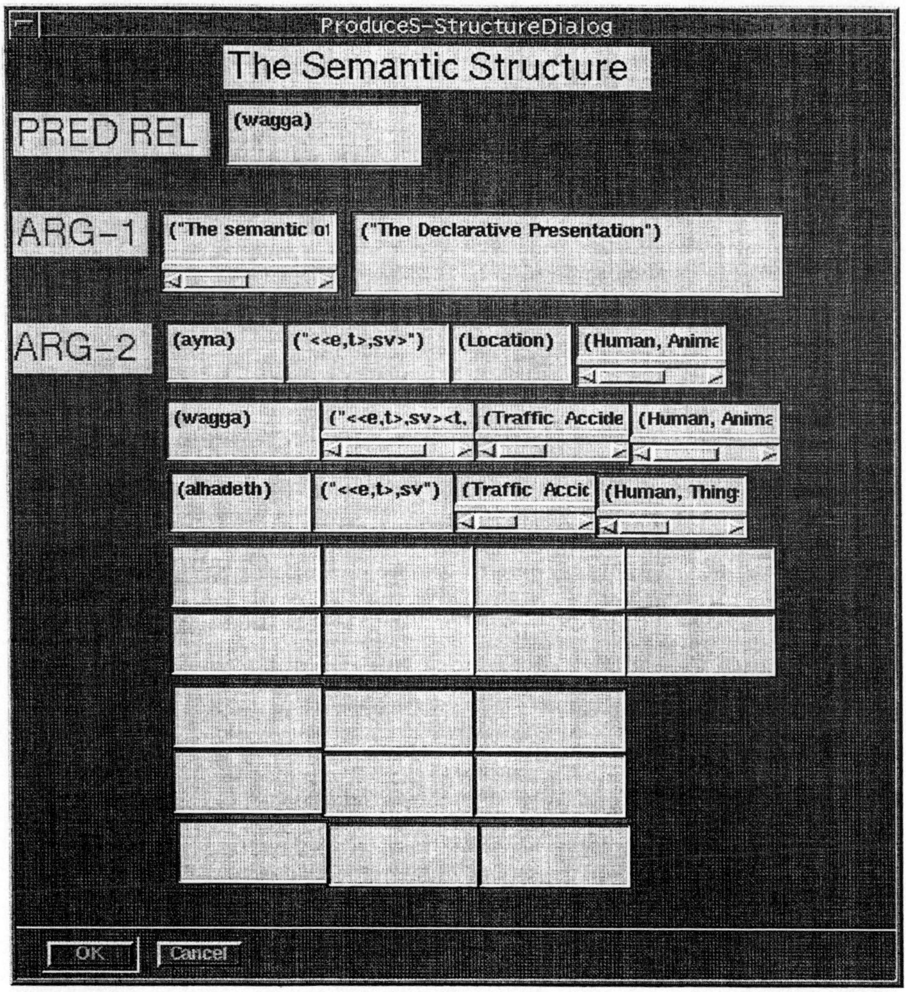

ProduceS-StructureDialog

The Semantic Structure

PRED REL (wagga)

ARG-1 ("The semantic o ("The Declarative Presentation")

ARG-2 (ayna) ("<<e,t>,sv>") (Location) (Human, Anima

(wagga) ("<<e,t>,sv><t, (Traffic Accide (Human, Anima

(alhadeth) ("<<e,t>,sv") (Traffic Accic (Human, Thing

OK Cancel

Fig. 7: The K-structure and results

Join Processing in Web Databases

S. S. Bhowmick W.-K. Ng E.-P. Lim S. K. Madria

Center for Advanced Information Systems, School of Applied Science,
Nanyang Technological University, Singapore 639798, SINGAPORE
{sourav,wkn,aseplim,skm}@cais.ntu.edu.sg

Abstract. Recently, there has been increasing interests in data models and query languages for unstructured data in the World Wide Web. When web data is harnessed in a *web warehouse*, new and useful information can be derived through appropriate information manipulation. In our web warehousing project, we introduce a new operator called the *web join*. Like its relational counterpart, web join combines information from two *web tables* to yield a new web table. This paper discusses various issues in web join such as join semantics, joinability, and join evaluation.

1 Introduction

Given the high rate of growth of the volume of data available on the WWW, locating information of interest in such an anarchic setting becomes a more difficult process everyday. Thus, there is the recognition of the undeferring need for effective and efficient tools for information consumers, who must be able to easily locate and manipulate information in the Web. We aim to build a web warehouse containing information extracted from the Web that may also interoperate with conventional data warehouses. To meet the warehousing objective, we materialize web information as a *web table* and define a set of web operators so as to equip the warehouse with the basic capability to manipulate web tables and correlate additional, useful, related web information residing in the web tables [7].

In this paper we focus on the web join operator. It serves two important purposes: First, like its relational counterpart, web join combines information from two web tables based on *some criteria* to yield a new web table. Second, this information can be stored in a separate web table and can be used for future queries. One of the objectives of web join is to capitalize on the reuse of retrieved data from the WWW in order to reduce execution time of queries.

Even though the notion of a web join is similar to that of a relational join, there are number of new challenges due to the richer nature of the web data model. For example, what exactly is a web join operation? How do we perform a

* This work was supported in part by the Nanyang Technological University, Ministry of Education (Singapore) under Academic Research Fund #4-12034-5060, #4-12034-3012, #4-12034-6022. Any opinions, findings, and recommendations in this paper are those of the authors and do not reflect the views of the funding agencies.

web join? What useful information can we gather if we perform a web join? Due to the graphical nature of the Web, the web join process is a much complicated and challenging problem than for relational join. In this paper, we address some of these challenges. In particular, our contributions are:

1. We formally define the notion of web join and discuss the necessity of join operation in a web database.
2. We determine the conditions required to perform a web join between two *web tables*.

2 Related Work

There has been considerable work in data model and query languages for the World Wide Web. But we are not aware of any work which deals with join operation in web databases. For example, Mendelzon, Mihaila and Milo [6] proposed a WebSQL query language based on a formal calculus for querying the WWW. The result of WebSQL query is a set web tuples flattened immediately to linear tuples. This limits the expressiveness of queries to a certain extent as complex queries involving operators such as web join are not possible.

Konopnicki and Shmueli proposed a high level querying system called the W3QS [4] for the WWW whereby users may specify content and structure queries on the WWW and maintain the results of queries as database views of the WWW. In W3QL queries are always made to the WWW. Past query result are not manipulated for the evaluation of future queries. This limit the usage of web operators like web join to derive additional information from the past queries.

Fiebig, Weiss and Moerkotte extended relational algebra to the World Wide Web by augmenting the algebra with new domains (data types) [3], and functions that apply to the domains. The extended model is known as RAW (Relational Algebra for the Web). Only two low level operators on relations, *scan* and *index-scan*, have been proposed to expand an URL address attribute in a relation and to rank results returned by web search engine(s) respectively. RAW provides minor improvement on the existing relational model to accommodate and manipulate web data and there is no notion of a join operation similar to ours.

Inspired by concepts in declarative logic, Lakshmanan, Sadri and Subramanian designed WebLog [5] to be a language for querying and restructuring web information. But there is no formal definition of web operations such as join.

Other proposals, namely Lorel [1] and UnQL [2], aim at querying heterogeneous and semistructured information. These languages adopt a lightweight data model to represent data, based on labeled graphs, and concentrate on the development of powerful query languages for these structures. Moreover, in both these proposals there is no notion of join operation similar to ours .

3 Background

In this section we describe our basic data model and web algebra and then provides the motivation.

3.1 Web Data Model(WDM)

We proposed a data model for a web warehouse in [7] and [8]. Our data model consist of hierarchy of web objects. The fundamental objects are *Nodes* and *Links*. Nodes correspond to HTML or plain text documents and links correspond to hyper-links interconnecting the documents in the World Wide Web. We define a Node type and a Link type to refer to these two sets of distinct objects. These objects consists of a set of attributes as shown below:

`Node` = `[url, title, format, size, date, text]`

`Link` = `[source-url, target-url, label, link-type]`

The WDM supports structured or topological querying; different sets of keywords may be specified on the nodes and additional criteria may be defined for the hyperlinks among the nodes. Thus, the query is a graph-like structure and it is used to match the portions of the WWW satisfying the conditions. In this way, the query result is a set of directed graphs consisting of nodes and links (called *web tuples*) reflecting the query graph. A collection of these web tuples is called a *web table*. If the web table is materialized, we associate a *name* with the table. A web table is associated with a schema and is formally defined as 4-tuple $M = \langle X_n, X_\ell, C, P\rangle$ where X_n is a set of node variables, X_ℓ is a set of link variables, C is a set of connectivities in CNF, P is a set of predicates in CNF. The web schema of a web table is the query graph that is used to derive the table. A set of web tables and a set of web schemas is called a *web database*.

We also proposed a *Web Algebra* for retrieving information from the Web and manipulating these information to derive additional information. The algebra provides a formal foundation for data representation and manipulation. We have defined a set of web operators with web semantics so as to equip the web database with the basic capability to manipulate web tables. These operators include *web select*, *web join*, *web union*, *web intersection* and so on. These operators build the foundation for the web algebra. For more details on WDM and web algebra and its motivation see[7]. We illustrate our Web Data Model with an example in the next subsection.

3.2 Motivating Example

Suppose, an user Bill, wishes to find all one bedroom and two bedroom apartments in Singapore whose monthly rent is between \$600—\$1,000 and \$1,000—\$1,200 respectively, and all areas in Singapore from which travel time to Raffles Place is around 20 minutes by bus.

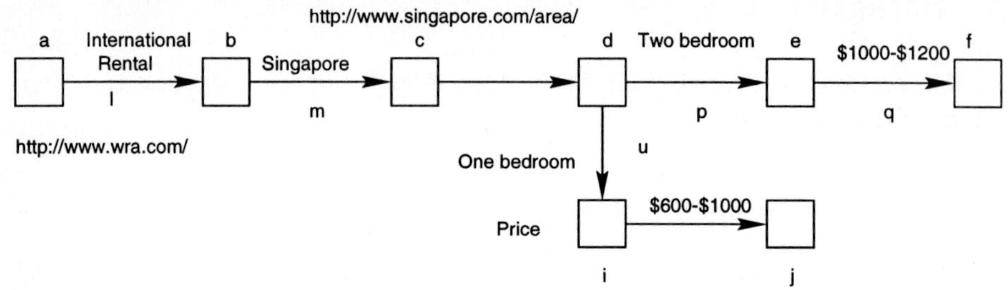

Fig. 1. Web schema(query graph) of Accommodation web table

Suppose, there are two web sites *World Rental Agency* (WRA) (`http://www.wra.com/`) and *World Transportation Agency* (WTA) (`http://www.wta.com/`) which provides apartment rental details and transportation details respectively for different countries in the world. From there, Bill figured there would be links with anchor labels 'International Rental', 'Singapore', 'Two bedroom', in WRA web site and 'International Transport', 'Singapore', 'Raffles Place', 'Bus' in WTA web site that might be used. For instance, in the WRA web site, the 'International Rental' link would point to a list of countries in the world. From this list the link 'Singapore' point to a web page containing list of residential areas in Singapore. From the hyperlinks associated with each area, he can probe further to find the list of one bedroom and two bedroom apartments with monthly rent between \$600—\$1,000 and \$1,000—\$1,200 respectively. With these web sites, Bill constructed the query graphs as shown in Figures 1 and 2.

When Bill's query is evaluated, he receives a set of web tuples each satisfying the query graphs. The result of each query is stored in the web tables `Accommodation` and `Transport` respectively.

The web schema of the web tables `Accommodation` and `Transport` is shown below in Examples 1 and 2 respectively. Note that the variables in the figures denote arbitrary instances of Node and Link. Observe that some of the nodes and links have keywords imposed on them. These keywords express the content of the web document or the label of the hyperlink between the web documents. Two special symbols `#` and `-` are used for those node and link variables which are not *bound* by the predicates of the schema.

Example 1. Find the list of all one bedroom and two bedroom apartments in Singapore whose monthly rent is between \$600—\$1,000 and \$1,000—\$1,200 respectively, starting from the home page of WRA.

Let the schema of the above query be $M_i = \langle X_{i,n}, X_{i,\ell}, C_i, P_i \rangle$ where $X_{i,n} = \{a, b, c, d, e, f, i, j\}$, $X_{i,\ell} = \{l, m, p, q, u, k\text{-}\}$, $C_i \equiv k_{i_1} \wedge k_{i_2} \wedge k_{i_3} \wedge k_{i_4} \wedge k_{i_5} \wedge k_{i_6} \wedge k_{i_7}$ such that $k_{i_1} = a\langle \ell \rangle b$, $k_{i_2} = b\langle m \rangle c$, $k_{i_3} = c\langle - \rangle d$, $k_{i_4} = d\langle p \rangle e$, $k_{i_5} = e\langle q \rangle f$, $k_{i_6} = d\langle u \rangle i$, $k_{i_7} = i\langle k \rangle j$ and $P_i \equiv p_{i_1} \wedge p_{i_2} \wedge p_{i_3} \wedge p_{i_4} \wedge p_{i_5} \wedge p_{i_6} \wedge p_{i_7} \wedge p_{i_8} \wedge p_{i_9} \wedge p_{i_{10}} \wedge p_{i_{11}} \wedge p_{i_{12}} \wedge p_{i_{13}} \wedge p_{i_{14}}$ such that $p_{i_1}(a) \equiv [a$`.url EQUALS "http://www.wra.com/"`$]$, $p_{i_2}(b) \equiv [b$`.title EQUALS "Country List"`$]$, $p_{i_3}(\ell) \equiv [\ell$`.label EQUALS "Internat-`

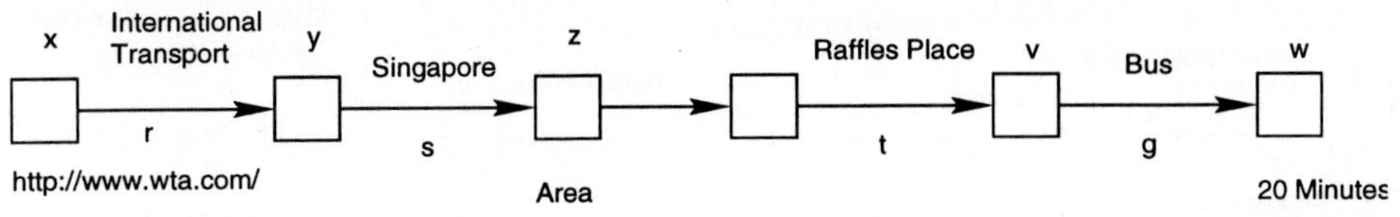

Fig. 2. Web schema(query graph) of Transport web table

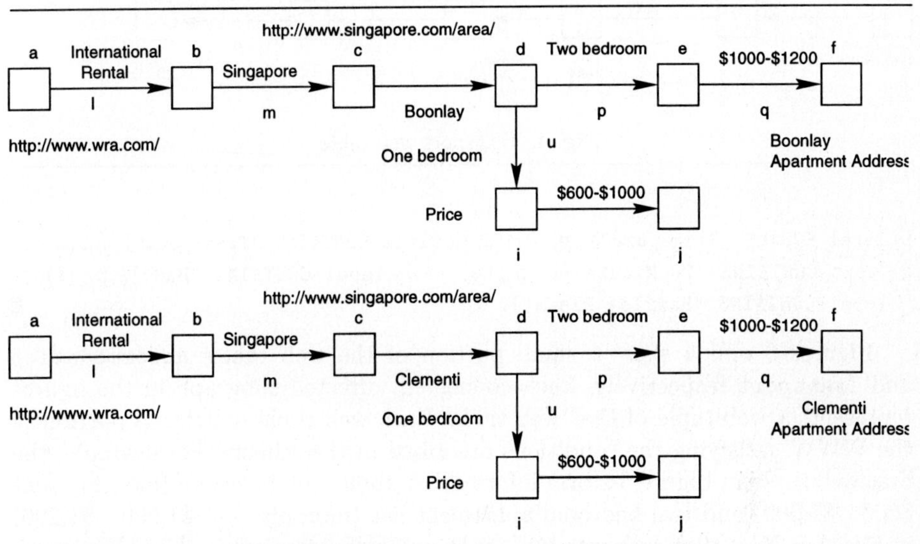

Fig. 3. Accommodation web table

-ional Rental"], $p_{i_4}(c) \equiv$ [c.url EQUALS "http://www.singapore.com/area/"], $p_{i_5}(m) \equiv$ [m.label EQUALS "Singapore"], $p_{i_6}(d) \equiv$ [d.title CONTAINS "Apartment- - Type"], $p_{i_7}(e) \equiv$ [e.title CONTAINS "Price"], $p_{i_8}(p) \equiv$ [p.label CONTAINS "Two bedroom"], $p_{i_9}(q) \equiv$ [q.label CONTAINS "$1000 - $1200"], $p_{i_{10}}(f) \equiv$ [f.text CONTAINS "Apartment Address"], $p_{i_{11}}(i) \equiv$ [i.title CONTAINS "Price"], $p_{i_{12}}(k) \equiv$ [k.label CONTAINS "$600 - $1000"], $p_{i_{13}}(j) \equiv$ [j.text CONTAINS "Apartment Add- -ress"]., $p_{i_{14}}(u) \equiv$ [u.label CONTAINS "One bedroom"]. ∎

Example 2. Find the list of all areas in Singapore from where travel time to Raffles Place is around 20 minutes by bus starting from the home page of WTA.

Let the schema of the above query be $M_j = \langle X_{j,n}, X_{j,\ell}, C_j, P_j \rangle$ where $X_{j,n} = \{x, y, z, v, w, \#\}$, $X_{j,\ell} = \{r, s, t, g, \text{-}\}$, $C_j \equiv k_{j_1} \wedge k_{j_2} \wedge k_{j_3} \wedge k_{j_4} \wedge k_{j_5}$ such that $k_{j_1} = x\langle r \rangle y$, $k_{j_2} = y\langle s \rangle z$, $k_{j_3} = z\langle \text{-} \rangle \#$, $k_{j_4} = \#\langle t \rangle v$, $k_{j_5} = v\langle g \rangle w$ and $P_j \equiv p_{j_1} \wedge p_{j_2} \wedge p_{j_3} \wedge p_{j_4} \wedge p_{j_5} \wedge p_{j_6} \wedge p_{j_7} \wedge p_{j_8} \wedge p_{j_9}$ such that $p_{j_1}(x) \equiv$ [x.url EQUALS "http://www.wta.com/"], $p_{j_2}(y) \equiv$ [y.title EQUALS "Country List"], $p_{j_3}(r) \equiv$ [r.label EQUALS "International Transport"], $p_{j_4}(z) \equiv$ [z.url EQUALS "http://www.singapore.com /area/"], $p_{j_5}(s) \equiv$

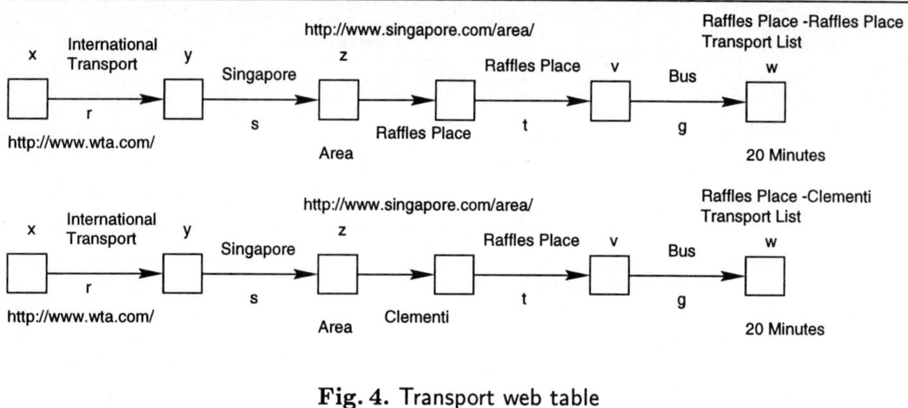

Fig. 4. Transport web table

[s.label EQUALS "Singapore"], $p_{j_6}(v) \equiv$ [v.title CONTAINS "Transport"], $p_{j_7}(w) \equiv$ [w.text CONTAINS "20 Minutes"], $p_{j_8}(g) \equiv$ [g.label CONTAINS "Bus"], $p_{j_9}(t) \equiv$ [t.label CONTAINS "Raffles Place"]. ∎

Figures 3 and 4 show a small portion of the web tables `Accommodation` and `Transport` respectively. Each connected, directed subgraph in the figures represents a web tuple of that web table. Each web tuple matches a portion of the WWW satisfying the conditions described in the schema. For example, the first web tuple in Figure 3 stores information about one bedroom (monthly rent \$600—\$1,000) and two bedroom apartment list (monthly rent \$1,000—\$1,200) in Boonlay. Note that each web tuple is structurally identical to the web schema.

In particular, Bill wishes to find out a list of one bedroom (monthly rent \$600—\$1,000) and two bedroom apartments (monthly rent is between 1,000-1,200 dollars), and from where the time taken to travel to Raffles Place by bus is around 20 minutes. In order to get this information Bill compares the `Accommodation` and `Transport` tables. For a reasonably small size of the web tables, browsing each web tuples and comparing them with that of other web table for information of interest is a feasible option. But just as browsing relational databases is often an ineffective way to retrieve information, the same holds for browsing web databases having web tables of significant size to gather composite information. Thus, what we need is a operator that allows to gather composite, relevant information from the two web tables `Accommodation` and `Transport`. In the next section we introduce the web join operator used to integrate information from two web tables.

4 Concept of Web Join

We now define a web join. We have two input web tables, `Accommodation` and `Transport` in the web database which we shall be using in the rest of the paper to illustrate web join. In the next section, we shall discuss the construction of joined schema and the joined web table.

We first introduce some terms we shall be using to explain web join in this paper.

- *Joinable nodes*
  We define joinable nodes as node variables participating in the join.
- *Join connectivity*
  Let $x\langle\rho\rangle y$ be the connectivity of a schema where x and y are node variables as defined in the schema. This connectivity is called a join connectivity if any one of the node variables participate in the web join. That is, $x\langle\rho\rangle y$ is a join connectivity if the join node of the schema is x or y.

The web join operator is used to combine two web tables by *concatenating* a web tuple of one table with a web tuple of other table whenever there exists joinable nodes. Let W_i and W_j be two web tables with schemas $M_i = \langle X_{i,n}, X_{i,\ell}, C_{i,p}, P_i\rangle$ and $M_j = \langle X_{j,n}, X_{j,\ell}, C_j, P_j\rangle$ respectively. Then W_i and W_j are *joinable* if there exist at least one node variable in M_i and in M_j which refers to identical (having the same URL) node or web document. Let us elaborate further. Consider the predicates of the node variables c and z as defined in the web schemas of `Accommodation` and `Transport` respectively in Examples 1 and 2:

$$p_{i_4}(c) \equiv [c.\texttt{url EQUALS "http://www.singapore.com/area/"}],$$
$$p_{j_4}(z) \equiv [z.\texttt{url EQUALS "http://www.singapore.com/area/"}]$$

Since the node variables c and z of M_i and M_j respectively refers to the same web document at url '`http://www.singapore.com/area/`', the web tables `Accommodation` and `Transport` are joinable. The joinable nodes are c and z. We store the joined web tuples in a separate web table. As one of the joinable nodes with identical URLs is superfluous, we remove any one of them in the joined schema. Thus, in the resulting web table, we keep only one joinable node variable (i.e, c or z). Formally, we express natural web join between two web tables as follows:

$$W = W_i \bowtie W_j$$

where W_i and W_j are the two web tables participating in the join and W is the resultant web table created by the join and satisfying schema $M = \langle X_n, X_\ell, C, P\rangle$. Let us illustrate with an example:

Example 3. Consider the `Accommodation` and `Transport` tables as described in Examples 1 and 2. Performing a web join on these web tables creates a joined web table (Figure 6). Due to space limitations, we only show a partial view of the joined web table. The schema of this joined web table is shown below (Figure 5). The construction details of the joined schema and the joined web table is explained in [9]. Let the joined schema be $M = \langle X_n, X_\ell, C, P\rangle$ where $X_n = \{a, b, c, d, e, f, i, j, x, y, v, w, \texttt{\#}\}$, $X_\ell = \{l, m, p, q, u, k, r, s, t, g, \texttt{-}\}$, $C \equiv k_1 \wedge k_2 \wedge k_3 \wedge k_4 \wedge k_5 \wedge k_6 \wedge k_7 \wedge k_8 \wedge k_9 \wedge k_{10} \wedge k_{11} \wedge k_{12}$ such that $k_1 = a\langle\ell\rangle b$, $k_2 = b\langle m\rangle c$, $k_3 = c\langle\texttt{-}\rangle d$, $k_4 = d\langle p\rangle e$, $k_5 = e\langle q\rangle f$, $k_6 = d\langle u\rangle i$, $k_7 = i\langle k\rangle j$, $k_8 = x\langle r\rangle y$, $k_9 = y\langle s\rangle c$, $k_{10} = c\langle\texttt{-}\rangle\texttt{\#}$, $k_{11} = \texttt{\#}\langle t\rangle v$, $k_{12} = v\langle g\rangle w$ and $P \equiv p_1 \wedge p_2 \wedge p_3 \wedge p_4 \wedge p_5 \wedge p_6 \wedge p_7 \wedge p_8 \wedge p_9 \wedge p_{10} \wedge p_{11} \wedge p_{12} \wedge p_{13} \wedge p_{14} \wedge p_{15} \wedge p_{16} \wedge p_{17} \wedge p_{18} \wedge p_{19} \wedge$

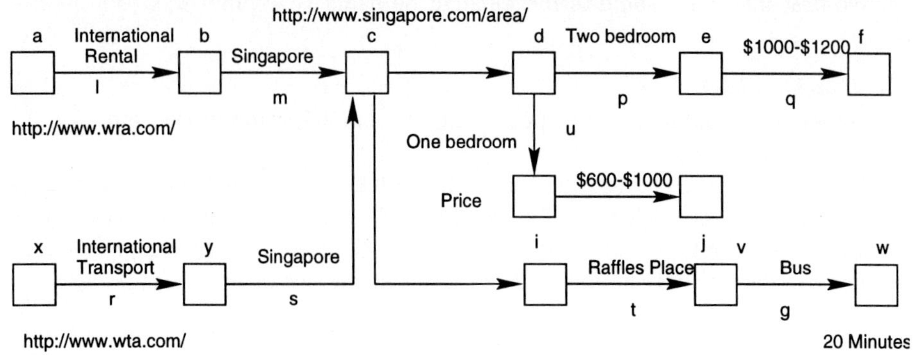

Fig. 5. Schema of the joined web table

$p_{20} \wedge p_{21} \wedge p_{22}$ such that $p_1(a) \equiv [a$.url EQUALS "http://www.wra.com/"], $p_2(b) \equiv [b$.title EQUALS "Country List"], $p_3(\ell) \equiv [\ell$.label EQUALS "International Rental"], $p_4(c) \equiv [c$.url EQUALS "http://www.singapore.com/area/"], $p_5(m) \equiv [m$.label EQUALS "Singapore"], $p_6(d) \equiv [d$.title CONTAINS "Apartment Type"], $p_7(e) \equiv [e$.title CONTAINS "Price"], $p_8(p) \equiv [p$.label CONTAINS "Two bedroom"], $p_9(q) \equiv [q$.label CONTAINS "$1000 - $1200"], $p_{10}(f) \equiv [f$.text CONTAINS "Apart--ment Add ress"], $p_{11}(x) \equiv [x$.url EQUALS "http:// www.wta.com/"], $p_{12}(y) \equiv [y$.title EQUALS "Country List"], $p_{13}(r) \equiv [r$.label EQUALS "International Tran--sport"], $p_{14}(s) \equiv [s$.label EQUALS "Singapore"], $p_{15}(v) \equiv [v$.title CONTAINS "Transport"], $p_{16}(w) \equiv [w$.text CONTAINS "20 Minutes"], $p_{17}(g) \equiv [g$.label CON--TAINS "Bus"], $p_{18}(t) \equiv [t$.label CONTAINS "Raffles Place"], $p_{19}(i) \equiv [i$.title CONTAINS "Price"], $p_{20}(k) \equiv [k$.label CONTAINS "$600 - $1000"], $p_{21}(j) \equiv [j$.text CONTAINS "Apartment Address"]., $p_{22}(u) \equiv [u$.label CONTAINS "One bedroom"]. ∎

5 Join Existence

Given two web tables, first we determine if these two web tables are joinable. Two web tables are joinable if there exist at least one web tuple in each web table which has a joinable node. We can identify these set of joinable node(s) from the schemas of the two web tables if the predicates in the two input schemas satisfy some *joinability conditions*. In this section, we determine what these conditions are. Given two web tables, we first inspect their schemas to find out whether they satisfy any of these conditions. If the schemas satisfy these conditions then a web join is possible between the two input web tables and the output of the join existence process is a set of joinable node variable(s). However, if we cannot identify a set of joinable node variable(s) from the schemas then we cannot perform web join.

Let us define some terms to facilitate our exposition. Given a web table W and its schema $M = \langle X_n, X_\ell, C, P \rangle$, let p be a predicate of P such that:

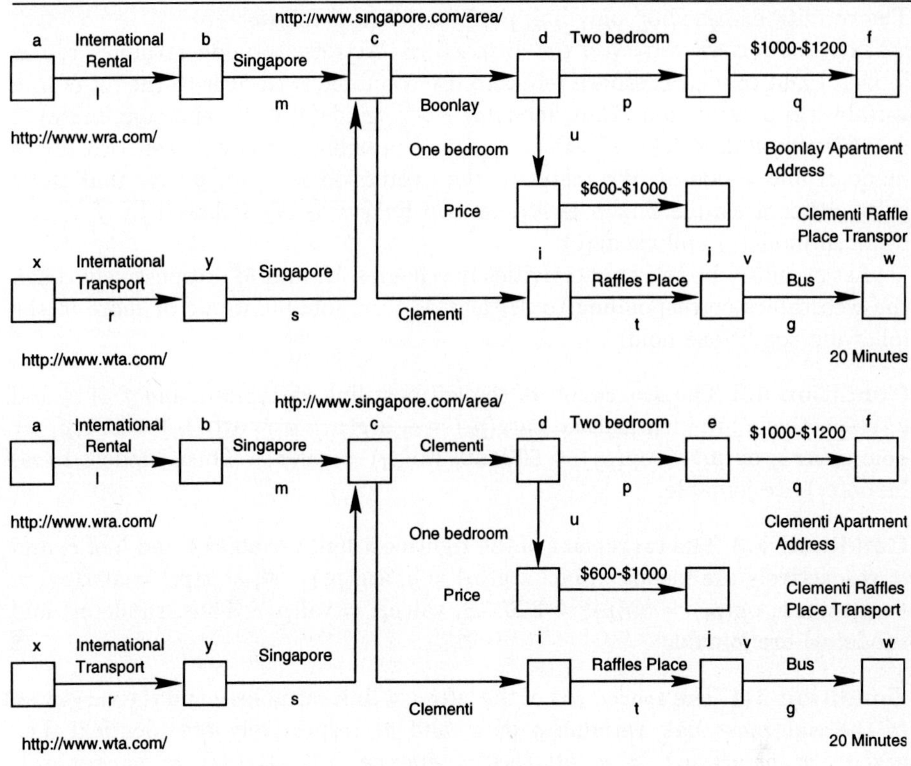

Fig. 6. Web join

- $\text{arg}(p) \in X_n \cup X_\ell$ is the argument of the predicate;
- $\text{attr}(p) \in$ {`url`, `text`, `title`, `format`, `date`, `size`} $\cup$ {`source_url`, `target_url`, `label`, `link_type`} is an attribute;
- $\text{op}(p) \in$ {`EQUALS`, `CONTAINS`} is the operator in the predicate; and
- $\text{val}(p)$ is the operand of the $\text{op}(p)$.

For example, for the predicate $p(x) \equiv$ [x`.url EQUALS "http://www.wta.com/"`], we have $\text{arg}(p) = x$, $\text{attr}(p) =$ `url`, $\text{op}(p) =$ `EQUALS` and $\text{val}(p) =$ `http://www.wta.com/`. Note that $\text{arg}(p)$ represents a node or link of the schema. Hereafter, we use $\text{arg}(p)$ to denote a node or link.

We now highlight the joinability conditions. The joinability conditions may be based on node predicates and/or link predicates of the input web schemas. The conditions for a web join based on node predicates is:

Condition 5.1 Two web tables are joinable if there exist at least a pair of predicates p_i and p_j belonging to schemas M_i and M_j respectively such that the node represented by the predicates have identical URLs. That is, $\text{attr}(p_i) = \text{attr}(p_j) =$ `url`, $\text{op}(p_i) = \text{op}(p_j) =$ `EQUALS`, and $\text{val}(p_i) = \text{val}(p_j)$. The joinable nodes are $\text{arg}(p_i)$ and $\text{arg}(p_j)$.

The conditions based on only link predicates are as follows:

Let c be a connectivity of the form $x\langle\rho\rangle y$. We refer to node variables x, y as lnode(c) and rnode(c) respectively, and use connlink(c) to refer to the set of link variables appearing in ρ. Thus, lnode(c) $\in X_n$, rnode(c) $\in X_n$ and connlink(c) $\subseteq X_\ell$. Clearly, c describes a path or a set of possible paths between two nodes lnode(c) and rnode(c). For instance, the expression $x\langle(ef|g)\rangle y$ says that there exist either a simple link $g \in X_\ell$, or two links $e \in X_\ell$ followed by $f \in X_\ell$, between lnode(c) and rnode(c).

Let c_i and c_j be two connectivities in schemas M_i and M_j respectively. Then the web tables corresponding to M_i and M_j are joinable if one or more of the following conditions hold:

Condition 5.2 The `source_url` of the leftmost link variables e and f of c_i and c_j respectively are identical, i.e., arg(p_i) = e, arg(p_j) = f, attr(p_i) = attr(p_j) = `source_url`, op(p_i) = op(p_j) = `EQUALS`, val(p_i) = val(p_j). Thus, lnode(c_i) and lnode(c_j) are joinable.

Condition 5.3 The `target_url` of the rightmost link variables g and h of c_i and c_j respectively are identical, i.e., arg(p_i) = g, arg(p_j) = h, attr(p_i) = attr(p_j) = `target_url`, op(p_i) = op(p_j) = `EQUALS`, val(p_i) = val(p_j). Thus, rnode(c_i) and rnode(c_j) are joinable. ∎

Condition 5.4 The `source_url` of the leftmost link variables e and the `target_url` of the rightmost link variable g of c_i and c_j respectively are identical, i.e., arg(p_i) = e, arg(p_j) = g, attr(p_i) = `source_url`, attr(p_j) = `target_url`, op(p_i) = op(p_j) = `EQUALS` and val(p_i) = val(p_j). Thus, lnode(c_i) and rnode(c_j) are joinable. ∎

The conditions based on node and link predicates are as follows:

Let p_i be a node predicate and p_j a link predicate in schemas M_i and M_j respectively. Then the web tables corresponding to M_i and M_j are joinable if any one of the following conditions hold:

Condition 5.5 The `url` of the node variable x and the `target_url` of the link variable g of p_i and p_j respectively are identical. Formally, arg(p_i) = x, arg(p_j) = g, attr(p_i) = `url`, attr(p_j) = `target_url`, op(p_i) = op(p_j) = `EQUALS` and val(p_i) = val(p_j). The joinable nodes are x and rnode(c_j). ∎

Condition 5.6 The `url` of the node variable x and the `source_url` of the link variable f of p_i and p_j respectively are identical. Formally, arg(p_i) = x, arg(p_j) = f, attr(p_i) = `url`, attr(p_j) = `source_url`, op(p_i) = op(p_j) = `EQUALS` and val(p_i) = val(p_j). The joinable nodes are x and lnode(c_j). ∎

6 Summary and Future Work

In this paper, we have motivated the need for a join operation for the web data model and we have introduced the notion of web join that enable us to combine web tuples from two web tables whenever joinable nodes exist. Please refer to [9] for detailed version of this paper.

Presently, we have implemented the first version of the web join operator and have interfaced it with other web operators. To explore different possible join conditions, we have created a synthetic database and have implemented the join operation for all joinability conditions using the synthetic database. The current web join operator can be used efficiently for simple web queries. Currently, we are in the process of extending the prototype of web join operator to support more complex web queries.

References

1. S. Abiteboul, D. Quass, J. McHugh, J. Widom, J. Weiner. The Lorel Query Language for Semistructured Data. *Journal of Digital Libraries*, 1(1):68-88, April 1997.
2. P. Buneman, S. Davidson, G. Hillebrand, D. Suciu. A query language and optimization techniques for unstructured data. *Proceedings of the ACM SIGMOD International Conference on Management of Data*, Canada, June 1996.
3. T. Fiebig, J. Weiss, G. Moerkotte. RAW: A Relational Algebra for the Web. *Workshop on Management of Semistructured Data (PODS/SIGMOD'97)*, Tucson, Arizona, May 16, 1997.
4. D. Konopnicki, O. Shmueli. W3QS: A Query System for the World Wide Web. *Proceedings of the 21st International Conference on Very Large Data Bases*, Zurich, Switzerland, 1995.
5. L.V.S. Lakshmanan, F. Sadri., I.N. Subramanian A Declarative Language for Querying and Restructuring the Web *Proceedings of the Sixth International Workshop on Research Issues in Data Engineering*, February, 1996.
6. A. O. Mendelzon, G. A. Mihaila, T. Milo. Querying the World Wide Web. *Proceedings of the International Conference on Parallel and Distributed Information Systems (PDIS'96)*, Miami, Florida,
7. W. K. Ng, E.-P. Lim, C. T. Huang, S. Bhowmick, F. Q. Qin. Web Warehousing: An Algebra for Web Information. *Proceedings of IEEE International Conference on Advances in Digital Libraries (ADL'98)*, Santa Barbara, California, April 22–24, 1998.
8. S. Bhowmick, W. K. Ng, E.-P. Lim. Web Information Coupling in Web Databases. *Submitted for publication*
9. S. Bhowmick, W. K. Ng, E.-P. Lim. Join Processing of Web Databases. *Technical Report - CAIS-TR-98-12, Centre for Advanced Information Systems, Nanyang Technological University, Singapore.*1998.

TENTACLE: A Database System for the World Wide Web

Marc Welz[1] and Peter Wood[2]

[1] University of Cape Town
Rondebosch, 7701 RSA
mwelz@cs.uct.ac.za
[2] King's College London
Strand, London, WC2R 2LS UK
ptw@dcs.kcl.ac.uk

Abstract. Currently most web-database interaction is loosely coupled: Usually database and web server employ different data models (the former is relational, the latter network based) necessitating a nontrivial translation effort. The translation tends to be inefficient, requiring gateways which may have to combine query and utility languages to extract and rewrite the database content resulting in the well known impedance mismatch. In this paper we describe TENTACLE, a database system which achieves a tighter integration between web server and database by implementing a web server in the TENTACLE database process itself. Since the system employs a graph-based model as its native storage representation and provides a combined (declarative) query and (procedural) programming language, it is possible to execute queries and present their results in a single phase, avoiding complex translations and performance penalties.

1 Introduction

The world wide web is the largest networked hypertext system. While it may be seen as a networked database in its own right, its interaction with more conventional databases has been surprisingly limited. Almost all hosts which constitute the world wide web store hypertext documents on a conventional file system and not in a database.

In the few cases where information is indeed stored in a database, extensive processing is usually required to transform the information from its internal storage representation to a form which is accessible to the end user. Essentially the databases commonly encountered on the world wide web are regular databases which are accessible through a web-based interface. In such cases the world wide web serves as a mere gateway to another database.

It would appear that there is scope for a closer integration between a database and the hypertext network that is the world wide web. In particular there seem to be a number of limitations in the storage representation currently employed which might be overcome by alternate storage and query subsystem designs [11].

One of the more obvious limitations of a typical web server is that there exists no easy means of querying the content of a set of hypertext documents on the server. In particular only a few systems exist which can take advantage of the structure of hypertext documents (examples include STRUDEL [5] and WebSQL [13]).

A further limitation is that each hypertext document is stored as a plain file and that in many instances a file is considered to be an atomic entity, even though the stored hypertext document has a structure, and components of such a document may be of interest individually. This lack of resolution of file-based storage has been identified in [6].

Another potential difficulty is that the mapping from the typical storage representation on the file system (the view of the hypertext author) to the structure as seen by the end user is not straightforward: the file system provides neither information about the structural detail between documents, nor does it record the existence of hyperlinks. This lack of link management has been addressed in hypertext systems such as HyperWave [10] and Microcosm [7].

Moving the hypertext into a typical relational database does not necessarily improve matters. While one might have gained the stability and security of a database, additional effort is required to extract the information from the database (see Fig. 1). Not only is the extraction process inefficient (involving a communications overhead between several processes), but there also exist significant mismatches: one is the classical impedance mismatch of embedding a query language (such as SQL) in a host language (such as C or PERL), while another is the mismatch between the relational model used by the database and the network model used by the world wide web.

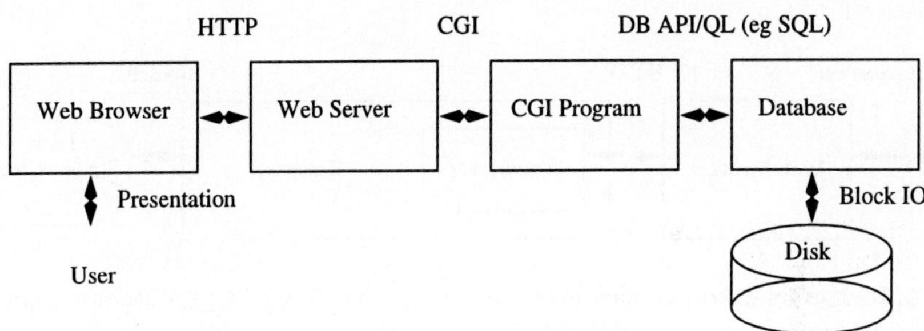

Fig. 1. Overhead involved in requesting information from a conventional database through the web.

The TENTACLE database system addresses the deficiencies described above as follows. We have chosen a graph-based model similar to the ones employed by LORE [12] and STRUDEL [5] to represent hypertext documents. Such a model is a natural representation for hypertext networks. In our system, hypertext documents or fragments of documents are represented as nodes, while hyperlinks or other associations are represented as labeled arcs. Such a representation is a reasonably direct model of the application domain and avoids the cumbersome and costly overhead of translating from one data representation to another.

TENTACLE provides a query language based on path expressions over the database graph. Since it is possible to represent both fragments of, as well as complete, hypertext documents as entities in the database, the system has sufficient resolution to query the structure of individual documents as well as the interrelationships among complete ones.

In an attempt to remove the impedance mismatch between classical query and host languages, TENTACLE provides an integrated language with both declarative querying capabilities as well as full procedural capabilities. As a result, it is possible to fold the querying and postprocessing phases into a single step, avoiding most of the impedance mismatch traditionally associated with a host and query language pair.

To improve performance, we have attempted to reduce the number of stages in the querying and rewriting process. In particular, we have removed the communications overhead between database and web server by moving the web server into the database itself. In other words, the web server is a program in our language and stored as a subgraph in the database. On receiving an incoming connection, the database interprets the web program in order to retrieve the requested pages or to execute a query. Since all this happens in a single process, there is no interprocess communications overhead. A further performance enhancement is that TENTACLE makes use of its own specialized storage layer, which has been designed to store and retrieve graph structures efficiently. Lack of space prevents us from describing the storage layer in this paper.

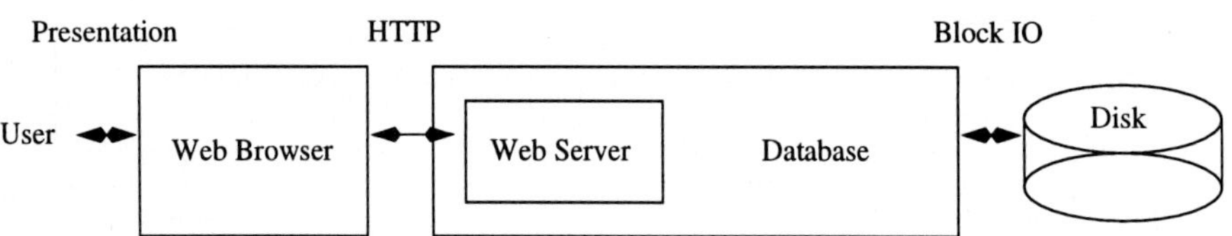

Fig. 2. Reduction of communications overhead in the TENTACLE database with web server capabilities (compare with Fig. 1).

In the next section, we describe the TENTACLE data model which enables us to provide a natural mapping from web documents to the database storage representation. Section 3 covers the declarative and procedural fragments of the graph-based data manipulation language provided by TENTACLE. These are used in Section 4 to show how a web server can be programmed to run as part of the database system. We present conclusions and possible directions for further work in Section 5.

2 TENTACLE Data Model

The data model underlying the TENTACLE database system is graph-based. Each entity is represented as a node in the system. A node can possess zero or more attributes, where each attribute consists of a name-value pair. The name part of the attribute serves to identify the attribute within the scope of a particular node, while the value part is either an atomic entity, or a reference to another node. In the latter case this attribute is equivalent to a labelled directed edge.

More formally, a TENTACLE database is a graph G which can be represented as a tuple

$$G = (N, r, A, E_n, E_a, \psi_N, \psi_A, \lambda_N, \lambda_A, T_n, T_a) \tag{1}$$

where N is the set of nodes, $r \in N$ is the root node, A is the set of atomic values, E_n is the set of node-to-node edges, and E_a is the set of node-to-atomic value edges. The function ψ_N is an incidence function from E_n into $N \times N$, ψ_A is an incidence function from E_a into $N \times A$, λ_N is a labeling function from E_n into T_n, and λ_A is the labeling function from E_a into T_a, where T_n and T_a are the sets of node-to-node labels and node-to-value labels respectively.

The emphasis on the distinction between nodes in N (compound entities) and atomic values in A is deliberate. While some semistructured data models do not draw a distinction between complex (nodes) and simple (atomic) entities, we feel that this distinction is useful since it highlights the difference between the identity of a node (usually opaque if not invisible to the user and thus not user-assigned) and the identity of an atomic value (visible and of meaning to the user). While reconciling these differences (by assigning a name to a node) may be acceptable in some circumstances, we chose to preserve these differences, in order to avoid difficulties encountered when 'renaming' or 'copying' a node.

Note that this data model is essentially untyped and thus bears a greater resemblance to systems such as LORE [12] rather than to strongly-typed graph databases such as GRAS [9] or the object reference graphs of conventional object databases such as O_2 [4].

Consider an example of three hypermedia entities consisting of an index and a first chapter referring to each other and both referring to an image. A simplified storage representation of these entities is given in Fig. 3.

In this example, the set of nodes $N = \{1, 2, 3\}$, while the set of atomic values A comprises the three strings starting "<html>...", "<HTML>..." and "\ff...". Node 1, the index page, is taken as the root node. The set of node-to-node labels T_n = { "Next", "See also", "Up", "Here" }, while the set of node-to-value labels T_a = { "text/html", "image/jpeg" }. The incidence and labeling functions can be determined in a straightforward way. As suggested above, we sometimes refer to edges leaving a node as attributes of the node. For example, node 1 possesses three attributes, one with name "text/html" and value "<html><head><title>Welcome ...", another with name "Next" and having as value a reference to node 2 (the first chapter), and a further attribute with name "See also" referencing node 3 (the image).

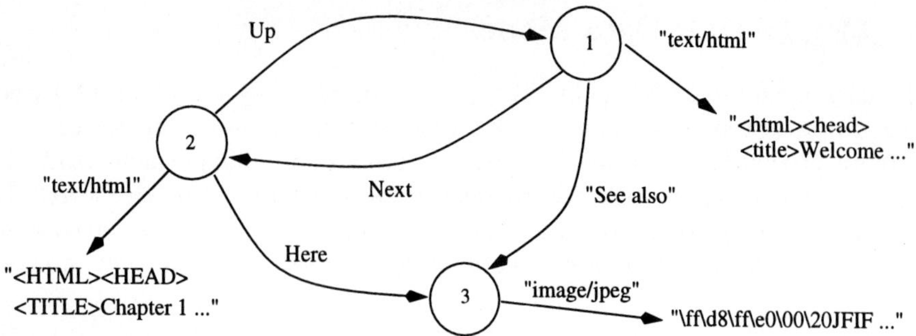

Fig. 3. Simplified hypertext represented using the TENTACLE data model.

3 The Querying and Programming Language

The language of the TENTACLE database system combines the conventional host and query language pair into a single coherent language. This combination provides both procedural constructs (`while,if else`) as well as declarative query expressions.

The query expressions are path expressions over the database graphs (similar to the ones of [3]) and resemble regular expressions over strings in several respects. In particular both systems rely on a matching process. In the case of path expressions in our system, an expression containing alternation, conjunction, concatenation and closure constructs, as well literals matching individual graph components, is matched against paths in a target graph.

Unlike conventional regular expressions which apply nondeterministically to any part of a target string, TENTACLE path expressions always have to be anchored. This means that either the expression supplies an initial node (or set of initial nodes) which is used as a starting point for the matching process, or the query system assumes that the query starts at the root node of the database.

The special tokens used to construct the path expressions are tabulated in Table 1. The example expressions match parts of the graph depicted in Fig. 3.

Name	Symbol	Syntax	Example	Precedence
Concatenation	.	path.path	`1.Next.2`	1
Conjunction	&	path&path	`1.Next.2&1."See also".3`	2
Alternation	|	path|path	`1.Next.2|1."See also".3`	3
Closure	*	[path]*	`1.[.]*."text/html"."<html>..."`	0 (explicit)
Override	[]	[path]	`1.[[Next.2.Here]&"See also"].3`	0 (explicit)

Table 1. Operators used in path expressions.

As an introductory example consider Fig. 3. Assuming that node 1 has been designated as the root node of the database, the expression

```
[.Next..Here.."image/jpeg"]
```

matches a path from node 1 to the attribute value of node 3 in the database graph of Fig. 3. Note that the token . serves to delimit graph components, that is, nodes and edges. An empty component, when occurring at the beginning of an expression, implies a match to the root node, and, when occurring anywhere else, implies a wildcard or don't-care match[1]. Thus the initial empty component delimited by [. will match the root node 1, while the empty component .. will match any node (in this particular case the only node satisfying the other constraints is node 2).

A more complex expression is [[.]*."text/html".], which matches the text of all documents reachable from the root. Here the construct [.]* matches zero or more concatenations of the path [.] (the latter matches any sequence of two components of the graph). Thus the expression matches, amongst others, the path [1."text/html"."<html>..."]. A search for JPEG images or (denoted by the token |) MPEG movies could be written as

```
[[.]*.["image/jpeg"|"movie/mpeg"].]
```

The procedural part of our language resembles a small subset of a language such as *C* [8]. Most of the complex syntactic constructs have been omitted in order to avoid confusion with the constructs used in the query component of the language. The coupling between the declarative and procedural components is achieved by allowing query expressions to appear in place of more typical R-values inside the procedural components. In such a case the value of the path expression is the set of graph components which match the last component of the path expression.

Combining both query and procedural components makes it is possible, for example, to locate the text of the first chapter (referring to Fig. 3) by using a query, and then to write the text to a network connection if it exists, or reporting failure otherwise:

```
if([.Next."text/html".]) write(connection,[.Next."text/html".])
else write(connection,"Could not find it\n")
```

The point of interest is that a path expression is used directly as argument of the condition and again as second parameter to the write() function — no special measures have to be taken to extract the information.

Not only is it possible to embed path expressions as R-values of procedural expressions, but it is also feasible to use variables and functions in path expressions. Consider the first example path expression (relating to Fig. 3) used above, namely, [.Next..Here.."image/jpeg"]. It is possible to replace literals such as Next in the expression with variables whose values will be automatically substituted. Hence the above expression can be rewritten as follows:

---

[1] The token * commonly used for this purpose was deliberately not chosen since it is used in closure expressions over graph components.

```
var n n=Next [.n..Here.."image/jpeg"]
```

Permitting functions inside path expressions makes it possible to synthesize more complex matching rules. Functions may appear in the same positions as variables inside path expressions. However, unlike a variable, where the dereferenced value must match the current position in the graph, it is sufficient for a function to return a non-null (true) result for a match to succeed. By using the special function `here()`, which returns the value of the current position in the graph[2], it also becomes feasible to incorporate function calls into query expressions for their side effects.

For example in conjunction with the `write()` function (which outputs its second and following arguments to the connection handle supplied as first parameter), it is possible to output paths as they are matched. Again consider the example in Fig. 3. To display the content of the index page the expression `[."text/html".write(connection,here())]` would be sufficient.

The full combination of path and procedural expressions makes it possible to present different views of the same document using a single query. Consider the hypothetical text in Fig. 4, which consists of document divided into three

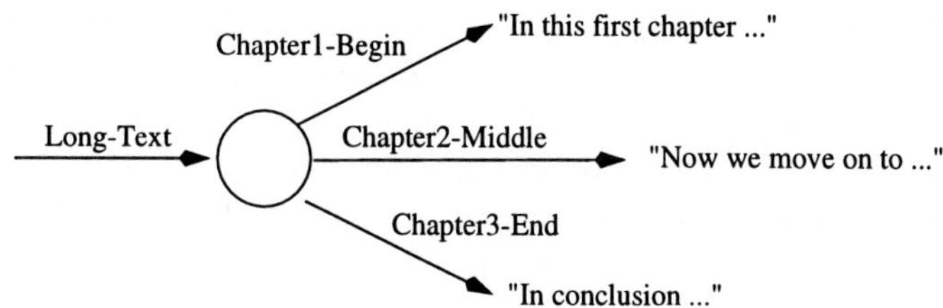

Fig. 4. Internal representation of a document of three chapters.

chapters. The document can be presented as either a single long piece of text, or as a table of content pointing to three chapters[3]. The expression to present the text as a single document would be

```
[.Long-Text..[write(connection,"\n<h1>",here(),"</h1>").
              write(connection,here())]]
```

This would output a document of the form

```
<h1>Chapter1-Begin</h1>In this first chapter ...
```

[2] There is a similarity in the reasons motivating the existence of `here()` and the `this` pointer as encountered in *C++*, but the actual structures are too different to bear the same name.

[3] The example has been simplified for the sake of clarity and brevity — the commands to emit the HTML header and footer have been omitted and the database graph has been simplified.

```
<h1>Chapter1-Middle</h1>Now we move on to ...
<h1>Chapter1-End</h1>In conclusion ...
```

To materialize the table of contents, one would use the expression

```
[.Long-Text..write(connection,"<a href=\"[.Long-Text..",here(),
          ".write(connection,here())]\">\n",here(),"</a>\n")]
```

resulting in a table of contents of the form

```
<a href="[.Long-Text..Chapter1-Begin.write(connection,here())]">
Chapter1-Begin</a>
<a href="[.Long-Text..Chapter2-Middle.write(connection,here())]">
Chapter1-Middle</a>
<a href="[.Long-Text..Chapter3-End.write(connection,here())]">
Chapter1-End</a>
```

Once again the above example has been simplified. It is usually not possible to encode such queries directly as an URL since that would violate the syntax rules imposed on URLs and break user agents which expect a simple file path component. Thus in the actual implementation, there is an intermediate step so that the URLs visible to the external world appear like conventional ones. Hence a proper query would emit regular URLs and the web server would use these to locate the appropriate chapters.

4 TENTACLE as a Web Server

In this section we briefly describe how our database system has been programmed to act as a web server. Note that the entire system runs as a single operating system process and thus interacts directly with both the web browser and the block storage abstraction provided by the OS (see Fig. 2).

On receiving an incoming request from the user agent, a specially tagged node attribute stored in the system is executed. This attribute contains the instructions (written in the combined query/programming language described previously) to process the HTTP [1] request.

Essentially the processing involves resolving the `/` delimited components of the request (the URL) and using the components to traverse the database resident graph. This may locate either a conventional static entity and return it to the user, or result in the evaluation of a query stored in the system which materializes hypertext entities.

For example, the database could store a query to materialize the complete text of a document (see Fig. 5) in the value of `[.Long-text..Complete-text]`. When the user requests the URL `/Long-text/Complete-text/` the system evaluates the query and returns the generated text. A naive user may thus be unaware of the fact that this information is materialized (that is, it is a view). Of course, sophisticated users can submit (`POST`) their own queries and even upload their own view descriptions.

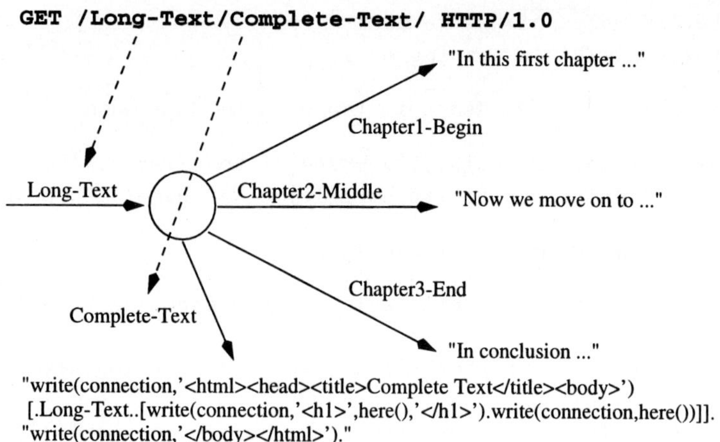

Fig. 5. Mapping from URL request to database graph.

Currently the database system only supports the querying of local documents. In future we might extend the web server to perform proxying tasks. In conjunction with a parser, it would then be feasible to decompose remote documents, store them locally as their components and formulate queries or define views on these. This would enable the system to build custom filters for the world wide web for tasks such as removing unwanted advertising from web pages, for example.

5 Conclusion and Future Work

We have described the TENTACLE database system and shown how it can be programmed to act as a web server. Using this approach (instead of separate web and database servers) allows us to eliminate intermediate representations and translation facilities. Since our data model matches the logical structure of documents more closely, document management should become easier, while the ability to define different views of the same documents should help reduce redundancy and assist in maintaining document integrity.

Currently the TENTACLE database is a research prototype. So far it has been programmed to interpret HTTP/0.9 and a subset of HTTP/1.0. Once a fully functional web server has been implemented, we will be in a position to test whether the suggested performance improvements of such an approach are borne out in practice.

In terms of further application of TENTACLE to data on the world wide web, it would be interesting to extend the system to store and interpret XML documents and VRML scenes. Once again, these formats can be naturally represented as graphs. Doing so potentially gives a user a uniform query language in which to query documents as well as other media.

There are a number of aspects of TENTACLE which could be explored further. It might be interesting to apply the system to other application domains which could benefit from a tighter coupling to a database. The graph-based model might be useful in poorly or semistructured application domains, in particular in cases where a natural representation of such information is a parse tree, since path expressions appear to be well suited to querying such structures.

Further application of TENTACLE could be as a graph storage system for other graph-based query languages. Examples include Hy$^+$ [2], which is presently implemented on a deductive database system, and Hyperlog [14], which is presently implemented on a functional database system.

References

1. T. Berners-Lee, R. Fielding, and F. H. Hypertext transfer protocol HTTP/1.0. http://ds.internic.net/rfc/rfc1945.txt, May 1996.
2. M. P. Consens, F. C. Eigler, M. Z. Hasan, A. O. Mendelzon, E. G. Noik, A. G. Ryman, and D. Vista. Architecture and applications of the Hy$^+$ visualization system. *IBM Systems Journal*, 33(3):458–476, 1994.
3. I. F. Cruz, A. O. Mendelzon, and P. T. Wood. A graphical query language supporting recursion. In *ACM SIGMOD Int. Conf. on Management of Data*, pages 323–330, May 1987.
4. O. Deux et al. The story of O_2. *IEEE Transactions on Knowledge and Data Engineering*, 2(1):91–108, March 1990.
5. M. Fernandez, D. Florescu, A. Levy, and D. Suciu. A query language and processor for a web-site management system. In *The Workshop on Management of Semistructured Data held in conjunction with ACM SIGMOD Int. Conf. on Management of Data*, May 1997.
6. H.-W. Gellersen, R. Wicke, and G. Martin. WebComposition: An object-orientated support system for the web engineering lifecycle. *Computer Networks and ISDN Systems*, 29(8-13):1429–1437, September 1997.
7. W. Hall, H. Davis, and G. Hutchings. *Rethinking Hypermedia - The Microcosm Approach.* Kluwer Academic Publishers, 1996.
8. B. W. Kernighan and D. M. Ritchie. *The C Programming Language: ANSI C.* Prentice Hall, 1988.
9. N. Kiesel, A. Schuerr, and B. Westfechtel. GRAS, a graph-oriented (software) engineering database system. *Information Systems*, 20(1):21–51, 1995.
10. H. Maurer. *HyperWave: The Next Generation Web Solution.* Addison-Wesley Longman, 1996.
11. H. Maurer. Web-based knowledge management. *IEEE Computer*, 31(3):122–123, March 1998.
12. J. McHugh, S. Abiteboul, R. Goldman, D. Quass, and J. Widom. LORE: A database management system for semistructured data. *SIGMOD RECORD*, 26(3):54–66, September 1997.
13. A. Mendelzon, G. Mihaila, and T. Milo. Querying the world wide web. *International Journal on Digital Libraries*, 1(1):54–67, April 1997.
14. A. Poulovassilis and M. Levene. A nested-graph model for the representation and manipulation of complex objects. *ACM Transactions on Information Systems*, 12(1):35–68, January 1994.

Workey: A Method and Tool to Build Web-Enabled Workflows

Jean-Loup Chappelet, André Le Grand

Institut de Hautes Etudes en Administration Publique
21 route de la Maladière, CH-1022 Chavannes-près-Renens, Switzerland
{Jean-Loup.Chappelet,Andre.LeGrand}@idheap.unil.ch

Abstract. Workflow management systems provide functions for process modeling, implementation and automation. Many systems do not allow modeling organizational goals and relating these goals with the processes which enable them. The method OSSAD provides models and project management guidelines to this effort. But this method is not sufficient to fully support workflow management. In order to do so, we define Workey as an extension of OSSAD, to enable workflow specification, implementation and automation for the web.

1 Introduction

Workflow management systems generally provide functions for process modeling, implementation and automation. The management of workflows involves [1]:

- *process modeling and workflow specification.*
  This phase requires models of workflow and methods to represent a process as a workflow specification,
- *process reengineering.*
  This phase requires methods for the optimization of processes and,
- *implementation and process automation.*
  This phase requires methods and technologies to coordinate systems and users to implement, plan, carry out and control the tasks of workflow such as they were specified.

The next subsections of this introduction describe the limits of current solutions according to the above topics. Then we discuss briefly the qualities and drawbacks of Internet for workflow applications. Thereafter we present the strong points of our contribution.

1.1 Process modeling

Following a recent workshop on workflows and process automation in information systems [2], some participants wrote a report describing the state of the art and the prospects for the field which they named "work activity coordination" [2]. This report enumerates the methodological points for which it is necessary to define a more rigorous framework, among those:

- the representation of process definitions,
- the modeling of coordination and control,
- the understanding of which methods and tools apply in which situation,
- and the consistent use of modeling concepts.

The formalism and the project management guidelines of OSSAD[1] [3] provide an interesting framework to address the above points [4][5] [2] . This method should however be extended to enable workflow specification and automation. The extensions of [4] aim to model the actors' responsibilities related to a workflow, and the circulation of documents. The models introduced in this extension do not provide a sufficiently formal specification from which a tool can automatically build a workflow application.

There are two paradigms of process modeling[6] : one based on the communication between people, the other based on the activities. The approach based on the communication comes from Workflow Action[7]. Its designers consider that the objective of reengineering is to improve customer satisfaction. Thus, every action is modeled as a loop of four phases of communication between a customer and a performer: preparation, negotiation, performance and acceptance [7]. Action Workflow is not always well adapted to the modeling of administrative workflows: many procedures cannot easily be modeled as a network of nested loops of customer - performer.

Activity-based methods aim at modeling the tasks and their ordering rather than the agreements between human actors in their communications. Most of workflow management systems are activity-based. Workey is also based on activities. Workey extends OSSAD to transform descriptions of procedures into specifications from which workflow applications on Internet are automatically implemented. An analysis is usually performed before the implementation of these specifications. The analysis results may lead to reengineering the processes.

1.2 Process reengineering

Process reengineering goal is to optimize processes with respect to criteria like customer satisfaction, cost reduction, or the introduction of new services. This reengineering is sometimes regarded as an art [1]. However, in order to imagine new solutions, methods and tools for process analysis –by providing qualitative and quantitative information on the execution or the runnability of the specifications– guide and stimulate creative thinking. According to [1], the capabilities for analysis, testing and debugging of specifications are insufficient in the current systems. They allow, for example, the animation of processes or simulation. These tests are carried out without requiring the effective implementation of the application to analyze. Additional tests can be carried out on the application when it is implemented. Pantha Rei [8], approach based on an extension

[1] Office Systems Support Analysis and Design. For a more complete list of reference about OSSAD, please see http://www.unil.ch/idheap/ossad/ossad.

[2] Workey is an extension of motown for web applications

of the PERT method, tries for instance, to anticipate the delays during the execution of processes. Even this approach is inapplicable if a process contains a loop, this system analyzes processes during their run, whereas others approaches analyze them before their implementation.

An OSSAD project incorporates a phase for the design of alternative solutions. Its purpose is to define other ways of realization of processes. These types of implementation of processes are called procedures in OSSAD. The confrontation of these alternative solutions is carried out by the project team on the basis of its experience (speculative mode). Workey supplements this mode with tools for qualititative analysis and simulations of time and cost [5].

These tools help for instance, to identify bottlenecks. The relevance of any simulation requires a rigorous and accurate quantification of the parameters it uses. This quantification involves considerable work. However, concrete values, extracted from the history of the real use of an application can be provided as input for simulation. Such simulations, even if they require a great effort of quantification, provide relevant information for process reengineering.

The results of analysis having guided the choice among these various alternatives of design, the implementation of an application can be performed. The application can in its turn provide real data for analysis and simulation.

1.3 Implementation and automation

Process implementation The implementation can be carried out, either by a team of developers starting from the specifications, or, and it is the more frequent case, by automatic generation of rules which are interpreted by the workflow management system.

In order to implement workflow applications, there are some myths about using Internet which should be carefully studied:

- the concept of "universal client" hides many and important disparities between the various browsers and their successive versions.
- there are several configurations for a single browser. Thus the storage and retrieval information on the client side of the connection ("cookies") can be enabled /disabled. An organization may impose a policy which cannot be changed for various reasons. The browser configuration may also prevent the handling (by script) of the history of previously accessed pages (in order to erase the already submitted pages).

Ultimately, the concept of "universal client" of a workflow management system for Internet is reduced to a small set of functions.

Process automation It concerns the planning and the control of the process executions. The automation of the processes is carried out according to the *push* or *pull* mode. In the push mode, the workflow management system dispatches the documents to users according to their workload. In the pull mode, the users themselves will seek the documents on which they have to work. In Workey, the default mode is pull. However, for particular operations, if specified in the process definition, Workey pushes documents towards one or more users (see concepts of selection and notification in section 2.3.).

For the workflow management system (in push or pull mode), using Internet as a client/server platform has undeniable qualities:

- easy deployment of the workflow applications within the organization,
- reduced training of the users (for the basic functions of the browsers),
- easier access to external clients,
- mobile computing, with machine and operating systems independence,
- inter-organizational workflows,

Using browsers as clients, however imposes more constraints than a proprietary client/server solution for which client-server relations can be tailored. Indeed the problems of security are then increased. Moreover the HTTP protocol which is state-less, limits the tailoring of these relations.

Inherent and specific to the use of browsers, the problems concerning the execution control of the workflows are primarily related to the actions "back" and "forward". These two actions give access to previously accessed pages in the same session of work. These pages display workflow documents which may have changed since they have been loaded. Therefore the double submission of the pages and loss of time due to a work performed twice by a user are to be avoided. It is then necessary, either to force the reloading of these documents by using HTML meta-tags (client-side solution), or to prevent double submission (server-side solution). These problems do not arise in proprietary solutions because the developers have the control of the dialogues between the clients and the server. Evolving from proprietary systems to Internet leads to the loss of control over the client configuration.

The next section draws the strong points of our contribution on the methodological and technical aspects.

1.4 Strong points of our contribution

In spite of the efforts of WfMC[3] , a rigorous conceptual framework is still missing for the modeling of workflows. OSSAD brings conceptual and methodological elements which are very useful and pertinent for organization modeling. Workey extends OSSAD to model, implement and automate workflows. Workey adds:

- a prescriptive level to OSSAD to specify workflow applications,
- a step by step guide to build specifications,
- time and cost simulation functions for the analysis of these specifications,
- an application builder for web-enabled workflow applications.

The rest of this article is organized as follows. Section 2 describes the modeling of the processes with Workey. This section introduce the various levels of modeling of OSSAD and presents the extensions for the modeling of workflows.

[3] workflow management coalition (http://www.aiim.org/wfmc)

The implementation and the architecture of the workflow management system are described in section 3. Section 4 describes the process automation. In these two sections, the use of Internet is compared with a proprietary solution. In conclusion, we present some research perspectives resulting from this work.

2 Process modeling

Processes are modeled at three levels: abstract, descriptive and prescriptive.

2.1 The abstract level

It describes the objectives, goals or missions of an organization, without taking into account the human and technical means necessary for their realization. These abstract models are generally invariants of a means reconception ("business process *redesign*"), but not of a major recasting of the activities of the organization ("business process *reengineering*"). The abstract level has a sole model whose components are *functions*, *sub-functions*, *packets* and *activities*.

A function is a subset of the organization with homogeneous objectives. Functions exchange data information, named packets (e.g. fig 1). Packets are not necessarily information related to the goals of the function. It is not the aim of finance and accounting to produce requirements, whereas the application development is to produce software products to the demanding function. Functions are not departments of a company. They describe a goal this enterprise has to achieve.

The functions can be broken down into sub-functions. The unbroken functions or sub-functions are called activities. These activities constitute the finest level of detail of the modeling of the objectives.

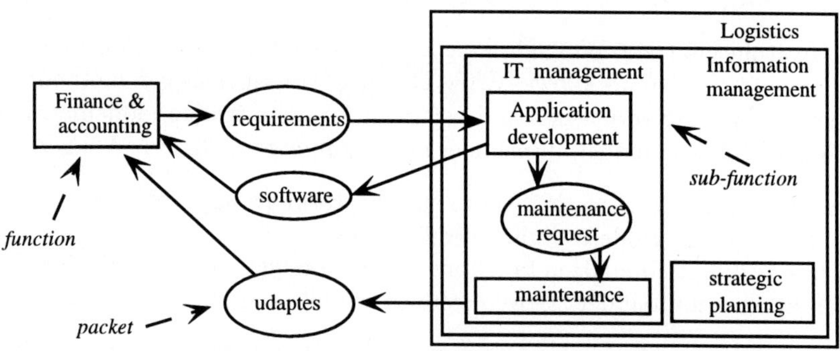

Fig. 1. abstract level: functions decomposition and packets

2.2 The descriptive level

The models of this level concern the human, technical and organizational support systems to achieve the objectives detailed in the form of activities. An activity in the abstract level maps onto a *procedure* in the descriptive level. A procedure is a coherent set of *operations*; it is carried out cooperatively by a set of *actors* to which *roles* are assigned. An actor may carry out several roles, a role may be carried out by several actors. A packet in the abstract level maps onto a set of information *resources* in the descriptive level. This level contains three models:

- the *procedure model* which describes the exchange of information between the procedures,
- the *role model* which describes the exchange of information between the roles and,
- the *operation model* which describes the flow of operations of a procedure.

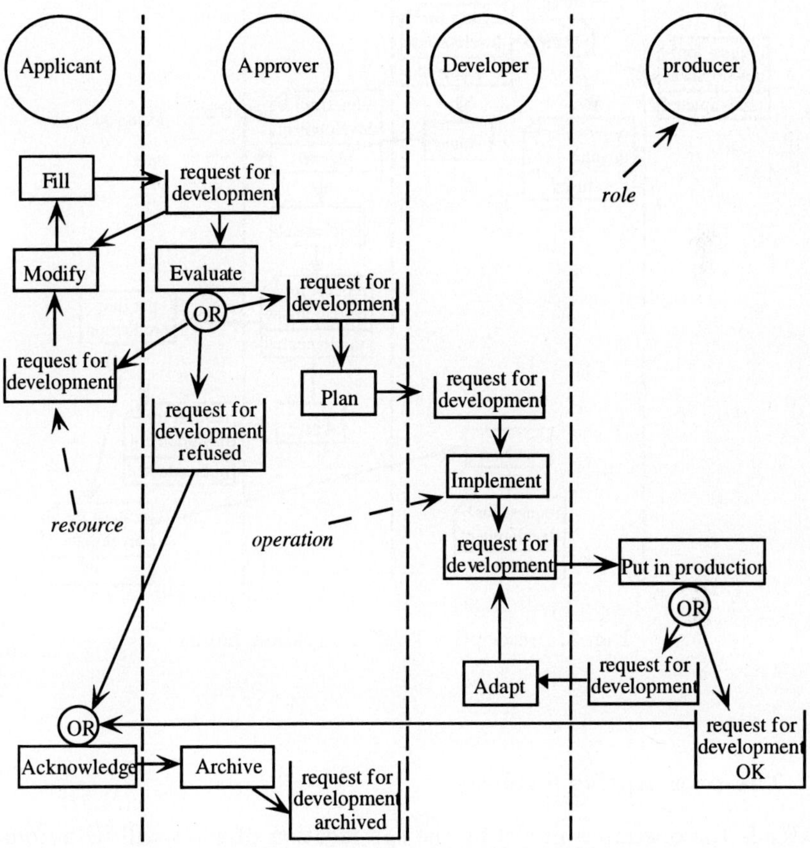

Fig. 2. descriptive level: operation model of a procedure

For example, fig. 2 displays the operation model of the procedure "application development". This procedure directly corresponds to the activity with the same name into fig. 1. Four roles are involved : Applicant, Approver, Developer and Producer. The *task* of a role is the set of operations which are placed in the role's column.

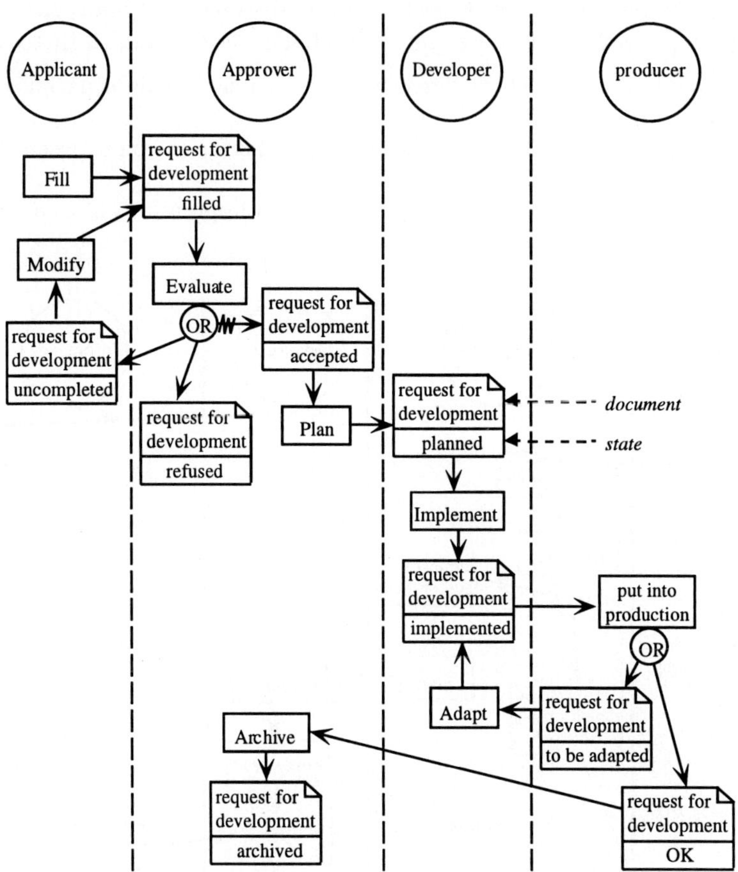

Fig. 3. prescriptive level: a workflow model

2.3 The prescriptive level

It extends the operation model by the specification of what will be automated in a workflow. To this end we introduced the following concepts:

- document,
- state of document,

- structure of document
- constraint of prohibition and obligation,
- selection, and,
- notification.

A *document* is a resource of the operations model which is computerized. The state of a document is used to indicate the document status within a flow. The *structure* of a document is a set of informational fields. *Constraints* between two operations can be defined: they oblige / prohibit a same actor carrying out these two operations on the same document.

> For instance (e.g. fig. 3), a prohibition constriant between the *Fill* and *Evaluate* operations will prevent the same actor to fill and positively evaluate his own requests, although he can still plan them.

The concept of *selection* is to choose a subset of the actors allowed to carry out the next operation.

> For example (e.g. fig. 3) when an actor of the *approver* role has *accepted* a *request for development*, he can choose a subset of actors of the developer role who are allowed to *plan* this request. For the other outputs of the *evaluate* operation, there is no selection.

The concept of *notification* is related to automation of a procedure. It indicates that the actors of a role must be notified by an electronic message when a document reaches a particular state and that the next operation belongs to the task of this role.

Fig. 3 displays the workflow model of fig. 2.

2.4 Steps of specification

The transformation of a descriptive model into a prescriptive model is done according to the following steps:

1. identify the information resources which will be computer supported, These resources become documents. When resources become documents, some "read" operations can be deleted since Workey lets users see the state of their documents within the flow, for instance, *acknowledge* on fig. 2.
2. specify the states changes of these documents (including computed changes),
3. specify the constraints between operations, if necessary,
4. determine the states for which it is necessary to select the actor or the actors having to carry out the following operation. This selection can be associated with a notification by an electronic message.
   The notifications are recommended either for occasional users of an application or for users working on several applications of workflow.
5. specify the structure (fields and sections) of the documents.

The following paragraph describes the transformation of these prescriptive models into an application.

3 Process implementation

The Workey application builder makes a workflow application based on Lotus Notes/ Domino. This application is a standard Notes base of documents to which we added a workflow engine that we developed. This target system provides a high level of security for access controls. The architecture which mixes Notes and Workey, is described in the next subsection.

3.1 Structure of Workey applications

Domino is a HTTP server which generates dynamically HTML pages from the documents stored in Notes bases. These bases are then accessible via browsers, while preserving their access rights. Domino and Workey are integrated in the following way (fig. 4):

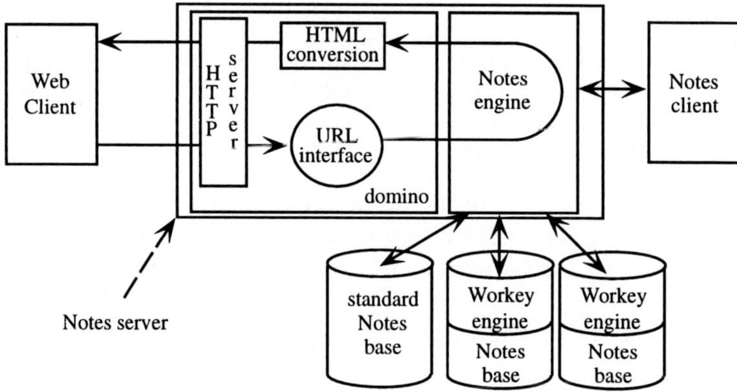

Fig. 4. Architecture of Workey applications with Lotus Domino

- the server is a Notes/Domino server.
- the clients are Web browsers or Notes clients,
- the workflow bases include the Workey workflow engine.

The same application can be accessed by a Notes client or a web browser. The users, whatever their client type is, can only access the bases for which they have rights.

The implementation does not amount to only adding a workflow engine to a Notes base. The following section presents the details of implementation.

3.2 Implementation of a workflow application

Fig. 5 describes the implementation procedure. It has two roles: designer and builder. Workey Builder carries out the builder role and generates a Notes base.

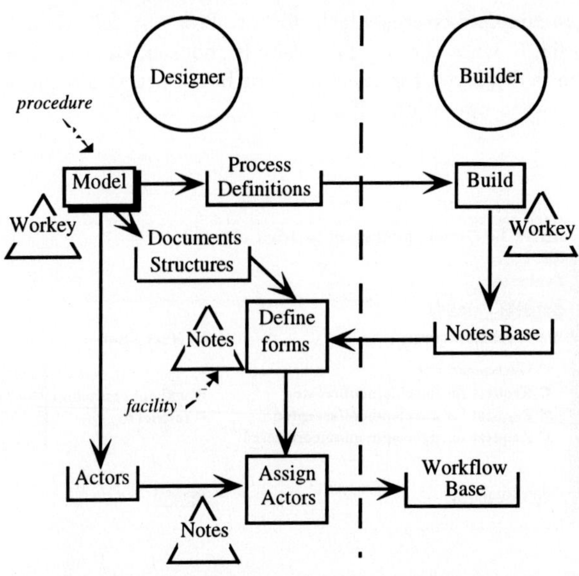

Fig. 5. implementation of a specification

This Notes base contains an workflow engine and the rules derived from the procedures specifications. The following section describes how the actors perform their work with Workey.

4 Process automation

The workflow engine works differently, depending on the type of client, since the HTTP protocol is state-less. The Notes/Domino server which recognizes the client type, controls the workflow engine in relation with its type. With a browser, the workflow engine is requested at each edition and recording of a document. When a document is queried for edition, the workflow engine adds a section to push or not the document one step further within a flow (e.g. fig. 6).

The "Workflow status" column is to specify whether the document moves or not within the flow. "Unchanged state" is to tell Workey that the modifications made during the edition do not lead to a new state (the current operation is not fully achieved). The other choices are to indicate the possible new states of the document. The "Next actors" column may enable a selection of the actors carrying out the role of the next operation. If there is no such specification at the prescriptive level, all the actors of this role are allowed to perform the next operation.

For a request of development in the *filled* state, the *Evaluate* operation leads possibly to various new states: *uncompleted*, *refused* or *accepted*. The actor has to tell Workey the effects of his changes on the document being edited, and then he has to push the *submit* button, to record the document. For the *refused* and *uncompleted* states which do not allow any selection, this column is empty. On fig. 6, since the *accepted* state is choosen, the list of actors of the *plan* operation is displayed for selection. The list of actors also depends on the constraints between operations, if any.

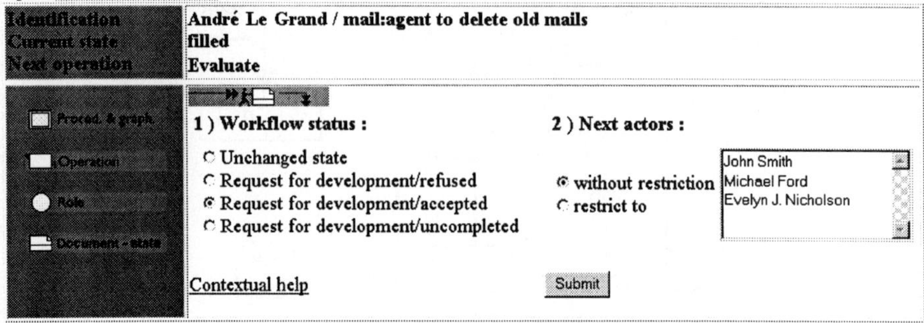

Fig. 6. selection of the next actors in relation with a new state

When the user submits the document, Domino requests the workflow engine to compute the document's update. If its state remains unchanged, the document is only recorded, if not, the document is updated according to its new state and the workflow rules.

The differences of interactions between the workflow engine and the client, according to its type, are summarized below:

- with a Notes client, the workflow engine only interacts with the client whenever an information about a document circulation is required [5].

  For instance, for a document in *filled* state, the workflow engine asks the actor to choose the new state. If the actor chooses *accepted* as new state of this document, since there is a selection specified (see fig. 3), then the workflow engine will transfer to the client the list of actors of the next operation. The actor, will then be able to select the next ones.

- with a browser, the workflow engine transfers to the client all the information. Then all the dialogues to specify the document circulation are made on the client-side.

The Domino servers do not have yet all the capabilities of the Notes servers. The administration of the Workey applications is thus carried out from a Notes Client software, like for instance, the policy of filing documents.

Moreover the roles and users administration, the evolution of the document forms and the management of evolving specifications are also performed inside Notes. These three functions cover the various changes which the modeling of a process can undergo. The management of this evolution is detailed in [5].

5 Conclusion

Our work consisted of extending an office work modeling method by the addition of workflow management capabilities. This extension consists in the definition of a third level of modeling to the OSSAD method, namely the prescriptive level. These ideas are implemented in a CABRE (Computer-Aided Business Re-Engineering) software which enables:

- modeling processes and procedures according to OSSAD and its prescriptive extension which is centered on the concept of document,
- carrying out qualitative and quantitative analysis of models,
- building web-enabled workflow applications from the procedures specifications. These applications are based on Lotus Notes/Domino and the Workey workflow engine.

This work revealed some perspectives which exceed the framework of our approach. The canceling of a procedure after it started is still in our view a research issue. On one hand, some models and tools to analyze how a procedure can be canceled are necessary to understand the cancellation effects, and on the other hand, workflow management systems should include functions to carry out properly these cancellations. Another interesting perspective concerns the management of process evolution: a method should provide guidelines to develop alternative designs in relation with the objectives of the evolution and the results of simulations.

References

1. Georgakopolous D., Hornik M., Sheth A.: An overview of workflow management: from process modeling to workflow automation infrastructure. Distributed and Parallel Databases, 3 (1995), 119-153.
2. NSF Workshop on Workflow and Process Automation in Information Systems: State-of- the-art and Future Directions, http://lsdis.cs.uga.edu/activities/NSF-workflow/proc_cover.html (1996)
3. Conrath D.W., Dumas P. et al.: Office Support Systems Analysis and Design: a Manual. Esprit Project 285. IOT, Munchen (1989).
4. Nurcan S. "Analyse et conception de systèmes d'information coopératifs. Technique et Science Informatique, vol. 15(9),(1996), 1287-1315.
5. Chappelet J-L., Le Grand A., Prevel M., Snella J-J.: Motown: a practical approach to workflows. proceedings of the 1st east-european symposium on Advances in Databases and Information Systems (ADBIS'97), St-Petersburg, Russia (1997).
6. Marshak R.: Software to support BPR- the value of capturing process definitions, Workgroup Computing Report, Patricia Seybold Group, vol. 17, no. 7 (1994).
7. Médina-Mora R., Winograd T., Flores R. et Flores F.: The action workflow approach to workflow management technology. Proceedings of the conference on Computer-Supported Cooperative Work, (1992).
8. Pozewaunig H., Eder J., Liebhart W.: ePert: extending pert for workflow management systems. Proceedings of the 1st east-european symposium on Advances in Databases and Information Systems (ADBIS'97),St-Petersburg, Russia (1997).

Attribute-Pair Range Rules

Jerome Robinson   Barry G. T. Lowden

Department of Computer Science, University of Essex
Colchester, Essex, CO4 3SQ, U.K.
{robij, lowdb}@essex.ac.uk

Abstract. This paper examines the properties of metadata in the form of IF THEN rules which contain two predicates on attributes of a relational database table. For example: a(15 .. 30) ⇒ d(243 .. 271), which means "if the value of attribute 'a' in a tuple is in the range 15 to 30 then the value of attribute 'd' will be in the range 243 to 271." Metadata of this kind is useful in Semantic Query Optimisation and Remote Cache Management. The two predicates (antecedent and consequent) in each rule are Selection Conditions or constraints of the type found in database queries. Each condition therefore denotes a subset of a database table. Rules can be cascaded, using subrange containment as the link between successive rules. The set of rules can therefore be regarded as a set of edges in a Condition Dependency Graph, and using the rule-set is path discovery in the graph. The purpose of the current paper is to introduce some of the properties of attribute-pair range rules.

1 Introduction

If data servers took more interest in their data they could be more helpful in their response to client queries. Metadata, in the form of pairs of range conditions from different attributes can be easily derived from the data, either by induction triggered by queries [4] or by systematic analysis [6]. The resulting attribute-pair rules can be used for Semantic Query Optimisation and cache management in remote clients.

Each Attribute Pair (AP) Rule is a *subset descriptor* for a database table, comprising a *set selector* (the antecedent) and a *set descriptor* (the consequent). Methods for choosing appropriate subsets include deriving rules by systematic analysis and set reduction as in [6], or by associating a rule with each bar of a histogram describing the table as in [7], or by recognizing subsets that are frequently used during database access. Some properties of AP Rules are now specified.

Each rule has the simple form: A ⇒ B, where antecedent A and consequent B are range constraints or *conditions* applied to attributes a and b respectively. 'Range' conditions include *equality* conditions, such as (a = n).

Range Conditions have two forms:

i) *single-test conditions:* (a θ n) where $\theta \in \{<, \leq, =, \geq, >\}$,
'a' is an attribute name, and n is a value of the same type as the attribute,

and ii) *double-test conditions:* $(n \leq a \leq m)$ where n and m are values, of attribute a's type. a(n .. m) is an *abbreviation* for $(n \leq a \leq m)$. We assume a(n .. m) denotes a *closed interval* (i.e. the values n and m are included in the range).

Rules are used by matching (comparing) condition A or B with another range condition such as a query condition or a condition in another rule. Two range conditions on the same database table are *comparable* if they have the same attribute name. Eg: b(5 .. 81), (b > 63), (b = 549) can all be compared because they all denote ranges for attribute b. Comparison is a test for *subrange containment.*

Set (A) is a subset of set (B) in the rule A $\Rightarrow$ B
The set selected by applying selection condition A is a subset of the tuples obtained by condition B. This is a necessary consequence of the assertion A $\Rightarrow$ B, which can be read as "all As are Bs". Furthermore, a rule partitions its database table into three disjoint subsets, corresponding to selection conditions: $A \wedge B$, $\neg A \wedge B$, $\neg A \wedge \neg B$. The significance of this table partition is discussed in [7].

Attribute Pair Rules are used as subset selector/descriptor pairs, and they are an exact description of the data rather than the probabilistic knowledge usually produced in KDD. A large amount of such metadata is desirable, for a full description of the data, but the rule set must be structured for fast access. Examination of the Hasse Diagram for the ordered set of attribute ranges (*e.g.* Figs. 2 and 3) identifies an efficient data structure, access strategy, and systematic rule discovery algorithm for arbitrary sets of range rules.

The structure of the rest of the paper is as follows. Section 2 introduces *Remote Cache Management* as an example of the use of attribute-pair rules. Section 3 describes the rule set as a *Condition Dependency Graph* (CD Graph) and mentions *Semantic Query Optimisation* [4, 8, 9, 10, 11] as a second application requiring these simple subset descriptors. Section 4 provides a data structure for range rule sets, which allows rapid *range matching*, since fast access to the rule base is important to its applications.

2 Remote Cache Management

A query-processing issue of current research interest [eg 1,2,3,5] concerns remote access, via wide area network, to the data server. Mediators, for example, are a local interface for clients to multiple remote data servers. They cache queries in order to reuse cached values to answer later queries. This provides faster query answering, achieves some degree of independence from network delays and breakdowns and helps reduce internet traffic congestion. Their problem is to identify queries that can be answered with locally-cached data. Query result containment by previous result sets, and overlap (partial containment) must be recognized. Existing attempts to solve this problem by query analysis suffer the same drawback as Conventional Query Optimisers: they are syntactic rather than semantic operations. Knowledge about the data can help.

For example: A query, Q1, selects all tuples in a table, where attribute b is greater than 27. The result set is cached. A new query whose selection condition is ($40 \leq b \leq 53$) can obviously be answered from set Q1. But query Q3, whose selection condition is ($21 \leq e \leq 33$) has no apparent connection with the cached set, since it refers to a different attribute. No amount of syntactic analysis will reveal any connection. But the data server may know that ($21 \leq e \leq 33$) $\Rightarrow$ ($b > 27$) *i.e.:* all tuples in that table with e column values in the range [21..33] have a value of the b attribute that is > 27. Therefore the result set for Q3 is *contained in* the cached set from Q1.

Two ways to use this knowledge of the data to assist remote cache managers are:

1. If the Mediator sent query Q3 to the data server, the server would recognize the connection with previous query Q1 and reply with a selection condition to apply to the specified cache set to obtain the new results. This short reply is a small single-packet message able to pass rapidly through the store-and-forward network, faster than the result set.

2. In the case of a *static* data repository (such as a Data Warehouse, Data Archive, or just stable data) the server could send relevant rules to the remote cache manager, so that it can supplement its decisions with knowledge of the data. Each query result set dispatched to a registered cache manager can be supplemented by a set of rules. N-1 rules for an N-ary database relation, one for each attribute other than the one in the current query.

For example: A cached result is for the range condition a(15 .. 30) on attribute 'a'. For each other attribute x_i in the table, produce a rule: range(x_i) $\Rightarrow$ a(15 .. 30). This means "all tuples with x_i value within the specified range(x_i) will have values of 'a' in the range [15..30] and are therefore in the local cache". Such rules can be obtained from the existing rule set, as follows.

Merging Rules

Each rule to be dispatched to the remote cache manager is obtained by *merging* cache-relevant rules from the server's rule set. There are 2 steps:

Step 1. Rules, in general, are classified according to the pair of attributes they contain. From the rules whose consequent condition refers to attribute 'a', and whose antecedent attribute is d, say, extract those with consequent range *within* [15 .. 30], *i.e.* [≥15 .. ≤30]. *E.g.* :

R1	d(46 .. 72) $\Rightarrow$ a(16 .. 25)
R2	d(53 .. 61) $\Rightarrow$ a(18 .. 22)
R3	d(55 .. 79) $\Rightarrow$ a(21 .. 30)

R1, R2 are *nested rules*, so R2 can be deleted from the set. It defines characteristics of a subset of the tuples covered by R1. R1 and R3 are *overlap rules*. These are the sort to merge, in step 2:

Step 2. From the selected set of $d(n_i .. m_i) \Rightarrow a(p_i .. q_i)$ rules, obtain $s = \min(n_i)$, $t = \max(m_i)$, $v = \min(p_i)$, $w = \max(q_i)$. The merged rule is: $d(s .. t) \Rightarrow a(v .. w)$ *i.e.*, the union of antecedent conditions implies the union of consequents. *E.g.* from the rules above, d(46 .. 79) $\Rightarrow$ a(16 .. 30). This means "all tuples selected by condition d(46 .. 79) will have attribute **a** values in the range [16 .. 30]".

Explanation: From R1, all tuples with d(46 .. 72) have a(16 .. 25); and from R3, all tuples with d(55 .. 79) have a(21 .. 30). Unioning the set selected by d(46 .. 72) with that selected by d(55 .. 79) produces the set selected by d(46 .. 79). This set inherits the consequents from the rules describing the smaller sets. Since no new tuples were added, all tuples selected by constraint d(46 .. 79) have (a(16..25) *OR* a(21..30)), *i.e.* all have a(16 .. 30). Consequent ranges must overlap if antecedents overlap [7].

Note that the consequent does not quite fill the cache range a(15 .. 30). If more rules had been available for merging, the consequent range might have been widened, in which case the antecedent range would necessarily increase and would then be able to capture a greater number of future queries.

2.1 Partial Containment by Cache

Current research on remote cache management [e.g. 1, 5] is interested in whether *some* of the answers to a current query are contained in the local cache. The user may not require more than the sample of results contained in the cache. But if the full set is needed, a request for a *smaller set* is made to the remote server, thereby reducing network traffic and also providing *immediate access* to some of the data. The smaller set complements the cached set to complete the query result set. The server can support partial containment by the cache as well as full containment. Full containment is expressed by a rule A ⇒ B, where A is a new query and B the old, cached, query condition. Partial containment can be indicated by rules in a number of ways. For example, a rule B ⇒ A means cached set B is a subset of new query result A. Partial overlap in condition ranges also represents partial containment in the cache. *Eg,* new query: a(15 .. 35), rule: a(25 .. 50) ⇒ B, where B is the cached set.

2.2 Conjunctive Conditions

The cached query may be the result of a conjunction of selection conditions on the table. E.g. (A & C), where A , C are constraints on two different database attributes. Two rules, B ⇒ A and B ⇒ C mean B ⇒ (A & C).

In practice, two rules with exactly the same antecedent, B, may not exist, so the *intersection* of antecedent ranges B' and B" from two rules B' ⇒ A' and B" ⇒ C" are used, where range(A) *contains* range(A') and range(C) *contains* range(C"). The intersection of B' and B'' provides the value of B in the rule B ⇒ (A & C).

For example: **cached query:** (c(15 .. 30) AND a(12 .. 20))

rules: b(3 .. 8) ⇒ c(17 .. 20)
b(4 ..9) ⇒ a(12 .. 18)

The first rule states: if attribute b has a value in the range [3 .. 8] then attribute c will have a value in [17 .. 20], which is therefore in the wider range [15 .. 30] used in the cache descriptor. Similarly, b(4..9) implies **a** is in [12 .. 18] and therefore in [12..20]. The rules therefore become: b(3 .. 8) ⇒ c(15 .. 30) and b(4 ..9) ⇒ a(12 .. 20).

(A rule means that all tuples matching the *antecedent* constraint will also obey the consequent constraint. It does not imply that values exist at all points on the number line interval denoted by the consequent range). From these rules it follows that b(4..8) ⇒ (c(15..30) AND a(12..20)) because if both rule antecedents are true (i.e. the *intersection* of their ranges) then both consequents are true. This rule does not claim to provide a *complete* description of the cached set, just *some* information rapidly available from currently held rules. The antecedent range [4..8] could no doubt be increased if the data itself, in the base relation, was examined.

2.3 Query Simplification

The remote cache manager labels each query result set with the query expression which produced the set [*e.g.* 2, 3]. The data server can use AP rules for semantic query reformulation, *e.g.* to eliminate redundant terms. *For example*, a query expression A & B is reduced to B by rule B ⇒ A. (A & B ≡ B if B ⇒ A, because set(B) ≡ set(A) ∩ set(B) when B ⇒ A). Eliminating terms from cache descriptor expressions allows them to subsume more queries in syntactic analysis, so cache management benefits from knowledge-based simplification of query expressions, using AP rules.

3 The Condition Dependency Graph (C D Graph)

It is useful to regard the set of rules as edges in a Condition Dependency Graph. Each rule is an edge, and rule composition produces paths of two or more edges which denote *transitive rules*. The first and last nodes in *any* path are antecedent and consequent in a rule, and can be linked directly by a single arc. These transitive rules identified by paths are no different in character from rules produced directly from data, e.g. by induction [4] or systematic analysis [6]. They denote a relationship between data values in two attributes. So although a path is a chain of deduction, it reveals a rule which is then independent of the inference path. Intermediate rules in the path could be deleted from the rule set without affecting the validity of the transitive rule.

Paths branch because a consequent range can imply many antecedent ranges in other rules; and because one antecedent condition can appear in several rules with consequents on different attributes. Branching is useful because transitive paths from a common antecedent can be *intersected* to produce a new, more specific rule.

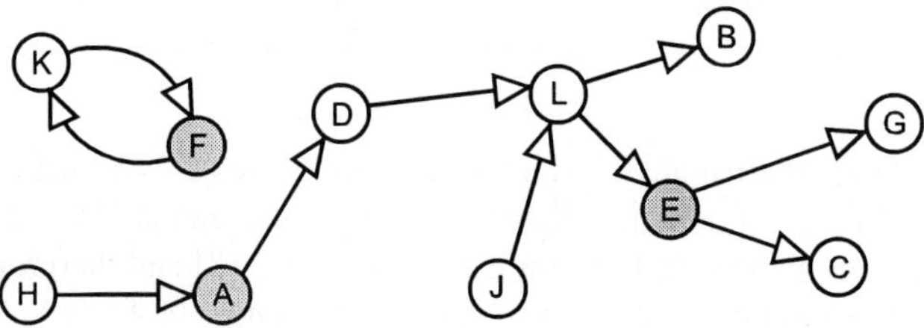

Fig. 1. Part of a Condition Dependency Graph including query conditions A, F and E.

Fig. 1 shows a second practical application of Attribute Pair rules, namely Semantic Query Optimisation (SQO), which involves path discovery in the Condition Dependency Graph. A query is a collection of conditions which query-result tuples must satisfy. The collection of query conditions is structured as a sum of products expression (i.e. a disjunction of conjunctive sub-queries). SQO rewrites *the sub-queries* in order to produce a query that can be processed faster. Fig. 1 shows three conditions, A, F and E in a conjunctive query have been matched with conditions in rules. The path from A to E means that condition E can be deleted from the query, because A ⇒ E so any tuples which satisfy condition A will also satisfy E, without being tested. The *cycle* containing condition F means F can be replaced *in the query* expression by K, if *equivalent condition* K is a faster test to apply to tuples. Equivalent conditions select the same set of tuples. If any of the conditions *implied by* A or E *contradict* condition F then the query will produce no results and can be answered immediately with the empty set without consulting any data (or if the conjunct $A \wedge E \wedge F$ is a *sub-query* it can be deleted from the larger query). *For example,* if F is the condition $(25 \leq d \leq 34)$ and a rule (*i.e.* path) $A \Rightarrow (45 \leq d \leq 63)$ exists, then no tuple can satisfy both conditions A *and* F as required by the query, because all tuples meeting condition A have attribute d values outside the range required by condition F.

3.1 Condition Matching

Matching conditions in the CD graph (e.g. query conditions to rule conditions, or consequent to antecedent when cascading rules) need not involve *exact match* if range conditions are involved. In fact, 'matching' is an inference process using *subrange containment* as the rule of inference. A range *implies* its super-ranges: [n .. m] ⇒ [≤n .. ≥m]. *e.g.* b(15..30) ⇒ b(12..40), meaning "if b is in the interval [15..30] it is also in [12..40]". Conditions denote *sets of tuples*, so set(b(15..30)) is *part of the set of tuples* with values in the range [12..40].

3.1.1 Query Condition/Rule Antecedent Matching

For comparable conditions, a query condition matches a rule antecedent if:

range(rule antecedent condition) *contains* range(query condition)

Reason: Query condition must *imply* rule antecedent. Implication is by subrange containment. Set(query condition) ⊆ set(rule antecedent condition).

3.1.2 Rule Consequent/Query Condition Matching

For comparable conditions, rule consequent matches query condition if:

range(query condition) *contains* range(rule consequent condition)

Reason: Consequent condition must imply query condition is true. (This ends a chain of inference from one query condition to another, through one or more rules).

Semantic Query Optimisation rewrites a query into a form which a Data Server can answer more quickly. SQO is a pre-processing stage between user and server, which intercepts and rewrites queries. It must therefore be *fast* to avoid delaying the query and so counteracting the benefits of the faster query it produces. Therefore it is important to pre-process the CD Graph, before a query arrives, so that transitive rules are ready to apply without having to build paths at query time. It is therefore useful to know (as discussed in the next section) whether there is a limit to the amount of pre-processing to be done, since full transitive closure is a significant workload.

3.2 Maximum Pathlength in the CD Graph

The maximum pathlength to be examined in the CD graph when deriving transitive rules is N edges, where N is the number of columns in the database table. Paths in the graph can be longer than N, but rule derivation need only examine paths to depth N. A path is a sequence of pairs of attribute conditions, formed by cascading attribute-pair rules. The longest useful path is one in which every attribute appears exactly *once.* When a path reaches a condition on the attribute from which it started, the node at the end of the path must denote a superset of the tuples denoted by the start of path condition. *Eg:* a(15..20) $\Rightarrow$ a(12..93). Paths such as a(15..20) $\Rightarrow$ a(23..32) or a(15..20) $\Rightarrow$ a(18..19) cannot be derived, since these rules are self-contradictory. A range can only imply a *super-range* of itself.

Consider the path: $A_1 \Rightarrow B_1 \Rightarrow C_1 \Rightarrow A_2 \Rightarrow C_2 \Rightarrow E_1$
where A_i denotes condition i on attribute a, B_i condition i on attribute b, etc.

Case 1: Nested paths with Shared Consequent
Three rules linking attributes a and c are shown: $A_1 \Rightarrow C_1$ $A_2 \Rightarrow C_2$ $A_1 \Rightarrow C_2$
But the second *subsumes* the third, since A_1 is a *subrange* of A_2 (because $A_1 \Rightarrow A_2$). *For example,* if A_1 = a(25 .. 31) and A_2 = a(21 .. 46) the information in the rule a(25 .. 31) $\Rightarrow C_2$ is only part of the information in the rule a(21 .. 46) $\Rightarrow C_2$.

Case 2: Absence of Consequent Attribute from the First Cycle
When a path reaches an attribute for the second time it starts a second cycle. Eg A_1 and A_2 in the path above start different 'cycles' through the database table's attribute set. Two rules link attributes a and e in the path above: $A_1 \Rightarrow E_1$ and $A_2 \Rightarrow E_1$
Since condition node A_1 does not imply any other condition on attribute e in the path, the rule $A_1 \Rightarrow E_1$ is the best rule in which condition A_1 implies a value range for attribute e. But it is a redundant rule, since it is subsumed by $A_2 \Rightarrow E_1$ because range(A_2) *contains* range(A_1), so set(A_1) $\subseteq$ set(A_2).

Therefore, although paths longer than N can be generated they are not useful. A second cycle can be treated as a SEPARATE path, providing information about a different subset of the database table. This is a superset of the tuples described by the first cycle, since the start node of the second path is a super-range of the first path's start node. (The start node is the *antecedent* of the rules in that section of the path, and *selects* the set of tuples described by the rules).

3.3 Merging Antecedent Ranges

The CD graph can therefore be seen as a collection of *separate,* but maybe concatenated, paths. So the maximum number of incoming edges to any node is N-1, representing each of the other columns of the database table. More than N-1 would denote redundant rules, since two rules have the same consequent, the same antecedent *column*, but different antecedent *range*. If those ranges are *nested* then the *subrange* rules are discarded. But if ranges *overlap*, they are *merged* during graph processing to produce a wider (more useful) range antecedent, as follows. Consider two incoming edges: a(15..20) ⇒ b(12..23) and a(17..23) ⇒ b(16..29) to the antecedent node of rule: b(10..31) ⇒ d(15..44). The two original rules are separate subset descriptors, with overlapping antecedent ranges. They can be combined, by unioning, to a single rule: a(15..23) ⇒ b(12..29) whose consequent assertion satisfies the antecedent constraint of b(10..31) ⇒ d(15..44) and therefore produces a new, transitive, rule: a(15..23) ⇒ d(15..44). A new antecedent node is thus added to the CD graph, for the condition a(15 .. 23), as the start of transitive rules.

3.4 Maximum Out-degree of Graph Vertices

When producing new edges to represent transitive paths, the number of *outgoing* edges from any node must be limited to N-1 (for an N-ary database relation) so that a node is only connected to the narrowest available range for each consequent attribute. Sequential and parallel paths can provide consequents. *Nested* consequent ranges are produced by successive 'cycles' in *sequential* paths, producing rules such as: a(15..23) ⇒ e(20..27), a(15..23) ⇒ e(10..49), a(15..23) ⇒ e(3..182). The *first* rule subsumes the others. The redundant rules are not produced if transitive path-length is limited as discussed in section 3.2.

Parallel paths produce *overlapping* consequent ranges, such as: a(15..23) ⇒ e(20..27), a(15..23) ⇒ e(24..31). Rule *intersection* provides an improved transitive rule, a(15..23) ⇒ e(24..27). Both original rules are *true*, but less informative than their intersection rule. Each consequent assertion is improved (made more specific) by information in another consequent, since only values common to *all* the overlapping consequent ranges can actually exist in the subset data they describe.

4 Rule or Condition Match Algorithms

The condition match problem is one that must be solved in any rule system which has a large number of rules. In a system that automatically increases the size of the rule set by discovery, there is a tendency for the rule system's performance to deteriorate as the set grows. The match phase *in production systems* (such as Expert Database Systems or C-A Rule support in Active Databases) is a very time-consuming component of rule use, in the continuous match-select-act cycle. It requires the use of discrimination networks such as RETE, TREAT or GATOR which store partial match results, in order to improve performance. However, attribute-pair range-condition rules are very different. Their structure and semantics allow rapid matching, by simple lookup algorithms. The algorithms, and the storage structure, are derived from the Hasse Diagram shown in Fig. 2, which denotes the ordered set of possible range conditions on an integer attribute whose extreme values are 10 and 20. But the diagram reveals the structure of any set of range conditions on any orderable attribute type. It is the position of certain *zones* on the diagram (those shown in Fig. 3) which suggests a suitable data structure and search algorithm for attribute-pair rules.

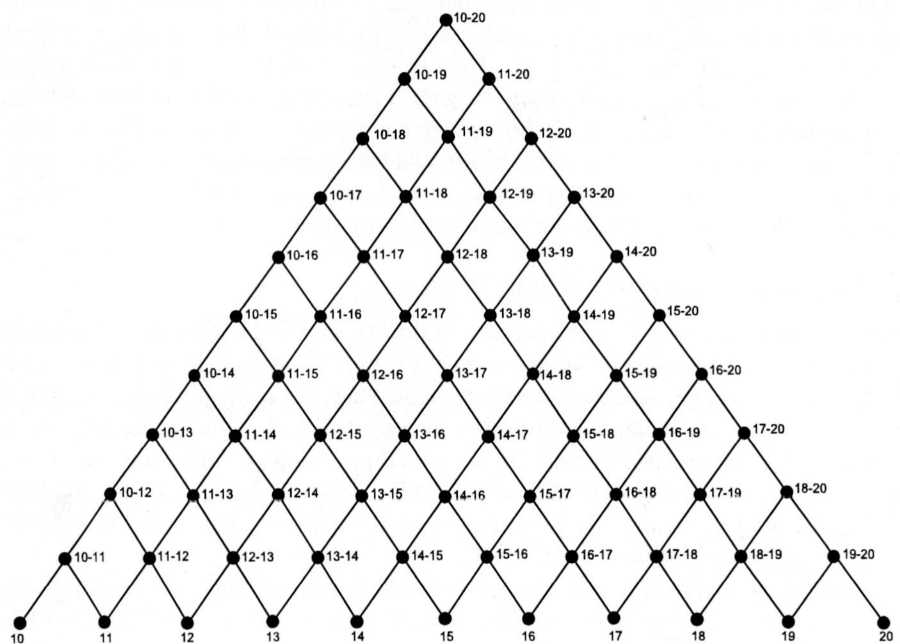

Fig. 2. Hasse Diagram for Range Conditions

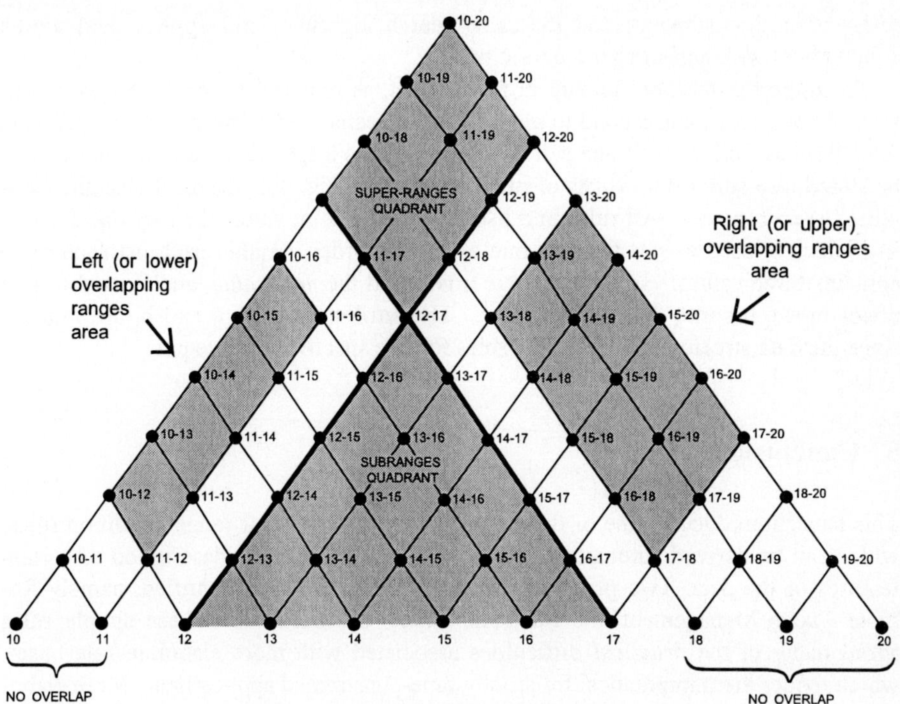

Fig. 3. Significant areas for range node 12-17

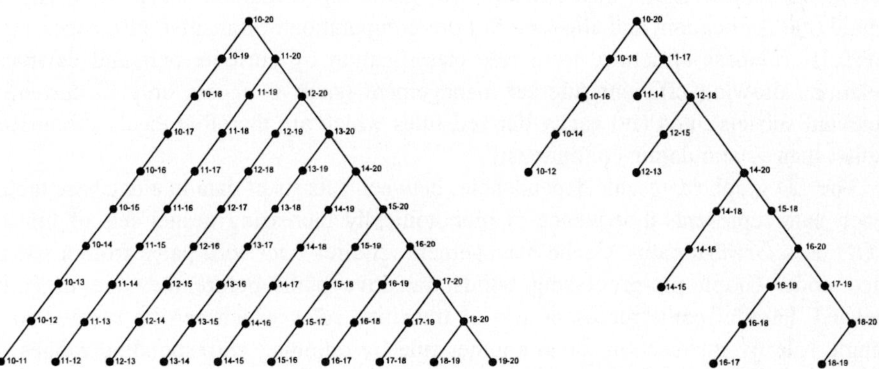

Fig. 4a. A Data Structure

Fig. 4b. Possible Version in Practice

Fig.4a shows a tree data structure derived from the Hasse diagram: a sequence of lists of nodes (range conditions). All nodes in a diagonal list have the same lower limit for their ranges (as shown in Fig. 2). This common value for a list is the *listvalue*. The *set of lists* is sorted by listvalue, so the sequence of diagonals in Fig. 4a is in ascending order of lower range limits. The nodes within each list are sorted in descending order of upper range-limit. This structure, corresponds to the diagonal rows in the Hasse diagram, and so allows early-terminating search algorithms to be easily specified for range match in any of the 'significant areas' in Fig. 3. In practice, nodes may be missing from the structure shown in Fig. 2, as indicated in Fig. 4b, but since the *order* of nodes is maintained the same search algorithm still applies, and works equally well with non-integer numeric types.

To support *antecedent* lookup in the rule set, as required for SQO, a Hasse Diagram whose nodes correspond to *antecedent* ranges is used. The structure represents the AP set associated with one pair of attributes from a specific table. The rule set can be stored as a sorted set of lists of rules, a shown in Fig. 4b. Each rule has the form a(m .. n) ⇒ b(p .. q). All rules in a list have the same m value, the *listvalue* for that list, which is used to sort the lists into ascending order. Within each list each node contains three values: <n, p, q> where n is called the *nodevalue*, and is used to sort nodes in the list into descending order. The attribute names, a and b, are implicit since the data structure contains only rules for one specific attribute pair.

5 Conclusions

This paper introduced some of the properties of Attribute-Pair range-condition rules, which can be derived automatically from data and constitute a description of certain features of the data. Two practical uses for these rules were identified, namely Remote Cache Management and Semantic Query Optimisation. These simple rules avoid many of the *practical* difficulties associated with more elaborate rule bases, which render them impractical for strictly time-constrained applications. More elaborate rule structures are more expressive, but lack benefits such as (i) fast access through a simple regular data structure, (ii) graph representation providing a map to guide rule application, and allowing full pre-computation of transitive inferences, (iii) modular rulebase structure, from rule classification by attribute pair and database relation, allowing efficient rule set management (such as access only to currently relevant subsets), and (iv) easily derived rules which are therefore easily discarded, rather than accumulating continuously.

The CD graph represents dependencies between subsets of data in a database table. Each path represents a sequence of monotonically increasing nested sets of tuples. SQO uses *forward* paths. Cache management requires *backward* paths from a specified node. Graph pre-processing builds transitive paths before they are urgently needed. Parallel paths represent sets of transitive rules which can be merged to a single rule by intersection, or to another rule by unioning corresponding ranges in rules. Unioning is useful in cache expression implication, and in broadening the antecedent range to enclose a given assertion range. Intersection narrows ranges to produce a more specific subset descriptor. Previous work in SQO has used rule sets which are an arbitrary collection of rule structures, not amenable to the graph representation for inference closure, and with inherently lower utility per rule in the applications we consider.

References

1. Adali, S., Candan, K. S., Papakonstantinou, Y., Subrahmanian, V. S.: Query Caching and Optimization in Distributed Mediator Systems. ACM SIGMOD Conf. (1996) 137-148.
2. Dar, S., Franklin, M. J., Jonsson, B. T., Srivastava, D., Tan, M.: Semantic Data Caching and Replacement, Proc. 22nd VLDB Conference (1996) 330-341.
3. Keller, A. M., Basu, J.: A Predicate-based Caching Scheme for Client-Server Database Architectures. VLDB Journal 5(1) 1996, 35-47.
4. Lowden, B.G.T., Robinson, J., Lim, K.Y.: A Semantic Query Optimiser using Automatic Rule Derivation. WITS'95, 5th Intl. Workshop on Information Technologies and Systems (1995) 68-76.
5. Qian, X.: Query Folding. 12th IEEE Intl. Conf. on Data Engineering (1996) 48-55.
6. Robinson, J., Lowden, B. G. T.: Data Analysis for Query Processing. 2nd Intl. Symposium on Intelligent Data Analysis (1997) 447-458. (LNCS 1280)
7. Robinson, J., Lowden, B. G. T.: Semantic Query Optimisation and Rule Graphs. KRDB'98, 5th International Workshop on Knowledge Representation meets Data Bases (1998).
8. Shekhar, S., et al.: A Formal Trade-off between Optimization and Execution Costs in Semantic Query Optimization. Proc. 14th VLDB Conference (1988) 457-467.
9. Shenoy, S. T., Ozsoyoglu, Z. M.: Design and Implementation of a Semantic Query Optimizer. IEEE Trans. Knowledge and Data Engineering, 1(3) 1989, 344-361.
10. Siegel, M.,et al.: A Method for Automatic Rule Derivation to Support Semantic Query Optimization. ACM Trans. Database Systems, 17(4) 1992, 563-600.
11. Yu, C., Sun, W.: Automatic Knowledge Acquisition and Maintenance for Semantic Query Optimization. IEEE Trans. Knowledge and Data Engineering, 1(3) 1989, 362-375.

Query-Driven Horizontal Class Partitioning for Object-Oriented Databases*

Ladjel Bellatreche and Kamalakar Karlapalem and Gopal K. Basak

University of Science and Technology Clear Water Bay Kowloon, Hong Kong
E-mail : {ladjel, kamal}@cs.ust.hk E-mail: mabasak@uxmail.ust.hk

Abstract. Horizontal partitioning (HP) technique is a logical database design technique first developed for distributed relational (record structured) databases. Though the main objective of HP is to reduce irrelevant data access, there has been very little work done in quantifying this by means of a cost model, and developing algorithms which derive the horizontal partitioning schemes. In this paper, we develop a cost model for query processing in object oriented databases (OODBs) for both unpartitioned and horizontally partitioned object oriented databases. The problem of coming up optimal HP scheme is NP-complete. Therefore, we present and evaluate two algorithms for coming up with optimal (based on exhaustive search) and/or near optimal (based on heuristics) HP schemes.

1 Introduction

OODB technology has matured enough to support modern applications such as CAM/CAD, software engineering and multimedia databases. HP is often used as a means to achieve better performance out of database systems by reducing irrelevant disk accesses for executing a set of queries [6]. A partial list of benefits of horizontal class partitioning include: 1) different queries access only the needed fragments of a class, so HP will reduce the amount of irrelevant data accessed by queries, 2) HP reduces the amount of data transfered when processing queries across multiple sites distributed [4], 3) the decomposition of a class into horizontal class fragments (HCFs), each being treated as a unit, permits queries to be executed concurrently, and 4) HP can be treated as an object-oriented database schema design technique, which takes a class and generates a class hierarchy of HCFs so as to increase the efficiency of query execution, while providing additional semantics for the OODB scheme.

There has been little work done on the *HP* in OODBSs [2, 4], in comparison to the relational model [3, 8, 7]. Ezeife et al. [4] presented a comprehensive set of algorithms for horizontally partitioning four class models: classes with simple attributes and methods, classes with complex attributes and simple methods, classes with simple attributes and complex methods, and classes with complex

* This research has been funded by RGC CERG HKUST747/96E

attributes and methods. They applied the concepts developed for relational models in [3, 8]. In [2] we presented primary and derived HP algorithms for generating HCFs of a given class. The primary algorithm is an adaptation of the horizontal partitioning algorithm proposed in the relational model [7]. The approach used is based on affinity between predicates, and we formalized "derived HP" concept and developed a scheme for generating derived HCFs. The work addressed in [2, 4] ignored the physical cost corresponding to the savings in the amount of irrelevant data accessed.

In this paper, we address the problem of HP, we show its utility for OODBs and finally, we present an algorithm for generating HCFs based on the cost model for executing a set queries. A major feature of this algorithm is that it minimizes the I/O disk accesses, and to the best of our knowledge, *it is the first algorithm* which uses the cost model for generating HCFs. The main contributions of this paper are:

1. Development of a mathematical formula to calculate the number of HP schemes for a given set of minterm predicates.
2. Development of a cost model for executing a set of queries on both horizontally partitioned classes and unpartitioned classes.
3. Development of two algorithms to achieve the horizontal class partitioning.

The rest of the paper is organized as follows : section 2 presents the cost model for unpartitioned classes and horizontally partitioned classes, section 3 presents two horizontal class partitioning algorithms an their evaluation, and section 4 presents a conclusion.

1.1 Basic Concepts

Definition 1. A *simple predicate* is a predicate defined on a simple attribute or a method and it is defined as [3]: *attribute/method operator* value, where operator is a comparison operator $(=, <, \leq, >, \geq, \neq)$. The value is chosen from the domain of the attribute or the value returned by the method.

Let $\Pi = \{p_1, p_2, ..., p_N\}$ be the set of all *simple predicates* defined on a class C. The set of *minterm predicates* $M = \{m_1, m_2, ..., m_z\}$ is defined as [3] : $M = \{m_i / m_i = \wedge_{p_k \in \Pi} \; p_k^*\}$, where $p_k^* = p_k$ or $p_k^* = \neg p_k$.

Definition 2. A path P represents a branch in a class composition hierarchy and it is specified by: $C_1.A_1.A_2....A_n$ $(n \geq 1)$ where : C_1 is a class in the database schema, A_1 is an attribute of class C_1, and A_i is an attribute of class C_i such that C_{i+1} is the domain of the attribute A_i $(1 < i \leq n-1)$. For the last class in the path C_n, you can either access an attribute A_n, or a method m_n that returns a value, or a set of OIDs. The length of the path P is defined by the number of attributes, n, in P. We call the first class C_1 the starting class and the last attribute (or method) A_n the ending attribute or method of the path. A predicate which is defined on path expression is called component predicate [2].

2 Cost Model for Horizontal Class Partitioning

Assume a database of object instances are stored on secondary memory which is divided into pages of fixed size. In this section, we present two analytical cost models of executing a set of k queries $\{q_1, q_2, ..., q_k\}$, where every query may contain a simple or component predicates. The first cost model is for executing these queries on unpartitioned classes (i.e., all classes in class composition hierarchy are unpartitioned), and second cost model is for executing the same queries on horizontally partitioned class(es) (i.e, we assume that there are some class(es) which are horizontally partitioned). The objective of our cost models is to calculate the cost of executing these queries, each of which accesses a set of objects. The cost of a query is directly proportional to the number of pages it accesses. The costs are calculated in terms of disk page accesses. The cost of executing a query is given by: **Total_Cost = IO_Cost + CPU_Cost + COM_Cost**, where *IO_Cost* is the input/output cost for reading and writing data between main memory and disk, *CPU_Cost* is the cost of executing CPU instructions, (for example, for evaluating predicate), and *COM_Cost* is the cost of network communication among different nodes. In this paper, we concentrate on the *IO_Cost* and disregard the *CPU_Cost* and *COM_Cost*. This is because for very large database applications with huge number of data accesses, the *CPU_Cost* contribution towards the *Total_Cost* will not be significant, and the database we consider is centralized, therefore the *COM_Cost* is not taken into account.

Cost Model Parameters

We can classify the parameters for the cost model into three categories: database, query and horizontal class fragments.

a- Database Parameters:

Cardinality of a class $C_i(||C_i||)$(i.e., number of objects), total number of pages occupied by the class $C_i(\ |C_i|)$, object length or size (in bytes) in the class collection $C_i(LC_i)$, and page size of the file system(in bytes)(PS).

b- Query Parameters :

Starting class of a component predicate $p_l(C_s^h)$, the number of object references for class C_i during the path evaluation process along the class composition hierarchy(REF_i), number of predicates used by all queries(N), selectivity of query $q_h(SEL_h)$, the fan-out for the class composition hierarchy from class C_{i-1} to C_i $(Fan(C_{i-1}, C_i))$, selectivity of predicate $p_l(sel_l)$, and the length of output result(L_{proj}).

c- Horizontal class fragments Parameters :

Number of HCFs of class $C_i(m_i)$, cardinality of a HCF $F_j(||F_j||)$(i.e., number of objects), total number of pages occupied by the HCF $F_j(|F_j|)$, the number of object references for HCF F_j during the path evaluation process along the class composition hierarchy(ref_j), selectivity of HCF $F_j(sel(F_j))$.

2.1 Cost of Executing a Single Query on Unpartitioned Classes

In order to make easier the formulation of the I/O cost model for both unpartitioned and horizontally partitioned classes, we develop it for a query q_h as shown Fig. 1, we assume that q_h contains one component predicate p_l. In the next subsection, we shall generalize this formulation for k queries. We assume that the starting class of component predicate as C_s^h and ending class as C_n^h. The length of path from C_s^h to C_n^h is n_h.

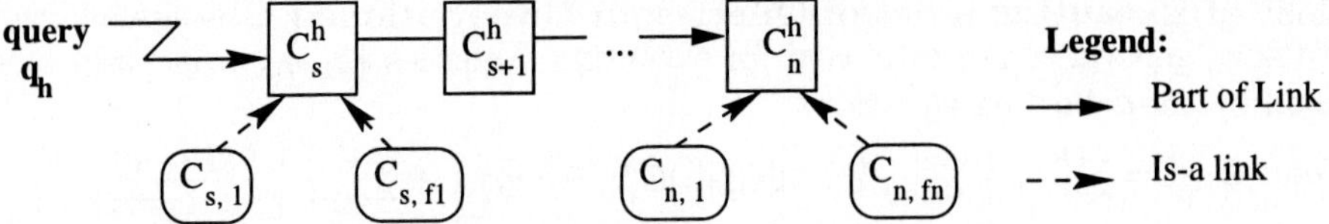

Fig. 1. Example of Unpartitioned Classes

Our cost model is based on [5]'s formulation. The cost for the query execution can be broken up into 2 components: the cost of evaluating a predicate(CEP), and the cost of building the output result(CBOR) which correspond to the number of pages to be loaded in order to evaluate a predicate, and the number of pages to be loaded to build the result, respectively.

Estimation of the Number of Pages in a Class Collection

Sequential scan and index scan are the two major strategies used for scanning a class collection. The objective of using an index is to attain faster instances access, while the objective of using horizontal class partitioning is to reduce irrelevant instances access. These two objectives are orthogonal and complementary. We concentrate on the sequential scan strategy; the use of index can also be incorporated into our model naturally as needed. We assume that the objects are smaller than the page size and do not to cross page boundaries. The total number of pages occupied by a class collection C is given by: $|C| = \left\lceil \frac{||C||}{\lfloor \frac{PS}{LC} \rfloor} \right\rceil$ where $\lceil\ \rceil$ and $\lfloor\ \rfloor$ are the ceiling and floor functions, respectively. The same formula can be used for a HCF F as follows: $|F| = \left\lceil \frac{||F||}{\lfloor \frac{PS}{LC} \rfloor} \right\rceil$

Estimation of the Number of Page Accesses for Predicate Evaluation

Let q_h be a query having a component predicate p_l with sel_l as its selectivity. We first define the number of distinct references involved in the path [5] $REF_i = (1 - Prob_i) \times ||C_i^h||$, where $Prob_i$ is the probability of an object of collection C_i^h not involved in the path, we have:

$$Prob_i = (1 - \frac{1}{||C_i^h||})^{(REF_{i-1} \times sel_l \times FAN(C_{i-1}^h, C_i^h))}, \text{ with } REF_1 = ||C_s^h||.$$

In order to estimate the number of page accesses in class collection C_i^h (see Figure 2) during the evaluation of a predicate, we use the Yao function [9]: given n records uniformly distributed into m blocks ($1 \leq m \leq n$), each contains n/m records. If k records ($k \leq n$) are randomly selected from n records, the expected number of page accesses is given by: $Yao(n, m, k) = m \times \left[1 - \prod_{i=1}^{k} \frac{n \times d - i + 1}{n - i + 1} \right]$ where $d = 1 - \frac{1}{m}$. We use the Yao's formula with $\mathsf{n} = ||\mathsf{C}_i^h||$, $\mathsf{m} = |\mathsf{C}_i^h|$ and $\mathsf{k} = \mathsf{REF}_i$ as defined above.

Cost Formulate for Query Execution

The total cost of executing the query q_h having a component predicate p_l defined on unpartitioned classes is given by the following equation:

$Total\_Cost = CEP + CBOR$, with: $CEP = \sum_{i=s}^{n} Yao(||C_i^h||, |C_i^h|, REF_i)$ and

$CBOR = \left\lceil \frac{SEL_h \times ||C_s^h||}{\lfloor \frac{PS}{Lproj} \rfloor} \right\rceil$

Cost of Executing a Set of Queries on Unpartitioned Classes
We now, generalize the total cost for executing k queries $\{q_1, q_2, ..., q_k\}$ which is given by the following equation:

$$Total\_Cost = \sum_{h=1}^{k} \left[\sum_{i=s}^{n} Yao(||C_i^h||, |C_i^h|, REF_i) \right] + \sum_{h=1}^{k} \left[\left\lceil \frac{SEL_h \times ||C_s^h||}{\lfloor \frac{PS}{Lproj} \rfloor} \right\rceil \right]$$

We note that all these equations are for queries having one component predicate. For a query having more than one predicate, we calculate the I/O cost for *each predicate* based on above equations, and finally we sum up all these I/O costs.

2.2 Cost of Executing a Single Query on Partitioned Classes

Let C_i^h be a class in the class composition hierarchy which is horizontally partitioned into m_i HCFs. Let us consider a query q_h having a component predicate invoking C_i^h as shown in Fig. 2. Before describing the cost on horizontally partitioned classes, we first estimate the number of page accesses in HCF F_j during the evaluation of a predicate. We can apply the same formula for unpartitioned class due to the representation of HCF as a class. Then the number of page accesses is given by: $\mathsf{Yao}(||\mathsf{F_j}||, |\mathsf{F_j}|, \mathsf{ref_j})$ where: $\mathsf{ref_j} = (1 - \mathsf{Prob_j}) \times ||\mathsf{F_j}||$ where $Prob_j$ is the probability of an object of HCF F_j to be not involved in the path, we have: $Prob_j = (1 - \frac{1}{||F_j||})^{(REF_{i-1} \times sel_l \times FAN(F_j^h, C_{i+1}^h))}$

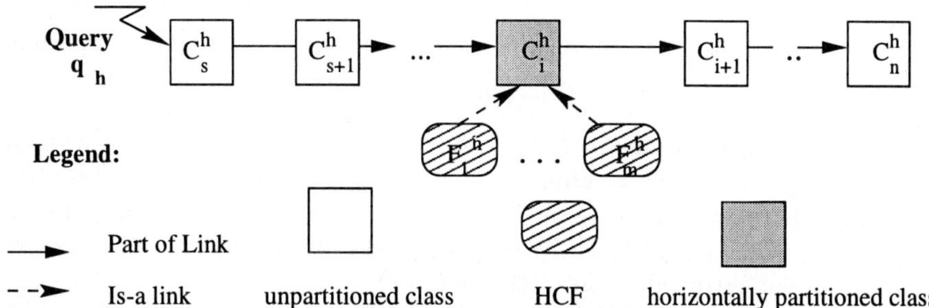

Fig. 2. Example Horizontal Class Partitioning

The predicate evaluation cost (CEP) is the sum of Yao's function over the classes involved in the query, but we need to consider the effect of HP of the class C_i^h which is represented by the binary variable $valid(p_l, F_j)$ that has the value 1 if the predicate p_l is valid in HCF F_j, 0 otherwise. That means we load only the HCFs which satisfy the predicates defined by the query:

$$CEP = \sum_{(i=s, i \neq h)}^{n} Yao(||C_i^h||, |C_i^h|, REF_i) + \sum_{i=1}^{m_i} valid(p_l, F_i) \times Yao(||F_i||, |F_i|, ref_i),$$

and the cost of building the output result is: $CBOR = \left\lceil \frac{SEL \times ||C_s^h||}{\lfloor \frac{PS}{Lproj} \rfloor} \right\rceil$

We generalize the above formulas for i ($i > 1$) classes which are horizontally partitioned. We introduce a binary variable H_i which is of value 1, if the class C_i is horizontally partitioned, 0 otherwise.
The predicate evaluation cost will be defined by the following equation:

$$CEP = \sum_{i=s}^{n} \left[H_i \times \sum_{j=1}^{m_i} (valid(p_l, F_j) \times Yao(||F_j||, |F_j|, ref_j) + (1 - H_i) \times Yao(||C_i^h||, |C_i^h|, REF_i) \right],$$

the CBOR is given by:

$$CBOR = (1 - H_s) \times \left\lceil \frac{SEL \times ||C_s^h||}{\lfloor \frac{PS}{Lproj} \rfloor} \right\rceil + H_s \times \sum_{j=1}^{m_s} (valid(p_l, F_j) \times \left\lceil \frac{SEL \times ||F_j||}{\lfloor \frac{PS}{Lproj} \rfloor} \right\rceil$$

Based on the cost model for both unpartitioned and horizontally partitioned, we can make the following comparison in order to show the utility of HP. In unpartitioned classes, all instances of these classes are loaded into main memory, but in horizontally partitioned classes; the query needs to load only the HCFs which contribute to the result, that it is done by the valid function. We note that $|F_j|$ is always less than $|C_i|$ for horizontally partitioned classes, and then $Yao(||F_j||, |F_j|, ref_j) < Yao(||C_i^h||, |C_i^h|, REF_i)$. In this case, the HP will always improve the performance of evaluating the predicate, but if the selectivity of the query is very high, which means all HCFs of the class C_i^h are relevant to the query, there is an extra overhead which is due to cost of applying the *union operation* to reconstruct the result of a query. This overhead may deteriorate the performance of the HP.

3 Horizontal Class Partitioning Algorithms

3.1 Cost-Driven Horizontal Partitioning Algorithm

We define that the result of the HP process as a partitioning *scheme* which represents a set of HCFs. We consider set of queries accessing C_h using N simple predicates $\{p_1, p_2, ..., p_N\}$. We assume that these simple predicates are *non-overlapping*, *complete* and *minimal* [8]. From these predicates, we generate the set $M = \{m_1, m_2, ..., m_z\}$ of minterm predicates. We note that a minterm or a combination of several minterms using disjunction connector ($\vee$) forms one HCF denoted by ( ). From the 8 minterm predicates, we have several possibilities of HP scheme of a given class. For example: $[(m_1 \vee m_2), (m_3), (m_4 \vee m_5), (m_6 \vee m_7), (m_8)]$ forms a scheme with 5 HCFs. The number of all possible HP schemes for a given z minterm predicates is given by the theorem 1.

Theorem 1. Let z be the number of minterm predicates and S_z be the all possible schemes. Then S_z is given by: $S_z = \sum_{k=1}^{z} S_z^k$, where: S_z^k represents all schemes defined for z minterm predicates having k HCFs, with $S_z^k = k * S_{z-1}^k + S_{z-1}^{k-1}$.

Proof. See [1]. □

We assume that the class C_h will be horizontally partitioned, and let $Q = \{q_1, q_2, ..., q_k\}$ be set of queries accessing a class composition hierarchy including the class C_h. From the set of simple predicates $P = \{p_1, p_2, ..., p_N\}$ defined on C_h, we generate all minterm predicates $\{m_1, m_2, ..., m_z\}$, after that, we exhaustively enumerate all possible schemes S_z (see Theorem 1). For each scheme, we calculate the cost of executing all these queries. Finally, the scheme with minimal cost gives the best HP scheme of the class C_h.

We note that this algorithm needs an exhaustive enumeration strategy to generate all schemes. For small values of minterms, this procedure is not computationally expensive. However, for large values of number of minterms, the computation is a very expensive, for example, for 15 minterms, the number of schemes is 1382958545.

3.2 Approximate Horizontal Class Partitioning Algorithm

We note that the cost driven algorithm has exponential time complexity to generate all schemes and that the predicate affinity algorithm(PAA) [2] is very efficient algorithm ($O(k * N^2)$, where N and k represent the number of queries and their predicates, respectively), but in most cases it does not give the optimal HP scheme that minimizes the total number of disk accesses to execute all queries. Therefore, we have developed an approximate algorithm which takes the advantages of both algorithms PAA and CDA. It is based on hill-climbing technique in order to find a near optimal solution. Before the introduction of the approximate algorithm, we consider some basic concepts.

Representation of Horizontal Class Fragments

We note that each attribute or method has a domain(dom), then when a class is horizontally partitioned, the predicates define partitions of domain of each attribute and method. The cross product of partitions of an attribute or method by all the predicates determine a partitioning of the domains of all the attributes or methods into sub_domains.

Fragment	Duration		Cost		Location	
	d_{11}	d_{12}	d_{21}	d_{22}	d_{31}	d_{32}
F_1	1	0	1	0	1	0
F_2	1	0	0	1	1	0
F_3	1	0	0	1	0	1
F_4	1	0	1	0	0	1

Table 1. Representation of Class Fragments Using Sub-Domains

Example We assume that class *Project* (given in reference [2]) has been horizontally partitioned into four HCFs as follows:
F_1 given by clause cl_1 : (Duration $\leq$ 4) $\wedge$ (Cost() $\leq$ 7000) $\wedge$ (Location = "CA"), F_2 given by clause cl_2 : (Duration $\leq$ 4) $\wedge$ (Cost() > 7000) $\wedge$ (Location ="CA"), F_3 given by clause cl_3 : (Duration$\leq$ 4) $\wedge$ (Cost() $\leq$ 7000) $\wedge$ (Location = "LA"), F_4 given by clause cl_4 : (Duration $\leq$ 4) $\wedge$ (Cost() > 7000) $\wedge$ (Location = "LA"). The domains of the attributes and return values of the method are: dom(Duration) =]0, 7], dom(Cost()) =]0, 20000], dom(Location) = {"CA", "LA"}. The partitioning of the attributes and methods defined in HCFs are as follows: dom(Duration) = $d_{11} \cup d_{12}$, where d_{11} =]0, 4], d_{12} =]4, 7], dom(Cost()) = $d_{21} \cup d_{22}$, where d_{21} =]0, 7000], d_{22} =]7000, 20000], dom(Location) = $d_{31} \cup d_{32}$, where d_{31} = "CA" and d_{32} = "LA". From sub-domains, we can represent all HCFs by a table whose rows and columns represent the HCFs and sub_domains respectively, as shown in Table 1. The value (F_i, d_{jk}) equals 1 if the HCF F_i is valid in sub-domain d_{jk}, otherwise, it is 0. For example, the value (F_1, d_{21}) is 1, because the HCF F_1 is defined by cost() $\leq$ 7000. From Table 1, we define two operations: shrink() and expand() as follows:

- **Shrink()**: If the HCFs F_i and F_j are defined by two clauses which differ in one predicate p_k and if there are some queries with high frequencies which do not access predicate p_k, then we shrink these two HCFs into one HCF without

p_k. For example, the HCFs F_2 and F_3 have the same two predicates, except one predicate which is defined on Location attribute, then we apply the shrink operation, and we obtain: F_{23}: (Duration ≤ 4) $\wedge$ (Cost > 7000).

• **Expand()**: If there is a HCF F_j of the HP scheme which is defined by a clause having f simple predicates, and if there is a query accessing the class using a clause with g, $(g > f)$ simple predicates, then we expand the clause of F_j by augmenting additional simple predicates defined on the new attributes or methods. For example, we suppose that there is a query accessing class *Project* (given in reference [2]) with the following clause: (Duration ≤ 4) $\wedge$ (Cost > 7000) $\wedge$ (Location = "CA"). Let F_j be a HCF defined by the clause cl : (Duration ≤ 4) $\wedge$ (Cost() > 7000). In this case, F_j can be expanded into two HCFs F_{j1} and F_{j2} defined by the clauses cl_{j1} and cl_{j2} which cover the location attribute (we note that the location attribute has domain ("CA" and "LA")).

cl_{j1} : (Duration ≤ 4) $\wedge$ (Cost() > 7000) $\wedge$ (Location = "CA").

cl_{j2} : (Duration ≤ 4) $\wedge$ (Cost() > 7000) $\wedge$ (Location = "LA").

We conclude that the two operations(Expand and Shrink) defined above are realized by processing Table 1, for details refer to the technical report [1].

Approximate Algorithm

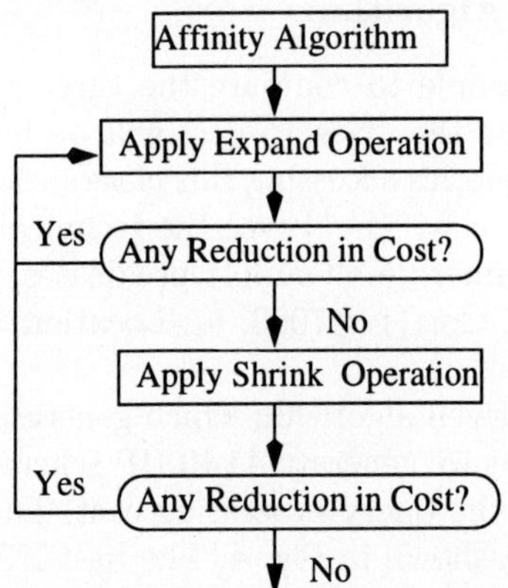

Fig. 3. The Steps of the Approximative Algorithm

We note that a hill-climbing technique needs four parameters: 1) the initial state, 2) how generate the next step, 3) determine the best state, and 4) stop test. The *initial state* is obtained by applying the affinity algorithm [2]. This is a good choice because the affinity algorithm is based on the best heuristic HP algorithm. We note that the result of this algorithm is a set of HCFs and each is HCF represented by one clause. In the *next step* a new scheme for HP is determined by applying the two operations (shrink and expand) described above. The *best state* is obtained by using the cost-driven approach's cost formulas to calculate the cost required for each of the new scheme to see if it is of lower cost than the cost of the current scheme. The *algorithm ends* if there is no new scheme with cost lower cost than the current scheme. The steps of this algorithm are shown in Fig. 3. In approximate algorithm, we apply expand() operation first, and then shrink() (see Fig. 3), because the application of expand() operation generates many HCFs, and a query accesses only those HCFs having relevant data. The disadvantage of this operation is generation of many HCFs and then an additional cost is occurred due to the union operation.

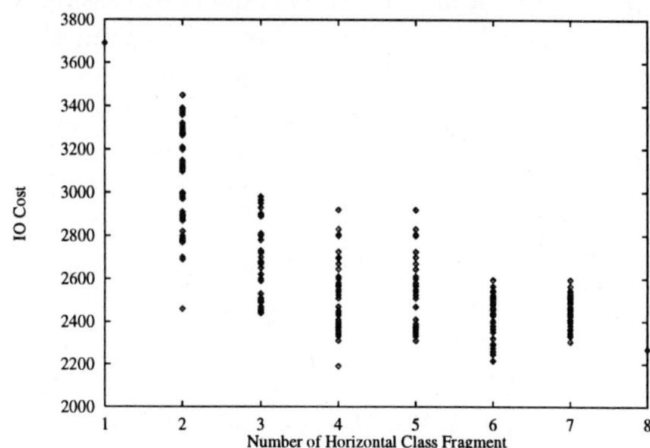

Fig. 4. Plot of Number of Horizontal Class Fragments vs. Total Cost

3.3 Evaluation of the Algorithms

We shall now take an example to compare the three algorithms: cost-driven, PAA, AA. We assume that the class *Project* will be horizontally partitioned, and we suppose there are queries accessing this class such as, $\{v.\text{PId}; v/\text{ Project}; v.\text{Duration} \leq 4 \wedge v.\text{Location} = \text{“CA”}\}$ (see the technical report [1] for details). From these queries, we enumerate all simple predicates, namely, : p_1: Duration ≤ 4, p_2: Cost() ≤ 7000, p_3: Cost() > 7000, p_4: Location = “CA”, and p_5: Location = “LA”.

First, we apply the Cost-driven algorithm which generates 8 minterms from the above predicates. After that we generate **4140** HP schemes(see Theorem 1). For each scheme, we calculate the query processing cost. The plot of the total cost against number of HCFs is shown in Fig. 4. The best HP scheme is:
CD_1: (Duration ≤ 4) $\vee$ [(Duration > 4) $\wedge$ (Cost() > 7000) $\wedge$ (Location =“LA”)], CD_2: (Duration > 4) $\wedge$ (Cost() ≤ 7000) $\wedge$ (Location = “CA”), CD_3: (Duration > 4) $\wedge$ (Cost() > 7000) $\wedge$ (Location = “CA”), CD_4: (Duration > 4) $\wedge$ (Cost() ≤ 7000) $\wedge$ (Location = “LA”) with cost 2190.

After that, we apply the predicate affinity algorithm. Following HCFs are got:
PA_1 with clause cl_1 : (Duration ≤ 4) $\wedge$ (Cost() ≤ 7000) $\wedge$ (Location = “CA”),
PA_2 with clause cl_2 : (Duration ≤ 4) $\wedge$ (Cost() > 7000) $\wedge$ (Location =“CA”),
PA_3 with clause cl_3 : (Duration≤ 4) $\wedge$ (Cost() ≤ 7000) $\wedge$ (Location = “LA”),
PA_4 with clause cl_4 : (Duration ≤ 4) $\wedge$ (Cost() > 7000) $\wedge$ (Location = “LA”),
PA_5 with clause cl_5 : Duration > 4.

The scheme obtained is one among those showed in Fig. 4 with cost 2830.

Finally, we apply the approximate algorithm which uses expand and shrink operations to HCFs generated by PAA so as to further reduce the total cost. The scheme obtained by AA has cost of 2520. We note that one shrink operation has been applied to the HCFs obtained by PAA. The HCFs produced by the

approximate algorithm are:
AA_1 with clause cl'_1 : (Duration $\leq$ 4) $\wedge$ (Location = "CA"), AA_2 with clause cl'_2 : (Duration$\leq$ 4) $\wedge$ (Cost() $\leq$ 7000) $\wedge$ (Location = "LA"), AA_3 with clause cl'_3 : (Duration $\leq$ 4) $\wedge$ (Cost() > 7000) $\wedge$ (Location = "LA"), AA_4 with clause cl'_4 : Duration > 4.

4 Conclusion

In this paper, we addressed the problem of horizontal class partitioning in object oriented databases. We developed the cost model for executing a query in both unpartitioned and horizontally partitioned class. We have developed two algorithms namely, a cost-driven algorithm that uses the cost model for query execution to exhaustively search all schemes to find the optimal HP scheme, and an approximate algorithm(AA), wherein an initial solution got by PAA is refined by using a hill-climbing technique. The preliminary results indicate that the HP is a good technique to optimize the query processing. Further, the approximative algorithm provides better quality solution in comparison with PAA, and has lot less computational complexity in comparison with cost-driven algorithm. Our future work is based on executing queries on both horizontally partitioned classes and unpartitioned classes, allocating these HCFs to different sites in a distributed environment.

References

1. L. Bellatreche, K. Karlapalem, and G. K. Basak. Horizontal class partitioning for queries in object oriented databases. Technical Report HKUST-CS98-6, 1998.
2. L. Bellatreche, K. Karlapalem, and A. Simonet. Horizontal class partitioning in object-oriented databases. *in 8th International Conference on Database and Expert Systems Applications (DEXA'97), Toulouse, Lecture Notes in Computer Science 1308*, pages 58–67, September 1997.
3. S. Ceri, M. Negri, and G. Pelagatti. Horizontal data partitioning in database design. *Proceedings of the ACM SIGMOD International Conference on Management of Data. SIGPLAN Notices*, pages 128–136, 1982.
4. C. I. Ezeife and K. Barker. A comprehensive approach to horizontal class fragmentation in distributed object based system. *International Journal of Distributed and Parallel Databases*, 3(3):247–272, 1995.
5. G. Gardarin, J.-R. Gruser, and Z.-H. Tang. A cost model for clustered object-oriented databases. *VLDB*, pages 323–334, 1995.
6. K. Karlapalem, S.B. Navathe, and M. M. A. Morsi. Issues in distributed design of object-oriented databases. In *Distributed Object Management*, pages 148–165. Morgan Kaufman Publishers Inc., 1994.
7. S.B. Navathe, K. Karlapalem, and M. Ra. A mixed partitioning methodology for distributed database design. *Journal of Computer and Software Engineering*, 3(4):395–426, 1995.
8. M. T. Özsu and P. Valduriez. *Principles of Distributed Database Systems.* Prentice Hall, 1991.
9. S. B. Yao. Approximating the number of accesses in database organizations. *Communication of the ACM*, 20(4):260, April 1977.

An Extended Meta Model for Conditional Fragmentation

J.A. Bakker
Department of Information Systems, Delft University of Technology
Zuidplantsoen 4, 2628 BZ Delft, The Netherlands
e-mail: J.A.Bakker@is.twi.tudelft.nl

Abstract. We discuss some weaknesses and limitations of an earlier semantic framework for the correctness of fragmentation schemes. For instance, this framework only supported conditional fragmentation based on single equality predicates. In order to solve these problems, we present a new meta model also allowing fragmentation based on a conjunction of less simple predicates.

1 Introduction

The application of fragmentation within databases enables us to distribute data so that the execution of many applications or queries is faster than in centralized systems. Another objective of fragmentation might be to distribute data complying with the local autonomy of organizational units (departments) in a geographically distributed organization. Both the advantages of data distribution, such as reliability, data availability and performance, and the disadvantages such as an increased complexity, are well known (Ceri and Pelagatti, 1984; Özsu and Valduriez, 1991). Schemes for fragmentation and allocation enable a distributed DBMS (D-DBMS) to hide the location of data for end users and applications. Such schemes are essential for a correct functioning of a distributed database system. Therefore they must be correct. Generally accepted criteria for the correctness of fragmentation and allocation schemes (Ceri and Pelagatti, 1984; Özsu and Valduriez, 1991) are:

Disjointness: Logical fragments do not overlap.
Completeness: If vertical fragmentation is not applied then each data element belongs to exactly one logical fragment.

Allocation: A logical fragment has at least one location.
Reconstruction: A tuple (instance) can be reconstructed from its allocated fragments.

In the context of the Xplain DBMS (Ter Bekke, 1980, 1992, 1994, 1995, 1996, 1997a, 1997b, 1997c; Rolland, 1998), the enforcement of correctness of fragmentation schemes could be based on a meta model and additional rules (Bakker, 1994). Only the following kinds of fragmentation for composite types (types having attributes) were allowed:

No-fragmentation (composite type as fragment)
Instance fragmentation (instance (tuple) as fragment)
Conditional fragmentation (restricted to single equality predicates)

The motivation was that associative data manipulation languages such as SQL (Date, 1995) and the Xplain language, offer too many possibilities for the specification of fragments. SQL even allows join operations that ignore the structure (semantics) of a data model (Ter Bekke, 1992, 1997b; Bakker, 1994). Although it is possible to specify fragmentation correctly by applying a (somewhat extended) data manipulation language, it remains possible to specify syntactically correct but semantically incorrect fragments and to forget some fragments. Moreover, generic rules for the disjointness and completeness of fragments valid for a whole class of data models cannot be specified using data manipulation languages. These languages can only apply the terms of a data model. Generic rules should be expressed in terms of concepts such as 'fragment' ('group') or 'instance' ('tuple') and allocation concepts such as 'node' and 'fragment location'. For example, without such concepts it is not possible to count fragments, which is essential for checking the completeness of fragmentation.

The previous approach restricted conditions to single equality predicates. Both primary and derived fragmentation could be specified through conditions using inheritance paths (links) built through a sequence of one or more attributes (Bakker, 1994). We did not propose any (analytical) method for the design of fragmentation, the objective only was to design a generic declarative solution for the correctness of data distribution schemes. The previous approach does not support global vertical fragmentation. However, *local* vertical partitioning remains possible as in Xplain by using attribute files (transposed files). In Xplain attribute values of an instance of a composite type are stored at a same relative *fixed* position, but in different 'parallel' files, which avoids the replication of object identifications.

Transposed files are described by Batory (1979), Batory and Gotlieb (1982), and by Teorey and Fry (1982). Transposed files can support a fast traversal of attribute paths circumventing indices by storing values (object identifications, attribute values) at *fixed* positions. So it is possible to replace a referring attribute value by the position of the referred object. Xplain uses one B-tree per composite type (B-trees: Bayer *et al.*, 1972, 1977; Comer, 1979).

Before discussing some weaknesses of the previous approach in section 3, we resume the applied semantic data modeling concepts in section 2.

2 Concepts for Semantic Data Modeling

An example of a semantic data model is shown in figure 1. This abstraction hierarchy (showing only composite types) is partly related to the model described by Ceri and Pernici (1985). It describes data in a geographically distributed company, assembling and selling computers. We assume each product assembled by one production department.

Sales departments send product orders to the production department responsible for an ordered product. Each department has a node and communicates with other nodes through a network (Tanenbaum, 1988). The previous paper presents a more complete model for this situation and also deals with the supply of materials and the composition of products.

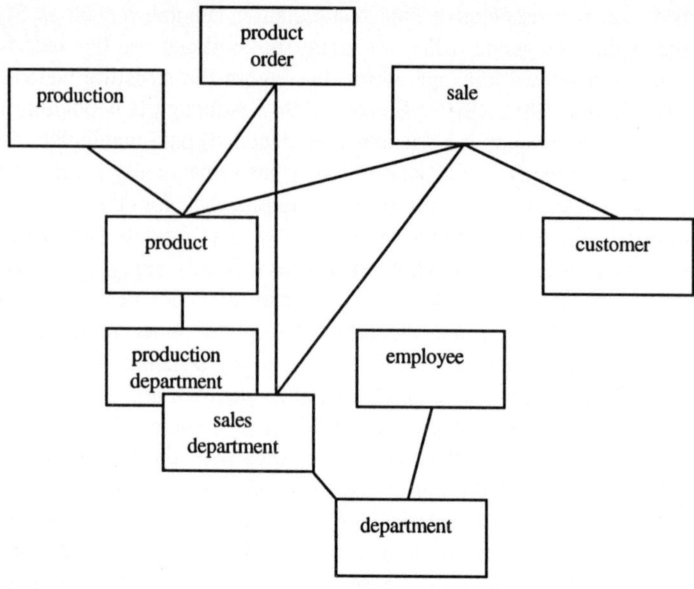

type department	=	department name, address, town, phone, region
type production department	=	[department], energy consumption
type sales department	=	[department], advertising budget
type employee	=	name, initials, address, town, function, phone, department
type product	=	product name, description, size, weight, price, stored_quantity, production department
type production	=	product, first_date, last_date, plan_quantity, real_quantity
type product order	=	product, ordered_quantity, date, sales department
type customer	=	name, address, town, region
type sale	=	product, sales department, customer, date, quantity, amount, delivery_date, status, /correctness/
assert sale *its* correctness (*true*)	=	(sales department *its* department *its* region = customer *its* region)

Figure 1. A data model in a distributed environment.

In figure 1 each line between rectangles represents a referring attribute. A line between corners of rectangles also represents the relationship between specialized object types and their generalization (Smith and Smith, 1977a, 1977b). We do not show the domain of types. The unique name of a composite type is written left of the '=' sign, whereas attributes are specified on the other side through the name of their type and are possibly preceded by a prefix (role). Square brackets indicate generalization.

Additional rules (static restrictions) are specified through a derived variable or attribute, possibly accompanied by a value restriction (controlled redundancy). For instance, a (business) rule that instances of the composite type 'sale' must refer twice to a same region can be specified through the derived attribute 'sale *its* correctness'. The concepts for data modelling, derived from Xplain, are shown in figure 2. Although 'type' denotes a conceptual entity, this entity also functions as a property in both 'attribute *its* type' and 'attribute *its* composite_type' (object relativity).

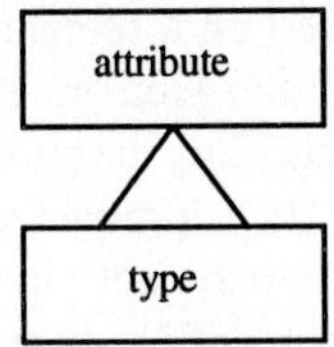

type type = name, domain, /composite/
type attribute = composite_type, type, role, kind
assert type *its* composite = *any* attribute *per* composite_type

Figure 2. Semantic data modelling concepts.

Figure 1 applies the concepts shown in figure 2. For example, 'department' and 'product' are instances of 'type'. Types without attributes, e.g., 'date' or 'region', are base types. Convertibility (Ter Bekke, 1980) requires that attributes of a composite type having the same (possibly another) type have different roles. E.g., both 'production *its* first_date' and 'production *its* last_date' denote attributes based on the aggregation of 'production' and 'date'. The property 'attribute *its* kind' enables us to distinguish aggregation ('A') and specialization ('S'). Table 1 and 2 show some composite types and attributes. The left columns contain object identifications (Khoshafian and Copeland, 1986).

type	name	domain
6	region	char6
7	department	int2
12	employee	int4
13	date	int8
16	product order	int5
18	sale	int7
20	sales department	int2
21	production department	int2
22	product	int3
23	production	int6
24	customer	int5

Table 1. Examples of types

attribute	composite_type	type	role	kind
7	21 {production department}	7 {department}	-	S
9	12 {employee}	7 {department}	-	A
10	22 {product}	21 {production department}	-	A
11	23 {production}	22 {product}	-	A
15	23 {production}	13 {date}	first	A
16	23 {production}	13 {date}	last	A
22	18 {sale}	20 {sales department}	-	A
23	18 {sale}	13 {date}	-	A
31	24 {customer}	6 {region}	-	A
32	16 {product order}	22 {product}	-	A
35	16	20 {sales department}	-	A

Table 2. Examples of attributes

Conditional fragmentation can be based on a semantic link (path of attributes) between types (Chang and Katz, 1989; Cheng and Hurson, 1992). Such a path might refer to a type representing an organizational unit. E.g., the path 'production *its* product *its* production department' ends with attribute '11': 'production *its* product', preceded by a first attribute '10': 'product *its* production department', in which 'production department' acts as inherited type. The previous approach will be discussed further in section 3.

3 The Previous Approach

In the previous approach conditional fragmentation is based on a meta model and a set of additional rules (section 3.1). Section 3.2 discusses problems related to this approach.

3.1 Fragmentation Based on Equality Predicates

The concepts of 'path attribute', 'instance' and 'group' were introduced previously (Bakker, 1992, 1994). Their definition and the related abstraction hierarchy are shown in figure 3. The concept of 'group' merges the concepts of 'predicate' and 'fragment': an equality predicate is specified through a 'last_path attribute' and a 'ref_instance'. This will be explained after figure 3. We do not discuss instance fragmentation and no-fragmentation because they are not involved in our problems.

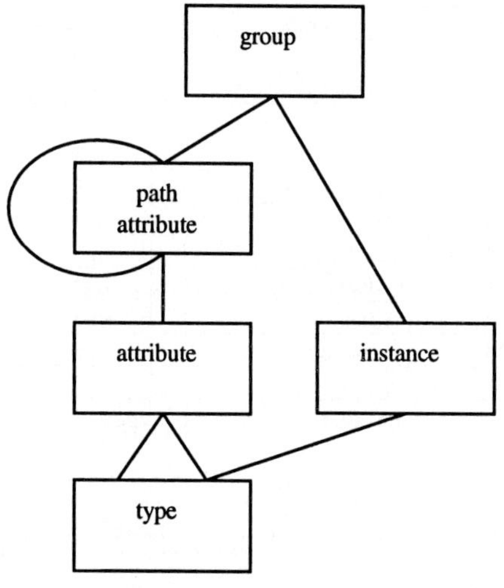

type type = name, domain, fragmentation
type attribute = composite_type, type, role, kind
type path attribute = attribute, preceding_path attribute
type instance = type, value
type group = last_path attribute, ref_instance

Figure 3. The previous meta model for conditional fragmentation

During data modeling different default values for 'type *its* fragmentation' should be applied because fragmentation within base types is not required.

For example: '+' for composite types and '-' for base types. After the completion of a data model but before the specification of fragments the '+' values must be substituted by one of the following values:

'C' : Conditional fragmentation (using only single equality predicates).
'I' : Instance fragmentation (instance as fragment).
'N' : No-fragmentation (composite type as fragment).

If 'type *its* fragmentation = 'C' ' then it is required to specify a correct number of fragments (groups). The members of a group are instances of a same composite type and inherit a same property through a path of attributes. E.g., a specific group of instances of 'production' share the property 'production *its* product *its* production department = 4':

group 'production 4' = production *where* product *its* production department = 4

The referred instance ('group *its* ref_instance') is 'production department 4'. The last path attribute is based on 'production *its* product', whereas 'product *its* production department' indicates the first path attribute and 'production department' functions as the common inherited type. Other groups of 'production' should refer to other instances of 'production department'. The number of these groups within 'production' must equal the number of production departments (completeness of fragmentation). The composite type of a group is found through 'group *its* last_path attribute *its* attribute *its* composite_type'. In the example it is the composite type 'production' of the last path attribute 'production *its* product'. The principle of convertibility (Ter Bekke, 1980) forbids more than one group referring to a same pair of 'last_path attribute' and 'ref_instance'. In this way, disjointness of groups can be enforced.

3.2 Some Weaknesses of the Previous Approach

Although the correctness of conditional fragmentation can be enforced partly through the meta model (figure 3) using the principle of convertibility, it remains possible to specify meta data complying with the meta model but still being incorrect. E.g., specified groups within a type without conditional fragmentation. Another example is a syntactically correct predicate using a path of attributes not linked to the involved composite type. In order to enforce correctness of specifications, a large number of additional restrictions were specified. Still there remain some flaws.

A *first* problem is that each composite type with conditional fragmentation must use one path. This requires counting last path attributes (path elements) per composite type. A path attribute functions as a last element if referred to by any group. However, the meta model does not require the completeness of groups (fragments). Therefore the previous approach started with enforcing the completeness of groups. Otherwise it would not be possible to base the completeness of paths per type on the following derivations:

assert path attribute *its* last = *any* group *per* last_path attribute

assert type *its* path_number (0..1) = *count* path attribute *where* last *per* attribute *its* composite_type

Types with conditional fragmentation should apply one path. Apparently, the completeness of paths depends on the completeness of groups. However, due to the meta model, groups have to be specified after path attributes. This dependency between the completeness of paths and the completeness of groups can be avoided by using:

type path = last_path attribute

Now the number of paths per type can be checked before any group is specified:

assert type *its* path_number (0..1) =
count path *per* last_path attribute *its* attribute *its* composite_type

Secondly, the previous approach restricts conditions to equality predicates:

type group = last_path attribute, instance

A solution is to separate the definition of 'condition' and 'fragment', whereas 'fragment' substitutes 'group' and 'range' replaces 'instance':

type range = preceding_range, type, min_value, max_value
type condition = path, range
type fragment = type, name

Now we can specify conditions based on either value ranges or single values (restriction: min_value = max_value) and guarantee mutual exclusiveness of ranges (section 4.2). Further it also becomes possible to apply a conjunction of predicates, which solves a *third* problem related to the previous approach.

4 An Extended Approach to Conditional Fragmentation

A new framework can be based on a modified meta model (section 4.1). It supports correctness of fragmentation based on either a single range predicate or the conjunction of predicates (section 4.2).

4.1 An Extended Meta Model

Figure 4 shows an improved meta model. The term 'path attribute' has been substituted by the more comprehensible term 'path element' (Ter Bekke, 1995). In the case of an equality predicate, 'condition *its* range *its* min_value' equals 'condition *its* range *its* max_value'.

The concept of 'type' has been extended with 'type *its* min_value' and ''ype *its* max_value'. This enables us to check that ranges comply with the values allowed for the involved type, found via 'range *its* type'.

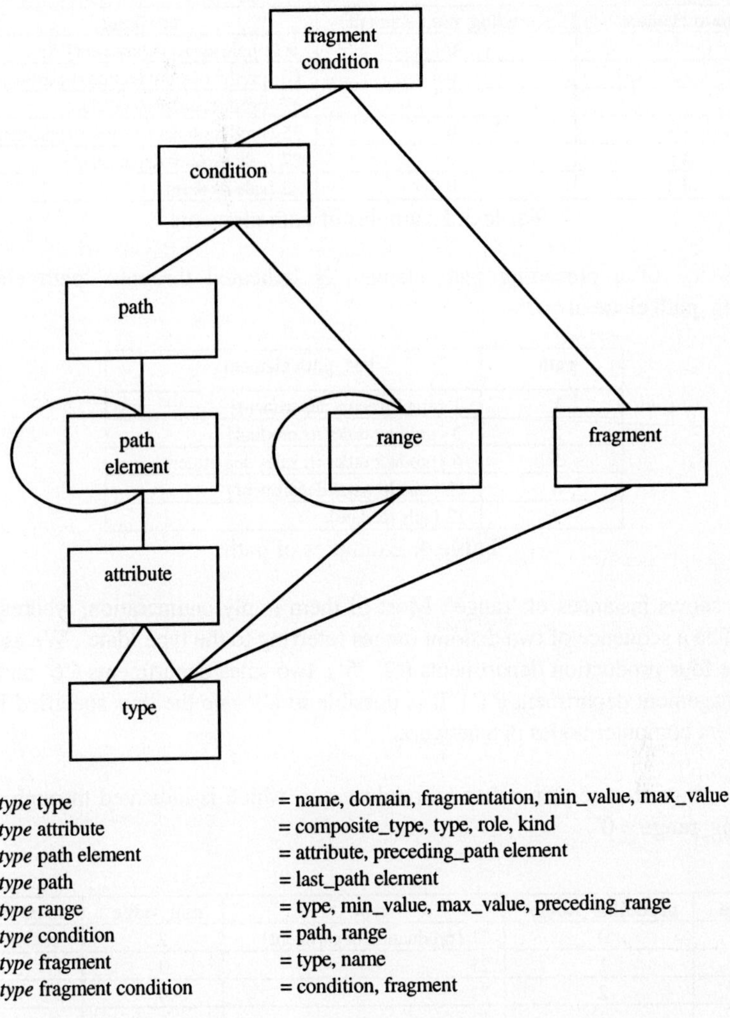

Figure 4. An extended meta model for conditional fragmentation

A type with conditional fragmentation is found through 'path *its* last_path element *its* attribute *its* composite_type'. For example, the following specification defines a fragment within the type 'product':

fragment 'product 2' = product *where* production department = 2

A path used by a condition is found through 'condition *its* path', whereas the associated value range is found through 'condition *its* range'. In this example, 'production department = 2' specifies a single value range.

The following tables are showing some meta data allowed by the new meta model.

path element	preceding_path element	attribute
1	0	9 {employee *its* department}
2	0	10 {product *its* production department}
3	2	32 {product order *its* product}
6	0	35 {product order *its* sales department}
11	0	22 {sale *its* sales department}
12	0	23 {sale *its* date}

Table 3. Examples of path elements

The absence of a preceding path element is indicated through: 'path element *its* preceding_path element = 0'.

path	last_path element
1	1 {employee *its* department}
2	3 {product order *its* product}
5	6 {product order *its* sales department}
8	11 {sale *its* sales department}
9	12 {sale *its* date}

Table 4. Examples of paths

Table 5 shows instances of 'range'. Most of them imply enumeration, whereas the last ones define a sequence of two disjoint ranges referring to the type 'date'. We assume that there are four production departments ('2'-'5'), two sales departments ('6' and '7') and one management department ('1'). It is possible to allocate the thus specified fragments to different computer nodes in a network.

The first range in a sequence has no predecessor, which is indicated through 'range *its* preceding_range = 0'.

range	preceding_range	type	min_value	max_value
1	0	21 {production department}	2	2
2	1	21	3	3
3	2	21	4	4
4	3	21	5	5
6	0	20 {sales department}	6	6
7	6	20	7	7
9	0	7 {department}	1	1
10	9	7	2	2
11	10	7	3	3
12	11	7	4	4
13	12	7	5	5
14	13	7	6	6
15	14	7	7	7
18	0	13 {date}	19580101	19901231
19	18	13	19910101	19991231

Table 5. Examples of ranges

Table 6 shows some conditions that can be applied to fragments.

condition	path	range
1	1	9 {employee *its* department = 1}
8	2	1 {product order *its* product *its* production department = 2}
9	5	6 {product order *its* sales department = 6}
15	8	7 {sale *its* sale department = 7}
16	9	18 {sale *its* date ≥ 19580101 *and* sale *its* date ≤ 19901231}
17	9	19 {sale *its* date ≥ 19910101 *and* sale *its* date ≤ 19991231}

Table 6. Examples of conditions

The tables 7 and 8 show fragments and applied conditions, corresponding with the following specifications:

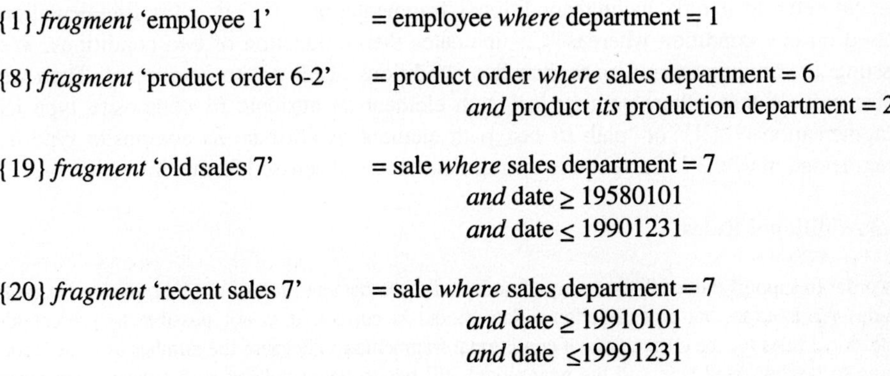

{1} *fragment* 'employee 1' = employee *where* department = 1

{8} *fragment* 'product order 6-2' = product order *where* sales department = 6
and product *its* production department = 2

{19} *fragment* 'old sales 7' = sale *where* sales department = 7
and date ≥ 19580101
and date ≤ 19901231

{20} *fragment* 'recent sales 7' = sale *where* sales department = 7
and date ≥ 19910101
and date ≤19991231

fragment	type	name
1	12 {employee}	employee 1
8	16 {product order}	product order 6-2
19	18 {sales}	old sales 7
20	18 {sales}	recent sales 7

Table 7. Examples of fragments

fragment condition	condition	fragment
1	1 {employee *its* department = 1}	1
13	8 {product order *its* product *its* production department = 2}	8
14	9 {product order *its* sales department = 6}	8
18	15 {sale *its* sales department = 7}	19
19	16 {sale *its* date ≥ 19580101 *and* sale *its* date ≤ 19901231}	19
20	15 {sale *its* sales department = 7}	20
21	17 {sale *its* date ≥ 19910101 *and* sale *its* date ≤ 19991231}	20

Table 8. Examples of fragment conditions

In the case of seven departments it would make sense to specify seven fragments within 'employee'. The required conditions apply the same path 'employee *its* department' but a different range, each representing another instance of 'department'.

When two organizational units want fast access to the same data, this can also be supported by the new meta model. E.g., both a sales department and a production department can be interested in the same product orders (figure 1).

This can be supported by fragmenting data on product orders on the basis of the conjunction of two equality predicates: one corresponding with a sales department, and the other with a production department. E.g., fragment 8 can be allocated to the nodes of the two mentioned departments (replication). We apply 'type *its* fragmentation = 'C2' ' to 'product order'. This means *N*M* fragments within 'product order'. We assume that *N* ranges refer to 'sales department' and *M* ranges related to 'production department'. The fragmentation of 'sale' in historical and recent data illustrates that the new meta model also can support a certain degree of query optimisation by placing these fragments at different nodes.

However, using the meta model alone it cannot be guaranteed that specifications are correct and that no specification is missing. For example, each path should refer to a type having conditional fragmentation: 'C1' denotes fragmentation based on one condition whereas 'C2' indicates the conjunction of two conditions. We assume the conjunction of more than two conditions needs not to be applied. Then we must enforce that either 'path *its* last_path element *its* attribute *its* composite_type *its* fragmentation = 'C1'' or 'path *its* last_path element *its* attribute *its* composite_type *its* fragmentation = 'C2''. Correctness of fragmentation is discussed further in section 4.2.

4.2 Additional Rules

In order to support the local autonomy of nodes, all meta data and rules must be replicated at each node. We assume that any underlying data model is correct. It is not possible to present all additional rules for the correctness of conditional fragmentation because the number of rules is too large to be discussed here and the new model still has to be completed with concepts for other kinds of fragmentation and allocation). We only discuss some of the rules. A first assertion derives whether or not a type is composite:

{1} *assert* type *its* composite = *any* attribute *per* composite_type

Before any other specification is made, the fragmentation of types must be correct:

{2} *assert* type *its* correct fragmentation (*true*) =
composite *and* (fragmentation = 'C1'*or* fragmentation = 'C2'
or fragmentation = 'I' *or* fragmentation = 'N') *or not* composite *and* fragmentation = '-'

Correctness of paths

Disjointness of path elements can be enforced using the principle of convertibility. Further, a path element must be correct: either it has no precursor or it refers correctly to a preceding element (see the examples in table 3):

{3} *assert* path element *its* correctness of references (*true*) =
preceding_path element = 0 *or* attribute *its* type =
preceding_path element *its* attribute *its* composite_type

The specification of paths is correct (and complete) if each path element is correct and if each composite type having conditional fragmentation 'C1' has exactly one path, whereas in the case of fragmentation 'C2' two paths must be specified. Further, each path must refer to a type having some kind of conditional fragmentation:

{4} *assert* path *its* correctness (*true*) =
    last_path element *its* attribute *its* composite_type *its* fragmentation = 'C1'
    or last_path element *its* attribute *its* composite_type *its* fragmentation = 'C2'

Completeness of paths requires a check of the number of paths per type:

{5} *assert* type *its* path_number (0..2) =
    count path *per* last_path element *its* attribute *its* composite_type

{6} *assert* type *its* completeness of paths (*true*) =
    fragmentation = 'C1' *and* path_number = 1
    or fragmentation = 'C2' *and* path_number = 2
    or (fragmentation = 'I' *or* fragmentation = 'N') *and* path_number = 0

Correctness of ranges
We must guarantee that each range is succeeded by at most one range, otherwise we cannot guarantee that ranges constitute a correct sequence:

{7} *assert* range *its* number of successors (0..1) = *count* range *per* preceding_range

{8} *assert* range *its* correctness of references (*true*) =
    max_value ≥ min_value
    and min_value ≥ type *its* min_value
    and max_value ≤ type *its* max_value
    and (preceding_range = 0 *or* type = preceding_range *its* type
        and min_value > preceding_range *its* max_value)

Completeness of ranges per type requires an inherited type to have at least one range:

{9} *assert* type *its* range_number = *count* range *per* type

We can derive whether or not a type functions as an inherited type:

{10} *assert* type *its* inherited = *any* path
    per last_path element *its* ..... *its* attribute *its* type

{11} *assert* type *its* completeness of ranges (*true*) =
    inherited *and* range_number > 0
    or not inherited *and* range_number = 0

Instances of 'range' can be derived from textually specified fragments, but it is also possible to design a dialogue supporting the separate specification of ranges. Assertion 9 illustrates why fragmentation should be based on a meta model. Without the concept of 'range', we cannot specify the counting of ranges per type. Consequently we also would not be able to specify a generic solution (independent of the underlying data model) for the completeness of ranges per type. Moreover, it would not be possible to enforce completeness of conditions: the number of conditions using a same path (*count* condition *per* path) must correspond with the range number of the inherited type. This range number can be found through 'path *its* last_path element *its* ..... *its* attribute *its* type *its* range_number'. Remember the fragmentation of 'employee' based on the path 'employee *its* department': for *N* departments we must specify *N* ranges and *N* conditions.

5 Discussion

The concept of 'path' improves the comprehensibility of the previous meta model and leads to a better separation of rules. As in the previous approach primary and derived fragmentation are treated uniformly. The first is based on a path containing a single path element, whereas the other is based on a sequence of two or more path elements.

A further improvement is the splitting of 'group' into 'condition','fragment' and 'fragment condition', which has the consequences that conditions are no longer restricted to single equality predicates and that conjunctive predicates can be supported. Moreover, it becomes possible to specify fragmentation based on value ranges and to support some kind of query optimization as shown by the fragmentation of data on sales.

Future work has to deal with the complete specification of rules for the correctness of conditional fragmentation. We also have to reconsider the concepts for instance fragmentation and allocation. Our objective is to design a more simple but versatile framework for the specification of correct data distribution schemes, whereas the previous framework is based on three fragmentation concepts.

REFERENCES

Bakker, J.A. (1992), A Unifying Approach to the Modelling of Object Association Based on a Common Property, in *Proceedings IEEE International Conference on Computer Systems and Software Engineering 'Compeuro 92'*, The Hague, P. Dewilde and J. Vandewalle (eds.), IEEE Computer Society Press, pp. 95-100.

Bakker, J. A. (1994), A semantic approach to enforce correctness of data distribution schemes, *The Computer Journal*, **37**, 7, pp. 561-575.

Bakker, J.A. (1996), Object-Orientation Based on Semantic Transformations, in *Proc .7th International Conference on Database and Expert Systems Applications DEXA 96*, Zürich, R.R. Wagner and H. Thoma (eds.), Lecture Notes in Computer Science, **1134**: pp. 163-176.

Batory, D.S. (1979), On Searching Transposed Files, *ACM Transactions on Database Systems*, **4**, pp. 531-544.

Batory, D.S. and C.G. Gotlieb (1982), A Unifying Model of Physical Databases, *ACM Transactions on Database Systems*, **7**, pp. 509-539.

Bayer, R. and McCreight, E. (1972), Organization and maintenance of large ordered files, *Acta Informatica*, **1**, pp. 173-189.

Bayer, R. and Unterauer, K. (1977), Prefix B-trees, *ACM Transactions on Database Systems*, **2**, pp. 11-26.

Ceri, S. and Pelagatti, G. (1984), *Distributed Databases: Principles and Systems*, New York, McGraw-Hill.

Ceri, S. and Pernici, B. (1985), DATAID-D: Methodology for Distributed Database Design, in *Computer-Aided Database Design: The DATAID Project*, A. Albano, V. De Antonellis, and A. Di Leva (eds.), Elsevier Science Publishers, pp. 157-183.

Chang, E.E. and Katz, R.H. (1989), Exploiting Inheritance and Structure Semantics for Effective Clustering and Buffering in an Object-Oriented DBMS, *SIGMOD Record*, **18**, pp. 348-357.

Cheng, J.R. and Hurson, A.R. (1992), Effective Clustering of Complex Objects in Object-Oriented Databases, *SIGMOD Record*, **20**, pp. 22-31.

Comer, D. (1979), The Ubiquitous B-tree, *ACM Computing Surveys*, **11**, pp. 121-137.

Date, C.J. (1995), *An Introduction to Database Systems*, Vol. I, 6th edition, Addison-Wesley.

Khoshafian, S.N. and Copeland, G.P. (1986), Object Identity, in *Proceedings ACM Conference. on Object-Oriented Programming Systems, Languages and Systems, SIGPLAN Notices*, **21**, pp. 11-20.

Özsu, M.T. and Valduriez, P. (1991), *Principles of Distributed Databases*, Prentice Hall.

Rolland, F.D. (1998), *The Essence of Databases*, Prentice Hall.

Smith, J.M. and Smith, D.C.P. (1977a), Database Abstractions: Aggregation and Generalization, *ACM Transactions on Database Systems*, **2**, pp. 105-133.

Smith, J.M. and Smith, D.C.P. (1977b), Database Abstractions: Aggregation, *Communications of the ACM*, **20**, pp. 405-413.

Tanenbaum, A.S. (1988), *Computer Networks*, Prentice Hall.

Teorey, T.J. and Fry, J.P. (1982), *Design of Database Structures*, Prentice Hall, pp. 201-211.

Ter Bekke, J.H. (1980), Convertibility in Databases, *Information Processing Letters*, **11**, pp. 168-171.

Ter Bekke, J.H. (1992), *Semantic Data Modeling*, Prentice Hall.

Ter Bekke, J.H. (1994), Complex values in databases, in *Proceedings International Conference on Data and Knowledge Systems for Manufacturing and Engineering*, Hong Kong, N. Chen (ed.), Chinese University of Hong Kong, pp. 449-455.

Ter Bekke, J.H. (1995), Meta Modeling for End User Computing, in *Workshop Proceedings 6th International Conference on Database and Expert Systems Applications, DEXA 95*, London, N. Revell and A. Min Tjoa (eds.), (1995), pp. 267-273.

Ter Bekke, J.H. (1996), Semantic Modeling of Successive Events Applied to Version Management, in Y. Kambayashi and K. Yokota, editors, in *Proceedings International Symposium on Cooperative Database Systems for Advanced Applications,* Kyoto, Advanced Database Research and Development Series, **7**: pp. 440-447, World Scientific, Singapore.

Ter Bekke, J.H. and J.A. Bakker (1996), *Manual of the Xplain-DBMS, version 5.2,* Delft University of Technology (in Dutch).

Ter Bekke J. H. (1997a), Comparative Study of Four Data Modeling Approaches, in *Proceedings Second CAiSE/IFIP 8.1 International Workshop on Evaluation of Modeling Methods in Systems Analysis and Design*, Barcelona, K. Siau, Y. Wand and J. Parsons (eds.), pp. B1-B12. Proceedings can be obtained by contacting: Dr. K. Siau, Dept. of Management, University of Nebraska-Lincoln, 209 College of Business Administration, Lincoln, NE68588-0491, U.S.A.

Ter Bekke J. H. (1997b), Can We Rely on SQL?, in *Proceedings of the 8th International Workshop on Database and Expert Systems Applications DEXA 97*, Toulouse, R.R. Wagner (ed.), IEEE Computer Society, Los Alamitos, California, pp. 378-383.

Ter Bekke J. H. (1997c), Advantages of a Compact Semantic Meta Model, in *Proceedings Second IEEE Metadata Conference,' Metadata 97,'* Silver Spring, Maryland (1997), available through: http://www.computer.org/conferen/proceed/meta97/list_papers.html

Query by Example for Nested Tables

Nikos A. Lorentzos, Konstantinos A. Dondis

Informatics Laboratory
Agricultural University of Athens
Iera Odos 75, GR 118 55 Athens, Greece
{lorentzos, ginf4dok}@auadec.aua.ariadne-t.gr

Abstract. QBEN, a *Query By Example* language for *Nested* tables, is described. QBEN is user-friendly and allows for the easy formulation of complex queries. At the same time, optimization techniques can be incorporated that enable the *global* optimization of a series of queries. QBEN is addressed both to non-experts and experts. Comparison with other approaches is also made.

1. Introduction

One primary requirement of the conventional Relational Model [1] is the satisfaction of the first as well as a number of other normal forms. This necessitates splitting an original table into many others. However, an undesirable side effect is that join operations, which are too expensive in terms of execution time, have to be issued very frequently. Because of this, many researchers were led to the definition of models that violate first normal form [5], [7], [10], [11], termed *nested models*. Textual query languages for these models have also been defined. However, a general remark is that even experts find it too difficult to use these languages. This same remark also applies to an extension of SQL2 [2], namely SQL3 [3], which is currently at the definition stage. On the other hand, variations of the *Query By Example* language [14] have been proposed, for distinct purposes: From these, [6], [13] restrict to tables which satisfy first normal form. The one defined in [9] aims only at the management of *summary tables*, hence it manages relations whose attributes can only be of order 0 or 1. Another language [4] is actually a generalization of that in [14], aiming at the management of data of either the relational or the hierarchical or the network model, and it was actually defined before the nested models appeared. Hence, [4] does not incorporate the inherent operations *Nest* and *Unnest* of the nested relational model defined in [5], [11]. Finally, a *Query By Example* dedicated to the management of nested relations is presented in [12], but only very simple examples of its functionality are given. Based therefore on these observations, in the present paper we propose QBEN, a *Query By Example* language for *Nested* tables. QBEN has similarities but it is *not* a generalization of the language proposed in [14]. It is rather a variation that takes advantage of the capabilities of modern software technology. The complete functionality of QBEN is given in [8].

The remainder of the paper is organized as follows. In section 2 we present briefly the structure of relations which can be handled by QBEN. The functionality of the language is described in section 3. In the last section we outline the advantages of QBEN, make comparison with other approaches, and report on further work.

2. Data Representation

The key characteristic of a nested relational model is that hierarchically ordered data is structured in a tabular way. Specifically, some of the attributes (columns) of a relation (table) R may be tables themselves and, by a finite recursion, the same may also be true for some of the attributes of one or more of these tables. R is a *table of order 0* and its attributes (tuples) are called *0 order attributes* (*tuples*). If R_1 is one of these attributes and it is also a table, it is called a *first order table.* The attributes of R_1 are called *first order attributes* of R. For some finite *n*, an *(n-1)-order attribute* R_{n-1} of R may be an *n-order table.* R is a *nested table*, called simply *table* in the sequel. If there is no table of order (n+1), then it is said that the *depth* of R *equals n.* For $i \geq 1$, R_i is called a *sub-table* of R. The tuples of R_i are called *sub-tuples* of R or *tuples of R of order i.* Two example nested tables are shown in figure 1.

DEPT					
Dno	Mgr	PROJECTS			
		Pno	Budg	MEMBERS	
				Eid	Sal
1	201	10	4,000,000	102	200.000
				131	130.000
				231	170.000
		11	3,000,000	101	250.000
				222	160.000
2	212	20	3,500,000	301	210.000
				302	120.000

EMPLOYEES		
Eno	LANGUAGES	
	Lang	Level
101	German	3
	English	2
102	German	1
	Italian	2
131	German	2
	French	2
201	German	3
	English	1
	Italian	3
231	German	1
	French	2

Fig. 1. Examples of nested tables

In table DEPT we record data for the departments of an organization. Specifically, for every department we are interested in the Department number (Dno), the Manager's number (Mgr), as well as the PROJECTS in which the department participates. Attribute PROJECTS is a sub-table of DEPT where we record, for each project, its number (Pno), Budget (Budg) and the MEMBERS of the organization who are dedicated to the project. Attribute MEMBERS is also a sub-table of DEPT where we record, for each employee, his number (Eid) and Salary. Table DEPT consists of two tuples, one for each of departments 1 and 2. Department 1 participates in two projects, one with code 10 and another with code 11. Under attribute PROJECTS, the first of these tuples is analysed into two sub-tuples of DEPT, one for each of the two projects. Similarly, under attribute MEMBERS each of these two tuples is also analyzed into other sub-tuples. In the second table, EMPLOYEES, for each employee we record his number (Eno) and the LANGUAGES he knows. For each language we are interested in the Language name (Lang) and the Level of its knowledge. As should be obvious, each of the tables in figure 1 constitutes a tabular representation of a hierarchically ordered data structure.

3. Query Language

In figure 2 we can see part of the screen for the formulation of queries in QBEN. Amongst others, it has a set of buttons that correspond to algebraic operations for nested tables. Except for SELECT/PROJECT, which corresponds to two operations, each of the remainder buttons corresponds to a single operation. Each table is associated with a *skeleton*. For example, the skeleton of table EMPLOYEES is shown in the middle of figure 2. As opposed to [14], however, the formulation of queries in QBEN makes use not only of the table skeletons but also of the buttons. The execution of every individual operation follows a 5-steps general algorithm. This algorithm is outlined below.

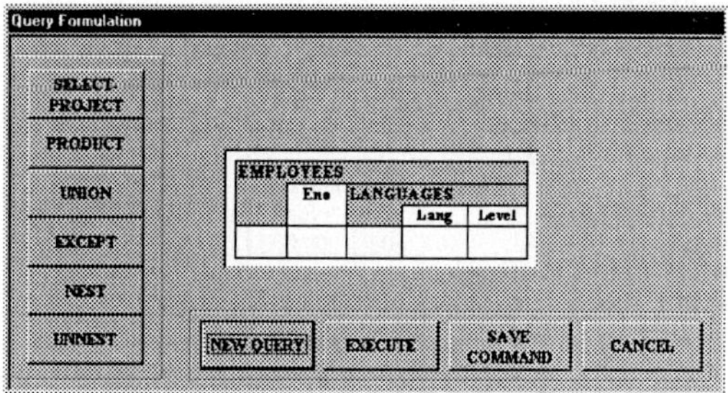

Fig. 2. Screen for query formulation

Step 1 (Selection of Current Table(s)): An operation is *unary* or *binary*, depending on the number of tables (one or two) to which it is applied. *Current* is (are) the table(s) which participate in an operation. Hence, there are at most two current tables at each time. At this step, the user selects the current table(s), i.e. the tables which participate in an operation. A table may be selected twice. Once a table has been selected, its skeleton appears on the screen. As will be seen in Step 3 and Step 4 below, this step is optional.

Step 2 (Query Preparation): Depending on the type of operation, the user must do some preparatory work. This work is described separately for each of the operations that are illustrated below.

Step 3 (Selection of Operation): This step aims at declaring to the system the operation that must be executed. (Note that the actual execution of the operation takes place at Step 5, described below.) This is achieved by pressing one of the buttons in figure 2. Then the system automatically assigns a name to the result table and displays its skeleton on the screen. If the particular operation causes the creation of new attributes, the system also assigns a name to each of them. Note that the name of each new table or attribute is different from all those assigned earlier. Once this step has been completed, the result table is the current table.

Step 4 (Renaming): This step is optional. It enables the user to change either the name of the result table or the name of its attributes. This renaming applies to all the names, not only to those assigned by the system. After this step, the result table is still the current table.

Step 5 (Execution of Operation): After the formulation of one or more queries, each of them consisting of Steps 1-4 above, the user can ask for their execution, by pressing button EXECUTE, shown in figure 2. In response, the system executes the operations, in the order they have been coded.

The functionality of each operation is illustrated next.

Select and Project

As opposed to [14], the combination of operations Select and Project makes use of only one current table. At Step 2 (Query Preparation) the user specifies the retrieval conditions either on the skeleton of the current table or in the *Condition Box*, in a way similar with that in [14]. He also declares the attributes whose content must be retrieved, by typing *P.* (*Print*) at the appropriate place. At Step 3 (Selection of Operation) he presses button SELECT/PROJECT, in which case the system displays the skeleton of the result table. This skeleton consists of all those attributes of the original table that have been associated with a *P.* As can be verified in the examples which follow, the QBEN selection and projection operations are functionally equivalent with those proposed in [6], [11].

Query 1 (Unconditional retrieval): *"Give the content of table EMPLOYEES."*

EMPLOYEES	Eno	LANGUAGES		
			Lang	Level
P.				

EMPLOYEES	Eno	LANGUAGES		
			Lang	Level
	P.	P.		

EMPLOYEES	Eno	LANGUAGES		
			Lang	Level
	P.		P.	P.

Fig. 3. Unconditional retrieval.

The query can be coded in any of the three ways shown in figure 3. This matches fully the functionality of *P.* in [14]. Notice that such an unconditional retrieval can be seen as a recursive retrieval of all the sub-tuples of a retrieved tuple.

Query 2 (Conditional retrieval): *"For each employee who knows English, give his id number, this language's name and the respective level of knowledge."*

The query formulation and the result table are shown in figure 4. The result table is also a nested table whose scheme matches that of EMPLOYEES. It consists of two tuples, one for Eno 101 and another for Eno 201. The value of each tuple of EMPLOYEES_1 for attribute LANGUAGES is a table that contains only one tuple. Similarly with the previous query, the same result can also be obtained in two more alternative ways. Note that a conditional retrieval also functions recursively: For each qualifying tuple, it fetches recursively only those sub-tuples that satisfy the condition.

EMPLOYEES				
	Eno	LANGUAGES		
			Lang	Level
	P.	P.	English	

EMPLOYEES_1		
Eno	LANGUAGES	
	Lang	Level
101	English	2
201	English	1

Fig. 4. Conditional retrieval.

Query 3 (Disjunction): *"For each employee who knows either English or Italian give the employee number and the respective level of knowledge of these languages."*

EMPLOYEES				
	Eno	LANGUAGES		
			Lang	Level
	P.	P.	English	
		P.	Italian	

EMPLOYEES_1		
Eno	LANGUAGES	
	Lang	Level
101	English	2
102	Italian	2
201	English	1
	Italian	3

EMPLOYEES				
	Eno	LANGUAGES		
			Lang	Level
P.			English	
P.			Italian	

EMPLOYEES_1		
Eno	LANGUAGES	
	Lang	Level
101	English	2
102	Italian	2
201	English	1
201	Italian	3

Fig. 5. Examples with a logical disjunction.

The formulation of the query and the result table are shown on the left part of figure 5. As in [14], the coding of the disjunction in table LANGUAGES is achieved by writing the alternative conditions in different rows of the table. From the way the query has been formulated, it is obvious that the two rows of LANGUAGES are associated with the same employee number. Hence, the result table contains exactly one tuple per qualifying employee.

The disjunction could alternatively be coded as is shown on the right part of figure 5. Recalling however how a recursive retrieval functions, now the first row of the query retrieves for each qualifying employee that tuple of LANGUAGES whose value for Lang equals English. The second row functions similarly. Hence, now the result table is the one shown on the right part of figure 5.

Query 4 (Conjunction): "For each employee whose knowledge of a language is better than that of employee 101 for English, give his number, the language and its level of knowledge."

EMPLOYEES				
	Eno	LANGUAGES		
			Lang	Level
	101		English	_x
	P.	P.		> _x

EMPLOYEES_1		
Eno	LANGUAGES	
	Lang	Level
101	German	3
201	German	3
	Italian	3

EMPLOYEES				
	Eno	LANGUAGES		
			Lang	Level
	P.		German	x
		P.		_x

EMPLOYEES_1		
Eno	LANGUAGES	
	Lang	Level
131	German	2
	French	2
201	German	3
	Italian	3

Fig. 6. Examples with a logical conjunction.

The query formulation and the result table are shown on the left part of figure 6. In analogy with the formulation of the query on the right part of figure 5, in this example it is clear that the example element *_x* associates the level of knowledge of English of employee 101, with that of the language(s) of (possibly) other employees. This way, we can associate sub-tuples of a table R that lay within distinct tuples of R.

Query 5 (Conjunction within a sub-table): *"For every employee who knows German, give all the languages which he knows equally well."*

The query formulation and the result table are shown on the right part of figure 6. Now the query is analogous with that on the left part of figure 5, it associates tuples of table LANGUAGES that refer to the same employee. Contrary therefore to the previous example, this one shows how it is possible to associate sub-tuples of a table R which lay within the same tuple of R.

Query 6 (Conjunction by using a *conjunction frame*): *"For every employee who knows both English and Italian, retrieve a single row with the level of knowledge of each of these languages."*

EMPLOYEES				
	Eno	LANGUAGES		
			Lang	Level
	P.	P.	English	
		P.	Italian	

EMPLOYEES_1		
Eno	LANGUAGES	
	Lang	Level
201	English	1
	Italian	3

Fig. 7. Logical conjunction by the use of frame.

Again, this query requires a logical conjunction between sub-tuples of the same tuple of a table. As is shown in figure 7, an easy way to formulate the query is to type the conditions which must be satisfied simultaneously in distinct rows of the same (sub-)table and enclose them in a *conjunction frame*. Note that if we were interested in retrieving only the sub-tuple for English, then *P.* in the sub-tuple for Italian would have to be removed. In the general case, more than one conjunction frame can be used in a query, and one such frame may be covering one or more others.

Query 7 (Conditional retrieval of the full content of a sub-table): *"Give full language details of every employee who knows French."*

EMPLOYEES				
	Eno	LANGUAGES		
			Lang	Level
	x		French	
	P. x	P.		

EMPLOYEES				
	Eno	LANGUAGES		
			Lang	Level
	P.		French	
		P.		

EMPLOYEES_1		
Eno	LANGUAGES	
	Lang	Level
131	German	2
	French	2
231	German	1
	French	2

Fig. 8. Alternative ways of conditional retrieval.

This particular query requires the retrieval of the *full* content of each employee's LANGUAGES table, assuming that some of the tuples of this table satisfy a condition. The query can be formulated in any of the ways shown in figure 8. In the second case, *P.* has been put before an empty row of table LANGUAGES. This indicates that for each employee who knows French we want to retrieve all the tuples of table LANGUAGES. Indeed, according to the explanation given in query 6 on the functionality of the conjunction frame, in this present query the two rows of table LANGUAGES are interpreted as the proposition "Lang = 'French' **and** TRUE". This is equivalent to proposition "Lang = 'French' ". Hence, for every employee the system tests whether he knows French. If this is true for some employee, the system retrieves for this employee the whole content of the respective table LANGUAGES, because *P.* has been put before an empty row of this table.

Cartesian Product

Query 8 (retrieval from two tables): *"Give the Cartesian product of each sub-table MEMBERS (of table DEPT) with the EMPLOYEES table, as well as all the respective data in table DEPT."*

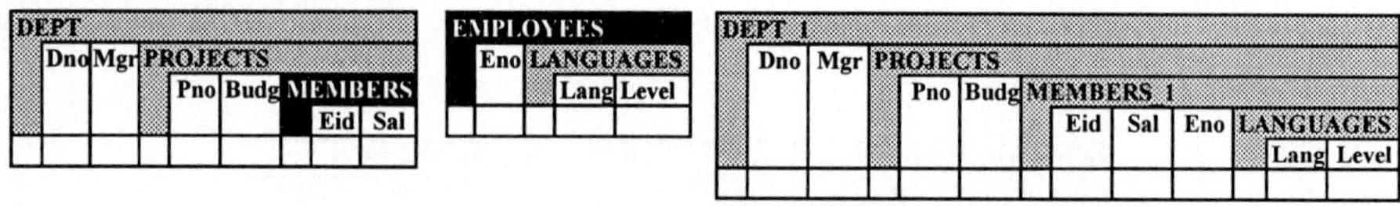

Fig. 9. Retrieval of Cartesian Product.

This operation matches the one defined in [7]. In Step 2 we *mark* sub-table MEMBERS and table EMPLOYEES, as is shown in the two first skeletons of figure 9. In Step 3 we press button PRODUCT and the system produces the skeleton of the result table DEPT_1. Note that in this query the system assigns *two* default names, one to the result table (renamed to DEPT_1 at Step 4) and another to the Cartesian Product of MEMBERS with EMPLOYEES (renamed to MEMBERS_1 at Step 4). In case the next query is a selection, the result obtained is equivalent to joining the two initial tables, as demonstrated in the next example.

Query 9 (Join of tables): *"Give per department and per project a list of the languages of every employee."*

DEPT_1

Dno	Mgr	PROJECTS: Pno	Budg	MEMBERS_1: Eid	Sal	Eno	LANGUAGES: Lang	Level
P.		P.		P._x		_x	P.	

DEPT_2

Dno	PROJECTS: Pno	MEMBERS_1: Eid	LANGUAGES: Lang
1	10	102	German
			Italian
		131	German
			French
		231	German
			French
	11	101	German
			English

Fig. 10. Example of a Join.

Once the system has produced the skeleton of DEPT_1, the user can formulate on it a selection, as is shown in figure 10. This yields the skeleton of a new scheme, DEPT_2. Upon execution of the two queries, the content of DEPT_2 is the one shown in figure 10. We notice that one requirement, to join two or more tables in QBEN, is to initially obtain the skeleton of their Cartesian product. Clearly, this is a deviation from the way a join can be formulated in [14]. There is however a good reason for not adapting accordingly the technique proposed in [14], our investigation has shown that in numerous cases it can be prohibitively difficult for the user to formulate correctly a join between distinct nested tables. This difficulty increases further in joining sub-tables of a nested table R with other sub-tables of R of a different order.

Unnest

Operation Unnest [5], [11] removes a sub-table and its attributes become at the same time columns of the directly lower order table (see section 2). The data of the nested table is restructured accordingly. For example, unnesting sub-table LANGUAGES of DEPT_2 in figure 10 yields table DEPT_3 in figure 11. To illustrate this, consider the following query:

Query 10 (Table unnesting): *"For each project within DEPT_2, list separately every pair of employee and language."*

In Step 2 we mark column LANGUAGES at the skeleton of table DEPT_2 (figure 11). In step 3 we press button UNNEST and after the execution we obtain DEPT_3.

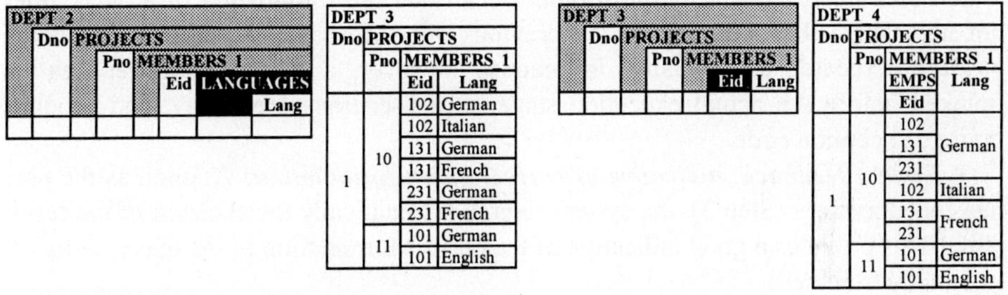

Fig. 11. Examples of Unnest and Nest.

Nest

In operation Nest [5], [11] one or more attributes are grouped below a newly created sub-table with a simultaneous increase of their order (see section 2), by one. Again, the data of the table is restructured accordingly. As an example, consider table DEPT_3 in figure 11. Then nesting on column Eid of sub-table MEMBERS_1 yields table DEPT_4 on the right part of figure 11. To achieve this, consider the following query:

Query 11 (Table nesting): *"For each project within DEPT_3 list all the employees per language."*

In Step 2 we mark column Eid in the skeleton of table DEPT_3, in Step 3 we press button NEST and after the execution we obtain table DEPT_4 on the right part of figure 11.

Union and Except

The functionality of Union and Except is described in [8]. Although no examples of these operations are given, it is worth noting that they are recursive and more general that the respective operations defined in [10].

4. Conclusions

We described the functionality of QBEN, a *Query By Example* language for the management of nested tables. QBEN has a number of advantages:

1. Easy formulation of queries: Complicated queries can be formulated as a series of simple, easily coded queries. As an example, the query *"for each department and for each project within a department, give a list of the employees who know each distinct language"* can be expressed as a series of queries, specifically queries 8-11 of the previous section. Relatively to this, it should be noted that a user is tempted to code a number of simple queries rather than a single complicated.

2. Potential for global optimization: Recall that the formulation of a query does not necessitate the execution of the previous one. Moreover, a batch of queries is *virtually* executed sequentially. In practice however, a *global* optimizer can be invoked before the actual execution stage, in a user-transparent way, and produce optimal execution code.

3. System feedback, indicative of correct query formulation: As soon as the user has coded a query (Step 3), the system returns automatically the skeleton of the result table. This provides a good indication of the correct formulation of the query, before it is actually executed.

Although QBEN has similarities with Zloof's QBE [14], it is *not* generalization of it. However, it can also be applied to tables, which do satisfy first normal form. Compared with other query languages, it might be argued that QBEN reminds of an algebraic rather than a calculus-based language in that (i) operation buttons are associated with relational algebra operations and (ii) a complex query has to be split into a series of simple queries. The counter-argument is as follows: Firstly, even the most recent version of standard SQL [2] also contains keywords which are associated to relational algebra operations, as it is for example UNION, EXCEPT, CROSS JOIN etc. Secondly, our experimentation has shown that formulating queries in QBEN is simple even for a non-expert. Formulating the equivalent queries in any of the non-first normal form calculus-based query languages, which have been proposed so far, can be penalizing even for experts.

To our knowledge, only one more QBE-like language dedicated to the management of non-first normal form relations has been proposed [12]. The two approaches differ in the following: (i) The skeleton table in [12] differs than that of the present paper. Due to this, it is not clear how certain QBEN queries can be formulated in [12]. (ii) In [12] the formulation of a query requires the prior execution of the previous query. Hence [12] is addressed only to non-experts and does not make provision for global optimization.

The use of scalar and aggregate functions within QBEN as well as the maintenance operations (insert, delete, update) are described in [8]. Further work concerns a subsequent extension for the management of temporal data.

Acknowledgement

This work has been supported by the European Union (project CHOROCHRONOS, FMRX-CT96-0056), by the Research Committee of the Agricultural University of Athens, and by the Greek National Scholarships Foundation.

References

1. E. F. Codd, *A Relational Model of Data for Large Shared Data Banks*, Communications of the ACM 13(6), 377-387, 1970.
2. ISO (1992), The International Organization for Standardization, *Database Language SQL*, ISO 9075:1992(E).
3. ISO (1996), *Database Language SQL/Foundation (SQL3)*, ISO/ DBL MCI-004C and ANSI X3H2 96-059C (ISO/ANSI Working Draft), March 1996.
4. B. E. Jacobs, C. A. Walczak, *A Generalized Query-by-Example Data Manipulation Language Based on Database Logic*, IEEE Transactions. on Software Engineering SE-9(1), 40-56, 1983.
5. G. Jaeschke, H.-J Schek, *Remarks on the Algebra of Non First Normal Form Relations*, Proc. ACM SIGACT/SIGMOD Symposium on Principles of Database Systems, 124-138, 1982.
6. A. Klug, *Abe-A Query Language for Constructing Aggregates-by-Example*, Proc. 1st Int. Workshop on Statistical Database Management, 190-205, 1981.
7. H.-C. Liu, K. Ramamohanarao, *Algebraic Equivalences among Nested Relational Expressions*, Proc. 3rd Int. Conference on Information and Knowledge Management, 234-243, 1994.
8. N. A. Lorentzos, K. A. Dondis, *A Query Language for Nested Tables*, Technical Report, Informatics Laboratory, Agricultural University of Athens, 1997 (in Greek).
9. G. Ozsoyoglu, V. Mattos, Z. M. Ozsoyoglu, *Query-Processing Techniques in the Summary-Table-by-Example Database Query Languages*, ACM Transactions on Database Systems 14(4), 526-573, 1989.
10. M. A. Roth, H. F. Korth, A. Silberschatz, *Extended Algebra and Calculus for Nested Relational Databases*, ACM Transactions on Database Systems 13(4), 389-417, 1988.
11. H.-J. Schek, M. H. Scholl, *The Relational Model with Relation-Valued Attributes*, Information Systems 11(2), 137-147, 1986.
12. L. Wegner, S. Thelemann, S. Wilke, *QBE-like Queries and Multimedia Extensions in a Nested Relational DBMS*, Proc. Int. Conference on Visual Information Systems, 1996.
13. S. B. Yao et al., *Formanager: An Office Forms Management System*, ACM Transactions on Office Information Systems 2(3), 235-262, 1984.
14. M. M. Zloof, *Query-by-Example: A data base Language*, IBM Systems Journal 4, 324-343, 1977.

A New Heuristic for Optimizing Large Queries*

Leonidas Fegaras

Department of Computer Science and Engineering
The University of Texas at Arlington
416 Yates Street, P.O. Box 19015
Arlington, TX 76019-19015
fegaras@cse.uta.edu

Abstract. There is a number of OODB optimization techniques proposed recently, such as the translation of path expressions into joins and query unnesting, that may generate a large number of implicit joins even for simple queries. Unfortunately, most current commercial query optimizers are still based on the dynamic programming approach of System R, and cannot handle queries of more than ten tables. There is a number of recent proposals that advocate the use of combinatorial optimization techniques, such as iterative improvement and simulated annealing, to deal with the complexity of this problem. These techniques, though, fail to take advantage of the rich semantic information inherent in the query specification, such as the information available in query graphs, which gives a good handle to choose which relations to join each time. This paper presents a polynomial-time algorithm that generates a good quality order of relational joins. It is a bottom-up greedy algorithm that always performs the most profitable joins first. Our heuristic is superior to related approaches in that it generates bushy trees, it takes into account both the sizes of intermediate results and the predicate selectivities, and it always updates the query graph to reflect the new sizes and the new selectivities.

1 Introduction

One of the most important tasks of a relational query optimizer is finding a good join order to evaluate an n-way join. Since a DBMS typically provides binary physical algorithms to evaluate joins, a relational optimizer must map an n-way join into a sequence of binary joins. To find the best join sequence, an optimizer needs to consider many different join orders, various physical algorithms, and all the available access paths. A naive generate-and-test approach would require exponential time ($\mathcal{O}(n! \times k^n)$ for an n-way join and for k different ways of evaluating a join), which becomes infeasible for large n. The bottom-up approaches adopted by commercial relational optimizers (mostly based on the dynamic programming approach of System R [13]) are better than the generate-and-test approach, but they are still exponential ($\mathcal{O}(2^n)$ in the worst case). As

* This work is supported in part by the National Science Foundation under grant IRI-9509955.

the result of that, most commercial systems cannot handle joins of more than ten tables.

Even though queries of more than ten tables do not appear very often in traditional database applications, there are some emerging applications, such as decision support systems and on-line analytical processing (OLAP) for analyzing data warehouses, that require the use of complex queries with aggregates. In addition, many recent DBMSs are in fact object-oriented (OODBs), object-relational, or deductive database systems, and they support many advanced modeling capabilities. Queries expressed in these systems, when evaluated, often require a large number of implicit joins, which the programmer may be unaware of. For example, most modern OODB languages, such as ODMG-93 OQL [1], support an SQL-like interface for associative access of data. The best way to evaluate a path expression in an OODB query is to use pointer joins between the type extents of the objects involved in the path expression [2]. This approach requires that a cascade of n projections in a path expression be mapped into a join of n extents. An alternative is to use a naive pointer chasing, which resembles the query evaluation in network databases and does not leave many opportunities for optimization. In addition, OODB queries can be arbitrarily nested. Some forms of query nesting can be avoided by using outer-joins combined with grouping [10]. In most OODB algebras, where grouping is an explicitly supported operator and can appear in any place in an algebraic form, any form of query nesting can be unnested by promoting the inner queries one level up in the query nesting hierarchy [5]. This results to a large flat join, which is the concatenation of all the joins from every level in the nested query. Other sources of implicit operations include views and methods, which are often expanded during query optimization.

There is a number of heuristics already proposed in the literature for optimizing large relational queries, even though most of them deal with acyclic query graphs and generate deep-left join trees only [14, 9]. As it is widely believed now in the database community, the goal of an optimizer is not to find the best evaluation plan to execute a query, since this is infeasible for non-trivial queries, but to avoid the worst plans. Cost-guided searching based on combinatorial optimization techniques, such as iterative improvement and simulated annealing [8], can be used to extract a solution in a fixed amount of time. Unfortunately, none of the cost-based searching methods proposed so far actually takes advantage of the semantic information inherent in queries, such as the information available in the query graphs, which gives a good handle to choose which relations to join each time. We believe, that a heuristic algorithm, mostly based on the semantic knowledge inherent in the query graphs, and to a lesser extent on a cost-based searching, would be a more appropriate choice than cost-based searching alone.

This paper presents a polynomial-time heuristic algorithm, called *GOO*, that generates a "good quality" order of relational joins. GOO is a bottom-up greedy algorithm that always performs the most profitable joins first. The measure of profit is the size of the intermediate results, but GOO can be easily modified to use real cost functions. GOO manipulates query graphs and takes into account both the sizes of the joins constructed in earlier steps and the predicate selectivities. It generates bushy join trees that have a very low total size of intermediate results. The difference between our algorithm and other related bottom-up heuristics is that, after two nodes are selected from the query graph to be joined, our algorithm always updates the query graph to reflect the new sizes and the new predicate selectivities.

GOO has complexity $\mathcal{O}(n^3)$, where n is the number of relations, but it can derive a join order for 100 joins in 32 milliseconds. When compared to iterative improvement (II), GOO is far superior and considerably more stable and consistent.

The paper is organized as follows. Section 2 presents our polynomial-time heuristic that finds a join order with a low total size of intermediate results. Section 4 compares the performance of our join ordering algorithm with that of the iterative improvement algorithm. Finally, Section 5 compares our work with related work. An extended version of this paper [4] extends our join ordering algorithm to handle OODB query graphs, which may include unnest and nest operators along with joins.

2 The Join Ordering Algorithm

We are interested in optimizing simple SQL queries of the form:

$$\textbf{select} \cdots \textbf{from } r_1, r_2, \ldots, r_n \textbf{ where } p_1 \textbf{ and } p_2 \textbf{ and} \cdots \textbf{and } p_m$$

This query uses n (not necessarily different) relations $r_1, \ldots, r_n$ and m uncorrelated (independent) predicates $p_1, \ldots, p_m$. A predicate p_k is either:

1. a *local predicate* on r_i, if it references the relation r_i only, or
2. a *join predicate* between r_i and r_j, if it references r_i and r_j only.

Our join ordering algorithm considers join predicates only, since any local predicate p_k on r_i can be safely ignored if we replace r_i by $\sigma_{p_k}(r_i)$. Thus, we represent a query Q as a pair $(\mathcal{R}, \mathcal{P})$, where $\mathcal{R} = \{r_1, r_2, \ldots, r_m\}$ is the set of relations referenced in Q and $\mathcal{P} = \{p_1(r_{11}, r_{12}), p_2(r_{21}, r_{22}), \ldots, p_m(r_{m1}, r_{m2})\}$ is the set of the join predicates in Q where $r_{ij} \in \mathcal{R}$.

The *selectivity* of a join predicate $p_k(r_i, r_j) \in \mathcal{P}$ is defined as follows [13]:

$$\text{selectivity}(p_k(r_i, r_j)) = \frac{\|r_i \bowtie_{p_k(r_i,r_j)} r_j\|}{\|r_i\| \times \|r_j\|}$$

where $\|X\|$ is the cardinality of X. Selectivities range between 0 and 1 (the predicate *true* has selectivity 1 while the predicate false has selectivity 0). For uncorrelated predicates p_1 and p_2, a good approximation of the selectivity of $p_1 \wedge p_2$ is [13]:

$$\text{selectivity}(p_1 \wedge p_2) = \text{selectivity}(p_1) \times \text{selectivity}(p_2)$$

For example, if 50% of the tuples satisfy p_1 and 60% satisfy p_2, then 30% (which is the 50% of 60%) of the tuples will satisfy both p_1 and p_2. The predicate P_{ij} and its selectivity S_{ij} between two relations r_i and r_j in Q is defined as follows:

$$P_{ij} = \bigwedge_{p_k(r_i,r_j)\in\mathcal{P}} \text{selectivity}(p_k(r_i,r_j))$$
$$S_{ij} = \text{selectivity}(P_{ij})$$

If there is no $p_k(r_i,r_j) \in \mathcal{P}$, then P_{ij} = true and $S_{ij} = 1$.

An *operator tree* P has the following syntax:

$$P ::= r_i \qquad \text{or} \qquad P ::= P_1 \bowtie_{pred} P_2$$

where P_1 and P_2 are operator trees and *pred* is either true or is a conjunction of join predicates that reference the relations in P_1 and P_2 exclusively.

A *valid operator tree* for a query $Q = (\mathcal{R},\mathcal{P})$ is an operator tree that uses each relation $r_i \in \mathcal{R}$ exactly once and each join predicate in $\mathcal{P}$ at least once. We do not allow node sharing in operator trees, even though a tree with shared nodes may result to better performance.

The size of an operator tree node is defined by the following equations:

$$\begin{aligned} \text{size}(r_i) &= \text{the cardinality of } r_i \\ \text{size}(P_1 \bowtie_{pred} P_2) &= \text{size}(P_1) \times \text{size}(P_2) \times \text{selectivity}(pred) \end{aligned}$$

That is, the size of a tree node is the size of the intermediate result produced by the operation of this node.

The *capacity* of an operator tree is the sum of size($P_1 \bowtie_{pred} P_2$) for every node $P_1 \bowtie_{pred} P_2$ in the tree:

$$\begin{aligned} \text{capacity}(r_i) &= 0 \\ \text{capacity}(P_1 \bowtie_{pred} P_2) &= \text{capacity}(P_1) + \text{capacity}(P_2) + \text{size}(P_1 \bowtie_{pred} P_2) \end{aligned}$$

In database terminology, this is the total size of the intermediate results. Note that trees that are equal modulo commutativity have equal capacities.

A *tree of minimum capacity* for a query Q is a valid operator tree for Q that has the least capacity among all valid operator trees for Q. Our goal is to construct an operator tree for Q that has very low capacity, preferably a minimum capacity.

3 The GOO Algorithm

Our join ordering algorithm is called *GOO*, which stands for a Greedy Operator Ordering algorithm. It is a greedy bottom-up algorithm, similar to Kruskal's minimum spanning tree algorithm. The main data structure that GOO uses is the *query graph* of a query Q. In the query graph of Q, each relation r_i corresponds to a node i and each join predicate P_{ij} between i and j corresponds to a graph edge between i and j. Each node i is labeled by the size of i and each

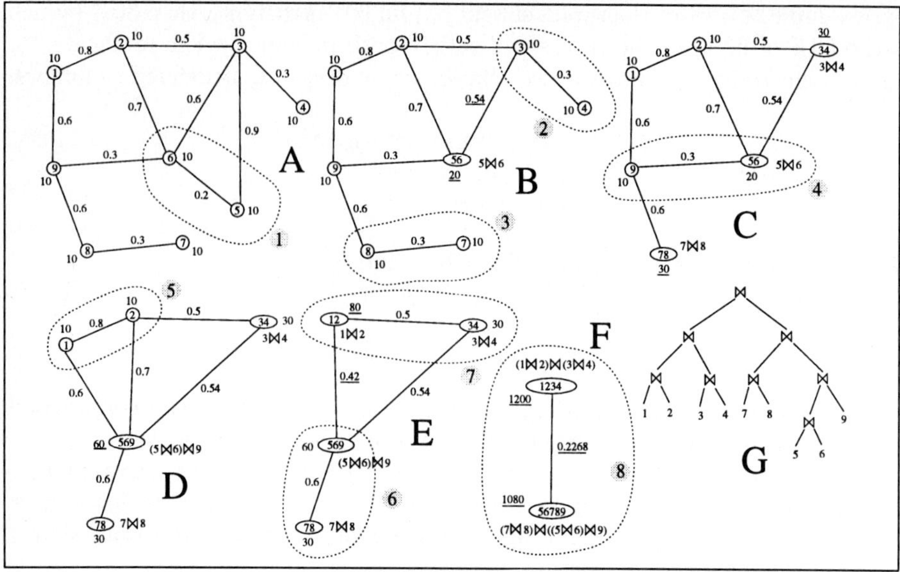

Fig. 1. Example of Join Ordering

edge between i and j is labeled by S_{ij} (the selectivity of P_{ij}). Edges of $S_{ij} = 1$ are not displayed in the graph. For example, Figure 1.A shows a query graph with 9 relations.

The GOO algorithm constructs the optimal operator tree by merging pairs of graph nodes, as it is shown in the following figure:

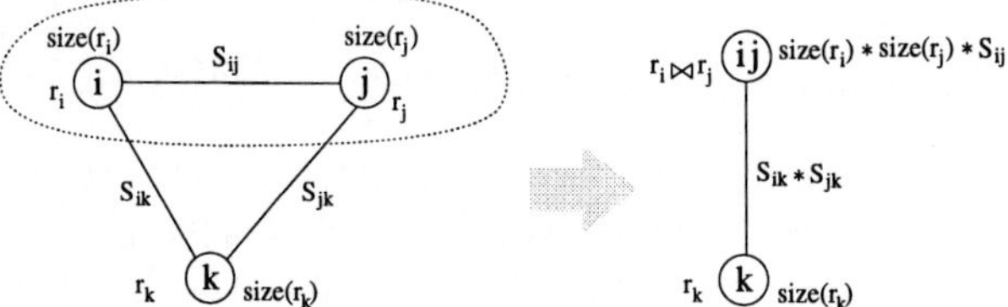

At each step of the algorithm, we select two nodes i and j that have a minimum value of size$(r_i) \times$ size$(r_j) \times S_{ij}$. Then we merge these two nodes into a new node ij. The size of ij is size$(r_i) \times$ size$(r_j) \times S_{ij}$ and its operator tree is $r_i \bowtie r_j$. In addition, for each node k connected to both i and j, the weight of the edge between k and ij becomes $S_{ik} \times S_{jk}$.

For example, in Figure 1.A the nodes i and j that have the minimum value size$(r_i) \times$ size$(r_j) \times S_{ij}$ (equal to $10 \times 10 \times 0.2 = 20$) are 5 and 6. Therefore, in Figure 1.B we merge 5 and 6 into the node 56, which has size 20 and operator tree $5 \bowtie 6$ (a shorthand for $r_5 \bowtie_{P_{56}} r_6$). At the same time, the selectivity of the edge between 3 and 56 becomes $0.6 \times 0.9 = 0.54$. Next, in Figure 1.B, we group together the nodes 3 and 4 and then the nodes 7 and 8, yielding the graph in Figure 1.C. We continue this process until we are left with one node only. The operator tree of the final node is the resulting operator tree (shown in Figure 1.G).

Algorithm 1 (GOO)
Input:

N	*number of relations*
predicate$[i, j]$	*the predicate, P_{ij}, between r_i and r_j (default is true)*
$S[i, j]$	*the selectivity, S_{ij}, of* predicate$[i, j]$ *(default is 1)*
tree$[i]$	*the operator tree for r_i (initially r_i)*
size$[i]$	*the size of r_i*

Output: *A valid operator tree with low capacity.*

Algorithm:

(1) **for** $n \leftarrow N \ldots 2$ **do**
(2)   **find** $i, j \in [1 \ldots n],\ i \neq j$: size$[i] \times$ size$[j] \times S[i, j]$ *is minimum*
(3)   tree$[i] \leftarrow [\![$tree$[i] \bowtie_{\text{predicate}[i,j]}$ tree$[j]]\!]$
(4)   size$[i] \leftarrow$ size$[i] \times$ size$[j] \times S[i, j]$
(5)   **for** $k \leftarrow 1 \ldots n,\ k \neq i$ **do**
(6) $S[i, k] \leftarrow S[k, i] \leftarrow S[i, k] \times S[j, k]$
(7)   predicate$[i, k] \leftarrow$ predicate$[k, i] \leftarrow [\![$predicate$[i, k] \wedge$ predicate$[j, k]]\!]$
(8)   **for** $k \leftarrow 1 \ldots n,\ k \neq j$ **do**
(9) $S[j, k] \leftarrow S[k, j] \leftarrow S[n, k]$
(10)   predicate$[j, k] \leftarrow$ predicate$[k, j] \leftarrow$ predicate$[n, k]$
(11)   tree$[j] \leftarrow$ tree$[n]$
(12)   size$[j] \leftarrow$ size$[n]$
(13) **return** tree$[1]$

Fig. 2. The GOO Algorithm

The pseudo code of the GOO algorithm is given in Figure 2. The semantic brackets $[\![\ldots]\!]$ are used to construct operator trees and predicates. Information about graph nodes is given in a form of one-dimensional vectors while information about edges is given in a form of adjacency matrices. The algorithm starts with a query graph of N nodes, where N is the number of relations and, at each iteration of the loop (1) through (13), the graph shrinks by one node. Line (2) finds two nodes i and j with minimum value size$[i] \times$ size$[j] \times S[i, j]$. Lines (3) through (7) merge nodes i and j and replace node i with the new merged node. Lines (8) through (12) copy the last node n to node j, so that the graph shrinks by one node.

The complexity of this algorithm is $\mathcal{O}(N^3)$. In contrast to Kruskal's minimum spanning tree algorithm, we cannot use a heap to speed up the extraction of the minimum in line (2) because the weights of the edges that are connected to both i and j nodes are modified at each iteration. Nevertheless, the GOO algorithm can derive a join order for 100 joins in 32 milliseconds (more performance results are given in Section 4).

The GOO algorithm is not optimal. The following example illustrates a case where our algorithm derives a suboptimal join tree:

A B C

The query graph is given in Figure A above and the join tree derived by GOO is given in B. The capacity of this tree is $20 + 30 + 36 = 86$. The optimal tree is given in C. It has capacity $25 + 24 + 36 = 85$.

4 Performance Evaluation

In this section we evaluate the performance of the GOO algorithm. The query graphs used in our experiments varied in two parameters: the number of relations and the maximum allowable number of edges attached to a node (called *fan-out*). We require that each node be attached to at least one edge and the query graph be connected. The size of a relation associated with a node has a uniform distribution between 1 and 100 blocks and the value $-\log s$ of the selectivity s associated with an edge has a uniform distribution between 0 and 5.

We compared three different algorithms in our performance evaluation: GOO (the GOO algorithm), II (the iterative improvement method that applies the downhill improvement phase to various random joins), and GOOI (the GOO algorithm followed by a downhill improvement phase).

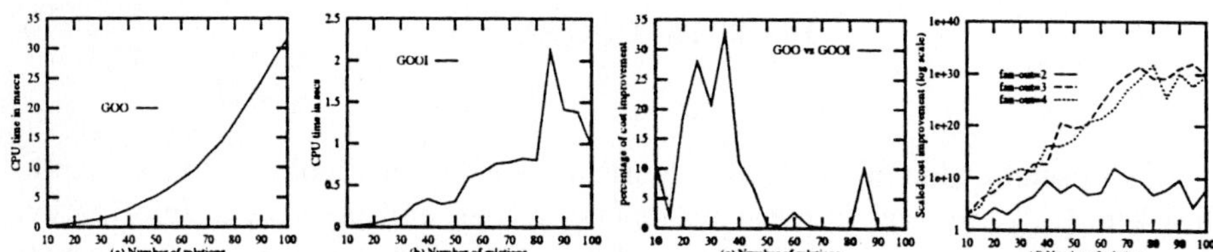

Fig. 3. Performance Results

Figure 3.a gives the running time performance (in milliseconds) of the GOO algorithm for query graphs of $10 \leq n \leq 100$ relations. The construction of the join from a query graph is also included in the time computation. Each point on a curve represents the average time of ten experiments (over different random graphs). Figure 3.b gives the running time performance (in seconds) of the GOOI algorithm for query graphs of $10 \leq n \leq 100$.

In our experiments, we used only two types of joins: nested-loops joins and merge joins. The cost model we used to evaluate performance is described in detail in the full version of this paper [4]. Even though our cost model is very simple, it still gives a good approximation of the I/O cost of the evaluation algorithms found in commercial databases.

As a first experiment, we compared GOO with GOOI (Figure 3.c). The values in Figure 3.c represent percentage of cost improvement: if t_1 is the cost of the plan produced by GOOI and t_2 is the cost of the plan produced by GOO, then the table entry is $(t_2 - t_1) * 100/t_1$. Like before, each value is the average value of ten experiments. We can see that GOOI results to at most 30% cost improvement but it requires at most 100 times more CPU time.

As another demonstration of the effectiveness of our algorithm, we compared the quality of the produced plans with the quality of the plans produced by the iterative improvement method (II), when the latter is allowed to run ten times longer than GOO (Figure 3.d). The II algorithm works as follows: a random join is selected and it is improved by the downhill improvement phase. When no improvement can be made to any node, the iterative improvement algorithm chooses another random plan and performs the same process. This task is repeated until the total running time of II exceeds the specified time limit (ten times the running time of GOO). At the end, the best plan found during all iterations is returned. The values in Figure 3.d represent scaled costs: if t_1 is the cost of the plan produced by GOO and t_2 is the cost of the plan produced by II, then the table entry is $(t_2 - t_1)/t_1$. Like before, each value is the average value of ten experiments. We can see that GOO clearly beats iterative improvement despite the time advantage given to II.

5 Related Work

Many heuristics have been proposed in the literature on join ordering for large relational queries, even though most of them deal with acyclic query graphs and generate deep-left trees only [9, 17]. A comparison between these heuristics as well as between various randomized algorithms can be found in [14]. Most commercial relational optimizers are based on the dynamic programming approach of System R [13] and they cannot handle queries of more than ten tables. A notable exception is Starburst [11], which uses various polynomial algorithms based on the query graph shape (such as, for linear queries) and is able to optimize queries containing up to 110 tables. For other shapes, their proposed dynamic algorithm becomes exponential ($\mathcal{O}(2^n)$).

The only heuristic join ordering algorithm for general (cyclic) graphs that we are aware of is the KBZ algorithm by Krishnamurthy, Boral, and Zaniolo [9], which in turn is based on the IK algorithm of Ibaraki and Kameda [6]. The IK algorithm finds the optimal deep-left tree of an acyclic graph under certain cost functions in polynomial time by assigning ranks to relations and ordering the relations according to rank. The KBZ algorithm is an $\mathcal{O}(n^2)$ heuristic that finds the minimum spanning tree of a cyclic graph and applies the IK algorithm to the resulting tree. The minimum spanning tree used in this algorithm considers the minimum product of edge weights (selectivities) rather than the minimum sum.

We believe that our join ordering algorithm is superior to the KBZ algorithm because it does not pose any restrictions to cost functions, it generates bushy trees, and it considers sizes of intermediate results instead of selectivities only. Recently, the KBZ algorithm has been extended by Scheufele and Moerkotte to include expensive predicates [12].

In a previous work [3], we have presented a top-down heuristic for ordering joins. It applies the min-cut algorithm recursively to split the query graph into two query subgraphs each time so that the product of selectivities between the relations of these two subgraphs is maximum. For each such cut, the algorithm generates a join. That way, selective joins are done as early as possible while non-selective joins (such as cartesian products) are left for the end. Our new algorithm is superior to this algorithm, because it considers cardinalities. In addition, our new algorithm is more efficient than the old one.

Ioannidis and Kang [8, 7] proposed various combinatorial optimization techniques for large relational queries based on iterative improvement and simulated annealing. Iterative improvement consists of a number of local optimizations, where each local optimization starts at a random state and performs downhill moves until it reaches a local minimum. Simulated annealing starts at a random state and proceeds by random moves, but if the move is uphill it is accepted by a certain probability, which decreases over time. The iterative improvement method does not consider states that are promising as starting points, while the simulated annealing method does not address the problem of selecting a random uphill state at each state transition. For both algorithms, the quality of the plan found at each iteration depends in a great extent on the quality of the initial state. In addition, there is no guarantee that a random initial state will not fall in the neighborhood of a previously examined state, thus resulting to the same local minimum. To be effective, a large number of initial states should be tried as starting points so that the computed local minima would include a fair number of deep minima. Alternatively, a good quality starting point generated by a heuristic algorithm can be used that promises a deep local minimum. The work by Swami and Gupta [16, 15] compares various heuristics and combinatorial algorithms. Their experiments suggest that iterative improvement is the best combinatorial optimization technique.

6 Conclusion and Future Work

We have presented a polynomial-time heuristic algorithm that generates good quality plans for OODB queries. The algorithm has been tested on various random relational query graphs. Our preliminary results show that our method is clearly superior to the iterative improvement method. As a future work, we are planning to incorporate this algorithm to the experimental query optimizer for OQL being developed at the University of Texas at Arlington. We are also planning to combine this algorithm with a local search technique, which improves small fragments of the query plan by performing a real cost analysis.

References

1. R. Cattell. *The Object Database Standard: ODMG-93*. Morgan Kaufmann, 1994.
2. S. Cluet and C. Delobel. A General Framework for the Optimization of Object-Oriented Queries. *Proceedings of the ACM-SIGMOD International Conference on Management of Data, San Diego, California*, pp 383–392, June 1992.
3. L. Fegaras. Optimizing Large OODB Queries. In *Fifth International Conference on Deductive and Object-Oriented Databases, Montreux, Switzerland*, December 1997.
4. L. Fegaras. A New Heuristic for Optimizing Large Queries (extended paper). Available at `http://www-cse.uta.edu/~fegaras/order.ps.gz`, February 1998.
5. L. Fegaras. Query Unnesting in Object-Oriented Databases. *ACM SIGMOD International Conference on Management of Data, Seattle, Washington*, June 1998.
6. T. Ibaraki and T. Kameda. Optimal Nesting for Computing N-Relational Joins. *ACM Transactions on Database Systems*, 9(3):482–502, September 1984.
7. Y. Ioannidis and Y. Kang. Randomized Algorithms for Optimizing Large Join Queries. In *Proceedings of the 1990 ACM SIGMOD International Conference on Management of Data, Atlantic City, NJ*, pp 312–321, May 1990.
8. Y. Ioannidis and Y. Kang. Left-deep vs. Bushy Trees: An Analysis of Strategy Spaces and its Implications for Query Optimization. *Proceedings of the ACM-SIGMOD International Conference on Management of Data, Denver, Colorado*, 20(2):168–177, May 1991.
9. R. Krishnamurthy, H. Boral, and C. Zaniolo. Optimization of Nonrecursive Queries. In Y. Kambayashi, editor, *Proceedings of the Twelfth International Conference on Very Large Databases, Kyoto, Japan*, pp 128–137, August 1986.
10. M. Muralikrishna. Improved Unnesting Algorithms for Join Aggregate SQL Queries. In *Proc. Int'l. Conf. on Very Large Data Bases*, page 91, Vancouver, BC, Canada, August 1992.
11. K. Ono and G. Lohman. Measuring the Complexity of Join Enumeration in Relational Query Optimization. In *Proceedings of the 16th Conference on Very Large Databases, Morgan Kaufman pubs. (Los Altos CA), Brisbane*, August 1990.
12. W. Scheufele and G. Moerkotte. Efficient Dynamic Programming Algorithms for Ordering Expensive Joins and Selections. *International Conference on Extending Data Base Technology, Valencia, Spain*, March 1997.
13. P. Selinger, M. Astrahan, D. Chamberlin, R. Lorie, and T. Price. Access Path Selection in a Relational Database Management System. *Proceedings of the ACM-SIGMOD International Conference on Management of Data, Boston, Massachusetts*, pp 23–34, May 1979.
14. M. Steinbrunn, G. Moerkotte, and A. Kemper. Heuristic and Randomized Optimization for the Join Ordering Problem. *VLDB Journal*, 6(3):191–208, 1997.
15. A. Swami. Optimization of Large Join Queries: Combining Heuristics and Combinatorial Techniques. In *Proceedings of the ACM-SIGMOD International Conference on Management of Data, Portland, Oregon*, pp 367–376, May 1989.
16. A. Swami and A. Gupta. Optimization of Large Join Queries. *Proceedings of the ACM-SIGMOD International Conference on Management of Data, Chicago, Illinois*, 13(3):8–17, September 1988.
17. K. Youssefi and E. Wong. Query Processing in a Relational Database Management System. In *Proceedings of the Fifth International Conference on Very Large Databases*, pp 409–417, 1979.

Discovery of User-Interests from Range Queries

Xiaoyong Du, Zhibin Liu, Naohiro Ishii

Department of Intelligence and Computer Science
Nagoya Institute of Technology, Nagoya, Japan
E-mail:{duyong, zhibin, ishii }@egg.ics.nitech.ac.jp

Abstract. This paper proposes a new application for data mining. It is discovery of user-interests from the user queries. Since queries themselves represent users' interests in nature without knowing the query results, we can discover user-interests from the users' queries. The user-interests plays an important role in improving the quality of information servers, and database performance tuning. In this paper, we focus on range queries on a continuous attribute. We propose an effective iterative algorithm to discover the most interest range, in the sense that the range is accessed by enough users, and is covered by the users' queries largestly on the average.

1 Introduction

Data mining aims at discovering patterns of interests from databases. Various methods like classification, regression, clustering and summarization are developed for data mining. Many applications have been benefited from data mining. For example, discovering the buying patterns of the customers from a database of sales transactions [1, 2]; identifying interested objects or events from image databases[8]; finding rules in data for semantic query optimization [6]. In this paper, we propose a new application of data mining. It is discovery of user-interests from user queries.

Recently, information server on the Internet has become more and more popular. The "quality" of the information server becomes more and more important. Among various meanings of "quality', it is the most important that the users can get what they want. Therefore, it is necessary to know the interests of the users. However, the Internet is open, it is not so easy to investigate the user-interests.

In this paper, we propose a new way to analyze the user-interests. It discovers the user-interests from their queries. The database in the information server is accessed frequently by users in queries. These queries written in some query language reflect the users' interests in nature. For example, consider a web-site for used-cars. Assume there is a relation used-cars in the database in which each tuple records the manufacturer, mode, price etc. of a used-car. A user can pose a SQL query like

SELECT * FROM used-cars WHERE price is between 3,000 and 4,000

This query itself says that the user is interested in those used-cars whose price is between 3,000 US$ to 4,000 US$, even if the query result is an empty set. If we record these queries, we can find some patterns from them. For example, the used-cars in the rank of 3,000 to 6,000 US$ are the most popular.

Based on the discovered user-interests, one can improve the quality of the information server, for example, by preparing more used-cars between 3,000 and 6,000 US$.

Discovery of users-interests plays also an important role in database tuning. One of the important step in database design is query analysis. The analysis results guide the design of a physical database that can response users' requests efficiently. However, in the Internet environment, it is difficult to catch the patterns of the user queries in advance. Discovery from queries provides a feasible way to do query analysis. Based on discovered knowledge, we can tune or reorganize the database.

In this paper, we focus on range queries on a continuous attribute. They can be represented as a pair of ordered values. We are interested in finding a range which is accessed by enough users and is covered by user queries largestly on the average. Moreover, we propose an $O(n)$ iterative algorithm to find such a range efficiently.

2 Preliminaries

Assume there are n range-type data on a continuous attribute A, stored in a relation R. Each range can be represented as $[l_i, u_i]$, where l_i and u_i are the lower and upper bound of the range, respectively. In this paper, we do not distinguish a closed range with an open range. It is because all ranges are from a continue attribute and we are interested in finding a continue range also. It is meaningless to say a point is interested. Similarly, the range [10,20] and range [20,30] are not considered as intersection. We are interested in finding a pattern from R which is the most "interesting" for the users.

The existing measures for patterns of interests are commonly based on the frequency with the pattern appeared in the databases. For example, for a database of sales transactions, one usually measures a buying pattern $A \Rightarrow B$ (it means that users who buy item A almost always buy item B) by two measures[1, 2]. One measure is ***support*** which says how many percent of the users who buy both item A and B. The other is *confidence* which says how many percent of the users who buy the item A also buy item B. Since the attribute in this example is a categorical attribute, we need only to check if a value is the member of a specified set.

Some complex cases like quantitative attribute (ordered discrete attribute) and continuous attribute, are also considered [7, 5]. The measures for the patterns of interests are revised correspondingly. For example, if the attribute is a quantitative one, we have to consider whether a value is contained in a given range [7]. If the attribute is a continous one, we have to consider both the membership and distance of a value in the database to a given range [5].

In this study, we consider a more complex case in which a datum is a range. In this case, it is not enough to measure the rank of a pattern by only frequency.

We have to consider the distance of the two ordered values (i.e. the length of the range) as well as the percentage of the intersection of a given range with others.

Definition 1 . Let $r_i = [l_i, u_i]$ be a range in R, $C = [L, U]$ a given range. The support of range C by R, denoted by $\alpha_R(C)$, is defined as the percentage of ranges that are intersected with C.

$$\alpha_R(C) = \frac{|\{r_i \in R | r_i \cap C \neq \phi\}|}{|R|} \tag{1}$$

where $|\cdot|$ represents the size of a set.

The measure $\alpha_R(C)$ defines how many percentage of ranges in R which are intersected with the given range C. For example, if the support $\alpha_R(C) = 0.1$, it means that there are 10% ranges in R which are intersected with C. It also means that there are 10 % users who are interested in the data in C.

However, the measure α_R considers only if a range is intersected with the given range C. The bigger of the C, the bigger of the $\alpha_R(C)$. Hence only $\alpha_R(C)$ is not enough to define the interested range. We have to consider how many percentage of the C is covered by the ranges on the average.

Definition 2 . Let $r_i = [l_i, u_i]$ be a range in R, $C = [L, U]$ a given range we considered. The intensity of range C with respect to R, denoted by $\beta_R(C)$, is defined as

$$\beta_R(C) = \frac{\Sigma_{r_i \in R} \beta(C, r_i)}{|\{r_i \in R | r_i \cap C \neq \phi\}|} \tag{2}$$

where $\beta(C, r_i) = \dfrac{||C \cap r_i||}{||C||}$ and $||\cdot||$ is the length of the range.

While the measure α reflects how many user queries are interested in the given range, the measure β reflects how many percentage of the given range is covered by the user queries on the average. Moreover, the smaller of the C, the bigger of the $\beta_R(C)$.

Example 1 . Assume $R = \{[0,8], [0,5], [5,10], [8,10], [7,15]\}$. Consider the following ranges $C_1 = [5,10]$ and $C_2 = [0,10]$, respectively. Then, we have $\alpha_R(C_1) =$ 80%, and, $\beta(C_1, [0,8]) = 0.6; \beta(C_1, [0,5]) = 0; \beta(C_1, [5,10]) = 1; \beta(C_1, [8,10]) = 0.4; \beta(C_1, [7,15]) = 0.6$. Hence $\beta_R(C_1) = 0.65$. Similarly, we have $\alpha_R(C_2) =$ 100%, and $\beta_R(C_2) = 0.46$. The intensity of C_1 is larger than that of C_2.

Definition 3 . A range C is called an interest range if the support $\alpha_R(C)$ is not less than a given minimum support threshold and the intensity $\beta_R(C)$ is not less than a given minimum value. We call a range C is optimized interest range if it is an interest range and has a maximal intensity $\beta_R(C)$.

Example 2 . Assume we have 100 range [10,20] and 900 range [100,110]. We consider 6 ranges [10,20],[10,100],[10,110],[20,100],[20,110],and [100,110] The values of α_R and β_R are listed in the following table. If we require that the least support and intensity of range is 50%, the range [100,110] is then the optimized interest range.

	[10,20]	[10,100]	[10,110]	[20,100]	[20,110]	[100,110]
α_R	0.1	0.1	1	0	0.9	0.9
β_R	1	0.11	0.1	0	0.11	1

For a given range, we can evaluate the two measures by scanning the database one time. However, we meet two difficults when computing the optimized interest range on a continuous attribute:

1. There are possibly infinite ranges which need to be checked. We can not check in practice all of them to decide which is the optimized one;
2. For a data mining problem on a huge database, it is unacceptable to scan the database many times.

Fortunately, an approximate optimized range is enough for practical applications. In the next section, we propose an efficient approximate solution to this problem. The main contribution is that a set of iterative formulas in lower complexity is derived for evaluating the measures of all possible ranges.

3 The Algorithms

Our algorithm is based on a special bucketing technique. The domain of the continuous attribute A is divided into a sequence of intervals. From these intervals, we construct a set of buckets. Every range in database is then distributed into one and only one bucket. We first give a naive algorithm to evaluate the measures based on the buckets. Then we present an efficient iterative algorithm.

3.1 Bucketing

Let MAX and MIN be the maximum and minimum bound of the continuous attribute A. Assume the range [MIN,MAX] is divided into a set of equi-length intervals $I_1, I_2, \cdots, I_m$, where $I_i = [x_{i-1}, x_i]$ and $x_i - x_{i-1}$ is a constant for all $1 \leq i \leq m$. From the interval set $\{I_1, \cdots, I_m\}$, we construct a set of buckets $B_{s,t} = \cup_{s \leq k \leq t}(I_k)$, where $1 \leq s, t \leq m$. We call $B = \{B_{1,1}, B_{1,2}, \cdots, B_{m,m}\}$ a bucket set. The bucket set can be organized as a lower triangle

$$\begin{Bmatrix} B_{1,m} & & & \\ B_{1,m-1} & B_{2,m} & & \\ \cdots & \cdots & \cdots & \\ B_{1,1} & B_{2,2} & \cdots & B_{m,m} \end{Bmatrix}$$

A range $[l, u]$ is distributed to bucket $B_{s,t}$ if and only if $B_{s+1,t-1} \subset [l, u] \subseteq B_{s,t}$. Ranges in the same bucket are treated as the same. The length is treated as equal as the length of the corresponding bucket. All ranges in the database can be distributed into the bucket set by scanning the database in one pass. The size of a bucket $B_{s,t}$, denoted by $u_{s,t}$, is defined as the number of ranges in the bucket. Combining a set of consective intervals $I_s, I_{s+1}, \cdots, I_t$ creates a large interval $[x_{s-1}, x_t]$, denoted by $I_{s,t}$. Obviously, the interval $I_{s,t}$ corresponds to the bucket $B_{s,t}$. In this paper, we consider all $I_{s,t}$ as candidates of the optimized range.

3.2 Naive Algorithm

First, we give a set of formulas to evaluate the measures for all candidates.

Property 4 . For any possible interval $I_{s,t}$, we have,

$$(1)\ \ \alpha_R(I_{s,t}) = \frac{1}{|R|}\Sigma_{1\leq k\leq t}\Sigma_{max(s,k)\leq l\leq m}(u_{k,l})$$

$$(2)\ \ \beta_R(I_{s,t}) = \frac{1}{|R|\alpha_R(I_{s,t})}\Sigma_{1\leq k\leq t}\Sigma_{max(s,k)\leq l\leq m}(\frac{||I_{s,t}\cap I_{k,l}||}{||I_{s,t}||}u_{k,l})$$

Proof. The buckets that are intersected with $I_{s,t}$ are those in the polygon $P = B_{1,s}B_{s,s}B_{t,t}B_{t,m}B_{1,m}$ (Figure 1).That is the buckets in $\{B_{k,l}|1 \leq k \leq t, max(k,s) \leq l \leq M\}$. From the definition, we can prove the property directly.

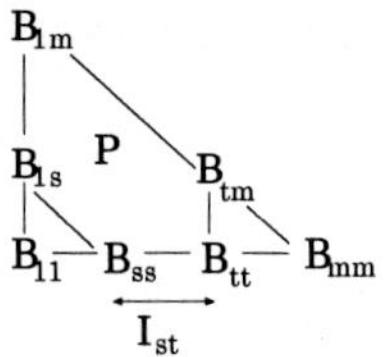

Fig. 1. Buckets intersected with $I_{s,t}$

After evaluating the measures of all candidates, the optimized interest range can be discoveried by the following algorithm.

Algorithm 5 . (Evaluating the optimized ranges)

s1: for $(1 \leq s \leq t \leq m\ )$ do {
    for $(1 \leq k \leq t\ )$ do {
        for $(max(s,k) \leq l \leq m)$ do {
            $\alpha_R(I_{s,t}) += u_{k,l}$;
            $\beta_R(I_{s,t}) += u_{k,l} * (||I_{s,t} \cap I_{k,l}||)$;
        };
    };
    $\beta_R(I_{s,t})/ = \alpha_R(I_{s,t}) * ||I_{s,t}||$;
    $\alpha_R(I_{s,t})/ = |R|$;
    if $(\alpha_R(I_{s,t}) \geq \theta_s \wedge \beta_R(I_{s,t}) \geq \theta_i\ )$ then
        insert $(I_{s,t}, \alpha_R(I_{s,t}), \beta_R(I_{s,t}))$ into table T;
};
s2: Evaluating I_{s^*,t^*} such that $\beta_R(I_{s^*,t^*}) = max_{I_{s,t}\in T}(\beta_R(I_{s,t}))$;

Theorem 6 . *The complexity of algorithm 5 is $O(n^2)$, where n is the number of the buckets.*

Proof. The most expensive step is obviously the step s1. We count the number of arithmetical operations in the step s1.

For an arbitrary interval $I_{s,t}$, the polygon P in Figure 1 contains $mt - t(t-1)/2 - s(s-1)/2$ buckets, where m is the number of the intervals. From the evaluation formulas of α_R and β_R, we know that the number of the arithmetical operations is the constant times of this number. Hence, the complexity of evaluating all the measure α_R and β_R in the step s1 is,

$$\begin{aligned}
&\Sigma_{1\le s\le t\le m}(mt - \frac{t(t-1)}{2} - \frac{s(s-1)}{2}) \\
&= \frac{m-1}{2}\Sigma_{1\le i\le m}(i^2) + \frac{m(m+1)^2}{4} \\
&= \frac{m-1}{2}(\frac{(m+1)^3}{3} - \frac{3m^3+5m+2}{6}) + \frac{m(m+1)^2}{4} \\
&= O(m^4) = O(n^2).
\end{aligned}$$

However, $O(n^2)$ is too complex for a data mining algorithm over a huge database. In the next subsection, we derive a set of efficient iterative formulas for evaluating α_R and β_R.

3.3 Iterative Algorithm

For reducing the complexity of the algorithm, we first derive a set of iterative formulas from the formulas in Property 4 .

Property 7 . Let $U_{s,t}$ be defined as the number of ranges in the database that are contained in the interval $I_{s,t}$. That is, $U_{s,t} = |\{r \subseteq I_{s,t} | r \in R\}|$. Let $W_{s,t}$ be defined as the sum of the percentage of the interval $I_{s,t}$ that are covered by the ranges in the database. Then,

$$\begin{aligned}
&(1)\ U_{s,t} = \Sigma_{s\le k\le l\le t}(u_{k,l}) \\
&(2)\ W_{s,s} = \Sigma_{1\le k\le s}\Sigma_{s\le l\le m}(u_{k,l})
\end{aligned}$$

Proof (1) Since $B_{k,l}$ are pairwise disjoint, we have

$$\begin{aligned}
U_{s,t} &= |\{r \subseteq I_{s,t} | r \in R\}| = |\{r \subseteq I_{s,t} | r \in B_{k,l}, 1 \le k \le l \le m\}| \\
&= |\{r \subseteq I_{s,t} | r \in B_{k,l}, s \le k \le l \le t\}| = \Sigma_{s\le k\le l\le t}(|\{r \subseteq I_{s,t} | r \in B_{k,l}\}|) \\
&= \Sigma_{s\le k\le l\le t}(u_{k,l})
\end{aligned}$$

(2) Since the interval $I_{s,s}$ is unit interval, any range intersected with $I_{s,s}$ covers it also. Hence, $W_{s,s}$ is equal to the number of ranges in that database that are intersected with $I_{s,s}$.

$$\begin{aligned}
W_{s,s} &= \Sigma_{r\in R}(|\{r \cap I_{s,s} \ne \phi\}|) = \Sigma_{1\le k\le l\le m}\Sigma_{r\in B_{k,l}}(|\{r \cap I_{s,s} \ne \phi\}|) \\
&= \Sigma_{1\le k\le s}\Sigma_{s\le l\le m}(u_{k,l})
\end{aligned}$$

The property says that $U_{s,t}$ ($W_{s,s}$) is the sum of the sizes of the buckests in the area P_1 (P_2) in Figure 2 (a) (Figure 2 (b)).

Property 8. Assume $U_{s,t}$ and $W_{s,t}$ are defined as above. We have

$$(1)\ U_{s,t} = \begin{cases} u_{s,s} & t = s \\ U_{s,t-1} + U_{s+1,t} - U_{s+1,t-1} + u_{s,t} & t > s \end{cases}$$

$$(2)\ W_{s,t} = \begin{cases} \Sigma_{1\le l\le m}(u_{1,l}) & t = s = 1 \\ W_{s-1,s-1} + (\Sigma_{s\le l\le m}(u_{s,l}) - \Sigma_{1\le l\le s-1}(u_{l,s-1})) & t = s > 1 \\ \dfrac{W_{s,t-1} + W_{t,t}}{t-s+1} & t > s \end{cases}$$

Proof (1) From Property 7, we know that $U_{s,t}$ is the sum of the sizes of all buckets in the lower triangle of $B_{s,t}$ in Figure 2(c). Hence, we have

$$\begin{aligned} U_{s,t} &= \Sigma_{s\le k\le l\le t}(u_{k,l}) \\ &= \Sigma_{s\le k\le l\le t-1}(u_{k,l}) + \Sigma_{s+1\le k\le l\le t}(u_{k,l}) - \Sigma_{s+1\le k\le l\le t-1}(u_{k,l}) + u_{s,t} \\ &= U_{s,t-1} + U_{s+1,t} - U_{s+1,t-1} + u_{s,t} \end{aligned}$$

(2) The case $t = s$ is a formula transformation of $W_{s,s}$ in Property 7. Consider an arbitrary bucket $B_{k,l}$ in the polygon $B_{1,m}B_{1,s}B_{s,s}B_{t,t}B_{t,m}$ in Figure 2(d). If it covers the interval $I_{s,t}$ (those buckets in area P_1), it contributes to every $W_{i,i}(s \le i \le t)$. If it is intersected with $I_{s,t}$ (those buckets in area P_2, P_3 and P_4), it contributes to those $W_{i,i}$ which are contained in both $I_{s,t}$ and $I_{k,l}$. Hence, each bucket contributes $W_{s,t}$ as the same times as the $t-s+1$, that is, the length of the interval $I_{s,t}$. Hence, $W_{s,t} = \Sigma_{s\le k\le t}(W_{k,k})/(t-s+1) = W_{s,t-1} + W_{t,t}/(t-s+1)$.

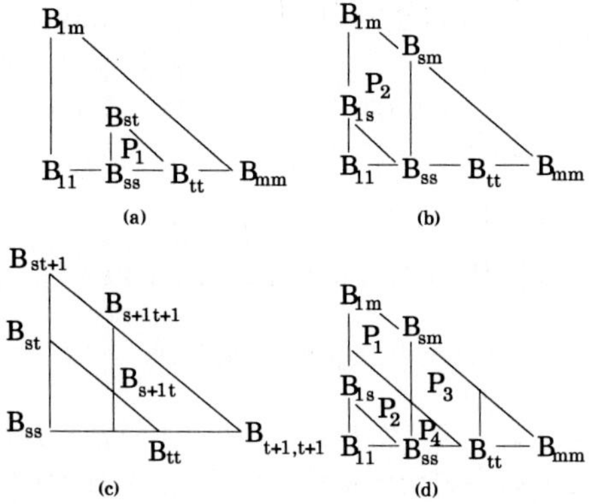

Fig. 2. Buckets Area: (a) buckets contributing to $U_{s,t}$; (b) buckets contributing to $W_{s,s}$; (c) buckets that contained in $B_{s,t+1}$; (d) Buckets that cover $I_{s,t}$

For convenience of evaluation, let $U_{s,t}$ and $W_{s,t}$ be equal to 0 when $s < t$.

Property 9. For arbitrary interval $I_{s,t}$, we have

$$(1)\ \alpha_R(I_{s,t}) = \frac{1}{|R|}(U_{1,M} - U_{1,s-1} - U_{t+1,M})$$

$$(2)\ \beta_R(I_{s,t}) = \frac{1}{|R|\alpha_R(I_{s,t})}(W_{s,t})$$

Based on these iterative formulas, the algorithm that evaluates α_R and β_R for each $I_{s,t}$ can be revised as follows.

Algorithm 10 . (Evaluating the optimized ranges)

s1: evaluating $U_{s,t}$ and $W_{s,t}$ by the formulas in Property 8 ;
s2: evaluating $\alpha_R(I_{s,t})$ and $\beta_R(I_{s,t})$ by the formulas in Property 9 ;
s3: if $(\alpha_R(I_{s,t}) \geq \theta_s \wedge \beta_R(I_{s,t}) \geq \theta_i$) then
insert $(I_{s,t}, \alpha_R(I_{s,t}), \beta_R(I_{s,t}))$ into table T;
s4: Evaluating I_{s^*,t^*} such that $\beta_R(I_{s^*,t^*}) = max_{I_{s,t} \in T}(\beta_R(I_{s,t}))$;

Theorem 11 . *The time complexity of the algorithm 10 is $O(n)$.*

Proof. We count the number of arithmetical operations in the algorithm as measure of the time complexity. First, consider the complexity of evaluating all $U_{s,t}$ and $W_{s,t}$ by the formulas in Property 8 . For $U_{s,t}$, it is $4m(m+1)/2 = 2m^2 + 2$; for $W_{s,s}$, it is m^2; and for $W_{s,t}(t > s)$, it is $2m(m-1)/2 = m^2 - m$. Hence, the complexity is $(2m^2+2) + m^2 + (m^2 - m) = 4m^2 + m$. Next, consider the complexity of evaluating all α_R and β_R by the formulas in Property 9 . It is a constant times of $m(m+1)/2$. Hence, the total is $O(m^2) = O(n)$.

3.4 Some Considerations

The following two points should be considered in practice.

(1) The number of the optimized ranges is possibly more than one. In this case, we have to consider their relation. If one optimized range is contained into another, only the bigger one is the solution. Otherwise, we list all of them and leave the judgement to analysts.
(2) The optimized range is dependent upon the given thresholds for α and β. What thresholds are appropriate dependents on the practical application.

4 Experimental Results

The proposed algorithm is implemented in C language on the Sun Sparc Workstation 5/110 with SunOS 4.1.4. Three sets of experiments are designed to test the accuracy, effectiveness and efficiency of our iterative algorithm. Each data set contains 10000 tuples which are generated randomly in average and normal distribution. The domain of the continue attribute is the integer in [0,1000].

The first set of experiments aims at showing the accuracy of the bucketing technique proposed in this paper. For a given range C, the measure $\alpha_R(C)$ and $\beta_R(C)$ can be evaluated by our iterative algorithm, or by their definitions directly. We compare the values of the measures for the same ranges that evaluated by different ways. Table 1 shows that the difference is very small, and becomes smaller when the number of intervals is increased. The result shows that the bucketing is reasonable and effectiveness.

Table 1: Accuracy of the bucketing

No. Intervals	100	200	500	1000
difference of α_R	0.0033	0.0015	0.0003	0
difference of β_R	0.00194	0.00083	0.00016	0

The second set of experiments aims at showing the effectiveness of the algorithm. That is, whether the algorithm can correctly find out the pattern while there is exactly a pattern in the data set.

We choose an arbitrary range, say [100,150], as the pattern. Then we duplicate the pattern 10, 100, and 1000 times respectively into the random data set with 10000 tuples to generate 3 new datasets, DS1, DS2 and DS3, respectively. By comparing the optimized range that extracted from the various datasets by the algorithm with the given pattern, we see whether the extracted optimized range becomes more and more near to the given pattern when we increase the number of the pattern. Table 2 lists the test results.

Table 2: Effectiveness of the approximate algorithm

No. Intervals	100	200	500	1000
DS1	(670,670)	(195,190)	(198,194)	(191,187)
DS2	(0,0)	(5, 0)	(2,-6)	(0, -9)
DS3	(0, 0)	(0, 0)	(0, 0)	(0, 1)

In the dataset DS1, there are only 10 tuples of [100,150]. The test showed that it is not the optimized range. While we increase the number of tuple [100,150], the extracted optimized range becomes nearer to the pattern. When we duplicate 1000 times of the pattern, the extracted optimized range is almost the same as the expected one in all bucket sets. This result shows that the iterative algorithm can find effectively the pattern in the dataset.

The third set of the experiments aims at showing that the running time of the iterative algorithm is much better than the naive one. Both algorithms run on the same datasets and the same thresholds for α_R and β_R. The results in Table 3 shows that the iterative algorithm is much faster than the naive one.

Table 3: Runing Time (in 1/60 seconds)

No. Intervals	100	200	500
Naive Algorithm	1959	30855	1673479
Iterative Algorithm	23	58	157

5 Comparisons and Concluding Remarks

First, this paper arises a new application of data mining, that is, query analysis. It is very important for improving quality of information server. As we know, query analysis is an important phase in database design. However, for internet databases, it is impossible to know exactly the user requirements before runing the databases. This study provides a way to do query analysis for designing internet databases.

Second, compared with the existing methods of finding summarization rules, our method processes a new type of objective data set, that is range data set.

Here we review briefly the work in the discovery of associated rules. Given a huge database, an association rule is a relationship between two conditions C_1 and C_2 such that if a tuple meets the condition C_1, then it also satisfies the other condition C_2 with a probability (called confidence), denoted by $C_1 \Rightarrow C_2$.

Agrawal et al[1, 2] considered the boolean-type data in their study of finding association rule from a huge database of sales transactions. An unordered attribute (also called categorical attribute) can be translated into this case by treating each value of the attribute as a new attribute. In this case, only the membership of specified data to a given set is necessary in defining the measure of the interest patterns. Srikant and Agrawal [7] studied a more complex case that the attribute may be a quantitative one. A quantitative attribute is an ordered discrete one, but the separation between two neighbour values has no meaning. In this case, whether a specified datum is in a given range need to be considered. Minker and Yang [5] and Fukuda et al [3] further consider more general case that the data is interval, that is, ordered data for which the separation between data points has meaning. In this case, the distance between data should be considered in addition. Our paper discusses the processing of the range-type data. Hence the overlap between two ranges should be considered. Our method provides a way to process this new type data. It is possible to extend the existing algorithm for finding association rules to the range data set.

Third, an efficient iterative formula is derived for evaluating the measure α_R and β_R. It reduces the time complexity from $O(n^2)$ to $O(n)$, while the space complexity is as the same $O(n)$ as the naive one.

References

1. Agrawal, R., Imielinski, T., Swami, A.: Mining Association Rules between Sets of Items in Large Databases, *Proc. SIGMOD*, pp.207–216 (1993)
2. Agrawal, R., Srikant, R. Fast Algorithms for Mining Association Rules, *Proc. VLD-B*, pp.487–499 (1994)
3. Fukuda, T., Morimoto,Y., Morishita, S., Tokuyama, T.: Mining Optimized Association Rules for Numeric Attributes *Proc. PODS*, pp.182–191 (1996)
4. Fayyad,U., Piatetsky-Shapiro, G., Smyth, P., and Uthurusamy R.: Advances in Knowledge Discovery and Data Mining *AAAI press/MIT press* (1996)
5. Miller, R.J., Yang, Y.: Association Rules over Interval Data *Proc. SIGMOD*, pp. 452–461 (1997)
6. Robinson,J., Lowden B.G.T: Data Analysis for Query Processing *Proc. 2nd Int'l Symp. on Intelligent Data Analysis, pp. 447–458 (1997)* LNCS 1280
7. Srikant, R., Agrawal, R: Mining Quantitative Association Rules in Large Relational Tables, *Proc. SIGMOD*, pp.1–12 (1996)
8. Smyth, P., Fayyad,U., Burl, M., Perona, P.: Modeling Subjective Uncertainty in Image Annotation, *in "Advances in Knowledge Discovery and Data Mining", edited by Fayyad,U., et al* , AAAI press/MIT press (1996)

Database Architecture for Data Warehousing: An Evolutionary Approach

José Samos[1], Fèlix Saltor[2], Jaume Sistac[2], and Agustí Bardés[1]

[1]Winterthur Ibérica, Informática Ibérica, Barcelona, Spain
jsamos@computer.org, abt@arrakis.es
[2]Departament de Llenguatges i Sistemes Informàtics,
Universitat Politècnica de Catalunya
{saltor, sistac}@lsi.upc.es

Abstract. In recent years, data warehouses have reached a prominent position in the database field, especially in the database industry. There are many issues in common between data warehouses and other database fields such as federated databases; in our opinion this fact has not been explored in its entirety. In this paper, an integrated database architecture in which data warehouses are part of the database is put forward. Instead of having data warehouses built using a database, we propose to have data warehouses defined as part of the database architecture; this architecture is defined as an extension of a federated database architecture.

1 Introduction

The main motivation of this paper is to put data warehouses in the context of other database research areas; and to benefit from developments in those areas.

In section 2, some database architectures are reviewed: the ANSI/SPARC three-level architecture; and two schema architectures for federated databases. In section 3, the most representative data warehouse architectures are presented. In section 4, our proposal of an integrated database architecture for data warehousing is put forward. Finally, some conclusions and future work issues are put forward in section 5.

2 Database Architectures

2.1 The ANSI/SPARC Three-Level Architecture

The ANSI/SPARC *three-level schema architecture* classified *database management system* data in physical, logical, and external levels [21]; information at these levels is represented by the *internal, conceptual,* and *external schemas* respectively. According to the ANSI/SPARC framework [1], the systems of schema definition are based on a *data dictionary*; its universe of discourse is all the information relevant to the management and use of the database system —including the schemas.

The ANSI/SPARC three-level architecture and framework have been widely applied in *relational databases*, but not so much in *object-oriented databases* (OODB). In [16], [17], [18] a new *external schema definition methodology* according to the ANSI/SPARC architecture and framework has been defined: an external schema may include classes defined in the conceptual schema just as it may also contain *derived classes* —directly or indirectly defined on the basis of conceptual schema classes— that do not necessarily need to be included in the conceptual schema; derived classes are defined and included in the data dictionary.

2.2 Architectures for Federated Database Systems

A *federated database system* (FDBS) is formed by different *component database systems*; it provides integrated access to them: they cooperate (inter-operate) with each other to produce consolidated answers to the queries defined over the FDBS. Generally, the FDBS has no data of its own, queries are answered by accessing the component database systems.

Many FDBS architectures have been proposed to support integrated access; two of them are reviewed in this section.

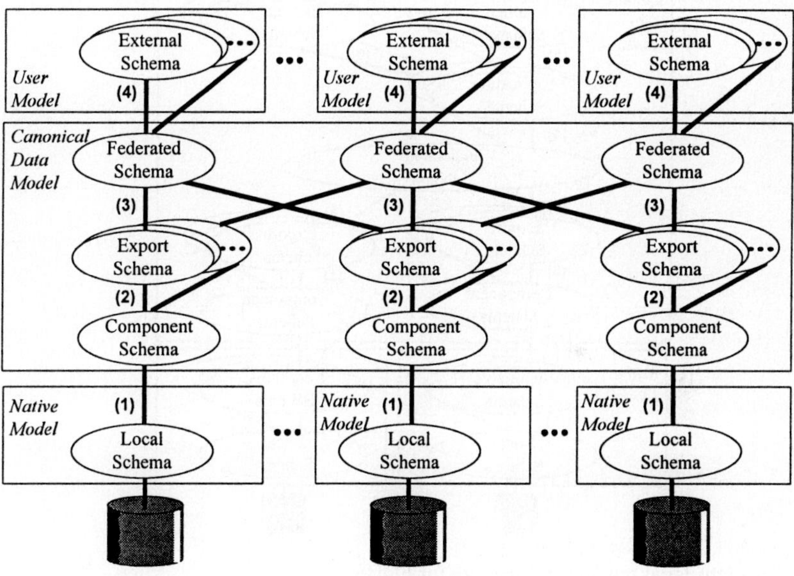

Fig. 1. The five-level schema architecture for FDBS. Three types of sections are defined (*surrounded by boxes*), each corresponding to a kind of data model: component databases (native models), FDBS (canonical data model) and external schemas (user models).

The Five-Level Architecture. The Sheth & Larson five-level architecture [19] is very general and encompasses most of the previously existing architectures (Fig. 1). In this architecture three types of data models are used: first, each component database can have its own *native model*; second, a *canonical data model* (CDM) which is adopted in the FDBS; and third, external schemas can be defined in different *user models*. Besides, three basic mechanisms are used to define the schemas in the different levels from schemas in their immediate lower level, namely: *translation of models* (between the CDM and other models), *integration of schemas* (all of them defined using the CDM), and *definition of derived schemas* from a schema.

As shown in Fig. 1, each component database system has its *local schema* defined in a native model. Local schemas are translated (tag 1) to obtain *component schemas* defined using the CDM. Each database negotiates which of its own data it makes accessible, therefore, from each component schema different *export schemas* can be defined using the derived schema definition mechanism (tag 2), each export schema represents the result of a negotiation. Export schemas are integrated (tag 3) to form a *federated schema*. From each federated schema, external schemas can be defined in different models using both the derived schema definition and translation of model mechanisms (tag 4).

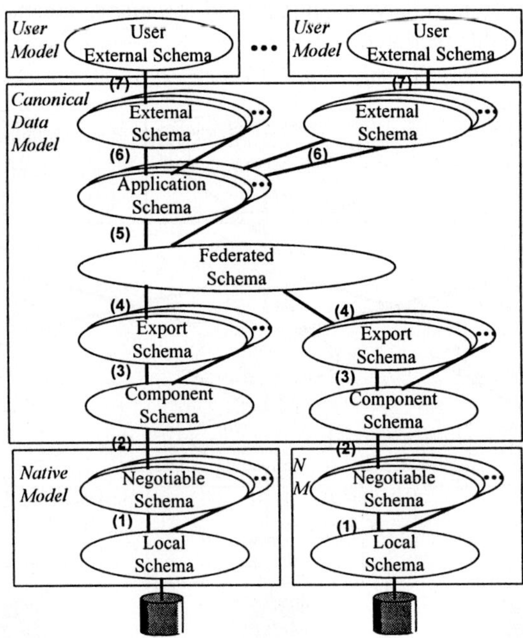

Fig. 2. The eight-level schema architecture for FDBS.

The Eight-Level Architecture. The eight-level architecture (Fig. 2), defined by Saltor et al. [15], is an extension of the five-level architecture with three new schema levels that deal with three issues that do not fit well within the five-level architecture:

component databases of several federations; external schemas in user models different from the CDM; and multiple semantics at the federated schema level. Therefore, the following schema levels are defined:

- The *negotiable schema*: this is defined from the local schema in each component database using the derived schema definition mechanism (tag 1), both the local schema and the negotiable schemas are defined in the same native model. Thus, it is the negotiable schema which is translated to form the component schema (tag 2). Using the negotiable schema, the local schema can have private elements not exportable to any federation.
- The *user external schema*: external schemas are defined in the CDM using the derived schema definition mechanism (tag 6); thus, each external schema can be translated to a user external schema, in its own user model, using the translation of model mechanism (tag 7). In the five-level architecture, the definition of external schemas and the translation to some user model were made in only one step.
- The *application schema*: a federated schema can support multiple semantics (see [15], [19] for details), while each application schema reflects just one semantic, common to one or more applications, and its scope is a general universe of discourse (like the scope of the federated schema). Therefore, instead of having external schemas directly defined from a federated schema, external schemas are defined from an application schema (tag 6) using the derived schema definition mechanism. Due to their scope characteristics, application schemas are defined from the federated schema using the derived schema definition mechanism with some limitations (tag 5).

The CDM used in [15] is the BLOOM model [4], an object-oriented model. Therefore, a derived schema mechanism for OODB like the one defined in [16], [17], [18] has to be used in tags 3, 5 and 6 of Fig. 2.

3 Data Warehouse Architectures

Inmon [10] defined a *data warehouse* as "a subject-oriented, integrated, time-variant, non-volatile collection of data in support of management's decision-making process." A data warehouse is a database that stores a copy of operational data whose structure is optimized for query and analysis. The scope is one of the data warehouse defining issues: it is the entire enterprise. Related to a more reduced scope, a new concept is defined: a *data mart* is a highly focused data warehouse whose scope is a single department or subject area. The data warehouse and data marts are usually implemented using relational databases [2], [7], [8], [13], [23] defining multi-dimensional structures.

3.1 Data Warehouse-Centered Architecture

In the *data warehouse-centered architecture* or simply the *data warehouse architecture* (Fig. 3), legacy system information is obtained from the operational systems and is integrated in a data warehouse: it contains summary data as well as detail. The data warehouse data model is obtained from the involved legacy system models [9]. The data warehouse is the basis of *executive information systems* (EIS), *decision support systems* (DSS), and other data querying and tools of analysis.

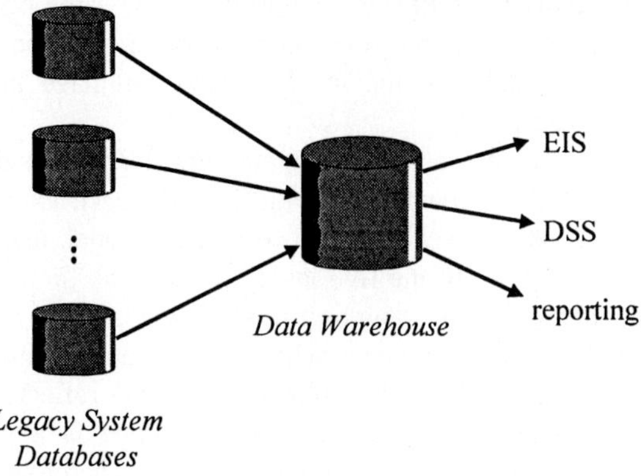

Fig. 3. The data warehouse-centered architecture.

3.2 Operational Data Store / Data Warehouse Architecture

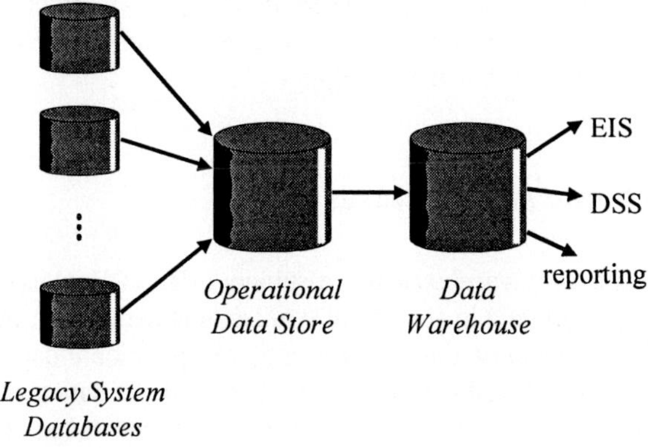

Fig. 4. The operational data store / data warehouse architecture.

The *operational data store / data warehouse architecture* (Fig.4) is an extension of the data warehouse-centered architecture [11]. Inmon [12] defined an *operational data store* (ODS) as " a subject-oriented, integrated, volatile (i.e., able to be updated), current or near-current collection of data in support of day to day operational decisions." In the ODS / data warehouse architecture, legacy system information is obtained from the operational systems and is integrated in the ODS; it is then transferred to the data warehouse when needed.

To define the ODS from the operational system databases a schema integration mechanism, like the one used in FDBS to define the federated schema from export schemas, may be used.

3.3 Data Warehouse / Data Marts Architecture

The only difference between a data warehouse and a data mart is the scope. In some cases, various data marts are constructed in an isolated way, then they are integrated in a corporate-wide data warehouse. An alternative architecture consists of having data marts derived from an enterprise-scale data warehouse.

Like in the ODS case, an integration mechanism may be used to define the data warehouse from various data marts (Fig. 5.A). On the other hand, to define data marts from the data warehouse (Fig. 5.B) an derived schema definition mechanism with additional features may be used.

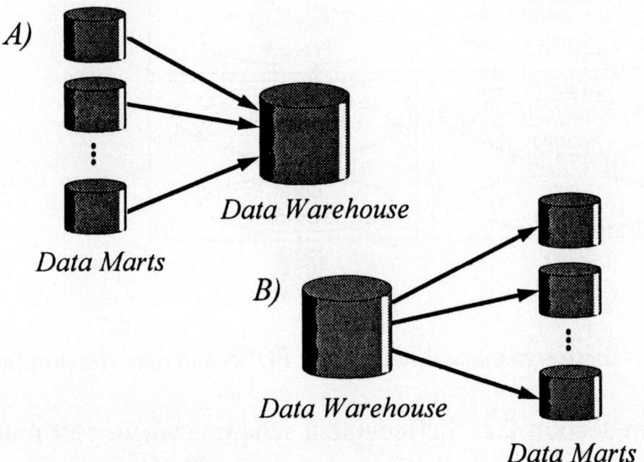

Fig. 5. Data warehouse / data marts architecture.

4 An Integrated Database Architecture for Data Warehousing

4.1 The Schema Architecture

There are similarities between FDBS and data warehouses. For example, the relationship between the legacy system databases and the data warehouse (Fig. 3) in some points is quite similar to the one between component database systems and the FDBS. This likeness with FDBS is more clear in the case of the relationship between the legacy system databases and the ODS (Fig. 4). A similar resemblance can be found in the relationship between data marts and the data warehouse as shown in Fig. 5.A. In addition, the relationship between the data warehouse and the data marts, as shown in Fig. 5.B, is similar to the one between the application schema (or the federated schema) and external schemas in FDBS. In this sense, a database schema architecture can be defined for data warehouses as has been defined for FDBS. Our proposal of integrated database architectures for FDBS and data warehouses can be seen in Fig. 6.

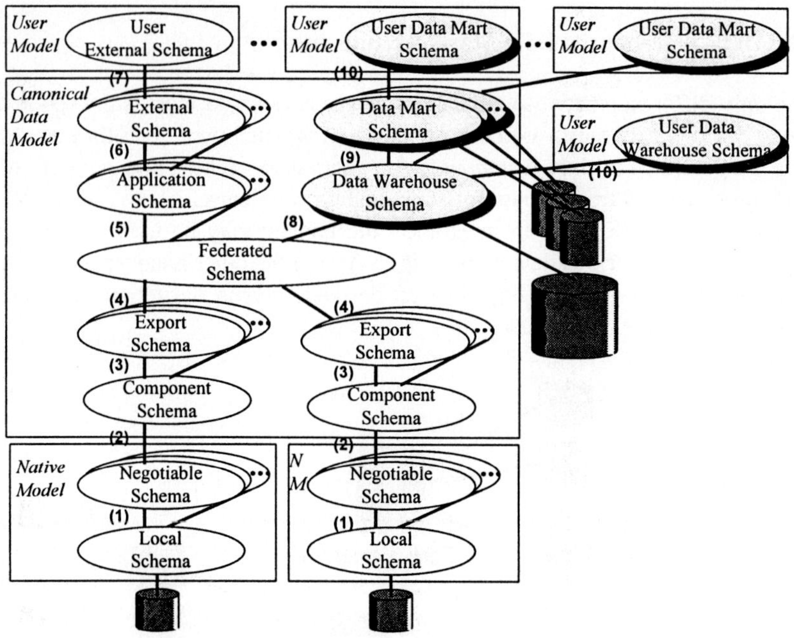

Fig. 6. Integrated database schema architecture for FDBS and data warehouses

As explained in section 2.2, the federated schema can support multiple semantics, each application schema reflects just one semantic, common to one or more applications, and its scope is a general universe of discourse (like the scope of the federated schema). In this sense, the data warehouse schema is like the application schema: it reflects just one semantic, and its scope is a general universe of discourse. Therefore, as can be seen in Fig. 6, the data warehouse schema is defined from the federated schema (tag 8) using a schema derivation mechanism similar to the one used to define application schemas (some extensions are required). In the same way, data mart schemas are defined from the data warehouse schema (tag 9) using a mechanism also similar to the derived schema definition one.

In some cases, the application schema and the negotiable schema can be considered unnecessary in the FDBS architecture (from our point of view, the distinction between external schemas and user external schemas is absolutely necessary). Therefore, an alternative integrated database architecture with two less levels can be considered, but the relationship between the federated schema and the data warehouse schema does not change. The key point here is that *the data warehouse and data marts are part of the database, they are a database feature* instead of being an independent system, built using a database. The number of schema levels is a secondary issue.

4.2 The Data Warehouse Data Model

In FDBS, application schemas are derived from a federated schema; in the same way, external schemas are derived from the corresponding application schema. All these derivations are performed using just one model, the CDM. In our architecture, the data warehouse schema is derived from a federated schema too (Fig. 6, tag 8), and therefore it is convenient to use the same CDM. Data marts are defined from the data warehouse (Fig. 6, tag 9) using the CDM. An object-oriented CDM is well suited for these definitions. Even if data warehouse and data marts are defined using the CDM, they can be translated to other user models (Fig. 6, tag 10) as can external schemas.

In the case of the data warehouse schema, data in the warehouse has been derived at a particular moment in time from data in the federated schema (time-variance): "data warehouse data is, for all practical purposes, a long series of snapshots [10]." Data mart data is derived from data warehouse data. In the definition of the data warehouse model, the definition of temporal views over non-temporal schemas has been studied for relational models [25]. In our view, it has to be studied also for object-oriented models used as CDM. The result will be the enhancement of the derived schema definition mechanism used to define application schemas from the federated schema to fit better with the definition of the data warehouse schema from the federated schema; this mechanism also has to be adapted to the data mart specific characteristics.

The CDM used in [15] is the BLOOM model [4], a semantically rich object-oriented model. This is also our proposal: to use for the definition of the data warehouse and data mart schemas an object-oriented model (the BLOOM model or the ODMG model) as CDM, enhanced with temporal features to define loading the data warehouse and the data marts.

4.3 Data Warehouse Data

Generally, the FDBS has no data of its own, queries are answered by accessing the component database systems. In the data warehouse or data mart cases, data obtained from the component databases has to be stored locally (Fig. 6) because of their time-variance characteristics. The ODS —not explicitly represented in Fig. 6— is like an application schema but, due to performance requirements, it can also contain local data. Data marts can also have local data, or their data can be obtained from the data warehouse data (like external schema data is obtained from application schema data). Therefore, this new feature has to be added to the original FDBS to fulfil the data warehouse and ODS requirements.

The data warehouse contains a historical, static perspective of integrated corporate data. Therefore, component database updates do not have to be transmitted immediately to the data warehouse. Due to the data warehouse characteristics, data is usually loaded in a massive way (from a log or audit file, snapshots, or any other method [9]). ODS data usually is loaded in shorter periods than data warehouse data. In the data warehouse and ODS definition this fact has to be taken into account.

In the case of the architecture presented in Fig. 5.A (integration of data marts in the data warehouse), data from the different data marts can be loaded in the data warehouse in the moment of the data warehouse definition; the rest of the updates can be loaded in the data warehouse directly from the component databases or from the data marts like common updates (also in a massive way).

Data warehouse or data mart local data is not updated (it is "non-volatile"), therefore usually there are no modifications to transmit from the data warehouse to the component databases.

Our proposal for an integrated database architecture (Fig. 6) conveniently supports the definition of all these issues.

4.4 The Database Data Dictionary

The schemas of the database (FDBS, data warehouse and data marts) are defined by the various database administrators and stored into the data dictionary along with the corresponding mappings. The universe of discourse of the data dictionary is all the information relevant to the management and use of the database (including all the elements of the data warehouse and data marts). The only schema whose definition is not included in the data dictionary is the local schema: it is not defined because it is a private schema in the component database systems; instead, the negotiable schemas are imported into the data dictionary from the component databases. If negotiable schemas are not considered, the local schemas have to be imported into the data dictionary (since they are not private schemas in the component database systems).

The data warehouse and data marts have became part of the database: their definition is a new database feature (like, for instance, the definition of external schemas). Therefore, the database data dictionary contains all the elements needed to define them. In particular, all the elements not needed previously for FDBS (i.e., the way data is loaded from the component databases) have to be defined.

Until now, to build a data warehouse from legacy system databases, application programs had to be developed or external tools had to be used to obtain and integrate the data into the data warehouse. Usually, to have enough flexibility, this process was based on a data warehouse definition repository or data dictionary. In our proposal, the definition of the data warehouse is part of the database definition (like external schemas are too), therefore it is carried into the database data dictionary.

5 Conclusions and Future Work

In this paper, a new general data warehouse architecture and definition framework have been defined. Data warehouses have been related to other database research areas like FDBS or OODB to benefit from developments in those areas.

We propose that data warehouses should be included *inside* the database, as a *database feature.* It is much like the external schemas case, they can be implemented as separated databases whose data is obtained from the database that represents the conceptual schema, or they can be a database feature which is the way they are defined in the ANSI/SPARC three-level schema architecture.

There has been an evolution, from local databases to FDBS. FDBS allow us to define queries over an integrated model of the corporation. The data warehouse allows us to analyze the evolution of the corporation data as a database feature.

Until now, most of the proposed data warehouse conceptual data models were relational or multi-dimensional. In this paper the use of an object-oriented model has been proposed; moreover, the data warehouse or data mart data model can be translated to different user data models.

Related to the data warehouse framework defined in this paper, our future research issues include the following:

- To study the use of a *temporal object-oriented model* [3], [5], [6], [14], [20], [24] to define the data warehouse and data mart data models.
- To extend the derived schema definition mechanism for object-oriented databases defined in [16], [17], [18] to include the functions required to define data warehouses and ODS from the federated schema, and data marts from the data warehouse.
- To restudy the research problems in data warehousing [22] (i.e., change detection in component databases, self-maintainability of views, etc.) from the new point of view offered by this paper.
- To define and develop a data warehouse definition system in the environment presented in this paper.

Acknowledgements

The work of F. Saltor and J. Sistac was partially supported by the Spanish CICYT (project TIC96-6903).

We would like to thank the anonymous reviewers for their helpful comments on earlier versions of this paper.

References

1. ANSI/X3/SPARC Database System Study Group: Reference Model for DBMS Standardisation. ACM SIGMOD Record, Vol. 15, No. 1 (March 1986) 19-58
2. Baralis, E., Paraboschi, S., Teniente, E.: Materialized View Selection in a Multidimensional Database. Proc. 23rd VLDB Conf. (Athens, 1997), Morgan Kaufmann, 156-165
3. Bertino, E., Ferrari, E., Guerrini, G.: T_Chimera: A Temporal Object-Oriented Data Model. TAPOS, Vol. 3, No. 2 (1997) 103-125

4. Castellanos, M., Saltor, F., García, M.: A Canonical Model for the Interoperatibility among Object Oriented and Relational Models. In: Ozsu, T. et al. (eds.): Distributed Object Management (Edmonton, 1992), Morgan Kaufmann (1994), 309-314
5. Chu, W., Ieong, Y., Taira, R., Breant, C.: A Temporal Evolutionary Object-Oriented Data Model and Its Query Language for Medical Image Management. Proc. 18th VLDB Conf. (Vancouver, 1992), Morgan Kaufmann, 53-64
6. Fauvet, M., Canavaggio, J., Scholl, P.: Modeling Histories in Object DBMS. In: Hameurlain, A., Tjoa, A. (eds.): Proc. 8th Int'l. Conf. DEXA (Toulouse, 1997), LNCS 1308, Springer-Verlag, 112-121
7. Hammer, J., García-Molina, H., Widom, J., Labio, W., Zhuge, Y.: The Stanford Data Warehousing Project. IEEE Data Engineering Bulletin (June 1995)
8. Harinarayan, V., Rajaraman, A., Ullman, J.: Implementing Data Cubes Efficiently. Proc. of ACM SIGMOD Conf. (Montreal, 1996)
9. Inmon, W.: Building the Data Warehouse. Wiley-QED (1992)
10. Inmon, W.: What is a Data Warehouse?. PRISM Tech Topic, Vol.1, No.1 (1992)
11. Inmon, W.: Information Architecture for the 90's: Legacy Systems, Operational Data Store. Data Warehouse. PRISM Tech Topic, Vol.1, No.13 (1993)
12. Inmon, W.: The Operational Data Store. PRISM Tech Topic, Vol.1, No.17 (1993)
13. Labio, W., Quass, D., Adelberg, B.: Physical Database Design for Data Warehouses. Proc. Int'l. Conf. on Data Engineering (Birminghan, 1997), IEEE, 277-288
14. Pissinou, N., Makki, K., Yesha, Y.: On Temporal Modeling in the Context of Object Databases. ACM SIGMOD Record, Vol. 22, No. 3 (Sep. 1993) 8-15
15. Saltor, F., Campderrich, B., Rodríguez, E., Rodríguez, L.: On Schema Levels for Federated DB Systems. In Yetongnon & Hariri (eds.): Proc. of the ISCA Int'l. Conf. on Parallel and Distributed Computing Systems (Dijon, 1996), ISCA, 766-771
16. Samos, J.: Definition of External Schemas in Object Oriented Databases. In: Murphy, J., Stone, B. (eds.): Proc. Int'l Conf. on Object Oriented Information Systems (Dublin, 1995), Springer-Verlag, 154-166
17. Samos, J., Saltor, F.: External Schema Generation Algorithms for Object Oriented Databases. In: Patel, D. et al. (eds.): Proc. Int'l Conf. on Object Oriented Information Systems (London, 1996), Springer-Verlag, 317-332
18. Samos, J., Saltor, F.: Integration of Derived Classes in Object Schemas. IADT'98 – Int'l. Workshop on Issues and Applications of Database Technology (Berlin, July 1998)
19. Sheth, A., Larson, J.: Federated Database Systems for Managing Distributed, Heterogeneous and Autonomous Databases." ACM Computing Surveys, Vol. 22, No. 3 (Sep. 1990)
20. Snodgrass, R.: Temporal Object-Oriented Databases: A Critical Comparison. In: Kim, W. (ed.): Modern Database Systems, ACM Press (1995) 386-408
21. Tsichritzis, D., Klug, A. (eds.): The ANSI/X3/SPARC Framework. AFIPS Press, Montvale, N.J. (1978)
22. Widom, J.: Research Problems in Data Warehousing. Proc. of the Int'l. Conf. on Information and Knowlege Management (Baltimore, 1995)
23. Wiener, J., Gupta, H., Labio, W., Zhuge, Y., García-Molina, H., Widom, J.: A System Prototype for Warehouse View Maintenance. Proc. of the ACM Workshop on Materialized Views: Techniques and Applications (Montreal, 1996) 26-33
24. Wuu, G., Dayal, U.: A Uniform Model for Temporal Object-Oriented Databases. Proc. IEEE Data Engineering Conf. (Feb. 1992)
25. Yang, J., Widom, J.: Maintaining Temporal Views over Non-Historical Information Sources for Data Warehousing. Technical note, Stanford University, 1997.

An Integrated Platform for the Evaluation of Spatial Query Processing Strategies*

Christophe Gurret and Philippe Rigaux

CEDRIC/CNAM
292 rue St Martin, F-75141 Paris Cedex 03, France
{gurret,rigaux}@cnam.fr

Abstract. We present in this paper a platform which integrates the necessary tools for the performance evaluation of various query processing strategies in multidimensional databases, and proposes a simple interface for the specification of spatial benchmarks.
In its current setting, our platform is focused on 2-dimensional operations: several kinds of spatial indices and spatial join algorithms have been implemented and their performance compared. We give these first results and discuss their relevancy.

1 Introduction

Traditionally, database management technology has been applied to business applications. One of the main features of such applications is the simplicity of data representation: objects are usually represented as points (tuples) in a n-dimensional space, each dimension corresponding to an attribute. The relational data model is essentially sufficient to meet these requirements. In addition, queries over relational databases are greatly simplified by the possibility to consider separately each dimension and to exploit the natural ordering of the underlying domain (mainly strings and numbers).

With the emergence of new application that manipulate multi-dimensional data, these nice properties do no longer hold, mostly because of the lack of ordering. This gave rise during the ten past years to specialized techniques for processing spatial queries [2,3], among which one can roughly distinguish the design of new data structures and the adaptation of well-known join strategies. to the particular requirements of spatial joins.

Many propositions have been made in the past few years [4–8] but many of them have been validated through experiments that run on different platforms, with various datasets and implementation choices. This renders difficult a fair comparison among the numerous techniques which have been advocated, and to draw sound conclusions regarding the strategies that should be handled by a query optimizer in a Spatial Database Management System.

In this paper, we propose an integrated platform as a solution to this problem. This platform provides basic services such as I/O's and buffer management,

* Work partially supported by the ESPRIT TMR Chorochronos network.

a set of representative spatial index structures and a toolkit to facilitate the implementation of join algorithms and their integration in complex query execution plans (QEP). By using this toolkit, one can easily define a benchmark by specifying QEPs, setting the query processing environment and getting the results.

An important underlying motivation to this work is to enrich classical query optimizers with techniques supporting multidimensional data access and processing. This leads us to consider data structures and algorithms which are simple, robust and general enough to support a wide range of situations. As a consequence, our implementation of some important algorithms found in the literature does not provide advanced optimization relying on sophisticated data structures or buffer management techniques.

To validate our approach, we have conducted as a first experiment a systematic evaluation of basic strategies for the filter step of spatial joins, applied to two kinds of index: a R*-tree and a grid-like structure. We discuss the main results of this study.

The paper is organized as follows. Section 2 briefly recalls the main features of the spatial data structures and summarizes related work. Section 3 presents the platform. Section 4 describes the experiment on spatial join algorithms. Section 5 concludes and outlines future work.

2 Background and related work

Spatial indices organize collections of spatial objects in searchable structures which rely on an approximation of the actual geometry, usually the minimal bouding box (*mbb*). They can be separated in two families. First *space-driven structures* partition the indexed dataset according to some predefined scheme. They can be roughly compared to hashing in traditional databases. For instance the *grid file* [9] consists of a regular decomposition in *cells*. An object is assigned to those cells which overlap its *mbb*.

Data-driven structures on the other hand try to adapt to the data distribution while preserving some nice properties such as balanced tree-like shapes and dynamic behavior. The most prominent index of this family is the R-Tree [10] and its variants [11, 12]. Each node is characterized by a rectangle which is the bounding box of all the objects contained in the node's subtree and which is used during index traversal.

The spatial join between two relations R_1 and R_2 is the set of tuples from $R_1 \times R_2$ such that some predicate θ (usually *intersect*) holds between the spatial attributes [13]. Spatial joins usually operate in two steps: the *filter step* uses an approximation of spatial objects (most often the *mbb*) to eliminate objects which cannot meet the join criteria. It delivers a superset of the result which is further processed during a *refinement step* to produce the exact result by considering the actual geometry of spatial objects.

Spatial joins that rely on grid-files were proposed in [4, 5, 14, 15]. They try to exploit the order of the grid cells during query processing, for instance in mapping the 1-dimensional representation of the grid onto the B-tree of a DBMS.

Partitioning techniques are also the basis of two recent algorithms [7, 8]. In [8], both datasets are partitioned such that each couple of buckets fit simultaneously in main memory. In [7], an explicit comparison with hash-join algorithms is made, and a customization of the hash-join framework to spatial data is proposed.

A second family of join algorithms uses hierarchical structures as a primary support [6, 16, 17]. The standard R-tree based join algorithms is the *Synchronized Tree Traversal (STT)* [6] which presumes the existence of an R-tree on each dataset. The algorithm consists in a synchronized and depth-first traversal of both indices. When only one index exists, the simplest strategy is a variant of the nested loop algorithm which scans the non-indexed collection and accesses the other one through the R-tree. The high efficiency of the STT algorithm suggests that the "on-the-fly" construction of a second index, followed by the STT, could compete with nested loop. This idea has inspired the join algorithm of [18] which takes advantage of the existence of the first R-tree R_1 to construct a so-called *seeded-tree* R_2 which is a R-tree whose first levels match exactly those of R_1. An alternative is to build a *packed R-tree* by using bulk-load insertions [19, 20].

The complexity of the spatial join operation and the numerous parameters which are involved make difficult a comparison between the various proposals briefly sketched above. Some experiences already attempted to validate these various propositions in a uniform framefork [21], but the structures and algorithms were built upon an existing DBMS, a design which makes difficult a precise analysis. In the same spirit, the platform described in the next section proposes a fully customizable architecture which makes explicit all the parameters involved in an experiment.

3 The platform

The architecture is shown on Fig. 1. It basically consists in three modules. First the buffer manager provides basic and standard low-level services such as pages read and write and the management of pages in main memory according to a replacement policy. The query processing module provides the necessary components for spatial queries support. Finally the toolkit interface is a set of functions which allow to specify easily a benchmarking experiment.

The platform has been implemented in C under UNIX. The design of the low-level modules is quite classical: datasets and spatial indices are stored in binary files divided in pages whose size is chosen at file creation (we experimented 1K, 2K and 4K page sizes). Each page is identified by its offset with respect to the beginning of the file, and is accessed through the `read` and `write` UNIX primitives.

The buffer manager associates with each opened file a buffer pool whose size (expressed in number of pages) is initially given as a parameter to the function which opens the file. The buffer pool is a cache with LRU or FIFO replacement policy (LRU by default). Pages can be *pinned* in memory. A pinned page is never

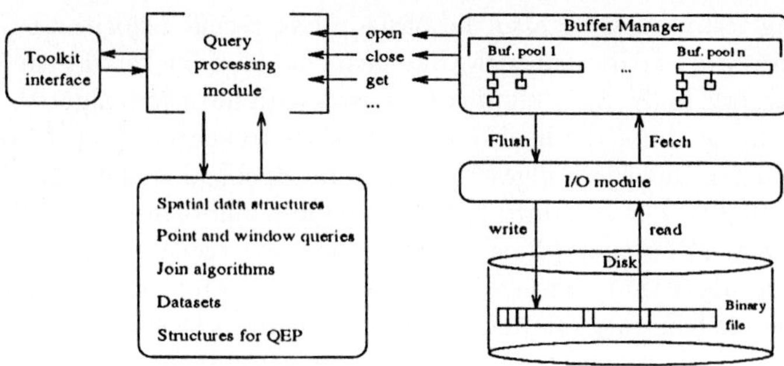

Fig. 1. Platform architecture

flushed until it is unpinned. This can be important for specific pages (such as the root of a tree or the directory of a hash table) which must reside in memory.

The main operations are summarized below: an index or a dataset is opened with **`open(fname, bufsize):bufid`** where **`bufsize`** stands for the number of pages initially allocated to the buffer pool, **`get(bufid, pageid)`** asks the buffer for a page using its *id*, `new(bufid):pageid` adds a page to the file associated with the buffer `bufid`. Page pinning is managed through the `pin(bufid,pageid)` and `unpin(bufid,pageid)` functions.

All algorithms and data structures which need to read from or write on secondary storage uniformly access pages through the interface provided by the buffer manager. This means in particular that spatial join algorithms share this module and therefore cannot rely on a tailored main memory management or a specialized I/O's policy which is not already supported.

The query processing module consists of all the technical components which are necessary to construct an experiment, namely the data structures and algorithms, the datasets and the toolkit to specify the parameters, input and output of a benchmark.

In the current setting, the spatial data structures are a grid file, an R-tree, a R*-tree and a packed R-tree [20] which allows an efficient construction of static data collections. Based on these indices, several spatial algorithms are available. Apart from the standard point query and window query algorithms, several join strategies have been implemented that will be further detailed in the next section.

We use in our experiments synthetic and real life datasets. Synthetic datasets were created by using the rectangle generator implemented by ENST in France [21]. This tool[1] produces a set of rectangles (bouding boxes) according to a statistical model whose parameters (size, coverage, distribution) can be precisely described. The following statistical models proposed in [21] were used: *Biotopes* is a uniform distribution of rectangles, whose coverage with respect to the whole space is 200% (hence a limited overlapping is allowed). *Cities* simulates the distributions of cities: the map contains many small and dense rectangles. The real life

[1] Available at `http://www-inf.enst.fr`.

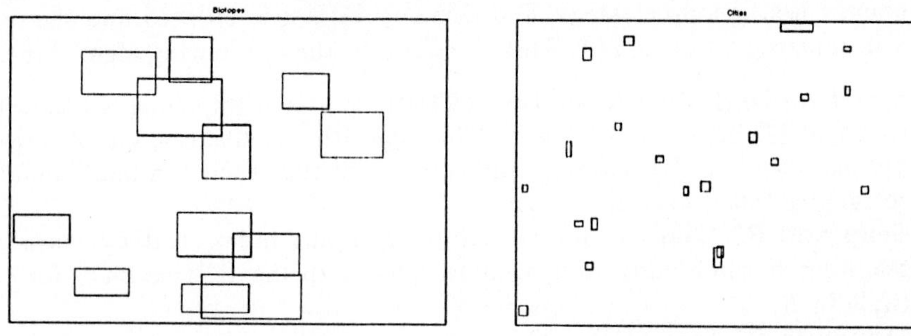

Fig. 2. Samples of the biotopes and cities statistical models

dataset collection is extracted from the Tiger files [23] for the north-east part of United States. Fig. 2 displays two samples of *biotopes* and *cities*: we shall use these statistical models throughout the experiment presented in Section 4.

An important feature of the query processing module is the possibility to specify easily new benchmark experiments. To this end it provides a uniform interface for all the algorithms (point queries, window queries and spatial join) listed above. This interface uses as a common structure *iterators* [1] which can be simply seen as small processors which can be included in a query execution plan to carry out some unary or binary operation with input and output data flows.

Iterators are instanciated through a small set of functions which constitutes the toolkit interface for spatial benchmarking. This design greatly simplifies the specification of each experiment: in the current setting, a few lines of C code are sufficient to carry out a set of measurements involving varying datasets, buffer sizes or join algorithms.

4 An experiment with spatial join algorithms

We next illustrate the functionalities of the platform with a comparison of the spatial join algorithms which are currently available in our implementation. The study is based on the following restrictions. First we limit ourselves to the *intersect* predicate, and consider only the filter step. Second we assume that each dataset is indexed on the spatial attribute, and that each query is processed by an optimizer which tries to use as much as possible existing spatial indices when generating Query Execution Plan (QEP). As a consequence, each join in the QEP accesses at least one based relation and can therefore take advantage of the existing index.

Given this context, the join algorithms involved in a comprehensive study can be divided as follows: (i) both datasets R and S are indexed and the algorithm relies on the two indices, (ii) one dataset is indexed and the algorithm follows an indexed nested-loop strategy, and (iii) one dataset is indexed and the other index is constructed on the fly. This gives rise to the 6 following algorithms.

1. **Synchronized Tree Traversal (STT)**. We have implemented the algorithm of [6] in a standard way. This algorithm delivers a set of object's *oid* pairs (oid_1, oid_2) without duplicates, such that their minimal bounding rectangles (*mbr*) overlap.
2. **Scan and R*-tree (SAR)** The simple scan-and-index strategy consists in scanning R while addressing window queries to the R*-tree on S for each tuple in R.
3. **Dynamic R*-tree (DR)**. This algorithm implements another solution to the previous situation: in the presence of two collections with only one index, a packed R-tree[2] is constructed dynamically on the non-indexed collection and the STT algorithm is then carried out.
4. **Synchronized Grid Scan (SGS)** The existence of a grid on each collection and the ordering among the cells of each grid gives rise to a merge-like strategy by applying a synchronized scan of both grids.
5. **Scan and Grid (SAG)** The idea is similar to that of the scan-and-index based on R*-tree: the first (non-indexed) collection is scanned, and each of its tuple is used to probe the grid structure.
6. **Dynamic Grid (DG)** The last algorithm partitions first the non-indexed collection in order to apply the **SGS** strategy in a second phase. Since one might expect to get optimal results when both partitioning functions are identical, the already existing grid is used a the pattern for the partition function [7].

We now compare the six previously described algorithms regarding only two parameters: the buffer size and the datasets size. All the other parameters have been fixed as follows: the page size has been set to 1K, the buffer replacement policy is LRU and the two statistical models are *Biotopes* and *Cities* as described in the previous section. We consider only the number of I/O's and not the CPU time. The machine used throughout the experiments is a SUN SparcStation 5 with 32 MB of memory, running SunOS 4.1.

Dataset	Nb pages	Nb levels
BIO20	571	3
BIO40	1 118	3
BIO60	1 676	3
BIO80	2 238	4
BIO100	2 792	4
CIT20	139	2
CIT40	276	3
CIT60	413	3
CIT80	561	3
CIT100	698	3

Table 1: R*-tree

Dataset	C × L	Nb Pages	Over. pages
BIO20	25 × 25	1 162	537
BIO40	35 × 35	2 310	1 085
BIO60	43 × 43	3 490	1 465
BIO80	49 × 49	4 568	2 167
BIO100	55 × 55	5 750	2 725
CIT20	25 × 25	644	19
CIT40	35 × 35	1 276	51
CIT60	43 × 43	1 915	66
CIT80	49 × 49	2 543	142
CIT100	55 × 55	3 206	181

Table 2: Grid

[2] We use the STR algorithm of [20].

For each of the statistical models *Biotopes* and *Cities*, 5 datasets have been generated, with a size ranging from 20 000 to 100 000 objects. A grid and a R*-tree have been constructed on each dataset: the following tables show their characteristics (BIO20 stands for *Biotopes* with population 20 000).

For the grid files, the following choices have been made: the minimum number m of cells has been estimated for each collection (each page of 1K can store 45 couples (mbr, oid)). The final number of cells has been obtained as $\lceil \sqrt{m} \times 1.33 \rceil$, the 1.33 factor being on account of skewed data.

Observe that for the *biotopes* collection, the size of the grid file is 85 % higher than the initial allocation of cells. This is mostly explained by the duplicates consecutive to the large rectangles of this statistical model (see Fig. 2). The small size of the page (1K) makes the problem even worse.

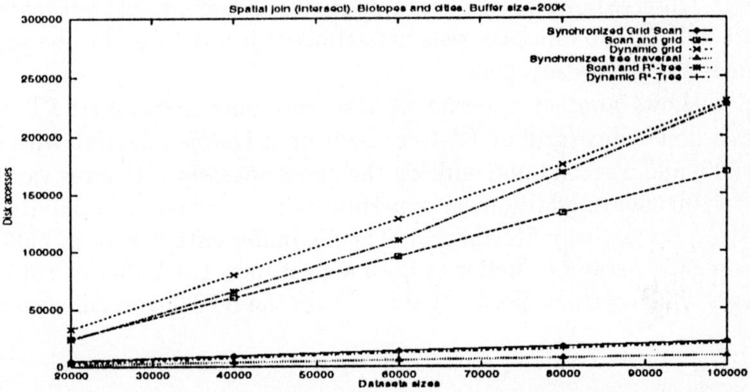

Fig. 3. The six join algorithms, with a fixed buffer size of 200K

The first experiment, whose measures are shown on Fig. 3 fixes the buffer size to 200K and lets the datasets size vary: the join is performed for couples (*biotopes, cities*) with equal size values ranging from 20 000 to 100 000. Except in the case of the DG algorithm where the construction of the missing grid is rather costly, there are several orders of magnitude in favor of the synchronization of two indices, either when these two indices pre-exist or when one of them is constructed dynamically. In addition, the STT algorithm appears to be better than the SGS one. The fact deserves some comments because this is a situation where the SGS is really optimal: since both datasets have the same size *and* the same partitioning function, there is an exact matching between pairs of cells during the scan. Each page is thus exactly read once. Despite this advantage, the grid suffers from its large size compared with the R-tree (see Tables 1 and 2). Observe also that the dynamic R*-tree competes with SGC, due to the fast construction of the packed R-tree and to the efficiency of the STT algorithm.

The simple scan-and-index strategy seems to be far more costly than the other ones, because of the random seeks which result in several fetches of the

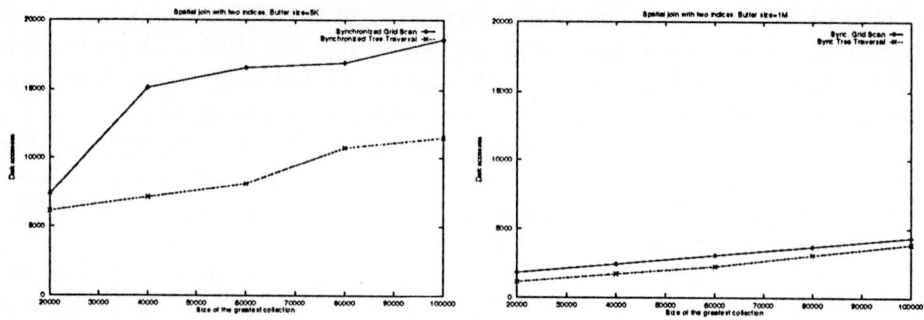

Fig. 4. A comparison of STT and SGS with various buffer sizes (5K and 1M)

same page. Observe however that the result is in that case a set of pairs (*object*, *oid*): therefore half the job which consists in fetching objects on disk for the subsequent refinement step is already done.

Fig. 4 shows another experiment involving only SGS and STT. The join involves a first index (grid or R*-tree) built on a *biotopes* dataset with constant size 20 000, and a second one built on the *cities* datasets with sizes varying from 20 000 to 100 000. In addition the experiments are made with two quite different buffer sizes, respectively 5K and 1M. The 5K buffer entails a lot of buffer misses and a somehow erratic behavior of both algorithms. The buffer of 1M smoothes the curves which are now perfectly linear. Still the STT algorithm appears to be better.

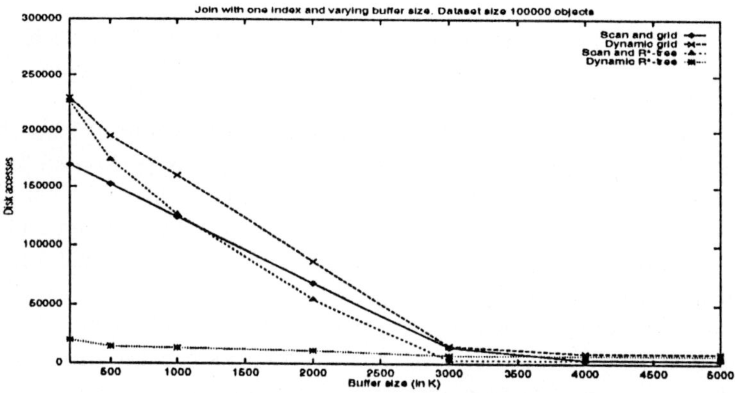

Fig. 5. A comparison of join strategies with varying buffer size

If one keeps these four algorithms and try to evaluate their robustness with respect to variations of the buffer size, one obtains the results of Fig. 5 which once more exhibit a better behavior of R-tree-based algorithms. This experiment involves two datasets of equal sizes (biotopes and cities, population 100 000) and a buffer whose size vary from 200K to 5M. The dynamic R-tree algorithm takes quickly advantage of the buffer size increase and is steadily better than the other strategies. For large buffer sizes, the whole index fit in memory and the query processing no longer encouters buffer misses: the cost becomes constant, with a small advantage remaining for R-trees whose size is smaller than the size of the equivalent grid.

In summary, the algorithms which rely on R-trees seem to behave better than those which use the grid partitioning. This seems surprising at first glance since some recent works [7, 8] advocate the partitioning scheme as superior to the other approaches. However these papers mostly focused on handling join processing whith no pre-existing index. Moreover, the implementation of join algorithms in [7] for instance rely on algorithmic and I/O optimisations (sequential reads for multiple pages for instance) which were deliberately omitted in our platform.

We plan to optimize the construction of the grid in order to improve the behavior of the dynamic partitioning algorithm. Forthcoming experiments should also involve fetching the objects themselves on disk, so as to obtain fully comparable results between the scan-and-index strategy and the other ones.

5 Conclusion and future work

We have described in this paper an integrated platform which aims at providing a rich and consistent set of tools to evaluate and compare the relative performances of multidimensional data strutures and algorithms. In its current setting, the platform is strongly focused on spatial access methods and on spatial join algorithms: this already allows a performance comparison of some basic spatial join strategies, as illustrated in the previous section.

We proceed currently with the integration of our work with others contributions in the context of the CHOROCHRONOS project. Future work will mainly consist in introducing new data structures and algorithms in order to extend the scope of the experiments to emerging multidimensional applications such as temporal and spatio-temporal databases.

Acknowledgments

The authors wish to warmly thank Michel Scholl for his careful reading and valuable comments. We are also indebted to Apostolos Papadopoulos for many fruitful discussions on spatial benchmarking.

References

1. G. Graefe. Query evaluation techniques for large databases. *ACM Computing Surveys*, 25(2):73–170, 1993.
2. R.H. Güting. An Introduction to Spatial Database Systems. *The VLDB Journal*, 3(4), 1994.

3. M. Scholl and A. Voisard, editors. *Proc. Intl. Symp. on Large Spatial Databases (SSD).* LNCS No. 1262. Springer-Verlag, 1997.
4. J. Orenstein and F. Manola. PROBE: Spatial Data Modeling and Query Processing in an Image Database Application. *IEEE Transactions on Software Engineering*, 14(5):611–628, 1988.
5. J. A. Orenstein. Redundancy in Spatial Databases. In *Proc. ACM SIGMOD Symp. on the Management of Data*, 1989.
6. T. Brinkhoff, H.-P. Kriegel, and B. Seeger. Efficient Processing of Spatial Joins Using R-Trees. In *Proc. ACM SIGMOD Symp. on the Management of Data*, 1993.
7. M.-L. Lo and C.V. Ravishankar. Spatial Hash-Joins. In *Proc. ACM SIGMOD Symp. on the Management of Data*, pages 247–258, 1996.
8. J.M. Patel and D. J. DeWitt. Partition Based Spatial-Merge Join. In *Proc. ACM SIGMOD Symp. on the Management of Data*, pages 259–270, 1996.
9. J. Nievergelt, H. Hinterger, and K.C. Sevcik. The Grid File: An Adaptable Symmetric Multikey File Structure. *ACM Transactions on Database Systems*, 9(1):38–71, 1984.
10. A. Guttman. R-trees : A Dynamic Index Structure for Spatial Searching. In *Proc. ACM SIGMOD Intl. Symp. on the Management of Data*, pages 45–57, 1984.
11. N. Beckmann, H.P. Kriegel, R. Schneider, and B. Seeger. The R*tree : An Efficient and Robust Access Method for Points and Rectangles. In *Proc. ACM SIGMOD Intl. Symp. on the Management of Data*, pages 322–331, 1990.
12. T. Sellis, N. Roussopoulos, and C. Faloutsos. The R+Tree: A Dynamic Index for Multi-Dimensional Objects. In *Proc. Intl. Conf. on Very Large Data Bases (VLDB)*, pages 507–518, 1987.
13. O. Günther. Efficient Computation of Spatial Joins. In *Proc. IEEE Intl. Conf. on Data Engineering*, pages 50–59, 1993.
14. L. Becker, K. Hinrichs, and U. Finke. A New Algorithm for Computing Joins with Grid Files. In *Proc. IEEE Intl. Conf. on Data Engineering*, 1993.
15. M. Scholl, G. Grangeret, and X. Rehse. Point and window queries with linear spatial indices: An evaluation with O_2. *Communication of the ACM*, 19–.
16. E.G. Hoel and H. Samet. Benchmarking Spatial Join Operations with Spatial Output. In *Proc. of Intl. Conf. on Very Large Data Bases*, 1995.
17. Y.-W. Huang, N. Jing, and E.A. Rudensteiner. Spatial Joins Using R-trees: Breadth-first Traversal with Global Optimizations. In *Proc. of Intl. Conf. on Very Large Data Bases*, 1997.
18. M.-L. Lo and C.V. Ravishankar. Spatial Joins Using Seeded-Trees. In *Proc. ACM SIGMOD Symp. on the Management of Data*, 1994.
19. N. Rossopoulos and D. Leifker. Direct Spatial Search on Pictorial Databases Using Packed R-Trees. In *Proc. ACM SIGMOD Symp. on the Management of Data*, 1985.
20. S. Leutenegger, J. Edgington, and M. Lopez. STR: A Simple and Efficient Algorithm for R-Tree. In *Proc. IEEE Intl. Conf. on Data Engineering (ICDE)*, pages 497–507, 1996.
21. O. Gunther, V. Oria, P. Picouet, J.-M. Saglio, and M. Scholl. Benchmarking Spatial Joins *À La Carte*. In *Intl. Conf. on Scientific and Statistical Databases (SSDBM'98)*, 1998.
22. D. Kerr, A.N. Papadopoulos, and Y. Manolopoulos. The BASIS System: a Benchmarking Approach for Spatial Index Structures. In *Submitted to publication*, 1998.
23. US Bureau of The Census. Tiger Line files, Technical Documentation, 1995.

On Updating the Data Warehouse from Multiple Data Sources

Kouba Zdeněk, Matoušek Kamil, Mikšovský Petr, Štěpánková Olga

The Gerstner Laboratory for Intelligent Decision Making and Control
Faculty of Electrical Engineering
Czech Technical University
Technická 2
166 27 Prague 6
Czech Republic
Phone: +420 2 24357379, Fax: +420 2 24357224,
e-mail: {kouba, matousek, xmiksovs, step}@labe.felk.cvut.cz

Abstract. The paper discusses various problems related to feeding the data warehouse with data originated in various data sources. The main focus is concentrated on describing and handling of uncertainty, which comes from merging imperfect data sources. Uncertainty measures and their implementation approaches are suggested.

1 Introduction

The data warehouse problem area is explored quite well on the levels of data presentation and aggregated data storage, while the data warehouse updating unfortunately lays behind. No real data warehouse can do without its input data. An experienced knowledge engineer - data analyst should be able to find the relationships in operational data sources and to transform them into the data warehouse structure. However, lot of his work is repeated case by case, and so it seems to be adequate to suggest some automation of this process. Moreover, data warehouses are very often built in (database) environment, which cannot be accessed by a common user. He has to ask the vendor company to develop (not cheaply) the entire system. If occasionally only partial changes in the structure or in other parameters of some data sources are made, it is necessary to ask the professionals again.

Our interest is focused on a general approach to the problem - we try to unify the entire process of data warehouse design and updating. A brief analysis of current problems of data warehouses can be found in [1].

The model case described later is artificial and has been constructed just to enable the reader to understand the motivation of the research. Nevertheless, the authors tried to construct the model case in a realistic way. Therefore its artificial character consists rather in non-realistic cumulating of problems in one model case than in dealing with artificially constructed problems.

Let us imagine a pharmaceutical company (producer) operating on an international market. It sales its products through a network of distributing companies (distributors). The distributor has its own network of dealers selling products of various producers.

The producer needs to know the sale amount of particular products in various geographical areas in given periods to modify its commercial policy. Let us suppose that the producer has a data warehouse and the distributors provide him with appropriate data in proper time periods.

The cardinality of the relationship between the producer and the distributor entity sets is "many to many". The distributor's data model must be compliant with requirements of all his partners - producers. That is why the producer can not prescribe the data model of the distributor's operational (transaction processing) database.

We can imagine each distributor as a data source. The producer's data warehouse will be kept up-to-date by incorporating data from data sources each time the particular data source issues a new batch of data.

2 Problems of Updating

By data warehouse updating we mean a periodical data gathering, transformation and its addition into a data warehouse. It consists of data extraction, data transformation, data consolidation and data cleaning phases. In the present contribution, we discuss some problems of this process and we suggest their solution.

2.1 Data Extraction

The task of data extraction is to acquire „fresh" data from the data sources. Basic approaches according to [2] are following:

1. The application, which uses the data source, is modified in order to be able to send the updates into the data warehouse.
2. The relevant changes are searched for in system log files. These files are used for recovery option, so this approach needn't demand any changes in the user application.
3. The changes are derived comparing current view of the data source with the previous one. In literature, this problem is called „snapshot differential problem". Detailed analysis of this approach and suggested algorithms for its implementation can be found in [2].

2.2 Data Transformation

In general there exist two basic transformation conflicts: missing data and redundant data. When less or more data than necessary is available quite similar conflicts arise. In fact, the resulting value is uncertain.

2.2.1 Missing Data

The missing data problem appears, first, if in certain moment of data request some of the required data is not available in a given data source. Secondly, such a situation is also formed, when data in different data sources is available in different moments and some of this data must be necessarily presented sooner than it becomes available. The "moments" here are meant macroscopic relatively to the data warehouse updating intervals. Also the data transformation supervisor, i.e. a person or some automatic checking mechanism, can decide to invalidate some of the data. In these cases, according to the circumstances, one of the following options can be chosen:

- Find the data in another data source
- Use the data available in current moment for calculating the missing values
- Approximate the missing values using interpolations/extrapolations from data, which is available in data warehouse.

For instance following the motivation example, the distributor's computer has broken down, which causes that data from this distributor is not available in time for updating the data warehouse. In this case there is no possibility to find the data in another data source. Neither the data warehouse itself can yield the requested data. The only the last options

2.2.2 Redundant Data

If, in certain moment of data request, some of the data is available concurrently in more data sources and its values are distinct, it is necessary to decide what value will be used for the respective data warehouse update. The possible solutions of this problem are following:

- Introduce a priority of data sources, which will provide a choice of the value from a preferred data source, in which case other data sources will not be reflected
- Discover the same meaning of differently represented data and transform it into a standard form
- Calculate the value from the data in available data sources, e.g. an average of the values
- Previous methods can be combined with consistency check with respect to other data. This can result in confirmation of only some of the concurrent values and so reducing redundancy.
- In addition, some measure for evaluating our belief in given data or in given data sources, respectively, can be introduced and exploited to calculate a more exact value.

3 Data Approximations

In order to provide the data warehouse with the data, which is not available in data sources, it is often necessary to extrapolate or interpolate from the data, which is available in data sources and in the data warehouse itself. Let us note here that we cannot rely on the availability of historical data in operational data sources.

If approximated data is used for data warehouse updating, it is meaningful to attach this data with a credibility value. Then the user can be provided with calculated information about the total credibility of the data just being presented.

If data is not available during several periods of data updating, it is often suitable to revalidate the approximate data depending on new data – new knowledge - available. It means to replace the value in data warehouse and the value of its credibility measure might also be changed.

3.1 Credibility Measures

3.1.1 AM - Approximation Measure

For exact data, i.e. the one coming directly from the data source or being exactly calculated, the *AM* is zero. For the approximate data the *AM* measure takes value of one.

When processing a query, we determine the resulting approximation measure according to:

$$AM = \frac{O}{C} \tag{1}$$

where O is the number of values approximated and C is the total number of values, that participated in forming the query response. C is always positive, so the value of *AM* remains between zero and one.

An advantage of this measure resides in its applicability to any data type.

When approximating the facts from the data warehouse fact table, it makes sense to consider only the data types, to which some of the aggregation functions can be applied. To these data types, following measures are applicable, too.

3.1.2 RAM - Relative Approximation Measure

To introduce a relative approximation measure, we are motivated by our intention to consider the influence of the magnitude of the approximate values on a value, which is derived by their aggregation with some other data. For individual exact value, i.e. the one directly coming from a data source or the one being exactly calculated, *RAM* is zero again. Similarly, for an approximate value, *RAM* is one. The difference between *RAM* and *AM* appears, when calculating *RAM* value from more *RAM* values. For continuation, we need to distinguish among the data types and the aggregation types.

E. g. for SUM, AVG, MAX and MIN functions, we can state the following rule:

$$RAM = \frac{F(O)}{F(C)}, \quad F \in \{SUM, AVG, MAX, MIN\} \tag{2}$$

where O represents a vector of absolute values of approximated data, while C is a vector of absolute values of all the data, which participates in the query response, and F is the aggregation function being used.

The COUNT function has different characteristics than previous functions and respective derivation rule must be different. We exactly know the number of values, i.e. RAM equals zero, if the COUNT expression is not constrained by the values in the fact table while aggregating. Otherwise we could e.g. form a query to the number of facts with a certain value, which can be based on approximate sub-data. Then RAM is positive.

C is always positive:

$$C \geq 0 \quad \rightarrow \quad RAM \in \langle 0;1 \rangle \tag{3}$$

As a derivation rule, an exponential function can be also used:

$$RAM1 = e^{\frac{F(O)}{F(C)}}, \quad F \in \{SUM, AVG, MAX, MIN\} \tag{4}$$

3.1.3 B - Belief in Data

$$B \in \langle 0;1 \rangle \tag{5}$$

The advantage of using the measure of belief is the possibility of introducing subjectivity in data transformation, its calculation can demand more effort and more disk space, however. The total belief of a derived value must be calculated similarly as in probabilistic approach; it is closely related to the rule contributions merging problem in expert systems.

If the data is independent, we can use the rule, by which we calculate the product of the belief of all uncertain data:

$$B = \prod_j B(C_j) = \prod_i B(O_i) \tag{6}$$

3.2 Credibility Representation

Data warehouse metadata should contain the credibility model of the data. Generally it can be stored on the level of sub-cubes of data warehouse. To achieve fast operations and calculations using the credibility measure, convenient "cube" algebra can be used.

3.3 Data Checking

Data entering the data warehouse can be to a certain extent co-related. This can be useful for checking its consistency. We can distinguish between two kinds of data dependency, which can be used for these checks – the data dependency and the time dependency.

4 Data Predictions

One of the data warehousing dogmas states, that in data warehouse only historical aggregated data should be stored, which is why this data is already exact and is not subject to change. Due to this reason, until now, the prediction was studied mainly in the area of data warehouse data exploitation (OLAP, data mining). From previous paragraphs it can be derived, that a part of a universal data warehouse should represent a tool for individual data credibility storing. The approximate data in its substance do not differ from the data predicted. In both cases, some credibility measure can be assigned to this data.

A useful equipment of a predictive data warehouse is also current moment tracking in time dimension, which enables to distinguish between historical data and the predictions in future.

5 Parameterized Data Forgetting

The data warehouse updating consists not only of adding „new“ historical data, but also of removing data, which, by its significance, already passed over a defined horizon and which would further only slow down the data access and consume the space in storage media. Possible approaches are:

- Defining a time horizon for older data removal
- Defining distinct time horizons for various levels of data
- More sophisticated method can be based also on finding less used data, e.g. track the query frequency and the level of details of respective responses

Note: In this paragraph we mention data „removal“, which means data deleting or back up. The important fact is that this data does not remain in the data warehouse itself any longer.

6 Agent-Based Implementation

The agent approach is based on interconnection of two parts (see the figure below). The *Real data* part (represented by the data cube) contains only the real data and the data pump updates it. The *Uncertain data* part consists of agents and their control engine. The agents represent uncertain data that has been calculated.

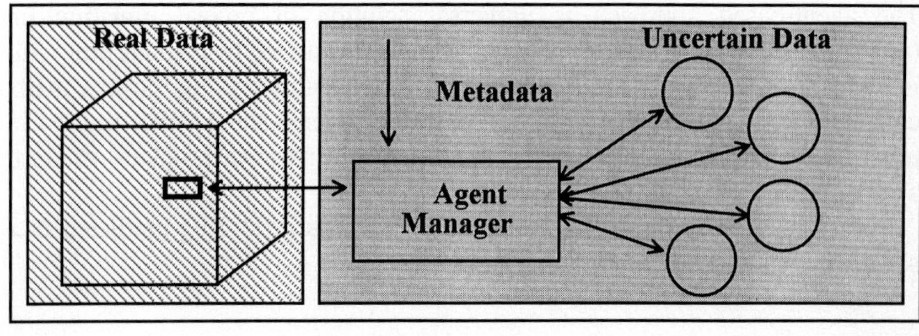

Fig. 1. Agent-based implementation.

6.1 Approach Description

The solution extends the aggregation processes in OLAP by the uncertain data calculation. There are two types of uncertainty handling:

- *Long time uncertainty* - During updating process the OLAP pre-calculates aggregations. If real data is missing the OLAP contacts Agent Manager for calculating a substitute. Agent Manager looks for an existing agent, which corresponds to the request. If there is not such an agent the new one is created. The creation of the agent and calculation of uncertain data is always driven by metadata. Because the pre-calculated aggregations remain in OLAP at least until the next update, the agent should not be destroyed. When the next updating process occurs the Agent Manager is called for updating existing agents. Agents are updated or replaced by the real value.
- *Temporary uncertainty* - If a user invokes an ad-hoc query on some sub-cube where the data is missing the Agent Manager creates a temporary agent with limited live time.

While long time uncertainty agents are usually generated during the transformation process, the temporary uncertainty agents are created as consequences of some ad-hoc queries.

The solution is based on use of the credibility as a measure of data quality. In this sense the credibility is the key parameter to judge the correctness of results.

6.2 Features

The agent-based approach is universal solution of crucial updating problems (missing data, redundant data). Each agent is represented by a small program, which is specialized for one solution of the problem. It allows using various methods for calculating and judging the uncertain data. The agents should have unified interface to allow user to create his custom agent. If some unknown problem occurs the new agent type can be developed to solve it.

As it is shown on the figure the approach can ensure storing predicted data in the same data warehouse with the real data.

7 Summary

The paper discussed the problems arising when updating the data warehouse with data coming from various data sources. It showed that some means for uncertainty handling were needed. Several useful uncertainty measures were proposed. We presented the new ideas of data forgetting and data recalling. We also presented an agent approach to the implementation of a data warehouse with incorporated uncertainty description.

The further research should be concentrated on several directions: first we need to confirm by the implementation the efficiency of credibility measures being presented. Secondly, we will explore in a detailed way the implementation approaches. Particularly, the focus will be oriented on the agent-based approach, because of its promising features.

To practically implement the concepts stated in the text, the new functionality must be contained in data warehouse structure description, i.e. in the metadata. It intermediates the necessary information to OLAP engine, which must be able to exploit it, consequently.

Especially credibility measure must be represented and it should be stored with maximal savings, but it should be also quickly accessible, not to slow down common functions of data warehouse OLAP kernel too much. The credibility values can be stored generally on the level of data warehouse sub-cubes. OLAP should be able to derive the total credibility of the answers of the queries and to provide the user with an option to chose the minimal acceptable credibility value of presented responses.

Defined horizons of data forgetting should also take part in metadata of data transformation. Data integrator must be controlled by this metadata.

8 Acknowledgment

The paper introduces results of a research done by closely co-operating teams of the Gerstner Lab for Intelligent Control and Decision-Making at the Czech Technical University of Prague and the Institute of Software Technology at the Vienna University of Technology. This research work is funded by the research project of the Fund for University Development of Czech Ministry of Education, Youth and Sport, FRVŠ no. 1245 – Data Warehouses.

References

1. Matoušek, K., Mikšovský, P.: Current Problems of Data Warehouses, Proc. of Workshop '98, 1998, CTU Prague
2. Labio, W. J., Garcia-Molina, H.: Efficient Snapshot Differential Algorithms for Data Warehousing
3. Labio, W. J., Quass, D., Adelberg, B.: Physical Database Design for Data Warehouses
4. Kurz, A., Tjoa, A M.: Data Warehousing within Intranet: Prototype of a Web-based Executive Information System. Proc. of the 8th Int. Workshop on Database and Expert Systems Application, 1997, IEEE Computer Press
5. Kirkgoeze, R., Katic, N., Stolba, M., Tjoa, A M.: A Security Concept for OLAP. Proc. of the 8th Int. Workshop on Database and Expert Systems Application, 1997, IEEE Computer Press
6. Mařik, V., Štěpánková, O., Lažanský, J., (eds): Artificial Intelligence I.,II. (in Czech), 1993, 1997, Academia, Prague
7. Matoušek, K., Mikšovský, P.: Problems of Data Warehouse Updating, Proc. of Poster '98, 1998, CTU Prague

Concurrent Warehouse Maintenance Without Compromising Session Consistency

Michael Teschke, Achim Ulbrich

[1]University of Erlangen-Nuremberg, Dep. of Database Systems, Martensstr. 3, D-91058 Erlangen, Germany
{teschke, ulbrich}@informatik.uni-erlangen.de

Abstract. To achieve acceptable query response times in data warehouse environments, the data have to be pre-aggregated according to the need of the applications and stored redundantly. These materialized views must be kept up to date, to assure their usability. In this paper we present an algorithm which improves the maintenance of materialized views in two ways. In the first place, the maintenance process is accelerated by supporting different maintenance strategies for individual views. Thus, views which do not need to be up to date can be maintained in a deferred or periodical way. In the second place, the algorithm provides *session consistency*, assuring that during an OLAP-session the underlying data do not change from the user's point of view. The algorithm facilitates high flexibility and performance of view maintenance without compromising session consistency.

1 Motivation

Data warehousing has become a major research issue of the database community in the last years [3]. To improve query performance in data warehouses (DWH) with a typically very high data volume, two major aspects must be considered. First, raw data access is accelerated by recently developed index and join techniques like bitwise join-indexing [10]. Second, pre-aggregation of the raw data according to the need of the applications and their redundant storing in the warehouse offers a high potential of performance increase for OLAP queries [8]. Another term for such a pre-aggregate is *materialized view* (MV), which is used throughout this paper (or just *view*). To remain useful for OLAP-queries however, MVs must incorporate updates of the source databases of the data warehouse eventually. In commercial systems, this is typically achieved by taking the warehouse off-line, maintaining the MVs and going on-line again. If it is unacceptable to take the warehouse off-line (e.g. when 24h availability is needed), the maintenance must take place concurrently to user queries. This may lead to data inconsistencies, if no strategies for concurrent access are applied.

Common approaches assume that all the changes of the data sources (*updates*) have to be incorporated in one single task. They do not take into account that most users do not need the latest data (relative to the warehouse), but would accept *user defined consistency*. For example, a user could specify a maximum difference he wants to tolerate between the most current data in the warehouse (the warehouse base relations, which contain the mirrored sources) and the views used to generate the query results. Or a user could state that the views he wants to access must not be older than three versions (relative to source updates propagated to the warehouse). Thus, when accessing a view within the user's tolerance, no deferred view maintenance has to be done. As a consequence, the maintenance granularity is no longer the warehouse itself but the maintenance of single views is possible. The time consuming process of warehouse maintenance occurring in certain intervals can be divided according to user queries. Traditional algorithms can not be adopted, because these expect the warehouse to be maintained as a whole. When providing user defined consistency and a finer granularity of warehouse maintenance, a new consistency aspect, the *session consistency*, has to be considered.

Example 1: The Problem of Session Consistency

Imagine a warehouse with a hierarchy of materialized views (Figure 1). Views MV_1 and MV_2 cover the sales figures of products for north and south Germany, respectively. On top of these, MV_3 is defined to contain the sales figures grouped by product groups for Germany. In a typical OLAP-session, a user could first examine the nation-wide sales figures and then drill-down to regional figures if he wants to investigate certain figures in more detail. Our example user is concerned about his data being consistent, but last weeks' figures are actual enough for him. Session consistency in this case comprises two aspects: All updates that affect both source views of MV_3 must be incorporated in both views or none of them. [14] refer to this problem as the *multiple view consistency problem*. The second aspect occurs, if the warehouse is maintained at relation level: if the views are updated, *after* the user has read MV_3, but *before* he drills down to views MV_1 and MV_2, the detailed data he investigates does not correspond to the aggregated data of MV_3 which can lead to incorrect results. Note that in our example the user does not require his data to reflect the latest data of the warehouse. It would be sufficient for him to read the old sales figures of MV_1 and MV_2, which would be consistent with MV_3.

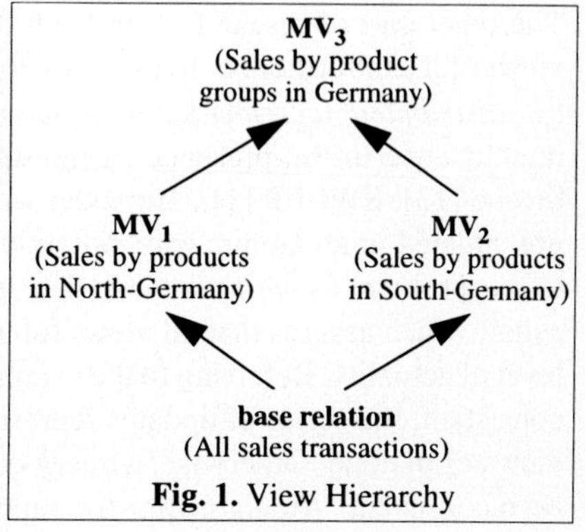

Fig. 1. View Hierarchy

As Example 1 and the discussion above have shown, an algorithm is required which

- allows different maintenance strategies for the data in the warehouse and
- prevents the user from seeing any inconsistent data within his user session, unless the user explicitly allows that for performance reasons.

The remainder of this paper is structured as follows. At first, we discuss related work dealing with consistency of materialized views in the warehouse context. We will show that, to the best of our knowledge, no algorithm provides the properties postulated above. In Section 3, the basic architecture and assumptions of our approach are discussed, before the algorithm is detailed in Section 4. A short summary and possible extensions of our approach conclude the paper.

2 Related Work

A series of algorithms concerning the maintenance of materialized views have recently been published. They can be divided into two classes. The first group of approaches provides algorithms for efficient update of single views, e.g. making them self-maintainable or using auxiliary views to avoid base relation access [5][11]. Another way to minimize the down-time during the view update is to prepare this step as far as possible. [9] therefore separate the update into a *propagation step* where the effects of an update for each view are calculated and a *refresh step* where the actual view update takes place.

The other part of research deals with data consistency in the presence of materialized views and can further be divided into three categories. One group of approaches tackles the *distributed incremental view anomaly* and assures consistent incremental view maintenance in the presence of multiple data sources and overlapping updates. (e.g. Strobe [13], SWEEP [1]). But even when assuring this level of consistency, views are not updated in an atomic way, possibly leaving views mutually inconsistent. [14] refer to this problem as *multiple view consistency* (Example 1). The authors present an algorithm, which assures that all views referenced by a user in a single query have the same level of actuality. Referring to the example of Figure 1, MV_1 and MV_2 are multiple view consistent, if a series of updates representing yesterday's sales are incorporated in both views or in none. Otherwise, a query comparing north with south German sales, would be inconsistent. An algorithm for supporting multiple view maintenance strategies in the DWH is presented in [4]. Views that have to be mutually consistent are grouped together (*viewgroups*) and maintained as a whole. Although this facilitates a higher flexibility of view maintenance, still session consistency is not supported.

The third category of papers dealing with consistency tries to assure *session consistency*, which is the main focus of this paper. Long running sessions of OLAP-queries (called *reader-sessions* in [6]) must be coordinated with *update sessions* to provide session consistency. Taking the whole data warehouse off-line for view maintenance has been shown to be unacceptable in Section 1. [12] propose a two-version no-locking algorithm (2VNL). When using two versions for each view, it is possible for a reader session to continue reading a view while the update session is already writing the new version of the view. But if the reader sessions are too long or if update sessions occur frequently, two versions are not enough and user sessions must be aborted or accept inconsistent data. Although [12] claim their algorithm to be extendable to n-versions, this approach is not satisfying for two reasons. On the one hand, it is impossible to state the sufficient number of versions in advance. On the other hand, providing a very high number of versions is generating space overhead. In the nVNL algorithm, the relational schemes are statically extended to contain all versions in a single tuple. As a consequence, space is wasted if not all versions are needed for all tuples. A general problem of the algorithms is that they only support the whole warehouse as maintenance and consistency granularity and are unable to support individual maintenance strategies.

Multi-version algorithms handle versioning by providing a tuple for each version [2]. Although they enable the warehouse to store as many versions as necessary, session consistency can only be guaranteed if each view is updated in an immediate manner. If individual update strategies for views or groups of views are to be applied, still session inconsistency can occur. Imagine that MV_1 in Figure 1 is maintained immediately whereas MV_2 is maintained periodically. A user reading the data of MV_1 (which has the highest level of actuality due to immediate refresh), will still see inconsistent data if he accesses MV_2, because here updates are not applied until refresh time has come.

In the next two sections, we will present our approach of providing session consistency, even in the presence of multiple view maintenance policies. In Section 3 the general idea and the assumptions of our approach are sketched. A more detailed discussion and some implementation issues follow in Section 4.

3 The DYVER Approach

The DYVER approach (*DYnamic VERsioning in data warehouses with individual maintenance strategies*) combines the advantages of viewgroups and multi-version concurrency control. We propose an algorithm that:

- allows readers and maintenance transactions to run concurrently without blocking,
- allows readers to see a consistent database state throughout an entire session, and
- allows to maintain every materialized view in the DWH individually.

With this algorithm it is possible to make a DWH available for analysis 24 hours a day. The algorithm is a multi-version concurrency control algorithm, based on the multi-version mixed method in [2]. The major extension of our algorithm is the possibility to generate older versions of tuples if necessary to assure session consistency.

As explained above, for session consistency the same state of the MVs has to be provided for analysis during a user session. As the queries a user will submit are typically unknown at the beginning of an OLAP-session, the whole DWH has to be in a consistent state during an active session. Furthermore, our algorithm allows active user sessions while maintaining the DWH. Thus, maintenance transactions and queries can run concurrently. Instead of changing the data of the MVs, the maintenance transactions generate new versions of the views. The read-only transactions use time-stamps to access the required versions. Instead of using a static number of available versions, the maintenance transactions produce new versions only when they are needed. The DYVER algorithm checks every accessed MV, whether the required version exists. If not, the requested version will be created. Note that this could be an older version of a view than the most current one.

Individual maintenance policies enable the system to maintain only the necessary data in the DWH instead of maintaining the whole DWH. Maintenance on such a fine granularity can be split into multiple active maintenance transactions. To coordinate these potentially conflicting maintenance transactions, we use some sort of blocking to order conflicting maintenance transactions (e.g. which would generate the same version of the same view). So the DYVER algorithm leads to a better maintenance performance and availability for readers without compromising session consistency.

As older versions should be reproducible, even the maintenance modifications have to be signed with time-stamps. All modifications that lead to a certain state of a MV get the same time-stamp. After maintaining a MV, the new version of the view gets the time-stamp of the modifications. At the beginning of a session the reading time-stamp is calculated from the degree of actuality a user demands. During a reader session the algorithm checks every requested relation, whether a version with the reading time-stamp exists. If this version exists, access is allowed. Otherwise a new version with this time-stamp has to be produced.

In order to understand the assignment of time-stamps to modifications, the underlying data warehouse model has to be explained. The main aspects of our warehouse model are sketched in Figure 2. One basic assumption is to store a layer of self-maintainable relations in the DWH, called *base relations*. They are also MVs and can be thought of as the cleaned and filtered source data required in the DWH.

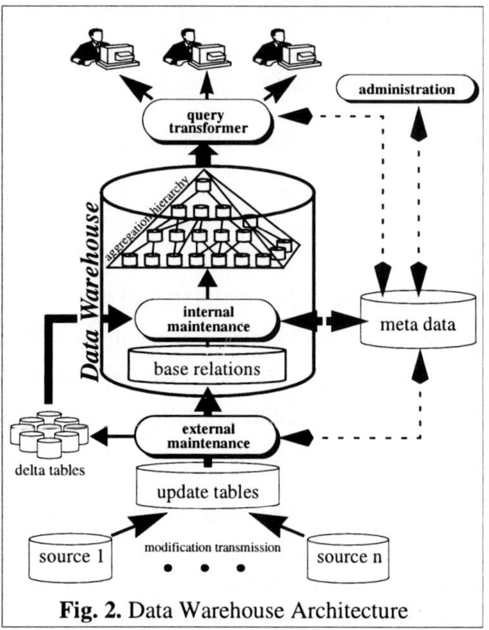

Fig. 2. Data Warehouse Architecture

All the other MVs base on these relations and can be maintained without querying the sources. This leads to a distinction between two kinds of maintenance. *External maintenance* (EM) stands for the maintenance process between the sources and the warehouse. *Internal maintenance* (IM) describes the process of maintaining the pre-aggregations in the warehouse. As changes to the source data in most cases are transmitted periodically to the warehouse, EM can only be done periodically, too. After the transmission, the modifications are stored in *update tables* to separate the moment of transmission from the moment of maintenance. Instead of maintaining the whole DWH, only the relevant data for running user queries have to be maintained. Base relations are used as a consistent layer for the other MVs and are the sole relations that have to be maintained during the EM process. Beside the update tables, *delta tables* are used to store the modifications to be applied to the MVs in the DWH. For simplicity, we assume to have an extra delta table for each MV. Using delta tables, external and internal maintenance can be separated from each other and the pre-aggregations of the DWH only need to be maintained when necessary.

4 The DYVER Algorithm

In this section we present some components of the DYVER algorithm. First we explain the modification of the relation scheme to support more than one version and further data structures necessary for the algorithm. Secondly the external and internal maintenance process and the query execution are described. The garbage collection minimizing the number of versions in the DWH has to be left out due to space constraints.

4.1 Modifying the relation scheme and meta data

Each materialized view in the DWH has to be extended by two additional attributes. Let $R(P_1, P_2, ..., P_k, A_1, A_2, ..., A_n)$ be the relation scheme for a relation R. $\{P_1, P_2, ..., P_k\}$ is the set of primary key attributes. The extended scheme of R is $R(tupleSN, P_1, P_2, ..., P_k, operation, A_1, A_2, ..., A_n)$, where *tupleSN* represents the sequence number and $operation \in \{insert, update, delete\}$ records the logical operation of the modification that created this version. Note that in order to handle more than only one version of a tuple, the logical operation described is not necessarily the same as the physical operation performed by the maintenance transaction (Section 4.2).

In Section 3 we explained that for IM the modifications have to be signed with sequence numbers to generate a specific version of the table. For that reason, also the relation scheme of the delta tables has to be modified. Let $\Delta R(operation, P_1, P_2, ..., P_k, MA_1, MA_2, ..., MA_m)$ be the relation scheme of R's delta table. $operation \in \{insert, update, delete\}$ records the logical operation of the modification. $\{P_1, P_2, ..., P_k\}$ is the set of primary key attributes identifying the tuple that has to be maintained. The set of modification attributes $\{MA_1, MA_2, ..., MA_m\}$ contains the changes to the attribute values. The number of modification attributes depends on the definition of R. Normally, m is equal to n, but if the definition of R contains a join, additional attributes may be necessary. Due to space constraints we will not detail this aspect any further. To store the sequence numbers of the modifications we extend the scheme of the delta table to: $\Delta R(modificationSN, operation, P_1, P_2, ..., P_k, MA_1, MA_2, ..., MA_m)$. The additional attribute *modificationSN* records the sequence number of the modification. We assume that for every tuple in a pre-aggregation there is at most one entry in the delta relation with the same modification sequence number. A way to combine several modifications is described in Section 4.2.

```
a) SEQUENCENR(SN, time)
b) TABLEVERSION(tableID, versionSN,
                maintenanceActive)
c) SESSIONS(sessionID, readingSN)
```

Fig. 3. Meta tables

The additional relations necessary to manage the versions are depicted in Figure 3. To record all sequence numbers that are available for the readers we use the table *SEQUENCENR*. *SN* is the sequence number of the EM process that executed at the moment *time*. The attribute *time* is used to calculate a reading sequence number from the user-defined actuality requirements.

The IM process creates a new version of a table even if only a few tuples are changed. To record all existing versions of a table, the relation *TABLEVERSIONS* is used. The attribute *tableID* identifies the MVs in the DWH, whereas *versionSN* stores the sequence number of a view version. The flag $maintenanceActive = \{false, true\}$ indicates an active maintenance transaction for this version. The flag is necessary to manage concurrent IM transactions (Section 4.2.1).

To administrate the active reading sessions we introduce the relation *SESSIONS*, which contains an identification (*sessionID*) for every active session. *readingSN* records the reading sequence number for this session. To guarantee session consistency, every query has to access the versions of the relevant relations with *versionSN* = *readingSN*. As mentioned above, *readingSN* results from the user-defined actuality requirements for the session.

4.2 Maintenance

As explained in Section 3 we have to distinguish between the external and internal maintenance process. Both maintenance processes have in common that new versions of tuples have to be inserted into the maintained relations to preserve the older ones. So the logical maintenance operations in the update tables may be different from the physical operations on the tuples. For example, when the logical operation is a deletion, the tuple is not physically deleted from the database because older versions might be needed by readers. Instead a new version of the tuple is produced. To indicate that this tuple does not belong to the current version, the *operation* is set to "delete". Nevertheless the reading algorithm has to be adapted to ignore tuples with *operation=delete*.

In order to reduce the storage required for the delta relations and to speed-up maintenance, all modifications of the same tuple with the same sequence number are compressed to a single operation. Therefore, for every tuple in a pre-aggregation there is at most one modification stored in the delta relation with the same modification sequence number. For example, an insertion followed by an update on the same tuple can be replaced by a modified insertion, two different updates can be integrated to a single update transaction and an insertion followed by a deletion neutralize each other. The modification compression is used for IM as well. In this case, modifications of different maintenance processes are compressed to calculate a new version (thus possibly leaving out a version).

In the following, a maintenance transaction is depicted as *m[O, TS]*, stating that object *O* (a view or a relation) is maintained to reflect time-stamp *TS*.

4.2.1 External Maintenance

The algorithm of the EM process (sketched in Figure 4) is activated by the DWH. At the beginning of the EM the new sequence number *newSN* has to be computed from the sequence number of the last EM process. Then the modifications belonging to the same tuples in the update tables are compressed to a single logical maintenance operation (Section 4.2). Instead of changing the tuples in the base relations, a new version is generated for these tuples. The tuple sequence number (*tupleSN*) is set to the sequence number of the maintenance process and the type of the logical operation is stored in the *operation* attribute. After the base relations are maintained, the delta tables have to be filled. With the use of the modification compression we reduce the number of modifications in the delta tables. The modification sequence number (*modificationSN*) is set to the maintenance sequence number and the *operation* attribute results from the logical operation. To release the new versions of the base relations to the readers, a new tuple for every base relation with the new sequence number is added to *TABLEVERSIONS*. Finally, the new sequence number has to be stored in the *SEQUENCENR* table and the update tables are cleared.

4.2.2 Internal Maintenance

Internal maintenance is started by the system according to a special maintenance policy or implicitly by the user to guarantee session consistency and the required level of actuality. In the latter case, the sequence number of the new table version depends on the reading sequence number of the session, otherwise the sequence number of the last EM procedure is used.

Figure 5 describes the IM process to maintain a materialized view MV to the actuality level of a given maintenance sequence number (*maintenanceSN*). First it has to be checked, if the requested level of actuality can be created at all (1). Step (2) detects the latest version of the view that has to be updated. If *maintenanceSN* exists in *SEQUENCENR*, the sequence number (*lastSN*) and the status of the last version of MV with $versionSN \leq maintenanceSN$ have to be detected. The flag *maintenanceActive* is used as a semaphore to synchronize the maintenance processes. If another maintenance process is active, we wait until *maintenanceActive* = *false*. It would also be possible to select an earlier version with *maintenanceActive* = *false* and run both maintenance processes concurrently, but sequential work is more efficient because otherwise some of the modifications are considered twice. Afterwards a new tuple is inserted into *TABLEVERSIONS* to indicate the activity of the maintenance process (*maintenanceActive* = true, Step 3). If MV is not self-maintainable, its reference relations have to be accessed (4). These are the relations referenced in the view definition of MV. We have to use the version of the reference relations with *versionSN* = *maintenanceSN* to guarantee consistency. So possibly some of the reference relations have to be maintained before maintaining MV. The major work is done in step 5. The maintenance process generates a single logical maintenance operation *OP* based on all the modifications in the update tables with $lastSN < modificationSN \leq maintenanceSN$ that change the same tuple in

(1) Get the new sequence number *newSN*:
 newSN = max(*SN* in SEQUENCENR) +1;

(2) Generate the logical maintenance operations from the tuples in the update tables:
 Compress all modification operations $m[R, t]$ that modify the same tuple t in the same base relation R to a single logical maintenance operation $m[R, t']$.

(3) Maintain the base relations:
 For every $m[R, t']$ insert a new tuple t' in the base relation with *tupleSN* = *newSN* and *operation* resulting from the logical maintenance operation.

(4) Generate the modifications for the delta tables:
 For every materialized view MV in the DWH that has to be maintained because of $m[R, t']$, generate $m[MV, t]$. For all $m[MV, t]$ that change the same tuple in MV, insert a new entry in the appropriate delta table with *modificationSN* = *newSN*, *operation* and the modification attributes resulting from $m[MV, t]$.

(5) Announce the new versions:
 For every base relation insert a new tuple in TABLEVERSION with *tableID* resulting from the base relation, *versionSN* = *newSN* and *maintenanceActive* = false.

(6) Announce the new sequence number:
 Insert a new tuple in SEQUENCENR with *SN* = *newSN* and *time* = actual local time.

(7) Clear the update tables.

Fig. 4. External Maintenance

MV. The type of the operation results from the modification compression (Section 4.2). The operation sequence number (*operationSN*) is the maximum of the sequence numbers of all the summarized modifications. After computing the changes to the updated tuple a new version t' is inserted into MV with *tupleSN* = *operationSN* and *operation* is set to the logical operation type. Note that *tupleSN* is set to the maximum sequence number of all compressed modifications and not to the maintenance sequence number. For this reason it is possible that another maintenance transaction has already produced this version. So before the insertion takes place, the algorithm has to check whether the new version already exists. After generating all the new tuple versions the maintenance process is completed by updating the *TABLEVERSIONS* entry for the new version of MV to indicate that the maintenance process has finished (*maintenanceActive=false*, step 6).

4.3 Querying

During reader sessions the appropriate versions of the views have to be extracted to assure session consistency. The general idea is that the user is explicitly starting a session and all queries during the session are computed with the same version of the data. The reading sequence number results from the user-defined actuality requirements. The algorithm for the readers is straight-forward and omitted here due to space constraints.

Input: materialized view MV and the sequence number *maintenanceSN*
Output: new version of MV with the sequence number *maintenanceSN*

(1) Check *maintenanceSN*:
IF max(*SN* in SEQUENCENR) < *maintenanceSN* THEN BREAK;

(2) Get last version of MV (*lastSN*):
$lastSN = max(\{versionSN\ \textit{from TABLEVERSIONS with}\ tableID = MV\})$;
IF *maintenanceActive* = *true* THEN WAIT for *maintenanceActive* = *false*;
IF *lastSN* = *maintenanceSN* THEN BREAK;

(3) Announce maintenance activity:
INSERT(MV, *maintenanceSN*, *true*) into TABLEVERSIONS;

(4) Check self-maintainability of MV:
IF MV is not self-maintainable THEN
FOR all relations RR referenced in the view definition of MV DO $m[MV, maintenanceSN]$;

(5) Generate new versions for the changed tuples:
FOR all modifications in ΔMV with $lastSN < modificationSN \leq maintenanceSN$, that changes the same tuple t DO:
Compress the modifications to a single logical operation OP with:
$operationSN = max(\{modificationSN\ \textit{of the compressed modifications}\})$;
operationType results modification compression;
Compute the changed tuple t' from tuple t;
/* if MV is not self-maintainable the access to the reference relations of MV is needed to compute t' */
IF $(operationSN, operationType, t') \notin MV$ THEN
INSERT(*operationSN*, *operationType*, t') into MV;

(6) Finish maintenance:
UPDATE(MV, *maintenanceSN*, false) in TABLEVERSIONS;

Fig. 5. Internal Maintenance

5 Conclusion

In this paper we have presented an algorithm for providing session consistency even in the presence of concurrent maintenance transactions. The DYVER approach bases on multi-versioning, but offers the advantage to generate older versions subsequently, if this is required to assure consistency for a user's session. In addition to the consistency aspect, multiple maintenance strategies can be applied without readers blocking maintenance processes and vice versa. This facilitates high flexibility and reduces query and maintenance times at the expense of higher storage requirements.

The DYVER algorithm is currently being implemented. Based on the performance and space requirement figures from the prototype, we intend to improve the approach in two ways. First, the garbage collection mechanism is to be improved to minimize space overhead. Secondly, we hope to establish trade-off rules, stating in which cases older versions should be deleted (saving space and query time) at the risk of generating them again using the delta tables, if this is required to assure session consistency.

References

1. Agrawal, D.; Abbadi, A.; Singh, A.; Yurek, T.: Efficient View Maintenance at Data Warehouses. In: *Proc. of the ACM Int. Conf. on Management of Data*, 1997
2. Bernstein, P.; Goodman, N.: Multiversion Concurrency Control - Theory and Algorithms. In: *ACM Transactions in Database Systems*, Vol. 8, No. 4, 1983
3. Chaudhuri, S.; Dayal, U.: An Overview of Data Warehousing and OLAP-Technology. In: SIGMOD Record 26(1), 1997
4. Colby, L.; Kawaguchi, A.; Lieuwen, D.; Mumick, I.; Ross, K.: Supporting Multiple View Maintenance Policies. In: *Proc. of the ACM Int. Conf. on Management of Data*, 1997
5. Gupta, A.; Mumick, I.: Maintenance of Materialized Views: Problems, Techniques, and Applications. In: IEEE Data Engineering Bulletin, 18(2), 1995
6. Kawaguchi A.; Lieuwen D.; Mumick, I.; Quass, D.; Ross, K.: Concurrency Control Theory for Deferred Materialized Views. In: Proc. of the 6th Int. Conf. on Database Theory, 1997
7. Lamport, L.: Time, Clocks and the Ordering of Events in a Distributed System. In: *Communication of the ACM, 21(7)*, 1978
8. Lehner, W.; Ruf, T.; Teschke, M.: Improving Query Response Time in Scientific Databases using Data Aggregation - A Case Study. In: *Database and Expert Systems Applications*, 1996
9. Mumick, I.; Quass, D.; Mumick, B.: Maintenance of Data Cubes and Summary Tables in a Warehouse. In: *Proc. of the ACM Int. Conf. on Management of Data*, 1997
10. O'Neil, P.; Graefe, G.: Multi-Table Joins Through Bitmapped Join Indices, SIGMOD Record 24(3), 1995
11. Quass, D.; Gupta A.; Mumick, I.; Widom, J.: Making Views Self-Maintainable for Data Warehousing, In: *Proc. of Parallel and Distributed Information Systems*, 1996
12. Quass, D.; Widom J.: On-Line Warehouse View Maintenance. In: *Proc. of the ACM Int. Conf. on Management of Data*, 1997
13. Zhuge, Y.; Garcia-Molina, H.; Wiener, J.: The Strobe Algorithms for Multi-Source Warehouse Consistency. In: *Proc. of Parallel and Distributed Information Systems*, 1996
14. Zhuge, Y.; Wiener, J; Garcia-Molina, H.: Multiple View Consistency for Data Warehousing. In: *Proc. of the 13th Int. Conf. on Data Engineering*, 1997

Mining Flexible Multiple-Level Association Rules in All Concept Hierarchies
(Extended Abstract)

Li Shen and Hong Shen

School of Computing and Information Technology
Griffith University, Nathan, QLD4111, Australia
{L.Shen, H.Shen}@cit.gu.edu.au

Abstract. We introduce the problem of mining FML (flexible multiple-level) association rules in all concept hierarchies related to a set of user-interested database attributes, as interesting association rules among data items may occur at multiple levels of multiple relevant concept hierarchies. We present a complete classification of all FML rules and show that direct application of previous research can find only a small part of strong FML rules. We propose an efficient method to generate all strong FML rules in all concept hierarchies.

1 Introduction

Association discovery is one of the most important problems in data mining. Previous research emphasized techniques for mining association rules at a *single* concept level [1, 2, 6–8, 10]. Some works extended this paradigm to mining rules at *generalized* abstract levels [9] or at *multiple* levels [4]. However, they can only find multiple-level rules in a *fixed* concept hierarchy. Our study is motivated by the goal of mining *more flexible* multiple-level association rules in *all* concept hierarchies related to a set of user-interested attributes.

We assume that the database contains two parts: (1) an item data set I and a database relation containing the description of each item in I; (2) a transaction data set T, which consists of a set of transactions $< T_i, a >$, where T_i is a transaction identifier and $a \subseteq I$. The *support* of an itemset a ($\subseteq I$) in T, $\sigma(a/T)$, is the ratio of the number of transactions (in T) containing a to the total number of transactions in T. An *association rule* is an expression $a \Rightarrow b$, where $a, b \subseteq I$ and $a \cap b = \emptyset$. The *confidence* of $a \Rightarrow b$ in T is the ratio of $\sigma(a \cup b/T)$ to $\sigma(a/T)$. We use minsup and $\mathsf{minconf}$ to denote the user-specified minimum support and confidence respectively. An itemset a is *large* if $\sigma(a/T) \geq \mathsf{minsup}$; an association rule $a \Rightarrow b$ is *strong* if $\sigma(a \cup b/T) \geq \mathsf{minsup}$ and $\frac{\sigma(a \cup b/T)}{\sigma(a/T)} \geq \mathsf{minconf}$. The task of mining association rules is to generate all *strong* association rules.

Clearly, the above problem statement doesn't consider the possible concept hierarchies implied by the description relation of I. Since interesting associations may occur in these concept hierarchies, in this paper, we propose the problem of mining FML association rules in all concept hierarchies related to a set of user-interested database attributes and present an efficient solution for that.

2 Problem Description

Given a set of user-interested database attributes and some query, we can generate an attribute-information-encoded and task-relevant set of transactions (called *encoded transaction table*) instead of the original database, see [4] for details. Table 1(b) is an abstract example, where any item is encoded by the attribute-code relations based on Table 1(a). For example, '121' denotes an item with attribute values {apple, large, Queensland} because the first digit, '1', represents 'apple' corresponding to the first attribute *content*, the second digit, '2', represents 'large' corresponding to the second attribute *size*, and the third digit, '1', represents 'Queensland' corresponding to the third attribute *producing-area*. Our study will be based on the encoded transaction table.

Table 1. (a) Attribute-code table (left) **(b)** Encoded transaction table (right)

attribute-code	content	size	producing-area
1	apple	huge	Queensland
2	banana	large	Victoria
3	pear	big	New-South-Wales
...	...	...	...

TID	Items
T_1	{111, 121, 211, 221}
T_2	{111, 211, 323}
T_3	{111, 122, 211, 221, 413}
...	...

A concept hierarchy can be defined on a set of database attribute domains such as $D(a_1), \cdots, D(a_n)$, where, for $i \in [1, n]$, a_i denotes an attribute and $D(a_i)$ denotes the domain of a_i. The concept hierarchy is usually partially ordered according to a general-to-specific ordering. The most general concept is the null description *ANY*; whereas the most specific concepts correspond to the specific attribute values in the database. Given a set of $D(a_1), \cdots, D(a_n)$, we define a concept hierarchy H as follows: $H^n \to H^{n-1} \to \cdots \to H^0$, where $H^i = D(a_1^i) \times \cdots \times D(a_i^i)$ for $i \in [0, n]$, and $\{a_1, \cdots, a_n\} = \{a_1^n, \cdots, a_n^n\} \supset \{a_1^{n-1}, \cdots, a_{n-1}^{n-1}\} \supset \cdots \supset \emptyset$. Here, H^n represents the set of concepts at the primitive level, H^{n-1} represents the concepts at one level higher than those at H^n, etc., and H^0, the highest level hierarchy, may contain solely the most general concept *ANY*. We also use $\{a_1^n, \cdots, a_n^n\} \to \{a_1^{n-1}, \cdots, a_{n-1}^{n-1}\} \to \cdots \to \{a_1^1\}$ to denote H directly, and H^0 may be omitted here. For example, there are 6 concept hierarchies related to the attribute set {content, size, producing-area}. Based on Table 1(a), every hierarchy of them implies a concept tree like Fig. 1. For more details about concept hierarchies, see [5].

We introduce FML items to represent concepts at any level of any hierarchy. We regard $*$, called *trivial-digit*, as a special digit and insert it into the set of all digits. An FML item is defined as a sequence of digits (may include $*$), in which $*$ means that we don't care about its corresponding attribute value. For example, 12$*$, representing {apple, large, *trivial*}, means large apples. Thus, any concept at any level of any concept hierarchy can be represented by an FML item. For simplicity, any item (or itemset) mentioned later always refers to an FML item (or itemset).

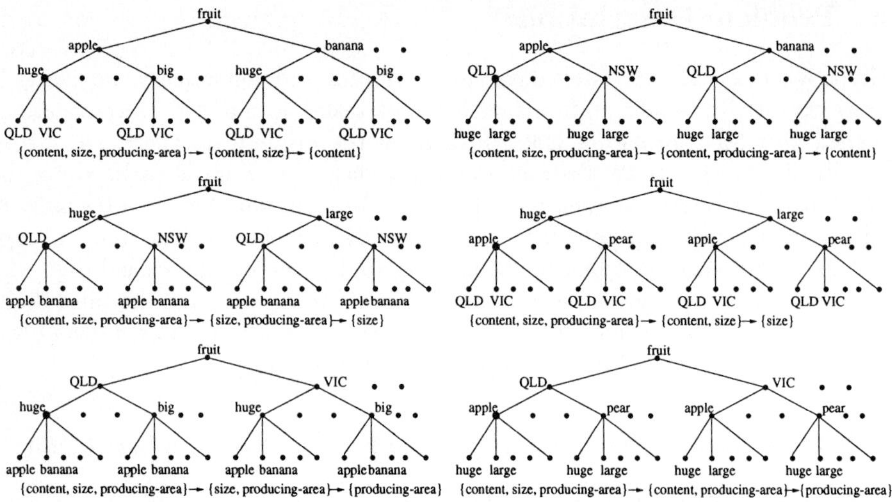

Fig. 1. Concept hierarchies related to attribute set {content, size, producing-area}

Given an item $x = x_1 x_2 \ldots x_n$, we define its *flat-set* $S_f(x) = \{(i, x_i) \mid i \in [1, n] \text{ and } x_i \neq *\}$. Given two items x and y, x is called a *generalized-item* of y if $S_f(x) \subseteq S_f(y)$, which means that x represents a higher-level concept which contains the lower-level concept represented by y. Thus, $*5*$ is a generalized-item of $35*$ due to $S_f(*5*) = \{(2,5)\} \subseteq S_f(35*) = \{(1,3),(2,5)\}$. If $S_f(x) = \emptyset$, x is called *trivial-item*, which represents the most general concept ANY.

2.1 FML Itemsets and FML Rules

Let T be an encoded transaction table, t a transaction in T, x an item, and c an itemset. We say that: (1) t *supports* x if there exists an item y in t such that x is a generalized-item of y; (2) t *supports* c if t supports every item in c. The *support* of an itemset c in T, $\sigma(c/T)$, is the ratio of the number of transactions (in T) which support c to the total number of transactions in T. Given a minsup, an itemset c is *large* if $\sigma(c/T) \geq \text{minsup}$, otherwise it is *small*.

Let $c_1 = \{12*, 23*\}$ and $c_2 = \{12*, 23*, 1**\}$. Note that $1**$ is actually a redundant item in c_2 because it can not provide any specific information due to the existence of $12*$. Every transaction supporting $12*$ must also support $1**$ and so the supports of c_1 and c_2 are always the same. As a result, c_1 and c_2 have the same meaning in our study. Given an itemset c, we define its *simplest-form* $F_s(c) = \{x \in c \mid \forall y \in c, S_f(x) \not\subset S_f(y)\}$, and its *complete-form* $F_c(c) = \{x \mid S_f(x) \subseteq S_f(y), y \in c\}$. Since an item in an itemset is redundant iff it is an generalized-item of another item in the same itemset, the following three statements about two itemsets are equivalent to each other: (1) they have the same meaning in our study, (2) their simplest-forms are the same, (3) their complete-forms are the same. Thus, itemsets with the same simplest (or complete) form will not be distinguished in our study. We usually use the simplest-form to denote an itemset. For c_1 and c_2 mentioned above, $F_s(c_1) = F_s(c_2) = \{12*, 23*\}$ and $F_c(c_1) = F_c(c_2) = \{12*, 23*, 1**, 2**, *2*, *3*, ***\}$. So we treat c_1 and c_2 as one itemset, which can be denoted by $F_s(c_1)$ or $F_s(c_2)$.

Given two itemsets c_1 and c_2, we define: (1) $c_1 \sqsubseteq c_2$ if $F_c(c_1) \subseteq F_c(c_2)$; (2) $c_1 \sqsubset c_2$ if $F_c(c_1) \subset F_c(c_2)$. We say that c_1 is a *generalized-subset* of c_2 if $c_1 \sqsubseteq c_2$, and a *proper generalized-subset* of c_2 if $c_1 \sqsubset c_2$. For example, $\{12*, *23, 2*1, *3*\}$ is a generalized-subset of $\{123, 2*1, 23*\}$. Clearly, every transaction supporting an itemset must also support all of its generalized-subsets. Hence, all generalized-subsets of a large itemset must also be large.

Direct application of previous research [1] is not suitable for our problem description because some more specific FML rules can be generated in our study. For example, assume that $\{*34, 2**\}$ is a large itemset, besides generating the rule $\{*34\} \Rightarrow \{2**\}$, it could be informative to also show that $\{*3*\} \Rightarrow \{*34, 2**\}$. To include the latter rule, we present a new description of all the desired FML rules. Let l be an itemset and $a \sqsubseteq l$. An *FML association rule* is an expression $F_s(a) \Rightarrow F_s(F_c(l) - F_c(a))$, denoted by $r(l, a)$. FML association rules are also called rules directly. Given a minsup and minconf, a rule $r(l, a)$ is *strong* if $\sigma(l/T) \geq$ minsup and $\frac{\sigma(l/T)}{\sigma(a/T)} \geq$ minconf, otherwise it is *weak*. The problem of mining FML association rules is to generate all *strong* FML rules, which can be decomposed into two parts: (1) finding all large FML itemsets, (2) finding all strong FML rules from all large FML itemsets.

We classify all itemsets c's into three types as follows according to whether they are associated with a single hierarchy or a single level. (1) *SHSL (Single-Hierarchy-Single-Level)*: all items in c can be confined to a fixed level of a fixed hierarchy, e.g. $\{1**, 2**\}$ and $\{111, 232\}$. (2) *SHML (Single-Hierarchy-Multiple-Level)*: all items in c can be confined to a fixed hierarchy, but not to any fixed level of the hierarchy, e.g. $\{11*, 2**\}$. (3) *MHML (Multiple-Hierarchy-Multiple-Level)*: all items in c can not be confined to any fixed hierarchy[1], e.g. $\{11*, **2\}$.

Let $r(l, a)$ be a rule. If $a \subseteq l$, $r(l, a)$ is called a *basic* rule; otherwise, it is an *extensive* rule. We classify all rules $r(l, a)$'s into five types as follows. (1) *BSHSL (Basic-SHSL)*: $r(l, a)$ is basic and l is SHSL, e.g. $\{1**\} \Rightarrow \{2**\}$ and $\{111\} \Rightarrow \{232\}$. (2) *BSHML (Basic-SHML)*: $r(l, a)$ is basic and l is SHML, e.g. $\{11*\} \Rightarrow \{2**\}$. (3) *BMHML (Basic-MHML)*: $r(l, a)$ is basic and l is MHML, e.g. $\{**2\} \Rightarrow \{11*\}$. (4) *ESHML (Extensive-SHML)*: $r(l, a)$ is extensive and l is SHSL/SHML[2], e.g. $\{1**\} \Rightarrow \{12*\}$. (5) *EMHML (Extensive-MHML)*: $r(l, a)$ is extensive and l is MHML, e.g. $\{1**, **2\} \Rightarrow \{12*\}$.

Previous studies can only generate either some strong BSHSL rules at the primitive level [1,2,6–8,10], or some strong BSHSL rules in a fixed concept hierarchy [4,9]. Han and Fu presented a discussion in [4] about some more flexible rules, however, this only covers a small part of strong BSHML rules in a fixed

[1] This statement implies that c is related to at least two different concept levels so that no Multiple-Hierarchy-Single-Level itemsets exist in this classification.

[2] Since any extensive rule is always associated with at least two concept levels, no Extensive-SHSL rules exist in this classification.

concept hierarchy. We will propose an efficient approach to generate all strong FML rules. We summarize the relevant notation in Table 2, where some concepts will be introduced later.

Table 2. Notation used in this paper

T	Encoded transaction table	$O(l)$	Set of all outcomes of l
$\sigma(c/T)$	Support of itemset c in T	$O_k(l)$	Set of all $\|k\|$-outcomes of l
$S_f(x)$	Flat-set of item x	$O^e(l)$	Set of all elementary outcomes of l
$F_s(c)$	Simplest-form of itemset c	$O^e_k(l)$	Set of all elementary $\|k\|$-outcomes of l
$F_c(c)$	Complete-form of itemset c	C_k	Set of candidate $[k]$-itemsets
$r(l,a)$	$F_s(a) \Rightarrow F_s(F_c(l) - F_c(a))$	L_k	Set of all large $[k]$-itemsets
$\hat{r}(l,o)$	$F_s(F_c(l) - o) \Rightarrow F_s(o)$	H_m	Set of candidate $\|m\|$-outcomes of l_k
$F_o(l,a)$	$F_c(l) - F_c(a)$	U_m	Set of all strong $\|m\|$-outcomes of l_k
$G_k(c)$	Set of all $[k]$-generalized-subsets of itemset c		
$V_m(a,l)$	Set of all $\|m\|$-suboutcomes of a versus l		
$E_r(a)$	Extension-result of self-extensive $[2^m - 1]$-itemset a, where $m > 1$		

3 Finding Large FML Itemsets

Given an itemset c, we call the number of elements in $F_s(c)$ its *size*, and the number of elements in $F_c(c)$ its *weight*. An itemset of size j and weight k is called a *(j)-itemset*, *$[k]$-itemset* or *$(j)[k]$-itemset*. Let c be a $(j)[k]$-itemset. We use $G_i(c)$ to indicate *the set of all $[i]$-generalized-subsets of* c, where $i \leq k$. Thus the set of all $[k-1]$-generalized-subsets of c can be generated as follows: $G_{k-1}(c) = \{F_s(F_c(c) - \{x\}) \mid x \in F_s(c)\}$, and the size of $G_{k-1}(c)$ is j. Hence, for $k \geq 1$, c is a (1)-itemset iff $|G_{k-1}(c)| = 1$. With this observation, we call a $[k-1]$-itemset a *self-extensive* if there exists a $(1)[k]$-itemset b such that $G_{k-1}(b) = \{a\}$; at the same time, we call b *the extension-result of* a. Thus, all self-extensive itemsets a's can be generated from all (1)-itemsets b's as follows: $F_c(a) = F_c(b) - F_s(b)$.

Let b be a (1)-itemset and $F_s(b) = \{x\}$. By $|F_c(b)| = |\{y \mid S_f(y) \subseteq S_f(x)\}| = 2^{|S_f(x)|}$, we have that b is a $(1)[2^{|S_f(x)|}]$-itemset. Let a be the self-extensive itemset generated by b, i.e., a is a $[2^{|S_f(x)|}-1]$-itemset such that $F_c(a) = F_c(b) - F_s(b)$. Thus, if $|S_f(x)| > 1$, there exist $y, z \in F_s(a)$ and $y \neq z$ such that $S_f(x) = S_f(y) \cup S_f(z)$. Clearly, this property can be used to generate the corresponding extension-result from any self-extensive $[2^m - 1]$-itemset, where $m > 1$. For simplicity, given a self-extensive $[2^m - 1]$-itemset a, where $m > 1$, we directly use $E_r(a)$ to denote its extension-result. For example, $E_r(\{12*, 1*3, *23\}) = \{123\}$.

Our algorithm makes multiple passes over the data. In the first pass, we count the supports of all [2]-itemsets and then select all large ones. In pass $k-1$, we start with L_{k-1}, the set of all large $[k-1]$-itemsets, and use L_{k-1} to generate C_k, a superset of all large $[k]$-itemsets. We call elements in C_k *candidate itemsets*. We count the support for these itemsets during the pass over the data. At the end of the pass, we determine which of these itemsets are actually large, and obtain L_k for the next pass. This process continues until no new large itemsets are found. Not that $L_1 = \{\{\text{trivial-item}\}\}$ because {trivial-item} is the unique [1]-itemset and supported by all transactions.

Algorithm 1. *Finding all large FML itemsets.*
Input: *(1) T, an encoded transaction table, (2)* minsup*, the minimum support.*
Output: *L, a set of all large FML itemsets.*

```
L_1 :={{trivial-item}};                                   /* σ({trivial-item}/T) = 1 */
L_2 := {a | a is a [2]-itemset and σ(a/T) ≥ minsup};      /* the first pass */
for (k := 3; L_{k-1} ≠ ∅; k++) do {                       /* pass k − 1 */
  C_k :=getcanditemset(L_{k-1});
  for each transaction t in T do {
    C_t := {c ∈ C_k | t supports c};
    for each candidate c in C_t do c.support++;
  }
  L_k := {c ∈ C_k | (σ(c/T) := c.support/|T|) ≥ minsup};
}
L := ∪_k L_k;

function getcanditemset(L_{k-1} : set of all large [k − 1]-itemsets) {
  C_t := {c | c = F_s(l_1 ∪ l_2), c is a [k]-itemset, l_1, l_2 ∈ L_{k-1}};   /* join */
  for every c ∈ C_t do if G_{k-1}(c) ⊈ L_{k-1} then delete c from C_t;      /* prune */
  if (log_2 k) is not an integer then C_k^1 := ∅;
  else C_k^1 := {E_r(l) | l is self-extensible, and l ∈ L_{k-1}};            /* self-extension */
  return C_t ∪ C_k^1;
}
```

It is obvious that the main procedure of Alg. 1 employs the idea described before. Now we focus on the function *getcanditemset*, which generates a superset of all large [k]-itemsets from L_{k-1}, the set of all large [$k-1$]-itemsets.

The key observation of our method is that all [$k-1$]-generalized-subsets of a large [k]-itemset must also be large. So a necessary condition for a candidate [k]-itemset c is $G_{k-1}(c) \subseteq L_{k-1}$. Furthermore, it is easy to see that the following two properties for $G_{k-1}(c)$ and $k \geq 3$ hold: (1) if $|G_{k-1}(c)| > 1$, then there exist $a, b \in G_{k-1}(c)$ such that $F_s(c) = F_s(a \cup b)$; (2) if $|G_{k-1}(c)| = 1$, then c is a (1)[2^m]-itemset, where $k = 2^m$, and so there exists a self-extensive [$2^m - 1$]-itemset[3] a such that $G_{k-1}(c) = \{a\}$ and $F_s(c) = F_s(E_r(a))$. For example, given [9]-itemset $\{123, *3*\}$ and [8]-itemset $\{123\}$, we have $G_8(\{123, *3*\}) = \{\{123\}, \{12*, 1*3, *23, *3*\}\}$ and $G_7(\{123\}) = \{\{12*, 1*3, *23\}\}$.

With the above observation, the function *getcanditemset* uses three steps to generate the desired result from L_{k-1}. In the *join* step, the function joins L_1^{k-1} with L_1^{k-1} to obtain a superset of $C_k - C_k^1$, where C_k^1 denotes the set of candidate (1)[k]-itemsets. The itemset $F_s(l_1 \cup l_2)$ is inserted in C_t if it is a [k]-itemset and $l_1, l_2 \in L_{k-1}$. In the *prune* step, the function deletes all itemsets $c \in C_t$ such that some [$k-1$]-generalized-subset of c is not in L_{k-1}. In the *self-extention* step,

[3] $k \geq 3$ implies $m > 1$ for $k = 2^m$.

C_k^1 is generated independently. Since only $[2^m - 1]$-itemsets can be self-extensive itemsets, where m is an integer, L_{k-1} contains self-extensive itemsets only when $\log_2 k$ is an integer. Thus, in this step, if $\log_2 k$ is an integer, the extension-result of each self-extensive itemset in L_{k-1} is inserted into C_k^1; otherwise, C_k^1 is empty. Finally, the function returns $C_t \cup C_k^1$, a superset of all large $[k]$-itemsets.

We evaluate the computation cost of Alg. 1. An algorithm for finding all large FML itemsets always needs to count supports for a set of *candidates*. Hence, its computation cost can often be denoted by $O(\sum_{c \in C}(g(c) + s(c)))$, where C is the set of all candidates, $g(c)$ is the cost for generating c as a candidate, $s(c)$ is the cost for counting the support of c. Since obtaining the support of c requires a scan of a very large data set, $s(c)$ is often much greater than $g(c)$. So the above computation cost can be simplified as $O(\sum_{c \in C} s(c))$.

A small itemset is *adjacent* if all its proper generalized-subsets are large. Thus itemsets can be divided into 3 types: (1) large, (2) small and adjacent, (3) small and not adjacent. For any itemset of Type 3, we can determine that it is small by finding out some of its small generalized-subsets. But for any itemset of Types 1 and 2, we can not determine if it is small or large unless we get its support. Hence, for completeness, the set of all candidate itemsets C must contain all Types 1 and 2 itemsets. Furthermore it is obvious that for any small $[k]$-itemset, it is adjacent iff all its $[k-1]$-generalized-subsets are large. Thus Alg. 1 generates the smallest C, which precisely consists of all Types 1 and 2 itemsets. Hence, if the method of support-counting is fixed, Alg. 1 with cost $O(\sum_{c \in C} s(c))$ is optimal for solving this problem because C contains only those necessary candidates.

4 Finding Strong FML Rules

As mentioned before, we use $r(l, a)$ to denote rule $F_s(a) \Rightarrow F_s(F_c(l) - F_c(a))$, where l is an itemset and $a \sqsubseteq l$. Now we use $F_o(l, a)$ to denote $F_c(l) - F_c(a)$, and say that $F_o(l, a)$ is an *outcome-form* of l or the *outcome-form* of $r(l, a)$. Note that $F_o(l, a)$ represents only a specific form rather than a meaningful itemset so that it is not equivalent to any other itemset whose simplest-form is $F_s(F_o(l, a))$. Outcome-forms are also called *outcomes* directly. Clearly, the corresponding relationship between rules and outcomes is one-to-one. An outcome is *strong* if it corresponds to a strong rule. Thus, all strong rules related to a large itemset can be obtained by finding all strong outcomes of this itemset.

Let l be an itemset. We use $O(l)$ to denote the set of all outcomes of l, i.e, $O(l) = \{F_o(l, a) \mid a \sqsubseteq l\}$. Thus, from $O(l)$, we can output all rules related to l: $F_s(F_c(l) - o) \Rightarrow F_s(o)$ (denoted by $\hat{r}(l, o)$), where $o \in O(l)$. Clearly, $r(l, a)$ and $\hat{r}(l, o)$ denote the same rule iff $o = F_o(l, a)$.

Let $o, \hat{o} \in O(l)$. We say that (1) o is a $|k|$-*outcome* of l if o exactly contains k elements; (2) $\hat{o}$ is a *suboutcome* of o versus l if $\hat{o} \subseteq o$. We use $O_k(l)$ to denote the set of all $|k|$-outcomes of l, use $V_m(o, l)$ to denote the set of all $|m|$-suboutcomes of o versus l. Let o be an $|m+1|$-outcome of l and $m \geq 1$. If $|V_m(o, l)| = 1$, o is called an *elementary* outcome; otherwise, o is a *nonelementary* outcome.

Let o be an elementary $|m+1|$-outcome of l. In this case, there exist $\hat{o} \in O_m(l)$ and $x \in F_c(l)$ such that $V_m(o,l) = \{\hat{o}\}$ and $\hat{o} \cup \{x\} = o$, which implies $o = \{y \in F_c(l) \mid S_f(y) \supseteq S_f(x)\}$. We use $P_u(l,x)$ to denote $\{y \in F_c(l) \mid S_f(y) \supseteq S_f(x)\}$. Thus, the set of all elementary outcomes of l, denoted by $O^e(l)$, equals $\{P_u(l,x) \mid x \in F_c(l)\}$. We also use $O^e_k(l)$ to denote the set of all elementary $|k|$-outcomes of l.

Let o be a nonelementary $|m+1|$-outcome of l. In this case, we have $|V_m(o,l)| > 1$. Furthermore, for any $o_1, o_2 \in V_m(o,l)$ such that $o_1 \neq o_2$, we have $o = o_1 \cup o_2$.

Let $r(l,a)$ and $r(l,b)$ be two rules. We say that $r(l,a)$ is an *instantiated-rule* of $r(l,b)$ if $b \sqsubseteq a$. Clearly, $b \sqsubseteq a$ implies $\sigma(b/T) \geq \sigma(a/T)$ and $\frac{\sigma(l/T)}{\sigma(a/T)} \geq \frac{\sigma(l/T)}{\sigma(b/T)}$. Hence, all instantiated-rules of a strong rule must also be strong. Let l be a large itemset, $o_1, o_2 \in O(l)$, $o_1 = F_o(l,a)$ and $o_2 = F_o(l,b)$. It is straightforward to get that (1) $F_o(l,a) \subseteq F_o(l,b)$ iff $b \sqsubseteq a$; (2) $\hat{r}(l,o_1) = r(l,a)$; and (3) $\hat{r}(l,o_2) = r(l,b)$. Therefore, $\hat{r}(l,o_1)$ is an instantiated-rule of $\hat{r}(l,o_2)$ iff $o_1 \subseteq o_2$, which implies that all suboutcomes of a strong outcome must also be strong.

This characteristic is similar to the property that all generalized-subsets of an large itemset must also be large. Hence, from a large itemset l, we first generate all strong rules with $|1|$-outcomes[4]. We then use all these strong $|1|$-outcomes and the function *getcandoutcome* described below to generate all possible strong $|2|$-outcomes of l, from which all strong rules with $|2|$-outcomes can be produced, etc. An algorithm using this idea is presented below.

Algorithm 2. *Finding all strong FML rules from all large FML itemsets.*
Input: *(1) L, a set of large FML itemsets, (2)* minconf, *the minimum confidence.*
Output: *R, a set of all strong FML rules.*

```
R := ∅;
for every large [k]-itemset l_k ∈ L, k > 2 do {
  H_1 := {{a} | a ∈ F_s(l_k)};
  R_t :=getrules(l_k, H_1);
  R := R ∪ R_t;
}

function getrules(l_k: large [k]-itemset, H_m: set of candidate |m|-outcomes of l_k) {
  R_1 := ∅;
  for every h_m ∈ H_m do {
    conf:= σ(F_s(l_k)/T) / σ(F_s(F_c(l_k) − h_m)/T);
    if (conf ≥ minconf) then insert rule F_s(F_c(l_k) − h_m) ⇒ F_s(h_m)
      with confidence=conf and support=σ(F_s(l_k)/T) into R_1;
    else delete h_m from H_m;
  }
  R_2 := ∅;
  if (k > m + 1) and H_m ≠ ∅ then {
      H_{m+1} :=getcandoutcome(l_k, H_m);
      R_2 :=getrules(l_k, H_{m+1});
```

[4] We ignore the $|0|$-outcome $\emptyset$, which only corresponds to all trivial strong rules: $F_s(l) \Rightarrow \emptyset$ for every large itemset l.

```
    }
    return R_1 ∪ R_2;
}

function getcandoutcome(l_k: [k]-itemset, U_m: set of all strong |m|-outcomes of l_k) {
    U_t := {o | o = o_1 ∪ o_2, o ∈ O_{m+1}(l_k), o_1, o_2 ∈ U_m};                    /* join */
    U_t := U_t ∪ O^e_{m+1}(l_k);                                                 /* elementary */
    for every o ∈ U_t do if V_m(o, l_k) ⊈ U_m then delete o from U_t;              /* prune */
    return U_t;
}
```

This algorithm uses every large itemset to generate the desired rules. Let l_k be the current large itemset considered by the algorithm. We use H_m to denote the set of candidate $|m|$-outcomes of l_k, which is a superset of all strong $|m|$-outcomes of l_k. Note that H_1 should exactly contain all $|1|$-outcomes of l_k so that it equals $O_1(l_k) = \{\{a\} \mid a \in F_s(l_k)\}$. Thus, it is easy to see that the main procedure and function *getrules* in Alg. 2 employ the idea described before.

Now we focus on the function *getcandoutcome*. It takes two arguments: l_k, a large $[k]$-itemset, and U_m, the set of all strong $|m|$-outcomes of l_k. It returns a superset of all strong $|m+1|$-outcomes of l_k. The key observation is that all suboutcomes of a strong outcome must also be strong. Thus a necessary condition for a candidate $|m+1|$-outcomes o is $V_m(o, l_k) \subseteq U_m$. Furthermore, as we have shown, for $m \geq 1$: (1) if $|V_m(o, l_k)| > 1$, then there exist $o_1, o_2 \in V_m(o, l_k)$ such that $o = o_1 \cup o_2$; (2) if $|V_m(o, l_k)| = 1$, then $o \in O^e_{m+1}(l_k)$. With this observation, the function *getcandoutcome* generates all elementary candidate $|m+1|$-outcomes of l_k and all nonelementary candidate $|m+1|$-outcomes of l_k respectively. In the *join* step, the function joins U_m with U_m to obtain a superset of all strong and nonelementary $|m+1|$-outcomes of l_k. The form $o_1 \cup o_2$ is inserted in U_t if it is an $|m+1|$-outcome of l_k and $o_1, o_2 \in U_m$. Next, in the *elementary* step, the function merges $O^e_{m+1}(l_k)$, the set of all elementary $|m+1|$-outcomes of l_k, into U_t to obtain a superset of all strong $|m+1|$-outcomes of l_k. Then, in the *prune* step, the function deletes all outcomes $o \in U_t$ such that some $|m|$-suboutcome of o versus l_k is not in U_m. Finally, the function returns U_t, which is a superset of all strong $|m+1|$-outcomes of l_k.

We evaluate the computation cost of Alg. 2. The computation cost of an algorithm for generating all strong FML rules from all large FML itemsets can be denoted by $O(|C|t + |C|s)$, where C is the set of all candidate rules, s is the average cost for generating one element in C, and t is the average cost for computing the confidence of one element in C. In Alg. 2, $|C| = \sum_{l \in L} |H(l)|$, where $H(l)$ is the set of all candidate outcomes of l. If we use the *hashing* technique described in [1] to search itemsets efficiently, both costs t and s can be limited. Hence, it is reasonable to take $O(|C|)$ as the main cost of Alg. 2.

A weak rule is *adjacent* if all its instantiated-rules but itself are strong rules. Thus rules can be divided into 3 types: (1) strong, (2) weak and adjacent, (3) weak and not adjacent. For any rule of Type 3, we can determine its weakness by finding out some of its weak instantiated-rules. But for any rule of Types 1 and 2, we can not determine if it is strong or weak unless we get its confidence.

Hence, for completeness, the set of all candidate rules C must contain all Types 1 and 2 itemsets. A rule is called a $|k|$-rule if its outcome is a $|k|$-outcome. Clearly, for any weak $|k|$-rule, it is adjacent iff all its $|k-1|$-instantiated-rules are large. Thus Alg. 2 generates the smallest C, which precisely consists of all Types 1 and 2 rules. So Alg. 2 with cost $O(|C|t + |C|s)$ is optimal for bounded costs t and s.

5 Conclusions

We have extended the study of mining multiple-level association rules in a fixed hierarchy to mining FML (flexible multiple-level) rules in all concept hierarchies related to a set of user-interested database attributes. We have classified all FML rules into five types and observed that the direct application of the existing algorithms can generate only a small part of strong Basic-Single-Hierarchy-Single-Level rules, which are confined in a fixed hierarchy. To generate all strong FML rules, we propose efficient algorithms for finding all large FML itemsets and for finding all strong FML rules from large itemsets respectively. Our performance study shows that the computation costs of both algorithms are near optimal.

Acknowledgments

The second author was supported by Australian Research Council (ARC) Large Grant A849602031. We thank Prof. Paul Pritchard for his useful comments.

References

1. Agrawal R., Mannila H., Srikant R., Toivonen H., Verkamo A.: Fast Discovery of Association Rules. In: Advances in Knowledge Discovery and Data Mining. AAAI/MIT Press (1996)
2. Agrawal R., Imielinski I., Swami A.: Mining Associations between Sets of Items in Massive Databases. In: Proc. of ACM SIGMOD Conf., Washington D.C. (1993)
3. Chen M., Han J., Yu P.S.: Data Mining: An Overview from Database Perspective. In: IEEE Transactions on Knowledge and Data Engineering, Vol.8, No.6 (1996)
4. Han J., Fu Y.: Discovery of Multiple-level Association Rules from Large Databases. In: Proc. of the 21st VLDB Conference, Zurich, Switzerland (1995)
5. Han J., Fu Y.: Dynamic Generation and Refinement of Concept Hierarchies for Knowledge Discovery in Databases. In: AAAI'94 Workshop on Knowledge Discovery in Databases (KDD'94), Seattle, WA (1994) 157-168
6. Park J. S., Chen M., Yu P. S.: An Effective Hash-Based Algorithm for Mining Association Rules. In: Proc. of ACM-SIGMOD Conf., San Jose, CA (1995)
7. Savasere A., Omiecinski E., Navathe S.: An Efficient Algorithm for Mining Association Rules in Large Databases. In: 21st VLDB Conf., Zurich, Switzerland (1995)
8. Srikant R., Agrawal R.: Mining Quantitative Association Rules in Large Relational Tables. In: Proc. of ACM SIGMOD Conf., Montreal, Canada (1996)
9. Srikant R., Agrawal R.: Mining Generalized Association Rules. In: Proc. of the 21st VLDB Conf., Zurich, Switzerland (1995)
10. Zaki M. J., Parthasarathy S., Li W.: A Localized Algorithm for Parallel Association Mining. In: 9th Annual ACM Symposium on Parallel Algorithms and Architectures, Newport, Rhode Island (1997)

A Framework for Temporal Data Mining

Xiaodong Chen [1] and Ilias Petrounias [2]

[1] Department of Computing & Mathematics, Manchester Metropolitan University, John Dalton Building, Manchester M1 5GD, UK
X.Chen@doc.mmu.ac.uk
[2] Department of Computation, UMIST, P.O. Box 88, Manchester M60 1QD, UK
ilias@sna.co.umist.ac.uk

Abstract. Time is an important aspect of all real world phenomena. Any systems, approaches or techniques that are concerned with information need to take into account the temporal aspect of data. Data mining refers to a set of techniques for discovering previously unknown information from existing data in large databases and therefore, the information discovered will be of limited value if its temporal aspects, i.e. validity, periodicity, are not considered. This paper presents a generic definition of temporal patterns and a framework for discovering them. An architecture for the mining of such patterns is presented along with a temporal query language for extracting them from a database. As an instance of generic patterns, temporal association rules are used as examples of the proposed approach.

1. Introduction

Over the past decades, a great amount of temporal data has been stored in different databases. Examples range from transaction databases in the health care and insurance, stock exchange and consumer goods market sectors, to scientific databases in geophysics and astronomy areas. In many application domains, temporal data are now being viewed as invaluable assets from which hidden knowledge can be derived, so as to help understand the past and/or plan for the future. The growth of research and applications of temporal databases has motivated an urgent need for techniques to deal with the problem of knowledge discovery from large temporal databases.

In most application areas that have been studied for data mining, the time that something happened is also known and recorded (i.e. the date and time that a point-of-sale transaction took place, or a patient's temperature was taken). However, most data mining techniques treat data in temporal databases at best as data series in chronological order and ignore time values which the data are stamped with. If data mining is to be used as a vehicle for better decision making, the existing approaches will in most cases lead into not very significant or interesting results. Consider, for example, a possible association -concerning a supermarket's transactions- between butter and bread (i.e. people who buy butter also buy bread). If someone looks at all the supermarket transactions that are available, let's say for the past ten years, that association might be -with a certain possibility- true. If, however, the highest concentration of people who bought butter and bread can be found up to five years ago, then the discovery of the association is not significant for the present and the future of the supermarket organisation. Similarly, if someone looks at the rule "over a year 50% of people buy umbrellas" this may be true. However, if the periodic pattern "*during autumn* 85% of people buy umbrellas" is true, then it is certainly more interesting to a company making or selling umbrellas, since it also tells them when and how often the highest concentration of people buying umbrellas can be found.

It has been recognised recently [4], [12] that such temporal patterns or rules should be investigated and discovered from temporal databases, since they can provide accurate information about an evolving business domain, rather than a static one. Data mining has been regarded as a field which potentially offers additional knowledge for a particular application domain. The existing approaches, however, take into account all available data (or a subset of them) and provide a static view of an application domain. Application domains, however, do change constantly, customers change their habits and things that may have been true in the past are not applicable any more. Temporal data mining can provide a model of an evolving business domain. It can uncover patterns that are applicable during certain time periods or during certain times within a particular time framework (e.g. summer within a year). Modelling techniques, like enterprise modelling provide a model of an organisation, the way it works, its goals and business objectives. They do not provide, however, any indication about whether or not the organisation is operating in an efficient manner, is adaptable to changes and to changing customer needs. Temporal data mining can provide that missing component and therefore, can initiate business process change and redevelopment activities in order for an organisation to adopt to changes within its operating area.

The work presented in this paper presents a framework for temporal data mining. It does so, by providing a simple, generic definition of a temporal pattern and then as an instance and example of that presents temporal association rules. It is believed that the process of knowledge discovery should consist of several interactive and iterative stages [5]. To find useful knowledge, the user of a KDD system has to select the relevant data subset, identify suitable classes of patterns and define good criteria for interestingness of the patterns. To help users achieve this, it is expected that powerful languages can be used to express different ad hoc data mining tasks [7]. Following this idea, the paper also proposes -as part of the above mentioned framework- a query language to support the expression of temporal data mining tasks. The proposed language is also a consistent extension to SQL2 and TSQL2 [10]. The rest of the paper is organised as follows. A framework for mining temporal patterns in temporal databases is given in section 2, including the definition of temporal patterns, the description of the temporal mining problem, and the description -based on these definitions- of temporal association rules. A temporal query and mining language (TQML) is presented in section 3, followed by a prototype system architecture described in section 4. Conclusions and future work will be discussed in section 5.

2. Mining Temporal Patterns

2.1 Temporal Patterns

To specify temporal features of patterns in which users may be interested within different application domains, calendar time expressions [3] are used in this paper. A calendar time expression is composed of calendar units in a specific calendar and may represent different time features, such as an absolute time interval over the time domain, a periodic time over the time domain, or a periodic time within a specific time period. The following is an example of the calendar time expression:

Weeks·Days(2)·Hours(12:13)*during*[Years(1993)·Months(5),Years(1996)·Months(8)]

In the above expression "Weeks", "Days", "Hours", "Years", and "Months" are calendar units in the Gregorian calendar. "Weeks·Days(2)·Hours(12:13)" is a *calendar periodic expression*, describing *a periodic time* which consists of a series of periodic intervals (Monday's lunchtime) on a repeated cycle (week). "Years(1993)·Months(5)" and "Years(1996)· Months(8)" are two *calendar interval expressions*, describing two time intervals which are respectively the starting interval and ending interval of a specific contiguous time framework (from May 1993 to August 1996). The whole expression represents the statement "the lunch time of every Monday during the time period between May 1993 and August 1996".

Generally, a time expression represents a set of periodic intervals during a specific contiguous time interval. The notion of periodicity [11] is an important temporal feature in the real world. A series of repeated occurrences of a certain type of event at regular intervals is described as a periodic event, which exists in many temporal applications. We use $\Phi(TimeExp) = \{ p_1, p_2, \ldots, p_n \}$ to denote the interpretation of a time expression *TimeExp*, where p_i is a time interval over time domain. In the case that people are only interested in an absolute time interval over the time domain, the first part of the time expression (Weeks·Days(2)·Hours(12:13) in the above example) can be omitted and its interpretation contains only one element.

Definition 1: *A temporal pattern* is a pair < *Patt*, *TimeExp* >, where *Patt* is a general pattern which may be a trend, a deviation, a classification rule, an association rule, etc., and *TimeExp* is a time expression. It expresses that *Patt* holds during each interval in $\Phi(TimeExp)$.

For any temporal pattern of the form < Patt, *TimeExp* >, if $|\Phi(TimeExp)| = 1$, it represents a pattern that refers to an absolute time interval, otherwise, it represents a periodic pattern with or without time limitation. The following are some examples of temporal patterns that refer to absolute time intervals or periodic times:

- <"(Emp#,=),(Rank,<)⇒(Salary,≤)",during[Years(1992)·Months(3), Years(1993)·Months(7)] >: describes that during the period between March 1992 and July 1993, if an employee's rank increases then his/her salary does not decrease.
- < "hiking_boots ⇒ outerwear", Years·Months(3:5) during [Years(1990), Years(1995)]> : shows that every Spring during 1990 to 1995 the shoppers who buy hiking boots, also buy outerwear at the same time;

- < "nausea → headache", Days·Hours(6:8) >: indicates that patients' nausea is followed by headaches from 6 to 8 o'clock every morning.

2.2 Mining Problem

Definition 2: Given a set ***D*** of time-stamped data over a time domain ***T***, we use ***D***(p) to denote a subset of ***D***, which contains all data with timestamps belonging to time interval p. For a time expression *TimeExp*, we define:

- *<Patt, TimeExp>* holds during interval p, p $\in \Phi$(*TimeExp*), if *Patt* satisfies all relevant thresholds in ***D***(p).
- *<Patt, TimeExp>* satisfies all relevant thresholds with respect to the frequency *f* % in the dataset ***D***, if *<Patt, TimeExp>* holds during not less than *f* % of intervals in Φ(*TimeExp*).

Definition 3: Given a time-stamped dataset ***D*** over a time domain ***T*** and a time expression *TimeExp*, the problem of mining temporal patterns is to discover all patterns of the form *<Patt, TimeExp>* in ***D*** that satisfy all the user-specified thresholds with respect to the user-specified minimum frequency *min_f* %.

In this definition, frequency is introduced for measuring the proportion of the intervals, during which *Patt* satisfies all relevant thresholds, within the intervals in Φ(*TimeExp*). It is required that the frequency of any temporal pattern *<Patt,TimeExp>* should not be smaller than the user-specified minimum frequency which is a fraction within [0,1]. In the case that $|\Phi(TimeExp)|=1$, Φ(*TimeExp*) just includes a single interval so that any non-zero minimum frequency has the same meaning, that is, *Patt* must satisfy all the relevant thresholds during this single interval.

2.3 An Example of Temporal Patterns: Temporal Association Rules

The problem of finding association rules [1] was motivated by analyses of sales data. Given a set of transactions, where each transaction is a set of items, an association rule is an expression of the form X⇒Y, where X and Y are sets of items, and indicates that the presence of X in a transaction will imply the presence of Y in the same transaction. Consider a supermarket database where the set of items purchased by a customer is stored as a transaction. A possible example of the association rule is: "60% of transactions that contain bread and butter also contain milk; 30% of all transactions contain both of these items." Here, 60% is called the confidence of the rule and 30% the support of the rule. The problem of mining association rules is the attempt to find all association rules that satisfy the user-specified minimum support and minimum confidence. As an example of temporal patterns, according to the definitions in the previous paragraph, temporal association rules are presented below.

Let $\boldsymbol{I}=\{i_1, i_2, \ldots, i_l\}$ be a set of literals which are called items. A set of items $X \subset \boldsymbol{I}$ is called an itemset. Let ***D*** be a set of time-stamped transactions. Each time-stamped transaction S is a triple tuple <tid, itemset, timestamp>, where S.tid is the transaction identifier, S.itemset is a set of items such that S.itemset $\subseteq \boldsymbol{I}$, and S.timestamp is a primitive time interval which the transaction S is stamped with, such that S.timestamp $\in T$. We say a transaction S contains an itemset X if $X \subseteq$ S.itemset.

Definition 4: *A temporal association rule* is a pair < *AssoRule, TimeExp* >, where *AssoRule* is an implication of the form $X \Rightarrow Y$, such that $X \subset I$, $Y \subset I$ and $X \cap Y = \emptyset$, and *TimeExp* is a time expression. We define:

- The rule has confidence *c%* during interval p_i, $p_i \in \Phi(TimeExp)$, if not less than *c%* of transactions in $\boldsymbol{D}(p_i)$ that contain X also contain Y.
- The rule has support *s %* during interval p_i, $p_i \in \Phi(TimeExp)$, if not less than *s%* of transactions in $\boldsymbol{D}(p_i)$ contain $X \cup Y$.
- The rule has confidence *c%* and support *s%* with respect to the frequency *f%* in the transaction set ***D*** (or saying the database ***D***) if it has confidence *c%* and support *s%* during no less than *f %* of intervals in $\Phi(TimeExp)$.

Example 2 from the previous section is an example of temporal association rules. The mining problem for temporal association rules can be stated as follows: Given a set ***D*** of time-stamped transactions over a time domain ***T*** and a time expression *TimeExp*, the problem of mining temporal association rules is to discover all rules of the form <$X \Rightarrow Y$, *TimeExp*> in ***D*** that satisfy the user-specified minimum support *min_s%* and confidence *min_c%* with respect to the user-specified minimum frequency *min_f%*.

3. A Temporal Discovery Language

From the point of view of database systems, knowledge discovery is the process of interactively and iteratively querying patterns. To a greater or lesser extent, data mining is application-dependent and user-dependent. Therefore, it is important that KDD systems supply users with flexible and powerful descriptive languages to express data mining tasks. Some SQL-like data mining languages have been suggested in the literature to describe non-temporal mining tasks ([6], [9]). We focus on the need and requirements for querying a database for the mining of temporal patterns and suggest a Temporal Query and Mining Language (TQML) with the ability to express the task of temporal data mining by extending of SQL2/TSQL2. TQML can be used to express several aspects of temporal data mining tasks: query demand (the data relevant to the mining task), mining demand (identification of different types of patterns) and presentation demand (i.e. discovered knowledge could be presented as tables, graphs, etc.)

3.1 Brief Syntax of TQML

The syntax of the TQML language is briefly defined as follows in the BNF grammar:

```
<TQML> ::=    Mine <Pattern-Form>
              [ With Periodicity(<PT>, <time-variable>) ]
                        [ Where <interval-relation-expression> ]
```

[Having Thresholds <threshold-expression-list>]
[Shown As <display-form>]
In Select <relevant-attribute-list> From <relation-list>
[Where <condition-expression>]
[Group By <group-attribute-list>
[Having <condition-expression>]]

In the above definition, <pattern-form> gives the form of patterns which users would like to discover and it may be "Trend", "Classification_Rule", "Association_Rule", etc. The temporal feature of the expected patterns can be expressed with the With-Where clause, where *PT* is a calendar periodic expression as discussed in the previous section and <time-variable> indicates the time attribute which users are concerned with in the database. The time value of a time variable is a primitive time interval which is stored in a database and may be "Transaction_Time", "Valid_Time" or user-defined time, as defined in the temporal databases literature [10]. <interval-relation-expression> is the expression of predicates in the forms of "<time-variable> <time-comparison-operator> *CI*", where *CI* is a calendar interval expression which represents a calendar interval, such as a year, a month, a day, an hour, etc. <time-comparison- operator> can be any of the possible relationships between time interval, firstly identified in [2] and later extended in [8]. They are: before/after, starts_before/starts_after, ends_before/ends_after, costarts/coends, overlaps/overlapped_by, during/contains, same_as.

The With-Where clause describes the periodicity that mining users are interested in, with or without a specific time framework. The With clause can also be omitted when users are just interested in non-temporal rules or rules that refer to an absolute time period. Thresholds can be stated in the Having-Threshold clause and presentation demands can be stated in the Shown-As clause. The data relevant to the data mining task can be stated in the Select-From-Where-Group clause. The Select subclause indicates attributes which are relevant to the mining task. The attribute in <relevant-attribute-list> is an attribute existing in the tables appearing in the From clause, an aggregate function (such as Max, Sum, etc.), or a set function which forms an attribute of a nested relation. Each attribute in <relevant-attribute-list> may also be followed by a descriptor, which is relevant to a specific mining model for a certain kind of pattern that the mining user is interested in. The From-Where clause has the same syntax and semantics as SQL2, constituting a basic query to collect the set of relevant data. The Where subclause can also contain time-related conditions. The selected data can also be grouped by <group-attribute-list>, being presented in the form that mining algorithms expect. The Having clause can be used to filter groups which users want to consider.

3.2 An Example: Mining Temporal Association Rules

Consider a Sales database containing two relations Items and Purchase as shown in Figure 1. The following is an example of a mining task for finding temporal association rules that convey purchase patterns every summer (assuming that summer starts from the sixth month of each year) between July 1990 and June 1996, with the thresholds of support, confidence and frequency being 0.6, 0.75 and 0.8, respectively. In this example, we are only concerned for items whose retail prices are not less than £10 and transactions in which the number of purchased items is greater than 3.

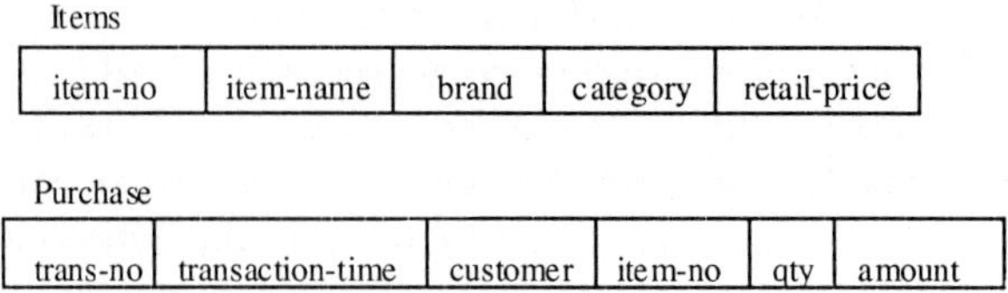

Fig. 1. Relation Schemes in Sales Database

Mine Association_Rules
    With *Periodicity(Years·Months(6:8), transaction_time)*
        Where *transaction-time* Costarts *Years(1990)·Months(7)*
        and *transaction-time* Coends *Years(1996)·Months(6)*
    Having Thresholds support = 0.6, confidence = 0.75, frequency = 0.8.
In
    Select *trans-no: TID, Set(item-name): ItemSet*
    From purchase, items
    Where purchase.item-no = items.item-no and items.retail-price ≥ £10
    Group By purchase.trans-no Having Count(*) > 3

In the above example, the "Select-From-Where-Group" part expresses a basic data query demand. The result of data query is a nested relation, forming the relevant data set to this mining task. "TID" and ItemSet are descriptors which indicate the "trans-no" and "Set(item-name)" as the "tid" and "itemset", respectively, in the mining model for temporal associations. The "transaction-time" in the database is chosen as the time-stamp. The first part of the statements, the one concerned with the mining task, depends on the type of patterns that one is interested for. For example, if one is looking for sequences, then the first two thresholds used in the above example (support and confidence) will not be applicable any more. The second part of the language, after the 'select' keyword will still follow the same SQL2-like syntax.

4. A Prototype System Architecture

Figure 2 shows a prototype system architecture for mining temporal patterns in temporal databases which includes five modules.

Task Analysis: It syntactically and semantically analyses the mining task which is submitted by data mining users and expressed in the temporal query and mining language TQML. This module generates the query for relevant data, which is represented in an SQL2-like language and will be processed by the data access module. It also extracts relevant information according to the patterns expected by the user, such as the form of patterns and thresholds. It generates the internal representation of the mining problem according to different mining models. During the course of analysis, it calls the time support module to construct the time expression by handling time-related components in the mining task. Based on the result of analysis, it successively invokes the data access, pattern search and pattern presentation modules with query demand, mining demand and presentation demand, respectively.

Data Access: With the query demand generated by the "task analysis" module, it queries the database to select data relevant to the mining task and organises the selected data in the format which is required by the mining algorithms. The actual query is basically generated by the data query part of the description of the mining task in TQML. Additionally, the temporal aspects in the mining target will also be considered. Considering the above example, the generated query may semantically be expressed in the SQL2-like intermediate language as follows:

```
Select trans-no, transaction-time, set(item-name)   From  purchase, items
      Where purchase.item-no = items.item-no And items.retail-price >= £10
            And Periodicity(Years·Months(6:8), transaction-time)
            And transaction-time Costarts "July, 1990"
            And transaction-time Coends "July, 1996"
      Group By purchase.trans-no Having Count(*) > 3
```

The data access module uses services supplied by the time support module to interpret time-related components, such as periodic predicates and interval comparison predicates in the generated data query.

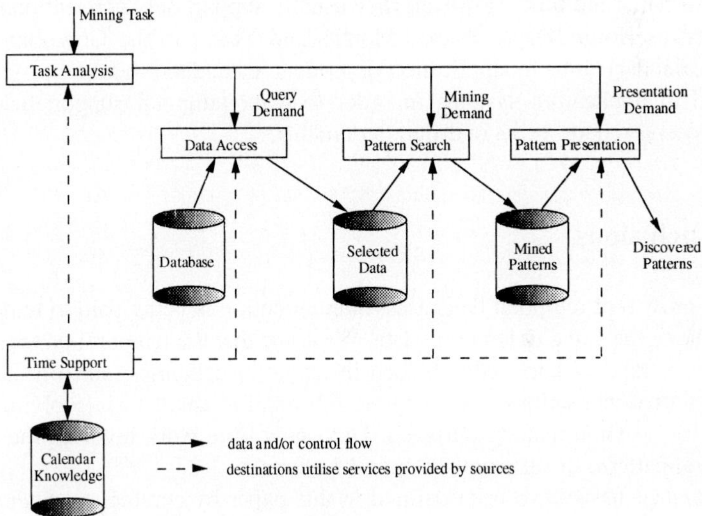

Fig. 2. A Prototype System Architecture

Pattern Search: According to the mining demand, it chooses and runs the relevant algorithm which will pass through the selected data to search for interesting patterns. The mining demand indicates the kind of knowledge which the user wants to find, and specifies the thresholds given by the user. With these demands and the data set selected by the data access module, the rule search module executes the algorithm and stores the searched rules in the internal form in a rule base. Discussion on search algorithms for temporal patterns is beyond the scope of this paper. The description of a pair of algorithms for mining temporal association rules can be found in [3]. Obviously the performance of any search algorithm attempting to identify temporal patterns will be worse than the performance of one that does not take into account the time component. However, the information provided is more accurate and more interesting and the authors believe that most organisations would be happier with more interesting and accurate information, even if more time is required in order to produce it.

Pattern Presentation: In terms of different presentation demands, it displays the discovered knowledge in different forms. For example, the patterns may be expressed by tables, graphs, etc. Sometimes, it may present rules with their thresholds.

Time Support: This is a key module for supporting temporal data mining. It supplies time support for all other modules. Any expression in the temporal query and mining language will be passed to the time support module in order to identify temporal aspects in the mining task. All other modules utilise its services when they need to deal with a time issue, such as constructing time expressions for task analysis, evaluating periodic predicates and interval comparison predicates when accessing data, and interpreting time expressions while performing pattern searching, etc. The time support module maintains and uses the calendar knowledge base which includes definitions of all relevant calendars. Currently, some commercial DBMSs provide support for dates and time. However, they usually support only conventional calendar units, such as Hours, Days, Weeks, Months and Years, in the Gregorian calendar. Special calendar units in application-dependent calendars should be defined and supported in application systems in order to offer temporal support according to different users' requirements in different domains.

5. Conclusions

With the growth of temporal databases, more attention is being paid to temporal data mining due to the value of temporal data. We argue that the temporal pattern or rule is an important kind of knowledge hidden in temporal databases, since it can provide companies or organisations with accurate information about their evolving business domains for decision making purposes. Until now little work involves the discovery of temporal patterns or rules with temporal features.

Temporal patterns have been defined in this paper by combining general patterns with temporal features which are represented by calendar time expressions. Three different types of temporal patterns and rules are identified in this paper: those that refer to absolute time values, those that refer to periodic time and those that refer to periodic time but within a specific time framework. These are the only types of temporal patterns that can exist in an application domain. For evaluating the significance and interestingness of mined temporal patterns, the minimum frequency is introduced as the threshold which can be specified by users in terms of different requirements. An architecture for temporal data mining has been proposed, along with an SQL-like mining language TQML with the ability to express the task of temporal data mining. The language can accommodate all different types of time that have been identified in the temporal database literature.

Current work is concentrating on the extension of the temporal discovery language to support the mining of temporal features of time related patterns (i.e. periodicity) and the extension of calendar support beyond that of the Gregorian calendar. Also work is being carried out in order to enhance the language so that it can be used both as a fully fledged temporal and data mining language. Finally, we are focusing on the effects of changes of business rules on temporal patterns.

References

1. Agrawal, R., Imielinski, T., and Swami, A., 1993, *"Mining Associations between Sets of Items in Massive Databases"*, Proceedings of ACM SIGMOD International Conference on Management of Data, Washington D.C., May 1993.
2. Allen, J., 1983, "*Maintaining Knowledge about Temporal Intervals"*, Communications of ACM, 26(11), Nov. 1983.
3. Chen, X., Petrounias, I., and Heathfield, H., "Discovering Temporal Association Rules in Temporal Databases", to appear in Proceedings of International Workshop on Issues and Applications of Database Technology (IADT'98), Berlin, Germany, July 1998.
4. Golan, R. and Edwards, D., 1994, "Temporal Rules Discovery Using Datalogic/R+ with Stock Market Data", Proceedings of the International Workshop on Rough Set and Knowledge(RSKD'93), Banff, Alberta, Canada, pp.74-81.
5. Fayyad, U, Piatetsky-Shapiro, G., Smyth, P., Uthurusamy, R., 1996, "*Advances in Knowledge Discovery and Data Mining"*, The AAAI Press/The MIT Press, 1996.
6. Han, J., Fu, Y., Koperski, K., Wang W., and Zaiane, O., 1996, "DMQL: A Data Mining Query Language for Relational Databases", 1996 SIGMOD'96 Workshop on Research Issues on Data Mining and Knowledge Discovery (DMKD'96), Montreal, Canada, June 1996.
7. Imielinski, T., and Mannila H., 1996, "A Database Perspective on Knowledge Discovery", CACM, Vol.39, No.11, Nov. 1996.
8. LOKI, 1986, *A Logic Oriented Approach to Knowledge and Databases Supporting Natural Language User Interfaces,* ESPRIT Project 107 (LOKI), Institute of Computer Science, Research Centre of Crete, Greece, March 1986.
9. Meo, R., Psaile, G., and Ceri, S., 1996, "*A New SQL-like Operator for Mining Association Rules"*, Proceedings of 22nd VLDB Conference, Bombay, India, 1996.
10. Snodgrass, R. T., (ed), "*The TSQL2 Temporal Query Language*", Kluwer Academic, Norwell, MA, 1995.
11. Tuzhilin, A. and Clifford, J., 1995, "*On Periodicity in Temporal Databases"*, Information Systems, Vol.20, No.8, pp.619-639,1995.
12. Weiss, S. and Indurkhya, N., 1998, "*Predicitve Data Mining*", Morgan Kaufmann Publishers, Inc., San Francisco, USA, 1998.

KD in FM: Knowledge Discovery in Facilities Management Databases

G. Goulbourne, F. Coenen, P. Leng

Department of Computer Science, The University of Liverpool,
Chadwick Building, P.O. Box 147, Liverpool L69 3BX, England.
graham_g@csc.liv.ac.uk,
WWW home page: http://www.csc.liv.ac.uk/~graham_g/

Abstract. The KD in FM project aims to investigate how Knowledge Discovery in Databases (KDD), and particularly data mining, techniques can be applied to the distributed, heterogeneous and autonomous data sources found in the Facilities Management (FM) environment. The problems associated with multiple disparate databases are examined as is recent research in heterogeneous database mining. Finally, we describe the architecture of a system for KDD in this environment and suggest some suitable data mining techniques.
Key words: Data mining, Heterogeneous databases, Facilities management.

1 Introduction

Knowledge Discovery in Databases (KDD) has, in recent years, generated much interest for the database community. KDD, and the related concept of data mining, are concerned with the extraction of previously unrecognised and "interesting" information contained within (usually large) data repositories. "Interest" is of course a subjective concept, and a definition of what is interesting is required: it is usually taken as an overall measure of pattern value, combining validity, novelty, usefulness and simplicity (Fayyad [7]). Given that many data mining techniques have been developed, the first question faced by the practitioner is, which of these are most likely to be effective in producing interesting information within necessary limitations of time, budget and resources. The answer to this question is context-dependent; it will depend on the nature of the data being examined, the form(s) in which it is represented, and the objectives of the organisation seeking the information.

In this paper we consider the application of KDD to the Facilities Management (FM) function of an organisation. Facilities Management is characterised by a great diversity of function, most of which is only peripherally related to the core objectives of the organisation, and elements of which are essentially unrelated to each other. This diversity of function is reflected in a corresponding diversity of information and data organisation. Further, many of these information systems are likely to be *legacy* systems in that they have evolved within the organisation over a long period of time; as such they tend to be large, developed using old technology, complex and critical to the organisation's day-to-day working. KDD in this context poses particular challenges, both in identifying objectives for information discovery and, especially, in dealing with the issues raised by this extreme heterogeneity. A second question, therefore, facing practitioners wishing to apply KD techniques to FM (and a necessary prerequisite to data mining) is how to address the problems associated with the distributed, heterogeneous and autonomous nature of the data sources that characterise the FM environment. These problems raise issues of database interoperability, but with the distinctive feature that, for KDD, we are concerned only with the retrieval of data; we do not wish to update it.

The KD in FM project thus has two aims; to investigate: (1) which data mining techniques are best suited to the FM operation, and (2) what are the most appropriate mechanisms to address the problems associated with the nature of the data sources to be accessed. These two interlinked questions are considered in this paper and some answers suggested. We commence, in Section 2, with a review of the facilities management application domain and consideration of the broad features and characteristics of KDD with respect to FM. Issues arising in KDD in a multi-database setting are reviewed in Section 3. In Section 4 we examine problems of heterogeneity, and present a proposed architecture of a system for KD in FM. Section 5 presents our overall conclusions and the current status of the KD in FM project.

2 Facilities Management

The FM operation of a company can be defined as an integrated approach to operating, maintaining, improving and adapting the buildings and infrastructure of an organisation in order to create an environment that strongly supports the primary objectives of that organisation (Further Education Funding Council [8]). Businesses may have already considered the distinction between their core and non-core businesses, as part of a drive to achieve better value for money and customer satisfaction.

Essentially, therefore, FM attempts to bring together under one organisational heading a number of operations which are largely functionally independent. These operations, for an organisation whose core business is (say) retailing of goods and services, might include: planning and design of premises; estate management; building maintenance; catering; staff travel and accommodation; car fleet management; printing services; and any other activities which are not intrinsic to the principal business function. In practice, within most large organisations, it will be necessary for each such operation to be managed separately. As an example, the Fleet Unit within an FM operation would be responsible for all aspects of vehicle policy within the company including types of vehicle available, delivery times, breakdown and recovery service, and maintenance; in fact, every aspect of running a fleet of perhaps 5000 or more vehicles. The scale and scope of this operation demands in itself a substantial organisational infrastructure which may be quite separate from that of the parent business. This tends to militate against holistic approaches to customer service, financial management, and other issues which are orthogonal to the functional organisation of the business. It is this problem which Facilities Management seeks to address.

Inherent in the nature of the FM operation is the likelihood that the information being considered will be:

1. *Distributed* among a number of separate databases each belonging to an individual area within FM: e.g. fleet DB, catering DB, print DB, etc. In many cases these databases will also be geographically distributed.
2. *Heterogeneous* in that they are likely to have been developed and be maintained independently; possibly using different platforms, DBMS, schemas and query languages, and to exhibit both structural and fundamental semantic heterogeneity (Colomb [3]).
3. *Autonomous* in that they are all managed and maintained independently of each other.

Note that: Structural semantic heterogeneity refers to differences in the representation of equivalent information in different databases: for example, differences in terminology used. Fundamental semantic heterogeneity occurs when the representations used in different databases do not allow identification of common information. The problems raised by both aspects of heterogeneity are, in our view, the central issues of KD in FM, and will be discussed more fully in section 5. We first review some of the techniques used in data mining, with this context in mind.

3 KDD in a Multi-database Environment

Methods used for KDD when multiple databases are involved, (such as the FM environment), may be broadly viewed under three headings:

1. Application of KD techniques to each database separately; an example of this would be inducing a set of rules and applying some interestingness measure to them. Such work is found in Silberschatz [13], Kamber and Shinghal [10] and Dzeroski and Grbovic [5].
2. Selection of a number of related, although not necessarily homogeneous databases, such as, premises - planning and design, estate management, and building maintenance, and integrating them for the purpose of data mining. Such work is found in McClean and Scotney [14], Levy [11] and Ganesh et al. [9].
3. Creation of a data warehouse and integrating all the databases, either for the purposes of mining the warehouse or to establish data marts for independent mining activities [16].

Application of KD techniques to each database in turn clearly poses fewest problems in dealing with heterogeneity. Unfortunately, the problems which KDD seeks to address in FM are essentially those which involve interactions between separate operations and hence associations between the corresponding databases. The underlying hypothesis is that some aspect of (say) building maintenance has an unsuspected influence on (say) the cost of the print operation, and that it may be possible to infer this relationship from some examination of the two (or more) corresponding databases. We therefore need to consider methods involving the integration of information from multiple, disparate, sources. Two relevant techniques are reviewed;

1. Entity integration techniques.
2. Query language extensions (e.g. SchemaSQL).

3.1 Entity integration techniques

Identification of records that represent the same real world entity is an important task in the database integration process. When a common identification mechanism for similar records across heterogeneous databases is not readily available, entity integration can be performed by examining the various attribute values among the records. The distances between attribute values can be used as a measure of similarity between the records they represent. Record matching conditions can, for entity integration, then be expressed as constraints on the attribute distances. KD techniques can be used to automatically derive these conditions, (expressed as decision trees) directly from the data, using a distance based framework [9].

The process of integration requires two distinct tasks: schema integration and entity identification. The former resolves mismatches such as homonyms (the same name for different attributes), and synonyms (different names for the same attributes). The removal of these inconsistencies allows the creation of a global schema, making it possible to treat all the records uniformly for further processing. The mapped global database may contain multiple instances of the same real world entity, therefore the identification of distinct entities is the is the purpose of the entity identification phase.

3.2 Query language extensions

SQL is the most common language for the extraction of information from databases. An extension of SQL, (SchemaSQL) has been developed, [19] that offers the capability of uniform manipulation of data and meta-data in relational multi-database systems. Interoperability in multiple databases is the ability to share, interpret and manipulate information in component databases. Factors influencing interoperability can be classified into semantic issues (interpreting and cross-relating information in different databases), syntactic issues (heterogeneity in schemas, data models and query processing) and systems issues (operating systems, communication protocols, security management etc.). SchemaSQL deals with the syntactic issues; its development is aimed at extracting information from relational databases storing semantically similar data in structurally different ways.

The architecture for implementing SchemaSQL builds on the existing database architecture in a non-intrusive manner. The SchemaSQL system is built on top of the existing SQL systems. A SchemaSQL server communicates with local databases in the federation. Local meta-information, database names, names of attributes and relations, are stored on the SchemaSQL server in the form of a table called the Federation System Table. Global queries are submitted to the SchemaSQL server which determines the queries to submit to the local databases. The server then collects the answers and executes a final series of SQL queries to produce an answer to the global query.

4 An Architecture for Mining Heterogeneous Databases

In seeking to apply data mining techniques in the field of Facilities Management, we require in particular to consider methods by which the relevant data can be made available for mining. This requires us to consider ways of integrating information held in a number of databases which are heterogeneous, geographically distributed, and autonomously maintained. The usual solution recommended in this situation is to establish a data warehouse, within which data extracted from all the relevant databases is stored in a common format.

There are a number of reasons why this approach may be unsuitable in the environment we are considering. The number of databases involved may be relatively large, and their structural heterogeneity very great, leading to significant problems and costs in establishing a common data representation. The costs of storing a large volume of integrated data, and of updating this when required from the diverse distributed sources, may be significantly high. Many attributes in the larger data set will be irrelevant to the current knowledge discovery task and therefore make the extraction of useful knowledge more difficult and computationally more expensive. There may also be ethical and even legal objections to integrating data which may include, in some of the databases, personal information which is held subject to the proviso that it is maintained securely. Finally, an integrated data warehouse is always liable to be undermined by the operational autonomy of the contributing databases; each organisational change may require a corresponding reorganisation of the warehouse to accommodate it.

The alternative approach is to organise the contributing databases into a multidatabase system, through which it is possible to access data from all sources using some unifying schema. Multidatabase architectures typically use a Canonical (Common) Data Model (CDM) where schemas are expressed in a common Data Definition Language (DDL). Each local schema associated with a component databases, and expressed in a local DDL, is mapped onto a component schema which represents the same information in terms of the CDM and common DDL. A query against a component schema is translated into queries against the underlying schema. The results of such queries are then processed to form an answer to the initial query. Typically component schemas are integrated into a multiple component schema referred to as a federated schema, also expressed in the common DDL, which is then the user's first point of contact. A query against a federated schema is translated into queries against the underlying component schemas and then on to the local schema. The software which co-ordinates, i.e. facilitates the integration of, a number of component databases in a multidatabase is referred to as a Federated Database Management System (FDBMS).

Architectures for multidatabase systems are reviewed by Fahl [6]. Four alternative models are identified:

1. Global Schema Architectures: In this approach all component schemas are integrated into a single federated schema. This is in principle the simplest approach, but shares some of the disadvantages we have ascribed to data warehousing solutions. To be effective, a global schema may need to undermine the autonomy of the component systems. The most serious drawback, however, is the need for all conflicts between component schemas to be resolved. This is unlikely to a a feasible option in the highly heterogeneous context we are considering.
2. Multiple Integrated Schema Architectures: Here a number of federated schemas are supported, each of which integrates a particular set of parts of the participating component schemas. Note that overlap between groups of component schemas is allowed. The advantage is that less integration of component schemas is required, and not all information need be included. This approach is appropriate when particular needs can be identified which can be addressed by a partial integration of the available data.
3. Federated Schema Architectures: This is similar to the multiple integrated approach except that each user site has its own dedicated federated schema. The distinction between this and the previous architecture is sometimes expressed using the terms tightly coupled and loosely coupled. In the previous case the federated schemas are maintained by a "multidatabase" administrator (tight coupling), while here the integrated schemas are the responsibility of individual users (loose coupling).
4. Multidatabase Languages Architectures: This last approach is different from the foregoing in that users do not access data through an integrated schema. Instead a data manipulation language is used that provides constructs to access component schema and consequently combine data from the component databases making up the multidatabase.

Global schema integration poses what may be unresolvable problems of reconciling cases of semantic heterogeneity. Conversely, methods involving partial integration of schemas bypass these problems by recognising that in particular applications, total integration may be unnecessary. In the KDD context, however, avoiding integration of problematic data runs the risk of losing vital information: because we are (by definition) searching for relationships which are not immediately apparent, we cannot a priori eliminate any data from our search.

Fortunately, the requirements of a system to support KDD across multiple databases are less demanding than in the general case of a multidatabase architecture. First, KDD requires only read access to data, without the need to

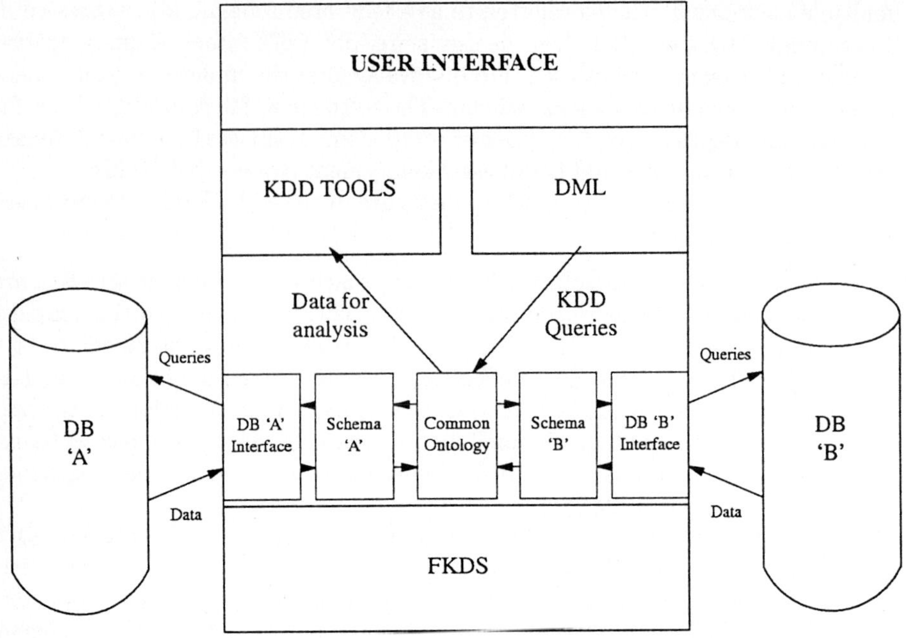

Fig. 1. A Conceptual view of the FKDS architecture

update it. Secondly, and in our view most significantly, it may be possible to draw "interesting" inferences from data even when this cannot be integrated in the strict sense usually required of a federated DBMS. For example, a Personnel database may contain records of all employees, and another database, records of payments made for staff travel and hospitality. It may be impossible reliably to match records in the two data, for various reasons; for example, there may be cases of payments being made to individuals who are not employees, or the attributes of the payment records may not enable reliable identification of the payees. This is, therefore, an instance of fundamental semantic heterogeneity which would normally prevent a full effective integration of the databases. However, it may be that there is, in practice, a very significant relationship between the two databases; it may be known that in almost all cases, recipients of travel payments are current employees, so a search for interesting patterns within the two sets of data may proceed on the assumption that this is the case. For this purpose we do not require a complete integration of the component schemas; it may be sufficient to define approximate relationships between entities, sufficient to enable heuristic searches for interesting patterns. Because of the relaxation of the requirements for integration, and the absence of a requirement for data updates, it is inappropriate to refer to this kind of system as a Federated Database Management System: we will instead describe it as a Federated Knowledge Discovery System (FKDS). The appropriate model for this is the Multidatabase Language Architecture. We postulate a Data Manipulation Language which provides constructs to access and combine data from component databases, including constructs which reference data in terms of the imprecise relationships which may exist between imperfectly matched entities. The principal elements of the FKDS (Figure 1) are:

1. A common Data Definition Language, in which schemas of all the participating component databases are expressed.
2. A common ontology, within which relationships between the component databases are described. For the reasons discussed above, the requirements of this ontology are less exacting than would be the case for a federated schema.
3. A Data Manipulation Language, the semantics of which enable queries formulated for knowledge discovery purposes to be translated via the shared ontology into queries to the component databases.
4. Tools for Knowledge discovery. In the generic FKDS model, these may include tools making use of genetic algorithms, neural networks, or any other chosen methods which can be applied to data extracted and combined using the DML.
5. Interfaces to the component databases. Because of the autonomy, geographical distribution, and technological diversity of the component databases, these interfaces may need to be very specialised; their purpose is to translate queries expressed in terms of the common DDL into queries expressed in the form required by the component database, and vice versa for responses. They may also include filters to prevent access to confidential or sensitive data when necessary.
6. A user interface to enable application of the available KD tools and the formulation of KD queries using the DML.

The FKDS architecture is generic, in that it provides a framework for KDD within a heterogeneous context, without defining which specific techniques of knowledge discovery will be used. We see this as an essential attribute of a system for KD in FM, as the diversity of the FM function may require a range of different techniques to be applied.

5 CURRENT STATUS AND FUTURE PLANS

In this paper we have considered the issues of data mining with respect to the FM environment and particularly the distributed, autonomous and hetereogeneous nature of the sources involved. We have presented a model for a generic system for Knowledge Discovery amongst such data sources, which we call a

Federated Knowledge Discovery System. Work is currently in progress to develop a prototype demonstration of a system with this architecture. This is to be achieved initially by developing a "test harness" using a number of different databases founded on different platforms and using different operating systems and DBMS e.g. Ingres on a UNIX platform, MS Access on a PC platform etc.. The FKDS will then be implemented using a WWW type interface supported by CGI scripts to achieve the desired connectivity. The "test harnes" will then be used to evaluate ideas regarding common ontalogies. When established this ontology will be use as the basis to define a Data Manipulation Language which will include constructs to allow for the manipulation of data which need not be precisely matched. The aim is to develop ways of extracting potentially interesting information from data even when the fundamental heterogeneity of this makes formal integration impossible. Work is currently in progress and the research team have been greatly encouraged by the results to date.

6 ACKNOWLEDGEMENTS

The KD in FM project is funded by Royal Sun Alliance FM. For further information see: http://www.csc.liv.ac.uk/research/kdfm.html.

References

1. Augier, S. Venturini, G. Kodratoff, Y. (1995). Learning First Order Rules with a Genetic Algorithm. Proceedings of the First International Conference on Data Mining and Knowledge Discovery, AAAI Press 1995, pp 21-26.
2. Ciampi, A. and Lechevallier, L. (1995). Designing Neural Networks from Statistical Models: A new Approach to Data Exploration. Proceedings of the First International Conference on Data Mining and Knowledge Discovery, AAAI Press, pp 45-50.
3. Colomb, R.M. (1997) Impact of Semantic Heterogeneity on Federating Databases, The Computer Journal, 40(5), pp235-244.
4. Domingos, P. (1996). Linear-Time Rule Induction. Proceedings of the Second International Conference on Data Mining and Knowledge Discovery, AAAI Press, pp 96-101.
5. Dzeroski, S. and Grbovic, J. (1995). Knowledge Discovery in a Water Quality Database. Proceedings of the First International Conference on Data Mining and Knowledge Discovery. AAAI Press 1995, pp 81-86.
6. Fahl, G. (1994). Object Views of Relational Data in Multidatabase Systems. Studies in Science and Technology, Sweden.
7. Fayyad, U., Piatetsky-Shapiro, G. and Smythe, P. (1996). Knowledge Discovery and Data Mining: Towards a Unifying Framework. Proceedings of the Second International Conference on Data Mining and Knowledge Discovery, AAAI Press, pp 82-95
8. Further Education Funding Council (1997) Effective Facilities Management: A Good Practice Guide. Her Majesty's Stationery Office.
9. Ganesh, M., Sirvastava, J. and Richardson, T. (1996). Mining Entity-Identification Rules for Database Integration. Proceedings of the Second International Conference on Data Mining and Knowledge Discovery, AAAI Press 1996, pp291-294.

9. Ganesh, M., Sirvastava, J. and Richardson, T. (1996). Mining Entity-Identification Rules for Database Integration. Proceedings of the Second International Conference on Data Mining and Knowledge Discovery, AAAI Press 1996, pp291-294.
10. Kamber, M. and R. Shinghal, R. (1996). Evaluating the Interestingness of Characteristic rules Proceedings of the Second International Conference on Data Mining and Knowledge Discovery, AAAI Press, pp 263-266.
11. Levy, A. (1996). Obtaining Complete answers from Incomplete Databases. Proceedings of the 22nd Conference on VLDB, VLDB 1996, pp 402-412.
12. Schafer, G. (1976). A Mathematical Theory of Evidance. Princeton University Press, Princeton, New Jersey.
13. Silberschatz, A. and Tuzhilin, A. (1995). On Subjective Measures of Interingness in KD. Proceedings of the First International Conference on Data Mining and Knowledge Discovery. AAAI Press, pp 275-281.
14. Toivonen, H. Klemettinen, M. Ronkainen, P. Hätönen, K. Mannila, H. Pruning and Grouping Discovered Association Rules. Working paper, Dept. of Computer Science, University of Helsinki.
15. Gill, H.S., Rao, P.C. Computing Guide To Data Warehousing. Que Corp. 1996. ISBN 0-7897-0714-4.

CIA's View of the World and What Neural Networks Learn from It: A Comparison of Geographical Document Space Representation Metaphors

Dieter Merkl and Andreas Rauber

Institut für Softwaretechnik, Technische Universität Wien
Resselgasse 3/188, A–1040 Wien, Austria
{dieter, andi}@ifs.tuwien.ac.at

Abstract. Text collections may be regarded as an almost perfect application arena for unsupervised neural networks. This because many operations computers have to perform on text documents are classification tasks based on noisy patterns. In particular we rely on self-organizing maps which produce a map of the document space after their training process. From geography, however, it is known that maps are not always the best way to represent information spaces. For most applications it is better to provide a hierarchical view of the underlying data collection in form of an atlas where starting from a map representing the complete data collection different regions are shown at finer levels of granularity. Using an atlas, the user can easily "zoom" into regions of particular interest while still having general maps for overall orientation. We show that a similar display can be obtained by using hierarchical feature maps to represent the contents of a document archive. These neural networks have a layered architecture where each layer consists of a number of individual self-organizing maps. By this, the contents of the text archive may be represented at arbitrary detail while still having the general maps available for global orientation.

1 Introduction

Today's information age may be characterized by constant massive production and dissemination of written information. Powerful tools for exploring, searching, and organizing this mass of information are needed. Particularly the aspect of exploration has found only limited attention. Current information retrieval technology still relies on systems that retrieve documents based on the similarity between keyword-based document and query representations.

The map metaphor for displaying the contents of a document library in a two-dimensional map has gained some interest [4, 5, 6, 7, 8]. Maps are used to visualize the similarity between documents in terms of distances within the two-dimensional map display. Hence, similar documents may be found in neighboring regions of the map display.

The map metaphor, however, has its limitations in that each document is represented within a single two-dimensional map. Since the documents are described in a very high-dimensional feature space, the two-dimensional map representation has necessarily some imprecisions. In much the same way as we are showing the world on different pages in an atlas where each page contains a map showing some portion of the world at some specific resolution, we suggest to use a kind of atlas for document space representation. A page of this atlas shows a portion of the library at some resolution while omitting other parts of the library. As long as general maps that provide an overview of the whole library are available, the user can find her way along the library chosing maps that provide the most detailed view of the area of particular interest.

A comparison with traditional document archives reveals that these archives are usually organized into hierarchies according to the subject matter of the various documents. This observation has stimulated research in the direction of using hierarchical clustering techniques based on statistical cluster analysis. The specific strengths and weaknesses of these approaches are well explored [11, 12]. An interesting recent approach is Scatter/Gather that relies on clustering during query processing [1].

In this paper we argue in favor of establishing a hierarchical organization of the document space based on an unsupervised neural network. More precisely, we show the effects of using the *hierarchical feature map* [10] for text archive organization. The distinguished feature of this model is its layered architecture where each layer consists of a number of independent *self-organizing maps* [2]. The training process results in a hierarchical arrangement of the document collection where self-organizing maps from higher layers of the hierarchy are used to represent the overall organizational principles of the document archive. Maps from lower layers of the hierarchy are used to provide fine-grained distinction between individual documents. Such an organization comes close to what we would usually expect from conventional libraries. As an important benefit from the unsupervised training process we have to note that the library organization is derived solely from the document representation. No semantic labeling such as labels of subject matters and the like is necessary.

The remainder of this paper is organized as follows. In Section 2 we give a brief description of the architectures and the training rules of the neural networks used in this study. Section 3 is dedicated to a description of the text documents that constitute our experimental document library. Sections 4 and 5 provide the experimental results from document classification. The former describes the results from using the self-organizing map, i.e. library organization according to the map metaphor. The latter gives results from using the hierarchical feature map, i.e. library organization according to the atlas metaphor. Finally, in Section 6 we present some conclusions.

2 Topology preserving self-organizing neural networks

2.1 Self-organizing maps

The self-organizing map [2, 3] is one of the most prominent artificial neural network models adhering to the unsupervised learning paradigm. The model consists of a number of neural processing elements, i.e. units. Each of the units i is assigned an n-dimensional weight vector m_i. It is important to note that the weight vectors have the same dimensionality as the input patterns.

The training process of self-organizing maps may be described in terms of input pattern presentation and weight vector adaptation. Each training iteration t starts with the random selection of one input pattern $x(t)$. This input pattern is presented to the self-organizing map and each unit determines its activation. Usually, the Euclidean distance between weight vector and input pattern is used to calculate a unit's activation. The unit with the lowest activation is referred to as the *winner*, c, of the training iteration, i.e. $m_c(t) = \min_i ||x(t) - m_i(t)||$. Finally, the weight vector of the *winner* as well as the weight vectors of selected units in the vicinity of the *winner* are adapted. This adaptation is implemented as a gradual reduction of the component-wise difference between input pattern and weight vector, i.e. $m_i(t+1) = m_i(t) \cdot \alpha(t) \cdot h_{ci}(t) \cdot [x(t) - m_i(t)]$. Geometrically speaking, the weight vectors of the adapted units are moved a bit towards the input pattern. The amount of weight vector movement is guided by a so-called learning rate, α, decreasing in time. The number of units that are affected by adaptation is determined by a so-called neighborhood function, h_{ci}. This number of units also decreases in time.

This movement has as a consequence, that the Euclidean distance between those vectors decreases and thus, the weight vectors become more similar to the input pattern. The respective unit is more likely to win at future presentations of this input pattern. The consequence of adapting not only the *winner* alone but also a number of units in the neighborhood of the *winner* leads to a spatial clustering of similar input patters in neighboring parts of the self-organizing map. Thus, similarities between input patterns that are present in the n-dimensional input space are mirrored within the two-dimensional output space of the self-organizing map. The training process of the self-organizing map describes a topology preserving mapping from a high-dimensional input space onto a two-dimensional output space where patterns that are similar in terms of the input space are mapped to geographically close locations in the output space.

Consider Figure 1 for a graphical representation of self-organizing maps. The map consists of a square arrangement of 7×7 units, shown as circles on the left hand side of the figure. The black circle indicates the unit that was selected as the *winner* for the presentation of input pattern $x(t)$. The weight vector of the *winner*, $m_c(t)$, is moved towards the input pattern and thus, $m_c(t+1)$ is nearer to $x(t)$ than was $m_c(t)$. Similar, yet less strong, adaptation is performed with a number of units in the vicinity of the *winner*. These units are marked as shaded circles in Figure 1. The degree of shading corresponds to the strength of adaptation. Thus, the weight vectors of units shown with a darker shading are moved closer to $x(t)$ than units shown with a lighter shading.

2.2 Hierarchical feature maps

The key idea of hierarchical feature maps as proposed in [10] is to use a hierarchical setup of multiple layers where each layer consists of a number of independent

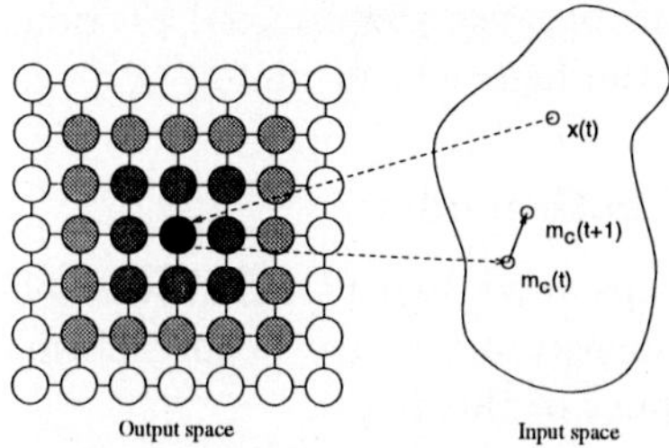

Fig. 1. Architecture of a 7 × 7 self-organizing map

self-organizing maps. One self-organizing map is used at the first layer of the hierarchy. For every unit in this map a self-organizing map is added to the next layer of the hierarchy. This principle is repeated with the third and any further layers of the hierarchical feature map. In Figure 2 we provide an example of a hierarchical feature map with three layers. The first layer map consists of 2 × 2 units, thus we find four independent self-organizing maps on the second layer. Since each map on the second layer consists again of 2 × 2 units, there are 16 maps on the third layer.

Fig. 2. Architecture of a three-layer hierarchical feature map

The training process of hierarchical feature maps starts with the self-organizing map on the first layer. This map is trained according to the standard training process of self-organizing maps as described above. When this first self-organizing map is stable, i.e. only minor further adaptation of the weight vectors are recorded, training proceeds with the maps of the second layer. Here, each map is trained with only that portion of the input data that is mapped on the respective unit in the higher layer map. By this, the amount of training data for a particular self-organizing map is reduced on the way down the hierarchy. Additionally, the vectors representing the input patterns may be shortened on the transition from one layer to the next. This shortage is due to the fact that some input vector components can be expected to be (almost) equal among those input data that are mapped onto the same unit. These equal components may be omitted for training the next layer maps without loss of information. There is no loss of information because the omitted portions of the input vector are already represented by the higher layer unit.

2.3 Comparison of both models

Hierarchical feature maps have two benefits over self-organizing maps which make this model particularly attractive in an information retrieval setting as described in the remainder of this paper.

First, hierarchical feature maps have substantially shorter training times than self-organizing maps. The reason for that is twofold. On the one hand, there is the obvious input vector dimension reduction on the transition from one layer to the next. Shorter input vectors lead directly to reduced training times because of faster *winner* selection and weight vector adaptation. On the other hand, and even more important, the self-organizing training process is performed faster because the spatial relation of different areas of the input space is maintained by means of the network architecture rather than by means of the training process. A more detailed treatment of this issue may be found in [9].

Second, hierarchical feature maps may be used to produce disjoint, clusters of the input data. Moreover, these disjoint clusters are gradually refined when moving down along the hierarchy. Contrary to that, the self-organizing map in its basic form cannot be used to produce disjoint clusters. The separation of data items rather is a tricky task that requires some insight into the structure of the input data. What one gets, however, from a self-organizing map is a sort of overall representation of input data similarities. In this sense we may use the following picture to contrast the two models of neural networks. Self-organizing maps can be used to produce maps of the input data whereas hierarchical feature maps produce an atlas of the input data. Taking up this metaphor, the difference between both models is quite obvious. Self-organizing maps, in our point of view, provide the user with a single picture of the underlying data archive. As long as the map is not too large, this picture may be sufficient. As the maps grow larger, however, they have the tendency of providing too little orientation for the user. In such a case we would advise to change to hierarchical feature maps as the model for representing the contents of the data archive. In this case, the data is organized hierarchically which facilitates browsing into relevant portions of the data archive. In much the same way as one would probably not use the map of the world in order to find one's way from *Schönbrunn* to *Neustift* one would probably not use a single map of a document archive to find a particular document. Conversely, when given an atlas one might follow the hierarchy of maps along a path such as *World* → *Europe* → *Austria* → *Vienna* in order to finally find the way from *Schönbrunn* to *Neustift*. In a similar way an atlas of a document archive might be used.

3 Document representation

For the experiments presented thereafter we used the 1990 edition of the *CIA World Factbook* (http://www.odci.gov/cia/publications/factbook) as a sample document archive. The *CIA World Factbook* represents a text collection containing information on countries and regions of the world. The information is split into different categories such as *Geography*, *People*, *Government*, *Economy*, *Communications*, and *Defense Forces.*

We used full-text indexing to represent the various documents. The complete information on each country is used for indexing. In other words, for the present set of experiments we refrained from identifying the various document segments that contain the information on the various categories. In total, the 1990 edition of the *CIA World Factbook* consists of 245 documents. The indexing process identified 959 content terms, i.e. terms used for document representation. During indexing we omitted terms that appear in less than 15 documents or more than 196 documents. These terms are weighted according to a simple $tf \times idf$ weighting scheme [11]. With this indexing vocabulary the documents are represented according to the vector-space model of information retrieval. The various vectors representing the documents are further used for neural network training.

4 A map of the world

Based on the document description as outlined above, we first trained a 10×10 self-organizing map to represent the contents of the document archive. Figure 3 gives a graphical representation of the training result. For ease of identifying the various rows of units in the graphical representation, we separated these rows by horizontal lines. Each unit is either marked by a number of countries (or regions) or by a dot. The name of a country appears if this unit serves as the *winner* for that particular country (or, more precisely, for the input vector representing that country). A dot appears if the unit is never selected as *winner* for any document.

Figure 3 shows that the self-organizing map was quite successful in arranging the various input data according to their mutual similarity. It should be obvious that in general countries belonging to similar geographical regions are rather similar with respect to the different categories described in the *CIA World Factbook.* These geographical regions can be found in the two-dimensional map display as well. In order to ease the interpretation of the self-organizing map's training result, we have marked several regions manually. For example, the area on the left hand side of the map is allocated for documents describing various islands. We should note, that the *CIA World Factbook* contains a large number of descriptions of islands. It is interesting to note, that the description of the oceans can be found in a map region neighboring the area of islands.

In the lower center of the map we find the European countries. The cluster representing these countries is further decomposed into a cluster of small countries, e.g. *San Marino* and *Liechtenstein*, a cluster of Western European countries, and finally a cluster of Eastern European countries. The latter cluster is represented by a single unit in the last row of the output space. This unit has as neighbors other countries that are usually attributed as belonging to the Communist hemisphere, e.g. *Cuba*, *North Korea*, *Albania*, and *Soviet Union.* At

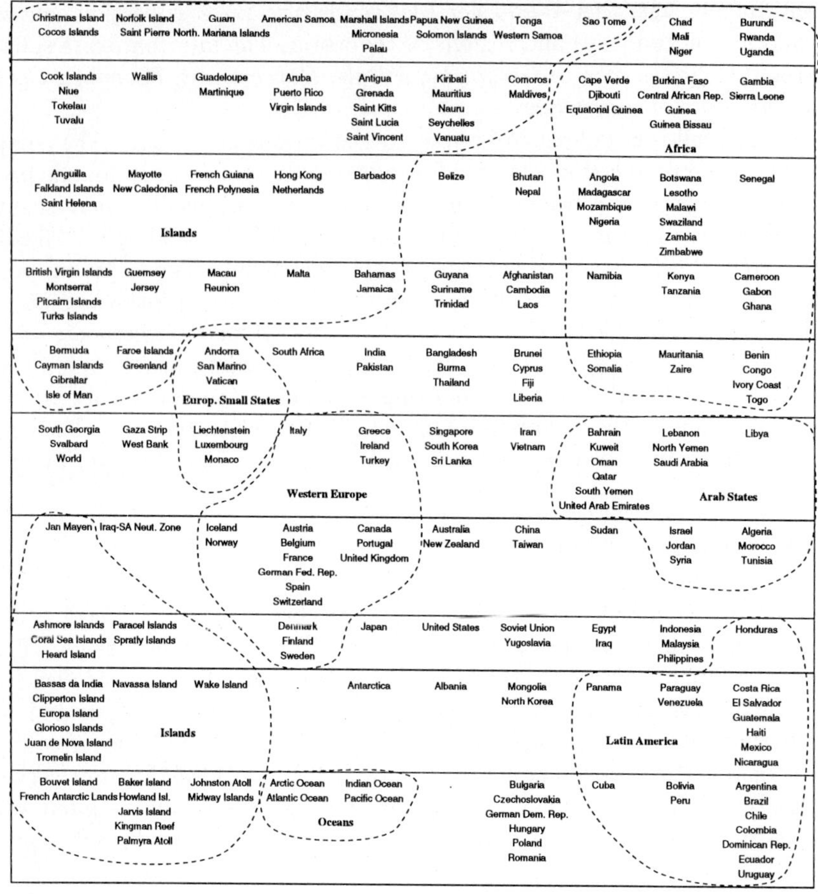

Fig. 3. 10 × 10 map of the world

this point it is important to recall that our document archive is the 1990 edition of the *CIA World Factbook*. Thus, the descriptions refer to a time before the "fall" of the Communist hemisphere.

Other clusters of interest are the region containing countries from Latin America (lower right of the map), the cluster containing Arab countries (middle right of the map), or the cluster of African countries (upper right of the map).

Overall, the representation of the document space is highly successful in that similar documents are located close to one another. Thus, it is easy to find an orientation in this document space. The negative point, however, is that each document is represented on the very same map. Since the self-organizing map represents a very high-dimensional data space (959 index terms) within a two-dimensional display it is only natural that some information gets lost during the mapping process. As a consequence, it is rather difficult to identify the various clusters. Imagine Figure 3 without the dashed lines indicating cluster boundaries. Without this information it is only possible to identify, say, African countries when prior information about the document collection is available.

5 An atlas of the world

In the previous section we have described the results from using self-organizing maps with the data of the *CIA World Factbook*. The major shortcoming of this neural network model is that the various documents are represented within only one two-dimensional output space making it difficult to identify cluster boundaries without profound insight into the underlying document collection.

The hierarchical feature map can provide essential assistance in isolating the different clusters. The isolation of clusters is achieved thanks to the architecture of the neural network which consists of layers of independent self-organizing maps. Thus, in the highest layer the complete document archive is represented by means of a small map (in terms of the number of neural processing elements). Each unit is then further developed within its own branch of the neural network.

For the experiment presented thereafter we used a setup of the hierarchical feature map using four layers. The respective maps have the following dimensions: 3×3 on the first layer, 4×4 on the second layer, and 3×3 on the third and fourth layer. This setup has been determined empirically.

Figure 4 presents the contents of the first layer self-organizing map. In order to keep the information at a minimum we refrained from typing the names of the various countries in this figure. We rather present some aggregated information concerning the geographical location of the various countries.

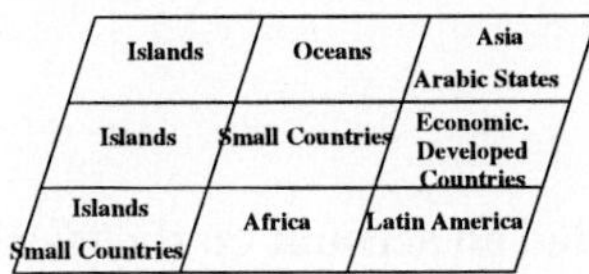

Fig. 4. Hierarchical feature map: First layer

In the remainder of this discussion we will just present the branch of the hierarchical feature map that contains what we called *economically developed countries*. The other branches cannot be shown in this paper because of space considerations. These branches, however, are formed quite similarly.

In Figure 5 we show the arrangement of the second layer within the branch of *economically developed countries*. In this map, the various countries are separated roughly according to either their geographic location or their political system. The clusters are symbolized by using different shades of grey.

Finally, Figure 6 shows the full-blown branch of *economically developed countries*. In this case it is straight-forward to identify the various cluster boundaries

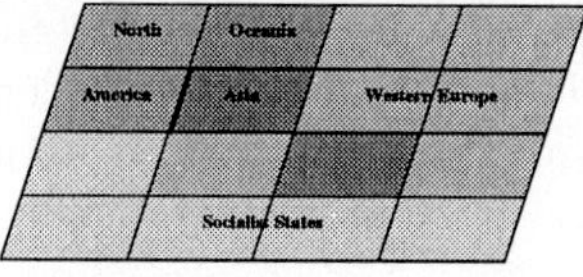

Fig. 5. Hierarchical feature map: Second layer

in that each cluster is represented by an individual self-organizing map. Higher level similarities are shown in higher levels of the hierarchical feature map.

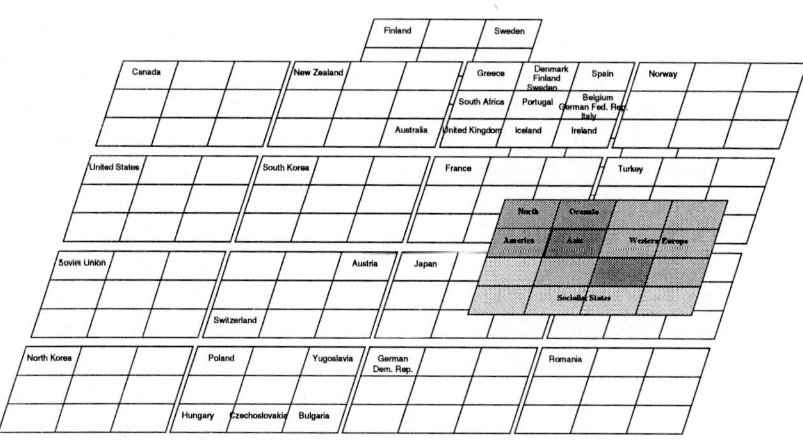

Fig. 6. A subset of the world map: Economically developed countries

6 Conclusions

In this paper we have provided an account on the feasibility of using unsupervised neural networks in a highly important task of information retrieval, namely text classification. As an experimental document collection we used the description of various countries as contained in the 1990 edition of the *CIA World Factbook*. For this document collection it is rather easy to judge the quality of the classification result. For document representation we relied on the vector space model and a simple $tf \times idf$ term weighting scheme.

We demonstrated that both the map and the atlas metaphor are highly useful for assisting the user to find her orientation within the document space. The shortcoming of the map metaphor, however, is that each document is shown in one large map and thus, the borderline between clusters of related and clusters of unrelated documents are sometimes hard to find. This is especially the case if the user does not have sufficient insight into the contents of the document collection.

The atlas metaphor overcomes this limitation in that the clusters of documents are clearly visible because of the architecture of the neural network. The document space is separated into independent maps along different layers in a hierarchy. The user thus gets the best of both worlds. The similarity between documents is shown in a fine-grained level in maps of the lower layers of the hierarchy while the overall organizational principles of the document archive are shown at higher layer maps. Since such a hierarchical arrangement of documents is the common way of organizing conventional libraries, only small intellectual overhead is required from the user to find her way through the document space.

References

1. M. A. Hearst and J. O. Pedersen. Reexamining the cluster hypothesis: Scatter/Gather on retrieval results. In *Proc Int'l ACM SIGIR Conf on R&D in Information Retrieval (SIGIR'96)*, Zurich, Switzerland, 1996.
2. T. Kohonen. Self-organized formation of topologically correct feature maps. *Biological Cybernetics*, 43, 1982.
3. T. Kohonen. *Self-organizing maps.* Springer-Verlag, Berlin, 1995.
4. T. Kohonen, S. Kaski, K. Lagus, and T. Honkela. Very large two-level SOM for the browsing of newsgroups. In *Proc Int'l Conf on Artificial Neural Networks (ICANN'96)*, Bochum, Germany, 1996.
5. K. Lagus, T. Honkela, S. Kaski, and T. Kohonen. Self-organizing maps of document collections: A new approach to interactive exploration. In *Proc Int'l Conf on Knowledge Discovery and Data Mining (KDD-96)*, Portland, OR, 1996.
6. X. Lin, D. Soergel, and G. Marchionini. A self-organizing semantic map for information retrieval. In *Proc Int'l ACM SIGIR Conf on R&D in Information Retrieval (SIGIR'91)*, Chicago, IL, 1991.
7. D. Merkl. A connectionist view on document classification. In *Proc Australasian Database Conf (ADC'95)*, Adelaide, SA, 1995.
8. D. Merkl. Exploration of document collections with self-organizing maps: A novel approach to similarity representation. In *Proc European Symp on Principles of Data Mining and Knowledge Discovery (PKDD'97)*, Trondheim, Norway, 1997.
9. D. Merkl. Exploration of text collections with hierarchical feature maps. In *Proc Int'l ACM SIGIR Conf on R&D in Information Retrieval (SIGIR'97)*, Philadelphia, PA, 1997.
10. R. Miikkulainen. Script recognition with hierarchical feature maps. *Connection Science*, 2, 1990.
11. G. Salton. *Automatic Text Processing: The Transformation, Analysis, and Retrieval of Information by Computer.* Addison-Wesley, Reading, MA, 1989.
12. P. Willet. Recend trends in hierarchic document clustering: A critical review. *Information Processing & Management*, 24, 1988.

Learning Concepts From Databases

Takao MIURA † and Isamu SHIOYA ‡

† Hosei University, Faculty of Engineering, Kajino Cho 3-7-2, Koganei, Tokyo, Japan
‡ SANNO College, Kamikasuya 1573, Isehara, Kanagawa, Japan
E-mail: miurat@k.hosei.ac.jp, shioya@sanno.ac.jp

Abstract. In this investigation, we discuss how to make *conceptual formation* from databases as background knowledge. Given a set E of objects $e_1, .., e_n$, we generate *conceptual description* to capture the meaning that E has. Database schemes contain common knowledge that are carried by all the instances. Since they had been designed much before various instances are generated, the schemes sometimes couldn't capture the *current* meaning of the instances.
To adjust such conceptual differences, we utilize relevant information (attributes, attribute values) to make suitable conceptual description by means of database schemes and their expression on. In this work, we introduce *Conditional Sum of Product* (CSOP) expressions on object types and we discuss how to generate conceptual description based on extended *decision tree* technique. We show some experimental results.

1 Introduction

One of the most important goals of information processing is to extract useful information from data in secondary storage upon requests. Users want to obtain not only stored data in databases but also what the data mean or sometimes what the users should ask.

In this investigation, we propose a learning method to capture concepts for a given set of objects in a database, by utilizing knowledge in the database and some description languages. Traditionally such kinds of research topics have been called *Knowledge Acquisition* or *Machine Learning* where databases have been regarded as just efficient storages or *repository*. Our work has sharp distinction from them since we consider databases not as storage repository but as *background knowledge*.

Databases have been constructed based on *schemes* such as *types* by which all the informations are classified into appropriate clusters and managed consistently. We should define schemes *first*, then we can populate them. These facts mean schemes could be seen as *common knowledge* among the instances while each instance carries its individual aspect of information. *Integrity constraints* are defined over schemes where all the instances should satisfy them. In short, *knowledge* in databases means schemes and the instances satisfying constraints. There is no reason why knowledge learning processes don't utilize schemes heavily. In almost all companies and organizations, a lot of large databases have been designed, constructed and managed for a long time in a consistent manner. These provide us with good knowledge bases, information sources for model candidate selection and for validation of learning results.

To capture what a set E of objects does mean, it seems natural to describe E as a expression κ in terms of schemes. Moreover the expression κ should be verified whether

κ could capture the full or enough semantics of E by using database instances. In this investigation, we regard the generation process of κ as *concept formation* and both the formation and the verification as *concept learning from databases.*

Unlike traditional research activities as machine learning, we assume databases are *dynamic.* Many databases have long life-cycle, say more than 10 years. Since they were born, database schemes have been re-designed and re-organized many times to follow *current world of interests,* but still it is hard to describe the exact meaning of the instances. This is because databases are still lack of flexibility and their reconstruction is not easy task even right now[19]. Then *new* kind of information are sometimes managed within individual data instead of database schemes. Thus many people believe there must exist some semantic gap between schemes and the instances in long-life databases. Our problem is not a toy issue against small databases, but the one how we can complement lost aspects of the schemes, i.e., one of the big problems of database life-cycle. An issue to be attacked is how we can describe *concepts,* what kinds of languages we can adopt for this purpose, and how we can generate suitable expressions to capture the meaning. In this investigation we introduce *Conditional Sum Of Product* (CSOP) expressions over types and discuss how to generate them.

In the following we discuss reasoning why database can be seen as knowledge description in section 2. Section 3 contains basic definitions of databases and related concepts such as type hierarchy. Also we discuss primary approach to concept learning from databases and clarify the issues to be overcome. In section 4, we define CSOP expression and show how they are useful to the issue. Then we discuss how we can generate CSOP expression to capture sets of objects as concept learning from databases. Section 5 contains some experimental results and the evaluation. Related research are summarized in section 6. Finally we conclude our investigation in section 7.

2 Databases as Knowledge

In this section, we discuss some assumptions that databases have and the goals of this investigation in order to clarify our issue. We will develop our methodology for concept learning in the subsequent sections.

2.1 Databases as Background Knowledge

For a given background knowledge, we recognize what a set E of objects in a database does mean based on the knowledge, then all of the quality, efficiency and reasoning of the recognition depend heavily on the background knowledge, the characteristic items and how E is described. In the following, we discuss how we can regard databases as knowledge.

A database is a set of information systematically modeled, abstracted and coded based on a given classification defined *in advance.* Such classification is called a *database scheme* (or just a scheme) and each coded data is called an *instance.* Schemes could be seen as knowledge extracted from the world of interests. Each instance carries its own meaning *and* it follows the meaning of the scheme at the same time.

Data independence means a property that information should be described independent of how they are utilized. Because of the historical reasons, all the databases should follow data independence, putting it into other words, it should have declarative property. Generally databases are formally described based on sorted first order predicate logic: a scheme is defined by means of a set of sorts (types) T and a set of sorted predicates P, and each instance is described as a ground term or a ground atom. A set IC of integrity constraints consists of closed formulas, and finally we call $\langle T, P, IC \rangle$ a *scheme system*. A database D could be seen as an interpretation over T, P satisfying IC. Data manipulation, called a *query*, is described as an (open) formula, and the answer is nothing but the first order calculation of the formula based on D.

We assume each instance in a database may have more than one (but finite number of) types, thus we don't introduce many sorted logic strictly but the one based on sorted terms. We don't develop formal theory on databases any more but see [13] for more detail.

Whenever we talk about databases for knowledge acquisition, we can fully utilize the consistent and high quality of knowledge of schemes consisting of general predicates and types, associated characteristic items, well-designed details and integrity constraints that all the instances satisfy.

However, when a new kind (not described in a scheme) of information arises, it could be stored not as a common knowledge but as an individual data where the new meaning is embedded. Eventually the scheme becomes useless as a common knowledge.

Originally concept learning from databases is the process to obtain alternative scheme systems keeping D as an interpretation[1]. Therefore, the learning could also be regarded as one of the re-engineering process to adjust current interests of the world, and the result should be put back into a new scheme. In this work, we are suspicious that scheme information is not enough to capture the semantics of E, since the scheme has been designed before. The learning process should have provide high level of conceptual languages as well as scheme information.

2.2 Concept Learning from Databases

Now let us formalize our issue to be addressed here. According to notational convention of databases, we denote E by a finite set of objects in a database: $E = \{e_1, .., e_n\}, \infty > n > 0$. Each $e_i \in E$ is an object in a database, and our goal is what the collection E does mean. The meaning of E should be captured as an expression κ based on a scheme system in an exact, formal and concise manner.

An expression κ is a formula constructed from a scheme system, and it is suitable that the interpretation $[\kappa]$ is exactly equal to E, but $[\kappa] \supseteq E$ seems reasonable since κ covers E. In the this case, we say κ describes E. When there exists big differences, we can say κ is too general to capture the semantics E. To evaluate the learning results, we introduce a notion of *degree of description* defined as $\mid E \mid / \mid [\kappa] \mid$. Note the degree of 1.0 says κ describes E exactly and correctly. But, κ may have much longer description which hurts *simplicity* or understandability.

It seems reasonable that expressions are constructed from scheme information, since the details are well-known to the users. Possible candidates are closed/open first order formulas and specifically arranged languages.

In database research activities, *intensional answers* have the similar goals[19]. By the answers, a huge amount of the instances are summarized as a high level of conceptual description in a form of (another) query. The technique could be also useful to optimize access plans to the answers and helpful to general database query processing.

It seems a good idea to consider the techniques of intensional answers as conceptual learning from databases. In fact, by considering E as a set of answer of a query Q, we

---

[1] We don't generate *models* for scheme systems like inductive logic programming.

try to generate a *better* query Q' from Q. However the process to obtain an original Q from E is indispensable, thus learning results depend on such process as well as syntax and expressive power of the languages for queries.

In the following sections, we translate E into κ directly in an effective and efficient manner.

3 Concept Formation from Databases

In this section, we give the definition of databases to introduce a notion of conceptual formation from databases. Then, to investigate our issue, we discuss the concept formation without any other knowledge than types. Introducing description of the concepts by Sum-Of-Product over types, we discuss how we have to extend the expression.

3.1 Databases and Type Hierarchy

Typically a *data model* consists of *objects* (or *entity*) and *association*[6]. The former is a surrogate to represent a *thing* in a real world of interests defined independent of how that are described, what kinds of properties they have and so on. The latter is to capture individual relationship among objects, each relationship in a real world is represented as an association. Objects have *types* which are intensional concepts to capture common properties in objects of the class, then an object called to have a type.

Generally an object e may have more than one type t. In the followings, let $\mathcal{E}$ be a finite set of objects, $\mathcal{T}$ a finite set of types. Let $\Gamma(t)$ be a set of objects that have a type t, called an interpretation of t. We assume a special type `@E` whose interpretation is $\mathcal{E}$ if otherwise stated. In a similar manner, we assume *predicates* which are intensional concepts to capture common properties of associations. We assume every association $p(e_1...e_n)$ of a predicate p is typed, i.e., every component of each association has a common type. Especially in a predicate $f(E_1 E_2)$ over E_1, E_2, E_2 is called an *attribute* of E_1 if the interpretation of f is a function from $\Gamma(E_1)$ to $\Gamma(E_2)$. For more detail, see [13].

For an object e, we denote a (finite) set of types that e has by $\tau(e)$, called *type scheme* of e : $\tau(e) = \{t \in \mathcal{T} \mid e \in \Gamma(t)\}$. All the $\tau(e)$ constitute typing of a database, called a type scheme of the database.

To keep database consistent, database systems have to manage all the type schemes according to all the changes, thus eventually the systems must have a lot of inefficient and complicated jobs. Also each object should be managed in a lengthy and complicated manner, sophisticated and unified mechanism should be introduced such as knowledge control. Among others, it should be useful to simplify individual type schemes $\tau(e)$.

EXAMPLE 1 Let us consider some Asian countries as our running example[16]. And we will discuss this database. Here we assume there are 8 sub-types which describe Asian area: Country (C), FarEastAsia (FE), WestAsia (W), SouthEastAsia (SE), Asia (A), Oceania (O), Pacific (P) and Kanji (K) where their meanings are self-explanatory

There are 14 countries (objects) in Asian area over 7 types (other than C) in the left part of figure 1. □

object	type scheme
Japan(J)	FE,A,P,K
Korea(K)	FE,A,P,K
Taiwan(TW)	FE,A,P,K
China(C)	A,K
HongKong(H)	SE,A,P,K
Philippines(PH)	SE,A,P
Singapore(S)	SE,A,P
Malaysia(M)	SE,A,P
Indonesia(IS)	SE,A,P
Thailand(TH)	SE,A
Australia(A)	O,P
New Zealand(NZ)	O,P
India(IN)	W,A
Pakistan(PK)	W,A

types	objects	$\Gamma(types)$
FE,K	J,TW,K	
K	C	C,J,TW,K,H
SE,P,K	H	
SE,P	PH,S,M,IS	
SE	TH	TH,PH,S,M.IS,H
O	A,NZ	
W	IN,PK	
P		J,TW,H,PH,S, M,IS,A,NZ

Fig. 1. Asian Area

One of the typical examples is *generalization* or sometimes called ISA. For two types t_1, t_2, we say t_2 is a generalization of t_1 (or t_1 ISA t_2) if an integrity constraint $\Gamma(t_1) \subseteq \Gamma(t_2)$ is posed. We say t_1 ISA t_2 holds if a database satisfies the constraint. By applying ISA in a repeated manner, we have reflective and transitive closure, called ISA *hierarchy* (or type hierarchy). By this notion, we can *deduce* ISA correctly. For instance, both t_1 ISA t_2 and t_2 ISA t_3 implies t_1 ISA t_3. For types t_1, t_2, we say t_2 is a *direct generalization* (or a direct parent) of t_1 if we have t_1 ISA t_2 and there exists no t_3 in the hierarchy such that t_1 ISA t_3 and t_3 ISA t_2.

Note we may have more than one direct parents thus the hierarchy is really Directed Acyclic Graph (DAG). But because of the historical conventions, we say parents, children, ancestors and descendants and so on.

For a type t that is a common ancestor of t_1, t_2, t is called *least general* of the two if, for every common ancestor t' such that t' ISA t, t' is identical to t. In a similar manner we can define a *least general* type of three types. For a set of types $V = \{t_1, .., t_k\}$, we denote all the least general types of $t_1, .., t_k$ by $LG(V)$, and we denote all the types that are never ancestors from the elements in V by $LF(V)$: $\{t \in V \mid \text{there is no } t'\texttt{ISA}t \text{ in } V\}$. Finally let $LGF(T)$ be $LG(LF(T))$.

When an object e has a type t and t ISA t', we should say e has t' too. In other words, we say a type scheme $\tau(e)$ is *consistent* if both $t \in \tau(e)$ and t ISA t' implies $t' \in \tau(e)$. Here, in this investigation, we assume such *type consistency* everywhere.

EXAMPLE 2 In ISA hierarchy of EXAMPLE1 readers can see 9 parents (i.e.,direct generalizations) and each type has up to 2 direct generalization. Figure 2 shows the ISA hierarchy.

Then we generate $LF(\tau(e))$ for each object e using the ISA hierarchy. Then we collect objects in such a way that the objects have same leafs. Note each object that has all of the types can be deduced by means of ISA hierarchy. See the right part of figure 1. □

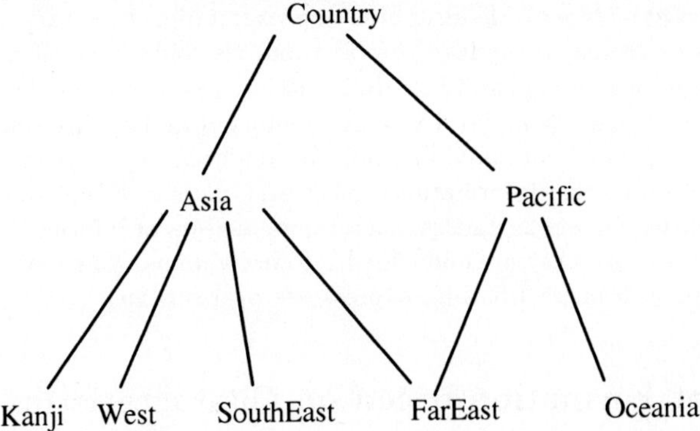

Fig. 2. ISA Hierarchy of Country

3.2 Concept Formation by SOP Expressions

Now let us develop our theory to make concept formation from databases. First of all, let us try to generate an expression κ in a form of Sum-Of-Product over types to describe $E = \{e_1, .., e_n\}$.

For types $t_1, .., t_m$, a conjunction $t_1 \wedge ... \wedge t_m$ is called a *Product* (P) expression over types. By using $\Gamma(t_i)$, we define the interpretation as $\bigcap_{i=1}^{m} \Gamma(t_i)$. Then, for a set $c = \{t_1, .., t_m\}$, we denote $t_1 \wedge ... \wedge t_m$ by $\wedge c$. For product expressions $c_1, .., c_m$, a disjunction $c_1 \vee ... \vee c_m$ is called a *Sum-Of-Product* (SOP) expression over types. The interpretation is defined as $\bigcup_{i=1}^{m} \Gamma(c_i)$ by means of $\Gamma(c_i)$. For a set $c = \{c_1, .., c_m\}$, we denote $c_1 \vee ... \vee c_m$ by $\vee c$. All these are defined by using $\wedge$ and $\vee$ and preserve intuitive meaning. When discussing P/SOP expressions, *degree of simplicity* of the expressions corresponds to the length of the description.

In our databases, each element $e_i \in E$ has a type scheme $\tau(e_i)$ individually, and the type scheme has all the types that e_i has. Then the interpretation of our goal κ, $[\kappa]$, should be defined as $\Gamma(\kappa)$. Our expression must describe E, i.e., $\Gamma(\kappa) \supseteq E$, have the good degree of description and must be simple, i.e., short.

Can we find just P or SOP expressions to describe E ? For example, $\tau(e_1) \cap ... \cap \tau(e_n)$ contains all the types that every object in E shares. Remember @E is included in all the type schemes, thus the result can't be empty. To obtain shorter description while keeping the identical interpretation, we define $\kappa_1 = LF(\tau(e_1) \cap ... \cap \tau(e_n))$ and then the P expression $\wedge\kappa_1$ describes E. What are types that each element in E shares ? As @E says, they may be general enough to describe large set of objects. Also common types may discard characteristic aspects (details) of E, and the degree of description should become lower.

Then let us simplify each $\tau(e_i)$ and combine them. To describe $\Gamma(LF(\tau(e_i)))$, it seems better to define $\wedge LGF(\tau(e_i))$, because the degree of decrease may decrease but simplicity increases. In fact, every type in $LGF(\tau(e_i))$ is the least general element of $LF(\tau(e_i))$ and, in an appropriate type hierarchy, $\wedge LGF(\tau(e_i))$ might be simple. Then our candidate is $\kappa_2 = (\wedge LGF(\tau(e_1))) \vee ... \vee (\wedge LGF(\tau(e_n)))$ which describes E.

Such a process is really intuitive, procedural and easy to understand. Users are possible easily to validate the results obtained. If database schemes are really effective to describe *current* instances, the proposed approach might be rather useful. Since the procedure goes by means of Boolean combination, we could have efficient processing.

However, SOP processing can't be suitable to learn new concepts from type schemes of E and the type hierarchy in databases. Remember that database schemes can't capture exact meaning of current individual information because of the database paradigm, and that sets of individual informations may carry more rich meaning than schemes. Without inspecting current instances, such (new) aspects of information can't be processed properly because they are embedded into individuals. Now our *true* issue is how we can translate such inspection into expressions over schemes.

4 Concept Formation based on Characteristics

In this section, we assume each object in E has a common set of characteristic items $A_1, .., A_m$, and by analizing the characteristic values, we discuss how to learn concepts that E carries. It is common that each object in E shares a set of characteristic items $A_1, .., A_m$. For example, a predicate $p(EA_1...A_m)$ defined on types $E, A_1, .., A_m$ corresponds to the interpretation of associations in a form of $\langle e, a_1, .., a_m \rangle$. From *relative* point of view, each e has one or more tuples $\langle a_1, .., a_m \rangle$ where each A_i has a_i. Another example says that, for types $t, t_1, .., t_m$ where t ISA $t_i, i = 1, .., m$, an attribute A_i of t_i is inherited to t, thus every element in E has all the $A_1, .., A_m$ values if $E \subseteq \Gamma(t)$ is satisfied.

In the following, we will develop our theory where E is described by means of Conditional Sum-Of-Product (CSOP) expressions over types, and according to the expression, E is decomposed to generate the expression in a recursive manner. Characteristic items are utilized to create *conditions*.

4.1 Conditional Sum-Of-Product Expressions

Now we develop our learning algorithm. Our idea is based on *decision tree* which generates branches based on characteristic values. Decision tree is a procedure to classify given set of information into one of the solutions based on item values. The tree consists of internal nodes representing branch process and leaf nodes representing one of the solutions attached as labels.

On an internal node, some characteristic item is examined and according to the values, one of the branches is selected. We start with the decision process at the root node in a recursive manner to get to one of the leaf node.

When generating the tree from a set of information E, we create a leaf node of a label c if all the set of the information to be processed have the identical solution c. Otherwise, we create an internal node with an characteristic item and the branches with the values. We repeat the process to all the values in E. Several algorithms such as ID3 and C4.5 propose which items should be selected based on *entropy* theory[22, 23].

During the generation of a tree, a path from root to a leaf represents one of conjunctive conditions on characteristic items. That is, for each internal node with a label A has a branch with a value a, we generate a condition $A = "a"$, denoted by σ. Then a path represents a conjunctive condition α where α means $\sigma_1 \wedge ... \wedge \sigma_k$. If a leaf label is a solution c, the path is described as $\alpha : c$. Since branching means disjunction, a decision tree is represented totally as $\alpha_1 : c_1 \vee ... \vee \alpha_m : c_m$. This kind of form is called *Conditional Sum Of Product* (CSOP) expression, and we utilize this class of expression for concept formation. It is quite true that a CSOP expression is a restatement of decision trees.

The interpretation of a CSOP expression $\alpha_1 : c_1 \vee ... \vee \alpha_m : c_m$ is defined as all the union of the interpretations $[\alpha_i : c_i]$ where $[\alpha : c]$ means all the elements of $\Gamma(c)$ satisfying a conjunctive condition α. It is straightforward to extend c as a set of solutions.

By the definition of decision tree, a set of paths decompose all the information E into sets where each component is described by $[\alpha_i : c_i]$.

4.2 Processing Concept Formation

For a while, we assume all the $\tau(e_i)$ is a singleton $\{c_i\}$ for simplicity. Then $e_i \in E$ can be described by means of sequences of characteristic values and c_i, $(a^i_1, ..., a^i_m, c_i)$.

If all of $c_1, .., c_n$ is identical to c, we say *degree of generality* is 1.0 and E can be described by c^2.

Let $T_c = \{d_1, .., d_k\}$ be a set of least general elements of $c_1, .., c_n$, i.e, $LG(\{c_1, .., c_n\})$. Then, if T_c has the degree of generalization more than a threshold ρ, we say E can be described by T_c where the degree of generalization of T_c is defined as $| \bigcup_{i=1,..,n} \Gamma(c_i) | / | \bigcap_{j=1,..,k} \Gamma(d_j) |$. Note the degree should be less than or equal to 1.0.

Otherwise, we select one, say A_1, of the characteristic items that is not processed yet. And we make grouping E by A_1, and finally, for each group, we do our process in a recursive manner. If there remains no item, we can say E can't be described by c.

Then which items should be selected ? Our basic idea is to utilize a notion of *coverage*. Grouping E by one item A into $E_1, ..., E_j, ..., E_l$, then, for each j, we obtain the degree of generalization g_j and the number of elements of E_j, and finally we calculate $g_1 \times k_1 + .. + g_l \times k_l$, called *coverage* of E by A.

This notion of coverage is really useful to decide characteristic items. In fact, the degree of generalization means how many information is lost at generalization step, and by multiplying with the number of the elements, we could obtain the weighted number of the elements in the abstraction hierarchy. By calculating all the coverages, we select the item which has the maximum number to reduce the information lost. Note entropy technique can't be applied directly since T_c depends on how groups are generated.

Let us consider what we obtain as a result. "E can be described by T_c" means is that every grouping component describes part of E in a manner more than the threshold ρ. Also it means that all the union of them are combined into a CSOP expression $\alpha_1 : c_1 \cup ... \cup \alpha_m : c_m$ which describes E. And finally the interpretation of this CSOP expression is defined as $\Gamma(\alpha_1 : c_1) \cup ... \cup \Gamma(\alpha_m : c_m)$ where $\Gamma(\alpha : c)$ is a set of elements in $\Gamma(c)$ satisfying α : $\Gamma(\alpha : c) = \{e \in \Gamma(c) \mid e \text{ satisfies } \alpha\}$.

Readers might say our proposed algorithm is similar to ID3 or the equivalent. In fact, we create one internal nodes based on a characteristic item and we go in a recursive manner. But our discussion differs from two important points. One is we utilize type hierarchy as the convergence condition, and another point is we select items based on coverage but not on entropy.

It is straightforward to extend $\tau(e_i)$ as a set. In fact, for $\tau(e_i)$, we take $c_i = LF(\tau(e_i))$. When every element in E has identical set of types c, we have done.

Let $T_c = \{d_1, .., d_k\}$ be a set of least general types of $c_1, .., c_n$, i.e., $LG(c_1 \cup ... \cup c_n)$. If the degree of generalization of T_c is more than a threshold ρ, we say E can be described by T_c where the degree is defined as $| \bigcup_{i=1,..,n} \Gamma(c_i) | / | \bigcap_{j=1,..,k} \Gamma(d_j) |$.

[2] In fact, c could be seen as a generalization of c itself.

EXAMPLE 3 Let us continue our example 1 of Asian countries. Here are some characteristic information of our countries: the major religion and the location of the tourist office in Tokyo where *location* means office location, B means Buddism, H Hinduism, M Muslim, F Confucianism and C Christian.

object	religion	location
Japan(J)	B	Ginza
Korea(K)	F	Ginza
Taiwan(TW)	B	UchiSaiwai
China(C)	F	ToranoMon
HongKong(H)	B	MarunoUchi
Philippines(PH)	C	NampeiDai
Singapore(S)	C	UchiSaiwai
Malaysia(M)	M	Ginza
Indonesia(IS)	M	Akasaka
Thailand(TH)	B	Ginza
Australia(A)	C	KioiCho
New Zealand(NZ)	C	Shinjuku
India(IN)	H	Ginza
Pakistan(PK)	M	Azabu

Then the set $E_2 = \{J, IN, A\}$ is clearly described by means of CSOP: $(L = "Ginza" \wedge R = "B" : \{FE, K\}) \vee (L = "Ginza" \wedge R = "H" : \{W\}) \vee (L = "KioiCho" : \{O\})$ where the first, the second and the last terms correspond to J, IN and A respectively. In the case of a set $E_3 = \{J, K, TH\}$ with a small ρ, we have a CSOP expression of $(R = "B" : \{A\}) \vee (R = "F" : \{FE, K\})$ where the fisrt and the second terms correspond to $\{J, TH\}$ and K respectively.

Let E_4 be a set of $\{J, K, C\}$ and $\rho = 0.5$. These objects have different type schemes and the common least general type *Asia* contains 12 countries in our example. Then we make group on L then a group of $L = "Ginza"$ contains J, K with the common type scheme FE, K and the degree of generalization is 1.0. So does true for another group C thus the coverage becomes 3.0. When we make group on R then a group of $R = "F"$ contains K, C with the type schemes FE, K and K. Since the least general type of the two is *Asia*, the degree of generalization now becomes 5/12.0. Another group J becomes closed and the coverage becomes 1.83. So our choice is the first and the result CSOP expression is $(L = "Ginza" : \{FE, K\}) \vee (L = ToranoMon" : \{K\})$. See figure 3. □

4.3 Algorithms

Let us summarize our procedure as an algorithm. We assume every type scheme $c_1, .., c_n$ is replaced by $LF(c_1), .., LF(c_n)$ respectively.

(1) If all of $c_1, .., c_n$ are identical to c, E is described by c with the degree 1.0. And we have done.
(2) Otherwise, find a set T_c of least general types of $c_1, .., c_n$, i.e., $LG(\{c_1, .., c_n\})$, and let T_c be $\{d_1, .., d_k\}$. Calculate the degree $\mid \bigcup_{i=1,..,n} \Gamma(c_i) \mid / \mid \bigcap_{j=1,..,k} \Gamma(d_j) \mid$, and if the value is more than ρ, we have done.
(3) Otherwise, we select a characteristic item A to make grouping. By grouping E by A, we generate components of E. For each component, we do the process in a recursive manner.. If there remains no other item, E can't be described.

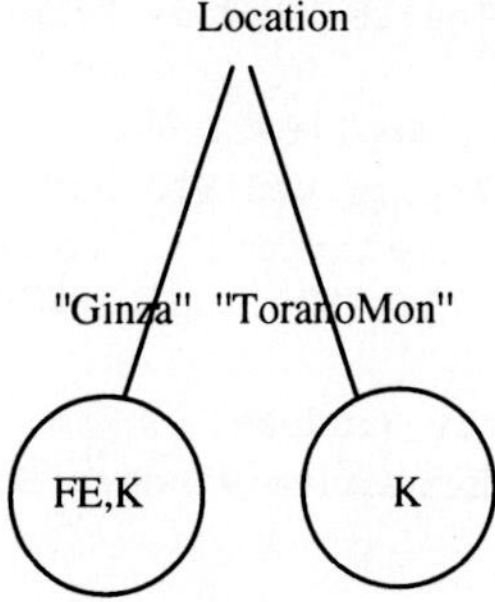

Fig. 3. CSOP expression

To select one of characteristic items, we do the followings:

(1) For every unprocessed characteristic item A, we make grouping of E by A and generate $E_1, ..., E_l$. For each group, we calculate the degree of generalization and the number of the elements. Then we obtain the coverage of E by A.
(2) Select the item which has the maximum coverage.

5 Experimental Results

Here we give experimental results of the CSOP algorithm. In this experiment, we utilize `Nikkei Byte Article Keyword Index` for `NIKKEI BYTE` magazines from 1985 until 1994. The index contains a collection of 2315 articles. Each record contains titles, year/number, pages, topics and keywords, and each article is considered as an objects of a type `ARTICLE` but also of which we regard the specified keywords as types. 198 keywords are defined in the index, and they appear 2792 times in total[3].

```
.....
(134) PART III 3.0 vs. 3.1 - Comparison of Windows3.1 at Graphics:
       1993.07:no.114:p.146:Topics:Windows:Benchmarktest
.....
(431) Small with Standard Keyboard - 2 IBM PC compatible at Printer port:
       1992.07:no.101:p.233:Survey:Keyboard:Smallcomputer
.....
(488) GUI based DTP softwares on Unix/Windows:1992.04:no.98:p.148:
       Product Report:DTP:GUI:UNIX:Windows
.....
(580) Demonstrating by IBM and MS - OS,Multimedia,Pen:
       1991.12:no.93:p.144:Trends:OS Trends:Multimedia:Pen computer
.....
(666) Page Printer on Windows - PART III Basic Benchmark - Graphics:
       1991.09:no.90:p.256:Topics:Windows:Printer:Benchmarktest
(667) Page Printer on Windows - PART IV Application Benchmark:
```

[3] Originally the index is in Japanese but it is translated in English in this paper.

```
      1991.09:no.90:p.274:Topics:Windows:Printer:Benchmarktest
.....
(965) Multiple Fonts - PART I Applications:
      1990.06:no.72:p.256:Topics:WYSIWYG:OutlineFont
(966) Multiple Fonts - PART II Platform - Environments for Apple and
      Microsoft:1990.06:no.72:p.270:Topics:WYSIWYG:OutlineFont
.....
(1140) 286/386 Performance for Windows:
      1989.09:no.63:p.233:Benchmark:Windows:Benchmarktest
.....
```

In this information, we have type schemes constructed by 198 keywords. There actually 146 keywords appear in the index and 52 keywords do not.

As for ISA hierarchy of the NIKKEI index, the hierarchy is described as a set of pairs ⟨ keyword, parent ⟩. There are 288 parents (i.e.,direct generalizations) in the hierarchy, and each item has up to 4 direct generalization. Next shows a part of the hierarchy.

```
....
x86 MicroProcessor:MicroProcessor
A/D converter:Component
AI:@E
APL:language
AX:IBM compatible:Personal computer
Ada:language
Apple II:Apple product:Personal computer
Apple product:@E
B16/32:HITACHI product:Personal computer
BASIC:language
C/C++:language:Object oriented
CD-ROM:Storage:ReadOnly
CG:@E
COBOL:language
CP/M:OS:Personal computer
CPU:Component
....
```

In Figure4, we summarize the index of article.

Num of Keywords	Num of Articles
0	304
1	1371
2	513
3	106
4	18
5	1
(Total)	2313

Fig. 4. NIKKEI index summary

In our experiment, we employ the attributes as topics field, year firld, the first keyword and the second keyword. And, also we choose a set of objects to be learned from `Keyword Index` such as articles those which contain the word `software`, in this case 233 articles are found. For an example, the article 1044 has the attributes separated by semicolon as

```
Byte network: 1989: Word processor/word processor software:
   Table calculator software
```

The next is keywords that the article has.

```
LAN: Word processor/Word processor software: Table calculator
   software
```

The keywords appear in E consisting of

```
Application linkage, Benchmark test, Communication software,
C/C++, Data exchange, Database management software, DTP, Editor,
Extended Memory, Facsimile adapter, FEP, File management software,
File format, Graphical software, Hypertext, Idea processor,
LAN, Macintosh, Music software, Mouse, OS/2,
Personal computer communication, Table calculate software,
Translation software, Unify software,
Utility software, Windows, Word processor/Word processor software
```

We set $\rho = 0.5$, and we ignore (or *delete*) 14 keywords in E, shown in the following, because the degree of generalization of E is required to be greater than the threshold ρ.

```
Application linkage, Benchmark test, C/C++、 Data exchange,
Editor, Extended memory, Facsimile adapter, FEP, File format,
Hypertext, Idea processor, Mouse, OS/2, Translation software
```

Other 14 keywords remain in the objects E as

```
Communication software, Database management software, DTP,
File management software, Graphic software, LAN, Macintosh、
Music software, Personal computer software, Table calculate software,
Word processor/Word processor software, Unify software,
Utility software Windows、
```

By the attribute "the first keyword", E is grouped and their characteristic items are shown in the following.

```
Communication software, Database, Database management software,
DTP, Editor, Facsimile adapter, File format,
File management software, Graphics software, Hypertext,
LAN, Mouse, Macintosh, Music software, Table calculate software,
Translation software, Unify software, Utility software,
Windows, Word processor/Word processor software
```

The set of objects grouped by the characteristic item `Database management software` makes the groups by the attribute "Topics".

```
Byte network, Byte report, Byte seminar, Introduction, Product file,
Product report, Review, Special issue, Survey, Trend, U.S.Insight
```

The set of objects grouped by the characteristic item `Byte network` make 6 groups by attribute "Year".

> 1984, 1985, 1986, 1987, 1988, 1989

The set of objects grouped by `1989` make 3 groups by the attribute "the second keyword".

> Database management software, Table calculate software, Word processor/Word processor software

By this experiment, E is well described.

In the second experiment, we set $\rho = 0.1$ in this case. We can find a set of objects of which two distinct objects have the same characteristic items (attribute values) but have different types. So, E can not be described. For example, two objects of which one object has a type `LAN` and another `Database management software` have the same characteristic items.

Throughout our experiments, we summarize following observations.

1. During the computation process of least generalization over types, we sometimes obtain the root `@E` as least general one. `@E` means typing is useless so that we regard the result as failure of description. On the other hand, the lower degree of generalization also causes the failure of the description, because of insufficient attributes.
2. To achieve high degree of generalization, we ignored (or *deleted*) some types in E. Rather, the CSOP expression could become shorter, and also the degree of description could become smaller. Conversely, the lower degree of generalization makes the approximation of E suitable, but sometimes it falls into failure of description.
3. Without ignoring types in the objects, we might get in trouble with the fact that we encounter the objects that have the same characteristic items and distinct types. So, sometimes we could not describe E.

6 Related Works

Concept learning from databases is one of the major research topics at the intersection of both databases and knowledge processing. As the work developed here, learning concepts by examining descriptions becomes one of the major techniques and much attention is paid[1, 2, 3, 4, 7, 8, 9, 21, 24]. For more detail, see Prof.Mannila's survey[12].

Traditionally the research topic as *scheme evolution* in databases means how to obtain *flexible* mechanism of databases at re-design in a top-down manner[5]. Clearly more substantial technologies are needed to capture feed-back from database instances to adjust schemes suitable for *current* databases.

Knowledge acquisition processes could be captured as general framework for meta-model manipulation[11]. Rules queries on databases are interpreted as rules/constraints discovery and knowledge acquisition as scheme discovery. Then very ambitious paradigm might be established and applied to wide range of applications.

Statistical methods such as clustering analysis, are useful to analyze instances and to deduce general directions in a quantitative manner[2, 10]. On the other hand, *qualitative analysis* provides us with schematic type generations by examining database schemes.

Sometimes an object type constitutes the description of the world of interests not only by type hierarchy and general type constraints but also in cooperation with predicates. When analyzing the description extensively, we might generate new types. Such knowledge discovery process considered databases as description of the meaning is called *scheme discovery in databases*. Such generation could be based on *grouping*. By utilizing multiple attributes, we can refine the classification. *Decision tree* is one of the ways of type generation[22, 23, 25].

It is said that machine learning, especially inductive inference has the strong relation with KDD[20, 24]. However utilized is only the scheme information but not characteristics of instances nor domain-specific knowledge.

A notable approach is found in [9, 21] to extract new predicates (relational schemes) from instances (tuples) by utilizing `ISA` hierarchy. But one of the deficiencies is that it concerns only on tuples but not domain values.

Our series of works show how to obtain new database schemes that are suitable for current database instances. We have developed the theories based on a general paradigm[16] from the view point of types[14, 15],predicates[17] and complex objects[18].

7 Conclusion

In this investigation, we have proposed a new method of concept learning from databases. Our approach is similar to machine learning investigated so far, but essentially different from utilizing databases as background knowledge but not as storage repository. We put our attention on the fact that databases have common knowledge in form of schemes as well as individual informations of the instances and that all the instances are consistent with respect to a scheme system consisting of types, predicates and integrity constraints.

To achieve our goal, we have defined a notion of Conditional Sum-Of-Product (CSOP) expressions over types and we have shown how to generate conceptual descriptions to a given set of objects E by means of CSOP expressions and database schemes. The proposed algorithm is heuristic but some experimental result shows it is useful and efficient. The results generated could be put back into database schemes as an important source of database re-engineering process.

Acknowledgement
The authors are grateful to Prof.Kambayashi (Kyoto Univ., Japan) Prof.Masunaga (Univ.if Library and Science, Japan), Prof.B. Thalheim (Technical Univ. of Cottbus, Germany) and Prof. S. Navathe (Georgia Institute of Technology, USA). This research was supported by Grant-in-Aid for Scientific Research on Priority Areas (09230219).

References

1. Agrawal, R., Ghosh, S. et al.: An Interval Classifier for Database Mining Applications, *Very Large DataBase* (VLDB), pp.560-573 (1992)
2. Agrawal, R., Srikant, R.: Fast Algorithms for Mining Association Rules, *Very Large Database* (VLDB), pp.487-499 (1994)
3. Cai, Y., Cercone, N. and Han, J.: An Attribute-Oriented Approach for Learning Classification Rules from Relational Databases, *Intn'l Conf. on Data Eng.* (ICDE), pp.281-288 (1990)

4. Cai, Y., Cercone, N. and Han, J.: An Attribute-Oriented Induction in Relational Databases, in [24], pp.213-228
5. Elmasri, R. and Navathe, S.B.: Fundamentals of Database Systems, *Benjamin* (1989)
6. Embley, D. et al.: Object Oriented System Analysis, Yourdon Press (1992)
7. Frawley, W.J., Piatetsky-Shapiro, G. and Matheus, C.J.: Knowledge Discovery in Databases – An Overview, in [24], pp.1-30
8. Fayyad, U.M., Piatetsky-Shapiro, G., Smyth, P. and Uthurusamy, R. (Eds): Advances in Knowledge Discovery and Data Mining, *MIT Press* (1996)
9. Han, J., Cai, Y. and Cercone, N.: Knowledge Discovery in Databases : An Attribute Oriented Approach, *VLDB*, pp.547-559 (1992)
10. Han, J. and Fu, Y.: Discovery of Multiple-Level Association Rules from Large Databases, *VLDB*, pp.420-431 (1995)
11. Imielinski ,T. and Mannila, H.: A Database Perspective on Knowledge Discovery, *CACM* 39-11, ACM, pp.58-64 (1996)
12. Mannila, H.: Methods and Problems in Data Mining, *Intn'l Conf. on Database Theory* (ICDT), pp.41-55 (1997)
13. Miura,T: Database Paradigms Towards Model Building, *Object Roll Modelling*, pp.228-258 (1994)
14. Miura, T. and Shioya, I.: Mining Type Schemes in Databases, *Conference and Workshop of Database and Experts Systems Applications* (DEXA), pp. 369-384 (1996)
15. Miura, T. and Shioya, I.: Knowledge Acquisition for Classification Systems, *Tools with Artificial Intelligence*(ICTAI), pp.110-115 (1996)
16. Miura, T. and Shioya, I.: Paradigm for Schema Discovery, *Intn'l Symposium on Cooperative Database Systems for Advanced Applications*(CODAS), pp.101-108 (1996)
17. Miura, T. and Shioya, I.: Differentiation for Schema Discovery, *Intn'l Database Workshop*, pp.62-77 (1997)
18. Miura, T. and Shioya, I.: Examining Complex Objects for Type Schema Discovery, *Conference and Workshop of DEXA*, pp.462-477 (1997)
19. Motro, A.: Intensional Answers to database Queries, *IEEE Trans. Knowledge and Data Engr.* 6-3, 444-454 (1994)
20. Muggleton,S.: Inductive Logic Programming, *Inductive Logic Programming*(ed. S.Muggleton), Academic Press, pp.3-27 (1992)
21. Ng, R. and Han, J.: Efficient and Effective Clustering Methods for Spatial Data Mining, *VLDB*, pp.144-155 (1994)
22. Quinlan, R: Induction of Decision Trees, *Machine Learning* 1-1, pp.81-106 (1986)
23. Quinlan, R: Learning Logical Definition from Rules, *Machine Learning* 5-3, pp.239-266 (1990)
24. Piatetsky-Shapiro, G. and Frawley, W.J. (Eds): Knowledge Discovery in Databases, *MIT Press* (1991)
25. Wu, X.: Knowledge Acquisition from Databases, Ablex Publishing (1995)

Rule Extraction Using Rough Sets When Membership Values Are Intervals

A. de Korvin[1]

College of Sciences & Technology
University of Houston –Downtown
One Main Street, Houston, TX 77002, USA
Internet: dekorvin@dt.uh.edu

G. Quirchmayr

Institut fur Angewandte Informatik und Informationssysteme
Universitat Wien
Liebiggasse 4, A-1010 Wien, Austria
Internet: Gerald.Quirchmayr@univie.ac.at

S. Hashemi

College of Business
University of Houston –Downtown
One Main Street, Houston, TX 77002, USA
Internet: Hashemi@dt.uh.edu

R. Kleyle

Department of Mathematical Sciences
Indiana University – Purdue University
402 North Blackford Street, Indianapolis, IN 46205-2820, USA
Internet: rkleyle@math.iupui.edu

Abstract: As corporate data is more and more becoming an invaluable asset for decision makers, technologies such as data warehouses and data mining are an essential part of a company's information infrastructure. Methods for mining corporate data and extracting rules from it are well established for crisp and traditional fuzzy data. This paper aims at extending the traditional fuzzy approach for situations where membership values are intervals.

[1] The research of this author was partially supported by grants from the National Science Foundation CDA-9522157 and the Army Research Office DAAH-0495-10250.

1. Introduction

Corporate data is more and more becoming an invaluable asset in an increasingly competitive world. That is why technologies such as data warehouses and data mining today are an essential part of a company's information infrastructure (cf. the approaches described in [Komorowski, J. and Zytkow 1997], [Caben, Hadjinian, Stadler, Verhees and Zanasi] and [Groth]). The analysis of data stored in data warehouses delivers the basis for trend analysis, management and executive information systems and ultimately for enterprise resource planning. Together with corporate Intranets (see [Bernard], [Guengerich, Graham, Miller and McDonald], [Griswold] and [Kyas]), data warehouses (see [Hammergren]) have revolutionized information management.

Most of the existing approaches do however focus on the analysis of crisp and consistent data, i.e. data being provided by accounting systems, sales statistics and the like. When analyzing customer behavior, contradicting and missing data sometimes makes it difficult to apply traditional statistical methods. Outliers are an additional problem which statistical analysis usually cannot cope with. That is why in the process of "data cleaning" contradictory data and outliers are removed and missing data is interpolated, thereby deleting information which could be vital in discovering newly developing trends or customers with especially interesting profiles.

As inconsistency and incomplete information are occurring in business processes far more frequently than expected, a different solution has to be found, which, as a substantial amount of research has shown, could be based on fuzzy systems and rough sets. Traditional rough sets however are not capable of dealing with membership values that are intervals, which makes them to a certain degree inapplicable for such essential procedures as the extraction of rules from advanced customer profiles.

2. Background

A lot of effort has recently been devoted to studying the problem of knowledge acquisition under uncertainty, which arises in many situations. It may be caused by the ambiguity in the terms used to describe a specific situation, the skepticism of rules used to describe a course of action or by missing and conflicting data. For a small sample of work done in the area, the reader is referred to [Bobrow, Mittal and Stefik 1986], [Cheeseman 1986], [Wiederhold, Walker, Blum and Downs 1986], [Yager 1984] and [Zadeh 1983].

To deal with uncertainty, techniques other than classical logic need to be developed. Statistics is the best tool available for handling likelihood, but in many situations it is required to estimate probabilities, sometimes without even the resource to relative frequencies. Estimates then are typically very inaccurate. The Dempster-Shafer theory of evidence gives useful measures for the evaluations of subjective certainty and has gained in popularity. Fuzzy set theory is another tool used to deal with uncertainty where ambiguous terms are present. Other methods include rough sets, the theory of endorsements and nonmonotonic logic.

For a sample of works using the Dempster-Shafer theory see [Shafer 1976], [de Korvin, Kleyle and Lea 1990], [Kleyle and de Korvin 1990], [Strat 1990] and [Yager]. Articles in [Zadeh 1979]. [Zadeh 1981], [Zadeh 1983] illustrate the numerous works carried out in fuzzy sets. The work on rough sets is illustrated in [Fibak, Slowinski and Slowinski 1986], [Gryzmala-Busse 1988], [Mrozek 1985], and [Mrozek 1987]. Numerous applications to many different areas of science and industry have been studied [Pawlak 1981b], [Pawlak 1983], [Mrozek 1985], and [Arciszewski and Ziarko 1986]. Finally, we refer to [Mamdani, Efstathiou and Peng 1985] for a study on the limitations of statistical methodology.

3. Rule extraction under uncertainty

A traditional way of acquiring knowledge is based on learning from examples. The methodology is described in [Gryzmala-Busse 1988]. In this work the values of attributes are crisp values as are the conclusions drawn. Possible and certain rules are extracted and a measure of how much the values of attributes determine the conclusion (decision) is established. However, in many cases the values may fail to be crisp. Thus, a customer might be classified as belonging to .4/Group_A + .8/Group_B.

Most of the formal concepts used in our approach are discussed in [Gryzmala-Busse 1988], additional work on rough sets can be found in [Pawlak 1981a], [Pawlak 1982] and [Pawlak 1985].

Let U be the universe. Let R be an equivalence relation on U. Let X be any subset of U. If $[x]$ denotes the equivalence class of x relative to R, then we define $\underline{R}(X)=\{x\in U | [x]\subset X\}$ as lower approximation of X and $\overline{R}(X)=\{x\in U | [x]\cap X\neq\Phi\}$ as upper approximation of X, with $\underline{R}(X)\subset X\subset\overline{R}(X)$ of course holding true. If $\underline{R}(X)=X=\overline{R}(X)$ then X is called definable.

An information system is a quadruple (U,Q,V,ρ) where U is the universe, $Q=C\cup D$ where $C\cap D=\Phi$. The set C is called the set of attributes, D is called the set of conclusions. We assume that Q (called the set of attributes) is a collection of attributes denoting an entity (C could e.g. be a customer's preferences, the frequency of his purchases, ...). The set V stands for the value and ρ is a function from $U\times Q$ into V where $\rho(u,q)$ denotes the value of attribute q for element u (e.g. the frequency of purchases q for customer u. The set C induces naturally an equivalence on U by partitioning U into sets over which all attributes are constant. The set X is called roughly C-definable if $\underline{R}(X)\neq\Phi$ and

$\overline{R}(X) \neq U$. It will be called internally C-undefinable, if $\underline{R}(X) \neq \Phi$ and $\overline{R}(X) = U$. It will be called totally C-undefinable, if $\underline{R}(X) = \Phi$ and $\overline{R}(X) = U$.

In reality, decision situations are characterized by C and D failing to partition the set into well-defined classes and some overlap will always be present. We do e.g. not have sharp boundaries between high and low. The best we can hope for is that high and low are "sort of partitioning the universe" by not overlapping "too much".

We recall that a fuzzy subset A of U is defined by a membership function $A: U \rightarrow [0,1]$. The notation $\sum_i a_i / x_i (0 \leq a_i \leq 1)$ denotes a fuzzy set whose membership function at x_i is a_i. Finally, we recall that if A and B are fuzzy subsets, $A \cap B$, $A \cup B$ and $\neg A$ are defined by $Min\{A(x), B(x)\}$, $Max\{A(x), B(x)\}$ and $1 - A(x)$. The implication $A \rightarrow B$ is defined by $\neg A \cup B$. The corresponding membership function is $Max\{1 - A(x), B(x)\}$. Fuzzy set $A \subset B$ when $A(x) \leq B(x) \forall x \in U$.

We now define two functions on pairs of fuzzy sets that will be of key importance in this work:

$$I(A \subset B) = \operatorname*{Min}_{x} \operatorname{Max} \{1 - A(x), B(x)\} \tag{1}$$

$$J(A \# B) = \operatorname*{Max}_{x} \operatorname{Min} \{A(x), B(x)\} \tag{2}$$

Here A and B denote fuzzy subsets of the same universe. The function $I(A \subset B)$ measures the degree to which A is included in B in the sense that it minimizes the degree to which A implies B. $J(A \# B)$ measures the degree to which A intersects B.

Indeed, if A and B are crisp sets, it is easy to establish that $I(A \subset B) = 1$ if and only if $A \subset B$, otherwise $I(A \subset B) = 0$. Also in the case of crisp sets, $J(A \# B) = 1$ if and only if $A \cap B \neq \Phi$, otherwise it is 0. It is clear that I and J can be expressed as $I(A \subset B) = \operatorname*{Min}_{x} (A \rightarrow B)$ and $J(A \# B) = \operatorname*{Max}_{x} (A \cap B)$. In addition the following relation holds: $I(A \subset B) = 1 - J(A \# \neg B)$.

The functions defined in (1) and (2) were first proposed by Zadeh ([Zadeh 1979], [Zadeh 1981]) in the content of his work on information granularity and the theory of possibility. He defined expected possibility and expected certainty by

$$E\ \pi\ (B) = \sum_i m(A_i)\ \sup\ (B \cap A_i)\ \text{and}$$

$$E\ \subset\ (B) = \sum_i m(A_i)\ \inf\ (B \Rightarrow A_i).$$

We use Zadeh's definition in our present work by defining $I(A \subset B) = \inf(A \Rightarrow B) = \underset{x}{\text{Min}}\,\text{Max}\,\{1 - A(x), B(x)\}$ and $J(A\#B) = \sup(B \cap A) = \underset{x}{\text{Max}}\,\text{Min}\,\{A(x), B(x)\}$.

4. The formal model and its application

We now go through an example and show how fuzzy certain and possible rules can be extracted from raw data. In many situations, it might, as previously stated, be difficult to determine the exact membership value.

For example, instead of stating that an airline customer prefers .2 economy class and .9 business class, the marketing analyst may only be able to judge that the customer preference is between .1 and .3 economy class and between .7 and .9 business class. This new type of uncertainty need not, of course, be limited to the attribute values, but might also be present in the conclusion drawn from these values (i.e. the decision inferred). Thus the analyst may believe that the customer, being characterized by a certain frequency of booking and his preference, books his flight early with a degree of belief between .2 and .4 while he books his flight late with a belief between .5 and .7.

This case introduces a new type of uncertainty, where the membership value is some subinterval of [0, 1]. Symbolically, such a set can be written as $A = \sum_i < a_i, b_i > /\ x_i$, indicating that A is a fuzzy set whose value at x_i is the interval $< a_i, b_i >$, also called Fuzzy Set of Type II.

Following the ideas expressed in the previous section, the "pure type" attributes and the decisions should have the above form. This leads to the question which "the right definitions" of operators I and J, in fact which the "right definitions" for Min, Max and 1- A, should be. In a very natural way the following definitions generalize the previous case:

$$1 - A = \sum_i < 1 - b_i, 1 - a_i > /\ x_i$$

$$\overline{\text{Max}}\{< a_i, b_i >, < a_j, b_j >\} = < \text{Max}(a_i, a_j), \text{Max}(b_i, b_j) >$$

$$\overline{\text{Min}}\{< a_i, b_i >, < a_j, b_j >\} = < \text{Min}(a_i, a_j), \text{Min}(b_i, b_j) >$$

This leads to the definition of operators I and J. Specifically, if A and B are fuzzy sets whose values are subintervals of [0,1], then

$$\bar{I}(A \subset B) = \overline{\underset{x}{\text{Min}}\,\text{Max}}(1-A(x),B(x)) \text{ and}$$

$$\bar{J}(A\#B) = \overline{\underset{x}{\text{Max}}\,\text{Min}}(A(x),B(x)).$$

It should be noted that $1\text{-}A$ is an interval as is $B(x)$. Thus $\overline{\text{Max}}(1-A(x),B(x))$ is some interval depending on x and $\bar{I}(A \subset B)$ then is some interval (independent from x). The same observation applies to $\bar{J}(A\#B)$. Thus the degree to which A is a subset of B, or more accurately, the degree to which A implies B, is interval-valued as is the degree to which A possibly implies B.

Rules generated by these definitions will have the following format: *If the booking frequency is low and the airline customer prefers economy class with a degree between a_1 and b_1 or if the booking frequency is low and the airline customer prefers business class with a degree between a_2 and b_2, then the airline customer will book early with a degree between a_3 and b_3.*

We now demonstrate the technique in the case where we have two conditions: the frequency of a customer's booking (low or high) and the preferred class (economy or business). The marketing analyst can then decide whether a customer will book early or late.

Customer	**Frequency of Booking**	**Preferred Class**	**Estimated Time of Booking**
x_1	<.2,.4>/low + <.7,.9>/high	<.1,.3>/economy + <.8,1>/business	<.2,.4>/early + <.5, .7>/late
x_2	<.3,.5>/low + <.6,.8>/high	<.9,.1>/economy + <.6,.9>/business	<.6,.9>/early + <.4, .6>/late
x_3	<.6,.9>/low + <.2,.5>/high	<.5,.7>/economy + <.5,.7>/business	<.5,.6>/early + <.8, .9>/late
x_4	<.7,.8>/low + <.4,.6>/high	<.2,.4>/economy + <.7,.8>/business	<.5,.8>/early + <.1, .2>/late
x_5	<.1,.4>/low + <.6,.7>/high	<.1,.2>/economy + <.5,.9>/business	<.3,.4>/early + <.1, .2>/late

We then get the following fuzzy sets:

Low = $<.2,.4>/x_1 + <.3,.5>/ x_2 + <.6,.9>/ x_3 + <.7,.8>/ x_4 + <.1,.4>/ x_5$
High = $<.7,.9>/ x_1 + <.6,.8>/ x_2 + <.2,.5>/x_3 + <.4,.6>/x_4 + <.6,.7>/x_5$
Economy = $<.1,.3>/x_1 + <.9,.1>/x_2 + <.5,.7>/x_3 + <.2,.4>/x_4 + <.1,.2>/x_5$
Business = $<.8,1>/x_1 + <.6,.9>/x_2 + <.5,.7>/x_3 + <.7,.8>/ x_4 + <.5,.9>/x_5$

Early = $<.2,.4>/ x_1 + <.6,.9>/x_2 + <.5,.6>/x_3 + <.5,.8>/x_4 + <.3,.4>/x_5$
Late = $<.5, .7>/x_1 + <.4, .6>/x_2 + <.8, .9>/x_3 + <.1, .2>/x_4 + <.1, .2>/x_5$

The interpretation of these equations is straightforward. For example, it says that x_1 is an example of Low rated between .2 and .4 (not a very good example), while x_1 is far more representative of high since the rating is between .7 and .9.

We now compute

Low $\cap$ Economy =

$$<.1,.3>/x_1 + <.3,.5>/x_2 + <.5,.7>/x_3 + <.2,.4>/x_4 + <.1,.2>/x_5$$

Low $\cap$ Business =

$$<.2,.4>/x_1 + <.3,.5>/x_2 + <.5,.7>/x_3 + <.7,.8>/x_4 + <.1,.4>/x_5$$

Similarly, expressions for High $\cap$ Economy and for High $\cap$ Business can easily be computed.

From $1 - A = \sum_i <1-b_i, 1-a_i> / x_i$

and $\overline{\text{Max}}\{<a_i, b_i>, <a_j, b_j>\} = <\text{Max}(a_i, a_j), \text{Max}(b_i, b_j)>$

we obtain $\overline{\text{Max}}(1 - \text{Low} \cap \text{Economy}, \text{Early}) =$

$$<.7,.9>/x_1 + <.6,.9>/x_2 + <.5,.6>/x_3 + <.6,.8>/x_4 + <.8,.9>/x_5.$$

From $\bar{I}(A \subset B) = \overline{\underset{x}{\text{Min}}\,\text{Max}}(1 - A(x), B(x))$

it follows that $\bar{I}(\text{Low} \cap \text{Economy} \subset \text{Early}) =$

$$\overline{\underset{x}{\text{Min}}\,\text{Max}}(1 - \text{Low} \cap \text{Economy}, \text{Early}) = <.5,.6>.$$

Similarly,

$\overline{\text{Max}}(1 - \text{Low} \cap \text{Business}, \text{Early}) =$

$$<.6,.8>/x_1 + <.6,.9>/x_2 + <.5,.6>/x_3 + <.5,.8>/x_4 + <.6,.9>/x_5.$$

Thus $\bar{I}(\text{Low} \cap \text{Business} \subset \text{Early}) = <.5,.6>.$

The corresponding extracted rule then reads: *if the booking frequency is low and the customer prefers economy class or the booking frequency is low and the customer prefers business class then the customer will book early [.5 .6].*

It should be noted that the set (Low and Economy) or (Low and Business) is not identical with the set Low. The membership of x_3 in Low is <.6,.9>; however its membership in $(\text{Low} \cap \text{Economy}) \cup (\text{Low} \cup \text{Business}))$ is <.5,.7>.

Moreover, in the crisp case, an equivalence class is the union of intersections of the form (Frequency = v_1) and (Preference = v_2) where v_1 and v_2 are possible values of these attributes. The above format is then truly a generalization of the concept of equivalence classes generated by combinations of attribute classes. One should resist making any inference, for example, as to how much a low frequency implies early booking.

We now use $\bar{J}(A\#B) = \overline{\underset{x}{\text{Max}}\text{Min}}(A(x), B(x))$ to compute possible rules.

For example, $\overline{\text{Min}}(\text{Low} \cap \text{Business}, \text{Early}) =$

<.2,.4>/x_1 + <.3,.5>/x_2 + <.5,.6>/x_3 + <.5,.8>/x_4 + <.1,.4>/x_5 and

$\text{J}(\text{Low} \cap \text{Business}\#\text{Early}) = \overline{\underset{x}{\text{Max}}\text{Min}}(\text{Low} \cap \text{Business}, \text{Early}) =$ <.5,.8>.

Similarly $\text{J}(\text{Low} \cap \text{Economy}\#\text{Early}) =$ <.5,.6>.

The corresponding possible rule can then be written as: *if the booking frequency is low and the customer prefers business class, then the customer will possibly book early [.5 .8], but if the booking frequency is low and the customer prefers economy class, then the customer will possibly book early [.5 .6].*

In the present example one would of course have additional rules by considering High and Economy, High and Business, and also by considering late bookings as well as early ones. To reduce the number of rules, we may consider a threshold $0 < \alpha < 1$ and not use rules where the right ends of the corresponding intervals fall below α.

When introducing the extracted rules into a knowledge-based system, the rules can serve as input for the knowledge acquisition system, the intervals can be used to determine the firing strength of the respective rules. Also note that the presented method incorporates outliers into the computations. Case x_1 seems to imply that high and business would favor late while x_2 seems to indicate that high and business could well lead to early. Instead of ignoring outliers, we incorporate them into our computations.

5. Conclusion

This work offers a methodology for extracting rules when membership functions are not completely known. The membership value is known to be some interval range only. The conclusion is in the form of a fuzzy set whose membership values are known to lie in some interval range.

This methodology was applied to the analysis of airline customer behavior with partial knowledge of booking frequency and preferred class and the conclusion drawn from these two attributes pertained to estimate the time of booking. Of course no known formula relates the two.

References

[Arciszewski and Ziarko 1986] Arciszewski, T. and Ziarko, W., Adaptive expert system for preliminary engineering design. Proc. 6th International Workshop on Expert Systems and their Applications, Avignon, France, 1(1986), 696-712.

[Bernard] Bernard, R., The Corporate Intranet, Wiley & Sons.

[Bobrow, Mittal and Stefik 1986] Bobrow,G.G., Mittal, S. and Stefik, M.J., Expert systems: perils and promises, Com. ACM 29(1986), 880-894.

[Caben, Hadjinian, Stadler, Verhees and Zanasi] Caben, P., Hadjinian, P., Stadler, R., Verhees, J. and Zanasi, A., Discovering Data Mining, Prentice Hall.

[Cheeseman 1986] Cheeseman, P., Induction of models under uncertainty. Proc. ACM SIGART Internat. Symposium on Methodologies for Intelligent Systems, Knoxville, Tennessee, (1986), 130-144.

[Fibak, Slowinski and Slowinski 1986] Fibak, J., Slowinski, K. and Slowinski, R., The application of rough set theory to the verification of indications for treatment of duodenal ulcer by HSV, Proc. 6th International Workshop on Expert Systems and their Applications, Avignon, France, 1(1986), 587-599.

[Griswold] Griswold, S., Building a Corporate Intranet, Prima Publishing.

[Groth] Groth, R., Data Mining, Prentice Hall.

[Gryzmala-Busse 1988] Gryzmala-Busse, J.W., Knowledge acquisition under uncertainty – rough set approach, Journal of Intelligent and Robotic Systems 1(1988), 3-16.

[Guengerich, Graham, Miller and McDonald] Guengerich, S., Graham, D., Miller, M. and McDonald, S., Building the Corporate Intranet, Wiley & Sons.

[Hammergren] Hammergren, T., Data Warehousing, Thomson Computer Press.

[Kleyle and de Korvin 1990] Kleyle, R. and de Korvin, A., A unified model for data acquisition and decision making, The Journal of the Amer. Soc. For Info. Science 15(1990), 149-161.

[Komorowski, J. and Zytkow 1997] Komorowski, J. and Zytkow, J. (eds.), Principles of Data Mining and Knowledge Discovery, Proc. of 1st European Symposium, PKDD '97, Springer 1997.

[de Korvin, Kleyle and Lea 1990] de Korvin, A., Kleyle, R. and Lea, R., An evidential approach to problem solving when a large number of knowledge systems are available, The Itern. Journal of Intelligent Systems 5(1990), 293-306.

[Kyas] Kyas, O., Corporate Intranets, Thomson Computer Press.

[Mamdani, Efstathiou and Peng 1985] Mamdani, A., Efstathiou, J. and Peng, D., Inference under uncertain expert systems, Proc. 5th Tech. Conf. BCS, SIG Expert Systems (1985), 181-194.

[Mrozek 1985] Mrozek, A., Information systems and control algorithms, Bull. Polish Acad, Sci., Technical Sci. 33(1985), 195-204.

[Mrozek 1987] Mrozek, A., Rough sets and some aspects of expert system realization, Proc. 7th International Workshop on Expert Systems and their Applications, Avignon, France, 1(1987), 597-611.

[Pawlak 1981a] Pawlak, Z., Rough sets. Basic Notions, Institute Comp. Sci., Polish Acad. Sci. Rep No. 431, Warsaw (1981).

[Pawlak 1981b] Pawlak, Z., Classification of objects by means of attributes, Institute Comp. Sci., Polish Acad. Sci. Rep No. 429, Warsaw (1981).

[Pawlak 1982] Pawlak, Z., Rough sets, Int. J. Information Computer Sci. 11(1982), 341-256.

[Pawlak 1983] Pawlak, Z., Rough classifications, Int. J. Man-machine Studies 20(1983), 496-483.

[Pawlak 1985] Pawlak, Z., Rough sets and fuzzy sets, Fuzzy sets and systems, 17(1985), 99-102.

[Shafer 1976] Shafer, G., Mathematical Theory of Evidence, Princeton University Press, (1976).

[Strat 1990] Strat, T.M. Decision analysis using belief functions, Int. J. of Approximate Reasoning 4(1990), 291-417.

[Wiederhold, Walker, Blum and Downs 1986] Wiederhold, G.C. Walker, M., Blum, R. and Downs, S., Acquisition of knowledge from data, Proc. ACM SIGART Int. Symp. On Methodologies for Intelligent Systems, Knoxville, Tennessee, (1986), 78-84.

[Yager 1984] Yager, R.R., Approximate reasoning as a basis for rule based expert systems, IEEE Trans. On Systems, Man and Cybernetics 14(1984), 635-643.

[Yager] Yager, R.R., Decision making under Dempster-Shafer uncertainties, Iona College, Machine Intelligence Tech. Report MII-915.

[Zadeh 1979] Zadeh, L.A., Fuzzy sets and information granularity, Advances in Fuzzy Set Theory and Applications (1979), 3-18.

[Zadeh 1981] Zadeh, L.A., Possibility theory and soft data analysis, Mathematical Frontiers of the Social and Policy Sciences, Eds. L. Cobb and R.M. Thrall, 1981, Westview Press: Boulder, Colorado.

[Zadeh 1983] Zadeh, L.A., The rule of fuzzy logic in the management of uncertainty in expert systems, Fuzzy Sets and Systems 11(1983), 119-227.

Using Semantic Links for Reuse in Knowledge Base Systems

Karima MESSAADIA Mourad OUSSALAH

LGI2P/EMA-EERIE
Parc scientifique Georges Besse - 30000 Nimes, France
Email : messaadi@ecrie.fr, oussalah@eerie.fr

Abstract. Constructing Knowledge Base Systems using pre-existing generic components rather than from scratch is a promising way to minimise their development time and facilitate their evolution and maintenance. The concepts commonly used in describing KBS are tasks, PSMs and domains. Developers have to select them from a library, adapt and link them so that they fit their specific needs. In order to help developers to quickly understand, find, and configure the components[1] best suited to their applications, we need to specify languages for describing tasks, PSMs and domains plus the different interactions between them. In this paper, we describe a methodology for structuring a library which integrates different components and relationships defined through levels of description: conceptual, ontological, object and implementation. In order to clarify the kinds of relationship, we propose to introduce at the conceptual level two other *new* concepts: *inter-concept* and *intra-concept links*. The former refer to relationships between different concepts, the latter between similar concepts. We propose to use ontologies to describe these concepts, improving thus their reusability and sharing. We use semantic and transfer links, often applied in databases systems and object modelling, to specify inter- and intra-concept links.

Keywords : AI methodologies, reuse, semantic links, transfer links, ontology.

Introduction

The notion of *knowledge level,* introduced by Newell [17] as separate from *symbol level,* allowed the describing of knowledge independently from the implementation adopted. Thus, the concept of task has been used to describe KBS reasoning independently from application knowledge in terms of three concepts: a task to be solved; a problem solving method (PSM) describing how to solve a task; finally, domain knowledge defining particular domains. The PSM is often described in the task body [19] [27]. As many studies show that a task can be realised by different PSMs and that a PSM can solve many tasks, separating these two notions leads to greater reusability. For example, a *diagnosis* task can be realised by either *heuristic classification* or *abduction* PSM, and a *classification* PSM can be used for either *diagnosis* or *design* tasks. Current work is directed towards reuse and the construction of KBS from reusable predefined components rather than from scratch.

---

[1] We use components refering to the concepts task, PSM, domain, and links and for their specialisation.

In this paper we present a methodology for KBS library development employing several levels of abstraction: conceptual, ontological, object and implementation. The library relies upon independent and generic descriptions of PSMs, tasks and domains using formal ontologies. In order to clarify the different kinds of relationships between these three concepts, we introduce two other new concepts: the *inter-concept link* and the *intra-concept link.* An inter-concept link describes relationships between concepts of different sort: task/PSM, PSM/domain or task/domain. An intra-concept link describes the ones between two concepts of the same sort: task/task, PSM/PSM and domain/domain. For example, the literature shows that a generic PSM becomes more specific either by linking it to a task or domain, or by specialising it through inheritance [8]. The inter-concept link can be used for relating a PSM with a task or a domain, and an intra-concept link for specialising it. This paper is organised as follows: in the next section we give a brief description of related work then introduce the semantic and transfer links and follow the library through a life cycle. We illustrate our model with an example and finally, we conclude and give an outline of future perspectives.

Related work

Many methodologies for KBS construction have been developed. Examples are: KADS [27], Role Liming Method [13] and its evolving CRLM [22], Component of expertise [21], TASK [18], ProtégéII [23], and KSM [14]. Some describe KBS following a life cycle like the Task methodology; others, consider the KBS construction as a reuse of interconnected components as in ProtégéII: all however share the principles of *knowledge level* description, using generally task, PSM, and domain concepts to describe a KBS. Some are flexible enough to allow a task to be realised by different PSMs and a PSM to be applied for different tasks like the Task Structure, others insists upon predefined task/PSM associations as does RLM. Among these studies, some are oriented towards the construction of reusable PSM libraries similar to the component-based approach used in Software Engineering. In this respect, different approaches leads to library organisation (generally PSM libraries) like : Generic Task and Task Structure[5], CommonKADS library [25], the diagnosis library of Benjamins [4], [8], and [16]. PSMs in these libraries are often described using task-specific terms like the CommonKADS library and Benjamins library for diagnosis, or domain-specific terms like the Generic Task library. Task specific and domain-specific PSMs are less reusable than generic ones. This is known as the reusability/usability trade-off [11]. Other studies focus on ontology portability in order to construct libraries of reusable PSMs, tasks and domains. Ontologies were initially used to *formally* describe generic model of domains which can be reused to describe different specific domains sharing the same structure. As we can reuse tasks and PSMs, the notion of task ontology and PSM ontology appeared in recent works [5] [8] [15] referring to independent descriptions of tasks and PSMs. The problem of these libraries is that there is no methodology clarifying their relationships at different levels of abstraction. Comparative studies can be found in [15] [19]. We propose in this paper, the use semantic and transfer links commonly applied in data base systems and object modelling like OMT or UML, to specify the relationships which can hold between the different concepts.

Semantic and transfer links

A semantic link [12] is used to relate concepts. It defines its own semantic and behaviour allowing the concepts it relates to communicate and collaborate. It can be enriched by using semantic properties which may reinforce its expressiveness and simplify its manipulation. These properties can be *exclusivity/sharing,* expressing that a concept referenced by an exclusive semantic link cannot be referenced by another semantic link of the same type. *Cardinality* expresses the number of target concepts that can be associated with a source concept and *inverse Cardinality* expresses the number of source concepts that can be associated with a target concept. *Predominance/non-predominance* specify whether or not the existence of a source concept of dependent semantic links depends on the existence of its target concept. A transfer link[20] expresses the transferability of information. It may also have transfer functions used to transform the information it transports between source and target concepts. A transfer is composed of a set of translators describing information propagation between the concepts concerned. Each translator defines information propagation between the attributes of linked concepts and specifies the transfer function used to translate the information being sent. The links are defined at class level but operate effectively at instances. In order to clarify them, we will pursue them through the life cycle of a library.

Library life-cycle development

A task oriented KBS can be described in terms of four levels of abstraction (Figure1). Each level reinforces the preceding one by adding new specifications up as far as implementation. The conceptual level defines the basic concepts used to describe a KBS structure independent of its implementation. At this level, we identify generic types of concepts, and relations between these concepts in terms of: task, PSM, domain, inter-concept and intra-concept links. These concepts and links will then be set forth at the ontological level.

The ontological level enables the specification of tasks, PSMs, domains, inter and intra-concept links and the introduction of a formal dimension in order to reduce ambiguities which could occur at the first level. It can be decomposed into different ontological layers according to the degree of specificity of the concepts. These specifications are then represented in the object level, which transforms them into a set of classes, attributes and methods. Finally, the implementation level implements object specification, translating it into internal structures such as: lists, tables, etc. To represent the ontological level, we choose an *object level* for its notions of reusability in the form of inheritance, encapsulation, modularity, etc. It can be replaced by any other level, such as frame or logical ones.

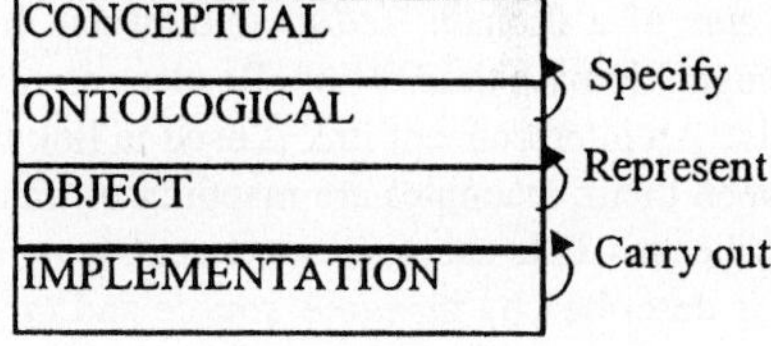

Fig. 1. Abstract levels

The conceptual level

The three main concepts used by the majority of methodologies to describe KBSs are: task, PSM and domain. In order to have independent descriptions, a task should be represented without any information about its method of resolution or the domain where it will be applied; similarly, a PSM should be described using generic terms independent of the task it will realise or the domain in which it will figure; finally, domain description must also be generic and independent of application domains. For keeping their descriptions separate, we introduce two other concepts: inter-concept and intra-concept links. We will see these links in more detail in the next section.

The ontological level

We use the ontological level to explicit the different *types* of concepts, inter-concept and intra-concept links. Thus, we define descriptive languages for the five concepts. Then, we use these languages to define the different types of each concept. We have split this ontological level into two sub-levels (layers) : *ontology of generalisation* representing descriptive languages of the different concepts, and *ontology of specialisation* specialising the generalisation ontology in order to define their different kinds.

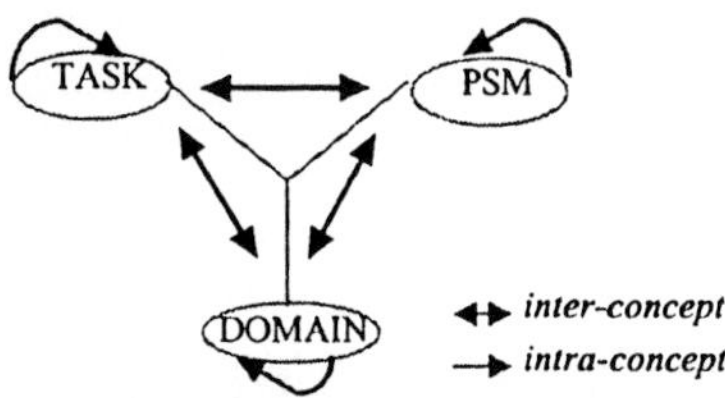

Fig. 2. The ontological level : the Y model

Ontology of generalisation

Ontology of generalisation permits to defining of concept ontologies. A task ontology is specified by its *name* which is a unique term designing it, its *input/output*, and the *goal* it is to reach; while a PSM ontology is specified by its *name, input/output*, and its *competence* to solve tasks. Domain ontology which have received much the most attention, have to be described through different levels of genericity for increasing its reusability. It can be specified by *concepts* of a domain, *relations* between these concepts and their *characteristics* allowing a leveraged domain description. Reader can refer to [26] for a categorisation of domain ontology levels. An inter-concept link is used to link two different concepts and can transfer information between them; examples are mapping or transferring information between tasks and PSMs. We describe this link using inter-concept *semantic* and *transfer* links. An inter-concept semantic link is described by its *name, source* and *target* concepts and may have formal rules requiring, for example, that its source and target concepts be different. It has also by default *semantic attributes* such as : shared and predominant. An inter-concept transfer link is defined by its *name*, the concepts it links (*from* and *to*) and its *semantic attributes* and *transformation functions*. Intra-concept semantic and transfer links are described the way inter-concept ones are, but with formal rules specifying that the concepts they link are of the same sort.

Ontology of specialisation

We can specialise concepts using the ontology of generalisation. Tasks, PSMs and domains can be seen at this level as an extended Y-shape with several branches shown in fig. 3 Task branches describe types of tasks, such as: *diagnosis, configuration, conception.* PSM branches describe PSM types, such as: *classification, abduction, qualitative simulation;* domain branches describe different domains such as: *networks, medicine, cardiology.* Task T1 for instance is specialised into T'1 as design and parametric design. Semantic and transfer links are specialised according to the sorts of concept pairing they do, amongst them: task/PSM, PSM/domain, task/domain, task/task, PSM/PSM and domain/domain.

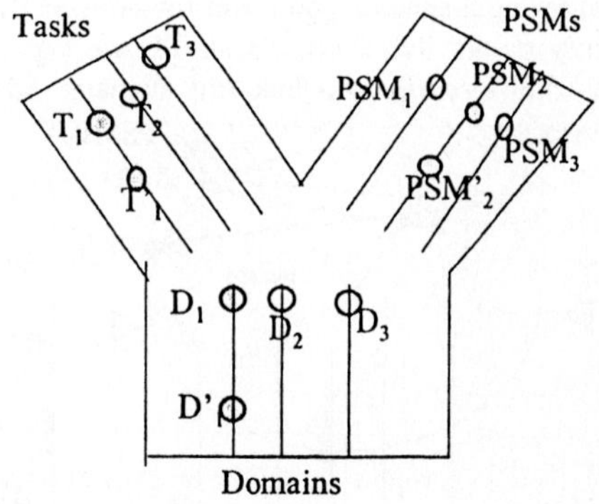

Fig. 3. The extent Y model

Inter-concept semantic links can be:

- PSM/domain: Defining the association of a PSM with a domain, describing the knowledge that the former requires from the latter. In order to consider a PSM as a black-box, its knowledge requirements are specified using *assumptions* [2]. We use *association links* to represent it.

Definition of an association link: An association link is a sort of semantic link. Borrowed from the entity-relationship (ER) modelling, it declares a connection between instances of associated concepts. It can store features shared by its associated concepts.

- Task/domain: This describes the association of a task with a domain in terms of knowledge requirements. We use an association link as defined below to specify it.
- Task/PSM : A task can be *realised-by* either one or several PSMs and each PSM can *decompose* a task into sub-tasks. These in their turn, are *realised-by* sub-PSMs, until reaching terminal and non-decomposable PSMs. We define two *new* semantic links expressing the task/PSM relations. We refer to them as: *realised-by* and *composed of* (figure 6).
    - The *realised-by link*: It allows relating a task to the different PSMs helping to solve it.
    - The *composed of link*: It expresses the decomposition of the PSM into different sub-tasks.

In addition to these links, the user can extend them by specifying its own semantic links via the *user inter-concept semantic* link (Figure 7).

Inter-concept transfer links : They allow defining the information propagation between concepts (Figure 4) and can be:

- Task/PSM: Expressing data transfers between tasks and PSMs, as well as their inter-ontology mapping [23].

- Task/domain: Expressing their inter-ontology mapping.
- PSM/domain : Expressing their inter-ontology mapping.

In this figure, the full circle represents a chosen task T1 which is *realised-by* PSM1 and PSM3 following a specific control in the domain D2. In this extended Y model, we can take various entry points: for a given task T1, we can find: the PSMs which can solve it through the task/PSM *realised-by* link; the domains where it can be applied through the task/domain association link (fulfilling its knowledge requirements). We can also take a given PSM such as PSM1, and find its sub-tasks through the *composed of* link and the domains to which it applies (in this example, T1 and D2). We can also take a domain as an entry point (D2) and find the tasks and PSMs where it can be used (in this example T1, PSM1 and PSM2).

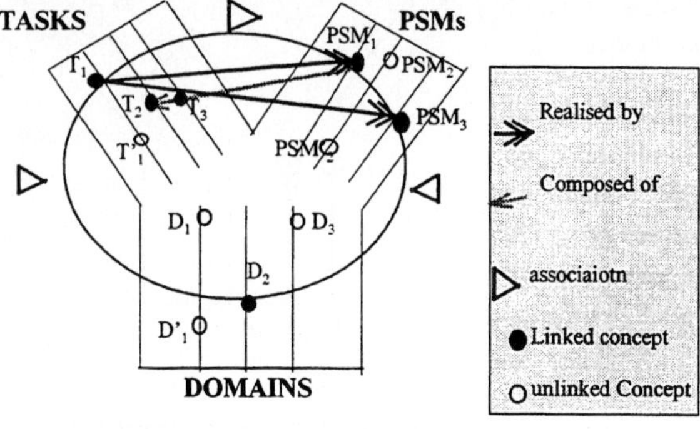

Fig. 4. The different types of inter-concept links

Intra-concept semantic links : we have identified the various sorts of intra-concept semantics links by their semantics, as:

- *Specialisation* (*is-a* relation): it is used to specialise a task, a PSM, a domain or a link.
- *Control*: it specifies the order of invocation of tasks, PSMs, or the union of two domains.
- *Strategy*: this specifies the strategic knowledge used when there is a choice to be made among PSMs, tasks, or domains.
- *User intra-concept link*: as for inter-concept links, the user can extend the links we have identified by defining his/her own intra-concept link.

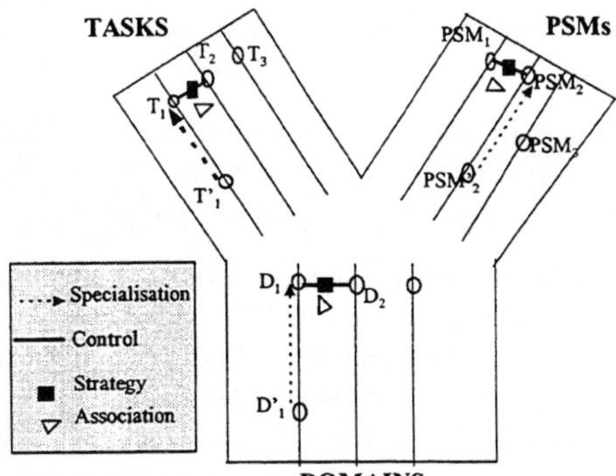

Fig. 5. Intra-task, intra-PSM and intra-domain links

Intra-concept transfer link :Transfer links allow the propagation of information between related concepts: task/task and PSM/PSM used in the decomposition/realisation graph (figure 6); and domain/domain for a mapping between domains sharing common structures such as: electrical and telecommunication networks.

Re-use of task/PSM/Domains/Links:

The library's components can be reused at the different levers of abstraction.
The task can be re-used :

- in various domains using a task/domain transfer *link* (inter-ontology mapping) and an *association* link specifying knowledge requirements.
- in the decomposition of various PSMs, by the use of an *association* link specifying task/PSM assumptions, a *realised-by* and a *task/PSM transfer* link for mapping and information propagation.
- in the description of different tasks using a *task/task specialisation* link.

The PSM can be re-used:

- in various domains by the use of an *association* link expressing its knowledge requirements and a *transfer* link for their ontology mapping.
- in different tasks by the use of a *composed of* link and a *transfer link* for data transfer.
- in various PSMs by using a *PSM/PSM specialisation* link.

The domain can be re-used:

- in different tasks the use of a *transfer link* for inter-ontology mapping.
- in different PSMs using a *transfer link* (inter-ontology mapping).
- for modelling various domain applications through the *domain/domain specialisation*.

The links : Inter-concept and intra-concept links can be re-used by the *specialisation* link in for instance the specialisation of adapters [8].

The concentrator location problem

The example we describe is about the optimization of the concentrator location in an access network. The concentrator location problem aims to find the number of concentrators, their locations, and the connection of terminals to concentrators. We can use a simulated annealing algorithm to find the optimal configuration. As this PSM is often used for many other problems, we need to describe a generic simulated annealing and optimization task using terms such as realizable solution, optimal solution, rather than concentrators, terminals; etc. Then transfer links are used for terminology mapping. The figure above gives the Task/PSM decomposition of this problem.

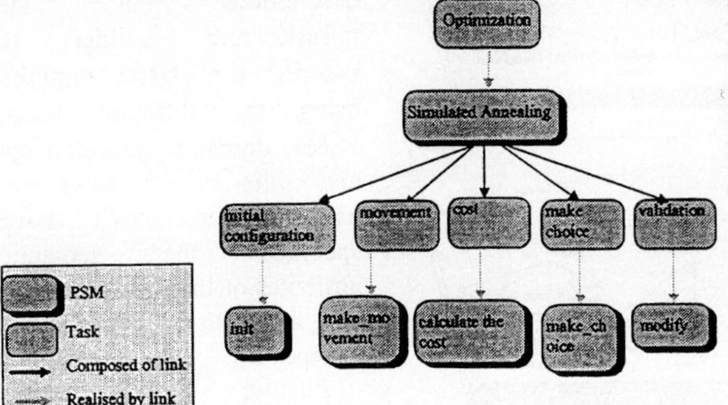

Fig. 6. The decomposition/ realisation graph

Object level

In order to represent the task, the PSM and the domain, we have used the concept of class to optimise reusability through specifying these three concepts independently of one another. The inheritance graph enables us to maintain the levels of abstraction previously defined. We have structured the semantic and transfer links at the ontological level as first level classes; semantic and transfer link types as second level classes. Control is represented by a class.

By reifying the control, we can specify it independently from the task-class and the PSM-class, allowing to re-use or modification, if necessary, without modifying task and PSM descriptions. We have used the concept of active object[24] to represent the strategy. Thus PSM/task, task/domain, PSM/domain, task/task, PSM/PSM and domain/domain links as third level and a user will choose among them, to construct their KBS. These are a specialisation of semantic and/or transfer links.

The library: Multi-hierarchical Y model

The library that we have presented, comprises PSMs, tasks and domains plus their various links at conceptual, ontological and object levels. It can be represented using a multi-hierarchical model [20] incorporating these three levels of abstraction. These, reference three kinds of user. First, the infrastructure builder who describes concepts aimed at modelling task-oriented knowledge bases. Then the application builder using the descriptions of the infrastructure builder to describe the classes required using the different tasks, PSMs, domains, inter-concept and intra-concept links we have defined. We have specified the semantic attributes of links *by default* so that they can be changed for exceptions.

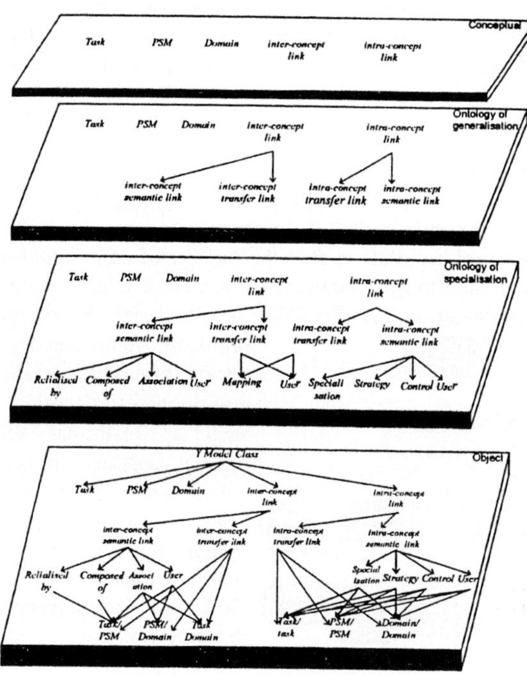

Fig. 7. The multi hierarchical Y model

Finally, the user instanciating these defined classes to solve a particular problem. The point of entry to the library can be either a task, a PSM, or a domain (Figure 3) or some mixture of them such as: domain plus task with task/domain links. The figure shows, for reasons of place, some of the classes, specified in an incremental manner through hierarchies.

Conclusion

We have described in this article a library which can model any task-oriented knowledge base while offering the re-use of tasks, PSMs, domains, and their inter-concept and intra-concept links. This library is structured in a multi-hierarchical model allowing the integration of reusable description concepts. It also allows modelling of various existing components used in knowledge engineering and knowledge representation. Our work approaches that in [16] in its reuse of tasks, PSMs and domains by means of an adapter to bind them. Our model can be seen as a fine-grained description of the adapter (section 4.2.2) in terms of its functionality.

Concerning the task/PSM decomposition, and the use of ontology, our work has some similarities with ProtégéII [14]. It differs from it in its use of an explicit control, rather than, as in ProtégéII, a hard-wired one and the use of semantic and transfer links. We have based our studies on work done in many fields: software engineering, object modelling, KE, and knowledge representation. The main contribution of our work is the explicit description it offers of the different concept interactions (relationships) by means of two new concepts, intra- and inter-concept links defined through different levels of description; secondarily, the use of object modelling concepts for representing them employing semantic and transfer links. Our purpose was to give a precise specification of descriptive languages and not a completely formal language. Our future work will concentrate on formalising concepts and links. We intend to develop this framework for an application concerning re-use of tasks and PSMs in the telecommunications domain.

Bibliography

[1] J. Angele, D. Fensel & R. Studer, Domain and Task Modelling in MIKE, Proc. IFIP WG. Joint Working Conference, Geneva. Chapman & Hall 1996.

[2] R. Benjamins & C. Pierret-Golbreicht, Assumptions of Problem Solving Method. in 8th European Knowledge Acquisition workshop, EKAW-96, Springler-Verlag, 1996.

[3] R.Benjamins & G. Van heijst, Modelling Multiple Models, In proceeding of CESA96, IMACS Multiconference, 1996.

[4] P. Beys & R. Benjamins & G. van Heijst, Remedying the Reusability-Usability Tradeoff for Problem-solving Methods, proceedings of (KAW'96), Banff, Canada, Novembre 9-14, 1996.

[5] B. Chandrasekaran & T.R, Josephson, The Ontology of Tasks and Methods. Symposium on ontological Engineering, AAAI Spring Symposium Series, Stanford, CA. 1997.

[6] B. Chandrasekaran, T.R, Johnson & J.W Smith, Task-Structure Analysis for Knowledge Modelling, Communication of the ACM, 35(9) :124-137, 1992.

[7] E. Coelho & G. Lapalme, Describing Reusable Problem- Solving Methods with a Method Ontology, proceedings of (KAW'96), Banff Alberta, Canada, Novembre 9-14, 1996.

[8] D. Fensel : The tower of adapter Method for developing and reusing problem solving methods. In E. Plaza & al (eds.), *Knowledge acquisition, modeling and management*, (LNAI), 1319, Springler-Verlag, Berlin, 1997.

[9] D. Fensel, H. Erikson, M. Musen & R. Studer, Conceptual and Formal Specifications of Problem-Solving Methods. In International Journal of Expert Systems, 9(4), 1996.

[10] T. R. Gruber: A Translation Approach to Portable Ontology Specifications, Knowledge Acquisition, 5(2), 1993.

[11] G. Klinker & Al, Usable and Reusable Programming Constructs, Knowledge Acquisition, 3:117-136, 1991.

[12] M. Magnan, Objets complexes, In Oussalah & Al (Eds): Ingénierie objet concept et techniques, InterEditions, Masson, (in French) 1997.

[13] J. McDermott, Preliminary steps towards a taxonomy of problem solving methods, in S. Marcus edt, Kluwer academic publisher, Boston 88.

[14] M. Molina, Y. Shahar, J.Cuena, & M. Musen, A Structure of problem-Solving Methods for Real-time Decision Support : Modelling Approaches Using PROTEGE-II and KSM. proceedings of (KAW'96), Banff Alberta, Canada, Novembre 9-14, 1996.

[15] E. Motta, Trends in knowledge modelling: Report on 7th KEML Workshop. The Knowledge Engineering Review, Volume 12/Number 2/June 1997.

[16] E. Motta & Z. Zdrahal, An Approach to the organisation of a Library of Problem-Solving Methods which integrates the search paradigm with task and method ontologies, International Journal of Human Computer Studies, July 1997.

[17] A. Newel, The knowledge level, artificial Intelligence 18, 1982, 87-127.

[18] C. Pierret-Golbreich, TASK MODEL: A Framework for the Design of Models of Expertise. and Their Operationalisation. KAW'96. Banff, Alberta, Canada 1994.

[19] C. Pierret-Golbreich, TASK un environnement pour le developpement de systèmes à base de connaissances flexibles, habilitation à diriger les recherches, (in French) LRI, Orsay, 1996.

[20] C. Oussalah & al, A framework for modeling the structure and behavior of a system including multi level simulation, IASTED INT. Symp. On Applied Simulation an Modeling, ASM, Grindelwald, Switzerland, February 1988.

[21] L. Steels, component of expertise, AI magazine, 11(2), 28-49, 1990.

[22] K. Poeck & U. Gappa, Making Role limiting shells more flexible. In Aussenac & AL. Edts, EKAW93 Toulouse, lecture notes in AI 723, Springler-verlag 1993.

[23] R. Studer, H. Eriksson, J.H. Gennari, S.W. Tu, D. Fensel & M. Musen, Ontologies and the Configuration of Problem-Solving Methods, proceedings of (KAW'96), 9-14, 1996.

[24] A. Tchounikine, Activité dans les bases de données objets : le concept de Schéma Actif, thèse , University of paul sabatier, (in French)Toulouse 1993.

[25] A. Valente, J. Breuker & B. Bredeweg, Integrating Modelling Approaches in the CommonKADS Library, In proceedings of the AISB93, 121-130, IOS Press, Amterdam, 1993.

[26] G. Van Heijst, A.Th Shreiber & B.J Wielinga, Using explicit ontologies in KBS development, International Journal of Human-Computer Studies, 46(2/3):128-292, 1997.

[27] B. Wielinga, A. Schreiber & J. Breuker, KADS: A Modelling Approch to Knowledge Engineering. Knowledge Acquisition. 4, 5-53. 1992.

Incremental Updating of Classification Rules

J. Shao

Department of Computer Science
Cardiff University
United Kingdom
e-mail j.shao@cs.cf.ac.uk

Abstract. Rough sets theory provides a powerful framework for inducing classification knowledge from databases. In [11] we introduced a classification induction algorithm which is based on rough sets theory and derives classification rules according to two user specified criteria. This paper is a follow-up of [11] and will discuss how the derived rules may be updated incrementally when new data is observed.

1 Introduction

Among many KDD (Knowledge Discovery in Databases) problems [4], learning *classification* is the one which has received extensive study. Let O be a set of data objects. Each $o \in O$ is labelled with a class value and is described by a set of features. The task of learning classification from databases is to search for rules $F \rightarrow C$, where F is a combination of some feature values and C is the class value, such that the set of objects matching F is contained, according to certain measure, in the set of objects matching C [1].

Rough sets theory provides a powerful framework for inducing classification knowledge from databases. A number of methods have been developed for learning classification rules based on the rough sets theory [3, 5, 7, 9, 12, 10]. Most of these methods derive classification rules based on an application independent criteria for simplifying information in O. In [11], we introduced an algorithm which derives classification rules according to two user specified criteria: support and confidence. Given a rule $F \rightarrow C$, the *support* for the rule is the number of cases in the database that match $F \wedge C$ and the *confidence* for the rule is the ratio of the number of cases matching $F \wedge C$ to the number of cases matching F [2]. Our approach only derives the rules that have the required support and confidence. This is advantageous as users can specify different levels of noise to be tolerated and reliability required for different applications.

An important problem in the application of KDD is the maintenance of the derived knowledge. It is often necessary to update the derived knowledge when new data is observed. Most of the classification methods based on rough sets focus on the generating of best rules from data, and few have the incremental learning capability [8]. In this paper, we discuss how classification rules derived by our algorithm introduced in [11] may be updated incrementally.

The rest of this paper is organised as follows. In Section 2, we briefly outline how classification rules are induced by the algorithm given in [11]. This is to make this paper self-contained. Section 3 introduces our approach and explains how incremental updating of classification rules is carried out. Conclusions are given in Section 4.

2 Rough Sets Based Classification

We use a simple example shown in Table 1 to explain our algorithm briefly. The table contains information about a collection of cars.[1] Most of the attributes are self-explanatory, except for CN which is used as a shorthand to indicate the number of the same tuples occurred in the table.

Table 1. A Relation of Car Information

Id	Model	Fuel	Disp	Weight	Cyl	Power	Turbo	Comp	Trans	Mileage	CN
1	USA	EFI	Medium	Light	6	High	Yes	High	Manu	High	1
2	Japan	EFI	Small	Medium	4	Low	No	High	Manu	High	1
3	Japan	EFI	Medium	Light	4	Medium	No	Medium	Manu	High	1
4	Japan	EFI	Small	Medium	4	High	Yes	High	Manu	High	1
5	Japan	2-BBL	Small	Medium	4	Low	No	Medium	Manu	High	1
6	Japan	2-BBL	Small	Light	4	Low	No	High	Manu	High	1
7	Japan	EFI	Small	Medium	4	Medium	No	High	Manu	High	1
8	USA	EFI	Small	Medium	4	Medium	No	High	Manu	High	2
9	USA	EFI	Medium	Medium	6	High	Yes	High	Auto	Medium	1
10	USA	EFI	Medium	Medium	6	High	No	Medium	Manu	Medium	3
11	USA	EFI	Medium	Heavy	6	High	No	High	Manu	Medium	1
12	USA	EFI	Medium	Medium	6	High	No	High	Manu	Medium	2
13	USA	EFI	Medium	Medium	4	Medium	No	Medium	Auto	Medium	2
14	USA	2-BBL	Small	Medium	4	Low	No	High	Manu	Medium	1
15	USA	2-BBL	Small	Medium	4	Medium	No	High	Auto	Medium	1
16	USA	EFI	Medium	Medium	4	High	Yes	Medium	Manu	Medium	1
17	USA	EFI	Medium	Medium	6	High	No	Medium	Auto	Medium	1
18	USA	EFI	Medium	Medium	4	High	No	Medium	Auto	Medium	1
19	USA	EFI	Medium	Heavy	4	High	No	Medium	Manu	Low	1
20	USA	EFI	Medium	Heavy	6	High	No	Medium	Auto	Low	1

Our task is to discover a set of classification rules which will identify the features of a car that determine its mileage. There is a trivial solution to this problem. We can simply use each tuple in Table 1 as a classification rule. However, such rules are too specific and has little value in classifying unseen data.

2.1 Rough Sets and Information Reduction

Rough sets theory was introduced by Pawlak [6]. It provides a theoretic framework for studying how information may be reduced in order to induce general classifications. Informally, *information reduction* is the problem of searching for a minimal subset of information from which we can induce rules which have the same ability to classify data as those induced from the full set of information. Different techniques have been developed to search for reducts from a given set of data [9, 5, 12]. Once a reduct is obtained, the generation of classification rules from the reduct is straightforward.

[1] This table is largely extracted from [9], with minor changes to the values in order to illustrate our approach.

2.2 Finding Reducts with User Specified Criteria

In [11], we introduced an algorithm for finding a reduct of T with two user specified criteria: support and confidence. The user specifies a minimum level of support σ_m and confidence δ_m that classification rules must satisfy, and our algorithm will only derive the rules that satisfy this requirement.

In the following we outline the algorithm briefly, and the reader is referred to [11] for details. The algorithm makes multiple passes over T. At the start of pass i, we have a set of *seeds* $S_{i-1} = \{s_1, s_2, \ldots, s_k\}$ which are generated from pass $i-1$ ($S_0 = \{\}$). Each $s_j = (< f_{j1}, v_{j1} >, < f_{j2}, v_{j2} >, \ldots, < f_{ji-1}, v_{ji-1} >)$ is a sub-tuple of some tuple in T which has sufficient support but not sufficient confidence. We use $\sigma_T(t)$ to denote the support and $\delta_T(t)$ to denote the confidence for t w.r.t. T. Thus, if s_j is a seed, then $\sigma_T(s_j) \geq \sigma_m$ and $\delta_T(s_j) < \delta_m$. We call the number of $< f, v >$ pairs in s_j the *size* of s_j, denoted by $|s_j|$.

During pass i, we first expand some seeds with one more $< f, v >$. The expanded seeds are called *candidates.* Not every seed can be expanded into a candidate because a candidate must satisfy the following condition: if *cr* is a candidate at pass i, then all its sub-tuples of size $i-1$ must be in S_{i-1} [11]. Note that expanding a seed this way may reduce its support and increase its confidence.

Once a set of candidates CR_i is generated, T is scanned to count the actual support and confidence for each $cr \in CR_i$. The result of this counting will partition CR_i into 3 disjoint sets.

1. If $\sigma_T(cr) \geq \sigma_m$ and $\delta_T(cr) \geq \delta_m$, then *cr* is part of the reduct. It will not participate in any future passes as further expansion on them will only make them less general.
2. If $\sigma_T(cr) \geq \sigma_m$ and $\delta_T(cr) < \delta_m$, then *cr* becomes a seed for the next pass and go through the process we outlined above.
3. If $\sigma_T(cr) < \sigma_m$, then *cr* will not be considered in future processing because further expansion on it will never increase its support to meet the required minimum.

This process is continued until no more seeds may be generated. All the candidates satisfying $\sigma_T(cr) \geq \sigma_m$ and $\delta_T(cr) \geq \delta_m$ make up the final reduct.

We now explain our algorithm using Table 1 as an example. Assume that $\sigma_m = 6$ and $\delta_m = 76\%$. In the following, we explain how the reduct is derived for class $Mileage(High)$. Reducts for other classes can be derived in a similar way.

First Pass The seed set $S_0 = \{\}$. Our algorithm expands S_0 with all the possible $< f, v >$ pairs that can be found for $Mileage(high)$ in T, and then counts their support and confidence. This gives us Table 2.

Each entry in Table 2 should be seen as a rule. For example, the first entry represents $Model(USA) \rightarrow Mileage(High)$. The class value ($Mileage(High)$) is not shown because it is the same for all the entries. Recall that for each

Table 2. Calculations from the first pass

Id	CR_1	$\sigma_T(cr)$	$\delta_T(cr)$	R_1	S_1
1	$(< Model, USA >)$	3	19		
2	$(< Model, Japan >)$	6	6	✓	
3	$(< Fuel, EFI >)$	7	21		✓
4	$(< Fuel, 2-BBL >)$	2	4		
5	$(< Disp, Medium >)$	2	16		
6	$(< Disp, Small >)$	7	9	✓	
7	$(< Weight, Light >)$	3	3		
8	$(< Weight, Medium >)$	6	19		✓
9	$(< Cyl, 6 >)$	1	10		
10	$(< Cyl, 4 >)$	8	15		✓
11	$(< Power, High >)$	2	14		
12	$(< Power, Medium >)$	4	7		
13	$(< Power, Low >)$	3	4		
14	$(< Turbo, Yes >)$	2	4		
15	$(< Tubor, No >)$	7	21		✓
16	$(< Comp, High >)$	7	13		✓
17	$(< Comp, Medium >)$	2	12		
18	$(< Trans, Manu >)$	9	18		✓

rule $r : cr \rightarrow Mileage(High)$ in Table 2, its support is defined as $\sigma_T(r) = ||cr \wedge Mileage(High)||_T$ and its confidence as $\delta_T(r) = ||cr \wedge Mileage(High)||_T/||cr||_T$, where $||A||_T$ is the number of cases in T that match A. For convenience of our discussion, we record $||cr \wedge Mileage(High)||$ as $\sigma_T(cr)$ and $||cr||$ as $\delta_T(cr)$. The actual confidence for r can easily be worked out from $\delta_T(cr)$.

It is clear that by the end of this pass, candidates $\{2, 6\}$, where the numbers are the *row* numbers in Table 2, have sufficient support and confidence, and they become part of the reduct (R_1). Candidates $\{3, 8, 10, 15, 16, 18\}$ become the seeds (S_1) for the next pass as they have sufficient support, but not enough confidence. Others are ignored by the following passes as they do not have sufficient support.

Following Passes The computation in the following passes is the same as in the first pass, except that a set of candidates are generated from the seeds rather than from T. The result is given in Table 3.

Table 3. Calculations from the following passes

Id	CR_2	$\sigma_T(cr)$	$\delta_T(cr)$	$R_{2,3}$	$S_{2,3}$
1	$(< Fuel, EFI >, < Weight, Medium >)$	5	16		
2	$(< Fuel, EFI >, < Cyl, 4 >)$	6	11		✓
3	$(< Fuel, EFI >, < Tubor, No >)$	5	17		
4	$(< Fuel, EFI >, < Comp, High >)$	6	10		✓
5	$(< Fuel, EFI >, < Trans, Manu >)$	7	15		✓
6	$(< Weight, Medium >, < Cyl, 4 >)$	6	12		✓
7	$(< Weight, Medium >, < Tubor, No >)$	5	16		
8	$(< Weight, Medium >, < Comp, High >)$	5	10		
9	$(< Weight, Medium >, < Trans, Manu >)$	6	13		✓
10	$(< Cyl, 4 >, < Tubor, No >)$	7	13		✓
11	$(< Cyl, 4 >, < Comp, High >)$	6	8		✓
12	$(< Cyl, 4 >, < Trans, Manu >)$	8	11		✓
13	$(< Turbo, No >, < Comp, High >)$	5	10		
14	$(< Tubor, No >, < Trans, Manu >)$	7	15		✓
15	$(< Comp, High >, < Trans, Manu >)$	7	11		✓
16	$(< Fuel, EFI >, < Cyl, 4 >, < Comp, High >)$	5	5		
17	$(< Fuel, EFI >, < Cyl, 4 >, < Trans, Manu >)$	6	8		✓
18	$(< Fuel, EFI >, < Comp, High >, < Trans, Manu >)$	6	9		✓
19	$(< Weight, Medium >, < Cyl, 4 >, < Trans, Manu >)$	6	8		✓
20	$(< Cyl, 4 >, < Tubor, No >, < Trans, Manu >)$	7	9	✓	
21	$(< Cyl, 4 >, < Comp, High >, < Trans, Manu >)$	6	7	✓	

Final Reduct The final reduct for $Mileage(High)$ is the union of reducts found at each pass, and it is shown in Table 4.

Table 4. Final Reduct

Model	Disp	Cyl	Turbo	Comp	Trans	Mileage	σ	δ
Japan						High	6	1.00
	Small					High	7	0.78
		4	No		Manu	High	7	0.78
		4		High	Manu	High	6	0.86

Generating classification rules from the reduct is straightforward. For example, the first entry in Table 4 produces the following rule

$$Model(Japan) \to Mileage(High)$$

These rules are much more general than the rules from Table 1 directly and all have sufficient support and confidence specified by the user.

3 Updating Derived Rules

We now discuss how the derived rules may be updated when new data is observed. Clearly, updating rules implies the updating of candidates. So we discuss how the candidates are updated in this paper.

We first introduce some notation. We say that "a contains b", denoted by $a \succ b$, if every $< f : v >$ pair of b is an $< f : v >$ pair of a. Let cr be a candidate, cr_f be the feature part of cr and cr_c be the class part of cr (note that cr_c is implicit in the tables shown in the previous section). We observe the following effect on cr when a new tuple d is obtained[2] ($\delta_T(cr)$ is interpreted as in Table 2).

1. If $d_f \succ cr_f$ and $d_c \succ cr_c$, then d increases both support and confidence for cr. That is

$$\sigma_{T \cup d}(cr) = \sigma_T(cr) + 1 \qquad \delta_{T \cup d}(cr) = \delta_T(cr) + 1$$

   We say that d covers cr in this case.
2. If $d_f \succ cr_f$ and $d_c \not\succ cr_c$, then d decreases confidence for cr. That is,

$$\sigma_{T \cup d}(cr) = \sigma_T(cr) \qquad \delta_{T \cup d}(cr) = \delta_T(cr) + 1$$

   Note that increasing $\delta_T(cr)$ without increasing $\sigma_T(cr)$ will effectively decrease the confidence for cr. We say that d does not cover cr in this case.
3. If $d_f \not\succ cr_f$, then d has no effect on either support or confidence for cr. That is,

$$\sigma_{T \cup d}(cr) = \sigma_T(cr) \qquad \delta_{T \cup d}(cr) = \delta_T(cr)$$

   We say that d is irrelevant to cr in this case.

[2] The discussion here can easily be generalised to a set of new tuples.

These conditions determine how the candidates' support and confidence are updated. Once the candidates are updated, they may result in new candidates begin generated and existing ones being invalidated. The following section discusses in detail how our algorithm updates, generates and invalidates candidates when new data is observed.

3.1 Updating Candidates

We first assume that all the candidates generated at the induction stage (i.e. $CR = CR_1 \cup CR_2 \cup CR_3$) are available. Our algorithm for updating a set of candidates is shown in Figure 1, which makes 3 passes over the candidate set CR.

```
Algorithm Update Candidates
  begin
    for each cr ∈ CR do update(cr)
    k ← 1
    repeat
      for each updated cr ∈ CR and |cr| = k do
        if σ_{T∪d}(cr) ≥ σ_m and δ_{T∪d}(cr) ≥ δ_m and δ_T(cr) < δ_m then
          CR ← CR − invalidate(cr)
      k ← k + 1;
    until k = maximum(|cr|
    k ← 1
    repeat
      for each updated cr ∈ CR and |cr| = k do
        if σ_{T∪d}(cr) ≥ σ_m and σ_T(cr) < σ_m then
          CR ← CR ∪ generate(cr)
      k ← k + 1;
    until k = |d_f| or seed = φ
  end
```

Fig. 1. Algorithm for Updating Candidates

The first pass is an *updating* pass. During this pass, the *update*(cr) function updates the support and confidence of cr according to the conditions given earlier. For performance reasons, updated candidates are marked.

The second pass is an *invalidating* pass. This pass is necessary due to the following observation. If d covers cr and updates cr from $\sigma_T(cr) \geq \sigma_m$ and $\delta_T(cr) < \delta_m$ to $\sigma_{T \cup d}(cr) \geq \sigma_m$ and $\delta_{T \cup d}(cr) \geq \delta_m$, then any candidate c which contains cr as a sub-tuple should be invalidated. This is because c now becomes less general than cr. The *invalidate*(cr) function finds all the candidates which contains cr as a sub-tuple and eliminates them from CR.

The third pass is the *generating* pass. This pass is required due to the following observation. If $\sigma_T(cr) < \sigma_m$ and $\sigma_{T \cup d}(cr) \geq \sigma_m$, then it is possible to use cr as a seed to generate new candidates. The $generating(cr)$ function is essentially the process we described in Section 2.2 for generating candidates at the induction stage.

3.2 An Example

To show how this algorithm works, we consider the following example. Suppose that we have obtained the following new data (values correspond to the attributes in Table 1)

$$d =< USA, EFI, Small, Medium, 4, Medium, No, High, Manu, High >$$

and we wish to update the candidate set $CR = CR_1 \cup CR_2 \cup CR_3$.

The updating pass The first pass updates the support and confidence for the relevant candidates. This gives us Table 5. The $\sigma_{T \cup d}(cr)$ and $\delta_{T \cup d}(cr)$ columns indicate the updated support and confidence for each $cr \in CR$. If the values for these two columns are blank, then d is irrelevant to cr. Note that Table 5 is for class $Mileage(High)$ only. If there are other reducts for other classes, e.g. $Mileage(Medium)$, then d is used to update the candidates for those classes too.

The invalidating pass The second pass starts with all the candidates of size 1 and terminates when the maximum size of candidates is reached.

- *Iteration 1*
  None of the candidates of size 1 (rows 1 to 18 in Table 5) satisfies the condition $\sigma_{T \cup d}(cr) \geq \sigma_m$, $\delta_{T \cup d}(cr) \geq \delta_m$ and $\delta_T(cr) < \delta_m$, so the $invalidate(cr)$ function returns an empty set. Nothing is removed from CR.
- *Iteration 2*
  For candidates of size 2 (rows 19 to 33 in Table 5), we found that ($< Cyl, 4 >$, $< Comp, High >$) (row 29) is the only candidate that satisfies the condition. We therefore use it to invalidate candidates that contain it as a subtuple. We found ($< Fuel, EFI >, < Cyl, 4 >, < Comp, High >$) (row 34) and ($< Cyl, 4 >, < Comp, High >, < Trans, Manu >$) (row 39), and they are removed from CR.
- *Iteration 3*
  Since the maximum candidate size in CR is 3, the invalidating pass terminates.

The generating pass The third pass again starts with all the candidates of size 1, but this time we seek to generate new candidates. This continues until no more new candidates can be generated.

Table 5. After the updating pass

Id	CR	$\sigma_T(cr)$	$\delta_T(cr)$	$\sigma_{T\cup d}(cr)$	$\delta_{T\cup d}(cr)$
1	$(< Model, USA >)$	3	19	4	20
2	$(< Model, Japan >)$	6	6		
3	$(< Fuel, EFI >)$	7	21	8	22
4	$(< Fuel, 2-BBL >)$	2	4		
5	$(< Disp, Medium >)$	2	16		
6	$(< Disp, Small >)$	7	9	8	10
7	$(< Weight, Light >)$	3	3		
8	$(< Weight, Medium >)$	6	19	7	20
9	$(< Cyl, 6 >)$	1	10		
10	$(< Cyl, 4 >)$	8	15	9	16
11	$(< Power, High >)$	2	14		
12	$(< Power, Medium >)$	4	7	5	8
13	$(< Power, Low >)$	3	4		
14	$(< Turbo, Yes >)$	2	4		
15	$(< Tubor, No >)$	7	21	8	22
16	$(< Comp, High >)$	7	13	8	14
17	$(< Comp, Medium >)$	2	12		
18	$(< Trans, Manu >)$	9	18	10	19
19	$(< Fuel, EFI >, < Weight, Medium >)$	5	16	6	17
20	$(< Fuel, EFI >, < Cyl, 4 >)$	6	11	7	12
21	$(< Fuel, EFI >, < Tubor, No >)$	5	17	6	18
22	$(< Fuel, EFI >, < Comp, High >)$	6	10	7	11
23	$(< Fuel, EFI >, < Trans, Manu >)$	7	15	8	16
24	$(< Weight, Medium >, < Cyl, 4 >)$	6	12	7	13
25	$(< Weight, Medium >, < Tubor, No >)$	5	16	6	17
26	$(< Weight, Medium >, < Comp, High >)$	5	10	6	11
27	$(< Weight, Medium >, < Trans, Manu >)$	6	13	7	14
28	$(< Cyl, 4 >, < Tubor, No >)$	7	13	8	14
29	$(< Cyl, 4 >, < Comp, High >)$	6	8	7	9
30	$(< Cyl, 4 >, < Trans, Manu >)$	8	11	9	12
31	$(< Turbo, No >, < Comp, High >)$	5	10	6	11
32	$(< Tubor, No >, < Trans, Manu >)$	7	15	8	16
33	$(< Comp, High >, < Trans, Manu >)$	7	11	8	12
34	$(< Fuel, EFI >, < Cyl, 4 >, < Comp, High >)$	5	5	6	6
35	$(< Fuel, EFI >, < Cyl, 4 >, < Trans, Manu >)$	0	8	7	9
36	$(< Fuel, EFI >, < Comp, High >, < Trans, Manu >)$	6	9	7	10
37	$(< Weight, Medium >, < Cyl, 4 >, < Trans, Manu >)$	6	8	7	9
38	$(< Cyl, 4 >, < Tubor, No >, < Trans, Manu >)$	7	9	8	10
39	$(< Cyl, 4 >, < Comp, High >, < Trans, Manu >)$	6	7	7	8

- *Iteration 1*
  None of the candidates of size 1 satisfies $\sigma_{T\cup d}(cr) \geq \sigma_m$ and $\sigma_T(cr) < \sigma_m$, so the *generating*(cr) function returns an empty set. Nothing is added to CR.
- *Iteration 2*
  For candidates of size 2, we found candidates $\{19, 21, 25, 26, 31\}$ satisfy the condition. We use this set as seeds, as we did at the induction stage, and expand them into new candidates. This gives us Table 7. Note that for these candidates, it is necessary to scan the database to obtain their support and confidence.

Table 6. New candidates of size 3

Id	CR	$\sigma_{T\cup d}(cr)$	$\delta_{T\cup d}(cr)$
1'	$(< Fuel, EFI >, < Weight, Medium >, < Cyl, 4 >)$	6	10
2'	$(< Fuel, EFI >, < Weight, Medium >, < Tubor, No >)$	5	14
3'	$(< Fuel, EFI >, < Weight, Medium >, < Comp, High >)$	6	9
4'	$(< Fuel, EFI >, < Weight, Medium >, < Trans, Manu >)$	6	12
5'	$(< Fuel, EFI >, < Tubor, No >, < Comp, High >)$	5	8
6'	$(< Fuel, EFI >, < Tubor, No >, < Trans, Manu >)$	6	13
7'	$(< Fuel, EFI >, < Tubor, No >, < Cyl, 4 >)$	6	10
8'	$(< Weight, Medium >, < Tubor, No >, < Cyl, 4 >)$	6	11
9'	$(< Weight, Medium >, < Tubor, No >, < Comp, High >)$	5	9
10'	$(< Weight, Medium >, < Tubor, No >, < Trans, Manu >)$	6	12
11'	$(< Weight, Medium >, < Comp, High >, < Trans, Manu >)$	6	9
12'	$(< Turbo, No >, < Comp, High >, < Trans, Manu >)$	6	10

- *Iteration 3*
  From the new candidates of size 3 in Table 6 and those of the same size in Table 5, we can generate only one candidate of size 4. This is shown in Table 8.

Table 7. New candidates of size 4

Id	CR	$\sigma_{T\cup d}(cr)$	$\delta_{T\cup d}(cr)$
1'	$(<Fuel, EFI>, <Weight, Medium>, <Comp, High>, <Trans, Manu>)$	6	8

- *Iteration 4*
  No more new candidates may be generated from Table 8, so the generating pass terminates.

This completes the entire candidate updating process. The candidates with sufficient support and confidence make up the updated reduct (or the updated rules). This is shown in Table 8. Note that two rules in Table 4 are replaced by a new and more general rule after the update. In addition, two new rules are generated, due to the increased support for them.

Table 8. The updated Reduct

Model	Fuel	Disp	Weight	Cyl	Turbo	Comp	Trans	Mileage	σ	δ
Japan								High	6	1.00
		Small						High	8	0.80
				4		High		High	7	0.78
		EFI		4			Manu	High	7	0.78
			Medium	4			Manu	High	7	0.78
				4	No		Manu	High	8	0.80

We end this section with two comments on our algorithm. Firstly, our algorithm is efficient and does not re-discover the rules found during the induction. The updating pass and the invalidating pass are linear in the size of candidates. Only a sequential scan of the candidate set and a simple term matching against d, the new data, are necessary. The generating pass has the same complexity as that of the induction algorithm. However, it should be noted that the generating function is only applied to the candidates which were not computed as seeds during the induction. In other words, if d were available at the time of induction, then all the new candidates generated during the updating process would have been generated during the induction. So our algorithm does not perform any redundant computation during updating.

Secondly, although our algorithm is introduced as an updating algorithm, it is in fact an incremental classification learning algorithm. This is because the generating pass of our algorithm is essentially the induction algorithm we described in Section 2.2. So, in theory, it is possible to learn classification case by case with our updating algorithm. Also, it is not difficult to see that our algorithm is capable of updating candidates with a set of new cases, not just a single one.

4 Conclusions

In this paper, we have introduced an algorithm for updating classification rules. The algorithm is designed within the framework of rough sets theory and updates the rules derived by a method introduced in [11]. One of the most useful features of our algorithm is its incremental updating capability. It makes full use of the information generated during induction and does not re-discover or regenerate the same information again during updating. As a result, our algorithm is efficient and is useful for applications where new data is observed frequently.

The proposed algorithm assumes some storage for intermediate results which could be potentially large. This problem can be tackled by using storage/efficiency trade-off, probabilistic estimation or data warehousing techniques. We plan to investigate the use of these techniques in the near future.

References

1. R. Agrawal, T. Imielinski, and A. Swami. Database Mining: A performance perspective. *IEEE Transactions on Knowledge and Data Engineering*, 5(6), 1993.
2. R. Agrawal and R. Srikant. Fast algorithms for mining association rules. In *Proceedings of International Conference on VLDB*, pages 487–499, 1994.
3. J.S. Deogun, V.V. Raghavan, and H.Sever. Exploiting Upper approximation in the rough set methodology. In *International Conference on Knowledge Discovery and Data Mining*, pages 69–74, 1995.
4. U.M Fayyad, G Piatetsky-Shapiro, P Smyth, and R Uthurusamy. *Advances in Knowledge Discovery and Data Mining.* AAAI/MIT Press, 1996.
5. Z. Pawlak. Rough classification. *International Journal of Man-Machine Studies*, 20:469–483, 1984.
6. Z. Pawlak. *Rough Sets: Theoretical Aspects of Reasoning About Data.* Kluwer Academic Publishers, 1991.
7. Z. Pawlak, S.K.M. Wong, and W. Ziarko. Rough Sets: Probabilistic versus Deterministic. In B.R. Gaines and J.H. Boose, editors, *Machine Learning and Uncertain Reasoning*, pages 227–241. Academic Press, 1990.
8. N. Shan and W. Ziarko. An Incremental Learning Algorithm for Constructing Decision Rules. In *International Workshop on Rough Sets and Knowledge Discovery*, pages 326–334, 1993.
9. N. Shan, W. Ziarko, H.J. Hamilton, and N. Cercone. Using rough sets as tools for knowledge discovery. In *International Conference on Knowledge Discovery and Data Mining*, pages 263–268, 1995.
10. J. Shao. Using rough sets for rough classification. In *Proceedings of International Workshop on Database and Expert Systems Applications*, pages 268–273, 1996.
11. J. Shao. Finding reducts with user specified criteria. In *Proceedings of International Workshop on Database and Expert Systems Applications*, pages 352–357, 1997.
12. R. Slowinski. *Intelligent Decision Support: Handbook of Applications and Advances of the Rough Sets Theory.* Kluwer Academic Publishers, 1992.

Declarative Semantics for Active Rules*

Sergio Flesca and Sergio Greco

DEIS
Università della Calabria
87030 Rende, Italy
{ flesca, greco }@si.deis.unical.it

Abstract. In this paper we analyze declarative deterministic semantics for active rules. In particular we consider deterministic (partial) stable model semantics previously defined for deductive rules such as well-founded, max-deterministic, and unique total stable semantics. The semantics of an active program $\mathcal{AP}$ is given by first rewriting it into a deductive program $\mathcal{LP}$, computing the model M defining the declarative semantics of $\mathcal{LP}$ and, finally, applying 'consistent' updates contained in M to the source database.

1 Introduction

Active databases is an emerging technology combining techniques from databases, expert systems and artificial intelligence. Active databases support the automatic 'triggering' of rules in response to events. Automatic triggering of rules can be useful in different areas such as integrity constraint maintenance, update of materialized views, knowledge bases, expert systems [12].

Active rules follow the so called *Event-Condition-Action* (ECA) paradigm; rules autonomously react to events occurring on the data, by evaluating a data dependent condition, and by executing a reaction whenever the condition is true. Active rules consist of three parts: *Event* (which causes the rule to be triggered), *Condition* (which is checked when the rule is triggered) and *Action* (which is executed when the rule is triggered and the condition is true). Thus, the semantics of a single active rule is that the rule reacts to a given event, tests a condition, and performs a given action. However, since the semantics of active rules are usually given in terms of execution models, understanding the behavior of active rules, especially in the case of rules each other interacting, is very difficult, and often the actions performed are not the expected ones. A very important issue in active databases is the development of tools which help in the design of programs with clear and intuitive semantics [3].

Two main properties have been identified for active rules: termination and confluence [1].

* Work partially supported by a MURST grant under the project "Interdata". The second author is also supported by ISI-CNR.

[1] A third important property is observable determinism. This property is not relevant in our framework since we consider as actions only insertion and deletion of tuples.

Consider for instance the following program $\mathcal{AP}$ where $+\mathtt{a}$ (resp. $-\mathtt{a}$) in the head of the rule means that, if the body is true, the atom a is inserted (resp. deleted) from the databases.

$-\mathtt{a} \leftarrow +\mathtt{a}.$
$+\mathtt{a} \leftarrow -\mathtt{a}.$

Assume also that the initial update is $\delta = \{+\mathtt{a}\}$. Thus, the meaning of the first rule is that if the atom a has been inserted, then it will be deleted (it defines a sort of constraint stating that "the atom a cannot be inserted"). The procedural evaluation of this active program applies alternatively the first and second rule deleting and inserting repeatedly the atom a. Thus, a procedural semantics could be not desirable since it is possible to generate infinite loops. A second problem dealing with active programs is that the future state of the database depends on the way active rules are fired. So, under procedural semantics, the behavior of active rules is not easy to understand and predict.

Several techniques have been designed to check if termination and confluence can be guaranteed. These techniques are mainly based of the definition of 'compile-time' sufficient conditions. However, there are terminating and confluent programs which cannot be identified by these techniques.

Different solutions to these problems have been proposed in [1], where a declarative semantics is associated to active rules, and in [13, 6], where active rules are modeled by means of deductive rules with an attribute denoting the state of the computation.

The solution proposed by Bidoit and Maabout [1] is based on the computation of the well-founded semantics of a Datalog$^{\neg}$ program derived from the rewriting of the active program. The merits of this approach are that the semantics of programs is well-defined and the computation guarantees both termination and confluence in the general case.

However, the approach proposed in [1] is not completely satisfactory since in many cases it does not capture the intuitive meaning of the active program. Consider for instance the following rule and the initial update $\delta = \{+\mathtt{p}\}$.

$-\mathtt{p} \leftarrow \neg + \mathtt{p}.$

Since the atom $+\mathtt{p}$ is inserted in the database, this rules will not be fired; therefore the atom p is not removed from the database. However, the semantics proposed in [1] is not able to deduce this fact and it concludes that p is undefined in the updated database. There are two problems with this semantics: the first is in the rewriting of active rules into deductive ones and the second is that the well-founded semantics in many cases is not satisfactory.

To overcome these problems we review their technique by defining a different rewriting method and proposing in addition to the well-founded, other confluent declarative semantics.

2 Preliminary definitions

2.1 Active and deductive rules

We assume finite countable sets of constants, variables and predicate symbols. A *term* is either a constant or a variable. A (standard) *atom* is of the form $p(t_1, ..., t_n)$ where p is a predicate symbol and $t_1, ..., t_n$ are terms. A *literal* is an atom A or its negation $\neg A$. Predicate symbols can be either *base* (EDB) or *derived* (IDB). Atoms and literals are either base or derived accordingly to their predicate symbols. An *update atom* (resp. literal) is of the form $+A$ or $-A$ where A is a base atom (resp. literal).

A *rule* is of the form

$$\mathtt{A} \leftarrow \mathtt{B_1, ..., B_n, C_1, ..., C_m}.$$

where A is an atom, $B_1, ..., B_n$ are update literals and $C_1, ..., C_m$ are standard literals. Rules can be either active or deductive. *Active rules* have in the head an update atom whereas *deductive rules* have in the head a standard atom. A deductive rule is said $\mathtt{DATALOG}^\neg$ *rule* if the body does not contain update literals. A rule is said to be positive if it is negation free. Positive $\mathtt{DATALOG}^\neg$ rules are called $\mathtt{DATALOG}$ rules. Let r be a rule, $H(r)$ and $B(r)$ represent, respectively, the head and the body of r. A ground $\mathtt{DATALOG}$ rule with no goals is called a *fact.* An *program* is a set of rules. A program $\mathcal{AP}$ is called *active* if it contains at least one active rule otherwise is said *deductive.* A deductive program is said $\mathtt{DATALOG}^\neg$ if does not contain update literals.

EDB predicate symbols form a relational database scheme $\mathcal{S}$, thus they are also seen as relation symbols. The set of all databases on a given schema $\mathcal{S}$ is denoted by $\mathbf{D}$. A database $D = \langle D^+, \overline{D}\rangle$ on $\mathcal{S}$ is a set of pairs of finite relations $\langle D^+(r), \overline{D}(r)\rangle$ on a countable domain U (database domain), one for each r in $\mathcal{S}$ such that $D^+(r) \cap \overline{D}(r) = \emptyset$. D^+ denotes the set of true facts in D whereas $\overline{D}$ is the set of unknown facts in D. Moreover, we denote with D^- the set of false facts in D, that is the set of facts which are not in the database. Observe that databases may contain, besides true facts, also facts which are unknown. The reason to consider also unknown facts will be clear in the next sections. A database D on $\mathcal{S}$ is said to be *total* if $\overline{D} = \emptyset$, i.e., there are no unknown facts in D.

An *update program* $\mathcal{UP}$ is a pair $\langle \delta, \mathcal{AP}\rangle$, where δ is a set of update facts and $\mathcal{AP}$ is an active program. The set δ contains the *input update set* which is used to fire the active rules. An update program $\mathcal{UP}$ defines a mapping from $\mathbf{D}$ to $\mathbf{D}$. Thus, the application of an update program $\mathcal{UP}$ to a database D_1 on $\mathcal{S}$, denoted $\mathcal{UP}(D_1)$, gives a new database D_2 on $\mathcal{S}$.

An update program $\mathcal{UP}$, on a database scheme $\mathcal{S}$, is a recursive (i.e., computable) function from $\mathbf{D}$ to $\mathbf{D}$. In addition to be computable, every update $\mathcal{UP}$ is required to be *C-generic*, i.e., for any D on $\mathcal{S}$ and for any isomorphism ρ on $U - C$, $\mathcal{UP}(\rho(D)) = \rho(\mathcal{UP}(D))$, where the domain C denotes the set of constant in the program. Informally speaking, the output of a program does not depend on the internal representation of the constants in the database not appearing in the program.

2.2 Semantics of DATALOG$^\neg$

P-Stable Models Given an atom A, $\neg\neg A$ denotes A. Let I be a set of ground literals; then $\neg I$ denotes the set $\{\neg A | A \in I\}$, and I^+ (resp., I^-) denotes the set of all atoms (resp., negated atoms) in I. Given a DATALOG$^\neg$ program $\mathcal{LP}$ and a database D, we denote with $\overline{I} = B_{\mathcal{LP}_D} - (I^+ \cup \neg I^-)$ the set of facts in the Herbrand base which are undefined in the interpretation I. I is a *(partial) interpretation* of $\mathcal{LP}_D$ if it is *consistent*, i.e., $I^+ \cap \neg I^- = \emptyset$. Moreover, if $I^+ \cup \neg I^- = B_{\mathcal{LP}_D}$, the interpretation I is called *total*.

Given an interpretation I, $X \subseteq B_{\mathcal{LP}_D}$ is an *unfounded set w.r.t. I* if for each rule $r \in ground(\mathcal{LP}_D)$ with $H(r) \in X$, $G(r) \cap (\neg I \cup X) \neq \emptyset$, i.e., there is a literal in the body which either is false in I or is contained in X. The union of all unfounded sets w.r.t. I is also an unfounded set w.r.t. I and is called the *greatest unfounded set* ($\mathbf{U}_{\mathcal{LP}_D}(I)$).

Let M be an interpretation of the program $\mathcal{LP}_D$. Let $pos(\mathcal{LP}_D, M^-)$ be the positive program obtained from $ground(\mathcal{LP}_D)$ by deleting (a) each rule that has a negative goal that is not in M^-, and (b) all negative goals from the remaining rules. Then M is *founded* if and only if $\mathbf{T}^{\infty}_{pos(\mathcal{LP}_D, M^-)}(\emptyset) = M^+$, where the operator $\mathbf{T}$ is the classical *immediate consequence transformation*.

An interpretation M of $\mathcal{LP}_D$ is a *P-stable* model if (*a*) it is founded in $\mathcal{LP}_D$ and (*b*) $\neg M^-$ is the greatest unfounded set w.r.t. M in $\mathcal{LP}_D$. A P-stable model M of $\mathcal{LP}_D$ is (i) *T-stable* (*total stable*) if it is a total interpretation of $\mathcal{LP}_D$, and (ii) *well-founded* if it is the intersection of all P-stable models of $\mathcal{LP}$ [4, 11].

Deterministic P-Stable Models. The notion of max-deterministic model has been first introduced in [9] and its relevance has been also discussed in [10, 5]. Let $\mathcal{LP}$ be a DATALOG$^\neg$ program, D be a database on $\mathcal{S}$ and M be a P-stable model of $\mathcal{LP}_D$. M is *deterministic* if for each other P-stable model N of $\mathcal{LP}_D$, M and N are not contradictory, i.e., $M \cup N$ is an interpretation. As proven in [10], two deterministic P-stable models are only an expression of assorted degrees of undefinedness inasmuch as there exists a P-stable model which includes both models.

The well-founded model is obviously a deterministic model — actually, as it is the intersection of all P-stable models, it is the minimum deterministic model. The family of deterministic models, denoted by *DM*, has an additional property: there exists a maximum element in the family, the *max-deterministic model*, which includes all other deterministic models and, therefore, can resolve all differences among them.

Observe that for every DATALOG$^\neg$ program $\mathcal{LP}$, $\langle DM, \subseteq \rangle$ is a complete lattice such that the bottom is the well founded model and the top is the max-deterministic model. [10] Thus, deterministic P-stable models trade off minimal undefinedness to achieve determinism, but in different degrees. At the bottom, we find the well-founded model, which ensures better computability at the expense of more undefinedness. At the top, we find the max-deterministic model, whose clear semantic advantages are counterbalanced by computational drawbacks, as it is stated next.

3 Desirable properties of active programs

Several desirable properties for active rules have been introduced in the literature. The most important properties are termination and confluence.

Termination is the property which guarantees that the execution of active programs terminates in a finite number of steps. It is a crucial problem in active databases since rules may trigger each other recursively, and consequently, nontermination of active rules is a permanent threat.

Confluence is the property that the execution of active programs produces a final state (updated database) independent on the order of execution of (not priorized) rules. In general, confluence is a desirable feature since the behavior of rules with a unique final state can be more easily understood.

In this paper we consider a different framework based on the use of declarative deterministic semantics. These semantics guarantee both termination and confluence since they are based on finite domains and semantics which identify univocally a particular model.

For declarative semantics, several other desirable properties have been proposed. A first requirement is that any semantics must be *founded*, that is, the set of (positive and undefined) atoms in the model must be derivable from the program. A second requirement is that the set of updates to be applied to a given database must be consistent.

Definition 1. A set of update literals δ is said to be

1. *conflict free* if it does not contains two update facts of the form $+A$ and $-A$;
2. *consistent*[2] if for each atom $+A \in \delta$ (resp. $-A \in \delta$) is $\neg - A \in \delta$ (resp. $\neg + A \in \delta$). ■

Finally, we consider a property of knowledge ordering among databases (i.e., set of atoms which can be either true or undefined).

Definition 2. Given two databases D_1 and D_2, we say that D_1 is not more informative than D_2 ($D_1 \preceq D_2$) if for each $A \in \overline{D}_2$ is $A \in \overline{D}_1$. ■

This property is very important since we are interested in databases having maximal sets of true and false facts, and, therefore, our transformations should minimize the set of unknown facts.

4 Declarative Semantics for Update Programs

As discussed in the Introduction, the semantics proposed in [1] is not able to capture the intuitive meaning of all programs. Thus, in this paper we propose different deterministic semantics for active rules. More specifically, we consider a different rewriting of active rules into deductive ones and analyze several confluent partial stable semantics.

Let us start by introducing how sets of updates are applied to databases.

[2] This property has been called *well founded* in [1].

Algorithm 1 *Rewrite update programs.*
Input *Update program $\mathcal{UP} = \langle \delta, \mathcal{AP} \rangle$;*
Output DATALOG$^\neg$ *program $st(\mathcal{UP})$;*
Method

1. *insert into $st(\mathcal{UP})$ the deductive rules in $\mathcal{AP}$;*
2. *For each active rule $+a(t) \leftarrow B$ (resp., $-a(t) \leftarrow B$) in $\mathcal{AP}$ insert into $st(\mathcal{UP})$ the rule $+a(t) \leftarrow B, \neg ck\_a(t)$ (resp., $-a(t) \leftarrow B, \neg ck\_a(t)$) where ck_a is a new predicate symbol;*
3. *For each rule r in $st(\mathcal{UP})$ replace each update atom $+p(t)$ (resp. $-p(t)$) in the body with $+p(t) \vee p'(t)$ (resp., $-p(t) \vee p''(t)$), where p' and p'' are new IDB predicate symbols;*
4. *For each new predicate symbol ck_a with arity n, introduced in Step 2, add a rule $ck\_a(X_1, ..., X_n) \leftarrow +a(X_1, ..., X_n), -a(X_1, ..., X_n)$;*
5. *For each update atoms $+p(t)$ (resp. $-p(t)$) $\in \delta$ insert into $st(\mathcal{UP})$ the fact $p'(t)$ (resp., $p''(t)$) (introduced in the body of rules in Step 3);*
6. *Rewrite the program in clausal form by eliminating disjunctions;*
7. *Return $st(\mathcal{UP})$ where every update atom $+a(t)$ (resp., $-a(t)$) is interpreted as a standard atom, i.e., $+a$ and $-a$ are new standard predicate symbols.* ∎

Fig. 1. Rewriting of update programs

Definition 3. Let $D = \langle D^+, \overline{D} \rangle$ be a database and let δ be a consistent set of update literals. Then, the application of δ to D, denoted $\delta(D)$, gives a new database D_1 defined as follows:

1. $p \in D_1^+$ if $+p \in \delta$ or ($p \in D^+$ and $\neg - p \in \delta$);
2. $p \in \overline{D}_1$ if one of the following conditions is true
   (a) $p \in \overline{D}$ and $+p, -p \notin \delta^+$;
   (b) $p \in D^+$ and $-p \in \overline{\delta}$;
   (c) $p \in D^-$ and $+p \in \overline{\delta}$.

∎

Thus, an atom p is undefined in the new database D_1 if (1) it was undefined in the old database D and there is no evidence about its insertion or deletion, or (2) it was true (resp. false) in D and there is no evidence about its deletion (resp. insertion). The following algorithm rewrites an update program $\mathcal{UP}$ into a deductive program denoted as $st(\mathcal{UP})$. The derived program contains update literals which are interpreted as standard ones (i.e., an update atom $+p(t)$ will be interpreted, in the rewritten program, as a standard atom with predicate symbol $+p$). The declarative semantics of the rewritten deductive program $st(\mathcal{UP})$ gives a set of literals containing also elements with predicate symbols of the form $+p$ and $-p$; these atoms will be next interpreted as insertions and deletions to be applied to the source database.

Essentially, the algorithm rewrites update atoms taking into account information contained in the input update δ, and adds 'temporary' rules which are used to guarantee consistency of the model, i.e., any model containing an atom of the form $+a(t)$ must contain also the literal $\neg - a(t)$. In particular, for each update $+a(t)$ (resp. $-a(t)$) in δ a fact $a(t)'$ (resp. $a''(t)$) is added to the program (Step 5) and every update atom $+a(u)$ (resp. $-a(u)$) in the body of a rule is replaced by a disjunction $+a(u) \vee a'(u)$ (resp., $-a(u) \vee a''(u)$) which takes into account that the insertion of an atom can be derived from the program or is contained in the input update set δ (Step 3). Moreover, programs are subsequently rewritten in standard form by eliminating disjunctions.

Example 1. Consider the update program of Example 1 where $\delta = \{+a\}$ and $\mathcal{AP}$ consists of the following two rules

$$+\mathtt{a} \leftarrow -\mathtt{a}. \qquad\qquad -\mathtt{a} \leftarrow +\mathtt{a}.$$

The deductive program derived from Algorithm 1 before rewriting disjunctions is

$$\begin{array}{ll} +\mathtt{a} \leftarrow (-\mathtt{a} \vee \mathtt{a}''),\ \neg\mathtt{ck\_a}. & \mathtt{a}'. \\ -\mathtt{a} \leftarrow (+\mathtt{a} \vee \mathtt{a}'),\ \neg\mathtt{ck\_a}. & \mathtt{ck\_a} \leftarrow +\mathtt{a},\ -\mathtt{a} \end{array}$$

The standard program $st(\mathcal{UP})$ is

$$\begin{array}{ll} +\mathtt{a} \ \leftarrow \mathtt{a}^-,\ \neg\mathtt{ck\_a}. & \mathtt{a}^- \leftarrow -\mathtt{a} \\ -\mathtt{a} \ \leftarrow \mathtt{a}^+,\ \neg\mathtt{ck\_a}. & \mathtt{a}^- \leftarrow \mathtt{a}'' \\ \mathtt{a}'. & \mathtt{a}^+ \leftarrow +\mathtt{a} \\ \mathtt{ck\_a} \leftarrow +\mathtt{a},\ -\mathtt{a} & \mathtt{a}^+ \leftarrow \mathtt{a}' \end{array}$$

Observe that the predicates a^+ and a^- and the rules defining them are introduced in the rewriting of the program in clausal form by eliminating disjunctions in the body of rules (Step 6 in Algorithm 1). ∎

In the following we will consider only (partial) stable model semantics which identify a unique particular model; we denote such semantics as *confluent* and denote any generic confluent stable model semantics with $\mathcal{XS}$.. Well-founded and max-deterministic semantics are two examples of confluent semantics.

Given an update program $\mathcal{UP}$ and a database D. Then, we denote with $SEM_{\mathcal{XS}}[\mathcal{UP}, D]$ the model of $st(\mathcal{UP})_D$ under the confluent $\mathcal{XS}$ semantics. Moreover, given a set of literals M, we denote with $\hat{M}$ the set of update literals in M. The following definition introduces the application of an update program $\mathcal{UP}$ to a database D.

Definition 4. *Let $\mathcal{UP} = \langle \delta, \mathcal{AP} \rangle$ be an update program and let D be a database. Then, the application of $\mathcal{UP}$ to D under stable model semantics $\mathcal{XS}$ denoted $\mathcal{UP}_{\mathcal{XS}}(D)$, is defined as $\Gamma_{\mathcal{XS}}(\delta(D))$ where $\Gamma_{\mathcal{XS}} = \widehat{SEM}_{\mathcal{XS}}[\mathcal{UP}, D]$.* ∎

The application of $\mathcal{UP} = \langle \delta, \mathcal{AP} \rangle$ to D is carried out into three steps: (i) first compute the set of update atoms which are derived from the standard version of $\mathcal{UP}$ applied to D, (ii) next, apply δ to D and, finally, (iii) apply the set derived update atoms to the current database. Observe that in the application of an update program $\mathcal{UP}$ to a database D, we first apply the input updates δ and next the updates derived from the active program $\mathcal{AP}$. Thus, we give priority to the active program since it defines a sort of constraints which must be satisfied — updates in δ could be nullified by the rules in the program.

Proposition 1. *Let $\mathcal{UP}$ be an update program and let D be a database. Then, $\widehat{SEM}_{\mathcal{XS}}[\mathcal{UP}, D]$ is consistent for every confluent stable model semantics $\mathcal{XS}$.* ∎

Corollary 1. *Let $\mathcal{UP}$ be an update program and let D be a database. Then, for each confluent semantics $\mathcal{XS}$, $\widehat{SEM}_{\mathcal{XS}}[\mathcal{UP}, D]$ is conflict-free.* ∎

4.1 Well-founded semantics

We consider here the well-founded semantics and compare it with the semantics for update programs proposed by Bidoit and Maabout [1]. The two semantics differ in the rewriting of the source program and in the application of the input update to the source database.

We first recall how programs are rewritten in [1]. Given an update program $\mathcal{UP}$ denote with $st_{[BM]}(\mathcal{UP})$ the standard DATALOG$^{\neg}$ program obtained from $\mathcal{UP}$ by (1) replacing each rule of the form $+A \leftarrow Body$ (resp., $-A \leftarrow Body$) in $\mathcal{AP}$ with a rule $+A \leftarrow Body, \neg - A$ (resp., $-A \leftarrow Body, \neg + A$) and (2) inserting, for each update atoms $+A \in \delta$ (resp. $-A \in \delta$), a rule of the form $+A \leftarrow \neg - A$ (resp., $-A \leftarrow \neg + A$). The following example shows the different behavior of the two rewritings.

Example 2. Consider a database D and the update program $\mathcal{UP} = \langle \delta, \mathcal{AP} \rangle$ where $\delta = \{+p\}$ and $\mathcal{AP}$ consists of the rule

$$-\mathrm{p} \leftarrow \neg + \mathrm{p}.$$

The rewritten program $st(\mathcal{UP})$ consists of the rules

$$\mathrm{p}'.$$
$$-\mathrm{p} \leftarrow \neg + \mathrm{p},\ \neg \mathrm{p}',\ \neg \mathrm{ck\_p}.$$
$$\mathrm{ck\_p} \leftarrow +\mathrm{p},\ -\mathrm{p}.$$

where the fact p$'$ takes into account the content of δ. The standard program $st_{[BM]}(\mathcal{UP})$ contains the rules

$$+\mathrm{p} \leftarrow \neg - \mathrm{p}.$$
$$-\mathrm{p} \leftarrow \neg + \mathrm{p}.$$

The well founded models of $st(\mathcal{UP})_D$ and $st_{[BM]}(\mathcal{UP})_D$ are, respectively, $M_1 = \{p', \neg - p, \neg ck\_p, \neg + p\} \cup D$ and $M_2 = D$ (all derived atoms are undefined). Therefore, the application of δ to D, followed by the application of $\hat{M}_1$ gives a new database containing the atom p with truth value *true*. However, the application of $\hat{M}_2$ to D gives a new database with p undefined. Our semantics concludes that p is inserted in the database with value *true* and, therefore, produces a more informative database. ∎

Theorem 1. $\mathcal{UP}_{\mathcal{WS}[BM]}(D) \preceq \mathcal{UP}_{\mathcal{WS}}(D)$. ∎

Thus, the rewriting here proposed is more intuitive and also leaves less atoms undefined.

4.2 Max-deterministic semantics

The well-founded semantics is not able to catch the intuitive meaning of all programs. We show this by means of an example.

Example 3. Consider a database D and the update program $\langle \delta, \mathcal{AP} \rangle$ where $\delta = \{+p\}$ and $\mathcal{AP}$ consists of the rules

$$\begin{array}{lll} \mathtt{c} \leftarrow \neg \mathtt{d}, +\mathtt{p}. & +\mathtt{a} \leftarrow \mathtt{c}. & +\mathtt{a} \leftarrow \neg - \mathtt{a}. \\ \mathtt{d} \leftarrow \neg \mathtt{c}, +\mathtt{p}. & +\mathtt{a} \leftarrow \mathtt{d}. & -\mathtt{a} \leftarrow \neg + \mathtt{a}. \end{array}$$

The application of the well-founded semantics gives an empty model, i.e., all derived atoms are undefined. However, the intuitive meaning of the first two rules is that if p is inserted either c or d should be true, and the third and fourth rules say that a must be inserted if c or d is true. Thus, it seems more intuitive to deduce that a should be inserted into the database independently on the particular values of c and d. This 'intuitive' meaning is captured by the max-deterministic semantics which gives, for the rewritten program, a model where the atom +a is true, the atoms c and d are undefined and the atom −a is false. ∎

Thus, the max-deterministic model is more informative than the well-founded model. The next proposition shows that this is true in the general case.

Proposition 2. $\mathcal{UP}_{\mathcal{WS}}(D) \preceq \mathcal{UP}_{\mathcal{MD}}(D)$ ∎

4.3 Total deterministic semantics

In this section we consider a total deterministic semantics for update programs. The idea is to consider only update programs which generate total database and to consider as 'wrong' programs which introduce unknown facts into the database.

Definition 5. Let D_1 be a total database and let $\mathcal{UP}$ be an update program. Then, the application of $\mathcal{UP}$ to D_1 under total well-founded semantics (resp. max-deterministic semantics), denoted $\mathcal{UP}_{\mathcal{TWS}}(D_1)$ (resp. $\mathcal{UP}_{\mathcal{TMD}}(D_1)$), is equal to $D_2 = \mathcal{UP}_{\mathcal{WS}}(D_1)$ (resp., $D_2 = \mathcal{UP}_{\mathcal{MD}}(D_1)$) if D_2 is total otherwise is equal to D_1. ∎

Observe that the condition of totality of the semantics is on the mapping and not on the model of the rewritten program. We next introduce necessary and sufficient conditions which guarantee that the mapping $\mathcal{UP}$ applied to a total database gives a total database.

Proposition 3. *Let $\mathcal{UP}$ be an update program and let D be a total database. Let $M = \mathcal{SEM}_{\mathcal{XS}}[\mathcal{UP}, D]$. Then, $\mathcal{UP}(D)$ is total iff at least one of the following conditions is true*

1. *M is total, or*
2. *for each atom $+p \in \bar{M}$ is $p \in D^+$, and for each atom $-p \in \bar{M}$ is $p \in D^-$.* ∎

Observe that the application of the program of Example 3 is not total under well-founded semantics whereas is total under max-deterministic semantics.

4.4 Unique total stable model semantics

We consider now a different semantics which is not based on deterministic models. A Datalog program may have associated zero, one or more total stable models. A possible declarative semantics for a program can be given by the unique total stable model semantics. Thus, we give semantics only to programs which have a unique total stable model (programs with zero or more than one total stable models are rejected). It is obvious that this semantics, as well as the previous ones, guarantees termination and confluence. The unique total stable model semantics will be denoted bt $\mathcal{UTS}$.

Definition 6. Let D_1 be a total database and let $\mathcal{UP}$ be an update program. Then, the application of $\mathcal{UP}$ to D_1 under unique total stable model semantics, denoted $\mathcal{UP}_{\mathcal{UTS}}(D_1)$, is equal to $D_2 = \hat{M}(\delta(D_1))$ if M is the unique total stable model of $st(\mathcal{UP})_{D_1}$, otherwise is equal to D_1. ■

Example 4. Consider a database D and the update program $\langle \delta, \mathcal{AP} \rangle$ where $\delta = \{+p\}$ and $\mathcal{AP}$ consists of the rules

$$\mathtt{c} \leftarrow \neg \mathtt{d}, +\mathtt{p}. \qquad +\mathtt{a} \leftarrow \mathtt{c}.$$
$$\mathtt{d} \leftarrow \neg \mathtt{c}, +\mathtt{p}. \qquad -\mathtt{a} \leftarrow +\mathtt{a}.$$

The program $st(\mathcal{UP})_D$ has a unique total stable model containing the atoms $\neg\mathtt{c}, \mathtt{d}, \neg + \mathtt{a}, \neg - \mathtt{a}$. ■

References

1. Bidoit, N., and S. Maabout. A Model Theoretic Approach to Update Rule Programs. in: *proc. Int. Conf. on Database Theory*, 1997, 173-187.
2. Buccafurri F., Greco S., and D. Saccà, "The Expressive Power of Unique Total Stable Model Semantics", in *Proc. ICALP*, 1997.
3. Ceri S., and P. Fraternali, *The IDEA Methodology*, Addison Wesley, 1997.
4. Gelfond M., and V. Lifschitz, "The Stable Model Semantics for Logic Programming", *Proc. 5th Int. Conf. on Logic Programming*, 1988.
5. Greco S. and Saccà D., "Complexity and Expressive Power of Deterministic Stable Model Semantics", *Proc. DOOD Conference.* 1997.
6. Lausen G., B. Ludascher, and W. May. On Logical Foundations of Active Databases. *Technical Report*, 1997.
7. Lloyd J.W., *Foundations of Logic Programming*, Springer-Verlag, Berlin, 1987.
8. Picouet P., and V. Vianu, Semantics and expressiveness issues in Active Databases, *Principles of Database Systems*, 1995.
9. Saccà D. and C. Zaniolo, "Stable Models and Non-Determinism in Logic Programs with Negation", *Proc. ACM PODS Symp.*, 1990, pp. 205-218.
10. Saccà D. and C. Zaniolo, "Deterministic and Non-Deterministic Stable Models", *Journal of Logic and Computation*, (to appear) 1997.
11. Van Gelder A., Ross K. and J.S. Schlipf, "The Well-Founded Semantics for General Logic Programs", *Journal of the ACM 38*, 3, 1991, pp. 620-650.
12. Widom, J., and S. Ceri (eds.), *Active Databases: Triggers and rules for Advanced Database Processing*, Morgan-Kaufman, 1996.
13. Zaniolo, C., Active Database Rules with Transaction-Conscious Stable-Model Semantics. *Proc. DOOD Conference.* 1995.

Towards Visual Schemas in Deductive Databases

Jordi Puigsegur[1,2], Jaume Agustí[1], and Joan A. Pastor[3]

[1] Artificial Intelligence Research Institute, CSIC
Campus UAB, 08193 Bellaterra, Catalonia, European Union
{jpf,agusti}@iiia.csic.es
[2] Visual Inference Laboratory, Indiana University
Lindley Hall 215, Bloomington IN 47405, USA
[3] Software Department, Technical University of Catalonia
Campus Nord UPC, 08034 Barcelona, Catalonia, European Union
pastor@lsi.upc.es

Abstract. We present a visual language expressive enough to capture an important subset of First Order Predicate Logic. We use the diagrams of our language to represent all the components of a deductive database schema: base predicates, derived predicates with their deductive rules, and integrity constraints. Our diagrams are grounded on two powerful visual metaphors: Venn/Euler diagrams and graphs, familiar to most designers. They are formal and independent of the application domain; they emphasize basic forms of logic description, the diagrammatic syntax being closer to the semantics; and they have a simple translation to Horn clauses. Thus, we aim at a situation where the generality of deductive databases would be fostered by the expected greater usability of visual schema languages in the hands of a wider group of practitioners.

1 Introduction

Deductive databases, also known as logic databases, result from decades of research in the areas of logic, databases, logic programming and artificial intelligence. Fortunately, they seem to be evolving from a research concept into a practical tool. Indeed, the large amount of theoretical research devoted to this field has not only penetrated current relational DBMSs, but is also inspiring several of their future extensions. Furthermore, this research is now materializing in some deductive DBMS prototypes and commercial products. Deductive databases extend relational databases by allowing for the representation and management of more general forms of 'application semantics'. Besides data explicitly stored in base predicates, comprehensive views permit the handling of additional forms of derived data, and more powerful integrity constraints can be used to care for overall data consistency. This generality of deductive databases is a consequence of their underlying theory: First Order Predicate Logic.

However, it is precisely for this same reason that deductive databases share with other areas, such as logic programming, an important problem: the inherent difficulty that many practitioners encounter when working directly with logical expressions. In fact, we believe that this may have been one of the main reasons for their slow diffusion. Certainly, few people in industry enjoy working directly with logic and, hence, we need more natural forms of communication which can be translated (sometimes automatically) into logic. In this way, both generality and usability may be obtained. This paper aims to be a first step towards this goal within the context of deductive databases, where we explore the visual definition of their schemas. In doing so, we draw from our prior results —here adapted and extended— regarding the definition of a visual logic programming language [1, 9]. Visual languages offer a completely new way to interact with computers that may now also be applied to existing paradigms like logic programming and deductive databases. We aim at languages that are independent from any particular application domain and which emphasize visually some semantic and pragmatic features of logic instead of its mathematical syntax patterned after Boolean algebra.

In this paper we propose a visual language expressive enough to capture the logic-based paradigm of deductive databases. We use the diagrams of our language to represent all the components of a deductive database schema: base predicates, derived predicates with their deductive rules, and integrity constraints. These diagrams are grounded on two powerful visual metaphors: Venn/Euler diagrams and graphs, familiar to most designers; they are formal —that is, unambiguously defined and interpreted—, independent of the application domain and have a simple translation to Horn clauses.

The paper is organized as follows. After this introduction, Section 2 introduces the kind of deductive database schemas that we address with the visual schema language presented in Section 3. Next, Section 4 discuses other research work that may be related to our approach, while in Section 5 we present both our conclusions as well as our ideas for further work. In an extended version of this paper [11], we also formalize the translation of visual into textual schemas and describe our visual environment prototype.

2 Deductive Databases Schemas Considered

We introduce here the kind of deductive database schemas addressed in this paper. We assume the reader is familiar with most of the basic concepts of deductive databases [6, 8], and therefore we only do a brief overview of the different parts involved in a schema.

We use first order logic as the main convention. Thus we consider a first order language with a set of constants, a set of variables, a set of predicate names and no function symbols. In formal definitions we will use names beginning with a capital letter for predicate symbols and names with lower-case letters for terms (variables and constants). *Atoms* and *literals* are defined as usual.

Since we concentrate on the visual representation of the database schema, irrespective of any particular database contents, we find convenient to clearly separate the definitions of database contents and database schema. Facts are considered to be explicitly stored in the database, and are modeled in the database schema through some *base predicate* (scheme). A *derived predicate* (or *view*) is a scheme representing information which is not stored in the database but can be derived using deductive rules. Formally, a deductive rule is of the form:

$$D(t_1, ..., t_m) \leftarrow L_1 \wedge ... \wedge L_n \qquad\qquad with\ m \geq 0$$

where the derived predicate appears as the head.

Finally, we also consider (*state*) *integrity constraints.* Formally, a state integrity constraint is a closed first-order formula defined in terms of base and/or derived predicates, that the database is required to satisfy. We deal of constraints that have the form of a denial:

$$\leftarrow L_1 \wedge ... \wedge L_n \qquad\qquad with\ n \geq 1$$

We associate with all integrity constraints an inconsistency (derived) predicate Ic_n, with or without terms, and, thus, they take the same form as deductive rules. We call them integrity rules.

In the rest of this paper we will use the example deductive database schema of Fig. 1. This example is (part of) a database for the *Human Resources Unit* of a hierarchically-structured organization. Besides enforcing such an organizational structure, the database is to keep track of the employees and managers assigned to the different units, and of arranged interviews between job applicants and units. Furthermore, for legal reasons, it also keeps track of residential status and the existence of criminal records for the people administered by them. Rather than to represent a real application domain, we regard this database schema as a representative example of the situations that we are able to represent with our visual schema language. We will focus on the two components that usually have more complex definitions: *derived predicates* and *integrity constraints.* We try to obtain visual representations of these components that are more visually compelling than their textual equivalents, while still completely formal. Fig. 1(a) presents the base predicate schemes corresponding to the database schema example, together with their intended meaning.

Fig. 1(b) shows the six derived predicates of our example with their corresponding deductive rules. Employees are those people working for some unit, and are defined with a single rule having an existential variable. Two derived predicates, each one with a rule, are used to know those units having some manager and those ones with some employee who is not a manager. Subordination among organizational units is modeled with a derived predicate recursively defined with two rules, respectively dealing with direct and indirect reporting. The right-of-residence status of a person is defined using two deductive rules without any existential variable. A single rule with an existential variable is used to define job candidates.

In our example we use the seven state integrity constraints shown in Fig. 1(c). The set of employees is a subset of the set of legal residents (Ic_1), and is disjoint with the set of applicants (Ic_2), which is a superset of candidates (Ic_3). While employees must only work for units (Ic_4), units with employees must have some manager (Ic_5). Finally, the organizational structure must be hierarchical (Ic_6 and Ic_7).

Base pred.	Base predicate meaning
$Unit(u)$	'u' is a unit in the organization
$Reports(u, u1)$	Unit 'u' directly reports to unit 'u1'
$Works(p, u)$	'p' works for unit 'u', i.e. 'p' is employee of 'u'
$Mng(p)$	'p' is a manager
$App(p)$	'p' is a job applicant
$Intw(p, u)$	'p' has a job interview with unit 'u'
$Cit(p)$	'p' is a citizen
$Ra(p)$	'p' is a registered alien
$Cr(p)$	'p' has some criminal record

(a) Base predicates

Derived pred. + Deductive rules	Derived predicate meaning
$Emp(p) \leftarrow Works(p, u)$	'p' is an employee because s/he works for some unit 'u'
$HasMng(u) \leftarrow Works(p, u) \wedge Mng(p)$	Unit 'u' has some manager because at least its employee 'p' is a manager
$HasEmp(u) \leftarrow Works(p, u) \wedge \neg Mng(p)$	Unit 'u' has some non-manager employee because at least its employee 'p' is not manager
$Subordinate(u, u1) \leftarrow Reports(u, u1)$ $Subordinate(u, u1) \leftarrow Reports(u, u2)$ $\wedge Subordinate(u2, u1)$	Unit 'u' is subordinate to unit 'u1' because it either directly reports to 'u1' or it reports to some unit 'u2' which is subordinate to 'u1'
$Cand(p) \leftarrow Intw(p, u) \wedge Unit(u)$	'p' is considered a job candidate when s/he has an interview with some unit 'u'
$Rr(p) \leftarrow Ra(p) \wedge \neg Cr(p)$ $Rr(p) \leftarrow Cit(p)$	'p' has right-of-residence if s/he is either a registered alien with no criminal record or a citizen

(b) Derived predicates and deductive rules

Integrity rules	Integrity constraint meaning
$Ic_1(p) \leftarrow Emp(p) \wedge \neg Rr(p)$	Every employee must have right-of-residence, i.e. it is inconsistent to have an employee without right-of-residence
$Ic_2(p) \leftarrow Emp(p) \wedge App(p)$	No employee may also be applicant, i.e. it is inconsistent to have someone being both employee and applicant
$Ic_3(p) \leftarrow Cand(p) \wedge \neg App(p)$	Every candidate must be applicant, i.e. it is inconsistent to have a candidate who is not an applicant
$Ic_4(p, u) \leftarrow Works(p, u) \wedge \neg Unit(u)$	Employees must work for units, i.e. it is inconsistent to have someone working for some area which is not considered an organizational unit
$Ic_5(u) \leftarrow Hasemp(u) \wedge \neg Hasmng(u)$	Every unit with some employee must have some manager, i.e. it is inconsistent that a unit with assigned employees does not have some manager
$Ic_6(u) \leftarrow Reports(u, u1) \wedge$ $Reports(u, u2) \wedge u1 \neq u2$	No unit may report to two different units, i.e. it is inconsistent that a unit directly reports to more than one unit
$Ic_7(u) \leftarrow Subordinate(u, u)$	No unit may be subordinate to itself, i.e. it is inconsistent that a unit directly or indirectly subordinates to itself

(c) Integrity constraints

Fig. 1. Deductive Database Schema: textual definition

3 Our Visual Schema Language

The visual representation used is based on a set metaphor: we use Venn/Euler-like diagrams, representing sets as square boxes, and then using the graphical inclusion relation to represent set membership and set inclusion. A predicate (either base, derived or inconsistency predicate) can be seen extensionally as a set, i.e. a set of n-tuples where n is the arity of the predicate. We use this property to visually represent predicates as boxes and then define them by means of graphical tuples included in them.

We consider a visual language semantically equivalent to the textual one defined in Section 2. Terms are either variables or constants. A variable is always represented as a circle (without any name). In a diagram —as we will see— there is no need to give names to variables, which distinguishes their role from that of constants. Constants are represented as rounded boxes with a constant symbol inside, its name.

We follow the same convention as in Section 2: we use names beginning with lower case letters for constant symbols and names beginning with upper case letters for predicate symbols.

A visual *positive literal* is thus a square box with a predicate symbol P in one of its corners (inside the box) and one or several n-ary Tuples included in the box, where n is the arity of the predicate symbol P. Variables and constants can be included in the box on their own when the arity of the predicate symbol is 1. A tuple is represented as a partitioned rounded box, where each partition contains a label and a term (i.e. a variable or a constant). An important difference with textual literals is that visual terms are labeled and therefore the order in which they appear in the tuple is irrelevant. This makes the syntax clearer and more flexible.

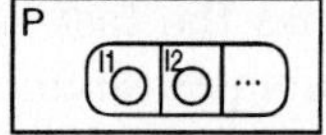

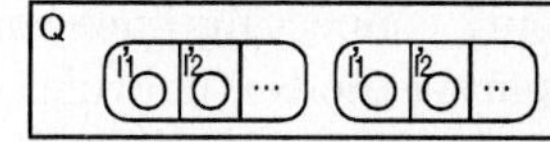

A visual *negative literal* is defined as a visual positive literal where the box is shadowed.

A negative literal represents the membership of the tuple to the complementary set of the predicate intension, which is equivalent to the negation of the membership.

Finally we need to define another type of literals, *visual evaluable literals.* They are used to indicate a relationship between two terms, like equality, inequality, comparison, etc. For example to represent variable equality (resp. inequality) we use a straight line (resp. a crossed straight line) joining both variables:

Other evaluable literals such as comparison are defined similarly.

3.1 Visual Base Predicates

Visual base predicates are represented using a visual literal with one tuple included, where all terms are variables. The following are examples of the visual predicate schemes corresponding to some of the base predicates introduced in Fig. 1(a):

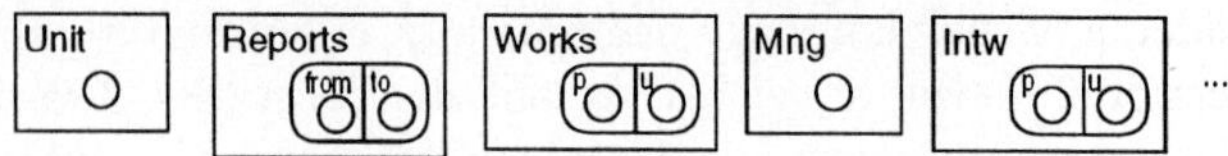

For instance, the visual predicate schema corresponding to *Works* indicates that its arity is two and its two terms are labeled 'p' and 'u' (referring to 'person' and 'unit'). The rest of base predicates are visually represented in the same straightforward way.

3.2 Visual Derived Predicates and Visual Deductive Rules

Visual derived predicates are defined using *visual deductive rules* (*diagrams*). A visual deductive rule (like its textual counterpart) contains one and only one conclusion visual predicate, and one or more condition visual literals. The conclusion literal is always a box (no evaluable literals), which contains one and only one tuple and it is distinguished from the others by drawing it using thick lines. Furthermore, each diagram (visual deductive rule) is graphically enclosed in a square box to delimit its syntactical scope.

In Fig. 2 we find the derived predicates of our example deductive database schema. We would like to note some properties of the visual language. First, the fact that variables do not need to have names assigned and that variable equality is expressed using connecting lines simplifies the task of reading the rules. For instance, comparing the textual rules defining *Subordinate* with their visual counterparts: the textual ones are difficult to understand at first sight because it is necessary to follow the different variables, while in the visual ones these relations are evident. Other features of deductive rules like existential variables are also more clearly visualized using these diagrams. For instance: in the definition of $HasMng$ or $HasEmp$ in Fig. 2 one can see that the existential variables are the ones not attached to any variable included in the box corresponding to the conclusion.

3.3 Integrity Constraints

As we said in Section 2, in this paper we restrict ourselves to *state integrity constraints* expressed as denials. An integrity constraint in our visual language is a diagram (a visual deductive rule) defining an *inconsistency predicate* (Ic_n). Whenever a Ic_n predicate holds then the consistency of the deductive database has been violated. The box corresponding to the conclusion literal of a visual integrity constraint rule represents the set of elements that violate that integrity constraint. The database is consistent when all Ic_n boxes represent empty sets.

In Fig. 3 we find the visual integrity constraints equivalent to those defined textually in Fig. 1(c). Notice how negations are expressed using the notion of complementary set in Ic_1, Ic_3, Ic_4 and Ic_5. Notice also the Ic_6 definition: we refer to two instances of the *Reports* predicate and then use inequality to indicate that they must be different instances.

However, the main strength of our approach to visualize database schemas comes from the set metaphor we use, i.e. from representing predicates as sets

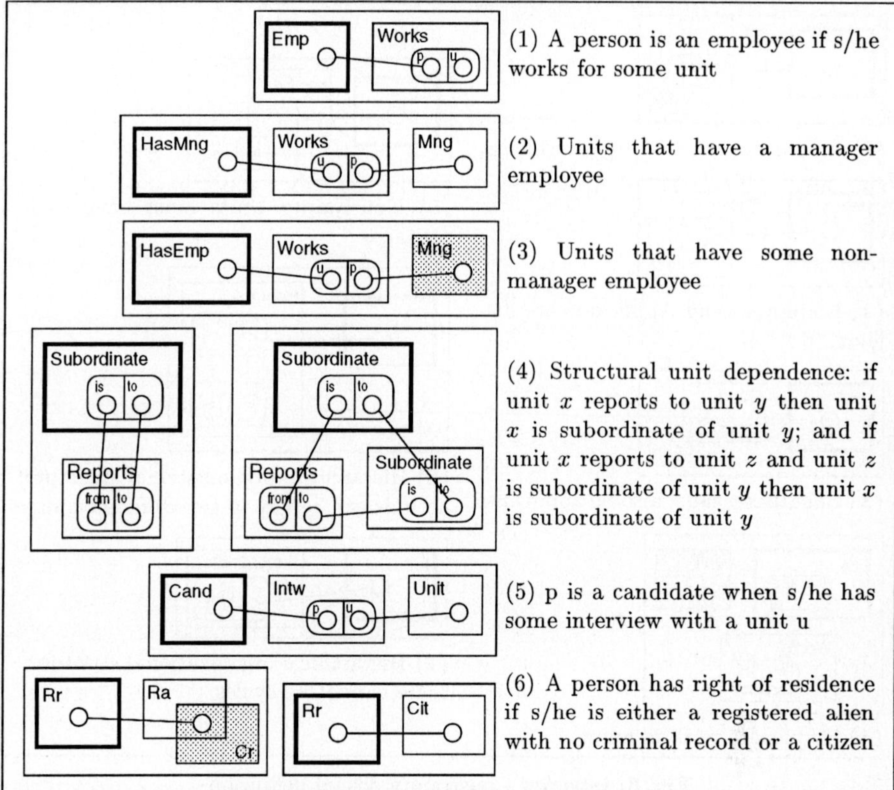

Fig. 2. Derived Predicates: visual definition

of tuples. Difficult rules with various literals corresponding to the same predicate, like the one defining Ic_6, are clearly represented using sets. In other more complicated real-world schemas these advantages would be even more apparent.

3.4 Other Features

There are other expressive potentialities of our diagrams —not used in the example used up to now— which can be useful in other situations. The most obvious of these visual constructs is graphical inclusion of boxes (sets) representing the logical implication. The unrestricted use of inclusion in our diagrams correspond to the unrestricted use of the corresponding connective (implication) and it would lead us outside the limits of deductive database schemas. Then to keep the simplicity of the computational interpretation of our diagrams we have to restrict the use of this visual construct (see [1]). In this section we show its utility by means of a different example. First we introduce a functional-like representation of predicates, alternative to the one defined up to now and then exemplify the use of inclusion.

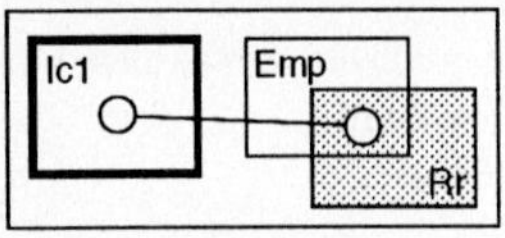

(1) Employees must be legal residents

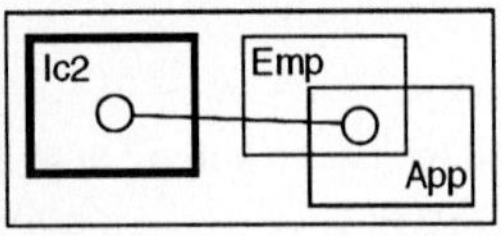

(2) Employees and Applicants are disjoint

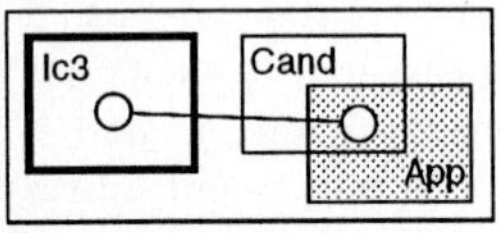

(3) Candidates must also be applicants

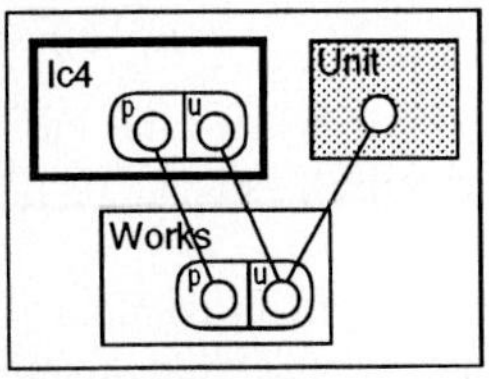

(4) Employees work in units

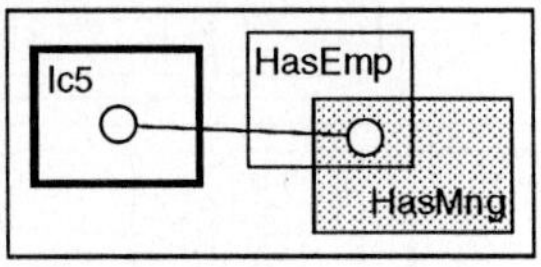

(5) Non-Empty Units must have some manager

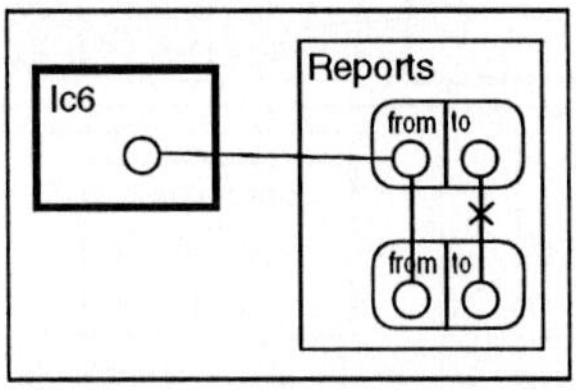

(6) Hierarchical organizational structure: no unit can report to two different units

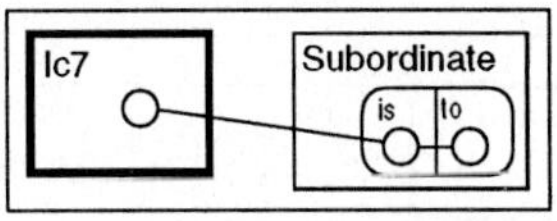

(7) Hierarchical organizational structure: there cannot be cycles

Fig. 3. Integrity Constraints: visual definition

The alternative visual representation of predicates is based on the observation that some predicates are better understood as nondeterministic functions (each input can have one or more outputs) than as relations without any preferred directionality (input / output). For instance, given a genealogical database, some predicates, like *Ancestor*, are easier to see as a function that gives us the ancestors (output) of any given person (input). In the inverse case the predicate even has a different name, that is, *Descendant*. Then it seems natural in these cases to distinguish the set of outputs (results) named by the predicate from the inputs.

Compare the alternative representations of the predicate scheme *Ancestor* in the two visual representations on the right. The left box is supposed to represent the set of ancestors of a person represented by a variable united to the box by an arrow. The right box represents the set of tuples constituted by descendant-ancestor pairs.

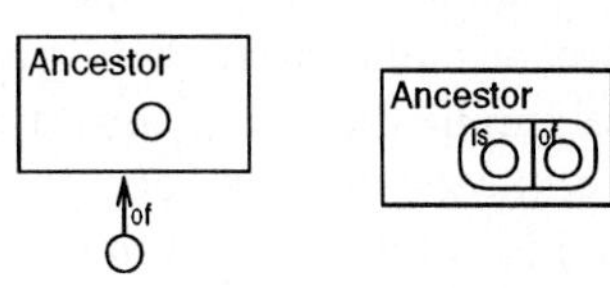

The functional representation favors the use of box (set) inclusion. For instance, the deductive rules representing that the parents of someone are his/her father and mother:

$$Parent(x,y) \leftarrow Father(x,y)$$
$$Parent(x,y) \leftarrow Mother(x,y)$$

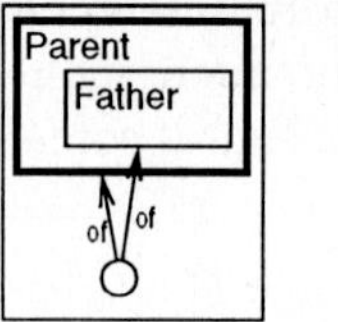

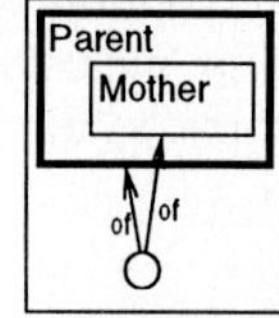

Fig. 4. Parent definition

can be represented by box inclusion as shown in Fig. 4. The box inclusion corresponds to the implication: every element of the *Father* / *Mother* boxes (sets) must belong to the *Parent* box. As it was explained before, other boxes corresponding to condition visual literals can be added to the diagrams, but no box inclusion between these boxes is allowed in order to keep the visual language expressive power within computational tractable limits.

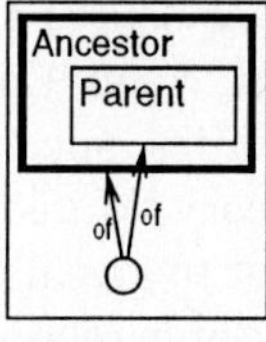

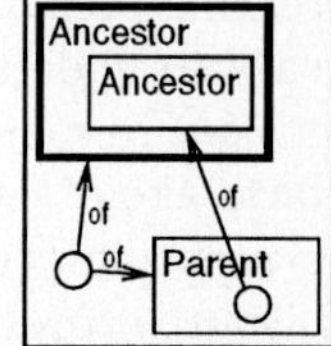

Fig. 5. Ancestor definition

This functional representation also allows to make more evident the *recursivity* of some predicates and predicate composition in some definitions. For instance, Fig. 5 presents the deductive rules for ancestor. The recursivity is shown by including ancestor inside itself. The composition of *Parent* and *Ancestor* (ancestors of parents are ancestors) is made evident by the graphical structure of the diagram itself.

4 Related Work

Previous work of our group has focused on the design of a visual logic programming language, first as a Prolog front-end [10, 1], and later as a logic programming language with its own visual operational semantics [12, 9]. The starting point of the work of our research group in the visual languages area was diagrammatic reasoning as presented by Jon Barwise's group [2]. However our goals differ from those of the diagrammatic reasoning community. Our use of Venn/Euler diagrams is centered on their computational aspects. We want to focus on simple diagrams with a clear computational interpretation, avoiding as many logical symbols as possible. A complete study of other existing visual declarative programming languages can be found at [1, 9].

Some few visual formalisms have made their way through wide industrial software practise; entity-relationship and data-flow diagrams (in many versions) being among the most popular ones [15]. There are also plenty of research proposals offering various forms of visual languages for representing software systems and their application domain, from conceptual modeling [3] to business requirements engineering [7] and enterprise modeling [4]. The *existential graphs* of Charles S. Peirce [13], a full First-Order-Predicate-Logic diagrammatic reasoning system, are of great interest and a source of inspiration of our research, together with John Sowa's *conceptual graphs* [14] modeled after Peirce's diagrammatic approaches to predicate logic. Our approach differs from that of conceptual graphs mainly on the type of visual representations used, being the main difference our option to represent relations (sets of tuples) by set operations (membership, inclusion, union, intersection) instead of their explicit representation of the corresponding logical connectives (implication, disjunction and conjunction).

5 Conclusions and Further Work

The visual language we have presented here is a complementary alternative (although not empirically tested) to conventional textual languages. While being *completely formal*, we believe that it permits to visualize deductive database schemas in a *simple, concise and elegant way.* The graphical metaphor of representing predicates as sets of tuples —the key-point of this work— is, we claim, easy to understand. Venn/Euler diagrams are one of the most used visual notations in mathematics, specially at elementary school when learning the basic facts about set theory. Moreover, as we have pointed out before, using a visual syntax allows us not to give names to variables, using instead a graph-like mechanism to express variable relationships, simplifying the comprehension of the rule. In [11] we developed other aspects of the language, as well as its translation into textual schemas and the environment we are currently implementing.

Recent studies stress the fact that, well used, visual languages might give better empirical results than textual ones. For instance in [5] an empirical study shows that the performance of a visual query language based on the well known Entity-Relationship model is better than SQL. However, our implementation of the language is still on its early stages and we have performed only limited tests with subjects outside the development group. A *full empirical study* of the language is planned once a full implementation is available.

Up to now we have concentrated our efforts on studying the basic problems of deductive database schema visual definition. However, we have not addressed the question of how to visually define *transition integrity constraints*, nor *updates.* Both are goals to be pursued in the future. Our work in visual logic programming languages, and specially that of [9], gives us the bases to think that it is possible to visually define *queries* and visualize their *answers* using our visual language. We have found that our visual syntax allows us to represent query answers showing different alternative solutions in a single diagram together with their trace (i.e. how the solutions have been obtained).

We also want to study how different *properties of deductive database schemas* (like being *allowed* or *stratified*) can be represented or even defined in a visual way. A drawback of deductive databases presented by means of a set of deductive rules is its flat character, the lack of explicit connections between the same predicates in different rules. This has been addressed by representation of dependency graphs in some environments (i.e. LPA MacProlog). We are considering similar ways of reflecting the global structure of the intensional component of the database. It is also interesting to study how to combine our formalism with other existing ones, like for instance the Entity-Relationship model for base predicates.

Acknowledgments

Part of the work has been done while the first author was visiting the Visual Inference Laboratory of the Indiana University supported by a doctoral grant of the *Direcció General de Recerca* (*Generalitat de Catalunya*). The first and second authors have been partially supported by the MODELOGOS project TIC97-0579-C02-01, and the third author has been partially supported by the PRONTIC program project TIC97-1157.

References

1. J. Agustí, J. Puigsegur, and D. Robertson. A Visual Syntax for Logic and Logic Programming. *Journal of Visual Languages and Computing*, 1998. To appear.
2. G. Alwein and J. Barwise, editors. *Logical Reasoning with Diagrams*. Oxford University Press, New York, 1996.
3. M. Borman, J. A. Bubenko, P. Johannensson, and B. Wangler. *Conceptual Modelling*. Prentice Hall, 1997.
4. J. A. Bubenko. Extending the scope of information modelling. In *Proc. Fourth Int. Workshop on the Deductive Approach to Information Systems and Databases*, pages 73–98, Lloret, Catalonia, 1993.
5. T. Catarci and G. Santucci. Diagrammatic vs Textual Query Languages: A Comparative Experiment. In Stefano Spaccapietra and Ramesh Jain, editors, *Proc. of the 3rd IFIP 2.6 Working Conference on Visual Database Systems*, 1995.
6. H. Gallaire, J. Minker, and J.M. Nicolas. Logic and databases: A deductive approach. *ACM Computing Surveys*, 16(2):153–185, 1984.
7. IBM Business Systems Development Method Technical Description. Technical Report Tech. Reps. GE19-5387, SC19-53(09,10,12,13), International Business Machines Corporation, 1992.
8. J.W. Lloyd. *Foundations on Logic Programming, 2nd. ed.* Springer, 1987.
9. J. Puigsegur and J. Agustí. Visual Logic Programming by means of Diagram Transformations. In *Proc. of APPIA-GULP-PRODE Joint Conference in Declarative Programming*, La Coruña, Spain, July 1998.
10. J. Puigsegur, J. Agustí, and D. Robertson. A Visual Logic Programming Language. In *Proc. of the 12th IEEE Symposium on Visual Languages*, Boulder, Colorado, September 1996.
11. J. Puigsegur, J. A. Pastor, and J. Agustí. Defining and Translating Visual Schemas for Deductive Databases. Research Report LSI-98-31-R, Department of LSI, Technical University of Catalonia, 1998.
12. J. Puigsegur, W. M. Schorlemmer, and J. Agustí. From Queries to Answers in Visual Logic Programming. In *Proc. of the 13th IEEE Symposium on Visual Languages*, Capri, Italy, September 1997.
13. D. D. Roberts. *The Existential Graphs of Charles S. Peirce*. Mouton and co., The Hague, 1973.
14. J. F. Sowa. *Conceptual Structures. Information Processing in Mind and Machine*. Addison Wesley, 1984.
15. R.J. Wieringa. *Requirements Engineering: Frameworks for Understanding*. Willey Publ., 1995.

Papers [1, 9–12] are available at the following URL:
`http://www.iiia.csic.es/~jpf/publications.html`

Incorporating Methods and Encapsulation into Deductive Object-Oriented Database Languages

Mengchi Liu

Department of Computer Science,
University of Regina
Regina, Saskatchewan, Canada S4S 0A2
mliu@cs.uregina.ca

Abstract. This paper presents an approach to incorporating rule-based methods and encapsulation of such methods into DOOD languages. The main novel feature of this approach is the simple and intuitive logic-based semantics that cleanly accounts for all important object-oriented features such as object identity, complex objects, typing, methods, encapsulation, class hierarchy, multiple structural and behavioral inheritance with overridden, and schema definition. Besides, the set-at-a-time semantics that is natural for database updates is also novel.

1 Introduction

In the past decade, a number of deductive object-oriented database languages have been proposed to combine the best of deductive database languages and object-oriented database languages, such as O-logic [19], revised O-logic [16], IQL [2], LOGRES [11], Datalog^{meth} [3], LLO [18], CORAL++[22], DLT [5], Gulog [13], F-logic [15], Rock & Roll [6] and ROL [17]. However, most of them are only structurally object-oriented. Important behaviorally object-oriented features such as methods and encapsulation common in object-oriented database languages are not properly supported. A few of them that support methods and encapsulation limit the methods to be deductive only so that updates cannot be performed. Some of them that are both structurally and behaviorally object-oriented simply provide two kinds of incompatible languages: rule-based declarative language for deduction and query, and imperative language for data definitions and manipulations, and complex tasks, which suffer various degree impedance mismatch and lack logic-based semantics.

In [8], general rule-based methods that can perform deduction as well as updates and encapsulation of these methods are discussed informally. The proposal is in the spirit of Prolog++ [20] in which Datalog facts and rules with action predicates of LDL [21] for specific objects are encapsulated together. However, proper syntax and semantics for the proposed framework are not defined. In Transaction F-logic [14], it is proposed to use F-logic [15] to model the structural aspect and Transaction Logic [9] to model the behavior aspects. Methods for updates can be supported but not the encapsulation. The reason is that there is no clear separation between the notions of schema and instance.

In this paper, we propose an approach to incorporating rule-based methods and encapsulation into deductive object-oriented database languages. The proposal is based on F-logic and ROL. The main contribution of this paper is the simple and intuitive logic-based Herbrand model semantics that cleanly accounts for all fundamental object-oriented features such as object identity, complex objects, typing, methods, encapsulation, class hierarchies, multiple structural and behavioral inheritance with overriding, and schema definition. The proposed approach can be used for other deductive object-oriented database languages as well. For simplicity of presentation, we focus on rules that can only perform updates rather than deduction.

This paper is organized as follows. Section 2 introduces the syntax of our framework. Section 3 defines the semantics. Section 4 concludes the paper. For lack of space, we omit the proofs of our results presented here.

2 Syntax

In this section, we define the formal syntax. We assume the existence of the following pairwise disjoint sets:

(1) a set of value class names $\mathcal{B} = \{integer, real, string, void\}$;
(2) a set $\mathcal{C}$ of object class names;
(3) a set $\mathcal{A}$ of attribute labels;
(4) a set $\mathcal{M}$ of method names with arity $n \geq 0$;
(5) a set $\mathcal{D}$ of values which is the union of the set $\mathcal{I}$ of integers, the set $\mathcal{R}$ of reals, the set $\mathcal{S}$ of strings, and the set $\{nil\}$;
(6) a set $\mathcal{O}$ of object identifiers (oids);
(7) a set $\mathcal{V}$ of variables.

A database consists of two parts: a schema and an instance. The schema contains structural and behavioral information about classes, while the instance contains extensional information about objects. We first define the schema.

The *classes* are defined as follows:

(1) elements of $\mathcal{B}$ are *value* classes;
(2) an object class name $c \in \mathcal{C}$ is an *object* class;
(3) if c is a class, then $\{c\}$ is a *set* class; c is the *component* class of $\{c\}$.

Classes denote collections of objects that share common signature and methods. Based on the definition, three kinds of classes are distinguished: value classes, object classes, and set classes. The collections which value classes denote are fixed. In details, *integer*, *real*, *string*, *void* denote $\mathcal{I}$, $\mathcal{R}$, $\mathcal{S}$ and $\{nil\}$ respectively. The collections which object classes denote depend on the instance. The collections which set classes denote depend on the collections which the component classes denote.

If c and c' are object classes, then c *isa* c' declares c to be an *immediate subclass* of c' and c' to be an *immediate superclass* of c.

For example, *student isa person* declares that the class *student* is an immediate subclass of the class *person*.

In the object-oriented paradigm, the signature of a class specifies the names of attributes and the classes of the attribute values and the names of methods that are applicable to objects of this class, the class of arguments each method takes and the class of the results it returns. We formalize this notion as follows.

Let c be an object class, c' a class, and l an attribute label. Then $c\ [l \Rightarrow c']$ is an *attribute signature* for the attribute l of c. Let c be an object class, $c_1, ..., c_n, c_r$ classes, and m an n-ary method name with $n \geq 0$. Then $c\ [m(c_1, ..., c_n) \Rightarrow c_r]$ is a *method signature* for the method m of the class c. If c_r is *void*, we can simply use $c[m(c_1, ..., c_n)]$ instead.

Unlike other proposals, the methods in our framework are rule-based and have to be encapsulated in class declarations. In what follows, we define terms, atoms, method rules and class declarations.

A *term* is defined recursively as follows:

(1) a variable is either a *value* term, an *oid* term, or a *set* term depending on the context;
(2) a value is a *value* term;
(3) an object identifier is an *oid* term;
(4) a set of values or object identifiers is a *set* term;

A term is *ground* if it has no variables. The set of all ground terms is denoted by $\mathcal{O}^*$ which is our Herbrand Universe.

There are six kinds of atoms based on terms: attribute atoms, method atoms, oid assignment atoms, oid membership atoms, action atoms, and arithmetic and set-theoretic comparison atoms.

Let O be an oid term, l an attribute label, and O' a term. Then $O[l \rightarrow O']$ is a positive attribute atom and $O[not\ l \rightarrow O']$ is a negative attribute atom.

Let O an oid term, m be an n-ary method name, and $O_1, ..., O_n, O_r$ terms with $n \geq 0$. Then the *method atoms* are defined as follows.

(1) $O[m(O_1, ..., O_n) \rightarrow O_r]$ is a *positive* method atom; if O_r is *nil*, we can use $O[m(O_1, ..., O_n)]$ instead.
(2) $O[not\ m(O_1, ..., O_n) \rightarrow O_r]$ is a *negative* method atom; if O_r is *nil*, we can simply use $O[not\ m(O_1, ..., O_n)]$.

If $O[V_1]$, ..., $O[V_n]$ are attribute atoms or method atoms, then $O[V_1, ..., V_n]$ is a *composite* atom; if $O[V_1]$, ..., $O[V_n]$ are all positive, then $O[V_1, ..., V_n]$ is positive.

Let c be a class and O an oid term. Then $c : O$ is an *oid assignment atom* and $c : *O$ is an *oid membership atom.*

In the object-oriented paradigm, an immediate instance of a subclass is also an instance of its superclasses. Here we use : to represent immediate instances of a class and : $*$ to represent both immediate and inherited instances of a class.

Let ψ be an attribute or oid assignment atom. Then *ins* ψ and *del* ψ are *action atoms.*

Action atoms are used to perform primitive updates to the database. We can use an action atom to insert/delete oids in a class or insert/delete attribute values of objects.

$$
\begin{array}{l}
\mathit{class\ person}\ [\\
\quad \mathit{name} \Rightarrow \mathit{string}; \mathit{address} \Rightarrow \mathit{string}; \mathit{spouse} \Rightarrow \mathit{person}; \mathit{marry}(\mathit{person}); \mathit{divorce}();\\
\quad X[\mathit{marry}(Y)] \text{ :- } X[\mathit{not\ spouse} \rightarrow Z, \mathit{gender} \rightarrow G],\\
\qquad\qquad\qquad Z[\mathit{not\ spouse} \rightarrow Z1, \mathit{not\ gender} \rightarrow G],\\
\qquad\qquad\qquad \mathit{ins}\ X[\mathit{spouse} \rightarrow Y], \mathit{ins}\ Y[\mathit{spouse} \rightarrow X];\\
\quad X[\mathit{divorce}] \text{ :- } \mathit{del}\ X[\mathit{spouse} \rightarrow Y], \mathit{del}\ Y[\mathit{spouse} \rightarrow X]]\\
\mathit{class\ employee\ isa\ person}\ [\\
\quad \mathit{worksin} \Rightarrow \mathit{dept}; \mathit{salary} \Rightarrow \mathit{integer};\\
\quad \mathit{raise}(\mathit{integer}); \mathit{transfer}(\mathit{dept});\\
\quad X[\mathit{raise}(Y)] \text{ :- } \mathit{del}\ X[\mathit{salary} \rightarrow S_1], S_2 = S_1 + S_1 * Y, \mathit{ins}\ X[\mathit{salary} \rightarrow S_2];\\
\quad X[\mathit{transfer}(Y)] \text{ :- } \mathit{del}\ X[\mathit{dept} \rightarrow Z], \mathit{ins}\ X[\mathit{dept} \rightarrow Y]]\\
\mathit{class\ student\ isa\ person}\ [\\
\quad \mathit{takes} \Rightarrow \{\mathit{course}\};\\
\quad \mathit{enroll}(\mathit{course}); \mathit{drop}(\mathit{course});\\
\quad X[\mathit{enroll}(Y)] \text{ :- } \mathit{del}\ X[\mathit{takes} \rightarrow C_1], \mathit{del}\ Y[\mathit{has} \rightarrow S_1], C_2 = C_1 \cup \{Y\}, S_2 = S_1 \cup \{X\},\\
\qquad\qquad\qquad \mathit{ins}\ X[\mathit{takes} \rightarrow C_2], \mathit{ins}\ Y[\mathit{has} \rightarrow S_2];\\
\quad X[\mathit{drop}(Y)] \text{ :- } \mathit{del}\ X[\mathit{takes} \rightarrow C_1], \mathit{del}\ Y[\mathit{has} \rightarrow S_1], C_2 = C_1 - \{Y\}, S_2 = S_1 - \{X\},\\
\quad \mathit{ins}\ X[\mathit{takes} \rightarrow C_2], \mathit{ins}\ Y[\mathit{has} \rightarrow S_2]]\\
\mathit{class\ wstudent\ isa\ student}, \mathit{employee}\ [\\
\quad \mathit{raise}(\mathit{integer});\\
\quad X[\mathit{raise}(Y)] \text{ :- } \mathit{del}\ X[\mathit{salary} \rightarrow S_1], S_2 = S_1 + 100 + S_1 * Y, \mathit{ins}\ X[\mathit{salary} \rightarrow S_2]]\\
\mathit{class\ dept}\ [\\
\quad \mathit{dname} \Rightarrow \mathit{string}]\\
\mathit{class\ course}\ [\\
\quad \mathit{cname} \Rightarrow \mathit{string}; \mathit{has} \Rightarrow \{\mathit{student}\};\\
\quad \mathit{add}(\mathit{student}); \mathit{del}(\mathit{student});\\
\quad X[\mathit{add}(Y)] \text{ :- } Y[\mathit{enroll}(X)]\\
\quad X[\mathit{del}(Y)] \text{ :- } Y[\mathit{drop}(X)]]
\end{array}
$$

Fig. 1. A Sample Schema

Arithmetic and set-theoretic comparison atoms are defined in the usual way.

We next introduce method rules. For simplicity, we do not consider deduction method rules in this paper. Instead, we focus on *update* method rules.

A *method rule* of the class c is of the form $c[A \text{ :- } L_1, ..., L_n]$ where the head A is a positive method atom, the body $L_1, ..., L_n$ with $n > 0$ is a sequence of atoms and at least one of them is an action atom or a method atom.

Method rules are used to perform complex updates which are composed of primitive updates.

A class contains three kinds of information: immediate superclasses, signatures, and method rules.

A *class declaration* is an expression of the following form:

$$\mathit{class}\ c\ \mathit{isa}\ c_1, ..., c_l\ [S_1; ...; S_m; R_1; ...; R_n]$$

where $c, c_1, ..., c_l$ $(l \geq 0)$ are distinct object classes, $c[S_1], ..., c[S_m]$ $(m \geq 0)$ are distinct signatures, and $c[R_1], ..., c[R_n]$ $(n \geq 0)$ are distinct method rules with distinct method names in the head of the rules such that for every method rule $c[R_i]$, there is a method signature $c[S_j]$ with the same method name and vice versa.

```
employee : tom[name → "Tom";
               worksin → cpsc;
               spouse → pat;
               salary → 20K]
employee : sam[name → "Sam";
               worksin → math;
               salary → 21K]
employee : ann[name → "Ann";
               worksin → cpsc;
               salary → 15K]
wstudent : pat[ name → "Pat";
               worksin → math;
               spouse → tom;
               takes → {ai, db};
               salary → 10K]
student : pam[ name → "Pam";
               takes → {ai, db, pl}]

dept : cpsc[ dname → "CPSC"]
dept : math[ dname → "Math"]
dept : phys[ dname → "Physics"]

course : ai[ cname → "AI";
             has → {pat, pam}]
course : db[ cname → "DB";
             has → {pat, pam}]
course : mis[cname → "MIS";
             has → {}]
course : os[ cname → "OS";
             has → {}]
course : pl[ cname → "PL";
             has → {pat}]
```

Fig. 2. A Sample Instance

A *schema* is a set of class declarations that can be represented abstractly as a tuple $K = (C, isa, \sigma, \mu)$ where C is a finite set of object classes, isa is a finite set of immediate subclass declarations, σ is a finite set of signatures, and μ is a finite set of method rules.

We note $\sigma(c)$ and $\mu(c)$ the set of all method signatures and the set of all method rules in σ and μ for the class c respectively.

Figure 1 shows a sample schema which we shall use as our running example. Note that the class *wstudent* overrides the inherited method *raise*.

We impose more syntactic constraints on the schema later in Section 3 to capture the intended semantics of multiple inheritance with overriding and to guarantee the termination of query evaluation.

We now define oid assignments, attribute assignments, object declarations, and instances.

A ground oid assignment atom $c : o$ is an *oid assignment.* It is used to specify that the oid o is an immediate instance of the object class c.

For example, *student* : *pam* specifies that the oid *pam* is an immediate instance of the class *student*.

A ground positive attribute atom $o[l \rightarrow o']$ is an *attribute assignment* for the oid o. It assigns the value o' to the attribute l of o.

An *object declaration* is an expression of the form:

$$c : o[A_1, ..., A_n]$$

which stands for the oid assignment $c : o$ and attribute assignments $o[A_1], ..., o[A_n]$.

An *instance* I is a set of object declarations which can be partitioned into two disjoint sets $I = (\pi, \Sigma)$ where π is a set of oid assignments and Σ is a set of attribute assignments.

Figure 2 shows a sample extensional instance.

Finally, we define the notions of database and query.

A *database* is a tuple $DB = (K, I)$, where K is a schema and I is an extensional instance.

For example, the schema in Figure 1 and the instance in Figure 2 form a database.

A database can be queried and manipulated using queries.

A *query* is a sequence of atoms.

Based on the database shown in Figures 1 and 2, we can use the following queries to manipulate the database.

Transfer Tom's wife to his department:

$$?\!-\ tom[worksin \rightarrow Y, spouse \rightarrow Z], Z[transfer(Y)]$$

As a result of the query, *tom*'s wife *pat* is also working in the department *cpsc*.

Give every employee a 10% salary increase:

$$?\!-\ employee : *X, X[raise(0.1)]$$

Here $employee : *X$ means that X is an immediate or non-immediate instance of *employee*. Therefore, not only *tom*, *sam*, *ann* but also *pat* get salary increase. When X is substituted to *pat*, the overrided method *raise* in the class *wstudent* is used to perform the operation instead. This accounts for late binding in the object-oriented paradigm.

Insert a new student Tom with oid *tom*:

$$?\!-\ ins\ student : tom[name \rightarrow \text{“}Tom\text{”}, takes \rightarrow \{\}]$$

This example shows how to create an object in our proposal.

Drop all the courses that *pat* enrolls:

$$?\!-\ pat[takes \rightarrow C], X \in C, pat[drop(X)]$$

Let *sam* marry to *ann*.

$$?\!-\ sam[marry(ann)];$$

Delete all the courses that has no students enrolled from the database.

$$?\!-\ del\ X[has \rightarrow \{\}], del\ X[name \rightarrow Y], del\ course : X$$

Delete the course with oid *ai* from the database

$$?\!-\ ai[has \rightarrow S], X \in S, ai[del(X)], del\ ai[name \rightarrow Y], del\ ai[has \rightarrow Z], del\ course : ai$$

Note that updates in our proposal are always set at a time.

3 Semantics

In this section, we define the semantics of the schema, instance and query.

Let $K = (C, isa, \sigma, \mu)$ be a schema. We note isa^* the reflexive transitive closure of *isa*, which captures the general subclass relationship among object classes. The *isa* relation is *well-defined* iff there do not exist distinct c and c' such that $c\ isa^*\ c'$ and $c'\ isa^*\ c$.

Let s_1 and s_2 both be sets of signatures (or method rules). We note $s_1 - s_2$ the set of signatures (or method rules) in s_1 which do not share the attribute/method names with the signatures (or with the head of method rules) in s_2.

We define multiple method signature and rule inheritance with overriding using the notions σ^* and μ^* as follows:

(1) if there does not exist a class c' such that c *isa* c', then $\sigma^*(c) = \sigma(c)$ and $\mu^*(c) = \mu(c)$;
(2) if c *isa* $c_1, ..., c_n$, then
$\sigma^*(c) = \sigma(c) \cup (\sigma^*(c_1) - \sigma(c)) \cup ... \cup (\sigma^*(c_n) - \sigma(c))$
$\mu^*(c) = \mu(c) \cup (\mu^*(c_1) - \mu(c)) \cup ... \cup (\mu^*(c_n) - \mu(c))$

The set σ is *well-defined* iff there do not exist two distinct signatures $c[S_1] \in \sigma^*$ and $c[S_2] \in \sigma^*$ and such that S_1 and S_2 have the same name.

Note that if two superclasses has distinct methods with the same method name, then the subclass inherits both methods and a conflict occurs. In this case, the set σ is not well-defined. The user has to redefine the method for the subclass so that the new method overrides the inherited ones as in O_2 [12].

For a class to override an inherited signature (or the corresponding method rule), we can simply introduce a new signature (or a method rule) for this class. Consider the following two class declarations taken from [10]:

$class\ patient\ [treatedBy \Rightarrow physician]$
$class\ alcoholic\ isa\ patient\ [treatedBy \Rightarrow psychologist]$

They define that patients are treated by physician and alcoholics are patients who are treated by psychologist. But psychologists usually are not physicians. Hence, the subclass *alcoholic* overrides the attribute signature *treatedBy* inherited from *patient* by introducing a new one.

In a schema, not all method rules are meaningful. For example, consider a schema with the following two method rules for classes *student* and *course* respectively.

$X[enroll(Y)] :- Y[add(X)]$
$X[add(Y)] :- Y[enroll(X)]$

Let ?– $sam[enroll(ai)]$ be a query. Then the termination of the query evaluation cannot be guaranteed. Therefore, we impose the stratification restriction on a schema. The notion of stratification has been used to deal with negation and sets in several deductive languages such as Prolog [4], COL [1], LDL [7] and ROL [17]. We present a similar notion here.

Let $K = (C, isa, \sigma, \mu)$ be a schema and M denote the set of the update method names in method rules in μ. We define an ordering $>$ on M as follows.

For two update method names $m_1 \in M$ and $m_2 \in M$, $m_1 > m_2$ if there is a method rule $c[R] \in \mu$ such that m_1 is in the head and m_2 is in the body.

We say μ is stratified if there do not exist a sequence of update method names $m_1, m_2, ..., m_n$ in M such that $m_1 > m_2 > ... > m_n > m_1$.

A schema $K = (C, isa, \sigma, \mu)$ is *well-defined* iff (1) the *isa* relation is well-defined; (2) the set σ is well-defined; (3) the set μ is stratified.

Therefore, the tuple (isa^*, σ^*, μ^*) gives the semantics to a well-define schema $K = (C, isa, \sigma, \mu)$.

Let K be a schema and $I = (\pi, \Sigma)$ an instance. The *instances* of classes in I (denoted by $: *$) are defined as follows:

(1) For a value class c and a value v, $c : *v$ iff v is an element in the collection which c denotes.
(2) For an object class c and an oid o, $c : *o$ iff there exists a c' such that c' isa^* c and $c' : o \in \pi$.
(3) For a set class $\{c\}$ and a set $\{o_1, ..., o_n\}$, $\{c\} : *\{o_1, ..., o_n\}$ iff for each o_i where $1 \leq i \leq n$, $c : *o_i$.

Let K be a schema and $I = (\pi, \Sigma)$ an instance. An attribute assignment $o[l \rightarrow o']$ is *well-typed* with respect to K iff (1) there exists an object class c such that $c : o \in \pi$; (2) there exists an signature signature $c[l \rightarrow c'] \in \sigma^*(c)$; and (3) $c' : *o'$.

The well-typeness of a method assignment is defined similarly.

Note that we only require attribute/method assignments of an oid to be well-typed with respect to the attribute/method signatures of its immediate class.

Let K be a schema and $I = (\pi, \Sigma)$ an instance. Then Σ is *consistent* if it does not contain a pair of attribute assignments $o[l \rightarrow o']$ and $o[l \rightarrow o'']$ or method assignments $o[m(o_1, ..., o_n) \rightarrow o']$ and $o[m(o_1, ..., o_n) \rightarrow o'']$ such that $o' \neq o''$.

Let K be a schema and $I = (\pi, \Sigma)$ an instance. Then I is *well-typed* with respect to K iff the following holds: (1) for each oid o occurring in Σ, there exists a unique object class c such that $c : o \in \pi$ (unique immediate class); (2) each attribute or method assignment in Σ is well-typed with respect to K; (3) Σ is consistent.

In what follows we discuss how a query can be satisfied by a database with a well-defined schema and a well-typed instance.

A *ground substitution* θ is a mapping from $\mathcal{V}$ to $\mathcal{O}^*$. It is extended to terms and atoms in the usual way.

Let K be a schema and I a well-typed instance with respect to K. The notion of satisfaction of non-action atoms (denoted by $\models$) and its negation (denoted by $\not\models$) are defined as follows.

(1) For a ground positive attribute atom $o[l \rightarrow o']$, $I \models o[l \rightarrow o']$ iff $o[l \rightarrow o'] \in \Sigma$.
(2) For a ground positive method atom $o[m(o_1, ..., o_n) \rightarrow o_r]$, $I \models o[m(o_1, ..., o_n) \rightarrow o_r]$ iff $o[m(o_1, ..., o_n) \rightarrow o_r] \in \Sigma$.
(3) For a ground negative method atom $o[not\ m(o_1, ..., o_n) \rightarrow o_r]$, $I \models o[not\ m(o_1, ..., o_n) \rightarrow o_r]$ iff $I \not\models o[m(o_1, ..., o_n) \rightarrow o_r]$.
(4) For a ground oid assignment $c : o$, $I \models c : o$ iff $c : o \in \pi$.
(5) For a ground oid assignment $c : *o$, $I \models c : *o$ iff $c : *o$ in I.
(6) For a ground arithmetic or set-theoretic comparison expression ψ, $I \models \psi$ iff ψ holds in the standard arithmetic or set-theoretic interpretation.

Let $K = (C, isa, \sigma, \mu)$ be a schema, I a well-typed instance with respect to K and $Q = L_1, ..., L_n$ a query. Then Q is *satisfiable* by a set Θ of ground substitutions with a sequence of instances $I_0 = II_1, ..., I_n$ denoted by $I_0, I_1, ..., I_n \models_\Theta Q$, iff the following hold:

(1) if L_i is an attribute atom, then $I_i = I_{i-1}$ and for each ground substitution $\theta \in \Theta$, $I_i \models L_i\theta$;

(2) if L_i is an action atom *ins* B, then
$I_i = I_{i-1} \cup \{B\theta \mid \text{for each ground substitution } \theta \in \Theta\}$ if I_i is well-typed with respect to K;
(3) if L_i is an action atom *del* B, then
$I_i = I_{i-1} - \{B\theta \mid \text{for each ground substitution } \theta \in \Theta\}$ if $I_{i-1} \models B\theta$ and I_i is well-typed with respect to K;
(4) if L_i is an update method atom, then there exists a method rule $A :- L'_1, ..., L'_m$ in μ such that L_i and A unify for every $\theta \in \Theta$, $L_i\theta$ is ground, and there are a set of ground substitution Θ' and a sequence of instances $I'_{i_0}, ..., I'_{i_m}$ with $I'_{i_0} = I_{i-1}$, and $I'_{i_m} = I_i$, such that $I'_{i_0}, ..., I'_{i_m} \models_{\Theta'} L'_1\theta, ..., L'_n\theta$

Note that the satisfaction of a query is defined in a top-down fashion and updates must be performed set at a time. The order of atoms in a query and method rule is important. A query with actions in this notion of satisfaction is a transaction, it either succeeds or fails. If it succeeds (satisfiable), it causes the database to change from state I_0 to state I_n. If it fails (not satisfiable), it won't leave any residue in the database. Each method rule if called is also a transaction and is nested in the query transaction.

Consider the sample database with schema K shown in Figure 1 and instance I shown in Figure 2. The query

$$?\!-\ tom[worksin \to Y, spouse \to Z], Z[transfer(Y)]$$

is satisfiable by $\Theta = \{\theta_1\}$ where $\theta_1 = \{Y/cpsc,\ Z/pat\}$ with the following sequence of instances:

$$I_0 = I,\ I_1 = I,\ I_2 = I - \{pat[worksin \to math]\} \cup \{pat[worksin \to cpsc]\}$$

Similarly, the following query is satisfiable by $\Theta = \{\theta_1, \theta_2\}$ where $\theta_1 = \{C/\{ai, db\}, X/ai\}$ and $\theta_2 = \{C/\{ai, db\}, X/db\}$:

$$?\!-\ pat[takes \to C], X \in C, pat[drop(X)]$$

with the following sequence of instances:

$$I_0 = I,\ I_1 = I,\ I_2 = I$$
$$I_3 = I - \{pat[takes {\to} \{ai, db\}], ai[has {\to} \{pat, pam\}], db[has {\to} \{pat, pam\}]\} \cup \{pat[takes \to \{\}], ai[has \to \{pam\}], db[has \to \{pam\}]\}$$

However, the following query is not satisfiable as the result of the insertion causes the database instance to be inconsistent with existing method assignment $tom[worksin \to cpsc]$:

$$?\!-\ ins\ tom[worksin \to math]$$

The set Θ of ground substitutions and the sequence of instances for a query may not be unique as some subset of Θ may also be satisfiable. For example, the second query above is satisfiable by $\Theta' = \{\theta_1\}$ where $\theta_1 = \{C/\{ai, db\}, X/ai\}$ with the following sequence of instances:

$$I_0 = I, I_1 = I, I_2 = I$$
$$I_3 = I - \{pat[takes \to \{\}], ai[has \to \{pam\}]\}$$

We have the following property.

Proposition 1. Let K be a schema, I a well-typed instance with respect to K and Q a satisfiable query. Then there exists a maximum set of ground substitutions such that all other sets of ground substitutions that can satisfy the query are subset of.

Proposition 2. Let K be a schema, I a well-typed instance with respect to K and Q a query. If Θ is the maximum set of ground substitutions that satisfy Q. Then the sequence of instances associated with Θ is unique.

Let K be a schema, I a well-typed instance with respect to K and Q a query. Then the *answer* to Q is the maximum set of ground substitutions that satisfies the query.

The notion of satisfaction of a query in fact specifies how to find all answers to a query and how to modify the database from current state to a new state through a number of intermediate states.

4 Conclusion

This paper presents an approach for integrating methods and encapsulation in deductive object-oriented database languages. As in the relational and object-oriented models, there is a clear separation between the notions of schema and instance. The schema not only contains the information about the structure of objects but also about the behavior of objects in the database. Multiple structural and behavioral inheritance with overriding in a uniform rule-based framework is supported. It is so far the only approach that has a well-defined logic-based semantics that cleanly accounts for all important object-oriented features such as object identity, complex objects, methods, encapsulation, multiple inheritance with overriding of both method signature and implementation.

The approach discussed here has been incorporated into the latest version of the ROL system (Version 3), which is available over the Internet from the web home page at `http://www.cs.uregina.ca/~mliu/ROL/`. The new ROL system supports not only method rules for updates as discussed here but also method rules for deduction with powerful set manipulation mechanisms.

There are several open issues which we still need to address. First, we have a notion of well-typedness. However, it does not apply to method rules. Second, we like to investigate query optimization techniques for the method rule evaluation.

References

1. S. Abiteboul and S. Grumbach. COL: A logic-based language for complex objects. *ACM TODS*, 16(1):1–30, 1991.
2. S. Abiteboul and P.C. Kanellakis. Object identity as a query language primitive. In *Proceedings of the ACM SIGMOD International Conference on Management of Data*, pages 159–173, Portland, Oregon, 1989.
3. S. Abiteboul, G. Lausen, H. Uphoff, and E. Waller. Methods and rules. In *Proceedings of the ACM SIGMOD International Conference on Management of Data*, pages 32–41, Washington, D.C., 1993.

4. K.R. Apt, H.A. Blair, and A. Walker. Towards a theory of declarative knowledge. In J. Minker, editor, *Foundation of Deductive Databases and Logic Programming*, pages 89–148. Morgan Kaufmann Publishers, 1988.
5. R. Bal and H. Balsters. A deductive and typed object-oriented language. In S. Ceri, K. Tanaka, and S. Tsur, editors, *Proceedings of the International Conference on Deductive and Object-Oriented Databases*, pages 340–359, Phoenix, Arizona, USA, 1993. Springer-Verlag LNCS 760.
6. M. L. Barja, A. A. A. Fernandes, N. W. Paton, M. H. Williams, A. Dinn, and A. I. Abdelmoty. Design and implementation of ROCK & ROLL: a deductive object-oriented database system. *Information Systems*, 20(3):185–211, 1995.
7. C. Beeri, S. Naqvi, O. Shmueli, and S. Tsur. Set construction in a logic database language. *J. Logic Programming*, 10(3,4):181–232, 1991.
8. E. Bertino and D. Montesi. Towards a logical object-oriented programming language for databases. In *Proceedings of the International Conference on Extending Database Technology*, pages 168–183, Vienna, Austria, 1992. Springer-Verlag.
9. A.J. Bonner and M. Kifer. Transaction logic programming. In *Proceedings of the International Conference on Logic Programming*, pages 257–279, Budapest, Hungary, 1993. MIT Press.
10. A. Borgida. Modeling class hierarchies with contradictions. In *Proceedings of the ACM SIGMOD International Conference on Management of Data*, pages 433–443, Chicago, Illinois, 1988.
11. F. Cacace, S. Ceri, S. Crepi-Reghizzi, L. Tanca, and R. Zicari. Integrating object-oriented data modelling with a rule-based programming paradigm. In *Proceedings of the ACM SIGMOD International Conference on Management of Data*, pages 225–236, 1990.
12. O. Deux et al. The O_2 system. *Communications of the ACM*, 34(10):35–48, 1991.
13. G. Dobbie and R. Topor. On the Declarative and Procedural Semantics of Deductive Object-Oriented Systems. *Journal of Intelligent Information System*, 4(2):193–219, 1995.
14. M. Kifer. Deductive and object data language: A quest for integration. In T. W. Ling, A. O. Mendelzon, and L. Vieille, editors, *Proceedings of the International Conference on Deductive and Object-Oriented Databases*, pages 187–212, Singapore, 1995. Springer-Verlag LNCS 1013.
15. M. Kifer, G. Lausen, and J. Wu. Logical foundations of object-oriented and frame-based languages. *Journal of ACM*, 42(4):741–843, 1995.
16. M. Kifer and J. Wu. A logic for programming with complex objects. *J. Computer and System Sciences*, 47(1):77–120, 1993.
17. M. Liu. ROL: A deductive object base language. *Information Systems*, 21(5):431 – 457, 1996.
18. Y. Lou and M. Ozsoyoglu. LLO: A deductive language with methods and method inheritance. In *Proceedings of the ACM SIGMOD International Conference on Management of Data*, pages 198–207, Denver, Colorado, 1991.
19. D. Maier. A logic for objects. Technical Report CS/E-86-012, Oregon Graduate Center, Beaverton, Oregon, 1986.
20. C. Moss. *Prolog++*. Addison-Wesley, 1994.
21. Shamim Naqvi and Shalom Tsur. *A Logical Language for Data and Knowledge Bases.* Computer Science Press, 1989.
22. D. Srivastava, R. Ramakrishnan, D. Srivastava, and S. Sudarshan. Coral++: Adding object-orientation to a logic database language. In *Proceedings of the International Conference on Very Large Data Bases*, pages 158–170, Dublin, Ireland, 1993. Morgan Kaufmann Publishers, Inc.

Author Index

Springer and the environment

At Springer we firmly believe that an international science publisher has a special obligation to the environment, and our corporate policies consistently reflect this conviction.

We also expect our business partners – paper mills, printers, packaging manufacturers, etc. – to commit themselves to using materials and production processes that do not harm the environment. The paper in this book is made from low- or no-chlorine pulp and is acid free, in conformance with international standards for paper permanency.

Lecture Notes in Computer Science

For information about Vols. 1–1397

please contact your bookseller or Springer-Verlag

Vol. 1398: C. Nédellec, C. Rouveirol (Eds.), Machine Learning: ECML-98. Proceedings, 1998. XII, 420 pages. 1998. (Subseries LNAI).

Vol. 1399: O. Etzion, S. Jajodia, S. Sripada (Eds.), Temporal Databases: Research and Practice. X, 429 pages. 1998.

Vol. 1400: M. Lenz, B. Bartsch-Spörl, H.-D. Burkhard, S. Wess (Eds.), Case-Based Reasoning Technology. XVIII, 405 pages. 1998. (Subseries LNAI).

Vol. 1401: P. Sloot, M. Bubak, B. Hertzberger (Eds.), High-Performance Computing and Networking. Proceedings, 1998. XX, 1309 pages. 1998.

Vol. 1402: W. Lamersdorf, M. Merz (Eds.), Trends in Distributed Systems for Electronic Commerce. Proceedings, 1998. XII, 255 pages. 1998.

Vol. 1403: K. Nyberg (Ed.), Advances in Cryptology – EUROCRYPT '98. Proceedings, 1998. X, 607 pages. 1998.

Vol. 1404: C. Freksa, C. Habel. K.F. Wender (Eds.), Spatial Cognition. VIII, 491 pages. 1998. (Subseries LNAI).

Vol. 1405: S.M. Embury, N.J. Fiddian, W.A. Gray, A.C. Jones (Eds.), Advances in Databases. Proceedings, 1998. XII, 183 pages. 1998.

Vol. 1406: H. Burkhardt, B. Neumann (Eds.), Computer Vision – ECCV'98. Vol. I. Proceedings, 1998. XVI, 927 pages. 1998.

Vol. 1408: E. Burke, M. Carter (Eds.), Practice and Theory of Automated Timetabling II. Proceedings, 1997. XII, 273 pages. 1998.

Vol. 1407: H. Burkhardt, B. Neumann (Eds.), Computer Vision – ECCV'98. Vol. II. Proceedings, 1998. XVI, 881 pages. 1998.

Vol. 1409: T. Schaub, The Automation of Reasoning with Incomplete Information. XI, 159 pages. 1998. (Subseries LNAI).

Vol. 1411: L. Asplund (Ed.), Reliable Software Technologies – Ada-Europe. Proceedings, 1998. XI, 297 pages. 1998.

Vol. 1412: R.E. Bixby, E.A. Boyd, R.Z. Ríos-Mercado (Eds.), Integer Programming and Combinatorial Optimization. Proceedings, 1998. IX, 437 pages. 1998.

Vol. 1413: B. Pernici, C. Thanos (Eds.), Advanced Information Systems Engineering. Proceedings, 1998. X, 423 pages. 1998.

Vol. 1414: M. Nielsen, W. Thomas (Eds.), Computer Science Logic. Selected Papers, 1997. VIII, 511 pages. 1998.

Vol. 1415: J. Mira, A.P. del Pobil, M.Ali (Eds.), Methodology and Tools in Knowledge-Based Systems. Vol. I. Proceedings, 1998. XXIV, 887 pages. 1998. (Subseries LNAI).

Vol. 1416: A.P. del Pobil, J. Mira, M.Ali (Eds.), Tasks and Methods in Applied Artificial Intelligence. Vol.II. Proceedings, 1998. XXIII, 943 pages. 1998. (Subseries LNAI).

Vol. 1417: S. Yalamanchili, J. Duato (Eds.), Parallel Computer Routing and Communication. Proceedings, 1997. XII, 309 pages. 1998.

Vol. 1418: R. Mercer, E. Neufeld (Eds.), Advances in Artificial Intelligence. Proceedings, 1998. XII, 467 pages. 1998. (Subseries LNAI).

Vol. 1419: G. Vigna (Ed.), Mobile Agents and Security. XII, 257 pages. 1998.

Vol. 1420: J. Desel, M. Silva (Eds.), Application and Theory of Petri Nets 1998. Proceedings, 1998. VIII, 385 pages. 1998.

Vol. 1421: C. Kirchner, H. Kirchner (Eds.), Automated Deduction – CADE-15. Proceedings, 1998. XIV, 443 pages. 1998. (Subseries LNAI).

Vol. 1422: J. Jeuring (Ed.), Mathematics of Program Construction. Proceedings, 1998. X, 383 pages. 1998.

Vol. 1423: J.P. Buhler (Ed.), Algorithmic Number Theory. Proceedings, 1998. X, 640 pages. 1998.

Vol. 1424: L. Polkowski, A. Skowron (Eds.), Rough Sets and Current Trends in Computing. Proceedings, 1998. XIII, 626 pages. 1998. (Subseries LNAI).

Vol. 1425: D. Hutchison, R. Schäfer (Eds.), Multimedia Applications, Services and Techniques – ECMAST'98. Proceedings, 1998. XVI, 532 pages. 1998.

Vol. 1427: A.J. Hu, M.Y. Vardi (Eds.), Computer Aided Verification. Proceedings, 1998. IX, 552 pages. 1998.

Vol. 1429: F. van der Linden (Ed.), Development and Evolution of Software Architectures for Product Families. Proceedings, 1998. IX, 258 pages. 1998.

Vol. 1430: S. Trigila, A. Mullery, M. Campolargo, H. Vanderstraeten, M. Mampaey (Eds.), Intelligence in Services and Networks: Technology for Ubiquitous Telecom Services. Proceedings, 1998. XII, 550 pages. 1998.

Vol. 1431: H. Imai, Y. Zheng (Eds.), Public Key Cryptography. Proceedings, 1998. XI, 263 pages. 1998.

Vol. 1432: S. Arnborg, L. Ivansson (Eds.), Algorithm Theory – SWAT '98. Proceedings, 1998. IX, 347 pages. 1998.

Vol. 1433: V. Honavar, G. Slutzki (Eds.), Grammatical Inference. Proceedings, 1998. X, 271 pages. 1998. (Subseries LNAI).

Vol. 1434: J.-C. Heudin (Ed.), Virtual Worlds. Proceedings, 1998. XII, 412 pages. 1998. (Subseries LNAI).

Vol. 1435: M. Klusch, G. Weiß (Eds.), Cooperative Information Agents II. Proceedings, 1998. IX, 307 pages. 1998. (Subseries LNAI).

Vol. 1436: D. Wood, S. Yu (Eds.), Automata Implementation. Proceedings, 1997. VIII, 253 pages. 1998.

Vol. 1437: S. Albayrak, F.J. Garijo (Eds.), Intelligent Agents for Telecommunication Applications. Proceedings, 1998. XII, 251 pages. 1998. (Subseries LNAI).

Vol. 1438: C. Boyd, E. Dawson (Eds.), Information Security and Privacy. Proceedings, 1998. XI, 423 pages. 1998.

Vol. 1439: B. Magnusson (Ed.), System Configuration Management. Proceedings, 1998. X, 207 pages. 1998.

Vol. 1441: W. Wobcke, M. Pagnucco, C. Zhang (Eds.), Agents and Multi-Agent Systems. Proceedings, 1997. XII, 241 pages. 1998. (Subseries LNAI).

Vol. 1442: A. Fiat. G.J. Woeginger (Eds.), Online Algorithms. XVIII, 436 pages. 1998.

Vol. 1443: K.G. Larsen, S. Skyum, G. Winskel (Eds.), Automata, Languages and Programming. Proceedings, 1998. XVI, 932 pages. 1998.

Vol. 1444: K. Jansen, J. Rolim (Eds.), Approximation Algorithms for Combinatorial Optimization. Proceedings, 1998. VIII, 201 pages. 1998.

Vol. 1445: E. Jul (Ed.), ECOOP'98 – Object-Oriented Programming. Proceedings, 1998. XII, 635 pages. 1998.

Vol. 1446: D. Page (Ed.), Inductive Logic Programming. Proceedings, 1998. VIII, 301 pages. 1998. (Subseries LNAI).

Vol. 1447: V.W. Porto, N. Saravanan, D. Waagen, A.E. Eiben (Eds.), Evolutionary Programming VII. Proceedings, 1998. XVI, 840 pages. 1998.

Vol. 1448: M. Farach-Colton (Ed.), Combinatorial Pattern Matching. Proceedings, 1998. VIII, 251 pages. 1998.

Vol. 1449: W.-L. Hsu, M.-Y. Kao (Eds.), Computing and Combinatorics. Proceedings, 1998. XII, 372 pages. 1998.

Vol. 1450: L. Brim, F. Gruska, J. Zlatuška (Eds.), Mathematical Foundations of Computer Science 1998. Proceedings, 1998. XVII, 846 pages. 1998.

Vol. 1451: A. Amin, D. Dori, P. Pudil, H. Freeman (Eds.), Advances in Pattern Recognition. Proceedings, 1998. XXI, 1048 pages. 1998.

Vol. 1452: B.P. Goettl, H.M. Halff, C.L. Redfield, V.J. Shute (Eds.), Intelligent Tutoring Systems. Proceedings, 1998. XIX, 629 pages. 1998.

Vol. 1453: M.-L. Mugnier, M. Chein (Eds.), Conceptual Structures: Theory, Tools and Applications. Proceedings, 1998. XIII, 439 pages. (Subseries LNAI).

Vol. 1454: I. Smith (Ed.), Artificial Intelligence in Structural Engineering. XI, 497 pages. 1998. (Subseries LNAI).

Vol. 1456: A. Drogoul, M. Tambe, T. Fukuda (Eds.), Collective Robotics. Proceedings, 1998. VII, 161 pages. 1998. (Subseries LNAI).

Vol. 1457: A. Ferreira, J. Rolim, H. Simon, S.-H. Teng (Eds.), Solving Irregularly Structured Problems in Prallel. Proceedings, 1998. X, 408 pages. 1998.

Vol. 1458: V.O. Mittal, H.A. Yanco, J. Aronis, R-. Simpson (Eds.), Assistive Technology in Artificial Intelligence. X, 273 pages. 1998. (Subseries LNAI).

Vol. 1459: D.G. Feitelson, L. Rudolph (Eds.), Job Scheduling Strategies for Parallel Processing. Proceedings, 1998. VII, 257 pages. 1998.

Vol. 1460: G. Quirchmayr, E. Schweighofer, T.J.M. Bench-Capon (Eds.), Database and Expert Systems Applications. Proceedings, 1998. XVI, 905 pages. 1998.

Vol. 1461: G. Bilardi, G.F. Italiano, A. Pietracaprina, G. Pucci (Eds.), Algorithms – ESA'98. Proceedings, 1998. XII, 516 pages. 1998.

Vol. 1462: H. Krawczyk (Ed.), Advances in Cryptology - CRYPTO '98. Proceedings, 1998. XII, 519 pages. 1998.

Vol. 1464: H.H.S. Ip, A.W.M. Smeulders (Eds.), Multimedia Information Analysis and Retrieval. Proceedings, 1998. VIII, 264 pages. 1998.

Vol. 1465: R. Hirschfeld (Ed.), Financial Cryptography. Proceedings, 1998. VIII, 311 pages. 1998.

Vol. 1466: D. Sangiorgi, R. de Simone (Eds.), CONCUR'98: Concurrency Theory. Proceedings, 1998. XI, 657 pages. 1998.

Vol. 1467: C. Clack, K. Hammond, T. Davie (Eds.), Implementation of Functional Languages. Proceedings, 1997. X, 375 pages. 1998.

Vol. 1468: P. Husbands, J.-A. Meyer (Eds.), Evolutionary Robotics. Proceedings, 1998. VIII, 247 pages. 1998.

Vol. 1469: R. Puigjaner, N.N. Savino, B. Serra (Eds.), Computer Performance Evaluation. Proceedings, 1998. XIII, 376 pages. 1998.

Vol. 1470: D. Pritchard, J. Reeve (Eds.), Euro-Par'98: Parallel Processing. Proceedings, 1998. XXII, 1157 pages. 1998.

Vol. 1471: J. Dix, L. Moniz Pereira, T.C. Przymusinski (Eds.), Logic Programming and Knowledge Representation. Proceedings, 1997. IX, 246 pages. 1998. (Subseries LNAI).

Vol. 1473: X. Leroy, A. Ohori (Eds.), Types in Compilation. Proceedings, 1998. VIII, 299 pages. 1998.

Vol. 1475: W. Litwin, T. Morzy, G. Vossen (Eds.), Advances in Databases and Information Systems. Proceedings, 1998. XIV, 369 pages. 1998.

Vol. 1477: K. Rothermel, F. Hohl (Eds.), Mobile Agents. Proceedings, 1998. VIII, 285 pages. 1998.

Vol. 1478: M. Sipper, D. Mange, A. Pérez-Uribe (Eds.), Evolvable Systems: From Biology to Hardware. Proceedings, 1998. IX, 382 pages. 1998.

Vol. 1479: J. Grundy, M. Newey (Eds.), Theorem Proving in Higher Order Logics. Proceedings, 1998. VIII, 497 pages. 1998.

Vol. 1480: F. Giunchiglia (Ed.), Artificial Intelligence: Methodology, Systems, and Applications. Proceedings, 1998. IX, 502 pages. 1998. (Subseries LNAI).

Vol. 1482: R.W. Hartenstein, A. Keevallik (Eds.), Field-Programmable Logic and Applications. Proceedings, 1998. XI, 533 pages. 1998.

Vol. 1483: T. Plagemann, V. Goebel (Eds.), Interactive Distributed Multimedia Systems and Telecommunication Services. Proceedings, 1998. XV, 326 pages. 1998.

Vol. 1487: V. Gruhn (Ed.), Software Process Technology. Proceedings, 1998. VIII, 157 pages. 1998.

Vol. 1488: B. Smyth, P. Cunningham (Eds.), Advances in Case-Based Reasoning. Proceedings, 1998. XI, 482 pages. 1998. (Subseries LNAI).